The Mormon Hierarchy

EXTENSIONS OF POWER

D. Michael Quinn

Signature Books
in association with Smith Research Associates
Salt Lake City

To my Mormon mentors
(Leonard J. Arrington, Davis Bitton)
and my non-Mormon mentors (Howard R. Lamar,
Jan Shipps) for twenty years of patiently encouraging
me to bring this study to conclusion.

With special honors to Janice Darley Quinn,
Yale University, the Mrs. Giles Whiting Foundation, Everett
L. Cooley, the National Endowment for the Humanities,
Martin B. Hickman, Gregory C. Thompson, George Miles,
George D. Smith, Martin Ridge, the Henry E. Huntington
Library, the Giles Mead Foundation,
John Netto, the Glen W. Irwin Foundation,
Ken Verdoia, the Dorothy Collins Brown family,
Milo Calder, Joyce C. Nye.

And to the memory of my son Adam

Jacket design by O'Very/Covey

The Mormon Hierarchy: Extensions of Power was printed on acid-free paper meeting the permanence of paper standard of the American National Standard for Information Services

02   01   00   99   98   97   6   5   4   3   2   1

Library of Congress Cataloging-in-Publication Data
Quinn, D. Michael.
    The Mormon hierarchy : extensions of power / by D. Michael Quinn.
        p.   cm.
    Includes bibliographical references and index.
    ISBN 1-56085-060-4
    1. Mormon Church—History.   2. Mormon Church—Government—History.
  3. Authority—Religious aspects—Mormon Church.   I. Title.
    BX8611.Q55   1997
289.3—dc20
                                                    95-7798R
                                                    CIP

TABLE OF CONTENTS

More than twenty-five years have passed since I began research in the historical archives of the Church of Jesus Christ of Latter-day Saints. As a graduate student at the University of Utah in the spring of 1971, I sat next to non-Mormons who were researching the archival files of the church's First Presidency. In what began as a teenage hobby, I had been studying the highest leadership of my church from printed sources for more than a decade. In 1962 I typed the first summary of my historical research on "the General Authorities."

But in 1971 I was at the Mecca of my research dreams, and began my first day by taking extensive notes on the diary of one of Mormonism's apostles. For the next fifteen years of research, every day was Christmas. There have been many changes at the LDS archives and in my own life since then, but I have always felt that same sense of awe as I have surveyed my research files in the hope of communicating to others my understanding of a remarkable leadership group.[1]

These primarily Utah-born men[2] now give guidance to a worldwide population of Mormons who constitute the fifth largest denomination in the United States. In addition, the LDS church is the first or second largest in nine western states.[3] Although a demographer wrote in 1995 that "Mormonism seems likely to remain a largely American or an Intermountain West [U.S.] faith,"[4] two facts of Mormon population indicate its larger significance. Twelve countries and one Canadian province have a higher percentage of Mormons in their populations than does the United States. Also, more than half of the LDS church's 9.5 million members currently reside outside the U.S.A.[5]

My historical knowledge of this Mormon hierarchy[6] has grown over the decades in expected and unexpected ways. I found much to admire in the personal lives and private councils of "the Brethren," and these findings reinforced my youthful conviction of their divine callings. I also discovered stark evidence of their human qualities. In diaries, letters, and personal statements to church members, these Mormon leaders expressed no apology for describing matters that others might now regard as negative or "too revealing" for an image-conscious, contemporary Mormonism. However, that earlier candor was also evident in the official minutes of the LDS church's various organizations, whose records were once available to outside researchers (non-Mormons and rank-and-file Mormons) at the church's history archives.[7]

Since the 1980s LDS leaders have ended access to such documents and have insisted that Mormon historical inquiry is legitimate only if it tells pleasant, "faith-promoting" stories while reinforcing current policies and definitions.[8] Although I understand the motivation of such expectations, I have tried to be true to the spirit of candor I found in the spoken and written records of the Mormon hierarchy. This study (now in its second volume) also examines the evidence of historical process and institutional change over time, rather than selecting evidence to reinforce current definitions and policies. That single-minded determination on my part led to conflicts with LDS leaders. I am now a believer outside the church for which I still have affection and fond hopes.[9]

Including this study's first volume, I have described Mormonism during 176 years. Like the first volume, this book's "Selected Chronology" has multiple functions which would suggest that the reader begin with that appendix. First, it allows readers to see how the close analysis of leadership topics fits within other developments of Mormondom. Second, it provides a guide to the diversity, continuities, and discontinuities of the Mormon experience. There are multiple dimensions of the Mormon experience that are worth examining but no space to do so here. Still the chronology emphasizes Mormon women far more than possible in chapters about male-only hierarchy. Third, in keeping with this volume's subtitle, the chronology shows how Mormon power in the twentieth century has extended beyond the LDS hierarchy to a growing influence of rank-and-file Mormons nationally and internationally. Most of these influential people regard Mormonism as central to their self-identity, feel connected with all other Mormons, and look to the LDS hierarchy for inspiration and direction. Although my analysis emphasizes the formal leadership of Mormonism, "power" takes many forms, both institutional and personal.

Mormon culture is remarkable by any standard, yet aspects of this narrative may not be pleasant for some readers. However, I believe my approach can be faith-promoting for believers seeking to understand their religious community as led by fallible humans who struggle to achieve God's will. For religious believers who do not view the LDS church and its leadership through the lens of faith, I hope they will read this study with the charity they expect others to give to the humanness of leaders in their own religion's history. I would also expect secular readers not to hold LDS leaders to a standard of infallibility which secularists deny to everyone else.

Charity is a virtue I have often found among secular humanists as well as among believers in various religious traditions. It has been my guide in appreciating an extraordinary people and in restraining personal judgments about many matters I have examined. "Of course, there are aberrations in our history," current LDS president Gordon B. Hinckley has publicly stated. "There are blemishes to be found, if searched for, in the lives of all men, including our leaders past and present. But these are only incidental to the magnitude of their service and to the greatness of their contributions."[10]

LDS encounters with the divine have been as transcendent as those in other religions, while Mormon culture's missteps are on a far smaller scale than those of other religious cultures. Yet that analogy requires me to give some explanation for the lack of comparative analysis in this study.

Some of my other publications have examined the Mormon experience in relation to American culture, cross-cultural comparisons, and interdisciplinary studies. In the early 1970s my original plan was to examine the Mormon hierarchy with respect to elite theory in political science and by comparison with group biographies of elites in various enterprises and cultures. In addition, James G. Clawson suggested that I also use theories and studies of organizational behavior, while Lawrence Foster urged me to employ anthropology and the sociology of religion, whereas Jan Shipps recommended that I place my findings within the context of recent work in religious studies.

However, I believe that it is necessary to establish the data before seeking larger contexts, and that was an enormous task. The bulk of my research explored uncharted terrain of the Mormon hierarchy's experience. Eventually I realized it would require more than one volume just to present the evidence I had uncovered. Significant comparative analysis became impossible because I was unwilling to trim the data. Nor did I want to imply that scattered sentences and a few footnotes equalled a comparison or defined a context. Although there are interpretations and analysis in these volumes on the Mormon hierarchy, my study is primarily descriptive. I leave it to others to provide the comparative analysis and new insights.

During three decades of research about the Mormon hierarchy, I received significant support and assistance of one kind or another from many sources. I wish to acknowledge the following people and organizations, with special thanks to those who aided me during the preparation of this volume: K. Haybron Adams, Roger J. Adams, Sydney E. Ahlstrom, Stan L. Albrecht, Marilyn and Thomas G. Alexander, Renee and James B. Allen, the American Academy of Arts and Sciences, the American Council of Learned Societies, Devery S. Anderson, Lavina Fielding Anderson, Lynn Matthews Anderson, Grace Fort Arrington, Harriet Horne Arrington, Leonard J. Arrington, Don R. Austin, Valeen Tippetts Avery, Pat Bagley, Will Bagley, Ian G. Barber, Alan Barnett, Steven Barnett, Bruce Bastian, Irene M. Bates, Lorette Bayle, Maureen Ursenbach Beecher, the Frederick W. Beinecke family, the Beinecke Rare Book and Manuscript

Library of Yale University, Jay Bell, the Samuel F. Bemis family, Curt
Bench, Steve Benson, Gary James Bergera, Davis Bitton, Ron Bitton, Scott
Blaser, Alan Blodgett, David F. Boone, George T. Boyd, Mary Lythgoe
Bradford, Don Bradley, Martha Sonntag Bradley, the Dorothy Collins
Brown family, L. Madelon Brunson, Frederick S. Buchanan, Mariel Budd,
Gary Burgess, Cecelia Warner Burnard, Alfred L. Bush, Milo Calder,
Thomas E. Caldwell, David Callahan, Beth and Eugene E. Campbell, Greg
Campbell, Donald Q. Cannon, Kenneth L. Cannon II, Mark W. Cannon,
Barbara and Ray Chandler, Steven F. Christensen, Howard A. Christy,
Lyndon W. Cook, Everett L. Cooley, F. Alan Coombs, Kathleen and Roy
M. Darley, George Daul, Robert Dawidoff, Mario S. DePillis, the Dialogue
Foundation, Connie Disney, Ken Driggs, John Charles Duffy, Elizabeth G.
Dulany, G. Homer Durham, Lowell M. Durham, Jr., Paul Durham, Della
Dye, Arden Eby, Steven Eccles, Paul M. Edwards, the George W. Egleston
family, Andrew F. Ehat, Maria and S. George Ellsworth, Jessie L. Embry,
Lee Erickson, Max J. Evans, Oakley Evans, Richard Fernandez, J. Arthur
Fields, Edwin Brown Firmage, Chad J. Flake, Jani Fleet, Craig L. Foster,
Rodney P. Foster, Vincent R. Frey, Juana Frisbie, Kent Frogley, Richard
Galbraith, Margaret L. Gardner, Alison Bethke Gayek, Elizabeth and Van
Gessel, Charlie Gibbs, Donna R. Glunn, L. Brent Goates, Leo Goates,
Duffy Goble, Lorine S. Goodwin, Sarah Barringer Gordon, Claude
Grenier, Victoria Grover-Swank, C. Jess Groesbeck, Rick Grunder, Donald
R. Gustavson, Chuck Hamaker, Marion D. Hanks, Maxine Hanks, Klaus
J. Hansen, B. Carmon Hardy, Michael Harris, William G. Hartley, Jay M.
Haymond, Harvard Heath, Martin B. Hickman, Alice Hill, Jane Hill,
Wayne K. Hinton, the history departments of Yale University and Brigham
Young University, Mervin B. Hogan, Erik Holdaway, Patricia and David
Honey, David S. Hoopes, Shauna and Richard G. Horne, Dawn House,
Richard P. Howard, J. Preston Hughes, the Henry E. Huntington Library,
the Glen W. Irwin Foundation, T. Harold Jacobsen, Duane E. Jeffery,
Warren S. Jeffs, Richard L. Jensen, R. Hal Jenson, Dean C. Jessee, Clifton
Holt Jolley, Greg Jones, Keiko Jones, Walter Jones, Brian Kagel, Lisa
Lineback Kamerath, Gregory A. Kemp, Scott G. Kenney, Camilla, Edward
L. and Spencer W. Kimball, Stanley B. Kimball, Mark Edward Koltko,
Ogden Kraut, KUED-TV of Salt Lake City, the LDS Historical Depart-
ment's current staff members who gave me their assistance and friendship
during a time they were free to do so, Shirley and Howard R. Lamar, Mary
and Richard N. W. Lambert, Laura Nguyen Lang, Stan Larson, Bill
Laursen, James B. Lavenstein, the Lee Library of Brigham Young University, Margaret D. Lester, Kirk and Becky Linford, J. Farrell Lines, Jr., Lee
Lucas, Steven Lucas, David Luciano, E. Leo Lyman, the T. Edgar Lyon
family, the McAdams family (Michael, Ruby, and Sylvia), Yvonne Zimmer

McBride, Judith and James W. McConkie, W. Grant McMurray, Sterling M. McMurrin, Brigham D. Madsen, Carol Cornwall Madsen, Gordon A. Madsen, Mark J. Malcolm, the Marriott Library of the University of Utah, Betty Ann Marshall, Martin E. Marty, Ray Matthews, the Giles Mead Foundation, Brent L. Metcalfe, George Miles, Henry Miller, Ronald W. Miller, Cindy Morgan, the Mormon History Association, the Mormon History Trust Fund, Douglas L. Morton, the National Endowment for the Humanities, John Netto, Linda and Jack Newell, Joy and Vaude Nye, Moyne Oviatt Osborne, Richard D. Ouellette, David Pace, D. Gene Pace, Wayne Parker, Max H. Parkin, Gary L. Parnell, Boyd Payne, Carol Lynn Pearson, Elbert Eugene Peck, Robert S. Perkins, Rinehart Lee Peshell, Lezann Pilgrim, Richard D. Poll, Perry Porter, Tom Portlock, Steven Pratt, Brian Preece, Ronald Priddis, Gregory A. Prince, Beverly and Donald Peña Quinn, Janice Darley Quinn, Carol Quist, John Quist, Will Quist, Tim Rathbone, P. T. Reilly, A. Hamer Reiser, the Religious Studies Center of Indiana University-Purdue University at Indianapolis, Marcia Rice, Martin Ridge, the B. H. Roberts Society, Cecile Rodrigue, Ronald E. Romig, William H. Rose, Dennis Rowley, William D. Russell, Roger Salazar, Susan Lucas Sceranka, Peter Schmid, Donald T. Schmidt, Gene A. Sessions, Jan Shipps, John R. Sillito, Erin R. Silva, Barnard S. Silver, A. J. Simmonds, Roy W. Simmons, Robert E. Simpson, Jr., Robert Allen Skotheim, Andrew F. Smith, Elizabeth Shaw Smith, E. Gary Smith, George D. Smith, James E. Smith, Melvin T. Smith, Robert J. Smith, Smith Research Associates, Stephanie and John Sorensen, William R. Spence, Peggy Fletcher Stack, Kathryn Quinn Jenson Standish, Martha R. Stewart, Ernest Strack, Lorie Winder Stromberg, William E. Stuckey, the students of Brigham Young University, the students of the Claremont Graduate School, the students of Snow College, the students of Southern Utah University, the students of the University of Utah, the students of Weber State University, the students of Yale University, the Sunstone Foundation, George S. Tanner, Raymond W. Taylor, Samuel W. Taylor, Linda Thatcher, Gregory C. Thompson, Gary Topping, Margaret Merrill Toscano, Paul Toscano, Mark N. Trahant, Grant Underwood, J. Brandon Valentine, Jeanie Hanks Van Amen, Richard S. Van Wagoner, Ken Verdoia, Dan Vogel, Fred Voros, Jr., Doris and Ted J. Warner, Bryan Waterman, Sam Weller, Tony Weller, Hugh S. West, Alan Whitesides, Lynne Kanavel Whitesides, the Mrs. Giles Whiting Foundation, the John Whitmer Historical Association, David J. Whittaker, Anne Wilde, J. D. Williams, Val Wilson, Wendy Winegar, Henry J. Wolfinger, Jeff Wood, Margery Ward Wood, the Workman family (Coila, Darlene, Della, Donna, Frank J., Frank L., Joseph Alma, Joyce, Norma, Pam, Ruben, and Toni), Nancy Young, and my children Mary, Lisa, Adam, and Paul Moshe.

Also I express special thanks to the following persons who critiqued preliminary versions of this volume in part or whole during the past twenty-five years: Linda Hunter Adams, Gordon Burt Affleck, Sydney E. Ahlstrom, Thomas G. Alexander, James B. Allen, Byron Cannon Anderson, Lavina Fielding Anderson, Leonard J. Arrington, Irene M. Bates, Louise Clark Bennion, Gary James Bergera, Davis Bitton, Jeff D. Blake, Mary Lythgoe Bradford, Martha Sonntag Bradley, Greg Campbell, Adrian W. Cannon, Howard A. Christy, J. Reuben Clark III, James G. Clawson, Curt E. Conklin, Brent D. Corcoran, Kathleen Latham Darley, Scott C. Dunn, Andrew F. Ehat, Richard G. Ellsworth, Ronald K. Esplin, Lawrence Foster, Frank W. Fox, Maxine Hanks, Klaus J. Hansen, William G. Hartley, Martin B. Hickman, Norris Hundley, Howard W. Hunter, Jeffery O. Johnson, G. Kevin Jones, Lynne Watkins Jorgensen, Brian Kagel, Scott G. Kenney, Howard R. Lamar, Stanford J. Layton, James Wirthlin McConkie II, Mark J. Malcolm, David E. Miller, Thomas S. Monson, Miriam B. Murphy, L. Jackson Newell, Linda King Newell, Elbert Eugene Peck, Richard D. Poll, Ronald Priddis, Daniel H. Rector, Allen D. Roberts, Richard W. Sadler, Patricia Lyn Scott, Marianne Clark Sharp, Jan Shipps, E. Gary Smith, Peggy Fletcher Stack, Susan Staker, Charles D. Tate, Jr., Robert K. Thomas, S. Lyman Tyler, Laura Wadley, Bryan Waterman, Jean Bickmore White, David J. Whittaker, R. Hal Williams, and Larry Wimmer. They have not always agreed with my conclusions, and I have not always accepted their critiques, but this is a better study because of the dialogue between us. Nevertheless, I alone am responsible for the content and interpretations of this study.

Salt Lake City
November 1996

CHAPTER 1

The Twin Charges
of the Apostleship

Conflict between any religion's spiritual aspirations and its day-to-day institutional functioning is inevitable. Mormonism is no exception, as stated in the authorized biography of a president of the Church of Jesus Christ of Latter-day Saints: "With the kind of strong-minded men called as General Authorities, differences of opinion [are] inevitable."[1] The necessary compromises and complexities are most evident where the most important decisions are made: the quorums of the First Presidency and Twelve Apostles. But occasional conflict also affects other councils throughout the church generally, regionally, and locally.

This chapter deals with the potential tension and conflict inherent in the charismatic calling of the Quorum of the Twelve as special witnesses of the risen Christ and the requirement that they should be united in all of their decisions. Discussed briefly here, but in greater detail in subsequent chapters, is how this dual charge of charisma and unity works itself out in the day-to-day operations of the church.

Special Charismatic Witnesses

In 1835 Joseph Smith and Oliver Cowdery emphasized to the newly organized Quorum of the Twelve Apostles that their calling was charismatic, evangelical, and also institutional. Of the three, the charismatic definition of the apostleship was the earliest, going back to 1829.[2] Cowdery told the new apostles: "It is necessary that you receive a testimony from heaven for yourselves; so that you can bear testimony to the truth of the Book of Mormon, and that you have seen the face of God." Then he continued, "That is more than the testimony of an angel. . . . Never cease striving until you have seen God face to face."[3] Cowdery acknowledged that most of the new apostles had depended on visions of others for their faith and suggested that some might even be skeptical of visions. Thus it was not necessary to see Jesus to be chosen as an apostle. However, once ordained each man had a lifelong obligation to seek this charismatic experience: a vision of deity. Some apostles from 1835 onward reported having had such visions before their ordination. Apostles in the nineteenth century referred publicly to their visionary witness.

1

The obligation to seek visionary confirmation continued throughout the nineteenth century. Abraham H. Cannon wrote in 1889 that the "charge" given him and two other new apostles included "the privileges of having the ministration of angels, and of seeing the Savior Himself; of hearing the voice of God as audibly as we hear a man's voice . . ."[4] A year later Lorenzo Snow said the apostles "should, if we sought it, live to see the Savior in the flesh."[5] As a result of this consistent emphasis in the nineteenth century, some LDS apostles, including Orson Pratt and Heber J. Grant, felt inadequate because they had not had such encounters.[6]

In the twentieth century, charismatic apostleship changed in several ways. First, the "charge" at ordination no longer obligated apostles to seek visions. Second, the Presidency and apostles began down-playing the importance of these experiences. Third, apostles began speaking of a non-visionary "special witness of Christ" by the Holy Ghost in terms which allowed listeners to conclude that the apostles referred to an actual appearance of deity. Fourth, apostles were reluctant to discuss their visionary experiences publicly. Fifth, evidence indicates that a decreasing number of apostles experienced visions before or after ordination.

The change in the apostolic "charge" apparently began with the appointment of Reed Smoot as an apostle in 1900. General church authorities had long regarded him as "reliable in business, but [he] has little or no faith."[7] President Lorenzo Snow blessed him to receive "the light of the Holy Ghost" so that he could bear testimony of Jesus Christ and Joseph Smith. That was an extraordinary departure from the apostolic charge as given since 1835.[8]

The lessening of charismatic obligation continued during Joseph F. Smith's administration. In 1903 the "charge" to new apostle George Albert Smith spoke of his obligations to attend quorum meetings, to sustain the First Presidency and Twelve's leadership, to express his views "boldly" in quorum meetings, and to lead an exemplary life. There was no mention of visions. In 1907 Francis M. Lyman instructed newly ordained Anthony W. Ivins: "The Twelve are the Special witnesses of Jesus Christ & should be able to testify that he lives even *as if* he had been seen by them" (emphasis added).[9]

Twentieth-century apostles began applying this "as if" approach to their spoken testimonies. Usually this involved wording their "special witness" of Christ in a way that encouraged listeners to assume the leader has had a more dramatic encounter with the divine than actually claimed. Apostle Boyd K. Packer acknowledges that some Mormons have become impatient with those carefully worded apostolic testimonies and ask: "Why cannot it be said in plainer words? Why aren't they more explicit and more descriptive. Cannot the Apostles say more." He dismisses this objection as seeking "for a witness to be given in some new and dramatic and different way."[10]

Sometimes LDS leaders made specific claims for charisma that exceeded their experiences. As early as 1860 Apostle Orson Hyde had claimed that upon organizing the First Presidency in 1847, all the apostles heard the voice of God which produced a physical "shock that alarmed the neighborhood." By contrast, Apostle Wilford Woodruff "did not remember any particular manifestations at the time of the organization of the Presidency."[11] As church president after 1918, Heber J. Grant told general conferences that as a newly ordained apostle, "I seemed to see, and I seemed to hear" a heavenly meeting involving his deceased father and Joseph Smith.[12] However, decades earlier Grant told the Twelve privately that "although he had always desired to see his father in a dream or vision that he had never been allowed to enjoy this privilege." Concerning Grant's public claims while church president, his scholarly biographer has noted that Grant later acknowledged: "I really saw and heard nothing."[13] Making "faith-promoting" claims that exceeded actual experience became such a problem in the twenty-five-year service of general authority Paul H. Dunn that the First Presidency required him in 1991 to make a public apology.[14]

Like the charge to Apostle Smith in 1903, the charge to newly ordained Hugh B. Brown in 1958 omitted any reference to a charismatic witness:

> Later, the president gave me what is known as the "charge to the apostles." That charge included a commitment to give all that one has, both as to time and means, to the building of the Kingdom of God; to keep himself pure and unspotted from the sins of the world; to be obedient to the authorities of the church; and to exercise the freedom to speak his mind but always be willing to subjugate his own thoughts and accept the majority opinion—not only to vote for it but to act as though it were his own original opinion after it has been approved by the majority of the Council of the Twelve and the First Presidency.[15]

Likewise there was no encouragement to obtain a visionary witness in the "fourfold charge" given in 1959 to new apostle (and later LDS president) Howard W. Hunter.[16] Unlike the nineteenth-century apostles, modern LDS apostles have no obligation to seek a visionary witness of Jesus Christ. In place of the instruction to seek a vision of Deity is a lengthy charge for modern apostles to be submissive to the majority of the Twelve.

Therefore, the twentieth-century hierarchy began publicly downplaying the necessity of apostolic visions. By the time he became church president, Heber J. Grant had overcome the guilt he had felt as an apostle for not having had a vision. "I have never prayed to see the Savior," he told a tabernacle meeting in 1942. "I have seen so many men fall because of some great manifestations to them."[17] He came to deny knowledge of such experiences for his colleagues: "I know of no instance where the Lord has appeared to an individual since His appearance to the Prophet Joseph Smith."[18] In fact, rather than qualifying a man as a special witness and apostle, visions made one vulnerable to apostasy in Grant's view. His first counselor, J. Reuben Clark, went so far as to dismiss visions as "testimonies of the flesh."[19] On the other hand, Grant's second counselor, David O. McKay, reported many spiritual manifestations, including a dream-vision of Christ.[20]

The twentieth-century Mormon suspicion of charisma is reflected in the LDS church's *Encyclopedia of Mormonism,* which cautions: "It is vital to distinguish authentically revealed visions from self-induced imaginings, wish-fulfilling dreams, errors of perception, satanic deceptions, and pathological hallucination, all of which have been abundant in human history." As an inadvertent comment on Oliver Cowdery's apostolic charge ("Never cease striving until you have seen God face to face"), the article notes: "Spurious visions result from seeking 'signs'; authentic visions usually come unbidden."[21]

Joseph Fielding Smith, the LDS church's apostolic theologian of the twentieth century, redefined the meaning of the "special" witness:

> Every member of the Council of the Twelve Apostles should have, and I feel sure have had, the *knowledge of the resurrection of Jesus Christ.* This does not have to come by *direct visitation* of the Savior, but it does come from the testimony of the Holy Ghost. . . . *The testimony of the Holy Ghost is the strongest testimony that can be given. It is better than a personal visit* [emphasis in original].[22]

This was consistent with Oliver Cowdery's original statements about pre-ordination experiences of Mormon apostles. However, it was a retreat from the charge given at ordination to the apostleship throughout the nineteenth century.

Instead, twentieth-century apostles have maintained that an inward prompting by the Holy Ghost is sufficient basis for their being special witnesses of Christ. For example, Joseph Fielding Smith's own apostolic charge in 1910 made no reference to seeking a visionary special witness.[23] It is rare for a modern LDS apostle to claim a special witness more dramatic than the impressions of the Spirit.

By the early 1980s authorized LDS history reflected this diminished apostolic requirement. In 1983 Deseret Book Company published a history by a Brigham Young University professor of religion who wrote that Cowdery instructed the apostles "to gain a powerful conviction of the divinity of the Savior."[24] Cowdery would not recognize that weak paraphrasing of his actual words: "Never cease striving until you have seen God face to face." The following year, in his 1984 general conference sermon, "Special Witnesses for Christ," First Presidency counselor Gordon B. Hinckley said that each apostle "knows that Jesus is the Christ, the Redeemer and the Savior of mankind. They know these great salient truths because of the power of the Holy Ghost which bears individual witness to them."[25]

This change in emphasis on apostolic visions is evident in the *Encyclopedia of Mormonism*. There is no reference to Cowdery's "charge" to the apostles in articles about him or about the calling of the Quorum of the Twelve in 1835 or about the process of appointing a new apostle. After lengthy discussion of the Twelve's duties, the article makes this comment about charisma: "Members of the Twelve are 'special witnesses' of the name of Jesus Christ in all the world; they possess a knowledge, by revelation, of the literal resurrection of Christ and a knowledge that he directs the affairs of his Church today. That shared conviction unites the Twelve in a bond of unity and love."[26] Repeatedly, the message of the twentieth-century LDS church is that inward conviction rather than outward vision is the basis for being a special witness of Jesus.

The twentieth-century change in charismatic emphasis has directly affected the willingness of recent apostles to speak publicly about their visionary experiences. In the nineteenth century, apostles openly proclaimed their visionary experiences. "I know that Jesus lives, for I have seen him," George Q. Cannon told a general conference in 1896.[27] Before his death in 1901 Lorenzo Snow told his granddaughter that he "actually saw the Savior here in the Temple and talked with Him face to face." The church's official magazine published that testimony.[28]

But by the mid-twentieth century LDS apostles were reluctant to discuss visions. For example, Apostle Marion G. Romney wrote in his diary during the 1960s: "I don't know just how to answer people when they ask the question, 'Have you seen the Lord?' I think that the witness that I have and the witness that each of us [apostles] has, and the details of how it came, are too sacred to tell. I have never told anybody some of the experiences I have had, not even my wife."[29] Nevertheless, as recently as 1989 Apostle David B. Haight publicly affirmed that during "days of unconsciousness" stemming from a health crisis, he had a vision of Christ's crucifixion and resurrection.[30] However, according to his official biography in 1995, whenever asked if he has seen Jesus Christ, Apostle Boyd K. Packer's response is: "I do not tell all I know. If I did, the Lord could not trust me." Such a standard would put Lorenzo Snow, George Q. Cannon, David O. McKay, and David B. Haight under divine condemnation for telling their visionary experiences.[31]

Hugh B. Brown privately related a charismatic experience which seems unprecedented among twentieth-century apostles. Following a decade of service as a counselor in the First Presidency, Brown was released in

1970 and resumed his position in the Quorum of the Twelve. In physical decline and unhappy at his release from the Presidency, Brown had an experience which he related to his nephew:

> He said it was not a vision, but the Lord appeared to him, very informal, the same as I was sitting talking to him. The Lord said, "You have had some difficult times in your life." Uncle Hugh responded, "Yes, and your life was more difficult than any of us have had." In the conversation Uncle Hugh asked when he would be finished here, and the Lord said, "I don't know and I wouldn't tell you if I did." Then He said, "Remain faithful to the end, and everything will be right."[32]

Brown was the only twentieth-century appointee to the Quorum of Twelve to describe a charismatic witness of Christ as a waking appearance. The few others who have reported such experiences have described them as dreams, "night visions," or visions while unconscious with a physical disability.[33] Brown received his "special witness" without a charge or obligation to obtain such at his ordination.

Another explanation for the decreased emphasis on visionary witness is the hectic life of LDS apostles in the late-twentieth century. "Before I became a General Authority I pictured the Brethren sitting at their desks studying the scriptures, writing books, and having hours at a time to meditate upon matters of the kingdom," said Apostle David B. Haight. Instead he discovered "the reality of back-to-back committee assignments; preparation of talks and remarks to be given in various parts of the world to many types of gatherings, as well as those assigned for general conferences; frequent (and often far-flung) travel to stake, region and area conferences; quorum and First Presidency council meetings; incoming calls; interviews; correspondence; emergencies; and ongoing special assignments that make up the regular schedules of the Brethren." Likewise, as an apostle, Gordon B. Hinckley "routinely lamented that he needed more time to think, ponder, and study, and only on rare weekends home could he indulge in such reflection. For the most part, however, he raced from one assignment, appointment, committee, or board meeting to another."[34] With little opportunity for the contemplative life of traditional mystics, LDS apostles currently have limited time in which to follow Oliver Cowdery's original charge: "Never cease striving until you have seen God face to face."

The Requirement for Unanimity

In 1835, the same year Cowdery gave the "general charge" to the new apostles, Joseph Smith received a revelation for all members of the presiding quorums of the church:

And every decision made by either of these quorums, must be by the unanimous voice of the same; that is, every member in each quorum must be agreed to its decisions, in order to make their decisions of the same power or validity one with the other. . . .

The decisions of these quorums or either of them, are to be made in all righteousness, in holiness and lowliness of heart, meekness and long-suffering, and in faith, and virtue, and knowledge, temperance, patience, godliness, brotherly kindness, and charity; because the promise is, if these things abound in them they shall not be unfruitful in the knowledge of the Lord.[35]

The requirement for unanimous decision-making is the administrative application of an earlier revelation on the latter-day economic order: "If ye are not one, ye are not mine" (D&C 38:27).

This 1835 revelation does not advocate compromise or accommodation to achieve a unanimous vote. Instead it mandates a spiritual oneness whereby "the knowledge of the Lord" is obtained. Theoretically, spiritual inspiration and divine revelation prevent conflict within the presiding quorums.

The requirement for administrative harmony was no less binding on apostles than Cowdery's charge for charismatic witness. Just as some LDS apostles have attained the visionary "special witness" and some have not, at times the presiding quorums have functioned in harmony and at other times they have not. Nevertheless, Mormon general authorities regard spiritual unity as a constant goal. As a result, processes which enable single, unanimous decisions have evolved within high-level quorums.

The minutes of presiding quorums available since 1835 show that religious context is pervasive. First, each deliberative meeting (or "council") begins with prayer—sometimes fasting and prayer—for God's guidance. For example, one new apostle reported, "After dressing in temple clothes and forming a prayer circle around the altar, they changed into street clothes and conducted business."[36] Second, in council meetings authorities often quote the injunction of Matthew 6:33 to "seek ye first the Kingdom of God and his righteousness." Third, they remind themselves of their obligations to learn God's will, to receive inspiration and revelation, to unselfishly seek the welfare of the Latter-day Saints, and to arrive at a unanimous decision. "We are not infallible in our judgment, and we err," first counselor J. Reuben Clark told a general conference, "but our constant prayer is that the Lord will guide us in our decisions, and we are trying so to live that our minds will be open to His inspiration."[37]

The hierarchy has developed a variety of strategies to encourage unanimous voting. One important context for all decisions is flexible deference, but not slavish devotion, to precedent. But despite the importance of precedent and the existence of verbatim minutes, authorities rarely ask a quorum secretary to consult long-distant minutes. Instead, they rely on their own memories of previous discussions. With life tenure, quorum members have the benefit of decades of decision-making, "the *unwritten* history of the Church and the workings of government in the minds and experiences of Church leaders."[38]

The dependence on collective memory can lead to redundant decisions. The best example involved the central question of rank in the Quorum of Twelve Apostles. On 5 April 1900 the First Presidency and Twelve decided that apostolic seniority should come from entry into the quorum and not from the date of ordination as an apostle. Because of this decision Joseph F. Smith moved ahead of Brigham Young, Jr., for the first time in thirty-two years and, as a result, became church president instead of Young in 1901.[39]

This 1900 decision repeated the same decision two decades earlier on 29 November 1880. Joseph F. Smith himself recorded in 1880: "it was unanimously agreed that members of the Council of the Twelve should rank according to their ordination into the Council, & not by age nor previous ordination." It is a puzzle why the ranking of the two apostles remained unchanged for nearly twenty years, as if this 1880 decision had never occurred.[40] Nevertheless, the presiding quorums usually prefer to risk redundant decision-making rather than postpone decisions on myriad topics until a secretary can look up previous references.

Respect for precedence is paralleled by deference to authority and seniority, which are similarly conducive to unanimity. This deference is encouraged by a process of open and sometimes protracted discussion. If unanimity is particularly difficult to achieve, such discussions continue for months or years prior to a decision. Each member of the Quorum of the Twelve, as in other quorums, can express his views fully about any matter under discussion. By the time all present have voiced themselves in support or opposition to a measure, voting preferences have usually emerged before the formal call for a vote. If disagreements have surfaced, those in opposition have already been able to recognize that they are a minority and that they should vote contrary to their views to achieve unanimity. But the snowball effect takes place even in preliminary discussions where members speak in order of seniority.

The emphasis on the prerogatives of seniority has increased over time. The Twelve sit in order of rank at their weekly meetings in their council room in the Salt Lake temple as well as on the stand of the tabernacle for semi-annual general conferences.[41] In contrast to their former preeminence as local stake presidents, newly appointed apostles often experience abrupt subordination: "Being a junior member of the Twelve, both in terms of service and age, he at first often drew the most strenuous and, in the eyes of many, less desirable assignments, jeeringly characterized by some of those who followed him in the apostleship as the 'Phoenix in summer and Alaska in winter' cycle."[42]

The formality of ranking carries over into informal situations. Beginning in 1904 the church president instructed apostles to walk through doorways in order of seniority. This then became the practice for entering and exiting elevators and airplanes, as well.[43] In 1993 Apostle Russell M. Nelson told general conference listeners that this doorway-deference is part of "proper priesthood protocol."[44]

It is not surprising that apostles usually speak in order of seniority in council meetings, beginning with the most senior. For example, a church administrator who attended several "temple council" meetings between 1969 and 1985 commented that "there tended to be deference to the senior person who would take a position."[45]

Junior members are subtly encouraged to tailor their comments to coincide with views already expressed. As an apostle Hugh B. Brown "was critical that Brother [Richard L.] Evans did not take a firm stand on anything, [but] he wanted to see which way the majority was going to vote."[46] The more outspoken Marion G. Romney, appointed a general authority in 1941, indicated the frustration of a junior in decision-making: "Some [general authorities], it seemed, were not inclined to yield at all, especially to the reasoning and suggestions of a relatively young Assistant to the Twelve."[47] Also, "because he expressed himself so forcefully as a very junior member of the Council of the Twelve, Henry D. Moyle experienced some gentle chastising from President George Albert Smith" not long after Moyle's 1947 ordination. By contrast, of his service in the Twelve during the 1960s Gordon B. Hinckley has commented: "I was free to speak on any issue, despite the fact that I was a junior member."[48]

In fact, subordinates are not powerless and on occasion have swayed their superiors. As a junior apostle while Ezra Taft Benson was president of the Twelve from 1973 to 1985, Boyd K. Packer said: "You could disagree with President Benson without worrying that there was anything personal to it. We had full discussions on matters without worrying what his viewpoint might be." The most junior apostle in 1985 added that as the Twelve's president, Benson "*listened* to counsel" from his subordinates.[49]

Less often the presiding officer will ask apostles to speak in reverse order, beginning with the most junior member. This encourages greater candor, which was what Harold B. Lee wanted in January 1970 when he asked the apostles to speak in reverse order on whether to set aside automatic succession of the senior apostle to become president of the church.[50]

Negative as well as positive consensus emerges through this process of discussion. Overwhelming opposition is not a problem if the presiding officer is uncommitted to the proposal. He then can call for a vote in such a way that predisposes a unanimously negative outcome. For example, Joseph Smith did this in a meeting with the apostles in 1842: "Moved by the Prophet that all those who are in favor of assisting Bro Robinson in printing the Book of Mormon . . . manifest it by the usual signs, not a hand raised, but every hand was raised in the negative."[51] A unanimously negative vote in the presiding quorums fulfills what a First Presidency secretary calls "the principal [sic] of apostolic unity."[52]

Even a process encouraging consensus and unanimity involves differing views. Unanimity is easiest when there are few alternatives or when the outcome does not appear momentous. Few alternatives can imply that general authorities are acting on insufficient information. After ten years of administrative meetings with the hierarchy, a Brigham Young University president observed: "The main difficulty with the way the brethren make decisions is that they generally operate after having only one side of the story."[53] Notable exceptions were two men who served as counselors to several presidents, J. Reuben Clark and N. Eldon Tanner, who methodically studied various options of any proposal before arriving at decisions.[54]

In order to head off disagreement, general authorities may begin to persuade fellow council members in advance of a meeting. This unofficial lobbying can achieve a unified coalition and streamline formal discussion. It also avoids the risk of unexpected opposition.

In September 1942 after a ten-year dead-lock over which of two men to appoint as Presiding Patriarch, President Heber J. Grant met privately with each of the apostles. He wanted to see if they would agree to end the stand-off by accepting his nomination of a previously unmentioned candidate. Grant obtained individual approval from each member of the quorum and then formally presented this new nomination at the temple meeting, which unanimously accepted the new patriarch.[55]

In January 1980 Apostle Gordon B. Hinckley (then ranked fifth in the quorum) arranged for such pre-vote lobbying concerning a church pamphlet against the Equal Rights Amendment. He and Apostle David B. Haight headed a committee of staff members from the *Ensign* and *New Era* magazines which prepared and revised several drafts of the pamphlet. The night before the Quorum of Twelve was to discuss and vote on the pamphlet, Hinckley had copies delivered to apostles Ezra Taft Benson, Mark E. Petersen, Bruce R. McConkie, and Boyd K. Packer. Hinckley regarded this pre-vote lobbying as necessary because of the magazines' tight printing schedule. The next day the quorum voted to accept the draft and have the pamphlet inserted into the February issues of the magazines.[56]

Strategies for a unanimous vote sometimes fail to eliminate differences. "Even among the Lord's chosen," observed BYU's president after many meetings with church leaders, "there are sometimes sharp divisions of opinion."[57] When open discussion shows marked division of views, the presiding officer may respond in several ways. First, he may take a decided position and then extend the discussion, perhaps into other meetings. This strategy delays a vote until he has succeeded in marshalling unanimity.[58] Second, he may not call for a vote and allow the matter to die, at least for the time being. For example, in 1887 presiding apostle Wilford Woodruff "stated that he should not call a vote on the question, as our quorum was divided right in the middle."[59]

Even strong-willed Brigham Young explained privately in 1865 "that whenever a proposition met with any opposition in the Council he dropped it as not being right to carry out. Unanimity must be had to give any matter force." This is noteworthy in a church leader who publicly claimed that no one "has a more indomitable and unyielding temper than myself."[60]

Tabling items due to dissent continues to be a pattern in the contemporary church. A church administrator commented on his experience from 1969 to 1985:

> If there was controversy, if it was an issue where there was a strong dissent—I didn't see this very often but I did see occasion where there would be a strong dissent on the part of someone. Particularly if it was someone senior that had a strong dissent, normally the item wouldn't be passed with a negative vote. It would be either tabled or deferred until such time as it could be re-addressed with the unanimous support by the entire group.[61]

After Apostle Howard W. Hunter had presided over meetings of the Twelve for nine years, his biographer observed in 1994: "If consensus isn't reached or anyone in the group still has strong feelings about a matter, he will table it rather than force a vote."[62]

Third, the presiding officer may change his own vote to achieve unanimity. As president of the Quorum of Twelve, George Albert Smith did this when the other apostles "overruled" him about a matter in 1944.[63] Fourth, if someone votes against an otherwise unanimous decision, the presiding officer will either ignore the opposing vote or ask the dissenter to join the rest of his quorum on a re-vote.[64]

Fifth, the presiding officer may choose to override in one way or another expected or expressed opposition to his proposal. For example, the First Presidency wanted to make a major change in the church's program for Native Americans but knew Apostle Spencer W. Kimball would oppose it. Therefore, the Presidency waited until the summer of 1969 when Kimball was out of the country on assignment in order to obtain the approval from the rest of the Twelve. At the first temple meeting Kimball attended following his return, first counselor Hugh B. Brown "singled him out for praise of his devotion and service. Elder Kimball decided later the compliments were intended to soften the impact of the decision which had been reached while he was away."[65]

Sixth, a presiding officer may use humor to relax a potentially divisive meeting. For example, David O. McKay had aggravated the "combative" Apostle Harold B. Lee for several years by cutting back on the Welfare Program. Lee, Apostle Marion G. Romney, and the new managing director of the Welfare Program walked into the church president's office without an appointment in 1959 to ask his approval to make an expensive land purchase for the Welfare Program. McKay exclaimed: "Hell's a poppin! What's up, Brethren?"[66]

Throughout the hierarchy's history, presiding officers have adopted each of these six strategies. Sometimes a presiding quorum responds similarly toward a dissenting subordinate quorum.

On occasion church authorities have praised a presiding officer's ability to achieve unanimous votes despite differing opinions. Of Ezra Taft Benson's service as president of the Quorum of the Twelve from 1973 to 1985, Apostle Howard W. Hunter said that Benson "knew how to get open and frank discussion from [the] Brethren and [was] able to direct and control it and arrive at a unanimous decision with everyone united."[67] However, throughout Mormon history some general authorities have regarded such "control" as manipulative.

A unanimous vote may give only superficial fulfillment to the requirement for unanimous agreement. Of his own grudging assent to the wishes of the church president, Counselor J. Reuben Clark said that "'compliance' was not 'unity.'"[68] The more important a general authority regards the subject of his vote, the more difficult it is for him to vote against his convictions. Tension is greatest in the two presiding quorums because decisions here have the greatest impact on the church. But other quorums experience internal dissent, as well, even though they share the obligation of "apostolic unity."

With the pressure for unanimity so great, general authorities sometimes vote against their conscience. For example, when Bishop Newel K. Whitney expressed opposition to an 1846 proposal, Brigham Young related a dream in its support and called for a unanimous vote. The church historian privately noted: "w[h]ether Bishop Whitney's doubts were removed or not, after hearing the dream, [he] voted to [support Young]."[69] In 1887 apostles Wilford Woodruff, Joseph F. Smith, and Franklin D.

Richards admitted "they voted against their own judgment at one of our recent meetings."[70] In 1907 recently appointed David O. McKay described a meeting where "my feelings and will had to submit to those of the majority."[71] Seventy's president J. Golden Kimball remarked that he had to "go right along with the authority, ask no question and await the results," or else "be under the ban."[72]

At the extreme general authorities feel compelled to make their understanding of God's will secondary to their obligation to support their quorum. In a 1900 meeting Apostle Abraham Owen Woodruff observed that church president Lorenzo Snow made a motion he expected to be unpopular. The president had the motion "seconded[,] and again without any chance to express our feelings and judgment[, we] were forced to sustain a motion that some of us were opposed to or be out of harmony with our brethren."

This happened on two matters at the same combined meeting of the Presidency and apostles. In each instance Snow had the controversial motion moved, seconded, and voted on without opportunity for discussion. Of this second occurrence in 1900, Woodruff wrote, "I felt forced to sustain this motion and that is why I did it, knowing that if it were not right the responsibility would not rest on me." In 1902 Woodruff found himself in a conflict of conscience with President Joseph F. Smith. Woodruff told the temple meeting: "I will vote for this because it is the Presidency's wish, not because it is my judgment."[73]

Harmony and unanimity became so important to the twentieth-century hierarchy that some authorities have even assented to what they regarded as violations of God's will. Seventy's president J. Golden Kimball wrote in 1904, "Decadence is taking place in the Church of Jesus Christ of Latter Day Saints and innovations are creeping in which annul the word of God to us." He remained in the hierarchy until his death thirty-four years later.[74] Apostle LeGrand Richards also wrote in 1967: "I always say I am not half as much concerned about pleasing the Lord as I am about pleasing all of the Brethren."[75]

A dramatic example of this occurred during the presidency of David O. McKay. On 12 November 1969 Stanford University refused to participate in athletic competitions with BYU because of the church's refusal to ordain blacks. First Counselor Hugh B. Brown had been on record for six years as favoring an end to this ban.[76] In 1969 he wrote of the denial of priesthood to those of black African ancestry:

> Personally I doubt if we can maintain or sustain ourselves in the position which we seem to have adopted but which has no justification as far as the scriptures are concerned so far as I know. I think we are going to have to change our decision on that. The President says that it can come only by

revelation. If that be true then it will come in due course. I think it is one of the most serious problems confronting us because of course it affects the millions of colored people.

This matter "caused many tense moments, tremendous debate, and unrest," Harold B. Lee's biographer acknowledged, "particularly in the Church leadership ranks." A First Presidency secretary also noted that this Stanford situation "touched off another round of debates as to whether this policy was based on principle or was merely a practice."[77]

In November 1969 Brown privately lobbied Stanford University to delay their decision to boycott BYU. The night before Stanford's announcement, Brown told the university's vice-president that he expected the church to drop this restriction.[78] Shortly after Stanford's decision Brown "was able to get a proposal allowing full priesthood for Blacks approved by the Quorum of the Twelve Apostles." With church president David O. McKay unable to function, the way was now open for the two counselors and the Quorum of Twelve to issue a joint declaration granting priesthood to those of black African ancestry. Second counselor N. Eldon Tanner confided to BYU's president Ernest Wilkinson on 3 December 1969 that "a special committee was to report on the Negro situation." Wilkinson labeled his memorandum of the conversation as "*ULTRA CONFIDENTIAL*." Apostle Harold B. Lee, an increasingly powerful member of the Twelve, was absent during his quorum's decision and rejected it upon his return.[79] Lee not only opposed giving priesthood to blacks, he also held "the traditional belief as revealed in the Old Testament that the races ought to be kept together."[80]

Lee persuaded the Quorum of Twelve to rescind its vote. Then he pressured the first counselor to sign a statement which reaffirmed the priesthood restriction on blacks "in view of confusion that has arisen." Brown's grandson relates how the first counselor surrendered his deeply felt convictions to Apostle Lee:

> Grandfather managed to add language to Elder Lee's statement endorsing full civil rights for all citizens, but he still resisted signing the statement. However, he suffered from advanced age and the late stages of Parkinson's disease and was ill with the Asian flu. With Grandfather in this condition, Elder Lee brought tremendous pressure to bear upon him, arguing that with President McKay incapacitated Grandfather was obligated to join the consensus within the Quorum of the Twelve. Grandfather, deeply ill, wept as he related this story to me just before he signed the statement that bore his and President Tanner's names.

Lee's reaffirmation of the restriction was a collaborative effort involving Neal A. Maxwell, Gordon B. Hinckley, and G. Homer Durham. To this committee-produced document, Brown made his addition which endorsed civil rights. Dated 15 December 1969, this extraordinarily important First Presidency document was signed only by the two counselors.[81]

Brown did not accept gracefully the defeat of his effort to reverse the church's ban against African Americans. Less than a week after he had reluctantly signed Lee's statement, Brown told a San Francisco newspaper reporter that the church's priesthood ban against blacks "will change in the not too distant future." Known for "his fiery temper," Lee privately exploded on 27 December, saying that Brown had been "talking too much."[82]

Lee's biographer observes that because "misleading announcements in the media caused much confusion during the Christmas holidays of 1969, the statement, which earlier had been circulated to Church leaders in missions, stakes, and wards, was released nationally. It appeared in print for the Latter-day Saints to read in the *Church News*, on Saturday, January 10, 1970."[83] The most recent "misleading announcement" was a published claim that Harold B. Lee was responsible for the Presidency's statement. Brown was probably also the source for that disclosure.[84] Unaware of all these discussions due to his mental incapacity, President McKay died a week after the statement's publication.

Not surprisingly, there was no change in this policy of priesthood restriction during the presidencies of McKay's two successors. Lee was first counselor to McKay's immediate successor Joseph Fielding Smith, and Lee the set the administrative agenda. When asked about the priesthood restriction against blacks on the day he became LDS president in July 1972, Harold B. Lee announced that he "intended to stand by and wait until the Lord speaks."[85] That passivity did not result in a revelation, and Lee's support of racial segregation did not predispose him to actively seek such a revelation.

Five years after Lee's death, church president Spencer W. Kimball in June 1978 extended priesthood ordination to all Mormon men of black African ancestry.[86] For decades he had been troubled about this racial restriction,[87] and was among the apostles who unsuccessfully voted for this proposal eight-and-a-half years earlier. This change in LDS policy was unique in two respects: the length of time it took for the church president to indicate his intentions to his associates in the hierarchy; and the care with which he obtained their gradual assent before he actually put the proposal to a vote.

As recently revealed by a secretary to the First Presidency, in early 1977 Kimball began "to focus on it intensely" and then decided to end the priesthood restriction in the near future. Remarkably, the church president indicated this to a faithful Mormon of black African ancestry, but not to any of his associates in the LDS hierarchy.

At the cornerstone-laying ceremony for the Brazilian temple on 9 March 1977, Kimball privately told Helvecio Martins to prepare himself to receive the priesthood. He pointedly asked if Martins "understood the implications of what President Kimball had said," and the African-Brazilian "said he understood."[88] Kimball waited more than a year before he informed any general authority of his intentions.

Although he was keeping his own counsel, Spencer W. Kimball began laying the groundwork for ending the priesthood ban. On 22 February 1978 he issued a First Presidency letter to all stake and mission leaders: "If there is no evidence to indicate that a man has Negro blood, you would not be justified in withholding the priesthood and temple blessings from him, if he is otherwise worthy."[89] This stopped denial of priesthood merely on the basis of black African "appearance," yet only the church president and a Brazilian black Mormon knew that this was a prelude to ending the ban entirely—and soon.

On 23 March 1978 "President Kimball advised his counselors that he had had a wakeful night struggling with the question of priesthood restrictions and felt they should be lifted." He and his counselors discussed the matter for a month before he informed the Twelve. He asked them to join the First Presidency in prayer as a group and individually about the matter. Kimball met privately with individual apostles who expressed their "individual thoughts" about his suggestion to end the priesthood ban.[90]

After discussing this in several temple meetings and private discussions, Kimball wrote a statement "in longhand removing all priesthood restrictions on blacks" and presented it to his counselors on 30 May. He then asked his counselors and the apostles "to fast and pray that the Lord would make his mind and will clear in this matter" at their temple meeting on 1 June. At the temple council that day "the feeling was unanimous that the time had come to lift the restrictions."[91] In the prayer circle of the men on this occasion, Apostle Bruce R. McConkie testified that "we all heard the same voice, received the same message, and became personal witnesses that the word received was the mind and will of the Lord," while Apostle David B. Haight affirmed: "Each was witness to a transcendent heavenly event." Gordon B. Hinckley added this clarification: "No voice audible to our physical ears was heard. But the voice of the spirit whispered into our minds and our very souls." [92]

On 7 June 1978 Kimball informed his counselors that "through inspiration he had decided to lift the restrictions on priesthood." In the meantime he had asked three apostles (including Boyd K. Packer) to prepare "suggested wording for the public announcement of the decision."[93] The First Presidency used the three documents to prepare a fourth preliminary statement which was "then reviewed, edited, and approved by the First Presidency. This document was taken to the council meeting with the Twelve on Thursday, June 8, 1978." The apostles made additional "minor editorial changes" in the nearly final statement which was then presented to all general authorities the next day, just hours before its public announcement.[94]

It had been an extraordinary administrative journey for a momentous change in the LDS church. The Presidency's secretary adds that when the general authorities ended this race-based restriction, "it seemed to relieve them of a subtle sense of guilt they had felt over the years."[95]

However, the hierarchy's decision-making has not always been unanimous or pleasant. In the nineteenth century apostles exchanged accusations of "sycophants & todyism."[96] At the turn of the century J. Golden Kimball candidly complained that among the general authorities, "some men will *kiss* a mans *ass* to get to suck a sugar *tit*. I would rather have Courage to express my honest convictions."[97] In 1939 first counselor J. Reuben Clark bluntly opposed this fawning sycophancy in the hierarchy: "I admonished President Grant that people were prone to say to him what people thought he wanted to hear." Whether out of a sincere desire to please or for self-advancement, flattery and sycophancy continue to influence decision-making.[98]

In contrast, some equally devout general authorities have maintained solitary, if usually fleeting, dissent against the rest of their quorum. In 1897 J. Golden Kimball complained that senior president Seymour B. Young "stood out for an hour, and rather unwillingly succumbed" to the expressed views of the rest of the First Council of Seventy.[99] Young himself reported in 1903 that B. H. Roberts cast the first negative vote in the history of the First Council of Seventy since its establishment in 1835.[100] In 1893 Apostle Francis M. Lyman's dissent blocked a decision by the Quorum of the Twelve for seven-and-a-half hours.[101]

Loyal dissent continued as the church began massive expansion following World War II. After his appointment to the First Council of Seventy in 1945, S. Dilworth Young stated his philosophy: "You must work through the Spirit. If that leads you into conflict with the program of the Church, you follow the voice of the Spirit."[102] After Spencer W. Kimball and Mark E. Petersen had cast the only dissenting votes in a 1946 temple meeting, Kimball moved to make the vote unanimous. "I am swallowing my pride and disappointment," he confided to his diary.[103] In a 1952 joint meeting of the First Presidency and Quorum of Twelve, Apostle Henry D. Moyle was the lone voice against adding lace to temple garments for women. He also later changed his vote.[104] When the First Presidency proposed extending federal Social Security coverage to church employees in 1957, Apostle

Harold B. Lee "created tension" by voting against the proposal, and Moyle privately criticized his friend for being "in rebellion."[105]

Dissent has also occurred within the First Presidency. During a temple meeting in 1900 second counselor Joseph F. Smith voted against the rest of the First Presidency and full Quorum of Twelve Apostles.[106] During the presidency of David O. McKay, first counselor J. Reuben Clark occasionally cast the only negative vote, "after which President McKay asked for another vote of all those who would be willing to make it unanimous. On this vote President Clark voted in the affirmative."[107] Of this grudging compliance Clark told secretaries in the First Presidency's office: "I know who the President of the Church is, I know what his authority is, I know what he wants and that is what he shall have, even if I don't like it."[108]

General authorities sometimes pay a price for candor when a presiding officer resents contrary views. In an 1882 council meeting President John Taylor "then went for those [apostles] who had spoken against his article [in the council meeting] the day before and he showed much feeling."[109] At a meeting in 1899 church president Lorenzo Snow told Apostle Abraham Owen Woodruff, "Never mind [–] you are a young man yet, let some of your seniors speak." Apostle Anthon H. Lund commented: "It was a hard rebuke for poor Owen. He is such a good fellow and what he said he meant, but not in a way to go against the President."[110] Woodruff wrote: "Prest. Snow gave me about the most complete sitting down I ever got in my life because he misunderstood me."[111] In 1908 the Twelve's president and the church president "severely reproved" apostles Hyrum M. Smith and Orson F. Whitney for dissenting from a decision that had been jointly approved by the First Presidency and rest of the apostles.[112]

Subordinates have sometimes been assigned to implement decisions they previously opposed and only reluctantly assented to—perhaps as an incentive for future acquiescence. For example, Apostle Orson Pratt repeatedly opposed organizing a new First Presidency in November-December 1847. Brigham Young had him make the public announcement regarding the new presidency.[113] When the Presidency assigned Apostle Mark E. Petersen in 1960 to form the stake he voted against organizing, Second Counselor Henry D. Moyle quipped: "Funny church, isn't it?"[114]

A presiding officer's quiet disapproval of dissent or his open censure of subordinates is an obvious restraint on "open" discussion in presiding quorums. Therefore church authorities sometimes decline to speak or even vote in council meetings. This abstention avoids the necessity of choosing among voicing unpopular views, casting the only negative vote, or voting against conscience. "I had previously stated plainly my objections," Joseph F. Smith wrote in 1880 concerning a proposal by church president John Taylor to the apostles, "so now I held my peace."[115] Faced with Brigham Young Jr.'s refusal to vote on a motion to hire a non-Mormon professor at Brigham Young Academy in Provo in 1896, Counselor Smith "moved to make the vote unanimous" in a temple meeting, but Young again abstained. "It is the first time I have failed to go with my leaders," he wrote. "I went my way sorrowfully." However, the next day, the First Presidency reversed the decision because church president Wilford Woodruff admitted that "he felt just as Bro Young did all the time the subject was under consideration."[116] First counselor Anthon H. Lund wrote in 1917, "I did not render a decision as I would not like to be opposite in opinion to my fellow-counselor."[117] During two Presidency meetings in 1933 newly appointed counselor J. Reuben Clark declined to voice strenuous disagreement with first counselor Anthony W. Ivins.[118]

Abstentions continue into contemporary church administration. Hugh B. Brown noted that several apostles abstained from voting in 1965 when President David O. McKay presented Thorpe B. Isaacson as an extra counselor without previously consulting his other counselors or the Quorum of Twelve. This occurred again in 1967 when McKay announced he was ordaining Alvin R. Dyer an apostle without having consulted the Quorum of Twelve in advance.[119]

During the 1960s and 1970s many authorities abstained from participation. Harold B. Lee and Boyd K. Packer, two strong-willed church leaders, sometimes abstained when they disagreed with the rest of the hierarchy. Lee even "intentionally stayed away" from meetings where he knew he would be outvoted.[120] After the sharp-tongued Lee became a First Presidency counselor in 1970, other authorities declined to express their views "because the Brethren were afraid that the First Presidency might think otherwise."[121]

Abstaining is only partially successful in avoiding confrontation. Apostle John Henry Smith noted, "Prest. Geo. Q. Cannon spoke to me today about my not voting with my quorum on many occasions and thought I was not doing right."[122] Ironically, two years later Cannon refused to vote on a matter: "Prest. L[orenzo]. S[now]. ordered a piece into [the Deseret] 'News' [newspaper] last evening *without his 1st Counselor's vote* but *with the votes of all others present.*"[123]

The presiding quorums have sometimes tailored their minutes to fulfill the requirement of unanimous voting. Personal diaries are usually the only source for instances in which general authorities have abstained from voting or have voted in dissent. It is easier to sanitize minutes than for general authorities to contain their anger after losing a vote. When President George Albert Smith vetoed Apostle Harold B. Lee's attempted "correlation" of church programs in 1948, Lee ridiculed the church president's views as "sentimental objections."[124] After a 1963 council meeting which voted against one of his proposals, Boyd K. Packer spoke "with venom in his voice, trembling."[125] While they acknowledge that Packer previously was "less than diplomatic," "dogmatic, bigoted," "offended people," and got "agitated and lashed out" as a church administrator, his biographer and Apostle Neal A. Maxwell have recently said that Packer "has grown" out of such behavior. Apostle Dallin H. Oaks adds that Packer "exerts his personal authority and influence in a leadership way that is very much felt in the Council of the Twelve." Packer is currently acting president of the Twelve.[126]

In fact, Boyd K. Packer is a modern example that subordinate general authorities are far from powerless. Since his appointment as an Assistant to the Twelve Apostles in 1961, Elder Packer has been a strident and persuasive voice at LDS headquarters. A member of the Quorum of Seventy described Boyd K. Packer as "vindictive" toward subordinates who challenged his views during deliberative meetings. After one such episode, Elder Packer thereafter was barely civil toward the other general authority. Five years later Packer publicly humiliated this man during a mission presidents' seminar, indicating that their previous encounter in the council meeting was the reason.[127] In 1983 Howard W. Hunter (then one of the senior apostles) said that he sometimes acquiesced to the strident views of unnamed junior members of the Quorum of the Twelve. Described by his biographer as "a modest man, unassuming and undemanding," Elder Hunter said he preferred not to express even deeply held convictions about a matter, rather than disrupt the spirit of a temple council meeting by "tangling" with such "zealots" among his subordinates.[128] Apostle Hunter did not identify which apostles he regarded as combative, but in 1993 Apostle Oaks called Apostle Packer "a grizzly bear" as a church administrator.[129] As of 1995 his official biography acknowledged that some of his associates at LDS headquarters still regard Packer "only as stubborn and immovable."[130]

Despite such conflicts, church leaders regard the final result of their deliberations as revelation. Counselor Hugh B. Brown once explained:

> When a question arises today, we work over the details and come up with an idea. It is submitted to the First Presidency and Twelve, thrashed out, discussed and rediscussed until it seems right. Then, kneeling together in a circle in the temple, they seek divine guidance and the president says, "I feel to say this is the will of the Lord." That becomes a revelation. It is usually not thought necessary to publish or proclaim it as such, but this is the way it happens.[131]

Because the final decision is revelation by definition, a First Presidency secretary has explained that the authorities "are silent thereafter about any contrary opinions expressed during the discussion."[132]

CHAPTER 2

Tensions among the First Presidency and Quorum of the Twelve

Through revelation Joseph Smith defined the duties and jurisdiction of the LDS hierarchy's presiding quorums. He also provided context for their work: revelation, harmony, and unity. But as one observer noted, whereas Joseph Smith formed a hierarchy to "spread the honors and responsibilities," he "soon found himself in the center of an internecine battle for power."[1] One thinks of the disputes between ancient apostles Paul and Peter (Gal. 2:11-14). As a product of human relationships, conflict is inevitable in any institution.

While ego and disaffection can create tension, disruptions often result from conscientious differences. When the hierarchy is in disagreement, church authorities on every side feel the support of God, the scriptures, or necessity of circumstances.

But conflict provides insight into the nature of an institution. Dispute indicates areas that are still being negotiated. Personality differences can intensify doctrinal and jurisdictional ambiguities.

This approach may leave the false impression that the presiding councils of the LDS church are in a constant state of disagreement. On the contrary, an equally comprehensive and representative study could be titled "Harmony" or "Camaraderie" that would just as accurately illustrate those qualities among the general authorities. For example, Apostle John Taylor wrote in his diary in 1845: "I meet with many things in the world that have a tendency to depress me; but when I meet with my brethren, I feel well, for there is the spirit of God, the spirit of Peace, and the spirit of union."[2] A century later recently appointed apostle Ezra Taft Benson wrote in his diary: "I don't think there's a body of men anywhere on the face of the earth who are as close to one another as the Twelve. We have differences of opinion, certainly, yet there's such a spirit of oneness and unity. It's impossible to describe."[3] Likewise Apostle Howard W. Hunter's 1967 diary recorded that "there is kindness, unity and love" in "the meeting of this council in the temple."[4]

21

Traditional Mormon histories have emphasized the hierarchy's harmony with little or no reference to conflict. The explicit intent of such histories is to make the Mormon experience "faith-promoting," but they do so by sanitizing it of human realities.[5] An extreme but significant example is the church's *Encyclopedia of Mormonism* which gives virtually no information about the processes by which the presiding quorums arrive at decisions.[6] On the other hand, this study emphasizes less explored dimensions of a complex dynamic.

The Church President and His Counselors

Usually comprised of only three men, the LDS First Presidency has experienced open conflict among its members. Only four months after Joseph Smith first chose counselors in 1832, a significant disruption occurred. While the oldest (and first) counselor Jesse Gause was on a mission and the church president was away from Kirtland, Ohio, second counselor Sidney Rigdon evidently tired of being third in command. The diary of Reynolds Cahoon described Rigdon's unsuccessful effort to seize control of the church: "Thursday 4 Oclock Met with some of the Br for Meting [sic] and at the meting Br Sidney remarked that he had a revelation from the Lord & said that the kingdom was taken from the Church and left with him [—] fryday Br Hiram went after Joseph[.] When he came he affirmed that the kingdom was ours & never should be taking [sic] from the faithful."[7] Smith disfellowshipped Rigdon (deprived him of all church privileges) on 6 July 1832. He ordained Rigdon to the high priesthood "the Second time" on 28 July after he had "repented like Peter of old."[8]

Ten years later polygamy put Smith in conflict with every other member of the First Presidency. Assistant president John C. Bennett's free-love arrangements exceeded Smith's authorization, and Smith publicly excommunicated him in 1842. First counselor Rigdon withdrew into sullen inactivity for two years after Smith unsuccessfully proposed polygamy to his daughter and then published affidavits that she had been immoral with Bennett. Rigdon's estrangement nearly lost him his position in 1843.[9]

Associate President Hyrum Smith was so opposed to his brother's polygamy that he sought to entrap him in a compromising situation. Only a few months after Hyrum became reconciled in May 1843, polygamy alienated Smith's second counselor William Law. Law's disaffection contributed to the murder of both Smiths in 1844.[10] No other president of the LDS church had such troubled relationships, but tensions have occurred.

For reasons still unclear Brigham Young distanced himself from his lifelong friend and first counselor Heber C. Kimball during the 1860s. Evidence of this distance can be seen in a prayer circle meeting of the First Presidency and apostles in January 1860. Kimball remarked, "I never saw T[homas]. D. Brown in that Circle but what I felt sorry to see him there. President Young said He would never have been there If you had not Recommended him for I had not Confidence enough in him." Then Young and others laughed at him.[11] By 1862 Kimball sought personal revelation that he would not be removed as first counselor.[12] Four years later in 1866 when Young and four members of the Quorum of Twelve ordained Kimball's step-son Joseph F. Smith an apostle, Young temporarily withheld knowledge of the ordination from his first counselor.[13]

The third and fourth presidents of the LDS church had very different relationships with their counselors. John Taylor bristled at anything less than submission from his counselors. During one meeting of the First Presidency, his second counselor Joseph F. Smith said, "I have my opinion." "Have it," Taylor snapped, "but keep it to yourself."[14] After Taylor's death his former first counselor, George Q. Cannon, said "he could not influence the ideas or opinions of Prest Taylor." Joseph F. Smith similarly remarked that "there was no power on earth that could bend the will of John Taylor."[15]

In contrast the next church president Wilford Woodruff was totally compliant with these same two men. Apostle John W. Taylor startled a congregation in 1895 by saying, "As well might a baby be placed at the head of the Church as Pres. Woodruff without the aid of Presidents Cannon and Smith."[16]

Fifth church president Lorenzo Snow chose Cannon and Smith in 1898, but they were in quiet conflict with him on two matters. Snow rapidly locked horns with Cannon over church finances. Less than three months after becoming president, Snow felt it necessary to repudiate his counselor's activities in front of the Quorum of the Twelve: "President Lorenzo Snow did take Bro. Geo. Q. Cannon to task for over hopefull [sic] Manner in which he had spoken of our financial Condition."[17] Four months later Snow restated his dissatisfaction with Cannon's handling of church monies.[18] Cannon's son later referred to the "enmity of Pres. Snow, who accused him [George Q. Cannon] of being the cause of the Church's financial difficulties." As the ultimate evidence of tension in Snow's presidency, he publicly denied at Cannon's 1901 funeral that the first counselor had influenced recent church decisions.[19]

Snow did not perceive himself in conflict with his second counselor Joseph F. Smith. However, from 1900 to 1901 Smith secretly authorized the performance of new plural marriages which church president Snow refused to permit.[20] Six months after Snow's death, "Prest Smith gave his experience with the different Presidents. He had been warmly attached to all of them but would not say that about President Snow who had constantly kept him at arm's length."[21]

When sustained as church president in 1901, Joseph F. Smith made the unusual public promise to include his two counselors in all his decisions and not ignore them as he said other church presidents had. General authority J. Golden Kimball, Smith's step-brother, took offense at those remarks: "To publicly arraign and criticize men that are his superiors in every way is to me a great mistake and will not add one cubit to his strength or height."[22]

In most respects Smith and succeeding presidents Heber J. Grant and George Albert Smith fully involved their counselors in all decision-making. In fact, George Albert Smith unassumingly walked from his own office down the hall to his first counselor's office to ask advice, and Counselor J. Reuben Clark had to remind him, "President Smith, you don't come to me, I come to you. You are the president and I am the counselor. When you want me, you call me."[23] Nevertheless, George Albert Smith was not totally deferential to his first counselor's judgment. On at least one occasion he immediately countermanded instructions Clark had just given to the apostles during a temple meeting.[24]

However, a more significant issue arose because George Albert Smith allowed his strong-willed daughter, Emily Smith Stewart, to function as his *ersatz* counselor in decision-making. Sometimes she even sat by the president's side and openly prompted his decisions. An LDS president, assistant secretary in the Presidency's office, and family member later confirmed that this irritated Counselor Clark.[25]

One matter revealed Stewart's sense of her own administrative powers. In 1947 she by-passed the First Presidency's financial secretary, the church purchasing agent, the Presidency counselors, and the entire Quorum of the Twelve by ordering four Persian carpets ($33,675) for the offices of the First Presidency and Quorum of Twelve. No one but Stewart and President Smith knew of the purchase until ZCMI delivered the first carpet to the church office building. Clark objected that "we had no right to spend the tithing of the people for these expensive rugs." To bolster that argument he also told Smith that the carpet's colors were dull. The parsimonious counselor cancelled the order. Nevertheless, two years later Clark accepted defeat when Stewart again by-passed the committee on tithing expenditures by ordering a Persian carpet for the First Presidency's office. He drew the line at her demand to receive half of the ZCMI salesman's 1 percent commission.[26]

Tensions involving Stewart were tame compared to the situation following George Albert Smith's death in 1951. The new church president, David O. McKay, often ignored his counselors totally in decision-making. In April 1951 McKay began his presidency by demoting J. Reuben Clark from first to second counselor. "How could any mortal take a blow like that and stand?" wrote Apostle Spencer W. Kimball of Clark. "But he did."[27] Before the public announcement some apostles worried that "it will kill Brother Clark," and that "the people will not be reconciled" to Clark's demotion. McKay publicly denied that the change was a demotion or that there was "any rift" between them. However, church leaders and bureaucrats knew that Clark had been demoted because of the disagreements they had experienced for years as First Presidency counselors.[28]

It was not long before this tension became public knowledge. Nationally-syndicated newspaper columnist Drew Pearson interviewed prominent Utahns and published this assessment: "Today, at the age of 80, Clark is the most reactionary apostle in the Mormon church—so reactionary that when McKay became president he promptly demoted Clark from his place as No. 1 counselor."[29] Years later McKay responded to a complaint about Clark's negativism with the comment: "How do you think I have gotten along with him? If I ever had any inspiration it was when I selected Stephen L Richards as my first counselor, against all precedent."[30] For sixteen years McKay had been subordinate to then first counselor Clark, but "their roles of domination and subordination had been reversed."[31] Now McKay was in charge.

Church finance was the area of sharpest conflict between the new McKay presidency and its hold-over counselor Clark. For years Clark had prided himself in reining in church investments and expenditures, yet both accelerated as soon as McKay became president. By the early 1950s Clark adopted a glum resignation in discussions with other members of the Presidency. In a typical comment Clark said: "If you two brethren feel that way, of course I will go along with you. I am not going to stand out. If you feel that way, I will go along." In April 1955 he reluctantly agreed to allow McKay and Richards to invest in municipal government bonds, even though he regarded this as a speculative use of tithing funds.[32]

In September 1956 Clark was not subtle about his opposition, since the church's investment in government bonds suffered a $1 million loss in just a few months. He told Richards that "he knew I never had approved of the investment of Church funds in Governments or in other securities; but that I had gone along with him and Brother McKay on this matter." Then Clark said simply that he would not oppose the rest of the Presidency in approving a contract to set aside two-thirds of tithing income for continued investment, despite the recent losses. By 1959 Clark's festering dissatisfaction led him to make this extraordinary statement to the April general conference: "wherever you begin to make great expenditures of money, there is always some lack of wisdom, sometimes a lack of foresight, occasionally, oh so occasionally in this Church, a lack of integrity."[33] Conflict over changes in the church's Welfare Program also aligned second counselor Clark, Apostle Harold B. Lee, and Apostle Marion G. Romney against first counselor Richards.[34]

It is not surprising that McKay excluded his dissenting counselor as much as possible from decision-making. That exclusion was nearly total during the last two years of Clark's life. "I don't have any influence in the Church any more," Clark told the non-LDS governor of Utah.[35] Clark's successor, Hugh B. Brown, echoed that observation: "President Clark had been severely tried by the fact that President McKay was making a number of decisions without referring to him in any way."[36]

However, McKay was occasionally at odds with nearly all of his counselors. His closest friend was Richards, with whom, it was said, he shared the love of David and Jonathan.[37] Still in 1957 Richards was "quite incensed" that McKay claimed he favored a decision the president alone had made. Richards added that McKay's published statement was "the silliest thing I ever heard."[38]

In the early 1960s McKay became alienated from his strong-willed counselor Henry D. Moyle. Appointed as second counselor in 1959, Moyle assumed direction of church finances and promoted massive church spending, as well as a worldwide missionary baseball program to convert teenage boys. Fellow apostle Harold B. Lee described him as "an aggressive mover."[39] Moyle's former mentor, Clark, unsuccessfully opposed Moyle's expenditures. McKay and Moyle brushed aside Clark's caution about the missionary program in April 1961: "We should not become too engrossed in the number of baptisms to the expense of actual conversions."[40] Clark sometimes described himself as "a croaking raven" because of his pessimism, but his dire warning about Moyle's programs was confirmed less than two years after Clark's death.

The church issued its last public statement of expenditures at the April 1959 conference two months before Moyle's appointment. As soon as he was a counselor, Moyle set aside the current budget and launched a massive increase, especially in the construction of new buildings. Six months later the church had spent $8 million more than it had received in all of 1959—an extraordinary development compared to its $7 million surplus at the end of 1958. Because the published report of expenditures included the building program, Moyle persuaded McKay not to publish even an abbreviated accounting of church spending. There has been no itemized financial report since.[41]

This policy reversed Clark's insistence on full financial disclosure to the public. He had announced to general conferences that the church had spending deficits of $100,000 in 1937 and nearly $500,000 in 1938. In his view, voluntary disclosure of deficits encouraged greater austerity on the part of leaders at headquarters and elsewhere.[42]

What his former protégé Moyle did with church finances in the remaining two years of Clark's titular counselorship went far beyond his ability to control or comprehend. Even the powerful apostle Harold B. Lee waged a losing battle in what he called "my stubborn resistance to the principle of 'deficit spending,' supposedly justified in the hope of increasing the tithing of the Church to cover the deficit."[43]

Moyle could not understand those who lacked his expansive vision. The managing director of the church's Financial Department observed that "deficit spending did not concern President Moyle as long as the Church had the resources and so long as needed facilities were being constructed."[44] Nevertheless, his plan to "finance such spending by selling Church securities for the next fifty years" was defeated in May 1962. A few months later several members of the Quorum of the Twelve indicated that "the First Presidency has been profligate in its spending."[45]

Moyle was so frustrated at this opposition that he told a group of LDS institute teachers during a dinner in Logan, Utah, in December that he was being "'restrained' by some of the more 'conservative' brethren who think they should retain this money 'for a rainy day.'" One of these institute teachers added: "From the sound of his talk he must be quite unhappy with the restraint."[46]

In February 1963 Moyle sought allies outside the hierarchy. He met in New York City with the Lochinvar Club of wealthy Mormons and asked what they thought of his proposal to spend $40 million to purchase a chain of radio and television stations. Like the Quorum of the Twelve, these businessmen balked at such expenditures.[47]

Moyle's financial program was fundamentally linked with his missionary program. First, he expected a major increase of tithing revenues from a significant rise in convert baptisms. Second, he was convinced that massive increases in church membership meant there would soon be a thousand Mormons in towns and cities where a year before there had been only a few dozen. Therefore, Moyle ordered the church building program to construct meeting houses for projected growth rather than for current needs. In effect, this left the church's financial future directly in the hands of nineteen- to twenty-one-year-old missionaries. To get more convert baptisms from LDS missions he visited, Moyle "interviewed, encouraged, challenged, cajoled and scolded the missionaries, as he felt the situation warranted."[48]

In this pressured context LDS proselytizing entered a *New Era,* the title of the British Mission magazine under Moyle's protégé, mission president T. Bowring Woodbury. The term "new era" was first used in the context of church finances, which underscores how intertwined financial and missionary goals were under Moyle. The First Presidency's financial secretary wrote, in assessing projected tithing revenues: "A new era in the financial history of the Church began in 1950-51!"[49] By 1961 this New Era involved six memorized proselytizing lessons (with a "challenge" for baptism at the end of the first), baptism quotas, and emphasis on baptizing young males, who were expected to become tithe-paying, bread-winning heads of LDS families.[50]

In tandem with the missionary work, another of Moyle's protégés, Wendell Mendenhall, chaired the church building committee, and he accelerated church construction worldwide beginning in 1959: "Mendenhall became President Moyle's *alter ego* in the field."[51] For example, in 1960 the two men addressed a meeting of mission presidents, missionaries, and local leaders in Manchester, England. They praised the missionaries for implementing baseball instruction to baptize young boys and for accepting goals to double the current year's number of baptisms. They explained that this rate of growth required that the church complete a new meeting house every day in Great Britain alone.[52] Moyle regarded this as simply expanding the missionary challenge McKay gave in 1958: "If you double the membership of the London branch in two years we'll build a chapel here."[53] On 15 December 1960 Moyle told the First Presidency and Twelve about the baseball approach to proselytizing.[54]

To assist this accelerated building effort in 1960, the church began having young men serve two-year labor missions in Britain and continental Europe.[55] But even with voluntary labor, the construction of new meeting houses almost single-handedly pushed the church to a $32 million deficit for 1962. Moyle's building program assumed long-term population growth, but paying for it required immediate tithing increases. By the end of February 1963 revenues were already lagging behind expenditures by $5 million.[56] The LDS church was teetering on the edge of a crisis by 1963.

Moyle's emphasis on baptism quotas and youth baptisms had also careened out of control. Convert numbers soared, but many authorities had misgivings, especially about Britain where several apostles had served missions. Baptisms per British missionary jumped from one or two annually to dozens. Some missionaries now baptized hundreds. Soon missionaries were not only competing with each other to achieve quotas, but mission presidents throughout the world were competing to have the highest numbers of baptisms. By May 1961 most of the apostles were "gravely concerned about the pressures being put on missionaries to baptize to fill a quota of baptisms."[57] When McKay appointed Hugh B. Brown as a special counselor to the First Presidency in June, the church president explained he "needed help in controlling a counselor who showed maverick tendencies."[58]

Rather than consider the merits of such criticisms, Moyle publicly counter-attacked. In August 1961 he had the *Church News* publish the full text of his defense of the "New Era" missionary program. He lashed out against people who "sow doubt or uncertainty about any phase of missionary work," which equalled "criticism of our Head, Jesus Christ, the son of God." He denied that missionaries were being overworked but then instructed parents and others to ignore youthful missionaries who complained about any aspect of the new proselytizing program.

So that no one would misunderstand, Moyle referred to "these teenage baptisms, about which there seems to have been so much talk." He said it was no one's business to complain if a boy chose to be baptized the "first day or the first week or the first month or the first year of contact with him concerning the Church." A few months later Moyle's annual report of missionary baptisms had the same tone of defensive defiance: "President Henry D. Moyle of the First Presidency, who, under the assignment of President David O. McKay, directs the great world-wide missionary effort of the Church, feels 1962 will record another 100 per cent increase as did 1961."[59] As Moyle's biographer noted, "backlash only stiffened his resolve."[60]

As the apostles suspected, however, there was a dark side to the so-called "New Era" of LDS missionary work. Mission presidents and missionaries regarded convert baptisms like scores in athletic competition.[61] With little or no gospel instruction, pre-adolescent and teenage boys were joining by tens of thousands in order to play baseball or other sports. LDS missionaries, under enormous pressure to achieve ever-spiralling quotas, often told boys that the baptism ceremony was an initiation into the LDS sports program. If missionaries could not find a teenager receptive to the sports program, they scoured underclass neighborhoods for eight-year-old boys.[62]

Among others, Elder Spencer W. Kimball derided this New Era as the "kiddie baptism program." According to Kimball, he and fellow apostles Joseph Fielding Smith, Harold B. Lee, and Mark E. Petersen were particularly opposed to it. Petersen complained that "'baseball baptisms' were being made whereby youngsters were baptized into the Church without any instruction and sometimes without the knowledge or consent of their parents." Missionaries blamed their mission presidents for the abuses, but the hierarchy saw it as Moyle's program and his responsibility.[63]

By 1963 the church was in a crisis, which resulted in Moyle's downfall. Less than a decade before, Zion's National Bank alone had $70 million in the church's once-secure reserves. Now finances were so strained that church "financial officers wondered if they would be able to meet the payroll."[64] Moyle's biographer noted that LDS headquarters now regarded the "horrible examples" of abuses in the baseball baptism program "as representative outcomes" of Moyle's emphasis on baptism quotas.[65] As a result, David O. Mckay stripped the first counselor of his two major responsibilities: direction of church finances and of the missionary program ("his portfolio," as one journalist put it).[66] Moyle said privately: "I have been relieved of every responsibility but my title," and his biographer notes that Moyle never attended another meeting of the Missionary Committee.[67]

The *New York Times* reported in May 1963 that the Church of Scotland officially condemned the baseball baptism program as the LDS church's "most insidious approach."[68] By July the president of the Quorum of the Twelve, Joseph Fielding Smith, openly expressed distaste for "the spending proclivities of President Moyle, also concerning the unorthodox way with which youngsters had been baptized in the Church and the manner in which President Moyle got recruits on his side among the General Authorities by helping them financially."[69]

Brown reported that Presidency meetings became tense in 1963 because "President Moyle was usually in hot water with President McKay." On one occasion Moyle even feigned illness as an excuse for abruptly leaving a First Presidency meeting where McKay was giving him a tongue-lashing.[70] In Brown's view, Moyle "died of a broken heart as a result of" this "down grading." His coronary occurred in September.[71]

The first counselor's downfall did not damage the future church careers of the pointmen in his building and missionary programs. Wendell Mendenhall later became a Regional Representative of the Twelve, and T. Bowring Woodbury became a member of the church's missionary committee.[72]

Hugh B. Brown succeeded Moyle as first counselor. Like all three senior counselors before him, Brown also conflicted with President McKay. Within a year-and-a-half the church president "seriously rebuked him so much so that Brother Brown almost threatened to resign." By 1968 Brown expressed resentment about McKay's lack of confidence in him.[73] Brown himself commented in 1969: "Recently there have been times when, in contact with the president of the church, I could have lost my temper and said things for which I would never have been entirely forgiven."[74]

A secretary to the First Presidency acknowledged that McKay enjoyed being "recognized, lauded, and lionized."[75] Therefore, the church president was easy to influence with flattery or criticism. It was also difficult for him to maintain his own views in the face of contrary views from his counselors. In 1956 Ernest L. Wilkinson critically noted that Stephen L Richards influenced McKay to oppose Wilkinson's proposal, "although instinctively his [McKay's] feelings were otherwise." Two years later Wilkinson basked in "the strong support of President Richards, who knows how to handle President McKay."[76] The church president disliked getting the contrary advice his counselors sometimes had to give him, but he enjoyed being unofficially lobbied by those who were eager to give him the "celebrity status" McKay liked.[77]

Therefore, general authorities and bureaucrats began making what they called "end runs" around the counselors to see McKay privately.[78] The church president then made decisions and commitments without consulting or informing his counselors, which created "uncomfortable and sometimes embarrassing situations."[79] This private lobbying sometimes led to the occasions when McKay "reverse[d] decisions made by the counselors when he felt they were wrong or ill advised."[80] At times McKay distanced himself from his colleagues in another way. If a First Presidency decision was unpopular, McKay defended himself by claiming that "he had been imposed upon by his counselors."[81] As a First Presidency secretary acknowledged, "President McKay was, in a sense, the antithesis of the traditional 'organization man.'"[82]

Under these circumstances, counselors Hugh B. Brown and N. Eldon Tanner felt especially frustrated at the administrative power of Thorpe B. Isaacson in the mid-1960s. Isaacson was a counselor in the Presiding Bishopric from 1946 to 1961 and was then made an Assistant to the Twelve.[83] Shortly after Moyle's death in September 1963, McKay began turning to Isaacson as his unofficial "executive assistant." In March 1964 Isaacson moved into J. Reuben Clark's former office, symbolically closer to McKay's office than the offices of the first and second counselors. A First Presidency secretary explained that, despite his lack of an official position in the Presidency's office, Isaacson "became the Prophet's eyes and ears, reporting to and receiving instructions from him directly."[84]

It infuriated counselors Brown and Tanner that Isaacson had more influence with McKay than they did. In February 1965 Isaacson commented that the first and second counselors "resent very much the fact that he can see President McKay any time he wants to and they don't know what business is transacted." Brown told others that he thought Isaacson "bugged" his office telephones.[85]

He also opposed Isaacson's formal advancement nine months later as an extra counselor to McKay. Brown later spoke with grim satisfaction about Isaacson's official appointment: "within a matter of days he was stricken with a stroke and has not been able to function in any respect since his appointment."[86] Actually Isaacson served for over three months before the stroke completely disabled him. He then remained non-functioning throughout the remaining four years of McKay's presidency.[87]

On 15 April 1966, two months after Isaacson's stroke, McKay recorded in his diary that he "would have to appoint another counselor," and on this day Alvin R. Dyer began the first of many closed-door meetings with the church president. Dyer had been an Assistant to the Twelve since 1958. A cousin of McKay's powerful "executive secretary," Clare Middlemiss, Dyer now became McKay's chief, though unofficial, adviser.[88] Second counselor N. Eldon Tanner felt growing frustration that Dyer "was taking matters directly to President McKay that probably should be considered by the entire council of the First Presidency." Finally Tanner "took it upon himself to speak rather directly to President McKay about the matter." Tanner was so emphatic and McKay's response was so negative that for several hours the second counselor "felt he might possibly be released because of the strong position he had taken."[89]

In the twenty-six years since 1970 smoother relationships have characterized the president and his counselors. This harmony was possible primarily because no church president has been as vacillating as McKay. Age has been another factor.

McKay's immediate successor was ninety-three years old and "delegated broadly to his counselors from the outset."[90] The three most recent church presidents were in their mid-eighties when they ascended to office: Ezra Taft Benson at eighty-six in 1985, Howard W. Hunter at eight-six in 1994, and Gordon B. Hinckley at eighty-four in 1995. Televised general conferences demonstrate how solicitous the relatively younger counselors are to the aging church presidents.

In 1972-73 N. Eldon Tanner demonstrated that a capable counselor who was especially deferential could achieve remarkable harmony with a church president known for his "combativeness" and "fiery temper."[91] When Joseph Fielding Smith's death made Harold B. Lee's presidency imminent, Tanner volunteered to be released permanently as a counselor.[92] Lee said he wanted Tanner to continue in the Presidency with the new counselor Marion G. Romney who had greater seniority than Tanner as an apostle. Tanner immediately offered to be second counselor despite his years of service in two presidencies as Romney's administrative superior. Lee wrote: "I felt certain that despite the difference in [apostolic] seniority, President Tanner had earned the right for this advancement [to first counselor] in my judgment, and I feel with the Lord's sanction, after having spent an hour or more in the temple in prayerful meditation."[93] Although Tanner had greater experience as a financial administrator than Lee, he accepted without question the new president's assumption of all financial decision-making. Lee soon recognized his first counselor's superior skills in directing church finances and returned them to Tanner's direction within months.[94]

Also, after Lee's death in 1973 President Spencer W. Kimball led by consensus and love. His twelve-year presidency achieved an unusual degree of harmony.[95]

Nevertheless, Kimball also demonstrated that even the most harmonious counselors may unite in vigorous disagreement with their beloved president. In 1978, for example, "against the strong recommendation of his counselors to the contrary, he directed the sale of the Laguna Beach, California, cottage that had been used for several decades by Presidents of the Church as a hideaway."[96]

First Presidency Counselors

The first known conflict between counselors in the First Presidency occurred during Brigham Young's presidency. Coarse and painfully aware of his limited education, Heber C. Kimball may have been the highest-ranking leader with the lowest self-esteem in Mormon history. Three weeks before he became first counselor in 1847, Kimball complained that apostles "Parley [P. Pratt] & [John] Taylor has [sic] treated me as if I was not a man of sense—they av come to the Quorum & importuned them that I shod. not preach because I am so simple."[97]

Seven years as first counselor did not heal Kimball's fragile ego. He told the Utah legislature in 1854: "I can speak now as an Elder in Israel and I want to speak and not be here like a Dumb Dog. I am ignorant of many technicalities, but when you come to the truth I know that as well as Professor Carrington, Professor Pratt, Professor Smith, P[rofessor]. Woodruff."[98] Constantly on guard, from 1857 on Kimball saw himself in silent combat with the newly appointed second counselor Daniel H. Wells.

Rather than choose a member of the Quorum of Twelve as a counselor in January 1857, Brigham Young appointed "Squire" Wells, who had a distinguished background of civil office. Seven months later Kimball worried about "a Collission between him & Daniel H. Wells," and Kimball recorded his festering resentment in 1859: "I was told by the Lord that those that had sought my hurt and had caused me to be cast off by his servant Brigham should see sorrow and be removed out of their places." He then listed "Daniel H. Wells[,] Albert Carrington, Joseph A Young and others, and they should be spoiled in all their evil designs."[99]

Less than three months later Kimball expressed his worries to rank-and-file Mormons. He told a group in the Salt Lake Endowment House that some with high church positions "think as to Brother Heber he is of No account . . . & they try to make a division between the First Presidency of the Church."[100] This was not merely Kimball's imagination. For example, when Young took a small group to see his new paper mill in 1861, he included Wells but excluded Kimball.[101]

During the early 1860s Kimball felt increased antagonism. He recorded a revelation that "Daniel Wells Should See Sorrow Even as he had caused Sorrow to come on his servent HCK becaus[e] he sat on me and oppressed me when he had power to do me good." Another of Kimball's entries complained that Wells "held him at a distance."[102] There is no record whether Wells perceived himself in conflict with the first counselor. Kimball spent the last ten years of his life convinced that he had lost a struggle for prestige and for influence with Young. Kimball died in 1868.

Another pair of counselors had much in common. George Q. Cannon and Joseph F. Smith were nephews of church presidents (John Taylor and Joseph Smith, respectively). They had served as missionaries in Hawaii and as assistant counselors to Brigham Young at different times. Then they served together as first and second counselors to John Taylor (1880-87), Wilford Woodruff (1889-98), and Lorenzo Snow (1898-1901).

Nevertheless, personality differences created tensions between them. Smith told apostles in 1891 that fellow counselor Cannon had "not shown me that confidence and love which I was entitled to receive."[103] From 1891 on there was evidence of specific administrative conflict between them.

At issue was their differing response as counselors to President Lorenzo Snow's effort to end all polygamous cohabitation and new plural marriages. As early as 1891 the two counselors disagreed on the nature of the 1890 Manifesto, which had officially ended plural marriage. Cannon argued that because it was inspired, the Manifesto was "a revelation from God." When an apostle asked the second counselor at the same meeting if the Manifesto was a revelation, "President Smith answered emphatically no."[104]

A decade later the conflict erupted during a temple meeting. Cannon supported Snow's intent to end cohabitation. Smith shocked the apostles by the fury of his words toward Cannon. At a meeting with the Quorum of Twelve two days later Snow required Smith to apologize for the outburst.[105] Two months later Cannon died.

The longest-standing tension between First Presidency counselors involved first counselor J. Reuben Clark and second counselor David O. McKay from 1934 to 1951. Their disagreements surfaced publicly in a *Time* magazine article in 1942. Clark noted in 1944: "Had conference with D.O.M. [—] we ironed out some differences."[106]

Opposite in personality and administrative style, the two men polarized other general authorities and bureaucrats into "Clark men" and "McKay men" for decades.[107] Clark's closest supporters were Joseph Fielding Smith, John A. Widtsoe, Charles A. Callis, Albert E. Bowen, Harold B. Lee, Spencer W. Kimball, Ezra Taft Benson, Mark E. Petersen, Matthew Cowley, Henry D. Moyle, Marion G. Romney, and LeGrand Richards of the Quorum of the Twelve, and Joseph L. Wirthlin of the Presiding Bishopric. Lee, Moyle, and Romney openly acknowledged Clark as their mentor. McKay's closest supporters were Stephen L Richards, Adam S. Bennion, and Hugh B. Brown of the Quorum of the Twelve; Thomas E. McKay, Alvin R. Dyer, and N. Eldon Tanner of the Assistants to the Twelve; Marion D. Hanks of the First Council of Seventy; and Thorpe B. Isaacson, a counselor in the Presiding Bishopric during Clark's tenure.

Even kinship and philosophical similarity did not prevent tension between counselors Hugh B. Brown and N. Eldon Tanner from 1963 to 1970. In 1965 Tanner was surprised to learn that his uncle had intentionally withheld information from him that the first counselor obtained during a private consultation with McKay. In 1969 Tanner said that "no one should let his emotions get control of them as Brown and Lee did" in angry outbursts against Ernest L. Wilkinson at a BYU Board of Trustees meeting. Seven years later, when Wilkinson declined to donate to a university chair named in Brown's honor, Tanner said: "Well, are you going to allow yourself to stoop to the level of Hugh Brown?"[108] This apparently referred to Brown telling BYU's president: "You are a cross between a crook and a skunk."[109]

From McKay's death in 1970 until his own death in 1982, Tanner continued to distinguish himself as an indispensable, non-combative, emotionally contained "McKay man" in successive presidencies of "Clark men." Presidents Joseph Fielding Smith, Harold B. Lee, and Spencer W. Kimball had long been closely aligned to each other and to Marion G. Romney, the other counselor until 1985. Also closely aligned with Clark's philosophy, Ezra Taft Benson presided over the church from 1985 to 1994 with counselors Gordon B. Hinckley and Thomas S. Monson. Hinckley and Monson combined "McKay man" N. Eldon Tanner's moderation and calmness with "Clark man" Harold B. Lee's administrative tutelage, qualities that served them throughout the presidency of Benson's successor, Howard W. Hunter, 1994-95.[110]

The First Presidency and Quorum of the Twelve

The First Presidency and the Quorum of Twelve share an affinity based on power. When a lesser unit of the hierarchy asserts its prerogatives against the Twelve, for example, the First Presidency almost always aligns itself with the apostles. The Twelve is equally protective of the First Presidency. Nevertheless, because they share this concentration of power, the Presidency and Twelve have sometimes been at odds with each other.

Within the first year of its organization, the Quorum of the Twelve was in ecclesiastical conflict with the First Presidency. Commenting on this early dynamic, Brigham Young reminisced: "T[homas]. B Marsh [president of the Twelve from 1835 to 1839] once said He did not know what Joseph Called the Twelve for[,] without it was to abuse them. I told him if the Twelve were faithful they would soon see the day that they would have all the influence they could wield."[111] Feeling that the Presidency was bypassing their rights, the Twelve requested a joint meeting on 16 January 1836. The apostles aired their grievances "in a very forcible and explicit manner, yet cool and deliberate." As a result each member of the First Presidency apologized for insulting the apostles, and Smith declared that the Quorum of the Twelve was subject only to the First Presidency.[112] Later Heber C. Kimball referred to this incident "of the Twelve Apostles being called home through prejudice, and how by their unity they rendered Joseph powerless to subvert them."[113] Nevertheless, strains continued between these two quorums. In the 1830s the apostles complained to each other, "our influence is nothing. why dont Joseph give us the power that belongs to us?"[114]

In April 1842 Smith criticized a third of the twelve apostles in remarks to the female Relief Society of Nauvoo. He said that Parley P. Pratt, Orson Pratt, Orson Hyde, and John E. Page were "aspiring—they could not be exalted."[115] Since he did not explain further, he left the women to wonder whether the four were *con*spiring as a group or simply proud and individually ambitious. In any event, on the eve of the open disruption with his assistant counselor John C. Bennett, the president's remarks could not have given a reassuring view of the church's administration.

Within weeks Bennett's apostasy put Smith in conflict with the Quorum of Twelve's president. Because of his younger brother William's complicity in Bennett's seductions,[116] Smith instructed Brigham Young to prefer charges against the wayward apostle. Then Smith inexplicably acted as if Young was using the trial to humiliate the entire Smith family. Joseph Smith interrupted the church court: "Bro. Brigham, I will not listen to this abuse of my family a minute longer. I will wade in blood up to my knees before I will do it!"

Of this Apostle Lorenzo Snow later commented: "A rupture between the two greatest men on earth seemed imminent. But Brigham Young was equal to the danger, and he instantly said 'Bro. Joseph, I withdraw the charge.' Thus the angry passions were instantly stilled."[117] However, this left a known adulterer in the Quorum of the Twelve Apostles from 1842 until 1845. His cousin, Apostle George A. Smith, later commented about "Wm Smith Commit[t]ing iniquity & we have to sustain him against our feelings."[118]

Although Smith gave the Twelve increased financial responsibilities in 1841, he antagonized the apostles at general conference on 6 April 1843 by requiring bonds to avoid misuse of donations they collected. This was consistent with Smith's earlier requirement for the Nauvoo Temple Committee to give "bonds to him to the amount of $12000 for a faithful dis-charge of all duties devolving upon them as a Committee."[119] Nevertheless, at the 1843 conference the official history records that "Elder Brigham Young objected, and said he should never give receipts for cash, except such as he put into his own pocket for his own use." He then demanded to know if anyone was charging the apostles with dishonesty, "to which the Twelve responded, Amen." The history gives the impression that Smith was immediately able to smooth over these objections.[120]

Instead Apostle Franklin D. Richards explained that Young left the morning session of general conference in a fury. "If the brethren could not trust him he would not go out to collect," the Quorum of Twelve's president fumed. In the afternoon meeting Young refused to join the presiding officers on the stand and instead sat in the congregation. He was not easily reconciled and did not sign his $2,000 bond until 30 May. Four months later Young put the best face he could on his requirement to pay a bond and told Mormons in Boston that "this is unheard of—I glory in it."[121]

In most respects, however, there was little conflict between the two quorums during the latter part of Smith's presidency. He gave the Twelve increasing status publicly and power privately. In fact they eclipsed the importance of the First Presidency counselors, who were excluded from knowledge and participation in polygamy until May 1843. From 1841 to 1843 a polygamous shadow government emerged that involved Smith, Apostle Young (who performed most of the prophet's polygamous marriages), and apostles Heber C. Kimball and Willard Richards (who each gave relatives to the prophet as plural wives).[122] Nevertheless, Young said, "while Joseph lived the Twelve dwelt under his Shadow."[123]

With the formation of an apostolic presidency of three men after Smith's death in 1847, the relationship between the two quorums changed markedly. Originally, the Quorum of the Twelve was a creation of the First

Presidency, but after 1847 exactly the reverse was true. The First Presidency became an extension of the Quorum of the Twelve, though virtually independent and exercising the prerogatives of the pre-1844 presidency.[124]

The Twelve knew that they surrendered administrative primacy in creating a new presidency. This is why several apostles opposed the move in late 1847. For more than three years the Twelve had ruled the church. In 1847 Brigham Young began a thirty-year erosion of the authority and prestige of that body.

By calling apostles on missions outside Utah or to preside over remote settlements of the church, Young removed them from prominence at headquarters. As a result, although active in ecclesiastical affairs, nine members of the Quorum of the Twelve lived in virtual exile during Young's presidency.

Orson Hyde spent nineteen years presiding over remote settlements between 1854 and 1877. Orson Pratt was on missions (primarily foreign) for eleven years during a twenty-two-year period (1848-70). John Taylor spent six years on missions. Amasa M. Lyman served two years on missions and six years presiding over remote settlements during a twenty-year period. Ezra T. Benson spent three years on missions and nine years presiding over isolated settlements. Charles C. Rich was away from Salt Lake City for twenty-three years between 1849 and 1877, while he presided over remote settlements. Lorenzo Snow served three years on foreign missions and presided for twenty-four years over a settlement distant from church headquarters. Erastus Snow spent eight years on missions and sixteen years presiding over remote settlements. Franklin D. Richards was on missions for seven years.

These absences from LDS headquarters were consistent with the 1835 calling of the Twelve to serve among the nations and peoples of the earth. From that perspective it might not seem unusual. Thus two scholars noted these absences and simply remarked that Young waited until the year of his death before he allowed "the Twelve to have full involvement in the administration of general church affairs on a regular basis."[125]

But some of the Twelve felt Young used mission assignments as punishments. Erastus Snow remarked to fellow apostles, "In the days of Brigham Young some men felt that they were sent on missions because of some private spite."[126] For example, in 1856 Young said Orson Hyde "is a stink in my norstrels" and then kept Hyde on a mission to preside over southern Utah settlements until his death. In 1860 Young vowed to get Ezra T. Benson out of Salt Lake City and called him to preside over northern Utah settlements until his death.[127] At April conference that year

Young commented, "We have at times sent men on missions to get rid of them, but they have generally come back."[128]

Apostle Joseph F. Smith became a missionary-exile for opposing Young's appointment of his son John W. Young as first counselor in 1876. Brigham condemned Smith's opposition and called him on a foreign mission for "not less than five years." The Twelve rescinded this mission-exile after Young died in 1877. Of this incident a counselor in the Presidency later wrote, "Truly man proposes and God disposes."[129]

Three months before Young's death a New York City newspaper referred to Orson Pratt's exile. The article quoted Pratt's son that he "has been repeatedly banished as a missionary to various countries of Europe and the East." The reason was his well-known doctrinal disputes with Young.[130] The cumulative effect of such exile was a lessening of the Twelve's status as a presiding quorum at church headquarters.

In addition to locating most apostles away from Salt Lake City, Young also publicly criticized and demeaned them when they were at home. This was already one objection to his 1847 proposal to organize a presidency.[131] At various times Young publicly berated at least nine members of the Quorum of the Twelve Apostles: Orson Hyde, Amasa M. Lyman, Orson Pratt, Parley P. Pratt, Franklin D. Richards, George A. Smith, Erastus Snow, John Taylor, and Wilford Woodruff.[132] As president of the Twelve and then church president, he had the right to criticize, but his doing this so often publicly diminished the entire Quorum of the Twelve.

Young was also adamant that the Twelve not infringe on his prerogatives as church president. In 1856, for example, he declared from the pulpit: "*The Twelve have no right* to ask the Presidency why they do this or that or why they tell the Twelve to do this or that [—] ownly go & do as they are told."[133] Most apostles were deferential to Young, but sometimes they inadvertently challenged his concept of authority.

For example, during the April 1861 general conference Young revealed how sensitive he was to any administrative intrusion. After waiting several minutes for the First Presidency to arrive, Apostle Orson Hyde (as acting president of the Quorum of Twelve) decided not to delay the opening of general conference any longer. Hyde began the meeting with remarks, prayer, and congregational singing.

Young and his counselors arrived shortly thereafter. Immediately following the meeting, Young amazed the Quorum of the Twelve by accusing them of undermining his authority: "Now I will ask all of you[,] how would you feel if you had a work to do which God & the heavens held you responsible for & just as you was about to step forth to do it another man should rise up & take it out of your hands Before the people[,] as though you was not qualifyed to Do it or was neglecting your duty. You would not like it. You would feel Chagrined and so did I." On the contrary, Wilford Woodruff noted that "it did not enter the mind of any of the Twelve but what it was right at the time."[134] This incident showed the extent to which Young guarded his own prerogatives while limiting those of the Quorum of the Twelve Apostles.

When Young used the title "Prophet, Seer, and Revelator" at the April 1851 general conference, he formalized the disparity between himself and the rest of the Twelve. Joseph Smith was the original Prophet, Seer, and Revelator at the organization of the church in 1830. A conference sustained Smith's counselors and the Quorum of the Twelve as "Prophets, Seers, and Revelators" on 27 March 1836. A written revelation gave that title to the Presiding Patriarch in January 1841. However, neither the apostles nor the church patriarch had been publicly sustained with that title at any other conference. When Young and his two counselors adopted this title, they did not extend it to the Twelve or to the church patriarch. Moreover, at every conference from April 1873 until his death in 1877 Young was the only church officer sustained as Prophet, Seer, and Revelator.[135]

It is understandable that most members of the Quorum of the Twelve Apostles were not anxious to organize another First Presidency after Young's death on 29 August 1877. Less than a week later nine members of the Quorum and Young's former counselors met to discuss the situation. "Came to an understanding on the question of responsibility and authority to guide the Church[—It] was determined and settled to devolve upon the Twelve and 2 Counsellors assisting, and John Taylor was sustained as president of the Twelve & Counsel [Council]." Even though Young's former counselors Daniel H. Wells and John W. Young had been ordained apostles, they were not admitted to the quorum but served as counselors to it.[136]

For thirty years the prestige of the Quorum of the Twelve had declined, and the apostles were in no mood to perpetuate the trend. As an obvious rebuff to Young's application of the title only to himself, the Twelve had themselves sustained as "Prophets, Seers and Revelators" at the general conference of 6 October 1877. The Twelve rarely allowed another general conference to pass without this formal acknowledgement of that status.[137]

George Q. Cannon described this feeling among the apostles after Brigham Young's death:

> Some of my brethren, as I have learned since the death of President Brigham Young, did have feelings concerning his course. They did not approve of it, and felt opposed, and yet they dare not exhibit their feelings to him, he ruled with so strong and stiff a hand, and they felt that it would be of

no use. In a few words, the feeling seems to be that he transcended the bounds of the authority which he legitimately held. I have been greatly surprised to find so much dissatisfaction in such quarters.[138]

Of the apostles who had followed Young, only Orson Pratt had challenged his autocracy. Pratt expressed his dissent in administrative terms in 1847 and in theological terms beginning in 1852.[139] As a result Young called Pratt on one mission after another for eleven out of twenty-two years. Young's death allowed the apostles to return home, consolidate their positions, and criticize his rule without fear of reprisal.

In this context Franklin D. Richards described the administrative challenges. On 3 and 4 October 1877, less than two months after Young's death, Richards noted in his diary that "Counsellor D. H. Wells gave us one of his *once again* speeches about Joseph F. Smith." Richards later explained: "When Bro Young died Counselor Daniel H. Wells said that Joseph F. Smith should be chosen to be the President of the Church, but the apostles did not accept of [sic] this and it was some time before there was a perfect union so that the Presidency could be organized."[140] Wells had never been a member of the Quorum of the Twelve, but he had been a counselor in the First Presidency for twenty years. His entire ecclesiastical orientation centered on the First Presidency, and his loyalty was not with the Twelve's prerogatives. The efforts of Wells in 1877 indicated some of the tension that had developed between the two presiding quorums during the previous decades.

After the Quorum of the Twelve led the church for two years following Young's death, senior apostle John Taylor became impatient to form a separate presidency. He exerted his authority as quorum president as early as April 1879 when he insisted on Moses Thatcher as the new apostle instead of Francis M. Lyman, who was the majority's choice.[141] The rest of the Twelve accepted Taylor's ruling then, but not six months later.

On 6 September 1879 the apostles voted against Taylor's suggestion for organizing a First Presidency. They regarded it "as altogether uncalled for & unbefitting of the Church [—] The 12 ought first attain a full unity with each other & people first."[142] Still anxious to avoid a second loss of their prerogatives, the Quorum of the Twelve resisted appointing the senior apostle as an independent president with counselors.

Taylor renewed his effort on 6 October 1880. "I was astounded and entered my humble objection," wrote Apostle Joseph F. Smith. The Quorum of Twelve debated the proposal nearly four hours that day. Most apostles were opposed because "the Saints were not only satisfied but happy under the administration of the Twelve." Smith added that "he for one did not want to live to see repeated what had occurred in the Church [under Brigham Young], in ignoring the quorum of Apostles and other quorums of the Church." In an obvious effort to dispel that impression, Taylor's choices for two apostles at this conference included Francis M. Lyman, the quorum's unsuccessful 1879 nomination.[143]

Wilford Woodruff wrote that after general conference meetings on 8 October 1880, the apostles again "debated upon the propriety of Organizing the first Presidency. We had held several Councils upon this subje[c]t and we finally left the Subje[c]t untill another Meeting."[144] Wells renewed his argument that the apostles should have organized a separate First Presidency "long ago." But Wells adamantly denied the assertion that Young had wanted Taylor to be his successor.[145] Taylor would remember that candor when the apostles recommended Wells to become a member of the Quorum of Twelve.

From noon until 2:00 p.m. the following day the Twelve was still divided over Taylor's proposal. That evening they finally assented. Taylor chose as first counselor his nephew George Q. Cannon, who had consistently supported Taylor's call for a new presidency.[146]

Taylor's choice for second counselor signaled reconciliation. He selected Joseph F. Smith, who had expressed opposition to a new presidency only three days earlier. Because Taylor had equally suffered under what Cannon called Young's "stiff hand," the apostles expected Taylor not to repeat that subjugation of the Quorum of Twelve.

However, within two years Taylor was in conflict with the Twelve. The dispute began on 7 April 1882 when the quorum unanimously voted that Counselor Daniel H. Wells and stake president Jesse N. Smith fill the two vacancies in the Twelve. Taylor said he preferred other men and mentioned stake president George Teasdale as one choice. He then asked that the vote be deferred until Cannon returned from the Eastern states. When some apostles protested the delay, Taylor said he would not cooperate. Hoping to avoid a confrontation, Woodruff and others urged that they defer the matter until the First Presidency presented it for discussion at a combined meeting. That vote was unanimous.[147]

When Taylor renewed the question on 3 October 1882, he argued that he was not bound by the unanimous vote of the apostles for Wells and the stake president. Apostle John Henry Smith wrote: "President John Taylor gave us his views on the duties of the first Presidency and the duties of the Twelve and showed by statistics that it was the prerogative of the president of the church to select candidates for the apostleship, and the Council of the apostles to confirm. I beleive [sic] it is the twelve's right to confirm or reject."[148] Thinking that Taylor objected only to their previous choices, the apostles voted again on 6 October for new quorum members.

This time the apostles scattered their ballots among twelve men. Eventually, there were six votes for Junius F. Wells and five for Matthias F. Cowley, the quorum's two new recommendations. Stung that not one apostle voted for his previously named preference, George Teasdale, Taylor left the October 1882 general conference without presenting any new apostles.[149] On 13 October he announced a written revelation which named George Teasdale and Heber J. Grant to fill the vacancies in the Quorum of the Twelve Apostles.

This 1882 revelation resolved the impasse about nominating new apostles, but Apostle John Henry Smith thought Taylor simply out-maneuvered the Quorum of Twelve. The church president had signaled his preference for Teasdale the previous April and in June had nominated Teasdale and Grant to fill vacancies in the theocratic Council of Fifty.[150] The revelation confirmed what Taylor had wanted for six months.

John Henry Smith found the 1882 revelation unconvincing. He regarded Teasdale as a sycophant and Grant as weak in faith. He wrote on the day of their ordination: "I am satisfied that before another President over our Church is sustained The Twelve apostles will be compeled [sic] to have an understanding in relation to the duties of their respective quorums. The first President takes the whole business in his hands."[151] They might have obtained that understanding with relative ease had the hierarchy been able to function normally during the rest of Taylor's administration. External forces soon disrupted the entire church.

For decades Americans had been suspicious of the church's virtual theocracy in the West. The practice of polygamy was offensive to the nation's Victorian sensibilities.[152] Desultory efforts at suppressing polygamy began with the 1862 Morrill Act, but the real momentum began after the U.S. Supreme Court ruled in the Reynolds decision of 1879 that the Morrill Act was constitutional.[153] U.S. president Rutherford B. Hayes expressed the governing attitude in 1880:

> Now the territory [of Utah] is virtually under the theocratic government of the Mormon Church. The Union of Church and State is complete. The result is the usual one [—] usurpation or absorption of all temporal authority and power by the Church. Polygamy and every other evil sanctioned by the Mormon Church is the end in view. This requires agitation. The people of the United States must be made to appreciate[,] to understand the situation. Laws must be enacted which will take from the Mormon Church its temporal power. Mormonism as a sectarian idea is nothing, but as a system of government it is our duty to deal with it as an enemy to our institutions, and its supporters and leaders as criminals.[154]

Mormon polygamy revolted most Americans even before federal law made its practice illegal in Utah and other territories. Mormon theocratic power (although not illegal) worried all Americans.

Theocratic power was the real target of the federal government, but polygamy was the more vulnerable. Unintentionally Mormons identified that vulnerability by claiming that the church would sooner give up anything else. A frequent advocate of that theme was Apostle Wilford Woodruff. He sermonized on one occasion that if Mormons gave up polygamy, "then we must do away with prophets and Apostles." A decade later he told Mormons, "Were we to compromise this principle by saying, we will renounce it, we would then have to renounce our belief in revelation from God."[155] Aware of that fact, the federal government used anti-polygamy laws to attack Mormon political, economic, and ecclesiastical power.[156]

For the hierarchy and regular Mormons alike the 1880s became the decade of the "Raid." In 1882 the Edmunds Act provided fines and imprisonment for men convicted of polygamy or the related crime of "unlawful cohabitation" with plural wives. To attack Mormon political power, the act also disenfranchised polygamists and removed them from public office and jury duty. Federal deputies scoured Mormon settlements for polygamist husbands and wives.[157]

By 1885 the threat of arrest and imprisonment chased Taylor and first counselor Cannon into hiding on the "Underground" in Utah. Second counselor Joseph F. Smith fled to Hawaii (then an independent kingdom). Hundreds of prominent Mormons, including most of the hierarchy, likewise disappeared or left on foreign missions to escape arrest.[158]

Faced with such defiance, the federal government enacted the Edmunds-Tucker Act in 1887. This disincorporated the church and provided for the confiscation of its money and property. The act disenfranchised Utah's women, who (to the puzzlement of most Americans) had consistently voted Mormon polygamists into civil office after the territory enfranchised women in 1870.[159]

With members of the Twelve widely scattered, it was difficult and dangerous for them to meet. Therefore, from 1885 to 1887 Taylor and Cannon ruled the church virtually alone. This situation reinforced Taylor's sense of the autonomy of the First Presidency and the apostles' feeling of almost total alienation. "We have no Council meetings, no Circle meetings," groused Apostle John Henry Smith in 1885, "so I am but little posted in regard to policy."[160]

Even when Taylor and Cannon consulted with apostles, they brushed aside contrary views. Early in 1886 John Henry Smith complained, "The Chief [John Taylor] sits still and does nothing and wont let anyone else."

Later that year four apostles met with Cannon and Taylor to discuss the church's entry into mining. John Henry Smith noted, "All of the Brethren expressed themselves as opposed to mining but the President." Still Taylor obtained a unanimous vote on his proposal for the church to invest $100,000 in the Bullion, Beck, and Champion Mining Company.[161]

Taylor's death on the Underground on 25 July 1887 raised a new question about the relationship between the First Presidency and Twelve. After George Q. Cannon and Joseph F. Smith became Taylor's counselors, apostles filled their places in the Twelve. With the church president's death, the remaining apostles had to decide whether to accept them back into the quorum and increase its size beyond twelve members. If readmitted would Cannon and Smith retain their former ranking or would it be based upon their re-entry date? The apostles voted on 3 August to receive Cannon and Smith back to their original positions in the quorum.[162] Although unprecedented, this reflected the view that the First Presidency after 1847 was an extension of the Quorum of the Twelve Apostles.[163]

Taylor's death automatically raised the issue of forming a new First Presidency. The most serious confrontation at this time centered on Daniel H. Wells, just as it had a decade before. Always an advocate of the unilateral authority of the First Presidency, Wells maintained that the Quorum of Twelve Apostles did not have the right to preside over the church: "No! not for twenty-four hours, or for ten minutes."[164]

His claim astounded the Twelve. When asked by what authority the Twelve presided over the church from 1844 to 1847, Wells replied that the "mantle" of Joseph Smith fell only on Brigham Young at the August 1844 conference. In his view, Young (not the Twelve) was the only presiding authority from 1844 to 1847.[165]

Wells claimed that God had revealed to him that the quorum did not have the right to preside: "it was as clear as the noon day sun that it was God's will that the Twelve have no business to act in the shoes of the First Presidency."[166] No member of the Quorum of Twelve agreed with Wells, and on 3 August 1887 the quorum began to direct the affairs of the church without an organized First Presidency.[167]

Although convinced of the Twelve's right to preside, senior apostle Wilford Woodruff shared the desire of Wells to organize a new First Presidency quickly. But the council meetings of August and September revealed ill feelings against Cannon, who had been Taylor's counselor. Among the complaints was that for years the first counselor had enjoyed access to temples without a recommend, while the apostles had to obtain and show a recommend for each entry.

On 4 August 1887 the Twelve adopted a sharply worded resolution that it "be distinctly understood that it is the inherent right of the Twelve Apostles and their counselors or any one of them, to be admitted into any of the Temples of the Lord without question or the need of a recommend." Cannon offered this motion but did not overcome resentment from the other apostles.[168]

Cannon was popularly regarded as the "power behind the throne" and "Mormon Premier." He admitted to the apostles that because of Taylor's physical decline, he "had virtually been the President of the Church for four months prior to the death of Prest Taylor."[169] For apostles whose resentment had festered for years, Cannon's admission vindicated their animosity. In 1886 John Henry Smith wrote second counselor Joseph F. Smith concerning the latter's Hawaiian exile: "I fully beleive [sic] it was G. Q. move to keep you out of the way so he could manipulate matters."[170]

Before Woodruff could propose organizing a First Presidency, he had to reconcile these feelings about the previous presidency's autocratic rule. Therefore, on 5 October 1887 he asked the apostles to discuss openly any objections they had. He thought that if the meeting resolved the misunderstandings, a presidency could be organized immediately. Instead, in one meeting after another, half the Quorum of Twelve Apostles blocked his effort. The dissenting apostles assumed (rightly it would turn out) that the new presidency would again include Cannon as first counselor.

Instead of providing reconciliation, Woodruff's invitation in October 1887 opened a Pandora's box of recrimination, bitterness, suspicion, and jealousy. Unknown to Woodruff, two weeks before the meeting junior apostle Heber J. Grant had coordinated forces against the former first counselor: "I want us one and all to have the moral courage to tell *all* we have in our hearts against George Q. when this matter comes up again and not say we are satisfied with his explanations unless we are."[171]

During the 5-6 October council meetings five apostles marshaled themselves against Cannon—senior apostle Erastus Snow and junior apostles Moses Thatcher, Francis M. Lyman, John Henry Smith, and Heber J. Grant. Franklin D. Richards regarded Grant and Thatcher as the ring-leaders of this attack.[172]

The five apostles had multiple charges against Cannon. Among their objections were that Cannon had concealed financial affairs from the Twelve, that he had snubbed the apostles and shown disdain for their authority, that he had purposely exiled them from church headquarters, that he had ruled over the church as an autocrat, that he had given preferment to his relatives in church matters, and that he aspired to be church president in power if not in fact.[173] L. John Nuttall wrote, "I never attended such a meeting," and Woodruff described the confrontation as "painful."[174] Nuttall had been secretary to John Taylor since 1879 and was current secretary to Woodruff.

At the conclusion of the 6 October meeting, the Twelve voted to forgive one another and establish harmony. Nevertheless, the issues behind the confrontation were nowhere near resolved in the minds of Cannon's opponents.

Although the apostles directed their complaints against George Q. Cannon personally, these members of the Twelve were actually attacking the deceased church president through his first counselor. Joseph F. Smith said he "felt many things were attributed to Geo Q. that should be attributed to Prest Taylor." Apostle Thatcher also "expressed his regrets that these kinds of matters had been left until after the death of Prest Taylor and felt that we should have had the courage to demand what were our rights while he was living."[175] Still Cannon represented both the autocratic rule of previous years and the likelihood for a repetition of that experience in a new First Presidency.

When Woodruff openly attempted to organize a First Presidency on 20 March 1888, the apostles showed that their opposition to Cannon was in reality opposition to forming a new presidency. Curiously Woodruff's diary claimed Brigham Young, Jr., supported his proposal. In fact Young dissented with this explanation: "If Brother Woodruff were to be President and Brother Cannon be a counselor, Brother Cannon would have the credit of presiding *defacto*, although Brother Woodruff would be nominally so."[176] During the next two days Erastus Snow, Moses Thatcher, Francis M. Lyman, John Henry Smith, and Heber J. Grant resurrected complaints and dissatisfaction that they had agreed to forgive the previous October.

Cannon regarded the dissident apostles as tools of the "schemes of the Adversary." The mild-mannered and sensitive Brigham Young, Jr., retreated from his initial criticism of Cannon and wrote that there was a "Continuation of charges and refutations until I am sick at heart." Woodruff recorded: "We had a vary [sic] unpleasant day. I could not Sleep at night." In October 1888 Woodruff's secretary blamed apostles Thatcher and Grant for the "apparent disunion in the council." Apostles Lyman and John Henry Smith were not far behind. On 23 March 1889 Woodruff conceded that "the more we tryed to get together the wider apart we were," and he withdrew the motion to organize the First Presidency.[177]

This bitter opposition was agonizing for the kindly, octogenarian senior apostle. Even though Erastus Snow's death in May removed the only high-ranking apostle in dissent, Woodruff did not propose a First Presidency for the October 1888 general conference. In February 1889 he indicated to his secretary how deeply the Twelve had lowered his morale:

"Prest Woodruff said to me, he would about as soon attend a funeral as one of our council Meetings."[178]

The hold-outs became convinced of Woodruff's personal need for reconciliation and finally approved a new presidency on 5 April 1889. Woodruff nominated Cannon as his first counselor, the inevitability against which half of the quorum had battled for a year-and-a-half. However, the intransigence had spent itself, and only Thatcher offered a tentative objection. Joseph F. Smith was called as second counselor. The apostles voted unanimously to sustain this First Presidency. Heber J. Grant decided not to say he was voting to sustain Woodruff's choice of counselors despite Grant's lack of confidence in Cannon.[179]

Traditional histories have implied that these long periods without an organized presidency were happenstance due to external factors. In reality these periods were evidence of power struggles between the Twelve and First Presidency. The apostles refused to form a new presidency because they did not want to surrender their own authority.

Less than seventeen months after the apostles finally allowed Woodruff to organize his First Presidency, he circumvented them by publishing his Manifesto on plural marriage without the full quorum's consultation or approval. In December 1888 he had presented a similar document, which the apostles overwhelmingly rejected.[180] In September 1890 federal officials were preparing to seize the temples, Congress was about to disenfranchise all Mormons, and Woodruff decided to act quickly.

While the rest of the apostles were away from Salt Lake City on conference assignments, Woodruff invited responses from only four apostles about his proposed repudiation of polygamy. Lorenzo Snow and Franklin D. Richards had consistently supported him in his earlier administrative conflicts with the Twelve. He also invited response from his recent appointee, Marriner W. Merrill, who had not been involved in the quorum's opposition to the Presidency. Woodruff did consult one of his previous opponents in the Twelve, Moses Thatcher. However, Thatcher was not expected to oppose the 1890 Manifesto since he had preached for four years that the Millennium would occur in 1891. The rest of the Twelve read the Manifesto in the newspapers as they returned to Salt Lake City. Had Woodruff wanted the prior consent of the full Quorum of Twelve, he needed to wait only a few days. However, rather than risk a repetition of the Twelve's rejection of such a proposal, Woodruff made public abandonment of plural marriage a *fait accompli*.[181] An administrative irony involved in Wilford Woodruff's publishing the 1890 Manifesto was that he asked three non-apostles (including one non-general authority) to do pre-publication revisions of this crucial document about which the majority of the Twelve knew nothing.[182]

At the first council meeting of the entire Quorum of Twelve to consider the already-published Manifesto, the openly expressed misgivings of the apostles indicate that they would not have approved its publication. Although the after-the-fact vote was unanimous, some apostles assented grudgingly.[183]

Haunted by the specter of his own difficulty in forming a presidency, Woodruff in December 1892 urged second-ranked Apostle Lorenzo Snow to immediately organize upon Woodruff's death. When Snow asked in surprise if this was a revelation, Woodruff replied that he regarded it as such. Woodruff added: "Now Brother Snow do not neglect to organize as I have told you, it may prevent much trouble."[184] Since Woodruff's death in September 1898, the Quorum of the Twelve has made it a practice to endorse a new presidency within days after the church president's death.

Woodruff's personal victory in 1889 did not end tensions between the Quorum of the Twelve and First Presidency. Woodruff allowed Cannon to dominate the financial affairs of the church without consulting the apostles. Cannon said the apostles criticized him when the president's policy was the actual source of their discontent. "Why," Cannon asked the apostles in 1891, "should I be blamed for keeping secrets, when Pres. Woodruff knows them and could tell them if he desired?"[185]

The Woodruff presidency continued to shut out the apostles from decision-making. At a meeting of the Presidency and apostles seven months after Cannon's comment, Francis M. Lyman complained the Presidency left the apostles "in partial or total ignorance." At an 1894 quorum meeting "John W. Taylor said he did not feel under obligations to sustain the Presidency in anything about which they did not consult him and the Twelve."[186] At a private meeting of Lorenzo Snow, Brigham Young, Jr., Heber J. Grant, and John Henry Smith in December 1897, "We also determined to insist that under existing conditions that the Councilors of the President must consult the Apostles on leading questions."[187]

By 1898 some apostles renewed the decade-old battle against Cannon. At a quarterly conference of apostles on 4-5 January, John Henry Smith accused Cannon of being the real power in the First Presidency, and Marriner W. Merrill said Cannon "is virtually at the head of the Church today." Brigham Young, Jr., suggested that it was the Twelve's duty to remove Cannon as counselor before Woodruff's death. Nothing came of this proposal.[188]

This apostolic conference became a venue for discussing the larger question of jurisdiction. John Henry Smith noted, "We spent the day talking over the Relative positions of the first Presidency and Twelve Apostles on all great questions in the Church. All spoke and gave their views." United in their own position, the Twelve confronted the First Presidency on 6 January 1898:

> all of the first Presidency came in. President Lorenzo Snow [of the Quorum of the Twelve] asked the Presidency as to the duties of the Apostles in Connection with the Presidency in the financial affairs of the Church. All of the Apostles present spoke very plain and Elder Brigham Young made a very sweeping statement in which he said President Geo. Q. Cannon was the cause of the great indebtedness of the Church.
>
> All three of the Presidency said it was their view that the two Quorums should be united in the consideration of the more weighty problems that affect the whole Church.

Young even directly accused Cannon "of taking on himself too much of presidential authority." The next day, the Presidency and apostles agreed to "forgive each other for Harsh words spoken."[189]

This reconciliation lasted little more than a year. After a temple meeting of the Presidency and Twelve in March 1899, apostles John Henry Smith and Heber J. Grant "came near boiling over for fancied or real wrongs inflicted on them by Pres. C[annon]."[190] Until his death in 1901, several apostles harbored personal and jurisdictional complaints against Counselor Cannon.

To his credit Lorenzo Snow began his presidency in 1898 committed to avoiding the jurisdictional mistakes he felt the three previous church presidents had made. Two days after Woodruff's death, Snow said "that he wanted the Apostles to know how everything stood. He himself had not been taken into the counsels of the First Presidency any more than the rest of us." Apostle John Henry Smith responded "for him to take the Apostles into his confidence and they would back him."[191]

Still, most apostles opposed Snow's efforts from 1898 to 1901 to end polygamous cohabitation and to prohibit new marriages. During Quorum of Twelve meetings in July 1899, some apostles openly criticized the church president. Others voiced their concerns directly to the First Presidency during meetings in December 1899.[192] After Snow published a statement against cohabitation in January 1900, the Twelve discussed it and several expressed discomfort with the president's position.[193]

Nearly all the apostles privately demonstrated the extent of their opposition to Snow. Brigham Young, Jr., John W. Taylor, Marriner W. Merrill, Matthias F. Cowley, and Abraham Owen Woodruff married new plural wives. In addition, Francis M. Lyman and Heber J. Grant fathered polygamous children; John Henry Smith cohabited with his wives; and George Teasdale advised men to marry additional wives.[194] So in the personal lives of general authorities the Snow presidency was the most dramatic twentieth-century confrontation between the apostles and the church president.

Snow's final administrative act stunned the apostles as arbitrary. "Prest. Snow chose as his *2nd* Councillor Apostle Rudger Clawson with[out] consulting the Twelve Apostles," one quorum member wrote. "We knew nothing of it until his name was read off in the meeting" at October 1901 general conference. Snow died before he could set apart the new counselor, and Clawson became the only man sustained to the First Presidency without ever actually serving there.[195]

The longest administrative conflict occurred during the presidency of Heber J. Grant. On 4 February 1932 Presiding Patriarch Hyrum G. Smith died. Grant told the apostles in 1932 that he wanted to change the patrilineal descent to the Joseph F. Smith family and specifically to Grant's own son-in-law, Willard R. Smith.[196]

After making his own feelings clear, Grant invited the Twelve to submit a recommendation to him. He expected them to do what he could not bring himself to do—nominate his own son-in-law to be the new Presiding Patriarch. Instead the Twelve unanimously recommended the former patriarch's son, Eldred G. Smith. Grant responded, "I think the Quorum of the Twelve Apostles has made a mistake."[197]

Grant had three reasons to consider the quorum's recommendation. First, he had led the 1887-88 confrontation between the Twelve and the First Presidency and did not want to nullify the Twelve's prerogatives that he had fought for then. Second, he did not want to be accused of nepotism. Third, although Grant wrote that he could not get inspiration to accept Eldred G. Smith, he expressed frustration at having no inspiration to nominate anyone else.[198]

Thus at the centennial of the organization of the First Presidency, the church's two highest quorums were at an impasse. Either together or separately the two presiding quorums discussed this problem prior to general conference for ten years. Each time the church president and the apostles maintained their opposing views.[199]

In April 1937 four members of the Twelve tried to side-step Grant's choice for his son-in-law to be the new patriarch. They voted for him as their first choice to be a new apostle. Instead Grant felt "strongly impressed" to call another man as apostle. He continued to hope the Quorum of Twelve would change its 1933 recommendation for the Presiding Patriarch and instead accept his son-in-law.[200] During this ten-year deadlock, other men not in the patrilineal line served as "Acting Patriarch to the Church."[201]

In the midst of this stand-off, Grant publicly humiliated Apostle Richard R. Lyman concerning administrative differences about missionary work. In June 1937 the church president "raked Elder Lyman over the coals pretty firmly in front of a group of missionaries." Afterward Grant asked newly installed mission president Hugh B. Brown: "Hugh, what do you think of the way I took care of Richard?" Brown replied, "Perhaps what you said needed to be said, but here's a man that I've got to uphold as my leader, and you demeaned him in front of all his subordinates."[202]

After a decade the Twelve finally supported Grant's patriarchal proposal. At the apostles' quarterly meeting in July 1942, Apostle and Acting Patriarch George F. Richards reminded them that "for ten years the President has waited for us to reconsider," giving them a detailed justification for complying. That August Grant told the apostles that he "was not ready or willing to recommend" Eldred Smith for the position. It was obvious there would never be a new patriarch if the Twelve insisted on its recommendation.[203]

The next month Grant began meeting with the apostles one by one with a compromise proposal. Dropping his recommendation for his son-in-law, Grant sought their support individually for Joseph F. Smith (b. 1899) as the new patriarch. Smith was the oldest son of Hyrum M. Smith, a deceased member of the Quorum of the Twelve Apostles.

Grant's individual lobbying amounted to a divide-and-conquer approach to the Twelve's stonewalling. On 14 September he told Joseph Fielding Smith that he was "the only member of the Twelve holding out against the appointment of Joseph F. Smith as Patriarch." In fact, Grant had not even met with apostles Richard R. Lyman, Sylvester Q. Cannon, and George Albert Smith.[204] During these private meetings President Grant may have told each apostle that he was the last hold-out. In any event, one by one the apostles pledged to support Grant's new nomination. The Twelve's president, George Albert Smith, was absent.

Not surprisingly, Grant officially obtained the unanimous vote of the Twelve at the temple meeting of 17 September 1942. He called for this vote while George Albert Smith (one of Eldred's strongest advocates) was out of town and unaware of what was happening. Grant's diary noted that George Albert "heartily approved" of the council's vote upon his return. However, George Albert's reaction was different. "I am very much disappointed that Eldred will not be sustained," he wrote. "But the President is assuming the responsibility and I will sustain the appointment."[205] George Albert Smith simply acquiesced to an appointment made in his absence and contrary to his preference. Still Grant was understandably pleased at his success in overcoming unanimous opposition. He later wrote, "I was very glad that I stood out for ten years."[206] Such a stalemate is evidence of the inevitability of disagreement.

Grant's resolution of his patriarchal dispute with the Twelve was also a mid-twentieth-century example of what one apostle described as "unthinkable" in the LDS hierarchy. Boyd K. Packer has said: "It would be unthinkable deliberately to present an issue in such a way that approval depended upon how it was maneuvered through channels, who was presenting it, or who was present or absent when it was presented."[207] As indicated, the 1890 Manifesto and the 1969 changes regarding Indians and blacks depended on "who was present or absent" (above, chap. 1).

In a similar manner, from 1951 until incapacitated in the late 1960s, church president David O. McKay frequently made administrative decisions without consulting the Twelve and sometimes did not even inform them until after they had learned about the decisions from rank-and-file members.[208] Despite being the Twelve's president since 1951, Joseph Fielding Smith knew only "bits and pieces" about the church's finances and occasionally learned about major financial decisions from newspaper reports.[209] Even when he did consult the Twelve, McKay sometimes let them know he that expected no discussion, "phrasing his motion in such a way as to make it difficult for the rest of the brethren not to support him."[210] Prior to his appointment as a counselor in 1959, Apostle Henry D. Moyle complained that the Presidency did not tell the Twelve what they "should have known" about the church's finances, but once he became a counselor, Moyle "carried on [in] same way," according to the president of the holding company for church properties.[211]

It is therefore not surprising that Harold B. Lee reported in 1959 that the Twelve and the First Presidency "were farther apart now than ever."[212] Lee's biographer notes that until the 1960s the First Presidency "didn't delegate even to the Quorum of the Twelve any decision-making in regard to Priesthood matters." That began to change as Lee increasingly implemented the "Correlation Program" which his biographer called Lee's "powerful, controlling Correlation Department."[213] However, while Counselor Moyle was "widely perceived to be 'running the Church'" from 1959 through 1962, "members of the Council of the Twelve who had known Apostle Henry Moyle to be a strong advocate of council participation in policy making now found themselves more than ever excluded from First Presidency decisions."[214]

Nevertheless, even vast differences in seniority and philosophy did not alienate senior apostle Joseph Fielding Smith from junior apostles who became his administrative superiors through appointment as counselors in the First Presidency. Smith had nearly fifty years of apostolic seniority over Hugh B. Brown and the two "were not kindred spirits." However, when Brown became a presidency counselor in 1961, "Joseph Fielding Smith could not have treated him with greater deference." In fact, it made Brown uncomfortable that "Pres. Smith would step back to let President Brown go ahead" when they were walking together.[215]

However, in 1962 the Quorum of Twelve began to assert its rights against the jurisdiction of first counselor Henry D. Moyle over missionary work. Moyle was "holding special instructional and motivational meetings throughout the Church with missionaries, mission presidents, and other leaders." The Twelve resented this intrusion on its role as the general missionary committee: "This concern prompted two ranking [senior] members of the Twelve to discuss the matter privately with President McKay on August 7, 1962." Two days later McKay instructed Moyle to discontinue these missionary meetings and to stop using an apostle as his junior companion.[216]

McKay's mental condition declined in the last five years of his presidency. In July 1965 his secretary Clare Middlemiss confided that he was "slowly deteriorating" and "does not remember anything after conferences had with him unless he has a written memorandum on it." Two months later she commented that McKay's "partial disability" was the cause of "unfortunate cross-currents going on among the General Authorities."[217] In February 1966 several general authorities informed Utah's Mormon senator that "President McKay is senile."[218] By August 1967 McKay was "somewhat confused" in administrative meetings and "had to be guided largely by his counselors."[219]

Without consulting the Twelve in advance, McKay simply announced that Alvin R. Dyer would be ordained a special apostle in September 1967. As McKay's unofficial adviser, Dyer had antagonized the Presidency's official counselors as well as the Twelve. Several apostles refused to raise their hands to sustain Dyer at this temple meeting and were no happier when required to formally sustain him as a special counselor in 1968.[220] Not surprisingly, following McKay's death the Twelve did not nominate Dyer to fill a vacancy in their quorum. A First Presidency secretary has noted that this was a "wrenching" disappointment to Dyer who resumed his former role as an Assistant to the Twelve. Dyer died as the only twentieth-century apostle who was not admitted to the Quorum of Twelve.[221]

From 1967 until McKay's death in January 1970, LDS administration was in quiet disarray. Neither first counselor Hugh B. Brown nor second counselor N. Eldon Tanner ruled with the strong hand of George Q. Cannon or J. Reuben Clark under similar circumstances.[222] A major reason for that weaker position of Brown and Tanner was extra counselor Alvin R. Dyer who had independent access to the church president for private meetings and authorizations about which Brown and Tanner learned only from Dyer. In his nineties, extra counselor Joseph Fielding Smith was also unable "to carry much of the administrative load of the First Presidency."[223] Into this leadership vacuum came strong-willed apostles, including Harold B. Lee, Mark E. Petersen, and Ezra Taft Benson, who had competing agendas. By 1969 BYU's president observed that there was "complete turmoil" at church headquarters where various general authorities were "sparring for the ascendancy" of their own ideas.[224]

At McKay's death it is understandable that some apostles preferred not to organize a First Presidency at all as the easiest way to prevent ninety-three-year-old Joseph Fielding Smith from becoming church president since he was "so elderly."[225] Similar to the position of half the Twelve in 1887-89, this would allow the Twelve as a body to resume control of the church after years of being ignored. Although Harold B. Lee successfully persuaded the apostles to reorganize the First Presidency in January 1970 and allow Smith to head an independent presidency, Lee later acknowledged the Twelve's other option: "they could take no action and allow the Quorum of the Twelve to govern the Church as was happening at that moment."[226]

After its low ebb during the McKay presidency, the administrative role of the Twelve grew with each successive church president. A secretary to the First Presidency notes that after McKay's death, there "was the effort to involve the Quorum of the Twelve more directly in the decision-making process."[227] Apostles were more involved under presidents Joseph Fielding Smith (1970-72) and Harold B. Lee (1972-73). In the judgment of general authority Neal A. Maxwell, the presidency of Spencer W. Kimball (1973-85) included the Quorum of Twelve more fully than any previous church presidency of which he had knowledge.[228]

At least once during the 1980s the Twelve's ascendancy over-stepped its bounds. For decades Mark E. Petersen had distinguished himself as an apostle who "seemed to appoint himself a doctrinal watchdog." His daughter continues that when Petersen became "aware that any of the General Authorities or Regional Representatives might be preaching doctrine not in harmony with Church teachings, he never hesitated to point out the error in their thinking."[229] In 1983 the First Presidency was stunned to learn that Petersen was leading other members of the Twelve in conducting their own inquisition of Mormon intellectuals. This included Brigham Young University professors and Mormons in four western states who were editors and contributors to Mormon journals *Dialogue* and *Sunstone*. Counselor Gordon B. Hinckley instructed the apostles involved to cease the interrogations immediately.[230]

It is worth noting that there has been no known friction between the contemporary Twelve and First Presidency during the years one counselor alone led the First Presidency. This occurred for the first time from 1942 to 1945, due to President Heber J. Grant's relapse from a stroke, plus his second counselor's illnesses and trips out of Utah. "J. Reuben Clark was the *de facto* President of the Church," a secretary in the First Presidency's office commented, "and President Grant not only knew it but allowed it."[231]

Second counselor N. Eldon Tanner carried most of the administrative burden of the First Presidency from 1966 to 1968. Utah's senator wrote in March 1966: "We have [an] intolerable situation at the top now. President McKay is senile, President Joseph Fielding Smith is senile, President Brown is ill and can't be in his office much of the time, President Thorpe Isaacson has suffered a stroke and is unable to speak and is paralyzed on one side, so we really have only Eldon Tanner to carry the load. He does his best, but he has an impossible assignment."[232] Tanner's burden was lessened by the appointment of Alvin R. Dyer as a special counselor to the First Presidency in April 1968, although that involved the previously discussed problems.[233]

One of Hugh B. Brown's biographers described McKay as "often physically and mentally incapable of seeing the real issues and acting on them. Some days the aging president was bright and alert and on other days he had difficulty remembering decisions made a few minutes previous."[234]

The situation improved only slightly when ninety-three-year-old Joseph Fielding Smith became church president in January 1970 with Harold B. Lee as first counselor. The managing director of the church's financial department observes: "President Lee was the administrative president of the church during the years that Joseph Fielding Smith was president." The church's chief financial officer during this period adds: "As far as the administrative affairs, I didn't see that he [Joseph Fielding Smith] contributed, or was involved, in any significant way during his presidency. President Lee universally assumed that responsibility."[235]

The next period a single counselor was *de facto* church president was 1981 to 1985. President Spencer W. Kimball appointed Gordon B. Hinckley as an extra counselor in July 1981 because Parkinson's disease had incapacitated both first counselor N. Eldon Tanner and second counselor Marion G. Romney. By the end of 1981 Kimball was disabled after his third (and unsuccessful) brain surgery to relieve a subdural hematoma. Hinckley became second counselor after Tanner's death in 1982, a month after which first counselor Romney was *non compos mentis*.[236] An assistant secretary in the First Presidency also acknowledged that "President Kimball was not lucid, and so President Hinckley in fact was carrying the full burden." His official biographer dates this five months before Tanner's death: "By mid-1982 the day-to-day responsibilities of the First Presidency had shifted almost entirely to President Hinckley."[237]

In 1984 Hinckley told a general conference that there was "an active First Presidency" as long as one counselor could function.[238] "President Hinckley was conscientious in bringing matters to the Twelve," Apostle Neal A. Maxwell noted, "some of which he probably didn't need to. He went the extra mile in sharing things [with the apostles] that were well within his prerogative as the surviving counselor to handle on his own." While still vigorous, Kimball promoted harmony and consensus in the hierarchy. With Hinckley's carefully-studied stewardship that consensus endured the difficult last four years of Kimball's presidency. In April 1984 Hinckley described the LDS hierarchy without exaggeration: "there has never been greater unity in its leading councils and the relationships of those councils one to another, than there is today."[239]

The consensus continued with the presidency of Ezra Taft Benson beginning in November 1985. The *New York Times* accurately commented that Benson "spawned controversy in the church for 20 years."[240] However, by the time he became president, eighty-six-year-old Benson's drive was tempered by memory loss and physical frailty. In January 1986 he had a fainting spell and ten months later received a surgically-implanted heart pacemaker. In 1987 he had a mild coronary which kept him from active participation for more than two months.[241]

Benson's ill health enhanced the moderating influence of his counselors. First counselor Gordon B. Hinckley's careful leadership had already endeared him to the hierarchy and church at large during the four years that he was *de facto* church president. Second counselor Thomas S. Monson, an equally careful yet powerful administrator, likewise typically sought consensus rather than confrontation and imposition. Although conservative, Hinckley and Monson never shared Benson's embrace of ultra-conservative politics.[242]

By May 1989 the counselors felt it necessary to execute legal documents giving them Ezra Taft Benson's "power of attorney [which] shall not be affected by his disability" or "incompetence." However, Benson was already affected by that "disability." Despite a notarized statement by the First Presidency's secretary, President Benson did not sign those documents himself. A signature machine produced Benson's identical signatures on these legal documents.[243]

Without public acknowledgement, this machine-signed document formally ended an official provision for dissolving the First Presidency that had been in print for ninety years. Since 1899 the book *Articles of Faith*,

"Written By Appointment; and Published By the Church," had specified
that the "First Presidency is disorganized through the death or disability
of the President."[244] However, this 1989 document specified that the
counselors would not dissolve the First Presidency or surrender their
powers despite the fact of the church president's "disability" or "incompetence." The current apostles have supported this policy, even though the
officially published *Articles of Faith* continues to specify that when there is
"disability of the President, the directing authority in [church] government
reverts at once to the Quorum of the Twelve Apostles."[245]

Counselors Hinckley and Monson were now in the familiar role of
leading the church due to a president's incapacitation. Benson was too
weak to address the April 1990 general conference. He entered the
hospital the following June for an infection and in September had two
separate brain surgeries for subdural hematomas. Like his predecessor
Benson was severely incapacitated thereafter.[246] At the October 1992
general conference Hinckley specifically commented about the administrative effects of President Benson's incapacitation. He denied that "the
Church faces a crisis," just because he and Counselor Thomas S. Monson
were the "backup system" for the incapacitated President Benson.[247]

In July 1993 the First Presidency's spokesman claimed that "the typical
faithful Mormon" already knew that Ezra Taft Benson's mental condition
prevented the church president from participating in decision-making.[248]
Hinckley and Monson maintained the same consensus and relative harmony with the Twelve that Hinckley alone had preserved during the years
when the Presidency's assistant secretary acknowledged that "President
Kimball was not lucid." Following Benson's death in 1994, the new church
president was the physically frail Howard W. Hunter. Again the same two
counselors served as the "backup system" while Hunter was incapacitated
for the last third of his nine-month presidency.[249]

Six months after Gordon B. Hinckley became LDS president in March
1995, there was oddly public evidence of disagreement between an apostle
and the First Presidency. In September the church's official *Ensign* magazine published a "First Presidency Message" by newly-appointed second
counselor James E. Faust who denounced "the false belief of inborn
homosexual orientation." The Presidency's message continued: "No scientific evidence demonstrates absolutely that this is so. Besides, if it were
so, it would frustrate the whole plan of mortal happiness." The next month
the *Ensign* published an article by Apostle Dallin H. Oaks who seemed to
challenge that absolute denial. Oaks wrote that there is "some evidence
that inheritance is a factor in susceptibilities to various behavior-related
disorders like aggression, alcoholism, and obesity. It is easy to hypothesize
that inheritance plays a role in sexual orientation." The apostle, a former

president of BYU and former justice of the Utah Supreme Court, then cited studies supporting the biological origin of same-sex desire, as well as contrary views.[250] There has been no official explanation why the church's magazine published this apostolic revision of an unconditional statement of doctrine by the First Presidency only a month earlier.

However, regarding the day-to-day administrative realities at LDS headquarters, a First Presidency secretary's recent description of the relationship between these two presiding quorums is inadvertently revealing.

> While the Twelve confer regularly with the First Presidency in their weekly temple meetings, they usually are not privy to the wide range of Church responsibilities discharged by the latter, matters pertaining to finances, physical facilities, personnel, temple work, public relations, and the myriad activities carried on under the umbrella of the Corporation of the President—or, in earlier years, the Trustee in Trust.[251]

Throughout Mormon history, those in the First Presidency's office (including its secretaries) have regarded it as impractical to involve the apostles in its "myriad activities." However, as the previous examples demonstrate, there has been tension between the Quorum of Twelve and First Presidency whenever the apostles felt they were not sufficiently "privy to the wide range of Church responsibilities discharged" by the church president and his counselors. Those differing perspectives guarantee periodic tensions between the LDS church's two highest quorums.

The Quorum of the Twelve Apostles

Until 1976 the Twelve was the largest presiding quorum of the church. A century after its 1835 organization, a total of fifty-eight men had been admitted as members. Thirty-four additional men have joined the quorum since the mid-1930s to fill vacancies from death or other causes. With twelve different personalities voting on crucial decisions, the potential for tensions is high, yet the apostles seek to minimize their differences as much as possible. The following discussion gives a chronological summary of a few areas that have been problematic.

As the most cultured apostle to join the Twelve during Joseph Smith's lifetime, John Taylor antagonized Brigham Young, who believed his own talents were superior to Taylor's. "Just as quick as he was in the Quo[rum of Twelve]," Young later told the apostles, John Taylor said "you r my niggers & you shall black my boots." Young mockingly described Apostle John Taylor to others as "Prince John."[252]

Young leveled accusations against Taylor that would have been difficult for anyone to bear without lasting resentment. On one occasion he accused Taylor of trying "to gull every Sov[ereign]. & Shil[ling] in England." He refused to reimburse Taylor's expenses for establishing a sugar refinery for the church with the explanation that Taylor had "ruined many, and many a poor family" as a businessman. Taylor replied that he would not allow Young "to cram a thing down my throat that is not so."[253] Young had serious disputes with Orson Pratt, yet both seemed to genuinely respect each other. By contrast, Young and Taylor privately detested each other.[254]

Understandably, Taylor tried to downplay the significance of his conflict with the church president. "When Prest. Brigham Young was alive," Taylor reminisced to the apostles, "there were some things in which my views differed from his."[255] Yet from April 1875 onward, Young had publicly indicated the depth of his disapproval of Taylor. According to Taylor, Young had "stated that John Taylor was the man that stood next to him; and that where he was not, John Taylor presides."[256] To the contrary, when this claim was reported barely a month after Young's death, Young's first counselor Daniel H. Wells told the apostles that it was absolutely false: "Elder Wells said that he did not believe that any man ever heard president Young say that, for *he* knew, that he never thought so."[257] In support of that statement, Young had never presented Taylor for a sustaining vote in general conference as the Twelve's president and instead left the position vacant.[258]

On 1 April 1877 the Young-Taylor conflict erupted during a congregational meeting at St. George, Utah. Apostle Wilford Woodruff recorded in shorthand that President Young "reproved the 12 [apostles] for not uniting into the United Order [an economic enterprise] more than they had." The diary entry was in shorthand because, as Lorenzo Snow later explained, it was Taylor whom Young "terribly scourged" and gave an "awful thrashing." Brigham Jr.'s diary noted that his father warned that "the Twelve must take a different course—that is some of them—or they would lose the Crown and others would take what they might have had." Rather than commending Taylor as his probable successor, Young warned that he was on the verge of losing his "Crown" or apostleship altogether.[259]

Young was angry enough to cancel the assignment he had given Taylor two days earlier to organize nearby stakes with Lorenzo Snow. Instead Young said that Taylor "had better return home and make wagons until he knew what was right." Snow regarded Young's public attack as "uncalled for" and delivered "unjustly," but Snow finally intervened to persuade Taylor to apologize to Young. Snow was convinced that Taylor would "never" be church president if he left St. George without apologizing.[260]

In nearly forty years of apostolic association, every reconciliation between Young and Taylor was tense and temporary. Four months after their public confrontation, Young died. This left Taylor as senior-ranked apostle without the kind of endorsement he would have liked and later claimed.

In the 1860s Orson Pratt and Erastus Snow experienced deep tension as they jointly presided over Mormons in southern Utah. Anthony W. Ivins later commented that Snow, his father-in-law, was the better administrator of the two, even though Pratt was the senior apostle. Pratt and his family were offended that Snow made no secret of his contempt for Pratt's leadership. This quiet stress surfaced when Orson Jr. publicly claimed Snow was "a secret influence working against" his father and said he wanted nothing to do with a church that allowed such behavior. Pratt and his family left southern Utah shortly after his son's excommunication.[261]

Apostle Joseph F. Smith wrote that during a council meeting in the Endowment House in 1880, Erastus Snow "threw out an insult to me and M. Thatcher. But we let it pass." At the council meeting the next day, Snow repeated the insults but then apologized.[262] At another meeting three years later, quorum counselor Daniel H. Wells and Apostle Brigham Young, Jr., "had some *words*." A week later Wells refused to shake hands with Young, who then declined to join the prayer circle with Wells.[263]

Erastus Snow had a long-standing conflict with Wilford Woodruff. First, they had "an altercation" over finances during a council meeting in 1883.[264] Relations became even more strained due to Snow's opposition to a Woodruff presidency. In a council meeting in March 1888 Snow accused Woodruff and George Q. Cannon of being "men worshippers[,] sycophants & [guilty of] todyism." The normally placid Woodruff said, "it Stird my blood," and lashed back in kind. Then Woodruff lamented, "I think I done wrong & went to[o] far in the matter."[265]

By the 1890s general authorities were involved with so many businesses that competition was common. In April 1890 Brigham Young, Jr., lamented how business conflicts were fragmenting the apostles: "Our Quorum represents firms whose employees are at swords points and all claiming to be brethren, too." He added a month later that "even the members of the Twelve represent businesses which are jealous of each other and almost ready to fight each other."[266] The most divisive was the Bullion, Beck, and Champion Mining Company. Eight general authorities stood on both sides of hostile take-overs and threatened lawsuits.[267]

In 1894 Marriner W. Merrill said "he had not felt well towards Bro. [Brigham] Young [Jr.] for years" over a family dispute. There was such bitterness that Young wrote in 1900 that he "did not believe" the religious testimony Merrill shared during a temple meeting of the apostles. In 1901

Apostle Anthon H. Lund observed that "Bro. Merrill feels hurt" because Young publicly criticized him. Lund commented: "The words of Brigham have no doubt hurt him deeply. I hope he may be wise enough not to show any resentment on that score."[268]

At the turn of the twentieth century, apostolic conflict sometimes occurred during general conference. "There was a conflict between two Apostles on the stand before 10,000 people," general authority J. Golden Kimball wrote in October 1898. He immediately added: "I am grateful that I know that the gospel is true."[269]

Apostle Francis M. Lyman gradually discovered that he was the center of a perplexing conflict from 1890 to 1906. Most of the apostles were secretly entering, performing, or encouraging new plural marriages during the fourteen years between 1890 and the so-called "Second Manifesto" of 1904. Until then Lyman was the only apostle who tried to actively enforce the 1890 Manifesto against polygamy. Lyman felt he was consistently implementing the published statements and official declarations of three church presidents.

However, the other apostles followed secret authorizations of these church presidents and their counselors. Particularly from 1900 to 1904, most of the Twelve regarded Lyman as an enemy of the "Principle."[270] For example, in November 1903 Apostle Matthias F. Cowley told a local church officer that "Pres. Lyman's views & teachings on the Manifesto given by Pres. Woodruff were incorrect and not endorsed by the First Presidency & Apostles."[271] Lyman was the Twelve's president. This was an undercurrent in every council meeting from 1890 to 1906.

Most church members regarded the 1905 resignations of apostles Matthias F. Cowley and John W. Taylor as casualties of post-Manifesto polygamy. In contrast, Francis M. Lyman saw the resignations as his personal vindication. After he announced these resignations for the first time at the April 1906 general conference, Lyman told the general priesthood meeting: "I do not want it whispered that I am not in harmony with Prest. Smith or that he is not in accord with me." Lyman became emotional as he reminded local priesthood leaders that "some of us had doubted him."[272] This was the dramatic resolution of more than fifteen years of a fundamental conflict among the apostles.

Ironically, in 1911 Matthias F. Cowley again divided the Twelve. At the quorum's request he made a detailed statement of his polygamous activities from 1890 to 1906. Apostles Lyman, Charles W. Penrose, and George F. Richards wanted to disfellowship Cowley. The other seven apostles regarded his several-hour testimony as humble and contrite. This majority said Cowley had been punished enough and did not deserve to be disfellowshipped.

After two days of discussion and no change in views, the three apostles refused to defer to the majority. Lyman, president of the Twelve, finally won over the more forgiving apostles with a compromise motion. Cowley would be deprived of the right to exercise the priesthood but would not be formally disfellowshipped. That meant he would retain other church privileges. After more discussion the apostles unanimously voted for this motion as the only way out of the two-day deadlock.[273]

As an apostle-senator for thirty years, Republican Reed Smoot was sometimes at odds with his quorum about political matters. In 1905 he was so angry at Democratic apostle Charles W. Penrose that Smoot said that he "will not forgive Penrose." The senator's LDS secretary thought a church court might be necessary to resolve "such bitter feelings."[274]

Smoot's next conflict involved his opposition to statewide prohibition of alcohol. This pitted him against apostles Heber J. Grant, Hyrum M. Smith, and David O. McKay. These three regarded Smoot as "not in harmony with the Quorum" and routinely snubbed him at meetings in the Salt Lake temple.[275] When some of the same general authorities disagreed over a tax proposal in 1918, first counselor Anthon H. Lund commented: "I woke in the night and thought of the bitterness that can arise among brethren when they can not see eye to eye."[276]

Smoot's position on the League of Nations in 1919-20 was similarly divisive. Smoot opposed the league, as did Apostle Joseph Fielding Smith, though for different reasons. Both found themselves at odds with the rest of the Twelve and First Presidency, who were promoting in every way they could ratification of the Versailles Treaty and League of Nations. One historian observes that apostles Anthony W. Ivins and Stephen L Richards "were particularly vehement" against Smoot for acting contrary to "the decision of the Council." Ardent Democrat Charles W. Penrose joined fellow Democrats in criticizing Smoot, who was among the U.S. senators who helped defeat ratification of the League of Nations.[277]

Another controversy emerged in 1923 when the First Presidency and Twelve decided that the endowment undergarment worn outside the temple would be different from the undergarment worn inside the temple. The new "street" garment had buttons instead of the traditional strings, no collar, and sleeves above the elbow instead of at the wrist. It was knee-length instead of ankle-length and closed-crotch rather than open as had been the tradition. George Albert Smith and Joseph Fielding Smith remained opposed to this change but supported the decision of the First Presidency and rest of the Twelve.[278]

George Albert Smith's biographer documented an apostolic conflict involving Smith's oldest daughter, Emily Smith Stewart, a decade later. Her disagreements with the president of the church's Primary Association for children led to her abrupt release from the Primary General Board in 1932. She then secured her father's support for her immediate reinstatement. After attending the council meeting which discussed the conflict on 17 November, George Albert wrote: "Am sad to know there is so much misunderstanding among some of our leaders."[279] His biographer notes: "In the Emily Stewart affair, however, the pursuit of sincere but conflicting views divided the Quorum of the Twelve, with some members concurring in the dismissals and others standing with the Smith family. At one point two neutral members of the Twelve were asked to look into the dispute and seek a solution, but nothing came of it." Smith was convinced that his colleagues were not interested in his family's welfare. His estrangement became so severe by March 1933 that President Heber J. Grant did not want to join him in temple prayer circles. Grant ended the dispute by declaring the absolute finality of Emily's release.[280]

For almost twenty years Apostle Joseph Fielding Smith was at odds with more scientifically oriented apostles over his rejection of organic evolution and the age of the earth. The controversy originally involved Smith and B. H. Roberts of the First Council of Seventy, but it soon expanded to include to varying degrees apostles James E. Talmage, John A. Widtsoe, and Joseph F. Merrill. After Roberts, Smith, and Talmage publicly refuted each other's views, President Grant imposed a moratorium on public expression concerning the topic.[281]

Longevity gave Smith the last word. He outlived Talmage and Roberts (d. 1933), Grant (d. 1945), and Widtsoe and Merrill (d. 1952). As sole survivor of the controversy, Smith told a quarterly meeting of apostles in 1953 his version of "Pre Adam-theorist-Talmage-Widtsoe and others." Without consulting new church president, David O. McKay, in 1954 the Twelve's president published his anti-evolution *Man: His Origin and Destiny.*

This book was a comprehensive attack on organic evolution and geology. Later that year the First Presidency refused to allow the book to be used as a text in LDS seminaries and institutes. McKay explained verbally and in writing that Smith's book "was not published by the Church, and is not approved by the Church." Concerning this and other doctrinal questions, J. Reuben Clark commented, "some matters have come to my attention where the Brethren not only differ among themselves, but where they differ with the First Presidency."[282]

Even the closest personal friends and administrative allies in the Quorum of Twelve were sometimes in sharp conflict in the post-World War II period. Harold B. Lee became an apostle in 1941, Henry D. Moyle in 1947, and Marion G. Romney in 1951. The three were close friends, associates in the church's welfare program, and were protégés of Clark.

Nevertheless in 1963 Lee acknowledged, "Often we disagreed, sometimes violently, but I think no three men ever had greater respect for each other than we did for each other."[283] Lee's biographer also acknowledged that "his fiery temper . . . had offended people," while a First Presidency secretary wrote of Lee's "combativeness" and that his "relationship with Brother Moyle was not always placid."[284]

And, of course, there were inevitable personality conflicts and inadvertent insults among the modern apostles. For example, Spencer W. Kimball (who stood 5'6") was deeply offended during a temple meeting in 1951 when a "tall and handsome" apostle described a local leader as "a little runt." Kimball never forgave his fellow apostle for that remark: "I've always held that against him a bit."[285]

During this same post-war period another strong personality was often at the center of conflict: Ezra Taft Benson. The issues he combatted demonstrate many of the strains which have developed within the church's highest quorums. In this sense the stormy career of Ezra Taft Benson is a valuable case study of how the institution deals with conflict.

CHAPTER 3

Ezra Taft Benson: A Study of Inter-Quorum Conflict

From the 1950s to the 1980s Apostle Ezra Taft Benson occupied center stage in a series of political conflicts within the LDS church. Though in 1943 he became an apostle, with President David O. McKay's permission he served as Secretary of Agriculture to U.S. president Dwight D. Eisenhower from 1953 to 1961. His autobiography and official biography detail the national controversies involved with his service as Secretary of Agriculture.[1]

Less known was the quiet conflict between the agriculture secretary and politically conservative LDS administrators and general authorities. As early as 1953 First Presidency counselor J. Reuben Clark said he was "apprehensive of Bro Benson in Washington." By 1957 Clark and Apostle Mark E. Petersen instructed the church's *Deseret News* to "print the adverse comment" about Benson's government service.[2]

During 1958 several church leaders expressed opposition to Benson. In March Apostle Harold B. Lee said that Benson needed "humbling" in order to serve "properly . . . as a member of the Council of the Twelve."[3] In July 1958 Ernest L. Wilkinson, Brigham Young University president, wrote that Benson "espouse[s] certain principles which are utterly inconsistent with the feeling of the Brethren."[4] During the next several months Apostle Hugh B. Brown campaigned for the Democratic candidate in Utah's senatorial race, against Benson's support for the incumbent Republican.[5]

Criticism of Benson even occurred within the First Presidency. In 1958 Clark said, "I did not think the Secretary of Agriculture would yield to argument"—this in conversation with the chair of the Utah Cattlemen's Association and with the chair of the National Wool Growers Association. Two years later Clark complained that "Sec'y Benson's policies have about extinguished the small farmer and small cattleman."[6] That view was shared by the other counselor in the First Presidency, Henry D. Moyle.[7] In 1961 Wilkinson observed that "President McKay for the moment is displeased with some things that Brother Benson has done."[8]

It is unclear whether Benson even knew that his fellow general authorities disapproved his policies. For example, Clark concealed his feelings in public statements about Benson. In conversations and correspondence with Benson, Clark also muted his dissent.[9] As for apostles Lee and Petersen, in 1953 Lee had publicly "scolded" Mormons who criticized recently appointed Secretary Benson, and Petersen had privately encouraged Benson to ignore his critics.[10] They apparently did not tell him of their growing dissatisfaction with his policies.

On the other hand, almost as soon as Benson returned to Utah in 1961, he became involved in a well-known conflict with senior members of the hierarchy. His official biographer declined to write about this controversy, and that silence remains in the biographies of other general authorities who were prominently involved.[11] Despite this conflict's significance, it is either absent or muted in histories of the LDS church. Because these matters directly relate to the internal dynamics of the modern LDS hierarchy, I will closely examine Benson's conflicts with other general authorities which began in the 1960s.[12]

At issue was Benson's anti-Communist crusade and his unrelenting effort to obtain or imply LDS endorsement of the John Birch Society. Founded in December 1958, the Birch Society was named for an American soldier killed by Chinese Communists ten days after the end of World War II.[13] Philosophical heir of the House Un-American Activities Committee (HUAC) and of U.S. senator Joseph McCarthy, the Birch Society became the most significant grass-roots organization to express the "Great Fear" of Communist triumphs internationally and of Communist subversions in America after World War II.[14] As Secretary of Agriculture, Benson reflected that concern in his *The Threat of Communism [and] World Brotherhood*, published by the church's Deseret Book Company in 1960.

Benson described the Birch Society as "the most effective non-church organization in our fight against creeping socialism and godless Communism." He added, "I know their leaders, I have attended two of their all-day Council meetings. I have read their literature. I feel I know their program."[15] On the other hand, even such well-known political conservatives and anti-Communists as Barry Goldwater, William F. Buckley, Russell Kirk, and Ronald Reagan described the Birch Society as "ultra-conservative," "right-wing," "extremist," "paranoid," "fanatic fringe," or "lunatic fringe."[16]

Anti-Communist activism polarized American conservatives from the 1950s onward. The Birch Society became an important manifestation of that conservative split.[17] In the early 1960s national officers, council members, "Endorsers," and editorial staff of the Birch Society were also directors of twenty-one conservative organizations.[18]

Less than a year after the Birch Society's founding, Benson was in close association with at least one of its highest leaders. In September-October 1959 Benson took Thomas J. Anderson with him as a member of his entourage on an official trip to Europe, including a visit to the Soviet Union. At that time Anderson was publisher of *Farm and Ranch* magazine as well as an influential member of the new Birch Society. By the time he accompanied Benson on a trip to the Far East in November 1960, Anderson was a member of the national governing council of the Birch Society.[19] By 1961 Benson had established an association with the Birch Society and would soon refer to its founder Robert H. Welch affectionately as "Dear Bob."[20]

This association with "Birchers"[21] represented a reversal of the position Benson took during his early years as U.S. Secretary of Agriculture. In 1954 he publicly condemned "the hysterical preachings of those who would destroy our basic freedoms under the guise of anti-communism." This was generally understood to be Benson's attack on Senator Joseph R. McCarthy.[22] Within a few years, however, Benson wrote that McCarthy "rendered a service in emphasizing the insidious threat of the Communist influence in government."[23] Secretary Benson's odyssey from anti-McCarthyism to neo-McCarthyism is beyond the scope of this chapter, but it is necessary to recognize that he made such a transition. Although Benson was never a member of record, his wife Flora and sons Reed and Mark all allegedly joined the John Birch Society.[24]

Immediately after his official trip with the Birch council member in 1960, Benson proposed to BYU president Ernest L. Wilkinson that his son Reed be used for "espionage" on the church campus. To Apostle Harold B. Lee, Reed explained that as a BYU faculty member "he could soon find out who the orthodox teachers were and report to his father." After resisting Benson's proposal for Reed's employment, Wilkinson countered that "neither Brother Lee nor I want espionage of that character."[25]

Reed had already organized student surveillance at the University of Utah during the 1959-60 school year. For example, he asked a conservative freshman to provide him with the names of students who were active in liberal causes on campus. This student enrolled in a political science course taught by J. D. Williams in order to monitor this liberal Democrat's classroom statements. The student-spy added that "I transferred to Brigham Young University, where I was involved in the same sorts of things."[26] Along with several other student-spies, he was active in BYU's Young Americans for Freedom.[27]

Apostle Benson's suggestion in November 1960 for "espionage" at BYU reflected two dimensions of the national Birch leadership. First, their long-time preoccupation with university professors as Communist-sympathizers ("Comsymps").[28] Second, the Birch program for covert "infiltration" of various groups.[29] Benson's suggestion would finally be implemented during the 1960s and 1970s by members and advocates of the Birch Society.

As early as the fall of 1961 some rank-and-file Mormons learned that Benson's anti-Communism had created a rift within the Mormon hierarchy. Benson proclaimed to October 1961 general conference: "No true Latter-day Saint and no true American can be a socialist or a communist or support programs leading in that direction."[30] Upon inquiry by a politically liberal Mormon, Counselor Hugh B. Brown replied in November that a Mormon "can be a Democrat or a Socialist and still be a good church member." Brown added that "he had just had a talk with Bro Benson" who was "on the carpet in regard to his political sallies of late."[31]

In December 1961 conservative BYU president Wilkinson noted that Benson was privately criticizing "the socialistic tendencies" of Brown. Wilkinson added that the two general authorities were already in "a vigorous dispute" about Communism.[32]

That same month the *Church News* printed Benson's talk in which he affirmed that "the internal threat to the American way of life is in the secret alliance which exists between the more advanced Social Democrats and the hard-core Communist conspiracy." He claimed that there was an "insidious infiltration of communist agents and sympathizers into almost every segment of American life." Benson added that "Social Democrats" in America were "in government, education, communications and policy-making bodies. There they remain today, occupying some of the highest offices in the land."[33] Prior to the talk, Benson also told reporters that current U.S. president John F. Kennedy was "very soft in dealing with the Communist threat."[34]

Immediately after the press reports of Benson's talk, Brown asked the editor of the *Deseret News* to write him a detailed briefing on the Birch Society.[35] Two weeks later Brown responded to an inquiry about the Birch Society by writing that "we [the First Presidency] are definitely against their methods." On the heels of Benson's widely publicized talk, Brown continued that "we do not think dividing our own people, casting reflections on our government officials, or calling everybody a Communist who do[es] not agree with the political views of certain individuals is the proper way to fight Communism." He added that LDS "leaders, or even members, should not become hysterical or take hasty action, engage in discussions, and certainly should not join these [anti-Communist] groups, some of whom, at least, are in for the money they can make out of it."[36]

The last week of February 1962 Benson cancelled at the last minute his appearance on a television program titled "Thunder on the Right." Some credited this to Brown's influence.[37] The presidency's counselor wrote a Mormon on 2 March about "the unwise actions of some of our people with respect to the extreme right activities. Many of us have been trying to counter this and I think at last have succeeded in removing some of the agitators."[38]

In fact, the conflict between Brown and Benson became a running battle in the Mormon hierarchy. In rebuttal to the publicity of Benson's remarks the previous December, Brown instructed the general priesthood meeting in April 1962: "The degree of a man's aversion to communism may not always be measured by the noise he makes in going about and calling everyone a communist who disagrees with his personal political bias." In a more direct allusion, Brown said, "There is no excuse for members of this Church, especially men who hold the priesthood, to be opposing one another over communism . . ." He concluded: "Let us not undermine our government or accuse those who hold office of being soft on communism. . . . [or] by destroying faith in our elected officials under the guise of fighting communism."[39]

Brown's rebuttal came directly from the newspaper reports of Benson's December 1961 talk. One Mormon wrote that "Bro. Brown certainly was talking to Benson when he warned the Priesthood Saturday about the dangers of extremism & of charging our leaders as dupes of the Communist conspiracy."[40] Of his April 1962 conference remarks, Brown confided: "While we do not think it wise to name names in our statements of Church policy, the cries which come from certain sources would indicate that somebody was hit by some of our statements and that was what we hoped would be the result."[41] Almost immediately Benson renewed his public statements about Communist influence in the United States.[42]

Because of this Brown-Benson dispute, BYU president Wilkinson told church president McKay in June 1962 that "President Brown is giving aid and comfort to the enemies of what should be sound basic Mormon philosophy."[43] In October first counselor Henry D. Moyle said that second counselor Brown spoke to a Democratic convention in Utah only "because Brother Benson had given a political tirade that needed answering."[44] A few days after Benson endorsed the Birch Society, Brown wrote that he was "disgusted" by Benson's activities "in connection with the John Birch Society," and if they did not cease, "some disciplinary action should be taken."[45]

Transcending personality, the Benson-Brown conflict reflected deep political divisions in the church and in the more diverse nation at large during the tumultuous 1960s.[46] Both men had a political stand.[47] However, Benson was notable for the manner in which he tried to mobilize both the LDS church president and general membership behind his own political agenda.

In the midst of the Cuban Missile Crisis of October 1962, Benson's son Reed became coordinator for the Birch Society in Utah. His announcement was coupled with his father's first public endorsement of the Birch Society.[48] The day before this announcement, President McKay gave Reed Benson permission to accept the Birch position.[49] Seven months earlier a ward bishop had complained that Reed violated the First Presidency's policy against political use of chapels by speaking to a stake meeting about the "currently popular, militantly anti-communist movement of which the speaker is the leading spokesman."[50]

Such activity infuriated both counselors to McKay. "It is certainly regrettable," Brown wrote in November 1962, that Reed Benson "is permitted to continue to peddle his bunk in our Church houses. The matter was brought sharply to the attention of the President by Brother Moyle during my absence."[51] That same month Henry D. Taylor, an Assistant to the Twelve Apostles, said that "in his judgment [Reed] Benson was the laughing stock of Salt Lake" for his Birch activism.[52] While speaking at a stake conference in the Assembly Hall on Salt Lake Temple Square, Counselor Moyle also "denounced tactics of Reed Benson and upheld J. D. Williams as a bishop without mentioning names."[53]

Nevertheless, the Birch Society's Utah membership tripled in the next six months after Reed Benson's appointment as state coordinator. A year later Reed also became coordinator for the Mormon counties of southern Idaho. Two years after his initial appointment the younger Benson left Utah to become the Birch coordinator in Washington, D.C. Eventually, Reed became the national director of public relations for the entire society.[54] In addition to introducing Birch beliefs to Mormons, Reed convinced the national Birch Council to open its meetings with prayer.[55]

Meanwhile, Ezra Taft Benson unsuccessfully tried to get President McKay's approval for the president of the Birch Society to speak at a session of LDS general conference.[56] Failing that, Benson endorsed the Birch Society during his talks at stake conferences and preached Birch themes in his general conference sermons.[57] In fact, Benson's official biographer calculated that during the decade of the 1960s "fifteen of his twenty general conference addresses focused on one or more of these [political] topics."[58]

By October 1962 these partisan talks at general conference were resulting in public dissent by LDS university students. In response to Benson's conference statement that "No true Latter-day Saint can be a socialist or a communist," a University of Utah student from Norway countered that "more than half" of Norwegian Mormons vote for the socialist Labor Party. This student concluded: "I am glad the president of the Church has taken a stand against Communism. But I do not think it is the responsibility of any other speaker in the tabernacle to give his own political opinions regarding welfare states." In equally public responses, other LDS students attacked such Mormons for criticizing Benson.[59]

Although the Benson-Brown controversy was less public at BYU, it was equally intense. By the fall of 1962 members of the Birch Society's national council and editorial advisory committee had been speakers at BYU's "Forum" assemblies which were attended by the majority of students. This reflected the pro-Birch sentiments of BYU's president. At the same time faculty members formally complained to Brown.[60] On one occasion Brown intervened directly to veto Benson's instructions that Wilkinson convene a special assembly at BYU to host the Birch president who was "staying at the Hotel Utah" in anticipation of the opportunity.[61]

After giving a "political" talk to a multi-stake meeting of BYU students in November 1962, religion professor Glenn L. Pearson told one of his students that Benson's support of the Birch Society was a mission from God. Then this religion professor, described by BYU's president as "the most untactful person I have heard," told his student that Brown was "a Judas in the First Presidency." The student concluded that a church court should be convened to excommunicate Brown.[62]

Such controversy on Utah's campuses appalled general authorities who did not want young Latter-day Saints to regard the Birch Society or its philosophy as a measure of one's faith. However, Benson skillfully created a public environment which left the First Presidency and his fellow apostles only five difficult options: remain silent, privately rebuke him, publicly endorse his views, publicly repudiate his views without naming him, or publicly repudiate him by name. On various occasions from the 1960s to early 1980s the hierarchy ambivalently adopted each possible response to Benson's political crusade. These "seemingly conflicting actions," the *Wall Street Journal* observed, "at different times have given comfort to both pro-Birch and anti-Birch Mormons."[63]

In January 1963 the First Presidency broke its silence. Their announcement stated: "We deplore the presumption of some politicians, especially officers, co-ordinators and members of the John Birch Society, who undertake to align the Church or its leadership with their political views."[64] This was a not-too-subtle reference to Benson's son Reed, the Utah Birch coordinator. Three days after the First Presidency announcement, Benson spoke at a rally endorsed by the Birch Society in Boston. Newspapers reported this as a defiant embarrassment to the LDS church.[65]

Mormon members of the Birch Society directly criticized the First Presidency for its January 1963 statement. For example, one pro-Birch Mormon informed McKay that she loved him as a prophet, but that the church president had inadvertently "given much aid and comfort to the enemy." She concluded that "this statement by the First Presidency regarding the John Birch Society and Reed Benson . . . might have an ill effect on the Missionary work."[66] Such letters stunned the normally hard-crusted first counselor Henry D. Moyle who wrote: "When we pursue any course which results in numerous letters written to the Presidency critical of our work, it should be some evidence we should change our course." Only five days after the statement's publication, Moyle had second thoughts about the First Presidency's anti-Birch approach.[67]

It is not surprising that McKay (always sensitive to criticism) also expressed concern by 31 January that "the First Presidency probably went a little too far" in its Birch statement. His secretary confided that McKay was disturbed by "at least 25 letters vigorously protesting the statement of the First Presidency on the John Birch Society—many of them very intelligent letters."[68]

Two weeks later the church president instructed his secretary Clare Middlemiss to send a reply to Mormon Birchers. The letter affirmed: "The Church is not opposing the John Birch Society or any other organization of like nature; however, it is definitely opposed to anyone using the Church for the purpose of increasing membership for private organizations sponsoring these various ideologies."[69]

On the other hand, Brown felt the presidency had not gone far enough in its January 1963 statement. The Birch Society's *Bulletin* for February 1963 gave Brown an additional reason for that view. The last "agenda" item was titled, "Write to President McKay." The *Bulletin* urged Mormon Birchers to write letters (in envelopes marked "Personal and Confidential") explaining why they had joined the Society. The Birch *Bulletin* further suggested that the letters thank McKay for his own anti-Communist statements and praise "the great service Ezra Taft Benson and his son Reed (our Utah Coordinator) are rendering to this battle, with the hope that they will be encouraged to continue."[70] The Birch Society saw this as a defensive response to the First Presidency's recent statement. Anti-Birch Mormons saw the February *Bulletin* as an effort to subvert the LDS presidency.

Benson added an ironic personal touch to the February Birch announcement. That same month he sent newly-called apostle N. Eldon Tanner a copy of Benson's *The Red Carpet: A Forthright Evaluation of the Rising Tide of Socialism—the Royal Road to Communism.*[71] As a Canadian cabinet officer, Tanner had been a member of the Social Credit Party, which advocated the "alleviation of poverty" through "redistribution of income" and government establishment of "a just price for all goods."[72] As a general authority in Utah, Tanner was a Democrat.[73]

Brown, Tanner's uncle, did not appreciate what appeared to be snide humor directed at Tanner. In March 1963 Brown told reporters that Benson was not "entitled to say the church favors the John Birch Society." Brown added that "we [the First Presidency] are opposed to them and their methods."[74] Barely a week later Benson published an acknowledgement that his support of the Birch Society was "my personal opinion only." Benson's statement went on to quote the church president as being "opposed to anyone's using the Church for purposes of increasing membership" of the Birch Society or other anti-Communist organizations.[75]

Benson was obviously under orders to publish this March 1963 statement. Aside from Brown's well-known criticism, Moyle said Benson "just didn't have any reason" in his anti-Communist crusade.[76] Benson's March 1963 disclaimer was contrary to his efforts before and after that date. A week after his letter newspapers reported that more than 1,000 LDS members had written church headquarters with complaints or requests for clarification. The media may have obtained that information from McKay's secretary, who supported the Birch Society.[77] In fact, her pro-Birch orientation became the source of complaints by other rank-and-file Mormons to the First Presidency.[78]

By March 1963 most Utah Mormons knew that Benson was at the center of a controversy with both of the president's counselors. This disturbed those who were accustomed to reassurances of harmony and unity among general authorities. Public evidence of this conflict was especially confusing to those who shared Benson's enthusiasm for the Birch Society. As one of Brown's biographers wrote, "in the minds of quite a number of the Church members the goals of the Church and the John Birch Society were identical and they joined the John Birch Society feeling that they were in a religious crusade against communism and had the blessing of the President of the Church and other Church leaders in so acting."[79] Bishops and other local LDS officers who were Birchers had circulated petitions in church in support of the proposal to impeach Chief Justice Earl Warren and remove him from the U.S. Supreme Court.[80]

By April 1963 the Benson controversy was also creating dissent among European Mormons. An LDS bishop visiting from Scotland was "shocked at Ezra Taft Benson's attack on socialists." He said, "If socialists are the same as communists, then all we're left [in Britain] is the Tories." The bishop vowed "to tell the people in Scotland about Ezra's comments."[81]

Although Mormon Birchers later became famous for "espionage" at BYU, anti-Birchers were involved in similar subterfuge. LDS bishop and political scientist J. D. Williams referred in May 1963 to "one of my 'spies' in the local Birch Society in Salt Lake City." He felt justified in this approach toward "Birchers, who hate me . . ."[82] As previously indicated, Reed Benson had already targeted Williams for surveillance.

For Mormons on both sides the controversy became poisonous. One of the directors of an LDS institute of religion wrote: "May a dumb spirit possess Bro. E. T. B."[83]

In September 1963 Benson gave a talk in Los Angeles praising Birch Society founder Robert H. Welch. Unlike his earlier praise for Welch, Benson delivered these remarks to a meeting officially sponsored by the Birch Society and attended by 2,000 Birchers.[84] He began his talk by saying: "I am here tonight with the knowledge and consent of a great spiritual leader and patriot, the President of the Church of Jesus Christ of Latter-day Saints, President David O. McKay." The Birch Society reprinted Benson's talk.[85]

Welch had just published his most controversial book, *The Politician*. It accused former U.S. president Dwight D. Eisenhower of being "sympathetic to ultimate Communist aims, realistically and even mercilessly willing to help them achieve their goals, knowingly receiving and abiding by Communist orders, and consciously serving the Communist conspiracy, for all of his adult life."[86] Benson publicly implied endorsement of the allegation. Privately, he had sent copies of the book to general authorities such as Apostle Joseph Fielding Smith, the Twelve's president.[87]

Benson's public praise for the Birch president brought the church controversy into national attention. Congressman Ralph R. Harding (D-Idaho) publicly condemned the apostle, telling colleagues that Benson was "a spokesman for the radical right" who used his apostleship to give an untrue impression that the LDS church and its people "approve of" the Birch Society.[88] Harding also privately lobbied Mormons to "let President McKay and the other leaders of the Church know of your opposition to Ezra Taft Benson's activities on behalf of the Birch Society."[89] Dwight Eisenhower then entered the controversy by praising the congressman's criticism of the apostle. Benson's support of the Birch Society was now a national issue.[90]

Anti-Birch Mormons were not comforted when McKay confirmed to the media that he had given Benson permission to speak at the Welch testimonial.[91] "President McKay may have given Ezra Benson consent to make the speech," Counselor Brown responded in an effort to undercut that acknowledgement, "but he did not know in advance what Benson's remarks would be."[92]

BYU's former student body president, Rex E. Lee, wrote in September 1963 about the difficulty of separating Benson's partisan statements from his church position. He observed, "It is regrettable, however, that Brother Benson has detracted from his effectiveness as a Church leader through his active support of the John Birch Society." This future president of BYU continued, "I have found myself periodically called upon to remind my friends, usually without success, that when Elder Benson acts to promote the ends of extremist organizations and leaders he is not declaring Church doctrine." In October a BYU professor of English wrote: "Even my conservative friends on the faculty are disturbed by Elder Benson's Birch activities."[93]

With all the national publicity of the Birch controversy, the conflict intensified at BYU. In October the Missionary Training Institute president (a son-in-law of Apostle Harold B. Lee) expressed concern about covert efforts to convert LDS missionaries to the Birch Society. He indicated that "he will resist efforts on the part of some of the young zealots among the missionaries to indoctrinate their colleagues in political extremism."[94] A month later a BYU student criticized the Birch Society while getting a haircut and was verbally attacked by Birchers who happened to be in the barber shop. Afterwards they reportedly harassed this student with phone calls and vandalism.[95]

Benson used the October 1963 general conference to further defy his critics. Right after Brown was sustained as first counselor, Benson's conference sermon relayed a covert subtext. On the surface the talk simply referred to the excommunication of early church leaders and warned of the need to detect error: "For even the Master followed the will of the Father by selecting Judas." In warning Mormons not to be deceived, Benson quoted Brigham Young against deception by persons "speaking in the most winning tone, attended with the most graceful attitudes." Benson warned against those who "support in any way any organization, cause or measure which, in its remotest effect, would jeopardize free agency, whether it be in politics, government, religion, employment, education, or any other field." He concluded with a long plea against the threats of socialism and Communism. Benson regarded his remarks as "what the Lord and his mouthpiece, President McKay would have me do."[96]

Wilkinson felt that "Judas" referred to Brown, known as an eloquent speaker and as a defender of liberalism and socialism. Brown also recognized Benson's subtext. "I don't think I'm going to be excommunicated," he told Wilkinson right after the conference session ended. Wilkinson saw Benson's talk as further evidence of animosity between Brown and Benson. "The feeling is very intense between them," he wrote, whereas Brown wrote of being "surrounded by enemies or opponents."[97]

Benson urged his conference audience to "come to the aid" of anti-Communist "patriots, programs and organizations." Three weeks later the First Presidency announced that they were assigning Benson to preside over the church's European mission beginning in December. The media immediately described this as a "reprisal" or "exile" for Benson's virtual endorsement of the Birch Society at general conference.[98]

Brown gave the public good reason to regard the mission call in that light. The day after the announcement Brown warned a BYU audience against "extremists and self-styled patriots who label all those who disagree with them as Communists." In a more obvious allusion to Benson, Brown said that the First Presidency "deplore any attempt made by individuals to ascribe to the Church personal beliefs which they entertain." Newspapers observed that Brown's "remarks were taken as a rebuff to Mormon apostle Ezra Taft Benson who has repeatedly expressed his admiration for the John Birch Society and its founder, Robert Welch."[99]

Two days after Brown's published criticism Benson publicly reasserted his support for the Birch Society. In an address to the New Orleans Stake on 27 October, Benson condemned U.S. presidents Eisenhower and Kennedy for sending federal troops to aid school integration in the South, then praised the Birch Society.[100] A few days later Congressman Harding gloated to the press: "The leadership of the Church was inspired in this calling. I think he'll make a wonderful mission president if he can get away from the Birch Society."[101] Harding privately wrote that "prospects in the Church do look brighter with the assignment of Ezra Taft Benson to Europe."[102]

This foreign mission only added to the controversy swirling around Benson. He told reporters that the assignment was not a "rebuke," and McKay eventually released an official denial that this mission was "because of Elder Benson's alleged activities with the John Birch Society."[103] However, leaders at church headquarters revealed that the intent of this mission was in fact to remove Benson from the American political scene.

McKay's son was the first to indicate that Benson's mission was a censure. Robert McKay wrote to Harding: "We shall all be relieved when Elder Benson ceases to resist counsel and returns to a concentration on those affairs befitting his office. It is my feeling that there will be an immediate and noticeable curtailment of his Birch Society activities." Robert was his father's secretary during trips to stakes and missions outside Utah and would later read the ailing president's talks to general conferences.[104] "The letter in no way reflects my view that Elder Benson is not a good apostle of the church," Robert explained after newspapers published his letter. He added that "in my own opinion Elder Benson would be better able to serve the church when he is free of Birch Society ties."[105]

A week after Robert McKay's letter, U.S. Under-Secretary of State W. Averill Harriman asked Hugh B. Brown how long Benson would be on this European mission. Brown reportedly replied: "If I had my way, he'd never come back!"[106] In introducing Harriman to BYU students, Brown also took a swipe at Birch employee Reed Benson. The *Deseret News* published his comment: "A lot of this nonsense gets disseminated by the professional, self-styled anti-Communists who make a comfortable living scaring people all over the country and who have a financial stake in making the Communists look stronger than we."[107]

Joseph Fielding Smith then identified Benson's mission as intentional exile. The Quorum of the Twelve's president wrote to Harding on 30 October: "I think it is time that Brother Benson forgot all about politics and settled down to his duties as a member of the Council of the Twelve." Smith concluded this letter, "He is going to take a mission to Europe in the near future and by the time he returns I hope he will get all of the political notions out of his system."[108]

The same day as Smith's letter, student conflict erupted at the University of Utah over Benson's speech to the New Orleans Stake. One of Benson's defenders accused the university's newspaper of an "anti-rightist crusade." For almost a month the *Utah Chronicle*'s editorial page was dominated by the Benson controversy, until President John F. Kennedy's assassination in November superseded it.[109] On 22 November Hugh B. Brown privately wrote that Reed Benson "is entirely out of order, does not represent the Church's position, although he claims to do so because his father has the position he has."[110]

By the eve of Benson's departure for Europe in December 1963, the bitterness over his banishment was public property. Some rank-and-file Mormons threatened to picket Benson's farewell talk at the LDS tabernacle in Logan, Utah, because his remarks "will most likely be an attempt to again build up the John Birch Society."[111] When stake leaders "became skittish" about letting him use the tabernacle for this talk, Benson said he would "hold the meeting in a tent, if need be."[112]

As his critics anticipated, his talk was an endorsement of the Birch Society. Early in his remarks he referred to the "Communist attack on the John Birch Society."[113] An analysis reveals that, without citing his source, 24 percent of Benson's talk quoted verbatim from the *Blue Book of the John Birch Society* and another 10 percent paraphrased this publication.[114] Benson's talk repeated such views as the American civil rights movement was "phony" and actually "part of the pattern for the Communist take over of America."[115] In contrast, the next year J. Edgar Hoover of the Federal Bureau of Investigation would publicly state: "Let me emphasize that the American civil rights movement is not, and has *never* been, dominated by the communists."[116]

Benson's statements worsened the church's public image during the 1960s. Most Americans regarded Mormons as racists because of the church's refusal to confer priesthood on anyone of black African ancestry.[117]

Benson's parting message at the Logan tabernacle even sounded inflammatory. The apostle predicted that within ten years the United States would be ruled by a Communist dictatorship which "will include military occupation, concentration camps, tortures, terror and all that is required to enable about 3% of the population to rule the other 97% as slaves." He promised such dire consequences "unless we join with those small but determined and knowledgeable patriots." He added: "Words will not stop the communists." Benson said that the U.S. government was becoming so infiltrated that American citizens "can no longer resist the Communist conspiracy as free citizens, but can resist Communist tyranny only by themselves becoming conspirators against established government."[118]

Nationally-syndicated newspaper columnist Drew Pearson quoted that breath-taking phrase and interpreted it as Benson's invitation "for Americans to overthrow their government."[119] One editorial claimed that "Drew Pearson wronged the former agriculture secretary by misinterpreting what he said at Logan."[120] However, Pearson's quote was accurate and his interpretation fit the context of Benson's extraordinary farewell talk which rallied Americans to battle Communism "even with our lives, if the time comes when we must . . . before the Godless Communist Conspiracy destroys our civilization."[121]

Utah's Democratic senator Frank E. Moss, a Mormon, described Benson's Logan address as "a disgraceful talk." Moss complained to Brown that Benson had arranged for copies of the talk to be distributed from his office at church headquarters.[122] Other Mormons wrote the Presidency with complaints that this "literature [is being] mailed from 47 East South Temple."[123]

As for the mission call itself, at a church farewell on 14 December Reed Benson complained that his father had been "'stabbed' in the back."[124] The Twelve's president was present to hear the younger Benson's remark. Nine days later Joseph Fielding Smith wrote: "I am glad to report to you that it will be some time before we hear anything from Brother Benson, who is now on his way to Great Britain where I suppose he will be, at least for the next two years. When he returns I hope his blood will be purified."[125] Recently appointed First Presidency counselor N. Eldon Tanner expressed a more charitable view at a congregational farewell: "I really know of no more courageous and capable proponent of any cause which he thinks is right than Brother Ezra Taft Benson."[126] Two months later, in February 1964, newspapers printed Smith's caustic assessment, and the Quorum of the Twelve's president made a public disclaimer which actually verified the political motivations for Benson's assignment to Europe: "I meant that when he returned he would be free of all political ties."[127]

Louis Midgley, a BYU political scientist, published an anti-Birch editorial in the school's *Daily Universe* in May 1964. He concluded: "It is little wonder that the First Presidency has taken steps to warn Church members not to try to align the Church or its leadership with the partisan views of the Welch-Birch or any similar monstrosity." This resulted in McKay's instructions to stop future discussion of the Birch Society in the *Universe*.[128]

Church leaders overestimated the foreign mission's moderating influence on Benson's political zeal. While there Benson authorized the Birch Society to publish a talk he prepared as an endorsement of the society. In addition, he authorized the society to publish his photograph for the cover of its magazine in October 1964. This issue of the Birch organ favorably reviewed Benson's just-published *Title of Liberty* and observed that he "is a scholar and a patriot, [but] he is primarily a man of God." Benson allowed the Birch magazine to publish his "The Christ and the Constitution" in December.[129] At the same time Reed Benson increased his role as his father's surrogate for the society and published full page ads in Idaho of Apostle Benson's endorsement of the Birch Society.[130]

Benson's other son advanced his father's anti-Communist and pro-Birch crusade publicly during this mission-exile. In 1964 Mark A. Benson compiled a collection of his father's talks for a Deseret Book Company publication. Nearly every talk referred to the threat of Communism, and the book also mentioned the Birch Society's president five times. By contrast, before their mutual involvement in the Birch Society, Reed Benson had compiled a book of his father's sermons which discussed Communism only three times.[131]

The November 1964 election in Idaho is one measure of the effect of the Benson controversy on the mass of faithful Mormons. U.S. representative Ralph Harding, who had condemned Benson in Congress, publicly gloated over his exile to Europe, and circulated the anti-Benson letters of church leaders, was defeated that fall for re-election. Harding and others saw his defeat as a result of his criticism of an LDS leader and as evidence of Birch Society influence.[132] After all, Harding had publicly condemned the Birch Society as "rotten to the core."[133]

To the contrary, an analysis of election returns from 1960 to 1964 shows that Harding overwhelmingly retained the support of Mormon voters. In fact, in Madison County with its 91.7 percent Mormon population, Harding's votes actually increased from 1960 to 1964, despite his criticism of Benson.[134] In other words, public criticism of Benson in the 1960s seems not to have alienated a large majority of faithful Mormon voters. They may have shared Harding's dismay at the apostle's endorsement of the Birch Society.

By January 1965 nationally prominent Mormon journalist Jack Anderson was reporting that the First Presidency was exasperated with Reed Benson's role as his father's surrogate for the Birch Society.[135] In response to an inquiry by a Mormon Bircher about this allegation, Clare Middlemiss replied that "neither Elder Ezra Taft Benson of the Council of the Twelve nor his son, Reed Benson, have been rebuked by the church." Barely concealing her own pro-Birch sentiments, the president's longtime personal secretary added: "Reed Benson, a member of the church in good standing, used his own intelligence and free agency in accepting his position with the John Birch Society." The Mormon Bircher released this endorsement to the press.[136]

Although out-flanked by the church president's secretary in this instance, Brown resumed his philosophical battle with Benson a month later. "All of us are one hundred percent against Communism in all its phases," Brown wrote in February 1965, "but the leaders of the Church are not convinced that any conspiracy exists within our own country."[137]

In contrast, while visiting Utah in April 1965 Benson reemphasized to general conference that there was a national conspiracy focused in the civil rights movement. This was in obvious response to the call of the National Association for the Advancement of Colored People (NAACP) for a prayer march in Salt Lake City "to ask the LDS Church to use their influence for moral justice in regards to civil rights."[138] Benson told general conference:

> Before I left for Europe I warned how the communists were using the civil rights movement to promote revolution and eventual takeover of this country. When are we going to wake up? . . .
>
> Now, Brethren, the Lord never promised there would not be traitors in the Church. We have the ignorant, the sleepy and the deceived who provide temptations and avenues of apostasy for the unwary and the unfaithful.

Newspapers regarded Benson's statement as a challenge to Brown's endorsement of "full civil rights for any person, regardless of race, color or creed."[139] Asked about Benson's talk, Brown replied "tartly" to reporters that the apostle "speaks strictly for himself. My statement is the official Church position. It was personally approved by President McKay."[140] The official publication of conference talks deleted Benson's reference to LDS "traitors," as well as his assessment of the civil rights movement as Communist and revolutionary.[141]

While in Utah Benson complained to BYU's president that "many of our political science and economics teachers are teaching false doctrine." This was a month after the Provo "section leader" of the Birch Society began receiving reports from a Birch student majoring in economics about his "covert surveillance" of BYU's "liberal professors," including professor Richard D. Poll. Wilkinson concluded that Benson had received this information through his son Reed.[142] The Bensons, Wilkinson, and BYU's student-spies were unaware that Professor Poll currently had a national security clearance. In 1958 he began ten years of extracurricular service at BYU as a "University Associate" of the Central Intelligence Agency (CIA).[143]

In 1965 Wilkinson was receiving separate reports from this same student-spy about Poll.[144] Poll had already published a scorching review of W. Cleon Skousen's anti-Communist book, *The Naked Communist*. Aside from skewering Skousen, Poll called America's anti-Communist movement "an evangelical blend of fear, hatred and pulse-pounding enthusiasm."[145]

Unknown to the public, Hugh B. Brown had encouraged Poll to prepare this critique of Skousen's book "in the hope that we may stem this unfortunate tide of radicalism."[146] This despite the fact that McKay had already recommended *The Naked Communist* to a general conference: "I admonish everybody to read that excellent book of [Salt Lake City Police] Chief Skousen's."[147]

Poll also joined twenty-one other BYU professors to publicly condemn John A. Stormer's *None Dare Call It Treason* as "this piece of fanaticism."[148] At the time Stormer's book was "in sales and in loans, the most popular book" within the Birch Society.[149] On 27 April 1965 Wilkinson wrote to Benson's son Mark for "any specific information that will be helpful to me respecting Richard Poll and his associates."[150] This demonstrates Wilkinson's belief that Mark was involved with his brother Reed in the kind of campus espionage their father had proposed five years earlier.

That same day Poll recorded that student Lyle Burnett had admitted on tape that he was "urged by Benson to write letters about the liberals at BYU," recommending that a specific professor be fired.[151] Burnett was a member of the campus chapter of Young Americans for Freedom, which would become the seedbed of next year's spy ring.[152]

However, in April 1965 the central figure of this letter-writing campaign was Stephen Hays Russell, a recently returned missionary "who is an avowed John Bircher and is trying to organize a letter-writing campaign on campus." Poll added that Russell "boasts of frequent meetings with ETB in the last month, and on the authority of [Jerreld L. Newquist's] *Prophets, Principles, and National Survival* and [statements by] ETB,

[Russell] is telling students that they should join the Birch Society as a religious obligation. ETB has told him that the reported restrictions on Birch activity on campus are false." Apostle Benson also told Russell during one of their private meetings that Poll "shouldn't be on the BYU campus."[153]

Meanwhile Benson's conference talk created another outburst at the University of Utah. One LDS student wrote a letter to the *Utah Chronicle* that Benson "told a damned lie" when he instructed LDS general conference that Communists controlled the NAACP. This caused a predictable backlash by students loyal to the Birch Society or to Benson.[154]

Benson's conference remarks as well as his alleged role in the Birch student letter-writing campaign at BYU led to Harold B. Lee's warning to students at the BYU devotional in May 1965: "Beware of that clever advocate, even in high places in the government, or in the Church, who deals in cunning half-truths, or endeavors to win his purposes by twisting the facts and so seeks for decisions based upon half-falsehoods." In a more obvious reference to Benson's invoking McKay's name when speaking to Birch-sponsored meetings, Apostle Lee added: "So often men of authority in the Church seek to buttress their position by making it appear that they speak for the highest Church authorities."[155]

A few weeks after general conference Reed Benson publicly endorsed Robert Welch's accusation that U.S. president Eisenhower had been a Communist agent.[156] Then the loyal son probably consulted Benson in advance about his apparent plan to use the Birch Society to spread rumors of a violent demonstration by African-Americans at the next general conference. Ezra Taft Benson's official biography is silent about this but observes that in 1965-66 Reed "continued to be involved in the fight for freedom which his father supported."[157]

Three factors led to Reed's apparent plan for October 1965 conference. First, he wanted to demonstrate the truth of his father's censored statement about the civil rights movement. Second, the annual convention of the NAACP in July 1965 passed a unanimous resolution asking all Third World nations "to refuse to grant visa to missionaries and representatives of The Church of Jesus Christ of Latter-day Saints . . . until such time as the doctrine of non-white inferiority is changed and rescinded by that church and a positive policy of support for civil rights is taken."[158] To the father and son, this proved the civil rights movement was evil. In May the Salt Lake City chapter of the NAACP had called for this national resolution in apparent response to Benson's statement a month earlier.[159] As the final catalyst for Reed's plan, the Watts riots erupted in Los Angeles in mid-August 1965.[160]

Reed escalated both the Birch conflict and racial tensions in Mormonism with a memorandum to all Birch Society chapters in Utah on 2 September 1965:

> It is common knowledge that the Civil Rights Movement is Communist controlled, influenced and dominated. . . . Our founder and guide, Mr. Robert Welch, has instructed us that when necessary we must adopt the communist technique in our ever present battle against Godless Communism. It is urged that in the coming weeks the Utah Chapters begin a whispering campaign and foster rumors that the Civil Rights groups are going to organize demonstrations in Salt Lake City in connection with the forthcoming LDS conference. . . . A few well placed comments will soon mushroom out of control and before the conference begins there will be such a feeling of unrest and distrust that the populace will hardly know who to believe. The news media will play it to the very hilt. No matter what the Civil Rights leaders may try to say to deny it the seed will have been sown and again the Civil Rights movement will suffer a telling blow.[161]

President McKay's nephew, Quinn McKay, recognized the letter's signature and regarded it as genuine. During a four-month period he attempted several times to get a statement from Reed denying that he was the author of this September 1965 letter: "Two-and-a-half weeks ago I wrote a third letter, stating that if I heard nothing from him I could only arrive at one conclusion. I have heard nothing."[162]

Reed's instructions to the "Utah Chapters" of the Birch Society were only one part of the society's effort in August-September 1965 to use the Watts riots as a way to undermine the American civil rights movement. On 17 August the society's "Major Coordinators" sent instructions to all the Birch officers in California to take "immediate action" to "expose the so-called Civil Rights Movement." On 1 September 1965, the day before Reed Benson's letter, a follow-up letter instructed Birch Society leaders in Los Angeles County to "take advantage of the current situation" as a means of repudiating civil rights activism.[163]

Reed's instructions were consistent with the cover story of *The John Birch Society Bulletin* for September 1965: "Fully expose the 'civil rights' fraud and you will break the back of the Communist Conspiracy!" Robert Welch concluded the article: "And we repeat once more: It is on the 'civil rights' sector of their total [Communist] front that we now have the best chance there has been since 1952 of setting them back with some really effective blows. Let's put our best into the job."[164]

The strategy of the Birch Society succeeded in creating near-hysteria in Utah during September 1965. One study observes that "hysterical rumors swept the Utah community, concerning the imminence of demonstrations and riots" at the upcoming LDS general conference.[165] The biography of Harold B. Lee, then an apostle, notes that "there were rumors of blacks invading Salt Lake City to take vengeance upon the Saints and the Church."[166]

Soon the stories claimed that African-American terrorists had targeted all of Salt Lake City. Reflecting Reed Benson's instructions to Utah members of the Birch Society, one rumor claimed that "2,000 professional demonstrators and Black Muslims will be imported to this area under NAACP sponsorship." Other widely circulated stories were that "all plane flights from Los Angeles to Salt Lake [had been] chartered by 'Watts Negroes'" and that "3500 'transient Negroes' have already arrived in Salt Lake." As a result, the Utah National Guard began "riot control" maneuvers.[167]

The NAACP issued an official statement which tried to instill calm in Utah and accurately identified Birchers as responsible for the race-war hysteria in Utah. "The NAACP deplores the malicious and totally irresponsible rumors circulating in many sections of the state to the effect that Negroes are planning a riot at the LDS conference," the statement began. Then the statement continued that the NAACP had "reason to believe the rumors started with certain right-wing societies that make a practice of scaring people."[168] The Anti-Defamation League of B'nai B'rith specifically condemned the Birch Society's "despicable actions" in seeking to inflame anti-black fears "while southeast Los Angeles was aflame in mid-August, 1965."[169]

Although there were no race riots or demonstrations at general conference, the Birch Society's role in fomenting this race-paranoia turned some Mormons implacably against the organization. At the time, the Birch Society's official magazine made no comment about the effort to disrupt LDS conference. However, after giving Reed Benson's perspective on the Watts riot, the Birch Society's October magazine referred to all black immigrants to the United States as "Savages" in a separate article.[170] *The John Birch Society Bulletin* for October 1965 also referred to civil rights activists and Martin Luther King as "the animals."[171] Later that month Utah's Republican U.S. senator, Wallace F. Bennett, publicly repudiated the Birch Society.[172] This was a significant change from Bennett's more sympathetic position two years earlier, when he inserted into the *Congressional Record* the letter from President McKay's secretary: "The church is not opposing the John Birch Society."[173]

Nevertheless, early in December 1965 McKay's secretary, Clare Middlemiss, endorsed Benson's continued anti-Communist crusade. She wrote a church member: "President McKay has further instructed me to tell you that Elder Ezra Taft Benson has not been rebuked by the Church . . . and, since Communism is a definite threat to the eternal principle of free agency, it cannot be considered that he is 'out of line' when discussing it in talks."[174] That was all Benson needed to justify his renewal of strident anti-Communist activism upon returning from his European mission. According to a pro-Birch interpreter of the Benson controversy, "Ezra Taft Benson returned to Salt Lake and continued his conservative patriotic speeches and his close association with the John Birch Society."[175]

By the end of December 1965 other general authorities vetoed an effort by one of Benson's intermediaries to have the Birch Society's president speak at BYU. Those voting against the proposal were apostles Joseph Fielding Smith, Harold B. Lee, Delbert L. Stapley, Marion G. Romney, and LeGrand Richards. That vote reflected N. Eldon Tanner's statement to a political science professor: "We certainly don't want the Birch Society to get a hold on the BYU campus."[176]

In January 1966 Benson endorsed the Birch Society and its program at stake conferences and at the LDS institute in Logan, Utah.[177] This disturbed Senator Bennett, who urged David O. McKay's son to persuade the church president to disassociate himself from Benson's "very clever statement about your father which would seem to give your father's endorsement" to the Birch Society.[178] At the end of the month the Birch Society released its *Bulletin* announcing that Benson would speak at a testimonial for Robert Welch in Seattle in February "with the full approval of President McKay of the Mormon Church."[179]

A week before attending that Birch meeting, Benson spoke about the Birch Society to a standing-room-only crowd at the Assembly Hall in Salt Lake City. He charged that "a minority bloc of American liberals [had] formed a propaganda coalition with the Communists . . . [and] drew the line of fire away from the Communist Conspiracy and to focus the heat of attack on the patriots." Benson added that this conspiracy of liberals and Communists "decided to level practically their entire arsenal on The John Birch Society."[180]

These remarks had been published by the Birch Society's national headquarters two years before Benson delivered them on Temple Square. They were a verbatim restatement of a speech Benson had prepared for an Idaho "Freedom Forum" as he was about to depart for his European Mission presidency in December 1963.[181] By repeating these words about the Birch Society in his February 1966 talk, Benson indicated that his mission exile had not taken "the political notions out of his system," as the Quorum of the Twelve's president had hoped.[182]

Benson then told this February 1966 meeting on Temple Square that he had read the Birch Society's *Blue Book,* Robert Welch's *The Politician,* and recommended that the audience subscribe to the society's official magazine *American Opinion.* He even included the mailing address. Of his support for the Birch Society, the *Deseret News* added Benson's comment:

"It has been very unpopular to defend this group," he said. "But I can remember when it was unpopular to defend my own church."[183]

Such equations of the Birch Society with the LDS church were part of what antagonized general authorities like Brown, Tanner, Smith, Lee, and Petersen. On 18 February, a week after Benson's Assembly Hall talk, the First Presidency ruled that the picture "of Pres. McKay [is] not to appear on cover of American Opinion Magazine."[184] Prior to his talk Benson had arranged for the church president's photograph to grace the cover of the April issue. The presidency thought that their mid-February decision would end the matter. It did not.

During a visit at church headquarters the last week of February, Senator Moss found "a number of the Brethren boiling pretty good" about Benson's recent talk. These general authorities "decided that Brother Benson's Assembly Hall speech should not be printed in the Church News. This was the decision until it was found that President McKay had already approved its printing and his office had directed the Deseret News to print it."[185]

However, Benson's opponents did manage to delete "without permission" the Birch Society references from the version published in the *Church News*.[186] Nevertheless, Brown and his allies were unable to prevent the television broadcast of Benson's Assembly Hall speech. This broadcast converted some Mormon viewers to assert: "No longer do we question the motives of the John Birch Society."[187]

To provide a context for the hierarchy's reactions to Benson's 1966 activities, the evaluation of two of his supporters is helpful. BYU's president Wilkinson had already attended three days of private indoctrination by the president of the Birch Society, and Wilkinson resolved "to press forward for more training along this line at the BYU." Fellow conservative W. Cleon Skousen had already published a defense of the society and was an official Birch speaker in 1966, even though he was not a member.[188]

In April 1966 Wilkinson and Skousen conversed about the Birch Society: "We would probably agree with 90% of their principles but we both believe that Ezra Taft Benson has made some tactical or procedural errors in trying to vouch President McKay in everything he has done . . ."[189] Even his authorized biography refers to the apostle's "single-minded concerns and convictions."[190] These reservations by Benson's supporters give better perspective for the position of those who did not share his views about the Birch Society.

Wilkinson's reference to Benson's "tactical errors" involved the apostle's effort to align the church with the Birch Society during the April 1966 general conference. Early that year Benson secured McKay's permission to introduce the Birch Society president as keynote speaker in the church's

Hotel Utah during general conference. This resulted in developments which shocked members of the First Presidency.

First, on 2 March they learned that the society's March *Bulletin* encouraged members to write to McKay and his two new counselors, Joseph Fielding Smith and Thorpe B. Isaacson.[191] The next day Benson notified the Twelve's president that McKay had approved invitations for Benson to speak at testimonials for Birch Society president Robert Welch. "I feel no compunction to make the Church popular with liberals, social- ists, or communists. I do feel responsible to tell the truth," Benson wrote. Of the fact that Mormons were joining the Birch Society and Birchers were becoming Mormons, he added: "and those who love the truth will embrace it without compromise and that is exactly what is happening."[192] On that same day the entire First Presidency decided that "Elder Benson [is] to be told not to mention [the] Birch Society."[193]

On 8 March J. Reese Hunter, chair of the Welch dinner meeting, mailed a "Dear Brethren" letter to stake presidents and bishops inviting them to attend "with your counselors and wives." Hunter had introduced Benson's February speech on Temple Square.[194] Then the Presidency learned that despite its mid-February decision, the Birch Society's maga- zine was going ahead with its plans for President McKay's photograph. In March the Birch magazine sent a letter to all of its Utah subscribers that its upcoming cover photograph of McKay was intended "to favorably impress your Mormon friends."[195] It is not clear whether the Presidency had instructed Benson to inform the Birch Society of this decision or had notified the society directly. Either way, the decision was ignored.

In early March anti-Birch Mormons were outraged to learn of these developments. A proposal was soon circulated urging the "removal of Benson from the Quorum of the Twelve." According to this "OPERA- TION CHECKMATE" handout, Benson's transgressions were "flagrant insubordination," "pulpit misuse," and "demeaning the President of the Church by callously taking advantage of his advanced years."[196]

By 15 March 1966 the First Presidency defined the situation as "a crisis." Second counselor N. Eldon Tanner, the Twelve's president Joseph Fielding Smith, and Apostle Mark E. Petersen held an emergency meeting with David O. McKay at his home in Huntsville, Utah. Tanner read the Hunter letter and observed that "KSL, at the request of the John Birch Society, was rebroadcasting the address given recently by Brother Benson in the Assembly Hall, in which address he gave strong endorsement to the John Birch Society." The church president said that it was necessary to issue a statement disassociating the church from these activities. Then "President McKay suggested that Elder Benson might not be assigned to stake conferences if he referred to the John Birch Society. The President then said that Elder Benson should be instructed not to discuss the Birch Society in any meeting, and that he should not advocate this group."[197]

Two days later the First Presidency publicly denied sponsorship of the Welch dinner and emphatically stated that "the Church has no connection with the John Birch Society whatever."[198] McKay stopped publication of his photograph in the Birch magazine and withdrew his permission for Benson to introduce the president of the Birch Society at its meeting during April conference.[199] Undeterred, Benson had the Birch magazine print a photograph of deceased first counselor J. Reuben Clark. The Birch organ stated that Clark was "one of the earliest and most outspoken 'alarmists' in America concerning the menace and the progress of the Communist Conspiracy."[200]

Benson attended the Birch Society dinner in April 1966 without speaking, although his name was on the program as a speaker. Others at the dinner gave him a standing ovation. The *Salt Lake Tribune*'s report included a photograph of Benson sitting next to the Birch president. BYU's president declined the invitation to substitute for Benson in introducing Welch. Even Benson's muted attendance at the dinner infuriated anti-Birch Mormons, including the wife of Utah's incumbent Democratic governor.[201]

Welch praised Benson as "one of the really great men of our times." In describing the Birch Society's "recruiting efforts," he said that "we have no better members, or more permanently dedicated members of the Society, than those who owe their first loyalty to the Mormon Church."[202] Of this, newspapers reported that the Birch Society regarded Mormons as "a very good recruiting ground."[203]

To counter such a perception, McKay, at the emergency council meeting on 15 March, authorized one of Benson's opponents in the Quorum of Twelve to publicly attack the Birch Society.[204] Mark E. Petersen (widely known as the unsigned editorial writer for the *Church News*) had criticized the Birch Society for years without actually naming it.

"From time to time organizations arise ostensibly to fight communism, the No. 1 opponent of the free world," Petersen had written in 1961, but concluded that "it is not good for citizens to align themselves with flag-waving groups which may bring them into difficulty." Three months later he had more directly alluded to the Birch Society and its attack on President Eisenhower as a Communist agent:

> Some groups and persons have attacked certain Americans . . . by casting doubt on their loyalty . . . they have set themselves up as judges of who is loyal and who is "un-American." They have accused certain men of being "unconscious [sic] agents of communism" . . . they have attributed national blunders not to errors in judgment but to evil motives. . . . [and] by blaming our

problems on certain scapegoats, they can keep us from manfully recognizing the real problems—internal as well as external.[205]

Less known was the fact that Brown had collaborated with Petersen in the 1961 editorials against the anti-Communist movement.[206]

Now in March 1966 Petersen's editorial proclaimed that the church had "nothing to do with racists, nothing to do with Birchers, nothing to do with any slanted group." This 1966 editorial further warned Mormons to "avoid extremes and extremists."[207]

The response of society members was predictably negative. A former LDS mission president and current "section leader" of the Birch Society hand-carried a letter to McKay that "many people are confused and shocked by the recent editorial in the Church News, entitled: 'Politics and Religion.'"[208] A Bircher in Arizona wrote a letter to "all of the General Authorities," which said, "Brother Petersen's article was a tragic and regrettable mistake." He added a few lines later that the "Communists and their dupes have directed their attacks and smear campaign against the John Birch Society . . ." Petersen's editorial was "a shocking smear I'm sure the Church doesn't condone," according to a "Letter to the Editor" which the *Deseret News* refused to print. This letter concluded: "Elder Petersen owes an apology to the readers of the Church News for the unwarrantable and unauthorized innuendos."[209]

Instead of offering an apology, Apostle Harold B. Lee continued the anti-Birch assault during the April 1966 general conference. Six years earlier he had publicly endorsed Benson's campaign against "radical and seditious voices."[210] However, Benson's alignment with the Birch Society had turned Lee into one of the Twelve's most determined critics of Benson. In 1963 he had privately said that Benson labelled as a Communist "anyone who didn't agree with Brother Benson's mind."[211]

In his April 1966 general conference talk Lee said, "We hear vicious attacks on public officials without the opportunity being given to them to make a defense or a rebuttal to the evil diatribes and character assassinations." He added "that the sowing of the seeds of hatred, suspicion, and contention in any organization is destructive of the purpose of life and unbecoming to the children of God."

Even more stunning, Lee then publicly criticized Benson. Without naming his apostolic subordinate, Lee continued, "I would that all who are called to high places in the Church would determine, as did the Apostle to the Gentiles, to know and to preach nothing save Jesus Christ and him crucified." He darkly added: "The absolute test of the divinity of the calling of any officer in the Church is this: Is he in harmony with the brethren of that body to which he belongs? When we are out of harmony, we should look to ourselves first to find the way to unity." Apostles Smith, Lee, and

Petersen had already indicated that Benson was not in harmony with his quorum.

Lee concluded this address with a devastating assessment of the unnamed Benson. "A President of the Church has told us where we may expect to find false leaders: First, the hopelessly ignorant, whose lack of intelligence is due to their indolence and sloth." "Second," he continued, "the proud and self-vaunting ones, who read by the lamp of their own conceit; who interpret by rules of their own contriving; who have become a law unto themselves, and so pose as the sole judges of their own doings."[212] This "insinuation" (as Lee's biographer called it) was a far more direct condemnation of Benson than Benson's "Judas" allusion to Brown less than three years before.[213] Brown had immediately recognized the personal reference in Benson's remarks; no doubt Benson was equally astute.

Within days after this controversial conference, the son of a previous First Presidency counselor publicly called Benson "the most divisive influence in the church today."[214] A few weeks later the nationally distributed *Parade* Sunday supplement observed: "Ezra Taft Benson has consistently supported the John Birch Society's recruiting drives among Mormons." Without exaggeration, *Parade* informed its millions of readers that Benson's political activism "has introduced as a result a divisive element in the Church of Jesus Christ of Latter-day Saints."[215]

The Mormon hierarchy's divisions over the Birch Society were the subject of a remarkable panel discussion at BYU on 25 April 1966. A "standing-room-only audience" listened as McKay's nephew referred to the recent Welch banquet as a "gathering of the clan" and referred to the "Dear Brethren" letter promoting it as "a deceitful device." Alluding to the controversies of the previous month, Professor Quinn McKay observed: "What do we do when General Authorities do not see eye to eye on political issues? Which do we follow? If each of the General Authorities were to speak on 'The Contributions of the John Birch Society' you would no doubt hear some rather contrasting views. Then which apostle would one quote?" McKay's nephew also referred to the Reed Benson letter which had ignited the race hysteria preceding the October 1965 conference.[216]

The role of Benson and the Birch Society in the tense atmosphere of the two previous general conferences led to a blistering condemnation by a nationally known Mormon in May 1966. Robert H. Hinckley, former assistant secretary of the U.S. Commerce Department, chair of the Civil Aeronautics Administration, and vice-president of the American Broadcasting Company, criticized the Birch Society in an address to students of the University of Utah. He lambasted the society's "collective slander, which now seems to have become standard operating procedure for some Birchites," and also "the semi-secret chapters that parallel Communist cells, the use of front groups, the tactics of infiltration, [and] the use of the big lie." Hinckley identified Benson as part of the "leadership of the Right Wing" in America. The full text of this assessment appeared in the *Congressional Record* in June 1966.[217]

Nevertheless, Benson shrugged off criticism from regular Mormons and even from his fellow apostles. As early as 1952 he had confided to his diary: "If I come in for criticism, so be it," when he gave a political talk at general conference.[218] McKay's address at April 1966 conference left church members "free to participate in non-Church meetings which are held to warn people of the threat of Communism."[219] The Birch Society's *Bulletin* later published this statement.[220] In Benson's eyes, McKay's statement was a personal vindication by the only church leader who mattered.

Moreover, some of his apostolic associates expressed support for his partisan views, while others praised his ability as a senior statesman to open doors for Mormonism with "U.S. Ambassadors, consular officials, governors, mayors, and other public officials." In the latter regard Apostle Gordon B. Hinckley wrote shortly after this general conference that "no one among the Brethren is as well equipped as you for this facet of our work." Despite their opposition to allowing the Birch Society's national president speak at BYU, Delbert L. Stapley defended Benson's conservative talks in a letter to one Mormon, while LeGrand Richards also encouraged Benson to send copies of one talk to the White House and to U.S. military leaders.[221]

Although Benson waited six months to respond to his critics in the hierarchy, some Mormon Birchers felt that the negative publicity of April 1966 conference required a rapid response. Members of the Birch Society in Seattle released a statement which addressed such questions as "Is the Church opposed to the John Birch Society?", "Has Brother Benson been rebuked by the Church?", "Is Brother Benson out-of-line in discussing communism in Church talks?", and "Has Reed Benson been rebuked by the Church?" To each of these questions, the Seattle Birchers responded in the negative.[222] Two months before April conference, Benson had spoken at a Welch testimonial in Seattle "with the full approval of President McKay of the Mormon Church."[223]

On the other hand, some liberal Mormons saw Lee's conference talk as a sign of a termination of Benson's political activism. "When Pres. McKay dies Ezra Taft won't last a year," a bishop from Logan, Utah said. "Pres. Smith or Elder Lee will not hesitate to put him in his place if he continues his political preaching." "If this happens," the bishop predicted, "it may turn out that Benson will refuse to give up his Americanism campaign and will be dropped or resign from the Quorum."[224]

Two weeks after the "crisis" in Salt Lake City, a Birch crisis of a different kind was developing fifty miles south in Provo, Utah. On 19 April 1966 Ernest Wilkinson asked his administrative assistant to organize a group of "conservative" students to "monitor" professors who were regarded as Communist sympathizers. Nearly all of these professors had publicly condemned the John Birch Society. Among them was political scientist Louis Midgley whose anti-Birch article in the *Daily Universe* had resulted in a muzzling of the newspaper two years earlier. Several of these professors had signed the public condemnation of the Birch best-seller *None Dare Call It Treason*. For a year Stephen Hays Russell, student-leader of this "spy ring," had already been reporting to the local Birch Society chapter and to Wilkinson about some of these professors.[225]

On 20 April Russell organized ten to fifteen other Birch students in a room of BYU's Wilkinson Center. A non-student chapter leader of the society acted as guard.[226] This room was the regular meeting place for BYU's Young Americans for Freedom, and each prospective spy was invited to this "special YAF meeting, to be held at the regular place, 370 ELWC."[227] These students included the president of BYU's Young Americans for Freedom and Cleon Skousen's nephew Mark. Academically, their majors included economics, political science, history, Asian studies, math, and zoology.[228] What linked these students was their participation in the Provo chapter of the Birch Society and the BYU chapter of Young Americans for Freedom.[229]

Before their involvement in the 1966 spy ring, several of these students had been vocal critics of Professor Richard Poll. One student helped monitor Poll in 1965 and had publicly accused him at that time of having a Communist subversive speak to his classes. Another had complained to Wilkinson in 1965 about Poll's negative reviews of Skousen's *Naked Communist*. Still another had recently complained to President McKay that Poll was "the most vocal leader of this opposition" to "Bro. Skousen and Elder Benson."[230] In spring 1966 their "covert surveillance" included efforts to extract "pro-Communist" views from their professors. Some students used hidden tape recorders to document their "evidence."[231]

The student organizer emphasized his association with Benson. "On one occasion, the head of the John Birch Society in Utah County took me to the Church Office Building at Salt Lake City to meet Apostle Ezra Taft Benson," Russell later wrote. "I was introduced to Brother Benson as a 'key conservative student at Brigham Young University.'"[232] At the group's initial meeting Russell told his associates that "the General Authorities" authorized this espionage. Later he specified several times that "Brother

Benson was behind this."[233] According to someone who was at LDS headquarters in 1966, Russell occasionally reported directly to Benson.[234]

On 29 April 1966 Wilkinson privately acknowledged the first "voluntary report from certain students" about "certain liberals on the campus."[235] After later discovering the details of this spy ring from its participants and from meetings with Tanner and Lee, one of BYU's vice-presidents confided that "the real home of the group was ETB."[236]

By the end of September 1966 the BYU operation had unraveled as its principal members confessed their participation to BYU faculty, administrators, bishops, and to general authorities. Due to their belief that Benson was involved, general authorities such as Tanner and Lee declined to pursue the matter rigorously.[237] They rejected demands for Wilkinson's resignation and merely asked him to apologize privately to the professors targeted for this espionage.[238] The media coverage of the scandal was already embarrassing enough to the LDS church.[239] This was the best-known manifestation of Benson's six-year-old encouragement of "espionage" at BYU. It was not the last.

Benson used October 1966 general conference to begin an extraordinary response to his critics at the previous conference. "There are some who apparently feel that the fight for freedom is separate from the Gospel. They express it in several ways, but it generally boils down to this: Just live the gospel; there's no need to get involved in trying to save freedom and the Constitution or stop communism." In an obvious reference to himself and other general authorities, Benson said: "Should we counsel people, 'Just live your religion—there's no need to get involved in the fight for freedom?' No we should not, because our stand for freedom is a most basic part of our religion." He added: "We will be given a chance to choose between conflicting counsel given by some," and observed: "All men are entitled to inspiration, but only one man is the Lord's mouthpiece. Some lesser men have in the past, and will in the future, use their offices unrighteously. Some will, ignorantly or otherwise, use it to promote false counsel; some will use it to lead the unwary astray; some will use it to persuade us that all is well in Zion; some will use it to cover and excuse their ignorance."[240] At least one in the congregation believed this "refer[s] to Hugh B. Brown."[241]

The church Presidency and Twelve's president regarded Benson's conference sermon as a criticism of every general authority except David O. McKay. "From this talk," Counselor Tanner noted, "one would conclude that Brother Benson and President McKay stand alone among the General Authorities on the question of freedom." Joseph Fielding Smith "agreed heartily with Tanner's objections to the talk in general." Brown added that Benson's "talk is wholly objectionable because it does impugn the rest of us and our motives when we have advised the people to live their religion and stay away from extremist ideas and philosophies." Benson had asked for approval to "mimeograph his talk for wider distribution" which the First Presidency disapproved.[242] Nevertheless, the presidency ultimately allowed the official report of conference to print Benson's talk virtually unchanged.[243]

Such publication was by no means certain when Benson addressed students at BYU's "devotional" meeting on 25 October. Because BYU devotional talks were separately broadcast and published, he decided to repeat his conference talk and expand upon its criticisms of unnamed members of the hierarchy.

Benson made it plain that the context for his remarks was the anti-Birch statements of anyone besides McKay. "Do we preach what governments should or should not do as a part of the Gospel plan, as President McKay has urged? Or do we refuse to follow the Prophet by preaching a limited gospel plan of salvation?" Alluding to disunity in the hierarchy, Benson affirmed: "We cannot compromise good and evil in an attempt to have peace and unity in the Church any more than the Lord could have compromised with Satan in order to avoid the War in Heaven."

He quoted the church president's April conference statement in favor of anti-Communist organizations, and observed: "Yet witness the sorry spectacle of those presently of our number who have repudiated the inspired counsel of our Prophet . . . It is too much to suppose that all the Priesthood at this juncture will unite behind the Prophet in the fight for freedom." Rather than ascribing this disunity to honest differences of opinion, Benson described his church opponents as inspired by Satan:

> Now, Satan is anxious to neutralize the inspired counsel of the Prophet, and hence, keep the Priesthood off-balance, ineffective, and inert in the fight for freedom. He does this through diverse means, including the use of perverse reasoning. For example, he will argue: There is no need to get involved in the fight for freedom. All you need to do is live the Gospel. . . . It is obvious what Satan is trying to do, but it is sad to see many of us fall for his destructive line.

He then tightened his reference more clearly to the presiding quorums. "As the Church gets larger, some men have increasing responsibility, and more and more duties must be delegated. . . . Unfortunately some men who do not honor their stewardships may have an adverse effect on many people. Often the greater the man's responsibility, the more good or evil he can accomplish. The Lord usually gives the man a long enough rope . . . There are some regrettable things being said and done by some people in the Church today."

After quoting the warning by J. Reuben Clark about "ravening wolves" who "wear the habiliments of the priesthood," Benson made clear his reference to fellow apostles: "Sometimes from behind the pulpit, in our classrooms, in our Council meetings, and in our Church publications we hear, read or witness things that do not square with the truth. This is especially true where freedom is involved." He concluded: "Some lesser men [have] in the past, and will in the future, use their offices un-righteously. Some will lead the unwary astray . . ."

At the conclusion of his talk Benson let the BYU students know he was referring to general authorities below the church president in author-ity. "Learn to keep your eye on the Prophet," Benson concluded. "Let his inspired words be a basis for evaluating the counsel of all lesser authori-ties." He closed with the only understatement of his talk: "I know I will be abused by some for what I have said."[244] The censored publication of his talk retained many of the critical allusions to the First Presidency counsel-ors and apostles.[245]

BYU professor Midgley called Benson's address "a really violent anti-Lee talk," and even pro-Birch Wilkinson regarded the talk as "a little extreme."[246] This counter-assault was even more extraordinary than Lee's conference remarks against Benson.

Benson gave this talk in the midst of a public effort to elect Benson and Thurmond. Three weeks after the April 1966 general conference, a national committee announced that it was preparing this campaign. This committee nominated Strom Thurmond, U.S. senator from South Caro-lina, as Benson's vice-presidential running mate.[247]

To Mormon liberals and non-racist conservatives this was a grotesque announcement with nightmarish consequences for LDS public relations. Americans were being asked to support a U.S. presidential team com-prised of a high-ranking leader of the only church that denied priestly ordination to African-Americans and a racial segregationist who had stridently (and unsuccessfully) opposed Congressional enactment of the Civil Rights Acts of 1957, 1960, 1964, and the Voting Rights Act of 1965.[248]

A former state coordinator wrote that Birch president Robert Welch "was the guiding light behind" this election committee.[249] National Birch leaders comprised 59 percent of the committee, including its chair and two vice-chairs. Most other committee members were probably lower-rank-ing Birchers.[250] This was a classic demonstration of Welch's philosophy of creating "fronts"—organizations that merely had the appearance of independence from the Birch Society.[251]

On 9 August 1966 Brown told two BYU professors that Benson had "a letter from President McKay endorsing his candidacy." Brown said "it would rip the Church apart" if Benson released the letter to the public as part of the presidential campaign.[252] This was the day after a front-page article in the *Wall Street Journal* referred to McKay's letter, which actually read: "Elder Benson has discussed this with me and to whatever extent he may wish to become receptive of this movement, his doing so has my full approval."[253] Although Mormon liberals might have been mystified by the church president's endorsement of Benson joining forces with a racial segregationist, this reflected McKay's private views: "the South knows how to handle them and they do not have any trouble, and the colored people are better off down there."[254]

Of this, Benson's biographer tells the following. As early as October 1965 Benson had asked the church president for permission to campaign as U.S. presidential candidate. McKay told him not to campaign actively but did not require him to decline the efforts of others to draft him. Benson decided to withhold these discussions from his own quorum which learned of his possible candidacy from the newspaper announcement in May 1966.[255]

In contrast to his private request of McKay which led to the draft movement, Benson told the *Boston Globe*'s religion editor: "It is strictly a draft movement about which I am personally doing absolutely nothing." The *Church News* immediately reprinted this.[256] Benson told newspapers in March 1967 that he regarded the draft movement as "almost frightening, yet humbling." He informed reporters in March 1967, "I have no desire to run for political office."[257] Coincidental with this Birch-led effort to elect Benson and Thurmond, a month later Mark E. Petersen editorialized in the *Church News*: "Political extremists sow seeds of hate and discord. Extremism among them can hardly be less dangerous on one hand than on the other. Both can lead to dictatorship."[258] However, within a few months Benson's supporters began circulating petitions to place his name on the ballot for the upcoming national election.[259]

In the midst of these presidential draft activities, the First Presidency and apostles were critical of Benson's association with such ultra-conservatives as Billy James Hargis. In an early report of their joint participation in anti-Communist rallies, even the *Deseret News* had identified Hargis as one the nation's "segregationist leaders."[260] Brown informed a church member in May 1967 that "numerous others" had complained about Benson's continued association with Hargis and the apostle's implied endorsement of his views. The Presidency "are taking it to the Twelve as soon as Brother Benson returns from Europe as we prefer to have him present when the matter is discussed." Brown reassured rank-and-file Mormons that Benson's "activities in this connection will be curtained [curtailed]."[261]

Nevertheless, Benson continued to preach Birch doctrine at LDS meetings. In a thinly disguised reference to the criticism against his political talks, Benson instructed the "Christian constitutionalists" at April 1967 conference: "Today you cannot effectively fight for freedom and not be attacked . . . [yet] a man is a coward who refuses to pick up a cross that clearly lies within his path." Apostle Lee dryly commented: "Ezra Taft Benson gave his usual eloquent oration on an old theme."[262] In the Salt Lake Tabernacle in September, Benson said that "the so-called civil rights movement as it exists today is a Communist program for revolution in America." He repeated that assessment in his general conference talk the next month.[263]

In 1967 Benson also approved the use of a recent talk as the foreword to an overtly racist book which featured the decapitated (and profusely bleeding) head of an African-American on its cover. The authors of *The Black Hammer: A Study of Black Power, Red Influence and White Alternatives, Foreword by The Honorable Ezra Taft Benson* wrote that the apostle "has generously offered this address as the basis for the introductory remarks to 'The Black Hammer.'"[264] Benson had given this talk at the anti-Communist leadership school of segregationist Hargis who had published it in his magazine.[265]

Although they did not identify themselves as Mormons, *The Black Hammer*'s authors (who lived in the San Francisco Bay area) referred on the dedication page to "all the Elders of the California North Mission for their interest and prayers." Their bibliography listed seven anti-Communist books including ones by Benson and W. Cleon Skousen. Two of *Black Hammer*'s pro-Communist sources were cited as reprints by the John Birch Society's *American Opinion*, and page 78 encouraged readers to "pass on your current copy" of that Birch magazine. Page 91 also encouraged "every Negro" to study the "conservative philosophy" of Robert Welch.

Consistent with Benson's own statements, *The Black Hammer* dismissed as Communist-directed all organized efforts for civil rights. On pages 32 and 35 the book warned about "the violent revolt which is part of the 100 year-old Communist program for the enslavement of America," and about the "well-defined plans for the establishment of a Negro Soviet dictatorship in the South." On page 51 *The Black Hammer* said: "The media would have the American public believe that the Black Power movement, with all its 'militant overtones' (as the media so affectionately describes it) is frowned upon by the 'moderate civil rights leadership'—more specifically, Martin Luther King. This is pure hogwash." Page 83 referred to "the Negro's need for complete subservience to the Great White Fathers in Washington." However, the authors insisted on page 90 that they were "ready and willing to take any Negro by the hand and help him into an era of self-proprietorship that every deserving American can achieve."

It does not seem coincidental that Benson endorsed this book in the midst of the Birch Society's effort to put him on the presidential ticket with racial segregationist Thurmond. In January 1967 thousands of "households nationwide" had received packets "promoting Ezra Taft Benson for president and Strom Thurmond for vice-president."[266] In addition, Benson may have endorsed *The Black Hammer* to provide leverage with another presidential aspirant, George C. Wallace, the segregationist governor of Alabama.

Not until McKay specifically instructed him to do so in February 1968 did Benson report to the Twelve about his presidential candidacy because "it might be interpreted that I was soliciting their support."[267] This was more than two years after he began exploring this possibility with McKay and with the national leaders of the Birch Society who headed his proposed election committee.[268] This was consistent with an assistant Secretary of Agriculture's observation that as an administrator Benson "asked advice from no mortal person."[269]

It is unclear whether Benson informed fellow apostles on 15 February 1968 of the most recent twist of his aspirations regarding the U.S. presidential campaign. Lacking sufficient support from the Republican leadership, Benson had negotiated to become the vice-presidential candidate in Wallace's third-party challenge. Wallace formally announced his candidacy on 8 February, but as early as November a vice-president of the Birch Society's "publishing and distribution arm" had resigned that position "to actively campaign for George Wallace." The *Christian Science Monitor* reported that Benson also supported Wallace.[270]

On 12 February Wallace formally wrote McKay asking for his "permission and blessings" and "a leave of absence" for Benson to be Wallace's vice-presidential candidate. This was the day the apostle and his son Reed met privately with Wallace in Alabama. Two days later McKay sent a "confidential" letter denying Benson's request and pointedly telling Wallace that "you no doubt have received word from Ezra Taft Benson as to my decision."[271]

From the Quorum of the Twelve's perspective, all this appeared as his defiant answer to Lee's address at April 1966 conference. Just three weeks after that rebuke, the apostles learned from newspapers that Benson was a likely presidential candidate. That impression was heightened by Benson's October counter-attack on his apostolic critics.

Benson continued his remarkable silence with the other apostles for two more years. He attended their weekly meetings without once mentioning the efforts being made to propel him out of quorum activity and into the White House. What the apostles learned about Benson's candidacy, they read in the newspapers. When he finally informed a quorum meeting of those efforts in February 1968, he made it clear he did so only upon McKay's insistence.[272] That was the day after the president had privately ended Benson's political hopes by denying permission to run with Wallace. It is difficult to see any deference or collegiality in these obviously strained relations.

Two months after McKay quashed Benson's hopes of being Wallace's running mate, America's most famous black civil rights leader, the Reverend Martin Luther King, Jr., was assassinated. In response to U.S. president Lyndon Johnson's designation of 7 April as a national day of mourning, Benson immediately prepared a statement for distribution which complained that "the Communists will use Mr. King's death for as much yardage as possible." Benson's hand-out continued that "Martin Luther King had been affiliated with at least the following officially recognized Communist fronts," and listed three organizations. Benson was simply repeating the Birch view of King.[273] Asked about this hand-out, Brown replied that Benson's "views do not coincide with the opinion of the majority of the General Authorities and we regret that they are sent out." The first counselor added: "However in President McKay's state of health we cannot get a retraction and must, I suppose, await a change in leadership before definite instructions can be given regulating such items of interest."[274] Nevertheless, no LDS leader took the opportunity to express regret or condolences at the April 1968 conference, an official silence which was widely "criticized for its indifference" to the assassination of America's best known African-American leader, an ordained minister.[275]

Added to the hierarchy's silence Benson expanded his attack on the civil rights movement. In his BYU devotional talk of May 1968 he accused the U.S. Supreme Court of treason and added that "a prerequisite for appointment to high government office today is one's past affiliations with communist fronts or one's ability to follow the communist line." Benson quoted three times from the Birch Society's official magazine, including references to "black Marxists" and "the Communists and their Black Power fanatics."[276] A month earlier he had written a warning to the First Presidency and Twelve that "increased racial unrest and violence" was the first of the "dangers he foresaw the United States facing in the coming years."[277] A Mormon who had taught religion in the LDS institute program for forty-one years condemned this devotional sermon: "Elder Ezra Taft Benson is at it again spreading his hate and fear campaign."[278]

In response to the BYU talk, the father of one BYU student complained to the First Presidency that Benson had turned devotionals "into a sounding board for vicious, political interests."[279] In 1968 this father was typical of most church members. A survey of more than 700 Mormons that year showed that 58 percent regarded the Birch Society as "not supporting Declaration of Independence principles."[280] Brown replied to the student's father: "We have had many such letters protesting the speech made at the B.Y.U. recently and we are trying to offset and curtail such expressions."[281]

Brown then delivered a BYU commencement address that attacked Benson's sermon only ten days earlier. "Beware of those who feel obliged to prove their own patriotism by calling into question the loyalty of others," Brown began. As clear response to Benson's quotes about African-Americans, Brown concluded: "At a time when radicals of right or left would inflame race against race, avoid those who preach evil doctrines of racism."[282] To many Mormons it was no doubt a disturbing situation for a First Presidency counselor to publicly advise Mormons to "beware" and "avoid" the unnamed Apostle Benson.

Brown's general assessment restated the views of FBI director J. Edgar Hoover who told Congress that "extremist organizations parade under the guise of patriotism, anticommunism and concern for the destiny of the country." However, "behind this veneer" the FBI director found deeply felt racial hatreds and anti-Semitism. Hoover continued: "While pretending to formulate their own particular theories for improving our Government in solving complicated social, political and economic problems, the extremists merely offer emotionally charged solutions to the gullible and unthinking person who craves for the simple answer. They call for improved government, yet continually defame those in high office."[283] Although the FBI director did not name the Birch Society, Mormon liberals like Brown and moderate conservatives like Utah's Senator Bennett felt the description applied.

In August 1968 counselors Brown and Tanner joined apostles Lee and Petersen in treating a local leader as Brown wanted to deal with Apostle Benson. The stake president "admits he is a member of the John Birch Society and we think it will be necessary to release him as stake president."[284]

Despite the controversy, Benson continued to attract national respect as an "elder statesman." One of his 1968 talks on government was published by the influential periodical *Vital Speeches of the Day*. It was republished in an academic journal, and fifteen of his post-Cabinet speeches appeared in the *Congressional Record*.[285]

Several months after McKay's initial decision against Benson joining Wallace's 1968 campaign, Benson again tried to persuade the church president to allow him to be the segregationist's vice-presidential candidate. Of this second effort to persuade McKay, Benson wrote in his diary: "I only want to do what the Lord would want me to do, as revealed through His mouthpiece."[286]

Brown continued to "offset" Benson's political talks at BYU, and Mormons of the 1960s often witnessed Brown following Benson's talks with rebuttal sermons.[287] While that gave grim satisfaction to some liberals, Wilkinson expressed a sentiment shared by Mormons of various political views: "If President McKay was vigorous enough to do it, I am sure he would call both of them in and talk to them about this, and especially President Brown for his critical personal [a]llusions."[288]

It is true that Brown barely concealed his antagonism for Benson in the sermons he delivered in response to the apostle.[289] His private statements and letters showed deep hostility toward Benson, which he even expressed to non-Mormons. Benson was more circumspect. One close associate affirms: "I doubt you could find anybody who ever heard Brother Benson speak negatively about Hugh B. Brown."[290]

But in his public comments Benson continued to be blunt. He told April 1968 conference: "If America is destroyed, it may be by Americans who salute the flag, sing the national anthem, march in patriotic parades, cheer Fourth of July speakers—normally good Americans, but Americans who fail to comprehend what is required to keep our country strong and free."[291] He described U.S. government "welfare-state programs" as a "Communist-planned program of deception" in his October 1968 conference talk.[292] The Mormon director of a government welfare program complained to the First Presidency, to which Brown replied: "Others of us feel much the same as you do but the President has not seen fit to check or refute the statements by the person involved and our hands are therefore tied. Be assured, however, of this, that what this man said does not represent the position of the Church with respect to the subject of government aid, etc."

Brown emphasized that Benson's "statements do not represent the position of the Church, but I am handicapped in that I cannot refute them because the President feels that each one should be free to express his own opinions. This seems to be unfortunate because, speaking from that pulpit and as one of the general authorities, each of us is supposed to represent the Church. There will be a change in this whole situation, we hope, before too long."[293]

However, Brown's hope for an official rebuke remained unfulfilled during the declining year of McKay's life. Benson's October 1969 conference sermon warned against "Communist conspiracy, fellow travelers, and dupes." Those remarks appeared in the official report of the conference.[294]

Earlier that year Benson was involved in another effort at espionage at BYU. In February 1969 W. Cleon Skousen, whom Benson had unsuccessfully tried to transfer from the religion faculty to the deanship of the College of Social Sciences,[295] allegedly asked a niece to recruit students as informants. A student herself, she told a political science major that her uncle "had discovered there was an active communist cell on campus whose goal it was to destroy this university by 1970." This student testified that she asked him to infiltrate BYU's Young Democrats. Anti-Birch professor Louis Midgley was among the faculty "'high on the list' of suspects as being communist sympathizers on this campus and her words were that I was to 'talk with them and to try to get them to commit themselves.'" Cleon Skousen relayed the information "to his 'superior' in Salt Lake City."[296]

Skousen's efforts at campus espionage in 1969 collapsed after a faculty member wrote a memo urging him "to give *the lie* to this rumor . . . that you have organized a 'spy' ring to check on the alleged pro-Communist sympathies of professors."[297] The political science student had confessed. He found no Communist sympathizers at BYU, and "I decided that I was involved in a questionable activity and that I should withdraw and cease to function as an agent in any way."[298] Again, this was not the last instance of Benson's support for spying on BYU professors.

Benson may not have been the only general authority who supported academic spying this year. In April 1969 the director of the church's seminary and institute program learned that a teacher in the LDS institute at Weber State College "has spied on his fellow teachers and then gone to the Church Office and reported to Alvin Dyer and some of the others." Alvin R. Dyer was the First Presidency's special counselor, and "the others" receiving these faculty-spying reports were "Ezra T. Benson and perhaps Mark E. Petersen."[299] The teacher's report about other institute faculty originally went to Benson who forwarded it to Dyer who ordered an investigation of those who allegedly criticized the recent conference talks of Dyer, Benson, and Petersen.[300] The faculty-spy's written defenses referred to "a friend of mine who happens to be one of the General Authorities," and to this teacher's own affiliation with the Birch Society.[301]

This Ogden Institute spying backfired even worse than it had at BYU the same year. In December 1969 the teacher wrote a long letter to Benson describing his likely termination by the "liberals" of the Church Educational System as an example of a Mormon Marxist dialectic: "We think we are doing wonderfully well [in the LDS church], while in fact all we are doing is slavishly following a dialectical program we neither understand nor know anything about. At the same time the liberal sees where we are and where it is he wants us to be, and then he devises several easy steps for us to take in getting there—with seemingly logical reasons for taking each one." Following a conversation two months later about this former instructor's sixteen-page, single-spaced essay "Dialectical Materialism—the Religion of Satan," Benson wrote that "I would like to suggest again that you consider preparing material for publication. That Dialectical Materialism [essay] particularly should make a choice little booklet for college and high school students. If I can help let me know."[302]

Benson apparently never actually asked McKay for permission to advocate the Birch Society or to engage in Birch-inspired activities but merely asked permission to speak about and promote "freedom." In Benson's thinking there was no distinction among the principles of freedom, the mission of the church, and the teachings of the Birch Society. He sincerely felt he had "a mandate from the prophet" for all of his political speeches and activities.[303]

On the other hand, Brown regarded Benson's private meetings with McKay as manipulative. Brown's grandson and biographer notes:

> As President McKay became increasingly impaired by age, some church functionaries, with allegiances to the radical political right, tried to influence the president in ways that Grandfather [Hugh B. Brown], President [N. Eldon] Tanner, and Elder Harold B. Lee thought unwise and improper. These three men—Grandfather in particular—were often but not always successful in blocking those efforts to influence church policy.[304]

There is no question that Benson made "end runs" to obtain McKay's encouragement. However, this was relatively common practice during the McKay presidency.[305] Brown's perspective on Benson's lobbying was itself a partisan overstatement.

McKay's amenability to Benson was not simply a result of the president's physical and mental decline. Less than a year after the organization of the Birch Society, McKay told a general conference: "The conflict between Communism and freedom is the problem of our times. It overshadows all other problems. This conflict mirrors our age, its toils, its tensions, its troubles, and its tasks. On the outcome of this conflict depends the future of mankind."[306] From that perspective, there was no extremism in Benson's campaign against what he perceived as Communist influence in America.

However, as soon as the Birch Society became an LDS controversy in 1961, McKay felt torn between his strong anti-Communist convictions and his desire to avoid entanglement with anti-Communist organizations.[307] As a First Presidency secretary has acknowledged, McKay "had some concerns about the John Birch Society."[308] Both Benson and his opponents in the hierarchy played upon that ambivalence for nearly nine years.

Nevertheless, Benson's political activism went into decline in the years following McKay's death in January 1970. McKay's successors were two apostles who had privately and publicly expressed their criticism of Benson, presidents Joseph Fielding Smith and Harold B. Lee. Of the two, Lee was more significant in restraining Benson.

For years Lee had overshadowed most of his fellow apostles in the Twelve. As early as 1942 J. Reuben Clark spoke of Lee as a future church president, and that was a common assumption. Marion G. Romney said that Lee "was the most influential man in the Twelve all the time that I was in the Twelve, from 1951 until 1970, when he came into the Presidency."[309] Lee's influence was greatest during the 1960s as he revolutionized the church with his "Correlation Program."[310]

With his sharp tongue, boundless energy, and strong will, Lee also overshadowed quorum president Joseph Fielding Smith and intimidated other apostles. By 1965 N. Eldon Tanner observed that other general authorities "were afraid to express their mind whenever Brother Lee spoke."[311] In the long run Lee's influence was greatest while he was a fellow member of the Quorum of Twelve Apostles (1941-70). In January 1970 he began twenty-nine months as first counselor to Joseph Fielding Smith and was the dominant voice of that administration. His seventeen-month service as church president from 1972 to 1973 is the second shortest in Mormon history.[312]

Due to Lee's influence as counselor and as church president, Benson's political activism was notably muted from 1970 to 1973.[313] This fulfilled Brown's hope in 1968 that "a change in leadership" would end Benson's ultra-conservative crusade.[314]

Not surprisingly, this turn of events appalled ultra-conservative Mormons. Some of them were outraged by the First Presidency's official condemnation of Mormons who had formed "Neighborhood Emergency Teams" in Utah. Benson announced that he had "no comment" about this March 1970 presidency statement.[315] Therefore, just a month before general conference, ultra-conservatives were convinced that an anti-conservative First Presidency had muzzled him.

Shortly after the presidency's statement against NET organizations, all local LDS leaders received an announcement which began: "There are dangerous sinister trends developing within the church due to the liberal factions gaining control." The announcement urged all "those of the conservative mind" to "cast a dissenting vote against the liberal factions" of "the First Presidency with its social-democrat thinking" when the church met on 6 April 1970. This would remove from office the new presidency of Joseph Fielding Smith, Harold B. Lee, and N. Eldon Tanner, all of whom opposed Benson's ultra-conservative activism. In their place, this proposal claimed that "Brother Benson will sound the trumpet [—] and thousands, yes tens of thousands, will heed his call and stand forth ready to sustain and support the fight for truth, right and liberty." Thus a general confer-ence vote of ultra-conservatives would propel Benson into the office of church president in place of the current president and ahead of other senior apostles.[316]

Rather than dismissing this document as the work of a lone crank and giving it no further attention, Lee publicly denounced it two days before the sustaining vote of April 1970 conference. He told the general priest-hood meeting that "there is one vicious story to the effect that one of our General Authorities is allegedly being urged to present himself to lead the Church contrary to the Lord's revelation and to make people think there is some division among the authorities of the Church." Lee indicated that this petition and its supporting documents "are finding their way into our Relief Society meetings, into priesthood quorums, firesides, institutes, and seminaries." That was an extraordinary acknowledgement of the threat he perceived from ultra-conservative Mormons.[317] By contrast, the First Presidency had not publicly criticized the anti-Birch effort four years earlier to have Benson expelled from the Twelve.

For the supporters of this right-wing petition, it would have been more significant for Benson himself to publicly repudiate it. However, Benson remained silent. "Despite continued threats of demonstrations," Lee's biography observes, "not a single hand was raised in opposition" to the First Presidency. After the vote Lee spoke against "the possibility of using political devices or revolutionary methods that could cause much confu-sion and frustration in the work of the Lord." The official photograph showing the Twelve's vote for the current First Presidency showed only three apostles, and the photograph centered on Benson.[318] Rank-and-file Mormons noted that for the first time "in many years" Benson gave "his first non-political sermon" at this tension-filled conference. They regarded this non-partisan talk as a result of specific instructions from the First Presidency.[319]

The newspaper published by Mormon members of the Birch Society was significant for what lay between the lines of its report of the confer-ence. The *Utah Independent* began with the comment that church members will remember this general conference "for decades to come" and noted:

"Despite persistent rumors to the contrary, no violence took place at the conference. No opposition was manifest by Church members when the names of general authorities were presented for sustaining." Of Lee's talk two days before this vote, the newspaper observed: "Special interest has centered around the talk given by President Harold B. Lee at the Saturday evening general priesthood session," and quoted excerpts. However, this Birch newspaper made no reference to the part of Lee's talk which referred to the ultra-conservative proposal to vote against "the First Presidency with its social-democrat thinking" and to substitute Benson as new church president.[320]

Not long afterward the author of this article lost his job in the LDS Publications Department. His supervisor told him that it was "inappropriate" for him to be a member of the Birch Society and a church employee. When informed of this by the state coordinator of the Birch Society, Benson said he could do nothing to remedy it.[321]

While Lee was in the presidency, he evidently gave an embarrassing rebuke to Benson during a meeting of general authorities in the Salt Lake temple. As reported by Henry D. Taylor, an Assistant to the Twelve, individual apostles were giving formal presentations on various subjects. Benson's assigned topic was the youth program, but he began presenting charts and quotes to show Communist influence in America and the need to teach anti-Communism to Mormon youth. Lee walked out while Benson was speaking, soon followed by the other apostles. Taylor and the other Assistants to the Twelve were the only ones who remained seated during Benson's presentation.[322]

However, as sharply as Lee criticized Benson's ultra-conservatism, he warmly expressed his personal friendship. As Presidency counselor Lee wrote: "I was profoundly moved by the feeling of sincerity conveyed in your message of brotherhood and fellowship."[323]

Wilkinson and Benson both indicated the frustration felt by ultra-conservatives during the Smith-Lee presidency. BYU's Wilkinson complained to Benson in April 1971 about not being able to establish "a chapter of the John Birch Society on our campus."[324] In April 1972 Benson told general conference listeners that "I would highly recommend to you the book *None Dare Call It Conspiracy* by Gary Allen." Allen was a member of the Birch Society and editor of its official magazine.[325] Benson's advice appeared in the report of his conference address by the *Utah Independent,* but the First Presidency deleted that recommendation from the official report of Benson's sermon.[326] Three months later he spoke at another Birch-sponsored rally and may have been the one who arranged for LDS missionaries to operate a booth there.[327]

President Joseph Fielding Smith died that July, followed in another seventeen months by the unexpected death of President Lee. Hugh B. Brown had already been released as counselor. With the deaths of Smith and Lee, the First Presidency's most strident voices against Benson's ultra-conservatism were stilled.

After Spencer W. Kimball became church president in December 1973, Benson's political crusade re-emerged. The two had been ordained apostles on the same day, and Benson was now president of the Twelve and next-in-line to become LDS president. During the next twelve years of presiding at the weekly temple meetings of the apostles, Benson shared his political views whenever he chose. His biography observes that he introduced "discussions on economics, social movements" and "also distributed pertinent materials to the Brethren."[328] This probably included the Birch materials he had been distributing and quoting for a decade.

In February 1974 Benson announced that the church might officially support political candidates. On the eve of the November election he publicly endorsed the ultra-conservative American Party and spoke at its rally on the Saturday before the election. This required the First Presidency to issue an immediate statement that "we take no partisan stand as to candidates or parties, and any person who makes representations to the contrary does so without authorization."[329] Despite that development and their own prior disagreements about the Birch Society, in October 1974 Mark E. Petersen published this remarkable statement about his fellow apostle: "He has faced severe opposition from political enemies who had no mercy and no discretion, but because of his integrity, his love of truth, and his faith that truth would prevail, he has come through with flying colors."[330]

In 1974 there was also a reversal of the policy against allowing BYU's *Daily Universe* to give any mention of the Birch Society. On 25 November the *Universe* published a favorable article. The Smith-Lee administrations had continued the policy established by McKay in 1964 against "allowing" such articles in the BYU newspaper. The newspaper's content was still monitored, but ultra-conservative partisanship no longer met the kind of First Presidency opposition that existed from Brown's appointment as counselor in 1961 to Lee's death in 1973.[331]

Still, there were limits to the Kimball administration's truce with ultra-conservatives. For example, Benson's resurgent activism was unsuccessful during 1975 in obtaining approval for the Birch Society's president to be a speaker at BYU.[332] Such a request would not have even been possible during the Smith-Lee presidencies. Nevertheless, Kimball's more relaxed approach gave Benson increased leverage at BYU. For example, in May 1976 he carefully questioned BYU president Dallin Oaks whether

BYU was "friendly to solid conservative constitutionalists." A few days later Oaks told fellow administrators about "BYU's tenuous position in the silent contest with extremists of the right wing."[333]

After a string of talks which echoed themes of the Birch Society,[334] Benson spoke at the dedication of W. Cleon Skousen's Freemen Institute at Provo, Utah, in September 1976.[335] Skousen named the organization after the *Book of Mormon*'s "freemen" and initially attracted Mormon members of the Birch Society. He later renamed it the National Center for Constitutional Studies and moved its headquarters to Washington, D.C., as an ecumenical effort to attract non-Mormons who were put off by the Mormon orientation. Within a few years the membership in this spin-off of Utah's Birch Society shifted from 90 percent Mormon to more than half non-Mormon.[336]

Former BYU president Wilkinson gave the invocation before Benson spoke at this dedicatory service. Skousen, Wilkinson, and Benson had been allied as advocates of the Birch Society for more than a decade. Now for the first time all three participated at an ultra-conservative political meeting also attended by the secretary to the LDS church president. The evident news black-out of this meeting in all the regular newspapers of Provo, Salt Lake City, and Ogden, Utah, apparently resulted from the fact that newspaper reporters were excluded. Even the Mormon-Birch *Utah Independent* reported only Benson's attendance at the dedicatory service.[337]

D. Arthur Haycock, President Kimball's secretary, specifically linked the Birch Society with this ceremony. After Wilkinson gave the prayer, Haycock confided to him that "nearly all of them [the general authorities] believed in the concepts of the John Birch Society."[338] Haycock was overstating the hope Benson had expressed seven years earlier: "Someday, more of us, in positions of [church] leadership will come to recognize the great contribution of the John Birch Society, its campaign to restore decency to America and the great fight it is making against the Communist conspiracy."[339] Haycock's statement showed that the society and Benson in particular had a partisan friend in the First Presidency's office. Haycock had been private secretary to Benson as Secretary of Agriculture and was a confidant and significant influence on President Kimball.[340]

Nevertheless, Kimball was not always willing to turn a blind eye to this ultra-conservative activism. Undoubtedly, Kimball's opposition was behind Benson's rejection of the U.S. presidential nomination from the Concerned Citizens Party in 1976. Involving former members of the American Party (which Benson had publicly endorsed) and LDS members of the Birch Society, the "Concerned Citizens party will be dedicated to individual rights under the Constitution," and proposed to bring God "back into government."[341] Benson declined as "impractical and impossible" efforts by "a resurrected" movement for him as vice-presidential candidate with former Texas governor John B. Connally.[342]

The last known instance of "espionage" at BYU and its promotion by Benson occurred in 1977. Some students in BYU's Washington, D.C., seminar were recruited to "spy" on professors there. One of the student reports intended for Benson's office instead ended up on the desk of Mark E. Petersen. After being informed of this "spy ring" by Petersen, Dallin Oaks angrily referred to "that Birch Mafia that surrounds ETB." Benson had put his own secretary, William O. Nelson, in charge of this most recent effort at BYU espionage.[343] Despite such intrusions of Petersen against his ultra-conservative activism, Benson later said of his fellow apostle: "I love this man as I have loved few men in this world!"[344]

Kimball resolved this "spy scandal" with a decisiveness lacking in the more famous episode of 1966. He issued the following statement to the school's Board of Trustees in December 1977: "We understand that a member or members of the Board directly, or through others, have sought evidence about alleged statements made by faculty members in courses taught on the BYU campus and have stated or implied that such evidence is to be used by a Church official in a so-called 'hearing.'" The church president condemned such "surveillance of BYU employees."[345] Although he did not name Benson as the trustee who had instigated this "surveillance," it was consistent with similar espionage attempts involving Benson for the previous seventeen years.

Barely a year later Kimball and his counselors found it necessary to counter the now-familiar pattern of Mormon ultra-conservatives to imply church endorsement. In February 1979 the First Presidency published a statement against "announcements [that] have been made in Church meetings of lectures to be given by those connected with the Freemen Institute."[346]

After another series of political talks Benson was sufficiently confident to authorize the Birch Society to publish one of his addresses in its February 1980 magazine.[347] At a meeting of the Freemen Institute on 23 February Benson gave a major address.[348] Then at BYU three days later he delivered a "devotional talk" which proclaimed the right of the LDS prophet to speak and act politically. The First Presidency immediately issued a statement that Benson was misquoted. However, it was difficult to finesse his words for the capacity BYU audience in the 25,000-seat Marriott Center or for the thousands of other Utahns who listened to the broadcast on radio and television of Benson's "Fourteen Fundamentals in Following the Prophets." To most observers, Benson's 1980 talk at BYU was an announcement of his own future intentions as church president.[349]

On 5 March the First Presidency released a statement "reaffirm[ing] that we take no partisan stand as to candidates or political parties, and exercise no constraint on the freedom of individuals to make their own choices in these matters."[350] The church's spokesperson claimed that "there is no connection between this [First Presidency] letter and a speech by Apostle Ezra Taft Benson to Brigham Young University" a few days before.[351] Those connected with LDS church headquarters knew otherwise.

Kimball's son affirms that the church president bore no ill feeling toward his longtime associate but "was concerned about Elder Benson's February 1980 talk at BYU." The president wanted "to protect the Church against being misunderstood as espousing ultraconservative politics, or—in this case—espousing an unthinking 'follow the leader' mentality."[352] A general authority revealed that although President Kimball asked Benson to apologize to the Quorum of the Twelve Apostles, they "were dissatisfied with his response." Kimball required him to explain himself to a combined meeting of all general authorities the following week.[353]

The entire Benson family felt anxious about the outcome of this meeting. They apparently feared the possibility of a formal rebuke. Benson's son Mark (the Freemen Institute's "Vice President in Charge of Development") wrote him a note that morning: "All will be well—we're praying for you and *know* all will be well. The Lord knows your heart." The meeting went well for Benson who "explained that he had meant only to reaffirm the divine nature of the prophetic call." Benson's biographer indicates that the most effusively supportive general authority in attendance was Apostle Boyd K. Packer: "How I admire, respect and love you. How could anyone hesitate to follow a leader, an example such as you? What a privilege!"[354] A few months later Benson wrote to his "Dear Friends" at the Birch national headquarters.[355]

By the time Benson himself became church president in 1985, he no longer acted as a standard-bearer of the anti-Communist movement. After all, at eighty-six he was the second oldest man to become LDS church president and already suffered dizzy spells, memory loss, and difficulty in public speaking.[356] Besides, the widespread paranoia and political passion of the 1950s and 1960s had died. Although still active in promoting anti-Communism in the 1980s, the Birch Society now seemed irrelevant.[357] In 1989 the Utah leader of the society reported 700 dues-paying members.[358]

Benson's ascension occurred in the middle of America's conservative "Reagan Revolution," which the church president saw as a personal vindication.[359] The former publisher of *American Opinion* and director of public relations for the Birch Society had already been appointed as one of U.S. president Ronald Reagan's special assistants.[360] Once Reagan was in the White House, Benson "continued to share his views with President Reagan."[361]

Non-Mormon journalists noted: "In the past Benson's heavy-handed political maneuvering has antagonized numerous members of the [LDS] church, leading to fears of a major schism if he became president."[362] When he ascended to that office in November 1985, church officials insisted that his political activism was "in the past." As Benson's biographer wrote, "the time for speaking out on political and economic ideologies was not right."[363] Four months later the *Salt Lake Tribune* observed that "President Benson's Fiery Conservatism Remains Quiet."[364]

Nevertheless, the Birch Society's new magazine immediately heralded the appointment of "the long-time Americanist patriot" as the new LDS president. "As in numerous past attempts to smear him and distract from his anti-Communist message, recent news articles have linked Benson to The John Birch Society," the magazine noted two weeks later in its regular "American Hero" section. The Birch magazine then mentioned Reed Benson's affiliation and quoted President Benson: "I do not belong to The John Birch Society, but I have always defended this group."[365] The new church president's son Mark was still on the board of the National Center for Constitutional Studies and remained there through December 1986.[366]

Many faithful Latter-day Saints had disagreed with Benson's advocacy of the Birch Society, but Benson himself had publicly announced how one could disagree with one's supreme file leader and still loyally sustain such a leader. "The American people can respect their President, pray for their President, even have a strong affection for him, and still have an honest difference of opinion as to the merits of some of his program," he once preached.[367] That was certainly true of his relationship with presidents Joseph Fielding Smith and Harold B. Lee. In addition, during the McKay presidency Benson had publicly dissented from the "program" of his file leaders in the Twelve.

Most important for the LDS hierarchy, however, during the 1980s-90s there were no political liberals for Benson as church president to combat in the First Presidency or Twelve. The lesson the hierarchy had learned from the public controversy was that if you appoint a political liberal as an apostle, you invite conflict within the politically conservative hierarchy, especially with a firebrand like Benson. Therefore, following the appointment of N. Eldon Tanner as an apostle in 1962, moderate church presidents McKay, Smith, Lee, and Kimball appointed no political liberals to the Twelve. The only Democrats, Boyd K. Packer and James E. Faust, were not known as liberals.[368] Benson's apostolic appointments, Joseph B.

Wirthlin and Richard G. Scott, lacked any background in ultra-conservative politics. His counselors Gordon B. Hinckley and Thomas S. Monson
were political moderates.[369]

One political loss to conservatives during the Reagan years was federal
adoption of Martin Luther King Day as a national holiday. In the 1960s
Benson had publicly identified King as a Communist.[370] A year after his
assassination, Benson wrote that "the kindest thing that could be said
about Martin Luther King is that he was an effective Communist tool.
Personally I think he was more than that."[371]

After Reagan signed the law for King Day, Cleon Skousen's Freemen
Institute observed that this national holiday honored "a man who courted
violence and nightriding and broke the law to achieve his purposes; who
found it expedient openly to collaborate with totalitarian Communism;
and, whose personal life was so revolting that it cannot be discussed."[372]
In deference to such views, conservative members of the Utah legislature
in 1986 refused to allow the state to call this national holiday by King's
name.[373] Although it is a state institution, the University of Utah's next
Catalog officially called the holiday by King's name, whereas BYU called
the holiday "Human Rights Day" until the fall of 1988.[374]

Like the Birch Society itself,[375] church president Benson continued
to preach a conspiratorial view of American society into the late 1980s. "A
secret combination that seeks to overthrow the freedom of all lands,
nations, and countries is increasing its evil influence and control over
America and the entire world," he told the October 1988 general conference.[376]

In view of his preoccupation with conspiracies, it is not surprising that
Benson's administration established a special committee to monitor and
maintain surveillance files on academics, intellectuals, and others assumed
to be critics of the church. William O. Nelson, a veteran of Benson's
abortive 1977 BYU spy ring, became the executive secretary of this
"Strengthening the Members Committee."[377] An assistant secretary in the
First Presidency's office from 1974 to 1981 never heard of such a committee during Kimball's presidency.[378]

In June 1989 the Birch Society held a dinner and meeting of its
national council in Salt Lake City but without the controversy of two
decades earlier. It was a sign of the times that the *Salt Lake Tribune* barely
mentioned the Birch council meeting, the first of its kind in Utah.
However, it published a long article that month titled, "Are We Hearing
[the] Death Rattle of Communism?"[379]

Two months later Republican U.S. president George Bush awarded the Presidential Citizens Medal to Benson, another personal vindication of Benson's decades of political activism.[380] Similarly, Mormon Birchers felt vindicated in Benson's advancement as church president.

In 1991 Utah membership of the Birch Society mushroomed as a result of U.S. president George Bush's proclamation of a "New World Order." As part of the Persian Gulf War, Bush adopted a phrase used by ultra-conservatives for decades to identify the "collectivist" goal of the international conspiracy. By May 1991 Utah had 1,000 Birchers, an increase of nearly 50 percent from two years earlier.[381] In 1990 apocalyptic-minded Mormon Birchers had organized "the American Study Group" which grew to 1,400 members within two months.[382]

This revitalization occurred while their presidential advocate was slipping deeper into the decay of old age. Benson was physically unable to speak at general conference from April 1990 onward. At his last public appearances in 1992 he was a frail shell of the strident partisan whom Mormons had known for decades in the center of controversy.[383]

By the fall of 1992 advocates of Benson's ultra-conservativism found themselves in a religious quandary. LDS church officers were suspicious of "those obsessed with the early speeches of LDS Church President Ezra Taft Benson and who believe the ailing, 93-year-old leader has been silenced because his opinions no longer are politically popular." Such ultra-conservative Mormons were being excommunicated or disciplined in Utah and surrounding states. One of them protested, "We support President Benson 100%," but "there are some brethren who speak 180 degrees against him."[384] Such anti-Benson influence characterized the hierarchy in the 1960s, but the scales had tipped dramatically by 1992. Based on the instructions of a general authority in October 1992, stake presidents prepared a list of twenty warning signs of apostasy. Third on this list was "John Birch membership or leanings."[385]

Such an indictment against the Birch Society was not even possible while anti-Birch men like Brown, Tanner, Smith, and Lee served in the First Presidency. During those years Benson was embattled but too influential to allow a linkage of Birchism with apostasy. This 1992 "Profile of . . . Troublesome Ideologies" was the ultimate evidence that Benson was incapacitated and had ceased to be the administrative leader of the LDS church.[386]

By Gordon B. Hinckley's own admission at October 1992 conference, the counselors had taken over the helm. He denied that "the Church faces a crisis" just because he and Thomas S. Monson were serving as Benson's "backup system."[387]

However, their caretaker presidency represented a crisis for ultra-conservatives. Hinckley and Monson were philosophical heirs of President Lee's conviction that ultra-conservatives are seditious and tend to brand anti-Birch general authorities as "Judases."[388] The church's "purge" of ultra-conservatives was an ironic thirty-year-anniversary of Ezra Taft Benson's first public endorsement of the Birch Society in October 1962.

The perspective of James "Bo" Gritz, a Mormon at the time, on this point is significant. As the ultra-conservative presidential candidate in the national election of 1992, most of the support for Gritz was in the "Mormon Culture Region"[389] centering on the state of Utah which alone gave him 28,000 votes.[390] Concerning pressures against Mormon ultra-conservatives, Gritz observed: "The critics I'm talking about are not little people but church authorities [who] have said what Ezra Taft Benson says before he was a prophet doesn't count."[391]

In the 1960s and 1970s the hierarchy wanted ultra-conservatives to ignore what Benson was saying. They did not. Beginning in the mid-1980s the hierarchy wanted them to forget what Benson had said. They would not and never will.[392] In May 1993 the national Birch president said: "Aided in part by Mormon ties, Utah and the Intermountain West still remain 'the most fertile area' for John Birch Society membership."[393]

For more than two decades as an apostle Benson had testified in the name of the Lord in support of the political views of the Birch Society. With the tacit, if not always informed, approval of President McKay, he preached the Birch message as his testimony. Also, while addressing congregations, Benson specifically praised Birch publications and endorsed membership in the society. He defined all of this as his personal mission from God.

On the other hand, his opponents in the hierarchy defined his support of the society and of ultra-conservatism as misguided personal opinion. For the rank-and-file who supported Benson's views, God resolved the controversy by making him the church's prophet and president. Within the context of LDS faith and priesthood, it is difficult to argue with that logic. After all, the First Presidency never publicly repudiated Benson while he was an apostle and instead permitted Deseret Book Company, the *Church News*, and official conference reports to print most of the partisan views he expressed.

Despite their dissent, politically moderate general authorities allowed Benson to become an enduring hero of ultra-conservatives. It seems ironic for them to punish "true believers" for emulating this apostle's thirty years of rejecting political moderation.[394] Yet that is the nature of the Mormon hierarchy, a group of well-intentioned, if not always unified, men who struggle to do God's will.

CHAPTER 4

Presiding Patriarch, Presiding Bishop, the Seventy, and an Expanding Bureaucracy

Jurisdictional tensions have been less extensive among members of the Mormon hierarchy's second tier than among the First Presidency and Quorum of the Twelve, primarily because these subordinate quorums have mutually exclusive duties for the most part. Still there have been conflicts and skirmishes. Also, the hierarchy has made various attempts to deal with the increasingly complex workload as the population of the church has grown in the twentieth century from 284,000 to 9 million. This growth has required certain revisions in the structure of the hierarchy. Some were uncanonical, such as Assistants to the Twelve, and some were provided by Joseph Smith, such as the First Quorum of Seventy.

The Presiding Patriarch

The one-man office of Presiding Patriarch has risen and fallen in status depending on the personality of each man in the position. Except for Joseph Smith, Sr. and his brother "Uncle" John,[1] every other Presiding Patriarch has been at odds with the rest of the hierarchy, though the causes for conflict have been different for each patriarch.

Patriarch Hyrum Smith was on the verge of a disastrous confrontation with his younger brother Joseph in 1843 over polygamy.[2] Brigham Young also reminisced, "Once Joseph told his Brother Hyrum if he would suffer him [Hyrum] to dictate him [Joseph] he [Hyrum] should lead the Church to Hell." Young added that the prophet "would frequently sit and sneer at the remarks of Bro Hyrum" in public meetings.[3] Nevertheless, the apostles acknowledged that the church patriarch ranked ahead of them.[4]

As soon as the apostles ordained William Smith as Presiding Patriarch in May 1845, he challenged the Twelve's jurisdiction. A recent study observes that because of the problem with Smith, Young eventually diminished the prestige of the patriarch. "Not only were the sealing powers thereafter disassociated with the office, there was also a perception of diminished importance, authority, and dignity."[5] Smith became a reference point for more than a century of misgivings that the Twelve had about the patriarch's potential as a rival.[6] However, Young did not diminish the office until a decade after his conflict with William Smith.

Two months after the conference dropped William from office, Heber C. Kimball called "Uncle" John Smith (b. 1781) "our patriarch."[7] Ordained a patriarch but not Presiding Patriarch in 1844, "Uncle" John's first book of patriarchal (predictive) blessings was volume 6 of the LDS church's records. William Smith's recorded blessings comprised volume 5.

The Twelve waited until 6 December 1847 to officially appoint John Smith "as the first patriarch over the whole Church." Although Smith was presiding over Mormons in the Salt Lake Valley, the apostles made this appointment the day after they organized the First Presidency. A conference at Kanesville (Council Bluffs), Iowa, on 27 December ratified Uncle John's position, and the general conference of October 1848 in Salt Lake City released him as stake president and then sustained him as "Patriarch over the whole Church of Jesus Christ of Latter Day Saints." In the presentation of officers he stood next to the First Presidency. Until his death in 1854, every general conference sustained the Patriarch ahead of the Twelve,[8] which was consistent with the patriarchal ranking before Joseph Smith's death.

On 1 January 1849 Brigham Young and his first counselor finally ordained "Uncle" John Smith to the presiding office he had filled since 1845. The words of the ordination were: "[we] ordain thee a Patriarch over the Church of Jesus Christ of Latter Day Saints & to hold the Keys Thereof . . . that thou mayest be a Counsilor to thy Brethren . . . that thou Mayest be a Presiding officer over this Priesthood."[9] These were the words William Smith had wanted to hear four years earlier. But Young distrusted William, while John Smith, by comparison, had served faithfully as an assistant counselor in the First Presidency from the Kirtland apostasy in 1837 to the Missouri expulsion in 1839, as acting patriarch to the church since 1845, and as Salt Lake Stake president (1847-48).[10] By 1849 Smith also ranked next to Young in the theocratic Council of Fifty.[11]

Brigham Young's reference to John Smith as "a Counsilor" was significant. As assistant counselor to the First Presidency in 1849, John Smith had the same position he had held under the founding prophet. Consistent with this position, ten months later he was given an assignment which had nothing to do with patriarchs or spiritual blessings. Young told him to select fifty men for a "Gold Mission" to California. Not only did Smith select these men, he soon received directly from them reports and gold dust from the California Gold Rush.[12] Therefore, Smith's position from 1849 until his death in 1854 mirrored the status of the first presiding patriarchs, Joseph Sr. and Hyrum Smith, who served simultaneously as church patriarchs and members of the First Presidency.

On 20 September 1853 John Smith laid his hands on the head of his son, Apostle George A. Smith: "I also seal upon you all the Keys of the Patriarchal Priesthood that ever was sealed upon any man on Earth." In John's view, George A. Smith was now his ordained successor as Presiding Patriarch.[13]

As John neared death the next year, Young asked him to give a message to the martyred founder when he entered the spirit world: "ask Joseph if all was Going right here & if not to Let him [Brigham] know." Smith agreed and then made a request of the church president: "I wish George A to carry the Blessing which I gave him ordaining him Patriarch & Read it at the Conference & tell them your feelings." Without responding, Young left on a trip.[14] John Smith died three weeks later. He had given 5,560 blessings in less than ten years since Joseph Smith ordained him in 1844.[15]

Despite the patriarch's long faithfulness, Young refused to acknowledge his death-bed request. Allowing a patriarch to name and ordain his successor would make him independent of the First Presidency and Quorum of the Twelve Apostles, even though in this case his intended successor was already an apostle.

Since Patriarch John Smith had been sustained ahead of the apostles at general conferences since 1847, Young and others feared that his patrilineally-ordained son or grandson might someday claim an unbroken chain of authority back to Joseph Smith that would bypass and conceivably supersede the Twelve's own authority. Prior to his 1849 ordination, "Uncle John" had served as the Presiding Patriarch for five years on the basis of his patriarchal ordination by Mormonism's founding prophet and "first patriarch," Joseph Smith, Jr.[16] Therefore, Young ignored George A. Smith's patrilineal ordination and instead selected John Smith, oldest son of the martyred Hyrum.

With John Smith (b. 1832) the status of the Presiding Patriarch's office changed markedly. Only twenty-two years old, John had never been a proselytizing missionary or served in public office or fulfilled any local presiding office in the church. Married barely a year at his ordination, John also had not entered the "patriarchal" covenant of plural marriage.[17] Moreover, Young had put Mormons under covenant in 1851 to observe the "Word of Wisdom" prohibition of tobacco and "strong drink,"[18] and John used both.

In fairness to young John, he was not the first Presiding Patriarch who was known for drinking alcohol. When Joseph Smith, Sr., gave his first patriarchal blessings in 1834, he praised his oldest son Hyrum's loyalty to his father despite his father's excesses: "Though he [Joseph Sr.] has been out of the way through wine, thou [Hyrum] hast never forsaken him nor laughed him to scorn," Joseph Sr. said referring to himself. This indicated that the recently published affidavits by New York neighbors about Joseph Sr.'s drunkenness were not total fabrications.[19]

However, one Palmyra neighbor defended Joseph Sr. against those extreme accusations. "The old man sometimes would drink until he felt quite happy at our log rollings and raisings," the neighbor admitted. However, he added, "It was rulable [customary] for people to drink at those times. The Smiths were no worse than others, and not as bad as some, but still they would take a drink."[20] Until the 1830s most Americans drank considerably. By the mid-1850s there was a major change in attitudes toward alcohol.[21]

Still, in Brigham Young's view this younger John Smith had none of the qualities that merited Uncle John Smith's expansive role as Presiding Patriarch from 1849 to 1854. Therefore, the young patriarch's ordination on 18 February 1855 was restricted: "we confirm thee to be the first in the church of Jesus Christ among the Patriarchs, to set apart, ordain, and confirm other Patriarchs, and bless the Fatherless and comfort the Saints." Unlike his ordination of Uncle John Smith, Young did not confer presiding authority, not even over local patriarchs whom Smith was to ordain. For the first time general conference sustained the church patriarch after the Twelve, not before.[22]

Nevertheless, Mormons in 1855 understood the presiding dimension of the church patriarch's office. The day after young John Smith's ordination, a returning mission president commented that Smith had been "ordained the previous evening to the Office of Presiding Patriarch to hold the Keys of that Office."[23]

Brigham Young began giving Smith opportunities to increase his status as a presiding officer. For example, he invited Smith to give the closing prayer at every general conference from 1855 to 1856, even though the shy young man "refused allmost every time Brother Brigham called on me to dismiss the conference." Young also allowed Smith to attend the prayer circle meetings of the First Presidency and Quorum of the Twelve until 1858.[24]

The church president must have been dissatisfied with Smith as early as 1858. In that year the Presiding Patriarch was allowed to have no prayer circle of his own and was excluded from his former attendance at the prayer circle of the First Presidency and Quorum of Twelve. Non-apostolic authorities who had attended that prayer circle before 1858 now presided over their own. Smith was a glaring exception. Instead he became one of the members of Apostle John Taylor's private prayer circle.[25]

By March 1862 Young dismissed the twenty-nine-year-old Presiding Patriarch as "given to rowdyism." He proposed calling him on a proselytizing mission so that Apostle George A. Smith could replace him. John's cousin George A. declined, but Young sent John on a two-year European mission anyway.[26] The patriarch manifested enough spiritual enthusiasm in the years immediately following this mission that Young allowed him to receive the second anointing, the church's highest ordinance, on 28 January 1867 at age thirty-four.[27]

However, John Smith did not become part of the theocratic Council of Fifty, which re-convened that same month for the first time in more than fifteen years. Under Young's leadership this revitalized council met periodically from 23 January 1867 until October 1868. During this time the council admitted every apostle ordained since its last meeting in 1851. It also admitted the new Presiding Bishop and thirteen non-general authorities but did not admit John Smith. That same pattern of patriarchal exclusion held true for the next and final period of the Fifty's activity, 1880-84. Smith was the only Presiding Patriarch of the nineteenth century who never became a member of this theocratic organization.[28]

In fact, for the balance of the nineteenth century Smith barely retained the office of patriarch. During this period he managed to alienate every member of the First Presidency and Twelve. Young refused to present Smith's name at the April 1873 general conference, and in October 1875 the entire First Presidency and Twelve voted to release him and appoint his brother Joseph F. Smith as Presiding Patriarch. Apostle Smith declined to become his half-brother's replacement and thereby saved John's position for the balance of Young's administration.[29]

Although the circumstances are unclear, in 1874 Young readmitted John Smith to the prayer circle meetings of the First Presidency and Quorum of the Twelve. He continued to attend these meetings from then until 1885.[30]

John Taylor began his administration as senior apostle by giving John Smith more opportunity to preside as patriarch. Smith had previously attended the private prayer circle of Taylor, who may have felt Young was unduly critical of the patriarch.

Taylor proposed on 31 October 1877 that all local patriarchs of the church form a single quorum over which Smith would have full presiding authority. Taylor first suggested this as an apostle in Nauvoo. "Magnify your calling and you will yet be a great man in Israel," Taylor told the Presiding Patriarch in 1877. "The spirit of your father and the spirit of the Lord will rest upon you if you seek for it, and the other patriarchs will seek counsel of you." Nevertheless, Smith was not enthusiastic about this new patriarchal quorum. He declined to keep a record book of the patriarchs because "it would be too much of a work."[31]

Smith's relations with the hierarchy worsened in the 1880s. One reason was the Presiding Patriarch's opposition to plural marriage. In 1857 he married a plural wife, who bore him one child, but they had separated during the 1860s.[32] In April 1880 Smith was the only general authority who objected to Apostle Wilford Woodruff's written revelation on the necessity of plural marriage.[33]

The patriarch's use of tobacco was the other cause of friction between him and the rest of the hierarchy. In 1883 his brother Joseph F. Smith prevented him from being admitted to the School of the Prophets. The reason was that John "smoked and, though having two wives, he lived entirely with one." Joseph F. asked the First Presidency and apostles if his half-brother should even continue as patriarch.[34] In his own defense, Patriarch Smith later claimed that "it was Heber C. Kimball, counselor in the First Presidency, who taught him how to chew tobacco." However, Kimball was dead by the time the patriarch was being criticized for using tobacco.[35]

In 1884 Taylor and Counselor Joseph F. Smith told John Smith it was dereliction of duty for him to neglect his plural wife and to use tobacco.[36] The patriarch's request to divorce his plural wife in 1886 outraged Taylor, his brother-counselor Joseph F., and cousin-apostle John Henry Smith.[37] This may have been why John Smith no longer participated in their prayer circle after 1885. Two years later he learned indirectly that he had been "debared the privileges of the Temple." The following year he met once with the Twelve who again instructed him to stop smoking.[38]

The decade of the 1890s was John's lowest point. Apostles Francis M. Lyman and Heber J. Grant complained that the Presiding Patriarch "was a notorious smoker, and also drinks sometimes." Even regular Mormons knew that Smith was "an inveterate smoker."[39] In response church president Wilford Woodruff publicly threatened at October 1894 general conference to drop him from office if he continued using alcohol and tobacco. However, Woodruff prefaced the public ultimatum by referring to the Presiding Patriarch "as the next man to him in authority in the Church."[40] This was small consolation for public humiliation. By 1899 the patriarch was so dispirited that he showed no interest in accompanying Apostle John Henry Smith to speak at stake conferences.[41]

For the last forty-five years of the nineteenth century, the patriarch chose not to preside in any way. Four church presidents and the apostles encouraged him to become Presiding Patriarch in the full sense of the term. Whereas William Smith had expected too much of the office, John Smith expected too little.[42]

The status of John Smith and of the Presiding Patriarch's office increased when his half-brother Joseph F. Smith became church president in 1901. The day before a special conference voted for him as president in November 1901, Joseph proposed that John be presented before the Twelve in the listing of officers. Although this would restore the order of patriarchal sustaining which had existed until 1855, first counselor Anthon H. Lund felt it would create a dangerous precedent:

> I had a private talk with the President and told him that I hesitated somewhat in making this change. While John Smith was a humble man[,] there might come a man who was ambitious and might cause us trouble. In case of the First Presidency being disorganized and the Apostles presiding[,] he might have to take a place behind them, and when the counselors and Apostles are put up for Prophets, Seers, and Revelators he would be passed. Bro. Smith said he would think about it.[43]

Neither Joseph F. Smith's counselors nor the apostles expected him to think out loud about the proposition. Nevertheless, he made the same suggestion at the special conference which sustained John for the first time as "Presiding Patriarch" rather than "Patriarch to the Church," and then the church president went beyond what he had proposed to his counselor.

He told the congregation that the correct procedure was to sustain the Presiding Patriarch ahead of the church president. "It may be considered strange that the Lord should give first of all the Patriarch; yet I do not know any law . . . from God to the contrary." President Smith added: "We will not make any change at present. But we will first take it into consideration." He then reaffirmed the once discredited argument of former counselor Daniel H. Wells that a new First Presidency should have been organized within twenty-four hours of Joseph Smith's death.[44]

The Twelve's worst fears were reflected in the reaction of one local patriarch to this talk of November 1901. Elias H. Blackburn (patriarch since 1889 in the town of Loa, Utah) concluded that Smith was promising "the day will come when this Church will be presided over by a *Patriarch*."[45] Thus Joseph F. Smith encouraged patriarchal views once promoted by William Smith and repudiated by Brigham Young.

In line with his thinking about the sustaining order, Joseph F. Smith then had the Presiding Patriarch set him apart as church president on 17 October 1901, the first and only church president to receive that ordinance from a patriarch. The ordinance presupposed that the Patriarch to the Church had authority at least equal to the church president's, which even exceeded Wilford Woodruff's comment about the office in 1894.[46]

President Smith sought in other ways to reassert the administrative power of the patriarch. After October 1901, for the first time in sixteen years, John Smith regularly attended the prayer circle and council meetings of the First Presidency and Quorum of the Twelve. The patriarch's participation included nominating men to fill vacancies in the Twelve. On 21 November Joseph F. Smith said that he wanted the Presiding Patriarch to speak at stake conferences. He re-established the quorum of patriarchs for John to preside over and instruct.[47]

At the next general conference President Smith renewed his intention to sustain the patriarch before the Twelve. His own second cousin, John Henry Smith, opposed the move as a threat to the apostles. Brigham Young, Jr., president of the Twelve in 1902, recorded this meeting and his own feelings:

> This question of the Patriarch Jno. Smith standing next to Presidency preceding the Twelve. Bro. Jno. H. S. said this might change succession of the president of twelve to presidency. I thought him unnecessarily exercised. Decision of Question was delayed for the present until we could look into it. I said Pres. Smith if the presidency will decide this question we will sustain your decision.[48]

At the quarterly meeting of the apostles the following June, John Henry restated his "anxiety" about that proposal.[49]

Facing opposition from his own counselors and the apostles, Joseph F. Smith hesitated to act. His public remarks in November 1901 showed how much he wanted to. Nevertheless, President Smith let the public know he regarded the patriarch as higher in authority than the counselors in the First Presidency. At the Salt Lake temple testimony meeting on 5 January 1902, he seated the "presiding Patriarch on his right [—] his first counselor on his left, 2nd counselor next [to] the Patriarch."[50] This symbol showed Joseph F. Smith's determination to place the patriarch on par with the president.

On 6 October 1902 President Smith obtained the acquiescence of his counselors and the Twelve in having the Presiding Patriarch sustained as "prophet, seer, and revelator." This was the first time since Hyrum Smith in 1841 that a patriarch was given such a title. Other general authorities expressed surprise at this change.[51]

During his ascendancy from 1901 until his death in 1911, Patriarch John Smith still used alcohol and tobacco. A grandson, only twelve when his grandfather died, remembered seeing the patriarch drink at the dinner table and roll his own cigarettes, though the grandson thought that he eventually quit smoking. After John's death the church's *Improvement Era* magazine re-emphasized the administrative role of the Presiding Patriarch: "It is his duty, also, to preside over all the evangelical ministers, or patriarchs, of the whole church."[52]

Church authorities passed over the deceased patriarch's son Hyrum F. Smith, who used tobacco and was separated from his wife. Instead the hierarchy chose Hyrum F.'s son Hyrum G. Smith. Some of Hyrum F.'s children were outraged, but Hyrum G. accepted the appointment despite conflicting loyalties.[53]

President Joseph F. Smith set Hyrum G. apart as "the Presiding Patriarch" on 9 May 1912. That was the first time this title appeared in the ordination words of the patriarch's office. Hyrum G. proved to be a vigorous patriarch. From 1912 onward he participated in temple council meetings, spoke at stake conferences, ordained and instructed local patriarchs, presided at and conducted meetings for all patriarchs at general conferences, ordained bishops, organized bishoprics, attended general board meetings of the Young Men's Mutual Improvement Association and of the Sunday school, performed temple marriage sealings, and gave patriarchal blessings. His personal conduct was exemplary.[54] Hyrum G. Smith was everything the apostles had asked of his grandfather John Smith.

In 1915 the patriarch cautioned a Mormon not to publish an outline which quoted the 1841 revelation to show that the Presiding Patriarch's office was above that of the church president. "While there is no discount or discredit upon the revelations quoted and referred to," he wrote, "yet I feel that this is a matter which concerns the First Presidency of the Church, and [will be] adjusted at a more opportune time." Significantly, Hyrum G. did not recognize the possible interest the Twelve might have in the matter.[55] Every time he entered the Salt Lake temple's council room, Patriarch Smith was reminded that he actually ranked ahead of the Twelve. His chair was situated immediately after the First Presidency's chairs and ahead of the senior apostle's chair.[56] John Smith had set apart Joseph F. Smith, which meant that the church patriarch had authority at least equal to his.

As Counselor Lund and Apostle John Henry Smith had feared, enhancing the patriarch's status led to a renewal of the patriarchal succession claim. When President Joseph F. Smith became seriously ill in 1918, Hyrum G. claimed he would automatically be the church's "presiding authority." Apostle Heber J. Grant, president of the Quorum of Twelve, expressed the predictable reaction:

> This morning, before going to the Temple, Joseph F. Smith, Jr., David O. McKay, and I called on Presidents Lund and Penrose, and stated to them that we understood that Brother Hyrum G. Smith, the Presiding Patriarch, held the idea that he was, in case of the death of President Smith, the presiding authority in the Church. We announced to the brethren [of the First Presidency] that all of the Council of the Twelve differed with Brother Hyrum G., and we did not care to have any controversy with him at all over a matter of this kind.

The counselors, still technically members of the Twelve, agreed with Grant's concern. They "said they did not think, in view of President Smith's ill health, that it would be a wise thing to bring this matter up for discussion before him."[57] That was an adroit way of avoiding a decision which might favor Hyrum G.'s claim—a claim that was disturbingly similar to William Smith's in 1845.[58]

Hyrum G. Smith may not have realized that his views (and those of President Joseph F. Smith) undermined apostolic succession to the church president's office. A recent study of the Presiding Patriarch's office affirms that "Hyrum G. Smith had no aspirations to be president of the church," yet the authors acknowledge that "Hyrum G. Smith might have suggested that the Patriarch might be the interim president after a president died and before a new one was chosen."[59] Was it reasonable to expect the Presiding Patriarch as chief "presiding authority" or "interim president" to be a mere rubber-stamp for the Twelve's decision to name its senior member as the new church president? What if the patriarch didn't approve of the senior apostle? What if he wanted to continue his own role as "presiding authority"? Of the Twelve's membership, only William Smith and Joseph F. Smith did not shrink from such prospects.

Apparently, Hyrum G. did not oppose Heber J. Grant's advancement as church president in November 1918. Nevertheless, within a month he said that he should be sustained above the Quorum of Twelve Apostles. Apostle James E. Talmage noted that Hyrum G. had made this claim "at intervals for years past" and "has repeatedly asked for a consideration of the matter." On 2 January 1919 the First Presidency ruled that the Presiding Patriarch ranked after the Quorum of the Twelve.[60] That was two steps below the ranking Joseph F. Smith had affirmed.

At this meeting Grant also deflated the status that Hyrum G. Smith had experienced under President Joseph F. Smith. He said that the patriarch attended the temple council meetings only "as a matter of courtesy." Grant said that the Presiding Patriarch's vote was insignificant and could not be a tie-breaker for "an even vote" of the presidency and apostles. He added that the Presiding Patriarch had no right to ordain patriarchs except by the courtesy of the First Presidency or apostles. An apostle pointed out that the patriarch's chair had always stood between the First Presidency's chairs and those of the apostles in the Salt Lake temple council room. Grant ordered the chairs moved so that the patriarch's chair came after the junior apostle's.[61] In Grant's view the patriarch had flown too high during Joseph F. Smith's administration. As new church president he was determined to clip the patriarch's wings.

Nevertheless, Hyrum G. remained a vigorous Presiding Patriarch despite Grant's lessening of the office's stature. Smith continued to attend temple council meetings. For example, Apostle George F. Richards wrote in 1922 that changes in the temple ceremony "have been approved of by the Council of the First Presidency, the Twelve and the Presiding Patriarch." Two years before his death the church's centennial history noted that the patriarch "presides over, instructs and directs the labors of all the patriarchs of the church."[62]

As Hyrum G.'s health deteriorated, Grant further undercut the patriarch's domain. On 2 June 1931 the hierarchy appointed James H. Wallis as a "traveling patriarch"—a new type of office—to give blessings in Great Britain, Canada, and in the United States where there were no stake patriarchs.[63]

In response, the Presiding Patriarch considered reasserting his primacy by privately ordaining his oldest son, Eldred G., as his successor. This was a right that President Grant had specifically denied to Hyrum G. Smith during a testimony meeting of the general authorities. Nevertheless, when the patriarch became gravely ill at the first of February 1932, "he asked his wife, Martha, to bring his eldest son to him so he could ordain Eldred to the office of Patriarch. Martha reproved Hyrum for imagining he was going to die (he was only fifty-two years old), and the Patriarch accepted her optimistic judgment. He died a few days later without ordaining his son." In nineteen years as church patriarch, Hyrum G. gave 21,590 blessings, nearly a thousand more than John Smith (b. 1832) gave during fifty-six years.[64]

Hyrum G. Smith's death began the twentieth-century decline of the patriarch's office. The longest example of tension between the First Presidency and the Quorum of the Twelve was their 1932-42 stalemate over whom to appoint. The Twelve proposed ordination of Eldred, but Grant resisted this. He wanted to appoint his son-in-law Willard R. Smith.[65]

This conflict fundamentally damaged the prestige and prerogatives of the Presiding Patriarch's office. First, the office went vacant for a decade. Second, the First Presidency and Twelve made it clear that there was no need to have a member of the Smith family fill the position which could be served for years at a time by "acting patriarchs" outside the Smith family.[66] Third, they redefined the patriarch's office while trying to reconcile differences about who should fill it.

In an unsuccessful effort to avoid confrontation with Grant, the Twelve as early as 1933 inadvertently undercut future patriarchal service. Both Grant and the apostles agreed that twenty-six-year-old Eldred was personally worthy of the office. Nevertheless, for ten years Grant persisted in calling him a "boy," even though Smith in 1933 was older than Grant when he became an apostle.[67] In a unanimous recommendation of 22 March 1933, the Twelve tried to deflect the age-objection by offering to limit the patriarch's responsibility to patriarchal blessings alone.[68] Grant regarded this as an admission that Eldred "was not the proper man." He added, "I feel that the Patriarch should be almost next, if not really and truly so, to the President." In contrast to his treatment of Hyrum G. Smith, Grant wanted a fully presiding Presiding Patriarch—his son-in-law.[69]

Grant refused to confer the patriarchal office on a descendant of John Smith (b. 1832) because John had used tobacco and alcohol, his oldest son had been unworthy of the office, and Hyrum G. had been aspiring. As Grant saw it, Eldred was the product of three generations of weakness and instability, and would revert to an inherent flaw in the John Smith family. Finally, Grant wanted the new patriarch to be a descendant of President Joseph F. Smith whom Grant had always admired and loved.[70]

Grant cited these reasons during a conversation with Eldred in 1942. He said, "Well, I just wanted you to know that I would not put in any descendant of John Smith—who didn't live the Word of Wisdom." Stunned, Eldred replied, "You mean to tell [me] that you penalize me because of something my great-grandfather did, whom I hardly knew, because I was only five years old when he died?" Grant answered, "Yes, you can put it that way if you want to."[71] However, Grant did not tell Eldred the final reason the office had been vacant for ten years: the Twelve had resisted Grant's preference for his son-in-law.[72]

Grant finally succeeded in changing the patriarchal line in 1942 from the descendants of Patriarch John Smith (b. 1832) to the descendants of President Joseph F. Smith. He gave up plans for his son-in-law and obtained the Twelve's approval for Joseph F. Smith, grandson of President Joseph F. Smith, son of Apostle Hyrum M. Smith, and nephew of Apostle Joseph Fielding Smith.[73] Patriarch Joseph F. Smith (b. 1899) immediately began instructing stake patriarchs and speaking at stake conferences. He also attended council meetings of the First Presidency and Twelve. On 20 January 1943 Joseph F. and his wife received their second anointing, one of very few couples since 1930 to receive this highest ordinance.[74]

After two years in office Joseph F. told the general conference that a patriarch "is not an administrative office, it is not an executive office, it is a spiritual office." Although this may have raised some eyebrows, his remarks simply reaffirmed a First Presidency circular letter regarding stake patriarchs. He was not describing his own functions, since, as Patriarch to the Church, he had participated in various administrative activities.[75]

Grant did not live to see the irony in his only patriarchal appointment. By May 1946 Joseph F. was incapacitated with a back injury, and the First Presidency asked three stake patriarchs to serve those seeking patriarchal blessings from the Presiding Patriarch.[76] This echoed the era of "acting patriarchs" appointed during the office's ten-year vacancy. His illness continued into the summer, but in July the hierarchy was stunned to learn that Patriarch Joseph F. Smith was homosexual. Publicly they cited "ill health" as reason for his resignation and released him at October 1946 conference.[77]

The former patriarch soon moved with his family to Hawaii. The First Presidency instructed the stake president there to prohibit him from speaking or engaging in other church privileges. Church president George Albert Smith continued the monthly allowance to the ex-patriarch and met with him in Hawaii in 1950 for a compassionate talk "with reference to his problems."[78]

The hierarchy did not allow Patriarch Smith to return to any church privileges for eleven years. Church president David O. McKay authorized the Hawaii stake president to rehabilitate Smith in 1957, and he soon became a member of the stake high council. He lived the remaining seven years of his life in full fellowship.[79]

Patriarch Smith's difficulties left the office vacant again in 1946. This time the hierarchy waited only six months to appoint a successor. President George Albert Smith ordained Eldred G. Smith on 10 April 1947.[80] Eldred's appointment fulfilled the Twelve's unanimous recommendation of 1933.

Nevertheless, Eldred began his service as patriarch with multiple disadvantages. The first three he knew already: the church president had left the office vacant for a decade rather than choose Eldred and then had passed him over in favor of another man. Now he was patriarch only because of the other's misfortune. Eldred did not know about his fourth disadvantage: he was ordained patriarch on the basis of the Twelve's recommendation fourteen years earlier that he be Patriarch to the Church without the status of a Presiding Patriarch.

Patriarch Eldred G.'s fifth disadvantage was his statement to the April 1947 general conference. He got a laugh from the knowing audience with his remark: "I was prepared to give a speech for this occasion fifteen years ago, but not today." This immediately offended the rest of the hierarchy. Their reaction grew worse as Eldred then continued for several minutes in rehearsing his frustration at not being ordained in 1932 and his dismay at Patriarch Joseph F. Smith's appointment in 1942. Eldred protested that he was worthy of the position all along. Thus Smith began his patriarchal service with a bad first impression.[81]

The day of Smith's ordination Apostle George F. Richards reduced the new patriarch to tears in front of the First Presidency and Twelve. Richards, who was publicly sustained as Acting Patriarch from 1937 to 1942, lectured Smith "that his attitude had been wrong in thinking that the office was his birthright." The others present congratulated Richards on this "masterful stroke."[82] The patriarch's 1947 conference remarks would remain a stain in the memories of the First Presidency and Twelve who had sat behind him as he spoke that day.[83] That memory became a self-fulfilling prophecy of difficult relations with Smith.

Eldred was not the only one to begin the association awkwardly. At his ordination the First Presidency and Twelve presented him with "a copy" of John Smith's 1855 ordination. They did not realize Smith already had a precise copy and could see that they had deleted the following phrase from his great-grandfather's patriarchal ordination: "we confirm thee to be the first in the church of Jesus Christ among the Patriarchs, to set apart, ordain, and confirm other Patriarchs." This "doctored" document struck an unpleasant note for the new patriarch.[84]

There was an administrative logic in acting as though those words never existed in the 1855 patriarchal ordination. The original text conferred status and authority on the patriarchal office which the apostles did not want to confer in 1947. It was, after all, consistent with a century-old pattern of reprinting original documents with unacknowledged changes to conform to current church definitions.[85]

Although no one realized it at the time, the office had begun a final descent into oblivion. Eldred's fifteen-year back-log of frustration grew each year after 1947. The First Presidency and Twelve repeatedly let him know in subtle and obvious ways that he was under constant scrutiny and condescension.

The apostles took him on local conference assignments occasionally but refused to let him join in the ordination and setting apart of officers or patriarchs. For several years the Twelve declined Smith's repeated requests to attend their temple council meetings, as had the three previous patriarchs. Even though church president George Albert Smith endorsed this request in 1949, the apostles replied: "His inclusion in the administrative meetings would seem to us to be somewhat confusing to the order of the Church." They even questioned how the patriarch could be considered a prophet, seer, and revelator like the apostles.[86]

For more than three decades Eldred G. Smith fulfilled his office to the best of his ability. Nevertheless, the hierarchy rebuffed his every request for the same privileges and responsibilities of patriarchs Joseph F. Smith, Hyrum G. Smith, and John Smith. Eldred did not seem to realize that his requests reminded the apostles of their heritage of difficulty with patriarchs. Of those earlier privileges, the hierarchy allowed Eldred only the second anointing ceremony and the right to perform temple sealings, neither of which had implications of presiding in the church.[87]

After 1947 the apostles usually had to be reminded that the church patriarch could even have a role in church administration. Without consulting Smith the Twelve scheduled meetings for local patriarchs at general conference, told him the meetings were not under his direction, and eventually added the church patriarch as a speaker only at his request. When he specifically asked why he was not allowed to be Presiding Patriarch in March 1953, President McKay permitted Smith to assist in setting apart high councilmen but not in ordaining bishops. Less than a year later the First Presidency had to remind the apostles to take the church patriarch with them to stake conferences, "since he feels left out."[88]

The problems ran deeper. At times the apostles scrutinized the blessings Smith gave for anticipated errors, only to report that the blessings were "quite satisfactory." At other times they asked him to prove to them that he was keeping busy. Smith let the apostles know he regarded these inquiries as inappropriate. Instead of consistently allowing the Patriarch to the Church to be the visiting patriarch in distant missions, the First Presidency sometimes assigned a stake patriarch to travel from Utah to give such blessings. The apostles even selected the patriarch's secretary without consulting him and instructed the church magazine in 1968 not to print its interview with him.[89]

However, not all the apostles were concerned about limiting the patriarch's administrative role. Richard L. Evans suggested that Eldred "ordain bishops and members of the Quorum of the Seventy," but the rest of the apostles and First Presidency overruled that proposal.[90]

In 1971 the Twelve allowed the patriarch to set apart missionaries, but he gave them new cause for concern. That year he seemed not to understand why apostles Spencer W. Kimball and LeGrand Richards bristled when Eldred told them that they would not be the ones to decide patriarchal succession because "if the Lord wants my son to succeed me, He'll take care of it." By 1975 Smith wrote in his diary: "Why do the brethren always keep me on the defensive?" He added: "Why, when I offer to help them with their tremendous load, do they continue to cut me lower and deeper, just because I wanted to help?" His discouragement continued to grow, as did the tension, and his stake conference assignments stopped in 1976, "without notice."[91]

Ultimately, the difficulties involving the Presiding Patriarch's office were unresolvable. Whenever a patriarch after 1844 tried to magnify his presiding office, the Twelve and First Presidency recoiled in apprehension. However, when individual patriarchs seemed to lack administrative vigor, the Twelve and First Presidency criticized them for not magnifying their office. Few men could successfully walk such an ecclesiastical tightrope.[92]

For various reasons the First Presidency and Twelve were in conflict with seven out of eight successors of the original Presiding Patriarch, Joseph Smith, Sr. The hierarchy finally resolved the situation on 6 October 1979 by making Eldred G. Smith an "emeritus" general authority without replacing him. This permanently "discontinued" the office of Patriarch to the Church. The First Presidency and Twelve announced there was no longer any need for the office, since there was a local patriarch in each of the organized stakes throughout the world. Eldred had given 17,517 blessings from 1947 until this retirement.[93] Ironically, the hierarchy discontinued the office but authorized the "emeritus" patriarch to continue giving patriarchal blessings in Salt Lake City just as he had before.[94]

Not all Mormons lived in organized stakes, so the hierarchy also made sure that fact could not be used as an argument for retaining the office of Patriarch to the Church. The First Presidency began appointing other men as "short term" patriarchs to give blessings "in specified sections of the world where stake patriarchs are not available."[95] Formerly that was the undisputed jurisdiction of the Patriarch to the Church.

Vacating the office in 1979 ended the conflicts. However, according to Brigham Young's instructions, the 1979 action made the church vulnerable: "It was necessary to keep up A full organization of the Church all through time as far as could be. At least the three first Presidency[,] quorum of the Twelve[,] Seventies, and Patriarch over the whole Church &c so that the devil could take no Advantage of us."[96] It is beyond the scope of this analysis to assess such metaphysical vulnerability. Administratively, however, the decision to leave the patriarch's office vacant after 1979 streamlined the hierarchy and removed a source of nearly constant tension.

The Presiding Bishopric

At Joseph Smith's death in June 1844 there were two semi-autonomous general bishops of the church, Newel K. Whitney and George Miller. Although Smith in 1841 provided for the office of Presiding Bishop, he never ordained anyone to that office. Also in 1841 he subordinated the economic prerogatives of the general bishops by appointing himself Trustee-in-Trust of the church and designating the Quorum of the Twelve to assist him. After Smith's death, a conference of 9 August 1844 appointed the two general bishops Whitney and Miller as joint Trustees-in-Trust. The October general conference honored Whitney as "first bishop" and Miller as "second bishop" on the basis of seniority.[97]

Following the exodus from Nauvoo, Illinois, in February 1846, Whitney gained increasing prominence and eventually became the church's sole Presiding Bishop. Miller resisted Brigham Young's leadership. When he refused to attend the 6 April 1847 general conference, Young dropped him from the list of officers. The conference sustained Whitney as Presiding Bishop, the first to function in that office.[98] By 1847 local bishops presided over the Aaronic priesthood and administered church finances in their respective wards. Thus members understood that the Presiding Bishop directed these functions for the entire church. However, there was no clear demarkation between the financial jurisdiction of the Presiding Bishop and that of the First Presidency.

Whitney was sole Trustee-in-Trust when he was sustained Presiding Bishop in 1847. Less than a year before Whitney's death, Apostle Orson Hyde published an early letter that emphasized the conflict of the founding prophet with the church's first bishop, Edward Partridge, who had sought "to steady the ark of God." In this 1832 letter, Hyrum Smith had written that Partridge accused "Brother Joseph in rather an indirect way of seeking after monarchial power and authority."[99] Publishing this after the October 1849 conference may have indicated that Presiding Bishop Whitney was involved in a similar jurisdictional dispute. At the next general conference on 7 April 1850 Brigham Young replaced Whitney as Trustee-in-Trust. Whitney died less than six months later, and from 1851 on the Presiding Bishop was by definition subordinate in financial matters.

Edward Hunter replaced Whitney as bishop and at first Young let Hunter serve as assistant trustee-in-trust. But in 1854 Young became sole trustee and remained so until 1873, when the Presiding Bishop was not among twelve newly appointed "Assistant Trustees." One scholar saw this as evidence of Young's "reluctance to accept Hunter as a partner in decision-making." Young told the October 1860 general conference that Hunter "is a good man but I do not admire his manner of doing business now." The president also dominated the bi-monthly meetings which Hunter conducted for the church's bishops.[100]

During the early years of Young's presidency, not only were issues of jurisdiction in flux but other details about the office of Presiding Bishop were as well. Whitney at first served without counselors. Then on 6 September 1850 Young and Heber C. Kimball became his counselors, a curious development since by then Young was church president and Kimball was his first counselor.[101] Whitney died two weeks later.

During the first five years of Hunter's tenure, there were erratic organizational developments. From his appointment on 7 April 1851 until 8 September 1851, Hunter served without assistants or counselors, then Young had Nathaniel H. Felt and John Banks sustained as "travelling

Presiding Bishops, under Bishop Edward Hunter."[102] The conference of 6 October 1851 voted to ordain Alfred Cordon as a third travelling bishop "to preside over other Bishops."[103] Official LDS histories still do not recognize these three men as general authorities. Nevertheless, in April and October 1852 and April 1853 the Presiding Bishopric was listed this way: "Edward Hunter was sustained as the Presiding Bishop to the Church; also Nathaniel H. Felt, John Banks, and Alfred Cordon, as Presiding, and Travelling Bishops among the people."[104] Though conferences from 1851 to 1853 sustained these three "traveling Presiding Bishops" as Hunter's assistants, in April 1852 Young and Kimball were sustained as Hunter's two counselors.[105] Then from 7 October 1853 until 1856 general conferences sustained Hunter as Presiding Bishop without counselors or assistants. On 6 April 1856 Hunter finally received regularly appointed first and second counselors, (Leonard W. Hardy and Jesse C. Lttle), after which the organization of the Presiding Bishopric was stable.[106]

Pioneer Utah also had local stake bishops and "regional presiding bishops."[107] For example, on 14 November 1859 "a Stake of Zion was partly organized in Cache Valley, Utah. Peter Maughan was appointed presiding Bishop in Cache Valley."[108] Similarly, Daniel D. McArthur was sustained in 1869 as "Presiding Bishop of St. George; Wm Carter and David H. Cannon, his counselors."[109] In addition, in 1871 Brigham Young appointed Elijah F. Sheets to act as traveling bishop to supervise the collection of tithing in various Utah counties, to counsel church members and ward bishops, and to ordain local officers.[110] In April 1876 the Twelve published a letter "To the Presiding Bishops Throughout The Territory."[111]

For a year beginning in August 1876 each issue of the *Deseret News* published a directory of "PRESIDING ELDERS AND BISHOPS of the Church of Jesus Christ of Latter-day Saints." The regional bishop with the most responsibility was William B. Preston, who presided over twenty-four wards in Cache County, Utah, and Oneida County, Idaho. Nineteen other men were listed as "presiding bishop" over regions with fewer wards. Only two wards fell under the jurisdiction of regional bishop John R. Murdock.[112]

Regional presiding bishops ended officially with a First Presidency announcement on 11 July 1877. However, within days general authorities began ordaining men who did not preside over ward bishops but were "bishop's agents" for regional tithing administration. These bishop's agents reduced the need for traveling bishops, which were eliminated as a church office by October 1880. The bishop's agents continued until March 1888.[113] Thus on the eve of the twentieth century there remained only two kinds of bishoprics: local ward bishops and the churchwide Presiding Bishopric.

Lacking Brigham Young's "stiff hand" after 1877,[114] the Presiding Bishop's office began to increase in status. In addition to overt administrative changes during the presidency of John Taylor, informal adjustments resulted from federal anti-polygamy laws. Taylor reappointed Edward Hunter as assistant trustee-in-trust for church finances, and five months after Young's death, "Prest. Taylor also said that Bishop Hunter frequently met with the Twelve in council, which he considered right and proper, as temporal and spiritual affairs were inseparable, and the representatives of both must act in unison and in concert."[115]

But the next year Taylor retracted this endorsement of the Bishopric's "temporal" jurisdiction because he felt they overstepped their prerogatives. On behalf of the Presiding Bishopric, Amos Milton Musser began publishing the periodical *Utah Farmer*. The Twelve, which had not yet organized a separate First Presidency, considered the situation:

> The Matter of the "Utah Farmer" was taken up and fully talked over and all deemed inexpedient to have this paper proceed further. The question as to the Bishops being the temporal heads of the Church was spoken of by Prest Taylor. (as Bro Musser had made that as his plea in not presenting the Matter to the Apostles). He said "Now what is the Office of Trustee-in-Trust for?" Joseph Smith was T. in. T. and Prest B Young also and now I am—we think it is to manage the temporal affairs of the Church.[116]

Taylor, however, did not resume Young's close supervision of the Presiding Bishop and did not even attend the Presiding Bishop's meetings after 1878. One researcher notes that Taylor "abandoned the basically unilateral decision-making practice of President Young."[117]

When the First Presidency went into hiding to evade arrest for polygamy from 1885 to 1887, the Presiding Bishopric (now under William B. Preston's direction) assumed unparalleled autonomy in conducting church finances.[118] Within a few weeks of Taylor's death in July 1887, the apostles took up a discussion of the "relative jurisdiction of Presidency & presiding Bishop."[119] It took two decades to resolve this question.

Although the First Presidency was not officially organized, in September 1887 Wilford Woodruff and his *de facto* counselors questioned the Bishopric's role in receiving and disbursing church money: "Pres Woodruff. Cannon & Smith at the office. Conversation was had with Bps Burton & Winder in regard to all the cash tithing & all cash received being collected & desbersed [sic] in & from Bishop's office. the Presiding Bishop having control of all cash receipts & disbursemts. Prest Woodruff was not satisfied with this method & said there must be some change."[120] Less than two years later the church president's secretary L. John Nuttall complained, "The Bishopric seem to be drawing away all the business from the Presidents office."[121]

The First Presidency and apostles renewed the question in October 1889. Woodruff noted that all church funds were entirely in the Presiding Bishop's control, saying that "the proper place for the funds of the Church was to have them under the control of the Presidency and the Apostles." First counselor George Q. Cannon said it was humiliating for the president to be required to apply to the Presiding Bishop for even "a dollar to mend a desk." Second counselor Joseph F. Smith countered that "he did not believe in ignoring the Presiding Bishopric any more than he did in having the Presidency of the Church ignored." The apostles agreed with Smith, commenting that it was no more humiliating to ask the Presiding Bishop to arrange for money than it was to ask a First Presidency clerk to arrange for it.[122] As a result of this split between the counselors, the status quo continued for another seven years, even though it irritated the church president.

Not until 2 April 1896 did the First Presidency and apostles jointly resolve the Bishopric's financial jurisdiction. Cannon rehearsed the same complaints of 1889 and concluded, "This was contrary to the custom in the Church from the beginning, and it placed the President of the Church in a fettered and limited position. He thought this was wrong, and that the matter should be set right during the life-time of President Woodruff, so that no precedent should be drawn from the present condition by the Church in future times." At this same meeting Apostle Heber J. Grant, who had been unsympathetic seven years earlier, now commented about "the greater prestige acquired by the Presiding Bishopric than by First Presidency in financial circles through the working of the present system." The apostles agreed to support changing the church's financial system.[123] By the end of 1897 meetings between Presiding Bishop William B. Preston and the First Presidency resulted in a change of procedures and ultimate financial control within the First Presidency.[124]

However, the apostles were dissatisfied that the Presiding Bishopric had more financial power than the Twelve. In 1901 they complained that the Presiding Bishop and his sons-in-law rode in church-owned vehicles, while senior apostle Brigham Young, Jr., used public transportation.[125] Heber J. Grant told Bishop William B. Preston, "I wish you would have me appointed as a counselor to the Presiding Bishopric." Grant explained, "I was kind of mad to think that as an Apostle I was a nonentity and that the funds of the Church were being controlled by the Bishopric."[126] In 1916 the Presiding Bishopric legally incorporated, and three years later Bishop Charles W. Nibley lobbied to "handle Church finances." New church president Heber J. Grant disagreed.[127]

As a result, Grant arranged for the First Presidency to have increased supervision of the Presiding Bishopric. Before 1919 the Presidency held meetings with the Presiding Bishopric when occasion required, sometimes once a quarter, sometimes several times a month, and the Bishopric provided detailed quarterly and annual financial reports to the First Presidency. Grant met with the Presiding Bishopric in regularly scheduled weekly meetings. Four years later Grant formed the Corporation of the President as the supreme organization of LDS finance.[128]

Evidence is not available until the twentieth century for personality conflicts involving the Presiding Bishopric. In 1914 Seventy's president Seymour B. Young noted that Bishop Charles W. Nibley "hates me most heartily" due to a business dispute.[129] In 1915 Bishopric counselor David A. Smith "got angry" at a clerk, John Wells, "and asserted that I would not do anything for him, and that everything he asked me to do I refused." Two years later the First Presidency chose this clerk to serve as a counselor in the Presiding Bishopric with Smith. They still did not get along, and in 1933 Wells spoke of resenting Smith's harassment. That year and the next, counselor Wells reported that Bishop Sylvester Q. Cannon also "shouted and scolded" at him over small matters.[130]

In fact, Cannon was at the center of one of the most significant conflicts between the Presiding Bishopric and First Presidency in the twentieth century. This involved a philosophical and political divergence during the 1930s. J. Reuben Clark came to the First Presidency in the middle of the Great Depression and was anxious to do something to remedy the economic position of Mormons. Years before, Clark had opposed the Bishopric's policy of encouraging needy members to accept financial aid from government agencies. Within months of his appointment in 1933, Clark was working on a proposal for a "Church Security Program." Clark wanted this plan to replace government aid and to offer an alternative to Franklin D. Roosevelt's Democratic New Deal.[131]

Presiding Bishop Sylvester Q. Cannon opposed Clark's security-welfare plan. Cannon was already miffed about a previous Presiding Bishopric priesthood plan that the First Presidency and apostles "changed over my protest in 1928."[132] Cannon had a civil appointment from Franklin D. Roosevelt, supported the New Deal, and resented Clark's effort to reverse decades of policies concerning church relief. His resistance was effective enough to block Clark's Welfare Plan for three years. Even after the First Presidency announced the plan in 1936, Cannon dragged his feet in implementing it and formally protested. Finally, Cannon's ill health allowed Clark to have him released and ordained a special apostle in 1938.[133]

On that occasion the First Presidency made an unprecedented change in the Presiding Bishopric. Until 1938 every newly appointed Presiding Bishop in Utah had continued to serve with the previous Bishop's counselors. However, Bishop Cannon's successor LeGrand Richards wanted to appoint new counselors, including his brother-in-law Marvin O. Ashton. The First Presidency acquiesced and released the former counselors.[134] This deeply offended David A. Smith, son of the former church president. Although he then served a six-year mission, "He wouldn't have anything else to do with the Church," and "died a bitter old man."[135]

Within five years of this Bishopric reorganization, Clark had also devised a program to reorganize the administration of church finances. First, in 1939 he began the policy of establishing an annual budget to define all church expenses for the coming year, rather than the former practice of accounting for *ad hoc* expenditures.[136] Second, in 1943 he proposed a structural reorganization of church finances.

At the center of Clark's proposal were two committees comprised of the First Presidency, two or three apostles, and the Presiding Bishopric. The Budget Committee devised the annual budget proposal, subject to approval by the temple council (First Presidency, Quorum of Twelve, and Presiding Patriarch). The Committee on Expenditures supervised all expenditures and made specific appropriations. After noting the Presiding Bishopric's previous control of church finances, the temple council approved this reorganization on 8 April 1943.[137]

After the reorganization, Presiding Bishop LeGrand Richards occasionally conflicted with the First Presidency. For instance, his official biography notes: "On one occasion, with typical frankness he questioned President Clark on a point. 'LeGrand, are you questioning my veracity?' the elder of the two asked. 'No, sir,' the Bishop respectfully answered, 'only your memory on the matter,' and it passed with no further comment."[138] Richards and his counselors expressed support for Mormons receiving federal aid contrary to the views of the Clark men.[139]

Bishop Richards occasionally disputed decisions of the Twelve. In 1946 Apostle Joseph Fielding Smith complained that the Twelve wasted an entire morning overcoming Richards and his counselors who opposed a lesson manual the apostles had approved. Three years later Richards objected to pre-publication censorship of his *Marvelous Work and a Wonder* by the Publications Committee of the Twelve.[140]

There are significant aspects to this friction of Bishop Richards with the Twelve from 1938 to 1952. First, he had the reputation of being inoffensive, accommodating, and universally loved within church administration, which itself is telling evidence of the inevitability of tension among church leaders. Second, those minor frictions did not lessen the esteem the First Presidency and Twelve had for him. Richards became an apostle and member of the Twelve in 1952. Seven years later Clark said no one was more spiritual than Richards. Apostle Richards later told a newly ordained apostle: "You can't always fix what you might want to fix. Remember, it's the Lord's Church. Let him worry about it!"[141]

Presiding Bishop Joseph L. Wirthlin, successor to Richards, experienced similar frustrations. For example, Presidency counselor J. Reuben Clark and Apostle Harold B. Lee unsuccessfully opposed the transfer of the Welfare Program back to the main jurisdiction of the Presiding Bishopric in the mid-1950s.[142] Wirthlin's first counselor Thorpe B. Isaacson had to apologize in 1959 "for talking back" to Clark.[143] In November 1960 Apostle Harold B. Lee wrote that the Quorum of Twelve resented the administrative powers exercised by Presiding Bishop Wirthlin. The apostles had "a very pointed discussion of the advisibility of the Twelve having more to do in working with the Presiding Bishopric in directing the ward teaching, as well as other programs, *which have been withheld from the Twelve*."[144] That echoed the early 1900s jurisdictional conflict between the apostles and the Presiding Bishopric. It is significant that Presiding Bishop Wirthlin was the center of this tension between the quorums in 1960, because he had distinguished himself previously as Bishopric counselor by saying if the First Presidency or Twelve "asked that we put the Presiding Bishop's Office up on Ensign Peak, there it would go."[145]

However, with the appointment of John H. Vandenberg as Presiding Bishop in 1961, his office achieved a remarkable harmony with the First Presidency. The church's chief financial officer during Vandenberg's service comments:

> He didn't appear to me to be a person who was trying to carve out a bigger niche for himself. He just wanted to try to do a good job of what he was doing. And during his administration, the role of the Presiding Bishop was pretty well defined, and didn't seem to be an area of any great controversy. . . . I didn't ever perceive him as trying to protect his role as the Presiding Bishop.

The only tension involved the Presiding Bishopric's supervision of the Aaronic Priesthood, held by teenage boys, which was eventually resolved in favor of the Bishopric.[146]

In 1972 harmony with the First Presidency increased noticeably following the appointment of Vandenberg's successor, Victor L. Brown. Brown demonstrated "profound devotion to President Tanner," who had direct oversight of church finances and was Brown's first cousin.[147] Brown and his counselors "were anxious to please the First Presidency with a type of devotion that I'd never seen," reported the managing director of the Financial Department. In his judgment they were "almost blindly loyal" to the First Presidency and did not give sufficiently independent counsel.[148] This harmony may have contributed to a major shift of responsibility to the Presiding Bishopric within five years of Brown's appointment: "Until 1977 the Financial Department was accountable to President Tanner, but in that year the Presiding Bishopric was reorganized to direct temporal aspects of Church administration."[149]

However, during Victor L. Brown's service from 1972 to 1985 the Presiding Bishop clashed with other presiding quorums. As the financial director observed: "It was between the Presiding Bishopric and the Quorum of the Twelve." The apostles had lost oversight of the building program, welfare, and corporate directorships and "found it difficult to give up some of those responsibilities."[150]

An assistant secretary in the First Presidency's office from 1977 to 1981 also noticed tension between the Bishopric and the recently formed Quorum of Seventy due to the latter's expanded administrative role. The Presiding Bishopric felt "frustrations" because they were limited to a role as "the temporal arm of the church. The First Presidency, the Twelve, the Seventy were the ecclesiastical arm, and they [the Presiding Bishopric] wanted to be both."[151]

The church's growth required a return to regional bishops. Even as the prerogatives of the Presiding Bishopric have been defined and circumscribed, its geographical jurisdiction has become ever more complex and extended. On 1 November 1975 the church announced the opening of three international offices of the Presiding Bishopric's administrative services division: Sao Paulo, Brazil; Mexico City, Mexico; and Lichfield, England. This led to a new bishopric position, the "Presiding Bishopric area supervisor," the first of whom began his work in Mexico City in January 1977. By that year there were nine Presiding Bishopric International Offices (PBIO). Far distant from Salt Lake City, a man in this position (later called "Area Director of Temporal Affairs," DTA) presided over a PBIO with an LDS population in the hundreds of thousands. In 1987 a former Area Director of Temporal Affairs was named a general authority and again in 1992.[152]

A First Presidency secretary reported that during the late 1970s:

DTAs started off with a very nebulous, vague mission of go down and take [charge] of the temporal affairs, but eventually it was streamlined . . . The general authorities who were area presidents came out, and they made a miniature church headquarters there. In other words, the general authority area president [from the Quorum of Seventy] would be like the ecclesiastical arm, and the DTA would be like the Presiding Bishopric arm. They worked in concert in that particular area, and then reported back through that section-of-the-world's member of the Twelve who brought it back to the First Presidency.[153]

By 1981 the next step above the DTA was the "Zone Administrator of Temporal Affairs." A single zone administrator supervised a jurisdiction such as the combined LDS membership of the Far East, Australia, New Zealand and the Pacific Islands. "Temporal affairs" for these zone administrators included "real estate, operations and maintenance, construction, finance, membership records and reports, Welfare Services, translation and distribution, and purchasing." In 1984 the zone administration was replaced by general authority Area Presidencies of the Seventy who "presently give direct supervision to directors for temporal affairs in international areas."[154] "Zone Supervisors" remain in the bureaucracy.

The Seventy

The First Council of Seventy experienced tensions with the First Presidency and Quorum of the Twelve for more than a century. These struggles centered in two characteristics of the First Council of Seventy. First, until Brigham Young's death the office of Seventy was termed an apostolic calling, the "seventy apostles." Second, according to Joseph Smith's revelations, seven presidents were to preside over a large group of sixty-three other men, the First Quorum of Seventy, which was equal in authority to the Quorum of the Twelve, which was equal in authority to the First Presidency.[155] Thus the Seventies felt that their authority was greater than the offices of bishop, elder, and high priest. In turn, the Quorum of Twelve wondered if the power of the Quorum of Seventy described in the 1835 revelation could threaten the Twelve's position.

The first conflict involved rivalry with high priests. After the First Council of Seventy's organization in 1835, some of the Seventies argued with some high priests over the question of who had greater authority. Joseph Smith ruled that one could not be a Seventy after ordination as high priest, implying that the latter superseded the former. He publicly criticized the First Council of Seventy in 1837 for ordaining men high priests. He then dropped five members of the First Council who had been high priests before their ordination as Seventies in 1835.[156]

This mystified the men who were dropped from the Seventy. Hazen Aldrich, senior president of the council from 1835 to 1837, left the church later that year. He never understood why the president dropped him and the other four: "Joseph first charged us to ordain the Seventies Highpriests [sic] & afterwards dropped 5 of us that was presidants [sic] because we were Highpriests or in other words ordained 5 others and left us: without giving any explination [sic] why he done so." Apostle Orson Pratt verified Aldrich's claim about Smith's 1835 instructions. They were to ordain Seventies to "the apostleship & [to be] High Priests of the 70s." Brigham

Young said that Smith instructed him to ordain Seventies first as high priests and then as "70 Apostles."[157]

Smith knew these five men were high priests before he ordained them Seventies and presidents. Four of them—Hazen Aldrich, Leonard Rich, Zebedee Coltrin, and Sylvester Smith—had served as pro-tem members in 1834 of high councils in Kirtland and Missouri. Smith was president of the Kirtland high council.[158]

Because of the ambiguities connected with this decision, Seventies and high priests continued to debate for decades which office had higher authority.[159] Young publicly denounced the 1837 decision as having "none of the whisperings of the spirit." He added that "it was the only time in my life that I ever heard Brother Joseph speak without bringing forth light and knowledge."[160]

In September-October 1844 Young put the First Council of Seventy in a curious situation. He greatly expanded their numbers, ordaining 400 men to that office on a single October general conference day, thereby dramatically increasing the statistical domain of the First Council of Seventy. However, less than a week earlier he had quietly transferred the sixty-three subordinate members of the First Quorum of Seventy (who were not general authorities) out of their quorum, appointing them as presidents of nine subordinate quorums of the Seventy. This left seven general authorities of the First Council of Seventy without their own quorum.[161] By vacating all except the seven presidents, Young ended its ability to function "as a quorum, equal in authority to that of the Twelve." Already battling schisms, his action in 1844 eliminated them as a succession rival.[162]

Nevertheless, Young did not diminish the status of the office. He and his fellow apostles reaffirmed that an ordained Seventy held an office of apostleship, and that Seventies could serve in bishoprics and high councils without high priest ordination.[163] As Young led most Mormons out of Nauvoo in February 1846, he and seven other apostles signed a certificate that the senior member of the First Council of Seventy, "Joseph Young who holds the Keys of the Apostleship in the City of Nauvoo, is duly appointed to preside over the Church during their stay in this place." This senior president of the Seventy dedicated the Nauvoo temple in 1846 in a private ceremony, a day before one of the Twelve dedicated it publicly.[164]

It was common for a local Seventy to preside over wards and stakes in early Utah. Before they became general authorities, Robert T. Burton, Charles W. Penrose, and John Henry Smith served in ward bishoprics or stake high councils as Seventies without high priest ordination. Members of the First Council of Seventy had done likewise from 1837 to 1847. Josiah Butterfield, Benjamin L. Clapp, James Foster, Jedediah M. Grant, Daniel

S. Miles, Albert P. Rockwood, and Joseph Young all served as bishop, high
councilor, or stake president without high priest ordination.[165]

Not until 1877 did Young give instructions that all bishops should be
ordained high priests.[166] Therefore, this diary entry in 1874 was typical:
"ordained Henry Chas. Barrell to the Apostleship and set him apart as a
member of the 27th Quorum of Seventies."[167] Because Young had defined
Seventies as ordained apostles, they served as bishops, bishopric counselors, stake presidents, and high councilmen without high priest ordination
before 1877. As a member of the Twelve, Young had done the same
without high priest ordination.

By 1901 the First Presidency and Twelve were no longer willing to
acknowledge the statements of earlier church presidents about "the seventy apostles." Although second counselor Joseph F. Smith retained his
certificate of ordination in 1858 "to the Apostleship of the Seventies," he
said the Seventies must be convinced that "they were simply elders with a
special calling" and that it was wrong to say "the Seventies were Apostles."[168]

Problems between these competing quorums of apostles had already
surfaced dramatically during the frenzied days of the Reformation in
Utah.[169] For instance, on 7 October 1856 Young asked for men to go on
proselytizing missions. When few Seventies responded, Young's second
counselor Jedediah M. Grant launched into a tirade against his previous
associates in the First Council of Seventy. According to the record:
"President Young was asked if it would not be well to send the Presidents
of seventies out. He said[,] No they would Preach the people to sleep &
then to Hell." Grant attacked each of the Council's seven presidents,
concluding, "you ought to be drop[p]ed." They protested their devotion,
and Benjamin L. Clapp commented wryly that if he had gone to sleep, it
happened during Grant's remarks.[170] Two months later the apostles asked
all but the senior member of the First Council of Seventy to resign, and
some did temporarily.[171]

"The first Quorum of Seventies, where are they?" Brigham Young
asked the April 1861 general conference. "Seven of them are here as First
Presidents of the Seventies, and sixty-three of them now stand at the head
of different quorums of seventies. Sixty-three of them have been made
presidents over quorums. It works very different to what it does in other
quorums in the Church."[172] The First Council of Seventy did not want
that difference to continue.

Beginning in 1880 the seven presidents discussed organizing their full
quorum so that it would exist in fact rather than in theory. They petitioned
the apostles and Presidency to do this in 1880, 1881, 1882, and 1883.[173]
In 1883 John Taylor dictated a revelation, which authorized their complete

organization, but even after this he left the quorum vacant except for its seven presidents. Taylor's revelation added little to Young's view that the presidents of the first local quorums of Seventy technically constituted the rest of the First Quorum of Seventy.[174]

The truth was that the First Presidency and Twelve did not want another quorum that was their equal. Occasionally individual apostles indicated this explicitly. In 1882 Apostle Franklin D. Richards wrote that the Twelve was concerned about "the true status of the '*Seventy*' whose decision is equal to that of the 12 Apostles."[175] Forty-four years later Apostle Reed Smoot wrote that the First Presidency would not admit the Seventy's claim that "they were a seperate body of the priesthood with authority equal to the 12."[176] It is true that some apostles saw no threat.[177] Nevertheless, for more than 130 years most apostles felt that a full quorum of Seventy would challenge their authority. Seventy's president J. Golden Kimball remarked in 1896 that the apostles "seemed afraid of us."[178]

During Wilford Woodruff's presidency relationships continued to deteriorate. On 12 December 1888 the First Council of Seventy wrote to Woodruff and the apostles, requesting re-organization and permission to send a letter to the Seventies regarding their duties. Both requests were refused. "The necessity for the epistle is not apparent to them in any way," Seventy's president Abraham H. Cannon wrote. "Altogether the letter was a severe rebuke to us."[179] In January 1896 George Q. Cannon invited the First Presidency, several apostles, the Presiding Bishopric, and the Salt Lake stake presidency to a social. He excluded both the Presiding Patriarch and all members of the Council of Seventy.[180]

Five months later Kimball recorded his dissatisfaction. "As the 1*st* Council of Seventy, we are under the direction of the Twelve Apostles, yet it is very seldom indeed that they ever direct us." In September he reported that the Twelve manifested "a lack of confidence" in them.[181]

This was confirmed when the Presidency and apostles publicly announced the appointment of a new member of the Council of Seventy in October 1897. The council had been neither consulted nor informed in advance of this appointment to their quorum. That same year Seymour B. Young publicly expressed his frustration "that of the first quorum of seventies there were only seven presidents and no members, so it is really not organized."[182]

Young symbolized the ongoing controversy over the administrative authority of the First Council of Seventy. From the 1880s onward apostles Lorenzo Snow, Moses Thatcher, John Henry Smith, and John W. Taylor had invited Young to ordain high priests, but in 1891 the First Presidency and Twelve decided "it was improper" and instructed that the men be re-ordained. Nevertheless, apostles Snow and Abraham Owen Woodruff asked Young to assist in ordaining high priests as late as 1896 and 1898.[183]

In 1899 the First Presidency and Twelve agreed that Apostle Anthon H. Lund erred in setting apart Joseph W. McMurrin as a president of Seventy in 1898, rather than ordaining him. However, they did not want to question the ordinances McMurrin had performed since then and let his position stand. Subsequent members of the First Council of Seventy were set apart rather than ordained. In 1900 Apostle Francis M. Lyman instructed them "that we should not ordain [local] Pres of Seventy, but to set them apart, although we have a ruling of the First Presidency, made Jan 23, 1898 that we were to ordain them." However, that was before their 1899 decision to let stand the setting apart of McMurrin to the First Council. In 1908 the First Presidency formally extended that change to presidents of local seventies quorums. The First Council of Seventy saw this as a further erosion of their prestige.[184]

However, as second counselor and then as church president, Joseph F. Smith enhanced the prestige of the Seventy. In 1900 he authorized Seymour B. Young to perform polygamous sealings for time and eternity in Mexico.[185] That same year Smith acknowledged: "High priests *have been* ordained by seventies."[186] As president, Smith authorized the First Council of Seventy to assist in ordaining high priests, bishops, and patriarchs but not "to be mouth" in the ordination.[187]

President Smith even challenged President John Taylor's 1883 definition of the First Quorum of Seventy. In July 1903 Smith told apostles that "the identity of this quorum is not recognized (or is practically lost) for the reason that they are never called together as a quorum, and it was a question in his mind whether these presidents of the first 63-quorums were aware of the fact that they constituted a part of the first quorum."[188] In October 1903 Smith instructed the general priesthood meeting that "a Seventy could ordain a high priest or vice-a-versa."[189]

From J. Golden Kimball's perspective, however, things got worse rather than better for the Seventy in the early twentieth century. In June 1900, the church president sent out 800 invitations for a wedding reception, "but I did not receive an invitation," Kimball wrote. "Some of our Council are afraid to assert their rights," he complained in May 1901, "but will surrender and cater for peace's sake." The next day not one member of the Twelve accepted an invitation to attend the Seventy's dedication of a monument for deceased council member John Morgan.[190]

The Quorum of Twelve's higher prestige undoubtedly intensified personality conflicts between apostles and a Seventy like J. Golden Kimball. While speaking at a stake conference in 1902, "Bro Hyrum M. Smith took me up on something I had preached and went wild and put his foot into it making an ass of himself. I said nothing but was angry." Concerning a congregational meeting five days later, Kimball's diary continued: "Because the people laughed at something I said Bro Smith had to air himself on the sin of loud laughter and preached himself hoarse on sobriety. He is too good for this earth. I was angry for days."[191] It does not seem coincidental that the most biting humor in J. Golden Kimball's published folkstories was directed at his superiors in the Mormon hierarchy.[192]

Not until 1902 did apostles invite the Council of Seventy to one of their socials. Kimball remarked that it was a pleasant change, "being treated as if we were not a rear guard to the Twelve Apostles." But in 1905 he groused that he was not allowed to take his wife on an excursion with the apostles and their wives. This caused him to comment on the "strong line of demarkation drawn between the Quorum of Apostles and the First Council of Seventy."[193] During the April 1912 conference Kimball complained to senior president Young that "the 70 are the dogs tail again cut off at the last moment at our recent conference."[194]

The Council of Seventy's members did not merely express their dissatisfaction among themselves during the Joseph F. Smith presidency. At the general conference of Seventies in October 1907, the first such conference in sixty-three years, B. H. Roberts was typically blunt. He told the assembled thousands that the Seventies quorums "have been forced to take nights of the week [for meetings] that happened to be left by organizations which received more favors and better advantages." Then he added, "Indeed, about the last consideration in Israel has been the advantage and the opportunities for the quorums of the Seventy." In his November letter to the First Presidency, Seymour B. Young also pointedly questioned "the elimination of our local Seventies' Councils from participating in the selection of the Elders to be ordained Seventies, for which we can see no good reason."[195]

The decline of their council's prestige during this period coincided with increased frictions among council members themselves. Of Roberts, Kimball wrote in 1898, "He was bitter and malicious . . . pompous, proud and defiant." Kimball added, "I noticed, as I had done several times before that Roberts breath was strong with liquor of some kind." Three weeks later Kimball complained, "[I] cannot not stand Roberts pompous manner of addressing me just as if I was his Servant." This assessment was consistent with that of an assistant church historian, whose 1901 diary described Roberts as an "officious fellow" who spoke "sneeringly" to those he considered his inferiors.[196]

His alcoholism continued to strain his relationships with fellow general authorities, and in 1901 Roberts confessed to the First Council "as to his violation of the word of wisdom." After the council had "a heart to heart talk" with him in 1906, Roberts traveled to Los Angeles for treatment. While Roberts was there John T. Caine (a member of the Council of Fifty and a fellow Democrat) told the California mission president that Roberts was there because of "a weakness for liquor." In 1908 Young wrote that council members "have had to take up a labor with" Roberts because he "has been many times much the worse for Liquor."[197]

These personality conflicts continued within the First Council of Seventy for decades. From 1901 to 1904 Kimball wrote that Young was "obstinate" and "in a quiet way snubs me," and that "Bro. McMurrin and I flashed up against each other & . . . will never agree."[198] In 1912 Young commented on the "bombastic talk" of Roberts and noted in 1921 that he "dominated" council meetings. Young wrote in 1920 that council member Joseph W. McMurrin had never given Kimball "the courtesy Brother Kimball is entitled to."[199]

However, by the 1920s the apostles no longer excluded the First Council socially as Kimball had complained two decades earlier. For example in 1922, apostles Joseph Fielding Smith, George Albert Smith, and James E. Talmage and their wives went to a swimming party with Seventy's presidents J. Golden Kimball and John H. Taylor and their wives. This party included Presiding Patriarch Hyrum G. Smith and his wife, and Bishopric counselors David A. Smith and John Wells and their wives.[200]

Nevertheless, the Seventy's administrative status was at its lowest during the 1920s and early 1930s. In 1920 the Council of Seventy was decimated by leaves of absence. That year senior president Seymour B. Young was the only functioning member.[201] In January 1923 a committee of the Quorum of the Twelve began deliberating about decentralizing supervision of local Seventies. In April the First Council again asked the First Presidency to organize the full quorum. President Heber J. Grant waited almost two years to reply, then predictably declined the request.[202]

In June 1926 the First Council formally protested their neglect. They had not even been invited to participate in discussions about their callings:

> Certainly it will not be necessary to enter into any argument in relation to the necessity or justice of granting this request. It ought to be sufficient that a Council of the Priesthood numbered among the General Authorities of the Church asks for such a hearing before matters are determined which vitally concern the quorum organization of the Priesthood which, by the revelations of God, they are appointed to choose and over which they are appointed to preside.

The council found that contemplated changes were "contrary to the revelations of God upon the subject." In October the Council of Seventy expressed opposition to the plan to give stake presidents jurisdiction over local Seventies. The First Council appointed B. H. Roberts as their spokesman.[203]

Roberts accused the Twelve of "tampering with their organization as God has given it." To the First Presidency in December 1926, the Twelve dismissed his comments as "contentious" and "uncharitable." The letter continued with a defense of their resolution to the problem of thousands of ordained Seventies who were unable or unwilling to fulfill their calling as proselytizing missionaries.[204]

By now the First Council of Seventy saw itself as an impotent presiding quorum. Senior president Roberts described the problem to fellow council members on 9 April 1931:

> To sum up, this is the situation, The word of the Lord provides that the first seven presidents of the seventy shall preside directly over their own quorum—The First quorum or council—which with them as presidents would constitute the first council of the seventy and the third great presiding council of the Church, and spoken of in the revelations as being "equal in power and authority with the Quorum of the Twelve"; but the practice is that for eighty years no first quorum has been permitted to exist, not even to be called together or function in any manner, therefore the seven presidents are presidents without any immediate quorum to preside over, and that is that. In the second place, the First Council is to be the authorities which shall choose and preside over all the other [seventies] quorums in the church, no matter how many of them there shall be, but in practice the administration in selecting and directing these quorums in their work is proclaimed to belong to the presidencies of stakes and such committees as they may choose to appoint; and again the authority and prerogative of the first seven presidents of the seventies [are] made null and void!

Roberts concluded that the 1835 revelation authorized "the First Council to do whatever the Apostles do *when necessary, and when appointed to do it.*" He tried to defend that view to President Grant in a circumspect letter which quoted statements by Joseph Smith and Brigham Young that the Seventies were in fact apostles.[205]

Grant instructed him to omit such quotes from the seventh volume of the official *History of the Church,* which he was editing for publication. Roberts was furious. He wrote President Grant in August 1932 that "while you had the physical power of eliminating that passage from the History, I do not believe you had any moral right to do so." In addition, Roberts refused to accept "any responsibility for the mutilating of that very important part of President Young's Manuscript." This censorship of church history caused Roberts to abandon any pretense of deference to the Twelve. A few months later he "astonished" the apostles by accusing them of acting as if the First Council of Seventy was "not competent to perform the functions of that office."[206]

His increasingly shrill arguments undoubtedly worsened the situation. Three years after Roberts died, the administrative role of the First Council of Seventy improved. In April 1936 it gained back supervision of stake missions and missionaries.[207]

Expanding the Hierarchy

Five years later President Heber J. Grant acknowledged that the apostles needed the help of other general authorities "to do what the Apostles do." All agreed with the First Presidency regarding the need but differed on the best approach. Instead of organizing the First Quorum of Seventy, they chose to exceed the provisions of the *Doctrine and Covenants*. This began a series of redefinitions which have continued to the present. Such expansions appear to be unprecedented, but they have historical antecedents. In 1880 Apostle Orson Pratt defended the prospect of open-ended change: "New circumstances require new power, new knowledge, new additions, new strengths, and new Quorums; not to do away with the old, but additional in their nature."[208]

In February 1941 J. Reuben Clark first suggested the idea of calling assistants to help the apostles. In a meeting with the Twelve on 13 March 1941, President Grant raised the issue. He wanted general authorities who could compensate for the inability of elderly and ill members of the Twelve to respond to the church's needs. He justified this by citing the precedent of Brigham Young ordaining apostles who were not members of the quorum.[209]

Five apostles wanted to accept the proposal. However, four apostles, led by Joseph Fielding Smith, feared the development was unscriptural. They also expressed concern that extra apostles would lessen the Twelve's prestige. These four dissenting apostles recommended that the assistants be high priests only, while five of the Twelve supported Grant's proposal to ordain extra apostles.[210]

Elder Richard R. Lyman proposed two other alternatives. First, retirement for apostles. Second, the addition of more Seventies as general authorities. Apostles Charles A. Callis and John A. Widtsoe supported Lyman's proposal, but the First Presidency and the other apostles feared both possibilities. It was easier to defer to the four apostles who wanted high priest assistants "in lieu of other plan."[211]

At the 6 April 1941 general conference the First Presidency announced the new calling of Assistants to the Twelve. The official statement reminded Mormons that special counselors had assisted church leaders in the past. Beyond the official notice, Apostle John A. Widtsoe acknowledged that there were now assistants because the "expanding Church has made it difficult, if not impossible, for the Council of the Twelve to perform, to their full satisfaction, the many duties placed upon them."[212]

The conference sustained five Assistants to the Twelve. A biography of one of the new appointees observes that "President Heber J. Grant set him apart as an Assistant to the Quorum of the Twelve Apostles with virtually the same authority of an apostle," except they could not ordain patriarchs or perform the second anointing ceremony.[213] A secretary to the First Presidency described this as "the most far-reaching organizational initiative" of Grant's presidency. The secretary regarded this as unequalled in importance from the time of Joseph Smith.[214]

During the next thirty-six years, thirty-eight men served in this new echelon of the hierarchy. Fifteen of these Assistants to the Twelve eventually became members of the Quorum of Twelve Apostles or of the First Presidency. One, Alvin R. Dyer, was ordained an apostle while still serving as an assistant. He then served as an extra counselor in the First Presidency from 1968 to 1970. After that, he returned to service as an assistant without ever becoming a member of the Twelve.[215]

The Assistants to the Twelve never formed a separate quorum. In fact, one of them observed that, as a group, they had almost no influence on policy or decision-making. Individual assistants had some administrative influence but not the group itself.[216]

From 1941 to 1975 the assistants were an administrative rival to the First Council of Seventy. As one official biography notes, "For some years, there was uncertainty about the respective roles of the Assistants and the members of the First Council of Seventy." For instance, the Seventy's presidents felt they should be sustained ahead of the assistants, but the First Presidency and Quorum of Twelve decided otherwise.[217] Assistant Alma Sonne was sensitive to the jurisdictional concerns of the First Council of Seventy "and deferred to them on many occasions."[218]

More fundamentally the First Council of Seventy resented the fact that they were denied their nineteenth-century administrative rights. New council member Oscar A. Kirkham apologized to President Grant for setting apart a bishop in 1942 before learning this was forbidden. Kirkham told Grant: "I wish the President and Apostles would give us the authority to attend to ordinations of that kind." He added that it was "humiliating" for the First Council of Seventy to attend stake conference without that opportunity. Curiously Grant expressed his own wish that the First Council could perform such ordinances for high priests, as though the Seventies never had done so before.[219] The First Council formally complained that the Assistants to the Twelve "performed the exact service as the revelations said belonged to the First Quorum of Seventy," but the Presidency and Twelve "ignored" that objection.[220]

When President David O. McKay allowed members of the Council of Seventy to perform similar functions as the assistants, he first ordained them to the office of high priest on 11 June 1961.[221] Ironically, this was the status for which founding prophet Joseph Smith dropped five members of the Council of Seventy in 1837.[222] McKay did not ordain Levi Edgar Young a high priest "inasmuch as he is not able to visit the stakes and wards at the present time due to his [physical] condition."[223]

In 1961 McKay diminished the Seventy's office in two ways. First, he ignored the apostolic nature of the Seventy's office, which President Joseph F. Smith had publicly reaffirmed in 1903: "A Seventy could ordain a high priest or vice-a-versa."[224] In 1961 McKay explained that, without high priest ordination, the first seven presidents "were unable to ordain High Priests to any position in the stake, or even assist in such ordinations." With this high priest ordination McKay said that the First Council of Seventy could ordain bishops. He seemed unaware that during Brigham Young's presidency local Seventies had served as bishops without high priest ordination. McKay also forgot that up to Grant's presidency members of the First Council ordained or assisted to ordain patriarchs. McKay had been both a Seventy and an apostle during that earlier period.[225]

Second, in 1961 McKay quashed the First Council's hopes for a full quorum. Seventy's president Antoine R. Ivins suggested on 14 June 1961 that it would be logical to merge the assistants with a First Quorum of Seventy. McKay answered that men who were already high priests would not be called to the First Council of Seventy. By McKay's definition, it would be a demotion for an already ordained high priest to serve as one of the Seventy's presidents. He added that the First Quorum of Seventy "has never been organized" and that he had no intention of doing so.[226] This indicates the degree to which the First Presidency and Twelve were unwilling to acknowledge the authority once envisioned for the Seventy.

The decision in 1941 to call Assistants to the Twelve was a conservative response to LDS population growth. At the beginning of the twentieth century, two or more general authorities had usually attended each quarterly conference of every one of the church's fifty stakes and sometimes visited conferences held by the church's 500 wards. By September 1949 even the assistants were unable to help maintain that tradition for 175 stakes.[227] Therefore, the hierarchy decided that year: "Due to the rapid increase in Church membership, General Authorities would attend stake conferences semiannually rather than quarterly."[228]

By the early-1960s church growth made it impossible to continue traditional patterns of church administration. The Twelve's president wrote in May 1962 "that it is very difficult to meet all conferences and many stakes have to go without [general authority] visitors."[229] The number of existing general authorities could not continue to set apart "by the laying on of hands" all full-time missionaries or to interview missionaries individually during visits at various mission headquarters. It was fast becoming an impossible burden to organize each stake presidency and ward bishopric throughout the world, plus ordain every bishop.

One response was to reduce local visitations even further. By the mid-1960s general authority visits to missions became rare and no longer involved personal interviews with missionaries. In 1975 the hierarchy discontinued the annual conferences of general auxiliary organizations that had required the presence of several general authorities. In 1978 stake conferences themselves were reduced from quarterly to semi-annual.[230]

Nevertheless, there were still not enough general authorities for even this reduced workload. The hierarchy chose not to increase the number of general authorities. Instead the First Presidency announced on 29 September 1967 the new administrative position of Regional Representative of the Twelve, an idea originated by Apostle Harold B. Lee nearly fifteen years earlier. Sixty-nine men initially served in that capacity.[231] Regional representatives lacked the status of general authorities but were soon performing functions once restricted to them. However, "because Regional Representatives do not preside as line officers, they serve without counselors."[232]

There was some precedent for this in the service of regional bishops from the 1830s to 1870s. However, only apostles serving as regional officers had performed the organizing functions that non-general authorities were doing after 1967.

The First Council of Seventy regarded this creation of regional representatives as another nonscriptural alternative to the provision in the *Doctrine and Covenants* for a full Quorum of Seventy who could serve as general authorities. Therefore, "in the last years of President McKay's administration," the First Council formally proposed that the Presidency and Twelve organize the full Quorum of Seventy and make the assistants part of the Quorum. To demonstrate that they were not seeking to increase their personal status, "the Seven Presidents stated their willingness to step aside and be [regular] members of the quorum if the Brethren preferred Assistants in the presidency." Again, the First Presidency and Twelve rejected this proposal. However, Apostle Harold B. Lee personally favored it, with the exception that he assured the First Council that former assistants would not supplant any of them as presidents of a fully organized Quorum of Seventy.[233]

By arrangement of Harold B. Lee, now first counselor, the Mormon hierarchy in 1971 took the extraordinary step of subjecting itself to an on-site analysis by the management consulting firm Cresap, McCormick, and Paget of New York City. The non-LDS firm's major criticism was that "the Twelve Apostles were doing 'staff' work assignments, rather than centering their efforts in broader policy-making functions." Consequent changes in the central bureaucracy occurred within months. However, it took years for LDS headquarters to implement some of the "major changes in the administrative functions of the General Authorities."[234]

In June 1972 regionalism extended to the role of the First Council of Seventy. The First Presidency called twenty-nine Mission Representatives. These men functioned "in mission districts in the same way regional representatives functioned in stakes" with "joint accountability to the Twelve and the First Council of Seventy." But within two years regional representatives absorbed the position of mission representative, and regional representatives were "chiefly under the direction of the First Council of Seventy."[235]

When recently sustained LDS president Harold B. Lee set apart Rex D. Pinegar as a member of the First Council of Seventy in October 1972, he reversed McKay's previous decision and did not ordain Pinegar as a high priest. Lee's successor Spencer W. Kimball also authorized Pinegar as a Seventy to ordain bishops and high priests. Kimball ordained Pinegar a high priest in 1974 only because a stake president objected that Pinegar should be a high priest if he was ordaining bishops and high priests. However, Kimball set apart Gene R. Cook, Charles Didier, William R. Bradford, and George P. Lee as general authority Seventies but did not ordain them high priests when he authorized them to perform high priest ordinations and temple sealings.[236]

Ultimately, massive growth has redefined the apostleship and lessened its status administratively. Necessity has reduced the number of ordinances and administrative acts that only the Twelve can do. The hierarchy has delegated those apostolic functions to assistants, to the Council of Seventy, to regional representatives, and ultimately to local stake presidents. Within a few years after the calling of regional representatives, the First Presidency authorized stake presidents to set apart full-time missionaries and to ordain bishops and patriarchs.[237]

These developments chipped away at the Twelve's traditional protectiveness of prerogatives and status. Finally, massive growth led to the one twentieth-century change in the hierarchy which the *Doctrine and Covenants* sanctioned. It was a change in the Seventy which the First Presidency and Quorum of Twelve had resisted for a century. On 3 October 1975 the First Presidency announced it was calling general authorities to a newly established First Quorum of Seventy. For the previous 140 years the Mormon hierarchy included only seven members of that body. Since 1975 more than half of those entering the Quorum of Seventy have first been regional representatives. Administrative logic then dictated the end of Assistants to the Twelve as a non-scriptural echelon, and they were absorbed into the First Quorum of Seventy on 1 October 1976.[238]

Only skyrocketing membership finally persuaded the First Presidency and Twelve to do what the First Council of Seventy had asked for over a century. The church "reconstituted" the quorum for the first time since the Mormon founder's death and made it part of the central hierarchy for the first time in LDS history.[239] In 1979 the church president said that this new quorum "will gradually do much of the work the Twelve has done up till now."[240] Even B. H. Roberts would be impressed by such extensive and far-flung administrative responsibilities as now shouldered by the Seventies.[241] However, this occurred with significant loss for the First Council of Seventy.

The demographic necessities of church growth did not lessen the Twelve's protectiveness, which required some means of diminishing the status of the seven presidents of what is now the largest presiding quorum of the church. In April 1976, "without saying anything to the First Quorum in advance, President [Spencer W.] Kimball called four new members to the Seventy."[242]

The First Presidency announced on 1 October 1976 that the First Council of Seventy was disorganized, that its presidents no longer had lifetime appointment, and that their ranking or rotation had nothing to do with seniority as Seventies or as general authorities.[243]

To demonstrate this new order, the First Presidency shuffled the previous membership of the First Council with the previous Assistants to the Twelve. Even as the Twelve released all of its assistants in 1976, it reaffirmed its supremacy over the first seven presidents of the Seventy. The hierarchy dropped senior president S. Dilworth Young into regular membership of the First Quorum and replaced him with the senior member of the now defunct Assistants to the Twelve. This was the kind of leadership change that the First Council of Seventy (including Young) had agreed to in theory a decade earlier.

However, this put LDS president Spencer W. Kimball "kind of on a spot," Young said privately, because "it looked like he was just dumping an old man."[244] After nine years as senior president Young suddenly ranked beneath twenty-three other men in the First Quorum of Seventy. He told the October 1976 conference: "A friend said to me last Friday, 'How can you bear what you have lost?' I replied, 'I have lost nothing, rather I have gained.'" The demoted Seventy's president then stoically explained, "I have gained a new group of close friends and associates." Of course, that statement would have been equally true had he remained president of the Seventy.[245] Two years later the hierarchy gave him emeritus status, which has yet to be applied to the Twelve or First Presidency. At eighty-one, Young was eleven years younger than Apostle LeGrand Richards who maintained his ranking in the Twelve.[246]

The excommunication of George P. Lee in 1989 provided another evidence of continued friction between the Twelve and the Seventy. As a Navajo, Lee's central objections were the church's changes in policy toward Native Americans. He also complained about personal injustices he felt he had suffered within the hierarchy. As one of the original members of the new First Quorum of Seventy, Lee referred to "double standards among the General Authorities" and to their "love of power, status, position,"[247] echoing J. Golden Kimball's observations at the beginning of the century. The ascendancy of the First Quorum of Seventy in 1975 did not end the pattern of tension between those general authorities comprising the Twelve and those comprising the Seventy.

However, the official 1993-94 LDS church almanac listed the First Council of Seventy before the Assistants to the Twelve for the first time in more than fifty years. Almost fifteen years after the assistants and the First Council had ceased to exist, the Seventy finally got the priority it had sought over the Twelve's assistants since 1941.[248]

Since the organization of the First Quorum of Seventy, growing regional hierarchy and bureaucracy have come to characterize the structure of relationships between church headquarters and local stakes. The office of Regional Representative continued until 1995, although "of the Twelve" was dropped from the title in 1979. That latter year "seven men were called to serve full time as Regional Representatives and to live within their assigned areas in Latin America or western Europe." This involved two firsts: the calling of regional representatives to full-time positions, and the relocation of some to the distant regions they supervised.[249]

Increased membership has resulted in changes every few years in titles, jurisdictions, and organizational structure. At present, each LDS "area" includes several regions and missions. A region includes several stakes, each of which includes several wards. A mission includes several "districts," each of which includes several "branches." Members of the Quorums of Seventy serve as each "Area Presidency" which now directs the non-general authority officers called "Area Authorities."[250]

This expansion made it difficult for even the most dedicated Mormon to know the names of all general authorities. For example, one Mormon observes, "When I was [assistant editor] at the *New Era* [in 1972] I knew every single general authority—his name, who he was, what he did, where he was." By the time he became president of the church-controlled ZCMI department store in the 1980s, there were so many general authorities that "there was no way I could have named them all or known what they did."[251]

By the mid-1980s Mormon headquarters culture had experienced a fundamental change. For more than a century, closer access to LDS leaders had been a magnet for Mormon immigrants to Utah. However, Mormons living in Salt Lake City now have no closer access to the LDS prophet than residents of the nation's capital have to the U.S. president. "Gone are the days when conversations with General Authorities could be held in your living room, or on the street at a chance meeting," wrote a prominent Salt Lake Mormon in 1985. "The type of intimacy between Church leaders and the people known [down to] the early 1950s seems forever lost."[252]

On the basis of doubling church membership every fifteen years or less, non-Mormon sociologist Rodney Stark estimates 265 million Mormons by the year 2080. Ten years after Stark made this prediction, he found the population actually ahead of his projections.[253]

The LDS hierarchy is now poised to expand numerically to cope with the Mormon population's extraordinary growth. The *Doctrine and Covenants* did not specifically limit general authority roles to the seven members of the First Council of Seventy. The revelation said there could be "seven times seventy, if the labor in the vineyard of necessity requires it" (D&C 107:93-6). At its most literal, this revelation allows for significant expansion to cope with enormous changes.

It is consistent with the *Doctrine and Covenants* to have seven general authority quorums of the Seventy, or 490 general authority Seventies, versus fewer than twenty men in the other presiding quorums. The First Presidency formed a Second Quorum of Seventy in 1989. Rather than life tenure, these appointments are for a five-year period after which the men return to the rank-and-file. If the First Presidency and Twelve are especially pleased with the service of a man in the Second Quorum of Seventy, he is appointed to one of the presiding quorums with life tenure.[254] If they are interested in life tenure as general authorities, this encourages members of the Second Quorum to be very solicitous to dominant members of the Twelve.

The First Presidency had announced in October 1986 the elimination of local Seventy's quorums and their incorporation into elders and high priests quorums. This step restricted the office of Seventy to general authorities for the first time in LDS history. Thus in the church's new *Encyclopedia of Mormonism*, "Seventy is a priesthood office in the Melchizedek Priesthood reserved since 1986 for General Authorities."[255]

The Bureaucracy

A final source of tensions over jurisdiction and power in the twentieth century has come from the increasing significance of the church's departmental bureaucracy.[256] One historian notes that even as late as 1930 the church was "prebureaucratic," because even the most routine matters required First Presidency approval.[257] Nevertheless, bureaucrats began with Joseph Smith's appointment of temple building committees in 1833 and in 1840.[258]

By the early 1900s general authorities had become the mainstays of general boards that governed the ecclesiastical auxiliaries of the church (such as Sunday schools). The hierarchy also headed various committees to oversee a welter of administrative functions. But within several decades there were too many committees and boards for general authorities to form a significant proportion of each. Instead they became the committee's highest-ranking members. For example, Apostle Henry D. Moyle's office calendar for 1956 listed "102 regularly scheduled committee meetings, not counting the weekly sessions of the First Presidency and Council of the Twelve."[259]

By the time the church completed its twenty-eight-story office building in Salt Lake City in 1972, bureaucrats already exceeded the building's capacity. The bureaucracy had become so large that general authorities could not govern it directly. In addition, there was a mitosis of committees and subcommittees, each of which was of interest to the hierarchy. General authorities began to realize that the geometric population growth created a geometric growth in personnel.

Now the hierarchy had to scurry just to keep abreast of what the bureaucracy was doing. Less than two decades after World War II, two members of the First Presidency expressed deep concern about the administrative influence of this growing infrastructure. J. Reuben Clark, Jr., predicted that they would be forced to make decisions about matters in which they had little or no experience. They would become more dependent on the church's technically trained bureaucrats. The result, he feared, would be abdication by necessity of the hierarchy's decision-making responsibilities. Technocrats would make many of the hierarchy's decisions for them and simply advise them of this necessity.[260]

President David O. McKay also expressed concern. He believed that the quorums were diminished by the existence of committees and departments which they merely presided over. "Be careful that you do not take away from the constituted authority of the Church the divine right by ordination and by setting apart and leave that to some committee," he warned the apostles. Then he added, "If we do that we will be running this Church by Committees, just as the Government has been running the country by Committees, and as it is being run now by Committees. You are the constituted Authority."[261]

Bureaucratic officials and committees are not the only incursions on the twentieth-century hierarchy's decision-making. Particularly in the First Presidency's office, secretaries can wield wide influence. By Heber J. Grant's administration (1918-45), the First Presidency received too much correspondence to be able to read efficiently. Even though he dictated letters at night, Grant fell months behind. In 1936 Clark began reading and answering these letters, which Grant merely signed. Grant's successor gave similar permission to his counselors.[262]

This developed into the practice of secretaries reading all incoming correspondence and preparing a cover-sheet summary of the contents. The summaries varied from a single sentence to a paragraph or more. Within a few years Presidency secretaries prepared cover-sheet summaries for official reports and correspondence from the bureaucracy and other presiding quorums. Eventually this became the practice for all the presiding quorums as well as for secretaries to individual general authorities.[263]

After World War II the administrative power of the secretaries (male and female) increased dramatically. This was most significant in the First Presidency's office. Secretaries began deciding which correspondence to present with cover-sheets to members of the First Presidency and which correspondence to read and answer themselves. For example, McKay's secretary Clare Middlemiss "draft[ed] suggested answers to letters for the Prophet's consideration before he had even read the correspondence."[264]

Middlemiss also decided who saw her employer and who did not. When A. Hamer Reiser began his ten-year service as an assistant secretary in the First Presidency's office in 1956, he "observed with disbelief the power exercised by Clare Middlemiss." She gave instant access to McKay for her favorite general authorities and department heads but put off the less favored, including members of the Twelve. Being on good terms with Middlemiss was necessary to achieve success with McKay. Flattery became the administrative lubricant of the McKay presidency.[265]

One of McKay's biographers referred to this "watchful diligence of the hovering Clare Middlemiss." A mixture of devoted friend, confidante, and executive secretary since 1935, Middlemiss said, "I have devoted my whole life to President McKay—I want nothing more."[266] During McKay's presidency (1951-70) she had her own private secretary, and Middlemiss was a force to be reckoned with. For example, one church administrator noted in 1962 that "through arrangement with President McKay's secretary whom I had converted to my side of this issue also, I went in to see President McKay."[267] For almost two decades after 1951, Middlemiss was a crucial ally, since McKay often made promises or decisions with those he met privately.

In 1966 general authorities informed Utah's senator that "one of the problems we have is that Miss Middlemiss runs the office of President McKay and often calls in his name to order things done."[268] A First Presidency secretary acknowledged that the administrative power of Clare Middlemiss "created some unintentional problems" involving "the historic differences between line and staff personnel."[269] In other words, she rivaled the authority of the Presidency counselors, and this created "problems" between Middlemiss and Counselor Hugh B. Brown.[270]

Since McKay's death in 1970 there has been an inevitable growth in secretarial significance. D. Arthur Haycock replaced Middlemiss as the church president's "executive secretary who could handle his correspondence, help plan his agenda, assist with routine procedural matters, serve as a buffer against unscheduled intrusions, and be available on call to assist the president in any other way." He served Joseph Fielding Smith, Harold B. Lee, Spencer W. Kimball, and (briefly) Ezra Taft Benson.[271] All secretaries at LDS headquarters have become "gate-keepers," abstractors of incoming documents, and semi-autonomous authors of out-going letters.

Secretarial influence at church headquarters increased in the 1970s when AUTO-PEN office machines began inscribing exact ink replicas of general authority's signatures for letters and other documents.[272] In 1993 a spokesman publicly acknowledged the First Presidency's use of the signature machine as "a common, efficient practice followed by leaders of many major organizations." He added that the LDS prophet's signature machine signs "thousands of documents and missionary assignments each year."[273] This improved upon a practice Grant described in 1898: "I had Francis Nelson sign about 90 [letters] for me as he can sign my name so nearly like my own signature that it is a very difficult matter to detect the difference."[274] Secretaries now decide whether a general authority even sees his incoming or outgoing correspondence, though drafts of replies are often reviewed by First Presidency members.[275] Arthur Haycock's biography noted that this secretary to the LDS president "represented the president and was acting in his behalf, a responsibility he never took lightly."[276]

By the mid-1980s the LDS bureaucracy had grown to a size that would have troubled the administratively cautious J. Reuben Clark. *The General Church Offices Telephone Directory* listed 2,971 employees in twenty-two departments as of January 1984. Total church membership as of 31 December 1983 was 5,351,724.[277] Thus LDS church headquarters in the mid-1980s had one bureaucrat for every 1,801 Latter-day Saints throughout the world. That number excluded the bureaucrats in the regional arms of these departments, and excluded such specialized bureaucracies as the administrative staffs of Brigham Young University and Ricks College, as well as the Church Education System (CES) administrators located primarily in the Western Hemisphere and Oceania. By contrast, at the same time the U.S. government had one federal bureaucrat per 108 persons of the total U.S. population.[278]

Now the central LDS bureaucracy is even leaner. Scattered in thirty-four buildings (including the twenty-eight-story Church Office Building and the Joseph Smith Memorial Building's 75,000 square feet of office space), the bureaucracy in Salt Lake City totalled 3,367 people in January 1996. Compared to the worldwide church population of 9,340,898 as of 31 December 1995, this equalled one bureaucrat for every 2,774 Mormons. This reflected the restraining influence during those years of Counselor Gordon B. Hinckley (LDS president since 1995): "As thrilling as [church] growth was, he abhored bureaucracy and at times felt himself swimming helplessly against a mounting tide [of it]."[279] In other words, although the central bureaucracy grew in absolute numbers by 1996, it declined by one-third in proportion to the growing church population. Rather than proportionately matching church membership since 1983, the LDS central bureaucracy became more efficient in responding to the challenges of more than 74.5 percent growth in population and 61 percent growth in stakes, wards, missions, and branches in twelve years.

However, decentralization was another factor in the relative decline of the central bureaucracy's size. By 1996 the LDS bureaucracy had "area offices" in forty-five countries and territories, as well as "administrative offices" of greater jurisdiction in fourteen countries. A typical Area Office has an extensive bureaucracy: area director of Temporal Affairs, assistant director of Temporal Affairs, zone supervisor for Temporal Affairs, regional manager for Temporal Affairs, membership records specialist, accounts payable specialist, distribution and purchasing supervisor, temple hotel administrator, systems manager, human resource specialist, construction supervisor, manager of physical facilities, construction supervisor, manager of physical facilities, physical maintenance supervisor, treasury supervisor, property supervisor, central services representative, motor pool coordinator, meeting house crew coordinator. Particularly outside the United States, ecclesiastical leadership is drawn from this bureaucracy of church employees, and "many Australian LDS are dismayed by the growth of the Church bureaucracy in the Australian Area Office."[280]

The Presiding Bishopric and the general authority Quorums of Seventy now divide the administrative supervision of the bureaucracy. The Presiding Bishopric supervises the "temporal" departments "which include finance and records, LDS Foundation, printing services, distribution of curriculum materials, purchasing, scripture and curriculum translation, temple clothing production, transportation, information systems and communications, security, investments, temples and special project construction and remodeling, real estate acquisitions and sales, meetinghouse construction, welfare production and processing, LDS Social Services, and property management." The Seventy preside over the ecclesiastical bureaucracy: "headquarters departments of the Church, such as operations related to Church history, curriculum, priesthood and auxiliary organizations, temples, family history, missionary work, and correlation."[281]

Smaller and more dedicated than the bloated federal bureaucracy, the bureaucracy of the LDS church is now an administrative partner of the Mormon hierarchy.[282] An insightful analysis observed in the mid-1980s:

> On the other hand, the [LDS] church, despite the predisposition of its bureaucracy, is not yet a corporate conglomerate in its leadership structures and decision-making procedures. It is, in many ways, a middle-management bureaucracy without an effective top-management layer, a bureaucracy that anticipates more than directs, whose sensitivities are most directed at what is happening at the top and what shifts, trends, or changes can be deciphered.[283]

The hierarchical presiding quorums of the church continue to direct its bureaucrats and apparently harbor suspicions of what the LDS president's official biography calls "the Church's burgeoning bureaucracy." Therefore, in all likelihood the church's central bureaucracy will retain the characteristics of middle-management.[284]

Conclusion

A devotional study of the hierarchy acknowledged: "Each time the First Presidency changed its members there would always be the occasional challenge of harmony among them, as indeed there would be among the Quorum of Twelve since, though servants of God, they were very human."[285] The hierarchy has long since learned to absorb its internal tensions as a matter of course. Lorenzo Snow once told the Quorum of Twelve Apostles: "I may criticize the actions of our leaders, but never do I question their authority. I saw Joseph the Prophet do and heard him say things which I never expected to see and hear in a Prophet of God, yet I was always able to throw the mantle of charity over improper things."[286] The general authorities expect church administrators and rank-and-file members to do likewise.

Nevertheless, conflicts can impede smooth progress in achieving God's will on earth. This occasional turbulence exasperated Brigham Young University president Ernest L. Wilkinson: "If the gospel were not true, some of the General Authorities with their internal disputes would have ruined it long ago."[287] However, tensions among leaders have never paralyzed the church, which Brigham Young liked to call the "old ship Zion."[288] Adopting that image, one can see that *Zion* has weathered its share of storms, as well as occasional grumbling from its officers and crew.

Organization of the LDS Church—31 December 1995

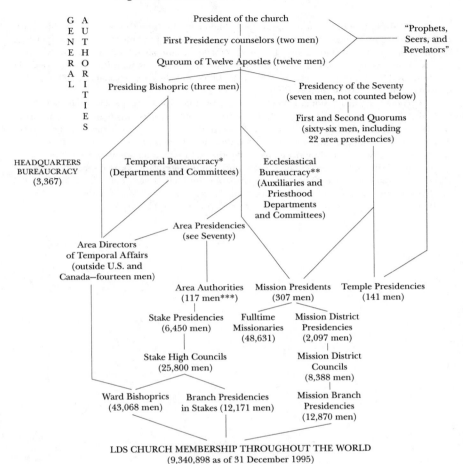

LDS CHURCH MEMBERSHIP THROUGHOUT THE WORLD
(9,340,898 as of 31 December 1995)

*The temporal bureaucracy has direct down-line relationships with the echelons listed here, excepting missionaries and general church membership.

**Every stake, ward, mission, district, and branch appoints male and female officers who implement the programs of the auxiliary organizations and priesthood departments and committees. Unnumerated here, the total number of these voluntary officers is approximately twenty times larger than this chart's numbers of presiding officers for those echelons.

***Number as of "First Presidency Names Area Authorities," *Deseret News* "*Church News,*" 5 Aug. 1995, 3.

Sources: *General Church Offices Telephone Directory, January 1996*; *Deseret News 1995-96 Church Almanac*; "Church Growth," *Deseret News* "*Church News,*" 3 Apr. 1996, 6; Ludlow, *Encyclopedia of Mormonism*, 3:1130, for Area Directors of Temporal Affairs; information from Public Communications, LDS headquarters, June 1996.

All these numbers will be significantly higher by the time the reader sees this chart. Females are included in the numbers for missionaries, the bureaucracy, and membership. The number of local leaders was calculated according to the norm of 3 men per presidency, 3 men per bishopric, and 12 men per council for 47 functioning temples, 2,150 stakes, 307 missions, 699 mission districts, 14,356 wards, 4,057 branches in stakes, and 4,290 branches in missions as of 31 December 1995.

There is no professional LDS clergy. Of more than 160,000 ecclesiastical leaders listed in the above chart as of the end of 1995, fewer than 500 received any living allowance from LDS church funds. Even those presently supported by a church living allowance were independently employed for years or decades prior to accepting such a church position (usually at great financial sacrifice). The majority of full-time missionaries are supported by personal savings or by their families. LDS church funds directly support a minority (probably no more than 10 percent) of missionaries from the United States and Canada. Full-time missionaries whose families live outside Canada and the United States (especially in "Third World" countries) receive most or all of their support from LDS church funds.

CHAPTER 5

Family Relationships

Of the social characteristics of the men who comprised the Mormon hierarchy during its first hundred years (1832-1932), the most complex and perhaps the most significant were the family relationships of these men. At a primary level were kinship ties. No less significant were marriage connections. These bonds fundamentally reinforced the religious affinity of men who shared a church calling. Convoluted relationships made the Mormon hierarchy an extended family, and extensive family connections persist among LDS general authorities today.

Kinship

There was theological rationale for the influence of kinship on appointments to the LDS hierarchy. One sociologist has commented: "Society in both the Book of Mormon and the Old Testament is conceived as an extended kinship group. All members thought of themselves as descended from a common ancestor."[1] This translated into an early Mormon concern for deceased ancestors. As early as 1835 Associate President Oliver Cowdery expressed this in a published letter: "Do our fathers, who have waded through affliction and adversity . . . [have] an inheritance in those mansions? If so, can *they* without *us* be made perfect?"[2] The implication was that Mormons had responsibility, as yet undefined, to secure the spiritual welfare of ancestors. Speaking further upon this question, Joseph Smith announced in 1838: "All those who have not had an opportunity of hearing the Gospel, and being administered to by an inspired man in the flesh, must have it hereafter, before they can be finally judged."[3] Without specific details, Smith reinforced Cowdery's view that mortals had a role in saving deceased ancestors. On 19 January 1841 Smith dictated a revelation about the nature of that role: baptism by proxy for the dead.[4] Mormons immediately began performing this ordinance for deceased relatives and friends, a practice which extended in the 1850s to other LDS ordinances such as priesthood ordinations, the endowment, and "celestial marriage." These practices resulted in an increasing emphasis on genealogical research.[5]

Smith also announced revelations that some men had the right to preside in the church by virtue of lineage (D&C 26:21, 36:8, 107:39-52, 113:8). As implied by some revelatory statements, this right extended beyond the lineal office of Presiding Patriarch. For example, in 1847

Brigham Young said: "I am entitled to the Keys of the Priesthood according to lin[e]age & Blood. So is Brother H. C. Kimball & many others."[6]
Several revelations indicated that the sons and other descendants of
current leaders would have significant roles in the church (D&C 86:10;
110;12; 124:58). These statements gave authority for the appointment of
relatives to the hierarchy.

Smith clearly established such kinship appointments as an accepted
practice. During his church presidency, he gave general authority positions
to his father, his uncle, two of his brothers, and his first cousin. Moreover,
the Quorum of the Twelve established in 1835 was intended to include
three sets of brothers, Orson and Parley P. Pratt, Luke S. and Lyman E.
Johnson, and Brigham and Phineas H. Young. This appears as a conscious
effort to duplicate Jesus' choice of twelve apostles who included three sets
of brothers (Matt. 10:1-4; Luke 6:13-16). However, the prophet decided to
drop Phineas Young from the proposed quorum, substituting his own
brother, William Smith.[7] In so doing Smith followed another biblical
precedent, since one of Jesus' brothers was appointed as an apostle
anciently (Gal. 1:19).

Later church presidents followed Smith's lead. In 1864, two months
after secretly ordaining three of his sons apostles and making them special
counselors in the First Presidency, President Brigham Young confided to
members of the Twelve: "I am going to tell you something that I have never
before mentioned to any other Person[.] I have ordained my sons Joseph
A.[,] Brigham & John W. Apostles and My Counsellors. Have you any
objections? J[ohn]. Taylor & G[eorge]. A. Smith said they had not, that it
was his own affair & they considered it under his own direction." Young
added: "In ordaining my sons I have done no more than I am perfectly
willing that you should do with yours. And I am now determined to put
my sons into active service in the Spiritual Affairs of the Kingdom and
keep them thare just as long as possible [–] you have the same privilege."[8]

Subsequent presidents advanced their own sons to various positions.
John Taylor (1877-87) appointed two of his sons to the hierarchy, Wilford
Woodruff (1887-98) one of his sons, and Joseph F. Smith (1901-18) three
of his sons. Only two presidents down to 1932 did not appoint immediate
family members: Lorenzo Snow (1898-1901), who made only two appointments during his brief presidency, and Heber J. Grant (1918-1945), who
had no living sons. Nor was this restricted to the sons of presidents. In all
twenty-nine sons of general authorities entered the hierarchy, accounting
for 23.6 percent of appointments between 1832 and 1932.

This should be put into perspective. After the 1840s the general
authorities married plural wives and therefore had more children than
would otherwise be expected. Young, for example, had fifty-seven chil-

dren.[9] Nine sons reached the age of twenty-five during their father's presidency, yet Young advanced only three to positions in the hierarchy. In short, the hierarchy produced more sons than vacancies.

If kinship relations involved only patrilineal appointments, they would be relatively easy to analyze. However, they included sons, brothers, nephews, uncles, first cousins, and distant cousins. Moreover, where brothers or cousins served in the hierarchy, oftentimes their sons were also appointed, thus establishing a complex series of connections involving distant cousin and nephew relationships to numerous other general authorities. In the resulting maze one might doubt whether it was significant or even recognized by a general authority that his grandnephew, third cousin, or more distant relative had joined him in the hierarchy.

Some have assumed that LDS leaders did not know the details of these distant relations, especially before the official encouragement of genealogical research.[10] Joseph Smith, however, had extensive knowledge of his ancestry. Two years prior to the revelation on baptism, his uncle John Smith recorded his own patrilineal ancestry back to his great-great-grandfather.[11] Thus in the 1830s Joseph Smith had personal knowledge of five generations of his own family. Moreover, he indicated an early awareness of the distant cousin relationships he sustained to the men he advanced. He told apostles Orson and Parley P. Pratt that by vision he had learned that their "fathers and his all sprang from the same man a few generations ago."[12] Smith and the Pratt brothers were sixth cousins.

LDS general authorities recognized and honored obscure family relationships that might seem inconsequential to others. This feeling of camaraderie is best shown in a "family meeting" held in Nauvoo on 8 January 1845. Assembled at this meeting were men and women who were as closely related as brother, sister, or first cousin and as distant as fourth, fifth, and sixth cousins. The remarks of John Haven set the tone for the meeting: "Brothers and Sisters, Cousins, Nephews and Nieces and all who are before me as such. I rejoice that I am connected with you as there are three branches here, descendants of Father Phinehas, and Mother Susannah Goddard Howe." At this meeting were four members of the Quorum of the Twelve, a member of the First Council of Seventy, the mother of Joseph Smith, Jr., and two future general authorities. Brigham Young's remarks indicated his regard for distant cousins: "When we come to the connections we discover that we all sprung back to the settlement of New England about 200 years ago. It is but a little more than that time when Father Smith, the Goddards, Richards, Youngs and Kimballs were all in one family—as it were. We are all relations. It is only three generations back that Brother Joseph Smith's family were related to this family."[13] Into the twentieth century, general authorities recognized these relationships, often referring to distant cousins as "kinsman," "uncle" (if older), "nephew" (if younger), or merely as "cousin." For example, in writing to his son in 1904 Apostle Francis M. Lyman referred to his fellow apostle as "Uncle John Henry Smith." Smith was Lyman's third cousin and through marriage was the first cousin once-removed of Lyman's son.[14]

The extent to which this allied the general authorities can best be illustrated through a diagram of one extended family group. This includes three of the families which assembled at the 1845 meeting (the Smiths, Youngs, and Richards) and also the Lyman family. General authorities are in bold face type.

To simplify this diagram, it is perhaps easier to focus first on each of the four immediate families. The Youngs, descended from John Young, provided seven patrilineal appointments between 1835 and 1909. The Richards family, descended from Joseph Richards, provided four appointments between 1840 and 1917. The descendants of Asa(h)el Smith provided fourteen patrilineal appointments between 1830 and 1912. The Lyman family, descended from Roswell Lyman, provided three appointments between 1842 and 1918.

Each of these families was in turn related to the others. Apostle Willard Richards was fourth cousin of Joseph Smith and first cousin of Brigham Young. Apostle Amasa M. Lyman was the first cousin once-removed of Counselor John Smith's wife and the second cousin of Apostle George A. Smith. The Smith family relationships are closer and more easily recognized. To avoid complexity, the diagram neglects Brigham Young's additional connection to Joseph Smith as a sixth cousin. Within this extended family, twenty-eight men became general authorities, accounting for 22.6 percent of the 124 members of the Mormon hierarchy, 1830-1932, including founder Joseph Smith.

One means of putting this maze into perspective is by analyzing the kinship relation to living general authorities that existed at the time men were appointed to the hierarchy. Of the 123 men appointed between 1832 and 1932, sixty-three (51.2 percent) were related as kin to one or more living general authorities. Several of these were distant cousin relationships, but of the 123 men, forty-seven (38.2 percent) were second cousins or closer. In three ten-year periods, the percentage of total kinship relations for new appointees was much higher than the 52.3 percent of the first decade: in 1856-66 it was 70 percent, in 1900-10 it was 64.3 percent, and in 1922-32 it was 100 percent.[15]

Reflecting the Mormon emphasis on ancestry, seven members of the Quorum of the Twelve (1835-1935) were sons of deceased apostles: Joseph F. Smith, Francis M. Lyman, John Henry Smith, Heber J. Grant, George F. Richards, Richard R. Lyman, and Joseph F. Merrill, and two (Orson F.

**Patrilineal Appointments in the Mormon Hierarchy, 1832-1932
from One Extended Family (Young, Richards, Smith, and Lyman)**

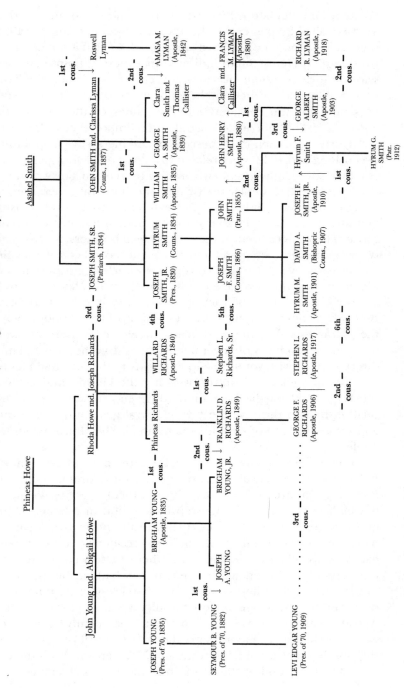

Whitney and Stephen L Richards) were grandsons of deceased apostles. That equalled 29 percent of the apostles appointed since 1849, the first time a new appointee was born late enough to be the son of an apostle.[16] Apostle John Henry Smith indicated that these appointments were conscious efforts to honor previous church leaders. When the Twelve discussed filling a vacancy in the quorum in 1901, Smith recorded: "I presented for the consideration the names of the sons of the dead apostles."[17] This, of course, magnified the importance of family ties.

Thirty-three men (26.8 percent of the hierarchy's appointments between 1832 and 1932) were related to at least one living general authority as father, son, brother, nephew, uncle, or first cousin. Forty-two appointees (34.1 percent) had similar ties (within one ancestral generation) to either living or dead church leaders. Of the total number of relationships each new appointee sustained to every other man in the hierarchy (current or former) there were twenty-nine sons, sixteen brothers, fourteen nephews, twelve grandsons, ten grandnephews, eight second cousins, six first cousins once-removed, five first cousins, two uncles, and one father.[18] The hierarchy was interconnected most densely at this level (i.e., within two ancestral generations of each general authority). Furthermore, of the twenty-five men under age thirty at the time of their appointment during the hierarchy's first hundred years, nineteen (76 percent) were sons, brothers, or nephews of general authorities. In other words, kinship was directly linked with youthful appointments to the Mormon hierarchy.

A final approach involves assessing the kinship impact on specific offices. By reducing the fluctuations to eleven-year intervals and restricting relationships to those within two ancestral generations, one can better appreciate the level of kinship penetration in the Mormon hierarchy (see Table 1).

Immediately apparent is the fact that the percentages almost exactly reflect the ecclesiastical status of the several quorums. Eliminating the Presiding Patriarch (which was a lineal office), the First Presidency had the highest percentage of kinship penetration in relation to the other quorums (except for 1855 and 1910). In the normative situation where there were three members of the First Presidency, two or three usually had kinship relations. In the years where there were more than three members of the Presidency, more than half had kinship relations within the hierarchy. Standing next to the First Presidency, both administratively and in percentage of close kinship, was the Quorum of the Twelve Apostles with 41.7 percent to 75 percent. Consistently behind the Twelve was its ecclesiastical subordinate, the First Council of Seventy, with kinship varying between 14.3 percent and 57.2 percent. With the exception of 1932, the Presiding Bishopric had the least percentage of kinship penetration. In other words, there apparently was a conscious effort to fill the hierarchy with relatives at the highest levels of ecclesiastical power, whereas there was less concern with family status in the lower echelons.

Table 1.
Percentage of Hierarchy Related by Kinship
within Two Ancestral Generations to Current or Former
General Authorities, 1833-1932

YEARS	FIRST PRESIDENCY	COUNCIL OF TWELVE	PRESIDING PATRIARCH	COUNCIL OF SEVENTY	PRESIDING BISHOPRIC	TOTAL HIERARCHY
April 1833	0.0%	*	*	*	*	0.0%
April 1844	75.0%	50.0%	100.0%	28.6%	*	50.0%
April 1855	33.3%	41.7%	100.0%	14.3%	0.0%	33.3%
April 1866	66.7%	50.0%	100.0%	28.6%	0.0%	44.8%
April 1877	57.2%	50.0%	100.0%	28.6%	0.0%	42.3%
April 1888	*	60.0%	100.0%	28.6%	0.0%	46.2%
April 1899	66.7%	58.3%	100.0%	42.9%	0.0%	50.0%
April 1910	66.7%	75.0%	100.0%	57.2%	33.3%	65.4%
April 1921	66.7%	58.3%	100.0%	57.2%	33.3%	57.7%
April 1932	100.0%	58.3%	100.0%	57.2%	66.7%	64.0%

Two ancestral generations include father, son, brother, nephew, uncle, first cousin, grandson, grandnephew, first cousin once-removed, and second cousin.

Excluded are relationships such as second cousin once-removed and beyond.

Men holding two positions in the hierarchy at one time (e.g., Hyrum Smith in April 1844 as Assistant President and also Presiding Patriarch) are included in the tabulation for each position but counted only once in the total.

*The quorum did not exist at this time.

Table 1 also identifies a chronological progression in kinship appointments. Throughout the nineteenth century the presence of close kinsmen in the hierarchy did not exceed the level at the time of the church founder's death. In the early decades of the twentieth century, the percentage of close kinship exceeded the level in 1844. This indicates that in making appointments after 1900, LDS presidents Joseph F. Smith and Heber J. Grant emphasized kinship appointments more than their predecessors. This is verified by Table 2.

Table 2 also shows that appointments involving distant ancestral relationships ceased to be important to LDS presidents after Brigham Young. Where kinship was involved, Young's successors appointed only men with close kinship relations to current or former general authorities. Aside from Wilford Woodruff, LDS presidents after Young also doubled his proportion of appointments with close kinship connections. Twenti-eth-century presidents Joseph F. Smith and Heber J. Grant more than doubled the founding prophet's proportion of appointments with close kinship to other members of the Mormon hierarchy.

Table 2.
Level of Kinship Relationships
to Current or Former General Authorities
by Appointees of LDS Presidents, 1832-1932

PRESIDENT	WITHIN TWO ANCESTRAL GENERATIONS	THREE OR MORE ANCESTRAL GENERATIONS	TOTAL MEN WITH KINSHIP RELATIONS	TOTAL APPOINTEES
Joseph Smith	13 (29.5%)	10 (22.7%)	23 (52.3%)	44
Brigham Young	7 (25.0%)	6 (21.4%)	13 (46.4%)	28
John Taylor	8 (53.3%)	0	8 (53.3%)	15
Wilford Woodruff	3 (30.0%)	0	3 (30.0%)	10
Lorenzo Snow	1 (50.0%)	0	1 (50.0%)	2
Joseph F. Smith	11 (61.1%)	0	11 (61.1%)	18
Heber J. Grant	4 (66.7%)	0	4 (66.7%)	6
TOTAL	47 (38.2%)	16 (13.0%)	63 (51.2%)	123

Two ancestral generations include father, son, brother, nephew, uncle, first cousin, grandson, grandnephew, first cousin once-removed, and second cousin.

Three or more ancestral generations include more distant relationships such as second cousin once-removed, great-grandnephew, or third cousin to a general authority.

Acknowledging that kinship was a theologically reinforced charac-teristic of the hierarchy, there still remains the question of the extent to which pedigree and its privileges created tension. For example, some general authorities were clearly disappointed that their sons, brothers, or other relations did not receive appointments to the church's highest leadership. "A great many people feel that Heber C. Kimball should be represented in the Quorum of the Twelve," wrote Seventy's president J. Golden Kimball. More blunt than other general authorities with similar dissatisfaction, he wrote that the deceased First Presidency counselor "has sons just as worthy and that have done more for the Church of Jesus Christ than any of the three last named Apostles" appointed during 1897-98. Kimball did not limit such candor to his diary, and five years later told a young elder that the First Presidency had not called Golden as an apostle because "my father was dead and I was not popular with the brethren."[19]

In 1835 family disappointment had even disrupted the process of apostolic appointment. Joseph Smith commissioned Oliver Cowdery and David Whitmer, witnesses to the *Book of Mormon,* to select the men who would comprise the Quorum of the Twelve Apostles. The selection included no close relation of Smith, and he countermanded their decision. The prophet removed one of the prospective apostles and substituted his own younger brother, William. In a letter to Brigham Young in 1848, Cowdery referred to this incident: "At the time the Twelve were chosen in Kirtland, and I may say before [this time] it had been manifested that Brother Phineas [Young] was entitled to occupy the station as one of the number; but owing to Brother Joseph's urgent request at the time, Brother David and myself yielded to his wish, and consented for William [Smith] to be selected, contrary to our feelings and judgment, and to our deep mortification ever since."[20]

Even those who followed their fathers into the hierarchy sometimes protested the appointment of other men's sons. Apostles Brigham Young, Jr., and Heber J. Grant (the latter's father had been a counselor to Brigham Young) voiced opposition in 1897 to the possibility that a son of First Presidency counselor George Q. Cannon might enter the Twelve. Young recorded that Grant was "cheerful but when I touched upon one of Bro Geo Q. C. sons being called to fill vacancy in our quorum he manifested stormy opposition. It is proposed to fill the 2 vacancies in the Twelve at this Conference." Young added: "I pray earnestly that I may be one with Prest. C. but I have much to contend with." Rather than choosing Cannon's sons, LDS president Wilford Woodruff filled the two vacancies with his own son and his grandnephew (by marriage). When Young learned of these appointments, he remarked: "I was much disappointed but prayed God would reconcile me which he did altho' I felt almost rebellious for a few minutes, but Thank God he gave me grace."[21]

General authorities themselves felt a certain amount of hesitancy in advancing their sons or other near relatives. Cowdery, for example, did not protest against Smith substituting his brother for Phineas Young in the quorum in 1835, because "Brother Phineas occupied at that time a relation [brother-in-law] to myself that caused me to feel delicate about urging his name."[22] When a vacancy occurred in the Quorum of the Twelve in 1867 due to the rejection of Apostle Amasa M. Lyman, Brigham Young wanted to replace Lyman with his own son Brigham Jr. but instead installed Joseph F. Smith. The younger Brigham explained why his father waited until the next vacancy to promote him: "Bro. Geo. A. Smith suggested that it might raise a question & comment if B. Y. Jr. was put in, in place of Bro A. M. Lyman apostatized; and if Jos. F. S. was now put in to the Quorum it could make no difference as I B. Y. Jr was ordained an

apostle [years before Joseph F. Smith] and would take ~~my~~ his place in the
Quorum according to that ordination."[23] George Q. Cannon indicated
this same discomfort in 1889 when the First Presidency counselor assured
his son Abraham H. that he had not been responsible for the son's
appointment as an apostle.[24]

As newly appointed church president in 1898 Lorenzo Snow was very
sensitive to possible criticism about giving preference to any of his sons.
He refused to appoint a son to the Twelve despite the recommendation
of several apostles. One of those who favored such an appointment was
Brigham Young, Jr., who wrote: "I seemed to have made a blunder in
suggesting all things being equal I would love to see President Snow
represented in the 12. Afterwards His Counsellors took me to task for such
an unwise suggestion [and] said it placed Pres. S in a very embarrassing
position. I could not see it."[25] However, someone as resentful as J. Golden
Kimball certainly saw a problem. When LeRoi C. Snow, "a boy of Pres
Snow's[,] was called up to speak" at a solemn assembly in the Salt Lake
Temple in 1899, Kimball wrote: "Some were amused and surprised. He is
a son of a favored [plural] wife and his father's pet." Then the Seventy's
president groused: "This young man will no doubt be an apostle, if Pres.
Snow has his way."[26]

Although Kimball's complaints could be dismissed as jealousy over
apostolic appointments denied to him and his brothers, Apostle John
Henry Smith was very forceful in opposing the appointment of his own
kinsman Hyrum M. Smith and his own son George Albert Smith to the
Quorum of the Twelve in 1901 and 1903.[27] As late as the 1920s and 1930s
President Heber J. Grant hesitated naming any of his sons-in-law as
Presiding Bishop, apostle, or Presiding Patriarch. He decided against
making such an appointment, despite his own desire to honor them and
despite strong recommendations from others in favor of his sons-in-law.
However, President Grant did apoint his son-in-law John H. Taylor as a
Seventy's president in 1933 and his son-in-law Clifford E. Young as an
Assistant to the Twelve in 1941.[28] LDS general authorities recognized that
by appointing near relatives they invited the charge of "nepotism."[29]

Even though Mormon theology encouraged this kind of favoritism,
LDS leaders themselves felt distinctly uncomfortable about it. When
Joseph F. Smith nominated his own son Hyrum as his first apostolic
appointment as new church president, Apostle John Henry Smith remarked: "I called attention to the charge that was likely to be made of
Nepotism and said I would bear my share of the responsibility and I
endorsed the selection."[30]

Because Joseph F. Smith appointed close relatives to the Quorum of Twelve and First Presidency from 1901 to 1910, faithful Mormons were extremely critical. When Hyrum M. Smith became the new apostle in 1901, J. Golden Kimball wrote: "I confess I am tried over this appointment." When George Albert Smith was announced as the new apostle at the 1903 general conference, Kimball wrote that "a cold wave passed over the congregation." The Seventy's president added that "many expressed themselves to me as disgusted. I confess myself to be among that number." This general authority concluded that "I question very much whether He [God] approves of it. It is nepotism of the strongest kind since the days of President Brigham Young."[31] A mission president also wrote in 1903: "The selection of Geo. A. Smith will be regarded by the critics as savoring too much of nepotism," yet noted that the newly appointed Smith "has the blood of the martyrs."[32] Actually, George Albert Smith was not a direct descendant of the martyred Joseph and Hyrum Smith, but their first cousin was his ancestor. This indicates the reverence felt by many Mormons for *anyone* born into that extended family descended from Asa(h)el Smith (b. 1744) and Mary Duty (b. 1743).

Nevertheless, disenchantment with LDS president Joseph F. Smith's "nepotism" reached a climax in 1910. He advanced Apostle John Henry Smith to be his counselor and filled the resulting vacancy in the Twelve with his own son Joseph Fielding Smith. A stake president spoke publicly about some Mormons "complaining on account of so many Smiths being chosen."[33] Joseph Fielding Smith's biography by his son comments that some regarded his father's appointment as "a heavy case of nepotism." A former secretary to the First Presidency has recently referred to "the blatant charges of nepotism that had surrounded his call to the Twelve."[34]

Nearly 40 percent of appointees during the Mormon hierarchy's first century were closely related by kinship, but disapproving general authorities faithfully set aside their objections to such appointments. For example, John Henry Smith wrote: "President Jos F. Smith said to me tonight that the mind of the spirit was that my son George Albert should fill the vacancy in the Apostles. I told him [that were] it a political office I would advise against it but I could not stand in the way of the suggestions of the spirit to him."[35] In other words, lineage was a factor in calls to the hierarchy, but not the decisive one in this faithful view.

In this regard, during 1859 Apostle Orson Pratt and President Brigham Young discussed the issue of what qualified men for the apostleship:

O. Pratt—"I would like to know on what principle men are to be selected: whether we are to suggest men of experience who have been tried and proven in many responsible positions, or those who are young, & have not been called to important trusts in the church, or if any qualifications are necessary [and] needed."

Pres. Y.—"I will answer your question Bro. Pratt to my own satisfaction. If a man was suggested to me of good natural judgment, possessing no higher qualifications than faithfulness and humility enough to seek to the Lord for all his knowledge and who would trust in him for his strength I would prefer him in preference to the learned and tallented."[36]

Cowdery's instructions to the apostles in 1835 indicated that an apostolic calling was independent of age, experience, or training but involved one's personal experiences with God.[37]

A non-kinship characteristic of Mormon family structure was the Law of Adoption, a practice that involved adopting individuals into one's spiritual family. Although not a literal process by which fatherless children were taken into other families, in a symbolic and religious sense that is exactly what happened. In order to complete the chain of family connections back to God the Father, grown men were spiritually adopted in a special ordinance to prominent church leaders. If the adopted man was a head of a family of wife and children, the entire family was considered linked to the earthly-spiritual father, usually an apostle. In 1894 President Wilford Woodruff described the discontinuation of this practice:

> In the commencement of adopting men and women in the Temple at Nauvoo, a great many persons were adopted to different men who were not of the lineage of their fathers. . . . When I went before the Lord to know who I should be adopted to (we were then being adopted to prophets and apostles) the Spirit of God said to me, "Have you not a father, who begot you?" "Yes, I have." I was adopted to my father, and should have had my father sealed to his father, and so on back; and the duty that I want every man who presides over a Temple to see performed from this day henceforth and forever, unless the Lord Almighty commands otherwise, is, let every man be adopted to his father. When a man receives the endowments, adopt him to his father; not to Wilford Woodruff, nor to any other man outside the lineage of his fathers.[38]

For fifty years prior to this announcement, adopted sons and families considered themselves under the dominion and protection of their surrogate father. In 1846-47 such spiritually-adopted sons often assumed the surname of their new father as their own, even though they themselves were grown men with children.[39]

Adoptions extended the family relationships for general authorities, but this practice had negligible effect on family relationships within the hierarchy. The apostles were usually the temporal apex of the system, so they were not adopted to each other. When adoptions occurred between hierarchical echelons, they tended to reinforce pre-existing kinship connections. For example, Albert P. Rockwood, a Seventy's president, became Apostle Brigham Young's adopted son but was also his fourth cousin.[40]

Apparently the only spiritual son of a living general authority to be advanced to the hierarchy was Apostle George Q. Cannon in 1860. He had been adopted to Apostle John Taylor in Nauvoo, and Cannon was already a nephew of Taylor's first wife. Before their appointment on the same day in 1882, two other apostles were considered sons of the deceased prophet Joseph Smith: Englishman George Teasdale, through an adoption ordinance, and Utah-born Heber J. Grant, whose mother had been "sealed by proxy" to the deceased Smith.[41] Although the practice of adoption had importance in the social structure of the Mormon community, it had little demonstrable significance in the family relationships between general authorities.

For more than half a century after 1932, the LDS hierarchy's new appointees continued to be close kin of general authorities, both living and dead.[42] Presented chronologically, the following examples do not include general authorities currently serving in 1996.

During the twenty years after the LDS hierarchy's first century, kinship distinguished eighteen of three dozen new appointments. In 1933 the new Seventy's president John H. Taylor was a grandson of former LDS president John Taylor. Ordained an apostle in 1934, Alonzo A. Hinckley was a third cousin of the Twelve's president, Rudger Clawson. At his appointment as Presiding Bishop in 1938, LeGrand Richards was a son of then-current apostle George F. Richards and grandson of deceased apostle Franklin D. Richards. In 1941 newly appointed apostle Harold B. Lee was a grandnephew of former Seventy's president Joseph W. McMurrin. Appointed to the newly created position of Assistant to the Twelve in 1941, Thomas E. McKay was a brother of then-current First Presidency counselor David O. McKay. Also appointed as one of the first assistants, Nicholas G. Smith was a brother of then-current apostle George Albert Smith, son of former apostle John Henry Smith, grandson of former apostle George A. Smith, and great-grandson of Presiding Patriarch John Smith (b. 1781). Still another of the Assistants to the Twelve in 1941, Clifford E. Young was brother of then-current Seventy's president Levi Edgar Young, son of former Seventy's president Seymour B. Young, and grandson of former Seventy's president Joseph Young.

Appointed Patriarch to the Church in 1942 after a ten-year vacancy in the office (see chaps. 2, 4), the closest kinship of Joseph F. Smith (b. 1899) was not to a former patriarch. He was the son of former apostle Hyrum M. Smith, whom the appointing president Heber J. Grant regarded as an adoptive kinsman. Great-grandson and namesake of a deceased apostle, Ezra Taft Benson became an apostle in 1943. Appointed on the same day as Benson, Apostle Spencer W. Kimball was first cousin of then-current First Presidency counselor J. Reuben Clark and grandson of founding apostle Heber C. Kimball. Appointed Seventy's president in April 1945, S. Dilworth Young was nephew of then-current Seventy's president Levi Edgar young, a nephew of then-current Assistant to the Twelve Clifford E. Young, a nephew of recently deceased apostle Rudger Clawson, a direct descendant of former Seventy's presidents Seymour B. Young and Joseph Young, and a direct descendant of former LDS president Brigham Young.

Recently appointed as LDS president, George Albert Smith's first selection of an apostle in October 1945 was Matthew Cowley, a son of former apostle Matthias F. Cowley. Appointed Seventy's president in 1946, Bruce R. McConkie was a first cousin once-removed of then-current Assistant to the Twelve Marion G. Romney. In addition to his lineal descent from patriarchs who served before 1942, at his appointment as Patriarch to the Church in 1947 Eldred G. Smith was also a direct descendant of former Seventy's president Salmon Gee. Appointed a First Presidency counselor in April 1951, Stephen L Richards was a grandson of former First Presidency counselor Willard Richards. At his appointment as Assistant to the Twelve in October 1951, Stayner Richards was a brother of recently sustained First Presidency counselor Stephen L Richards. First cousin of deceased Seventy's president Samuel O. Bennion, Adam S. Bennion became an apostle in 1953. Also appointed in 1953, Seventy's president Marion D. Hanks was a direct descendant of apostles Amasa M. Lyman and Francis M. Lyman.

Kinship was not an incidental consideration to the LDS presidents who made these appointments. President Grant told Ezra Taft Benson in 1943 that deceased apostle Ezra T. Benson "and other faithful progenitors were rejoicing at this appointment of a descendant to the apostleship."[43] Direct descendant of two former Seventy's presidents and of Brigham Young, at his setting apart in 1945 new Seventy's president S. Dilworth Young was instructed about the "'blood' in his veins 'of those who have served devotedly in the past.'"[44] Despite his own relationship to a former general authority, Apostle Harold B. Lee spoke sarcastically about "the church aristocracy that some *name* families in the Church have seemed to feel."[45]

After a five-year break in the appointments of close kin, in 1958 the new Seventy's president A. Theodore Tuttle was a first cousin once-removed of then-current Presiding Bishopric counselor Thorpe B. Isaacson. Theodore M. Burton became an Assistant to the Twelve in 1960 as a grandson of Presiding Bishopric counselor Robert T. Burton and first cousin of then-current First Presidency counselor Henry D. Moyle. Also appointed as an assistant in 1960 Franklin D. Richards was the namesake and grandson of a former apostle and was the first cousin of then-current apostle LeGrand Richards. Three months after the appointment of Hugh B. Brown as a counselor in the First Presidency in June 1961, his nephew Victor L. Brown became a counselor in the Presiding Bishopric. Bishopric counselor Brown was also a third cousin of Apostle Harold B. Lee. A year later Hugh B. Brown's nephew N. Eldon Tanner was advanced to the Quorum of the Twelve and began serving with his uncle as a counselor in the First Presidency in 1963. Appointed as a Seventy's president in 1964, Paul H. Dunn was a first cousin once-removed of then-current Assistant to the Twelve Henry D. Taylor. Son of a former counselor in the Presiding Bishopric, Marvin J. Ashton became an Assistant to the Twelve in 1969 and an apostle in 1971. When Victor L. Brown became Presiding Bishop in 1972 his first cousin Tanner was the First Presidency's counselor in charge of church finances. Bishop Brown chose as his own counselor H. Burke Peterson, Tanner's second cousin once-removed.

In the 1980s there were significant kinship relations for several of the short-term appointments to the expanding Seventy. Appointed to the First Quorum of the Seventy in 1984, Russell C. Taylor was a direct descendant of founding apostle Parley P. Pratt and 2nd-great-grandnephew of founding Seventy's president Sylvester Smith. Another direct descendant of Apostle Parley P. Pratt, Waldo P. Call became a member of the Seventy in 1985. Appointed in 1986, Francis M. Gibbons was a direct descendant of Vinson Knight who was appointed (but did not serve) as the first Presiding Bishop over all other bishops. Also sustained in 1986, George I. Cannon was a direct descendant of First Presidency counselors Jedediah M. Grant and George Q. Cannon, of LDS president Heber J. Grant, and of Apostle Abraham H. Cannon. Appointed in 1987, George R. Hill was a nephew of former LDS president David O. McKay. Appointed to the newly established Second Quorum of the Seventy in 1989, Richard P. Lindsay was a first cousin once-removed of former apostle Adam S. Bennion. In 1990 Brigham Young's direct descendant LeGrand R. Curtis also became a member of the Second Quorum.

None of the post-1932 appointees listed in the above paragraphs are currently serving the LDS church as general authorities. That discussion also did not include appointees without kinship ties but whose wives were "blood" relations to then-current or former members of the hierarchy.

A genealogist once described the general authorities as a "Race of Religious Leaders."[46] Another useful term to describe the LDS hierarchy is "Mormon dynasticism."[47] This dynasticism was limited in two ways: no single, nuclear family controlled the hierarchy's dynasty; and the preference for "blood" ties did not prevent the appointment of men who lacked kinship connections. Although general authorities and regular Mormons have used the word "nepotism" to criticize kinship appointments to the hierarchy, "dynastic appointment" is a nonjudgmental term that is more compatible with the theology behind such callings. A further characteristic of the general authorities is that marriage allied men who otherwise lacked natural kinship and also reinforced existing kinship connections within the hierarchy.

Marriage

The emphasis on leading families inevitably influenced Mormon thinking on marriage. During the 1830s Mormons began considering the possibility that marriage as an institution would have significance in the next life. Shortly after his arrival at Kirtland, William W. Phelps, a prominent Mormon editor and church officer, wrote his wife on 26 May 1835: "A new idea, Sally, if you and I continue faithful to the end we are certain to be one in the Lord throughout eternity." Joseph Smith was not yet ready to announce this "new idea" to the church as LDS doctrine. A month later in the church newspaper, Phelps cited the Bible (1 Cor. 11:11), instead of the LDS prophet, as the authority for a similar idea. However, the concept was becoming popular among Mormons, and in a letter from Kirtland in July 1835 John Corrill addressed his wife as "my companion forever."[48] Eight years later Joseph Smith privately taught that a special ordinance was necessary to "seal" couples together in marriage of eternal duration.[49]

Implicit in this doctrine was a concept far more revolutionary. If a man was sealed to a woman who later died, and the man was later sealed for time and eternity to another woman, theologically these ordinances would give him two wives in the eternities. Moreover, the earthly counterpart of this other-worldly polygamy was supported by biblical precedent (Gen. 16:1-3; 29:23-28; 30:3-4, 9-10; Ex. 21:10; Deut. 21:15; Judg. 8:30; 2 Sam. 12:7-8). From the 1830s onward Mormonism claimed to be a "restoration of all things," in other words the modern embodiment of ancient truths and practices of God's people.[50] Therefore, it is not surprising that polygamy was part of the latter-day restoration.

In 1830 the *Book of Mormon* contained injunctions against polygamy, with the theological basis for its resumption: "For if I will, saith the Lord of Hosts, raise up seed unto me, I will command my people; otherwise, they shall hearken unto these things."[51] Sixteen months after the publication of that statement, Smith confided a revelation which encompassed this possibility. An early defector from Mormonism, Ezra Booth, wrote in 1831 that Smith announced a revelation for married men serving as LDS missionaries among Native American tribes to take Indian women as wives.[52] Phelps, one of these missionaries, subsequently confirmed the

revelation and dated it as 17 July 1831.[53] Orson Pratt said he learned of
the revelation in 1832.[54] Since polygamy existed as a theoretical possibility
from the founding of the church, it is not surprising that Joseph Smith
later translated the theory into practice.

Although there is evidence that both Smith and Cowdery took plural
wives during the 1830s in Ohio,[55] polygamy as a general practice began in
the 1840s at Nauvoo, Illinois.[56] On 5 April 1841 a rank-and-file Mormon
secretly performed a ceremony uniting the man's sister-in-law Louisa
Be(a)man with the prophet. This is traditionally regarded as the first fully
dated of Smith's polygamous marriages. There has been disagreement
about the total number. In 1887 an assistant in the Church Historian's
Office published a semi-official list of twenty-seven wives the founding
prophet married during his lifetime. In 1905 another assistant church
historian reconfirmed that list. As of 1996 the LDS Ancestral File lists
twenty of those polygamous wives, with twenty "marriage" dates before
Smith's death and post-martyrdom sealing dates for twelve wives.[57] Other
researchers have provided more expansive lists, including my own tally of
forty-six women whom Joseph Smith secretly married from 1833 to 1844.[58]

The secrecy that surrounded polygamy in Nauvoo has continued to
obscure many of the details of this early departure from western norms.
The number of Smith's wives is a partially answered question, while the
number and identity of children born to these polygamous unions has
remained in obscurity. One of the women who was sealed to Smith during
his lifetime stated that three such children were born to him ("they told
me") and lived long enough in Utah to "go by other names" than Smith.[59]
One such child was Josephine Lyon, who bore the legal name of Smith's
polygamous wife who was married to Windsor P. Lyon at the time she
cohabited with the Mormon prophet. Toward the end of her own life,
Josephine's mother told this daughter of her true paternity.[60]

Smith dictated an explicit revelation on the subject in 1843 and began
urging his close associates to marry plural wives. Five years after Young
established LDS headquarters in Utah, he authorized the public acknowledgement of polygamy in 1852. This alternative lifestyle became an
integral part of Mormon society, a fact which most Americans condemned
as a threat to the Christian institution of marriage. Although Mormons
ridiculed that argument as an irrational response to a tiny minority, a
federal campaign resulted in the LDS church's public abandonment of
polygamy in 1890.[61]

Because of Mormon emphasis on the primacy of a woman's sealing to
one man despite her legal or "for time" marriage to another man (or men),
spiritual descendants of founder Joseph Smith have served in the Mormon
hierarchy during the twentieth century. This does not include men like

Heber J. Grant who were sons or descendants of women who lacked a marital relationship with Smith during his lifetime, having been sealed to the prophet only after his martyrdom. Nevertheless, in all cases, these general authorities trace their lineage to other marriages of women who were Smith's polygamous wives during his lifetime. In other words, because of the obscure identity of the prophet's polygamous children, none of his own direct descendants are known to have served in the LDS hierarchy.[62]

The first descendant of one of Joseph Smith's polygamous wives to become a general authority was Apostle Orson F. Whitney in 1906. He was a son of Helen Mar Kimball Smith Whitney. Appointed a Seventy's president in 1945, S. Dilworth Young was a direct descendant of Emily Partridge Smith Young. Appointed an Assistant to the Twelve in 1954, Sterling W. Sill was a direct descendant of Elvira Cowles Holmes Smith. Francis M. Gibbons, former secretary to the First Presidency and former Seventy's member, is a direct descendant of Martha McBride Knight Smith. Current apostle Robert D. Hales and Seventy's member Carlos E. Asay are direct descendants of Lydia Kenyon Carter Smith. Current Seventy's member William R. Bradford is a direct descendant of Patty Bartlett Sessions Smith.[63]

When considering the role of polygamy in the family structure of the hierarchy, it is also necessary to recognize that not all general authorities were polygamists. The practice was not available to the general membership at LDS headquarters until 1845. Even after the founding of Salt Lake City in 1847, monogamists received appointments as LDS general authorities (see Table 3).

Nearly 71 percent of all general authorities were monogamists at the time of their calling during the hierarchy's first hundred years. However, those who received these offices prior to 1842 and after 1889 did so at a time when polygamy was not an obligation of the hierarchy. From 1845 to 1888 only fourteen (31.8 percent of 44 appointees during that period) were monogamists at the time of their advancement. As long as polygamy was the norm in headquarters culture, there was an obvious preference for polygamist general authorities, since monogamist males were always the majority among the Mormons. However, rather than the 98 percent majority often claimed by Mormons today, monogamists accounted for only 60-80 percent of the married males in the Mormon culture region during the heyday of polygamy from the 1850s to the 1880s.[64] Despite their numerical minority, polygamists were far more likely to be advanced to leadership, both general and local.[65]

Table 3.
Monogamist and Polygamist Appointees
to the Hierarchy, 1832-1932

PERIOD OF APPOINTMENT	MONOGAMIST APPOINTEES	POLYGAMIST APPOINTEES	TOTAL APPOINTEES
1832-44	44	0	44
1845-55	8	8	16
1856-66	1	9	10
1867-77	0	2	2
1878-88	5	11	16
1889-99	6	4[*]	10
1900-10	12	2[**]	14
1911-21	7	0	7
1922-32	4	0	4
TOTAL	87	36	123

[*]Formerly a polygamist, Rudger Clawson had only one wife at his appointment in 1898.
[**]Formerly a polygamist, Orson F. Whitney had only one wife at his appointment in 1906. Both are counted here as monogamists.

As he encouraged or commanded the apostles to marry plural wives in 1842-43, Smith said that the kingdom of God could not advance without polygamous marriage. "What will become of those individuals who have this law taught unto them in plainness, if they reject it?" asked Orson Pratt at the official announcement of plural marriage as a doctrine and practice of the LDS church in 1852. One of the general authorities sitting behind the pulpit answered: "They will be damned," which Apostle Pratt underscored: "I will tell you: they will be damned, saith the Lord God Almighty, in the revelation He has given."[66] When church members seemed slack in their religious devotion, the First Presidency launched a reformation in 1855-57, with emphasis on polygamy.[67]

When the federal government began its anti-polygamy crusade, LDS president John Taylor counter-attacked. In 1879 he denounced the U.S. Supreme Court for ruling that anti-polygamy legislation was constitutional, and said that this decision placed Mormons "in a position a good deal like the Christians were in the days of Rome." In 1882 he published a revelation that required all priesthood officers to "conform to my law" of polygamy. This revelation was not canonized in the English language *Doctrine and Covenants,* which did not have a revised printing until after the LDS church officially abandoned polygamy. However, this 1882 revelation was canonized in five editions (Swedish, German, and Danish) of the *Doctrine and Covenants* published in Salt Lake City and Europe. In 1884 the First Presidency urged monogamists to resign their ecclesiastical offices.[68]

Although ten monogamist general authorities appointed between 1845 and 1899 married plural wives eventually, several took years to do so despite the social and ecclesiastical pressure. Prominent among the early procrastinators were the Presiding Patriarch John Smith (b. 1832), who waited exactly two years after his ordination to marry a plural wife, and Seventy's president Jedediah M. Grant, who delayed more than three years. Even more interesting was the fact that despite President Taylor's public demands, he advanced five monogamists to the hierarchy (Heber J. Grant, Seymour B. Young, John Q. Cannon, John W. Taylor, and William W. Taylor). By the 1882 revelation, President Taylor required Grant and Young to enter plural marriage, which they did within two years. However, Taylor's son William remained a monogamist from his appointment in 1880 until shortly before his death in 1884. Moreover, John Q. Cannon and John W. Taylor wanted to enter "the patriarchal order of marriage," but President Taylor refused to allow them to do so in order to protect them from the jeopardy of arrest. John W. Taylor did not marry polygamously until 1888, four years after his appointment as an apostle.[69]

With the exception of Apostle Anthon H. Lund, all of the pre-1890 appointees who remained monogamous had relatively short tenure as general authorities. Lund was an exception that proved the rule, because as a monogamist he was appointed to the hierarchy only a year before the LDS church publicly abandoned polygamy.

The last monogamist of the nineteenth-century hierarchy who married polygamously was Abraham Owen Woodruff. He became an apostle in 1897 and took an additional wife in 1901. This was more than ten years after his father, LDS president Wilford Woodruff, formally announced that there would be no more polygamous marriages. Apostle Woodruff was among the two hundred men who married new plural wives between the Manifesto of September 1890 and the so-called "Second Manifesto" of April 1904. This occurred by secret authorization of various members of the First Presidency.[70]

Appointed an apostle in 1898, Rudger Clawson was a special case. After the start of his four-year sentence as a "prisoner of conscience" in 1884, Clawson's legal wife divorced him, thus leaving him married only to his plural wife. A monogamist at his appointment to the Twelve, Clawson secretly married a new plural wife in 1904 in a ceremony performed by fellow apostle Matthias F. Cowley. This polygamous marriage occurred four months after the Second Manifesto and lasted until 1913.[71]

Clawson's was the first of about ten polygamous marriages that occurred after the Second Manifesto with the private approval of President Joseph F. Smith. At the same time Smith was emphatically assuring the public, his own counselors, and the Quorum of Twelve that there was absolutely no authorization for any new polygamous marriages. These president-authorized polygamous marriages overlapped with those performed by an emerging fundamentalist movement that did not claim the living LDS president's permission or authority. As a result, dozens of prominent Mormons were excommunicated or otherwise disciplined by the Quorum of Twelve from 1906 onward for performing or entering marriages similar to Clawson's, of whose marriage none of his fellow apostles were apparently aware. The murkiness and ambiguities of these authorized polygamous marriages after 1890 (and especially after 1904) guaranteed the growth of a polygamous underground that continues today in opposition to LDS church policy.[72]

The only twentieth-century appointee who definitely[73] entered polygamy was also a special case. Richard R. Lyman became an apostle in 1918, and seven years later began a totally unauthorized relationship which he defined as a polygamous marriage. Unable to trust anyone else to officiate, Lyman and this woman exchanged vows in a mutual covenant to establish a relationship known only to themselves. He had recently restored this woman's church privileges which had been taken away following her post-1904 polygamous marriage to another man. Her new marriage continued until discovered by the First Presidency in 1943, at which time Apostle Lyman and his secret wife were excommunicated. They were both in their seventies.[74]

Not all of the wives who were married or sealed to general authorities are presently recognized as having been wives, even though the data of their sealings/marriages seem conclusive. More than twenty of the general authorities were married to such lesser-known wives. To analyze the relationships within the hierarchy without including these women is to ignore in-law and other marriage connections that were significant.

Some writers have claimed that the ordinance of sealing a living man and woman did not always involve the physical union of marriage but sometimes solemnized a spiritual union that had reference only to life after death.[75] There is indirect support for such an interpretation. For example, it was common in the nineteenth century for living men to be sealed to deceased women to whom they had never been married in this life. Obviously these were not marriages in a literal sense.

However, there are clear problems of evidence in claiming that a relationship remained celibate for a man and woman who received an LDS sealing ordinance as living persons. First, the original records of sealings in the nineteenth century used variations of only two phrases to define each marriage: "for time and eternity," and "for time only," both of which gave the sanction of the church for sexual intercourse between the living persons thus sealed. If the phrase "eternity only" ever appeared in an *original* record of LDS sealing in the nineteenth century, I have not discovered it while examining thousands of such manuscript entries.

Second, a polygamist's children or other descendants are not reliable sources for determining whether a childless marriage sealing was also celibate. An archivist recently commented about such assumptions by Brigham Young's children: "This does not necessarily mean that he did not have conjugal relationships with some of the other thirty-nine wives, but the topic of where he spent his nights was apparently not a matter of household discussion."[76] For example, Susa Young Gates confidently asserted that Augusta Adams Cobb was "never father's wife in the real sense of the word."[77] However, a principal complaint of Augusta's private letters to Brigham eight years after their sealing was that he *no longer* fulfilled the husband's sexual obligation, and her letter of February 1850 asked him to spend the night with her.[78] Even statements by one wife are not reliable sources to determine the intimate dimensions of another wife's relationship to the husband. Claims for marital celibacy by children or other wives would be reliable only if reporting statements they themselves heard from the husband or particular wife.

A statement by the husband or the wife involved is the best evidence for marital celibacy of a childless wife of a polygamist or of lesser-known polygamous wives. For example, John D. Lee was sealed for time and eternity in Nauvoo to the mother of three of his wives. Twenty-seven years her junior, "Lee always insisted that although she was sealed to him to be a member of his family, she was never a wife in fact."[79] Some also regard the alleged remark of Heber C. Kimball that he had not seen some of his wives since the ceremony as evidence that these sealings were for celibate relationships with living women. However, his biographer regarded that as an exaggerated reference to the wives who had formally divorced him or simply deserted him (including the Cutler sisters who had given birth to Kimball's children).[80] Patty Bartlett Sessions later specified that she had been sealed to Joseph Smith "for Eternity" in an ordinance for which there is no original record. This would preclude the sexual cohabitation of a marriage "for time and eternity." Her sealing to the thirty-six-year-old living prophet occurred when she was forty-seven and cohabiting with her legal husband.[81]

Mary Elizabeth Rollins Lightner also claimed that she "was sealed to Joseph for Eternity." However, this statement for the public was an effort to conceal the polyandrous circumstances of her marriage to Smith at a time when the twenty-five-year-old woman was also married to Adam Lightner and cohabiting with both men. Nearly thirty years before her "for Eternity" description of her marriage to the prophet, she wrote a private letter to an LDS apostle (Smith's nephew) that "in the year 1842 in the month of February the Prophet Joseph Smith came to me and said he had received a direct command from God to take me for a wife for time and all eternity." Concerning the sexual implications (and resulting criticism she had experienced) "in regard to my living with Mr L, after becoming the *Wife of another*," Mary Lightner Smith told Apostle John Henry Smith that "I cannot explain things in this Letter." As a non-Mormon Mr. Lightner obviously did not give permission for his legal wife to be sealed "for time and all eternity" to Joseph Smith and later "for time" to Brigham Young. However, as the ultimate expression of his Mormon faith, Henry B. Jacobs allowed his beloved wife Zina D. Huntington to be similarly sealed to Smith and Young. During these polyandrous marriages Zina bore three children, but only the last is recognized as a prophet's (Young's).[82]

Although some lesser-known wives may not have been in a sexual relationship with their sealed husband, these sealings were significant in the familial relationships of those who entered them. Brigham Young, for example, is credited officially with twenty-seven wives, ten of whom are classed as wives "for eternity only" or "in name only." This classification has described those wives who bore him no children, apparently based on the questionable assumption that a childless marriage involved no physical union.[83] Since ten of Young's twenty-seven recognized wives are sometimes classed as wives "in name only," it would be equally consistent to give the title "wife" to nearly thirty other women who have been conclusively identified as married and/or sealed to him.[84]

Furthermore, when they were "sealed" to him five of Young's childless wives were from sixteen to nineteen years old; a dozen were in their twenties. Several formally divorced him and married someone else, as was the case with lesser-known wives of several general authorities. Since Young fathered children by wives who were sixteen years old at marriage, it is very unlikely that he maintained celibate relationships with the young wives who bore him no children. Like the known wives of Joseph Smith, most of Young's wives were under age forty.[85]

The "widows and elderly spinsters" argument of celibacy often expressed by Mormon apologists applies to only five or six of Young's scores of wives, and about the same number among the dozens Smith married. Such an argument assumes that a polygamist male avoids sex with middle-aged women, an assumption based on the prejudicial and misogynist view that widows and middle-aged women lack sexual attractiveness.

The marital experience of another general authority refutes the age prejudice which underlies those assumptions. As his third living polyga-mist wife, Seventy's president Brigham H. Roberts married physician Margaret Curtis Shipp, who was seven years his senior and in her forties. Dr. Shipp had borne the last of her children to a previous husband, and Roberts continued to father children by his younger wives, the second being fourteen years Margaret's junior. Even though she was older and childless like dozens of women whom writers assume were "wives in name only" for Joseph Smith and Brigham Young, Margaret's marriage to the much younger Roberts was clearly passionate.[86] In fact this middle-aged and childless wife immediately displaced his younger wives in Roberts's affections and attentions. "Aunt M. seems to be having a happy life with her admirer B.H.R.," wrote Maggie's former sister-wife Ellis Reynolds Shipp. "Report says his family are greatly grieved with his absence from home." One biographer noted that Margaret "had been his closest com-panion for a number of years" at her death in 1926, even though Roberts continued to express his love to his younger wives in letters.[87]

The verified details of the Roberts-Shipp marriage provide a realistic context for similar marriages of polygamous general authorities. For example, it is reasonable to conclude that Joseph Smith's marriages to teenage girls did not prevent him from having a passionate relationship with his middle-aged wives such as Eliza R. Snow. When Heber C. Kimball asked if she remained "a virgin" during her marriage to the prophet, Eliza replied: "I thought you knew Joseph Smith better than that."[88]

Admittedly, from age fifty onward Brigham Young was emotionally distant, sexually neglectful, and verbally cruel with many of his tradition-ally acknowledged wives, including some who had borne his children.[89] However, here are examples of letters concerning his childless and lesser-known wives. Readers can decide whether these sound like women who have a celibate relationship with their sealed husband. "I received your very welcome little note with heart felt pleasure," Augusta Adams Cobb wrote two years after Joseph Smith sealed her to Young. Despite her years of complaints about his emotional and physical neglect, she assured Brigham in 1850 that never "have I ever sought to tear myself from your embrace and give myself to another on the earth."[90] Seven months after Mary Ann Clark Powers was sealed to Brigham Young, she wrote about her legal husband's plan to move to Utah: "I often wish I knew what your feelings are about him coming there [—] he does not mistrust any thing of you yet." In asking for a divorce in 1851 because "you held me at a distance and treated me with so much indifference," Mary Ann assured Brigham: "You may think I have Betrayed my trust [to you] but this I have not done

[—] I have not been a Wife to Mr P since I left him at Montrose[, Iowa] five Years ago . . ."[91]

In 1847 James B. Woodward wrote that "I am the most miserable of mortals" because he had learned why Brigham Young refused, without explanation, to seal him and his wife in Nauvoo. Without his knowledge, Mary de la Montague Woodward had been sealed to Young in the Nauvoo temple. She deserted her legal husband with the explanation "that you [Brigham] came to her and asked her if she did not love you [—] She asked you would it not be a sin to love you [—] You told her no [—] you asked her whose wife she would be the best off as." Now this faithful Mormon husband wrote that his wife claimed "that I prevent you from having intercourse with her and raising up seed to her glory." Four years later Mary Woodward Young began a letter to Brigham: "I cannot describe to you my feelings to find my hand once more clasp'd in yours and to see that smile again." Of the rumor that she wanted "to be adopted to you as a daughter," Mary wrote Brigham that "my feelings for you were not the feelings of a child to a parent [—] they are the deep devoted love of a wife to one who she idolised . . ." Concerning Mr. Woodward, she assured the church president: "I here acknowledge no husband but you since I was sealed to you."[92]

In my view, the existing evidence does not support writers who assume that Young had a celibate, "eternity only" relationship with these dozens of wives who bore him no children. Many of Brigham Young's marriages eventually became celibate, but there is good reason to believe that most, if not all, of his marriages were sexually consummated shortly after the ceremony of sealing. In the lesser-known marriages, the sealing records specified either "for time and eternity" or "for time" only—no different from the record of sealing for polygamous wives who bore children. Modern embarrassment about pioneer polygamy has created an "eternity only" definition that was absent in the original records of these marriage ceremonies between living persons.

Compared with the convoluted relationships of kinship within the Mormon hierarchy, the relationships resulting from marriage were far more complex. With the practice of polygamy, the total number of fathers-in-law, mothers-in-law, sisters-in-law, and brothers-in-law of a general authority frequently exceeded one hundred. Young and Kimball had several hundred in-laws each. The large number of children born to general authorities provided a source for scores of additional marriage ties as the children married, often to kin of other general authorities. Whereas the geometric increase of kinship relations attained sizeable proportions only with the passage of several generations, polygamous marriage allowed a man within his lifetime to become aligned to an entire community. The resulting labyrinth of marriage almost defies analysis, but a starting point is the connection by marriage of general authorities at their entry into the hierarchy. However, "blood" relatives in the hierarchy often also shared marriage connections. Therefore, to assess the independent influence of marriage, it is necessary to discuss the appointment of men who had marriage connections but no kinship to other general authorities.

Among general authorities appointed from 1832 to 1932, kinship was far more significant than the marriage connections. There were more than twice as many men (sixty-three) with kinship connections to former or current general authorities than there were new appointees (twenty-four) with marriage connections alone. Moreover, the kinship relations were of a proportionally closer degree than those of marriage. Forty-seven (38.2 percent) were within two ancestral generations of kinship, whereas only twenty-four (19.5 percent) of the marriage ties were within two ancestral generations. No appointee had only distant marriage relationships to other members of the hierarchy—the new general authority had kinship relations or had only close family relations that included marriage. A new appointee who shared distant marriage relationships with another general authority was also related by kinship to the hierarchy. Although marriage ties were less significant than kinship, the combined effect of marriage and kinship gave an extensive familial character to the appointment of new general authorities (Table 4).

The lowest and highest periods of appointee relationship are contrary to what one might expect. Founding prophet Joseph Smith began the pattern of dynastic appointments, and his selection of near relations is well known. However, fewer of his appointees to the hierarchy were closely related by kinship or marriage than those of subsequent church presidents. At the other extreme, even though Lorenzo Snow declined to appoint his own sons, his only two appointments were closely related within the hierarchy. Likewise, because Heber J. Grant had no living sons, many people would not associate him with dynastic appointments. However, all but one of President Grant's appointments from 1919 to 1932 were closely related to current or former members of the hierarchy, and he appointed two of his own sons-in-law after 1932.

Family interrelationships did not end with a man's appointment to the hierarchy. The introduction of polygamy added a dimension unavailable to every other dynastic order of the western world. Through polygamy a Mormon general authority could himself marry the close relatives of his associates in the hierarchy, thus reinforcing preexisting kinship connections. This also introduced into the hierarchical family some men who were otherwise unrelated.

Table 4.
Level of Total Family Relationships
to Current or Former General Authorities
by Appointees of LDS Presidents, 1832-1932

PRESIDENT	UP-DOWN TWO GENERATIONS	UP-DOWN THREE+ GENERATIONS	TOTAL MEN WITH FAMILY RELATIONSHIPS	TOTAL APPOINTEES
Joseph Smith	17 men (38.6%)	10 men (22.7%)	27 men (61.4%)	44
Brigham Young	14 men (50.0%)	6 men (21.4%)	20 men (71.4%)	28
John Taylor	12 men (80.0%)	0	12 men (80.0%)	15
Wilford Woodruff	7 men (70.0%)	0	7 men (70.0%)	10
Lorenzo Snow	2 men (100%)	0	2 men (100%)	2
Joseph F. Smith	14 men (77.8%)	0	14 men (77.8%)	18
Heber J. Grant	5 men (83.3%)	0	5 men (83.3%)	6
TOTAL	71 men (57.8%)	16 men (13.0%)	87 men (70.7%)	123

Two generations up-down from the appointee include: father, step-father, son, step-son, brother, step-brother, nephew, uncle, first cousin, grandson, grandnephew, first cousin once-removed, second cousin, brother-in-law (including situations where two men marry sisters), son-in-law, father-in-law, first cousin of a general authority's wife, nephew of a general authority's wife, second cousin of a general authority's wife, grandnephew of a general authority's wife, the situation where an appointee's wife is a granddaughter of a general authority, the situation where an appointee has married the former wife of a general authority, and sibling exchange (an appointee's child is married to a general authority's child).

Three or more generations up-down include more distant relationships such as second cousin once-removed, great-grandnephew, or third cousin to a general authority or to his wife.

Joseph Smith began this process in 1833 when he married Fanny Alger, the first polygamous wife in the list prepared by the assistant church historian. At the prophet's request, her uncle Levi W. Hancock arranged for this polygamous marriage. Two years later Smith appointed Hancock as a founding member of the First Council of Seventy.[93] The prophet married dozens of wives between 1841 and 1844, among whom were close relatives of eight general authorities. In 1842 Smith married the widow of Seventy's president Lyman R. Sherman and the legal wife of Apostle Orson Hyde (who was absent on a mission). Smith also married the wife of Presiding Bishop-designate Vinson Knight (probably before Knight's death in July 1842 rather than a few weeks afterward, as usually assumed from the intentionally vague traditional dating of "the summer"). In 1843 Smith married a daughter of Apostle Heber C. Kimball (Smith's fifth cousin), a sister-in-law of Apostle Parley P. Pratt (Smith's sixth cousin), two stepdaughters of Seventy's president Josiah Butterfield, and sisters of apostles Brigham Young and Willard Richards (respectively Smith's sixth and fourth cousins). Thus distant cousins were now Smith's in-laws. He also allied himself to the ecclesiastically prominent first bishops of the church, Edward Partridge and Newel K. Whitney, with marriages to their daughters.[94]

Some of his proposals were unsuccessful. One that got extensive publicity in 1842 involved the daughter of his first counselor Sidney Rigdon.[95] That same year Smith told Sarah M. Granger Kimball (then married to a non-Mormon) that God commanded him to teach her polygamy and marry her himself. This devout Mormon woman later wrote: "I asked him to teach it to some one else."[96] In contrast to Sarah's faith and quiet resistance, the wives of his second counselor William Law and of Apostle Orson Pratt denounced the prophet for such proposals. This caused the apostasy of their husbands, even though Pratt became reconciled within six months.[97]

In addition, when some of his associates in the hierarchy agreed to let their wives secretly marry him, Smith said that his polygamous proposal was only "a test." This was the experience of apostles Heber C. Kimball and John Taylor in 1842 and of Apostle Brigham Young in 1843.[98] "Did the Prophet Joseph Smith want every man's wife he asked for?" asked First Presidency counselor Jedediah M. Grant in a Utah sermon. "He did not," Grant explained because "the grand object in view was to try the people of God, to see what was in them."[99]

Apostle Amasa M. Lyman (Smith's special counselor from January 1843 on) confided to a Utah congregation that LDS leaders "made many crooked paths" during the early years of introducing plural marriage.[100] However, the polygamous apostles did not regard Smith's practice of marrying the relatives of other general authorities as one of those "crooked paths." Utah's apostles married the daughters, nieces, and granddaughters of fellow members of the hierarchy. Marrying widows and divorced wives of general authorities was almost as common. Few other officers in the hierarchy entered into such marriages: only one Seventy's president and one Presiding Bishop did so.

A final means of reinforcing dynasticism was through the marriages of children and other relatives. This occurred on virtually every level of kinship conceivable and is too complex for a diagram or table. By selecting one type of such marriage, however, it is at least possible to suggest the general nature of such additional family ties.

Sibling exchange—marriages between children of two associates—had the obvious effect of uniting the respective members of the hierarchy in a significant way. This was an ecclesiastical version of the financially motivated marriages among Boston's merchant elite during the early nineteenth century: "Sibling exchanges could be used to cement partnership alliances with non-kin merchants. Persons from outside the circle of kin could be taken into partnership . . ."[101] This is not to say that there was a lack of significance to the other marriages involving children, nephews, and nieces in various combinations, but familial significance was obvious in the hierarchy's sibling exchange. Such marriages were in some ways an inevitable result of the social interaction which occurred between the families of general authorities (see Table 5).

Table 5.
Children of Living General Authorities
Who Married Children of Other General Authorities,
Living or Dead, 1843-1926

POSITION OF LIVING FATHERS	POSITION OF THE OTHER GENERAL-AUTHORITY FATHER						
	PRESIDENT	COUN-SELOR	PATRI-ARCH	APOSTLE	SEVENTY	PRES. BISHOP	P.B. COUNS.
Church president	—	1	—	4	2	—	—
Pres. Counselor	1	—	1	—	—	—	—
Patriarch	—	—	—	—	—	—	—
Apostle	3	1	—	9	3	2	—
Seventy	5	1	—	2	—	—	—
Presiding Bishop	—	—	—	2	—	—	—
Pres. B. Coun.	1	1	—	—	—	—	—

This table does not include children of a deceased general authority who married children of another deceased general authority.

Some general authorities purposely arranged or promoted sibling exchange as a means of uniting their families. One example is the marriage between a son of President Joseph F. Smith and a daughter of Apostle Heber J. Grant, as related by a granddaughter of the two general authorities:

> One day Mother was waiting for a street car on Main Street when President Smith came up to her and said, "Are you interested in my son?" And Mother said, "Well, I think he's very nice." Then President Smith said, "Well, you ought to marry him. I'll see that he asks you." Mother said she was very embarrassed.
> S: Was he just kidding?

J: No, he was very serious. These two men, Grandfather Smith and Grandfather Grant, were very close in the councils of the Church and had often talked about having one of their children marry. They saw this as the golden opportunity, I guess, and were both promoting it (laughter). So it wasn't long after that that they were married.[102]

Although such arranged marriages may have been infrequent, they were an extension of Mormon dynasticism. During its first century, the Mormon hierarchy was unquestionably an extended family (see Table 6).

Table 6.
Percentage of Hierarchy Related by Kinship or Marriage (within Two Generations) to Current or Former General Authorities, 1833-1932

YEARS	FIRST PRESIDENCY	COUNCIL OF TWELVE	PRES. PATRIARCH	COUNCIL OF SEVENTY	PRES. BISHOPRIC	TOTAL HIERARCHY
April 1833	0.0%	*	*	*	*	0.0%
April 1844	75.0%	75.0%	100.0%	71.4%	*	70.8%
April 1855	100.0%	91.7%	100.0%	57.2%	0.0%	79.2%
April 1866	100.0%	100.0%	100.0%	100.0%	66.7%	96.6%
April 1877	100.0%	100.0%	100.0%	100.0%	100.0%	100.0%
April 1888	*	93.3%	100.0%	85.0%	100.0%	92.3%
April 1899	100.0%	75.0%	100.0%	42.9%	100.0%	73.1%
April 1910	66.7%	75.0%	100.0%	57.2%	66.7%	69.3%
April 1921	66.7%	66.7%	100.0%	57.2%	66.7%	65.4%
April 1932	100.0%	75.0%	100.0%	57.2%	66.7%	72.0%

The relationships include: father, step-father, son, step-son, brother, step-brother, nephew, uncle, first cousin, grandson, grandnephew, first cousin once-removed, second cousin, brother-in-law (including situations where two men marry sisters), son-in-law, father-in-law, first cousin of a general authority's wife, nephew of a general authority's wife, second cousin of a general authority's wife, grandnephew of a general authority's wife, the situation where an appointee's wife is a granddaughter of a general authority, the situation where an appointee has married the former wife of a general authority, and sibling exchange (a general authority's child is married to the child of another general authority).

Excluded are relationships such as second cousin once-removed to a general authority or his wife, and more distant relationships of kinship and marriage.

Men holding two positions in the hierarchy at one time (e.g., Hyrum Smith in April 1844 as Assistant President and also Presiding Patriarch) are included in the tabulation for each position, but counted only once in the total.

*The quorum did not exist at this time.

The Hierarchy at Present

The ancestry of current general authorities emphasizes the hierarchy's Utah origins.[103] While more than half of these men were born in Utah, 78.2 percent have roots in nineteenth-century Utah. This early Utah ancestry accounts for all of the current First Presidency, all the Quorum of Twelve, all the Presidency of the Seventy, and all the Presiding Bishopric. Only in the lesser-status first and second quorums of the Seventy as of 1996 are there general authorities who have no ancestor from early Utah. Those with roots in pioneer Mormonism also have at least one ancestor who married a polygamous wife, although some of these current leaders are descended from the legal wife of their polygamous ancestor.

Pioneer Utah's "enforcers" (see chap. 7) are also represented among the Seventy in the hierarchy of 1996. First Quorum member John B. Dickson is a direct descendant of William A. Hickman. Howard Egan's descendants include First Quorum member Carlos E. Asay (made emeritus in October 1996) and the wife of Second Quorum member Gary J. Coleman. First Quorum member James M. Paramore's wife is a direct descendant of Ephraim K. Hanks. Second Quorum members John E. Fowler and Lowell D. Wood have wives who are descended respectively from Isaac C. Haight and Hosea Stout.

In addition to the polygamous ancestry of three-fourths of today's Mormon hierarchy, there has always been significant representation of post-Manifesto polygamists. From 1890 to 1943 there was at least one current general authority who had married a polygamous wife after the Manifesto of September 1890.[104] Despite the release of John W. Taylor and Matthias F. Cowley from the Quorum of the Twelve Apostles in 1906 for the public knowledge that they were "out of harmony" with the church's official position on the Manifesto,[105] from 1906 until 1945 current members of the Twelve or First Presidency had previously officiated in post-Manifesto polygamous marriages.[106] Ever since the appointment of Matthew Cowley as an apostle in 1945, the LDS hierarchy has also included sons and other descendants of those who married polygamously after the 1890 Manifesto, as well as general authorities married to women so descended. LDS headquarters has had continual representation of post-Manifesto polygamy from 1890 to the present.

Several general authorities or their wives in 1996 have ancestors who were post-Manifesto polygamists. Descended from men who married polygamous wives between the 1890 Manifesto and the 1904 Second Manifesto are: Apostle Henry B. Eyring, Seventy's president W. Eugene Hansen, First Quorum of Seventy member John H. Groberg, Second Quorum of Seventy member Jerald L. Taylor, Second Quorum of Seventy member Lowell D. Wood, the wife of Apostle Dallin H. Oaks, the wife of

Apostle Richard G. Scott, the wife of First Quorum of Seventy member Bruce C. Hafen, the wife of First Quorum of Seventy member Glenn L. Pace, the wife of First Quorum of Seventy member Robert E. Wells, the wife of Second Quorum of Seventy member W. Don Ladd, the wife of Second Quorum of Seventy member Lance B. Wickman, and the wife of Presiding Bishopric counselor Richard C. Edgley. Most of those 1890-1904 marriages occurred in Mexico, but some occurred in Salt Lake City and one in Canada.[107] Descended from men who married polygamously after 1904 are: Seventy's president W. Eugene Hansen, the wife of First Quorum of Seventy member Glenn L. Pace, and the wife of Presiding Bishop H. David Burton. Those post-1904 marriages occurred about equally in Mexico, Canada, and Utah.[108] None of these current general authorities and only one of their wives is a descendant of a post-Manifesto polygamous wife. In addition, current Seventy member Cree-L Kofford's wife is a great-granddaughter of Alexander F. Macdonald, who performed more than fifty polygamous marriages in Mexico from 1890 until his death in 1903.[109]

Thus, despite the official position of the LDS church against polygamy in the twentieth century, post-Manifesto polygamists have always been well represented in the Mormon hierarchy. Twelve years ago I explained the demographic basis for my estimate that there were then at least 50,000 living descendants of men who married polygamously after the 1890 Manifesto and by secret authorization of the church's presiding officers.[110] Today an even larger number of such Mormons can look for empathetic understanding from fifteen general authorities whose own family heritage allows them to give reassurances of the difference between LDS public policy and private realities concerning polygamy.

In certain respects the hierarchy's family relations as of 1996 are as low as one would expect in terms of the worldwide growth of the LDS church. By comparison with Table 1, these are the percentages of the hierarchy related by kinship within two ancestral generations to current or former general authorities: 33.3 percent of the First Presidency, 33.3 percent of the Twelve, 12 percent of all members of the Seventy, 33.3 percent of the Presiding Bishopric, and 15.8 percent of the entire hierarchy as of 1996. By comparison, Table 1 shows that the lowest level of this degree of kinship during the hierarchy's first century was 33.3 percent in 1855. In other words, today's level of close kinship for the entire hierarchy is half of the lowest level during the hierarchy's first century.

Nevertheless, current general authorities are concerned about accusations of "nepotism," even for appointments outside the hierarchy. First Counselor Gordon B. Hinckley opposed selection of his daughter as a counselor in the general presidency for Young Women because "he felt some concern that charges of nepotism might be leveled about her appointment and initially discouraged her call when Sister [Janette C.] Hales made the recommendation, but he was pleased that she was worthy and capable."[111]

If wives and marriage relationships (within two ancestral generations) are included for the hierarchy as of 1996, the level of close family relationships is still significantly lower than during the first century. By comparison with Table 6, these are the percentages of the hierarchy related within two generations of kinship or marriage to current or former general authorities: 33.3 percent of the First Presidency, 66.7 percent of the Twelve, 26.5 percent of all members of the Seventy, 66.7 percent of the Presiding Bishopric, and 32.7 percent of the entire hierarchy as of 1996. Again the lowest level (in April 1921) of similar relatedness during the first century was double the current level for the entire hierarchy.

However, a family relationship more distant than two generations is far more significant in the LDS church today. When the 1845 "family meeting" in Nauvoo celebrated such distant family relationships, the LDS church had no emphasis on genealogical research. By contrast, during the last thirty years LDS headquarters has periodically asked Mormons to research and submit pedigree charts and family group records for three or four generations of their ancestors. Hundreds of Mormon families have published books which show kinship and marriage interconnections of current Mormons extending back five or more generations. The one extended "family meeting" of Nauvoo has expanded in the twentieth century to annual reunions for hundreds of large family organizations in which it is common to meet one's second and third cousins. This extensive knowledge of family relationships is especially true for those with Utah pioneer heritage.[112]

By examining the family relationships of the current hierarchy back five generations, one discovers an extensive network of kinship and marriage relationships among current general authorities. This is the same extent of family research conducted for the Mormon hierarchy in the first century (see Appen. 4), with one exception. This current analysis does not include the marriage relationships among children of general authorities since 1932, because that information is not uniformly available. Therefore, this analysis does not assess the extent to which sibling exchange has occurred in recent decades among the children of LDS general authorities.

By examining the five ancestral generations often included in current Mormon family organizations, one gets a very different view of the current hierarchy's relatedness. First, these are the percentages of the hierarchy related by kinship alone to current or former general authorities: 100

percent of the First Presidency, 75 percent of the Twelve, 42.2 percent of all members of the Seventy, 66.7 percent of the Presiding Bishopric, and 48.5 percent of the entire hierarchy as of 1996. Second, by including wives, these are the percentages of the hierarchy related by kinship or marriage to current or former general authorities: 100 percent of the First Presidency, 100 percent of the Twelve, 66.3 percent of all members of the Seventy, 100 percent of the Presiding Bishopric, and 72.3 percent of the entire hierarchy as of 1996.

The data also demonstrate the persistence in 1996 of two patterns of family relationship observable for the hierarchy in 1832-1932. First, if an appointee was not himself related to the hierarchy, his wife often was. Second, family penetration still tends to correspond to the status of the presiding quorum. For example, the Second Quorum of the Seventy (which contains only temporary appointments as general authorities) consistently has the lowest levels of family relatedness. This is true for close kinship among current members of the hierarchy, for total kinship and marriage relationships among only current members of the hierarchy, for kinship to current and former general authorities, and for total kinship and marriage relationships to current and former members of the hierarchy. In that final category, for example, 54.5 percent of the current Second Quorum of the Seventy have family relationships, whereas 74.4 percent of the First Quorum of the Seventy (with its permanent status as general authorities) have such family relationships. By contrast, the administratively powerful First Presidency and Quorum of the Twelve today are 100 percent related in that last category.[113]

Conclusion

Such intricate kinship and marriage connections within the Mormon elite might be disconcerting to some people, but they are the logical extension of a theological framework that focuses on the family. Mormons have the responsibility of joining together on earth those who experienced the new covenant of the restoration of God's church. That responsibility extends to those who died without LDS membership. The heads of these spiritually organized families are kings and priests, queens and priestesses to their nuclear and extended families. Moreover, within the hierarchy these relationships have promoted additional unity, stability, and loyalty. The interwoven and replicating relationships could not be easily unraveled, and this provided an added layer of protection against high-ranking apostasy.

There are limits, however, to the influence of family ties. Even the closest relationships were not absolute assurance against friction and schism, as the periodic rebellion of Apostle William Smith against his brothers and cousins demonstrated. Moreover, extensive connections did not save general authorities from being disciplined or rejected for unacceptable conduct, as in the excommunications of William Smith, Amasa Lyman (brother-in-law of President Brigham Young), Albert Carrington (father-in-law of Apostle Brigham Young, Jr.), John Q. Cannon (son of Counselor George Q. Cannon), and Richard R. Lyman (second cousin of the Twelve's then-current president, George Albert Smith).

In addition, being closely related to a general authority who had disgraced himself did not prevent capable men from being advanced. This was demonstrated by the appointments of Henry Harriman (brother-in-law of excommunicated apostle John F. Boynton), Jedediah M. Grant (brother-in-law of excommunicated apostle William Smith), Francis M. Lyman (son of excommunicated apostle Amasa M. Lyman), and Matthew Cowley (son of Matthias F. Cowley, released from the Twelve for being "out of harmony"). Matthew Cowley's birth and apostleship were also the fulfillment of a prophecy by Apostle Moses Thatcher who was disfellowshipped by the Twelve a year after pronouncing this blessing.[114]

Although family connections have been important in new appointments, the overriding consideration to enter and remain in the LDS hierarchy is personal worthiness. Dynasticism in the hierarchy is partly a demonstration of theology, personal inclination, and administrative protectiveness.

In a fundamental way the hierarchy's composition continues to celebrate pioneer Mormon ancestry. The Utah birth of a majority of today's general authorities still understates their shared pioneer heritage. In 1992 a former First Presidency secretary publicly referred to "the unofficial and loosely structured Church family comprised of General Authorities and their kin."[115] Family interrelationships of Utah origin continue at extraordinary levels for the top leadership of a church whose membership resides primarily outside the United States.

CHAPTER 6

Church Finances

From the 1830s to the 1990s, LDS church finances have experienced many significant transitions.[1] This is an overview of highlights during 160 years of tithing, salaried ministry and voluntary service, business activity, revenues, personal use of church funds, church indebtedness, and public disclosure. This chapter shows that LDS finances have not always functioned as they do today and that the financial sacrifices of Mormons have been great, indeed.

To begin, by divine injunction since ancient times, God's disciples have seen themselves as "not of the world" (John 17:14). This has resulted in various religious communities regarding themselves as outside the ordinary definitions and expectations of society and of the world's leaders.[2]

Theologically, Mormonism has never accepted the "worldly" distinctions between secular versus religious, civil versus theocratic, mundane versus divine.[3] An 1830 revelation declared: "Wherefore, verily I say unto you that all things unto me are spiritual, and not at any time have I given unto you a law which was temporal; neither [unto] any man, nor the children of men . . ."[4]

In reaction to hostile critics, the First Presidency issued this formal statement in 1907: "The charge that the Church is a commercial rather than a religious institution; that its aims are temporal rather than religious; that it dictates its members in their industrial activities and relations, and aims at absolute domination in temporal affairs,—all this we emphatically deny."[5] The difficulty with such a denial is that LDS leaders were stating criticisms of their church in the categories and assumptions of non-Mormons, but answering them in the categories and assumptions of Mormonism. In Mormon terms the LDS church is not "a commercial rather than a religious institution," but the LDS church is commercial because it is religious. Likewise, Mormonism's aims are not "temporal rather than spiritual," but its aims are temporal because they are spiritual. And all questions of dictation and absolute dominion—economic or political—are based on the Mormon view of the supremacy of free will. In other words, whether it is the political dictates of Mormon leaders or the prosperity of an economic institution of the LDS church, Mormonism has dominion only insofar as Mormons choose to allow it (see chaps. 7-10).

Mormons have always been irritated by complaints and hand-wringing about "Mormon power" (whether financial, political, or social). In 1984, for possibly the first time, two non-Mormon writers declared the LDS perspective of the hierarchy's financial power: "These are money managers, but unlike any other kind of money managers. . . . The wealth and power, in the end, come down to the essentials: The church is in the business of expanding the church. . . . a temporal structure whose major goal is spiritual—the building of the Kingdom of God on earth in preparation for the millennial reign of Jesus Christ."[6]

There are both continuities and discontinuities in Mormon financial history since Joseph Smith, Jr., organized a new church on 6 April 1830. The most significant difference involves the definition of tithing.

Tithing

Since 1831 LDS bishop Edward Partridge and his counselors had presided over all Mormons in Missouri, which had equal status with church headquarters in Ohio.[7] In December 1837 they defined tithing as 2 percent of one's net worth, after deducting debts. "Believing that voluntary tithing is better than Forced taxes," the Missouri bishopric defined it as "two cents on the dollar or one fiftieth of what we are worth after deducting what we owe."[8] Until 1908 Mormons were allowed to pay tithing in labor, personal property, livestock, and produce in addition to cash.[9]

In July 1838 Joseph Smith dictated a revelation which required a more stringent financial sacrifice from Latter-day Saints. It defined the law of tithing as a donation of *all* the individual's "surplus property" at first, and then a tenth of annual income thereafter (D&C 119:1, 4). In November 1841 the Quorum of the Twelve made the first liberalization of the 1838 tithing revelation: the initial donation was reduced to only "one-tenth of all a man [possesses, and] 1/10 of increas[e]" afterwards.[10]

In August 1844 the Quorum of the Twelve Apostles issued an epistle which required all Mormons to immediately pay "a tenth of all their property and money . . . and then let them continue to pay in a tenth of their income from that time forth." There was no exemption for Mormons who had already paid one-tenth of their property upon conversion.[11] In January 1845 a Quorum of Twelve's epistle reemphasized "the duty of all saints to tithe themselves one-tenth of all they possess when they enter into the new and everlasting covenant: and then one-tenth of their interest, or income, yearly afterwards."[12] However, two weeks later the Twelve voted to exempt themselves, the two general bishops Newel K. Whitney and George Miller, and the Nauvoo Temple Committee from any obligation to pay tithing. This was due to their services to the church.[13]

Apostle John E. Page's enforcement of the full-tithing requirement for the rank-and-file led to his disaffection from his own quorum. Exempted from tithing himself, Page felt guilty about collecting tithing from others such as one Mormon who gave $4 which was "the tenth of all" the man and his impoverished family possessed. Upon abandoning the Quorum of the Twelve in 1846, Page complained that he "believes that many paid tithing & in consequence of [this, were in] want of money enough to procure misc. necessaries of life."[14]

Five years later Brigham Young provided a penalty for those Mormons who did not comply with the published definitions of the law of tithing. In September 1851 a special conference at Salt Lake City voted to accept excommunication as punishment for non-payment of tithing and non-observance of the Word of Wisdom's prohibition of tobacco and spirituous alcohol. Neither requirement was enforced consistently or often.[15] Nevertheless, in 1854 the *Deseret News* printed a notice by the bishop of the Salt Lake City Nineteenth Ward that Enoch M. King was disfellowshipped "for repeatedly refusing to conform to the rules of said Church, in the law of Tithing." In October 1858 a bishop's meeting asked Presiding Bishop Edward Hunter: "Are all to be cut off who do not pay their Tithing? Answer, deal according to circumstances, and the wisdom God gives."[16]

On this matter Apostle Erastus Snow was more zealous than most. In 1868 he gave orders to southern Utah bishops to excommunicate everyone "who will not keep the word of wisdom, Pay their Tithing & donate of their substance to help bring the Poor Saints from the old country." A local Mormon estimated that enforcement of Snow's instruction "would cause 3/4 of this community to be cut off from this church."[17]

For the church as a whole, Brigham Young publicly estimated that Latter-day Saints had paid less than 10 percent of their 10 percent tithing obligations from 1847 to 1870.[18] In other words, adult Mormons were contributing, on average, less than 1 percent of their net worth at conversion, less than 1 percent of their net worth upon arrival in Utah, and less than 1 percent of their annual income. However, pioneer definitions of tithing delinquency varied radically. In Cache Valley during the same period, local bishops concluded that 90 percent of people who could pay tithing were full-tithe payers. The difference in perspective was due to the fact that these Cache Valley bishops "excused" a large portion of the population from tithing due to poverty. The church president's report made no such distinctions.[19]

After President Young's announcement of tithing delinquency, LDS general authorities gave sermons to remind church members that the law of tithing was "one tenth of all we possess at the start, and then ever after one tenth . . ."[20] Apostle Erastus Snow even reinvoked the 1838 revelation's original requirement to donate all surplus property at first.[21] These sermons were futile efforts to reverse a nineteenth-century trend of financial non-compliance. Otherwise faithful Mormons withered before an overwhelming tithing obligation. Young told the October 1875 general conference that neither he nor anyone else "had ever paid their tithing as it was revealed and understood by him in the Doctrine and Covenants."[22]

John Taylor tried to increase church donations by liberalizing the law of tithing for the first time since 1841. On the fiftieth anniversary of the church's organization, he declared a biblical Jubilee Year in which he forgave *half* of the delinquent tithing and half of the debts owed to the Perpetual Emigrating Fund.[23] After the Jubilee year of 1880 failed to bring in the unforgiven half of delinquent tithing, the church president offered a carrot-and-stick approach to tithing in 1881. On 8 January 1881 Taylor said he did not care whether Mormons paid the "one-tenth of the property of the new comers" to Utah, as required by Brigham Young. However, the Presiding Bishopric's tithing clerk recorded that, on motion of the LDS president, the assembled priesthood holders voted unanimously to sustain the requirement of "one tenth of the property on entering the Church, and one tenth of the increase afterward."[24] At this stake conference in January and again at general conference in April 1881, President Taylor instructed stake presidents that church members now "must be tithe payers" in order to have recommends for temple ordinances.[25]

The early tithing requirements of Mormonism give added significance to the numbers of immigrants to Utah before 1881 and to the numbers of LDS converts prior to 1899. At a personal level, any Mormon who paid a full tithing by nineteenth-century definitions (like the man who gave $4 in 1845) was deserving of awe and veneration. Then in May 1899 Lorenzo Snow publicly announced a revelation which limited the law of tithing to one-tenth of annual income with no massive payment upon conversion. As an LDS church president, Snow is best known for his emphasis on observance of this new definition of tithing.[26] This was the last LDS liberalization of the 1838 revelation on tithing. From then until the present, Mormons have been allowed to decide whether to pay tithing on their gross income or net income.[27]

Lorenzo Snow's announcement was undoubtedly the cause for a significant increase in the percentage of Mormons who paid at least some tithing (see Table). In 1890, 17.2 percent of LDS stake membership had paid some tithing, and the percentage hovered around 15 percent for seven years. In 1898 the percentage of stake members who paid some tithing was only 1 percent higher than in 1890. In 1899, the year of Lorenzo Snow's announcement, the number of tithe payers in the stakes jumped to 25.6 percent.[28]

In early 1900 President Snow asked the Presiding Bishop to prepare
a list "of non-tithe payers and about 10,000 names were in the record."[29]
Snow told the apostles that non-payment of tithing "was worse than the
non-observance of the Word of Wisdom" prohibitions against tobacco
and alcohol. The time had long since passed when general authorities
were exempt from the obligation to pay tithing, and one apostle was
shocked to learn that Apostle John W. Taylor's "name is on the Non-
Tithing List!"[30]

In April 1910 the church president announced it was necessary to
comply with this greatly reduced law of tithing in order to have temple
recommends.[31] This 1910 announcement was a reincarnation of the
poorly enforced First Presidency announcement in 1881. Since 1910
bishops and stake presidents have given greater attention to the requirement of tithing for temple recommends. Higher expectations of tithing
compliance were possible because twentieth-century Mormons have had
it easy regarding their tithing obligations compared with nineteenth-
century Mormons.

Table 1.
LDS Stake Members Who Paid Some Tithing, 1890-1925
(per capita for total membership)

YEARS	TITHE PAYERS	YEARS	TITHE PAYERS	YEARS	TITHE PAYERS	YEARS	TITHE PAYERS
1890	17.2%	1900	27.0%	1910	21.6%	1920	21.9%
1891	15.1%	1901	28.9%	1911	21.0%	1921	20.7%
1892	15.8%	1902	28.2%	1912	20.6%	1922	28.4%
1893	14.9%	1903	28.5%	1913	21.0%	1923	27.3%
1894	15.7%	1904	27.6%	1914	20.1%	1924	25.1%
1895	15.3%	1905	26.4%	1915	20.0%	1925	25.3%
1896	15.1%	1906	26.1%	1916	20.1%		
1897	15.6%	1907	26.8%	1917	21.8%		
1898	18.4%	1908	26.0%	1918	21.3%		
1899	25.6%	1909	25.0%	1919	22.3%		

Of course the figures in this Table were significantly higher than the
percentage of stake members who paid a *full* tithing. During the pre-
Depression first quarter of the twentieth century, the highest percentage
of full-tithe payers was in 1910. In that year 16.5 percent of the church's
total stake membership of men, women, and children paid a full 10-per-
cent tithing.[32] However, neither of the above measures adequately assesses

individual compliance by Mormons concerning their church's requirement for tithing.

The annual reports did not regularly list the number of wage-earners
or consistently show the percentage of wage-earners who actually paid
tithing. The 54,346 full-tithe payers in 1910 were a much higher percentage
(though unquantifiable) of the wage-earners among Latter-day Saints in
the stakes that year. For example, in the very next year 59.3 percent were
full-tithe payers of the total wage-earners. Likewise, the highest percentage
(28.9 percent) who paid *any* tithing in that quarter-century amounted to
74,625 tithe payers in 1901. That had to be an impressive record for the
Mormon wage-earners in the stakes that year, for the lowest rate of tithe
paying during that quarter-century was 20 percent of total stake population in 1915. In that latter year 73 percent of wage-earners paid at least
some tithing.[33] The praise of Mormon leaders for the financial devotion
of LDS church members has never been exaggerated.

Tithing donations from the widow's mite to the rich man's abundance
have always been the essential source of LDS church revenues. When
Esquire magazine's August 1962 cover story claimed the church's revenues
were $1 million a day,[34] tithing revenues were actually about $100 million
that year instead of $365 million.[35] This 350+ percent error was due to
careless research and a wild guess by Salt Lake City's non-Mormon mayor,
J. Bracken Lee: "I do know that the net income exceeds a million dollars
a day."[36] With far more attention to available details, a carefully researched
estimate of 1991 was probably closer to the mark in claiming that the LDS
church received $4.3 billion in annual tithing revenue.[37] The accuracy of
this estimate is debatable, since recent tithing figures are unavailable for
research.

However, annual tithing revenues for the decade prior to the *Esquire*
estimate are helpful for estimating recent LDS church income. In 1962
tithing revenues were about $56.62 per capita for total LDS membership
that year, nearly double the per capita tithing revenues of $28.65 in 1952.
In real dollars (a term in economic history), the 1962 tithing equalled $253
per capita in 1990 dollars.[38] Therefore, assuming similar tithing observance in 1990 (without including the observable annual growth rate), this
would translate to $1.96 billion in tithing revenue during 1990. From that
perspective, LDS Public Affairs in 1991 rightly dismissed the estimate of
$4.3 billion of annual tithing income as "grossly overstated."[39] However,
by including the growth rate of the earlier reports by LDS headquarters,
it is difficult to regard $4.3 billion as a "grossly overstated" estimate of
annual LDS revenues in the 1990s.

A nearly 100 percent growth rate in the actual dollars of per capita tithing from 1952 to 1962 cannot simply be ignored when estimating the LDS church's present income. That decade included the explosive growth of LDS conversions outside the United States and Canada. There is no reason to discount similar growth in tithing rates during the three decades since 1962. With the 1952-62 period as a basis of comparison, the church's tithing revenues for 1990 would be far in excess of the estimate of $4.3 billion. From this perspective that estimate seems conservative.

However, it is important to recognize that tithing from Mormons outside the United States has rarely ever been transferred to church headquarters in America. Except for the early years of the British Mission (established in 1837) and of the Canadian settlements of Mormons (begun in 1887), Mormon tithing funds have remained in the countries of their origin. The first reason for this is that foreign outposts of Mormonism have been financial drains on the church's general funds, which typically supplement local tithing collected outside the United States. In the nineteenth century it was more practical to use foreign tithing for the immediate needs of the missions and branches in each country where it was collected. Physical transfer of overseas funds required months of travel to and from headquarters in the United States.

The second reason for keeping tithing in the country of its origin was that the church lost money in exchange fees for every transaction involving U.S. dollars and foreign currency. The third reason is that (particularly in the twentieth century) laws of some countries either complicated or prohibited transfers of tithing to the United States. The bottom line is that the net flow of tithing funds has been from Salt Lake City to other countries where Mormons have converted and eventually built chapels and temples.

Both the definition of tithing and the extent of its payment have evolved since 1831. The LDS church could not have become the international organization it is today without the development of regular tithe paying.

Paid Ministry and Voluntary Service

Even less recognized than the change in tithing definitions is the existence of a paid Mormon ministry. Before the church even had a tithing requirement, it had a paid ministry. In November 1831 a revelation declared: "He who is appointed to administer spiritual things, the same is worthy of his hire . . ." (D&C 70:12). This was the doctrinal basis for giving financial support to Joseph Smith, and later to a hierarchy of general authorities.

In May 1835 an official church council voted that the Quorum of Twelve Apostles and First Council of Seventy "have particularly to depend upon their ministry for their support, and that of their families; and they have a right, by virtue of their offices, to call upon the churches to assist them."[40] When Bishop Edward Partridge gave the first definition of tithing in December 1837, part of the tithing was for "remunerating the officers of the church for the time which they were necessarily employed in doing the business of the same." Six months later the stake high council voted "to instruct the Bishop to pay the First Presidency, J. Smith, & Sidney Rigdon, whatever sum they agree with them for." However, there was "such an uproar" over this decision that the First Presidency dropped its request for a fixed annual salary.[41]

For several decades only the patriarch had a set compensation, while other general authorities depended on haphazard donations from the rank-and-file or *ad hoc* appropriations from general church funds. In 1835 the Presiding Patriarch was authorized a salary of $10 a week, plus expenses.[42]

Both the Presiding Patriarch and local stake patriarchs charged a fee. In the 1840s the fee was $1 per patriarchal blessing at Nauvoo; by the end of the nineteenth century it had increased to $2 per blessing.[43] Joseph Smith, Sr., gave patriarchal blessings without payment of a fee, but would not record them.[44] "Uncle" John Smith commented that he "lived very Poor ever Since we Left Kirtland Ohio" in January 1838 until January 1844. Then his nephew Joseph Smith ordained him a patriarch "through which office I Obtained a Comfortable Living."[45]

Financial incentive is another explanation for the fact that individual Mormons received more than one patriarchal blessing in the nineteenth century, often at the invitation of the patriarch. In October 1877 John Taylor criticized the monetary motivation of some stake patriarchs. He said they were using their patriarchal office as "a mere means of obtaining a livelihood, and to obtain more business they had been traveling from door to door and underbidding each other in the price of blessings."[46]

In addition, patriarchs received fees for giving unrecorded blessings of healing to the sick. In fact, Apostle Francis M. Lyman commended Patriarch Elias Blackburn for "doing a great deal of good among the sick, without receiving very much pay for his services."[47]

Patriarchal blessing fees ended in 1902, although patriarchs were allowed to accept unsolicited donations.[48] Not until 1943 did church authorities prohibit patriarchs from accepting gratuities for giving blessings.[49]

In the nineteenth-century American West, local officers of the LDS church obtained their support from the tithing they collected. As early as 1859 Brigham Young wondered "whether a Stake would not be better governed when none of the officers were paid for their services."[50] During Young's presidency, ward bishops drew at will from the primarily non-cash tithing Mormons donated. He complained at October 1860 general conference "against a principle in many of the Bishops to use up all the Tithing they could for their own families."[51]

Even full-time missionaries benefitted from tithing funds in the nineteenth century. The senior president of the First Council of Seventy commented in 1879 that the families of married missionaries should be supported from tithing funds.[52] However, at best that practice barely kept struggling wives and children out of abject poverty while their husbands and fathers served two-year missions.

In 1884 church president John Taylor limited bishops to 8 percent of tithing they collected (now primarily cash), while stake presidents got 2 percent of tithing collected by all the bishops of the stake. In 1888 Wilford Woodruff established set salaries for stake presidents and provided that a stake committee would apportion 10 percent of collected tithing between the bishops and the stake tithing clerk. At April 1896 general conference, the First Presidency announced the end of salaries for local officers, in response to the decision of the temple meeting "to not pay Salaries to any one but the Twelve."[53]

Nevertheless, ending salaries to stake presidents in 1896 was temporary. For a while stake presidents and their counselors were allowed to draw "from the tithing fund . . . no more than the limit which had been previously specified, and not to entertain the idea that a stipulated compensation attached like a salary to certain offices in the Church." By April 1897 the First Presidency spoke about "the subject of compensation to presiding men" in a meeting with stake presidents and other local officers. The First Presidency urged "the brethren to give their services so far as possible to the church without remuneration." In 1898 "the regular 10% of tithing [was] allowed Bishops and clerks for handling the same," but the First Presidency balked at allowing even more to cover expenses for supplies.[54]

By 1904 set salaries were back again for stake presidents, who were allowed $300 per year.[55] As late as 1910, local officers continued to receive 10 percent of locally collected tithing "for handling tithes."[56] Recently a Mormon said that his father received a cash allowance as bishop in the 1920s, which was a later period of such compensation than my own research has verified.[57]

In addition, since the 1880s stake presidents and bishops of long tenure had received retirement allowances in monthly or annual payments.[58] In 1901 even the parsimonious church president Lorenzo Snow said that a financially struggling stake president "ought to receive his remuneration after he was released as well as before." Retirement allowances for stake presidents continued into the early 1900s.[59]

As previously mentioned, financial compensation for church officers began with the general authorities in the 1830s but did not become systematic until 1877. During these decades there was evidence of rank-and-file dissatisfaction with the Mormon hierarchy's financial privileges. In 1847 Brigham Young told a public meeting: "Be cont[e]nted with your lot and station and stop whining and babbling about the 12, saying that Brigham oppresses the poor and lives off their earning and that you can't see why you can't have some of his good living, and so on. Did Brigham Young ever get anything from you, did you ever help him to any of his fine living, you poor curses, or was it through Brigham's influence that thousands of the poor have been fed?"[60] After Young and the apostles spent the next twelve years directing the expanding settlements of the Great Basin, "Erastus Snow spoke Concerning the feelings of many of the people against seeing the Twelve prosper in Temperal things."[61]

Following discussion of this criticism in February 1859, the First Presidency and apostles restrained their financial activities. For the next five years Salt Lake County's annual assessments showed a steep decline in the wealth of Brigham Young, his counselors, and the apostles. By contrast the assessed wealth of the Presiding Bishop and his counselors initially increased and then only gradually tapered off during the same period. The rank-and-file expected the Presiding Bishopric to have extensive financial activity.[62] In fact the pendulum had swung so far that in December 1865 Apostle John Taylor "Prophesyed that the Twelve should be delivered from the bondage of poverty under which they have been weltering for years."[63]

Although the rate of this financial decline had been equivalent for the First Presidency and apostles, the burden was far less on Brigham Young and his counselors who had massive personal wealth compared to the apostles. In 1859 Young's own property assessments were only slightly below those of the entire church for Salt Lake County. Young's totalled $100,000, while the Trustee-in-Trust's was $102,250.[64] In 1860 first counselor Heber C. Kimball "observed that Mormonism had made him all that he was: he was worth $20,000 now; and if he had remained in the States he would have been a poor man to this day."[65] Brigham Young estimated his personal wealth at about $600,000 in a legal deposition of 1875. That was three years after he paid $100,000 in "the tithing of his own personal means."[66] By contrast, during Young's presidency the Twelve's average assessed wealth reached a high of $6,672 in 1874, and several apostles individually had only $500 to $2,000 in assessed wealth annually from 1860 to Young's death in August 1877.[67]

At the October 1877 general conference, the hierarchy announced a policy of "reasonable recompense for their services" to the Quorum of the Twelve Apostles and to the First Presidency, when organized. In John Taylor's view, this was actually a way of stopping the previous abuses in the personal use of tithing funds. "Some of my brethren, as I have learned since the death of President Brigham Young, did have feelings concerning his course," Apostle George Q. Cannon wrote. "It is felt that the funds of the Church have been used with a freedom not warranted by the authority which he held."[68] Of general authorities still living, Joseph F. Smith wrote in December 1877: "One man, for instance, who has drawn $16,000 per year from the tithing office for his support, has been cut down to 2,000 per year. Thus some of the leaks are plugged up and we hope to be able by and by to build the temple."[69] Smith was apparently referring to Brigham's son John W. Young, who served as his father's counselor for thirteen years (first secretly and later with public acknowledgement).

However, Taylor's "reasonable recompense" of 1877 did not cover the needs of the apostles. At an apostles meeting on 3 May 1880, "The question of over running salaries was brought up. Several of the brethren had overdrawn their allowance . . ." They voted to forgive the overdrafts and to increase their annual allowance. In addition, the apostles decided to give an allowance to the Presiding Patriarch in addition to his per-blessing fee.[70]

In September 1887 this became fixed allotments, which one apostle opposed with the comment: "it was repugnant to the people to have the 12 [apostles] draw a salary."[71] In April 1888 the First Council of Seventy also began receiving financial allowances, to which one council member replied: "I would prefer to receive no salary." A "permanent" allowance to members of the First Council of Seventy was not established for another decade.[72]

Nevertheless, LDS presidents themselves expressed discomfort about using their allowances. When the First Presidency and Twelve discussed the salary system again in 1896, President Wilford Woodruff said that he had not drawn money from the church until after 1877. Apostle Lorenzo Snow, Woodruff's presidential successor, said that despite the allowance system, he had not drawn from church funds for forty years.[73] This resistance to making personal use of church funds reached its climax in President Heber J. Grant, who rode public street cars rather than use tithing funds to have an automobile and chauffeur for the First Presidency.[74]

Despite discomfort over receiving tithing funds for living allowances, a salary system for LDS general authorities continued without significant interruption from 1882 on. As indicated by Joseph F. Smith's 1877 letter and by Wilford Woodruff's diary, the apostles received $2,000 to $2,500 annually during the first five years of the salary system. Then significant financial stratification occurred, with the senior apostle receiving $5,000 annually, apostles of middle seniority $3,000, and junior apostles $2,000. In September 1887 the apostles adopted a uniform compensation, with each receiving $3,000. Although there was not yet a fixed allowance for the First Council of Seventy, in 1888 the Presiding Patriarch's "annuity" increased from $1,000 to $1,250.[75]

By the turn of the twentieth century, the hierarchy's allowances were stratified by ecclesiastical position and seniority. In 1890 the monthly allowances of the Quorum of the Twelve and Presiding Bishop were identical, with the counselors in the First Presidency receiving $50 more a month and the church president receiving another $100 monthly. By 1907 the monthly allowances were stratified into a six-tiered system: (1) the lowest allowance for junior members of the Seventy, (2) the next higher allowance to mid-level members of the Seventy and the Presiding Patriarch, followed by (3) the eight junior members of the Twelve, (4) the Presiding Bishopric, two senior members of the Seventy, and four senior members of the Twelve, (5) the counselors in the Presidency, and (6) the president of the church. In those 1907 allowances, $100 monthly separated the top two tiers, and only $50 monthly separated each of the lower tiers. By 1932 there were only four strata in the monthly allowance system: (1) the lowest allowance was for counselors to the Presiding Bishop and for the entire Seventy, (2) an extra $50 monthly allotment for the Presiding Bishop, the Presiding Patriarch, and all members of the Twelve, (3) an additional increase of $100 monthly for counselors in the First Presidency, (4) and a $150 monthly bonus for the church president.[76] David O. McKay's presidency (1951-70) adopted uniform allowances for all general authorities, regardless of quorum or seniority.[77]

There were also miscellaneous fees which the general authorities collected for ecclesiastical services. Brigham Young charged men "ten dollars for each divorce" or cancellation of sealing, which policy continued until the end of the century.[78] In addition, until 1899 the general authorities charged a fee for setting apart all departing missionaries.[79]

Periodically the Mormon hierarchy has made a significant increase in monthly allowances to general authorities. In 1950, for example, there was a 30-percent increase.[80] Nevertheless, in view of the financial empire administered by the LDS general authorities, their compensation from church funds has always been paltry compared to the salaries and perks of corporate America. In 1949 First Presidency counselor J. Reuben Clark wrote that "the General Authorities of the Church get precious little from the tithing of the Church. They are not paid as much as a first-class, stenographic secretary of some of the men who run industry."[81] That disparity was probably the reason for the next year's increase in allowances to the general authorities.

For example, as a newly appointed Assistant to the Twelve in 1941, Marion G. Romney found that his church "allowance amounted to less than half of what he was earning from his law practice when he was called as a General Authority."[82] Appointed an apostle that same year, Harold B. Lee found that his financial allowance was less than the salary of some staff members at LDS headquarters.[83] As was true in the nineteenth-century hierarchy, a significant drop in income and personal wealth occurred when a man accepted the calling of LDS general authority.[84]

Although not a formal salary, general authorities can also receive significant income from the books they publish. When he published *The Way To Perfection* in 1931, Joseph Fielding Smith specified that all its future royalties would go to the LDS Genealogical Society. However, he was not as generous with the royalties from his dozens of other books. For example, when President Smith died in July 1972, his royalties from Deseret Book Company totaled $9,636 for the previous six-month period.[85] Presiding Bishop (and later apostle) LeGrand Richards set a remarkable example by accepting no royalties for his *Marvelous Work and a Wonder* which had sold 2 million copies by the time of his death in 1983. However, a president of the LDS church's publishing company has observed that very few general authorities have declined royalties for their books.[86] Mormons purchase books written by general authorities primarily because of the church office the author holds, rather than for the book's content. Although many general authorities do not write books, such royalty income is a direct consequence of being an LDS leader.

Speaking of LDS church-owned businesses and stock-portfolio in 1985, First Presidency counselor Gordon B. Hinckley said that "the living allowances given the General Authorities, which are very modest in comparison with executive compensation in industry and the professions, come from this business income and not from the tithing of the people."[87] However, tithing was the source of these "living allowances" from the 1830s until the church's corporate success in recent years.

Moreover, President Hinckley's description of the hierarchy's income as "very modest" depends upon one's own concept of wealth. For example, when Joseph Fielding Smith died at age ninety-five in 1972, he had worked nearly all his adult life at LDS headquarters, first as a paid employee in the Historian's Office and then as a general authority with a church living allowance. At his death, President Smith had $245,000 in bank deposits, $120,000 in cash, $120,574 in stocks/bonds, and $10,688 in uncashed checks (including Deseret Book royalties of $9,636). Even twenty-five years after his death, few rank-and-file Mormons have such "modest" amounts of cash and liquid assets available to them in old age.[88]

The LDS ministry is still a volunteer, lay ministry. In the twentieth century, church offices have become unpaid to a degree they never were in the nineteenth century. Of more than 160,000 ecclesiastical leaders at the beginning of 1996, fewer than 500 were authorized a living allowance from church funds.[89] Many of these LDS officials decline to use their authorized allowances.

However, on occasion church presidents have personally benefitted from church finances by simply cancelling their indebtedness to church funds. On 23 April 1834 a revelation ended the Kirtland United Order and distributed its real estate assets among Joseph Smith, Oliver Cowdery, Sidney Rigdon, Frederick G. Williams, Martin Harris, Newel K. Whitney, and John Johnson. The revelation said, "it is my will that you shall pay all your debts" (D&C 104:78). However, Joseph Smith privately required Whitney to balance "in full without any value recd." the $1,151.31 Whitney had loaned to the prophet, as well as $2,484.22 of the other men's debts to Whitney. Bishop Whitney had to personally absorb this loss "because Joseph said it must be done."[90]

The next two church presidents did likewise. Three weeks before he died in August 1877, Brigham Young obtained a cancellation of his debts in Ogden, Utah, extending back to 1849.[91] Despite the previously stated objections of his own counselor, John Taylor also persuaded the Quorum of Twelve Apostles in 1880 to allow him a $10,000 claim for sugar machinery, which claim Brigham Young had refused since 1853.[92]

By contrast, Wilford Woodruff, Lorenzo Snow, and Joseph F. Smith did not use their office as church president to cancel their personal indebtedness, yet they allowed tithing funds to serve as a loan pool for prominent Mormons. In a sharply worded report in 1911, the church auditors noted: "If certain members of the Church are entitled to borrow money for private ends, is this not a right of all members, for the same purpose? If this policy is admitted, would it not result in confusion, jealousy, loss and consequent wrong?" The committee observed that "the debtors frequently look upon their obligations as being due to a rich and indulgent relative, to be paid (if at all) at their own convenience." Among the debtors was Apostle Heber J. Grant for a "cash loan of $34,000." In 1913 the committee renewed the subject of church loans to individuals, and commented that "it is not within the purview of the Trustee-in-Trust to make advances of this kind . . . And any loans made on plain notes are legally uncollectible."[93]

It is important to recognize that general authorities borrowed from the church's general fund because their living allowances were insufficient to meet their needs. In 1910 Apostle Anthony W. Ivins recorded that the following members of the Twelve were in debt: Francis M. Lyman, George Albert Smith, Heber J. Grant, Rudger Clawson, Hyrum M. Smith, George F. Richards, and David O. McKay.[94] Grant was the most candid about his apostolic indebtedness: "A president of the stake begged and pleaded with me to quit paying tithing. He said I did not owe any tithing until I got out of debt. Would not that have been a fine record for a man who now stands as president of the Church, not to have paid tithing for thirty-two years?"[95]

Many general authorities repaid their debts after long years of effort, while others died in debt. On the other hand, some chose to declare legal bankruptcy. In 1842 Joseph Smith, his counselor Sidney Rigdon, Presiding Patriarch Hyrum Smith, and Presiding bishop-designate Vinson Knight sought relief from their indebtedness by filing for bankruptcy.[96] Seventy's president J. Golden Kimball was the next current general authority who filed for bankruptcy. In 1899 he had $11,126 in debts but only $2,031 in assets.[97] By 1902 the First Presidency was unwilling for a member of the Presidency or Twelve to declare public bankruptcy, and Apostle Reed Smoot quietly persuaded the creditors of John W. Taylor to settle the apostle's $140,000 debts at ten cents on the dollar.[98]

On 27 December 1919 recently sustained Heber J. Grant obtained the approval of his counselors to accept $30,000 worth of his stock (at par) in the Utah-Implement Vehicle Company to cancel loans he received as an apostle from the Trustee-in-Trust.[99] However, accepting stock to cancel personal loans caused enormous losses to the church during Grant's administration. In 1930 first counselor Anthony W. Ivins computed that the church lost $900,000 in personal loans to Presiding Bishop Charles W. Nibley. Upon his appointment as second counselor in the First Presidency in 1925, Nibley had used stocks and bonds to repay his indebtedness to the church.[100]

Public Disclosure

As early as January 1832, Missouri's regional bishop Edward Partridge gave a public accounting of church finances to a church conference. The meeting voted that each general conference receive "a regular account of moneys and properties received and expended for the use and benefit of this church." This continued until the Mormons were expelled from

Missouri in 1838, but apparently not during the remaining six years of Joseph Smith's life.[101]

Brigham Young gave financial reports periodically, rather than annually. For example, at October 1860 general conference, he observed: "By the cash manifest just read by brother John T. Caine, you perceive there has been expended, during the years 1857, 1858, 1859, and to October 4, 1860, $70,204 in excess of what has been received in money and Tithing." Then Young added with typical candor, "It has been rather difficult to raise the large amount of cash we have expended over the amount received on money-Tithing . . ."[102] Deficit spending was common in nineteenth-century Mormonism.

Following Brigham Young's death, John Taylor proposed in 1878 to make the financial report an annual event. "He expected to present before the people at least once a year, an account of what was done with their means."[103] However, as the U.S. government increased its anti-polygamy campaign against the LDS church, President Taylor stopped the annual financial report in April 1884 because "it is none of the business of outsiders to know about our financial matters."[104]

In 1899 the First Presidency and Twelve discussed resuming the public report of church income and expenditures. "President Young and President Taylor had both made it a practice to keep the people pretty well informed as to the general condition of the Church," senior apostle Franklin D. Richards observed. He thought such a public accounting should be "presented before the General Conference, thereby correcting false reports and bringing the people to share in the responsibility of the Church's business."[105]

Regular reports of general church finances did not begin until the 1900s, and they were as unrevealing as current financial reports. For example, the April 1907 general conference learned the following information from the General Church Auditing Committee's report to the First Presidency: "We have carefully examined the accounts of the Trustee-in-Trust, Presiding Bishopric, the Deseret News, the Latter-day Saints' hospital and other business concerns in which the Church is interested, for the year 1906. We find that the accounting in the various departments is properly done; every dollar received has been correctly entered and disbursements under your direction have been economically and wisely made for the exclusive benefit of the various interests of the Church. And we heartily endorse your judicious and conservative administration." The currently non-informative financial report reveals no less about church income and expenditures than was true of the bland reports of April general conference in the early 1900s.[106]

Detailed public reporting of church income and expenditures was of briefer duration than sometimes assumed today. Until April 1915, LDS church presidents made only occasional references to the dollar amounts of church income or revenues. In that year, however, the church released its first report to "show how the tithing of the Church for the year 1914 has been disbursed."[107] For the next forty-four years, those annual reports continued to show total dollars expended in selected categories.

Church Businesses

Almost from the beginning, the business of the LDS church has been business. Established in March 1832, the same month Joseph Smith organized the First Presidency, the church's "United Firm" included merchandizing, real estate, and publishing.[108] In 1841 Joseph Smith printed a revelation to establish a church hotel (D&C 124:59). In 1870 Brigham Young publicly announced a revelation for Mormons to invest in a railroad.[109] In 1881 John Taylor privately dictated a revelation to organize an iron company, and in 1883 another revelation to invest tithing funds in a gold mine.[110] In the 1890s the hierarchy gave certain men the religious "calling" or obligation to invest thousands of dollars each in a sugar company.[111]

During the first century of corporate Mormonism, current general authorities were partners, officers, or directors in nearly 900 businesses. Most, but not all, of these were church-owned, church-controlled, or church-invested businesses.[112] However, a hierarchy-managed business has not necessarily been church-owned, -controlled, or -invested. Also, general authorities have sometimes been absent from the board of companies owned or controlled by the LDS church. Furthermore, some directorships have been honorary and lacked significant influence on the company.

Nevertheless, during the first third of the twentieth century it was possible for Latter-day Saints in and near Salt Lake City to have a cradle-to-grave economic association with businesses managed by LDS general authorities. Many of these businesses were owned or controlled by the LDS church itself.

To demonstrate, let us suppose that when the First Presidency issued its 1907 statement a young man named Brown lived in Salt Lake City. In sketching the economic environment of this Everyman of the Mormon Culture Region at that time, each **BOLD-PRINT** enterprise was one in which general authorities currently served as officers or directors.

Shortly after the First Presidency denied seeking "absolute domination in temporal affairs," Brother Brown went on a proselytizing mission to the Eastern States, traveling there and back on the **UNION PACIFIC**

RAILROAD. Not long after his return from this mission, he bought his sweetheart an engagement ring at **DAYNES JEWELRY COMPANY.** The newlyweds spent their wedding night in the recently constructed **HOTEL UTAH.**

The Browns ate breakfast cereals from **UTAH CEREAL FOOD COMPANY,** with dairy products from **MUTUAL CREAMERY COMPANY** and sugar from either **AMALGAMATED SUGAR COMPANY** or **U AND I SUGAR COMPANY.** The **NEVADA LAND AND LIVESTOCK COMPANY** raised the beef the family ate for dinner, and Sister Brown purchased fruits and vegetables from **GROWERS MARKET.** This produce had been grown with the assistance of **INLAND FERTILIZER COMPANY,** harvested with equipment purchased from **CONSOLIDATED WAGON & MACHINE COMPANY,** on lands owned by **THE WASATCH LAND AND IMPROVEMENT ASSOCIATION,** and irrigated by the **RIVERSIDE CANAL COMPANY.** She carried groceries in sacks manufactured by **UTAH BAG COMPANY** and refrigerated perishables with ice from **ALASKA ICE AND STORAGE COMPANY.** The Browns used dishes and cutlery purchased from **ZION'S COOPERATIVE MERCANTILE INSTITUTION (ZCMI),** seasoned their food with salt from **INLAND CRYSTAL SALT COMPANY,** and ate bread made from flour of the **REXBURG MILLING AND ELEVATOR COMPANY.**

The Browns bought clothing manufactured by **SALT LAKE KNITTING WORKS** and **KNIGHT WOOLEN MILLS** and furniture from **GRANITE FURNITURE COMPANY.** For reading material, the Browns had the *DESERET NEWS* as a newspaper and bought books from **DESERET BOOK COMPANY.** Some of their books were also published by **ZION'S PRINTING & PUBLISHING COMPANY** in Missouri.

The Browns financed a new house with a mortgage loan from **HEBER J. GRANT & COMPANY.** It was built by the **UTAH CONSTRUCTION COMPANY** with materials from **UTAH LUMBER COMPANY, ENAMEL BRICK AND CONCRETE COMPANY, UNION PORTLAND CEMENT COMPANY, UTAH ONYX DEVELOPMENT COMPANY, SALT LAKE IRON AND STEEL COMPANY, UTAH LIME AND STONE COMPANY,** and **EMIGRATION CANYON ROCK COMPANY.** They insured it with **UTAH HOME FIRE INSURANCE COMPANY,** but later changed to a policy from **SOUTHWESTERN FIRE INSURANCE COMPANY.** The house was lighted by **UTAH POWER AND LIGHT,** heated first by coal from **SMOOT & SPAFFORD,** and later by gas from **U.S. FUEL COMPANY,** with phone service from **MOUNTAIN STATES TELEPHONE AND TELEGRAPH COMPANY.** Within a few years, the Browns decided that their house needed a better roof and insulation, so they turned to **LAMBERT ROOFING COMPANY** and the **INSULATION MANUFAC-**

TURING COMPANY. The Browns paid for all of these services from their checking account at **UTAH STATE NATIONAL BANK.**

For entertainment, the Brown family patronized the **ENSIGN AMUSEMENT COMPANY,** the **GIANT RACER COMPANY,** the **SALT LAKE DRAMATIC ASSOCIATION,** the **SALT LAKE THEATRE,** the **SALTAIR BEACH RESORT,** and **DESERET MUSEUM.** But often the Browns simply listened to radio station **KSL** or to phonograph records from **DAYNES-BEEBE MUSIC COMPANY.**

While using the streetcars of the **UTAH LIGHT & TRACTION COMPANY,** the Browns saved for an automobile by maintaining a savings account with **ZION'S SAVINGS BANK & TRUST.** They also made conservative investments in stocks and bonds through **KIMBALL AND RICHARDS SECURITIES.** Finally they were able to buy a Hupmobile in 1918 from **HYLAND MOTOR COMPANY,** then traded it in for a Ford in 1924 from **TAYLOR-RICHARDS MOTOR COMPANY,** then traded it in for a Nash auto in 1929 from **BALLARD-JACKSON NASH COMPANY.** For all their cars, Brother Brown purchased gasoline and oil processed at the **UTAH OIL REFINING COMPANY.**

As the Brown children grew, they attended **LDS HIGH SCHOOL** in Salt Lake City. After graduation, one daughter went to **LDS BUSINESS COLLEGE,** another daughter graduated from the **McCUNE SCHOOL OF MUSIC,** and a son went to **BRIGHAM YOUNG UNIVERSITY.** Those were church institutions, but one son received a scholarship from the **UNIVERSITY OF UTAH,** where a member of the Quorum of the Twelve served on the board of regents.

The Browns took a vacation to California in 1932 on the **WESTERN PACIFIC RAILROAD,** but soon returned because Brother Brown had contracted pneumonia. While being treated at the **LDS HOSPITAL,** he received oxygen from **WHITMORE OXYGEN COMPANY.** Despite the best efforts of his physicians, Brother Brown died and was buried in **WASATCH LAWN CEMETERY.** His widow collected his insurance policies from **BENEFICIAL LIFE INSURANCE COMPANY** and **CALIFORNIA WESTERN STATES LIFE INSURANCE COMPANY.**

However, the hierarchy's participation in this maze of corporations from the 1880s on did not please every general authority. In 1890 Apostle Brigham Young, Jr., wrote: "Bro Jno. H. Smith said our last U[nited]. O[ders]. resembled Communism to[o] much; thought present system of Corporations would unite the people better, perhaps. I could not agree with him but said nothing. There is too much time given to Corporations, stocks, bonds, politics, etc by our leaders to please me. We are in all kinds of business interests [—] even the members of the Twelve represent businesses which are jealous of each other and almost ready to fight each other."[113] In 1919 Apostle James E. Talmage wrote: "Today I was elected one of the directors of the Utah State National Bank, and this, to some degree, against my will." Two years later he wrote, "In consulting with President Heber J. Grant I was made glad by receiving his consent to my withdrawal as one of the Board of Directors of the Utah State National Bank."[114]

Apostle Talmage was willing to lose financially by withdrawing from participation in corporate Mormonism. By the twentieth century it was standard policy to give financial compensation to those serving as officers and directors of LDS firms. Such business leadership was primarily the privilege of the First Presidency, Quorum of the Twelve, and the Presiding Bishopric. Their corporate income continued the economic stratification of the hierarchy.

George Albert Smith was a good illustration of the corporate side of the hierarchy's income in the twentieth century. Appointed an apostle in 1903 without significant business experience, by 1915 he was a director of three church enterprises: Utah Savings and Trust Company, Utah Home Fire Insurance Company, and ZCMI, for which he received a total of $1,260 yearly in director's fees. His annual income that year was $5,088, of which only $1,800 came from his allowance as a general authority. The same proportion continued throughout his service as an apostle, but his income jumped more than 500 percent in the first year of his service as LDS president in 1945. This was a direct result of his advancement to corporate offices which were part of his new church position. An undated statement shows that before his death in 1951 President Smith's monthly income of $2,307 came from $650 in general authority's allowance and $1,657 in director's fees from nine LDS corporations.[115]

A decade after Smith's death, church corporations were providing some general authorities with very lucrative supplements to their church stipends. In 1963 Beneficial Life Insurance Company alone awarded $13,400 in director's fees to President David O. McKay, $6,750 to first counselor Henry D. Moyle before his death in September, $9,200 to Moyle's co-counselor Hugh B. Brown for service during the entire year, $1,700 to Moyle's replacement as counselor N. Eldon Tanner (who apparently accepted less than authorized) for his service from October to December 1963, and $6,200 to the Twelve's president Joseph Fielding Smith for a full year's service.[116]

Nevertheless, non-Mormons have almost always overlooked the reality that the LDS church has rarely had financial profit as the motive for starting even the most ambitious business. In fact, from 1933 to 1961 First Presidency counselor J. Reuben Clark continually cautioned against church enterprises making too much money. Why? Because that would be profiteering at the expense of those whom Mormon enterprises seek to benefit, the average Latter-day Saints.[117] Generally, church-owned or -controlled businesses have been a drain on its resources, often helping drive the church to the edge of bankruptcy. This happened first in 1837 during a national depression.

Various apostles (subsequently excommunicated) are traditionally blamed for the financial speculation in Kirtland which preceded the collapse.[118] However, Heber C. Kimball laid the responsibility directly on Joseph Smith. When the Quorum of Twelve returned to Kirtland from its first mission in September 1835, the prophet told the apostles, "Now, brethren, it is a good time to get property; now is the time for you to get rich." Kimball explained the consequences: "Well, it was one of the most trying times the Church ever saw. Most of the Twelve went into speculation, and half of them turned away [from the church]."[119] It is no coincidence that these times of severe Mormon financial crisis usually occurred during depressions in the national business community in 1837, in 1842-44, in 1873, in 1893, in the 1920s (in agriculture, mining, and manufacturing), and in the 1930s.[120]

While it may have worsened the church's financial panics, the weakened national economy did not create any of them. That was true in the 1830s and also in the 1890s. Official LDS histories describe the $2 million of church debts in the 1890s as a result of the federal raid which had confiscated church properties from 1887 to 1890.[121] Instead, the debts resulted from massive losses in the church's interlocked mining, sugar, real estate, banking, and investment firms.[122]

For example, despite a national economic depression, the First Presidency in 1894 used $217,000 in tithing funds to establish the Sterling Mining and Milling Company. Within four years the church lost its entire investment in this speculative mining venture.[123] In June 1899 recently sustained church president Lorenzo Snow told the apostles that "the Lord was displeased with us for borrowing or going into debt to the extent of nearly two millions of dollars for business enterprises."[124]

In 1927 first counselor Anthony W. Ivins calculated that the church had lost $526,900 in transactions involving the church's Utah State National Bank. Five years later second counselor J. Reuben Clark noted that those losses had increased to $1,374,900.[125] In 1930 first counselor Anthony W. Ivins cataloged the church's loss of "at least six million dollars" in stock and bond transactions during the previous decade.[126] A million dollars today is far less valuable in purchasing power than it was in the 1920s.

Deficit Spending and Modern Financing

The combination of bad financial investments, declines in church businesses, and the Great Depression once again pushed the LDS church into deficit spending. First counselor J. Reuben Clark announced to general conferences that the church had spending deficits amounting to $100,000 in 1937 to nearly $900,000 in 1938. In Clark's view, voluntary disclosure of regrettable deficits was a way to encourage greater austerity on the part of the leaders at headquarters and elsewhere. During the 1940s Clark allowed the church to spend only 27 percent of its annual tithing revenues. The rest went into bank savings accounts as a "reserve fund."[127]

Twenty years later the First Presidency's deficit spending caused the end of detailed financial reports regularly given to April general conferences since 1915. In the period of a few months in mid-1956, the church suffered a loss of $1 million of tithing funds invested in municipal government bonds, yet later that year the First Presidency committed two-thirds of church income to continued investment in municipal bonds.[128] The next annual financial report gave fewer details about expenditures of church funds, and the church published its last financial report in April 1959.[129]

By the end of 1959, the church spent $8 million more than its income that year. This was extraordinary in view of the fact that the church had surplus income of $7 million after 1958's expenditures.[130] To conceal the massive increase of building expenditures in the last half of 1959 which created that deficit, the church stopped releasing even abbreviated financial reports. At the close of 1961, Apostle Harold B. Lee expressed "my stubborn resistance to the principle of 'deficit spending,' supposedly justified in the hope of increasing the tithing of the Church to cover the deficit."[131] To no avail.

At the end of 1962 the church was deficit-spending $32 million annually. New York financiers had to advise against the First Presidency's proposal "to finance such spending by selling Church securities for the next fifty years."[132] The new year looked no better. By the end of February there was already a $5 million shortfall, and 1963 threatened to equal or exceed the spending deficit of 1962.[133]

Then in 1963 N. Eldon Tanner entered the First Presidency as the church was struggling to avoid the worst financial crisis of its history. By then, his biographer notes, the building program "had so drained Church reserves that at one point financial officers wondered if they would be able to meet the payroll" for church employees.[134]

Known as the church's modern financial wizard, President Tanner's legacy is an extraordinary success story which deserves separate discussion not possible here. In brief, he responded to Mormonism's financial crisis of 1963 by declaring "a moratorium" on the LDS building program and by halting investments "until a buffer reserve could be built up." Five years of deficit spending had wiped out the church's reserve fund, yet under Tanner's careful stewardship, "step by step the Church was introduced to corporate financing."[135] The task of rebuilding church finances was so daunting that not until 1966 did church administrators conclude that "the finances of the Church are now in a little better shape."[136] Once church finances were comfortably in the black again, there was no incentive to resume the detailed annual reports to general conference.

One example of that success story is the *Deseret News* purchase of a large bloc of *Los Angeles Times* stock in 1965. Four years later its valued had increased from less than $1 million to nearly $30 million.[137] Silence concealed massive church deficits for years, and later concealed massive financial successes that resulted from N. Eldon Tanner's impact on church finances.[138]

Outside observers often wonder why LDS church members do not criticize the end to public accounting of expenditures since 1959. The answer lies in the fact that since local and regional leadership of the LDS church rotates an average of every five years or less, literally millions of LDS men and women today have had experience as stewards over church funds. These Mormons have personal knowledge of the careful account-ability for these funds as overseen by superiors in the line of authority and by church auditors.[139] More important, these lay leaders in priesthood or auxiliary organizations have regarded their own financial stewardship—large or small—as a sacred obligation. Equally important, rank-and-file Mormons feel no need for public accountability for general church funds in view of the motto of the contemporary church: "When our leaders speak, the thinking has been done."[140]

The Hierarchy: From Corporate Management to the Sideline

"Breaking with tradition," in June 1975 Spencer W. Kimball withdrew as LDS president from being an officer or director of corporations in which the church had significant financial interest. The First Presidency explained: "Membership on the boards has required some time and the presidency has felt its time could be better utilized in building the kingdom." When the church president withdrew from corporate respon-sibilities, there were 3 million Mormons throughout the world.[141]

By implication such priorities applied equally well to Kimball's coun-selors, the apostles, and the Seventy. Their callings involved primarily spiritual ministry and ecclesiastical governance, in contrast to the financial domain that has defined the Presiding Bishopric since its beginning. However, not until January 1996 did the rest of the LDS hierarchy follow

Kimball's example by ending the role of all general authorities as officers or directors of any business. They had waited until church membership stood at more than 9 million.[142]

A profile of the corporate responsibility of the general authorities as of June 1984 helps to assess its impact on their time and attention "in building the kingdom" spiritually. Exactly nine years after Kimball's business withdrawal, this was about midway toward the decision of the entire hierarchy to accept the same inevitability. It was also seven months after the *Wall Street Journal*'s front-page headline: "Leaders of Mormonism Double as Overseers of a Financial Empire."[143]

From a variety of public documents,[144] this was the business world of the general authorities in 1984, beginning with the First Presidency. Despite his public withdrawal from corporate responsibilities, President *Spencer W. Kimball* (who had been physically incapacitated since 1982) remained a director of Bonneville International Corporation. His first counselor *Marion G. Romney* (also physically incapacitated for years) was still chairman of the board of Beneficial Development Co., of Beneficial Life Insurance Co., of LDS Social Services, Inc., and director of Bonneville International Corporation and of Deseret Management Co. The only functioning member of the First Presidency in 1984, second counselor *Gordon B. Hinckley* was chairman of the board of Deseret Management Corporation Foundation, and director of Bonneville International Corporation, of Deseret Management Corporation, of KIRO, Inc. of Seattle, of Utah Power and Light Co., and of Zion's First National Bank.

The Quorum of Twelve's president *Ezra Taft Benson* was a director of Beneficial Life Insurance Co. Apostle *Howard W. Hunter* was president of the Polynesian Cultural Center (Hawaii), and director of Beneficial Life Insurance Co., of Continental Western Life Insurance Co., of Deseret Federal Savings and Loan, of First Security Bank of Utah, of First Security Corp., of Heber J. Grant & Co., of PHA Life Insurance Co. (Oregon), of Watson Land Co. (Los Angeles), and of Western American Life Insurance Co. Apostle *Thomas S. Monson* was president and chairman of the board of Deseret News Publishing Co., vice-president of LDS Social Services and of Newspaper Agency Corp, and director of Beneficial Life Insurance Co., of Commercial Security Bank, of Commercial Security Bankcorporation, of Continental Western Life Insurance Co. (Iowa), of Deseret Management Corp., of IHC Hospitals, Inc., of Mountain States Telephone and Telegraph Co., of Murdock Travel, of PHA Life Insurance Co. (Oregon), of Pioneer Memorial Theater, and of Western American Life Insurance Co. Apostle *Boyd K. Packer* was chairman of the board of Utah Home Fire Insurance Co., while also director of Murdock Travel and of Zion's First National Bank. Apostle *Marvin J. Ashton* was president of Deseret Book

Co., chairman of the board of ZCMI, and director of Beneficial Development Co., of First Security Bank of Utah, of First Security Corporation, of Laie Resorts (Hawaii), and of Zion's Securities Corporation. Apostle *L. Tom Perry* was director of American Stores Co. (which operated Skaggs Drugs and Alpha Beta supermarkets), of ZCMI, of Zion's First National Bank, and of Jewel Companies, Inc. (Chicago), and trustee of LDS Social Services and of Nauvoo Restoration. Apostle *David B. Haight* was director of Bonneville International Corporation, of Deseret Management Corporation, of First Security Bank of Utah, of First Security Corporation, and of Valtek, Inc., while also a trustee of Deseret Management Corporation Foundation. Apostle *James E. Faust* was vice-president of Deseret News Publishing Co., director of Commercial Security Bank, and of Commercial Security Bank Corporation, while also a trustee of Ballet West and of LDS Social Services. Apostle *Neal A. Maxwell* was director of Mountain Fuel Resources, Inc., of Mountain Fuel Supply Co., and of Deseret News Publishing Co. Apostle *Russell M. Nelson* was director of Zion's First National Bank. Apostle *Dallin H. Oaks* was chairman of the Public Broadcasting System (national), while also director of O.C. Tanner Jewelry Co. and of Union Pacific Railroad.

Franklin D. Richards, senior president of the First Quorum of Seventy, was president of Laie Resorts, chairman of the board of Deseret Trust Co. and of Richards-Woodbury Agency, was director of Beneficial Development Co., of Deseret Management Corp., of Utah Home Fire Insurance Co., and of Zion's Securities Corp., while also trustee of Deseret Management Corporation Foundation and of Wasatch Lawn Cemetery Association. Seventy's member *J. Thomas Fyans* was trustee of LDS Social Services. *Carlos E. Asay* was director of Laie Resorts, while *M. Russell Ballard* was director of Deseret Book Co. Seventy's member *Royden G. Derrick* was chairman of the board of UI Group, Inc. (formerly U&I Sugar) and director of Utah Home Fire Insurance Co. *Paul H. Dunn* was director of Consolidated Capital Corporation. *Robert D. Hales* was president of Deseret Management Corporation and trustee of Deseret Management Corporation Foundation. *Adney Y. Komatsu* was a director of Laie Resorts. *Vaughn J. Featherstone* was director of Utah Home Fire Insurance Co. *Hugh W. Pinnock* was director of First Interstate Bank of Utah. *Ronald E. Poelman* was director of Consolidated Freightways and of Deseret Trust Co. *Robert L. Backman* was chairman of the Deseret Gymnasium.

Presiding Bishop *Victor L. Brown* was president of Deseret Title Holding Corporation, vice-president of LDS Social Services, chairman of the board of Deseret Trust Co. and of Utah Hotel Co., and director of Deseret Farms (Utah), of Deseret Farms of Texas, of Deseret Management Corporation, of Deseret News Publishing Co., of Deseret Ranches of

Florida, of O.C. Tanner Jewelry Co., of Pioneer Memorial Theater, of the Utah Symphony, and of Western Airlines. His first counselor *H. Burke Peterson* was vice-president of Beneficial Development Co., director of Zion's Securities Corp., and trustee of LDS Social Services. The Bishopric's second counselor, *J. Richard Clarke*, was chairman of the Board of Deseret Mutual Benefit Association, director of Deseret Healthcare, and trustee of LDS Social Services.

Emeritus general authority *Bernard P. Brockbank* was trustee of Wasatch Lawn Cemetery Association. *John H. Vandenberg* was trustee of Nauvoo Restoration, and emeritus *O. Leslie Stone* was director of Utah Opera Co.

That was the corporate world of the LDS hierarchy in 1984. Why would the First Presidency's two counselors (sometimes with only one or two able to function) and the twelve apostles (often with one or two incapacitated) continue to shoulder such enormous burdens of business administration while church membership tripled in the twenty years after 1975? There seemed to be three considerations—financial, personal, and administrative—which jointly operated to delay the hierarchy's surrender of corporate management. One factor may have weighed more heavily with an individual leader than another.

Those who had corporate positions did not want to give up the money. A general authority's 1992 biography stated that such management positions, even if honorary, "provided him with extra income to help augment the slender living allowance he received from the Church."[145] The unspoken inequity involved general authorities who had to support their families on "the slender living allowance," without the financial windfall of a corporate assignment. Thus the hierarchy's financial inequality continued on another basis for decades after the decision to give standardized allowances, regardless of quorum or seniority.

The other personal reason for clinging to these corporate positions was that many general authorities enjoyed the world of business management. For example, Gordon B. Hinckley's authorized biographer regards it as "a wonder that he accepted" one corporate directorship after another as an apostle in view of the fact that "he raced from one [church] assignment, appointment, committee, or board meeting to another." She the explains that Hinckley "did enjoy affiliating with businessmen of talent and influence and was eager to be tutored in the art of industry."[146] When another apostle's entry in *Who's Who in America* listed eight business corporations he was serving, this expressed status, not just activity.[147] Giving up the tokens of status is rarely easy for anyone.

There were two basic administrative factors which prolonged the hierarchy's role as business managers. As previously demonstrated (see chaps. 2 and 4), the Quorum of the Twelve, in particular, has never easily surrendered any of its privileges or functions. For example, at the formation of a new holding company for the church's income-producing properties in 1966, "There was criticism from members of the Twelve," second counselor N. Eldon Tanner commented, "because they couldn't see why the First Presidency would hand that [power] over to the Deseret Management Corporation."[148] Moreover, if the hierarchy gave up its role in the church's businesses, this would increase the power of the central bureaucracy. The First Presidency had expressed misgivings about the LDS bureaucracy since the late 1940s.[149]

At some point the crushing responsibilities for 9 million Mormons overwhelmed all other personal and administrative considerations within the hierarchy concerning the management of LDS businesses. The hierarchy resisted Spencer W. Kimball's example for twenty years, and only time will tell whether a new combination of the above factors will cause a return of at least some general authorities to business management.

Conclusion

The diverse and increasingly far-flung business world of the Mormon church has one real motivation. Viewing itself as surrounded by a hostile world, the church has used business as part of a multifaceted effort to provide security by controlling the environment in which Mormons live. Historian Marvin S. Hill has called this the Mormon flight from pluralism and "Quest for Refuge."[150]

In the nineteenth century this quest for security had five features. First, a coordinated and centrally-financed immigration to LDS headquarters which expanded to the entire Great Basin of the American West. Second, a church military force to provide physical security for Mormons and their communities. Third, control of elected political offices within this domain through bloc voting and central direction by the church hierarchy. Fourth, the creation and maintenance of Mormon economic and business structures to avoid, as much as possible, Mormon dependence on the economy of an alien world. Fifth, duplication of all the social and cultural structures of the outside world so that Mormon culture was outwardly similar to mainstream society, at the same time the internal dynamics of Mormon culture were alien to the larger society it mimicked.[151]

By necessity, much of this has changed. LDS church leaders have surrendered theocratic militarism to national sovereignties. Mormonism no longer has a central gathering place, but has redefined itself as a headquarters culture with national and international satellites of growing importance. Salt Lake City is no longer polarized between competing Mormon and non-Mormon social structures, but both camps have acquiesced to joint participation in a cultural life and social order which are infused with Mormon church influence. In the political realm, LDS general authorities no longer fill the Utah state legislature in person. Instead, the hierarchy orchestrates a political agenda through loyal Mormon proxies, as well as fellow-travellers of various religious persuasions who share specific political goals with the LDS hierarchy. Mormon lock-step partisanship and interfaith partnership also operate in every large satellite population of Mormonism throughout the United States. It will undoubtedly continue wherever international Mormons gain a population sufficient to wield political power within democratically governed regimes (see chaps. 9-10).

The Mormon hierarchy now uses its corporate influence more selectively and more influentially than ever before. It is difficult to examine the *Arizona Republic*'s two-page chart of the "Mormon Financial Empire" of the 1990s without a sense of awe.[152] Here there is no possibility of exaggeration, because these organizations are legally registered. LDS church-owned corporations in at least twenty states currently conduct everything from insurance to retail sales to broadcast to real estate.[153] That study excluded LDS church ownership of large blocs of stock in such enterprises as the *Los Angeles Times*. This analysis also did not even touch on the LDS church's non-U.S. corporations which are scattered on five continents and throughout the Pacific islands.[154]

To the eye of the unbeliever, the Mormon quest for security smacks of hegemony in the nineteenth century. On the eve of the twenty-first century, many outsiders in the United States and other countries regard the LDS church as engaged in colonialism and religious imperialism.[155] However, to the converted Mormon view, LDS finances are what the Lord has done for his people, church, and kingdom. The perspectives are irreconcilable.

CHAPTER 7

Post-1844 Theocracy and a Culture of Violence

Joseph Smith's theocracy received primarily local attention in Missouri and Illinois. The government Brigham Young subsequently established in Utah became a national embarrassment, "Uncle Sam's Abscess," as one author put it.[1]

Young both continued and departed from the theocracy of Joseph Smith. He maintained the founding prophet's views and publicized them relentlessly for four decades. Civil office and voting patterns in the Mormon West became a public testament of Smith's ideals for political control, including the involvement of a few friendly non-Mormons. However, unlike the founder, Young managed the Mormon territory with the proverbial iron fist. As his secretary George Q. Cannon put it, the apostles thought Young "ruled with so strong and stiff a hand."[2] Likewise, he severely diminished the theocratic status of Joseph Smith's Council of Fifty.

Young's public rhetoric and private actions were also more extreme than Smith's. This was the outgrowth of three factors: anti-Mormon mob violence during the founder's own lifetime, Mormon paranoia after Smith's murder in 1844, and the establishment in 1847 of a completely separate domain in the Great Basin centered in Salt Lake City.

Brigham Young's Government

In various ways Young's theocracy departed significantly from Smith's in structure and procedure. Unlike Smith, Young never fully trusted anyone and instead kept every subordinate on a short leash. Thus Young rejected Smith's inclusion of friendly non-Mormons in the innermost councils and barely tolerated them in public office. Structurally and theologically, Young undermined the Council of Fifty's revealed number of members. By initiating numerous extra members throughout his term of leadership, Young organized a "Kingdom" which was often led by a council of sixty men.

Young learned from the succession crisis following Smith's death never to allow the structures of Mormon theocracy to diminish the church hierarchy.[3] He made a special point of emphasizing the subordination of the Council of Fifty to the Quorum of the Twelve Apostles. No one could conclude that they had power independent of the hierarchy. It was no exaggeration for one writer to assert that Young "successfully throttled the Council of Fifty."[4]

Young waited six months to reconvene the Fifty after his arrival at Nauvoo in August 1844. The *Nauvoo Expositor* demonstrated that there was disloyalty within Smith's Fifty,[5] and Young was determined to root it out. For Young there were three tests of loyalty for the Fifty: loyalty to their original theocratic oath of secrecy, loyalty to Smith, and loyalty to the new presidency of the twelve apostles. A man did not remain a member of the Fifty long if he failed to meet any one of those tests.

During the five months after Young's return to Nauvoo, several members of the Council of Fifty were under suspicion of disloyalty. In August and September this included Sidney Rigdon, Samuel James, and William Marks, who supported Rigdon's bid to set aside the apostles and become the church's sole "guardian."[6] Alexander Badlam had proposed that the Fifty choose the new president, and his loyalty to the Twelve was now under suspicion.[7]

George J. Adams, accused of treachery after the martyrdom by fellow council member Lucien Woodworth, was under suspicion for declining to perform a mission for the apostles during the summer. Adams also promoted polygamy in the eastern states contrary to Young's instructions. By December 1844 Young believed Adams was "in opposition to the Twelve." This was true because Adams wanted Joseph Smith III to assume the presidency instead of the apostles.[8]

Other members of the Fifty came under suspicion. Lorenzo D. Wasson's role in persuading Smith to surrender for arrest was compounded by his association with his aunt Emma Smith (Joseph Smith's widow). By 27 August 1844 Emma had joined "some others [who] are trying to draw off a party. They say there is no church."[9] After September Fifty members Lyman Wight and James Emmett defied Young by taking as many Mormons as they could to explore and settle the West.[10]

In Nauvoo's first election after Smith's martyrdom, Young intended to avoid the impression that the Council of Fifty governed in Mormon political realms. At a meeting in January 1845 to nominate candidates for the upcoming local civil election, he announced that no member of the Twelve would accept nomination. Pressing church needs required this exclusion. The only general authorities who remained in Nauvoo's civil office were members of the First Council of Seventy. Albert Perry Rockwood retained the offices of assessor and fire warden, and Levi W. Hancock remained a member of Nauvoo's police. They had both served in those positions since 1843.[11]

A logical alternative (and powerful symbol for Mormonism's secret elite) would have been for Young to nominate Council of Fifty members for the 1845 election. Instead they were a minority on the roster. Only city mayor Orson Spencer, aldermen Newel K. Whitney and Charles C. Rich, and city counselors George Miller, William W. Phelps, and Samuel Bent were members of the Fifty. One elected Mormon would not join that council for almost four years, another did not for twenty-two years, and three of those elected would never be invited to become members.[12] Young made his point: in the absence of the apostles, the Council of Fifty was politically prominent but not dominant.[13]

When Young reconvened the Fifty on 4 February 1845 (the day after Nauvoo's municipal election), the Clerk of the Kingdom recorded that Young "reorganized" the council. First, "President B. Young [was] appointed standing chairman as successor to President Joseph Smith by unanimous vote."[14] There is no indication that Smith's instructions or the Fifty's pre-martyrdom minutes had named who should succeed Smith or how. The only known references which Smith made to theocratic succession involved his sons, Joseph III and David.[15] Therefore the Fifty's selection of a standing chairman in February 1845 was by default. The Council of Fifty's reorganization depended on the Nauvoo congregation's sustaining vote for the entire Quorum of the Twelve in August 1844 and on Young's adoption of the title "President of the Church" by December 1844.[16]

As the next order of business, Young expelled eleven members. They included religious and theocratic dissenters Rigdon, James, Marks, Badlam (temporarily), Adams, Wasson, Wight, and Emmett.[17]

With little or no evidence of disloyalty on their part, Young also dropped the three non-Mormons. Edward Bonney was the only "Gentile" member with any hint of disloyalty. Although Bonney acted as prosecutor in Smith's trial for the *Nauvoo Expositor*'s destruction, Smith continued to trust him. Smith appointed Bonney as his personal aide-de-camp on 28 June and called him as a defense witness on 26 June.[18]

Young apparently dropped Bonney for two reasons. First, Bonney disapproved of the *Expositor* action and prosecuted the case vigorously. Second, on 24 June he prevented a non-Mormon from seeing Smith contrary to the prophet's request. This action suggested disloyalty since the visitor was selling Texas lands which could be important to the Fifty's colonization plan.[19]

Bonney became hostile after his rejection from the Fifty in February 1845. He left Nauvoo in April and returned the next month to arrest two Mormons, the Hodge brothers, for murder in Iowa. Bonney encouraged the attempted arrest of Jackson Redden in October in connection with the

trial of Redden's father and brother for murdering George Davenport at
Rock Island, Illinois, the previous July. Another of the murderers con-
fessed that "in Joseph Smith's old council chamber in Nauvoo," Redden
and Orrin Porter Rockwell (a Council of Fifty member) helped plan the
Davenport robbery and murder. By the end of 1845 Apostle Heber C.
Kimball said it would be an "answer to prair" if Bonney were dead. Instead
Bonney lived another twenty years and wrote a book which condemned
Mormonism without acknowledging his participation in its theocratic
secrets.[20] However, Bonney's overt disloyalty began after the Fifty
dropped him, not before.

On the other hand, M. G. Eaton was loyal until Smith's death and
beyond. On 7 July 1844 he and Rockwell had to be restrained from killing
dissident Robert D. Foster for alleged involvement in the murder of the
Smith brothers.[21] When the Illinois governor enforced a New York
warrant for Eaton's arrest on counterfeiting charges in September, Eaton
apparently fled Illinois.[22] Eaton was absent from Nauvoo indefinitely and
was a criminal liability, so Young replaced him at the first opportunity.
There is no evidence that disloyalty preceded the rejection of this gentile.

The expulsion of Uriah Brown from the Fifty in February 1845 showed
that Young simply did not trust non-Mormons to be part of the secret
workings of his "reorganized" theocracy. Brown was not disloyal to the
Council of Fifty or to Mormonism. This is evident in his letter to Young
nine months after he was dropped and by the fact that other members of
the Fifty proposed readmitting him several years later. He lived more than
a day's travel from Nauvoo, but that was no reason for his expulsion.[23]
Benjamin F. Johnson lived almost an equal distance from Nauvoo, but this
nonresident retained his membership.

In other words neither Brown nor any other non-Mormon was welcome in Young's Council of Fifty. By his definition, gentiles could not be
loyal to the Twelve, so Young refused them access to his secrets. The inner
structure of Mormon theocracy ceased to have even a token appearance
of interfaith inclusiveness after Smith's death. In practical terms expelling
non-Mormons from the Fifty may have been a wise defensive measure for
the embattled Quorum of Twelve at Nauvoo, but this was a fundamental
departure from Smith's theology of a nonsectarian Kingdom of God.[24]

Young did retain in his 1845 Council of Fifty a few longtime Mormons
about whom there were suspicions of disloyalty. Most prominent among
them was Reynolds Cahoon, who had accused Smith of cowardice when
he tried to leave Nauvoo. At the end of October 1844, William Clayton
wrote that ten members of the Fifty expressed "considerable fears" that
Cahoon "is not true to us." They also felt that they had "good evidence"
that William W. Phelps and Almon W. Babbitt were "conspiring with the

mob to overthrow us."[25] Throughout the rest of 1844 Nauvoo was filled with suspicions of treachery, yet Young decided to trust Cahoon, Phelps, and Babbitt. Significantly, the official *History of the Church* would lead readers to believe that these three suspected traitors were "highly trusted after the martyrdom," in the words of one historian who has used that retroactively edited publication to deny post-martyrdom suspicions about Council of Fifty member Jonathan Dunham.[26] In their favor, Cahoon, Phelps, and Babbitt were members of Smith's secret Anointed Quorum[27] and had openly expressed support for the twelve apostles as the church's new presidency.

Young's decision not to drop Apostle William Smith from the Fifty in February 1845 was based on necessity, not merit. William's family relationship to Joseph Smith was all that had prevented Young from excommunicating the adulterous apostle for three years.[28] By December 1844 William was equally implicated with George J. Adams for being "in opposition to the Twelve."[29] However, in February 1845 Young could not risk further alienation of Mormons by dropping from the Council of Fifty the only surviving Smith brother. William had been in the eastern states on a mission since May 1844, and any discipline against him *in absentia* would give credence to Rigdonite charges that Young and his fellow apostles were tyrannical.[30]

On 1 March 1845 Young began introducing replacements into the Fifty. There were fourteen vacancies from Smith's Fifty: three deceased and eleven dropped. In addition, the February meeting noted that fifteen of the approved members were absent from Nauvoo. Instead of filling the fourteen actual vacancies, Young initiated nineteen new members before William Smith's return in May. Among these new initiates were three of the eight Mormons elected to municipal government the previous month, who were not yet affiliated with the Fifty.[31] From now on Young's council hovered around sixty members. Bishop George Miller, who ranked thirteenth in Smith's council, later complained: "This council, originally consisting of fifty three members, and some twenty of them gone on missions, and by death and other means absent, was now swelled to a great crowd under Brigham's reign."[32]

Because of the turmoil of the *Expositor* incident, the martyrdom, and the succession crisis since June 1844, the Council of Fifty as a body and its members individually had not completed their original assignments. These included the U.S. presidential campaign, exploration of the West, negotiations with foreign countries, and the establishment of colonies in Texas, Oregon, and California. One of the significant interpreters of the Fifty concludes that from the perspective of January 1845 "all of the special projects of the pre-martyrdom Council of Fifty had failed."[33]

That judgment is probably too harsh because it implies negligence or incompetence by the Fifty. Instead the death of its standing chairman necessarily ended the council's presidential campaign. Smith's death was no more evidence of failure than Robert F. Kennedy's assassination more than a century later meant that his bid failed as well. Death tragically ended both campaigns.[34] Smith's death also required a several-months' suspension of his other plans. By 1845 those who saw failure in this had been removed by death or expulsion from the Fifty.

Young was not going to suspend forever Smith's theocratic vision. On the day he began appointing new members, the Council of Fifty voted "to [ful]fill Josephs measures originally adopted in this Council by going West to *seek out a location* and a home where the Saints can dwell in peace and health and where they can erect the ensign and *standard of liberty for the nations,* and *live by the laws of God without being oppressed and mobbed under a tyrannical government,* without *protection from the laws*."[35]

This 1 March 1845 resolution contained the essentials of Smith's theology of government, which extended back to the 1833 revelation.[36] In the biblical tradition of "the last shall be first," the ultimate goal was "protection from the laws" of civil government. This was the context of the revelation (D&C 98:4-6) and of Smith's specific words to the preliminary meeting of his "special council" on 10 March 1844.[37] The prophet wanted the practical ability to ignore or repudiate secular laws that were obstacles to the Mormon kingdom.

By 1845 it was obvious that Mormons could not have "protection from the laws" if church headquarters remained in Nauvoo or anywhere under the rule of a secular, "tyrannical government." Thus seeking "a location" became the immediate goal of the Council of Fifty. Once established in a region allowing functional autonomy, Mormons could "live by the laws of God" in the Old Testament sense. Then the latter-day Kingdom of God could advertise itself as the interfaith "standard of liberty for the nations."

To get from Nauvoo to this as-yet-undecided location in the West required passage of several obstacles. First, Mormons would need to survive the murderous intent of antagonists surrounding Nauvoo and smaller settlements.[38] Second, they would be required to leave the United States and cross unsettled U.S. territory as an armed body of thousands on route to foreign lands.[39] Third, they would traverse an area inhabited by various tribes of Native Americans. Smith's martyrdom narrowed the odds of safe passage on route to a new gathering place.

In response to such danger and complications, Young appointed men with militant backgrounds to the Council of Fifty. At least seven of Young's twenty appointees in 1845 were former Danites (35 percent), and several of these were currently members of Nauvoo's police.[40]

After its initial reorganization at Nauvoo, Young convened the Council of Fifty frequently for two months. After its 4 February meeting, it did not meet again until 1 March, when Young initiated the first of the council's new members. The council met five more times in March, on the 4th, 11th, 18th, 22nd, and 25th; five times in April, on the 11th, 15th, 18th, 22nd, and 29th; twice in May, on the 6th and 10th; and did not reconvene again until four months later.[41]

In the meetings of 1 and 4 March, the Fifty discussed a proposed exploring party, known as the "Oregon Mission" whose main purpose was "to unite the Lamanites [Native Americans] and find a home for the saints." On 11 March the council prepared to defend against mob action, to complete the Nauvoo temple and Nauvoo House, and to write the Illinois governor about the prospects for the future. The 18 March meeting focused on the "western mission." On 22 and 25 March the Fifty discussed completion of the Nauvoo House, "organization of the City," and work on church history. In the 11 April meeting, they decided to move the printing office to the Masonic Hall, to increase the print shop, and to "do their utmost to sustain it." The 6 May meeting was preoccupied with countering threats by enemies and judicial officers. The 10 May meeting was indefinitely adjourned because of council member David D. Yearsley "of whom there is strong suspicions of treachery."[42]

During this intense activity from February to May, church authorities were making independent decisions on the same matters being discussed by the Fifty. For example, the theocratic council decided on 11 March to continue work on the Nauvoo House and the temple. Four days later, however, a church council comprised of the apostles, First Council of Seventy, temple committee, and church trustees (bishops Whitney and Miller) reversed that decision and decided to direct all building efforts on the Nauvoo temple alone. The next meeting of the Fifty on 22 March discussed the Nauvoo House again and plans for its construction under Council of Fifty direction were resumed temporarily.[43]

Suspicion of "treachery" by a council member does not adequately explain why Young did not convene the rest of the Fifty from early May until early September. Nor, as one author maintains, is the absence of some of the Fifty on an "exploring party" sufficient reason.[44] More significantly, Young was in hiding to avoid arrest from 13 to 24 May and again on 23 June.[45] After that he declined to summon the Fifty on matters even more central to its concerns.

Of special significance, on 2 and 4 August errant Fifty member James Emmett was interrogated by the apostles instead of by a convened meeting of the Fifty.[46] When formally discussing Emmett's rebellion five months earlier on 27 February, Young had likewise convened only a church hearing, even though there were sufficient members of the Fifty in Nauvoo two days later.[47] Another church tribunal—not the Fifty—sent Emmett to his emigrant company in August with instructions from "the authorities of the church."[48]

When the Fifty reconvened, the move west was at the top of the agenda. On 9 September they voted to send "a company of Saints to the West next spring" and to appoint a committee of five to begin preparations. The published *History of the Church* claims that this meeting specified the "Great Salt Lake valley" as the destination, but that is a retroactive addition. The Clerk of the Kingdom indicated the location as simply "the West." Apostle John Taylor wrote that this meeting of the Fifty discussed "California," and four days later Young referred to settling "on the California coast."[49]

By 30 September three of the five assigned members (none of whom were general authorities) had recruited nearly "one hundred families each" for the westward exodus. A fourth man "has got his company about full." Young appointed another five members of the Fifty (also non-general authorities) to begin their recruitment for the anticipated spring move.[50] The published *History of the Church* obscured the importance of the Fifty in these preparations, with this statement: "It was decided that all the council (i.e. of the Twelve) [sic] were to go west with their families, friends and neighbors."[51]

Still the significance of the Fifty in preparing for the western move can be legitimately downplayed. Young himself sometimes ignored the Council of Fifty as a whole, and even specifically excluded members of the Fifty from deliberations about the move West. The most significant example of this at Nauvoo occurred on 11 December 1845. The Fifty had not formally convened for more than two months. As twenty-three members of the council and their wives were in the Nauvoo temple for various temple ordinances that evening, Young received an urgent letter which warned that the U.S. government opposed the westward exodus of Mormons. Of the members of the Fifty present, Young asked only the apostles, the two general bishops, and his clerk to join him in his private room to consider this message, excluding the other twelve members of the Fifty present, even though the discussion involved the principal concern of the Fifty.[52] This December incident foreshadowed Young's later pattern of excluding the Fifty from decision-making about matters clearly within its mission.

The Fifty met on 18-19 January 1846 but not again for almost eleven months. After Mormons began leaving Nauvoo in February 1846, the Fifty had little direct supervision of the pioneer exodus. Because of their scattered condition along the pioneer trail, it was rare for council members to have the required majority present to convene formally.

As a result there was no council meeting of the Fifty to discuss or approve the next most important development of 1846, the Mormon Battalion. Young sent Jesse C. Little to ask U.S. president James K. Polk to hire the Mormons to build forts on the Oregon Trail. Young saw this as a way to obtain federal subsidy for the Mormon emigration. Although Polk had refused the request of the governor of Illinois in January 1846 to militarily prevent the Mormons from leaving the United States, the president was deeply suspicious of Young's motives. Little even warned the U.S. president not to "compel us to be foreigners." Polk finally authorized five hundred Mormons to volunteer for a U.S. army battalion to march along the Mexican border and engage in a war with Mexico that Polk had managed to provoke. On three different days in June, the U.S. president wrote that he allowed Mormons to form this battalion only to "prevent their becoming the enemies of the U.S."[53]

Brigham Young was appalled that Polk had turned his offer of carpenters into a requisition for a Mormon military force likely to involve wartime casualties. However, the church president was also convinced that U.S. troops would obstruct the Mormon emigration if he did not provide the men. Therefore, Young announced Polk's offer to the emigrant camp (without acknowledging that it came in response to his own prior request), promised the Mormon volunteers they would not have to shed anyone's blood in battle, and instructed the men to give their salaries to the church's general fund. This much-needed windfall exceeded $50,000. As promised, the Mormon Battalion had no military engagements and no battlefield deaths, even though disease took its toll.[54] However, as an indication of the low priority Young gave to this endeavor itself, he allowed neither apostles nor current members of the Fifty to join the Mormon Battalion. The only active general authority in this expedition was Seventy's president Levi W. Hancock who volunteered to serve as a musician.[55] Young would soon preach that President Polk (in collusion with Missouri's senator Thomas H. Benton) required the Mormons to enlist in the battalion as part of a plot for "the total destruction of every man, woman, and child" of the Mormon pioneers.[56]

During the balance of 1846-47 Young held "council" meetings on the trail with the apostles, the available members of the Fifty (who otherwise did not meet separately), and captains of the emigrant wagon train (most of whom were neither general authorities nor members of the Fifty).[57] For example, Apostle Willard Richards recorded in April 1846 that "a convention of the Council" included "of the 12—B Young[,] H. C. Kimball, P. P. Pratt, O. Pratt, & G. A. Smith. Pres[ent]. of the council of Y.T.F.I.F. [FIFTY spelled backwards] Bishop Miller, Chas Shumway, Shadrach Roundy, A. P. Rockwood Young[,] Benj F Johnson & J D Lee Young [and also] Capt

Stout[,] Hunter[,] Benson & others were present."[58] (Rockwood and Lee used the surname of their adopted, spiritual father; see chap. 5.) Scores of councils show this same pattern of apostles inviting members of the Fifty and others to make day-to-day decisions for the exodus to the Salt Lake Valley.

In these *ad hoc* council meetings in which there was neither a majority of apostles nor of the Fifty, Young sometimes invited enough emigrant leaders to imitate the required number for a theocratic council. Apostle Willard Richards wrote that one of these council meetings included "B. Young & Kimble [sic] P. P. Pratt & W. Richards[,] Bishops Whitney & Miller & 11 others of the council of (YTFIF) [FIFTY, plus] commandants of the Co*s* [companies] &c. in all 53."[59] That was the exact number of men Smith originally introduced into his Council of Fifty, and George Miller saw these *ad hoc* arrangements as lessening the Fifty's status.[60]

Not until 12 November 1846 was a minimal quorum (twenty-six members) able to convene a formal meeting of the Fifty. They promptly dropped former apostle John E. Page who had been disfellowshipped from the church in February and excommunicated by the apostles in June 1846. Otherwise "Prest Young said he had no business to lay before the council." The Fifty met again on 13 November and again on 25-27 December 1846. The council thus convened only a total of seven times during 1846.[61] It is little wonder that George Miller complained: "When we arrived at Winter Quarters the council convened, but their deliberations amounted to nothing."[62]

The Kingdom of God

In 1847, the year Young established headquarters at Salt Lake City, he and the apostles made important announcements about the "Kingdom of God." On 29 May he directed a sermon to non-Mormons in the emigrant camp. He affirmed that their rights were protected as long as they did not introduce wickedness. He promised that people of every nationality and religion ("Mahometan[,] Pagan or Jew") would find refuge among the Mormons as long as they acknowledged Jesus and his right to reign, even if they never converted to Mormonism. In this sermon Young also announced the Council of Fifty's revealed name (though without identifying it as such): "The Kingdom of God and His Laws with the Keys and Power[s] thereof, and Judgment in the Hands of His Servants, Ahman Christ."[63]

The Quorum of the Twelve Apostles published a more explicit proclamation about the kingdom's interfaith embrace in December 1847. The apostles invited Protestants, Catholics, Muslims, and pagans to partake freely of the new refuge in the Great Basin: "The kingdom which we are establishing is not of this world, but is the kingdom of the Great God."[64] They did not volunteer the fact that non-Mormons were now excluded

from theocratic governance. However, nineteenth-century Mormon congregations sang of those who were invited to embrace "Zion's standard
wide unfurled" in Utah: "Come, ye Christian sects, and Pagan,/ Pope and
Protestant and Priest;/ Worshippers of God, or Dagon,/ Come ye to fair
freedom's feast./ Come, ye sons of doubt and wonder,/ Indian, Moslem,
Greek, or Jew."[65]

Young originally intended the new refuge in the West to be foreign
territory—alien to the rule of the United States of America. In September
1845 he proclaimed that "I never intend to winter in the United States
[again]."[66] Although Mormons today prefer to emphasize the American
patriotism of their pioneer ancestors, even the official *History of the Church*
still publishes Orson Pratt's defiant farewell to the United States: "It is with
the greatest of joy that I forsake this republic; and all the saints have
abundant reasons to rejoice that they are counted worthy to be cast out as
exiles from this wicked nation."[67] The last editorial of the church's
newspaper in Nauvoo proclaimed: "All things are in preparation for a
commencement of the great move of the Saints out of the United States."[68]

Six months after Young founded Salt Lake City in July 1847, the Treaty
of Guadalupe Hidalgo ended the Mexican-American War. On 2 February
1848 the new Mormon gathering place became part of the United States
dominion. As usual Congress delayed providing governmental machinery
and legitimacy to settlers in the hinterland.[69]

In all this acquisition, transfer, settlement, and organization of lands,
the Native American Indians were an afterthought. Euro-American governments "discovered" new possessions, drew maps, founded settlements,
transferred vast domains through conquest or treaty, and "created" colonies or territories out of lands that had always belonged to native peoples.[70] Similar to European ideas of "the noble savage," Mormon theology
conferred the Hebraic status of God's chosen people ("Lamanites") upon
these first inhabitants of the lands coveted by Euro-Americans.[71] Brigham
Young sometimes achieved peaceful coexistence, and one scholar has written that Young's "philosophy toward the native inhabitants of the American West differed markedly from most western frontiersmen . . ."[72]
Nevertheless, Mormon settlement generally followed the national pattern
for native peoples who were there first: displacement, resentment, conflict,
killing of isolated settlers, retaliatory massacres by Anglo-Americans, and
subjugation.[73]

In December 1848 the Council of Fifty began gathering signatures
(eventually more than 2,000) for a yet-to-be-written petition to Congress
requesting territorial status for an area to be known as "Deseret," the *Book
of Mormon* name for honeybee, a derivative of the Egyptian word *dsrt*.[74]
The proposed boundaries included all of present-day Utah and Nevada,

half of Colorado, half of southern California, three-fourths of present-day Arizona, one-fifth of present-day Wyoming, and the western edge of present New Mexico. In sending Fifty member John M. Bernhisel with the petition to Washington, D.C., Willard Richards suggested increasing Deseret's boundary to include what is now southern Oregon and southern Idaho. In the words of one historian: "Covering the drainage system of the Great Basin from the Continental Divide to the Sierra Nevada-Cascade system and Colorado Plateau south to the Gila River, the [proposed] boundaries avoided the problems of landlocked commerce by gerrymandering itself into the superb harbor at San Diego."[75]

On 9 December "The council of YTFIF [FIFTY] again met at the House of H. C. Kimballs, & took into consideration the propriety of Petition[ing] Congress for a Territorial Government." Not content to wait for Congress, the Fifty established their own government with Young as governor and other civil officers drawn from the Fifty. On 4 March 1849 they publicly repeated these nominations as a *pro forma* prelude for Deseret's "first political election" on 12 March. This public event was merely a unanimous sustaining vote by the 674 Mormons who were able to assemble during a snow storm.[76] It was also the first example in Utah of what would become a pattern: repeating publicly what had previously been determined in private by secret council.

Despite these activities, on 1 July 1849 Council of Fifty member Almon W. Babbitt arrived in Salt Lake City and persuaded Young to abandon the territorial application and instead apply for statehood. But there was not enough time to involve the general populace (as required by Congress) in a constitutional convention and to send a ratified state document to Washington before Congress convened.

Therefore the Fifty began a series of meetings the day after Babbitt's arrival to draft a state constitution and to invent previous political activities which never actually occurred. Devised by the Fifty in July 1849, the printed *Constitution of the State of Deseret* presented fictitious minutes of a convention allegedly held on 5-10 March 1849. This nonexistent assembly met, according to the July publication, in response to a public notice of February (also invented) "for the purpose of taking into consideration the propriety of organizing a Territorial or State government." The July publication claimed that a public election of "state" officers had occurred on 7 May 1849, instead of the actual sustaining vote on 12 March. As presented in the July application, Deseret's alleged election seemed to have been spontaneously authorized by "the people" at a convention rather than by a theocratic body. All of these fictitious events and time intervals were consistent with Congressional expectations for statehood applications.[77]

In drawing up the 1849 *Constitution,* Young followed a precedent of retroactively adding crucial events to previously written revelations and historical documents.[78] What was customary in Mormon self-definition of scripture, history, and theocratic ethics, however, had not previously been applied to fabricating government documents and fictitious events. In 1849 Young and the Fifty committed a fraud on Congress.[79] Still this constitution was notable for giving "an explicit guarantee of religious freedom in its bill of rights."[80]

Though unaware of this deception, Congress declined the application and instead formed the "Territory of Utah" as part of the Compromise of 1850, the "Organic Act."[81] For his part Young maintained claim to an independent country, the sovereign state of Deseret, from March 1849 to 28 March 1851. Then Deseret's General Assembly voted to dissolve and accept U.S. territorial status. Until 1896 Utah remained a territory within the United States.[82] It would take Congress eleven years to annul the legalization of polygamy that the Mormons had discreetly included within the incorporation act of 4 February 1851 which gave the Church of Jesus Christ of Latter-day Saints the legal right "to solemnize marriage compatible with the revelations of Jesus Christ."[83]

In view of such developments, it is not surprising that the period from late 1848 to mid-1850 was the heyday of the Council of Fifty. In fact, the Fifty met in Salt Lake City at least once a month from December 1848 through March 1850, with its highest activity of six meetings in July 1849.[84]

After the 6 December 1848 meeting (the first since January 1847), John D. Lee wrote that the Council of Fifty "is the Municipal department of the Kingdom of God set up on the Earth, and from which all Law emanates, for the rule, government & controle of all Nations Kingdoms & toungs and People under the whole Heavens." Lee quickly echoed the qualifications his adopted father Brigham Young had appended to such expansive evocations: the Council of Fifty was "not to controle the Priesthood but to council, deliberate & plan for the general good & upbuilding of the Kingdom of God on the Earth."[85]

In 1848-49 the Fifty often referred to their organization as the "Legislative Council."[86] They dropped that name once Utah became a U.S. territory in 1850 since the "Legislative Council" was the upper chamber of the territorial legislature, according to congressional act.[87]

In one of the Council of Fifty's meetings during this period of expansive theocratic ambition between 6 December 1848 and 9 February 1849, the Fifty ordained Young as its king. In his next meeting with the Twelve on 12 February 1849, Young referred to himself as "King & Prest."[88] After predicting several years later that "brother Young will become President of the United States," his counselor Heber C. Kimball alluded to Young's theocratic kingship: "And I tell you he will be some-thing more; but we do not now want to give him the name: but he is called and *ordained* to a far greater station than that."[89]

It is thus no longer tenable to dismiss as mere invective or apostate misunderstanding the proclamation of former apostle William Smith in 1850: "The people of Salt Lake govern their church by a secret lodge of 50 men. It is in this lodge that Young is crowned a King, and is there seated upon a throne prepared for him."[90] The "throne" was a polemic invention, but not the kingly reference. In April 1844 Joseph Smith had been anointed and ordained "Prophet, Priest, and King" by the Council of Fifty, and Young's successor John Taylor would later be anointed and ordained by Council of Fifty members as "King, Priest and Ruler over Israel on the Earth."[91] By the time Young ordained new apostles into the Quorum of Twelve on 12 February 1849, he held this theocratic kingship.

While Young's council was operating at its zenith in Salt Lake City in 1849, other members of the Fifty at Winter Quarters expressed frustration at their subordination. These dissident members of the Fifty had followed Young and the apostles through the succession crisis of 1844 and the first stage of the Mormon exodus west. George Miller had already left there in a fury because the Fifty's meetings "amounted to nothing" under Young's rule. As a result Young also replaced Miller as bishop. By June 1849 Miller had begun publishing wistful letters about Smith's "council of 50."[92] Alpheus Cutler was likewise on the verge of forming his own theocratic commonwealth in Iowa to protest what he saw as Young's abandonment of the Fifty's original mission.[93]

In February 1849 Fifty member Peter Haws best expressed the view of these men about the way in which Young had elevated the Twelve and subordinated the Fifty. "Brigham had pledged himself to carry out the measures of Joseph . . . [but] it had not been done," Haws protested, and added: "Twelve men had swallowed up thirty eight." Apostle George A. Smith retorted in a way which only confirmed the criticism: "Elder G. A. Smith interrupted him by telling him that the fifty was nothing but a debating School."[94] That was the perspective of the apostles after 1844, but such a dismissal of the Fifty's significance seemed far from Joseph Smith's teachings.

Young demonstrated further disregard for the Fifty in 1851 through a restructuring of its functions. The council had not met since June 1850, then met seven times in August-October 1851, but ignored Utah's political affairs. "Quorum of 50" meetings were preoccupied with resolving dis-putes involving members. The Fifty's meeting of 13 September barely touched on the "bitter feeling" between Mormons and federally-appointed non-Mormon officials.[95] More than a century later a Brigham Young

University professor of church history referred to these federal officials as "foreign appointees."[96]

The lack of focus on political events was striking, since the antagonism became so intense that several of the federal officials had abandoned their Utah territorial posts and returned to Washington, D.C. Their scathing reports charged Mormons with attempting to establish a theocracy (which was real enough) and criticized LDS sermons against federal authority (which also occurred and could possibly be regarded as seditious). However, these "run-away" federal officers exaggerated, if not fabricated, claims that Young and other Mormon leaders committed treason against federal authority.[97]

If that conflict in Utah's civil government was an agenda item for the next scheduled meeting of the Fifty on 4 October 1851, the matter provoked little interest. Only nine of the Fifty showed up for the morning meeting which was adjourned to the afternoon in the hope of obtaining the necessary quorum of one-half of the council's membership. "Again met—roll called—not a quorum," the minutes read and ended: "on motion adjourned to the call of the President." Young showed as little interest in another meeting as its members had shown. He did not reconvene the Council of Fifty for more than fifteen years.[98]

Not until January 1854 did Mormons attempt to legally prevent Utah's federally appointed judges from applying the common law in their decisions. Appeals to common law could conceivably convict Mormons for polygamous marriage, even though neither bigamy nor polygamy was prohibited by federal statute. At the request of Governor Young, the Utah legislature decreed that "no laws nor parts of laws shall be read, argued, cited, or adopted in any court . . . except those enacted by the Governor and Legislative Assembly" of Utah.[99] As one legal analyst has written, "[S]entiment existed at the highest levels of the early LDS church for the supplanting of English common law with another jurisprudence they called mountain common law."[100]

During the Council of Fifty's fifteen-year vacation, Brigham Young decided in July 1855 to tell a congregation about the interfaith nature of this "actually organized" Kingdom of God: "A man may be a legislator in that body which will issue laws to sustain the inhabitants of the earth in their individual rights, and still not belong to the Church of Jesus Christ at all." Young did not volunteer the fact that he had removed all non-Mormons from this theocratic body ten years earlier or that he had recessed it indefinitely.[101]

The so-called "Utah War" provided the most striking example of Young's disinclination to convene the Council of Fifty or invite its input. Convinced that Young was leading an insurrection against the national government, the U.S. president secretly replaced him as governor and sent troops to forcibly suppress the alleged rebellion. Young learned of this "invasion" in July 1857.[102] The next month he spoke of establishing Utah as "an independent kingdom" and promised to secede from the Union if Congress revoked Utah's territorial status.[103]

In crucial "council" meetings during the Utah War, Young excluded most members of the Fifty. In the council meeting which proclaimed martial law on 14 September 1857, Young and the apostles invited only three other current members of the Council of Fifty (Elias Smith, George D. Grant, and Albert Carrington) and excluded twenty-six members who lived nearby. This was all the more striking since Young invited eight non-members of the Fifty.[104]

In a March 1858 "council of War," Young included only two non-hierarchy members of the Fifty (Albert Carrington and John S. Fullmer). Twenty-one men outside the Fifty were in attendance.[105]

A Culture of Violence

The descent of federal troops on Utah intensified a violent strain in Mormon culture. Although the founding prophet and early Mormons had sometimes endured anti-Mormon persecution without violent response, there were increasing attacks on anti-Mormons and church dissenters in the years following Joseph Smith's martyrdom.[106]

The culture of violence that reached its apex in pioneer Utah was rooted in fifteen years of suffering caused by anti-Mormons. The social and political causes of this religious persecution were irrelevant to the fact that anti-Mormons (often aided by civil officers and LDS apostates) forced the evacuation of Mormon communities of New York in 1830; Jackson County, Missouri in 1833; Clay County, Missouri, in 1836; northern Ohio in 1837-38; all of Missouri in 1839; and Hancock County, Illinois, in 1846. Some families had been forced to abandon their homes six times before reaching a secure haven in Utah. Mormons counted their martyrs as the murdered missionary Joseph B. Brackenbury in 1832, Joseph Smith's infant son during a mob attack in 1832, Andrew Barber at the "Battle of Blue River" in Missouri in 1833, Apostle David W. Patten at the "Battle of Crooked River" in Missouri in 1838, the murdered and mutilated men and boys at Haun's Mill, Missouri, in 1838, the Smith brothers at Carthage Jail in 1844, Edmund Durfee in front of his home at Morley's settlement in Illinois in 1845, Apostle Parley P. Pratt in Arkansas in 1857, and every other Mormon who suffered and died during these expulsions.[107] Mormons buried thousands of loved ones on the pioneer trail to Utah.[108] It would be the worst kind of distortion today to criticize Mormons of the past for harboring profound bitterness toward persons who "acted" or "sounded" anti-Mormon.

Because of the danger of these times, Joseph Smith had both volunteer and paid bodyguards from 1834 to his death in 1844. Brigham Young had personal bodyguards from 1844 on. After 1847 Young used several of these loyal and violent men as an internal security force of "enforcers" for the Mormon commonwealth centered in Utah.[109]

"Together they constituted a select task force of gutsy, frontier Mormon types who possessed the abilities and inclination to repeatedly place themselves as buffers between the Mormon 'kingdom' and the forces that threatened it," the LDS biographer of one of these enforcers has recently written. "While literally thousands of Mormons could claim some involvement in defending [Utah's pioneer theocracy], Warren Snow and such men as Daniel H. Wells, Lot Smith, Robert T. Burton, Porter Rockwell, Hosea Stout, Ephraim Hanks, Bill Hickman and William H. Kimball, often took leading roles in Mormon defensive efforts and seemed to specialize as protectors, playing extremely important roles that set them apart from the rank and file."[110] Concerning one of these men, Brigham Young's son wrote that Lot Smith "was the [most] violent man I ever associated with."[111]

Orrin Porter Rockwell, a former Danite and original member of the theocratic Council of Fifty, had killed an anti-Mormon militiaman in Illinois in 1845. By appointment in the 1849 State of Deseret and in the 1850 Territory of Utah, Rockwell had the lifelong position of deputy sheriff with unrestricted territorial jurisdiction. The subject of many comments by others, Rockwell left no record of his own activities or views.[112]

Some of Brigham Young's other enforcers specifically referred to their group identity and violent role as protectors of the Mormon "Zion" or Kingdom of God. When the Salt Lake high council investigated former Danite Hosea Stout for attempted murder in 1848, he said: "It has been my duty to hunt out the rotten spots in this K[ingdom] . . . even now I have a list [of] who will deny the faith." Stout added that "I av tried not to handle a man's case until it was right."[113] Ten years later Stout specifically referred to his associates Howard Egan, Porter Rockwell, and Ephraim Hanks as "some of the 'Be'hoys,'" an American slang term meaning "gang member" or "thug."[114] A BYU professor of religion has rendered this as "Brigham's Boys," and William A. Hickman also identified William H. Kimball (son of Brigham Young's counselor) and George D. Grant as members of the group. A former Danite like Rockwell, Grant was one of Brigham Young's appointments to the Council of Fifty before Mormons abandoned Nauvoo.[115]

Aaron Johnson later affirmed that "Brigham Young had men around him who aided in ridding Salt Lake City of gamblers and desperados." Another BYU professor of religion has acknowledged that Young "sanctioned at least some of their doings."[116] As editor of the *Deseret News* in 1859, judge Elias Smith (a former Danite and current member of the Council of Fifty) gave his own vindication of Aaron Johnson, bishop of Springville, Utah, on the charge of ordering the murder and throat-cutting of the apostate Parrish family members. Instead Elias Smith wrote that the murdered men simply "got into a row about matters best, if not only, known to themselves . . ."[117] On the other hand, a BYU professor of LDS history refers to this incident as the "Parrish-Potter religious murders."[118] This was an early example of the "suppression and shaping of news" by the LDS church's official newspaper. However, a researcher with the LDS Genealogical Society affirmed that "in the Mormon theocratic Kingdom few felt themselves unjustly coerced" by those journalistic lapses in the *Deseret News.*[119]

In July 1857 the widow Parrish told details of her family's murder to Brigham Young who said that "he would have stopped it had he known anything about it." He took no action against Johnson but wrote letters asking the bishop and one of the perpetrators to return to widow Parrish the horses confiscated from her murdered husband. Young explained to Bishop Johnson that she "apparently desires to serve the Lord[,] although her mind is necessarily somewhat harassed from events which have occurred." She later testified that Young "never wrote to me" about the horses. After months without an answer, she made several visits to the church president's office at 8 a.m., but Young refused to see her again even though she "sat there till 4 o'clock in the afternoon."[120] This was consistent with other examples of Brigham Young's supporting after-the-fact local leaders who committed bloody deeds without his personal authorization but whose acts had fulfilled Young's frequently expressed rhetoric of blood atonement (see below).

The *Deseret News* even emphasized that Mormon enforcers like Orrin Porter Rockwell could kill with impunity and immunity. In February 1860 it reported how Rockwell shot Martin Oats to death. After a scuffle in a hotel where the belligerent Oats was disarmed of his only weapon, a knife, Rockwell ordered some men "to take away the madman, as he did not want to hurt him." Later in the day Rockwell on horseback "overtook Oats" who "renewed his abuse and threats; whereupon Rockwell, after trying every expedient to make the fellow desist, and giving him proper warning of the consequence that would follow if he did not let him alone, shot the villain . . ." Although the *News* story showed that Oaks was disarmed before this final confrontation, the church newspaper reported that "the civil authorities" at Lehi (where Rockwell lived) "honorably acquitted [him]. The result seems to have given general satisfaction to all parties." Other versions of this incident were available, but editor-judge Elias Smith preferred his Mormon readers to understand that Rockwell killed an unarmed loudmouth who dared to insult a Mormon enforcer.[121]

Faithful Mormons understood the message. Thomas Jenkins, a former "minute man" against anticipated Indian attacks and himself a bishop in Salt Lake City from 1866 to 1875, later told his son-in-law that Rockwell was a "dreadfully bad man." He acknowledged that Rockwell had "a mission" from Joseph Smith and Brigham Young "to avenge our people on their enemies by the taking of life." However, Jenkins said that Rockwell eventually turned "on good men as well as bad," and "was going to shoot Bro. J. once." Jenkins observed that "the police never treated him [Rockwell] as they would have done any other criminal."[122]

The church newspaper continued to reenforce the view that criminals and anti-Mormons had good reason to be wary of Porter Rockwell. At his death the *Deseret News* noted that "he was under indictment for the killing of some [other] persons by the name of Aiken, in Juab County, over twenty years ago." The apostle-editors George Q. Cannon and Brigham Young, Jr., countered that Rockwell "was reported honorable in all his dealings, true to his friends and his word, firm in the faith of the gospel, and feared only by cattle-thieves and mobocrats and their supporters."[123] When the prosecutors sought to convict other Mormons for the Aiken murders, the same apostle-editors complained that the prosecutors were seeking "to make an attack on the faith of the bulk of the people in this Territory," and concluded "how singular it is that officers of the law should be so eager to hunt up cases that are musty with age . . ."[124] A devotional LDS writer has listed "Porter Rockwell and Bill Hickman" as "tough and ruthless men" who were in close association with Brigham Young.[125]

Of pioneer Utah's "Be'hoys," only William A. Hickman wrote a detailed account of his violent activities on behalf of LDS leaders. Most LDS writers and at least one non-Mormon historian have preferred to dismiss his published autobiography as an attempt to blame LDS leaders for his own crimes.[126] However, Hosea Stout's diary provides circumstantial verification of Hickman's detailed account of how he murdered Mormon apostate Jesse T. Hartley in 1854, allegedly by Apostle Orson Hyde's direct orders relayed from Brigham Young and approved afterwards by Stout.[127] It is unlikely that Hickman got his details of this incident from Stout's diary and less likely that he had read the high council's minutes of Stout's statement about his own "duty to hunt out the rotten spots in this K[ingdom]."

Moreover, prominent Mormons regarded some of Hickman's crimes as divinely sanctioned and church-sanctioned. In 1857 John Young (a member of the Council of Fifty) gave Hickman a patriarchal blessing: "You shall have power over all your enemies, even to set your feet upon their necks." This brother of Brigham Young also promised: "If you are faithful you shall assist in avenging the blood of the prophets of God . . ."[128] Salt Lake City's mayor Abraham O. Smoot (later a member of the Fifty) also accepted as a fact that Brigham Young used Hickman to kill the church's enemies. However, in 1860 Smoot complained that Hickman was freelancing against loyal Mormons. "Mayor Smoot had a conversation with the President about Wm. A. Hickman, observing people see him come in and out the office, and that leads them to suppose he is sanctioned in all he does by the President," began an entry in Brigham Young's office journal. Concerning Hickman, the mayor advised the church president that "dogs were necessary to take care of the flock, but if the Shepherd's dogs hurt the sheep it would be time to remove them."[129]

One member of Hickman's "gang" was George A. Stringham, who admitted involvement in the murder of U.S. Army sergeant Ralph Pike in 1859. Stringham's niece later "suggested with a frightened look" that he was also involved in the murder of anti-Mormon physician J. King Robinson in the 1860s. Hickman was known to be involved in Dr. Robinson's murder. The niece reported that Brigham Young once told Stringham, "I want you to choose better company." In view of Young's association with Hickman, Stringham told the church president: "I keep as good company as you do." His niece explained that in pioneer Utah "our problems were of the original savage kind," and that early Mormons were glad to have such "desperadoes" to take care of those problems without "hold[ing] too close to the observance of law."[130] George Stringham "was the type of rugged frontiersman necessary in his day and time," a family history stated less bluntly, "in running down outlaws and renegades preying upon the properties and liberties of those engaged in establishing and developing these Utah communities."[131]

Like Hickman, however, Stringham occasionally freelanced against fellow Mormons, and the *Deseret News* announced his excommunication in 1874. Civil authorities caught up with him a few years later and arrested him for horse theft. Although he occasionally committed lesser violations of the law into his old age, Stringham died peacefully out of jail.[132]

When John Bennion tried to excommunicate William Hickman in 1860, he learned that someone higher in authority had prevented another bishop from taking action. When Bennion held a church trial, Apostle Hyde came to Hickman's defense: "a man may steal & be influenced by the Spirit of the Lord to do it[,] that Hickman had done it in years past."

Hyde concluded that "he never would institute a trial against a brother for stealing from the Gentiles . . ." Because Bennion still intended to excommunicate Hickman, Hyde announced "it as the word of the Lord to set him free from the past." However, eight years later Hickman was summarily excommunicated after unsuccessfully attempting to blackmail Brigham Young with a threat to "disclose all" in a book about his various murders. Because Hickman turned against his prophet-benefactor and publicly revealed his own murders, traditional LDS history has not been kind to the memory of Mormonism's "Wild Bill."[133]

Another "Be'hoy," Howard Egan, provided lifelong security to the church president from the mid-1840s to his death. Apostle George A. Smith won Egan's acquittal of murder charges in 1851 when Egan returned from a proselytizing mission and shot to death an unarmed Mormon who had fathered a child by Egan's wife. Church authorities repeatedly published the full text of Smith's concluding argument that "the man who seduces his neighbor's wife must die, and her nearest relative must kill him."[134] According to a family biography, Egan "became a special guard for Pres. Brigham Young at the Lion House and Church Offices before and at the time of Pres. Brigham Young's last illness and acted as special nurse." From Young's death in August 1877 to his own death in 1878, Egan "was a special guard at his grave."[135]

During this period Brigham Young and other Mormon leaders also repeatedly preached about specific sins for which it was necessary to shed the blood of men and women. Blood-atonement sins included adultery, apostasy, "covenant breaking," counterfeiting, "many men who left this Church," murder, not being "heartily on the Lord's side," profaning "the name of the Lord," sexual intercourse between a "white" person and an African-American, stealing, and telling lies.[136]

Some LDS leaders have dismissed allegations about blood atonement as misunderstanding or misuse of earlier sermons concerning the atonement of Jesus Christ or the civil necessity of capital punishment.[137] Other Mormon leaders have continued to affirm that after committing "certain grievous sins," a person "must make sacrifice of his own life to atone—so far as in his power lies—for that sin, for the blood of Christ alone under certain circumstances will not avail."[138]

Some LDS historians have claimed that blood-atonement sermons were simply Brigham Young's use of "rhetorical devices designed to frighten wayward individuals into conformity with Latter-day Saint principles" and to bluff anti-Mormons. Writers often describe these sermons as limited to the religious enthusiasm and frenzy of the Utah Reformation up to 1857.[139] The first problem with such explanations is that official LDS sources show that as early as 1843 Joseph Smith and his counselor Sidney

Rigdon advocated decapitation or throat-cutting as punishment for various crimes and sins.[140]

Moreover, a decade before Utah's reformation, Brigham Young's private instructions show that he fully expected his trusted associates to kill various persons for violating religious obligations. The LDS church's official history still quotes Young's words to "the brethren" in February 1846: "I should be perfectly willing to see thieves have their throats cut."[141] The following December he instructed bishops, "when a man is found to be a thief, he will be a thief no longer, cut his throat, & thro' him in the River," and Young did not instruct them to ask his permission.[142] A week later the church president explained to a Winter Quarters meeting that cutting off the heads of repeated sinners "is the law of God & it shall be executed . . ." A rephrase of Young's words later appeared in Hosea Stout's reference to a specific sinner, "to cut him off—behind the ears—according to the law of God in such cases."[143]

In a November 1846 "council" meeting with the apostles, Howard Egan, and John D. Lee, the church president also applied this decapitating "law of God" to non-Mormon enemies. Informed that Lt. Andrew J. Smith was acting like "a poor wolfish tyranicle Gentile" as commander of the Mormon Battalion, Young asked Lee "why I did not take his head off then, and wished that his arm was long enough to reach the Bat."[144]

When informed that a black Mormon in Massachusetts had married a white woman, Brigham Young told the apostles in December 1847 that he would have both of them killed "if they were far away from the Gentiles." In 1848 Young "then swore with up lifted hands. that a theif [sic] should not live in the [Salt Lake] Valley," a faithful Mormon woman recorded, "for he would cut off their heads or be the means of haveing it done as the Lord lived." In 1849 the church president told a congregation of Mormons, "if any one was catched stealing to shoot them dead on the spot and they should not be hurt for it."[145]

Young's remarks in March 1849 showed that he expected members of the Council of Fifty to be one of "the means" for killing certain persons. On 3 March, at a meeting of the Fifty, he spoke concerning thieves, murderers, and the sexually licentious: "I want their cursed heads to be cut off that they may atone for their crimes." The next day the Fifty agreed that a man "had forfeited his Head," but decided it would be best "to dispose of him privately." Two weeks later Young instructed the Fifty regarding two imprisoned men (including the man discussed on 3 March): "he would show them that he was not affraid to take their Head[s] but do as you please with them." Instead, the Fifty allowed the two men to live.[146] From 1851 to 1888 Utah law allowed persons to be "beheaded" if found guilty of murder.[147]

Equally significant local sermons during the 1850s intensified the central hierarchy's emphasis on blood atonement. The Parrish murders of March 1857 were the subject of a sermon within days of the incident, and one man in the congregation of Big Cottonwood Ward, Salt Lake Valley, wrote that he "was glad to hear that the law of God has been put in force in Springville on some men who deserved it."[148] In May "Brother Ross" told a "fellowship meeting" of the Salt Lake City Fifth Ward that the "time is at hand when those who commit sins worthy of death will have to be slain by the Priesthood [leadership] that is directly over them." He included an obligation of parents to kill their "disobedient children." The "worthy of death" phrase was a quote from the blood-atonement sermon by First Presidency counselor Jedediah M. Grant three years earlier.[149] In Spanish Fork, fifty-three miles south of Salt Lake City, some speakers advised "if you should find your father or your mother, your sister or your brother dead by the wayside, say nothing about it, but pass on about your own business."[150] An LDS woman also confided to an assistant church historian that ward teachers advised Mormons in Cedar City, southern Utah: "If you see a dead man laying on your wood pile, you must not tell but go about your business."[151]

Mormons also privately indicated their belief in an obligation to kill non-Mormon enemies. "Avenging the blood of the Prophets" was part of the 1852 blessing given by Presiding Patriarch John Smith (senior member of the Council of Fifty) to his grandnephew.[152] In 1854 local patriarch Elisha H. Groves blessed William H. Dame: "thou shalt be called to act at the head of a portion of thy Brethren and of the Lamanites in the redemption of Zion and the avenging of the blood of the prophets upon them that dwell on the earth." Days later Patriarch Groves gave another resident of Parowan, Utah, a blessing with almost identical wording about "avenging." In less than four years, as commander of the militia in southern Utah, Dame ordered this man and about sixty other Mormons to join with local Indians ("Lamanites") in massacring a non-LDS wagon train of Arkansas families who had been joined by belligerent young men calling themselves "Missouri Wild Cats" and antagonizing every Mormon settlement they passed through. These people represented the two groups that Mormons blamed for shedding the blood of the prophets David W. Patten, Joseph and Hyrum Smith, and Parley P. Pratt.[153] Philip Klingensmith also received the following blessing from Patriarch Isaac Morley (a member of the Council of Fifty) barely three months before Klingensmith followed Dame's orders to kill men, women, and children: "Thou shalt yet be numbered with the sons of Zion in avenging the blood of Brother Joseph for thy heart and thy spirit can never be satisfied until the wicked are subdued."[154]

Several days after this Mountain Meadows Massacre, a member of the Council of Fifty discussed similar actions with a ward bishop hundreds of miles away in Salt Lake City on 21 September 1857: "Br. *P[hineas]. Richards* [a member of the Council of Fifty] spoke of coming in contact with our enemies. We have covenanted to avenge the blood of the Prophets and Saints. Why, then, should we hesitate to go forth and slay them—shed their blood—when called upon." The minutes of Bishop Samuel L. Sprague's prayer circle meeting continued: "Pres. *Sprague* spoke a few words in answer to the inquiry made by br. Richards; that the Lord had said 'vengeance is mine.' Nevertheless, we shall have blood to shed."[155] Concerning this early covenant of vengeance, First Presidency counselor George Q. Cannon told his son that "when he had his endowments in Nauvoo that he took an oath against the murderers of the Prophet Joseph as well as other prophets . . ."[156]

Mormons who had committed serious sins also expressed willingness to be blood-atoned by church leaders. In 1854 the criminal court of Parowan, southern Utah, tried George W. Braffit for adultery, with his wife Sarah as a co-defendant for helping him to obtain the woman. Instead of a civil trial, they "wanted to go to Brigham, confess, and have their heads taken off."[157] "The time we have prayed for so long has come," exclaimed William H. Dame to the congregation of Parowan on 19 October 1856: "Some that have sinned grievous sins are offering their lives at the feet of the Prophets as an expiation of them."[158] Ten days after this sermon, the stake's president Isaac C. Haight wrote Brigham Young and asked what to do with a man who was willing to be blood-atoned for having engaged in sexual intercourse prior to his marriage. Remarkably Young waited four months to respond with an allowance of forgiveness without blood atonement. What the man experienced in the interim is unknown, but Haight was not patient about such matters and subsequently ordered the Mountain Meadows Massacre without waiting for the authorization he had also sought from the church president.[159] The last known example of this willingness to be blood-atoned was in another part of Utah five years after Haight's inquiry.[160] Pioneer Mormons took blood-atonement sermons seriously and literally.[161]

Aside from sermons, this culture of violence was part of LDS congregational singing. In 1856 the *Deseret News* announced a new hymn which included the verse: "We ought our Bishops to sustain,/ Their counsels to abide/ And knock down every dwelling/ Where wicked folks reside."[162] Throughout the last half of the nineteenth century, Mormon congregations sang five hymns that mentioned vengeance and violence upon anti-Mormons. One such LDS hymn advised: "Remember the wrongs of Missouri;/ Forget not the fate of Nauvoo;/ When the God-hating foe is before ye,/ Stand firm, and be faithful and true . . . Our vows, at each pulse we renew,/Ne'er to rest till our foes are retreating," while another specified: "The blood of those who have been slain/ For vengeance cries aloud;/ Nor shall its cries ascend in vain/ For vengeance on the proud," and a third emphasized this theme of vengeance: "Though Zion's foes have counseled deep,/ Although they bind with fetters strong,/ The God of Jacob will not sleep; his vengeance will not slumber long." One hymn linked God's vengeance with Mormon priesthood: "Lo! the Lion's left his thicket;/ Up, ye watchmen, be in haste;/ The destroyer of the Gentiles/ Goes to lay their cities waste/ We're the true born sons of Zion," while another described the Mormons as agents of God's vengeance: "In thy mountain retreat, God will strengthen thy feet;/ On the necks of thy foes thou shalt tread . . . Thy deliverance is nigh, thy oppressors shall die,/ And the Gentiles shall bow 'neath thy rod." The hymn "Deseret" even referred to performing blood atonement on adulterers in Utah: "Where society frowns upon vice and deceit,/ And adulterers find Heaven's laws they must meet."[163]

LDS meetinghouses in Utah were also not free of violence that was approved, at least after-the-fact, by church authorities. In 1851 Brigham Young defended Madison D. Hambleton who shot and killed a man at LDS church services immediately after the closing prayer. The jury acquitted him for killing his wife's seducer. In 1868 the church newspaper praised "a couple of young men" for giving a "sound thrashing" to a gentile who attended an LDS meeting to see a young woman.[164] A year later Indians allegedly killed three men who had left John Wesley Powell's exploring expedition at the Colorado River, but a Mormon later wrote a private letter about "the day those three were murdered in our ward & the murderer killed to stop the shed[d]ing of more blood." The "our ward" referred to a building in either Harrisburg or Toquerville, small towns in southern Utah.[165]

Three men left Powell's group to go to "some Mormon settlements north of the river" and "get some grub and return to our boats and continue on down the river." On 7 September 1869 an unsigned telegram (with no place of origin given) informed Apostle Erastus Snow at St. George, Utah, of their deaths "5 days ago, one Indian's day's journey from Washington, [Utah]."[166] Washington was the town next on route to Harrisburg.[167] Powell's men expressed suspicion that Mormons were involved in these killings,[168] but the identity and motive of the killer(s) are still unclear.[169]

In the midsummer of 1857 Brigham Young also expressed approval for an LDS bishop who had castrated a man. In May 1857 Bishop Warren S. Snow's counselor wrote that twenty-four-year-old Thomas Lewis "has now gone crazy" after being castrated by Bishop Snow for an undisclosed sex crime. When informed of Snow's action, Young said: "I feel to sustain him," even though Young's brother Joseph, a general authority, disapproved of this punishment. In July Brigham Young wrote a reassuring letter to the bishop about this castration: "Just let the matter drop, and say no more about it," the LDS president advised, "and it will soon die away among the people."[170]

Just weeks after that letter, Mormons were stunned to learn during the pioneer celebration of 24 July 1857 that the U.S. president had secretly ordered 2,500 troops to "invade" Utah. Newly inaugurated President James Buchanan believed the Mormons were in actual insurrection as claimed by W. W. Drummond, the chief justice who had recently "escaped" from Utah. However, one historian has noted that "Drummond's tenure as Utah judge came to an end because of a personal feud with a Salt Lake Jewish merchant whom Drummond tried unsuccessfully to murder. When news of his bungled effort surfaced, Drummond left the territory quickly but not quietly."[171] Buchanan decided to send the largest U.S. military force yet assembled to restore federal authority to a territory he believed was in rebellion. With a personal vow to "fight until there is not a drop of blood in my veins," Brigham Young ordered the militia of every city and town in Utah to prepare for war. Young's immediate strategy was to assemble "a human wall of soldier-settlers to bar the federal army from entering the territory" from the east. If that failed, by August Young decided on a fallback strategy of abandoning Utah and leaving only smoking ruins where Mormon settlements had once been.[172] The Utah Reformation's religious frenzy was now joined with war hysteria.

In September 1857 Apostle George A. Smith told a Salt Lake City congregation that Mormons at Parowan in southern Utah "wish that their enemies might come and give them a chance to fight and take vengeance for the cruelties that had been inflicted upon us in the States." Smith had just returned from southern Utah where he had encouraged such feelings by preaching fiery sermons about resisting the U.S. army and taking vengeance on anti-Mormons.[173] Just days before his talk in Salt Lake City, members of Parowan's Mormon militia participated in killing 120 men, women, and children in the Mountain Meadows Massacre. After holding a prayer circle, stake president Isaac C. Haight had decided not to await word from Brigham Young about whether to help Indians kill the emigrants.[174]

For a decade the church president had threatened to use Native American Indians against other Americans. He warned Thomas L. Kane of this in August 1846, but was more specific in a letter to Kane in September 1857. "Day after day I am visited by their Chiefs to know if they may strike while 'the iron is hot,'" Young wrote. "My answer depends on Mr. Buchanan's policy—if he does not mete out justice to us, the war cry will resound from the Rio Colorado to the headwaters of the Missouri— from the Black Hills to the Sierra Nevada . . . It is peace and our rights—or the knife and tomahawk—let uncle Sam choose." Young wrote in his diary on 1 September 1857: "I can hardly restrain them from exterminating the 'Americans.'"[175]

Ironically, some LDS historians today are less willing to acknowledge that Mormons planned and carried out the Mountain Meadows Massacre than the official history of the church sixty-six years ago. In his biography of Brigham Young, a secretary of the First Presidency has written that the "white" perpetrators included "some members of the Church." In fact, all non-Indian perpetrators were Mormon, as acknowledged by the church's centennial history, a Brigham Young University Press book, a recent Deseret Book publication, and the church's 1992 encyclopedia. The latter source also refers to "the community guilt" of the "Mormon residents in and around Cedar City," who had "participated in the massacre . . ."[176]

In reporting the massacre to Brigham Young on 29 September, John D. Lee (who had persuaded the emigrants to surrender) claimed that the Indians "cut the throats of their women & Children." The LDS church's political newspaper later published Lee's statement that Young "wept like a child, walked the floor and wrung his hands in bitter anguish" at this report. Lee added that "all who participated in the lamentable transaction, or most of them, were acting under orders that they considered it their duty—their religious duty—to obey."[177] Although most accounts claimed that the militia killed only the adult males and let their Indian allies kill the women and children, perpetrator Nephi Johnson later told an LDS apostle that "white men did most of the killing." Perpetrator George W. Adair also told another apostle that "John Higbee gave the order to kill the women and children," and Adair "saw the women's and children's throats cut."[178] Slitting the throats of only the women and children seemed to be a special application of LDS teachings, as if the Missouri "Wild Cats" and Arkansas men did not deserve this rite of blood atonement. This was a pattern that would be repeated in a subsequent massacre committed by Mormon militiamen at Circleville in south-central Utah.

Although Brigham Young did not authorize the Mountain Meadows Massacre and had tried to prevent it,[179] he privately approved of it after the fact. Apostle Wilford Woodruff, the official church historian, re-corded that when Young first visited the mass burial site, he said that the memorial plaque should read: "Vengence is mine and I have taken a little." Five days later the church president spoke to a congregation filled with many of the participants in the massacre. "Pres. Young Said that the company that was used up at the Mountain Meadows were the Fathers, Mothe[rs], Bros., Sisters & connections of those that Murdered the Prophets; *they Merit[e]d their fate, & the only thing that ever troubled him was the lives of the Women & children, but that under the circumstances [this] could not be avoided.* Although there had been [some] that want[e]d to bet[ray] the Brethr[e]n into the hands of their Enemies, for that thing [they] will be Damned & go down to Hell. I would be Glad to see one of those traitors" (emphasis added).[180]

About October 1857 Cedar City's LDS bishop ordered the execution of a Mormon who had sexual intercourse with his step-daughter. "Reputable eyewitnesses" reported that the man consented to this theocratic death penalty "in full confidence of salvation through the shedding of his blood."[181]

On 30 November 1857 Brigham Young's counselor Daniel H. Wells ordered blood atonement for a sexual act. After Governor Young declared martial law for Utah at the approach of federal troops, Wells as commanding-general ordered the execution of a Mormon soldier for "committing the sin of Sodomy or Bestiality [sexual intercourse with an animal—] one of the most heinous crimes." The day after this court martial Wells assembled all his troops and required them to approve the judgment that twenty-one-year-old Willis Drake "be shot publicly & also the mare."[182] Despite the upraised hands of the entire company, Wells delayed the execution long enough for Young to instruct him "to release one Drake and give him [only] a severe reprimand . . ." Apparently his horse was not so lucky.[183]

In February 1858 Salt Lake City's police captain Hosea Stout described with no disapproval how Mormons "disguised as Indians" dragged a man "out of bed with a whore and castrated him by a square & close amputation." Parenthetically, a few of the Mormons "were all painted and disguised as Indians" before participating in the Mountain Meadows Massacre.[184] A few months later the non-Mormon federal judge asked Stout to investigate and bring to justice those who had castrated another man for committing adultery with a Mormon's wife. That was the last reference in Stout's diary to the case which he apparently ignored.[185]

Then in April 1858 the bishop of Payson, his brother (the sheriff), and several members of their LDS ward joined in shooting to death a twenty-two-year-old Mormon and his mother for committing incest. They also castrated the young man and killed the infant girl born of this incest.[186] A general authority resided in Payson at that time. Levi W. Hancock was a former member of the 1834 Zion's Camp, of the 1838 Missouri Danites, of the Nauvoo police, of the 1846-47 Mormon Battalion, a former member of the Utah legislature, and a senior member of the First Council of

Seventy. It is unlikely the bishop and sheriff would have committed this blood atonement without consulting with their prestigious uncle and fellow resident.[187]

Thirty years later the church's *Deseret News* expressed sympathy for those who had murdered "the brutal mother and son" because the Mormon community had been "disgusted and greatly incensed." The editorial claimed that the prosecution against "the antiquated Payson homicide" was anti-Mormon and unnecessary since the evidence of incest "was clear and indisputable" (through the birth of a child). The editorial did not mention the infant's murder. Ultimately, the sheriff was convicted of the murders, while the charges against the bishop were dropped.[188]

In the meantime, the federal invasion had been halted by a combination of factors that spelled humiliation for the U.S. military and President Buchanan. Young's strategy of preventing entry into Utah through Echo Canyon was initially so effective that commanding colonel Edmund B. Alexander led his U.S. troops into unmapped northern territory in an abortive effort to outflank Mormon defenses. Under military command of First Presidency counselor Daniel H. Wells, Lot Smith and other Mormon officers captured more than a thousand cattle and horses, burned enough supply trains to destroy 150 tons of food, and brought federal troops to the edge of starvation by the time General Albert Sidney Johnston assumed command at the start of a hard winter. This military paralysis allowed Thomas L. Kane, a longtime friend of the Mormons, to successfully conclude his self-appointed diplomacy between a hopeful Young, suspicious Johnston, and pessimistic Buchanan, who had nonetheless officially endorsed Kane's effort. Skillfully exploiting the criticism in Eastern newspapers against this use of U.S. troops against the Mormons, Young ordered the abandonment of all northern settlements, including Salt Lake City. As Eastern reporters described thousands of women and children huddled in misery at Provo, Utah, prior to another Mormon exodus to escape persecution, the Buchanan administration became eager for a peaceful solution to a public embarrassment. The result was the bloodless conclusion of the Utah War that provided for a presidential amnesty to all Mormon belligerents and peaceful entry of U.S. troops through a deserted Salt Lake City in June 1858 on route to establish Camp Floyd southwest of Salt Lake Valley.[189]

"What is gained?" General Johnston complained in a letter to his son on 4 September. "The theocracy [still] exists, the obligations to which are in as full force now as before, the people are as much bound to go by Council now as before . . ."[190] The Mormon culture of violence also continued despite federal troops and, in some instances, because of their presence.

On 12 September 1858 a clerk in the LDS Historian's Office recorded that U.S. soldiers discovered "this morning" a woman's decapitated head. This Mormon woman had left her Provo ward only a week earlier to live in the camp of U.S. soldiers.[191] Six weeks before that a dog in Utah Valley had found a different woman's decapitated head, "much dried and mummified . . ."[192] This was consistent with First Presidency counselor Heber C. Kimball's sermon that adulterers should be decapitated, and with his views of adulterous women: "We wipe them out of existence."[193] These women had evidently received retributive blood atonement from Mormons who took such sermons literally. Their severed heads, as well as the above cases prior to 1858, make it impossible to accept church historian Joseph Fielding Smith's rhetorical question: "Did you not know that not a single individual was ever 'blood atoned,' as you are pleased to call it, for apostasy or any other cause?"[194]

Aside from vigilante castrations for going to "bed with a whore," for adultery, and for incest, young Mormon males in the 1850s were also castrated for the accusation of bestiality. In March 1859 a U.S. soldier's diary recorded that "two youths" fled to the U.S. army camp after being "castrated by the Mormons." One "handsome young Dane" had been courting a girl whom an LDS bishop wanted. To dispose of his rival, the bishop claimed the young man "had committed bestiality and had him castrated."[195]

Brigham Young and other general authorities repeatedly emphasized that blood atonement was appropriate punishment for those who violated certain commandments. These sermons did not require nor advise Mormons to ask permission of ecclesiastical superiors before performing blood atonement on a person whose sin was "worthy of death." The only restraint appeared in first counselor Heber C. Kimball's 1861 sermon: "Do not fret yourselves; if any man has done a wrong deed, do not undertake to kill him without knowing whether he has done right or wrong; wait till you have ascertained the facts in the case." Even this caution did not require asking authorization from higher authorities, but only recommended that the individuals be certain before "cutting off a dead limb from a tree."[196]

In February 1862 Mormons knew "the facts" of a "wrong deed" and also had the church president's public endorsement for shedding the man's blood. Jean Baptiste, the city cemetery's gravedigger, had been robbing Mormon graves in Salt Lake City for years and stripping clothes and valuables from the corpses. After this was discovered, the Mormon judge Elias Smith wrote in his diary that "the people wo[u]ld have torn him in pieces," and Brigham Young preached: "To hang a man for such a deed would not begin to satisfy my feelings."[197] Because grave-robbing was not a capital offense in Utah's criminal code, the court gave Baptiste the unusual sentence Young recommended—banishment to a deserted island in the Great Salt Lake. His guards also cut his ears off and branded "Grave robber" on his forehead.[198] However, this may not have been sufficient for the "Be'hoys," and some Mormons later claimed that Ephraim Hanks killed Baptiste.[199] Thirty-two years later the *Salt Lake Herald* reported the discovery of a skeleton, manacled with a ball-and-chain, with its skull resting several feet away. Though disputed by the *Deseret News,* the *Herald* claimed these were Baptiste's decapitated remains.[200]

During the Black Hawk War in April 1866, the local militia committed a massacre at Circleville, Piute County, Utah. After capturing a group of Piede Indians, Mormon militiamen shot the hand-tied men, then slit the throats of their women and children one by one. Of this incident second counselor and commanding general Daniel H. Wells wrote that these "brethren" did what was necessary.[201]

In December 1866 Brigham Young, Jr., wrote that "a nigger" was found dead in Salt Lake City, with a note pinned to the corpse: "Let this be a warning to all niggers that they meddle not with white women." The non-Mormon newspaper identified the victim as Thomas Coleman, "a member of the Mormon Church."[202] Brigham Jr., then an ordained apostle and special counselor in the First Presidency, recorded no value judgment about this killing. It had fulfilled his father's public announcement three years earlier that for miscegenation (race-mixing with African-Americans), "the penalty, under the law of God, is death on the spot."[203]

As late as 1868 the *Deseret News* encouraged rank-and-file Mormons to kill anyone who engaged in sexual relations outside marriage. Concerning a man who "shot the seducer of his sister" in January, the church newspaper editorialized: "In this Territory we jealously close the door against adultery, seduction and whoredom. Public opinion here pronounces the penalty of death as the fitting punishment for such crimes." A few weeks later the church newspaper editorialized that "it is a pity" a father did not succeed in killing his daughter's seducer when the father "drew a revolver and shot him down in the court room."[204] In 1869 Apostle George Q. Cannon made the following statement in a sermon: "We close the door on one side, and say that whoredoms, seductions and adulteries must not be committed among us, and we say to those who are determined to carry on such things[:] we will kill you . . ."[205]

Under such circumstances the Mormon hierarchy bore full responsibility for the violent acts of zealous Mormon who accepted their instructions literally and carried out various forms of blood atonement.

"Obviously there were those who could not easily make a distinction between rhetoric and reality," a BYU religion professor has written.[206] For many Mormons, Brigham Young had published their sacred obligation: "Will you love your brothers or sisters likewise, when they have committed a sin that cannot be atoned for without the shedding of their blood? Will you love that man or woman well enough to shed their blood?"[207] It is unrealistic to assume that faithful Mormons all declined to act on such repeated instructions in pioneer Utah. It is also unfair and contrary to the evidence for LDS historians to dismiss such executioners as "misguided Mormon zealots" who misinterpreted "Church leaders' fulminations against malcontents."[208] A devotional history of the *Deseret News* acknowledged that its frequent publication of "speeches that approved of blood atonement" in the 1850s "may have unknowingly served to arouse some Mormons" to kill.[209]

For more than a decade after the Mormons arrived in 1847, the Salt Lake Valley and more distant settlements had a pattern of Mormons either murdering or castrating males for adultery and for sex with animals, to which law enforcement officers turned a blind eye or after which juries acquitted the Mormon perpetrators.[210] For Mormon females who were regarded as immoral, decapitation was the publicly advocated form of blood atonement, and there are two examples that this actually occurred.

There were relatively few instances of blood atonement (including castrations) by ecclesiastical authority in pioneer Utah, but these were not aberrations. Nor were the verified examples of blood atonement lessened by the numerous examples of Mormon adulterers who received forgiveness from LDS leaders without any punishment or by the long lives many apostates lived in Utah. Neither is it reasonable to assume that the known cases of blood atonement even approximated the total number that occurred in the first twenty years after Mormon settlement in Utah. During this period there were dozens of sermons by general authorities about blood atonement, untold numbers of talks and testimonials on the topic by local Mormons, no announced restraints on fulfilling the blood-atonement option, and abundant numbers of "grievous" sinners, apostates, anti-Mormons, and other enemies. There was also the practical option of concealing blood-atoned persons as straight-razor suicides, accidental shootings, victims of Indian attacks, self-defense killings, or missing persons in Utah's harsh terrain.

After a Mormon woman in 1858 "generally maintained silence, or answered evasively" about the above situation, she eventually told a federal officer that such people just "disappeared—'used up [killed] in the pocket of the Lord,' we call it." The man's diary also quoted this Welch convert's reference to "the Destroyers" who "murder you in canyons, and cut your throat from ear [to ear]."[211] Two years later the *Deseret News* also expressed indifference about certain kinds of unsolved murder. "Murder after murder has been committed with impunity within the precincts of Great Salt Lake City, till such occurrences do not seemingly attract much attention," the *News* editorialized, "particularly when the murdered have had the reputation of being thieves and murderers or of associating with such characters from day to day and whenever they had a chance."[212] John W. Christian, a pioneer physician in Beaver, Utah, wrote that "if men were found who were murderers and thieves and beyond the control of society and law[,] it would be better if they were disposed of."[213] Aside from the already cited references in diaries and private letters, the above circumstances suggest giving greater credence even to acknowledged apostates who referred to their knowledge of actual instances of blood atonement and "secret assassinations."[214]

A decade after religiously motivated killing ended in the Salt Lake Valley, that option still appealed to some Mormons in northern Utah's Cache Valley. In 1873 Mormons lynched accused murderer Charles Benson (apostate son of a deceased apostle) in Logan.[215] Two years later LDS apostate Aaron DeWitt was a principal witness in the murder trial of Thomas E. Ricks, Cache Valley's sheriff and high priest quorum president. Accused of murdering a horse thief in his custody as sheriff, Ricks was acquitted. Upon his return to Logan, DeWitt said that "the local Mormon leaders had threatened his life," and one account even claimed that "the [high] council decided to take his life, and appointed a time, but one of them proved traitor and went and told him [DeWitt], so he was on guard and thus saved his life."[216]

In December 1889 the First Presidency and Twelve published an official statement which denied that "our Church favors or believes in the killing of persons who leave the Church or apostatize from its doctrines."[217] Nevertheless, a year later the Twelve's president Lorenzo Snow, age seventy-six, privately told the apostles that he "expected to see the day when a man's blood will be shed for the crime of adultery."[218]

Aside from blood atonement, the church's official newspapers continued to endorse random violence against anti-Mormons until 1890. Without editorial comment, the *Deseret News* reported in 1878 that "unknown persons" attacked the editor of the anti-Mormon *Salt Lake Tribune* with "brass knuckles," breaking his nose. Several months earlier the *News* had reported that its editor George Q. Cannon said that the *Tribune* editor "deserves kicking."[219] In November 1884 the church's political newspaper reported that it was "a refreshing and pleasing sight to many," when Presiding Bishopric counselor John Q. Cannon assaulted a reporter for the anti-Mormon *Salt Lake Tribune*, then took out "a riding whip, and struck his victim a couple of times over the head. Then he knocked him down . . ." After giving a lengthy and heroic description of the assault on the reporter by "respectable citizen" Cannon, the *Deseret News* dutifully acknowledged that "no law-abiding citizen can countenance assault and battery." The *News* immediately added: "but to those conversant with the outrageous course which the *Tribune* and its editors have pursued for years, it is only surprising that such occurrences have not happened oftener."[220] A month later the LDS political newspaper praised another Mormon who gave a *Tribune* reporter "two ringing slaps, one on each ear," and then smashed his nose. The *Deseret News* also reported the story approvingly.[221] In 1886 the LDS political newspaper light-heartedly reported a Mormon legislator's slapping and punching of another *Tribune* reporter. After a judge fined the legislator for assault and battery, the *Deseret News* complained that "the only marks on [the assaulted reporter's] face were a swelling of the upper lip, and lump over the eye . . ."[222]

After years of publishing endorsements of Mormon attacks on their enemies, the *Deseret News* recoiled in horror in August 1883 when Mormons of Salt Lake City engaged in what a historian has called "one of the most extraordinary episodes of mob violence in the annals of the American West." The incident began when Salt Lake City's police chief Andrew Burt attempted to arrest Sam Joe Harvey, an African-American who then shot and killed Burt, who was also bishop of an LDS congregation. The other Mormon policemen disarmed Harvey and severely beat him with brass knuckles and billy clubs. Then the police simply handed the murderer over to a screaming mob which lynched him. Joined by hundreds of men, women, and children who had learned of Burt's death, a crowd of at least 2,000 cheered those who dragged Harvey's corpse through the streets.[223] Of this incident, Apostle Heber J. Grant wrote: "Learned that Bp Andrew Burt of the 21st Ward was shot & killed yesterday by a negro, and that the nigger that did the shooting had been hung by the citizens."[224] In 1889 the *Deseret News* applauded the acquittal of a Mormon for the decades-earlier murder of Sgt. Pike who "richly deserved his fate" for having physically attacked the young man previously.[225]

True, nineteenth-century American society was violent generally. Random murders and vigilante justice were especially common in the Far West where the institutions of civil government were weak.[226] "Vigilantes and supporters of vigilante movements included Presidents Andrew Jackson and Theodore Roosevelt, senators, congressmen, governors, literary luminaries, legal scholars, prominent lawyers, and businessmen, as well as representatives from practically every class of American society," an LDS interpreter has written. "It is from this perspective that the relatively few instances of extralegal violence in early Utah must be viewed."[227] For example, Texas, New Mexico, and Georgia also completely exonerated husbands for killing their wives' "paramours."[228]

In this regard, an LDS historian has recently warned that revisionist history can exchange the stereotype of pioneer Mormons as benign victims for a stereotype of early Mormons as "brittle, persecution-obsessed" and "fully capable of murder."[229] Because much of early Utah's violence seems similar to the rest of the West, even non-Mormon historians have discounted religious motivation, aside from the glaring example of the Mountain Meadows Massacre.[230] Another historian has added that despite an environment which promoted blood atonement and retribution, "the level of violence in Mormonism's frontier sanctuary was much lower than in other western regions."[231]

Nevertheless, Mormonism created different dimensions for the violence in early Utah. First, there was no absence of social order to attract criminals or require nonjudicial punishment by self-appointed vigilantes. LDS leaders established effective institutions of government and judiciary at the formation of nearly 340 pioneer settlements during Young's presidency.[232] However, LDS leaders publicly and privately encouraged Mormons to consider it their religious right to kill antagonistic outsiders, common criminals, LDS apostates, and even faithful Mormons who committed sins "worthy of death." Mormon theocracy created such a unique context for Utah violence that it will always be impossible to determine how many violent deaths occurred for theocratic reasons and how many merely reflected the American West's pattern of violence. As late as 1880-89, LDS leaders in San Juan County, Utah, were conducting "a church vigilance committee" that acted independently of civil officials.[233]

When religiously motivated executions were too well known to ignore judicially, pioneer Mormon judges typically dismissed the charges or LDS juries acquitted LDS defendants. From the arrival of federal troops in Utah in 1858 until 1889, non-Mormons initiated the few investigations and court cases that provided enduring evidence of such theocratic killings. LDS leaders and the church's newspaper typically condemned these murder investigations as anti-Mormon in motivation and conduct.[234] Despite their well-earned reputation for keeping detailed records of community life and personal experiences, Mormon diarists rarely wrote about these events and perpetrators. That silence engulfed the diaries of the entire southern Utah community involved in the Mountain Meadows Massacre.[235]

To prevent stereotyping the entire early Mormon community, every study of pioneer Utah should acknowledge that Mormons were diverse in their group dynamics and complex individually. Despite the suffering imposed by anti-Mormons on them, despite hearing repeated sermons about blood atonement, despite singing hymns of vengeance, despite receiving patriarchal blessings promising them the privilege of taking revenge on their enemies, the historical evidence indicates that most early Mormons avoided violence and were saddened by the news of such incidents. For example, recently excommunicated George A. Hicks insisted that no one was ever religiously executed in his hometown of Spanish Fork, Utah, despite sermons advocating blood atonement.[236] Some pioneer Mormons opposed retaliation and blood atonement even though they believed that such opposition jeopardized their own lives at the hands of Mormons obsessed with vengeance.[237] Nevertheless, it is equally true that other devout Mormons perpetrated violence in the name of religion or approved of such acts, and that those persons also demonstrated love, compassion, tolerance, and nonviolence in other circumstances of their lives.

Mormon theocracy was in part a response to anti-Mormon attacks, but it also spawned violence. In the founding years of their movement Mormons were most often the victims, but some became perpetrators of "us-them" violence while the Mormon kingdom was at its zenith in Utah. Although religiously motivated deaths virtually ended with the development of a significant gentile population in the late 1860s, religion and race continued to be factors of Mormon participation in lynchings. LDS publications applauded physical attacks on anti-Mormons until 1889, the year the First Presidency also publicly abandoned its ideals of a political theocracy.[238] The next year ushered in the official end of Mormon polygamy which led to the end of the church's political party (chap. 9). The year 1890 also signalled Mormonism's abandonment of its violent culture and the beginning of its selective memory of a turbulent past.

CHAPTER 8

Priesthood Rule and Shadow Governments

Rule by Priesthood Decree

Brigham Young preached that "the Priesthood will bear rule, and hold the government of the Kingdom under control in all things."[1] Nevertheless, his downplaying of the Council of Fifty (see chap. 7) did not mean that he had abandoned the idea of theocracy. In 1855 Apostle Franklin D. Richards editorialized: "There is one kind of government that will insure permanent prosperity and happiness, as long as the people will render willing obedience to it, and that is a Theocracy, or the government of God through His Prophet, Seer, and Revelator. . . . A Theocracy embodies the two extremes of absolute power and republicanism."[2] Young admired absolute power and criticized the tradition of limiting the U.S. president to specified terms. He argued that capable men should remain in civil office for life.[3]

Regarding even constitutional monarchies as weak, Apostle Richards affirmed: "Absolute power vested in one man is the best and most efficient human government, when that power is used in wisdom and righteousness . . ."[4] This enthusiasm was not unique to Mormon theocracy, and for decades English translations had proclaimed the popular view of French philosophers that "the happiest government would be that of a just and enlightened despot."[5]

"What do I understand by a theocratic government?" Brigham Young asked in 1859. "One in which all laws are enacted and executed in righteousness, and whose officers possess that power which proceedeth from the Almighty. That is the kind of government I allude to when I speak of a theocratic government, or the kingdom of God upon the earth. It is, in short, the eternal powers of the Gods."[6]

After the relatively peaceful conclusion of the Utah War, Young (now deposed as governor) wrote to non-Mormon confidant Thomas L. Kane in September 1858: "Trusting that the time is not far distant when Utah shall be able to assume her rights and place among the family of nations."[7] That dream endured among Mormons like William C. Staines, who wrote twenty years later that Utah "will become a nation, while they who lead this nation to day, go to hell, and the [U.S.] nation go to ruin."[8]

In anticipation of an independent theocracy, Young devised a flag for the Kingdom of God. He told a congregation in the Nauvoo temple that Joseph Smith had instructed him in the colors and design. Young intended to unfurl it in the "valleys that are within the Mountains."[9] Based on a Union model, the kingdom's flag had blue and white stripes and a field of twelve stars encircling one large star. Council of Fifty meetings probably displayed this banner privately. Mormon leaders publicly displayed the "Flag of Deseret" (and its variations) on a few known occasions: at Utah's first "Pioneer Day" celebrations from July 1849 to at least 1856, during the Las Vegas Mission in 1855, at Young's funeral in 1877, from the half-completed Salt Lake temple in 1880, and at Apostle Brigham Young Jr.'s funeral in 1903.[10]

These hopes for a fully independent Mormon nation must be placed in the context which encouraged such aspirations. Mormons first looked to the political Kingdom of God as protective refuge.[11] However, LDS leaders doggedly anticipated the day their theocracy would cease to be on the defensive. When that day came, they expected to expand the beneficent domain of their kingdom to an anxiously waiting and diversely religious world population.[12]

Nineteenth-century Mormon leaders argued that factionalism, contending political parties, and more than one candidate for political office were contrary to righteous political order. In the Kingdom of God people exercised freedom by sustaining their leaders' decisions and by voting unanimously for the candidates presented to them.[13] For example, the church's *Deseret News* editorialized:

> Suppose some leading men in the Church, then, select the candidates and tell the men and women whom to vote for. If those people of their own volition choose to accept those candidates and vote for them at the polls, should they not be allowed to do so without interference from their opponents? . . .
>
> Some people, however, cannot conceive of liberty without strife, nor freedom in acquiescence.[14]

At the election in 1878 a *Deseret News* editorial entitled "A Word of Warning" concluded: "One policy, one ticket, one ballot for all. 'Whatever is more or less than this cometh of evil.'"[15]

There is ample evidence of the nearly universal success of this political rule by priesthood decree. In the territory of Utah, where thousands of votes were cast, the degree of political unity was staggering. Between 1851 and the arrival of the railroad in 1869, the percentage of territorial votes against church candidates was almost negligible: none in 1851, .49 percent in 1852, less than .3 percent in 1861, less than 6 percent in 1862, less than 5 percent in 1863, less than .1 percent in 1864, less than .3 percent in 1865, less than .1 percent in 1867, less than .3 percent in 1868, and only forty-five contrary votes out of 11,000 votes in 1869.[16] In other words, until the arrival of the transcontinental railroad in 1869, more than 99 percent of Mormon voters supported church-approved candidates in all but one election. Even in that one discordant election, nearly 96 percent supported the candidates selected by the Mormon hierarchy. Not to quibble about less than 1 percent of opposition votes, the church's *Deseret News* typically announced that the voters "unanimously sustained" the church's candidates.[17]

Mormons continued to bloc-vote at extraordinary levels into the 1880s. In southeastern Idaho, where Mormons were members of the Democratic Party, 99.5 percent of Bear Lake County's votes went to Apostle Charles C. Rich for county commissioner in 1880, and no church-approved candidate received less than 98.8 percent.[18] The church's political newspaper reported that 82.6 percent of voters supported church-approved candidates in the 1882 Utah election.[19] In the 1880s Mormon bloc-voting in Arizona was defeated only through "ballot box stuffing" by the non-Mormon political "ring."[20]

Mormon bloc-voting for Democratic candidates in Idaho alienated non-LDS Democrats who formed their own Independent Party. By 1876 this "strictly anti-Mormon" political party joined with Idaho's Republicans to isolate and eventually disenfranchise virtually every Mormon in the state's southeastern counties. In the process, members of Utah's anti-Mormon Liberal Party moved to Idaho where they became governor and legislators.[21] Likewise, Nevada and Arizona disenfranchised Mormons temporarily.[22] However, the influx of non-Mormons into Utah after the arrival of the transcontinental railroad was not numerically sufficient to weaken Mormon political power there. In 1884 there were still less than 4,000 gentiles in Utah's population of 168,600.[23]

Ultimately, only the federal government was able to break the Mormon lock on Utah politics by passing anti-polygamy laws. "Laws must be enacted which will take from the Mormon Church its temporal power," U.S. president Rutherford B. Hayes explained. He added: "Mormonism as a sectarian idea is nothing, but as a system of government it is our duty to deal with it as an enemy to our institutions, and its supporters and leaders as criminals."[24] This was an echo of the complaint and determination expressed by "old residents" in Ohio, Missouri, Illinois, and Iowa who had battled the church's political power over bloc-voting Mormons.[25]

However, bloc-voting produced more apathy than elation among Utah Mormons. As early as 1862 the *Deseret News* commented on the "unusually small" voter turnout, which it described as "meagre" in 1878.[26] In 1880 the *Salt Lake Herald*, the church's political organ, was more precise: "not one-fourth of the registered voters" voted, and after the next year's election the *Deseret News* dismissed most Mormons as "too lazy or indifferent to walk or ride to the polls."[27] In 1884 the *Deseret News* complained "as a synonym for quietude and lackadaisical apathy, yesterday's election ought to be placed in the museum and handed down to succeeding ages."[28]

The church's political newspaper explained why three-fourths of registered Mormon voters did not participate in Utah's elections. In 1878 the *Herald* noted: "No apparent interest has been taken in the matter, one side resting serenely in the knowledge that it will be successful . . ."[29] Four years later the church's political organ summed up Mormon political power: "A nomination by the People's party is equivalent to an election . . ."[30] Since the result was guaranteed, most Mormons regarded their political participation as pointless before the 1890s.

Contributing to such near unanimity was the fact that until 1878 elections in Utah were either carried out by voice vote, numbered ballots, or ballots whose color indicated which party's candidates the voter selected.[31] This was typical of elections throughout the United States until the widespread adoption of procedures to guarantee a secret ballot for voters ("the Australian ballot") in 1888-90.[32] The *Salt Lake Tribune* also pointed out that the absence of a statutory time period for counting votes allowed dissidents to be persuaded to switch to the ballot of the church-approved candidates "before the vote is announced."[33]

Mormon leaders understandably opposed the non-Mormon governor's effort to introduce a secret ballot in Utah. "There is certainly greater irresponsibility, and in all probability greater fraud, connected with secret than with open voting," the *Deseret News* editorialized in 1876. The church newspaper added nearly two years later: "Why should a man be ashamed of the way he votes, any more than of his politics. . . . We can see no reason for it. People are said to shun the light and love darkness and secrecy when their deeds are evil."[34]

Concerning allegations that Mormons were ostracized for voting differently than instructed by LDS leaders, an editorial in the *Deseret News* acknowledged in 1878: "it cannot be expected that the dissenter will receive as much cordial friendship, countenance and support from his former fellow-partizans [sic] as those who remain in accord with them." The editors were apostles George Q. Cannon and Brigham Young.[35]

Not surprisingly, the hierarchy was conspicuous in public office until the end of the nineteenth century. In the State of Deseret, 1849-51, the president of the church was governor, his first counselor was chief justice and lieutenant governor, and his second counselor was secretary of state. The Presiding Bishop and an apostle were associate justices, and other general authorities comprised 19.2 percent of the House of Representatives and 21.4 percent of the Senate.[36]

Even after Congress created Utah territory in 1850, the president of the United States sanctioned this overlapping of church and state. Millard Fillmore agreed to appoint Young as governor of the territory and superintendent of Indian affairs between 1850 and 1857. In gratitude, Young named a central Utah county and town after the president, and Fillmore, Utah, was Utah's remote territorial capital from 1851 through 1858.[37]

Civil rule by the highest leaders of the Mormon church was not a transitory affair but permeated territorial, county, and municipal governments until the mid-1880s. The "people" elected general authorities to these civil offices as directed from LDS headquarters. For example, in 1857 Brigham Young instructed stake president Isaac C. Haight "to Send George A Smith from Iron County as Senator."[38] The extent of the hierarchy's civil service is best shown in their composition of the two chambers of the territorial legislature between 1851 and 1890.[39]

Table 1.
Hierarchy in the Chambers of Utah Territorial Legislature, 1851-90

	1851	1852	1853	1854	1855	1856	1857	1858	1859	1860
Upper	38.5%	46.2%	38.5%	30.8%	38.5%	30.8%	46.2%	46.2%	53.8%	38.5%
Lower	20.0%	23.1%	28.0%	24.0%	11.5%	11.5%	15.4%	19.2%	8.3%	12.0%

	1861	1862	1863	1864	1865	1866	1867	1868	1869	1870
Upper	53.8%	53.8%	69.2%	69.2%	76.9%	69.2%	69.2%	53.8%	53.8%	53.8%
Lower	12.0%	15.4%	19.2%	19.2%	19.2%	23.1%	23.1%	26.9%	23.1%	26.9%

	1871	1872	1873	1874	1875	1876	1877	1878	1879	1880
Upper	53.8%	38.5%	38.5%	23.1%	23.1%	30.8%	30.8%	36.4%	36.4%	30.8%
Lower	26.9%	26.9%	26.9%	24.0%	24.0%	19.2%	19.2%	19.2%	19.2%	11.5%

	1881	1882	1883	1884	1885	1886	1887	1888	1889	1890
Upper	30.8%	50.0%	50.0%	23.1%	23.1%	8.3%	8.3%	0	0	0
Lower	11.5%	11.5%	7.7%	0	0	4.2%	4.2%	0	4.2%	0

LDS general authorities were most dominant in the upper chamber, the Legislative Council. In the territorial legislature the council had the parliamentary status of the U.S. Senate in Congress. As Apostle Orson Pratt proclaimed in 1860: "Ours is an ecclesiastical Church and an ecclesiastical state."[40]

Although unanimous voting on legislation by territorial legislators was the rule in Utah until the 1880s, Mormon leaders tolerated a loyal opposition. The published minutes show that Mormon legislators in 1851 declined to vote for Apostle Wilford Woodruff as Speaker of the House, and instead installed William W. Phelps to that prestigious office. Although Phelps was a fellow member of the Council of Fifty, he was not a general authority. Perhaps to avoid similar embarrassments for defeated general authorities, the published minutes thereafter stopped listing the losing candidates for the legislature's administrative offices.[41]

Aside from that split vote about legislative officers, both houses of Utah's legislature voted unanimously until 13 January 1852. On that date five members of the upper chamber (including two general authorities and two current members of the Council of Fifty) voted in favor of tabling a petition, while five legislators (including one apostle and one current member of the Fifty) voted against the motion. The presiding officer, First Presidency counselor Willard Richards, broke the tie by siding with the negative voters. On 27 January Apostle Orson Pratt led an unsuccessful effort in the upper chamber to postpone "indefinitely" a bill authorizing any Utahn to purchase Indian slaves and register them legally as indentured servants for up to twenty years. Although Pratt supported the enactment of African-American slavery in Utah four days earlier, his opposition to legalizing the purchase and indenturing of Indians lost four votes to six. Two days later Pratt again voted against the majority along with Seventy's president Albert P. Rockwood because they felt a proposal "ought to be in the form of an act" rather than a mere resolution. On the other hand, Utah's House of Representatives voted unanimously on every motion in the 1851-52 session, and its only disruption occurred in a letter of 24 January 1852 from the upper chamber "to the effect that they had not concurred in the bill to create a county called Summit county, as it was not deemed expedient at present to divide Utah county. On motion, said bill was laid on the table."[42]

The unanimous voting in the Utah legislature's lower chamber during its first session showed that Seventy's president Jedediah M. Grant ran a tight ship as Speaker of the House. At the start of the legislature's second session of 1852-53, Grant explained his view of legislative theocracy: "The Speaker said during the last three days some of the members felt cramped in their feelings. I say unto them they will not violate any rule of Congress if they keep the power of the Holy Ghost, and act with the same conscientious feelings as if they were in a school of the Prophets." His message apparently reached the previously fractious upper chamber which now voted unanimously throughout all meetings of this legislative session.[43]

After the 1853-54 legislature also convened without a single dissenting vote, the next split vote occurred in the 1854-55 session of Utah's House of Representatives. On 9 January 1855 a motion passed with "eight voting in the affirmative, four voting in the negative." This split vote stood alone in the 1854-55 legislature. During the next twenty-five years, the only non-unanimous vote occurred when John C. James voted "in the negative on every motion" to incorporate a business in January 1861.[44]

With the exception of the split votes previously mentioned, for thirty years Utah's territorial legislators unanimously approved or unanimously disapproved every motion, tabled bills unanimously, and passed laws unanimously. Although verbatim transcripts are unavailable, this legislative unanimity was apparently accomplished by resolving all questions and disputes during the discussions-debates prior to the actual votes. Thus it is not sufficient to acknowledge that the legislature's sessions "of Brigham Young's administration enacted about all of his recommendations."[45] Utah had a legislative voting pattern unparalleled by any other western territory. In fact, it was without parallel in American legislative history since the establishment of England's colonial rule.

However, like the first example in January 1852, unanimous voting in one chamber of Utah's territorial legislature did not always agree with the unanimous voting in the other. In January 1866 the upper chamber sent the following message to the House: "The Council does not concur in your amendment to (C.F. No. 23.) in relation to Surveyor-General giving certificate of his surveys, etc., and respectfully ask your reconsideration of the bill."[46] Such were the only ripples in the placid minutes published by Utah's pioneer legislature.

January 1882 saw an explosion of dissent in the lower house of the Utah legislature. From then to March, there were split votes on forty-five different motions. As an evidence of real disagreement among LDS legislators, general authorities and current members of the Fifty were on both sides of nearly every vote. One possible explanation for this change is that the Mormon hierarchy intended this to bolster Utah's application for statehood in 1882 by signalling Congress that the legislature no longer moved in theocratic lockstep. However, that interpretation is undermined by the puzzling fact that the upper chamber continued to vote unanimously on every motion.[47]

Moreover, despite the failure of the 1882 statehood effort, in the next legislative session of January 1884 the upper chamber also began splitting votes on motions—thirteen in all. Although there were fewer splits than in the lower house's first experiment with dissenting votes, current members of the Fifty were on both sides of the split voting in the legislature's upper chamber in 1884. On one occasion the upper chamber's two general authorities were on different sides of a split vote.[48] Therefore, after 1881 the Mormon hierarchy participated in and allowed dissenting votes in the legislature, even though they vigorously promoted unanimous voting at elections for another decade.

However, during the decades of unanimous voting, real dissent occurred during the pre-vote discussions of the Utah territorial legislature. For example, the Church Historian's Office noted in 1862 that legislator Albert Carrington "allowed one bill (on attachments and garnishments) to *pass* the council [upper chamber], without any malicious alterations."[49] Carrington had been a member of the Council of Fifty since 1845 and later became a member of the Quorum of Twelve Apostles. However, general authority Albert P. Rockwood reminded a public meeting in 1859 that "all men holding the Priesthood employed in civil or military occupations were amenable to that priesthood for their acts."[50] In pioneer Utah a Mormon in civil office was really answerable only to Brigham Young.

Young's office was the center of power for pioneer Utah's civil government. For example, on 5 January 1861 various Utah legislators "called in and discussed a little Legislature Assembly business." Again in Young's office on 11 January he "discussed the doings of the L. Assembly with Hosea Stout and a few members of the Legislative Assembly." Stout was not yet a member of the Council of Fifty. Young's office journal then recorded in July: "First Presidency attended a meeting at the Historian's Office for the purpose of making nominations. J. M. Bernhisel was nominated for Delegate, and others for the [Utah] House of Representatives." Later his office journal recorded that Young "suggested" the men for appointive offices in Salt Lake City.[51]

By this time the secession crisis had brought the nation to the brink of civil war, and Brigham Young was using that as leverage for Utah's autonomy. A month after South Carolina seceded from the Union in November 1860, he instructed Utah's Congressional delegate William H. Hooper to "take some of our old memorials [seeking statehood], of which you have plenty, and alter the dates" for a new petition. He added that "if we are not admitted as a State during the present session, petition that we at least be privileged to elect our own Governor, Judges, and other Territorial Officers."[52] On 26 December 1860, the day before Young's letter, the *Deseret News* printed on its front page the following statement by an unidentified letter-writer from Washington, D.C.: "To be brief;—the thought is evidently in the minds of the leading politicians, that if now refused [statehood], Utah will be likely to take her own course, and set up an independent government."[53] That echoed the letter Hooper sent to England ten days earlier concerning the statehood application: if the United States "don't want us, we must then carve out our own future."[54]

Whether the *Deseret News* version was actually from Hooper or had been written at LDS headquarters, by January 1861 Young was also expressing a similar view. He first wrote Hooper to warn the Republican members of Congress that "in these hurrying times, Utah, after patiently waiting so long, may not feel disposed to again trouble Congress with a petition for admission [to the Union]." Young combined that dark warning with instructions to Hooper that Utah's governor Alfred Cumming "is anxious that Utah should have her quota of arms allowed by Government to the States and Territories." Young instructed Utah's delegate to arrange for immediate delivery of the requested arms to Mormon agents in Florence, Nebraska. Cumming would soon leave Utah with his nephew and namesake who returned immediately to Georgia and became an army general in the Confederate States of America. Governor Cumming returned to Washington, D.C., to make his final report to President Lincoln, only to be detained against his will for two years.[55] On 17 January Young instructed Hooper to warn Congress that "they had better admit Utah now while they have the opportunity."[56] This request to put weapons in Mormon control apparently raised concern among Union military leaders who instructed the army commander of Utah to destroy whatever supplies his troops could not take with them in abandoning this remote outpost.[57]

After five more southern states seceded in January 1861, Young's attitude toward the Union became correspondingly cavalier. On 7 February he made this remarkable statement to Utah's delegate: "We are very thankful that Congress has not admitted us into the Union as a State. However, we shall continue to tease them on that point so long as they even pretend to legislate for the past Union, but hope they will not admit us, unless they give us our present boundaries." The church president explained: "To be plain, the acts of that portion of Congress now operating are strictly illegal, being passed by Members from 27 instead of 33 States."[58]

Without providing documentation, a Brigham Young University professor wrote that "the Southern States made overtures for Utah's support of the rebellion."[59] Such an appeal from the Confederacy may have been why Young reassured the apostles on 10 March that "he did not wish Utah mixed up with the secession movement."[60]

Other manifestations of Mormon autonomy occurred in the first days of April 1861. On the 4th, a month after Abraham Lincoln's inauguration, Young instructed Utah's Congressional delegate to demand that the new U.S. president appoint Mormons as Utah's federal officials. Young's list included his own appointment as governor, with his son Joseph A. Young as territorial secretary.[61]

At general conference on 6 April 1861 Young announced his policy of bribing government officials. He preached that it was necessary to bribe officials "to grease the wheels." The church president described one instance in which he paid a $1,300 bribe. To demonstrate his contempt for the federal government, Young published these remarks.[62] Until the end of the nineteenth century, the First Presidency authorized the payment of bribes to editors of leading newspapers in New York City,[63] to members of Congress,[64] to deputy U.S. marshals,[65] to the U.S. marshal for Utah,[66] to Utah's prosecuting attorney,[67] to Utah's district court judges,[68] to U.S. Supreme Court justices,[69] and to the U.S. president's private secretary.[70] Church president John Taylor authorized Apostle Brigham Young, Jr., to take $25,000 to New York to bribe the newly elected president of the United States (Young was unsuccessful).[71] This was the Mormon hierarchy's response to the pervasive corruption in nineteenth-century U.S. government which typically required bribes. It was an era of "the most widespread and the deepest corruption that the federal government was ever to endure."[72]

Within five days after his public announcement about bribing federal officials, Young had second thoughts about putting too much pressure on Lincoln to appoint Mormon officers. "It will doubtless still be the best policy to patiently bide our time," he advised Utah's Congressional delegate on 11 April 1861. "Plausible pretexts against us would tend more than aught else to heal the present breach," he feared. Then the federal government and southern Confederacy would launch a joint military "crusade to Utah," rather than fight each other.[73] A Civil War historian has observed: "Young here expressed in a different context the idea that Secretary of State William H. Seward put forward, of picking a foreign war in order to bring the sections of the United States together in a common cause. But he [Young] showed, despite his perception, that he was out of touch with the seriousness of the North-South struggle."[74]

After a civil war began with the Confederate attack against Fort Sumter on 12 April 1861, Brigham Young decided to threaten Lincoln with Utah's secession. After all, Young had "correctly predicted" more than two months earlier that the civil war would begin "about the middle of April."[75] In February Young had publicly condemned secession as leading to anarchy, but he privately threatened it now that the federal government was fighting the Confederate military. If the U.S. president resisted appointing the requested Mormon officers for the territory, Young instructed Utah's Congressional delegate on 25 April to "hint that Territories as well as States are liable to become restive in these exciting times."[76] On 1 May 1861 Young confided that he was "pleased with the news which showed more and more secession, and each party was preparing for war, thus giving the Kingdom of God an opportunity of being established upon the Earth."[77] In August Apostle John Taylor said that "he had wished success to the Southern party but now they have got a little power he wished success to both parties."[78]

The Confederacy formally established its vast southwestern territory south of Utah on 1 August 1861. With the exception of one isolated post, all of the Southwest "from the Rio Grande to California, was free of Union troops."[79] Moreover, 40 percent of California's population came from slave states, and there were vocal secessionists in the southern half of California, despite the presence of Union troops.[80] In addition, Brigham Young and the Mormon legislature had legalized African-American slavery in 1852. Although free blacks lived in Utah during the 1850s, there were about seventy slaves in the territory.[81]

In view of that situation, Utah's acting governor reassured the nation's capital in September that Brigham Young had not "declared Utah independent" nor "appropriated" U.S. military supplies. Young's first message on the newly completed telegraph in October was more significant than most realize today: "Utah has not seceded, but is firm for the Constitution and laws of our once happy country." The church president, rather than the federally appointed governor of Utah, sent this reassurance of loyalty to the Union.[82] However, in the privacy of his office Young said that he "would be glad to hear that [Confederate] Genl. Beauregard had taken the [U.S.] President & Cabinet and confined them in the South."[83] That was one sentiment Young decided not to express publicly.

In fact, in December 1861 Mormons had an extraordinary confrontation with Utah's federal officials. Two days after newly arrived governor John W. Dawson refused to authorize a statehood convention, an unidentified person fired five "pistol shots" at associate justice Henry R. Crosby on Main Street in Salt Lake City. On Christmas day the *Deseret News* published the text of the governor's veto alongside his offer of a $100 reward for the assailant of the federal official.[84] By then the city was in an uproar over the report that Dawson had "made an insulting proposal" to a Mormon widow, and the *Deseret News* observed on 1 January 1862 that Utah's governor had hurriedly left for the East to "prevent his being killed or becoming qualified for the office of chamberlain [castrated eunuch] in the king's palace." The church newspaper claimed that Dawson hired as his "body guards" Lot Huntington, Moroni Clawson, and several others.[85] However, Dawson had asked Ephraim Hanks, one of Brigham Young's "Be'hoys," to escort him personally out of the territory. Instead, Hanks sent the other so-called bodyguards whom the *Deseret News* condemned as a "gang of thieves, who, at Hanks' station, beat him [the governor] in a most cowardly and dastardly manner." Although Dawson recovered sufficiently to return to his native Indiana, his official biography claimed he never fully recovered from the beating.[86] In choosing a protector, Governor Dawson obviously had not heard the report that Hanks recently helped an LDS policeman to slit a young thief's "throat from ear to ear."[87]

Despite their acquaintance with Hanks, these assailants were not Young's "Be'hoys" and had not acted with his approval. Young was furious that anti-Mormons could use this incident as an excuse to send troops to Utah and complained to Utah's delegate on 14 January 1862 that "all our efforts to legally rid ourselves of such characters have proved abortive."[88] Two days later Utah's deputy sheriff Orrin Porter Rockwell began solving that problem. He killed Lot Huntington while "attempting to escape" arrest for the Dawson beating. The LDS Church Historian's Office journal noted that Rockwell shot Huntington eight times in the stomach—difficult to do while someone is running away from the shooter. A day later Salt Lake City policemen killed the unarmed Moroni Clawson and John P. Smith for "starting to run" while being escorted to jail for the Dawson beating.[89] Decades later First Presidency counselor Joseph F. Smith acknowledged in a sermon that "a few horse thieves and murderers have perchance been summarily dealt with by officers of the law" in Utah.[90]

In real desperation, one of the surviving attackers sought to avoid that outcome by confessing to an LDS church court. Twenty-two-year-old Isaac Neibaur protested that he "never stole from a Mormon," asked forgiveness, but added that "if his Blood must atone he is willing to die." Church authorities did not require blood atonement. Thus one of the governor's assailants survived arrest long enough to receive a prison sentence.[91]

Claiming he could not remember appointing Dawson, Abraham Lincoln shrugged off the beating of Utah's governor.[92] However, after Utah's 1862 application for statehood,[93] Young publicly and privately expanded his original warning to Lincoln. On 26 February the *Deseret News* editorialized that "no one believes" the Confederacy "will soon be conquered, notwithstanding their recent [military] reverses . . ."[94]

Although confident of the Confederacy, the editors at that date were unaware that just five days earlier the Confederate army won the Civil War's first far western battle—at Valverde, New Mexico. Confederates occupied Tucson, Arizona that month, as well as Albuquerque and Santa Fe, New Mexico in early March.[95] Union generals recognized that the ultimate Confederate goal was to conquer California and draw Utah into the Confederacy.[96] The *Deseret News* did not immediately comment on these military developments close to Utah's borders, but the next issue of the church's newspaper published the full text of a Confederate "Address to the People of Georgia" to prepare for invasion by Union forces.[97]

On 12 March 1862 the *News* intensified veiled threats of secession by the "State of Deseret" if the federal government rejected the statehood application. By electing Brigham Young as governor of Deseret a few days earlier, the Mormon people "have declared their aversion to colonial servitude, tyranny and oppression," the editorial announced. If Congress rejected the statehood application, the last sentence of the editorial warned, "The sequel wise men may be able to predict."[98]

To underscore that warning, the first issue of the *Deseret News* in April 1862 printed the full text of the inaugural address by Jefferson Davis, president of the Confederate States of America, and also published his message to the Confederate Congress.[99] On 14 April Brigham Young learned that Utah's acting governor and chief justice had asked the U.S. Secretary of War "to raise and officer a regiment here, for three months, or until U.S. troops can reach here . . ." That same day Young's first message as "Governor" of the State of Deseret did not refer directly to this news, but he did "object to any action being taken in this or any other matter, except on the ground of right and justice, and in nowise as an evidence of our loyalty . . ." In response to the news of federal troops being sent to Utah, Young immediately signalled Congress that the Mormons were self-governing. The unstated implication was that if Utah did not receive statehood, the Mormons were prepared to assert their own form of self-government. As Young informed Utah's delegate Bernhisel on 15 April: "all the machinery [is] in readiness to be put in motion when the appropriate time shall arrive."[100]

In an effort to avoid Washington's plan of sending federal troops to Utah to guard the mail routes and "quiet the Indians," Young authorized Mormons on 25 April 1862 to serve as volunteers for such military service. Young put them under the general direction of his counselor Daniel H. Wells, commanding officer of Utah's militia, the Nauvoo Legion. Five days later the *Deseret News* told Mormons that Union troops from California had been ordered to Utah.[101]

Because of failures in the telegraph lines and not receiving mails (including eastern newspapers) for "nearly a month,"[102] Utahns did not learn until mid-May that the U.S. House of Representatives had overwhelmingly passed a bill to disincorporate the LDS church, invalidate certain laws passed by the Utah legislature a decade earlier, and "prevent and punish the practice of polygamy."[103] Representative Morrill of Vermont had introduced this bill repeatedly since 1858, but it had usually died in committee. Despite the negative vote of representatives from thirteen southern states, four midwestern states, two western states, and even scattered votes in opposition by four northern states, the House passed the Morrill bill in 1860. It died in the U.S. Senate where these southern, midwestern, and western states had equal representation, and their "popular sovereignty" views succeeded in killing the anti-polygamy bill in committee.[104] Only the secession of eleven states of the South now allowed Congress and President Lincoln to enact this invalidation of acts by Utah's elected legislators. After announcing this added insult by the Union, the next issue of the *Deseret News* published an article about "a strong secession feeling" in California and Nevada.[105]

By then Young had increased his thoughts of actual secession of Utah from the Union. On 30 May 1862 he instructed William H. Hooper to travel from Washington, D.C., to Philadelphia for a private meeting with an unnamed person whom Young fully trusted. One might assume it was his longtime confidant Thomas L. Kane, but Kane had been wounded six months earlier while commanding Union troops, was leading his men into battle at this time, and would soon be captured by the Confederates.[106] Now Hooper was no longer Utah's delegate to Congress, but was U.S. senator for the theocratic State of Deseret. Whatever the identity of his secret adviser, Young instructed Hooper: "Please whisper in his ear whether he thinks it possible for the union to be broken [between Utah and the federal government]," Young wrote. "Ask what he thinks about it."[107]

Since January 1861 Young may have confided these secession thoughts to no other Mormon than Hooper who was a slave owner. He had purchased an African-American slave in Utah as recently as 1859.[108] Young certainly did not even hint at the possibility of secession in his correspondence with Utah's official delegate to Congress, John M. Bernhisel, a member of the theocratic Council of Fifty from Pennsylvania.[109]

Whether or not the State of Deseret joined the Confederacy, the church president knew that Union generals would attempt to invade Utah if the Mormon commonwealth seceded. Ever since 1860 Young had reminded Hooper that "peaceable secession" from the United States was impossible.[110]

Young's secret inquiry in May was due to the fact that the Mormons needed to act quickly to prevent U.S. troops from entering Utah. Secession by the State of Deseret would be a desperate act of theocracy that depended on the Confederacy's military success in keeping Union forces at bay in the West. However, before Young received a reply from Hooper's secret consultation in Philadelphia, the Confederate army lost a decisive battle in the Far West and was retreating back to Texas. Union forces retook Tucson on 7 June.[111]

Within the week Utah's non-Mormon Chief Justice John F. Kinney asked the acting governor, also non-LDS, to authorize the forcible suppression of a group of Mormon schismatics who were resisting federal authority within Utah. A thousand Mormon artillerymen and infantry massed on the border between Weber and Davis counties, surrounding the refuge of those who had left Mormonism to follow the revelations of Joseph Morris. Shortly after the commanding officer Robert T. Burton gave the Morrisites an ultimatum to surrender, cannons fired on the congregation assembled in the middle of the fort. After three days of siege, the Morrisites surrendered and then witnessed their principal leaders being shot and killed as the Mormon posse entered their fort. Burton was later indicted for the alleged murders of Morris, his counselor, and a woman who cursed Burton as a coward for shooting her leaders. Her body fell to the ground, "holding in her arms the babe of the mother who had been killed by the first cannon ball fired into the camp." A counselor in the Presiding Bishopric at the time of his trial, Burton was acquitted by a Mormon jury.[112]

Although federal authority had helped the Mormons to suppress a schismatic movement, dreams of Confederate victory died hard. After all, representatives from these Southern states had voted against the original attempts in Congress to outlaw polygamy. Brigham Young wrote on 18 July 1862 that "the prospects of the North's conquering the South are much poorer than they have been at any time since the war began."[113]

Mormons lined the streets and watched in silence as Colonel Patrick E. Connor marched his California volunteer troops along Salt Lake City's East Temple Street (now Main Street) in October 1862. It was only fifteen months since federal troops had left Utah.[114] Soon the Irish-born Connor was angrily referring to "the real governor of this Territory, Brigham Young."[115] Less polite, Young told a meeting of the First Presidency, apostles, and Presiding Bishopric in October that federally appointed governor Stephen S. Harding was no better than "a sack [of] cow shit."[116] Connor stationed his troops on the city's eastern foothills within cannon-range of Young's official residence, the Beehive House.[117]

Ironically, one of Connor's officers was a former Danite who had abandoned Mormonism years ago. First lieutenant John Darwin Chase was severely wounded during the army's battle with the Shoshoni during which hundreds of women and children were massacred. He "begged" for a blessing of healing from two Mormons after Porter Rockwell took some of the wounded soldiers to Farmington, Utah. "I said I thought it would be the wrong thing to do," a Mormon wrote, "so he was not administered to" and died.[118]

Colonel Connor secretly petitioned his military superiors to send him siege cannons and 3,000 more troops as a prelude to declaring martial law in Utah "and put[ting] a brief end to the institution of polygamy." On almost a daily basis, at the least suspicion of trouble from the U.S. troops, Brigham Young summoned 1,500 men to surround his residence. In response, the commander of the army's Department of the Pacific vowed that "a day of retribution will come," and the commanding general of all Union forces promised massive reinforcements to Utah. But troops were needed elsewhere, and nothing happened to ignite the tinderbox in Salt Lake City.[119]

Young may have learned of these proposals, for he furiously told a public meeting on 3 March 1863: "They are trying to break up civil government in Utah and set up a military despotism, and woe be to that man who undertakes to introduce despotism in Utah; in such an attempt they will then learn who is Governor." The Salt Lake Tabernacle immediately erupted in "great applause."[120] Five days later Young told a congregation that he refused to allow any Mormons to serve in the Union military "to fight in the present battle-fields of the nation, while there is a camp of soldiers from abroad located within the corporate limits of this city."[121]

During the first half of the American Civil War, LDS authorities routinely condemned the Union's leaders and maintained a public attitude of aloofness. They awaited the outcome of a conflict they hoped would permanently cripple the federal government.[122] Utah also became a haven for draft-dodgers and deserters from the armies of both the Union and the Confederacy.[123] "The Gentile did not comprehend the fact that the Saints were committed to the [U.S.] constitution while not feeling committed to either the North or the South," a non-Mormon historian has written. The Mormon "attitude of loyalty to the Union while looking forward to its eventual downfall was not an easy position to make clear" to outsiders.[124]

However, the federal-Mormon conflict cooled down considerably in the summer of 1863. First, in response to complaints by the Mormons against Governor Harding, President Lincoln agreed in June to replace him and told Mormon emissary T. B. H. Stenhouse: "You go back and tell Brigham Young that if he will let me alone, I will let him alone." Aside from statehood for Utah, Lincoln's reassurance was all Young wanted, and LDS leaders stopped publicly denouncing the U.S. president as a tyrant.[125] Next Young arranged for John F. Kinney, a friendly non-Mormon and recently released federal judge, to be "unanimously" elected as Utah's delegate to Congress in August 1863.[126] Six months before this election a former federal judge told Congress that Kinney was the "creature and tool of Brigham Young."[127] Despite these developments, a history of the *Deseret News* regarded the church newspaper as "pro-Confederate" or at best neutral "until the summer of 1864 when it definitely turned pro-Union."[128]

Although Mormons elected a gentile as Utah's delegate to Congress, non-Mormons did not have equal rights in the territory. A legal historian has observed that in 1865 "the Mormon legislature" passed an act for incorporating irrigation companies that effectively disbarred non-Mormon enterprises. The act required that only "a majority of the citizens in a county or part of a county" was eligible to organize an irrigation company. Because of the Mormon majority in every county, this act "provided all the power necessary to consolidate Utah's water resources under Mormon control." Not until fifteen years later did the federally appointed judges on Utah's supreme court strike down this law. The court denounced the territorial legislature for turning Utah's irrigation companies into "engines of oppression."[129]

This was the background for the hierarchy's highest presence in the upper chamber of the Utah legislature from 1863-67. The so-called "ghost government" of the theocratic State of Deseret also passed its own laws (duplicates of what the same Mormon legislators had just done in the territorial legislature), held elections, and functioned until 1872. During this ten-year period of openly theocratic government, Brigham Young was the announced "governor," elected by ballots that had no force in Utah's civil government. He had not legally served as governor since 1857.[130]

At the bicentennial of the American nation, Utah's official history commented on this ghost government of Deseret. It was "in effect, a state-in-waiting, product of Mormon faith in the imminence of Christ's second coming and reflection of the Mormon yearning for self-government."[131] This understandably irritated Utah territorial governor James D. Doty, who complained to the U.S. secretary of state in January 1865 that there were "really four governments in Utah: the Church, the State of Deseret, the [U.S.] Army, and the federal officials."[132] Brigham Young controlled the first two, was carefully watched by the third, and often stymied the fourth. As one historian has written, "Brigham Young still ruled Utah and was conducting a brilliant, coordinated, unceasing, passive resistance movement unique in American history."[133]

On 6 March 1865 First Presidency counselor Heber C. Kimball reassured Apostle Wilford Woodruff: "The North will never have the power to Crush the South [—] No never. The Lord will give the South power to fight the North untill they will destroy Each other." At this time every major city of the South was in ruins or had been captured, and a month later the Confederacy surrendered unconditionally.[134]

Midway through the ghost government's public affront to Washington, D.C., Young privately reconvened the Council of Fifty on 23 January 1867. This was in the midst of the national effort to politically "reconstruct" the defeated Confederacy, and "Radical Republicans concerned with polygamy and court reform felt that they also had the power to use extraordinary measures to reconstruct Utah."[135] After noting that "the last meeting of the Council [was] on the 4th. October 1851," the Fifty's minutes for January 1867 demonstrated Young's continued lack of enthusiasm about a political role for the council: "the chairman stated that he was not aware of any particular business to be brought before the Council, further than to meet and renew our acquaintance with each other in this capacity."

At the opening of this 1867 meeting Young acknowledged that he had not consulted the Fifty as an organization for more than fifteen years. However, he observed that during those years "the members of this body had been selected as far as possible, to represent the people in the Legislative Assembly."[136] If that smacked of tokenism, none voiced the kind of criticism expressed two decades earlier by George Miller, Alpheus Cutler, and Peter Haws. Still, the true significance of Young's reassurance was that the church hierarchy, not the Council of Fifty, had "selected" members of the Fifty for civil office from 1851 to 1867.

Although the Fifty convened five times in 1867 and three times in 1868, its meetings were occupied with initiating new members and reminiscing about the council's Nauvoo origins. Even its vote on 9 October 1868 to establish Zion's Co-operative Mercantile Institution (ZCMI) was a rubber stamp. The *Deseret News* had announced this proposal on 3 October, and the church's general conference had already voted for this business association before the Fifty discussed it. Young never reconvened this theocratic body after its *pro forma* ratification of the ZCMI proposal.[137]

However, the formation of ZCMI demonstrated how Council of Fifty members persuaded themselves that the Fifty had a more significant administrative role than it actually possessed. On 13 October 1868 Fifty member Abraham O. Smoot told the Provo "School of the Prophets" that after the above conference, "the council of 50 met and while at that Meeting it was proposed that in organizing [sic] a Mercantile Cooperative association . . ." Therefore, Smoot knew that the Fifty's first discussion of ZCMI occurred after the announcement in the *Deseret News* and after the general conference's vote. Nevertheless, he told the bishops of Provo on 15 October that ZCMI "is a measure concocted by the Council of Fifty as suggested by the President."[138] Thus non-hierarchy members of the Fifty were able to persuade themselves that the Council of Fifty had supreme importance within days of events which demonstrated that the council was a rubber stamp for decisions previously made by the hierarchy and even by the public vote of a general conference.

The School of the Prophets

At the same time Brigham Young denied a significant political role to the Council of Fifty, he allowed the School of the Prophets to participate in Utah's shadow government. Established at Kirtland, Ohio, in 1833 as a pioneering adult education center for Mormon leaders,[139] Young reconstituted the School of the Prophets in Salt Lake City on 9 December 1867. More than 900 men belonged to the central school, and approximately 5,000 others joined branches in various communities throughout the Great Basin. Admission was by ticket only, thus providing control over attendance. In addition to theological discussions from 1867 to 1874, each school implemented political and economic policies.[140]

Concerning the political significance of the schools, one analyst has written:

> The two Schools of the Prophets organized by Young between 1867 and 1874 participated actively and enthusiastically in the planning, organization, and conducting of Utah Territorial political affairs. The various schools nominated and sustained local officials prior to their names being placed upon the election ballot, and these schools made the decisions and arrangements for protecting polling places and transporting voters to and from the polls.

This overestimates the extent to which the hierarchy was willing to allow democracy in Mormon theocracy. The schools were indeed a form of broader political participation, but they were controlled in a variety of ways. For instance, general authorities presided over schools in the most important population centers: The entire First Presidency in the School of the Prophets at Salt Lake City, Apostle Ezra T. Benson in Logan, Apostle Erastus Snow in St. George, and Apostle Charles C. Rich in Paris, Idaho.[141]

Moreover, when the school decided on nominations for Salt Lake City's elections, the nominating committee was comprised entirely of general authorities. On 29 January 1870, for example, the Salt Lake School of the Prophets was turned into a "caucus," and the nominating committee was Apostle Wilford Woodruff, Apostle George Q. Cannon, and Presiding Bishopric counselor Jesse C. Little.[142] General authorities were often a third of larger nominating committees. If only one general authority was on the "People's" nominating committee, that man was an apostle or a member of the First Presidency and chaired the committee. This pattern applied to nominations for territorial offices, as well.[143]

This control did not begin at the nominating committee, however, as demonstrated by the 1872 election in Salt Lake City. On 28 January the First Presidency and apostles held a "preliminary meeting" to select municipal candidates. On 3 February the School of the Prophets met and received the already approved nominations from the chair of the school's nominating committee, Apostle George Q. Cannon. He had obtained the list of names in his meeting with the First Presidency. The School of the Prophets unanimously voted for the nominations to be presented to the voters for a final, legal approval.[144]

In 1874 Brigham Young again referred to the Council of Fifty during a sermon. "I shall not tell you the names of the members of this kingdom," he said, "neither shall I read to you its constitution, but the constitution was given by revelation." Nor did Young volunteer that he had not convened a meeting of this theocratic council for nearly six years and had transferred its political role to the School of the Prophets.[145]

The hierarchy also flexed its power in non-institutional, *ad hoc* gatherings to arrange nominations. LeGrand Young, a Mormon, was invited to participate in one of these secret meetings in January 1878, even though he was not a member of the hierarchy nor of the Council of Fifty. His reaction was unfavorable:

> Met with several of the brethren this P.M. at the office of the president of the Twelve [apostles] to talk over the candidates for next term of the City Council. I must confess I am disgusted with what took place there. All the persons present were City Councilors except President Taylor and myself. Bro Taylor was called to the chair, and the rest proceeded to elect themselves to the new council.
>
> It was then arranged to have primaries and to send men to the convention to nominate city officers. Of course the names have been selected for them and when that august body meets it will have a committee of eight or ten, named by the chair who will withdraw and in all likelihood bring in the names of those previously selected.[146]

LeGrand Young's distaste for this informal manipulation of the nominating process would have changed to amazement had he known the extent to which he was involved in a charade.

The Quorum of the Twelve Apostles had already met three days earlier and selected candidates for the city election before this *ad hoc* meeting.[147] LeGrand Young and other non-apostles thought their own meeting was the shadow government behind the public convention. To the contrary, the hierarchy was behind every other shadow government. This secret meeting's outcome was merely an echo, and the political convention's outcome was an echo of an echo.

Up to 1890 general authorities were the source of first approval for every political nomination in Utah that they regarded as important. The hierarchy approved John M. Bernhisel, William H. Hooper, George Q. Cannon, and John T. Caine as Utah's delegates to Congress before any other echelon nominated these men.[148] The hierarchy not only initiated the nominations to the territorial legislature but also decided who would replace those who died during a legislative session, who would be elected as officers of the respective legislative chambers, and who would be recommended to the governor for territorial appointments.[149] The First Presidency and apostles regularly decided in advance who would be elected and reelected as mayor and city councilmen in Salt Lake City, Ogden, and Provo.[150] When Young toured distant settlements, he arranged for the selection of civil officers in those towns.[151]

Sometimes Young simply gave direct instructions on political matters to the School of the Prophets. In 1872 he sent a telegram to Parowan, Utah, to instruct the school which candidates to vote for. In the 1874 election Young left his list of political candidates for the Salt Lake school to approve while he was out of the city.[152]

Loyal Mormons knew of the charade and some did not like it. In 1878 J. M. Benedict, a member of Salt Lake County's central committee of the church's political party, complained that the public conventions were "influenced by previous manipulation."[153] At a public nominating convention in 1880 Bishop George Romney "reluctantly" explained why most Mormons were indifferent toward nominations and elections in Utah: "He did not believe that any four or five men should select the officers, but the people should do it. He believed that the reason the meetings are so thinly attended is because the people often do not endorse the nominees." Another Mormon delegate added that "for some years past the people have not been satisfied with the nominations made for officers, but they have been voted for, and by him, among others, because the people desire to be united and to keep the offices in the [church's political] party."[154] Such candor was not in evidence until after Brigham Young's death. However, it seems clear that many Mormons had understood the political charade for years, perhaps as far back as Joseph Smith's leadership. Nevertheless, they stoically (rather than enthusiastically) upheld the theocracy due to faith in LDS leaders and fear of Zion's enemies.

After the hierarchy placed its preferred candidates in public office, general authorities continued to advise and counsel them in the conduct of their offices. The LDS church president regularly instructed Utah's territorial delegates to Congress about how they should lobby at the nation's capital.[155] In the 1850s President Young, Counselor Willard Richards, and Apostle Ezra T. Benson participated in Salt Lake City Council meetings even though they were not members of that body. Apostle George A. Smith did the same in Provo during the early 1850s, and Apostle Ezra T. Benson continued the practice in Logan from its first meeting in 1868 until his death in 1869. When he knew he would be out of town, Young informed the mayor in advance of the agenda he wanted to be presented to the Salt Lake City Council.[156]

Young's consistent refusal to give the Council of Fifty a decision-making role during his thirty-year presidency is why it is misleading for historians to measure the council's significance by tallying up its members who held civil office.[157] A majority of these office holders were general authorities whose quorums met weekly during the years the Fifty itself never convened. The Fifty's non-hierarchy members fulfilled civil offices according to instructions of the First Presidency and Quorum of the Twelve.

There were also disparities in the Fifty's public service. Nearly 11 percent of its total members had no discoverable record of public office in politics, military, or civil service.[158] In part, this can be accounted for by men who left the church prior to the settlement of Utah. Yet even in Utah the following men apparently held no public office: Abraham H. Cannon, Amos Fielding, George F. Gibbs, Charles S. Kimball, and David P. Kimball. In addition, Levi Richards held no civil office in Utah, though he had in Nauvoo. Joseph Fielding, Philip B. Lewis, and John Young held civil office only in the legislature of the provisional State of Deseret (1849-51).[159]

The claim that the Fifty was a channel to political power becomes less convincing upon examination of the lives of council members who held public office. Nearly 69 percent of those who were politically active in Nauvoo and in Utah began civil service *before* they entered the council. Some served more than a decade in public office before becoming one of the Fifty. Most of these had loyally served the interests of the church in public office for years, and the Council of Fifty did not introduce them to a new world of office-holding. For these experienced public servants, membership in the Fifty did not alter their previous pattern of political devotion to the interests of Mormonism as directed by the First Presidency and the Quorum of the Twelve. The Council of Fifty introduced only a minority of its members to political life.

As was true during the Joseph Smith era, theocratic service in public office was conspicuously the domain of the First Presidency and Twelve. During the entire period 1851-83, as long as there was an organized First Presidency there was at least one counselor of the First Presidency serving in the Utah legislature. Aside from the years 1864-67 and 1872, a counselor in the Presidency was president of the upper chamber of the legislature. During much of the period from 1863 to 1873, either ten or eleven apostles were in the legislature each session. A member of the Quorum of the Twelve was president of the upper chamber during the period 1864-79, including periods when the same man served both in the Quorum of the Twelve and as an assistant counselor in the First Presidency. A member of the Quorum of the Twelve served as Speaker of the House in the Utah legislature's lower chamber from 1857 to 1883.[160] Moreover, during the period 1872-82 Apostle George Q. Cannon served as Utah's territorial delegate to Congress.[161]

Whereas the lower echelons of the hierarchy had virtually no role in the civil government of Nauvoo, they were frequently represented in Utah's territorial legislature. A total of eight members of the First Council of Seventy served in the Utah legislature between 1851 and 1879. Although Levi W. Hancock, William W. Taylor, Horace S. Eldredge, and Joseph Young served only a session or two, other men such as Jacob Gates, John Van Cott, and Albert P. Rockwood served in multiple sessions. Moreover, during the period 1852-54 a junior member of the First Council of Seventy, Jedediah M. Grant, served as Speaker of the House.[162]

The Presiding Bishop served in the Utah legislature only during 1851-52, but counselors in the Bishopric served periodically until the mid-1880s. Nathaniel H. Felt was in the first territorial legislature from 1851-53. Jesse C. Little served in the Utah legislature from 1856 to 1859, Robert T. Burton from 1875 to 1877, and John Q. Cannon in 1886.[163]

The two Presiding Patriarchs of territorial Utah had minimal experience in the legislature. The first, "Uncle" John Smith, had been a member of the legislature of the State of Deseret (1849-51), but served only as a chaplain in the territorial legislature until his death in 1854. His grand-nephew and successor, Patriarch John Smith (b. 1832), was never a member of the Utah legislature but often served as its sergeant-at-arms (1861-62, 1864-67, 1876-82).[164]

The year 1882 was both a high point and end point for general authority service in the legislature's administrative offices. For the first time in Utah history, the sergeant-at-arms of both houses of the territorial legislature in 1882 was a general authority (John Van Cott in the upper and Patriarch Smith in the lower house). However, an active general authority has never served as an administrative officer of the Legislature since then.[165]

The rapid decline of general authority presence after 1883 reflected the federal effort to restructure Utah's political life by disenfranchising Mormon polygamists. Congress enacted the Edmunds Law in 1882 to achieve that purpose.[166]

Nevertheless, even as the federal campaign against polygamy began chipping away at the theocracy, the hierarchy's political control was temporarily undaunted. When the 1882 Edmunds Law disqualified polygamists from holding public office, the First Presidency and Twelve decided which polygamists should resign from municipal and county offices. The hierarchy also decided which "faithful" monogamists would replace them.[167]

The remaining policy-making body at the territorial level was that of the convention, which periodically drafted proposed constitutions to be submitted to Congress for statehood consideration. In 1856, in the midst of a religious reformation and a year prior to federal troops descending upon Utah, general authorities comprised 18.4 percent of delegates to the constitutional convention. In subsequent years the proportion was less: in 1862, 10.8 percent; in 1872, 7.7 percent; and in 1882, only 2.8 percent. At the height of the federal campaign against Mormons in 1887, no general authorities were at the convention.[168]

The proportion of the hierarchy in these conventions was often one-half or one-third of their proportion in the territorial legislature. This was no accident of local politics even in counties hundreds of miles from church headquarters, because Brigham Young himself instructed local LDS leaders about the specific men to be nominated and elected as delegates from each county to these statehood conventions.[169] This control persisted after Young's death, and all delegates of the 1882 constitutional convention met with the First Presidency and apostles for instruction prior to the opening of the convention.[170] Until 1895 the work of these conventions was in vain, because neither Congress nor the president of the United States would give serious consideration to statehood applications submitted by an openly polygamous and theocratic territory.[171]

The membership of committees which drafted these proposed state constitutions indicated another side of the dynamics between the LDS hierarchy and the Council of Fifty. For the 1849 constitution the ten members of the drafting committee were all members of the Fifty (with four general authorities, all apostles). That participation of the Fifty was consistent with the high point of its formal meetings. Since the 1850 and 1856 constitutions were "in the main, a copy of the constitution of 1849," those conventions apparently served as a committee-of-the-whole for the constitutional revisions, with no separate drafting committee. In 1862, when the theocratic council had not met for a decade, four members of the Fifty sat on the drafting committee of five, and two of the Fifty were apostles. In 1872, when the theocratic council had not met in nearly four years, the nine-member drafting committee had two apostles and two other current members of the Council of Fifty (committee members John T. Caine and William Jennings would join the Fifty in later years).[172]

As the federal anti-Mormon campaign intensified, the proportion of the Fifty's participation declined and the hierarchy eventually disappeared from the drafting committees of these proposed state constitutions. In 1882 exactly one-third of the twenty-one-member committee on the constitution's final "revision and consolidation" were current members of the Fifty. Another committee member, Charles W. Penrose, joined the Fifty two months later. The only general authority on the committee was its chairman, Daniel H. Wells, former First Presidency counselor and current counselor to the Quorum of Twelve Apostles. Here the hierarchy apparently felt that "a little leaven leaveneth the whole lump" (Gal. 5:9).[173]

The 1887 convention for the first time included a significant percentage of friendly non-Mormons, while two of the Fifty (Franklin S. Richards and John R. Winder) were members of only one of the committees to draft the constitution, the Committee on Miscellaneous Powers and Amendments. However, this was the crucial committee which allegedly drafted an amendment in July outlawing polygamy, the text of which was approved for adoption in February by church president John Taylor. Although Winder was now a general authority, he had served on the 1882 drafting committee as a member of the Fifty.[174]

Also, members of these committees were not drafting entirely new constitutions. As an analyst of various Rocky Mountain territories has observed, "the 1856 and 1862 constitutions were similar to their first [of 1849 and 1850]. The 1872 Utah constitution used the Nevada constitution of 1864 as a reference. The 1882 constitution was essentially the same as the 1872 document, and the 1887 convention used the 1882 constitution as a model."[175]

Despite the theocratic context of Utah's constitutional conventions for the proposed "State of Deseret," real dissent occurred. The most significant example concerned the proposal to authorize slavery in the 1856 constitution, as it had been in Utah territorial law since 1852. On 21 March 1856 Apostle George A. Smith seconded a motion to add the following to the proposed constitution: "We recognize the right of the people of this State to adopt and regulate African Slavery, as they in their wisdom may deem proper." The proposal specified "African" slavery, because Utah territorial law prohibited the enslavement of Native American Indians. Apostle Orson Pratt immediately moved that this provision "be stricken out." When the thirty-five-delegate convention overwhelmingly rejected Pratt's motion, "the following members desired to have their names recorded in the Journal as having voted in favor of striking out the" provision: Orson Pratt, Parley P. Pratt, Samuel P. Hoyt, and Enoch Reese. Delegates who voted to authorize "African Slavery" in the proposed State of Deseret included First Presidency counselor Jedediah M. Grant, apostles George A. Smith, Ezra T. Benson, Lorenzo Snow, and Council of Fifty members Daniel H. Wells, Albert Carrington, Almon W. Babbitt, John D. Parker, John D. Lee, and Isaac Morley. At the close of this day's session, Apostle George A. Smith seconded a substitute motion that "the people of this State do adopt and will regulate African Slavery, as they in their wisdom may deem proper." This time pro-slavery delegates joined the anti-slavery delegates in defeating the motion. William H. Hooper explained that "if the question was for or against the principle of slavery they would have voted in favor of slavery," but Hooper and other pro-slavery delegates voted against allowing the slavery question to be decided by popular vote. As a result, the 1856 constitution made no direct reference to slavery.[176]

Since owning and purchasing African-American slaves was already legal in Utah, this decision of the 1856 convention was simply a diplomatic strategy to avoid mixing up the Mormon quest for statehood with the bitter conflict in Congress about slavery. Despite the absence of reference to slavery in the proposed constitution, the legalized slavery of African-Americans in Utah doomed this attempt for statehood. The *New York Times* published William H. Seward's furious reaction: "Utah, already organized as a Slave State, with her incestuous social system [of polygamy], is lying concealed and waiting, ready to demand admission so soon as Kansas shall have been received into the Union. The adoption of both, or even one of these States, will bear heavily, perhaps conclusively, on the fortunes of the entire conflict between Freedom and Slavery."[177] This statehood effort in 1856 failed, as did all others by the Mormons prior to 1894.

In the Mormon-gentile "era of reconciliation"[178] surrounding adoption of the 1895 constitution, the LDS hierarchy felt more confident about letting rank-and-file delegates vote according to their individual conscience. Aside from 1849-50, participation of the Council of Fifty's members in Utah's constitutional conventions did not reflect formal decisions of the Fifty, but resulted from the hierarchy's decision to allow participation by individual members of the Fifty.

General authorities occasionally held some of the miscellaneous territorial offices of Utah. Apostle Wilford Woodruff served as inspector of the Utah penitentiary during 1857-59. Bishopric counselor Jesse C. Little was the territorial assessor for the U.S. Internal Revenue Service (IRS) from 1863 to 1866. Seventy's president Albert P. Rockwood was the first territorial Fish Commissioner in 1855, and from 1855 until the 1870s he also served as inspector and warden of the Utah penitentiary. Seventy's president Horace S. Eldredge served as Utah territory's collector and assessor from 1852 to 1853. Seventy's president John Van Cott served from 1868 to 1875 as one of the three territorial commissioners to locate university lands (again, 1880-82). Apostle and church president John Taylor served as territorial superintendent of district schools from 1877 to 1881.

In contrast to their extensive involvement in municipal and territorial government, general authorities had relatively minimal service in county government. The only active general authority who served as a county selectman was Seventy's president Jacob Gates who served in Washington County in 1862-63 and 1870-71. County clerk positions were filled by Francis M. Lyman in Tooele County for three years following his appointment as an apostle in 1880 and by Brigham Young, Jr., in Cache County during 1873-75, when he was both a member of the Quorum of the Twelve Apostles and an assistant counselor to his father. Young was also county recorder (1874-77). Apostle Charles C. Rich served as the first treasurer of Bear Lake County, Idaho (1875-76), and then as county commissioner until 1880. Bishopric counselor Robert T. Burton was Salt Lake County assessor and collector in 1880.[179]

The one county office with particular impact on Mormon prerogatives was the county probate judge. Until the Poland Act of 1874, Utah's probate judges had both civil and criminal responsibility, and most were Mormon bishops who protected Mormons against non-Mormons.[180] General authorities sometimes filled this office as well. Apostle George A. Smith was "Chief Justice" in Iron County in 1851, Apostle Orson Hyde was the first probate judge in Carson County (now Nevada) in 1855-57. Apostles Charles C. Rich and Erastus Snow and Presiding Bishop Edward Hunter served as probate judges in 1857-58. Apostle John Taylor was probate judge for Utah County in 1868-70, possibly as insurance against the arrival of gentile railroad workers and immigrants. Once the railroad was completed with Ogden as its junction, Apostle Franklin D. Richards served as probate judge for the heavily non-Mormon Weber County from 1869 until 1883 and also as justice of the peace most of that time. In addition apostles Erastus Snow (1862-70) and Amasa M. Lyman (1866-67) served as "circuit judge" in the "ghost government" of Deseret.[181]

The hierarchy's domination of Utah's territorial government was closer to the extent and spirit of Nauvoo's theocratic city-state, but general authorities were also active in municipal office. For thirty-six years the hierarchy controlled the most important elective offices in Salt Lake City, although a comparison shows that their presence on the Salt Lake City Council was less than in Nauvoo.[182] From 1851 to 1866 the hierarchy was represented in the Salt Lake City Council by men of the lesser echelons: Benjamin L. Clapp, Zerah Pulsipher, and John Van Cott of the First Council of Seventy, and Nathaniel H. Felt and Leonard W. Hardy of the Presiding Bishopric. Although Leonard W. Hardy continued to serve the city until 1874, he was joined in 1866 by Apostle Joseph F. Smith and in 1872 by President Brigham Young.[183]

Table 2.
General Authorities in Salt Lake City Government, 1851-90

	1851	1852	1853	1854	1855	1856	1857	1858	1859	1860
Mayor	100%	100%	100%	100%	100%	100%	0	0	0	0
Council	22.2%	22.2%	22.2%	11.1%	11.1%	11.1	11.1	11.1%	11.1%	11.1%

	1861	1862	1863	1864	1865	1866	1867	1868	1869	1870
Mayor	0	0	0	0	0	100%	100%	100%	100%	100%
Council	1.1%	22.2%	22.2%	22.2%	22.2%	22.2%	22.2%	22.2%	22.2%	22.2%

	1871	1872	1873	1874	1875	1876	1877	1878	1879	1880
Mayor	100%	100%	100%	100%	100%	0	0	0	0	0
Council	22.2%	33.3%	33.3%	33.3%	33.3%	22.2%	22.2%	11.1%	11.1%	22.2%

	1881	1882	1883	1884	1885	1886	1887	1888	1889	1890
Mayor	0	0	0	0	0	0	0	0	0	0
Council	22.2%	22.2%	22.2%	11.1%	11.1%	33.3%	22.2%	0	0	0

From 1874 on the Salt Lake City Council was the domain of the First Presidency and Quorum of Twelve. The high point occurred during the years 1874-75 when the mayor was Brigham Young's first counselor Daniel H. Wells and the nine-member city council included Young, his assistant counselor and apostle Albert Carrington, and his former assistant counselor and present apostle Joseph F. Smith.

Smith became the focus of a disagreement during a Salt Lake City Council meeting in 1879. He successfully led the city council in adopting legislation which had been privately approved in advance by John Taylor, the church's presiding apostle (in the absence of an organized First Presidency). Council of Fifty member John Sharp accused Smith of "attempting to manipulate the city council,"[184] not knowing the extent to which their decisions were otherwise orchestrated.

Even after the Edmunds Law of 1882 disenfranchised polygamists, the hierarchy was able to continue its local rule for several years. Although he was a well-known polygamist, former mayor Daniel H. Wells served on the city council from 1882 to 1884. Wells was replaced by Apostle Heber J. Grant, a temporary monogamist who married two plural wives shortly after taking office in 1884 but remained in the city council until 1888. He was joined in 1886 by two monogamists, Apostle John W. Taylor and Bishopric counselor John Q. Cannon, though Cannon was excommunicated from the church later in the year. When these three men left the Salt Lake City Council on 28 February 1888, the hierarchy's presence in that body ended.

Although general authority domination of the Salt Lake City Council was the most prominent example of their service in municipal office, it did not end there. Presiding Bishop Newel K. Whitney was justice of the peace from 1849 until his death in 1850. From 1851 to 1853 one out of Salt Lake City's four aldermen was an LDS general authority. When Leonard W. Hardy and Jesse C. Little were appointed counselors to the Presiding Bishop in 1856, both had municipal offices which they continued to fill for several years. Hardy was captain of the Salt Lake City Police Department and city meat inspector. Little was chief of the Salt Lake City Fire Department. Seventy's president Henry Harriman served as a policeman at Winter Quarters (1846-47) and as a justice of the peace in Utah (1852-53). Apostle Orson Hyde was one of Salt Lake City's Board of Examiners (1855-56). Seventy's president Horace S. Eldredge began a two-year service as Sugar House constable in 1877 at age sixty-one.[185] After his appointment to the Council of Seventy, Seymour B. Young continued as Salt Lake City's quarantine physician from 1882 to 1886. After his appointment as a counselor in the Presiding Bishopric in 1886, John R. Winder served another year as Salt Lake City's water master.

Outside church and territorial headquarters in Salt Lake Valley, general authorities similarly served in municipal policy-making capacities. Apostles Amasa M. Lyman and Charles C. Rich consecutively served as mayor of San Bernardino, California, during the period 1854-56, and Seventy's president Jacob Gates served as mayor of St. George, Utah, 1866-70. Serving on city councils outside the Salt Lake Valley were Seventy's president Levi W. Hancock at Manti, 1852-54; Apostle George A. Smith at Provo, 1851-53; Seventy's president Jacob Gates at St. George, 1862-66; Apostle Wilford Woodruff and Joseph F. Smith at Provo, 1868-69; Apostle Brigham Young, Jr., at Logan, 1874-78; Apostle Erastus Snow at St. George, 1863-81; and Apostle Heber J. Grant at Tooele, 1882-83. In addition Seventy's president Jacob Van Cott was a Salt Lake City alderman in 1872-74. When the hierarchy felt the need for direct control of municipal government, they had ample opportunity.[186]

Moreover, as in Nauvoo,[187] general authorities in the Great Basin often held several civil offices at once. A total of twenty-one general authorities held public office in different political jurisdictions at the same time. The most common combination was to serve on a city council and in the Utah territorial legislature at the same time: John Q. Cannon, John W. Taylor, and Wilford Woodruff for one year; Nathaniel H. Felt, Daniel H. Wells, Jacob Gates, Heber J. Grant, George A. Smith, and John W. Taylor for two years; Erastus Snow for eight years; and Joseph F. Smith for thirteen years.

From 1851 to 1854 Willard Richards was Salt Lake City's postmaster and territorial secretary. From 1851 to 1856 Jedediah M. Grant served three years as both Salt Lake City mayor and Utah legislator. He held those civil offices while he was a counselor in the First Presidency. During the years Albert P. Rockwood served in the legislature from 1851 to 1879, he was also at various times Salt Lake City's supervisor of streets and penitentiary inspector and warden. While he was Salt Lake City's marshal, assessor, and fire marshal, Jesse C. Little served in the legislature to 1859. John Van Cott served as territorial land commissioner and city alderman for four years ending in 1874. Franklin D. Richards served as a county probate judge and then as a city justice of the peace while he served in the Utah legislature to 1875. William W. Taylor served as a territorial legislator and city constable in 1880. Francis M. Lyman was Tooele County's clerk-recorder while also in the legislature to 1882. Brigham Young, Jr., was county clerk during part of the time he served on the Logan City Council.[188] Serving in multiple civil offices at the same time also occurred in the territory of New Mexico.[189]

In some instances these men did not even reside in the multiple jurisdictions in which they were elected. In 1851-53 Apostle George A. Smith was chief justice of Iron County, postmaster of Centre Creek, and a territorial representative of Iron County, while at the same time he was a member of the Provo City Council in Utah County, more than 160 miles away. Smith overcame the inconvenient distances by attending Provo City Council meetings while he was on route between Iron County and Salt Lake City on church and legislative business.[190]

Four other apostles held offices in several jurisdictions simultaneously. In 1855-56 Orson Hyde was a member of Utah's territorial legislature and Salt Lake City's board of examiners, while he also served as county probate judge in Nevada. In 1868-69 Joseph F. Smith and Wilford Woodruff served on the Provo City Council and John Taylor served as Utah County probate judge. At the same time all three men were representing Salt Lake County (fifty miles distant) in the territorial legislature.

Before residency requirements were enacted, such arrangements reflected nearly a century of Anglo-American legal precedents. In 1774 an act of Parliament ended the long-ignored requirement for members of its lower house (the Commons) to reside in the boroughs from which they were elected. Likewise, a decade later the U.S. Constitution required the representatives of its lower house only to be state residents of their election districts. As a result some members of Congress, particularly in New York, never resided in the districts they represented.[191]

The blending of civil and religious authority can be further illustrated by two examples. Brigham Young delivered the word of the Lord to Mormons in sermons on doctrine, morality, and such mundane subjects as disciplining children and irrigating land. At the same time, as governor, he recommended and approved legislation, while he conducted the territorial policies toward the Native Americans as Utah's superintendent of Indian affairs. Mormons also came to Young for advice on family relations, disputes with neighbors, business ventures, and virtually any other subject.[192] Similarly, Apostle Joseph F. Smith officiated in marriages and other ceremonies performed in the Salt Lake Endowment House. He also drafted and voted on legislation for Utah territory and directed the municipal affairs of Salt Lake City.[193] The role of the hierarchy in providing social control was pervasive until the mid-1880s.

In fact, in the view of one local stake president, Joseph F. Smith's political rule was heavy-handed. George Teasdale, a freshman member of the legislature's upper chamber, started to speak in defense of a bill in January 1880, "when Counsellor Jos F Smith rudely interrupted me and called [the] question on motion." Taken aback, Teasdale wrote: "Feeling snubbed I sat down not being used to this kind of business or I should have demanded to have been heard." A month later the stake president noted that the upper chamber was in "a deadlock."[194] Thus the published minutes of unanimous voting concealed pre-vote fractures in Utah's legislative theocracy. Such conflicts among Mormon legislators may have caused John Taylor to reconvene the Council of Fifty as a harmonizing force through its pre-legislative meetings.

A Revitalized Council of Fifty

Two years before the hierarchy's active role in civil office ended, John Taylor revitalized the Council of Fifty. On 10 April 1880 Taylor reconvened the Fifty for the first time "since last met, in Oct. 68."[195] Under Taylor's direction, the council assembled for five consecutive years, a continuity which exceeded the Fifty's activity in pioneer Utah from 1848 to 1851. Nevertheless, they met only infrequently: four days in 1880, four days in 1881, ten days in 1882, eight days in 1883, and four days in 1884.[196] The Fifty was indeed functioning but less than any other civil or religious body in Utah during the 1880s.

Unlike the Fifty under Young's leadership, Taylor's council had a substantive role in discussing and implementing the political process in Utah and elsewhere. In October 1880 they considered whether to accept a tax-supported system for the public schools in Utah.[197] In May 1881 the council appointed its members to visit local communities to arrange for unanimous nominations of candidates approved by them. This theocratic lobbying continued for two months.[198]

In their meetings of April 1882, the Fifty debated whether to allow "minority representation" to non-Mormons in the convention for a proposed state constitution.[199] In June 1882 the council debated and defeated motions by members William H. Hooper and Apostle John Henry Smith to organize the Democratic Party as the church's new political party.[200]

Also in June the Fifty appointed committees "to see after Election affairs in Idaho Territory [and] in Nevada State," as well as to arrange for approved voter registration officers and election judges. The Fifty's emissaries (all apostles) for election matters outside Utah reported their work in October 1882.[201] At the April 1883 meeting, "*President Taylor* inquired if all the machinery were in proper shape for the next August election." John Sharp (member of the Fifty since 1867) answered that "all the committees that acted during the last election were still in power, none having been discharged." The group also heard a report of its assessments to all Utah counties for a "defence fund" for prominent men charged with polygamy.[202]

Taylor retired members who had become too old to function in the Council of Fifty. On 24 June 1882 he released seven men because of "age & infirmity & that their places be supplied with active able men." One of the released council members was in the Quorum of the Twelve Apostles; another lived twenty-eight years after being released.[203] This 1882 policy of releasing council members due to age or infirmity was particularly farsighted. A similar "emeritus" status for general authorities did not begin until 1978, and has not yet been applied to members of the Quorum of the Twelve or First Presidency.[204]

A revelation to the Fifty on 27 June 1882 underscored the fact that church office was a significant factor in being admitted to the council: "Behold you are my kingdom and rulers in my Kingdom and then you are also, many of you, rulers in my Church according to your ordinations therein. For are you not of the First Presidency, and of the Twelve Apostles and some Presidents of Stakes, and some Bishops, and some High Priests and some Seventies and Elders therein?"[205] From 1844 to 1884 the Council of Fifty included every member of the First Presidency except the disaffected William Law, every member of the Quorum of the Twelve, every Presiding Patriarch except John Smith (b. 1832), the principal members of the Bishopric except Jesse C. Little and the traveling bishops, and more than 44 percent of the First Council of Seventy.[206] Presiding church office was so identified with the Council of Fifty by 1883 that one of the Fifty called it "A Council of the Presiding Authorities of the

Church."[207] That designation would not have applied to Joseph Smith's Council of Fifty with its three non-Mormons.[208]

Membership in the Fifty could follow appointment to the hierarchy or immediately precede it. After the exodus from Nauvoo, recently appointed general authorities filled vacancies in the Fifty.[209] Young appointed Albert P. Rockwood and Horace S. Eldredge to the first vacancies which opened in the Council of Seventy after their admission to the Fifty.[210] In like manner President John Taylor admitted Francis M. Lyman, John Henry Smith, George Teasdale, and Heber J. Grant to the Fifty in apparent anticipation of his appointing them to the Twelve a few months later. This was consistent with the post-1844 subordination of the kingdom to the church and with Young's comment in 1855 that the church produced the government of the kingdom.[211]

Taylor, like his predecessor, maintained actual theocratic power in the First Presidency and Quorum of the Twelve. For example, when the Twelve considered who should fill vacancies in the soon-to-be-convened Council of Fifty in 1880, Moses Thatcher was among the apostles voting on the matter. Thatcher was not yet a member of the Fifty.[212] When the council reconvened on 10 April for the first time in nearly twelve years, the non-apostolic members of the Fifty had only a perfunctory role in selecting new members. The day before the Fifty met, the apostles had already notified the new initiates to attend this first meeting.[213]

Although the Council of Fifty was the logical body (theocratically) to select Utah legislative officers, Taylor made those selections in meetings of the hierarchy. For example, in January 1882 the First Presidency and apostles considered the "applicants for the officers of the Legislature" and then selected and "sustained" the men down to the legislative doorkeeper.[214]

The most striking example of the Fifty's rubber-stamp quality occurred in October 1882, when its political role was at its highest. The First Presidency and Twelve discussed on 4 October who should be the candidate for Utah's delegate to Congress and in the morning of 11 October selected John T. Caine. Three hours later the Fifty convened, and the motion to nominate a Congressional delegate "was fully discussed by many members of the Council" as if no choice had already been made by the hierarchy. Not surprisingly, at the direction of the church hierarchy, the Council of Fifty "nominated" John T. Caine and appointed a committee to inform the nominating committee.[215] In such a process the decision-making role of the Council of Fifty was clearly symbolic.

Outside the First Presidency or Twelve, other members of the Fifty may have been unaware of the extent to which general authorities manipulated meetings of the Fifty to arrive at predetermined decisions. On the other hand, awareness of this would explain the otherwise puzzling low attendance at Council of Fifty meetings.

Absences became a problem less than four years after Taylor revitalized the theocratic council. At the meeting on 12 January 1884, "no business [was] done on account of a majority of the members being absent."[216]

The apathy may have resulted from its meetings the previous October. Apostle Brigham Young, Jr., indicated that the Council of Fifty had degenerated into discussing matters unimportant to its theocratic mission. He reported that the Fifty's meetings of October 1883 focused "on observing laws of chastity" and "much discussion on minor matters."[217]

It is no coincidence that the most effusive descriptions of the Council of Fifty were written by John D. Lee, Benjamin F. Johnson, George Miller, and others who were not privy to orchestration of Fifty meetings by the First Presidency and apostles. Apostle Lyman Wight, who also exaggerated the Fifty's importance, was absent from Nauvoo during 1844 and 1845 and thus did not see the extent to which the Presidency and apostles constituted a shadow government behind the Fifty's shadow government. These overly enthusiastic members of the Fifty simply did not understand that the Mormon hierarchy after 1844 was supreme in both church and kingdom, and that it allowed no rival.[218]

This might not have been the case if there had been no 1844 succession crisis and if Joseph Smith had lived a full life. His governance of Council of Fifty meetings lasted only two months, and the prophet might have allowed real autonomy to the Fifty's decision-making. However, it took him almost six weeks to complete its organization.[219] The three remaining weeks of the Fifty's formal meetings did not allow enough time to assess whether Smith would have followed the pattern Young and Taylor later implemented of subordinating the Council of Fifty to the hierarchy.

In Smith's theology the Council of Fifty loomed as an awesome force, yet the council was prosaic in the hands of his successors. At the most practical level, after 1844 the Fifty was, as Apostle George A. Smith derisively termed it, a "debating School." Buttressed by oaths of secrecy, the Fifty was a forum to give the LDS hierarchy different views on pressing questions. Yet Young regarded even this contribution as negligible, since he refused to convene the Fifty for a total of twenty-five years after Utah became a territory. In fact, from 1850 to 1880 the Fifty met less than twenty-five times, despite Utah's active political life during those thirty years.[220] Even when the Fifty was functioning organizationally and its meetings were not pre-orchestrated, the opinions and recommendations of the Presidency and apostles carried conclusive weight.

Young and Taylor did honor members of the Fifty with positions of public prominence. This was a recognition of the special bond they shared through their theocratic oaths of secrecy and knowledge of such explosive secrets as the ordination of the standing chairman as king on earth. The Fifty provided more than two dozen non-general authorities who could be relied on to influence sectors that the hierarchy might not otherwise reach. However, neither Young nor Taylor allowed the Fifty itself to rival the hierarchy's power.

The Fifty had minimal political power but was a symbol of the yet-unattained goal of sovereign rule under a religious monarch. Like its economic counterpart, the United Order of Enoch and the Law of Consecration,[221] the Council of Fifty required greater subservience of individual ambition and more deference to authority. Created in a context of uncompromising millennialism, the Fifty's sporadic existence was often compromised by members for whom power and prestige became ends in themselves. Arguably those who most successfully fulfilled their roles saw in the Council of Fifty a potential of what could transpire when the hearts of a sinful world and imperfect church turned sufficiently to Christ the King.[222] Those who were least successful were men who regarded the Fifty too literally and became bitter at the disparity.

During the 1950s and 1960s some scholars also described the Fifty's influence beyond its reality. One interpreter claimed that "the Council of Fifty or General Council was the policy-making body for the civil government of Utah from 1848 to 1870, if not later"; another wrote that "the Council of Fifty was as important, if not more so, in building the temporal Kingdom than the Council of the Twelve Apostles."[223] The most influential interpreter claimed that "without the existence and activities of the Council of Fifty . . . Mormonism might well have failed to enjoy its present stature and prestige within the framework of accepted American religious values and persuasions."[224] The greatest weakness of this "Kingdom School" among historians has been the confusion of symbol and substance, failing to separate the temporal realities of the Mormon kingdom from its unachieved millennial anticipations.

The symbolic character of the Fifty is clearest in its most sensational dimension, the ordination of a king on earth. The non-revolutionary dimension of that office was demonstrated in its third incumbent, John Taylor.

After Taylor reestablished the Council of Fifty in 1880, he desired to receive the theocratic office to which Smith and Young had been ordained before him. In the 1880s at least one member of the Fifty regarded the kingship as literal and disliked it. George Q. Cannon observed that "the Council of Fifty met in the old City Hall [1880-81], and Moses [Thatcher] opposed the proposition to anoint John Taylor as Prophet, Priest and King, and Moses's opposition prevailed at that time."[225] Not until 1885, just days after the federal crusade against polygamy forced Taylor into exile,[226] did he receive this ceremony.

Franklin D. Richards wrote an account which is the most detailed description available of this kingship:

> Wednesday Feb 4*th* 1885-
> Prests. John Taylor & Geo. Q. Cannon having been secluded since Sunday evening [—] word had been given to L. Snow, E. Snow[,] F. D. Richards, A. Carrington, F. M. Lyman, H. J. Grant, John W. Taylor, to meet in Council this evening—Prests. W. Woodruff, George Teasdale[,] Moses Thatcher were oblivious to prevent arrest—B. Y. [Jr.] & J. H. Smith in N. York & Europe—
> Soon after 8. p.m. Prests Taylor & Cannon met the seven of the 12 first named at End[owment] house[.] Secretaries Geo. Reynolds and L. John Nuttall were present. After listening to some current items of news, President Taylor stated the object of the Council. directed Br Nuttall to read a Revelation which he said he received more than a year ago requiring him to be anointed & set apart as a King Priest and Ruler over Israel on the Earth—over Zion & the Kingdom of Christ our King of Kings. He also read some extracts from minutes of the Council of the Kingdom after which the President called for any remarks[,] when several spoke their mind and F. M. L. motioned that we proceed to obey the requirement of the Revelation, when we clothed in our Priestly attire. E Snow offered prayer, when after the usual ceremony F. M. Lyman prayed in the circle. L. Snow consecrated a bottle of oil. Counselor Cannon anointed President John Taylor and we all laid hands on the Prest. & Geo. Q. sealed the anointing according to a written form which had been prepared.[227]

Only the First Presidency, seven apostles, and two secretaries to the First Presidency attended the meeting, but both secretaries were members of the Council of Fifty. Someone in that otherwise trustworthy group talked outside the council about the ceremony, and the *Salt Lake Tribune* soon reported that Cannon had recently "assisted at the coronation of JOHN TAYLOR as king" of the Mormon commonwealth. John Henry Smith complained that the *Tribune* story showed "how sacred some things are to some persons . . ."[228]

This 1885 ordinance verifies the exclusively symbolic nature of the Fifty's king. Although Smith and Young became theocratic kings at the zenith of their achievements, Taylor received the ordinance at the lowest point in his life. The political kingdom was in disarray when the apostles and two other members of the Fifty anointed and ordained him. Twelve thousand polygamist men and women (accounting for most of the prominent political leaders of Mormonism) had been disenfranchised for three years.[229] Most of Mormonism's elite was in prison "for conscience sake," on missions of "exile," or hiding in the polygamist "underground" of Utah and the Mormon settlements in Idaho, Arizona, New Mexico, Nevada, Wyoming, Colorado, and northern Mexico.[230] After a four-year renaissance of limited significance, the Fifty could no longer convene because of the federal "raid," and the council started its final slide into oblivion. Only days before receiving this kingship, Taylor himself began a permanent exile to avoid arrest, and two weeks later there was an advertised reward for his capture.[231]

Ordaining Taylor as king in 1885 was a magnificent gesture, similar to the *Titanic*'s orchestra playing "Nearer My God To Thee" as the passenger ship plunged into the icy Atlantic. Taylor was anointed in a simple ceremony performed by a few members of the Fifty, and at a time when it was obvious that Mormon theocracy was in its death throes.

As God's representative on earth, Taylor was apparently satisfied that he had witnessed to God spiritually through a symbolic ordinance that it was the right of Christ to reign on the earth. Like the Fifty itself, the office of prophet-king was an ultimate symbol of a heavenly kingdom, which could only be foreshadowed on a corrupt world and in a temporal church.[232]

During the years of its sporadic activity, the Fifty was an open secret. Some knowledge came from unauthorized sources, such as the 1844 disclosures in the anti-Mormon press.[233] People known to be at odds with Young, such as William Smith, Charles B. Thompson, and William Marks, also published references to the Fifty.[234] It would have been easy for rank-and-file Mormons to ignore such allegations.

More often knowledge came to Latter-day Saints through official sources. In January 1846 the Fifty openly identified itself in a meeting with many others who were appointed to lead the exodus from Nauvoo.[235] In November 1849 Albert K. Thurber, an LDS convert of only two months, learned about the Council of Fifty when he was appointed on a "mission" to join the California Gold Rush to benefit the Mormon kingdom: "The California gold mines were attracting great attention and as [Benjamin F.] Johnson was of the council of 50, the president (B. Young) authorized them to send a few men, as Johnson told me, to prove them."[236] In June 1857 the *Deseret News* published the account of Joseph Smith's organizing this "special council." The following November Young handed the minutes of the Fifty to the church historian and "gave his Concent [sic] for us to publish an account of it so that the Saints might understand it (but not the world)."[237] In 1858 LDS publications began referring to the Fifty by name, and church leaders delivered sermons explaining that the Kingdom of God was an organization which had already been established among the Saints.[238]

In October 1868 Abraham O. Smoot told Provo's bishops and School of the Prophets about a recent meeting of the Council of Fifty. In December he told the bishops about the Fifty in Nauvoo.[239] In 1877 a *Deseret News* obituary referred to membership in the Fifty.[240] In 1880 council member John Pack told women of the Seventeenth Ward Relief Society: "Joseph organized and set up the Kingdom of God, in his day, with its officers and fifty members. . . . This Kingdom is still in existence."[241]

Nevertheless, members of the Fifty were undoubtedly stunned to learn on 15 May 1881 that the anti-Mormon *Salt Lake Tribune* was describing the Council of "the YTFIF," with long statements by "an old member of it." This was five weeks after the previous meeting of the Fifty. These were actually quotes from the diary of the deceased John D. Lee. Worse, in June the newspaper published the Lee diary's minutes about the Fifty's discussions of blood atonement in March 1849, including what the *Tribune* described as "the bombastic name of the Council."[242] In 1883 a local Mormon told a priesthood meeting in southern Utah about his assignment from "the Council of 50 in the days of Joseph."[243] In 1901 the assistant Church Historian matter-of-factly identified men as members of the Council of Fifty in his published biographies.[244]

Despite the availability of those sources as well as numerous scholarly studies already cited here, Fawn Brodie's widely published biography has perpetuated this exaggeration in its revised edition: "Few secrets in Mormon history have been better kept than the activities of this council [of Fifty]."[245] The Fifty was secretive in the same way that the Quorum of Twelve Apostles guarded the minutes of its own meetings, but the Council of Fifty was hardly a secret among the Mormons of the nineteenth century.

More Latter-day Saints would have known of the Fifty had it functioned in a lasting manner. After decades of sporadic activity, the council last convened on 9 October 1884. This is evident from the diaries of men such as Robert T. Burton, Abraham H. Cannon, Heber J. Grant, Franklin D. Richards, John Henry Smith, Wilford Woodruff, and Brigham Young, Jr., who regularly recorded attendance through 1884 but made no mention of such meetings during the decades after 1884.

The Fifty's inactivity troubled Apostle John W. Taylor who entered the council on its last meeting date in 1884. In October 1887, while the Quorum of the Twelve was in the midst of secret negotiations to obtain statehood for Utah, "John W. Taylor expressed it as his opinion that it would be much better if all of our business in relation to a State was transacted through the Council of Fifty. Prest Woodruff said it would be all right for the Council of Fifty to meet and attend to this matter but under existing circumstances it would not be safe to have them do so."[246] After

1884 members of the Fifty had occasional *ad hoc* meetings with the First Presidency and Twelve concerning statehood and other political matters, but that was a repetition of earlier periods in which the council itself was non-functioning.[247]

In 1888 the national platform of the Republican Party dedicated itself to the destruction of Mormon theocracy. "The political power of THE MORMON CHURCH in the territories, as exercised in the past, is a menace to free institutions," this plank of Republican platform began. The party pledged itself to obtain "legislation stringent enough to divorce the political from the ecclesiastical power, and thus stamp out the attendant wickedness of polygamy."[248] In December 1889 the First Presidency and Quorum of the Twelve issued a joint declaration that "this Church does not claim to be an independent, temporal kingdom of God . . ."[249]

Up to 1890 the First Presidency and Twelve arranged for municipal and territorial laws. Members of those quorums met with the Salt Lake City council and mayor about such matters as salaries, division of the city into districts, and municipal projects designed to promote the church's well-being.[250] The hierarchy also drafted legislation they wanted introduced in the territorial legislature. They met with individual legislators to discuss bills they wanted introduced, killed in committee, passed, or defeated.[251] As the church's *Deseret News* editorialized in 1889: "There is nothing in the Constitution or laws or institutions of our country which forbids a man who holds an ecclesiastical calling to counsel another as to political affairs."[252]

Even friendly non-Mormons were not free of the hierarchy's political manipulation. In 1889 Apostle Heber J. Grant drafted a petition as a protest by gentiles against the federal campaign against polygamy.[253]

Because such power brokering depended on voluntary assent, sincere debate often occurred at all stages of the process. There was loyal opposition to "approved" rulings, as well as defection from the theocracy itself. Mormon theology promoted the concept of voluntary assent rather than coercion. Therefore, theologians, historians, and political scientists have affirmed that Mormon culture was always politically democratic.[254] Nevertheless, when a small group of men (who hold non-civil offices for life) formulates the social and political policy for a people, presents for popular vote a pre-approved list of candidates, proclaims that contrary votes are destructive of the social order, and dominates the conduct of the elected civil officers, it is difficult to say that the resulting society is significantly democratic. It is certainly not pluralistic, even if the leadership tolerates a loyal opposition.

"The incompatibility of the Kingdom, if sovereignty is to be held by Christ, and a republican or democratic government did not seem to trouble Brigham Young," wrote a BYU political scientist. He explained that "Young's concept of theocracy portrays the Kingdom more as a republic, Christ more as a president than a king. This unique concept was not clarified in President Young's many discourses on the Kingdom."[255]

Politics After Statehood

The church hierarchy publicly repudiated theocratic prerogatives in 1889, but waited more than a year to dissolve its political party. Therefore, the hierarchy's activity in public office underwent alterations. General authorities did not abandon involvement in the political process altogether, but their actions no longer reflected the world view of the Council of Fifty. Mormon theocracy ceased functionally after John Taylor's death in 1887, and the hierarchy wrote its political obituary in 1891. Thereafter general authorities took political actions behind the scenes without publicly-endorsed church candidates and without consistent bloc-voting. Even the hierarchy itself was divided along national political lines and sometimes campaigned publicly against each other as individuals on partisan issues. (See chap. 9.)

By the time the First Presidency and Twelve had shepherded Utah into statehood in 1896, safety was no longer the reason for ignoring the Council of Fifty. It was obsolete even as a symbol. The theocracy of Utah had given way to factional politics, which divided church leaders and members alike. Two years later the hierarchy, with the exception of Apostle Brigham Young, Jr., enthusiastically supported the U.S. war with Spain. In effect, the War of 1898 represented the First Presidency's acceptance of national militarism and abandonment of theocratic "selective pacifism."[256]

The next national outcry about Mormon theocracy was the most spectacular and again it was linked with polygamy.[257] In 1903 the Mormon-dominated legislature elected Apostle Reed Smoot as a member of the U.S. Senate. The Salt Lake Ministerial Association filed a formal protest that Smoot was

> one of a self-perpetuating body of fifteen men who, constituting the ruling authorities of the Church of Jesus Christ of Latter-Day Saints, or "Mormon" Church, claim, and by their followers are accorded the right to claim, supreme authority, divinely sanctioned, to shape the belief and control the conduct of those under them in all matters whatsoever, civil and religious, temporal and spiritual, and who thus, uniting in themselves authority in church and state, do so exercise the same as to inculcate and encourage a belief in polygamous cohabitation; who countenance and connive at violations of the laws of the State prohibiting the same regardless of pledges made for the purpose of

obtaining statehood and of covenants made with the people of the United
States, and who by all the means in their power protect and honor those who
with themselves violate the laws of the land and are guilty of practices
destructive of the family and the home.[258]

An investigation of these allegations dragged on from 1904 to 1907,
and filled four volumes with 3,427 pages of testimony. Witnesses before
the U.S. Senate included President Joseph F. Smith, other LDS general
authorities, disaffected Mormons, current polygamists, long-time anti-
Mormon crusaders, and friendly gentiles. Ultimately a simple majority of
Smoot's colleagues voted in favor of his right to remain U.S. senator.[259]
A month after this vote the First Presidency issued a formal "address" as
a summary response to the objections raised during the Smoot Case. In
regard to charges of theocracy and the LDS church's political influence,
President Joseph F. Smith and his counselors declared:

> The Church of Jesus Christ of Latter-day Saints holds to the doctrine of
> the separation of church and state; the non-interference of church authority
> in political matters; and the absolute freedom and independence of the
> individual in the performance of his political duties. If at any time there has
> been conduct at variance with this doctrine, it has been in violation of the
> well-settled principles and policy of the Church.

The next general conference voted to accept this document, which "makes
the *Address* official doctrine, teaching, and viewpoint of the Church."[260]
Nevertheless, during the Senate's investigation, Utah anti-Mormons
formed another anti-church political organization, the American Party,
which controlled Salt Lake City's government from 1905 to 1911.[261]

Within this context Apostle John W. Taylor's February 1911 letter to
church president Joseph F. Smith seemed a curious anachronism. He
addressed Smith as "Prophet, President and King," even though there is
no evidence of any church president after John Taylor receiving this
ordination. Given the Fifty's history of subordination to the church
hierarchy, it was ironic that John W. would petition the president to
convene the Fifty to protect Taylor from the Twelve's discipline. However,
he had never seen the hierarchy's manipulation of the Fifty, because as a
newly appointed apostle John W. Taylor joined the Fifty on the last day it
ever convened. President Smith wrote on the letter: "*Not granted* [—] I think
the demand most absurd."[262]

Almost a year before Taylor's request, Smith had made a statement
which illuminates the spasmodic history of the Council of Fifty. On 7 April
1910 he stated: "This body of men, this Council of Presidency and
Apostles, compose the living constitution of the Church, with power to
legislate, judge and decide."[263] There is a crucial insight within Smith's
use of the Fifty's name, "Living Constitution,"[264] as a designation for the

church hierarchy. In theory, theology, and reality, the LDS presidency and apostles had always governed the Council of Fifty when it was functioning. When the Fifty was non-functioning, the Presidency and apostles continued to be the apex of both church and kingdom.

In January 1932 Heber J. Grant recorded that he and Franklin S. Richards were the only surviving members of the Council of Fifty. No one had been admitted since its last meeting in 1884.[265] Technically, LDS theocracy ended upon the earth at the death of the last surviving member of the Fifty, President Grant, on 14 May 1945.

In May 1955 church president David O. McKay inadvertently echoed the theocratic prerogatives claimed by Mormonism's first three presidents. During a formal dinner at the White House with various government officials, U.S. president Dwight D. Eisenhower asked McKay to offer prayer over the food. "Toward the end of the evening, President McKay, sensing that President Eisenhower was tired, suggested that the guests leave so as not to wear out their welcome." Eisenhower immediately replied that "it was his, not President McKay's, prerogative to indicate when the festivities were at an end." White House staffers retold this incident from one administration to another. At their first meeting in the nation's capital in 1964, U.S. president Lyndon B. Johnson humorously asked McKay not to adjourn any of the federal government's meetings while there.[266]

Church Security without Theocracy

Joseph Smith, Brigham Young, and John Taylor each had bodyguards during at least part of their presidencies.[267] However, just as Wilford Woodruff declined to convene a meeting of the Fifty or receive its theocratic office of "King over Israel on the Earth," he also abandoned the use of bodyguards six weeks after Taylor's death.[268]

For nearly fifty-five years after September 1887, no LDS president used a bodyguard, even though several incidents could have justified a resumption of security arrangements. In 1905 a man burglarized the bedroom of church president Joseph F. Smith while he and his wife slept. In 1910 labor radicals dynamited the construction site of the church's Hotel Utah due to its non-union policies. In 1911 someone fired a weapon at the Salt Lake temple, and a bullet "passed through one of the heavy window panes in the Celestial Room." In 1913 a man physically assaulted Seventy's president J. Golden Kimball on Salt Lake City's Main Street. In May 1919 labor radicals sent package bombs to Apostle-Senator Reed Smoot, his senatorial colleague William H. King, and former assistant U.S. attorney general Frank K. Nebeker, then living in Salt Lake City. The three prominent Mormons were not among those injured by the exploding bombs sent to prominent leaders throughout the United States.[269]

In the following decades, despite absence of security measures to protect LDS leaders and buildings, church headquarters implemented various security techniques against "Mormon Fundamentalists" who continued to perform plural marriages in violation of LDS policy.[270] In April 1921 Apostle George F. Richards "formulated a pledge of loyalty to the Church & authorities and to their attitude towards plural marriage for temple workers to sign."[271] By 1935 anyone suspected of Fundamentalist sympathies was required to sign the following statement: "I repudiate any intimation that any one of the Presidency or Apostles of the Church are living a double life," as well as the unconditional statement: "I denounce the practice and advocacy of plural marriage as being out of harmony with the declared principles of the Church at th[is] time." Refusal to sign was grounds for excommunication.[272] Eventually, a variation of this loyalty oath became one of the questions asked of every Mormon during the annual worthiness interview for a temple recommend.[273]

In addition to uncovering polygamist subversives, the First Presidency wanted information about Mormons who were affiliating with the Communist Party. On 3 July 1936 the Presidency published a "Warning to Church Members" (written by J. Reuben Clark) to avoid any association with Communism.[274] Although the statement claimed that "Communism is not a political party," the Communist Party during the 1930s was a legally registered political organization. Communist Party candidates had been on election ballots in various states since 1922, and in 1932 the Communist Party candidate for U.S. president received 102,221 votes. That year the Communist Party candidate got 772 votes in Utah, with nearly all Communist voters living in Salt Lake County.[275] Within weeks of the July statement Lester Wire, a Roman Catholic and chief of Salt Lake City's "subversive detail" of detectives, was sending to the First Presidency his reports on police surveillance and infiltration of the Communist Party in Utah. This transfer of confidential reports was undoubtedly authorized by police chief Harry L. Finch, a Mormon.[276] Also a week after Wire's first known report, Seventy's president Samuel O. Bennion, general manager of the *Deseret News,* assigned two reporters "who are new, and not known in Salt Lake City" to secretly infiltrate meetings of Utah's Communist Party. Bennion forwarded to the First Presidency the surveillance reports of the reporter-spies.[277]

In the November election 280 Utahns voted for the Communist Party's presidential candidate. Utah's Communist vote had plunged by almost 64 percent, while Communist votes nationally declined 22 percent.[278] The loss of Utah's Communist support was consistent with the national pattern in the massive reelection of Democratic Franklin D. Roosevelt in 1936, but Utah's greater percentage of decline may have been influenced by the First

Presidency's statement. However, because the number of Communist voters in Utah was small to begin with, the difference in rates of decline was probably not significant.

Until mid-1940 Detective Wire continued to provide Communist surveillance information to the First Presidency, either directly or through an ardent anti-Communist, Jeremiah Stokes.[279] However, this ended after Utah's Communist Party newspaper exposed the situation on 25 May 1940: "In Salt Lake City, for several years past, the situation has been so silly that one member of the city police force, Detective Lester Wire, has occupied himself with compiling a list of alleged communists, which he has taken, from time to time, not to his official superiors but to a messiah anointed by busybodies to save Utah from the Bolsheviks."[280]

After the United States declared war on Japan and Germany in December 1941, the First Presidency decided to adopt protective security procedures. In view of the successful air raid on Pearl Harbor, the First Presidency installed "bullet-proof glass" in the windows of its office in March 1942. Shortly afterward President Heber J. Grant employed a special bodyguard. As a private demonstration of his public statements that the First Presidency had no ill feeling toward the people of any nation, Grant's bodyguard in 1942 was Horst Scharffs, a German-born Mormon.[281] After the end of World War II in 1945, Grant's successor George Albert Smith dispensed with special bodyguards. His thirty-one-year-old secretary D. Arthur Haycock was the church president's constant companion when Smith, a widower, was away from home.[282] Such informal security arrangements continued for LDS presidents during the next twenty-five years.

In the meantime church headquarters continued its quiet campaign against polygamist Fundamentalists. In 1938 First Presidency counselor J. Reuben Clark commissioned stake president Lorenzo H. Hatch, Bishop Fred E. H. Curtis, former bishop Christian O. Jensen, and high priest quorum secretary George Lund to form a surveillance team in Salt Lake City to investigate suspected polygamists and their supporters.[283] Less than two years later Curtis was the principal director of the surveillance team, and Clark "told him we would like him to drop [his ward] Bishopric and help P.B.O. [Presiding Bishopric's Office] in new polygamy clean up." In October 1940 First Presidency counselor David O. McKay promised to obtain stake president Hatch's approval to "have the same men to help" Curtis. Two months later, concerned about reports that ordinance workers in the Salt Lake temple were involved with new polygamy, Clark decided "to appoint two people—one brother and one sister—who were thoroughly reliable, alert and not gullible, as workers here in the temple, and to watch and report to the First Presidency what they found to be going on in such matters." As further evidence of the overlapping jurisdictions in this religious counter-subversion, the LDS Genealogical Society organized its own surveillance squad whose report about forty-three suspected Fundamentalists arrived at the First Presidency's office in October 1940.[284]

By then Clark had obtained the cooperation of Salt Lake City's police chief Charles H. Olson in the LDS church's campaign against its polygamist Fundamentalists. On 16 October 1940 Clark began giving Curtis secret reports (transmitted through an unnamed third party) of surveillance conducted by two police detectives on suspected polygamists. Olson, a former FBI agent, assigned his men to conduct this surveillance on suspected polygamists. However, when Reed E. Vetterli, also a Mormon, became police chief two months later, he abruptly reassigned the two detectives and refused to furnish any more information to the First Presidency or its surveillance group.[285]

By January 1944 McKay noted that these "special missionaries" included Percy Kaspar Fetzer and Cornelius Zappey, respectively a stake leader of the young men's program and a stake director of the Welfare Program. The surveillance group's jurisdiction had also increased, and Clark told Curtis "to go after" residents of Ogden, Utah, who were suspected of "new polygamy."[286]

Curtis and his group continued their surveillance work until 1944, when more than twenty-two men and eleven women were arrested for unlawful cohabitation and conspiracy to commit polygamy. Apostle Mark E. Petersen announced that LDS headquarters furnished this evidence to state and federal law officers, and he referred to the "men who have been appointed by the Church to search out the cultists, turning over such information as they gather to the prosecution for their use . . ."[287]

However, this six-year program of surveillance was less discreet than the hierarchy had hoped. Almost immediately in 1938 the Fundamentalists identified those who attended meetings in order to "spy." By 1939 polygamist leader Joseph W. Musser described the surveillance group: "On the 2nd. at our con-joint class meeting held at the Cleveland home, 'peeping Toms' in the form of Bishops of two or three of the near-by wards, were on hand again, refusing to come in but peeping through the windows and taking notes of what was said." He added: "They take the numbers on the cars, and check for names, with a view of trying their own members on their fellowship if they dare to attend such meetings."[288]

Curtis and Fetzer testified at the 1944 trial with mixed results. The judge disallowed the testimony of former bishop Curtis whose testimony against members of his own ward involved "commitments and conversation [which] at that time were privileged." When a defense attorney referred to Fetzer as "an investigator," he insisted: "I am a missionary, not an investigator." He explained: "I was appointed by President McKay in the early spring of 1943 to serve as a missionary and my duty is to save souls." All defendants were convicted by a jury of Mormons who deliberated ninety minutes.[289] Fetzer later became one of the first Regional Representatives of the Twelve.[290]

After these polygamy convictions the hierarchy expanded the scope of its investigations. In November 1945 Presiding Bishop LeGrand Richards launched a continued surveillance of church-owned Belvedere Hotel and Temple Square Hotel to discover the "evil practices" of tenants. About this same time First Presidency counselor Clark asked former bishop Gordon Burt Affleck to organize a similar surveillance in the men's steamroom of the Deseret Gymnasium.[291]

In 1946, probably with Counselor Clark's encouragement, the presidency of George Albert Smith renewed the decade-earlier interest of Grant's presidency in obtaining lists of Mormon members of the Communist Party. In August the Smith presidency wrote U.S. Senator Elbert D. Thomas, a faithful Mormon, asking if he could obtain for them a copy of a Senate committee's secret "list of the Communists of the United States." With icy formality Thomas replied in September: "The Communist Party records in the states where the Communist Party is organized in America are open as are the Democratic and Republican Party lists." He also reminded the First Presidency that it was the responsibility of FBI director J. Edgar Hoover to keep track of suspected subversives.[292]

For the next twenty-five years, surveillance assignments were *ad hoc* activities of operatives commissioned by the Presiding Bishopric's Office or by Apostle Petersen. His self-appointed role as "a doctrinal watchdog" had the endorsement of the First Presidency, and he presided over a special committee to counsel Fundamentalist sympathizers, intellectuals, and coordinate surveillance files.[293] In 1959 Petersen's assignment was expanded to include LDS homosexuals.[294]

During the 1960s the hierarchy became concerned about their own physical security as social stability seemed to unravel nationally. In November 1962 a bomb blew out the doors and windows on the east side of the Salt Lake temple.[295] In September 1965 "hysterical rumors swept the Utah community, concerning the imminence of demonstrations and riots" at the upcoming general conference.[296] After the homes of several general authorities were burglarized while they and their wives were speaking at distant stakes, in September 1967 the *Church News* stopped its thirty-six-year practice of announcing in advance the hierarchy's speaking assignments at stake conferences. A year later Apostle Gordon B. Hinckley asked general conference to consider "if our society is coming apart at the seams."[297]

Shortly after Apostle Harold B. Lee became a counselor in the First Presidency in January 1970, he gave attention to the church's security arrangements. One biographer noted that "President Lee found that little had been done to safeguard the offices of the Church and to protect the sacred buildings on Temple Square and the homes of the Church leaders, in the event of a riot or a militant demonstration." That was of immediate concern after a BYU basketball game was disrupted on 5 February 1970 by a protest against the LDS church's policy of denying priesthood ordination to African-Americans. This policy had recently been the subject of a number of media articles, including one in *Sports Illustrated*. While 150 Colorado State University student demonstrators scuffled with campus police and twenty Fort Collins policemen during half-time, someone threw a Molotov cocktail on the playing floor. When the game resumed, spectators threw raw eggs at BYU's players. On 14 February the First Presidency and Presiding Bishopric launched the first organized effort to "provide sufficient security for the Church headquarters buildings." The next day Lee met with Salt Lake City officials "to discuss the coordination between Church security personnel and the city police in handling any emergencies that might arise."[298]

As an added incentive, demonstrations against the Vietnam War stunned Salt Lake City the following May. After the Ohio National Guard killed student protestors at Kent State University, hundreds of students seized the University of Utah's administration building and police arrested eighty-five "agitators." Three days later arsonists burned a vacant building on campus during another student demonstration, and on 12 May 1970 a bomb destroyed the offices of the Utah National Guard.[299]

The First Presidency and Presiding Bishopric jointly launched Mormonism's first effort in ninety years to protect headquarters culture "from enemies from the outside and from Judases within the church." Television monitoring equipment was installed in various buildings, "riot-proof glass was installed in the windows on the main floor" of the Church Administration Building at 47 East South Temple, and men who "had professional training in law enforcement work" replaced the previous security force, "some of whom were little more than night watchmen."[300]

In July 1972 "Security" appeared for the first time as an administrative department in the directory of LDS headquarters. Keith Nielsen was "Chief of Security," with four "Supervisors" of unspecified activities. In October the director of the Federal Bureau of Investigation (FBI), L. Patrick Gray, offered to give the LDS Security Department "the cooperation of his office in protecting against the assassination threats" against members of the LDS hierarchy. In addition, a secretary to the First

Presidency noted that church security personnel "for some time, had been working cooperatively with the Salt Lake City police force."[301]

Established in 1952, Brigham Young University's security police also had been maintaining contacts with the FBI since 1970. BYU's security chief publicly acknowledged in 1968 that the church school used "undercover agents" and a "lie detector" for students suspected of violating LDS standards of conduct. This included homosexuality.[302] When the polygraph did not succeed in reducing their numbers, BYU began an effort in January 1975 to expel all homosexual male students, including those who were celibate. BYU security officers interrogated young men who were majoring in fine arts or drama. Security operatives also took down license plate numbers of cars parked outside Salt Lake City's gay bars and cross-checked them with cars registered by current students. The national gay and lesbian magazine *The Advocate* published several articles about this "purge" and "inquisition."[303]

In connection with the publicity about this campaign against student homosexuals, "a former undercover agent for the Brigham Young University security force" revealed more of its methods in March 1975. He publicly charged that BYU operatives "used electronic devices to spy on students both on and off campus, in dormitories, private apartments, married student housing and in the streets." In response, BYU's security chief "denied that dormitories or other student housing facilities have been bugged per se, but he did admit that electronic recording devices have been planted on students in order to gather information on roommates and acquaintances." The security chief also acknowledged that "searches of dorms and other student housing units have taken place without bona fide search warrants." When reporters confronted BYU's president Dallin H. Oaks with these statements by the security chief, Oaks acknowledged the activities in general terms, including the targeting of suspected homosexuals. The BYU president eventually asked the Utah legislature to give the church school's security officers the legal powers of arrest and law enforcement throughout Utah, after which the *New York Times* headlined, "Brigham Young U. Admits Stakeouts on Homosexuals."[304]

A month after the publicity about the methods of BYU's security department, former Salt Lake City police chief J. Earl Jones became director of security arrangements at LDS headquarters. However, in 1976 an official spokesman denied that Church Security was using an "electronic surveillance system." At this time Jones was "manager" of the Security Department, with Brent L. Chandler as supervisor of "Investigations," and other supervisors of "Headquarters Services," of "Central

Services," of "Training Section," of "Executive Services," of "Information Section," of "Field Services," and of "Auxiliary Force."[305]

In 1979 director Jones stated that Chandler was "assigned to terrorism and its threat against the church." The Salt Lake County Sheriff Office's specialist on terrorism added that the LDS "Administration Building (47 East South Temple Street) is as secure as any building in the state, including Hill Field's [U.S. air force] security," and that the LDS church president was "the most protected man in the state." Gordon B. Hinckley had been a counselor in the First Presidency for fourteen years when he wrote: "Church Security has now surrounded me like a flock of eagles." He had just become presiding apostle/church president, and "they have taken from me all liberty to come and go."[306] By the 1980s news reporters routinely observed Church Security operatives using "bomb-finding dogs" before meetings in the Salt Lake Tabernacle.[307]

Although Director Jones had been a police chief, "a state department public safety officer," and once attended "an FBI training course,"[308] the professional status of the LDS Security Department increased with the appointment of J. Martell Bird. An FBI agent from 1942 to 1969, Bird was "managing director of Church security worldwide" from 1981 until his death in 1987.[309]

In 1988 LDS headquarters appointed Richard T. Bretzing as Bird's successor in the Security Department. A special agent with the FBI for twenty-seven years, at this appointment Bretzing headed the FBI's field office in Los Angeles. Previously he had led the unsuccessful FBI investigation of the disappearance of Mafia-connected union leader Jimmy Hoffa, directed the Bureau's highly successful security arrangements for the 1984 Olympics, and conducted the espionage investigation of Richard Miller, a Mormon and the first FBI agent convicted as a spy. By 1990 law enforcement officials were giving "cautious praise" to Bretzing for appointing "a retired bomb expert from the federal Bureau of Alcohol, Tobacco and Firearms, a former police academy instructor and a former FBI investigator" to the LDS Security Department.[310]

The security apparatus at LDS headquarters also changed significantly under the influence of Ezra Taft Benson. For decades as a Cold-Warrior apostle and supporter of the ultra-conservative John Birch Society, Benson had encouraged "espionage" on LDS professors he regarded as pro-Communist, socialist, or "liberal" at Utah's largest universities. For the first time in LDS history, "left wing" students also became the targets of surveillance. William O. Nelson, the apostle's secretary, was identified as directing one of the BYU student spy-rings in the mid-1970s, but similar surveillance was also occurring on Utah's other campuses (see chap. 3).

After Benson became church president in 1985, the hierarchy established a "Strengthening the Members Committee" which went far beyond the surveillance activities at LDS headquarters during the previous sixty years. Building on files created while Benson was an apostle, staff members of this now-centralized committee began maintaining files on every member of the church regarded as critical of LDS policies or as too liberal. The committee furnished information to local leaders to prepare them for taking disciplinary action against the targeted individuals. This committee's executive secretary was William O. Nelson.[311] During Benson's presidency, Church Security personnel also engaged in rigorous investigations of persons suspected of disclosing confidential information at LDS headquarters. One such "interrogation" of a female, who was not an LDS employee, lasted three-and-a-half hours.[312]

During the past decade this committee, whose total number of staff members and operatives is unknown, has staked out a daunting task. Its files include even a sentence regarded as controversial in an LDS member's writings about any Mormon topic for such independent publications as the academic *Utah Historical Quarterly*, *Dialogue: A Journal of Mormon Thought*, *Journal of Mormon History*, for the LDS magazine *Sunstone* with its open-forum and sometimes irreverent format, and for LDS feminist publications such as *Exponent II* and *Mormon Women's Forum*. This clipping service at LDS headquarters is also interested in published letters-to-the-editor in all Utah's newspapers, including the student publications of BYU and other Utah colleges. Statements considered controversial about LDS policy to national media are also targets for these files. In addition, the Strengthening the Members Committee uses operatives to obtain tape-recordings of every Mormon who gives presentations at public forums regarded as suspicious.[313] As a glimpse into the extent of these files, a history professor at Utah State University was informed during a meeting at LDS headquarters in 1990 that his surveillance file contained an anti-war statement he made as an undergraduate student in college.[314]

Rather than deny the existence of such files, the LDS hierarchy has publicly defended them. The First Presidency has stated that the committee is chaired by two members of the Quorum of Twelve Apostles. Nevertheless, editors of the *Deseret News* introduced the Presidency's statement as a response "to false accusations of so-called secret Church committees and files."[315] This "committee receives complaints from church members about other members," the official spokesman at LDS headquarters told the Religious News Service, adding that the Strengthening the Members Committee will "hear the complaints and pass the information along to the person's ecclesiastical leader."[316]

Following the pattern established by J. Reuben Clark, the LDS Security Department shares its "intelligence" information with law enforcement agencies.[317] The Strengthening the Members Committee also receives surveillance reports and other information about LDS members from the Correlation Department, Public Affairs Department, Church Security Department, security officers of ZCMI department store, and from BYU's Security, all of which also maintain their own files of original jurisdiction.[318]

As of 1996 the Church Security Department's central administration involves forty-five persons assigned to three divisions. These three divisions incorporate the functions previously performed by the more explicitly defined organizational chart published twenty years ago: Investigations, Headquarters Services, Central Services, Training Section, Executive Services, Information Section, Field Services, and Auxiliary Force. Bodyguarding for general authorities is now the main function of the Personal Protection division, while the Protective Operations division provides physical security for LDS buildings of special importance. The Confidential Services division conducts intelligence gathering, including surveillance. The total number of security operatives is unknown because they are not listed in the directory of church headquarters. Aside from female secretaries and one Hispanic male, nearly all the directors and administrative staff are North American "white" males.[319] However, by my personal observations at headquarters, the LDS security operatives "on the beat" include persons of both sexes from various racial and ethnic backgrounds. In addition, nine years ago LDS headquarters publicly acknowledged that "Church security [has] worldwide" jurisdiction,[320] and many of its international operatives probably look like natives of the countries where they serve.

Conclusion

Although Mormonism in its theological and ecclesiastical framework was an authoritarian system, the hierarchy always tried to work out the political implications of Mormon revelation within a framework which seemed both democratic and republican. Nevertheless, during most of the nineteenth century, Mormon theocracy functioned through a series of façades.

In every election from 1830 to 1890 Mormon voters participated in what appeared to be a democratic process. However, Mormon bloc-voting involved autocratic "counsel," supervision, and lock-step obedience. From the city-state of Nauvoo, Illinois, in the 1840s to the federal assault on the Great Basin Kingdom in the 1880s, Mormons of various backgrounds participated in what appeared to be a republican process but was actually an extension of a subterranean theocracy.

Up to the official abolition of polygamy in 1890, the LDS First Presidency and Quorum of the Twelve Apostles created Mormon political life and administered it monolithically. For both practical and symbolic reasons, the hierarchy established theocratic appendages such as the Council of Fifty and the School of the Prophets. Through these organizations a larger group of Mormons could feel that they were participating in affairs of state, even though they were subtly or openly under the supervision of the Mormon hierarchy.

Obviously general authorities did not constantly intervene in civil affairs in every town and hamlet of the Great Basin. Most often the ordinary operations of government were left to the established civil authorities who were under the watchful care of the local LDS ward bishoprics and stake presidents. Often these local LDS officers were also the civil authorities.[321] But whenever and wherever general authorities regarded control of politics as crucial, they subordinated all other institutions of Mormon theocracy. The secret *ad hoc* councils, the secret Council of Fifty, the semi-secret Schools of the Prophets, the closed caucuses, the public conventions, legislatures, individual office holders, and the ballot box amounted to performances of a symphony composed by the general authorities and orchestrated through a series of rehearsals.[322]

The role of the hierarchy in creating and supervising these political institutions was more monolithic than most people realized. However, anti-Mormons perceived enough of it to begin a national campaign to crush "Uncle Sam's Abscess." One analyst has observed that the American "state was religious in its nationalism; the saints were nationalistic in their religion. That paradox was the source of the trouble."[323]

During decades of bitter confrontation, both Mormons and anti-Mormons defined their goals within a dichotomy of extinction versus survival. Anti-Mormons claimed that if Mormon theocracy survived, it would lead to the extinction of American matrimonial and political institutions.[324] Mormons claimed that if their polygamous theocracy did not survive, Mormonism would become extinct.[325] Each side hoped that the other was right. It turned out both were wrong.

American institutions and Mormonism had vitality that was mutually underestimated. The former survived a civil war and the unrealistic constraints of the Victorian age; the latter survived abandonment of both polygamy and theocracy. As for the theocratic rule of the Mormon hierarchy, there was no necessity to alter the traditional reverence for republican government even though general authorities had to discover the painful limits that partisan politics imposed on them.

CHAPTER 9

Partisan Politics

By theology, religious observance, and political practice, Mormons of the nineteenth century were predisposed toward authoritarian control, supported by voluntary submission to "counsel."[1] But despite their religious faithfulness, Mormons occasionally banded together to challenge approved candidates for public office. This occurred in Davis County, Salt Lake City, Sanpete County, and Utah County in 1854; in San Bernardino, California, in 1855 and 1857; in Box Elder County, Davis County, and Salt Lake City in 1858; in Davis, Utah, and Weber counties in 1860; in Morgan, Salt Lake, Sanpete, and Tooele counties in 1862; in Tooele County in 1863; in Sanpete County in 1865 and 1866; in Salt Lake City and County in 1866, 1868, 1874, 1878, 1879, 1882, 1888; in Moroni, Utah, in 1868; in Ogden, Tooele, and Cache Valley, Utah, in the mid-1870s; in Beaver, Utah, in 1884; in Emery County in 1889; in Beaver, Logan, and Provo, Utah, in 1890; and in Brigham City in February-March 1891.[2]

The hierarchy responded with public criticism and active suppression. At Salt Lake City's School of the Prophets in February 1868, one of those present said that "some of the brethren voted the opposition ticket and those that had done it the President said they would sooner or later apostatize." Another added: "I am glad that I did vote for the ones that were approved by President Young."[3] At the school's next meeting First Presidency counselor Daniel H. Wells and Apostle George Q. Cannon made "full confession" for not "putting down the division at the polls." Several members of the school "made humble confessions" for their independent voting.[4] That same year Apostle Orson Hyde "condemned the course pursued in the recent Municipal Election in Moroni in opposing the nominations made by the priesthood."[5]

Understandably votes against a general authority were the rarest form of political dissent by loyal Mormons during these years. In the 1854 election eighty-three Mormons voted against Seventy's president Albert P. Rockwood. He was elected as the only candidate who received less than unanimous approval.[6]

The most significant incident of independent voting by otherwise loyal Mormons occurred in 1876, the year before Brigham Young's death. Many did not want to reelect Apostle Franklin D. Richards as Weber County's probate judge, and held an unauthorized political caucus which ratified and published a "REVISED" ballot that included every church-approved candidate except Richards. Thirty-nine percent of LDS voters supported the altered ballot with the unauthorized LDS candidate. The Mormon newspaper in Ogden editorialized: "But we do blame those of the 'Mormon' people who join with them [non-Mormons] in opposing that which their own delegates have agreed upon. We consider it wrong in principle and ruinous in policy." The editorial continued: "Our strength is in our union. If we suffer ourselves to be split into factions, our common enemies will step in and sweep the field. They care little for this measure or that man, at present. Their desire is to divide and weaken us. Persons who are openly and avowedly hostile to our cause, engineered and prosecuted the opposition of yesterday, and many of our own people followed their lead. Is this a safe policy?"[7]

Such responses support one interpreter's observation: "There was no loyal opposition within the kingdom of God. . . . Dissent meant defection."[8] However, despite tongue-lashings, the hierarchy rarely punished political dissenters who were otherwise loyal.[9] Moreover, up to 1890 the hierarchy's rejection of pluralism was more true in partisan politics than in doctrinal matters or in ecclesiastical governance. Beginning in 1891 the hierarchy abruptly accepted political pluralism and gradually moved toward the late-twentieth-century church's uncompromising insistence on conformity in doctrine and church government.

It was with a certain amount of pride that a committee of apostles in 1888 described the extent to which the First Presidency and Twelve controlled Mormon political life. At this date the apostles had not yet organized a separate First Presidency after the death of John Taylor:

> The great majority of the Saints respect the advice and counsel of this Quorum in political as in other matters, and obey it in most instances: at times even against their own judgment.
>
> In the opinion of your committee it is of the utmost importance that this influence for good be maintained and even increased, for upon it largely depends the political well-being of the Saints of GOD. Destroy the influence of the Priesthood in political affairs and the people fall victims here, as elsewhere, to the plans of unscrupulous rings, who make means of individual gain through personal advancement.[10]

In nineteenth-century Mormon theology and practice, partisan politics had no legitimate function within a community which sought to discourage political pluralism.

In that same context the hierarchy thought it could manipulate politics to benefit the Kingdom of God. The communitarian practice of "gathering" Mormon adherents gave the church increasing political importance in the voting districts where Mormons congregated. As a nineteenth-century LDS hymn stated: "A Church without a gathering is not the Church for me;/ The Savior would not own it, wherever it might be."[11] Although the hierarchy was unwilling to countenance factionalism; at times it solicited favors from competing political parties with the promise of bloc-voting. Thus general authorities felt the church could be political while keeping "the world" at arm's length.

Early Attempts at Manipulation

Efforts to manipulate political parties began in Kirtland, Ohio, less than four years after the church was organized. On 5 December 1833 Joseph Smith wrote that the church was going to establish a Democratic newspaper because "the influential men of that party have offered a liberal patronage to us, and we hope to succeed."[12] Although Jacksonian political favors did not descend upon the Mormons, the hierarchy established a Democratic newspaper at Kirtland in February 1835.

Edited by associate church president Oliver Cowdery and printed by second counselor Frederick G. Williams, the *Northern Times* advocated the election of Andrew Jackson's designated successor, Martin Van Buren.[13] If the First Presidency's establishment of an openly Democratic newspaper was not sufficient evidence of the hierarchy's political wishes, Cowdery ended all doubt when he attended the Democratic state conventions in 1835 and 1836 as a delegate from Geauga County.[14] A non-Mormon at Kirtland complained that the Mormons "now carry nearly a majority of this township, and every man votes as directed by the prophet and his elders."[15] Although Van Buren lost in Ohio and in Geauga County, the Mormon vote gave him a majority in Kirtland. The rest of the nation's voters did likewise.[16] Just before Van Buren's inauguration as U.S. president in March 1837, First Presidency counselors Oliver Cowdery and Sidney Rigdon signed a published announcement of a Democratic Party meeting in Kirtland.[17] Mormon bloc-voting was the chief cause of anti-Mormon sentiment in Ohio of the 1830s.[18]

Mormon leaders deserted Kirtland when the church splintered there, and bloc-voting again made the Mormons a divisive force at the church's new headquarters in Missouri.[19] When Mormons swept into virtually every office in Caldwell County, non-Mormons of Daviess County tried to prevent Mormons there from voting. The resulting melee in August 1838 left anti-Mormons in disarray and provided the catalyst for the mobbing and eventual expulsion of Mormons from the state.[20]

During a lull before the conflict escalated into civil war, one of the "old residents" of the state described the bloc-voting. "But when you get to the extreme part of the state, where Jo Smith and his Mormonites reside, nearly all the people are Van Burenites," he wrote in September 1838. Then he added, "Caldwell county, which is Smith's headquarters, gave but 2 Whig votes."[21] Smith's diary described the nearly unanimous vote but did not reveal that the paramilitary "Danites" had organized the Mormon vote.[22]

After Missouri's governor expelled the Mormons from the state, Joseph Smith expected a fair return for the LDS community's three years of loyally supporting Van Buren's Democratic presidency. Having lost property estimated at several millions of dollars, Mormons appealed to the U.S. Congress for compensation, knowing that Missouri would never consent to be sued for that amount. When Smith obtained a personal interview with President Van Buren on 29 November 1839, the chief executive infuriated the prophet by saying that he could do nothing about matters within Missouri as a sovereign state of the Union.[23]

Van Buren's rebuff, despite Mormon support for his election, soured the hierarchy on endorsing political parties even if their ideologies corresponded with Mormon philosophy. Throughout the rest of the nineteenth century the calculated *quid pro quo* ("exchange of favors") of *Realpolitik*[24] governed dealings of the hierarchy with national parties.

When the Mormons arrived in Illinois in 1839, the Whig-Democratic equilibrium allowed the bloc-voting Mormons to manipulate the two political parties.[25] Nevertheless, the only success the hierarchy had in exploiting the Whig and Democratic scramble for votes was in obtaining the Nauvoo Charter from the Illinois legislature. To a large extent, this initial triumph was the responsibility of Mormonism's only successful Machiavellian, John C. Bennett.[26]

Smith himself did considerably less well when he sought to bargain. From 1840 to 1841 Mormons voted for Whigs in a reflex response against Van Buren. Nevertheless, this pattern built up expectations of Whig leaders that they could count on the Mormon vote. In December 1841 Smith announced that Mormons "care not a fig for *Whig* or *Democrat*: they are both alike to us; but we shall go for our *friends,* our TRIED FRIENDS."[27] In the gubernatorial election of 1842 Mormons voted for Democrats again.[28] A Whig newspaper complained about "the CORRUPT BARGAIN between the leaders of the same [Democratic] party in Illinois and Joe Smith the Mormon Prophet, by which they have formed a league to govern the State. They gave him power and he gave them votes."[29]

This increased anti-Mormon feeling in Whigs and gave hope to Democrats.[30] However, Smith played his Whig card again in 1843 by privately assuring a Congressional candidate that he would vote for him. A Mormon dissenter informed inhabitants of Illinois what such a promise meant about the Mormon vote: "Let the ballot box, at every election where they have voted answer, and it will be found that they have voted almost to a man, with Smith."[31]

Two days before the 1843 election Hyrum Smith, Associate President and Presiding Patriarch, announced that he had a revelation that Mormons should vote Democratic. The day before the election Joseph Smith publicly stated that he had received no revelation about politics and deferred to Hyrum's inspiration. However, Joseph said he would keep his personal promise to vote for the Whig candidate. Mormons got the message, and Nauvoo voted for the Democrat.[32]

This clumsiness outraged Whigs who called Hyrum's revelation a "blasphemy." Joseph had now destroyed the faith of both parties. Mormons continued to bloc-vote, but neither party seriously courted them after the 1843 election. Mormon political power encouraged anti-Mormonism.[33]

The *Warsaw Signal* editorialized: "The Mormons have the control of our elections, and while they see proper to obey the dictates of one man in political matters, what necessity is there for the old citizens going to the polls? Joe Smith sitting on his throne at Nauvoo, can name our sheriff and our county commissioners, he can name his nimble 'cat's paws' for these important stations, and thus hold under his own thumb, the jury panel of our County." The editor concluded: "Is it possible, in this land of Republican liberty that free men shall live in peace and know that their dearest rights are subject to the control of one man?"[34]

By 1844 the LDS church's political newspaper regarded the Whig Party (ancestor of the future Republican Party) as anti-Mormon in every state of the Union. A year later the Mormon newspaper simply referred to "the Whig or anti-Mormon candidates."[35]

In 1844, after Mormons had alienated both political parties, Smith began an independent bid for the White House. The prophet sought the U.S. presidency under the banner of "Jeffersonian Democracy," which demonstrated the traditional Mormon preference for the Democratic Party.[36] After Smith's martyrdom, "the brethren all concluded to vote for Polk," the Democratic candidate.[37] A month after the election Brigham Young wrote: "The Democratic banner floats again triumphant over our country. God grant that it ever may." He signed the letter as "Prest of the Church of L.D.S."[38]

However, two weeks after Young's letter the church's New York newspaper warned Democrats not to take Mormon support for granted: "We want the broad mantle of the Constitution to extend itself across our shoulders, and if the Democratic party will not give it to us, we are bound to support that party that will!"[39] They made good on that threat in Iowa.

When Mormons left a hostile Illinois in 1846, they were welcomed temporarily in Iowa. There they again established a gathering place where Whig and Democratic parties were at equilibrium, and Mormons again held the balance of political power for an entire state. On 18 March 1848 the Whig State Executive Committee wrote a long letter to "Rev. Brigham Young," commiserating with previous Mormon sufferings and laying the responsibility on the Democratic parties of Missouri and Illinois. After several consultations the hierarchy issued a resolution on 27 March 1848 that Mormons in Iowa would vote for Whigs at the next election.[40]

Because Mormons had voted for Polk in 1844, Iowa Democrats may not have taken the pledge seriously. LDS voters obeyed the hierarchy's instructions, with a margin of 491 Whig votes to thirty-two Democratic votes. Democrats were enraged, and there was serious talk of driving all Mormons from the state. Instead, Democrats engineered irregularities in the vote count and disqualified the Mormon ballots. With control of Iowa's legislature, they came within one vote of passing a bill to abolish the Mormon-controlled Pottawattamie County and thereby disenfranchise the immigrants.[41]

Apostle Orson Hyde's Whig partisanship in Iowa led to bitter conflicts with Almon W. Babbitt, a Democratic member of the Council of Fifty. Brigham Young shrewdly advised Hyde: "Now we do not care about your political differences, but wish to say confidentially to [both of] you, keep them up, outwardly for that may be good policy." However, because Hyde had excommunicated his political opponent, the church president added: "Never, no never! no never!! again drag Priesthood into a Political gentile warfare."[42]

Hyde turned the church newspaper in Iowa, *The Frontier Guardian*, into a Whig political organ. He urged Mormons to remain true to the party whose members had opposed the anti-Mormon bill in the legislature. Despite Hyde's partisanship, Democrats moderated their antagonism and in the 1850 campaign again tried to court the Mormon vote. Nevertheless, in two separate elections Hyde succeeded in getting the Mormons of Pottawattamie to overwhelmingly support Whig candidates: 550 to four in a special election, and 446 to 82 in the general election. The rest of Iowa went totally Democratic.[43]

Although Mormons under Hyde's direction alienated only the Democratic Party, it was the party in control. One reason why Young had the Mormons of Iowa move to Utah before 1852 may have been his concern over the volatile political situation. There had already been mob action in Missouri and Illinois in response to Mormon political power. Young saw no reason to add Iowa to the list.

Likewise, by 1855 the bloc-voting San Bernardino Mormons "often held the balance of political power in southern California." Although they had bloc-voted for all but one Whig candidate three years earlier, the Mormons switched to the Democratic Party after their only elected Democrat persuaded the California legislature to create a Mormon-dominated county. In 1855 the resident apostles, Amasa M. Lyman and Charles C. Rich, rejected a $7,000 bribe to vote for the anti-Catholic Know-Nothing Party. Instead, 90.5 percent of Mormon voters supported Democratic candidates, but Californians elected a Know-Nothing governor that year. In 1856, 93.5 percent of Mormons in San Bernardino voted for Democratic presidential candidate James Buchanan. However, in the July 1857 election an anti-Mormon candidate defeated the Mormon candidate for the state senate. This political isolation doubly mimicked the Iowa situation— on 4 August 1857 Brigham Young advised the Mormons to abandon San Bernardino and move "to a place of safety." Although Young was preparing to resist an "invasion" by the U.S. army from the east, two-thirds of the 3,000 Mormons in Southern California dutifully sold their belongings at a loss and moved to Utah. For them it was a bitter irony that they had helped elect the U.S. president who ordered this military assault on the Mormon commonwealth.[44]

Political Leveraging in Utah Territory

After settling in the Great Basin, Young tried to leverage support in Washington, D.C. When Mormons sought statehood status in 1849, the administration was Whig, but Democrats controlled both houses of Congress. Therefore, Young sent John M. Bernhisel, a Whig, as a special emissary in May 1849. To cover all bases Young also arranged for the July election of Almon W. Babbitt, a Democrat, as the official delegate of the State of Deseret to Congress.[45]

Once Congress had created Utah territory, Orson Hyde, now an ardent Whig, wrote the First Presidency that Bernhisel should be Utah's delegate because "he not only makes friends at Washington, but retains their confidence and good will." Young obliged and arranged for Bernhisel's election. He was an able delegate, and the hierarchy kept him in office until after the conclusion of the Utah War.[46] That conflict began when Democrats controlled both houses of Congress and the White House.

From then on, Young switched Utah's delegates to match the political party in power in Washington. A year after Democratic president James Buchanan's 1858 amnesty to Mormons, Young responded in kind. He had Bernhisel retire and arranged the election of a Democrat, William H. Hooper. When the new Republican Party gained control of all branches of government in 1860 and 1861, it was Hooper's turn to retire. Bernhisel, whose Whig Party had been absorbed into the Republican, returned to Congress as Utah's delegate.[47]

Despite the 1856 Republican Party platform pledging to suppress polygamy in the territories, Mormons and Bernhisel himself felt confident. With the secession of the southern states, surely the Republican Congress would welcome Utah as a state. Instead, in 1862 Congress rejected Utah's petition and passed the Morrill Act. Aimed at Mormons, this act made "bigamy" a federal crime and disincorporated the LDS church.[48] Stung by this Republican affront, the Mormon hierarchy selected only Democrats to serve as Utah's Congressional delegates from Bernhisel's retirement in 1863 until 1895.[49]

In 1870 anti-Mormons transformed the dynamics of the territory's political life by organizing their own political party, the Liberal Party. On 9 February 1870 non-Mormons appointed a central committee to serve for a year, nominated "independent" candidates for the Salt Lake City municipal election, and called for a traditional "mass meeting" to ratify its candidates. In retaliation the church's *Deseret News* immediately invited every interested Mormon to attend the meeting "to see a good ticket nominated."[50]

Mormons jammed the dissident meeting and used parliamentary rules and voting majorities to take over. As a result this dissident mass meeting formally ratified its own opposition—a ticket of the already-announced candidates of the church's "People's Ticket."[51] The hierarchy used this identical tactic a century later to derail a women's convention which the general authorities disapproved (see chap. 10). Concerning the 1870 incident, an assistant LDS church historian would later write that this "was simply a practical joke."[52]

Unamused and undeterred, Salt Lake City's non-Mormons called for a territorial convention on 16 July 1870 of those "who are opposed to despotism and tyranny in Utah." In swift reaction the LDS church organized its own political organization, the People's Party, on 16 July, the same day anti-Mormons formed their statewide Liberal Party. Previously the hierarchy had announced its candidates under the banner of the "Union Ticket" or "People's Ticket," without a formally organized party.[53]

Although the Liberal Party elected a permanent Territorial Central Committee at its July convention, "the People's Territorial Convention" established no permanent officers or organizational structure. An early interpreter observed that at this point the People's Party "functioned without the appearance of leadership, an illusion which made the party appear to keep pace naturally with the needs of the people and the Church."[54] Instead, the convention chose a "nominating committee" of four general authorities and nine regular Mormon members. Their role did not extend beyond the convention. Everyone understood that the power behind the People's Party was the Mormon hierarchy.[55]

In 1872 LDS authorities involved themselves in politics as part of a tremendous effort to obtain statehood for Utah. For the first time non-Mormons were included in the convention which drew up the proposed state constitution. Non-Mormons were also among the proposed state officers. As a more startling element of the statehood effort, the 1872 constitution contained a provision that obliquely invited Congress to add to the state constitution a clause prohibiting polygamy.[56]

The 1872 petition and proposed constitution had barely been sent off to Washington when Mormons began to divide along national party lines. One analyst suggested that one purpose for support of national parties in Utah was to split the already fractionalized Liberal Party of anti-Mormons.[57] While this may have been true, the key objective was to obtain bipartisan Congressional support for statehood.

Because Republicans had traditionally opposed Mormons, the hierarchy sought reconciliation by overwhelmingly supporting the Republican Party in 1872. On 15 March First Presidency counselor Daniel H. Wells signed the call for a Republican mass meeting. At this 2 April mass meeting Wells was joined by Seventy's president Albert P. Rockwood and Presiding Bishopric counselor Jesse C. Little. Three apostles and the first counselor in the LDS First Presidency attended the territorial convention. Wells's colleague in the presidency, George A. Smith, was chosen as a delegate to the 1872 Republican national convention at Philadelphia. The territorial Republican Party was organized with the following officers: Apostle Franklin D. Richards as president and as vice-presidents George A. Smith and apostles Charles C. Rich and Erastus Snow.[58]

The church's political newspaper, *Salt Lake Herald,* made sure that the leadership of the Republican Party would not mistake the intentions of the Mormons. An editorial on 30 May 1872 noted: "The vote of Utah is over 25,000. Of this number not more than one-tenth are Gentiles. . . . If it is desired to encourage the Mormons to enter the Republican organization, the Philadelphia convention will admit the Salt Lake delegates."[59]

Although Mormons were courting the majority party of Congress and the White House, general authorities did not want to lose their Democratic friends in Congress, who had been cultivated through the efforts of Utah's territorial delegates up to 1872. With one exception general authorities were conspicuous by their absence in the organization of the Democratic Party in Utah. That exception was Apostle George Q. Cannon, who attended the territorial convention in July 1872. Cannon was elected a vice-president and was nominated as the Democratic candidate for the election of Utah's territorial delegate to Congress.[60]

The hierarchy reasoned that they could successfully enlist the support of both national parties. Massive public support by LDS authorities for the Republicans would contribute toward their approving the entry of a Republican state. At the same time Cannon could privately reassure Democratic Congressmen of Utah's future support once Congress granted statehood.

Unfortunately the hierarchy's lack of sincerity contributed to the defeat of the 1872 statehood effort. A rival non-Mormon delegation went to Philadelphia, where the Republican convention voted as a compromise to accept both delegations. George A. Smith refused to be seated with the gentile delegation in a self-inflicted prelude to the failure of the statehood petition. That ended the blossoming of general authority participation in the Utah Republican Party, even though local organizations met again in 1876.[61]

The hierarchy was obviously the moving force behind the People's Party which did not even have a territorial central committee until 1874.[62] No current general authorities were on this committee until 1876 when apostles Franklin D. Richards, Brigham Young, Jr., and Joseph F. Smith joined the territorial central committee.[63] As of the 1878 convention, the People's Party territorial committee had only one general authority (Richards) and two women (Bathsheba W. Smith and Emmeline B. Wells). That same year Salt Lake County's central committee had no general authorities and three women.[64]

Beginning in 1879 members of the territorial central committee were appointed to the Quorum of the Twelve. Committee member Moses Thatcher became an apostle in 1879, followed in 1880 by committee member Francis M. Lyman. From then until the 1882 Edmunds law, apostles Richards, Thatcher, and Lyman served on the central committee.[65]

From 1882 until 1886 there were again no general authorities on the territorial central committee of the People's Party. John R. Winder had joined the committee in 1874 as a non-general authority, became a member of the Presiding Bishopric in 1886, and chair of the territorial central committee from 1887 on. Although newly appointed general authority Winder was on the central committee as of October 1886, women were no longer committee members that month.[66]

Although the hierarchy was barely represented on the central committee of the People's Party, the First Presidency and apostles ran the show. In January 1890, a year before the dissolution of the church's political party, the presidency and Twelve "decided to leave it with the central committee to meet with the delegates who were elected at the People's Primaries last night and prepare a ticket, after the committee has met with us and got our ideas about the men who should be nominated."[67] Members of the People's Party central committee were simply relaying a message when they "counseled" delegates about persons to choose as candidates.

Other general authorities served on county or municipal central com-
mittees of the People's Party. Apostle Brigham Young, Jr., chaired the
Cache County party in 1874, Apostle Franklin D. Richards chaired Weber
County's central committee, and Apostle Orson Hyde chaired the Sanpete
County People's Party in 1878.[68] William B. Preston and Marriner W. Mer-
rill were apparently still chairman and member, respectively, of Cache
County's central committee when they became, respectively, Presiding
Bishop in 1884 and apostle in 1889.[69]

Other general authorities served as delegates to the People's Party ter-
ritorial, county, and municipal conventions from 1870 to 1890. These in-
cluded apostles Orson Hyde, Orson Pratt, George A. Smith, John Taylor,
Wilford Woodruff, Erastus Snow, Franklin D. Richards, George Q. Can-
non, Brigham Young, Jr., Joseph F. Smith, Albert Carrington, Moses
Thatcher, John Henry Smith, Heber J. Grant; the Twelve's counselor
Daniel H. Wells; Seventy's presidents Albert P. Rockwood, Horace S.
Eldredge, William W. Taylor, and Seymour B. Young; Presiding Bishop
Edward Hunter and his counselors Leonard W. Hardy and Robert T. Bur-
ton.[70]

The hierarchy's apolitical manipulation of partisan politics became apparent in the immediate wake of the organization of the two national parties in Utah during 1872. By the time Apostle George Q. Cannon took his
seat as delegate in the U.S. House of Representatives, the Republican Party
had gained majority control of both houses of Congress in addition to the
White House. Therefore, Cannon declared himself a Republican and sat
on the Republican side of the House, even though he had been elected as
the joint candidate of the People's Party and Democratic Party.[71] This political contradiction resulted in a caustic comment by the anti-Mormon *Salt
Lake Tribune*: "He now calls himself a Republican because there is a Republican majority in Congress. Had the Democrats been the stronger in numbers, our facile Delegate would have set himself down as a Democrat. But,
in simple truth, he belongs to neither of these two great political parties.
He is simply a son of the Church, a pliant tool in the hands of Brigham."[72]
Cannon himself provided ample support for this assessment after Democrats gained majority control of the U.S. House of Representatives in 1874,
1876, and 1878: he moved to the Democratic side of the House. In an 1878
newspaper interview Cannon stated: "The Mormons generally on national
issues are inclined to be Democrats, and all other things being equal, in the
respective candidates of the parties, would vote the Democratic ticket."[73]

Other general authorities demonstrated similar opportunism in the
1872 organization of Utah's Republican Party. Erastus Snow was the territorial vice-president of the Republican Party until 1876, when he became
chair of the Democratic Party for Washington County, Utah. In 1874 an-

other former Republican territorial vice-president, Charles C. Rich, presided over a Democratic county convention in the Territory of Idaho, where he was elected to office as a Democrat in 1876. The territorial president of the Republican Party in 1872, Franklin D. Richards, was a life-long Democrat but would not publicly demonstrate that commitment until 1891.[74] The organization of national political parties in Utah had not moved beyond Mormon theocracy. It was another two decades before the hierarchy would actively support the establishment of the two-party system.

The Waning of Mormon Political Supremacy

During the next fifteen years both national parties helped to dismantle Mormon political supremacy in Utah. In 1874 the Poland Act restricted Utah's judiciary and placed it more firmly under federal control. In 1879 the U.S. Supreme Court's famous *Reynolds v. United States* case declared polygamy to be a heathen threat to western marriage institutions and sanctioned the laws prohibiting it.[75] In 1880 the national convention of the Democratic Party refused to admit George Q. Cannon as a delegate, and in 1882 the U.S. House of Representatives voted to exclude Cannon despite his decade of service there.[76] In 1882 the Edmunds Act disenfranchised polygamists and provided for the reconstruction of Utah's political life.[77]

Just as Southern Democrats had opposed the first federal law against polygamy twenty-six years earlier, the proposed 1882 legislation against the political rights of polygamists was vigorously attacked by senators and representatives from every state of the South including Missouri, where the Mormons had once suffered at the hands of state and local officials. However, Democratic senators and congressmen from non-Southern states joined with the Republicans to make the Edmunds Act the law of the land. Nevertheless, the *Deseret News* still affirmed in 1884 that Idaho Mormons supported the Democratic Party because its principles were "fundamental to this republic."[78]

The final evidence of bipartisan repression of Mormon theocracy was passage of the Edmunds-Tucker Act in 1887. This reaffirmed the 1862 disincorporation of the LDS church and provided the machinery for confiscating its assets. In the political realm the act also disenfranchised Utah's women. This reduced the eligible Mormon vote by almost three quarters, since one quarter of the men were already disenfranchised for being polygamists. However, a feminist historian has observed that the Edmunds-Tucker Act "ultimately had unintended and ironic consequences" for Mormon women because "it also helped motivate Mormon suffragists to organize official suffrage societies and advance monogamist Mormon women as leaders." The Democratically-controlled House of Representatives approved this bill, and it became law with the silent acquiescence of Democratic president Grover Cleveland.[79]

Cleveland gave the Mormon hierarchy reason to support the national Democratic Party in June 1887 by personally providing them with an acceptably moderate provision outlawing polygamy for Utah's proposed state constitution. Church president John Taylor approved the provision, which was to be included in the constitution as though by independent action of constitutional delegates.[80] Moreover, in 1888 Cleveland appointed as Chief Justice for Utah a man favorable to Mormons who understood that he was to administer anti-polygamy laws leniently.[81]

Cleveland's efforts were responsible for a flurry of Democratic support by the Mormon hierarchy in the last year of his administration. In August 1888 John W. Young, counselor to the Twelve, urged the apostles to establish a Central Democratic Club in Salt Lake City and to buy up and reorganize the *New York Star* to support church political interests in New York City. Meanwhile, as the hierarchy's then-current agent for distributing bribes to federal officials, Young was requesting amounts like $15,000 "to keep [anti-Mormon Republican] Cullom quiet" on the U.S. Senate's Committee on Territories, and to pay Democratic senator Cushman K. Davis "to vote with us in Committee."[82] The apostles decided against Young's proposal for the *Star,* because he had already purchased the *New York Globe* five months earlier as part of that strategy. However, in September 1888 the Twelve (as the acting presidency) authorized a Mormon organization of Democrats in Ogden, Utah, as long as there was no separation from the People's Party of the church.[83]

The next month some overly enthusiastic, yet faithful Mormons formed a new Democratic Party with an extraordinary platform: "enforcement of all valid laws . . . the decision of the court of last resort is final, and should be accepted in good faith. . . . Equal and exact justice to all men, of whatever state, religious or political . . . Absolute separation of church and state."[84] This went beyond what the hierarchy could allow, and the *Deseret News* warned: "There is no need for any other organization at present than the People's Party . . ."[85]

Support for Democrats extended beyond Utah. In Arizona, Cleveland's appointment of a Mormon-friendly governor had already won the support of the Utah hierarchy, and LDS president Taylor instructed LDS leaders in Arizona to "get the Saints in the various Arizona Stakes in line to sustain the Democratic nominees," which they "overwhelmingly" did in 1886. In September 1888 the apostles instructed Mormons in Arizona to vote for the Democratic candidate for U.S. Representative but to choose Republicans as local officers.[86]

Later that month Idaho stake president William Budge astounded a Democratic justice on Idaho's supreme court by promising that Idaho Mormons would vote a straight Democratic ticket if the judge would agree to administer the anti-polygamy laws "justly and not oppressively." Although the state's Mormons had previously voted Democratic, Budge had already asked the First Presidency whether to give the LDS vote to the Republicans in view of the fact that Idaho's Democrats expelled Mormons in 1886. The Mormon newspaper in Idaho threatened this political reversal. Budge's offer of a political-judicial swap was not successful in persuading the judge to invalidate the Idaho law which disenfranchised Mormon voters. Although Budge had previously served as delegate to Democratic conventions, he soon became a Republican activist.[87]

Church authorities also publicized this message to Mormon voters. "Every true Democrat in Utah can vote for John T. Caine without going back on a single principle," the *Deseret News* editorialized. "He is the nominee of the People's Party, but the platform of that party is Democratic in every plank."[88]

Three things stopped the hierarchy's rush to support Democrats. First, the Democratic convention in Ogden refused to admit the four Mormon delegates. Second, the Democrats in Congress declined to fight for passage of Utah statehood. Third, Republicans swept the national elections in November 1888. For the first time since 1875 Republicans controlled both houses of Congress as well as the White House.[89] Daniel H. Wells, a counselor to the Twelve and ardent Republican, quietly dissented from the Twelve's tilt toward the Democrats until after the election. His son wrote the equally devout Republican Joseph F. Smith: "Of course father can't help giving the Democrats a 'dig in the ribs.'"[90] Smith, a counselor in the First Presidency, was in Hawaii to avoid arrest during this period.

Years of public and private support for the Democratic Party had failed to produce either statehood for Utah or an end to anti-Mormon legislation. Therefore, as the federal government reapplied its repressive force against polygamy in 1889, the hierarchy began a crucial tilt toward the Republican Party, the "Grand Old Party" (GOP). In May the newly-sustained church president instructed Apostle Heber J. Grant, a Democrat and president of the board of the Democratic *Salt Lake Herald,* to stop editorials critical of U.S. president Benjamin Harrison and other prominent Republican leaders. Grant met with the board of directors, and they agreed that such editorials "did us more harm than good."[91] In October the First Presidency and Twelve retracted its previous instructions to Arizona Mormons to vote for Democratic national leaders and told them instead to vote for "the best men" of each party.[92]

By July 1890 the political situation was desperate. The Republican Congress was preparing to disenfranchise all Mormons throughout the United States and to deny Mormons the right to homestead on public lands. Undoubtedly not by coincidence, James G. Blaine, U.S. Secretary of State in the Republican administration, privately announced to emissaries from the First Presidency that he was in favor of Utah statehood as the way "of securing Mormon votes."[93]

On 31 July the First Presidency assigned Apostle John Henry Smith to instruct Mormons in Wyoming "to vote the Republican State ticket." They gave Apostle Francis M. Lyman the same instructions for Mormons in Arizona. Apostle Abraham H. Cannon summarized this meeting: "Self protection demands that we look to the Republicans for relief, now that the Democrats have proved themselves cowards on our question." Two weeks later the entire First Presidency visited Arizona and "recommended the Saints in Arizona so far as practicable to affiliate with the Republican party."[94] Although stake president Budge carried out the First Presidency's decision to instruct Mormons not to vote in Idaho's first state election of 1890, the LDS newspaper there was advising them to abandon the Democratic Party.[95] About the same time Secretary of State Blaine advised an emissary of the First Presidency that he would arrange for fellow Republicans to allow the pending bills to fail passage. However, he advised that the church president should announce a revelation to abandon polygamy, and Blaine even provided a provisional draft of such an announcement.[96]

At the beginning of September 1890 federal officials indicated that the government was preparing to confiscate the Salt Lake temple. Church president Wilford Woodruff and his counselor George Q. Cannon immediately left for San Francisco, where they visited with prominent Republican leaders including Morris M. Estee. Estee was a California judge who had chaired the Republican National Convention during the successful candidacy of the current U.S. president.[97] Estee said he and the church's other influential Republican friends would do everything they could to help the cause of the church and Utah statehood, which were intertwined. However, the "permanent chairman" of the Republican Party's national convention said that it would be absolutely necessary "sooner or later" for the church to make an announcement "concerning polygamy and the laying of it aside." Unlike his similar discussions with non-Mormons in previous years, Cannon did not protest that it was impossible. Instead, on 12 September 1890 he spoke of "the difficulty there was in writing such a document—the danger there would be that we would either say too much or too little."[98]

Cannon's conversation with this national Republican leader was the most crucial turning point in the various concessions the Mormon hierarchy had gradually made about polygamy. For a year Woodruff had been willing to comply with federal law by stopping all plural marriages in the United States, but his counselor had resisted. Now Cannon accepted the need for a public announcement. Only the wording was a question for him. He and the church president spent more than a week at San Francisco in further discussions about the church's situation and in "negotiations" with Republican leaders in San Francisco.[99] On 25 September, three days after his return to Salt Lake City, Woodruff issued his famous Manifesto urging Mormons to comply with the "laws of the land concerning marriage."[100]

Polygamy had become symbolic of the chasm that separated Mormon culture from "American" society. In one sense polygamy was an inappropriate symbol because Mormons had been accused of being "un-American" long before polygamy became significant.[101] One historian concluded that Mormon "anti-pluralism was the main cause of persecution."[102] Even after Brigham Young gave institutional status to polygamy, it involved an elite minority. More than 95 percent of Utah's Mormons voted for church candidates, while only 20-40 percent of the male Mormon voters entered into polygamous marriages during this entire period. The polygamous rate for females was 10-15 percent higher, and plural wives sometimes exceeded the total number of monogamous wives in Utah.[103]

Although plural marriage was a non-essential of the Mormon commonwealth, it had become the central focus of anti-Mormon polemics. Polygamy assaulted the moral sensibilities of the majority of Americans for whom "the fear that Mormonism was corrupting the nation's homes overrode every other terror."[104] It was also an easy target and rallying cry against everything non-Mormons detested about Mormonism, especially its political power.[105] "Now the territory is virtually under the theocratic government of the Mormon Church," U.S. president Rutherford B. Hayes wrote concerning anti-polygamy legislation: "To destroy the temporal power of the Mormon Church is the end in view."[106] The Republican platform of 1888 specified this linkage in its anti-Mormon campaign: "to divorce the political from the ecclesiastical power, and thus stamp out the attendant wickedness of polygamy."[107]

In like manner polygamy had become the centerpiece of the Mormon defense of the church's mission. As federal pressures against polygamy increased after the death of Brigham Young, the hierarchy adopted a defensive stance that was the undoing of the commonwealth. Amid cries of "No compromise!" general authorities insisted that polygamy was an essential practice that could not be given up without destroying Mormonism.[108] Rather than discourage anti-Mormons, this claim inspired them to renewed efforts. When the church president capitulated to the supremacy of federal authority in 1890 by publicly abandoning polygamy, the surrender of more central features of the Mormon commonwealth would paradoxically become easier. As an early non-Mormon interpreter has written, "the frictions that made headlines were caused by a conflict of social orders and of cultures and not by a conflict over polygamy alone."[109]

There was no parallel anguish about giving up the Council of Fifty or the church president's office as theocratic king. Those features of the Mormon kingdom had gone into permanent disuse four years before the joint statement of the First Presidency and Twelve that "this Church does not claim to be an independent, temporal kingdom of God."[110] Those theocratic offices were a five-year-old memory when Woodruff officially announced the end of polygamy. As an early interpreter of the Fifty wrote, "Polygamy died with a bang, the political kingdom of God with a whimper."[111] However, the church experienced a wrenching change after the Manifesto as it surrendered Mormon unity at the ballot box.

Acceptance of political pluralism was the end of Mormon theocracy for those who knew little or nothing about the Council of Fifty. While this theocratic council had rarely met and remained largely symbolic even to its members (see chap. 8), for sixty years the civic life of most Mormons revolved around unanimous elections of political candidates chosen in advance by the LDS hierarchy.

By February 1890 the anti-Mormon Liberal Party had gained control of the municipal governments in Ogden and Salt Lake City.[112] Now that the church had officially abandoned polygamy, anti-Mormons advised the hierarchy to disband the People's Party. "When the Mormon Church shall have done this," the *Salt Lake Tribune* editorialized in November, "there will then no longer be any objection to the entrance of Utah to the Union. All then will be clear sailing."[113]

On 17 February 1891 Ogden Mormons asked the First Presidency what to do in view of the fact that the Liberal Party there seemed ready to divide along national party lines. Two days later the First Presidency, two apostles, and the Presiding Bishopric met with Ogden's political leaders and decided to organize national parties among Mormons. On 25 February the First Presidency instructed the presidency of Salt Lake Stake "to move quietly among the people and advise them cautiously of the changes pending in political affairs as to their becoming Republicans or Democrats."[114]

After more than fifty years of ridiculing political factionalism, the hierarchy moved carefully. In a meeting of 19 March 1891 the First Presidency, Quorum of the Twelve, and First Council of Seventy decided to restrict the political division of Mormons to Weber County, because "we desire to see first how the experiment will work there before we advise the adoption of a similar course elsewhere." Pleased with the outcome, "the Presidency and other brethren" decided on 25 May to instruct the leadership of the church's political party to consider a total division along national lines.[115]

As a result, the Central Committee of the People's Party submitted resolutions to precinct meetings on 29 May that called for the party's dissolution. It was another example of the hierarchy's political orchestration when the People's Party disbanded on 10 June and urged its members to join one of the two national parties.[116]

Adjustments to Partisan Politics

In 1890 Mormons voted as a bloc and had their own political party, but within half a century Mormons would be as politically independent as the rest of society. Between the division along political lines in 1891 and the emergence of the Democratic New Deal in 1932, Mormons experienced a difficult and often painful transition from the uncomplicated acceptance of theocratic rule to the ambiguous world of national politics. Caught between the necessity of encouraging political pluralism and a longing for the verities of the theocratic past, the hierarchy frequently exhibited an ambivalence that was both ironic and melancholy.

The first adjustment was the fragmentation of the hierarchy's political unity, which occurred almost immediately after the division along political lines. General authorities had kept themselves informed on issues to know how to exploit the political parties for the welfare of the Mormon commonwealth, while the average Mormon relied on their behind-the-scenes management and was obediently apolitical.[117] Yet the hierarchy itself, when freed of constraint, lacked political unity, as indicated by the following table.[118] (The years represent the period of service in the quorum indicated in the subheads.)

Table 1.
Affiliation of the Hierarchy in National Political Parties, 1891-1931

FIRST PRESIDENCY
Wilford Woodruff (1891-98), nominal Republican (former Democrat)
    George Q. Cannon (1891-98), ardent Republican (former Democrat)
    Joseph F. Smith (1891-98), ardent Republican
Lorenzo Snow (1898-1901), politically ambivalent to 1900; ardent Republican, 1900-1901
    George Q. Cannon (1898-1901), ardent Republican
    Joseph F. Smith (1898-1901), ardent Republican
    Rudger Clawson (1901), ardent Republican (former Democrat)

Joseph F. Smith (1901-18), ardent Republican
>   Anthon H. Lund (1901-18), ardent Republican
>   John R. Winder (1901-10), ardent Democrat
>   John Henry Smith (1910-11), ardent Republican
>   Charles W. Penrose (1911-18), ardent Democrat

Heber J. Grant (1918-1931+), nominal Democrat (formerly ardent)
>   Anthon H. Lund (1918-21), ardent Republican
>   Charles W. Penrose (1918-25), ardent Democrat
>   Anthony W. Ivins (1921-31+), ardent Democrat
>   Charles W. Nibley (1925-31), ardent Republican (former Democrat)

QUORUM OF THE TWELVE APOSTLES
(in order of seniority)

Lorenzo Snow (1891-98), politically ambivalent, but declared Democratic affiliation in 1895

Franklin D. Richards (1891-99), ardent Democrat (former Republican)

Brigham Young, Jr. (1891-1903), ardent Democrat in 1890s; ardent Republican in 1900s

Moses Thatcher (1891-96), ardent Democrat

Francis M. Lyman (1891-1916), ardent Republican

John Henry Smith (1891-1910), ardent Republican

George Teasdale (1891-1907), Republican

Heber J. Grant (1891-1918), ardent Democrat

John W. Taylor (1891-1906), nominal Democrat in 1890s; nominal Republican in 1900s

Marriner W. Merrill (1891-1906), ardent Republican

Anthon H. Lund (1891-1901), ardent Republican

Abraham H. Cannon (1891-96), nominal Democrat

Matthias F. Cowley (1897-1906), ardent Republican

Abraham Owen Woodruff (1897-1904), nominal Democrat until 1899; Republican in 1900s

Rudger Clawson (1898-1931+), ardent Democrat in 1890s; ardent Republican in 1900s

Reed Smoot (1900-1931+), ardent Republican

Hyrum M. Smith (1901-18), ardent Republican

George Albert Smith (1903-31+), ardent Republican

Charles W. Penrose (1904-11), ardent Democrat

George F. Richards (1906-31+), ardent Republican (former Democrat)

Orson F. Whitney (1906-31), ardent Democrat

David O. McKay (1906-31+), ardent Republican

Anthony W. Ivins (1907-21), ardent Democrat

Joseph Fielding Smith (1910-31+), ardent Republican

James E. Talmage (1911-31+), Republican

Stephen L Richards (1917-31+), ardent Democrat

Richard R. Lyman (1918-31+), ardent Republican (former Democrat)

Melvin J. Ballard (1919-31+), ardent Democrat

John A. Widtsoe (1921-31+), Republican
Joseph F. Merrill (1931-31+), ardent Democrat

PATRIARCH TO THE CHURCH
John Smith (1891-1911), Republican
Hyrum G. Smith (1912-31+), ardent Republican

FIRST COUNCIL OF SEVENTY
(in order of seniority)
Henry Harriman (1891), died before adoption of national parties
Jacob Gates (1891-92), ardent Democrat
Seymour B. Young (1891-1924), ardent Republican (former Democrat)
Christian D. Fjeldsted (1891-1905), ardent Republican (former Democrat)
John Morgan (1891-94), ardent Republican
Brigham H. Roberts (1891-1931+), ardent Democrat
George Reynolds (1891-1909), Republican
J. Golden Kimball (1892-1931+), ardent Democrat to 1905; then Republican
Rulon S. Wells (1893-1931+), ardent Democrat
Edward Stevenson (1894-97), Democrat
Joseph W. McMurrin (1897-1931), ardent Republican
Charles H. Hart (1906-31+), ardent Democrat
Levi Edgar Young (1909-31+), Republican
Rey L. Pratt (1925-31), Republican
Antoine R. Ivins (1931-31+), ardent Democrat

PRESIDING BISHOPRIC
William B. Preston (1891-1907), ardent Democrat
    Robert T. Burton (1891-1907), ardent Democrat
    John R. Winder (1891-1901), ardent Democrat
    Orrin P. Miller (1901-1907), ardent Democrat
Charles W. Nibley (1907-25), ardent Republican (former Democrat)
    Orrin P. Miller (1907-18), ardent Democrat
    David A. Smith (1907-25), ardent Republican
    John Wells (1918-25), Republican (former Democrat)
Sylvester Q. Cannon (1925-31+), nominal Republican
    David A. Smith (1925-31+), ardent Republican
    John Wells (1925-31+), Republican (former Democrat)

Before the People's Party disbanded in 1891, Wilford Woodruff told an apostle that he was Republican.[119] However, in 1892 when angry leaders of Utah's Democratic Party confronted the church president with charges that the First Presidency was using church influence for Republicans, Woodruff reportedly told them: "I'm a Dimicrat myself."[120] That was apparently a defensive response rather than his true political conviction. Nevertheless, a Democratic newspaper insisted in February 1895 that Wilford Woodruff "is a Democrat. He has said so repeatedly." With Apostle Heber J. Grant as its announced vice-president, the newspaper acknowledged, "yet this guileless old man was induced to vote [in 1894] for the political son [Republican Frank J. Cannon] of Mr. [George Q.] Cannon. He voted early in the morning publicly rejecting a Democratic ticket offered him and publicly voting the Republican ticket." In August 1895 a Republican newspaper claimed Wilford Woodruff as one of the Republican general authorities.[121] That was undoubtedly his actual affiliation. In addition to Woodruff's private admission of GOP affiliation in conversations with a Republican apostle, his administration consistently favored Republicans and restrained Democrats.[122] However, several church authorities were politically ambivalent.

Apostle Lorenzo Snow had avoided political involvement even in the church's People's Party, and after 1891 he was politically ambivalent. His sons included Republican activists and Democratic activists in the same town and county. Possibly to keep peace in the family, he did not participate in the political conventions of either party in his home town. However, in 1894 Snow went with one of his activist Republican sons to a victory party of Utah's Republicans. Understandably, in August 1895 a Utah Republican newspaper listed him as one of the Republican apostles.[123]

However, in October 1895 he attended Utah's Democratic convention with Apostle Brigham Young, Jr. and Presiding Bishop William B. Preston. At this convention Apostle Snow said that he "had come to the conclusion that he was a Democrat now that he had become stirred up."[124] In July Young had privately told the Twelve that "he was inclined to Democracy," and the following month Salt Lake's Democratic newspaper announced that Apostle Young "openly declares that he is a Democrat."[125] In 1896 Snow's youngest plural wife, Minnie Jensen Snow, the only wife Lorenzo now lived with, was a Democratic delegate to a local convention.[126] Undoubtedly she did so with his permission.

Shortly after becoming church president in 1898, Lorenzo Snow told Salt Lake City's Democratic newspaper: "I have never been in politics. I want to keep entirely out of it, and am not in now."[127] However, Snow publicly supported the Republican Party in 1900. Again, this was in response to national Republican politics.

The Republican Congress was once more threatening a constitutional amendment against Mormon polygamy.[128] This time ardently Republican apostle John Henry Smith reported to Snow that Republican president William H. McKinley privately assured Smith in February 1900 that "we should not be hurt." In return Apostle Smith "told him I would do all I could for him [in the upcoming election] but that he must not overestimate my strength." A month later President Snow sat on the stand at a Utah Republican convention, with both his counselors, four apostles, and two members of the Council of Seventy.[129]

As part of this political tradeoff to avoid a constitutional amendment against polygamy, the church president privately arranged for the election of Republican Thomas Kearns as Utah senator the following year.[130] Two of Snow's apostolic friends, the Twelve's recently ordained president Brigham Young, Jr., and recently ordained Rudger Clawson, followed the church president's abandonment of the Democratic Party and public embrace of the Republican Party, even though Young and Clawson had been Democratic partisans up to Snow's presidency.[131]

In 1891 Apostle Abraham H. Cannon said that "he had not as yet been able to make up his mind as to which party he should join." In 1892 the secretary of the First Council of Seventy listed Cannon among the hierarchy's Democrats. Abraham's diary indicated he was apolitical, and in response to a Republican newspaper's claim in August 1895, Abraham Cannon "entered a specific denial to the charge that he is a Republican."[132]

Apostle John W. Taylor expressed his continuing disdain for the political party system in 1892: "as for me I do not care which party is victorious." In April 1895 he added that no apostle should join a political party without the permission of the First Presidency, yet a Republican newspaper regarded John W. Taylor as a Democrat this year.[133] However, at best Taylor was a nominal Democrat in the 1890s, and his immediate family understood that he was a Republican by the 1900s.[134]

Apostle Abraham Owen Woodruff was allegedly identified by his father as a Democrat in 1895, and he voted for Democratic general authority Brigham H. Roberts in November 1898. However, in February 1899 he sat with partisan apostles Francis M. Lyman and Anthon H. Lund "in front seats near the speaker" at a Republican meeting. In 1900 Apostle Woodruff also attended the Republican state convention and actively worked for the election of Republican Senator Kearns in 1901. However, the next year Woodruff wrote to Democrat Heber J. Grant in criticism of the Republican candidacy of Owen's cousin Reed Smoot.[135]

Heber J. Grant was known as a Democratic apostle even before the disbanding of the People's Party, and he opposed the pro-Republican views of the First Presidency in the 1890s. When the First Presidency told a temple meeting that "the Republican ticket should win in the Territory" in 1894, Grant responded angrily and a fellow apostle wrote: "The warmth he showed astonished me very much."[136] However, Grant's views had become Republican by the time he was church president. He commented in 1920: "It is amusing for me to pose as a Democrat, and when I come to vote at our State elections and National elections divide my vote for a larger number of Republicans than Democrats." Eight years later Grant did not deny a published allegation that he had voted in the Republican primary, but denied a claim that he was one of "the leaders of the Republican party."[137]

In contrast to general authorities who were apolitical or politically ambivalent after 1891, other members of the hierarchy were ardently partisan. These political activists attended the conventions of their respective parties, publicly supported their party's candidates, and sometimes became candidates themselves.[138] In the politically tumultuous decades after Utah's adoption of national parties (to 1910), the hierarchy had a larger number of ardent Republicans, while the First Presidency and Quorum of Twelve had nearly twice as many ardent Republicans. Intense partisanship divided every quorum of the hierarchy, including the First Presidency after 1901 and the Presiding Bishopric after 1908.

Some general authorities formed political views long before the official division along national political lines. Joseph F. Smith voted for Abraham Lincoln in California in 1864, and thirty years later a fellow general authority wrote that Smith was "a very radical Republican."[139] Moses Thatcher was a Democratic delegate from Cache County during the 1872 organization of the Democratic Party in Utah. A fellow Democrat described his "dominating character," yet affirmed that "Thatcher, in fact, was as magnificent a Democrat as there was in the territory."[140] When there was no national party organization in Utah, Reed Smoot converted to the Republicans in 1884 and helped organize Utah's first Republican Club in 1888, three years before the First Presidency instructed Mormons to choose a national party.[141]

Other partisan members of the hierarchy adopted their politics in 1891. For example, John Henry Smith was the hierarchy's most active Republican in the 1890s and publicly claimed: "From my youth I have been a pronounced Republican." However, a decade earlier he unsuccessfully tried to persuade the theocratic Council of Fifty to disband the People's Party and adopt the Democratic Party as the church's official party.[142] Charles W. Nibley (later the church's Presiding Bishop) was a founding member of Utah's Lincoln Republican Club in 1891, but Democrats denounced his political conversion. The *Salt Lake Herald* dismissed Nibley as "a sort of blatherskite who for years has been figuring in politics in Idaho and Wyoming, sometimes as a Democrat, but this year as a Republican." The newspaper added that Nibley was a "smooth and cunning breed of demagogue."[143]

Although the political preferences of general authorities appointed prior to 1891 could not have been a factor in their selection, political affiliation may have influenced their selection after 1891. For the total number of appointees from 1892 to 1932 there does not appear to be a significant political demarcation. Of these thirty-two general authorities, eighteen (56.3 percent) were Republicans at the time of their appointment. When the new appointees are classed politically according to the echelons in the hierarchy, however, political affiliation seems more significant.

Of the eighteen appointees to the Quorum of the Twelve Apostles between 1897 and 1932, ten (55.6 percent) were Republicans at their appointment. During the administration of ardent Republican Joseph F. Smith, seven (63.6 percent) of his eleven new apostles were Republicans. The proportion might seem to reflect Utah's Republican population, except that of the eight appointees to the First Council of Seventy between 1892 and 1932, only three (37.5 percent) were Republicans. In other words, a Republican was far more likely to be appointed as an apostle rather than as a Seventy's president. This correlates directly with the dynamics of power in the two respective echelons. The Quorum of the Twelve, unlike its ecclesiastical subordinate, traditionally had a prominent role in the social, political, and economic life of Mormons.

Deference to the Republican Party was also reflected in the Presiding Bishopric. William B. Preston, a Democrat, had been appointed as Presiding Bishop seven years before the division along party lines. While he lived the entire Presiding Bishopric was Democratic. Preston's two successors as Presiding Bishop were Republicans, and they preferred fellow Republicans as counselors. Therefore, deaths of counselors allowed the composition of the Presiding Bishopric to shift to completely Republican by 1918.

The preference for Republicans in the hierarchy's quorums of economic and political power was consistent with the First Presidency's relationships with the national Republican Party. The trends of Republican dominance in the hierarchy are shown below (Table 2).

Table 2.
Percentage of Republicans in the Mormon Hierarchy[144]
November 1891-November 1931

	1891	1896	1901	1906	1911	1916	1921	1926	1931
Hierarchy	52.0%	48.0%	69.2%	61.5%	69.2%	69.2%	65.4%	69.2%	69.2%
Presidency	100.0%	100%	66.7%	66.7%	66.7%	66.7%	0	33.3%	66.7%
Twelve	41.7%	36.4%	*91.7%	75.0%	75.0%	75.0%	75.0%	75.0%	75.0%
Patriarch	100%	100%	100%	100%	100%	100%	100%	100%	100%
Seventy	66.7%	*42.9%	57.1%	57.1%	57.1%	57.1%	57.1%	57.1%	42.9%
Bishopric	0	0	0	0	66.7%	66.7%	100%	100%	100%

*one vacancy in the quorum before November.

Whether these partisan general authorities were early or late converts, the intensity of their political confrontations was unmistakable. In February 1892 Apostle Abraham H. Cannon recorded:

> I then went to the President's office where I remained a short time listening to the political talk of the brethren. I was surprised to see the warmth of feeling in John R. Winder when his Democratic principles were assailed, and he did not hesitate to oppose the expressions of Joseph F. Smith in favor of Republicanism. I very much fear that the politics which are being introduced among us will lead to a spirit of disregard and disrespect for the Priesthood. Such a feeling is already beginning to make its appearance in some places.[145]

Three months later prominent Mormon (and future apostle) James E. Talmage could hardly conceal his shock at the personal attacks published in newspapers by Republicans Joseph F. Smith and John Henry Smith against fellow general authority and Democrat Moses Thatcher.[146]

The novelty of partisan politics was not the sole reason for this hostility between general authorities, because political antagonisms continued into the twentieth century. When Apostle Reed Smoot returned to Salt Lake City in 1909 from his duties as U.S. senator, he felt his reception by three partisan members of the hierarchy "was rather cool."[147] When Democratic Seventy's president B. H. Roberts made a personal attack on Republican Senator Smoot in a 1910 political speech, Smoot said that Roberts was "a very contemptible man and dishonest in his life and utterances." A decade later, when the apostles discussed another public attack by Roberts on Smoot, Democratic apostle Anthony W. Ivins defended Roberts, so Smoot said he wanted to drop the subject.[148] Such partisan strife, as Abraham H. Cannon had feared in 1892, had a ripple effect in reinforcing the political autonomy of rank-and-file Mormons.

Political disunity was complicated by the tendency of general authorities to reassert their former ecclesiastical control over political activity, while at the same time denying that there was such a thing as "church influence" on the political process. In an interview with the *Salt Lake Times* (popularly regarded as a non-Mormon newspaper) in June 1891, President Wilford Woodruff and his counselor George Q. Cannon stated: "As officers of the Church we disclaim the right to control the political action of members of our body." Had the statement ended there, both Mormons and non-Mormons would have understood the message without ambiguity. But the interview moved into areas which would be interpreted differently by Mormons who had specific knowledge of the hierarchy's past subterranean political control. Woodruff and Cannon categorically stated: "There is, therefore, no foundation for the charge that the church brought about the dissolution of the people's party." They also disclaimed either past or present desires to unify church and state in Utah, and stated that the phenomenon of church authorities serving in Utah political office in the past was a coincidence. They claimed that Mormons chose for public office men of the "best talent," who just happened to be church leaders.[149]

The appearance of this interview in the "non-Mormon" *Salt Lake Times* was a truly ironic subterfuge. The First Presidency gave the impression that this was the product of tough, independent journalism rather than a carefully arranged statement by the Mormon hierarchy. Everyone would have assumed such journalistic collusion if the interview had been conducted by the church's known newspapers in 1891, the *Deseret News* and *Salt Lake Herald*. However, the First Presidency and Twelve had secretly purchased the *Salt Lake Times* in March 1891.[150] Nevertheless, this 1891 interview set the pattern for future denials by the First Presidency of efforts to direct the political decisions of voters or civil officers.[151]

After 1891 there were various specific issues which led to the hierarchy's intervention in politics. An overriding factor was the First Presidency's conviction that the welfare of Mormonism required support of the Republican Party's national organization. In July 1891 second counselor Joseph F. Smith informed the apostles that among prominent Republicans interested in Utah's welfare were Secretary of State James G. Blaine, national chair of the Republican Party; James S. Clarkson, former chair of the 1888 national Republican convention; California judge, Morris M. Estee; and U.S. senator Leland A. Stanford.[152]

When the *Salt Lake Tribune* learned of these negotiations, it published furious editorials about the hierarchy's "secret betrayals." The Mormon acceptance of national parties "was just a common, vulgar bargain

. . . to obtain Statehood for the Mormons," in exchange for giving support to the Republican Party. These mid-1891 editorials demonstrated that the *Tribune* valued its anti-Mormon origins more than its role as Utah's defender of the national Republican Party.[153]

In October 1891 Estee wrote Counselor Cannon that the national Republican chair believed that "if the Mormons are now properly handled they will make of Utah a Republican State."[154] One of the ironies of this period is that although non-Mormons had virulently opposed the political influence of the Mormon hierarchy before 1891, leaders of both national parties now expected the hierarchy to deliver voting majorities after 1891.[155] For example, when pressured to guarantee that Utah's first two U.S. senators would be Republican, Cannon replied: "I had said I could not give a pledge of that kind, and I did not know any one else that could. I would do anything in my power to have Utah admitted as a State and to have it Republican, but could make no pledge of that kind." With this understanding of earnest Republican intentions, national Republican leaders devoted several years of effort among Congressional friends to obtain statehood for Utah.[156] Republican support of Utah's statehood was part of the exchange of favors involved in the First Presidency's discussions with Republicans just days before the Manifesto publicly ended polygamy.

General authorities saw two major appeals in the national Republican Party. First, it alone offered substantive progress toward the hierarchy's decades-old goal of statehood. Second, and most important after statehood, the conservative tariff and business policies of the Republicans were more favorable to the hierarchy's involvement in banking, railroads, mining, sugar, and other industries.[157]

The question of statehood vis-à-vis the Republican Party was symptomatic of a more fundamental dilemma facing the hierarchy after 1890. On the one hand, political issues that general authorities regarded as crucial to the church's interests could fail without active support of the hierarchy. On the other hand, any time the Mormon hierarchy became involved in an issue (whether collectively or individually), both Mormon and non-Mormon partisans of the contrary view became alienated and accused the hierarchy of violating promises concerning the separation of church and state. Of this situation one historian has written: "Neither alternative was accepted as church policy and instead, a vacillating course between the two was pursued. Denials of the use of ecclesiastical influence followed hard upon decisions announcing the 'Will of the Lord' concerning political matters. The consequent confusion gave credence to the earlier charges of duplicity."[158]

Although members of the hierarchy, especially the First Presidency, often tried to avoid becoming involved in politics after 1891, the theology and tradition of monolithic political management acted as an incentive for intervention. When the need seemed sufficient, the church leadership involved itself, often clandestinely, in the new political world they entered after 1890.

Public Office and Politics after Statehood

Although the LDS church publicly abandoned polygamy in 1890 and its theocratic political party in 1891, not until October 1892 did the *Salt Lake Tribune* accept the fact that Utah's Mormons were sincerely in opposition to each other politically. Significantly the turning point was a published attack by First Presidency counselor Joseph F. Smith against a Democratic publication by Charles W. Penrose, counselor in the Salt Lake Stake presidency. The *Tribune* exulted that Republican Smith "fairly wipes the earth with the Elder." The hierarchy's former boast about political unity was now obsolete. Despite its previous complaints about the hierarchy's "vulgar bargain," the Republican newspaper in November 1892 recommended that Utah receive statehood because "the majority" of Mormons "voted the Republican ticket" in the recent election. However, entrenched anti-Mormons waited to disband the Liberal Party until 18 December 1893, just days after the U.S. House of Representatives approved an act to allow Utah statehood.[159]

This "enabling act" became law in 1894, and authorized Utah to hold a constitutional convention. In the convention of 1895 that drafted Utah's eventual state constitution, non-Mormons tolerated a swan song demonstration of general authority presence in territorial politics. Four general authorities were among the delegates to the convention (3.8 percent), and the president of the convention was Apostle John Henry Smith. However, Smith became convention president because Democratic delegate Anthony W. Ivins outmaneuvered the attempt of non-Mormon Republicans to force a roll-call vote that would have shown which LDS Democrats voted for Republican Smith. Instead, Ivins succeeded in obtaining a voice-vote.[160]

One unprecedented development was the frequency with which general authorities declined nomination to be candidates for public office. John Henry Smith declined nomination as a representative to the territorial legislature in 1893. Apostle Brigham Young, Jr., turned down offers to nominate him as Utah's first state governor in 1895. Apostle John Henry Smith refused the nomination as Utah's representative to Congress in 1896 and, after seeking the nomination of U.S. senator in 1898, withdrew from the race in favor of Counselor George Q. Cannon. Cannon himself had not accepted the nomination as Utah's first U.S.

senator in 1896, and Apostle Anthon H. Lund declined the nomination for U.S. representative in 1900. In 1909 Seventy's president Charles H. Hart withdrew as Democratic candidate for city attorney. In 1920, after announcing his intention to be a candidate for Utah's governorship, Seventy's president Brigham H. Roberts announced that he would not be a candidate. Though virtually guaranteed the Republican nomination to be the candidate as U.S. senator in 1934, First Presidency counselor J. Reuben Clark publicly declined to seek the office or accept a "draft" nomination by the convention.[161]

Where election defeats were rare for the nineteenth-century hierarchy, after 1891 general authorities experienced frequent defeats as candidates at various stages in their new political world. Barely a year after the dissolution of the LDS church's political party, the hierarchy suffered its first political defeats at the hands of Utah Mormons. A general authority had not served as a Utah legislative officer (such as chaplain, sergeant-at-arms, or doorkeeper) since 1882. Since non-legislators filled those positions, John Henry Smith apparently felt confident of being elected chaplain in the 1892 Utah legislature. Instead, Mormon legislators helped defeat Apostle Smith's candidacy to be the House's chaplain. After that stinging loss in 1892, for the next hundred years no general authority sought the chaplaincy or any of the other administrative offices of the Utah legislature.[162] Later in 1892 Apostle Anthon H. Lund also lost the election for the territorial legislature.[163]

The scope of the problem was clear by 1894 when three general authorities lost the elections of their respective parties for delegates to the momentous constitutional convention of 1895. Apostle Marriner W. Merrill lost in the balloting for Republican delegates, while Democratic voters rejected Presiding Bishopric counselor Robert T. Burton and Apostle Heber J. Grant. In the 1894 election Seventy's president Rulon S. Wells also lost as a Democratic candidate for the Utah legislature.[164]

In 1895 it was clear that the Mormon hierarchy could expect political defeats. Although Apostle Heber J. Grant and Presiding Bishop William B. Preston were favored as candidates for Utah's governorship in 1895, both men failed to receive the nomination. Despite their popularity, Seventy's president B. H. Roberts and Apostle Moses Thatcher also failed in their 1895 candidacies for the respective offices of U.S. representative and senator. In 1899 Counselor George Q. Cannon was defeated in the final vote for U.S. senator, at a time when the Mormon-dominated legislature elected U.S. senators.[165]

Only three general authorities were elected to public office after the Mormon acceptance of national politics in 1891. Utah elected Seventy's president B. H. Roberts in 1898 as its representative to Congress, but the U.S. House of Representatives voted in 1900 to exclude him due to his polygamous marriages.[166] Seventy's president Rulon S. Wells was elected to the Utah legislature in 1900 but lost his reelection bid in 1902. Then Wells won election to the Salt Lake City Council, where he served until 1908. Those two general authorities were Democrats. Most notably Republican apostle Reed Smoot was repeatedly elected to the U.S. Senate from 1903 until his defeat in 1932. Smoot blamed his defeat on the fact that President Heber J. Grant gave him only a personal endorsement without strongly urging Mormons to vote for him. Even that was undercut by Grant's cousin and Democratic counselor, Anthony W. Ivins, who persuaded the church president four days later to publish a statement of non-interference in politics. However, Apostle Smoot's real bitterness was toward the Mormon people: "The members of my Church were my principal opponents, some of them in high places."[167]

Faced with the likelihood of election defeats, other general authorities preferred appointive office in various governmental jurisdictions. For twentieth-century LDS church presidents, political appointments began with the Utah governor's selection of Grant as a member of the state's Committee for Armenian and Syrian Relief (1918-22). As an indication of Mormon demographic power, U.S. president Lyndon B. Johnson appointed LDS president David O. McKay to the National Citizens Committee for Community Relations in 1964. As an elder statesman, J. Reuben Clark had already enhanced the national status of the First Presidency when U.S. presidents appointed him as a delegate to the Pan-American Conference at Montevideo in 1933 and as general counsel, president, and director of the Foreign Bondholder's Protective Council from 1933 to 1953.[168]

During the twentieth century, counselors in the First Presidency and apostles had appointments on various state commissions. In October 1908 Utah's governor appointed recently-ordained apostle Anthony W. Ivins to membership on the State Conservation Commission. Counselor John Henry Smith served on the Utah State Capitol Commission in 1911 until his death, after which Counselor Anthon H. Lund served on that commission until 1914. Heber J. Grant and George Albert Smith were members of Utah's Council of Defense (1917-18). Smith also served as chair (1918-19) of the Utah Committee for Armenian and Syrian Relief (on which Grant, Reed Smoot, James E. Talmage, and John A. Widtsoe also served). Stephen L Richards became a member of the Utah State Board of Corrections two years after his appointment to the Quorum of the Twelve. Richard R. Lyman likewise served on a Utah water commission from 1922 to 1937, and John A. Widtsoe served on water and reclamation boards from his appointment as an apostle in 1921 until his death in 1952.[169]

In April 1931 Apostle David O. McKay was the general chairman of Utah state's official "White House Conference on Child Health and Protection." Held in Salt Lake City, this meeting adopted the name of the national meeting convened in 1930 by authority of the U.S. president. Although general authorities were apparently not delegates at the national meeting, McKay was joined in this state meeting by Presiding Bishop Sylvester Q. Cannon who served as a member of one of the Utah conference's "general" committees. McKay also chaired the Utah Council for Child Health and Protection (1932-33). As a counselor in the First Presidency, McKay was also a member of the Utah Centennial Exposition Commission (1938-47).[170]

Members of the lesser presiding quorums also served in appointive political office in Utah. Presiding Bishop Charles W. Nibley served on Utah's Council of Defense in 1917-18. His successor, Sylvester Q. Cannon, had the most diverse political appointments, serving on Salt Lake City's zoning commission, as supervisor of Salt Lake County's water district, Utah's flood commission, and ending with a national appointment as an advisor for the New Deal's Public Works Administration. Levi Edgar Young began the Council of Seventy's political appointments as a member of the Board of Governors for Utah state's Art Institute in 1913, followed two years later by his appointment as trustee of the State Industrial School for delinquent juveniles. In 1917 a newly-elected Democratic governor appointed B. H. Roberts to Utah's Board of Equalization. That same year fellow Democrat and Seventy's president Rulon S. Wells began four years as Utah State Commissioner of Insurance, during which time Young served on the Commission for the Education of Aliens. In 1925 Roberts chaired the Utah Commission for the Mormon Battalion Monument of which Seventy's president Charles H. Hart was also a member.[171]

After Congress authorized Utah's statehood, most of Utah's governors also made sure that the LDS hierarchy was represented on the boards of Utah's colleges and universities. From 1895 to 1969 the board of trustees of Utah Agricultural College (later Utah State University) included currently serving First Presidency counselors Anthony W. Ivins and David O. McKay, apostles Marriner W. Merrill, Anthony W. Ivins, Melvin J. Ballard, Matthew Cowley, LeGrand Richards, assistants to the Twelve Thorpe B. Isaacson and Alma Sonne, Seventy's president Brigham H. Roberts, and Presiding Bishopric counselor Thorpe B. Isaacson. From 1903 to 1993 the board of regents for the University of Utah included First Presidency counselor Anthon H. Lund, apostles David O.

McKay, Richard R. Lyman, Stephen L Richards, Adam S. Bennion, Thomas S. Monson, Neal A. Maxwell, Marvin J. Ashton, Seventy's presidents Richard L. Evans, Neal A. Maxwell, and W. Eugene Hansen, Presiding Bishop Robert D. Hales, and Bishopric counselor Thorpe B. Isaacson. From 1961 to 1969 the board of trustees for Weber State College (later University) included Apostle Mark E. Petersen, Seventy's president Marion D. Hanks, and Presiding Bishop John H. Vandenberg. From 1969 to 1993 general authorities on the State Board of Regents (Monson, Maxwell, Ashton, Hansen, Hales) presided over all of Utah's state schools of higher education, including the technical colleges. No current general authorities have served in these positions since 1993.[172]

Apostle Ezra Taft Benson's extraordinary appointment to U.S. president Dwight D. Eisenhower's cabinet introduced the hierarchy to national service in the second half of the twentieth century. Benson was the only cabinet member to serve both terms with Eisenhower (1953-61).[173] In 1955 Apostle Adam S. Bennion headed Utah's delegation to the White House Conference on Education, and three years later Seventy's president Marion D. Hanks was the first of several general authorities to serve on the U.S. President's Council on Youth and Fitness. In 1960 Hanks was a keynote speaker at the White House Conference on Children and Youth.[174]

Attempts to Control Partisan Politics

Most of the hierarchy's political involvement has been unofficial, including control of its newspapers' allegiances. On 19 February 1891 the hierarchy decided that the *Ogden Standard* would be a Republican newspaper and that the *Salt Lake Herald* would be Democratic. Five days later it decided that another Ogden newspaper, the *Commercial,* would be Democratic. This gave Ogden a church-supervised paper for both major parties, with sons of Counselor George Q. Cannon as the editor and manager of each.[175]

In Salt Lake City the church organ, *Deseret News,* announced itself as politically independent, and Apostle Heber J. Grant's *Salt Lake Herald* was Democratic. However, the hierarchy wanted the capital to have its own Republican newspaper under church control. Therefore, in March 1891 general authorities agreed to secretly purchase control of the *Salt Lake Times* to make it a Republican, "non-Mormon" newspaper, to reduce the influence of the Republican, anti-Mormon *Salt Lake Tribune.*[176]

Unlike the earlier Democratic *Northern Times* in Kirtland, Ohio, and the Whig *Frontier Guardian* at Council Bluffs, Iowa, the Mormon domination of partisan newspapers after 1891 became ambiguous. Control of newspapers on both sides of the national division was disruptive because it seemed insincere. Bipartisan control was especially at odds with the First Presidency's effort to enlist the aid of the national Republican Party.

After the Republican *Times* discontinued publication in 1892, the financially strained LDS presidency tried to increase the distance between itself and Democratic newspapers. They encouraged Grant to withdraw Mormon control from the *Salt Lake Herald* in 1896. In 1900 the Presidency refused to take over operation and financial responsibility for this Democratic newspaper.[177] However, Apostle John Henry Smith remained vice-president of the Republican newspaper in Provo, Utah, until 1903.[178]

More serious than the tactical error of providing initial support to papers of both parties was the hierarchy's inability to control the newspapers it did own. Although nominally independent, the *Deseret News* was editorially Democratic until well into the twentieth century. This fact both irritated and worried Republican members of the hierarchy.[179] The First Presidency also subsidized Apostle Reed Smoot's Republican newspapers: the *Inter-Mountain Republican* (1906-1909) and the *Herald-Republican* (1909-18), which later merged with the *Salt Lake Telegram* in 1918. However, there was almost as much frustration with their editorial independence as with the *Deseret News*.

Commenting on the *Inter-Mountain Republican*'s opposition to state-wide prohibition, Counselor Anthon H. Lund stated the problem directly: "I am a prohibitionist, but I told them it was folly for us to fight the paper we sustain with our money."[180] The confidence with which the hierarchy began its control of partisan newspapers deteriorated into an uncomfortable acceptance of the divisive influence of politics.

Another means of control after 1891 was the enlistment of authorities and other prominent Mormons to promote publicly an approved political view, while at the same time asking general authorities and others of a contrary persuasion to remain silent. In January 1892 Democratic apostles in the Quorum of the Twelve criticized Republican John Henry Smith for going "on the stump" for the Republican Party, and the decision of the Democratic president of the quorum, Lorenzo Snow, was that Smith should not be politically active. The next day, however, the Republican-inclined First Presidency met with the Quorum of the Twelve and authorized Smith to publicly promote Republicanism.[181] As the 1892 elections approached, Republican apostle Anthon H. Lund told an adjourned priesthood meeting of Arizona Mormons, "If I were an ardent Democrat I would lie low during this election at any rate." Shortly afterward, "despite strong loyalty to the Democratic party, many [Arizona] Mormons joined the Republicans."[182]

Predictably the partisan members of the hierarchy resisted limitations on their political activities. In the 1890s Apostle Moses Thatcher and Seventy's president B. H. Roberts got into difficulty because they openly rebelled against such impositions by the church presidency. In 1910

Republican Reed Smoot wrote that Democrats Grant and Ivins "talked wild on question of politics" in a meeting of the apostles, and "claimed Democrats had no show and were not treated with impartiality and he [Grant] was muzzled on the prohibition question." Apostle Smoot noted that Grant "had his say and no one answered him."[183]

When Democrat Heber J. Grant became church president in 1918, the situation was occasionally reversed. Now it was Republican Reed Smoot who complained that he was expected to remain silent even though he was a U.S. senator, while apostles without civil office were encouraged to work publicly for certain issues.[184] Despite the difficulties involved, the First Presidency continued to exercise selective restrictions on individuals whenever the circumstances seemed to require it and as long as the Presidency assumed that the men would be willing to acquiesce.

As an extension of this approach, after 1891 the church leadership frequently became involved in the effort to convert rank-and-file Mormons to the Republican Party. Although Mormons had traditionally favored the Democratic Party, the First Presidency privately expressed the desire that within the year there would be an equal number of Republicans and Democrats in Utah.[185] This obviously required many Democrats to become Republicans.

However, the First Presidency did not really want political parity, they wanted Republican domination. They were convinced that Republicans would support Utah's statehood, amnesty for polygamists, and the return of the church's confiscated property. Apostle John Henry Smith indicated this goal when he told Republican judge Charles S. Zane in 1891 that "I would go into the movement with the determined purpose of making Utah Republican."[186]

Republicans in the hierarchy were direct about trying to convert Mormons. Before the 1892 election, Counselor Joseph F. Smith published a pamphlet titled *Another Plain Talk: Reasons Why the People of Utah Should Be Republicans*. About the same time Apostle Francis M. Lyman told a Mormon priesthood meeting in southern Utah "that we had too many Democrats."[187] Some have said that Utah's political shift was consistent with the trend in most western states prior to the Democratic Party's silver issue in 1896.[188] This ignores the hierarchy's intense effort to encourage conversion to the Republican Party.[189]

The hierarchy's efforts in this direction did not cease with the supremacy of the Republican Party in Utah. In 1914 Apostle Francis M. Lyman, president of the Quorum of the Twelve Apostles and next-in-line to become church president, requested Nephi L. Morris to return to the Republican Party. Morris was a prominent leader in the Progressive Party and president of the Salt Lake Stake. For almost twenty-five years, Lyman and other Republican general authorities made similar demands on Mormons who would not have chosen to be Republicans if left alone. This stake president's written response is a rare glimpse into the inner turmoil and divided loyalties for some LDS church members.

> The request, though made in a kindly and brotherly spirit, is of great importance and must be regarded in a most serious light, since you place yourself and the first presidency on the Republican side of the question, and consider my attitude as being in conflict with yours. I use the word "conflict" because you ask me if I wish to fight you and the brethren. To be arrayed against the leaders of the Church is the one thing I have studiously avoided in the past, and have solemnly resolved never to do. * * *
>
> I have always believed in obeying the counsel of my file leaders, but when I have seen the counsel of my leaders disapproved by their successors in office, I have been perplexed beyond measure in determining how far a man is justified in surrendering his private judgment for that of others. Neither am I exactly clear as to how far a man may avoid responsibility for his acts when he thus surrenders his own opinions to his ecclesiastical superiors. These, I say, are the delicate phases and the perplexing problems that have confronted me for some time. Especially is the situation a trying one when I am asked by you to forsake the party that has my devotion, and come over into a party which has repudiated me and from which I have been for a long time completely divorced. Added to that requirement is an equally difficult one, in asking me to support Senator Smoot, whose policy and [news]paper and colleagues have been in conflict with all my activities for a number of years.
>
> When these requirements are made of me, I naturally wonder what meaning and force the public declarations of the Church can possibly have, wherein the Church has declared that all its members are politically free.
>
> After weighing the question with such feeble judgment as I have, I feel that my interests in and my love for the Church and Kingdom of God overwhelmingly [override] my interest in and devotion to political affairs.[190]

Despite the difficulty of this political conversion, Morris was true to his word. He absented himself from activity in the Progressive Party and conferred with his former adversary Reed Smoot in 1916 about uniting the Progressives and Republicans of Utah.[191] This is a classic example of the coerciveness of the hierarchy's "counsel" for devoted Mormons with differing political conscience.

Aside from total political conversion, the Mormon hierarchy wanted the electorate to vote as directed. Sometimes the message went out in what Utahns call a "whispering campaign." For example, in February 1892 the First Presidency sent its private secretary, George F. Gibbs, and one other man "to go quietly to Logan and work to make the Republican ticket successful in the approaching city election."[192] As often happened, Gibbs's effort backfired and brought accusations of "church influence" from an angry Democratic Central Committee. The *Salt Lake Herald* exposed this

"Church Influence at Logan" on the same page which listed Grant as the vice-president of the Democratic newspaper. Apostle Grant had been out of state for more than a week and was probably not consulted about the article.[193] The First Presidency issued a carefully worded statement which did not deny that the Presidency had sent Gibbs to influence Mormons to vote Republican but denied authorization "to use our names."[194]

Despite the frequent public embarrassment of being discovered, the First Presidency could not resist the temptation of authorizing these campaigns. LDS mission president Ben E. Rich and Apostle Matthias F. Cowley performed similar missions for the First Presidency in promoting Republican candidates in 1900. When Rich returned to the Presidency's office, he proudly claimed that their work had been so discreet that no trouble would result. President Lorenzo Snow's response was to show Rich a handful of telegrams protesting the church influence that Rich and Cowley had used.[195] Despite these perils, the hierarchy continued to leak their wishes to voters.

Another way to influence Mormon voters was to make their wishes a matter of public record. In the midst of Utah's prohibition controversy of 1909, President Joseph F. Smith told a general priesthood meeting of two thousand men "to send the right kind of men to the legislature and get what we want."[196] In the 1912 election President Smith published an article in the October *Improvement Era* in which he favored the election of William H. Taft. As a clear statement of Mormon peculiarity over regional interests, Utah was the only state to vote for Taft west of Vermont, the only other state that supported the incumbent president.[197] One analyst wrote of this period: "The Mormon Church was a major factor in creating and maintaining a Republican majority in Utah until 1912. The L.D.S. Church remained a 'sore spot' in state politics until 1918."[198]

In 1922 Heber J. Grant joined with LDS stake presidents and Protestant ministers in endorsing an independent candidate for sheriff, and the *Deseret News* instructed readers how to vote a party ticket and still scratch vote for the independent sheriff.[199] However, this was an exception to the general approach of the Grant administration during the 1920s: "the church leadership was generally reluctant to enter into politics and removed itself from some of the political involvement of previous years . . ."[200] In 1932 President Grant publicly stated his intention to vote for the reelection of Reed Smoot as U.S. senator but left Mormons to use their own judgment.[201]

Even before the ballot box, the Mormon hierarchy sought on occasion to influence the selection of candidates. The First Presidency felt that at a minimum it had jurisdiction in advising high Mormon ecclesiastics who

sought public office. Therefore, on 6 April 1896 the LDS general conference was presented with a "political manifesto" that stated in part:

> We have maintained that in the case of men who hold high positions in
> the Church, whose duties are well defined, and whose ecclesiastical labors are
> understood to be continuous and necessary, it would be an improper thing
> to accept political office or enter into any vocation that would distract or
> remove them from the religious duties resting upon them, without first
> consulting and obtaining the approval of their associates and those who
> preside over them.[202]

At face value that was not an unreasonable position. However, in the
context of the Presidency's efforts to encourage Republicans and "muzzle"
Democrats, this announcement created an uproar.[203]

By the end of September 1896 the First Presidency retreated from its
original intention. When a Republican stake president and a Democratic
bishop asked the Presidency on 29 September if they should accept nomination for political office, President Woodruff said that the manifesto applied only to general authorities. All other church officers were free to use
their own wisdom in accepting political nominations.[204]

The Case of B. H. Roberts and Moses Thatcher

Although this still put Democratic general authorities at a disadvantage, all but one of them were willing to accept this political constraint. To
this majority, asking the First Presidency's permission seemed a logical result of accepting the burdens and opportunities of a lifetime position of
presiding over the church. The lone dissenter in 1896 was Apostle Moses
Thatcher. His case is the most well-known instance of the use of ecclesiastical sanctions against political activity in the late nineteenth century.

The ecclesiastical approach to achieve partisan ends under the new
political arrangement began as early as February 1892. The First Presidency considered dividing a stake to prevent the Democratic stake president from influencing the Mormons of his stake away from the Republican
Party.[205]

Although general authorities had the freedom to speak and publish on
behalf of the Republican Party throughout most of 1892, the First Presidency and Quorum of the Twelve decided on 4 October that no general
authorities "should take the Stump to make political speeches."[206] Two
Democrats, Moses Thatcher and Brigham H. Roberts, felt that this ruling
was designed to aid Republicans. The two continued their political activity.

As a result the First Presidency punished the two renegades, as well as
Charles W. Penrose (Democratic editor of the *Deseret News* and a counselor
of the Salt Lake stake). On 23 March 1893 the Presidency forbade Thatcher, Roberts, and Penrose from attending the dedication of the Salt Lake

temple on 6 April unless they acknowledged their error. The three men held out until the night before the long-awaited event and then confessed their error.[207]

By 1895 the selective nature of restrictions on Democratic church leaders had become a publicly divisive issue. Although President Woodruff decided on 30 July 1895 that "the leading men" should not be active in the campaign, by 27 September Joseph F. Smith and George Q. Cannon had authorized Seventy's president Seymour B. Young to campaign for the Republicans.[208] For Thatcher and Roberts, such special preference was unacceptable.

Continuing to campaign for the Democratic Party, Thatcher and Roberts then accepted nominations for office. Counselor Joseph F. Smith publicly denounced them in October 1895 for not seeking the First Presidency's consent. The rest of the campaign was charged with acrimonious statements by Democrats about the separation of church and state.[209] The First Presidency waited to punish them until after Utah was admitted to the Union.[210] After President Grover Cleveland signed the statehood bill on 4 January 1896, the hierarchy prepared to deal with their wayward Democratic colleagues.

When Roberts refused to acknowledge any error in his activities during the previous campaign, he was dropped from the First Council of Seventy and deprived of the right to exercise his priesthood on 5 March 1896. The First Presidency stipulated that this action would become final if he did not recant within three weeks. Roberts decided to give up his position as a general authority. At the last moment he was persuaded to write a letter of apology by Republican apostle Francis M. Lyman and Democratic apostle Heber J. Grant. That letter and a subsequent apology by Roberts before the First Presidency and Quorum of the Twelve allowed him to function as a both a Democrat and a general authority. However, as always, this required the advice and consent of the Presidency.[211] A subsequent secretary to the First Presidency had a more charitable view of Roberts and Thatcher: "They had simply misread the signals when the Brethren had modified the rigid policy of 1892, believing that this left them free to seek political office [in 1895]."[212]

Moses Thatcher's case was less happy. Thatcher had been in periodic conflict with the First Presidency over economic, business, ecclesiastical, personality, and political differences for a decade before he refused to sign the political manifesto of 6 April 1896.[213] Even though current apostles had been aligned with him in some of these earlier difficulties, it was understandable that the hierarchy viewed Thatcher's 1896 rebellion as the culmination of spiritual disaffection.[214]

From April to October 1896 the hierarchy hesitated to force the issue because Thatcher's physical condition was precarious due to long illness and inadvertent morphine addiction.[215] Nevertheless, general authorities became enraged that Thatcher was conducting business and political activities at the same time he professed to be too ill to meet with them. Without the knowledge of the apostles, the First Presidency denied Thatcher entrance to the Salt Lake temple on 15 October 1896—the one occasion he tried to meet with apostles about this dispute. His political antagonist, Apostle John Henry Smith, disliked this rejection of Thatcher's one sign of cooperation: "I don't feel quite right about it."[216]

The relationship between Thatcher and his associates deteriorated to the point that they were convinced he wished only to embarrass the church in order to win the Democratic candidacy for the U.S. Senate. The situation transcended partisanship. Democratic apostles Heber J. Grant, Brigham Young, Jr., and Lorenzo Snow urged the Twelve to drop Thatcher from office, which they did on 19 November 1896.[217]

Probably due to the First Presidency's pressure against Democrats, for decades after 1891 there were more general authorities in Republican conventions than Democratic. From 1891 to 1932 twenty-one functioning general authorities were delegates at Republican conventions, sat on the stand of a Republican convention, or were committee members of the Republican Party: President Lorenzo Snow; counselors George Q. Cannon and Joseph F. Smith; apostles Brigham Young, Jr. (1900), Francis M. Lyman, John Henry Smith, Marriner W. Merrill, Anthon H. Lund, Abraham Owen Woodruff, Rudger Clawson, Reed Smoot, Hyrum M. Smith, George Albert Smith, and David O. McKay; Seventy's presidents Seymour B. Young, Christian D. Fjeldsted, John Morgan, and Joseph W. McMurrin; Presiding Bishop Charles W. Nibley, his counselor David A. Smith; and Presiding Patriarch Hyrum G. Smith. Thirteen functioning general authorities were delegates at Democratic conventions, sat on the stand of a Democratic convention, or were committee members of the Democratic Party: apostles Franklin D. Richards, Brigham Young, Jr. (1894-95), Moses Thatcher and Heber J. Grant; Seventy's presidents Jacob Gates, Brigham H. Roberts, J. Golden Kimball, Rulon S. Wells, and Charles H. Hart; Presiding Bishop William B. Preston, and his counselors Robert T. Burton, John R. Winder, and Orrin P. Miller. Only the Republican Party was represented by delegates from the First Presidency.[218]

Covert Intervention

Public and official influence in the process of candidate selection and nomination was circumscribed after 1890, but the actual influence of the hierarchy continued to be significant. Correspondence between mission president Ben E. Rich and Apostle John Henry Smith in 1902 shows how church leaders continued to discourage Democratic candidates in order to ensure Republican victories. In one letter Rich wrote Apostle Smith:

> I left a message for you by George [Albert Smith, the apostle's son], to the effect that Bassett [Thomas E. Bassett, president of the LDS Fremont Stake in Idaho] had said to some one that he intended to withdraw from the Democratic ticket if he found out he had not done right. If you have no time to see him I would suggest that you leave at the house a confidential letter to me, asking me to see brother Bassett and explain our promises to the Pres. [Theodore Roosevelt] &c. I will use it as a basis of talk. He might go and see Pres. Smith, therefore if you would drop him (Pres S) a note and tell him if Bassett comes to refer him to me, it would fix it. It might not be wise to ask them both [Bassett and Don C. Driggs, Democratic president of the LDS Teton Stake in Idaho] to get off, unless you think so, but if Bassett will do so (and I think he can find a way) I believe we can win. Fremont County is a large one and has four members of the legislature. Without it there is no hope of a Republican Senator.

In a subsequent letter Rich felt that both men should abandon the Democratic ticket and indicated more confidence about "Driggs' following advise" than Bassett. He complained about the possibility of the two Democrats getting contrary advice from "other apostles, who perhaps does [sic] not fully understand matters."[219] The Rich-Smith correspondence demonstrated the First Presidency's pattern in the twentieth century of using intermediaries to spread political wishes. This allowed "deniability" to the Presidency, which could then issue statements disavowing "church influence" when the occasion required.

For example, in 1916 LDS president Joseph F. Smith asked an Idaho stake president "to hint our wishes [about a possible Republican candidacy] to Bro Steele. He could not write to Steele as this might be found, and the Idahoans are so jealous of being dictated to from Salt Lake."[220] That caution reflected the embarrassing outcome a decade earlier when three LDS apostles privately lobbied legislators and voters of both parties to vote uniformly on matters of interest to the LDS hierarchy. In response, Idaho's Democratic chairman published a proclamation that "the men of Idaho become so docile in their subjection to [the political wishes of] Joseph F. Smith of Salt Lake."[221] Agreements with national Republican leaders, clandestine conversations and letters, and instructions relayed through intermediaries were all part of the hierarchy's difficult passage through divided loyalties into the non-theocratic world of Mormonism after 1890.

From 1896 to 1917 the hierarchy exerted behind-the-scenes influence on the election of U.S. senators. Until the ratification of the seventeenth amendment to the U.S. Constitution, state legislatures elected senators. The First Presidency realized that its political powers had been fragmented by the accommodations of 1890 and 1891 and that it could not automatically assume that legislators would elect the hierarchy's choice for U.S. senators.[222]

For example, in 1896 the Presidency and apostles feared that they could not persuade Utah's legislators to elect Counselor George Q. Cannon as U.S. Senator "without trouble." Therefore, they decided against his candidacy, despite President Woodruff's frequently expressed desire that he be U.S. Senator.[223] At the same time, the hierarchy was willing to do anything to stop the legislature from electing Moses Thatcher, which was a nightmarish prospect. He was a Democrat, a rejected apostle, and campaigned on an anti-church platform. Democrats controlled the Utah legislature.

To stop Thatcher the hierarchy was willing to support the election of non-Mormon Democrat Joseph L. Rawlins, the territory's last delegate to Congress before statehood. General authorities first began by having emissaries instruct legislators not to pledge themselves to any one candidate in order to avoid a stampede for the extraordinarily popular Thatcher. Then the First Presidency and apostles met with responsive legislators to promote Rawlins. After a heated contest in the Utah legislature, the Mormon hierarchy succeeded. Thatcher was defeated on the fifty-third ballot, and Rawlins became the legislature's choice as U.S. Senator.[224]

More confident by 1899, church authorities sought to persuade legislators to elect Counselor George Q. Cannon. Brigham Young, Jr., enthusiastically described "the plot" which the hierarchy used in getting Mormon legislators to vote as the First Presidency wished:

> The plot is working favorably. His servants know His voice. I consider Pres. Snow is brave and wise asking no man or bystander to vote for Pres. C[annon]. but stating that the Presidency and nine of the Twelve are a unit on this point and can elders think them wrong and party right[?] We want you to vote for Pres. C. but not unless you can see it [as] your duty to do so. You have agency and we cannot gain say it.[225]

This 1899 effort misfired because the hierarchy pitted Cannon against his own popular son Frank J. Cannon. In the deadlock between these two Republicans and six other candidates, the legislature adjourned without electing a senator. The office remained vacant in Congress.[226] Apostle Abraham Owen Woodruff blamed this on ten LDS legislators who refused to obey counsel to vote for the Presidency counselor, whereas Woodruff listed nine LDS legislators "who saw Prest. Snow and followed out his council by voting for Prest. Cannon."[227]

The election of Thomas Kearns two years later showed that Utah's Mormon legislators regarded the hierarchy's lobbying as spiritually coercive. Even Anthon H. Lund remarked "what a man to send east! It will be a bitter pill for many to swallow."[228] Nevertheless, President Lorenzo Snow had appointed Apostle Abraham Owen Woodruff to secure the non-Mormon's election, which Woodruff carried out successfully as "My mission."[229] Later Mormon legislator Nephi L. Morris lamented that his vote for Kearns was "a humiliating thing" which he did for only one reason: "An apostle [Abraham Owen Woodruff] of the Church made a positive command, in the name of the president of the Church, that I do that thing. To my remonstrances and protests and arguments there was only a threat—no man who went contrary to the wishes of the prophet would prosper."[230] Kearns bribed the legislators who were not persuaded by the hierarchy.[231]

Once men were elected, the hierarchy tried to continue its pre-1891 direction of civil officers and legislation. On the municipal level George Romney, a member of the Salt Lake City Council, felt it necessary in 1896 to confer privately with the First Presidency to explain the city council's action in not paying exorbitant utility bills and thus leaving the city in darkness at night.[232] "[T]o prevent as far as possible the passage of improper legislation," the First Presidency two years earlier had set up a committee comprised of two apostles and the church attorney "to revise the bills which are presented to the Legislature, and on which our people in that body may desire counsel, and report our findings and judgment to the Presidency."[233]

When a similar committee was publicly exposed, the First Presidency issued an emphatic denial. After loyal Mormon editor Richard W. Young consulted with the First Presidency, the *Salt Lake Herald* reported that "they had not appointed nor had they anything to do with the appointment of such a committee."[234] "The Mormon leaders were generally honorable and capable," an LDS historian has recently observed. "Can we defend their distortions during the highly charged 1890s? No. At least I cannot. Yet, I can try to understand."[235] Plausible denial would become a familiar refrain in Utah (and national) politics throughout the twentieth century.

However, such church-organized committees were rarely passive. In 1901 President Lorenzo Snow established a legislative oversight committee to produce specific legislation. One product of that committee was a bill designed to protect Mormon polygamists from criminal complaints. The First Presidency arranged for Abel John Evans, a Mormon in the Utah legislature, to introduce the bill. The "Evans bill" passed the legislature but was vetoed by the governor despite his promise to the hierarchy to sign it.[236] In 1909 the First Presidency and apostles also agreed that "every reasonable influence shall be used with the legislature to pass a prohibition law against the sale of liquor in the state," and apostles like Francis M. Lyman successfully lobbied Mormon legislators to do so.[237]

In 1915 Utah governor William Spry indicated how much power he thought the First Presidency had with Mormon legislators, when he asked them to instruct friendly legislators to sustain his veto of a prohibition bill that the First Presidency had initially encouraged. Presiding Bishop Nibley and First Presidency counselor Penrose feared that the bill would result in the formation of an anti-Mormon political party. To the objection that such a reversal would destroy confidence in the First Presidency, Governor Spry replied: "Oh, the people will do what you people want them to do!"[238]

Spry's assessment was accurate only for the nineteenth century, not for the first half of the twentieth. For example, when Governor Heber M. Wells reversed his agreement with Apostle John Henry Smith and vetoed the Evans bill, Utah legislators failed to override the veto. However, Wells paid the price for his independence. Four years later church president Joseph F. Smith said "he was not in politics," when approached by men seeking support for the re-election of Wells who was then defeated.[239]

Moreover, Apostle Reed Smoot was hardly a pliant tool in the hands of the First Presidency as U.S. Senator. In 1913 he voted to override President Taft's veto of an immigration bill, despite instructions from President Smith to sustain the veto. During his 1919-20 opposition to the League of Nations (for which he was severely criticized by the First Presidency and most of the Quorum of the Twelve), Smoot abruptly informed his associates in their weekly temple meeting: "I claim I have a right to vote on the League as my judgment dictates, and in conformity with my oath of office [as a U.S. Senator]."[240]

Although such independence disturbed the hierarchy, it was now a different political world. Dissent like Smoot's would have been grounds for dismissal from church service before 1891, but now a politically divided hierarchy had competing agendas. For example, Apostle Lyman rarely hesitated to use his church office to further the Republican cause, but in 1898 he objected to Grant's using church influence to support a Democratic candidate.[241] Likewise, when Smoot objected to church influence for statewide prohibition in 1909, President Smith commented: "He had no objection to Priesthood influence when he wanted to be elected. Then he said all they honored was power."[242]

Smoot welcomed and defended Smith's public endorsement of Republican William H. Taft for president in 1912. However, he criticized President Grant's 1922 endorsement of Democratic candidates.[243] Undoubtedly Democratic members of the hierarchy had opposite reactions to these endorsements. In the early decades of the twentieth century, it was a rare occurrence when church political influence could be exerted with unanimity in the hierarchy.[244]

Conflicting Loyalties

The extent to which general authorities sometimes became involved in contradictory issues of ethics and power became a factor in the decline of rank-and-file allegiance to political direction. Mormons were disturbed when the hierarchy supported the election of former anti-Mormons, who in the past had publicly stated their distaste for Mormon doctrine and practice. Other strains occurred when Mormons were asked to vote contrary to their conscience, as with Nephi L. Morris's explanation of his vote for Senator Kearns in 1901.

Apostles Grant and Smoot found themselves at opposite ends of several political disputes about ethics. In 1910 Grant threatened to prevent a Republican newspaper editor from being married in the temple if he did not retract an editorial criticizing Grant's Democratic remarks at a stake conference. In response, Smoot replied that if his fellow Republican were denied entry to the temple, he would perform the marriage in his own house.[245]

This see-saw continued even after Grant became church president. Smoot observed condescendingly that in 1922 Grant supported a local candidate, whom his own counselor in the First Presidency knew to be "dishonest and unclean." But his counselor was unable to stop the president's campaign in the man's favor. His counselor did succeed in having Grant sign the published endorsement alone rather than with the entire First Presidency. Paradoxically, Smoot was at the same time supporting "an unsavory machine politician" as a senatorial candidate.[246] Smoot completely abandoned his sense of moral superiority in 1928 when the general authorities objected to his promoting the same "unsavory" candidate. He was the nominee of the Utah Republican Party, and Smoot was a loyal Republican. "I did not sleep much last night. I hardly know just what action to take but I am not going to be a coward," Smoot wrote concerning the hierarchy's criticism. His conclusion: "I shall do my duty as a leading Republican no matter what happens."[247]

From the church president on down, the hierarchy had committed itself to the American system of politics in 1891. As a result, they were periodically trapped in the amoral convolutions of that system. One author claims: "By the 1920s church political activity had become non-partisan. Moral considerations rather than political partisanship became the basis for church involvement."[248]

But it has been difficult even for the hierarchy to separate the moral from the partisan. General authorities could defend Prohibition on moral grounds and as consistent with a revelation by God in the LDS "Word of Wisdom" that was a religious obligation. Nevertheless, in June 1933 the First Presidency and apostles made a decision that most Mormons today would find astonishing: "Decided at this meeting that the Church as an organization could not take part in the campaign for the repeal of the 18th Amendment since this was a partisan political question. It was hoped however that all L.D.S. would vote against repeal [of national Prohibition]."[249] By contrast, in recent years the hierarchy has launched political campaigns on "moral issues" that are less securely grounded in LDS doctrine than was Prohibition. In fact, a Mormon sociologist has recently written that "church leaders will sometimes speak out on what they call 'moral issues' as distinguished from 'political issues,' a distinction not valid to social scientists, of course."[250]

The low point of the hierarchy's influence was the twelve-year period beginning with the election of Franklin D. Roosevelt. Roosevelt's New Deal and proposal to repeal Prohibition drove church president Heber J. Grant to bolt from the Democratic Party in 1932.[251] Likewise, Apostle Joseph F. Merrill, formerly a Democratic leader and candidate, became a Republican in protest against the New Deal.[252] Although Grant had spoken for years at church meetings in favor of Prohibition, Utah Mormons overwhelming voted for anti-Prohibition candidates in 1933. Seventy's president B. H. Roberts was among those who supported the repeal of Prohibition. Utah was the swing state that ratified repeal of the Prohibition amendment to the U.S. Constitution.[253]

Despite the First Presidency's public opposition to Roosevelt, nearly 70 percent voted for Roosevelt and the New Deal in four presidential elections from 1932 to 1944. Mormons did this despite front page editorials in the church's *Deseret News* urging them against voting for Roosevelt and also first counselor J. Reuben Clark's active campaigning for his opponent.[254] Utah's Democratic leaders never forgave Grant's abandonment of the party. Although he had been a Democratic candidate and served as vice-president of the Democratic *Salt Lake Herald* until May 1896, Grant's name was absent from a 1942 list of "names of one hundred prominent Democrats who worked, unselfishly, and contributed, generously, for the party's success" to 1896.[255]

The church president's unpopularity was a significant factor in the widespread rejection of his political advice among faithful Mormons. Often criticized by otherwise loyal Mormons since he was a junior apostle, Heber J. Grant was the most unpopular church president in Mormon history. In 1889 he conscientiously recorded what his own mother told him: "it was the opinion of a great many of the Latter day Saints that I was filled with pride and that there was nothing in this life that I cared about so much as I did about making money," and that "I had no respect for the poor among the people." When he learned that Grant had become president in 1918, a faithful Mormon wrote about another set of objections: "I am quite sure that no matter how energetic and forceful Heber may have been in some of his political views and in his likes and dislikes[,] the Lord will modify and mellow him down . . ."[256] Twenty years later widespread criticism and disdain for Grant reached into the highest levels of church administration. "The word constantly comes back to us that some of our general boards and members are not loyal to President Grant," first counselor Clark told a meeting at church headquarters in 1938. "I am tired of the way people speak about him."[257] Therefore, most Mormons felt neither hesitation nor guilt about rejecting the church president's political statements.

At the beginning and end of World War II, the First Presidency opposed Congressional efforts to conscript ("draft") young men into the U.S. military. Just days after the U.S. declaration of war against Imperial Japan, Nazi Germany, and Fascist Italy, the Presidency asked all of Utah's members of Congress on 17 December 1941 to vote against "a new proposal to reduce the Selective Service age below its present level, possibly down to eighteen years."[258] On 2 February 1945, while U.S. troops were fighting in Europe and Asia, the First Presidency learned that both the Utah legislature and Congress were in favor of "legislation providing for compulsory military training after the war." Clark, a director of America's oldest pacifist organization, drafted a First Presidency statement against peacetime conscription. The First Presidency had Apostle Mark E. Petersen use this unpublished statement to lobby Utah legislators against their previous commitment to the draft.[259]

In June 1945 the First Presidency "counseled" Mormon members of Congress to support this anti-draft position, and Clark privately said that "he proposed to force the brethren to take a stand for or against the resolution." In December a three-page letter went to all "members of the Utah delegation in Congress as well as to the Congressional delegations from other states in which a considerable number of the members of the Church reside." The First Presidency presented seventeen arguments and concluded: "we have the honor respectfully to urge that you do your utmost to defeat any plan designed to bring about the compulsory military service of our citizenry."[260] In January 1946, after nearly a year of privately lobbying Mormon members of the Utah legislature and Congress, the First Presidency published its statement against "universal compulsory military service."[261] Although the LDS hierarchy acted alone, many churches, private organizations, and individual Americans publicly expressed equal opposition to a peacetime draft.[262]

On the eve of the 1950 election, the hierarchy's connection with a political action committee became public knowledge because someone was careless. A member of the Salt Lake County Law Observance and Enforcement Committee (LOEC) mistakenly mailed to bishops outside the county the written text of a "suggested talk" to be given from the pulpit on the Sunday before the election. The recommended talk's final sentence: "If you desire further advice as to candidates, it is suggested that you consult your Bishop, who is informed as to those candidates who will definitely support our principles." Accompanying this suggested talk was a list of the approved candidates for every office including county surveyor, judges, state legislators, as well as the approved candidate for the U.S. Senate and House of Representatives. The chair of this LOEC was manager of the church's holding company Zion's Securities Corporation and reported the political committee's activities directly to Apostle Spencer W. Kimball.[263] As a result of the uproar over these disclosures, church president George Albert Smith publicly disavowed the action of this committee. President Smith's announcement appeared in two non-LDS newspapers (morning and evening) before the church's own newspaper printed it on the evening of the next day. Allegedly Apostle Mark E. Petersen resisted publishing this retraction in the *Deseret News* which he edited. [264]

However, this did not impede Democratic and Republican apostles from fulfilling their assignment from the First Presidency to lobby Utah state legislators of both parties. Democrat Henry D. Moyle wrote that he and Republican apostles Albert E. Bowen and Harold B. Lee had an "assignment on the legislature." To fulfill this, Apostle Moyle obtained Counselor Clark's approval in January 1951 to hire two attorneys to draft bills for cooperative legislators to introduce. On 23 February 1951 Moyle and Republican apostle Matthew Cowley had a nighttime meeting in the "Church office building" with six Republican legislators and one Democratic legislator. At 7:45 the next morning apostles Moyle, Lee, and Petersen had a brief but confrontational meeting with a Republican state senator from Salt Lake County who "denied all charges and any interest in police bill." Fifteen minutes later the apostles went to Lee's office where they met with six Democratic legislators and four Republican legislators. On 1 March apostles Moyle and Bowen met in Bowen's office with a Republican state legislator from Utah County, after which Moyle lobbied by telephone with two Democratic legislators and two Republican legislators. The next day Moyle "spent balance of day on legislative matters [and] had telephone conversations" with a Democratic legislator and a Republican legislator.[265]

Following the election of Dwight D. Eisenhower ("Ike") as U.S. president in 1952, recently sustained LDS president David O. McKay seemed eager to express his lifelong Republican partisanship. The church president told the *Deseret News* that Eisenhower's election "is the turning point in United States, if not world history." At Ike's inauguration, McKay also offended some of his companions, who included Presiding Bishop Joseph

L. Wirthlin, when he light-heartedly criticized twenty years of the nation's New Deal rule that had come to an end.[266]

In 1953-54 general authorities made an abortive effort to influence Utah's 1954 vote on reapportioning the legislature. Apostle Henry D. Moyle said privately: "Brethren, don't you realize that if this proposal is passed that the Church will control twenty-six of twenty-nine [state] senators."[267] In the pattern established by Clark since the mid-1940s, Democrat Moyle and Republican apostle Harold B. Lee jointly lobbied the legislators of their respective parties and reported back to Clark and then to LDS president David O. McKay.[268] When asked privately by legislators about the First Presidency's views "about the proposed reapportionment," Clark typically replied in March 1953 that "Brother Moyle and Lee were handling these matters."[269]

The effort to control the 1954 reapportionment vote was not limited to lobbying. Ward bishops and stake presidents later acknowledged that "Church welfare trucks were loaded with pamphlets and sent to the various wards and stakes throughout the state [of Utah]. In many wards and stakes priesthood members were handed bundles of pamphlets and told to get them to every door in their areas." Bishops throughout Utah were asked to read statements at sacrament meetings in support of reapportionment. The effort failed when a Mormon political scientist complained to McKay about these activities, and McKay and his counselors issued a statement that "the Church takes no position" regarding Utah's reapportionment. Despite church influence in support, Utah's voters defeated it 142,972 to 80,044.[270]

Popular wisdom holds that McKay was unaware of the behind-the-scenes activity of apostles Moyle and Lee on behalf of reapportionment.[271] To the contrary, the two apostles reported their political lobbying to the First Presidency. For example, in January 1953 Moyle and Lee met with four members of the Utah legislature in the Church Administration Building and "discussed for an hour the proposed reapportionment bill." Then the two went to the joint meeting of the First Presidency and apostles in the Salt Lake temple and reported "our legislative activity in Utah, Idaho, Wyo."[272]

Lee and Moyle also reported directly to McKay. In March 1953 the president "suggested we keep on as we have been accustomed in the past. Both in city, county & state matters."[273] Of this meeting, McKay wrote: "They asked if they might have a meeting during Conference with men [i.e., Utah legislators] they have heretofore contacted. I said yes, but thought they should not attend it [themselves]. They thought probably they could coach Pres. Elggren and Brother Romney [about what to say at the meeting]."[274] Although the church president preferred several levels of intermediaries to separate him from the political lobbying done in his name, he was quietly involved from a distance.

The campaign for reapportionment in 1953-54 could not be justified as a moral issue. It was simply an effort to secure church "control of the [Utah] State Senate."[275] The campaign failed only because McKay was unwilling to accept public criticism for the private campaign he had been directing. The hierarchy would not repeat those mistakes in its campaign against the Equal Rights Amendment a generation later (see chap. 10).

Combined with its reapportionment campaign, the hierarchy suffered another loss when Utah's non-Mormon governor vetoed a Sunday-closing bill passed by the legislature. Apostles Lee and Moyle had lobbied Mormon legislators on the matter for two years, but the governor regarded the legislation as discrimination against Jews and Seventh-Day Adventists.[276] Hearing of the possibility of a veto, Clark telephoned Utah's governor to lobby him directly. When the governor explained that Sunday-closing laws discriminated against religious minorities, Clark shot back: "Suppose you had a group of harlots come in and object to any restrictions you might place on them." The First Presidency counselor questioned "whether the minority should control" Utah's Mormon community. Nevertheless, the governor vetoed the bill. A blistering editorial in the *Deseret News* urged Mormon legislators to consider only "the great majority of Utah's citizens," and override the governor. Instead the Mormon-dominated legislature sustained the veto.[277] This was a dramatic swan-song of political independence by Utah's Mormon legislators in opposition to clear signals from LDS headquarters.

Still another controversy during these years was the adoption of (and challenges to) release-time religious instruction in Utah during public school hours and the granting of high school credit for this religious coursework. The LDS hierarchy was both interested and involved in this matter. In January 1916 the Utah State Board of Education authorized release-time religious instruction and school credit for coursework on the Bible as history or as literature. Due to the overwhelming Mormon majority on the school board, Salt Lake City's school district adopted release-time religious instruction with school credit in the 1940s. In 1956 the school board stopped giving school credit for religion classes in Salt Lake City, but the practice continued in Logan and other outlying areas of Utah until a lawsuit resulted in a ruling by the U.S. District Court and by the U.S. Court of Appeals against allowing such credit.[278]

Conflicting partisanship between general authorities resurfaced in Utah's 1958 election for U.S. senator. Apostle Ezra Taft Benson, then serving as President Eisenhower's Secretary of Agriculture, actively campaigned for Arthur V. Watkins. Opposing Benson, Apostle Hugh B. Brown campaigned for Democrat Frank E. Moss, who won the election.[279]

Adoration of the LDS President

By the mid-1950s a change was underway in Mormonism that profoundly affected its political influence. The hierarchy and church publications encouraged an unprecedented adoration of church president David O. McKay. His "graceful, witty manner, his imposing physical appearance, his deep warmth, all made people see him as THE prophet, to be classed with Joseph Smith and Brigham Young."[280] Extensive television broadcasts of two general conferences annually after 1953 heightened McKay's personal and ceremonial impact on members of the church. By the late-1960s LDS publications and speakers routinely identified McKay as "the Prophet," "our Prophet," and "beloved Prophet." Those terms had previously applied to the martyred prophet, Joseph Smith, while the living LDS president had simply been "the President."[281]

That changing devotional status of the LDS president can be dated precisely through the official *Church News*. Published weekly by the *Deseret News* since 1931, every headline reference of *Church News* to each LDS president referred to him as "President" until 1955. During those twenty-four years no headline referred to the living LDS president as "prophet," and that term was used exclusively to refer to Joseph Smith or to prophets of the Bible and *Book of Mormon*. In February 1955 the *Church News* published the first headline reference to the living LDS president as the "Prophet."[282]

Concerning such "adulation," a First Presidency secretary acknowledged that McKay liked his "celebrity status," and wanted "to be recognized, lauded, and lionized."[283] However, that was something J. Reuben Clark had declined to give to any of the church presidents he had served as counselor since the 1930s, and he seemed to avoid calling anyone "the Prophet" except Joseph Smith. Rather than adulation, Clark reminded LDS religion teachers in July 1954 that "even the President of the Church has not always spoken under the direction of the Holy Ghost." The only known time Clark referred to McKay by any other title than "President" was in a letter to the church president's secretary about "your Chief."[284] Clark's influence may have been the reason why no other reference to McKay as "the Prophet" appeared in the *Church News* until after the counselor's death. Nevertheless, photo captions proclaimed: "Ever popular, President McKay is met by admiring members with cameras after each session of General Conference."[285]

Personal reverence for McKay was still insufficient to persuade many Mormons to follow his political wishes in the early 1960s. He publicly stated his support of Republican Richard M. Nixon for U.S. president in

1960, and the electoral votes of Utah and Idaho (like those of nearly all western states) went for Nixon.[286] However, 44 percent of Democratic Mormons and 15 percent of Republican Mormons disapproved of the church president making such a political statement, according to a survey of 265 actively participating members of the LDS church in Logan, Utah, Tucson, Arizona, and Washington, D.C. In addition, of 286 faithful Mormons, 43 percent believed that McKay "was not inspired" of God when the church president made this political endorsement.[287]

In fact, more than 100,000 Mormons in the Mormon culture region ignored the publicly stated view of the LDS president and voted instead for Democrat John F. Kennedy, who became the U.S. president. For example, in the twenty-five counties of Idaho, Nevada, and Utah with 90-100 percent LDS population, there were 98,451 votes for the Roman Catholic candidate in these virtually all-Mormon counties. Ten other counties with 80-89 percent LDS population in Idaho and Utah gave an additional 122,447 Democratic votes in the 1960 election. The aggregate statistics of voting, of course, cannot even approximate the number of Mormons who voted Democratic in U.S. counties without a dominant LDS population.[288] Apparently sensitive to the criticism of Democratic Mormons about his public endorsement of the Republican loser, McKay confided in 1961 that his choice of "two Democrats for counselors should be sufficient indication that the Democrats have a definite place in the Church."[289]

The next headline in the *Church News* referring to McKay as "the Prophet" did not occur until 7 September 1963, when the *Deseret News* published a special insert titled *President McKay Birthday Tribute,* with headline on page 2: "Portrait of a Prophet at 90," and caption on page 7: "Huntsville is the Prophet's birthplace." However, the *Church News* itself continued referring to McKay only as "President McKay" in headlines until 1965.

That year the First Presidency sent letters to eleven members of Congress from five states asking them to vote to retain the anti-union provisions in the Taft-Hartley Act. Seven Mormon congressmen drafted a joint answer: "While we respect and revere the offices held by the members of the First Presidency of the Church, we cannot yield to others our responsibilities to our constituency, nor can we delegate our own free agency to any but ourselves." In the face of adverse publicity about this in July-August 1965, McKay softened his position. Six of the Mormon Congressmen (all Democrats) voted with the majority of Congress, and one Congressman complained that the First Presidency had not advised the same Mormon Congressmen to support the Civil Rights Act for African-Americans.[290]

In apparent response to this "loyal opposition" against the First Presidency's political wishes, the *Church News* began emphasizing that David O. McKay was "the Prophet." On 11 September 1965 there was an article headline: "Honors For a Prophet," and within a year typical headlines proclaimed: "The Beloved Prophet, Seer, and Revelator, President David O. McKay."[291]

In 1968 the First Presidency had complete success in a political campaign against liquor-by-the-drink in Utah as a moral issue. McKay publicly urged Mormons "to take a stand against the proposal," but the church worked indirectly through an organization called "The Citizens for a Better Utah." In addition, a Presidency secretary has written: "At the same time, the Brethren openly authorized priesthood officers and quorums to distribute literature and to circulate petitions on the subject." Pre-election surveys showed only 11.9 percent of Mormons resisting the hierarchy's massive campaign against the initiative, and liquor-by-the drink failed to pass in 1968.[292] As a recent history by Deseret Book Company observes: "Significantly, opposition to the Church's stand [on liquor by the drink] was not construed as disloyalty to the Church."[293]

A week after the announcement on 23 January 1970 that the Twelve chose Joseph Fielding Smith as the new church president, a *Church News* editorial headline proclaimed: "Another Prophet Is Sent." After the solemn assembly sustained him to that position the following April, a *Church News* story about President Smith was headlined "The Prophet." Thus Joseph Fielding Smith was the first LDS president identified by headlines of the *Church News* as "The Prophet" throughout his administration.[294] This practice intensified for his successors.

Recently sustained president Harold B. Lee complained in 1972 about this "almost worshipful attitude, which I am trying earnestly to play down to a respectful and appropriate loyalty to their Church leaders."[295] Lee's brusque administrative style restrained sentimentality at LDS headquarters, and the *Church News* printed only one headline reference to him as "Prophet"—the day after he was sustained by the Twelve. The lack of similar headlines during the rest of his presidency was evidence of Lee's determination "to play down" such adoration. However, Lee's presidential tenure was too brief to reverse the accelerating adoration by the rank-and-file. The *Church News* published the second headline reference to Lee as "Prophet" when he could no longer prevent it—three days after his death.[296]

Lee's successor Spencer W. Kimball had struggled with lifelong feelings of inadequacy, even as an apostle. Appointed church president in 1973, he could not be expected to discourage effusive adulation by other general authorities or by the rank-and-file. It was also inevitable that Mormons felt special devotion for the new president because of his down-to-earth qualities, his open expressions of affection for people, and his example of unrelenting church service despite well-known physical challenges.[297]

A secretary to the First Presidency noted that the devotion of some Mormons "border[ed] on worship" for Spencer W. Kimball.[298] *Church News* headlines increasingly referred to Kimball as "Prophet," and by March 1976 multiple references to him as "Prophet" were appearing in the headlines of a single issue.[299] References to the living LDS president as "the Prophet" also became routine in LDS publications, sermons, and ordinary conversations. In the televised, twice-annual general conferences, it was not unusual for general authorities to express emotional tributes to President Kimball. "His faith and works are incomparable," one general authority told general conference in April 1976. "In my estimation he is as great as any prophet that preceded him since the time of Adam." This would, of course, include Elijah whose righteousness entitled him to be "translated" into God's presence "without experiencing mortal death."[300]

A side effect of this headquarters-encouraged adoration was increased political allegiance of rank-and-file Mormons to political direction by the First Presidency. It became more difficult for the majority of faithful Mormons to politically dissent from the Presidency than it had been in the first half of the twentieth century. For example, 88 percent of students at Brigham Young University in 1973 valued "obedience to [church] authority above own desires," compared with 41 percent of BYU students who held that view in 1935.[301]

Popular devotion for the church president renewed in Mormonism the kind of political unity that persecution and theocracy maintained in the nineteenth century. This adoration of the living LDS president coincided with an increased emphasis on the dictum of "Follow the Brethren," which a Mormon sociologist has noted "began receiving much greater emphasis after 1950 than in the generation immediately preceding."[302]

In 1981 the presidency of the much-adored Spencer W. Kimball was more successful at changing popular political views than the McKay presidency had been in 1965. After the death of pacifist counselor Clark, Mormons and the general public forgot that there was an anti-militaristic tradition in Mormonism.[303] It came as a shock to the national conservatism of Ronald Reagan's presidency and its supporters when the First Presidency issued a strongly-worded statement against the MX missile system in Utah and "the building of vast arsenals of nuclear weaponry."[304] A few weeks after the Presidency's statement, the *Deseret News* proclaimed that "MX opposition soars" among Mormons. However, four months later a survey of 600 Utahns by the church newspaper found that 31 percent of Mormons would "definitely support" the MX in Utah and 40 percent would "probably support" it.[305] At this time the Mormon hierarchy was nearing a successful conclusion to its nationwide campaign against ratification of the Equal Rights Amendment. The difference in the long-term response of Mormons to the MX statement and ERA statements of the First Presidency was probably due to the fact that the First Presidency made the MX statement only once, while the hierarchy expressed anti-ERA statements repeatedly during a five-year period (see chap. 10).

The ERA campaign also consolidated a new direction in Mormon political power—interfaith cooperation to achieve similar political goals. From the late 1970s to the present, the LDS hierarchy has joined with the American Catholic hierarchy and leaders of various Protestant fundamentalist and evangelical groups to share resources and strategy in political processes which all these groups have defined as moral issues.[306] However, this requires many Catholics and Protestant fundamentalists to "compartmentalize" their beliefs in order to avoid reminding their Mormon political allies how much these Christians detest the LDS church and its doctrines.[307]

Conclusion

Prior to 1890 the Mormon hierarchy unsuccessfully sought to manipulate the national political parties in a manner that seems clumsy from a current perspective. In part, their isolation in the Great Basin misled Mormons about the need of the national parties to court the favor of polygamous and theocratic Utah. Moreover, the hierarchy's ill-concealed contempt for American political parties doomed each effort at partisan manipulation.

Even the numerical success of the church's political party in Utah rang hollow. Sometimes 75 percent of LDS voters declined to vote in elections whose outcome was guaranteed. Also, the periodic rebellions of pioneer Utah Mormons against the People's Party is evidence of long smoldering dissatisfaction with politics-by-decree. Even among the LDS faithful, there was long-suppressed political independence which welcomed the end of theocratic control. That is why partisan politics became divisive so quickly among the Mormons of the 1890s.[308]

In the nineteenth century, when Mormons saw themselves as the only true Christian commonwealth in combat against a gentile world, it was easy to sacrifice individualism for political unity. But once crucial accommodations occurred, there was no longer a need to suppress individuality. Mormonism could now boast significant political accomplishments. The hierarchy obtained nearly everything it wanted from negotiations with the Republican Party, even avoiding constitutional amendments against polygamy.[309] Moreover, by the 1920s a Mormon apostle was a power within the national Republican Party, with his fellow senators, and with U.S. presidents who unsuccessfully invited him to join their cabinets. Senator Smoot declined to accept a Cabinet post because he thought he would lose power and prestige by leaving the U.S. Senate. Instead, Smoot helped the presidents select their cabinet members.[310] The Mormon hierarchy's political activity had been initially conceived as a defense against non-Mormons, but developed into a comparatively successful accommodation to the non-Mormon power structure.

But it took more than half a century to reconstitute Utah as the Mormon hierarchy's "pocket borough."[311] The First Presidency had done the theologically unthinkable by surrendering polygamy in 1890, and that lessened the rank-and-file's unthinking support of the Presidency's political decrees. The majority of rank-and-file Mormons often dissented politically from the LDS leadership until after World War II.

It is doubtful that the Mormon hierarchy realized in 1891 how thoroughly the abandonment of theocracy would undermine the ability of the First Presidency to control the political sphere. For decades public disavowals of church influence had an effect opposite from what the First Presidency desired. Non-Mormons saw duplicity, whereas Mormons became convinced that political statements by the First Presidency were merely advice or opinion.[312] In 1940 one political scientist observed without exaggeration: "The Church membership has not obeyed its leaders on any important political issue or candidacy during the last ten years. Only a small group of sincere members blindly follow the Church leaders."[313]

However, the hierarchy began to reverse that process in the 1960s. Crucial to a new pattern of Mormon political behavior, LDS leaders from the mid-1960s on encouraged popular adoration of whatever man filled the office of church president. In the secular world of politics, this is called "the cult of personality"; sociologists refer to this as "institutionalized awe."[314] Despite this tendency to adore the church president, and the interest of LDS headquarters to promote it, recently appointed president Gordon B. Hinckley has lashed out against such devotion: "Adulation is poison." Still, his statement appears in an official biography which indicates the determination of others at LDS headquarters to encourage adulation by the rank-and-file. The church's publisher presents as the biography's final illustration a color photograph that seems to surround the heads of President Hinckley and his wife with halos of light.[315]

Beyond this emphasis on the LDS president, general authorities have recently claimed virtual infallibility for all decisions of the LDS hierarchy, even though a First Presidency counselor affirmed half a century earlier: "We are not infallible in our judgment, and we err."[316] By contrast, in November 1994 Apostle M. Russell Ballard instructed 25,000 students at Brigham Young University: "We will not lead you astray. We cannot." He repeated those words to a similar meeting less than two years later. In April 1996 First Presidency counselor James E. Faust told general conference that the LDS president "will never mislead the Saints."[317]

This "de facto infallibility"[318] claimed by current general authorities further reduces the likelihood that faithful Mormons will even privately dissent from the political "counsel" of LDS headquarters. That also reduces the constraints on the hierarchy's political power recently itemized by a Mormon sociologist: "The political effectiveness of this leadership is constrained by its own dependence on open collegial consensus, by its commitment to partisan even handedness, or at least the appearance thereof, and by its manifestly shaky control over the voting tendencies of the church membership."[319] Such constraints were more significant from the 1890s to the 1950s than they are today.

With unintended irony the church-owned *Deseret News* demonstrated the hierarchy's political power in a 1993 article titled "LDS Church's Influence A Myth, Legislators Say." Since 86 percent of Utah's legislators are LDS, one Mormon lawmaker acknowledged that church headquarters has "a strong indirect influence" on the legislative process. However, the article then described political oversight that is far from indirect: "House and Senate leaders on both sides of the aisle routinely meet before general session with the Church's Public Affairs Committee, composed of four members of the Council of the Twelve Apostles . . ." The *News* defended this practice by observing that the legislature's Roman Catholics (two or three in all) also confer with Utah's Catholic hierarchy about upcoming legislation.[320]

A dramatic example of the political power of LDS headquarters occurred in June 1996. By making "a simple statement opposing firearms in chapels," LDS headquarters dealt a staggering blow to decades of entrenched opposition by the Utah legislature to any kind of gun control. The conservative Republican governor, a Mormon, quickly endorsed making that limitation a legal requirement, as did Democratic legislators. Even Utah's chief gun-rights lobbyist lamented, "I've never gone up against the LDS church on a political issue, and I hope I never have to." The only hope he expressed was to persuade LDS headquarters to announce a retraction or modification. Otherwise the National Rifle Association (NRA) is "looking ahead to what could well be its first defeat" in Utah. All because of a two-sentence statement issued by a spokesman at LDS headquarters.[321]

During the last half of the twentieth century, the hierarchy has also become a major player in the national political scene through demographic factors and public relations. As a result U.S. presidents have solicited the advice of LDS presidents and curry their support.[322] A First Presidency secretary has called this "opportunism on the part of politicians," and a Utah political scientist once analyzed "the sustained efforts over a period of years made by President Lyndon B. Johnson to cultivate a friendship with David O. McKay."[323] U.S. presidents have appointed general authorities to the Cabinet and various national advisory commissions. Rank-and-file Mormons have also served in the Cabinet, sub-Cabinet positions, as the national security adviser to the U.S. president, as some of the highest officers of the U.S. military, and as ambassadors to foreign governments, to the United Nations (UN), and to the North Atlantic Treaty Organization (NATO).[324] And in what the hierarchy sees as perhaps its finest hour, LDS headquarters coordinated a nationwide campaign which contributed significantly to the defeat of the proposed Equal Rights Amendment to the U.S. Constitution (see chap. 10). In 1996 the hierarchy is in the midst of another political campaign of national proportions.[325]

The contrasts in the hierarchy's political controls and successes before and after 1891 have resulted in a series of myths. One has been that the hierarchy has not involved itself in what one Utah political scientist described as the true nature of partisan politics: "an intricate labyrinth of intrigues and machination."[326] To the contrary, Mormon leaders were always involved in political intrigue, but the groups they alienated by these activities varied. Before 1891 it was primarily non-Mormons; after 1891 it was primarily Mormons who became disaffected.

A second myth holds that "Utah was for thirty years a pocket borough belonging to Reed Smoot."[327] The successes that Smoot and his fellow Republican advocates achieved were most often hard-won battles against dedicated Mormons of conflicting political persuasions, and Smoot sometimes opposed the rest of the Mormon hierarchy. One study estimated that "Senator Smoot, the Mormon apostle, never received a large majority of Mormon votes, except perhaps for 1926."[328]

A third myth is that the LDS church is an impersonal entity politically separate from the actions and statements of its general authorities.[329] This claim has opposite uses. For the hierarchy, it has been a convenient device for avoiding the charge of "church influence." Ironically, the loyal opposition among the LDS rank-and-file has used the same myth to reject the hierarchy's "whispering campaigns" and published statements about political matters. However, the commonly expressed argument fails to describe reality. Even when the hierarchy has been divided on a political issue, the church president has usually sanctioned one of the factions, and his view has been regarded by partisans in and out of the hierarchy as the church's view. The "Church" in Mormonism cannot be separated from the decisions of its highest leaders.

A Mormon sociologist has recently written, "Officially and unofficially, the Mormon church has always been an important political player in Utah and, to a much lesser extent, in the neighboring states." That same pattern has held true for national political issues throughout the twentieth century, and the LDS hierarchy's national political impact has grown substantially in the last third of the century.[330]

There is a curious corollary of the myth of the partisan-hierarchy-and-the-nonpartisan-church. LDS leaders expect that rank-and-file Mormons will not criticize members of the hierarchy who publicly advocate a political position. For instance, a First Presidency secretary noted that the hierarchy found it "galling" that Mormons publicly opposed the policies of Apostle Ezra Taft Benson while he was U.S. Secretary of Agriculture.[331] Ecclesiastical sanctions have occasionally been employed against Mormons who have publicly criticized a public official who was also a general authority. As one example, Nathaniel V. Jones published a pamphlet critical of Reed Smoot's political actions, and the hierarchy dropped Jones from his local LDS position because his publication "was making one of our brethren ridiculous before the world."[332] Although affirming that they act as private citizens when urging political positions, general authorities expect to be treated differently than private citizens in the political arena. This appeal to immunity is a throw-back to the days of nineteenth-century theocracy.

A fourth myth is that Mormons are "free" to accept, reject, or modify the political counsel of general authorities. The hierarchy has always regarded its political pronouncements as the will of God for the people. Mormons who use their freedom to reject such counsel choose the latter of Mormonism's ubiquitous dichotomy of obey or perish spiritually. In the LDS conception of "free agency," one is free only if one has a choice to obey or disobey a divine law, or to accept/reject an evil temptation.[333] In such a context political freedom has limited significance. The hierarchy has not always regarded political dissenters as loyal, even if acknowledging that they are faithful believers.

In April 1960 J. Reuben Clark explicitly stated the theocratic limits on individual freedom in Mormonism:

> I hope Brother [Mark E.] Petersen will pardon me—but this is not a democracy; this is not a republic; this is a kingdom of God. The President of the Church is his premier, if you will, his agent, his possessor of the keys. Our free agency which we have does not make us any more nor less than subjects of the Kingdom and subjects we are,—not citizens, Brother Mark.

Clark made this statement to a missionary meeting at general conference. He had given a less explicit statement of the notion at a general conference fifteen years earlier.[334]

The Mormon hierarchy has always been a political power structure. The men who direct that power—the First Presidency and Quorum of the Twelve Apostles—give legitimacy to all individual and collective functions of theocracy and political direction. The hierarchy's political accommodations of the 1890s made it possible for non-Mormons to have a greater share in the Mormon political pie. Nevertheless, to achieve success in Utah the most powerful non-Mormons and secular institutions still find it necessary to negotiate with LDS headquarters or take its views into consideration.[335]

As early as 1956 the non-LDS governor of Utah, J. Bracken Lee, was giving such advice to non-Mormons. "I said to them you are never going to have any success in Utah unless you let the leaders of the Church give you some advice. You better make it a point to talk with the Church officials to find out if they are going along with it or not." Governor Lee's biographer noted that the general authorities "prefer politicians who clearly recognize the role of the LDS church as Utah's most important interest group."[336] The national media highlighted an example of that power in 1983 when Salt Lake City's mayor made one phone call to LDS headquarters and got 2,000 volunteers within the hour to build emergency levees during a spring flood.[337]

Non-LDS politicians understandably become exasperated at the pervasiveness of LDS culture in the political life of ordinary Mormons. For example, at one meeting of the Salt Lake City board of education,

> an LDS bishop protested the closing of a school in his ward near "Swede Town" in the northwest section of the city. In his presentation, he referred to board members by their ecclesiastical titles: President Fetzer, President Burbidge, etc. Finally, Culp [a Freemason and non-LDS board member] could restrain himself no longer and spoke up: "What the hell is going on here? Is this a priesthood meeting?" Defusing the situation neatly, [T. Quentin] Cannon, himself a bishop, proposed that the board there and then sustain Glenn V. Culp as the "President of the Salt Lake Masonic Stake." The motion was seconded, carried and, according to Cannon, recorded in the official minutes of the board. Next day, Cannon was greeted with good-humored comments from approving Masonic business colleagues who enjoyed the appropriateness of the gesture.[338]

Whether in Utah, elsewhere in the United States, or in countries throughout the world, LDS office-holders see political life through an LDS lens and they "speak Mormon"[339] whenever they are together. Those facts require a certain amount of good-humored accommodation on all sides.

Although the general authorities are limited by political pluralism, they retain the theological sanction for political intervention. The Mormon hierarchy has simply adapted its methods to the American political system's public reverence for pluralism and private expectation of voter management.

CHAPTER 10

A National Force, 1970s-1990s

After the 1982 defeat of the proposed Equal Rights Amendment (ERA) to the U.S. Constitution, sociologist O. Kendall White wrote that "small Mormon minorities exerted disproportionate influence over the fate of the ERA in Virginia, Missouri, Florida, Illinois, and North Carolina." White, a Mormon who had favored ratification, concluded that Mormons had tipped the scales for the entire nation.[1] Yet two non-Mormon historians analyzing the ERA barely mentioned the LDS church.[2] And the church's almanac gives only one reference to the Equal Rights Amendment: the date of its defeat in June 1982.[3]

These contrasting views raise two questions: (1) Did the Mormon hierarchy conduct a significant national campaign against ratification of the ERA? Yes, the LDS church was part of a religious coalition which was decisive in bringing about its defeat. (2) In this campaign did the hierarchy "subvert" the American political process? White implies that it did, while non-Mormon sociologist Anson D. Shupe, who tends to see the LDS church in conspiratorial terms, made the charge explicitly.[4] In fact, the LDS hierarchy's grass-roots mobilization and high-pressure lobbying were typical of the American political system. Nevertheless, there are inherent costs for this kind of politicking, and the Mormon church paid a price for its involvement. Nor has the hierarchy come to terms with the ethical issues raised by the methods it employed.

The Equal Rights Amendment and Its Mormon Supporters

Almost from its settlement in 1847, Utah's women enjoyed equal access with men to institutions of higher education, the right to file for divorce on grounds of incompatibility, the right to own property, the right to engage in business, official encouragement to be trained as bookkeepers and to take care of family finances if husbands were inefficient, and official instruction to seek medical treatment from other women rather than from men. During the 1870s Mormon women voted, served on the central committee of the Mormon political party, edited a suffragist periodical, graduated with M.D. degrees from eastern medical schools, administered the first Mormon hospital, and became lawyers at the Utah bar. A Mormon in 1896 was the first woman elected as state senator in the nation.[5]

A nineteenth-century woman could also attack the Victorian cult of the family[6] and still be rewarded with high church office by the Mormon leadership. For example, as editor of the Mormon suffragist publication from 1875 on, Emmeline B. Wells publicly ridiculed the Victorian image of womanhood as being the equivalent of "a painted doll" or "household deity." Instead, she insisted that every married woman must be "a joint-partner in the domestic firm." The First Presidency appointed her president of the church's worldwide organization for women, the Relief Society. She served as president from 1910 until just weeks before her death in 1921.[7]

However, from the 1920s on, Mormon women experienced an erosion of their autonomy and status. In this complex development, general authorities increasingly adopted Victorian ideals of domesticity and ignored earlier teachings and examples of female autonomy.[8] Administratively, the process was complete by July 1970 when the First Presidency ended the financial autonomy of the Relief Society and dismissed the organization's traditional fund-raising bazaar as "a noisy, carnival-like or commercial atmosphere."[9]

Having become socially conservative in the twentieth century, the Mormon hierarchy spoke critically of "women's liberation" during the late 1960s and early 1970s. Coming on the heels of widespread anti-authoritarianism, the drug and "hippie" culture, the homosexual liberation movement, and a widespread rejection of traditional values, "equal rights" became a slogan which polarized Americans.[10] For example, in January 1971, before Congress passed the ERA, Joseph Fielding Smith's First Presidency publicly criticized "the more radical ideas of women's liberation." Each copy of the church's *Ensign* had a small vinyl recording of the message for easy home listening.[11] These conservative attitudes did not translate initially to opposition against the proposed Equal Rights Amendment, even within the First Presidency.

Although some Mormons became aware of the ERA only in the 1970s, it had attracted Congressional and First Presidency attention decades earlier. The National Woman's Party succeeded in introducing it for consideration in Congress in 1923. The Republican national platform officially endorsed the idea in 1940, followed by the Democratic Party in 1944. However, labor unions saw this as an elitist proposal that threatened existing protections and benefits of female blue-collar workers.[12]

On 25 January 1950 the U.S. Senate approved a carefully worded version of the amendment. Its first clause was identical to the proposed Equal Rights Amendment a generation later, but its text in 1950 had an additional clause that was later absent: "The provisions of this article shall not be construed to impair any rights, benefits, or exemptions now or hereafter conferred by law upon persons of the female sex." In 1950 Utah's two Mormon senators split their votes, Democrat Elbert D. Thomas for the amendment and Republican Arthur V. Watkins against.[13]

The Relief Society general presidency assumed that J. Reuben Clark would oppose this 1950 Equal Rights Amendment due to his strict constructionist views of the U.S. Constitution. Instead, on the day of the U.S. Senate's vote, Clark "suggested they [the Relief Society] keep out of it; there will be some of the women who think it is a fine thing."[14] The U.S. House of Representatives rejected this proposed amendment, and there is no way of knowing if the missing exemption clause would have affected Clark's support of the amendment in the 1970s. He died before the shortened version became a divisive national issue.

The Equal Rights Amendment was approved by the U.S. House of Representatives in October 1971 and by the U.S. Senate in March 1972, after which it began the ratification process by individual states. Without instructions from LDS headquarters, Mormon Congressmen voted their conscience across party lines, although Democratic Mormons tended to be more supportive. In the House the "aye" votes included Arizona's Morris K. Udall (D), and three Mormon representatives from California: Delwin M. Clawson (R), Richard T. Hannah (D), and John E. Moss (D). Two Mormon Republicans abstained from the vote: Utah's Sherman P. Lloyd and Idaho's Orval H. Hansen. Utah Democrat Gunn McKay was the only Mormon who voted against the ERA in the House. In the U.S. Senate Utah's Wallace F. Bennett cast his Republican vote against, while Utah's Democratic senator Frank E. Moss voted for, as did Nevada's Mormon senator Howard W. Cannon, also a Democrat.[15]

By December 1972 bipartisan action of twenty-two state legislatures ratified the proposed amendment. LDS legislators voted for the ERA in Hawaii, Idaho, Colorado, and California where Mormons had significant percentages of the population. In states without Mormon representation in their legislatures, rank-and-file Mormons encouraged ratification, especially in Maryland where "Belt Route" Mormons were prominent near the nation's capital, and in Massachusetts where there was a thriving Mormon community in the Boston area.[16] Idaho ratified the ERA in a landslide vote of 58-5 in the House and 31-4 in the state Senate, with the aye-vote of nearly every legislator from the Mormon counties of southeastern Idaho. "I don't believe in women's liberation," said Republican representative Elaine Kearnes of Idaho Falls, "but I will go along with the women on this issue."[17]

However, a few weeks later in 1973 "a John Birch Society-backed organization" successfully lobbied against ratification of the ERA in the Utah legislature.[18] Nevertheless, in September 1974 twenty-four female legislators of Utah publicly endorsed the ERA. Twenty-one of these current and former legislators were Mormon, eighteen Democrats and three Republicans.[19]

In fact, ERA support was dominant among Utah Mormons, despite the social turmoil of the 1960s and conservative criticism of the women's movement. In November 1974 the *Deseret News* published a survey showing that 63.1 percent of Utah Mormons favored ratification. Even 70.3 percent of southern Utah's conservative population wanted the ERA.[20] By 1974 thirty-three states had ratified, without a contrary word from LDS head-quarters concerning this support by two-thirds of the Union.[21]

Harold B. Lee was the principal reason for the First Presidency's silence on the ERA until after his death in December 1973. He regarded the national women's movement as the most serious challenge faced by the LDS church, but was apparently unwilling to engage in a head-on confrontation about issues which many LDS women supported.[22] His successor Spencer W. Kimball had different perspectives.

When Kimball spoke out against this constitutional proposal which had overwhelming support by Mormons, he had two advantages over church president Heber J. Grant in similar circumstances. Forty-one years earlier the often strident and personally unpopular Grant had unsuccess-fully tried to persuade Mormons to vote against repealing national Prohi-bition, even though it could be defended as a "moral issue." Grant also failed to persuade Mormons against voting for Franklin D. Roosevelt's New Deal in four elections. By contrast, the gentle and unassuming President Kimball had endeared himself personally to church members. More important, popular adoration of the church president as "The Prophet" had reached an unprecedented level by the time Kimball launched a campaign against the Equal Rights Amendment (see chap. 9).

Early Anti-ERA Activities

A recent history published by the church's Deseret Book Company observes that the "Special Affairs Committee, organized in 1974, gathered information on various questions that affected the Church and helped formulate a Church response."[23] Defeating the Equal Rights Amendment was apparently the specific reason for its organization when it began its behind-the-scenes activities a month after the *Deseret News* poll. Committee members Gordon B. Hinckley and James E. Faust, a Republican and a Democrat, asked the general president of the Relief Society to publicly oppose the amendment. The two apostles "instructed" Barbara B. Smith "on what to say" in her speech to the LDS institute of religion at the University of Utah.[24] "It is my considered judgment that the Equal Rights Amendment is not the way," declared the prepared text of her talk on 13 December 1974. She continued: "Once it is passed, the enforcement will demand an undeviating approach which will create endless problems for an already troubled society."[25]

For the time being, male leaders allowed Smith to be the proxy spokesperson for this policy. Although sources at LDS headquarters later verified that general authorities were already committed against the ERA before January 1975, Spencer W. Kimball "said the Church stays out of politics and thus has not taken a stand on the Equal Rights Amendment."[26]

A week after the LDS president's noncommittal statement, church headquarters gave the only signal necessary to defeat Utah's ratification of the ERA. An official editorial in the LDS *Church News* opposed ratification. Apostle Mark E. Petersen, who "had written the editorials since the beginning of the weekly publication in 1931," was assumed to be its author. The newspaper of Logan, Utah, predicted: "Church Stand Apparently Dooms ERA Amendment." Even more astute, considering its distance from the Mormon culture region, the *Washington Post* announced that the editorial "chills prospects for ERA in Utah."[27]

To no one's surprise, pro-ratification legislators switched sides to defeat the ERA in Utah, 54-21, on 18 February 1975. Bishop M. Byron Fisher, the legislator who had previously co-sponsored the Utah bill, explained that he now opposed it due to the church editorial: "It is my church and as a bishop, I'm not going to vote against its wishes."[28] An unsigned editorial in the *Church News* was not enough to discourage all pro-ERA Mormons in Utah. In May 1975 former legislator Beatrice Marchant organized the Equal Rights Coalition of Utah.[29]

By the fall of 1976 thirty-four states had ratified the ERA, only four short of the requirement for the proposal to become part of the U.S. Constitution.[30] Those at headquarters recognized that more would be necessary to stem the momentum, and on 22 October the First Presidency issued a formal statement against ratification. The amendment, they said, "could indeed bring them [women] far more restraints and repressions. We fear it will even stifle many God-given feminine instincts."[31]

Two months later on 29 December, Ezra Taft Benson, president of the Quorum of the Twelve, instructed all mission presidents and stake presidents: "As the Equal Rights Amendment issue is activated in some states, we suggest that you urge members of the Church, *as citizens* of this great nation, to join others in efforts to defeat the ERA."[32] Benson, a longtime ultra-conservative, took a strict stand on the Constitution. He also urged women to accept their traditional roles as full-time mothers and homemakers.[33]

In January 1977 Apostle Boyd K. Packer delivered a major address against the ERA in Pocatello, Idaho, days before Idahoans voted on a referendum to rescind ratification of the amendment. Although the legislature had sustained the ERA with a two-thirds majority, a simple majority of Idahoans was now able to rescind it.[34] Among many responses to this political move, Idaho's Secretary of State considered prosecuting Packer for allegedly violating the state's lobbyist registration law.[35] Despite this brief embarrassment, the church printed Packer's talk in the *Ensign*.[36]

Idaho's federal district judge Marion J. Callister, who eventually ruled on the constitutionality of rescinding ratification, was a Regional Representative of the Twelve and remained so until midway through the court case. Although the U.S. Justice Department and the National Organization for Women (NOW) both tried to remove him, he refused to disqualify himself. He eventually ruled that a state could rescind prior ratification but could not extend the ratification period. The U.S. Supreme Court issued an indefinite "stay" of Callister's order without overturning it.[37] One of Callister's three Mormon law clerks at this time was a son of Neal A. Maxwell, a member of the Special Affairs Committee in charge of the church's anti-ERA campaign. Maxwell's service on this committee probably contributed to his appointment to the Twelve when Gordon B. Hinckley advanced into the First Presidency.[38]

Six months after the Idaho vote, the church took on the broader feminist movement as embodied in the International Women's Year conferences in the summer of 1977. This episode was important in reinforcing the commitment of LDS leaders against what they perceived as a national feminist agenda, in testing political tactics that would be useful against state-level ratification efforts, and in proving how easily women could be mobilized for political causes that are defined as defending families and manifesting loyalty to the church.

The IWY State Conferences

When the International Women's Year state conference was scheduled for 24 June 1977 in downtown Salt Lake City, the hierarchy resisted requests for Mormon women to attend. Their attendance might be construed as an endorsement of feminism.[39] Then it occurred to one of them that a legion of loyal Mormon women could overwhelm the conference. A conservative Mormon majority could set aside the presumed feminist agenda of the Utah IWY meeting and act as a standard bearer of "traditional family values" to the national conference in Houston.

In early June 1977 five days of meetings began among a four-person strategy team: Oscar W. McConkie, Jr., senior partner of the LDS church's law firm; Wendell Ashton, director of the church's Public Communications Department; Georgia Bodell Peterson, president of the conservative "Let's Govern Ourselves" organization; and Young Woman's General Board member Moana Ballif Bennett, "a consultant in women's affairs for the Public Communications Department of the Church" and an occasional speech-writer for the Relief Society's general president. Together the four created a strategy for neutralizing the IWY conference and turning it to the church's advantage. During these meetings Ashton acted as liaison with the Special Affairs Committee.[40]

In early June 1977, by means of a telephone tree, Ezra Taft Benson communicated down the Mormon echelons of leadership in Utah to send ten conservative women from each ward to the upcoming IWY conference.[41] Expecting no more than 3,000 attendees, the IWY organizers were swamped with 13,867 women. This was more than twice the attendance at the IWY state meeting in California which had twenty times Utah's population.[42] Women were instructed "to attend the conference as a ward representative, to vote down the ERA and other feminist resolutions."[43]

Fourteen years later Belva Barlow Ashton, a member of the Relief Society General Board, said that these preparations for the IWY Conference in Utah occurred because LDS women in Hawaii and New York had reported to the Relief Society general leadership that feminists "railroaded" those IWY conventions "and they would not allow us to participate."[44] This was inaccurate; the Utah IWY conference occurred before the IWY meetings in Hawaii and New York and became the model for Mormon tactics in those conventions.

Before going to the IWY meeting in June, many of the Utah Mormon women attended anti-feminist, anti-ERA orientations by the Conservative Caucus of Utah, led by Mormon bishop Dennis R. Ker.[45] The most detailed study of the Utah IWY conference notes: "Ker and his group warned women about lesbian take-overs, unfair voting practices, and being subjected to pornographic films."[46] In one of those orientations, Amy Y. Valentine, a member of the Relief Society General Board, told the meeting that "she was voting against all the national resolutions. She said Barbara Smith took the same position, but couldn't say so publicly, and was letting it be known through the General Board members."[47] The John Birch Society newspaper in Utah editorialized that "every woman who is for motherhood and opposed to the E.R.A. [should] attend this meeting to select delegates to represent Utah."[48] A member of Georgia Peterson's conservative "Let's Govern Ourselves" organization claimed that Bircher women and men took over this pre-IWY orientation in 1977, often using the name of Peterson's group without her knowledge or authorization.[49]

In the scheduled workshops and voting at the Utah IWY conference, the conservative Mormon delegates shouted down women they identified as "feminist," sometimes calling them lesbians.[50] In the heated rhetoric and polarization of 1977, it was common for critics throughout the nation to accuse the IWY supporters of being lesbians.[51] The *Church News* itself had encouraged this association of the IWY with lesbianism when it published the invitation for Mormon women to attend the Utah meeting in the same issue as its article about the Relief Society general president's praise for Anita Bryant's campaign against lesbians and homosexuals.[52] Frequently coordinated by men with "walkie-talkies," these conservative women called for immediate votes on proposals without allowing discussion and, thanks to their stunning majority, rejected all forty-seven proposals of the national IWY leaders.[53]

Some were recommendations one would expect both conservative and liberal women to endorse. For example:

> Federal and State governments should cooperate in providing more humane, sensible, and economic treatment of young women who are subject to court jurisdiction because they have run away from home, have family or school problems, or commit sexual offenses.

* * *

> Federal and State laws relating to marital property, inheritance, and domestic relations should be based on the principle that marriage is a partnership, in which the contribution of each spouse is of equal importance and value.

* * *

> Alimony, child support, and property arrangements at divorce should be such that minor children's needs are first to be met and spouses share the economic dislocation of divorce.

* * *

> Medicare coverage should be liberalized and the use of generic drugs of certified equivalent quality should be allowed and encouraged, to reduce the cost of medicines.

* * *

> State and local governments should revise rape laws to provide for graduated degrees of the crime, to apply to assault by or upon both sexes; to include all types of sexual assault against adults; and to otherwise redefine the crime so that victims are under no greater legal handicaps than victims of other crimes.

* * *

> Homemakers displaced by widowhood or divorce should be helped to become self-sufficient members of society through programs providing job counseling, training, and placement; advice on financial management; and legal advice.[54]

Conference voters could accept any of the above proposals, while rejecting any disapproved item from the total list of national IWY recommendations. Nevertheless, these LDS women rejected all of the humanitarian proposals along with those that were controversial, liberal, or feminist. Utah's delegates to the national IWY conference repeated that unilateral rejection.[55]

The men of the Conservative Caucus and at least one Relief Society general board member had told these women to vote against every IWY proposal, no matter how good it might seem, and the women obeyed. The LDS women even rejected a resolution against pornography.[56] "When two such inflammatory issues as abortion and ERA were established as major goals of the IWY commission," a president of a stake Relief Society told the media, "how could IWY's leaders have expected all peace and love[?]"[57]

However, as chair of Utah's official anti-ERA delegation to the national IWY meeting in Houston, Georgia Peterson led her delegation in reversing one of the Utah meeting's negative votes. Although "the Utah delegation voted for a resolution its constituents did not support," Peterson obtained a unanimous approval of Utah's delegates "for an end to double discrimination suffered by non-Caucasian women." This included supporting provisions for bilingual education and community services, "culturally [non]biased educational, psychological and employment testing; protection of Indian hunting, fishing and whaling rights; extension of the 1972 Indian Education Act; equal opportunity for Hispanic people in media acquisition, training and hiring; [and concerning] the crisis of unemployment as it affects the Black community." For the other delegates at the national IWY convention, this was a stunning departure from Utah's negative votes on every other proposal. "Black, Indian, Hispanic and Asian women rushed forward and embraced members of the Utah delegation. Coretta King, wife of assassinated civil rights leader Martin Luther King, hugged Georgia Peterson. The [entire Houston] assembly chorused, 'We Shall Overcome.'"[58]

Nevertheless, profound bitterness remained about the conduct at Utah's IWY meeting. The state IWY leaders, many of them pro-ERA Mormons, protested that the conference takeover had been inspired by right-wing, John Birch Society elements within the LDS church.[59] The Relief Society general presidency, Barbara Bradshaw Smith, Janath Russell Cannon, and Marian Richards Boyer, issued a form letter on 11 July 1977 that referred to the Conservative Caucus: "Our [noncommittal] approach made some feel that they could contact Relief Society sisters without our tacit approval and imply that their information was Church sanctioned." Barbara Smith told the media that "the Relief Society had been used by the far right" in connection with the Utah IWY conference.[60] This public-relations approach allowed Smith to focus on the loose-cannon activities of Birchers and other ultra-conservatives without implicating the church's Special Affairs Committee, law firm, and Public Communications Department.[61]

LDS women attending Hawaii's IWY conference, scheduled for early July, received the following written instructions from their LDS leaders: "Report to Traditional Values Van, sign in, pick up dissent forms. Sit together. Stay together to vote on rules. Ask Presidency for help if needed."[62] Those in Honolulu car-pooled from the LDS stake parking lot; those at the Brigham Young University-Hawaii campus on the north shore were bussed to the meeting. The Honolulu newspaper reported that "a militant bloc of conservatives led by women of the Church of Jesus Christ of Latter-day Saints (Mormon) outnumber[ed] the more liberal faction about 2 to 1."[63]

However, two Mormon delegates wrote to the national IWY commission protesting an alleged feminist takeover of the Hawaii convention:

> The parliamentarian, Clara Kakalia, was also observed to be wearing a pro-E.R.A. wristband and she took visible satisfaction in rulings that went against the Women for Traditional Values group. . . . and there were complaints that she snatched lists of candidates from voters and ejected at least one Traditional Values woman from the polling place. . . . Through parliamentary maneuvering and obstruction, a small minority of pro-E.R.A. advocates was able to totally control Saturday and Sunday sessions to the almost complete exclusion of participation by anyone else.[64]

According to the *New York Times,* LDS women constituted half or more of the IWY attendance in Montana and Washington in early July. They controlled the conventions in both states even though they were a minority of each state's population. These women voted down "resolutions supporting the E.R.A."[65] At the Montana IWY there was the now-familiar sight of a Mormon man coordinating women delegates with a walkie-talkie.[66]

Mark Koltko, then an LDS convert of two years, was one of those who used walkie-talkies to coordinate women at the New York state IWY meeting in July. He described how two high councilors in Manhattan organized Mormons who were bussed from New York City to the IWY meeting in Albany, where they were joined by Mormons from throughout the state. An LDS observer with a walkie-talkie attended each IWY workshop and session. When a vote was about to occur, he notified his counterpart in the other sessions. These coordinators then told the women in their respective locations to rush to the site of the upcoming vote. Otherwise outnumbered, they used this method to overwhelm the feminists on each IWY vote,[67] though this walkie-talkie tactic succeeded better at some meetings than at others.

One LDS woman was so eager to join her Relief Society sisters in voting against the IWY proposals at the New York state meeting "that although only New York residents with valid drivers' licenses were allowed to register as voting participants, I felt compelled to borrow one of the member's license who would not be able to attend herself." She added that the women "were explicitly instructed not to mention our affiliation with the Church while attending the conference." She noted that in the "Women and the Family" workshop the remarks of law professor Judith T. Younger were "offensive" to the Mormon women who "booed the presentations, with the result that Ms. Younger stormed out of the room." Of this disclosure another LDS woman commented: "I find it strangely logical that she should choose not to question the clandestine nature of the Mormon involvement in the [New York IWY] conference, but only whether these unethical activities should be directed by the Priesthood [leaders] or the Relief Society."[68]

As in Utah, anti-ERA Mormons often derided the IWY organizers as lesbians. For example, on the Saturday before the IWY meetings in Hawaii, the Honolulu LDS stake held workshops for women assigned to attend the IWY. The first workshop had the following title: "Feminists—Consciousness raising (Homosexuality)." In the pre-convention workshops, Mormon women were warned that lesbians would be showing X-rated movies at the convention. In her description of the national IWY convention to an LDS ward in Las Vegas, Nevada Assemblywoman Karen Hayes, an LDS Democrat, used the words "lesbians," "lesbianism," "gay," "lesbian," or "dyke" forty-five times in three typed pages.[69] Hayes could be an outspoken feminist in her own right: "I don't think it's necessarily the church brethren," she later stated, but "of course we have chauvinists in the church."[70]

The IWY national commission was appalled by the Mormon takeover at several state conventions. The commission issued an official report which lumped the LDS church with the Ku Klux Klan and John Birch Society as "engaged in attacks to subvert the purposes of Public Law 94-167 and the goals of the national commission."[71] The LDS First Presidency issued a statement in reply: "The extent of the Church's involvement in International Women's Year activities has been to encourage its members, as part of their civic responsibilities, to participate in various state meetings."[72] The statement was technically true but beside the point.

During the IWY conferences in the summer of 1977, the LDS hierarchy learned a crucial lesson. With minimal direction from headquarters, women cooperated with male leaders to carry out a political agenda as far away as Hawaii or as close as Montana, even where Mormons were a small minority. The general authorities also showed themselves willing to accept two prices: the disaffection of some previously loyal Mormons and some scathing media coverage.[73] As a result, the LDS church's officially appointed "public communications coordinators" increased their efforts in what they called the "cultivation of media representatives."[74]

The LDS Church's National Anti-ERA Campaign

As of January 1977 thirty-five states had ratified the ERA.[75] This 70 percent approval reflected national support during the next five years, including polls of full-time housewives.[76] Ratification was now only three states short of the constitutional requirement. Opponents saw themselves in a last-ditch effort,[77] but by September 1977 a nationally syndicated newspaper story reported: "The Mormon presence helped defeat ERA resolutions in several states."[78]

Existing evidence verifies a centrally directed, locally implemented, and successful effort by the LDS church to prevent ratification in Arizona, Florida, Georgia, Illinois, Maryland, Missouri, Nevada, North Carolina, Oklahoma, South Carolina, and Virginia. Those combined losses guaranteed the defeat of the proposed amendment. In addition, LDS leaders publicly and successfully campaigned to rescind ratification in Idaho and supported successful rescission efforts in Kentucky, Nebraska, South Dakota, and Tennessee. A history of the rescission effort in South Dakota specifically mentioned the influence of Mormons, even though they comprised only 1 percent of the state's population.[79] In California, Hawaii, Iowa, Montana, Texas, and Wyoming, Mormons and their interfaith allies were unsuccessful in stopping or rescinding ERA ratification.[80]

One example of the central direction of this effort was a meeting in Salt Lake City for "all of Missouri and Illinois stake presidents and state[wide] ERA coordinators" on 5 October 1979, presided over by Apostle Gordon B. Hinckley. He instructed them:
1. People should not be set apart for this work
2. Should not use LDS in title of organizations
3. Church building[s] may be used for ERA education
4. Any and all Church meetings are appropriate forums for discussing ERA
5. Should not use church funds
6. Educating members on ERA issues [is appropriate]
7. Do not endorse political candidates—but publish incumbent voting record.[81]

Hinckley thus reversed the previous limitation imposed by Benson who had instructed stake and mission presidents "to join others in efforts to defeat ERA," but added: "Please keep in mind that Church buildings and organizations are not to be used for this or any other political or legislative purposes."[82] Regional representatives gave verbal instructions similar to Hinckley's to anti-ERA "coordinators" in their states, and ward houses became the staging ground for rallies.

Initially, the *Ensign* magazine published statements by Relief Society president Barbara B. Smith, church president Spencer W. Kimball, and Apostle Boyd K. Packer against ratification.[83] These were read over the pulpit in local LDS congregations, and copies were distributed to every Mormon's home before crucial elections or referendum votes. As of March 1980 this official distribution of anti-ERA materials included the *Ensign's* publication of a twenty-three page insert, *The Church and the Proposed Equal Rights Amendment: A Moral Issue.* Local LDS leaders organized pre-election distribution of these materials to members in such widely scattered states as Virginia, Florida, Nevada, and Missouri.[84]

Stake presidency counselor Charles Dahlquist introduced his anti-ERA talk to a Virginia ward by saying the people were "here tonight to be taught, not to contend with each other, not to debate, but to be taught." He said that the Equal Rights Amendment "can be summed up in just four words. Those four words: The Prophet has Spoken." He concluded: "President [N. Eldon] Tanner once said, 'Given a choice, I would rather proceed blindly following the Prophet than proceed on my own with little knowledge.' Nevertheless, each one of us has an obligation to gain for ourselves that unshakable testimony of the divine appointment of our Prophet." Local leaders gave similar talks to congregations in Georgia and elsewhere.[85] Likewise, Relief Society president Barbara B. Smith told the *New York Times* that "the Prophet can so see" all the future implications of the Equal Rights Amendment, "and if you know that, you know there is no further need for discussion."[86]

Mormon congregations received leaflets describing how to vote for referendums and sometimes for state legislators. Specific voting instructions were given in Virginia, Nevada, Arizona, and Georgia.[87] Some members expressed gratitude for this intervention. An ERA advocate in Nevada reported: "Ann Bryant of the 12th Ward told me that the [anti-ERA] Quest 'survey sheet' was distributed in her Sunday School Class. She believed that it was a nice gesture of someone to take the time to help her learn about the various candidates. I'm convinced that her reaction is typical of most faithful Mormons."[88] Estimates are that 90-95 percent of eligible Mormons voted on ERA referendums,[89] compared to 76.8 percent of Utah's registered electorate who voted in 1980, and a national average of 53.2 percent of the total American electorate who voted that same year.[90]

On crucial ERA referendums Mormon congregations tried to distribute anti-ERA leaflets to the doorsteps or car windshields of all eligible voters. Wards in Tempe, Arizona, made this pamphlet distribution an assignment for Aaronic priesthood boys ages fourteen to sixteen.[91] During the two days before the Nevada referendum, up to 9,000 Mormons telephoned every voter they knew and distributed anti-ERA pamphlets "on virtually every doorstep in Las Vegas the day before the election." Despite pre-election polls showing pro-ERA forces with a slight lead, Nevada voters overwhelmingly defeated the amendment. The official LDS magazine reported this activism in February 1979.[92]

Full-time missionaries sometimes became involved in this pre-election canvassing, as well. In Florida the effort was coordinated by LDS ward mission leaders, and the mission's zone leaders and district leaders told full-time missionaries that this anti-ERA activity was their "assignment."[93] Influencing the ERA vote in Virginia may have also been the unstated intent of the Washington, D.C., mission president's 1979 letter to his full-time missionaries: "I have been authorized to put a copy of the attached statement of the Church position on the ERA in the hands of each missionary to assist you in answering questions you may be getting. I know you will handle this matter prayerfully."[94]

In each state anti-ERA "civic" organizations of Mormons, sometimes of women only, were organized under the direction of Regional Representatives of the Twelve. The regional leaders acted under the direction of Gordon B. Hinckley, chair of the Special Affairs Committee at LDS headquarters.[95] For example, the Oakton Stake, Virginia, newsletter proclaimed in 1978:

> President Kimball recently asked President Julian Lowe, Regional Representative to the Council of the Twelve, to call a committee of Mormon women to work together against the passage of the Equal Rights Amendment.
> The resulting committee leaders include Beverly Campbell and Leila Horne of Oakton Stake and Elaine Nelson of Annandale. The four Stake Relief Society presidents of the region will also sit on the board, and three sisters will be asked to represent each ward. These three will serve as liaison officers, each organizing a group of ten women who will help in writing letters, making phone calls, and educating people in general. The resulting organization will form an impressive coalition of nearly 1,000 people.

There is no direct evidence that Kimball authorized this specific activity; rather Hinckley met with Lowe and others. The newsletter's perhaps innocent use of Kimball's name may represent the reflexive belief that any activity connected with the church would have the prophet's specific approval.

Another LDS newsletter described Hinckley's call to a priesthood leader "to coordinate the anti-ERA efforts in the state of Illinois."[96] Aside from newsletters, stake presidents sometimes instructed every ward bishop to read endorsements of these organizations over the pulpit at sacrament meetings.[97] Regional Representative W. Don Ladd acknowledged that the "line between [the Virginia Citizens] Coalition and Church [was] fine, but [he was] not concerned because of Pres. K[imball's]. commitment to defeating ERA."[98] This role of LDS headquarters in forming these local anti-ERA organizations was the unspoken context for the officially published *Encyclopedia of Mormonism*'s description of "significant local organizing by private Church members acting on their own accord against the amendment in Florida, Illinois, Maryland, Nevada, and Virginia."[99]

Mormon anti-ERA organizations bore such names as Arizona Home and Family Rally Committee, Citizens for Family Life (Iowa), Citizens Quest for Quality Government (Nevada), Families Are Concerned Today (Florida), *Hana Pono* ["Do What Is Right"] Political Action Caucus (Hawaii), Illinois Citizens For Family Life, Missouri Citizens Council, Pro-Family Coalition (California), Pro-Family Unity (South Carolina), Save Our Families Today (Tennessee), Standard of Liberty Political Action Group (California), and Virginia Citizens Coalition.[100] Mormons in North Carolina did not form their own organization but joined with members of the John Birch Society and fundamentalist Protestants in forming the North Carolinians Against ERA. The editor of the Baptist *Biblical Recorder* acknowledged that "there was a Mormon network at the core of the organization," and the head of the Charlotte chapter of NCAERA was president of the LDS stake's organization for young women. Likewise, Mormons in Tennessee's Save Our Families Today (SOFT) associated with the non-LDS, ultra-conservative Eagle Forum, and Mormons in Oklahoma did the same.[101]

In terms of prominent LDS leadership, the anti-ERA organization with the highest profile was California's Standard of Liberty Political Action Group. Its officers included former lieutenant-governor John L. Harmer and then-current Regional Representative Jay N. Lybbert.[102]

Although established through the LDS chain-of-command, the internal structure of these organizations sometimes mirrored a state's political sub-divisions, rather than the boundaries of wards and stakes. In an anti-ERA book published by Mormon women, the president of Pro-Family Coalition explained: "What we do is divide the state in 40 regions—Senate regions. Each region has a chairman and keeps its own identity—such as California Family Women. They do whatever they can in that area."[103] The result, and perhaps intent, of each group keeping "its own identity" was to obscure the fact that all forty anti-ERA groups in the state were actually branches of a single Mormon organization.

In Hawaii U.S. senator Orrin G. Hatch (R-Utah) and Ida Smith of the BYU Women's Research Institute spoke at anti-ERA meetings publicly sponsored by the Mormon group, *Hana Pono*. These meetings were held in non-religious sites such as public schools but were advertised through the local wards.[104]

In other cases speakers were scheduled in LDS chapels. In February 1978 Nevada representative Karen Hayes gave her lesbian-gay-dyke talk in an LDS chapel. She told the women assembled there how to join the Citizens for Responsible Government, which she described as follows: "And they do endorse candidates. They do help develop candidates." In November 1979 the Missouri Citizens Council advertised an anti-ERA meeting to be held "in the LDS Church on Clayton Road, Frontenac, Missouri." The principal speaker was Relief Society general president Barbara Smith whose announced topic was "How E.R.A. Will Affect the Family."[105] The church magazine endorsed membership in such organizations by praising Nevada Mormons for participating in "Citizens for Responsible Government, the Conservative Caucus, Citizens Quest, and Christian Coalition."[106]

BYU tried to maintain a policy of selective non-partisanship. For the most part, it limited anti-ERA speakers to general authorities and others with high church positions. In fact, in January 1980 the administration decided not to allow Beverly Campbell to address students about the amendment, even though she was an official LDS spokesperson. Dallin H. Oaks made this decision in order "to limit overt political activity and to eliminate excessive debate of political issues" at BYU. However, Apsotle Benson responded by arranging for the visit of nationally-known ultra-conservative Phyllis Schlafly to speak against the ERA on the church campus.[107]

In February 1979 Regional Representative Julian Lowe said that anti-ERA Mormons "have allied with other groups—whoever sees things the way we do—Catholic, Baptist . . ."[108] James I. Gibson, a regional representative and member of the Nevada state senate, introduced into the legislature an anti-ERA letter written by the highest-ranking Catholic in Nevada, the Most Reverend Norman F. McFarland.[109] Mormon bishops in various states distributed within LDS chapels the publications of such organizations as Phyllis Schlafly's Eagle Forum. Her STOP-ERA literature was displayed inside the distribution center for temple garments in Las Vegas, Nevada.[110] The Relief Society's general president Barbara Smith also spoke at anti-ERA meetings with Schlafly and publicly endorsed the ultra-conservative leader.[111]

Mormons in California were then asked to contribute to anti-ERA organizations in other states, such as Florida. Financial reports show that hundreds of Mormons donated, often ten to twenty dollars each, in one two-day solicitation that produced $13,000 for a single anti-ERA organization. John K. and Shirley Carmack were the largest single donors, contributing $3,000 each to Families Are Concerned Today. Carmack was then a regional representative in Southern California and is now a member of the First Quorum of Seventy. His specific role in coordinating those anti-ERA donations is presently unknown.[112] An article in the *Florida Historical Quarterly* noted: "Because the funds went to candidates or to the organization, 'Families Are Concerned Today,' as contributions from individual donors, they were not identified initially as part of an organized campaign."[113]

Florida's regional representative Jay N. Lybbert, a political scientist at Tallahassee Junior College, explained the anti-ERA donations from California by saying: "I just talked to a few of my friends." He did not volunteer that he was also an executive committee member of the California Mormon anti-ERA organization, Standard of Liberty Political Action Group.[114] In a surprisingly candid comment about these cross-state financial transactions, LDS spokesman Jerry Cahill told the media that "things undoubtedly were done that on review shouldn't have been done."[115] On the other hand, when asked about the financial contributions to Florida's FACT organization, Bill Evans, on the staff of the Special Affairs Committee, claimed he "doesn't know if money's being raised in other states to send to unratified states."[116]

There are few details of this cross-state financial activity because most of these organizations failed to register as lobbyists or to file the legally required reports of donations. For example, legal registration and financial reports were not produced in Virginia and Florida until the media exposed the Mormon group as an illegal political action committee (PAC).[117] Investigative reporting was less rigorous in the twenty other states where regional representatives had established these organizations.

The Mormon president of California's Pro-Family Coalition said in 1980: "We're hoping to raise $10,000 to give to Phyllis [Schlafly in Illinois]."[118] Schlafly's STOP-ERA organization in turn made donations of thousands of dollars each to Mormon anti-ERA organizations. Families Are Concerned Today showed that Schlafly's STOP-ERA organization in Illinois donated $3,000 to the Florida organization during September 1978 alone.[119]

In North Carolina an LDS bishop gave money to the ward's Relief Society president for transportation and motel rooms for ten women to attend an anti-ERA rally on the steps of the state legislature at Raleigh.

When she and her ten women arrived at the rally, they were joined by hundreds of other LDS women from every county of North Carolina. This Relief Society president was "thrilled" at how efficiently "the Church" had organized this statewide rally. She did not know whether the funds she received came from the ward budget or from private donations by the bishopric.[120] Nevada bishops who paid for anti-ERA activities insisted that the "money had been donated by members of the bishopric, *as private citizens.*"[121]

Meanwhile some local leaders posted anti-ERA petitions in the foyers of LDS chapels for Mormons to sign, while others passed the petitions among the congregation during sacrament meetings. This procedure was used in both Virginia and Georgia, and similar action probably occurred in other states where the LDS campaign operated.[122]

Local LDS leaders encouraged Mormons to write letters to state legislators or to sign pre-printed anti-ERA postcards. They were instructed not to identify themselves as Mormons. This occurred in every state where the Special Affairs Committee had commissioned the anti-ERA campaign.[123] In Georgia letter-writing occurred within the ward meeting houses.[124] One LDS woman described a social she held for other Mormon women at her home where they signed anti-ERA letters to Virginia legislators. She had already typed most of the letters or had already written them in longhand.[125] In Illinois the Relief Society president of Macomb wrote all women in her branch in 1978: "The First Presidency has asked that all of the stakes and the district in Illinois work toward its defeat by sending mailgrams to members of the state legislature and by going to Springfield on Wednesday, December 13th to campaign with the members of the legislature."[126]

Numerically, the results were staggering. The church's public relations coordinator for Las Vegas claimed that LDS leaders amassed 4,000 such letters within one day after receiving the assignment from Elder Boyd K. Packer in Salt Lake City.[127] Some estimates put 85 percent of the anti-ERA mail received by state legislators in Virginia as actually written by Mormons, though they comprised less than 1 percent of the state's population.[128] A study in North Carolina noted that "one woman walked into the General Assembly carrying five thousand letters to each legislator in her district. She came back later with fifteen hundred more." The study described this woman during its discussion of the "Mormon network" that was at the center of this campaign. Latter-day Saints were also less than 1 percent of North Carolina's population.[129] In Phoenix, Arizona, where Mormons comprised a large percentage of the population, the female anti-ERA coordinator presented a petition to Congress in February 1978 "signed by 70,000 Arizonans opposed to it."[130]

In June 1981 the *Boston Globe* headlined, "It's Do or Die for the ERA: Mormon Power Is the Key." In September a historian of American power and international relations wrote that "the Mormons display a very shrewd understanding of the kind of national power that can grow out of organizing a relatively small number of people in a specific region."[131]

Women were the main participants in all local activities against the Equal Rights Amendment. "Women opposed the ERA because it jeopardized a way of life they had entered in good faith," wrote one non-LDS author. "A critical reason for ERA's defeat was opposition from women."[132]

Yet only a minority of American women opposed the ERA. Shortly after the proposal's defeat in 1982, a Gallup poll showed that 61 percent of American women wanted Congress to reintroduce the amendment and begin the ratification process all over again.[133]

It is also misleading to suggest that Mormon women "became involved" in the anti-ERA campaign by happenstance.[134] In the Mormon way, the agenda and direction were male-authorized and hierarchical. The results demonstrated politically the view of one analyst that "the Mormon Church [is] a Central Command System."[135]

Tensions and Responses

Never before had LDS headquarters conducted a political campaign so vast in geography or participation. In states a thousand miles from Salt Lake City, political instructions flowed from regional representatives to stake presidents and mission presidents, to "state[wide] ERA coordinators," to bishops and branch presidents, to Relief Society presidents and missionary zone leaders, to rank-and-file Mormons. The resulting activism extended from small towns to state capitals. Whatever the outcome, all sides recognized that these headquarters-directed activities would have direct consequences on the political rights of non-Mormons. What was less clear was the cost in the moral authority of the First Presidency and its spiritual prerogatives.

Divisions among Mormons became public during the rancorous IWY conference in Utah in June 1977. As the official history of the Relief Society acknowledges, "some of the faithful Latter-day Saints among them [the IWY supporters] felt betrayed."[136] Anti-ERA legislator Georgia B. Peterson was also outraged. When she formed a national organization for politically conservative women three years later, she publicly specified that it would not admit any "extremist" women who "identify with the Eagle Forum," Phyllis Schlafly's national organization.[137]

In 1978 BYU president Dallin H. Oaks became the center of controversy over pro-ERA boycotts of Utah. On 27 April he officially protested
this "repressive tactic." He explained: "A boycott is an ugly instrument by
which to impose one's will upon others, since its efforts to penalize the
adversary necessarily inflict injury on the innocent." He condemned all
boycotts because their "morality is contemptible." The organizations he
addressed included the American Home Economics Association, American Political Science Association, American Psychological Association,
American Theatre Association, American Association of University
Women, the Organization of American Historians, and the Speech Communication Association. In a letter to each, Oaks threatened to withdraw
BYU's membership, an action which was ironically also a boycott.[138] Oaks
was at this time a regional representative,[139] all of whom had the responsibility of furthering anti-ERA efforts.

A few days later Sybel Alger, editor of BYU's *Daily Universe,* printed
the text of Oaks's letter along with comments by BYU faculty. Within the
week her signed editorial observed: "Apparently [President Oaks] does
not realize that boycotts are an accepted part of society. . . . One must
wonder why Pres. Oaks chose to protest this particular boycott." Oaks then
sent Alger a rebuke, claiming that her editorial "does not meet the
standard I have come to expect of *Universe* writers sufficiently experienced
to use a byline."[140]

Daily Universe editors subsequently published two letters from community members critical of Oaks's position. The first was from Loneta Murphy of the Utah League of Women Voters, who criticized Oaks, praised
Alger's editorial, and condemned the church's opposition to the ERA. The
second letter, by a husband and wife, observed that two days after Oaks's
letter to the faculty, the First Presidency had asked for a twenty-four-hour
"TV Boycott" to protest unacceptable network programming. Was Oaks
also saying the Presidency boycott's "morality is contemptible"?[141]

Privately Oaks instructed *Daily Universe* supervisors to "take whatever
steps are necessary" to prevent the future publication of similar letters
critical of his stance on the ERA. Alger's by-line did not appear on an
editorial for nearly three months.[142] Oaks then formally withdrew BYU's
membership from organizations which had boycotted Utah.[143]

Three months later the First Presidency issued its second official
statement against the Equal Rights Amendment, clearly labeling the issue
a "moral" one. Unlike the 1976 statement, this August 1978 document
detailed the religious, moral, legal, and political context, which one analyst
considers a response to LDS "radical feminist" Sonia Johnson's very public
criticism (including before the U.S. Senate) of the church-run campaign
in Virginia and elsewhere.[144]

The First Presidency's statement opened: "We believe ERA is a moral issue with many disturbing ramifications for women and for the family." It warned in dire terms against "the possible train of unnatural consequences which could result because of its very vagueness—encouragement of those who seek a unisex society, an increase in the practice of homosexual and lesbian activities, and other concepts which could alter the natural, God-given relationship of men and women."[145]

Homosexuality and lesbianism may have seemed tangential objections to the ERA, yet Kimball and his counselors were now giving specific endorsement to views in circulation among Mormons for nearly two years. General authority Neal A. Maxwell had sounded this warning in March 1977: "Would ERA confer upon homosexuals [any] privileges or status not intended[?]"[146] Briefings given at LDS meeting houses before the IWY conferences in 1977 also equated the ERA with homosexuality. Kimball's church assignment for decades had included counseling homosexual Mormons, and the topic was a personal preoccupation.[147] Likewise, two years later Rex E. Lee's legalistic rejection of the ERA gave six separate references to homosexuality in a booklet published by BYU.[148] Using homophobia as an anti-ERA argument was common nationally, especially among Protestant fundamentalists.[149]

The First Presidency also expressed concern that the ERA would lead to nontraditional families, increased divorce, and "challenge[s] to almost every legally accepted social custom." They feared nullification of the gender-discriminatory provisions in current laws to protect women.[150]

The First Presidency's statement silenced a previously pro-ERA publication, the Utah Order of Women Legislators' *Woman's Chronicler*. The organization dropped the ERA from its masthead and featured an article about anti-ERA legislator Georgia B. Peterson.[151]

However, the Presidency's statement galvanized opposition from Utah's League of Women Voters, staffed primarily by Mormons. In September 1978 the league published a pro-ERA pamphlet which quoted from prominent nineteenth-century Mormon women and general authorities who had "demanded equality under the law" for women. The pamphlet emphasized that Utah's League of Women Voters "has supported the ratification of the Equal Rights Amendment since 1972."[152]

In October 1978 the First Presidency distributed a follow-up letter: "We urge our people to join actively with other citizens who share our concerns and who are engaged in working to reject this measure on the basis of its threat to the moral climate of the future." While acknowledging "political processes, we are convinced that because of its predictable results the matter is basically a moral rather than a political issue." This significantly modified the First Presidency's statement less than two months earlier. In a question-answer format on 24 August, Kimball and his counselors had denied that the ERA was a political issue at all.[153]

In direct response, thirty-eight Mormons signed a pro-ERA pamphlet in 1979. Titled *Another Mormon View of the ERA,* this publication was a clear alternative to the official position. Signers included such distinguished Latter-day Saints as Lucybeth Rampton, wife of Utah's Democratic governor; Utah's Democratic U.S. Senator Frank E. Moss and wife Phyllis; Esther W. Eggertsen Peterson, former Assistant Secretary of the U.S. Labor Department; Jean M. Westwood, former national chair of the Democratic Party; and Christine Meaders Durham, now a Utah Supreme Court justice.[154] There were no sanctions against these individuals, despite their published dissent from the Presidency's publicly-defined "moral issue."

Nevertheless, this pro-ERA activism by devout Mormons was the unstated context for a statement in the August 1979 issue of the church's magazine. "When the prophet speaks the debate is over," wrote First Presidency counselor N. Eldon Tanner concerning "many issues under debate as controversies rage all around us." For fifteen years he had been widely regarded as a "liberal" Democrat, and Tanner's statement was apparently directed toward like-minded Mormons who dissented from Spencer W. Kimball's views of the Equal Rights Amendment.[155] The ERA debate was also the unstated context less than a year earlier when the Young Women's general president first coined the phrase: "When the prophet speaks, sisters, the debate is over."[156]

Two months after Apostle Hinckley's instructions in October 1979 to "state[wide] ERA coordinators" that they "should not use LDS in title of [their] organizations,"[157] a distressed Mormon in Missouri wrote a letter to Neal A. Maxwell of the Special Affairs Committee. "My concerns are not with that ultimate goal [of defeating the ERA], but with the methods the MCC [Missouri Citizens Council] uses to persuade members of the Church and to influence legislators," he began. "My first concern is with the surreptitious manner in which the group operates. The leaders of the MCC publicly deny being a Church sponsored organization, yet the facts indicate otherwise." The writer concluded that the Missouri Citizens Council "is and will be perceived as a Church sponsored organization and their denials will only invite criticism, anger, and ridicule from the public."[158] However, such concealment was consistent with Apostle Hinckley's instructions.

Concealment of finances created similar anxiety. Linda Goold, then a recent graduate of BYU's law school, became the legal counsel for the Virginia Citizens Coalition by request of Regional Representative Julian Lowe. She withdrew from the organization when its leaders declined to file legally required lobbying registration and financial statements.[159]

Sonia Johnson formed the national organization of "Mormons for ERA" (MERA) in Virginia in January 1978. Similar groups soon formed in Nevada, California, Arizona, Montana, and Washington state.[160] Utah Mormons for ERA (UMERA) fragmented within months due to personality conflicts and an internal dispute over admitting men to the board. The director resigned and men joined the board.[161]

At its peak, a thousand people belonged to Mormons for ERA.[162] That was a small number compared to the tens of thousands of Mormons whom LDS officials had organized into anti-ERA demonstrators, letter-writers, and voters. More significantly, of pro-ERA correspondence sent to Sonia Johnson, non-Mormon writers outnumbered LDS writers by four to one.[163] Pro-ERA Mormons were a marginal dimension of the LDS church yet gained attention from the nation at large. Ironically, the disproportionate influence of pro-ERA Mormons on non-Mormons mirrored the national impact of the Mormon hierarchy's organized effort to defeat the ERA among non-Mormons.

In December 1979 Sonia Johnson was excommunicated from the LDS church. To her supporters she was a national "martyr to LDS hierarchical power and a symbol of women's struggles inside the institution for greater equality."[164] LDS headquarters reinforced that view among her supporters by officially distributing copies of "Sonia's Bishop Was the Real Hero" to the public communications directors in every stake of North America. The article was written by Catholic ultra-conservative Patrick J. Buchanan.[165]

For those who supported the ERA, the collision between their religious ideals and political realism made continued participation in Mormonism painful. Within three years, 19.4 percent of the membership of Mormons for ERA had been "excommunicated by personal choice or by the church."[166]

There were exceptions to this unpleasantness. One of the most temperate expressions of opposition to the Equal Rights Amendment came from Belle S. Spafford in July 1974, before the *Deseret News* editorial against the ERA and before the First Presidency publicly declared its opposition. This former president of the National Council of Women and former president of the international LDS Relief Society said: "I am of the opinion that major advantages embodied in the proposed amendment could be achieved through regular channels of state and federal legislative action without raising questionable results." Unlike many of her anti-ERA associates, she predicted no dire results if the ERA or something like it eventually became the law of the land: "Legislation may make legal the total equality of the sexes, but it is my opinion that the different natures of man and woman will be the supreme law in dictating the divisions of labor to which each will be drawn in the work of the world." When BYU published this in 1980 as part of a two-volume collection of talks, it included Emma Lou Thayne's remarks about "the cat fight" among Mormons over the Equal Rights Amendment: "Must I declare a total opposition in order to take a faithful stand? Must any person sacrifice a belief in fair play or thoughtful discipleship for the sake of blind acceptance or absolute rejection of a cause?"[167]

As if in response, the pro-ERA *Exponent II,* "published by Mormon Women," printed a man's anti-ERA article that filled more than one full page in the twenty-page newspaper.[168] Also in 1980 Ann Terry, Marilyn Slaght-Griffin, and Elizabeth Terry published an anti-ERA book which included long and respectful interviews with ERA activists Sonia Johnson, Marilee Latta, and Nadine Hansen.[169] In 1981 the pro-feminist and pro-ERA Mormon journal *Dialogue* also published a woman's account of her anti-ERA views and activities, of which she wrote: "I for one am weary of the strife and the exaggerated promises on all sides of the ERA issue. I am eager to bind up the wounds they may have caused." Four years earlier she had publicly defended the animosity of LDS women at the IWY meetings.[170] However, for many people the ERA conflict was beyond conciliatory gestures.

By 1981 the church's coordinated campaign against the ERA resulted in a backlash from national feminist organizations. Eleanor Smeal, president of the National Organization for Women, explained: "We are carrying our fight for equal justice for women to the heart of the opposition, the Mormons." In May 1981 NOW began sending up to one hundred pro-ERA "missionaries" to canvass the cities of Salt Lake City, Ogden and Provo, because "the facts are clear that the Mormon Church has worked actively against ERA."[171]

This proselytizing increased the perception of many Latter-day Saints that Mormonism was under siege. The *Los Angeles Times* reported that during the Utah Pioneer Day parade in July 1981, "some spectators heckled, threw fruit and spat on ERA missionaries" who marched in the parade.[172]

Nevertheless, this concealed a curious fact about many Mormons' private views. More than half continued to support the content of the ERA, even after First Presidency statements in 1976, 1978, and 1980. Polls during the 1980s showed that 53 percent of Mormons who said they were opposed to the Equal Rights Amendment actually agreed with the phrase: "equality of rights under the law shall not be denied or abridged by the United States or by a state on account of sex" if presented to them without identifying it as the Equal Rights Amendment. In total, 69.3 percent of the Mormon sample in 1982 favored the text of the ERA. The Mormon hierarchy's official rejection was apparently what made the difference.[173]

That same year LDS college students received a manual which demonstrated why it was virtually impossible for most Mormons to dissent from Spencer W. Kimball's opposition to the Equal Rights Amendment. "The Lord Will Never Permit the Living Prophet to Lead the Church Astray," announced a bold-faced heading in this 1982 publication for twenty-year-olds. Other headings followed: "The Standard Works and Living Prophets Must Be Accepted or Rejected Together, What the First Presidency Says Is Scripture, Those Who Follow the First Presidency Will Never Go Astray, Truly Converted Latter-day Saints Sustain the Prophets, Prophets Are Rejected for Unsound Reasons, Those Who Oppose or Reject Counsel of Prophets Lose the Spirit of God, The Gates of Hell Will Not Prevail against Church Members Who Follow the Word of the Living Prophet, Those Who Follow the Prophet Will Obtain Eternal Life."[174] These are the slogans of contemporary Mormonism. LDS headquarters has given current Latter-day Saints good reason to feel that they would jeopardize their eternal welfare by exercising the kind of political independence that faithful Mormons demonstrated fifty years ago (see chap. 9).

Mormons and Jews were the only religious groups whose response to the ERA was overwhelmingly one-directional. A national study showed that 85.7 percent of Jewish women supported the ERA, compared with 25 percent of Mormon women. Likewise, 89.4 percent of Jewish men supported the ERA, whereas only 12.5 percent of Mormon men supported it. No other American religious groups had such unified responses.[175]

Extent and Limits of Official LDS Involvement

Throughout its campaign, LDS headquarters officially maintained that chapels should not be used for overtly political activities connected with ERA. Benson's letter of December 1976 emphasized this restriction. However, the use of meeting houses was encouraged in Hinckley's private instructions to regional representatives, stake presidents, and "state[wide] ERA coordinators."

However, when questioned about this political use of church buildings, church representatives claimed that these activities were sporadic and unauthorized. For example, Virginia's regional representative Julian C. Lowe commented in February 1979: "I personally advocated not doing those things in church bldg[s]. but some [local leaders] may have done them." Regional Representative W. Donald Ladd, now a general authority, concurred.[176] The First Presidency affirmed this in a letter read in all LDS sacrament meetings five months later.[177] In March 1980 the presidency reaffirmed: "It is, however, contrary to our counsel and advice that ward, branch or stake premises, chapels or other Church facilities be used in any way for political campaign purposes, whether it be for speech-making, distribution of literature, or class discussion."[178] These public statements were necessary to protect the tax-exempt status of LDS meetinghouses, yet LDS church "involvement in the ERA controversy may well have exceeded legal boundaries for tax-exempt institutions, at least in some states."[179]

In February 1978 Hinckley told the media: "If Mormons seem to have a cohesiveness, it springs from the convictions of basic Mormon principles." He said that the church does not tell a person specifically how to vote. "But," he admitted, "it is not unusual for Mormons to be of a like mind."[180] That was the vintage explanation for Mormon bloc-voting in the nineteenth-century West.

In a private meeting with Hinckley two years later, Sonia Johnson asked: "Did you meet with Regional Representative Julian Lowe to set up the Virginia Citizens Coalition?" Unaware that the Oakton Virginia Stake newsletter and Lowe himself had already described this authorization, Hinckley twice denied such a meeting. Johnson icily replied: "Gordon, [either] you're lying to me or else Julian Lowe is." The record of their interview continued: "Then he remembered he had met with Lowe."[181]

When asked, "Do the Brethren know what you've been doing?" Lowe replied in February 1979, "Oh, they know what's going on. We update them from time to time." Two regional leaders indicated that anti-ERA reports went to general authorities besides Hinckley, as well.[182] However, until July 1981 the First Presidency may not have been given detailed information.

During a candid interview, Rodney P. Foster, an assistant secretary in the First Presidency's office from 1974 to 1981, explained that he was not aware of the existence of the Special Affairs Committee until about 1977. This was three years after its formation. Foster said that the anti-ERA campaign was not referred to in the First Presidency meetings he attended. Nor did reports of local anti-ERA efforts appear in the detailed minutes he transcribed of First Presidency meetings he did not attend. "The actual grass-roots [anti-ERA] movement and working with regional representatives, and setting up meetings—that was all done under cloak of other authority," Foster said, "what they now call Special Affairs." In his view the committee purposely kept the LDS president and his counselors uninformed of its activities. He added that Kimball and his counselors may have preferred that.[183] In any event, apparently no one in the First Presidency's office knew details of the church's ERA campaign until Hinckley moved from the Special Affairs Committee to become a special counselor to the First Presidency in July 1981. By that time, Kimball and his first two counselors were severely limited by health problems.[184]

Despite the many published statements about Hinckley's activities, a recent 600-page biography (unauthorized) is completely silent about the Equal Rights Amendment. The biographer also made this single statement about Hinckley's role with the Special Affairs Committee: "Special liaison on governmental and political matters. It handled criticism of the Church, a First Presidency responsibility." His equally long official biography also mutes Hinckley's supervision of the ERA campaign. While spending three pages on his six-month role "in orchestrating the Church's opposition to" the Utah referendum on liquor-by-the-drink in 1968, it devotes one sentence to his five-year direction of the anti-ERA campaign: "Elder Hinckley acted several times as a Church spokesman on the matter."[185]

Church funds were apparently not used to support the anti-ERA campaign. Hinckley emphasized that restriction in his 5 October 1979 meeting. Alan Blodgett, the church's chief financial officer during the campaign, explained that LDS headquarters distributed no funds to the various political action committees. Lowell M. Durham, president of Deseret Book Company at the time, confirmed that LDS business corporations were not asked to donate funds. However, Blodgett understood that "someone" was arranging for individual donations from members.[186]

Implications of the ERA Campaign

The assertion that the LDS church's campaign was the final straw in breaking the back of ERA ratification is debatable. It may be true but is unverifiable. However, immediately after Mormon anti-ERA campaigns in several states, pro-ERA forces lost their slight edge of support among state legislators or among voters facing an ERA referendum. The Roman Catholic church and fundamentalist Protestant churches made similar last-ditch efforts.[187] At the least, it is fair to say that Mormons were significant players in the religious coalition which defeated the Equal Rights Amendment.[188]

ERA supporters and the national media often questioned the right of LDS leaders to conduct this political campaign and to conceal its central direction. Some Mormons and many non-Mormons simply ridiculed Hinckley's statement to the media: "We have construed that the ERA is a moral issue."[189] As sociologist Armand Mauss noted: "It is as though the Mormons spent the first half of the twentieth century striving to become more like Episcopalians, only to reverse course with the approach of the twenty-first century and begin emulating the Southern Baptists instead."[190]

In recent decades LDS leaders have often identified their political campaigns as a "moral issue," but not always. For example, in the midst of the church's campaign against the ERA the First Presidency asked all western Congressmen to vote against the deregulation of airlines, hardly a matter of faith or morals.[191]

Moreover, Mormon sociologist White's complaint is irrelevant when he decried "the whim" of Mormon leaders for mounting a political assault on the ERA as a "moral issue" in the 1970s-80s. He contrasted this with the general aloofness of most LDS leaders toward the civil rights movement of the 1960s because they defined that as "a political issue."[192] Nevertheless, every organization—secular or sacred—has the right to draw its own battle lines.

The LDS church, like other organizations, also has the right to impose whatever penalty it chooses upon members who dissent from such decisions, as long as the punishment does not violate the secular laws to which the church is also subject. From that perspective, Sonia Johnson was simply a casualty, not a martyr.

One can debate whether the LDS church's anti-ERA campaign weakened particular values or expectations of some of its members. Certainly, the Equal Rights Amendment helped the church grow stronger at a personal and institutional level. For the first time in their lives, thousands of Mormon women participated directly in the American political process. They were not only "good Mormon soldiers" in letter-writing campaigns and public demonstrations but were often also the local organizers and spokespersons in the anti-ERA campaign. Although LDS women were usually assigned to these activities by male priesthood leaders, for the most part these women enthusiastically participated in the anti-ERA campaign as an expression of their own deeply felt views. Two historians of the ERA's defeat have stated that female "Birchers, Mormons, and [other] right-wing women may have been new to the public forum, but they had as much right to it as their counterparts from a different political culture."[193]

Also, for the first time, the Mormon hierarchy planned and successfully administered a multi-directional political campaign in widely scattered states and in hundreds of cities and towns. Institutionally, the LDS church won a short-term battle in its century-old war with the federal government. "Opponents, even if they supported the objectives [of the ERA], felt that the federal government should not be involved," wrote two LDS historians.[194]

However, the hierarchy's campaign involved intangible costs, impossible to quantify, involving psychological and spiritual strain. Many Mormons realized that their political strategy required an amount of subterfuge, deceit, and misdirection to protect the church's direct involvement.[195]

Even though LDS leadership made a decision to combat a political cause supported by a majority of Americans (and initially) by most Mormons, this was not an aberration in the U.S. political system. The First Amendment limits governmental intrusions on religion and prevents government advocacy of religious groups, but the First Amendment does not limit religions from making non-coercive intrusions upon U.S. citizens.[196] The Equal Rights Amendment demonstrated that LDS leadership will use the political process to defend church policy, despite the effect on the lives of millions of non-Mormons who see things differently. Politically active churches and church-sponsored political organizations are simply examples of special-interest lobbying in the United States.[197] These are the costs and advantages of the democratic system.

However, churches must always decide whether a potential backlash is worth the effort. One legacy of the anti-ERA campaign is a widespread lack of credibility for the LDS church as an advocate for women.[198] This image persists despite numerous talks at LDS general conferences which honor women and their contributions, despite an outpouring of LDS books about women, and despite a higher public profile for the general presidencies of the women's auxiliaries in recent years.[199]

Beyond the historical facts of the anti-ERA campaign, the political activism of Mormon leaders is embedded in LDS theology and history (see chaps. 8-9). In the decade since winning its anti-ERA battle, the Mormon hierarchy has continued to intervene in a variety of political issues in Utah, such as a 1992 ballot initiative for pari-mutuel betting.[200]

A 1994 vote in Oklahoma, discussed in a *Church News* article, showed the decentralization and expansion of the Special Affairs Committee. Now there are permanent "Public Affairs Councils" of the church on an area, regional, statewide, and local level. This change occurred in 1991.[201]

Although "members of the Church in Oklahoma make up less than 1 percent of the state's population," they directed "a statewide campaign against the lottery, resulting in its defeat May 10 by a 60 percent to 40 percent vote," this article proclaimed. The campaign occurred "under direction of the North American Southwest Area presidency and local public affairs councils." The article identified two general authorities involved as Elders W. Mack Lawrence and D. Todd Christofferson of the area presidency. The article did not specify that the area presidency consulted with Public Affairs at LDS headquarters, but such stewardship is automatic for general authorities.

The article noted that prior to the church's involvement, "public opinion polls showed 75 percent for the initiative, 25 percent against." The *Church News* outlined the strategy to persuade 35 percent of a non-Mormon electorate to change their intended votes. "Two weeks before the vote,

Elder Christofferson . . . met with a local LDS public affairs council. Included in that meeting were members of a non-member organization, 'Oklahomans Against the Lottery.'" This centrally coordinated campaign included Southern Baptists, Methodists, and members of the Assembly of God. However, "the 'spinal cord' of the work," according to Oklahoma's statewide director of LDS Public Affairs, "was the network of LDS public affairs."[202]

With Public Affairs directors stationed across the United States, the Mormon hierarchy has both the will and the ability to intervene politically on any "moral issue" that involves Congress, state legislatures, county supervisors, local school boards, or city councils. In 1994 the LDS church began such a campaign nationally.

A New Crusade in the Mid-1990s

In February 1994 the First Presidency issued a statement against the legalization of same-sex marriages that echoed the announcement that had mobilized the anti-ERA campaign. Almost immediately, LDS congregations from Hawaii to Maryland began receiving fliers telling them how to get involved in the political action groups opposing same-sex marriages.[203] In California the area presidencies sent LDS congregations sample letters for lobbying state legislators to pass a law against giving legal recognition to same-sex marriages. The area presidencies instructed California Mormons to personalize these letters but not to mention their LDS membership.[204] As a reprise of denials during the ERA campaign, the regional representative in Hawaii insisted that "the effort is local," and a spokesman at LDS headquarters added that the general authorities "have not involved themselves" in these activities.[205]

A year later LDS officials petitioned the Hawaii circuit court to formally admit the LDS church as a co-plaintiff with the state attorney general in the suit against legalization of same-sex marriages. A regional representative in Hawaii told the media that "this initiative is our own," but acknowledged that "we have the approval and support of the Church." He insisted that "the Church has not attempted to oppose basic civil rights for homosexuals or any other group."[206]

In March 1995 the Utah legislature passed a bill "to strengthen Utah's ban on same-sex marriages and to deny recognition of such marriages performed elsewhere." Specifically aimed at the possibility that Hawaii may legalize same-sex marriages, this law also prohibited recognition of the same-sex marriages that have been legally solemnized for several years in Denmark, Norway, Sweden, and the Netherlands. This action by Utah's legislature (86 percent LDS) and by Utah's LDS governor had the appearance of serving the hierarchy's national campaign against same-sex marriages.[207]

After the circuit court judge in Hawaii denied the LDS church's petition in March 1995, an LDS stake president and two bishops appealed this decision to the state supreme court. The church newspaper observed that the petition "is based on the reasonable fear that the authority of Hawaii clergy to solemnize marriages could be lost if same-gender marriages are legalized and they (clergy) refused to perform them on the basis of their moral beliefs." The *Deseret News* report noted that "the church's leadership in Salt Lake City" had authorized this appeal to Hawaii's supreme court. LDS headquarters also formally offered to furnish Hawaii's attorney general with "additional legal manpower" to stop the same-sex marriages.[208]

However, during the last week of January 1996, Hawaii's supreme court denied this petition for the LDS church to join the lawsuit. Neither the Catholic church nor the LDS church had legal standing in the case because state law does not require clergy to perform any marriage.[209] For example, Catholic priests have traditionally declined to perform marriages involving non-Catholics and Catholics, just as LDS officers have traditionally exercised their right to decline the request of certain individuals for an LDS officer to perform their marriage. Since the hierarchies of both churches were well aware of this legal right of clergy to decline to perform civil marriages, the above judicial appeal had the appearance of being simply a delaying tactic.

A month after this decision by Hawaii's supreme court, Gordon B. Hinckley, now president of the LDS church, traveled there to confer with Honolulu's Catholic bishop Francis X. DiLorenzo. In contrast to his behind-the-scenes direction of the anti-ERA campaign, the *Deseret News* announced in February 1996 that Hinckley's purpose was to coordinate with the Roman Catholic hierarchy "as part of a grass-roots coalition opposed to same-sex marriage." Their meeting place was on LDS property in Laie on the north shore of the island of Oahu. The church newspaper also announced that the campaign was being spearheaded by Hawaii's Future Today, a "nondenominational organization of about 1,500 members. It is made up of the Catholic and LDS churches—the two largest denominations in Hawaii." This information was provided by "Elder Loren C. Dunn, a member of the LDS Church's First Quorum of the Seventy and president of the North America West Area."[210]

By June 1996 it became clear that the anti-ERA campaign has been the model for techniques of the LDS campaign against same-sex marriages. The co-chairs of Hawaii's Future Today deny that this political action committee has official connection with the LDS church's opposition to same-sex marriages in Hawaii. Such statements are consistent with the solemn denials concerning the origins of the anti-ERA organizations established nearly twenty years ago in various states by regional representatives acting on instructions from LDS headquarters in Utah. In addition, this current group's female co-chair works at the BYU-Hawaii campus, and the male co-chair is chief executive officer of Hawaiian Reserves Incorporated, the LDS church's holding company for properties surrounding its Polynesian Cultural Center at Laie. However, the most revealing continuity with the anti-ERA campaign comes from a recent financial report submitted by Hawaii's Future Today. One of the largest single contributors to this political action committee is *Hana Pono*.[211]

This organization's name is the Hawaiian translation of the LDS hymn "Do What Is Right," and its literature has proclaimed: "HANA PONO was founded in August, 1977, by a group of women who had participated in the Hawaii IWY convention the preceding month. They recognized a need for persons with similar moral values to become better informed regarding local and national issues in order to take a stand and become a positive force in the community." During the anti-ERA campaign, *Hana Pono* issued announcements for "OAHU BISHOPS TO READ" to LDS congregations. After *Hana Pono* incorporated its own "Political Action Caucus" in 1979, this organization printed pamphlets outlining for Hawaiians the "position" of the LDS church on various matters.[212] *Hana Pono*'s current involvement demonstrates the direct connection of the LDS campaign against same-sex marriages with the methods and even some of the organizations involved with the anti-ERA campaign.

Despite the 1994 denials of official connection with local political action committees opposed to same-sex marriages, in June 1996 LDS headquarters acknowledged that it has been "calling" married couples on short-term missions to aid these organizations. For example, in November 1995 general authority Dunn formally appointed a Salt Lake City advertising executive and his wife to do several months of volunteer work for Hawaii's Future Today organization. Although an official statement from LDS headquarters claims that such church members are simply "responding" to the First Presidency's general invitation to become involved as citizens, the LDS hierarchy is asking specific Mormons to perform this political service as a church calling.[213]

It remains to be seen whether the hierarchy's anti-gay political campaign will rival the success of its anti-ERA campaign. Except for the public acknowledgement of central direction for recent activities, the two crusades appear to share identical methods. The anti-ERA campaign seems to be the blue-print for the Mormon effort to prohibit same-sex marriages and to oppose any legislation favoring homosexuals. In fact, the LDS church's political activism against "gay rights" in any town, city, county, or state of the United States was inevitable because homophobia was central to the national ERA campaign. "The possibility cannot be avoided," the church's official pamphlet had warned in 1980 that "Passage of the ERA would carry with it the risk of extending constitutional protection to immoral same-sex—lesbian and homosexual—marriages."[214]

However, the current political campaign is vastly more difficult because there can be no decisive victory, as with ERA ratification or failure to ratify. Every state has its own laws, and each new session of a state legislature is a new opportunity for the losing side to renew the battle over a sexual minority's civil rights or "special rights." This is equally true for every county, city, and town.

For example, because Denver, Aspen, and Boulder, Colorado, passed local ordinances prohibiting civil rights discrimination against persons because of their sexual orientation, Colorado's voters approved a consititutional amendment which denied such rights for homosexuals and lesbians. The state supreme court ruled this as unconstitutional, after which supporters of the anti-gay amendment appealed the decision to the U.S. Supreme Court. LDS headquarters allowed BYU's president Rex E. Lee to serve as a legal counsel to aid the state of Colorado in this case.[215] This contradicted the recent claim from Hawaii's same-sex campaign that "the Church has not attempted to oppose basic civil rights for homosexuals or any other group."

Even a U.S. Supreme Court decision will not end the conflict if the LDS church and its interfaith allies are on the losing side of legalizing same-sex marriage. For example, in May 1996 the court's majority declared that Colorado could not deny homosexuals the protection of anti-discrimination laws because "a state cannot so deem a class of persons a stranger to its laws." Rather than publish its own editorial against the Supreme Court, the *Deseret News* reprinted nationally syndicated editorials against this decision. This again reflects the political style of President Hinckley who for two decades has advised against official LDS criticism of the U.S. Supreme Court.[216] If pressed, the next step of the LDS interfaith coalition will be to mount a national campaign to ratify a U.S. constitutional amendment against "special rights" for the small minority of Americans who define themselves as homosexual.

In this context it is noteworthy that a dozen countries and one Canadian province boast a higher percentage of Mormons than in the United States.[217] It seems likely that the LDS church will, sooner or later, take stands on the political life of other countries where Mormons have the demographics for political activism. At that time the Mormon hierar-

chy will become a political force internationally. The *Church News* announced the first significant evidence of that outreach in 1974: "David M.
Kennedy, former United States ambassador-at-large, ambassador to
NATO and Secretary of the Treasury, has been named special consultant
for diplomatic affairs for the church, the First Presidency announced April
5." This was the first time since Joseph Smith's 1844 theocracy that
Mormonism had an official ambassador to foreign governments, and the
church's official magazine echoed that theocratic context by calling Kennedy "Ambassador for the Kingdom."[218]

In July 1996 there was a dramatic demonstration of the international
impact of the LDS church's influence with the U.S. government. The
"security leader and de facto second in command" of the Russian Republic
publicly apologized a week after he referred to the Mormons in Russia as
"filth and scum." The LDS church has no more than 5,000 converts and
300 missionaries in Russia, but LDS members of the U.S. Senate had
"called on the Clinton administration to reconsider aid to Russia because
of [Alekandr] Lebed's stand."[219]

However, LDS headquarters will certainly make every effort to deny
U.S. direction of political campaigns being conducted by local Mormons
in other nations. This will be necessary to prevent difficulties in acquiring
missionary visas, as well as to avoid anti-American assaults against LDS
missionaries, against non-U.S. Mormons, and against American-looking
chapels.[220]

Then non-U.S. Mormons will face central questions of the LDS
campaigns against the ERA and against same-sex marriages in the United
States. Can a church improve public morality if its leaders and members
engage in ethical compromise during their involvement in the political
arena? Can a church suffer internal, spiritual decline by engaging in such
normative activities of the secular world? And perhaps most significant for
non-U.S. Mormons, can a minority church suffer a popular backlash by
taking actions which affect the political lives of millions of non-members?
Time will tell.

Three months after Joseph Smith organized a church in New York state in 1830, a local Protestant minister predicted that this Mormon "monstrosity" would soon be "given the stamp of oblivion."[1] Smith's refutation of that prophecy was so remarkable that after visiting him in May 1844, Boston's mayor Josiah Quincy reflected: "What historical American of the nineteenth century has exerted the most powerful influence upon the destinies of his countrymen? And it is by no means improbable that the answer to that interrogatory may be thus written: 'Joseph Smith, the Mormon prophet.'"[2] More than a century later a literary critic, Jewish biblical interpreter, and American religious historian wrote: "Whatever account of charisma is accepted, the Mormon prophet possessed that quality to a degree unsurpassed in American history." Harold Bloom added that "Mormonism is as much a separate revelation as ever Judaism, Christianity, and Islam were."[3]

Most people confuse Brigham Young with Mormonism's founder and know too little about Smith to have any opinions of him. Nevertheless, about 5 million Americans today applaud the perceptiveness of Quincy and Bloom. The Mormon prophet is equally revered by one-third of the population of some countries beyond the western hemisphere.

At the close of its second century, Mormons predict that their latter-day movement has just begun to spread. While the faithful have made that claim ever since the organization of their church in 1830, two non-Mormon scholars believe that Mormonism has achieved the critical mass for world-wide significance. American religious historian Jan Shipps has persuasively argued that Joseph Smith formulated far more than just another American sect. Instead, Mormonism is an alternative religious tradition on its way to becoming a world religion that stands in relation to Christianity as Christianity once stood to Judaism.[4] Based on LDS growth rates since 1950 and on a ten-year test that proved to be ahead of his original projection, American sociologist Rodney Stark predicts that Mormonism will have 265 million adherents worldwide before the end of the twenty-first century.[5]

Millions of dedicated believers are worthy of attention. Their movement is of special interest when the faithful follow directions from a centralized leadership whose spiritual domain encompasses the secular world.

My two-volume study has analyzed this Mormon hierarchy institutionally, chronicled it historically, described it biographically, and presented its relationships with outside power structures in both nineteenth and twentieth centuries. Because I believe that Mormonism has been defined

by its epiphanies, its theology, its leadership, and its people, I have tried
to give significant attention to all four. However, I have not given them
equal emphasis because my study reflects Robert Michels's thesis concerning the "Iron Law of Oligarchy." This German sociologist argued that no
matter how democratic and altruistic any movement is at its inception,
"Whoever says organization, says oligarchy."[6] Thus Mormonism became
"a democracy of participation and an oligarchy of decision-making and
command."[7]

Pioneer Utah's First Presidency

Brigham Young,
president (courtesy Utah
State Historical Society)

Heber C. Kimball,
first counselor (courtesy Utah
State Historical Society)

Willard Richards,
second counselor

Jedediah M. Grant,
second counselor (courtesy Utah
State Historical Society)

Daniel H. Wells,
second counselor (courtesy Utah
State Historical Society)

Other Counselors of Brigham Young to 1877

George A. Smith,
first counselor (courtesy Utah
State Historical Society)

John W. Young,
first counselor (courtesy Utah
State Historical Society)

Brigham Young, Jr.,
special counselor (courtesy Utah
State Historical Society)

Joseph A. Young,
special counselor (courtesy
Utah State Historical Society)

Albert Carrington,
special counselor (courtesy
Utah State Historical Society)

Diverse Apostles of Nineteenth-century Utah

Orson Pratt, mathematician

Erastus Snow, colonizer
(courtesy Utah State Historical Society)

Moses Thatcher, businessman
(courtesy Manuscripts Division,
University of Utah Libraries)

John W. Taylor,
"the prophet of the quorum"
(courtesy Utah State Historical Society)

Abraham H. Cannon,
newspaper editor

Patriarchs to the Church, 1855-1979

John Smith (b. 1832)
(courtesy Utah State
Historical Society)

Hyrum G. Smith
(courtesy Utah State
Historical Society)

Joseph F. Smith (b. 1899)
(courtesy Utah State
Historical Society)

Eldred G. Smith
(courtesy Manuscripts Division,
University of Utah Libraries)

Presiding Bishops, 1851-1952

Edward Hunter
(courtesy Utah State
Historical Society)

William B. Preston
(courtesy Utah State
Historical Society)

Charles W. Nibley
(courtesy Utah State
Historical Society)

Sylvester Q. Cannon
(courtesy Utah State
Historical Society)

LeGrand Richards
(courtesy Utah State
Historical Society)

Joseph L. Wirthlin
(courtesy Utah State
Historical Society)

The Mormon Hierarchy and Federal Law, 1886-89

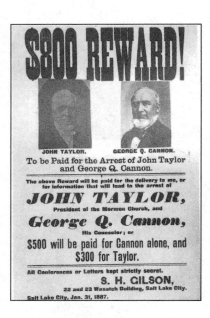

BELOW: Two imprisoned general authorities in 1889: Presidency counselor George Q. Cannon at center with bearded Apostle Francis M. Lyman, holding prison cap. (courtesy Utah State Historical Society)

The First Presidency
and Presidents of Seventy, 1890s

First counselor George Q. Cannon, President Wilford Woodruff, second counselor Joseph F. Smith (courtesy Utah State Historical Society)

Back row: Brigham H. Roberts, J. Golden Kimball, Rulon S. Wells; front row: George Reynolds, Seymour B. Young, Christian D. Fjeldsted, Edward Stevenson (courtesy Sunstone Foundation)

The Mormon Hierarchy Enters
the Twentieth Century

Back row: Apostles Anthon H. Lund, John W. Taylor, John Henry Smith,
Heber J. Grant, Francis M. Lyman, George Teasdale, Marriner W. Merrill;
center row: Apostle Brigham Young, Jr., first counselor George Q. Cannon,
President Lorenzo Snow, second counselor Joseph F. Smith, Apostle Franklin D.
Richards; front row: Apostles Matthias F. Cowley and Abraham Owen Woodruff.
Apostle Rudger Clawson was absent (courtesy Utah State Historical Society)

First counselor John R. Winder, President Joseph F. Smith,
second counselor Anthon H. Lund (courtesy Utah State
Historical Society)

Partisan Apostles in the Early 1900s

Reed Smoot,
Republican and U. S. Senator

Charles W. Penrose,
Democrat (courtesy Utah
State Historical Society)

George F. Richards,
Republican (courtesy Utah
State Historical Society)

Orson F. Whitney,
Democrat (courtesy Utah
State Historical Society)

Anthony W. Ivins,
Democrat (courtesy Utah
State Historical Society)

Presidents and Counselors in the Jazz Age, Great Depression, World War II, and Cold War to 1951

First counselor Anthony W. Ivins, President Heber J. Grant, second counselor Charles W. Nibley (courtesy Utah State Historical Society)

First counselor J. Reuben Clark, President George Albert Smith, second counselor David O. McKay (courtesy Manuscripts Division, University of Utah Libraries)

Activist Apostles, Mid-twentieth Century

Harold B. Lee,
architect of Welfare Plan and
Church Correlation (courtesy Utah
State Historical Society)

Ezra Taft Benson,
U.S. Secretary of Agriculture and
advocate of the John Birch Society

Mark E. Petersen
investigated polygamists,
dissidents, "extremists," and intellectuals
(courtesy Sunstone Foundation).

Richard L. Evans,
announcer for the "Spoken Word
from Temple Square" and president of
Rotary International (courtesy Utah
State Historical Society)

The First Presidency of an International Church

First counselor Stephen L Richards, President David O. McKay,
second counselor J. Reuben Clark (courtesy Utah State Historical Society)

First counselor Henry D. Moyle,
President David O. McKay,
second counselor Hugh B.
Brown (courtesy Utah State
Historical Society)

Thorpe B. Issacson,
special counselor (courtesy
Utah State Historical Society)

Alvin R. Dyer,
special counselor (courtesy
Utah State Historical Society)

Two First Presidencies, 1970-73

Second counselor N. Eldon Tanner, first counselor Harold B. Lee, President Joseph Fielding Smith (courtesy Utah State Historical Society)

First counselor N. Eldon Tanner, second counselor Marion G. Romney, President Harold B. Lee (courtesy Utah State Historical Society)

Outside the Hierarchy,
Inside the President's Office

L. John Nuttall,
secretary and confidant of
John Taylor and Wilford Woodruff
(courtesy Utah State
Historical Society)

George F. Gibbs,
secretary and confidant of
Lorenzo Snow, Joseph F. Smith,
and Heber J. Grant to 1923
(courtesy Utah State
Historical Society)

Joseph Anderson,
secretary and confidant of
Heber J. Grant from 1922 to
1945 (courtesy Utah State
Historical Society)

Emily Smith Stewart,
daughter and unofficial
adviser of George Albert Smith
(courtesy Manuscripts Division,
University of Utah
Libraries)

Clare Middlemiss,
executive secretary to David O.
McKay (courtesy Utah State
Historical Society)

Ernest L. Wilkinson,
BYU president and adviser to
David O. McKay

Joseph Anderson,
senior secretary to
Joseph Fielding Smith
and Harold B. Lee
(courtesy Utah State
Historical Society)

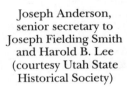

D. Arthur Haycock during his most
influential service as official secretary
to Spencer W. Kimball (courtesy
Utah State Historical Society)

Reed A. Benson, son and unofficial adviser of Ezra Taft Benson. He displaced
Haycock functionally and arranged for
his release (courtesy *Salt Lake Tribune*).

Formulators of LDS Theology, 1892-1992

James E. Talmage, apostle, author of *The Articles of Faith* and *Jesus the Christ* (courtesy Utah State Historical Society)

Joseph Fielding Smith, apostle and church historian, author of *Essentials in Church History, Answers to Gospel Questions* (5 vols.), *Doctrines of Salvation* (4 vols.), and *Man: His Origin and Destiny*

Bruce R. McConkie, seventy and apostle, author of *Mormon Doctrine* and *Doctrinal New Testament Commentary* (courtesy Sunstone Foundation)

Daniel H. Ludlow, former dean, BYU College of Religion; senior member, Correlation Committee; editor, general conference sermons; editor, 1992 *Encyclopedia of Mormonism* (courtesy *The Salt Lake Tribune*)

Three Church Presidents, 1973-95

Spencer W. Kimball
greeting Mormons
(courtesy Sunstone
Foundation)

Ezra Taft Benson
(center) in May 1992
(courtesy *The Salt
Lake Tribune*)

Howard W. Hunter
in October 1994
(courtesy Sunstone
Foundation)

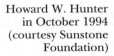

General Authorities, April 1996

THE FIRST PRESIDENCY

First Counselor
Thomas S. Monson

President
Gordon B. Hinckley

Second Counselor
James E. Faust

THE QUORUM OF THE TWELVE

Boyd K. Packer

L. Tom Perry

David B. Haight

Neal A. Maxwell

Russell M. Nelson

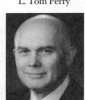

Dallin H. Oaks

M. Russell Ballard

Joseph B. Wirthlin

Richard G. Scott

Robert D. Hales

Jeffrey R. Holland

Henry B. Eyring

THE PRESIDENCY OF THE SEVENTY

Carlos E. Asay

L. Aldin Porter

Joe J. Christensen

Monte J. Brough

W. Eugene Hansen

Jack H. Goaslind

Harold G. Hillam

Quorums of Seventy and Presiding Bishopric, April 1996

FIRST QUORUM OF THE SEVENTY

Angel Abrea	Carlos H. Amado	Neil L. Andersen	Dallas N. Archibald	Ben B. Banks	Merrill J. Bateman	William R. Bradford	F. Enzio Busche	John K. Carmack
D. Todd Christofferson	J. Richard Clarke	Spencer J. Condie	Gene R. Cook	Robert K. Dellenbach	John B. Dickson	Charles Didier	Loren C. Dunn	Vaughn J Featherstone
John H. Groberg	Bruce C. Hafen	F. Melvin Hammond	F. Burton Howard	Jay E. Jensen	Marlin K. Jensen	Kenneth Johnson	L. Lionel Kendrick	Yoshihiko Kikuchi
Cree-L Kofford	Dean L. Larsen	Lynn A. Mickelsen	Alexander B. Morrison	Dennis B. Neuenschwander	Glenn L. Pace	James M. Paramore	Andrew W. Peterson	Rex D. Pinegar
Hugh W. Pinnock	Ronald E. Poelman	Cecil O. Samuelson Jr.	David E. Sorensen	Earl C. Tingey	Dieter F. Uchtdorf	Robert E. Wells	W. Craig Zwick	

SECOND QUORUM OF THE SEVENTY

Lino Alvarez	L. Edward Brown	C. Max Caldwell	Sheldon F. Child	Gary J. Coleman	Quentin L. Cook	Claudio R. M. Costa	Rulon G. Craven	Julio E. Davila
Graham W. Doxey	John E. Fowler	In Sang Han	Wm. Rolfe Kerr	W. Don Ladd	W. Mack Lawrence	Augusto A. Lim	John M. Madsen	James O. Mason
V. Dallas Merrell	Joseph C. Muren	Stephen D. Nadauld	Bruce D. Porter	Jorge A. Rojas	Sam K. Shimabukuro	Dennis E. Simmons	F. David Stanley	Kwok Yuen Tai
Jerald L. Taylor	Francisco J. Vinas	Lance B. Wickman	Richard B. Wirthlin	Lowell D. Wood				

PRESIDING BISHOPRIC

Richard C. Edgley	H. David Burton	Keith B. McMullin

The Halls of Power, 1850 - 1996

Council House, 1850-83
(courtesy Utah State
Historical Society)

Gardo House, 1882-93

Council room of the First
Presidency and Twelve, Salt
Lake Temple, 1893-present

Church Administration
Building, 47 East South
Temple, 1917-present
(courtesy Sunstone
Foundation)

NOTES

Notes to Preface

1. See also D. Michael Quinn, "The Rest Is History," *Sunstone* 18 (Dec. 1995): 50-57.

2. See *Deseret News 1995-1996 Church Almanac* (Salt Lake City: Deseret News, 1994), 14-41, for the Utah birth of the LDS leadership as constituted at the beginning of 1995: 66 percent of the First Presidency, 75 percent of the Quorum of the Twelve Apostles, 71 percent of the Presidency of the Seventy, 67 percent of the Presiding Bishopric, 51 percent of the First Quorum of Seventy (including Cecil O. Samuelson, Jr., whose Utah birth was inadvertently omitted from the almanac), and 36 percent of the Second Quorum of Seventy. From April 1995 to the present, 100 percent of the First Presidency was Utah-born. For these echelons of the Mormon hierarchy, see J. Lynn England and W. Keith Warner, "First Presidency," H. David Burton and William Gibb Dyer, Jr., "Presiding Bishopric," William O. Nelson, "Quorum of the Twelve Apostles," Dean L. Larsen, "Quorums of Seventy," in Daniel H. Ludlow, ed., *Encyclopedia of Mormonism: The History, Scripture, Doctrine, and Procedure of the Church of Jesus Christ of Latter-day Saints*, 5 vols. (New York: Macmillan, 1992), 2:512-13, 3:1128-30, 1185-89, 1303-1305; James B. Allen and Glen M. Leonard, *The Story of the Latter-day Saints*, 2d ed. rev. (Salt Lake City: Deseret Book Co., 1992), 89-91, 179, 213-16, 654-55; Davis Bitton, *Historical Dictionary of Mormonism* (Metuchen, NJ: Scarecrow Press, 1994), 85, 184-85, 210-11, 245-46; D. Michael Quinn, *The Mormon Hierarchy: Origins of Power* (Salt Lake City: Signature Books/Smith Research Associates, 1994), 39-77, 155-80, 246-52; and chaps. 1-2 and 4 of this volume.

3. Bernard Quinn et al., *Churches and Church Membership in the United States, 1980* (Atlanta: Glenmary Research Center, 1982), 10-11, 13-14, 18-21, 23, 25-27; D. Michael Quinn, "Religion in the American West," in William J. Cronon, George Miles, and Jay Gitlin, eds., *Under An Open Sky: Rethinking America's Western Past* (New York: W. W. Norton and Co., 1992), 160.

4. Lowell C. "Ben" Bennion, "The Geographic Dynamics of Mormondom, 1965-95," *Sunstone* 18 (Dec. 1995): 31; also Bennion and Lawrence A. Young, "The Uncertain Dynamics of LDS Expansion, 1950-2020," *Dialogue: A Journal of Mormon Thought* 29 (Spring 1996): 31, as conclusion to a sophisticated analysis (8-30) of LDS population trends and projections throughout the world.

5. While 1.8 percent of the U.S. population is Mormon, Tonga is 37 percent Mormon, Samoa 25 percent, Niue 17 percent, Kiribati 6.5 percent, Tahiti 6.4 percent, Cook Islands or Rarotonga 4.4 percent, Marshall Islands 4.2 percent, Chile 2.6 percent, New Zealand 2.3 percent, Micronesia 2.3 percent, Alberta province, Canada 2.2 percent, Palau 2.2 percent, and Uruguay 1.9 percent. See *Deseret News 1995-1996 Church Almanac*, 108, 192, 207, 216, 220, 231, 251, 256, 262, 265, 268, 292, 298, 302, 414-15, 417; LDS population of 4,719,000 in the United States as of 25 February 1996 in "More Members Now Outside U.S. Than in U.S.," *Ensign* 26 (Mar. 1996): 76-77; U.S. population of 264,349,000 as of 1 March 1996 in Bureau of the Census electronic publication, *Monthly Estimates of the United States Population: April 1, 1980 to June 1, 1996* (http://www.census.gov/population/estimate-extract/nation/intfile1-1.txt).

6. Although most Mormons do not identify the LDS general authorities in this way, "hierarchy" was used by First Presidency secretary Francis M. Gibbons to describe the presiding quorums in his *Heber J. Grant: Man of Steel, Prophet of God* (Salt Lake City: Deseret Book Co., 1979), 101.

7. For the perspective of an assistant church historian during that time, see Davis Bitton, "Ten Years in Camelot: A Personal Memoir," *Dialogue: A Journal of Mormon Thought* 16 (Autumn 1983): 9-35; for the gradual closing of LDS archives, see "Access to Church Archives: Penetrating the Silence," *Sunstone Review,* Sept. 1983, 7; for the significance of these developments as viewed by non-Mormon researchers, see Lawrence Foster, "A Personal Odyssey: My Encounter with Mormon History," *Dialogue: A Journal of Mormon Thought* 16 (Autumn 1983): 87-98; and Jan Shipps, "History as Text," in Shipps, *Mormonism: The Story of A New Religious Tradition* (Urbana: University of Illinois Press, 1985), 41-65.

8. The most articulate and extended expression of those views is Boyd K. Packer, "The Mantle Is Far, Far Greater Than the Intellect," *Brigham Young University Studies* 21 (Summer 1981): 259-78, reprinted in Boyd K. Packer, *Let Not Your Heart Be Troubled* (Salt Lake City: Bookcraft, 1991), 101-22.

9. "Apostles vs. Historians," *Newsweek* 99 (15 Feb. 1982): 77; "The World Is His Campus," *Sunstone* 12 (Jan. 1988):45; "LDS Church Turns Up Heat In Feud With Intellectuals," *Salt Lake Tribune,* 5 Oct. 1991, A-6, A-7; "Despite Growth, Mormons Find New Hurdles," *New York Times,* 15 Sept. 1991, 1; "Latter-day Skeptics: Liberal, yet loyal Mormon scholars are bringing long-kept secrets about Joseph Smith into the open," *Christianity Today* 35 (11 Nov. 1991): 30; "Professors' Freedom Questioned," *Brigham Young University Daily Universe,* 21 Nov. 1991, 1; "Editor's Introduction," in D. Michael Quinn, ed., *The New Mormon History: Revisionist Essays on the Past* (Salt Lake City: Signature Books, 1992), vii-xx; Quinn, "On Being a Mormon Historian (And Its Aftermath)," in George D. Smith, ed., *Faithful History: Essays on Writing Mormon History* (Salt Lake City: Signature Books, 1992), 69-111; "Historian: LDS Church Wants 'Cookie-Cutter' Members," *Salt Lake Tribune,* 6 Dec. 1992, C-3; "Apostasy Investigation Launched Against Historian," *Salt Lake Tribune,* 13 Feb. 1993, A-6, A-7; "Mormons Investigating Him, Critic Says," *Los Angeles Times,* 13 Feb. 1993, B-4, B-5; "Michael Quinn Investigated for Apostasy," *Sunstone* 16 (Mar. 1993): 69; "Historian Assails LDS Research Barriers: Quinn Contends 'Golden Age' of Access to Data By Scholars Has Come and Gone," *Standard-Examiner* (Ogden, UT), 15 May 1993, C-2; "Six Facing Censure Accuse Mormon Church of Purge," *Los Angeles Times,* 18 Sept. 1993, B-5; "Mormons Penalize Dissident Members: 6 Who Criticized Leaders or Debated Doctrine Await Sanctions by Church," *New York Times,* 19 Sept. 1993, 31; "Tempo Di Purghe Tra i Mormoni," *Correriere Della Serra,* 21 Sept. 1993, 9; "As Mormon Church Grows, So Does Dissent From Feminists and Scholars," *New York Times,* 2 Oct. 1993, 7; "'Loyal Opposition' Died Slow Death in 20th Century," *Salt Lake Tribune,* 16 Oct. 1993, B-3; "Hostile Bountiful Call Goes To the Wrong Man," *Deseret News,* 18 Oct. 1993, B-1; "Elders Banishing Dissidents In Struggle Over Mormon Practices," *Washington Post,* 26 Nov. 1993, A-3; "By the Book: Mormon Leaders Have Doggedly Fought Recent Attempts To Reinterpret Official Church History and Liberalize Its Doctrine," *Vancouver Sun,* 4 Dec. 1993, D-13; "Ex-Mormon Warns LDS Historians To Be Wary," *University of Utah Daily Utah Chronicle,* 9 Dec. 1993, 1; "Mormon Church Ousts Dissidents," *Los Angeles Times,* 30 Dec. 1993, E-2; "SUU Cancels Excommunicated LDS Historian's Talk," *Daily Spectrum* (Cedar City, UT), 6 Jan. 1994, A-3; "Historian To Speak On LDS Issues After All: Private, Faculty Funds Will Bring Quinn to SUU and Snow College," *Salt Lake Tribune,* 1 Mar. 1994, D-5; "Mormon Church Excommunicates Five Scholars Over Their Books," *Publishers Weekly* 241 (25 Apr. 1994): 12; Quinn, "Dilemmas of Feminists and Intellectuals in the Contemporary LDS Church," *Sunstone* 17 (June 1994): 67-73; "Losing His Religion," *Washington City Newspaper,* 15 July 1994, 30, 31-32; "Excommunicated Mormon Offers Statement of Faith," *Daily Herald* (Provo, UT), 20 Aug. 1994, A-3; "Those Disciplined Watch Their Families Feel Pressure," *Salt Lake*

Tribune, 16 Sept. 1995, D-2; Quinn, "Pillars of My Faith: The Rest Is History," *Sunstone* 18 (Dec. 1995): 50-57.

10. Sheri L. Dew, *Go Forward With Faith: The Biography of Gordon B. Hinckley* (Salt Lake City: Deseret Book Co., 1996), 391.

Notes to Chapter One

1. Edward L. Kimball and Andrew E. Kimball, Jr., *Spencer W. Kimball: Twelfth President of The Church of Jesus Christ of Latter-day Saints* (Salt Lake City: Bookcraft, 1977), 344.

2. D. Michael Quinn, *The Mormon Hierarchy: Origins of Power* (Salt Lake City: Signature Books/Smith Research Associates, 1994), 10-12. Unless otherwise indicated, consult either the above volume or the present volume for biographical sketches of the general authorities specifically named throughout this chapter.

For LDS general authorities customarily identified as either "President" or "Elder," I sometimes precede their names with their specific office in the hierarchy. This is not intended to be disrespectful of LDS protocol but to be helpful to readers who may not be readily acquainted with the church offices held by dozens of men cited in this study. See Russell M. Nelson, "Honoring the Priesthood," *Ensign* 23 (May 1993): 38; "Forms of Address," in Davis Bitton, *Historical Dictionary of Mormonism* (Metuchen, NJ: Scarecrow Press, 1994), 87-88.

3. Joseph Smith et al., *History of The Church of Jesus Christ of Latter-day Saints. Period I: History of Joseph Smith the Prophet, and . . . Period II: From the Manuscript History of Brigham Young and Other Original Documents,* ed. B. H. Roberts, 7 vols. (Salt Lake City: Church of Jesus Christ of Latter-day Saints, 1902-32; 2d ed. rev. [Salt Lake City: Deseret Book Co., 1978]), 2:195 (hereafter *History of the Church*).

4. Abraham H. Cannon diary, 7 Oct. 1889, copies at Department of Special Collections and Manuscripts, Harold B. Lee Library, Brigham Young University, Provo, Utah (hereafter Lee Library); at Manuscripts Division, J. Willard Marriott Library, University of Utah, Salt Lake City (hereafter Marriott Library); and at Utah State Historical Society, Salt Lake City.

5. Brigham Young, Jr., diary, 6 Aug. 1890, archives, Historical Department, Church of Jesus Christ of Latter-day Saints, Salt Lake City, Utah (hereafter LDS archives). It is possible that Snow was referring to the Second Coming of Christ, but his words were consistent with his emphasis a year before on the apostolic responsibility to see Jesus in vision or actual appearance.

6. Orson Pratt expressed this frustration in Scott G. Kenney, ed., *Wilford Woodruff's Journal: 1833-1898 Typescript,* 9 vols. (Murray, UT: Signature Books, 1983-85), 5 (6 Feb. 1859): 285, and spoke of it publicly in *Journal of Discourses,* 26 vols. (London and Liverpool: Latter-day Saints' Book Depot, 1854-86), 8:313 (O. Pratt/1860). Wilford Woodruff also referred to Pratt's inability to have a vision in Anthon H. Lund diary, 19 Apr. 1893, microfilm, LDS archives. Heber J. Grant expressed similar frustration in his journal, 30 May 1890, LDS archives. The Lund diary microfilm is available to all researchers at LDS archives by stipulation of its donor. Also, while "diary" is the standardized term I use to identify personal documents with daily entries, Grant kept several different kinds of such records, which must be identified separately in order to locate the quotations.

7. Francis M. Lyman to Joseph F. Smith, 17 Apr. 1888, my reconstruction of abbreviated transcription, fd 7, box 6, Scott G. Kenney papers, Marriott Library.

8. Reed Smoot ordination, 9 Apr. 1900, photocopy of original transcription, fd 1, box 7, Kenney papers.

9. Rudger Clawson diary, 8 Oct. 1903, in Stan Larson, ed., *A Ministry of Meetings: The Apostolic Diaries of Rudger Clawson* (Salt Lake City: Signature Books/Smith Research Associates, 1992), 664; George F. Richards diary, 6 Oct. 1907, LDS archives.

10. Lucile C. Tate, *Boyd K. Packer: A Watchman on the Tower* (Salt Lake City: Bookcraft, 1995), 179; *Deseret News 1995-1996 Church Almanac* (Salt Lake City: Deseret News, 1994), 17, for Packer.

11. *Journal of Discourses* 8: 234 (Hyde/1860); Abraham H. Cannon diary, 30 Aug. 1894; also other examples of Hyde claiming a charismatic exprience he did not have in Richard S. Van Wagoner, *Sidney Rigdon: A Portrait of Religious Excess* (Salt Lake City: Signature Books, 1994), 343, 350n98; Quinn, *Mormon Hierarchy: Origins of Power,* 393n117.

12. Francis M. Gibbons, *Heber J. Grant: Man of Steel, Prophet of God* (Salt Lake City: Deseret Book Co., 1979), 54; also Heber J. Grant to Don Carlos Young, quoted in L. Brent Goates, *Harold B. Lee: Prophet & Seer* (Salt Lake City: Bookcraft, 1985), 495.

13. Heber J. Grant 1889-1890 letterbook-journal, 382 (30 May 1890); Ronald W. Walker, "Heber J. Grant," in Leonard J. Arrington, ed., *The Presidents of the Church: Biographical Essays* (Salt Lake City: Deseret Book Co., 1986), 233.

14. Lynn Packer, "Paul H. Dunn: Fields of Dreams," *Sunstone* 15 (Sept. 1991): 35-44; *Deseret News "Church News,"* 26 Oct. 1991; "Elder Dunn Apologizes For Inaccuracies," *Sunstone* 15 (Nov. 1991): 60; *Deseret News 1995-1996 Church Almanac,* 65, for Dunn.

15. Edwin B. Firmage, ed., *An Abundant Life: The Memoirs of Hugh B. Brown* (Salt Lake City: Signature Books, 1988), 126-27; *Deseret News 1995-1996 Church Almanac,* 46, for Brown.

16. Eleanor Knowles, *Howard W. Hunter* (Salt Lake City: Deseret Book Co., 1994), 147; *Deseret News 1995-1996 Church Almanac,* 14, for Hunter.

17. Heber J. Grant journal sheets, 4 Oct. 1942, also 15 Mar. 1921. In support of this view Grant privately cited the problems of apostles he had once envied for their visions— Moses Thatcher, John W. Taylor, Marriner W. Merrill, and Abraham Owen Woodruff. See their biographical sketches in this study.

18. Heber J. Grant to Mrs. Claud Peery, 13 Apr. 1926, First Presidency letterbooks, vol. 72, LDS archives.

19. J. Reuben Clark's sacrament meeting talk, 23 Sept. 1928; J. Reuben Clark to W. D. LeCheminant, 19 Feb. 1946; Clark to Ira C. Fletcher, 15 Apr. 1949; Clark to Mrs. Francis Huntington-Wilson, 29 Mar. 1947; Clark to Cloyd H. Marvin, 2 Aug. 1957, Clark papers, Lee Library; *Deseret News 1995-1996 Church Almanac,* 46, for Clark.

20. Clare Middlemiss, comp., *Cherished Experiences From the Writings of David O. McKay* (Salt Lake City: Deseret Book Co., 1955), 14, 16, 18, 67, 73-78, 101-102, 145, 155, 161-63.

21. Allen E. Bergin, "Visions," in Daniel H. Ludlow, ed., *Encyclopedia of Mormonism: The History, Scripture, Doctrine, and Procedure of the Church of Jesus Christ of Latter-day Saints,* 5 vols. (New York: Macmillan Publishing Co., 1992), 4:1511. The *Encyclopedia of Mormonism* is an official product of the LDS church, not an independent work of scholars. At the outset it expresses gratitude (lxiii) to "the General Authorities of the Church for designating Brigham Young University (BYU) as the contractual Author of the *Encyclopedia.*" LDS apostles Neal A. Maxwell and Dallin H. Oaks supervised the endeavor with "special assignments" by four other general authorities. Despite an insistence that the encyclopedia's "contents do not necessarily represent the official position of The Church of Jesus Christ of Latter-day Saints," the church hierarchy had ultimate control over the project and final revision of its contents.

22. Joseph Fielding Smith, *Doctrines of Salvation: Sermons and Writings of Joseph Fielding Smith,* ed. Bruce R. McConkie, 3 vols. (Salt Lake City: Deseret Book Co., 1955), 3:153.

23. Francis M. Gibbons, *Joseph Fielding Smith: Gospel Scholar, Prophet of God* (Salt Lake City: Deseret Book Co., 1992), 152.

24. Milton V. Backman, Jr., *The Heavens Resound: A History of the Latter-day Saints in Ohio, 1380-1838* (Salt Lake City: Deseret Book Co., 1983), 250.

25. *Ensign* 14 (May 1984): 51; *Deseret News 1995-1996 Church Almanac,* 15, for Hinckley.

26. William O. Nelson, "Quorum of the Twelve Apostles," in Ludlow, *Encyclopedia of Mormonism,* 3:1185-89 (esp. 1189), also S. Kent Brown, "Apostle," in 1:59-61.

27. *Deseret News Weekly* 53 (31 Oct. 1896): 610; Jerreld L. Newquist, ed., *Gospel Truth: Discourses and Writings of George Q. Cannon,* 2 vols. (Salt Lake City: Deseret Book Co., 1974), 1:vi.

28. LeRoi C. Snow, "An Experience of My Father's," *Improvement Era* 36 (Sept. 1933): 677.

29. F. Burton Howard, *Marion G. Romney: His Life and Faith* (Salt Lake City: Bookcraft, 1988), 222; *Deseret News 1995-1996 Church Almanac,* 47, for Romney.

30. Sermon of David B. Haight in *Ensign* 19 (Nov. 1989): 59-60; *Deseret News 1995-1996 Church Almanac,* 17, for Haight.

31. Tate, *Boyd K. Packer,* 178.

32. G. Homer Durham et al., *N. Eldon Tanner: His Life and Service* (Salt Lake City: Deseret Book Co., 1982), 255-56.

33. Orson F. Whitney's dream of Christ in Andrew Jenson, *Latter-day Saint Biographical Encyclopedia,* 4 vols. (Salt Lake City: Andrew Jenson History Co. and Deseret News, 1901-36), 1:676 (should be 660); George F. Richards diary, 22 Mar., 26 July 1906; Bryant S. Hinckley, *Sermons and Missionary Services of Melvin J. Ballard* (Salt Lake City: Deseret Book Co., 1949), 156; Middlemiss, *Cherished Experiences From the Writings of David O. McKay,* 101-102; David B. Haight in *Ensign* 19 (Nov. 1989): 59-60.

34. Lucile C. Tate, *David B. Haight: The Life Story of A Disciple* (Salt Lake City: Bookcraft, 1987), 278; Sheri L. Dew, *Go Forward With Faith: The Biography of Gordon B. Hinckley* (Salt Lake City: Deseret Book Co., 1996), 303. See Perry H. Cunningham, "Area, Area Presidency," Douglas L. Callister and Gerald J. Day, "Region, Regional Representative," and Stan L. Albrecht, "Stake," *Encyclopedia of Mormonism,* 1:65-66, 3:1198, 1411-14; Bitton, *Historical Dictionary of Mormonism,* 26, 231-32.

35. *The Doctrine and Covenants of The Church of Jesus Christ of Latter-day Saints,* published at Salt Lake City in various editions, sec. 107:27, 30-31, hereafter cited in the text as D&C with numbers of section and verse(s).

36. Sheri L. Dew, *Ezra Taft Benson: A Biography* (Salt Lake City: Deseret Book Co., 1987), 190; also George S. Tate, "Prayer Circle," in Ludlow, *Encyclopedia of Mormonism,* 3:1120-21.

37. *April 1940 Conference Report* . . . (Salt Lake City: Church of Jesus Christ of Latter-day Saints, 1940), 14. The church's centennial history specifically denied that general authorities "are without faults or infallible" (B. H. Roberts, *Comprehensive History of the Church* . . . , 6 vols. [Salt Lake City: Church of Jesus Christ of Latter-day Saints, 1930], 1:viii).

38. Tate, *Boyd K. Packer,* 240.

39. Joseph Fielding Smith, *Life of Joseph F. Smith* . . . (Salt Lake City: Deseret News Press, 1938), 310-11; Francis M. Gibbons, *Joseph F. Smith: Patriarch and Preacher, Prophet of God* (Salt Lake City: Deseret Book, 1984), 205; Reed C. Durham, Jr., and Steven H. Heath, *Succession in the Church* (Salt Lake City, Utah: Deseret Book Co., 1970), 115.

40. Joseph F. Smith diary, 29 Nov. 1880, LDS archives, with transcriptions in Kenney papers.

41. Dew, *Ezra Taft Benson,* 190; Kimball and Kimball, *Spencer W. Kimball,* 207.

42. Gibbons, *Heber J. Grant,* 59; also Gibbons, *Joseph Fielding Smith,* 165.

43. Rudger Clawson diary, 7 Jan. 1904, in Larson, *A Ministry of Meetings,* 695; my interview on 1 Mar. 1980 with A. Hamer Reiser, former assistant secretary in the First Presidency's office; Lavina Fielding Anderson, "Leaders and Members: Messages from the *General Handbook of Instructions,*" *Dialogue: A Journal of Mormon Thought* 28 (Winter 1995): 154.

44. Russell M. Nelson, "Honoring the Priesthood," *Ensign* 23 (May 1993): 38, 40; *Deseret News 1995-1996 Church Almanac,* 18, for Nelson.

45. My interviews on 29-30 Aug. 1992 with Alan Blodgett, managing director of the LDS church financial department from 1969 to 1980 and managing director of the LDS church investment department from 1980 to 1985. Blodgett attended some joint meetings of the First Presidency and Quorum of the Twelve Apostles in the Salt Lake temple. For earlier examples of the apostles speaking about an agenda item in order of seniority, beginning with the most senior apostle, see L. John Nuttall diary, 5 Apr. 1889, copies at Lee Library, at Marriott Library, and at Henry E. Huntington Library, San Marino, California; Abraham H. Cannon diary, 5-6 Aug. 1890; minutes of the Quorum of the Twelve Apostles, 5 Jan. 1904, 13 Mar. 1941, LDS archives.

46. Charles M. Brown interview, 7 June 1973, page c-3-12, fd 25, box 48, Richard Douglas Poll papers, Marriott Library.

47. Howard, *Marion G. Romney,* 160.

48. Richard D. Poll, "Henry D. Moyle: Man of Action," unpublished 1983 biography, fd 16, box 67, chapter, "Missionary Apostle," 5, Poll papers; Dew, *Go Forward With Faith,* 302.

49. Dew, *Ezra Taft Benson,* 429-30; *Deseret News 1995-1996 Church Almanac,* 44, for Benson.

50. Quinn, *Mormon Hierarchy: Origins of Power,* 256-58, for extensive discussion of this situation; *Deseret News 1995-1996 Church Almanac,* 43, for Lee. He once explained that at the death of the president, "by revelation" the Quorum of Twelve "could choose any member of the Twelve if so directed by the Lord, to preside over a new First Presidency." See Goates, *Harold B. Lee,* 457, also 403-404 for the January 1970 situation.

51. Minutes of the Quorum of the Twelve Apostles, 17 Jan. 1842; *History of the Church,* 4:494.

52. Gibbons, *David O. McKay,* 405. Appointed a general authority in 1989, Francis M. Gibbons was secretary to the First Presidency for sixteen years. See *Deseret News 1991-1992 Church Almanac* (Salt Lake City: Deseret News, 1990), 30.

53. Ernest L. Wilkinson diary, 4 Feb. 1960, photocopy, Marriott Library.

54. Ibid., 11 Oct. 1963; D. Michael Quinn, *J. Reuben Clark: The Church Years* (Provo, UT: Brigham Young University Press, 1983), 45, 116; Durham, *N. Eldon Tanner,* 230-31, 303-304; *Deseret News 1995-1996 Church Almanac,* 46-47, for Clark and Tanner.

55. Heber J. Grant journal sheets, 12-17 Sept. 1942; Irene M. Bates and E. Gary Smith, *Lost Legacy: The Mormon Office of Presiding Patriarch* (Urbana: University of Illinois Press, 1996), 190.

56. My interview, 29 Sept. 1991, with a knowledgeable source who was at LDS headquarters in 1980, name withheld by request; *Deseret News 1995-1996 Church Almanac,* 55, 56, for Petersen and McConkie. See also chap. 10 for the Equal Rights Amendment campaign.

57. Ernest L. Wilkinson diary, 8 June 1955.

58. This is the one technique of decision-making acknowledged by Nelson, "Quorum of the Twelve Apostles," in Ludlow, *Encyclopedia of Mormonism,* 3:1189.

59. Heber J. Grant journal sheets, 12 Aug. 1887.

60. George Q. Cannon 1864-65 diary, 5 Nov. 1865, LDS archives; *Journal of Discourses* 11:290 (B. Young/1867).

61. My interviews, 29-30 Aug. 1992, with Alan Blodgett.

62. Knowles, *Howard W. Hunter,* 231.

63. J. Reuben Clark office diary, 11 Feb. 1944, Clark papers.

64. Quinn, *J. Reuben Clark,* 141.

65. Kimball and Kimball, *Spencer W. Kimball,* 377-78; *Deseret News 1995-1996 Church Almanac,* 44, for Kimball.

66. Henry D. Taylor, *Autobiography of Henry Dixon Taylor* (Provo, UT: Brigham Young University Press, 1980), 248, for McKay's words, 261, for Taylor's 1959 appointment as managing director; Goates, *Harold B. Lee*, 327-29, for Lee's concerns about McKay's attitude toward Welfare Program; Francis M. Gibbons, *Harold B. Lee: Man of Vision, Prophet of God* (Salt Lake City: Deseret Book Co., 1993), 159, for Lee's "combativeness."

67. Dew, *Ezra Taft Benson*, 430.

68. Harold B. Lee diary, 22 Apr. 1955, LDS archives.

69. Willard Richards diary, 27 Apr. 1846, LDS archives.

70. Heber J. Grant letterbook-journal, 21 Sept. 1887.

71. David O. McKay personal diary, 30 Jan. 1907, LDS archives.

72. J. Golden Kimball diary, 2 Aug. 1902, Marriott Library.

73. Abraham Owen Woodruff diary, 11 Jan. 1900, 6 Feb. 1902, Lee Library

74. J. Golden Kimball diary, 20 Apr. 1904.

75. LeGrand Richards to Ernest L. Wilkinson, 27 Dec. 1967, Wilkinson papers, Lee Library, with photocopy in my possession; *Deseret News 1995-1996 Church Almanac*, 56, for Richards; also Quinn, *J. Reuben Clark*, 48. In an untranscribed portion of his 1974 tape-recorded oral history (in LDS archives), Richards repeated this statement and added that he knew he would have to answer to God for compromising His will.

76. *New York Times*, 7 June 1963, 17; 13 Nov. 1969, 35.

77. Quoted in Eugene Campbell's typed draft of Hugh B. Brown biography, chapter titled, "Responsibility Without Authority—The 1st Counselor Years," 6, Campbell papers, Lee Library; Goates, *Harold B. Lee*, 378; Gibbons, *Harold B. Lee*, 417.

78. "Pres. Wilkinson Refutes Charge of Stanford," *Deseret News "Church News,"* 29 Nov 1969, 7; "Stanford Chief Explains BYU Action," *Salt Lake Tribune*, 18 Dec. 1969, B-12; Lester Kinsolving, "An Inconsistency? Stanford and the Mormons," *San Francisco Chronicle*, 20 Dec. 1969; "Wilkinson Claims Stanford Failed to Check Facts," *Salt Lake Tribune*, 23 Dec. 1969, 21; "LDS Leader Says Curb On Priesthood to Ease," *Salt Lake Tribune*, 25 Dec. 1969, D-4. For the LDS church's policy toward those of black African ancestry, see Dennis L. Lythgoe, "Negro Slavery in Utah," *Utah Historical Quarterly* 39 (Winter 1971): 40-54; Margaret Judy Maag, "Discrimination Against the Negro in Utah and Institutional Efforts to Eliminate It," M.S. thesis, University of Utah, 1971; Douglas Monty Trank, "A Rhetorical Analysis of the Rhetoric Emerging From the Mormon-Black Controversy," Ph.D. diss., University of Utah, 1973; Lester E. Bush, Jr., "Mormonism's Negro Doctrine: An Historical Overview," *Dialogue: A Journal of Mormon Thought* 8 (Spring 1973): 11-68; Ronald Gerald Coleman, "A History of Blacks in Utah, 1825-1910," Ph.D. diss., University of Utah, 1980; Lester Bush, Jr., and Armand Mauss, eds., *Neither White Nor Black: Mormon Scholars Confront the Race Issue in a Universal Church* (Salt Lake City: Signature Books, 1984).

79. Ernest L. Wilkinson memorandum, 3 Dec. 1969, in his diary; Edwin B. Firmage, ed., *An Abundant Life: The Memoirs of Hugh B. Brown* (Salt Lake City: Signature Books, 1988), 142.

80. Ernest L. Wilkinson diary, 3 Mar. 1965.

81. Firmage, *An Abundant Life*, 142; Goates, *Harold B. Lee*, 279-80; Dew, *Go Forward With Faith*, 295-96, which claims (without any support in source-notes) that the committee began drafting this document in October 1969; Hugh B. Brown and N. Eldon Tanner, "To General Authorities, Regional Representatives of the Twelve, Stake Presidents, Mission Presidents, and Bishops," 15 Dec. 1969 in *Priesthood Bulletin* 6 (Feb. 1970): 1-5, copy in fd 1, box 51, Poll papers; *Deseret News 1995-1996 Church Almanac*, 15, 18, 66, for Hinckley, Maxwell, and Durham.

82. Kinsolving, "An Inconsistency?"; "LDS Leader Says Curb On Priesthood to Ease," *Salt Lake Tribune*, 25 Dec. 1969; Ernest L. Wilkinson memorandum, 27 Dec. 1969, Wilkinson diary; Goates, *Harold B. Lee*, 618; Gibbons, *Harold B. Lee*, 493.

83. Goates, *Harold B. Lee*, 380; *Deseret News Church Section*, 10 Jan. 1970, 12. Goates claims the statement was "signed by all members of the First Presidency," but the manuscript and published versions bear only the signatures of first counselor Hugh B. Brown and second counselor N. Eldon Tanner. Missing from the reaffirmation on 15 December 1969 are the signatures of church president David O. McKay and assistant counselors Joseph Fielding Smith, Thorpe B. Isaacson, and Alvin R. Dyer. For the congregational meaning of LDS ward, see Bitton, *Historical Dictionary of Mormonism*, 251.

84. Gibbons, *Harold B. Lee*, 418, cited the *Salt Lake Tribune* of 1 Jan. 1970, but I could find no such statement in that newspaper from 1-18 January. Unless I overlooked it there, the statement probably appeared in the San Francisco newspaper that Gibbons also cited.

85. Goates, *Harold B. Lee*, 465, also 404 for Lee's administrative supremacy as first counselor.

86. Edward L. Kimball, ed., *The Teachings of Spencer W. Kimball* . . . (Salt Lake City: Bookcraft, 1982), 449-52; *Deseret News 1995-1996 Church Almanac*, 389; Alan Cherry and Jessie L. Embry, "Blacks," Warner, "Council of the First Presidency and the Quorum of the Twelve Apostles," Edward L. Kimball, "Spencer W. Kimball," in Ludlow, *Encyclopedia of Mormonism*, 1:126, 327, 2:789.

87. Kimball and Kimball, *Spencer W. Kimball*, 349.

88. Francis M. Gibbons, *Spencer W. Kimball: Resolute Disciple, Prophet of God* (Salt Lake City: Deseret Book Co., 1995), 293; and for dating this conversation, "Pres. Kimball to Place Brazil Temple Cornerstone," *Deseret News "Church News,"* 5 Mar. 1977, 4.

89. Spencer W. Kimball, N. Eldon Tanner, and Marion G. Romney to "Stake and Mission Presidents, District Presidents, Bishops, and Branch Presidents," 22 Feb. 1978, circular letter, LDS archives, photocopy in my possession, received from a local LDS leader.

90. Gibbons, *Spencer W. Kimball*, 293-94; Tate, *David B. Haight*, 279; also Knowles, *Howard W. Hunter*, 235: "Prior to the day the [1 June 1978] revelation was received, President Kimball talked at length over a period of several months, with the members of the First Presidency and the Quorum of the Twelve as a group and individually."

91. Gibbons, *Spencer W. Kimball*, 294-95.

92. Bruce R. McConkie, "The New Revelation," in *Priesthood* (Salt Lake City: Deseret Book Co., 1981), 128; Tate, *David B. Haight*, 280; Dew, *Go Forward With Faith*, 362; also Ezra Taft Benson diary, 1 June 1978, in Dew, *Ezra Taft Benson*, 457: "We took each other in our arms, we were so impressed with the sweet spirit that was in evidence. Our bosoms burned with the righteousness of the decision we had made."

93. Gibbons, *Spencer W. Kimball*, 295; Tate, *Boyd K. Packer*, 226.

94. Gibbons, *Spencer W. Kimball*, 295; Taylor, *Autobiography of Henry Dixon Taylor*, 386.

95. Gibbons, *Spencer W. Kimball*, 297. It is not clear from his phrasing whether he intended those words to apply to Mormons generally or to the hierarchy specifically, but the hierarchy would be included if Gibbons intended the phrase to refer to Mormons generally.

96. Kenney, *Wilford Woodruff's Journal* 8 (23 Mar. 1888): 491; Thomas G. Alexander, *Things in Heaven and Earth: The Life and Times of Wilford Woodruff, a Mormon Prophet* (Salt Lake City: Signature Books, 1991), 244.

97. J. Golden Kimball diary, 24 Nov. 1897.

98. J. Reuben Clark office diary, 10 July 1939; Quinn, *J. Reuben Clark*, 47.

99. J. Golden Kimball diary, 22 Oct. 1897.

100. Seymour B. Young diary, 7 Jan. 1903, LDS archives.

101. Francis M. Lyman diary, 29 Dec. 1893, LDS archives.

102. Benson Y. Parkinson, *S. Dilworth Young: General Authority, Scouter, Poet* (American Fork, UT: Covenant Communications, 1994), 297; *Deseret News 1995-1996 Church Almanac*, 68, for Young.

103. Kimball and Kimball, *Spencer W. Kimball,* 228.

104. Henry D. Moyle diary, 23 Oct., 4 Dec. 1952, LDS archives; Evelyn T. Marshall, "Garments," in Ludlow, *Encyclopedia of Mormonism,* 1:534; *Deseret News 1995-1996 Church Almanac,* 46, for Moyle.

105. Gibbons, *Harold B. Lee,* 348; Goates, *Harold B. Lee,* 329.

106. Abraham Owen Woodruff diary, 25 Jan. 1900.

107. Ernest L. Wilkinson diary, 9 Jan. 1960; Quinn, *J. Reuben Clark,* 141.

108. Quinn, *J. Reuben Clark,* 128.

109. John Henry Smith diary, 4 Jan. 1882, in Jean Bickmore White, ed., *Church, State, and Politics: The Diaries of John Henry Smith* (Salt Lake City: Signature Books/Smith Research Associates, 1991), 70.

110. Anthon H. Lund diary, 30 Dec. 1899.

111. Abraham Owen Woodruff diary, 30 Dec. 1899.

112. George F. Richards diary, 23 Dec. 1908.

113. Quinn, *Mormon Hierarchy: Origins of Power,* 247-50.

114. Ernest L. Wilkinson diary, 17 Apr. 1960; Quinn, *J. Reuben Clark,* 48.

115. Joseph F. Smith diary, 10 Nov. 1880.

116. Brigham Young, Jr., diary, 31 July, 1 Aug., 1896.

117. Anthon H. Lund diary, 8 Aug. 1917.

118. J. Reuben Clark office diary, 12-13 Sept. 1933; Quinn, *J. Reuben Clark,* 68.

119. Hugh B. Brown interview, 30 Nov. 1969, side 2 transcription, 8, 14, box 3, Edwin B. Firmage papers, Marriott Library; *Deseret News 1995-1996 Church Almanac,* 49-50, for Isaacson and Dyer.

120. Goates, *Harold B. Lee,* 383; Ernest L. Wilkinson diary, 3 July 1963, for an abstention by Boyd K. Packer, with Lee's abstentions on 7 June 1967, 3 Jan. 1968, and 4 Sept. 1969.

121. Ernest L. Wilkinson diary, 27 May 1971.

122. John Henry Smith diary, 21 May 1896, in White, *Church, State, and Politics,* 350.

123. Franklin D. Richards diary, 16 Dec. 1898, emphasis in original, LDS archives.

124. Gibbons, *Harold B. Lee,* 252; also Goates, *Harold B. Lee,* 365, 366 for 1948 dating.

125. Ernest L. Wilkinson diary, 27 June 1963.

126. Tate, *Boyd K. Packer,* 161, 262, 264. In contrast to these statements by fellow apostles in Elder Packer's authorized biography, President Gordon B. Hinckley told his official biographer: "There was never animosity in the council" (Dew, *Go Forward With Faith,* 302).

127. Related to the author by a member of the Quorum of the Seventy in February 1982, name withheld by request. I described this conversation in "On Being a Mormon Historian (and Its Aftermath)," in George D. Smith, ed., *Faithful History: Essays on Writing Mormon History* (Salt Lake City: Signature Books, 1992), 89-90.

128. Howard W. Hunter statement to the author, July 1983; Quinn, "On Being a Mormon Historian (And Its Aftermath)," 109n54; Knowles, *Howard W. Hunter,* 176.

129. "Cartoonist Says Oaks Lied To Protect Fellow Apostle," *Salt Lake Tribune,* 12 Oct. 1993, B-1. There was no reference to the "grizzly bear quote" in the clarifications and denials by Dallin H. Oaks in "I've Been a Victim of Double-Decker Deceit," *Salt Lake Tribune,* 21 Oct. 1993, A-19, reprinted with new material in *Sunstone* 16 (Dec. 1993): 68-69; also *Deseret News 1995-1996 Church Almanac,* 19, for Oaks.

130. Tate, *Boyd K. Packer,* 243.

131. Firmage, *An Abundant Life,* 125.

132. Gibbons, *David O. McKay,* 405.

Notes to Chapter Two

1. Paul Bailey, *The Armies of God* (New York: Doubleday and Co., 1968), 33-34. Unless otherwise indicated, consult either D. Michael Quinn, *The Mormon Hierarchy: Origins of Power* (Salt Lake City: Signature Books/Smith Research Associates, 1994), or the present volume for biographical sketches of the general authorities specifically named throughout this chapter.

2. Dean C. Jessee, ed., "The John Taylor Nauvoo Journal: January 1845-September 1845," *Brigham Young University Studies* 23 (Summer 1983): 78 (13 July 1845).

3. Sheri L. Dew, *Ezra Taft Benson: A Biography* (Salt Lake City: Deseret Book Co., 1987), 191; *Deseret News 1995-1996 Church Almanac* (Salt Lake City: Deseret News, 1994), 44, and chap. 3, for Benson.

4. Eleanor Knowles, *Howard W. Hunter* (Salt Lake City: Deseret Book Co., 1994), 226; *Deseret News 1995-1996 Church Almanac,* 14, for Hunter.

5. The most extensive argument for such an approach is Boyd K. Packer, "The Mantle is Far, Far Greater than the Intellect," *Brigham Young University Studies* 21 (Summer 1981): 259-78, reprinted in Packer, *Let Not Your Heart Be Troubled* (Salt Lake City: Bookcraft, 1991), 101-22.

6. In Daniel H. Ludlow, ed., *Encyclopedia of Mormonism: The History, Scripture, Doctrine, and Procedure of the Church of Jesus Christ of Latter-day Saints,* 5 vols. (New York: Macmillan Publishing Co., 1992), there is no article or even an index citation for decisions, decision-making, or any of their synonyms. There is no discussion of deliberative processes in most of the relevant articles, and W. Keith Warner, "Council of the First Presidency and the Quorum of the Twelve Apostles" (1:327), says: "The order and procedure of the Council are rarely discussed in public, but can be inferred . . ." William O. Nelson, "Quorum of the Twelve Apostles" (3:1189), gives only this information: "Church priesthood quorums strive for unanimity in their decisions in accordance with revelation [see *The Doctrine and Covenants of The Church of Jesus Christ of Latter-day Saints,* published at Salt Lake City in various editions, sec. 107:27, hereafter D&C with numbers of section and verse(s)]. Until agreement is reached, the Quorum of the Twelve takes no action. Instead, the President of the Twelve usually defers the matter for reconsideration. Unanimity among the presiding quorums provides the Church members with an assurance that 'the united voice of the First Presidency and the Twelve' will never 'lead the Saints astray or send forth counsel to the world that is contrary to the mind and will of the Lord' (Joseph Fielding Smith, *Ensign* 2 [July 1972]: 88)."

7. Reynolds Cahoon diary, 5-6 July 1832, archives, Historical Department, Church of Jesus Christ of Latter-day Saints, Salt Lake City, Utah (hereafter LDS archives).

8. Hyrum Smith diary, 28 July 1832, Department of Special Collections and Manuscripts, Harold B. Lee Library, Brigham Young University, Provo, Utah (hereafter Lee Library); Joseph Smith to William W. Phelps, 31 July 1832, in Dean C. Jessee, ed., *The Personal Writings of Joseph Smith* (Salt Lake City: Deseret Book Co., 1984), 247; Richard S. Van Wagoner, *Sidney Rigdon: A Portrait of Religious Excess* (Salt Lake City: Signature Books, 1994), 126-27; Quinn, *Mormon Hierarchy: Origins of Power,* 42, 161.

9. F. Mark McKiernan, *The Voice of One Crying in the Wilderness: Sidney Rigdon, Religious Reformer, 1793-1876* (Lawrence, KS: Coronado Press, 1971), 115-22; Richard S. Van Wagoner, *Mormon Polygamy: A History* (Salt Lake City: Signature Books, 1986), 30-32; Van Wagoner, *Sidney Rigdon,* 291-324; Quinn, *Mormon Hierarchy: Origins of Power,* 162-63.

10. James B. Allen, *Trials of Discipleship: The Story of William Clayton, A Mormon* (Urbana: University of Illinois Press, 1987), 136; Lyndon W. Cook, *William Law: Biographical Essay, Nauvoo Diary, Correspondence, Interview* (Orem, UT: Grandin Book Co., 1994), 12, 22-28, 46-47, 53, 127-29; Quinn, *Mormon Hierarchy: Origins of Power,* 53-54, 636.

11. Scott G. Kenney, ed., *Wilford Woodruff's Journal: 1833-1898 Typescript,* 9 vols. (Murray, UT: Signature Books, 1983-85), 5 (22 Jan. 1860): 418.

12. Revelation to Heber C. Kimball, 12 Jan. 1862, copy in J. Golden Kimball diary, after entry of 21 Feb. 1887, Manuscripts Division, J. Willard Marriott Library, University of Utah, Salt Lake City (hereafter Marriott Library).

13. Kenney, *Wilford Woodruff's Journal* 6 (1 July 1866): 290. In Quorum of the Twelve Apostles minutes, 5 Apr. 1900, 10, LDS archives, Joseph F. Smith referred to his unhappiness about having to conceal his apostleship from Kimball.

14. Joseph F. Smith diary, 2 Dec. 1880, LDS archives, with transcriptions of the diary in Scott G. Kenney papers, Marriott Library.

15. Heber J. Grant 1886-87 letterbook-journal, 538 (5 Oct. 1887), and journal sheets, 3 Aug. 1887, 329-30, LDS archives. While "diary" is the standardized term I use to identify personal documents with daily entries, Grant kept several different kinds of such records, which must be identified separately in order to locate the quotations.

16. Abraham H. Cannon diary, 3 Dec. 1895, copies at Lee Library, at Marriott Library, and at Utah State Historical Society, Salt Lake City.

17. John Henry Smith diary, 1 Dec. 1898, in Jean Bickmore White, ed., *Church, State, and Politics: The Diaries of John Henry Smith* (Salt Lake City: Signature Books/Smith Research Associates, 1990), 414. This edited version inadvertently omitted the word "did" from the original, a photocopy of which is in the George A. Smith Family papers, Marriott Library.

18. Brigham Young, Jr., diary, 21 Apr. 1899, LDS archives.

19. Georgius Y. Cannon interview by Mark W. Cannon, 10 Feb. 1955, LDS archives; Frank J. Cannon, *Under the Prophet in Utah* (Boston: C. M. Clark Publishing Co., 1911), 247.

20. D. Michael Quinn, "LDS Church Authority and New Plural Marriages, 1890-1904," *Dialogue: A Journal of Mormon Thought* 18 (Spring 1985): 83-87; Abraham Owen Woodruff diary, 30 Aug., 14 Oct., 30 Oct. 1900, LDS archives, with copy at Lee Library.

21. Anthon H. Lund diary, 7 Apr. 1902, microfilm, LDS archives, which is available to all researchers by stipulation of its donor.

22. J. Golden Kimball diary, 10 Nov. 1901; also James E. Talmage diary, 10 Nov. 1901, Lee Library; *October-November 1901 Conference Report . . .* (Salt Lake City: Church of Jesus Christ of Latter-day Saints, 1901), 80-81; Joseph Fielding Smith, *Life of Joseph F. Smith . . .* (Salt Lake City: Deseret News Press, 1938), 322.

23. Heidi S. Swinton, *In the Company of Prophets: Personal Experiences of D. Arthur Haycock with Heber J. Grant, George Albert Smith, David O. McKay, Joseph Fielding Smith, Harold B. Lee, Spencer W. Kimball, and Ezra Taft Benson* (Salt Lake City: Deseret Book Co., 1993), 32; *Deseret News 1995-1996 Church Almanac,* 46, for Clark.

24. L. Brent Goates, *Harold B. Lee: Prophet & Seer* (Salt Lake City: Bookcraft, 1985), 215.

25. My interview with Marianne Clark Sharp, 7 Nov. 1977; interview with Spencer W. Kimball, 2 Feb. 1979; interview with A. Hamer Reiser, 1 Mar. 1980; J. Reuben Clark office diary, 22 Jan., 26 Apr. 1949, Clark papers, Lee Library; and D. Michael Quinn, *J. Reuben Clark: The Church Years* (Provo, UT: Brigham Young University Press, 1983), 98. Francis M. Gibbons, *George Albert Smith: Kind and Caring Christian, Prophet of God* (Salt Lake City: Deseret Book Co., 1990), makes no comment on Emily Smith Stewart's administrative influence. Nevertheless, Gibbons (a secretary to the First Presidency) observes (34-35): "The elder girl, Emily, was so active and aggressive and filled with self-confidence, it was said of her later that had she been a boy, she surely would have risen to the presidency of General Motors or some other major enterprise."

26. J. Reuben Clark office diary, 7-8 May 1947, 15 Sept. 1949.

27. Edward L. Kimball and Andrew E. Kimball, Jr., *Spencer W. Kimball* . . . (Salt Lake City: Bookcraft, 1977), 268; *Deseret News 1995-1996 Church Almanac,* 44, for Kimball; also Joseph Anderson, *Prophets I Have Known* (Salt Lake City: Deseret Book Co., 1973), 82; Swinton, *In the Company of Prophets,* 44.

28. Dew, *Ezra Taft Benson,* 247; Goates, *Harold B. Lee,* 239; Quinn, *J. Reuben Clark,* 116, 118-19, 122, 141-42, 300n24, 301n43; *April 1951 Conference Report* . . . (Salt Lake City: Church of Jesus Christ of Latter-day Saints, 1951), 151. Francis M. Gibbons, *David O. McKay: Apostle to the World, Prophet of God* (Salt Lake City: Deseret Book Co., 1986), 278, repeats the official explanation that there was no rift in the First Presidency and that Clark's changed status was not a demotion. Nevertheless, Gibbons undercuts that explanation by saying McKay was wise to make "the selection of Elder [Stephen L] Richards as first counselor so that in the event the chemistry was wrong after the change, the administration of the Church would not suffer because of any differences between the Prophet and the one second in authority."

29. Utah newspapers refused to print that particular Drew Pearson, "Washington Merry-Go-Round," which was syndicated throughout the country, including *St. Louis Post-Dispatch,* 25 Feb. 1952, B-1. See also Tyler Abell, ed., *Drew Pearson Diaries, 1949-1959* (New York: Holt, Rinehart and Winston, 1974), 201.

30. Ernest L. Wilkinson diary, 28 Apr. 1960, photocopy, Marriott Library.

31. Gibbons, *David O. McKay,* 278.

32. Quinn, *J. Reuben Clark,* 127; Harold B. Lee diary, 22 Apr. 1955, LDS archives.

33. J. Reuben Clark memorandum, 21 Sept. 1956, Clark papers; *April 1959 Conference Report* . . . (Salt Lake City: Church of Jesus Christ of Latter-day Saints, 1959), 45.

34. Francis M. Gibbons, *Harold B. Lee: Man of Vision, Prophet of God* (Salt Lake City: Deseret Book Co., 1993), 288, 295, 297, for specific reference to Richards as the source of the conflict; Goates, *Harold B. Lee,* 327-29, for nonspecific reference to "the First Presidency" as source of conflict; *Deseret News 1995-1996 Church Almanac,* 43, 47, for Lee and Romney.

35. Dennis L. Lythgoe, *Let 'Em Holler: A Political Biography of J. Bracken Lee* (Salt Lake City: Utah State Historical Society, 1982), 101.

36. Edwin B. Firmage, ed., *An Abundant Life: The Memoirs of Hugh B. Brown* (Salt Lake City: Signature Books, 1988), 131; Quinn, *J. Reuben Clark,* 128, 141-42; J. Reuben Clark office diary, 17 Mar., 14 July 1953; Ernest L. Wilkinson diary, 22 May 1961; *Deseret News 1995-1996 Church Almanac,* 46, for Brown.

37. The comparison was Gordon B. Hinckley's in his "An Appreciation of Stephen L Richards," *Improvement Era* 54 (July 1951): 499; also Gibbons, *David O. McKay,* 277.

38. Ernest L. Wilkinson diary, 21 July 1957.

39. Gibbons, *David O. McKay,* 402; Goates, *Harold B. Lee,* 336; Gibbons, *Harold B. Lee,* 373; *Deseret News 1995-1996 Church Almanac,* 46, for Moyle.

40. Quinn, *J. Reuben Clark,* passim; Ernest L. Wilkinson diary, 24 Feb. 1960; J. Reuben Clark office diary, 19 May 1960, 13 Apr. 1962.

41. *April 1959 Conference Report,* 91-92; Ernest L. Wilkinson diary, 4 Dec. 1959; LDS church financial department's Condensed Financial Report to the Corporation of the President, 12 Apr. 1961 (for summary from 1950 to 1960), LDS archives. Wilkinson's diary, 4 Dec. 1959, said the budget committee announced "the Church last year had spent $8,000,000 in excess of its income," which leaves the impression that he referred to 1958. However, LDS church financial department reports show the deficit in 1959, which means Wilkinson's diary reference to "last year" referred to the year which was just ending in December 1959.

42. J. Reuben Clark remarks to presidencies and superintendents of all church auxiliaries, 1 Apr. 1940, Clark papers; also his less detailed reference in *April 1940 Conference Report* . . . (Salt Lake City: Church of Jesus Christ of Latter-day Saints, 1940), 14; Quinn, *J.*

Reuben Clark, 272. In Clark's office diary, 23 Jan. 1939, he confided to Brigham Young University's president that the church had spent "between $800,000 and $900,000 more than our revenues."

43. Quinn, *J. Reuben Clark,* 137; Goates, *Harold B. Lee,* 381. Lee's biography avoids identifying Moyle as the one who promoted this deficit spending.

44. J. Alan Blodgett, quoted in Richard D. Poll, "Henry D. Moyle: Man of Action," unpublished 1983 biography, fd 21, box 67, chapter, "Counselor in the First Presidency—I," 4, Richard Douglas Poll papers, Marriott Library.

45. Goates, *Harold B. Lee,* 382; Ernest L. Wilkinson diary, 5 Sept. 1962.

46. George S. Tanner journal, 51 (29 Dec. 1962), Marriott Library.

47. Ernest L. Wilkinson diary, 15 Feb. 1963.

48. Poll, "Henry D. Moyle: Man of Action," unpublished 1983 biography, fd 22, box 67, chapter "Counselor in the First Presidency—I," 26.

49. William F. Edwards, *Budget Preparation and Control Report to the First Presidency* (Salt Lake City: N.p., 21 Oct. 1955), 6, copy in LDS archives.

50. "Mission Presidents Get Uniform Plan For Teaching Gospel," *Deseret News "Church News,"* 1 July 1961, 3; "New Mission Plan Ready," *Deseret News "Church News,"* 19 Aug. 1961, 2; *A Uniform Plan for Teaching the Gospel* (Salt Lake City: Church of Jesus Christ of Latter-day Saints, 1961); James B. Allen and Richard O. Cowan, *Mormonism in the Twentieth Century* (Provo, UT: Brigham Young University Extension Publications, 1964), 140-41; Richard O. Cowan, *Church in the Twentieth Century* (Salt Lake City: Bookcraft, 1985), 281; James B. Allen, "David O. McKay," in Ludlow, *Encyclopedia of Mormonism,* 2:873.

51. Poll, "Henry D. Moyle: Man of Action," unpublished 1983 biography, fd 21, box 67, chapter, "Counselor in the First Presidency—I," 12.

52. Ibid., 13-14; *Deseret News "Church News,"* 29 Oct. 1960, 3; Henry D. Moyle diary, 26 Nov. 1960, LDS archives.

53. "Pres. McKay," *Deseret News,* 16 Sept. 1958, A-7.

54. Henry D. Moyle diary, 15 Dec. 1960.

55. *Deseret News 1995-1996 Church Almanac,* 385, for Jan. 1960; Cowan, *The Church in the Twentieth Century,* 298; Paul L. Anderson and Richard W. Jackson, "Building Program," in Ludlow, *Encyclopedia of Mormonism,* 1:237; Poll, "Henry D. Moyle: Man of Action," unpublished 1983 biography, fd 21, box 67, chapter, "Counselor in the First Presidency—I," 11-12, 14-15.

56. Robert Gottlieb and Peter Wiley, *America's Saints: The Rise of Mormon Power* (New York: G. P. Putnam's Sons, 1984), 101-102, 135; LDS church financial department's Condensed Financial Report to the Corporation of the President, 20 Dec. 1962, LDS archives; Ernest L. Wilkinson diary, 6 Mar. 1963; Kimball and Kimball, *Spencer W. Kimball,* 339, 340.

57. Ernest L. Wilkinson diary, 6 Sept. 1960, 11 May, 25 May 1961.

58. Poll, "Henry D. Moyle: Man of Action," unpublished 1983 biography, fd 24, box 67, chapter, "Counselor in the First Presidency—III," 4.

59. Henry D. Moyle, "Conversion to Gospel Comes When Spirit Touches Hearts of People," *Deseret News "Church News,"* 5 Aug. 1961, 14; *Deseret News "Church News,"* 30 Dec. 1961, 4.

60. Poll, "Henry D. Moyle: Man of Action," unpublished 1983 biography, fd 18, box 67, chapter, "Man of Action," 18.

61. As an example of this officially sponsored competitiveness, "Convert-Baptisms Reach All-time High of 47,912," *Deseret News "Church News,"* 9 Sept. 1961, 4, reported that so far in the year "the Northwestern States Mission leads the missions. . . . Samoan missionaries were in second place. . . . California Mission reported 2,138 converts to clinch third place." In "Spirit of Conversion Places 75,500 on Mission Records," *Deseret News "Church News,"* 30 Dec. 1961, 4, reported that the Scottish-Irish Mission's "baptisms could

well exceed 5,100 for the year—the highest of any mission. . . . The Northwestern States with 4,003 baptisms by the end of October will run the Scottish-Irish a close second with an estimated 4,900 to 5,000 for the year. . . . Contending for the third spot will be the Samoan Mission."

62. Interviews and research about the baseball baptism program are summarized in my oral history, 1973, LDS archives; James B. Allen and Glen M. Leonard, *The Story of the Latter-day Saints*, 2d ed. rev. (Salt Lake City: Deseret Book Co., 1992), 610; D. Michael Quinn, "I-Thou vs. I-It Conversions: The Mormon 'Baseball Baptism' Era," *Sunstone* 16 (Dec. 1993): 33-34, 37-38; Richard Williams, "Crying on Cue," *Sunstone* 17 (June 1994): 6-7; Michael Rayback, "Gospel As Commodity," *Sunstone* 17 (Sept. 1994): 7-8; C. LaVarr Rockwood, "1930s Baseball Baptisms," *Sunstone* 18 (Apr. 1995): 2; see also Derek A. Cuthbert, *The Second Century: Latter-day Saints in Great Britain, 1937-1987* (Salt Lake City: By the author, 1987), 52-53.

63. My interview with Spencer W. Kimball, 2 Feb. 1979; Peggy Petersen Barton, *Mark E. Petersen: A Biography* (Salt Lake City: Deseret Book Co., 1985), 122; *Deseret News 1995-1996 Church Almanac*, 55, for Petersen. Francis M. Gibbons, *Spencer W. Kimball: Resolute Disciple, Prophet of God* (Salt Lake City: Deseret Book Co., 1995), 250, claims that only unnamed "critics" of the LDS church use the term "baseball baptisms" and that LDS president Spencer W. Kimball "deplored the use of this term." However, Apostle Petersen used the term repeatedly in my presence while I was a missionary in England, and his use of the term appeared in his biography. In his interview with me President Kimball used the term "kiddie baptisms," which was even a more negative reference to this proselytizing program.

64. David O. McKay office diary, 13 Dec. 1957, LDS archives; G. Homer Durham et al., *N. Eldon Tanner: His Life and Service* (Salt Lake City: Deseret Book Co., 1982), 208.

65. Poll, "Henry D. Moyle: Man of Action," unpublished 1983 biography, fd 24, box 67, chapter, "Counselor in the First Presidency—III," 2.

66. Peter Scarlet, "Periodic Dissent at Top Big Part of LDS History," *Salt Lake Tribune*, 9 Aug. 1991, B-2; also Gibbons, *David O. McKay*, 408.

67. Marion D. Hanks interview, 9 Apr. 1981, fd 40, box 63, Poll papers; Poll, "Henry D. Moyle: Man of Action," unpublished 1983 biography, fd 18, box 67, chapter, "Man of Action," 19, and fd 24, box 67, chapter, "Counselor in the First Presidency—III," 8. Moyle made this remark while meeting in London with Apostle Mark E. Petersen and Hanks, a president of the First Council of Seventy.

68. *New York Times*, 13 May 1963, 31.

69. Ernest L. Wilkinson diary, 9 July 1963. However, Moyle's biographer gives a different perspective: "He was an impuls[ive] giver. For President Clark it was once a new Cadillac. For others among the General Authorities it might be shares of stock or an opportunity to participate in a rewarding investment" (Poll, "Henry D. Moyle: Man of Action," unpublished 1983 biography, fd 18, box 67, chapter, "Man of Action," 12).

70. Reported in Charles M. Brown interview, 7 June 1973, page c-1-2, fd 25, box 48, Poll papers.

71. Hugh B. Brown interview, 30 Nov. 1969, side 2 transcription, 21, Edwin B. Firmage papers, Marriott Library; also Alice Moyle Yeates interview, 17 June 1980, transcription, 21-22, fd 23, box 64, Poll papers: "It broke Daddy's heart. When Daddy died he didn't have any friends. They had taken all of his work away from him. . . . He was [still] in the First Presidency. He had some power, but every responsibility was taken from him."

72. "Regional Representatives: 7 Called To Serve The Church," *Deseret News* "*Church News*," 1 Aug. 1970, 5; and "T. B. Woodbury, Churchman, Dies," *Deseret News*, 18 Oct. 1972, B-5.

73. Ernest L. Wilkinson diary, 3 Feb. 1965, 29 May 1968.

74. Hugh B. Brown interview, 30 Nov. 1969, in Firmage, *An Abundant Life: The Memoirs of Hugh B. Brown*, 133.

75. Gibbons, *David O. McKay*, 263.

76. Ernest L. Wilkinson diary, 7 May 1956, 3 Nov. 1958, 28 July 1962.

77. Gibbons, *David O. McKay*, 263.

78. Specific use of "end run" terminology appears in J. Reuben Clark office diary, 22 May 1961; Ernest L. Wilkinson diary, 25 May 1967; Neal A. Maxwell oral history, 1976-77, 24-25, LDS archives.

79. Eugene Campbell's handwritten draft of Hugh B. Brown biography, chapter titled, "Responsibility Without Authority—The 1st Counselor Years," 2, Campbell papers, Lee Library; also Quinn, *J. Reuben Clark*, 128, 141-42; Jerry C. Roundy, "Ricks College: A Struggle for Survival," Ph.D. diss., Brigham Young University, 1975, 223, 231-47; Gary James Bergera and Ronald Priddis, *Brigham Young University: A House of Faith* (Salt Lake City: Signature Books, 1985), 25; David O. McKay office diary, 6 Dec. 1956; Ernest L. Wilkinson diary, 7 Dec. 1953, 12 July 1957, 25 June 1960, 22 May 1961.

80. Gibbons, *David O. McKay*, 417.

81. Ernest L. Wilkinson diary, 23 Nov. 1960, also 17 July, 21 July 1960.

82. Gibbons, *David O. McKay*, 401.

83. *Deseret News 1995-1996 Church Almanac*, 49.

84. Gibbons, *David O. McKay*, 411-13; *Deseret News 1995-1996 Church Almanac*, 46-47, 49, for Brown, Tanner, and Isaacson.

85. Ernest L. Wilkinson diary, 23 Feb. 1965.

86. Hugh B. Brown interview, 30 Nov. 1969, side 2 transcription, 14.

87. Durham, *N. Eldon Tanner*, 216; *Deseret News 1995-1996 Church Almanac*, 49; Francis M. Gibbons, *Joseph Fielding Smith: Gospel Scholar, Prophet of God* (Salt Lake City: Deseret Book Co., 1992), 438, 457.

88. Gibbons, *David O. McKay*, 415, 418-19. Alvin R. Dyer was a first cousin to the mother of Clarabel ("Clare") Middlemiss, who was therefore Dyer's first cousin, once removed. See Ancestral file, Family History Library, Church of Jesus Christ of Latter-day Saints, Salt Lake City, Utah (hereafter LDS Family History Library).

89. Durham, *N. Eldon Tanner*, 215. Durham did not specifically identify Dyer as the object of Tanner's complaint but described the incident after mentioning Isaacson and Dyer becoming extra counselors.

90. Gibbons, *Joseph Fielding Smith*, 457; also Quinn, *Mormon Hierarchy: Origins of Power*, 258.

91. The phrases are from Gibbons, *Harold B. Lee*, 159, and Goates, *Harold B. Lee*, 382. Gibbons also referred to "the few incidents when President Lee's temper flared" (493).

92. Durham, *N. Eldon Tanner*, 265.

93. Goates, *Harold B. Lee*, 462.

94. My interviews, 29-30 Aug. 1992, with Alan Blodgett, managing director of the LDS church financial department, 1969-80, and managing director of the investment department, 1980-85.

95. Dew, *Ezra Taft Benson*, 448; Neal A. Maxwell oral history, 83; also Kimball and Kimball, *Spencer W. Kimball*, portrays both his personal and administrative style.

96. Gibbons, *Spencer W. Kimball*, 286.

97. Quorum of Twelve Apostles minutes, 16 Nov. 1847.

98. Church Historian's office journal, 20 Dec. 1854, LDS archives.

99. Kenney, *Wilford Woodruff's Journal* 5 (11 Aug. 1857): 74; Heber C. Kimball memorandum book, 27 Dec. 1859, copied in J. Golden Kimball diary, after entry for 21 Feb. 1887; also published with variations in Stanley B. Kimball, *Heber C. Kimball: Mormon Patriarch and Pioneer* (Urbana: University of Illinois Press, 1981), 294-95; Stanley B. Kimball,

ed., *On the Potter's Wheel: The Diaries of Heber C. Kimball* (Salt Lake City: Signature Books/Smith Research Associates, 1987), 176.

100. Wilford Woodruff, "Historian's Private Journal" (1858-78), 14 Mar. 1860, LDS archives. This is not Woodruff's personal journal, nor is it the Church Historian's office journal, which covered the period 1858-78 in sixteen manuscript volumes.

101. Hosea Stout diary, 25 July 1861, in Juanita Brooks, ed., *On the Mormon Frontier: The Diary of Hosea Stout, 1844-1861,* 2 vols. (Salt Lake City: University of Utah Press, 1964), 2:711.

102. Statements in Heber C. Kimball memorandum book, 12 Jan. and 29 Mar. 1862, copied in J. Golden Kimball diary, after entry for 21 Feb. 1887; also Heber C. Kimball memorandum book, 29 Mar. 1862, [?] Mar. 1862. Kimball, *Heber C. Kimball,* 294-95, cites a similar entry for 12 January 1865.

103. Abraham H. Cannon diary, 29 Jan. 1891.

104. Excerpt from First Presidency office journal, 20 Aug. 1891, LDS archives. Compare with Paul H. Peterson, "Manifesto of 1890," in Ludlow, *Encyclopedia of Mormonism,* 3:852-53; also discussion of Manifesto, to follow.

105. Rudger Clawson diary, 28 Feb. 1901, in Stan Larson, ed., *A Ministry of Meetings: The Apostolic Diaries of Rudger Clawson* (Salt Lake City: Signature Books/Smith Research Associates, 1993), 250; Anthon H. Lund diary, 26 Feb. 1901; Abraham Owen Woodruff diary, 26 and 28 Feb. 1901; John Henry Smith diary, 26 Feb. 1901, in White, *Church, State, and Politics,* 477, referred to the "warmth" of the discussion but did not identify his kinsman.

106. "Mormon Mixup," *Time* 40 (19 Oct. 1942): 41; J. Reuben Clark office diary, 2 June 1944; Quinn, *J. Reuben Clark,* 118-19; Gibbons, *David O. McKay,* 201.

107. In response to Quinn, *J. Reuben Clark,* 115-16, 300n24, Francis M. Gibbons (secretary to the First Presidency) wrote in *David O. McKay,* 405-406n, about "some observers, unacquainted with the inner workings of the Church hierarchy" who use "generic terms 'McKay men' and 'Clark men.'" Those terms were not mine but were volunteered to me by church president Spencer W. Kimball, by second counselor Marion G. Romney, by an assistant secretary in the First Presidency's office, A. Hamer Reiser, by church purchasing director Gordon Burt Affleck, and others. Affleck and Counselor Romney each proclaimed themselves "a Clark man," and Reiser said he was "a McKay man." President Kimball did not identify himself in such a way but acknowledged the tendency for general authorities to be "Clark men" or "McKay men." He thought differences in emphasis were not extreme (my interviews with Spencer W. Kimball, 2 Feb. 1979; Marion G. Romney, 26 Oct. 1977; A. Hamer Reiser, 1 Mar. 1980; and Gordon Burt Affleck, 1978-80).

In casual conversations from 1967 onward, a decade before my research on Clark, church bureaucrats also volunteered to me the existence of "Clark men" and "McKay men." These LDS bureaucrats told me that "Clark men" and "McKay men" were tightly-knit and competitive with protégés of the other mentor.

108. Durham, *N. Eldon Tanner,* 10; Ernest L. Wilkinson diary, 3 Feb. 1965, 16 Apr. 1969, 8 Sept. 1976.

109. Charles M. Brown interview, page c-3-12.

110. "Benson Heads Mormons, Enlists 2 Key Moderates," *Los Angeles Times,* 12 Nov. 1985, I, 6; my interviews, 29-30 Aug. 1992, with Alan Blodgett; Gibbons, *Harold B. Lee,* 355-56.

111. Kenney, *Wilford Woodruff's Journal* 4 (31 Dec. 1852): 171.

112. Joseph Smith et al., *History of The Church of Jesus Christ of Latter-day Saints. Period I: History of Joseph Smith the Prophet, and . . . Period II: From the Manuscript History of Brigham Young and Other Original Documents,* ed. B. H. Roberts, 7 vols. (Salt Lake City: Church of Jesus Christ of Latter-day Saints, 1902-32; 2d ed. rev. [Salt Lake City: Deseret Book Co., 1978]), 2:372-75 (hereafter *History of the Church*).

113. Church Historian's office journal, 22 Oct. 1861.

114. Brigham Young statement in Willard Richards diary, 16 Feb. 1847, LDS archives.

115. Nauvoo Relief Society minutes, 28 Apr. 1842, microfilm, Lee Library, and typescript, Linda King Newell papers, Marriott Library.

116. Testimony of Sarah Miller on 24 May 1842 and of Catherine Fuller Warren on 25 May 1842, LDS archives; Quinn, *Mormon Hierarchy: Origins of Power,* 220.

117. Lorenzo Snow statement in Abraham H. Cannon diary, 9 Apr. 1890. Snow blamed Emma Smith for her husband's reversal, but the incident is consistent with many of Joseph Smith's other "tests" of his associates.

118. Kenney, *Wilford Woodruff's Journal* 4 (22 Dec. 1852): 157.

119. Book of the Law of the Lord, 28 Nov. 1842, in Dean C. Jessee, ed., *The Papers of Joseph Smith,* 2+ vols., with a different subtitle for each volume (Salt Lake City: Deseret Book Co., 1989-92+), 2:494; *History of the Church,* 5:197.

120. *History of the Church,* 5:332.

121. Franklin D. Richards statement to Quorum of the Twelve Apostles in Abraham H. Cannon diary, 9 Apr. 1890; *History of the Church,* 5:414; Brigham Young's statement in Boston conference meeting, 11 Sept. 1843, 16, LDS archives, which *History of the Church,* 6:28, changed to "heretofore unheard of in the Churchap."

122. Danel W. Bachman, "A Study of the Mormon Practice of Plural Marriage Before the Death of Joseph Smith," M.A. thesis, Purdue University, 1975, 348-52; George D. Smith, "Nauvoo Roots of Mormon Polygamy, 1841-46: A Preliminary Demographic Report," *Dialogue: A Journal of Mormon Thought* 27 (Spring 1994): 14-15; Linda King Newell and Valeen Tippetts Avery, *Mormon Enigma: Emma Hale Smith,* 2d ed. (Urbana: University of Illinois Press, 1994), 98-100, 141, 146; Quinn, *Mormon Hierarchy: Origins of Power,* 66, 148.

123. Willard Richards diary, 17 Mar. 1847.

124. For more extensive analysis of this transition, see Quinn, *Mormon Hierarchy: Origins of Power,* 57-67, 155-75, 245-52.

125. Leonard J. Arrington and Ronald K. Esplin, "The Role of the Quorum of the Twelve During Brigham Young's Presidency of The Church of Jesus Christ of Latter-day Saints," *Task Papers in LDS History,* No. 31 (Salt Lake City: Historical Department of The Church of Jesus Christ of Latter-day Saints, 1979), 51-53; also Leonard J. Arrington, *Brigham Young: American Moses* (New York: Alfred A. Knopf, 1985), 303; William G. Hartley, "The Priesthood Reorganization of 1877: Brigham Young's Last Achievement," *Brigham Young University Studies* 20 (Fall 1979): 3-36.

126. Heber J. Grant letterbook-journal, 8 Sept. 1887.

127. Kenney, *Wilford Woodruff's Journal* 4 (19 Oct. 1856): 477; Wilford Woodruff, "Historian's Private Journal" (1858-78), 14 Mar. 1860.

128. *Journal of Discourses,* 26 vols. (London and Liverpool: Latter-day Saints' Book Depot, 1854-86), 7:228-29 (B. Young/1860).

129. Charles W. Nibley, *Reminiscences of Charles W. Nibley* (Salt Lake City: The Nibley Family, 1934), 73-74; Smith, *Life of Joseph F. Smith,* 236.

130. Breck England, *The Life and Thought of Orson Pratt* (Salt Lake City: University of Utah Press, 1985), 265; Gary James Bergera, "The Orson Pratt-Brigham Young Controversies: Conflict Within the Quorums, 1853-1868," *Dialogue: A Journal of Mormon Thought* 13 (Summer 1980): 7-58.

131. Quinn, *Mormon Hierarchy: Origins of Power,* 247-48.

132. Kenney, *Wilford Woodruff's Journal* 4 (15 June 1851): 38, 5 (7 Apr. 1857): 45-46; Brigham Young office journal, 7 Apr. 1857, 28 Apr. 1861, copy of latter in Donald R. Moorman papers, archives, Donnell and Elizabeth Stewart Library, Weber State University, Ogden, Utah, and in H. Michael Marquardt papers, Marriott Library; *Journal of Discourses* 4:266-67 (B.Young/1857), 305 (B.Young/1857), 6:275 (B.Young/1852).

133. Kenney, *Wilford Woodruff's Journal* 4 (6 Jan. 1856): 382.

134. Ibid., 5 (6-7 Apr. 1861): 564.

135. *History of the Church,* 1:78, 2:417-18, 4:282, 286; Journal History of the Church of Jesus Christ of Latter-day Saints (1830-1972), 246 reels, microfilm, Special Collections, Marriott Library, 7 Oct. 1844-9 Oct. 1872; *Deseret Evening News,* 9 Oct. 1872, 9 Apr. 1873, 9 Oct. 1873, 9 May 1874, 10 Oct. 1874, 10 Apr. 1875, 9 Oct. 1875, 10 Apr. 1876, 9 Oct. 1876, 9 Apr. 1877. Young served as LDS president without being sustained as "Prophet, Seer and Revelator" until 7 April 1851 and he alone had that designation until 8 October 1855, when his counselors received that title. No one was presented with that title from 7 April 1859 until 9 October 1872, when the entire First Presidency was again so sustained. Young alone had that designation at general conferences from 9 April 1873 until his death in August 1877.

136. Franklin D. Richards diary, 4 Sept. 1877, LDS archives. Although *Deseret News 1995-1996 Church Almanac,* 45, 48, acknowledges this official position of "counselor to the Twelve Apostles," it is not acknowledged in Ludlow, *Encyclopedia of Mormonism,* 4:1679-80.

137. *Deseret Evening News,* 8 Oct. 1877, and every report of general conference afterward.

138. George Q. Cannon diary, 17 Jan. 1878, quoted in the official LDS magazine *Instructor* 80 (June 1945): 259.

139. England, *Life and Thought of Orson Pratt,* 189-90, 264; Bergera, "The Orson Pratt-Brigham Young Controversies," 7-58.

140. Franklin D. Richards diary, 3-4 Oct. 1877, and his remarks in Heber J. Grant journal, 4 Oct. 1898.

141. Joseph F. Smith diary, 6 Apr. 1879.

142. Franklin D. Richards diary, 6 Sept. 1879.

143. Joseph F. Smith diary, 6 Oct. 1880; Moses Thatcher 1880 diary, Oct. 1880, 120, Lee Library; George Q. Cannon diary, October 1880, summarized in *Instructor* 80 (Sept. 1945): 410; John Henry Smith diary, 9 Oct. 1880, in White, *Church, State, and Politics,* 53; Gary James Bergera, "Seniority in the Twelve: The 1875 Realignment of Orson Pratt," *Journal of Mormon History* 18 (Spring 1992): 54-56.

144. Kenney, *Wilford Woodruff's Journal* 7 (8 Oct. 1880): 594.

145. Moses Thatcher 1880 diary, Oct. 1880, 120.

146. Joseph F. Smith diary, 9 Oct. 1880; Kenney, *Wilford Woodruff's Journal* 7 (9 Oct. 1880): 595.

147. Kenney, *Wilford Woodruff's Journal* 8 (8 Apr. 1882): 94; L. John Nuttall's minutes of the Quorum of Twelve Apostles, 8 Apr. 1882, LDS archives; Francis M. Lyman diary, 8 Apr. 1882, LDS archives; John Henry Smith diary, 8 Apr. 1882, in White, *Church, State, and Politics,* 76.

148. John Henry Smith diary, 3 Oct. 1882, in White, *Church, State, and Politics,* 83.

149. Francis M. Lyman diary, 6 Oct. 1882.

150. Franklin D. Richards diary, 26 June 1882.

151. John Henry Smith diary, 16 Oct. 1882. His evaluation of the new apostles is in the entry of 13 October 1882. See White, *Church, State, and Politics,* 84-85.

152. B. Carmon Hardy, *Solemn Covenant: The Mormon Polygamous Passage* (Urbana: University of Illinois Press, 1992), 39-83.

153. Orma Linford, "The Mormons and the Law: The Polygamy Cases," *Utah Law Review* 9 (Winter 1964/Summer 1965): 308-70, 543-91; James L. Clayton, "The Supreme Court, Polygamy, and the Enforcement of Morals in Nineteenth-Century America: An Analysis of Reynolds v. United States," *Dialogue: A Journal of Mormon Thought* 12 (Winter 1979): 46-61.

154. T. Harry Williams, ed., *Hayes: The Diary of a President, 1875-1881* (New York: David McKay Co., Inc., 1964), 258-259, diary entry of 9 Jan. 1880.

155. *Journal of Discourses* 13:166 (Woodruff/1869), 22:147-48 (Wood-ruff/1881).

156. Klaus J. Hansen, *Mormonism and the American Experience* (Chicago: University of Chicago Press, 1981), 145, minimizes polygamy as the real target. Edward Leo Lyman, *Political Deliverance: The Mormon Quest for Utah Statehood* (Urbana: University of Illinois Press, 1986), 2, 23, sees polygamy as the real target.

157. Thomas G. Alexander, "Federal Authority versus Polygamic Theocracy," *Dialogue: A Journal of Mormon Thought* 1 (Autumn 1966): 85-100; Charles A. Cannon, "The Awesome Power of Sex: The Polemical Campaign against Mormon Polygamy," *Pacific Historical Review* 43 (Feb. 1974): 61-82; Joseph H. Groberg, "The Mormon Disfranchisements of 1882 to 1892," *Brigham Young University Studies* 16 (Spring 1976): 399-408; Melvin L. Bashore, "Life Behind Bars: Mormon Cohabs of the 1880s," *Utah Historical Quarterly* 47 (Winter 1979): 22-41; Kimberly Jensen James, "'Between Two Fires': Women on the 'Underground' of Mormon Polygamy," *Journal of Mormon History* 8 (1981): 49-61; Martha Sonntag Bradley, "Hide and Seek: Children on the Underground," *Utah Historical Quarterly* 51 (Spring 1983): 133-53; Rosa Mae McClellan Evans, "Judicial Prosecution of Prisoners for LDS Plural Marriage: Prison Sentences, 1884-1895," M.A. thesis, Brigham Young University, 1986; Sarah Barringer Gordon, "'The Twin Relic of Barbarism': A Legal History of Anti-Polygamy in Nineteenth-Century America," Ph.D. diss., Princeton University, 1994.

158. Gustive O. Larson, *The "Americanization" of Utah for Statehood* (San Marino, CA: Huntington Library, 1970); Ken Driggs, "The Mormon Church-State Confrontation in Nineteenth-Century America," *Journal of Church and State* 30 (Spring 1988): 273-89.

159. Leonard J. Arrington, *Great Basin Kingdom: An Economic History of the Latter-day Saints, 1847-1900* (Cambridge, MA: Harvard University Press, 1958), 353-79; Edwin Brown Firmage and Richard Collin Mangrum, *Zion in the Courts: A Legal History of the Church of Jesus Christ of Latter-day Saints* (Urbana: University of Illinois Press, 1988), 130-260; *Deseret News 1995-1996 Church Almanac,* 371-73; Ray Jay Davis, "Antipolygamy Legislation," William G. Hartley and Gene A. Sessions, "History of the Church: 1877-1898," Danel Bachman and Ronald K. Esplin, "Plural Marriage," and Paul Thomas Smith, "John Taylor," in Ludlow, *Encyclopedia of Mormonism,* 1:52-53, 2:625-26, 3:1094-95, 4:1440-41.

160. John Henry Smith to "J. Mack" [Joseph F. Smith], 28 Aug. 1885, John Henry Smith 1884-94 letterbook, 432, George A. Smith Family papers, Marriott Library.

161. John Henry Smith to "J. Mack" [Joseph F. Smith], 10 Feb. 1886 in ibid.; John Henry Smith diary, 27 Aug. 1886, in White, *Church, State, and Politics,* 153.

162. Franklin D. Richards diary, 3 Aug. 1887.

163. The only precedent was Amasa M. Lyman whose actual date of official entry into the Quorum of the Twelve was clouded by Joseph Smith's decision in 1843 that the excommunication of Orson Pratt by Brigham Young and two other apostles was invalid: "President Joseph Smith remarked that as there was not a quorum [i.e., at least six of the twelve apostles] when Orson Pratt's case came up before, that he was still a member. He had not legally been cut off" (Quorum of the Twelve minutes, 20 Jan. 1843, LDS archives). *History of the Church,* 5:255, deleted that statement from the manuscript minutes but included from the manuscript (with a slight variation) Smith's other statement about the legality of Quorum of Twelve actions: "Brigham Young said there was but 3 present when Amasa was ordained [an apostle]. Joseph said that was legal when no more could be had." The effect of his words in January 1843 was that there were now thirteen members in the Quorum of Twelve, since Pratt had "not legally" been removed, while Lyman had been legally ordained an apostle. Therefore Smith reinstated Pratt and made Lyman his counselor. No conference voted on Lyman's position before Smith's death, and the apostles in 1887 did not cite Lyman as a precedent for their decision to readmit Cannon and Smith.

This selective deletion in the official *History of the Church* supported Young's redefinitions of apostolic authority when he proposed to organize a separate First Presidency of three apostles in December 1847 (Quinn, *Mormon Hierarchy: Origins of Power,*

246-52). He was willing to have the other apostles scattered throughout the world on missions, to fulfill the missionary calling of the Twelve, while he and two others stayed at church headquarters and made decisions to guide the churchap. By printing only Smith's statement that an apostle's selection and ordination by three of the Twelve was "legal when no more could be had," the *History of the Church* gave the impression that the founding prophet meant three apostles could "legally" make any decision or perform any administrative act if the other apostles were unavailable. That was Young's view after 1847, but Smith's ruling in 1843 was that some actions (like excommunication) required the presence of at least six members of the Quorum of Twelve. Publishing Smith's statement would naturally lead to questions about what other administrative decisions or actions required the presence of half of the Twelve. Since Smith's words on this matter had become inconvenient to Young's presidency, they were absent in the official LDS history as prepared by the apostle-historians in pioneer Utah. For devotional and critical explanations of this pattern of changes in the published form of original LDS documents, see Quinn, *Mormon Hierarchy: Origins of Power*, 5, 156-57, 161.

164. Quorum of Twelve Apostles minutes, 3 Aug. 1887, 2-3.

165. Heber J. Grant journal-sheets, 3 Aug. 1887, 323. For my discussion and acceptance of Brigham Young's August 1844 "mantle" (or transfiguration) experience, see Quinn, *Mormon Hierarchy: Origins of Power,* 166-67; also the skeptical view of this reported experience in Van Wagoner, *Sidney Rigdon,* 343-45; Richard S. Van Wagoner, "The Making of a Mormon Myth: The 1844 Transfiguration of Brigham Young," *Dialogue: A Journal of Mormon Thought* 28 (Winter 1995): 1-24.

166. Heber J. Grant journal-sheets, 3 Aug. 1887, 325.

167. Franklin D. Richards diary, 3 Aug. 1887; John Henry Smith diary, 3 Aug. 1887, in White, *Church, State, and Politics,* 175.

168. Mark W. Cannon, "The Mormon Issue in Congress, 1872-1882, Drawing on the Experience of Territorial Delegate George Q. Cannon," Ph.D. diss., Harvard University, 1960, 255; Edward Leo Lyman, "The Alienation of an Apostle from His Quorum: The Moses Thatcher Case," *Dialogue: A Journal of Mormon Thought* 18 (Summer 1985): 69-88; Heber J. Grant journal sheets, 3 Aug., 9 Sept., 12 Sept., 21 Sept. 1887; Quorum of the Twelve Apostles minutes, 4 Aug. 1887.

169. Cannon, "The Mormon Issue in Congress," 4; Heber J. Grant 1886-87 letterbook-journal, 518-19 (5 Oct. 1887).

170. John Henry Smith to "J. Mack" [Joseph F. Smith], 10 Feb. 1886, John Henry Smith 1884-94 letterbook, 493.

171. Heber J. Grant to Moses Thatcher, 16 Sept. 1887, Grant papers, LDS archives. A decade later Grant and other apostles reinterpreted these events to cast an increasingly isolated Thatcher in the role of a rebellious maverick who spearheaded the opposition. See Journal History, 26 Nov. 1896, 2-4.

172. Franklin D. Richards diary, 5 Oct. 1887; also Thomas G. Alexander, *Things in Heaven and Earth: The Life and Times of Wilford Woodruff, a Mormon Prophet* (Salt Lake City: Signature Books, 1991), 244.

173. John Henry Smith diary, 5-6 Oct. 1887, in White, *Church, State, and Politics,* 181; Franklin D. Richards diary, 5-6 Oct. 1887; and Heber J. Grant letterbook-journal, 3 Aug., 5-6 Oct. 1887. Alexander, *Things in Heaven and Earth,* 244-45, limits the charges to Cannon's business dealings and his preferential treatment of his excommunicated son, John Q.

174. L. John Nuttall diary, 6 Oct. 1887, copies at Lee Library, at Marriott Library, and at Henry E. Huntington Library, San Marino, California (hereafter Huntington Library); Kenney, *Wilford Woodruff's Journal* 8 (5 Oct. 1887): 460.

175. Joseph F. Smith statement on 5 Oct. 1887, recorded in Heber J. Grant 1886-87 letterbook-journal, 565 (10 Oct. 1887); Moses Thatcher statement on 3 Aug. 1887 in Heber J. Grant journal sheets, 3 Aug. 1887, 310.

176. Quorum of the Twelve Apostles minutes, 20 Mar. 1888, 3; compare Kenney, *Wilford Woodruff's Journal* 8 (20 Mar. 1888): 489.

177. Abraham H. Cannon diary, 23 Mar. 1888; Brigham Young, Jr., diary, 21 Mar. 1888; Kenney, *Wilford Woodruff's Journal* 8 (20-23 Mar. 1888): 489-90; also Franklin D. Richards diary, 21-23 Mar. 1888; John Henry Smith diary, 20-26 Mar. 1888, in White, *Church, State, and Politics*, 194; Brigham Young, Jr., diary, 20-23 Mar. 1888; Quorum of the Twelve Apostles minutes, 20-23 Mar. 1888; L. John Nuttall diary, 5 Oct. 1888; also Steven C. Heath, "Notes on Apostolic Succession," *Dialogue: A Journal of Mormon Thought* 20 (Summer 1987): 47-48; Alexander, *Things in Heaven and Earth*, 244.

178. L. John Nuttall diary, 27 Feb. 1889.

179. Ibid., 5 Apr. 1889; Heber J. Grant letterbook-journal, 5 Apr. 1889. Alexander, *Things in Heaven and Earth*, 244, notes the unanimous vote but not the continued uncertainty of apostles Thatcher and Grant.

180. Quinn, "LDS Church Authority and New Plural Marriages, 1890-1904," 35-36; Lyman, *Political Deliverance*, 105-106. Alexander, *Things in Heaven and Earth*, 250-51, does not discuss this December 1888 meeting.

181. Quinn, "LDS Church Authority and New Plural Marriages, 1890-1904," 46-47; Hardy, *Solemn Covenant*, 127-33; Lyman, *Political Deliverance*, 124-36; Alexander, *Things in Heaven and Earth*, 261-66.

182. The three were Presiding Bishopric counselor John R. Winder, Seventy's president George Reynolds, and stake presidency counselor Charles W. Penrose (excerpts from George Q. Cannon diary, 24-25 Sept. 1890, LDS archives; excerpt from First Presidency office journal, 24 Sept. 1890; Quinn, "LDS Church Authority and New Plural Marriages, 1890-1904," 44-45).

183. Quorum of Twelve Apostles minutes, 30 Sept.-1 Oct. 1890, with excerpts in Kenneth W. Godfrey, "The Coming of the Manifesto," *Dialogue: A Journal of Mormon Thought* 5 (Autumn 1970): 22-23, and extensive quotations in Abraham H. Cannon diary and Heber J. Grant journal-sheets.

184. Kenney, *Wilford Woodruff's Journal* 9 (2 Dec. 1892): 228, refers to his meeting with Snow but gives no details; Lorenzo Snow statement, 3 [sic] Dec. 1892, copied by his wife Minnie Jensen Snow and also published in "Memorandum in the Handwriting of Lorenzo Snow," *The Elder's Journal of the Southern States Mission* 4 (1 Dec. 1906): 110-11.

185. Abraham H. Cannon diary, 29 Jan. 1891.

186. Ibid., 9 July 1891, 3 Oct. 1894.

187. John Henry Smith diary, 26 Dec. 1897, in White, *Church, State, and Politics*, 386.

188. Heber J. Grant journal sheets, 4-5 Jan. 1898; John Henry Smith diary, 4 Jan. 1898, in White, *Church, State, and Politics*, 387, where the discussion is referred to without detail.

189. John Henry Smith diary, 6-7 Jan. 1898, in White, *Church, State, and Politics*, 387-88; Brigham Young, Jr., diary, 6 Jan. 1898.

190. Brigham Young, Jr., diary, 4 Apr. 1899, with reference to temple meeting of 30 Mar.

191. Anthon H. Lund diary, 4 Sept. 1898.

192. Rudger Clawson diary, 11 July 1899, in Larson, *A Ministry of Meetings*, 77; Marriner W. Merrill diary, 12 July 1899, LDS archives; Anthon H. Lund diary, 30 Dec. 1899; Abraham Owen Woodruff diary, 30 Dec. 1899.

193. Heber J. Grant journal sheets, 9 Jan. 1900; Rudger Clawson diary, 9 Jan. 1900, in Larson, *A Ministry of Meetings*, 130; Anthon H. Lund diary, 10 Jan. 1900; Abraham Owen Woodruff diary, 29-30 Dec. 1899, 11 Jan. 1900; John Henry Smith diary, 9 Jan. 1900, in White, *Church, State, and Politics*, 443.

194. Ancestral file, LDS Family History Library; statement of John Henry Smith in *Proceedings Before the Committee on Privileges and Elections of the United States Senate in the Matter of the Protests Against the Right of Hon. Reed Smoot, a Senator from the State of Utah, to Hold His Seat,* 4 vols. (Washington: U.S. Government Printing Office, 1904-1907), 2:311; Kenneth L. Cannon II, "Beyond the Manifesto: Polygamous Cohabitation Among LDS General Authorities After 1890," *Utah Historical Quarterly* 46 (Winter 1978): 24-36; Hardy, *Solemn Covenant,* 186-227.

195. Abraham Owen Woodruff diary, 5 Oct. 1901; *Deseret News 1995-1996 Church Almanac,* 48.

196. Heber J. Grant journal sheets, 30 Mar. 1932.

197. First Presidency and Quorum of the Twelve meeting minutes, 3 Mar., 31 Mar., 7 Apr. 1932, 16 Mar. 1933, excerpts from First Presidency office journal; Heber J. Grant journal sheets, 23 Mar., 27 Sept. 1933, 7 Apr. 1937.

198. Heber J. Grant journal sheets, 7 Apr. 1937.

199. Irene M. Bates and E. Gary Smith, *Lost Legacy: The Mormon Office of Presiding Patriarch* (Urbana: University of Chicago Press, 1996), 173-91.

200. Heber J. Grant journal sheets, 7 Apr. 1937.

201. The three acting patriarchs during this period were Nicholas G. Smith (not a descendant of Joseph Smith, Sr.), John M. Whitaker, and Apostle George F. Richards. See this study's biographical sketches; also Bates and Smith, *Lost Legacy,* 180, 187; *Deseret News 1995-1996 Church Almanac,* 54.

202. Charles M. Brown interview, page c-3-11. This probably occurred at a missionary meeting in Paris, France, on 4 June 1937, which is referred to without any details in Hugh B. Brown's journal, box 49, Poll papers.

203. Heber J. Grant journal sheets, 4 Oct. 1933, 15 Mar., 5 Apr., 6 Sept. 1934, 7 Apr. 1937, 20 Aug. 1942; George F. Richards diary, 4 July, 10 July, 4 Sept., 6 Sept., 13 Sept., 8 Oct. 1942, LDS archives.

204. Quotation from Irene May Bates, "Transformation of Charisma in the Mormon Church: A History of the Office of Presiding Patriarch, 1833-1979," Ph.D. dissertation, University of California at Los Angeles, 1991, 323, paraphrased in Bates and Smith, *Lost Legacy,* 190; also Heber J. Grant journal sheets, 12-17 Sept., 1 Oct. 1942.

205. Heber J. Grant journal sheets, 17 Sept., 1 Oct. 1942; George Albert Smith diary, 1 Oct. 1942, George A. Smith papers, Marriott Library; Bates and Smith, *Lost Legacy,* 190.

206. Heber J. Grant journal sheets, 27 Feb. 1943; also Gibbons, *Joseph Fielding Smith,* 342.

207. Lucile C. Tate, *Boyd K. Packer: A Watchman on the Tower* (Salt Lake City: Bookcraft, 1995), 243.

208. Quinn, *J. Reuben Clark,* 116, 128, 132-33; Roundy, "Ricks College," 231-47; David O. McKay office diary, 6 Dec. 1956; Ernest L. Wilkinson diary, 17, 21 July 1957; Neal A. Maxwell oral history, 83; J. Reuben Clark memorandum, 8 May 1959, Clark papers. However, Gibbons, *David O. McKay,* 69, insisted: "While the Prophet, who holds all the keys, or his quorum, the First Presidency, possess the inherent authority to act independent of the Twelve, this occurs only infrequently and then, usually, only in cases where urgent necessity requires prompt action."

209. Gibbons, *Joseph Fielding Smith,* 438; my interviews with persons at LDS headquarters (names withheld by request).

210. Firmage, *An Abundant Life: The Memoirs of Hugh B. Brown,* 127.

211. J. Howard Dunn interview, 17 Nov. 1981, fd 36, box 63, Poll papers.

212. Ernest L. Wilkinson diary, 13 Aug. 1959.

213. My interview with L. Brent Goates, 27 Oct. 1992. For the significance of the Correlation Program, see Goates, *Harold B. Lee,* 363-77, 519; Allen and Leonard, *Story of the Latter-day Saints,* 596-606, 654; Gottlieb and Wiley, *America's Saints,* 15, 59-62, 81-82;

Cowan, *Church in the Twentieth Century,* 305-17; Peter Wiley, "The Lee Revolution and the Rise of Correlation," *Sunstone* 10 (1985), 1:19-22; Wilburn D. Talbot, *The Acts of the Modern Apostles* (Salt Lake City: Randall Book Co., 1985), 294-95; Frank O. May, Jr., "Correlation of the Church: Administration," James B. Allen and Richard O. Cowan, "History of the Church: 1945-1990," and L. Brent Goates, "Harold B. Lee," in Ludlow, *Encyclopedia of Mormonism,* 1:324, 2:642-43, 822; Jan Shipps, "Making Saints in the Early Days and the Latter Days," paper given in a plenary session of the Society for the Scientific Study of Religion, Salt Lake City, 27 Oct. 1989, in Marie Cornwall, Tim B. Heaton, and Lawrence A. Young, eds., *Contemporary Mormonism: Social Science Perspectives* (Urbana: University of Illinois Press, 1994), 77, 80.

214. Poll, "Henry D. Moyle: Man of Action," unpublished 1983 biography, fd 24, box 67, chapter, "Counselor in the First Presidency—III," 4 for first quote, 3 for extended quote.

215. Interview with Charles M. Brown and Zola Brown Hodson, 7 June 1973, pages c-3-17, c-3-18, fd 25, box 48, Poll papers.

216. Gibbons, *David O. McKay,* 407.

217. Ernest L. Wilkinson diary, 7 July, 20 Sept. 1965; also James B. Allen, "David O. McKay," in Ludlow, *Encyclopedia of Mormonism,* 2:874.

218. U.S. senator Frank E. Moss to U.S. representative Ken W. Dyal, 2 Mar. 1966, Moss papers, Marriott Library. Moss's assessment was based on conversations with "the Brethren" in Salt Lake City a week earlier.

219. Ernest L. Wilkinson diary, 19 Aug. 1967.

220. Hugh B. Brown interview, 30 Nov. 1969, side 2 transcription, 8, 14, box 3, Firmage papers.

221. Gibbons, *David O. McKay,* 415-16; Gibbons, *Joseph Fielding Smith,* 462; *Deseret News 1995-1996 Church Almanac,* 49-50.

222. Durham, *N. Eldon Tanner,* 230-31, 303-304; Firmage, *An Abundant Life: The Memoirs of Hugh B. Brown,* 141-42; previous discussion of Cannon and forthcoming discussion of Clark.

223. Gibbons, *David O. McKay,* 408, 413-14, 417.

224. Ernest L. Wilkinson diary, 8-9 Sept. 1969.

225. Kimball and Kimball, *Spencer W. Kimball,* 387; also Quinn, *Mormon Hierarchy: Origins of Power,* 256-58, for analysis of this situation in January 1970. However, in apparent response to the above discussions, Gibbons, *Spencer W. Kimball,* 258, has insisted: "There was speculation that he would not be selected because he was almost ninety-four years old . . . [but] there was no doubt among the Brethren that President Smith was the one."

226. Goates, *Harold B. Lee,* 457.

227. Gibbons, *Joseph Fielding Smith,* 465.

228. Neal A. Maxwell oral history, 83.

229. Barton, *Mark E. Petersen,* 167; for regional representatives, see chap. 4.

230. "Several LDS Writers Say Officials Caution Them to Promote the Faith," *Deseret News,* 23 May 1983, B-2; "LDS Church Telling Editors to Use Only 'Faith Promoting' Stories?" *Salt Lake Tribune,* 23 May 1983, A-10; "LDS Leaders Challenge Y Professors' Faith," *Provo Herald,* 25 May 1983, 3; "Mormon Brethren Silencing Scholars?: 'Inquisition' Reported," *Salt Lake Tribune,* 26 May 1983, B-4; *Utah Holiday* 12 (Aug. 1983): 77; Gottlieb and Wiley, *America's Saints,* 81-82.

231. My interview with A. Hamer Reiser, 1 Mar. 1980; Quinn, *J. Reuben Clark,* 91; also John Gunther, *Inside U.S.A.* (New York: Harper & Brothers, 1947), 202.

232. Senator Frank E. Moss to U.S. representative Ken W. Dyal, 2 Mar. 1966, Moss papers.

233. *Deseret News 1995-1996 Church Almanac,* 49-50; my interviews, 29-30 Aug. 1992, with Alan Blodgett.

234. Eugene Campbell's handwritten draft of Hugh B. Brown biography, chapter titled, "Responsibility Without Authority—The 1st Counselor Years," 1-2, Campbell papers.

235. My interviews, 29-30 Aug. 1992, with Alan Blodgett.

236. Durham, *N. Eldon Tanner,* 278-79; F. Burton Howard, *Marion G. Romney: His Life and Faith* (Salt Lake City: Bookcraft, 1988), 240; *Deseret News 1995-1996 Church Almanac,* 390; Edward L. Kimball, "A Time of Reaching Out: The Administration of Spencer W. Kimball," *Sunstone,* Mar. 1987, 8, 13-14; Sheri L. Dew, *Go Forward With Faith: The Biography of Gordon B. Hinckley* (Salt Lake City: Deseret Book Co., 1996), 385 (for Kimball's condition) 387, 393 (for Tanner's), 396, 399 (for Romney's). Gordon B. Hinckley's son, a local Salt Lake City LDS leader, described Romney's mental condition to me in 1983.

237. My interviews, 5-6 Sept. 1992, with Rodney Foster, an assistant secretary in the First Presidency's office from 1974 to 1981; Dew, *Go Forward With Faith,* 393; also Swinton, *In the Company of Prophets,* 55.

238. Gordon B. Hinckley, "The Sustaining of Church Officers," *Ensign* 14 (Nov. 1984): 4.

239. Dew, *Ezra Taft Benson,* 465; Dew, *Go Forward With Faith,* 397 (for Maxwell quote), also 401 (for Thomas S. Monson's perspective), 409, 413-14, 424, 434 (for Hinckley's own perspective); Gordon B. Hinckley, "Special Witnesses for Christ," *Ensign* 14 (May 1984): 51.

240. "For Benson, the Wait Is Nearly Over," *New York Times,* 8 Nov. 1985, A-22.

241. Dew, *Ezra Taft Benson,* 486-87; *Los Angeles Times,* 12 Jan. 1986, I, 5; *Deseret News "Church News,"* 19 Jan. 1986, 3; *New York Times,* 10 Nov. 1986, A-17; *Deseret News "Church News,"* 24 Oct. 1987, 3; *New York Times,* 26 Oct. 1987, A-17; *Deseret News "Church News,"* 12 Dec. 1987, 2.

242. Bob Gottlieb and Peter Wiley, "Mormons to the Right," *San Jose Mercury News,* 1 Dec. 1985, 9; Robert Lindsey, "The Mormons: Growth, Prosperity and Controversy," *New York Times Magazine,* 12 Jan. 1986, 46; Dew, *Go Forward With Faith,* 472-73; my interviews, 29-30 Aug. 1992, with Alan Blodgett; my interview, 2 Nov. 1992, with Lowell M. Durham, Jr., vice-president (and later president) of Zion's Co-operative Mercantile Institution (ZCMI), 1982-90. *Deseret News 1991-1992 Church Almanac* (Salt Lake City: Deseret News, 1990), 304-25, lists one public activity for Benson in 1986, two in 1987, two in 1988, four in 1989, and four in 1990.

243. Ezra Taft Benson, "Certificate of Authority" [to Gordon B. Hinckley], 23 May 1989; Benson, "Certificate of Authority" [to Thomas S. Monson], 23 May 1989; Frank M. Watson [F. Michael Watson] statement as Notary Public, 23 May 1989, all in Corporation File 016041, Corporation of the President of the Church of Jesus Christ of Latter-day Saints, Division of Corporations and Commercial Code, Utah Department of Commerce, Salt Lake City, with photocopies in my possession. For Watson as official secretary to the First Presidency, see *General Church Offices Telephone Directory: January 1990* (Salt Lake City: The Church of Jesus Christ of Latter-day Saints, 1990), 18. These documents and their machine-produced signatures were featured in "Documents Show Counselors Now Control LDS Assets," *Salt Lake Tribune,* 15 Aug. 1993, C-2.

244. James E. Talmage, *The Articles of Faith: A Series of Lectures On the Principal Doctrines of The Church of Jesus Christ of Latter-day Saints,* "Written By Appointment; and Published By the Church" (Salt Lake City: Deseret News, 1899), 213-14; Talmage, *A Study of the Articles of Faith: Being a Consideration of the Principal Doctrines of The Church of Jesus Christ of Latter-day Saints,* Missionary Reference Library edition (Salt Lake City: Deseret Book Co., 1990), 191.

245. Talmage, *Articles of Faith* (1899), 214; Talmage, *Articles of Faith* (1990), 191.

246. *Deseret News 1991-1992 Church Almanac,* 322, 324-25. Dew, *Go Forward With Faith,* 472-73. As early as September 1989 excommunicated general authority George Lee claimed Benson "was too feeble to make decisions," and that his counselors made all

important decisions for him. See "Mormons Oust First Indian in the Hierarchy," *New York Times*, 3 Sept. 1989, A-29.

247. Gordon B. Hinckley, "The Church Is On Course," *Ensign* 22 (Nov. 1992): 53.

248. Don LeFevre statements, quoted and paraphrased in "Mormons Split on Benson's Remarks," *Arizona Republic*, 13 July 1993, B-1. That acknowledgement resulted from public statements by the church president's grandson Steve Benson that his grandfather's mental incapacity made it impossible for him to participate in decision-making ("Aged Mormon Head Incapable of Church Role, Grandson Says," *Arizona Republic*, 9 July 1993, B-1, B-3; "Infirm Mormon Leader's Role Questioned," *Phoenix Gazette*, 10 July 1993, D-7). The *Arizona Republic* article's reference to "carefully staged photo sessions" was deleted from its reprinting in "Benson's Not Competent, Grandson Says: LDS Leader Struggles With Growing Senility," *Salt Lake Tribune*, 10 July 1993, E-1, E-3. That article and most others on this topic were not reprinted in the LDS church-owned *Deseret News*, even though First Presidency's spokesmen were being quoted in those articles.

249. "Pres. Hunter Remains Fair in LDS Hospital," *Deseret News*, 13 Jan. 1995, B-1; "President Hunter Resting Comfortably at Home," *Deseret News*, 7 Feb. 1995, B-1; Dew, *Go Forward With Faith*, 502-505.

250. James E. Faust, "First Presidency Message: Serving the Lord and Resisting the Devil," *Ensign* 25 (Sept. 1995): 5; Dallin H. Oaks, "Same-Gender Attraction," *Ensign* 25 (Oct. 1995): 10 for quote, 11-12 for studies; "Pres. Hinckley Ordained Prophet: Pres. Monson, Pres. Faust Are Called as Counselors," and "President Faust Never Looks Back After He Puts His Hand To the Plow," *Deseret News "Church News,"* 18 Mar. 1995, 3,5; *Deseret News 1995-1996 Church Almanac*, 19, Oaks.

251. Gibbons, *David O. McKay*, 170.

252. Brigham Young statement in Quorum of Twelve Apostles minutes, 16 Nov. 1847; Arrington, *Brigham Young*, 198; Samuel W. Taylor and Raymond W. Taylor, *The John Taylor Papers: Records of the Last Utah Pioneer*, 2 vols. (Redwood City, CA: Taylor Trust, 1984-85), 2:522.

253. Brigham Young statement in Quorum of Twelve Apostles minutes, 16 Nov. 1847; meeting minutes regarding the sugar company, 17 Mar. 1853, LDS archives; Samuel W. Taylor, *The Kingdom or Nothing: The Life of John Taylor, Militant Mormon* (New York: Macmillan Publishing Co., 1976), 171-72, for different quotes from this bitter confrontation.

254. Taylor, *Kingdom or Nothing*, 5, 159-74, and passim.

255. Minutes of a meeting in the First Presidency's office, 23 Feb. 1878, as quoted in Bergera, "Seniority in the Twelve," 53.

256. John Taylor, *Succession in the Priesthood: A Discourse . . .* (Salt Lake City: N.p., 1881), 17.

257. Wells statement as reported in Moses Thatcher 1880 diary, Oct. 1880, 120. There is no available record that Wells expressed any opinion regarding Taylor's 1881 publication which alleged Young's endorsement of Taylor.

258. Taylor and Taylor, *John Taylor Papers*, 1:346n11; Arrington, *Brigham Young*, 198; *Deseret Evening News*, 10 Apr. 1875, 9 Oct. 1875, 10 Apr. 1876, 9 Apr. 1877, compare to previous church conferences since 1835 in Journal History. *Deseret News 1995-1996 Church Almanac*, 42, 51, and Ludlow, *Encyclopedia of Mormonism*, 4:1638, 1648, both state that Hyde's seniority was changed in 1875 and that Taylor was not sustained as president of the Twelve until after Young's death in 1877. Bergera, "Seniority in the Twelve," 19, describes Taylor's later published interpretation of the 1875 change but does not discuss what happened to the office of president of the quorum from 1875 to 1877.

259. Kenney, *Wilford Woodruff's Journal* 7 (1 Apr. 1877): 342; Brigham Young, Jr., diary, 1 Apr. 1877.

260. Brigham Young, Jr., diary, 30 Mar. 1877; Lorenzo Snow statement in Abraham H. Cannon diary, 9 Apr. 1890, and in Heber J. Grant letterbook-journal, 9 Apr. 1890; Taylor, *Kingdom or Nothing*, 258-59.

261. Anthony W. Ivins, "Dixie Mission History," 1:47-52, Utah State Historical Society; James G. Bleak, "Annals of the Southern Utah Mission," typescript, 1:172-75, Lee Library, with copy of manuscript at Huntington Library; England, *Life and Thought of Orson Pratt*, 223.

262. Joseph F. Smith diary, 28-29 Apr. 1880. This was more than five months before Smith became a counselor in the First Presidency.

263. Ibid., 16 May (emphasis in original) and 23 May 1883; Brigham Young, Jr., diary, 23 May 1883.

264. Franklin D. Richards diary, 10 Jan. 1883.

265. Kenney, *Wilford Woodruff's Journal* 8 (23 Mar. 1888): 491; Quorum of the Twelve Apostles minutes, 23 Mar. 1888.

266. Brigham Young, Jr., diary, 29 Apr., 30 May 1890.

267. Heber J. Grant journal, 3 Dec. 1888; Abraham H. Cannon diary, 6-7, 13 Aug. 1889, 20 Jan., 4-5, 19 Mar., 8 Apr. 1890, 28 Jan., 2 Mar. 1891, 14 Sept. 1894; Journal History, 1 Oct. 1896, 4-6 Feb., 11 Feb. 1897, 2-4 Mar., 13 Mar. 1899, 3 Apr., 27 Apr. 1899, 2-7.

268. Abraham H. Cannon diary, 5 Apr. 1894; Brigham Young, Jr., diary, 5 Apr. 1900, also 7 July 1901; Anthon H. Lund diary, 24 Nov. 1901, also 9 July 1901.

269. J. Golden Kimball diary, 9 Oct. 1898.

270. Victor W. Jorgensen and B. Carmon Hardy, "The Taylor-Cowley Affair and the Watershed of Mormon History," *Utah Historical Quarterly* 48 (Winter 1980): 4-36; Kenneth L. Cannon II, "After the Manifesto: Mormon Polygamy, 1890-1906," *Sunstone* 8 (Jan.-Apr. 1983): 27-35; Quinn, "LDS Church Authority and New Plural Marriages, 1890-1904," 9-105; Thomas G. Alexander, *Mormonism in Transition: A History of the Latter-day Saints, 1890-1930* (Urbana: University of Illinois Press, 1985), 11-12, 62-66; Hardy, *Solemn Covenant*, 206-244 (esp. 207); Anthony W. Ivins statement to the Quorum of the Twelve Apostles in Heber J. Grant journal sheets, 2 Jan. 1917.

271. Joseph Eckersley diary, 9 Nov. 1903, 14 Apr. 1906, LDS archives.

272. Anthony W. Ivins diary, 9 Apr. 1906, Utah State Historical Society; Joseph E. Robinson diary, 9 Apr. 1906, LDS archives.

273. Charles W. Penrose diary, 10-11 May 1911, Utah State Historical Society; Heber J. Grant 1911 notebook, 10 May 1911; Joseph Fielding Smith diary, 10-11 May 1911, LDS archives; *Deseret Evening News*, 12 May 1911, 1.

274. Carl A. Badger to Rose Badger, 26 Nov. 1905, Badger letterbook 3:232, Lee Library. On the role of courts in mediating disputes, and the absence of such a role in the contemporary LDS church, see James H. Backman, "Courts, Ecclesiastical: Nineteenth-Century," and Bruce C. Hafen, "Disciplinary Procedures," in Ludlow, *Encyclopedia of Mormonism*, 1:329-30, 386.

275. Reed Smoot diary, 15 Feb., 10 Aug. 1909, 29 Sept. 1910, 4 Oct. 1911, copies in Lee Library and Marriott Library; also Brent G. Thompson, "'Standing between Two Fires': Mormons and Prohibition, 1908-1917," *Journal of Mormon History* 10 (1983): 35-52; Heber J. Grant journal sheets, 8 Jan. 1911.

276. Anthon H. Lund diary, 31 Oct. 1918.

277. Alexander, *Mormonism in Transition*, 52-53; James B. Allen, "Personal Faith and Public Policy: Some Timely Observations on the League of Nations Controversy in Utah," *Brigham Young University Studies* 14 (Autumn 1973): 77-98; Milton R. Merrill, *Reed Smoot: Apostle in Politics* (Logan: Utah State University Press, 1990), 256-66; Reed Smoot diary, 29 July, 5 Aug., 23 Oct. 1920; Anthon H. Lund diary, 5 Aug., 21 Oct. 1920.

278. Reed Smoot diary, 17 May 1923; Marshall, "Garments," in Ludlow, *Encyclopedia of Mormonism*, 2:534.

279. George Albert Smith diary, 17 Nov. 1932.

280. Merlo J. Pusey, *Builders of the Kingdom: George A. Smith, John Henry Smith, George Albert Smith* (Provo, UT: Brigham Young University Press, 1981), 288; George Albert Smith diary, 13 Jan., 3 May, 30 Dec. 1932, 2 Feb. 1933; David O. McKay office diary, 11-12 Jan. 1932; Heber J. Grant journal sheets, 15 Jan. 1932, 2-3 Feb., 21 Mar., 23 Mar., 1 Apr., 25 Apr. 1933; see also Glen R. Stubbs, "A Biography of George Albert Smith, 1870 to 1951," Ph.D. diss., Brigham Young University, 1974.

281. Duane E. Jeffery, "Seers, Savants and Evolution: The Uncomfortable Interface," *Dialogue: A Journal of Mormon Thought* 8 (Fall-Winter 1973): 41-75; Richard Sherlock, "A Turbulent Spectrum: Mormon Reactions to the Darwinist Legacy," *Journal of Mormon History* 5 (1978): 33-46; Sherlock, "'We Can See No Advantage to a Continuation of the Discussion': The Roberts/Smith/Talmage Affair," *Dialogue: A Journal of Mormon Thought* 13 (Fall 1980): 63-78; Truman G. Madsen, *Defender of the Faith: The B.H. Roberts Story* (Salt Lake City: Bookcraft, 1980), 344-45; Gibbons, *Joseph Fielding Smith,* 237-41; James E. Talmage diary, 2 Jan., 7 Jan., 21 Jan., 7 Apr., 5 Nov., 21 Nov. 1931; First Council of Seventy minutes, 20 Sept. 1928, 12 Feb., 9 Apr. 1931, LDS archives; Heber J. Grant journal sheets, 25 Jan., 23 Feb., 30 Mar. 1931; George F. Richards diary, 7 Apr. 1931.

282. Henry D. Moyle diary, 8 Apr. 1953; Joseph Fielding Smith, Jr., and John J. Stewart, *The Life of Joseph Fielding Smith . . .* (Salt Lake City: Deseret Book Co., 1972), 319; Gibbons, *Joseph Fielding Smith,* 240-42; David O. McKay office diary, 18 Aug., 29 Dec. 1954; David O. McKay to William Lee Stokes, 15 Feb. 1957, in "An Official Position," *Dialogue: A Journal of Mormon Thought* 12 (Winter 1979): 91; J. Reuben Clark to Harvey L. Taylor, 2 Jan. 1957, Clark papers; Quinn, *J. Reuben Clark,* 168.

Clark also disagreed with Smith, writing a lengthy letter on 2 October 1946 criticizing Smith's tendency "to give highly technical meanings to general terms" in LDS scripture concerning the earth's age and organic evolution. The disagreement was good-natured, however, and Smith sent a gift copy of *Man: His Origin and Destiny* to Clark with this inscription: "Hoping that you can tolerate a part of this if not all" (Quinn, *J. Reuben Clark,* 167-68; Clark to Joseph Fielding Smith, 2 Oct. 1946; inscribed copy of *Man: His Origin and Destiny,* Clarkana, Special Collections, Lee Library).

283. *Deseret News "Church News,"* 28 Sept. 1963, 6; Talbot, *Acts of the Modern Apostles,* 282. For the association of these three, see Marion G. Romney oral history, 1976, 4, 8, LDS archives; Quinn, *J. Reuben Clark,* 88, 137, 179, 271; Burton, *Marion G. Romney,* 167-69; Goates, *Harold B. Lee,* 177-79, 209, 311.

284. Goates, *Harold B. Lee,* 618; Gibbons, *Harold B. Lee,* 159, 176, also 176-77 which gave an excellent analysis of the differences in personality between Lee and Moyle.

285. Kimball and Kimball, *Spencer W. Kimball,* 275.

Notes to Chapter Three

1. *Time* 61 (13 Apr. 1953): cover, 13; *Time* 67 (7 May 1956): cover, 30; "GOP Committee Members Propose Benson Resign," *Arizona Republic,* 13 Dec. 1959, Sect. 2, 1; "Irate Benson Says He's Not About To Quit Job," *Arizona Republic,* 15 Dec. 1959, 3; Ezra Taft Benson, *Cross Fire: The Eight Years with Eisenhower* (Garden City, NY: Doubleday and Co., 1962); Sheri L. Dew, *Ezra Taft Benson: A Biography* (Salt Lake City: Deseret Book Co., 1987), 253-359; also Edward L. Schapsmeier and Frederick H. Schapsmeier, "Eisenhower and Ezra Taft Benson: Farm Policy in the 1950s," *Agricultural History* 44 (Oct. 1970): 369-78; Schapsmeier and Schapsmeier, *Ezra Taft Benson and the Politics of Agriculture: The Eisenhower Years, 1953-1961* (Danville, IL: Interstate Printers and Publishers, 1975); and Schapsmeier and Schapsmeier, "Religion and Reform: A Case Study of Henry A. Wallace and Ezra Taft Benson," *Journal of Church and State* 21 (Autumn 1979): 525-35.

2. Henry D. Moyle diary, 24 Mar. 1953, archives, Historical Department, Church of Jesus Christ of Latter-day Saints, Salt Lake City, Utah (hereafter LDS archives); J. Reuben Clark ranch diary, 29 Oct. 1957, Clark papers, Department of Special Collections and Manuscripts, Harold B. Lee Library, Brigham Young University, Provo, Utah (hereafter Lee Library).

3. Ernest L. Wilkinson diary, 7 Mar. 1958, photocopy in Manuscripts Division, J. Willard Marriott Library, University of Utah, Salt Lake City (hereafter Marriott Library).

4. Ibid., 7 July 1958; other criticisms of Benson's politics are in entries of 13 Sept., 11 Dec. 1957, 12 Feb., 2 May, 21-29 June 1958, 20 Oct. 1959, 29 Nov. 1960, and 13 May 1963.

5. F. Ross Peterson, "Utah Politics Since 1945," in Richard D. Poll, ed., *Utah's History* (Provo, UT: Brigham Young University Press, 1978), 516.

6. J. Reuben Clark, memorandum of conversation with "Chairman Hopkin," Don Clyde, Lawrence Johnson, Hugh Colton, Howard J. Clegg, Ted Crawford, and Art Woolley, 18 Apr. 1958; Clark farm diary, 5 June 1960; also more of Clark's criticism of Benson's policies appears in Clark office diary, 11 May 1953, 1 July 1957, 31 Mar. 1958, all in Clark papers.

7. Thomas G. Alexander, *The Forest Service and the LDS Church in the Mid-Twentieth Century: Utah National Forests as a Test Case* (Ogden, UT: Weber State College Press, 1988), 7-8, 20-21.

8. Ernest L. Wilkinson diary, 9 Aug. 1961.

9. J. Reuben Clark office diary, 9 Apr. 1953; Clark memoranda of his conversations with Benson, 21 Mar. 1955, 1 July 1957; Clark, remarks to special Welfare Plan meeting, 1 Oct. 1955; Clark to Benson, 21 Jan. 1953, 30 Sept. 1956, 19 July 1960, all in Clark papers. I tried unsuccessfully to obtain Benson's perspective on the hierarchy's criticism of his service. See n12.

10. Dew, *Ezra Taft Benson,* 285, 297.

11. Ibid., viii. The published biographies of David O. McKay, Joseph Fielding Smith, Harold B. Lee, Hugh B. Brown, N. Eldon Tanner, and Mark E. Petersen are either silent about the controversy or only indirectly allude to it.

12. Aside from Benson's public addresses, his statements to the media, and a few comments to his friends or associates, my analysis lacks Ezra Taft Benson's perspective about his controversies with other general authorities. I tried unsuccessfully to obtain from relevant sources Benson's personal perspectives in these matters. After considering my request for a week, Reed A. Benson declined on 25 November 1992 to provide his perspective and that of his father. Likewise, prominent Utah Birchers J. Reese Hunter and David B. Jorgensen decided against expressing their memories of these events. Also, on 15 January 1993 D. Arthur Haycock, former First Presidency secretary and longtime associate of Ezra Taft Benson, declined to discuss the apostle's support of the Birch Society and what Haycock described as "alleged differences between Brother Benson and the other Brethren." However, I quote views in defense of the Bensons and cite Birch advocates who responded to Benson's critics in the hierarchy. To the best of my ability, this chapter presents the varied perspectives of a controversial episode in American experience and Mormon history.

13. Robert H. Welch, *The Blue Book of the John Birch Society* (Belmont, MA: Western Islands, 1961), vii; Welch, *A Brief Introduction to the John Birch Society* (Belmont, MA: John Birch Society, 1962); John H. Rousselot, *Beliefs and Principles of the John Birch Society* (statement to Congress, 12 June 1962) (Belmont, MA: John Birch Society [1962]); "What Is the John Birch Society? The Truth May Surprise You!" (paid advertisement), *Salt Lake Tribune,* 11 Dec. 1965, 18; Welch, *What Is the John Birch Society?* (Belmont, MA: John Birch Society, 1970); Robert W. Lee, "The John Birch Society At Age 25," in the Birch Society's *American Opinion* 26 (Dec. 1983): 1; Susan L. M. Huck, "Founding of the Society," and

Robert W. Lee, "How Robert Welch Developed His Views on Conspiracy in America," *American Opinion* 28 (Mar. 1985): 16, 69-76, 153-72. For alternative views of John Birch's death, compare Welch, *The Life of John Birch* (Chicago: Regnery, 1954), with "Different Views on [John Birch's] Death," *New York Times,* 4 Apr. 1961, 18, "Who Was John Birch?" *Time* 77 (14 Apr. 1961): 29, and "How John Birch Died," *New York Herald Tribune,* 25 Nov. 1962.

The principal archival holdings on the Birch Society are at its archives in Appleton, Wisconsin, which has official documents as well as the personal papers of Robert H. Welch, the society's founder. However, research access is limited at the Birch archives, and the Welch papers are presently unorganized for researchap. Therefore, the most important archival resource for independent researchers interested in the Birch Society is the Conservative/Libertarian Manuscript Collection, Special Collections, Knight Library, University of Oregon at Eugene. The University of Oregon's collection includes the papers of such prominent Birchers as Thomas J. Anderson, T. Coleman Andrews, Augereau G. Heinsohn, and E. Merrill Root. Also, see the Knox Mellon Collection on the John Birch Society, Special Collections, Research Library, University of California at Los Angeles; William J. Grede papers (restricted until 1999), and Clark R. Mollenhoff papers, State Historical Society of Wisconsin at Madison; Sterling Morton papers, Chicago Historical Society.

14. For the general context of domestic fear of Communist subversion, see David Caute, *The Great Fear: The Anti-Communist Purge Under Truman and Eisenhower* (New York: Simon and Schuster, 1978); also Robert K. Carr, *The House Committee on Un-American Activities* (Ithaca, NY: Cornell University Press, 1952); Samuel A. Stouffer, *Communism, Conformity, and Civil Liberties: A Cross-section of the Nation Speaks Its Mind* (New York: Doubleday, 1955); Ralph S. Brown, *Loyalty and Security: Employment Tests in the United States* (New Haven: Yale University Press, 1958); John W. Caughey, *In Clear and Present Danger: The Crucial State of Our Freedoms* (Chicago: University of Chicago Press, 1958); Herbert L. Packer, *Ex-Communist Witnesses: Four Studies in Fact Finding* (Stanford, CA: Stanford University Press, 1962); Daniel Bell, ed., *The Radical Right* (New York: Doubleday, 1963); J. Allen Broyles, *The John Birch Society: Anatomy of a Protest* (Boston: Beacon Press, 1964); Richard Hofstadter, *The Paranoid Style in American Politics and Other Essays* (New York: Alfred A. Knopf, 1965); Donald J. Kemper, *Decade of Fear: Senator Hennings and Civil Liberties* (Columbia: University of Missouri Press, 1965); Earl Latham, *The Communist Controversy in Washington: From the New Deal to McCarthy* (Cambridge, MA: Harvard University Press, 1967): Walter Goodman, *The Committee: The Extraordinary Career of the House Committee on Un-American Activities* (New York: Farrar, Straus and Giroux, 1968); "The Era of the John Birch Society," in Seymour Martin Lipset and Earl Raab, *The Politics of Unreason: Right-Wing Extremism in America, 1790-1970* (New York: Harper and Row, 1970), 249-87; Murray Burton Levin, *Political Hysteria in America: The Democratic Capacity for Repression* (New York: Basic Books, 1971); Athan G. Theoharis, *Seeds of Repression: Harry S. Truman and the Origins of McCarthyism* (Chicago: Quadrangle Books, 1971); David Brion Davis, ed., *The Fear of Conspiracy: Images of Un-American Subversion From the Revolution to the Present* (Ithaca, NY: Cornell University Press, 1971), 327-48.

Richard M. Freeland, *The Truman Doctrine and the Origins of McCarthyism: Foreign Policy, Domestic Politics, and Internal Security, 1946-1948* (New York: Alfred A. Knopf, 1972); Eric Bentley, *Are You Now Or Have You Ever Been?: The Investigation of Show Business by the Un-American Activities Committee, 1974-1958* (New York: Harper and Row, 1972); Richard O. Curry, *Conspiracy: The Fear of Subversion in American History* (New York: Holt, Rinehart and Winston, 1972); Cedric Belfrage, *The American Inquisition, 1945-1960* (Indianapolis: Bobbs-Merrill, 1973); Robert Griffith and Athan Theoharis, eds., *The Spectre: Original Essays on the Cold War and the Origins of McCarthyism* (New York: New Viewpoints, 1974); F. Ross Peterson, "McCarthyism in the Mountains, 1950-1954," in Thomas G. Alexander, ed., *Essays*

On the American West, 1974-1975 (Provo, UT: Brigham Young University, 1976), 47-77; Michael R. Belknap, *Cold War Justice: The Smith Act, the Communist Party, and American Civil Liberties* (Westport, CT: Greenwood Press, 1977); Allen Weinstein, *Perjury: The Hiss-Chambers Case* (New York: Random House, 1978); Larry Ceplair and Steven Englund, *The Inquisition in Hollywood: Politics in the Film Community, 1930-1960* (Garden City, NY: Doubleday, 1980); Victor S. Navasky, *Naming Names* (New York: Viking Press, 1980); Stanley I. Dutler, *The American Inquisition: Justice and Injustice in the Cold War* (New York: Hill and Wang, 1982); Athan G. Theoharis, ed., *Beyond the Hiss Case: The FBI, Congress, and the Cold War* (Philadelphia: Temple University Press, 1982); Ronald Radosh and Joyce Milton, *The Rosenberg File: A Search for the Truth* (New York: Holt, Rinehart and Winston, 1983); Mark Alan Fuhrman, "Through the John Birch Society: An Historical and Participant Observational Analysis of Organizational Survival," M.A. thesis, University of Wisconsin, 1985; Peter L. Steinberg, *The Great "Red Menace": United States Prosecution of American Communists, 1947-1952* (Westport, CT: Greenwood Press, 1985); Ellen Schrecker, *No Ivory Tower: McCarthyism and the Universities* (New York: Oxford University Press, 1986); Thomas G. Patterson, *Meeting the Communist Threat: Truman to Reagan* (New York: Oxford University Press, 1988); M. J. Heale, *American Anticommunism: Combating the Enemy Within, 1930-1970* (Baltimore: Johns Hopkins University Press, 1990); Jeff Broadwater, *Eisenhower and the Anti-Communist Crusade* (Chapel Hill: University of North Carolina Press, 1992); Joel Kovel, *Red Hunting in the Promised Land: Anticommunism and the Making of America* (New York: Basic Books, 1994).

15. Benson's first official endorsement of the Birch Society appeared in "Reed A. Benson Takes Post In Birch Society," *Deseret News,* 27 Oct. 1962, B-5; "Reed Benson Takes Post With John Birch Group," *Salt Lake Tribune,* 27 Oct. 1962, 24; and was repeated in "Benson-Birch Tie Disturbs Utahans [sic]," *New York Times,* 4 Nov. 1962, 65; "Benson's Praise of the Birchers," *San Francisco Chronicle,* 14 Mar. 1963, 16; "Elder Benson Makes Statement," *Deseret News "Church News,"* 16 Mar. 1963, 2; *The Pink Book of the John Birch Society* (Belmont, MA: John Birch Society, 1963); "The John Birch Society: A Report," *Advertising Supplement to Los Angeles Times,* 27 Sept. 1964, 14; and "Socialism Warning Sounded: Elder Benson Hits Liberals," *Deseret News,* 12 Feb. 1966, B-1. His reference to Birch training seminars is in "LDS Apostle Backs Up Birch Group," *Salt Lake Tribune,* 16 Jan. 1966, B-14.

16. "Goldwater Disagrees With John Birch Theories, Is Impressed by Members," *Sacramento Bee,* 30 Mar. 1961, A-16; Russell Kirk's statement about "fanatic fringe" appears in his and Benjamin L. Masse, "The Birchites," *America: National Catholic Weekly Review* 106 (17 Feb. 1962): 643-45; Barry Goldwater introduced into *Congressional Record* 109 (1 Oct. 1963): 18453-55 a talk which lumped the Birch Society and the Ku Klux Klan with the "so-called radical right" (18454); "Barry Disagrees With 3 Bircher Stands," *Sacramento Bee,* 22 Oct. 1963, A-6; William F. Buckley, Jr., "Real Responsibility Lacking Still With Birchite Members," *Ogden Standard-Examiner,* 6 Aug. 1965, A-4 [which dropped "paranoid" from his description of Birch "drivel" in his syndicated column]; "Bouquet for Buckley," *Christian Century* 82 (25 Aug. 1965): 1028; Buckley [with supporting contributions by Goldwater, Kirk, and others], "The John Birch Society and the Conservative Movement," *National Review* 17 (19 Oct. 1965): 914-20, 925-29; Ronald Reagan's statement about the Birch Society's "lunatic fringe" is in "Reagan Criticizes Birch Society and Its Founder," *Los Angeles Times,* 24 Sept. 1965, I, 3, also quoted in Fletcher Knebel, "The GOP Attacks The John Birch Society," *Look* 29 (28 Dec. 1965): 74; Goldwater to Harvey B. Schechter, 31 Oct. 1966, endorsing Schechter's pamphlet *How To Listen To A John Birch Society Speaker,* copy in J. D. Williams papers, Marriott Library. These anti-Birch critics had established their anti-Communist credentials in Buckley and L. Brent Bozell, *McCarthy and His Enemies: The Record and Its Meaning* (Chicago: H. Regnery Co., 1954); Buckley, *The Committee and Its Critics: A Calm Review of the House Committee on Un-American Activities* (New York: Putnam, 1962);

Goldwater, *The Conscience of a Conservative* (Shepherdsville, KY: Victor Publishing Company, 1960); Russell Kirk, *A Program for Conservatives* (Chicago: H. Regnery, 1954); Kirk, *The American Cause* (Chicago: H. Regnery Co., 1957); Ronald Reagan, with Richard G. Hubler, *Where's the Rest of Me?* (New York: Duell, Sloan and Pearce, 1965), 157-84, 192, 199-200, 297-312. The books by Buckley, Kirk, and Goldwater appeared in the lists of "Approved Books" following *The John Birch Society Bulletin* (July 1961) in *The White Book of The John Birch Society for 1961* (Belmont, MA: John Birch Society, 1961).

17. Of the labels given by mainstream conservatives to the Birch Society, I use "ultra-conservative" and "right-wing" as the most neutral terms for a controversial movement, although these are usually resented by Birch advocates. See Buckley, "Birch Society Members Indignant at Buckley," *Ogden Standard-Examiner,* 17 Aug. 1965, A-4; *The John Birch Society Bulletin* (Dec. 1967): 24-25; Medford Evans, "Welch and Buckley" in the John Birch Society's *American Opinion* 28 (Mar. 1985): 89-106. W. Cleon Skousen wrote: "Very often it is popular to resist any Constitutional reform by calling it 'rightist' or 'ultraconservative.' However, it is obvious that the elimination of socialist principles from the American system and the re-establishment of the American eagle in the balanced center of the political spectrum is neither right-wing extremism nor ultra-conservatism" (Skousen, *What Is Left? What Is Right?: A Study of Political Extremism* [Salt Lake City: Freemen Institute, 1981], 22). See also Jerreld L. Newquist's specific denial that the John Birch Society is ultra-conservative or right-wing in Jerrald [sic] L. Newquist, "Liberty Vs. Creeping Socialism: Warns of Internal Threats," *Deseret News,* 21 Dec. 1961, A-12. See below for Ezra Taft Benson's association with Skousen and the Freeman Institute, for Newquist's edition of Benson's talks, as well as Skousen's association with the Birch Society.

18. These are: America's Future, American Committee for Aid to Katanga Freedom Fighters, American Security Council, Americans For Constitutional Action, Christian [Anti-Communism] Crusade, Christian Freedom Foundation, Church League of America, Citizens Foreign Aid Committee, Committee of One Million (Against the Admission of Red China to the United Nations), Conservative Society of America, Dan Smoot Report, For America: A Committee for Political Action, the Intercollegiate Society of Individualists, the International Services of Information, Liberty Lobby, Manion Forum, National Economic Council, National Education Program, Veritas Foundation, We, the People, and Young Americans for Freedom. See Douglas Kirk Stewart, "An Analysis of the Celebrity Structure of the American Right," M.S. thesis, University of Utah, 1962, 6, 11, 25-26; *The Patriots* (Cleveland, OH: Precis Press, 1963), 28; National Council of Civic Responsibility, Press Release, 22 Sept. 1964, 1-5, copy in Williams papers; Editors and Advisory Committee of the Birch Society's *American Opinion* (1961-64); also files on the above organizations in J. Bracken Lee papers, Marriott Library. Although not technically a member of the Birch Society, Bracken Lee became a member of the society's Committee of Endorsers in 1961 and a member of *American Opinion*'s Editorial Advisory Committee until November 1966. See Lee to Robert Welch, 19 Jan. 1961, Lee papers; *American Opinion* 9 (Nov. 1966): inside front cover. Lee was Utah's governor (1949-57) and Salt Lake City mayor (1960-72).

19. "Benson Took Birchite on Tours," *Washington Post,* 12 July 1961, D-11; "The Council," *The John Birch Society Bulletin* (Feb. 1960): 2. Neither Benson's *Cross Fire* nor Dew's *Ezra Taft Benson* says that Anderson was part of the secretary's entourage on these two trips. However, Benson prints (606-608) Anderson's account of their visit to Russia, and Dew quotes (344) part of that article.

20. See Ezra Taft Benson, "Biographical Notes," Dec. 1961, and Benson's "Dear Bob" letter, 10 Dec. 1970, Welch papers, archives, Birch Society, with photocopies in my possession.

21. "Bircher" and "Birchers" are terms that members of the Birch Society apply to themselves, as in *The John Birch Society Bulletin,* Oct. 1992, 6, 14, 20.

22. "Benson Aims New Blast At M'Carthy," *Salt Lake Tribune*, 23 June 1954, 1; also see "Joe" McCarthy, *McCarthyism: The Fight For America* (New York: Devin-Adair Co., 1952); Arthur V. Watkins [U.S. senator from Utah], *Enough Rope: The Inside Story of the Censure of Senator Joe McCarthy By His Colleagues: The Controversial Hearings that Signaled the End of a Turbulent Career and a Fearsome Era in American Public Life* (Englewood Cliffs, NJ: Prentice-Hall, 1970); Allen J. Matusow, *Joseph R. McCarthy* (Englewood Cliffs, NJ: Prentice-Hall, 1970); Thomas C. Reeves, *The Life and Times of Joe McCarthy: A Biography* (New York: Stein and Day, 1982); Robert Griffith, *The Politics of Fear: Joseph R. McCarthy and the Senate*, 2d ed. (Amherst: University of Massachusetts Press, 1987); Richard M. Fried, *Nightmare in Red: The McCarthy Era in Perspective* (New York: Oxford University Press, 1990); Diana Trilling, "How McCarthy Gave Anti-Communism a Bad Name," *Newsweek* 121 (11 Jan 1993): 32-33.

23. Ezra Taft Benson to H. Roland Tietjen, president of the Hawaiian LDS temple, 22 May 1962, Lee Library.

24. My telephone interview with Byron Cannon Anderson, 18 Jan. 1993. As an undergraduate, Anderson became a member of the Birch Society through his association with Reed Benson. However, Mark Benson's son Steve told me on 28 June 1993 that his father was a Bircher in philosophy without formal membership. That philosophical commitment was sufficiently ardent that Mark Benson provided his adolescent son with the society's *American Opinion* as well as tape recordings of speeches by its president and national council members.

25. Ernest L. Wilkinson diary, 29 Nov. 1960. Gary James Bergera and Ronald Priddis, *Brigham Young University: A House of Faith* (Salt Lake City: Signature Books, 1985), 203, mention Reed Benson's offer but do not refer to his father's support of the "espionage" proposal. Wilkinson's diary indicated that Ezra Taft Benson first made the proposal which Reed later outlined to Harold B. Lee.

26. Byron Cannon Anderson interview, 18 Jan. 1993; *Directory: University of Utah, 1959-1960: Faculty, Students, Employees* (Salt Lake City: University of Utah, 1959), 34; *Directory: University of Utah, 1960-1961 . . .* , 30; *Directory: University of Utah, 1961-1962 . . .* , 31; *Directory: University of Utah, 1962-1963 . . .* , 33. For his revision of statements to me in January 1993, see Byron Cannon Anderson, "'Spy' Reply," *Dialogue: A Journal of Mormon Thought* 26 (Winter 1993): ix-x, with my response and summary of his activities at BYU (x-xii).

27. *Banyan, 1965* (Provo, UT: Associated Students of Brigham Young University, 1965), 410. See discussion to follow.

28. For example, E. Merrill Root, *Collectivism on the Campus: The Battle For the Mind in American Colleges* (New York: Devin-Adair Co., 1955). Root became a founding member of the "Committee of Endorsers" for the Birch Society and an associate editor of the society's *American Opinion*. For professors as "Comsymps," see Robert Welch, "Through All the Days To Be," *American Opinion* 4 (June 1961): 34-35.

29. Max P. Peterson, "Ideology of the John Birch Society," M.S. thesis, Utah State University, 1966, 116, 132; also "Birchers Infiltrate Police, Trigger Freedom Issue," *Salt Lake Tribune*, 17 Nov. 1964, 13.

30. Ezra Taft Benson, "The American Heritage of Freedom: A Plan of God," *Improvement Era* 64 (Dec. 1961): 955.

31. Hugh B. Brown statements, as quoted and paraphrased in Frederick S. Buchanan diary, 27 Oct. 1961, photocopy in my possession. Buchanan walked into Brown's office just as Benson was leaving.

32. Ernest L. Wilkinson diary, 21 Dec., 29 Dec. 1961.

33. Ezra Taft Benson, "Is There A Threat To The American Way of Life?" *Deseret News "Church News,"* 23 Dec. 1961, 15, reprinted as *The Internal Threat to the American Way of Life . . . Talk given at the Shrine Auditorium, Los Angeles, California, December 11, 1961* (Salt Lake City: Bookcraft, 1961), 30-31, and in Roland L. Delorme and Raymond G. McInnis,

eds., *Antidemocratic Trends in Twentieth-Century America* (Reading, MA: Addison-Wesley Publishing Co., 1969). Benson quoted portions of his recent talk in an official statement, "Speech Misinterpreted By King, Benson Says," *Deseret News,* 16 Dec. 1961, B-5; "Benson Rips King 'Challenge,'" *Salt Lake Tribune,* 16 Dec. 1961, 7. Although his disclaimer said this referred to the Social Democratic Party of Russia in 1903, the *Church News* publication of his talk showed that he emphasized (15) the present American context: "Many people have wondered if the Marxist concepts of Fabian Social Democrats have deeply penetrated the United States. In truth they have. . . . There they remain today, occupying some of the highest offices of the land." He added that "the Communists and the Social Democrats don't want us to examine this internal threat, but I believe we should."

34. "Benson Says JFK Soft on Reds," *Los Angeles Herald and Express,* 12 Dec. 1961, A-3; also "Kennedy Aides Held Soft on Reds," *Los Angeles Times,* 12 Dec. 1961, Pt. III, 1; "U.S. Red Peril Emphasized By Elder Benson," *Deseret News,* 12 Dec. 1961, A-1, A-7; "Benson Warns of 'Secret Alliance,'" *Salt Lake Tribune,* 12 Dec. 1961, 3. Benson's talk itself made no reference to Kennedy.

35. O. Preston Robinson, editor and general manager of the *Deseret News,* to Hugh B. Brown, 14 Dec. 1961, "as per your request," in "Hugh B. Brown's File on the John Birch Society," box 48, Edwin B. Firmage papers, Marriott Library.

36. Brown to Mrs. Alicia Bingham, 28 Dec. 1961, carbon copy in "Hugh B. Brown's File on the John Birch Society."

37. Frederick S. Buchanan diary, 22 Feb. 1962.

38. Hugh B. Brown to L. Hyrum Coon, 2 Mar. 1962, photocopy in fd 4, box 41, Richard Douglas Poll papers, Marriott Library.

39. Hugh B. Brown, "Honor the Priesthood," *Improvement Era* 65 (June 1962): 450.

40. Frederick S. Buchanan diary, 7 Apr. 1962.

41. Hugh B. Brown to Harley Ross Hammond, 25 Apr. 1962, photocopy in fd 4, box 41, Poll papers, and in Williams papers.

42. "We Must Protect U.S.: Ezra Benson Sounds Warning," *U.S. News and World Report* 52 (23 Apr. 1962): 20.

43. Ernest L. Wilkinson diary, 3 June 1962, described a memorandum of what he was going to say privately to McKay on 6 June.

44. Ibid., 29 Oct. 1962, referred to a Democratic state convention "two years ago." In Buchanan diary, 27 Oct. 1961, Brown said that in response to Benson's conference address that month, "he'd be speaking to the States Democratic leaders in order to set them straight on the position of politics in the churchap."

45. Hugh B. Brown to Gustive O. Larson, 11 Nov. 1962, in answer to Larson's letter of 1 Nov., Larson papers, Lee Library. The letter did not name Benson specifically, but his identity is clear from the circumstances surrounding the correspondence. Larson's "outline diary" notes (fd 19, box 1) for 1962 referred to "Bensonizing & Skousenizing" before Brown's letter, and "Pres Brown and Birchers etc" after the letter. A carbon copy of Larson's original letter to Brown on 1 Nov. 1962 is in Eugene Campbell papers, Lee Library, and a photocopy in fd 1, box 51, Poll papers. Larson's letter referred to an unnamed member of the "L.D.S. officials" who was associated by a recent newspaper article with the Birch Society. This obviously was the newspaper report of Benson's formal endorsement of the Birch Society which appeared in "Reed A. Benson Takes Post In Birch Society," *Deseret News,* 27 Oct. 1962, B-5; "Reed Benson Takes Post With John Birch Group," *Salt Lake Tribune,* 27 Oct. 1962, 24.

46. For the national context, see Kenneth Keniston, *Young Radicals: Notes on Committed Youth* (New York: Harcourt, Brace, and World, 1968); Benjamin Muse, *The American Negro Revolution: From Nonviolence to Black Power, 1963-1967* (Bloomington: Indiana University Press, 1968); Theodore Roszak, *The Making of a Counter Culture: Reflections on the Technocratic Society and Its Youthful Opposition* (Garden City, NY: Doubleday,

1969); Philip Slater, *The Pursuit of Loneliness: American Culture at the Breaking Point* (Boston: Beacon Press, 1970); David Burner, Robert D. Marcus, and Thomas R. West, *A Giant's Strength: America in the 1960s* (New York: Holt, Rinehart and Winston, 1971); William L. O'Neill, *Coming Apart: An Informal History of America in the 1960's* (Chicago: Quadrangle Books, 1971); James A. Geschwender, *The Black Revolt: The Civil Rights Movement, Ghetto Uprisings, and Separatism* (Englewood Cliffs, NJ: Prentice-Hall, 1971); Thomas Powers, *The War at Home: Vietnam and the American People, 1964-1968* (New York: Grossman, 1973); Alexander Kendrick, *The Wound Within: America in the Vietnam Years, 1945-1974* (Boston: Little, Brown, and Co., 1974); Tom Shachtman, *Decade of Shocks: Dallas to Watergate, 1963-1974* (New York: Poseidon Press, 1974); Donald D. Warren, *The Radical Center: Middle Americans and the Politics of Alienation* (South Bend, IN: University of Notre Dame Press, 1976); Morris Dickstein, *Gates of Eden: American Culture in the Sixties* (New York: Basic Books, 1977); Charles R. Morris, *A Time of Passion: America, 1960-1980* (New York: Harper and Row, 1984); Allen J. Matusow, *The Unraveling of America: A History of Liberalism in the 1960s* (New York: Harper and Row, 1984); George C. Herring, *America's Longest War: The United States and Vietnam, 1950-1975* (Philadelphia: Temple University Press, 1986); Neil Sheehan, *A Bright Shining Lie: John Paul Vann and America in Vietnam* (New York: Random House, 1988); Kim McQuaid, *The Anxious Years: America in the Vietnam-Watergate Era* (New York: Basic Books, 1989); Charles DeBenedetti, *An American Ordeal: The Antiwar Movement of the Vietnam Era* (Syracuse, NY: Syracuse University Press, 1990); Patrick Lloyd Hatcher, *The Suicide of an Elite: American Internationalists and Vietnam* (Stanford, CA: Stanford University Press, 1990); Stanley Karnow, *Vietnam: A History*, rev. ed. (New York: Viking Press, 1991); Peter O. Whitmer, *Aquarius Revisited: Seven Who Created the Sixties Counterculture that Changed America: William Burroughs, Allen Ginsberg, Ken Kesey, Timothy Leary, Norman Mailer, Tom Robbins, Hunter S. Thompson* (New York: Citadel Press, 1991); Edward P. Morgan, *The 60s Experience: Hard Lessons About Modern America* (Philadelphia: Temple University Press, 1991); David Steigerwald, *The Sixties and the End of Modern America* (New York: St. Martin's Press, 1995).

47. The dimensions of Hugh B. Brown's agenda appear in Eugene E. Campbell and Richard Poll, *Hugh B. Brown: His Life and Thought* (Salt Lake City: Bookcraft, 1975); and Edwin B. Firmage, ed., *An Abundant Life: The Memoirs of Hugh B. Brown* (Salt Lake City: Signature Books, 1988).

48. "Reed A. Benson Takes Post In Birch Society," *Deseret News*, 27 Oct. 1962, B-5; "Reed Benson Takes Post With John Birch Group," *Salt Lake Tribune*, 27 Oct. 1962, 24; "Ezra Benson's Son Takes Birch Society Post," *Sacramento Bee*, 27 Oct. 1972, B-7; "Benson-Birch Tie Disturbs Utahans [sic]," *New York Times*, 4 Nov. 1962, 65; "LDS in Capital Rap Reed Benson Talk," *Salt Lake Tribune*, 15 Dec. 1962, 7; "Reed Benson Replies to News Dispatch," *Salt Lake Tribune*, 18 Dec. 1962.

49. Francis M. Gibbons, *David O. McKay: Apostle to the World, Prophet of God* (Salt Lake City: Deseret Book Co. 1986), 380.

50. Richard P. Lindsay, on letterhead of Taylorsville Second Ward Bishopric, to David O. McKay, Henry D. Moyle, and Hugh B. Brown, 20 Mar. 1962, carbon copy in Williams papers. Lindsay's handwritten note to Williams at the end of the carbon copy: "I'm sure this sounds soap boxish but the latter talk referred to cost me one whole night's sleep. Everyone seems to profit in the hard sell book business—One of these days write a sequel called 'Conscience of a Liberal,'" which referred to Goldwater, *Conscience of a Conservative*, cited above. For Lindsay's later appointment to the Second Quorum of Seventy, see *Deseret News 1995-1996 Church Almanac* (Salt Lake City: Deseret News, 1994), 74.

51. Hugh B. Brown to Richard D. Poll, 26 Nov. 1962, in response to Poll to Brown, 20 Nov. 1962, fd 15, box 39, Poll papers.

52. Henry D. Taylor's statement as reported in Richard M. Taylor to Richard D. Poll, 7 Nov. 1962, fd 15, box 39, Poll papers. Someone even burned a Nazi swastika in the lawn of Reed Benson's home shortly after his appointment as state coordinator for the Birch Society. See "Vandals, Reds, Loaded Queries Plague Utah's Bircher Benson," *Portland Oregonian*, 19 May 1963, 16, with photo of Reed beside the swastika vandalism.

53. Henry D. Moyle daybook, 11 Feb. 1962, typed notes in fd 24, box 62, Poll papers.

54. "Benson Son Leads Rightists in Utah," *New York Times*, 19 May 1963, 55; "Benson's Son Claims He Has Tripled Utah Birch Membership," *Washington Post*, 20 May 1963, A-1; T. George Harris, "The Rampant Right Invades the GOP," *Look* 27 (16 July 1963): 20; "Benson and Birch: Politics Or Religion?" *University of Utah Daily Utah Chronicle*, 3 Dec. 1964, 2; "Utahn Heads Birch Office in Capital," *Deseret News*, 16 Dec. 1964, A-13; Jules Witcover, "Bircher Benson," *The New Republic* 152 (8 May 1965): 8-9; "Washington Report . . . Birchers Settle In," *Life* 58 (18 June 1965): 43; "Birch Society Opens Washington Office Friday," *New York Times*, 14 Sept. 1965, 20; "John Birch Society Representative Reed Benson," *Ogden Standard-Examiner*, 19 Sept. 1965, A-6; "Mormons and Politics: Benson's Influence Helps Keep Growing Church on Conservative Track," *Wall Street Journal*, 8 Aug. 1966, 1; "Gets Birch Job," *Salt Lake Tribune*, 19 May 1967, B-4; Byron Cannon Anderson, "Church and Birch in Utah," senior paper, University of Utah, June 1966, 20, photocopy, Western Americana, Marriott Library; Reed A. Benson to Dean M. Hansen, 22 May 1967, in Dean Maurice Hansen, "An Analysis of the 1964 Idaho Second Congressional District Election Campaign," M.A. thesis, Brigham Young University, 1967, 50, 221.

55. Reed A. Benson to Tom Anderson, "*PERSONAL AND CONFIDENTIAL*," 3 July 1963, Anderson papers, Knight Library, University of Oregon at Eugene.

56. Minutes of a meeting, 15 Mar. 1966, with David O. McKay, N. Eldon Tanner, Joseph Fielding Smith, and Mark E. Petersen in Huntsville, Utah, LDS archives.

57. Anderson, "Church and Birch," 8-13; Alison Bethke, "BF [Before Falwell], EB [Ezra Benson]," senior paper, History 490, Brigham Young University, 9 Apr. 1984, 6, 8, photocopy in Williams papers.

As a graduate student Anderson was chair of a Birch Society spin-off group called Citizens for Honest Government (CHG). In my interview with him, 18 Jan. 1993, Anderson stated that he was an undergraduate when he joined the Birch Society and that the CHG was also led by such prominent Mormon Birchers as J. Reese Hunter and Mark E. Anderson. In 1970 Hunter and Cannon became founding editor and assistant editor of *The Utah Independent: The Conservative Marketplace of Utah*, written by and for Mormon Birchers. See Byron Cannon Anderson, "Open Letter to Utah Citizens," Mar. 1966, fd 5, box 184, Frank E. Moss papers, Marriott Library; "Young, But Eager, He Looks for Political Chance," *Deseret News*, 30 Sept. 1965, B-1; "Welch Raps 'Senseless' U.S. Policy," *Salt Lake Tribune*, 8 Apr. 1966, B-1; Anderson, "Church and Birch In Utah"; "David O. McKay: Prophet-Patriot," and staff list, *Utah Independent*, 12 Feb. 1970, 1-2; "Birch Society PR Speaker," *Utah Independent*, 9 Apr. 1970, 1; "What Is The John Birch Society," *Utah Independent*, 28 May 1971, 6-7, 9; "The Communist Attack on The John Birch Society," *Utah Independent*, 21 Apr. 1972, 4-7; "Birchers Ask Economic Sanctions on Communists," *Utah Independent*, 19 May 1972, 4; and the regular column from Birch headquarters in Belmont, Massachusetts, officially named "The Birch Log" as of *Utah Independent*, 5 Aug. 1976, 3. Also see Cannon's retractions about the CHG in "Spy Reply," x, and also "Quinn Responds," xii.

58. Dew, *Ezra Taft Benson*, 366-67. For an academic summary of Birch themes, see Peterson, "Ideology of the John Birch Society."

59. Kjell Nilsen, letters to the editor, *Daily Utah Chronicle*, 22 Oct. 1962, 2, and 26 Oct. 1962, 2, to which Allen Mickelsen and Jim Wanek responded in *Daily Utah Chronicle*, 24 Oct. 1962, 2, and 25 Oct. 1962, 2.

60. Richard D. Poll to Hugh B. Brown, 13 Dec. 1962, fd 15, box 39, Poll papers; "The Council," *The John Birch Society Bulletin*, Feb. 1960, 2; Birch Society's *American Opinion*.

61. C. LaVar Rockwood to D. Michael Quinn, 22 July 1993. Rockwood was BYU's assistant dean of students at the time and "served on the assembly committee with Herald R. Clark & hosted many of the forum & devotional speakers."

62. Ernest L. Wilkinson diary, 4 Nov. 1962; conversation reported to me by the student in November 1962, during which time I was enrolled in Pearson's missionary preparation course. The student supported the views of the Birch Society, of Benson, and of Pearson. Pearson's political tracts included *The Constitution versus the Bill of Rights* (Provo, UT: N.d.); *Freedom of Speech and Press* (Provo, UT: N.d.); *Socialism and the United Order or the Law of Consecration* (Provo, UT: 1962[?]); *The No-Plan Plan* (Provo, UT: [1967]); *Public School Philosophy–State Religion* (Provo, UT: 1967[?]); also Bergera and Priddis, *Brigham Young University*, 196, about Pearson. Benson made a public allusion to Brown as Judas in general conference a year after Pearson's remark. See discussion of October 1963 conference, below.

63. "Mormons & Politics," *Wall Street Journal*, 8 Aug. 1966, 12.

64. "Church Sets Policy on Birch Society," *Deseret News*, 4 Jan. 1963, B-1; also "Mormon Head Clarifies Stand on Birch Society: McKay Lashes at Those Who Try to Align Church With Group's Partisan Views," *Los Angeles Times*, 4 Jan. 1963, Pt. I, 5; "LDS Leaders Reject Any Idea of Link Between Church, Birch Society," *Sacramento Bee*, 4 Jan. 1963, A-10; "Birch Tie Flatly Denied By LDS," *Ogden Standard-Examiner*, 4 Jan. 1963; "Reprint of Statement From the First Presidency," *The Messenger: Distributed By the Presiding Bishopric of the Church of Jesus Christ of Latter-day Saints, Salt Lake City, Utah*, Feb. 1963, 1.

65. "Ezra Taft Benson Addresses Rally," *Deseret News*, 7 Jan. 1963, A-3; Drew Pearson, "Benson Embarrasses His Church," *Washington Post*, 22 Jan. 1963, B-23; "Church Embarrassed Over Ezra Taft Benson Stand," *Ogden Standard-Examiner*, 22 Jan. 1963, 4. Dew, *Ezra Taft Benson*, frequently referred to Benson speaking about "freedom" at "a convention" here or "a rally" there, but never mentioned the John Birch Society, and insisted (370): "He avoided speaking at partisan gatherings of any kind, but in nonpartisan settings he was anxious to teach that the principle of agency was a religious, not a political, issue."

66. Nancy Smith Lowe to David O. McKay, 10 Jan. 1963, LDS archives, photocopy in my possession.

67. Henry D. Moyle to J. D. Williams, 9 Jan. 1963, Williams papers. See also Frank H. Jonas, political scientist, University of Utah, typed document, 83, Jonas papers, Marriott Library. Liberals had long encouraged the First Presidency to issue a statement against the Birch Society (e.g., Richard D. Poll to Hugh B. Brown, 22 Jan. 1962, fd 15, box 39, Poll papers) but had not criticized the presidency for failure to do so.

68. Ernest L. Wilkinson diary, 31 Jan. 1963. Three weeks before learning this, he had already written that "I think you ought not to read too much in the statement of the First Presidency" (Wilkinson to Richard D. Poll, 7 Jan. 1963, fd 15, box 39, Poll papers); also Gibbons, *David O. McKay*, 381.

69. Clare Middlemiss to Nancy Smith Lowe, 15 Feb. 1963, LDS archives; identical statement in Middlemiss to Robert W. Lee, 1 Aug. 1963, in *Congressional Record* 109 (6 Aug. 1963): 14172; "Stand of LDS On Birch In 'Record,'" *Salt Lake Tribune*, 8 Aug. 1963, A-2; Anderson, "Church and Birch in Utah," 11. Before becoming Reed Benson's assistant in Washington, D.C., Robert W. Lee served as a chapter leader, section leader, and volunteer coordinator of the Birch Society in Salt Lake City. See "S.L. Man Takes Capital Post With Birchers," *Salt Lake Tribune*, 11 Nov. 1964, B-11. Dew, *Ezra Taft Benson*, 532, listed "Bob Lee" as a source for her discussion of Benson's post-Cabinet political speeches.

70. *The John Birch Society Bulletin*, Feb. 1963, 28-29; also summarized in George Rucker memorandum, 17 June 1963, fd 5, box 636, Moss papers.

71. Ezra Taft Benson, *The Red Carpet . . .* (Derby, CT: Monarch Books, 1963), inscribed to "Eldon" on 2-12-63, copy in Special Collections, Lee Library. The book was originally published in 1962 in Salt Lake City by Bookcraft.

72. G. Homer Durham et al., *N. Eldon Tanner: His Life and Service* (Salt Lake City: Deseret Book Co., 1982), 57-89; *Encyclopedia of Canada,* 6 vols. (Toronto: University Associates of Canada, 1948), 6:41; *Encyclopedia Canadiana,* 10 vols. (Ottawa: Canadiana Co./Grolier Society of Canada, 1957-58), 9:353.

73. Richard D. Poll, "Henry D. Moyle: Man of Action," unpublished 1983 biography, fd 21, box 67, chapter, "Counselor in the First Presidency—I," 2, Poll papers.

74. "'LDS Oppose' Birch Group," *Salt Lake Tribune,* 5 Mar. 1963, 5; "Brown Says Church Opposed To Birch Society, Methods," *Provo Daily Herald,* 5 Mar. 1963, 12.

75. "Benson Declares His Birch Society Support Has No Bearing on Church," *Sacramento Bee,* 14 Mar. 1963, A-2; "Elder Benson Makes Statement," *Deseret News "Church News,"* 16 Mar. 1963, 2.

76. Ernest L. Wilkinson diary, 13 May 1963.

77. "Benson Clarifies Views On Birch Society Stand," *Salt Lake Tribune,* 21 Mar. 1963, A-11; Anderson, "Church and Birch In Utah," 10-11; U.S. senator Frank E. Moss to U.S. representative Ken W. Dyal, 2 Mar. 1966, fd 5, box 184, Moss papers.

78. "CROSS REFERENCE SHEET," Mrs. Joyce M. Sowerwine letter, 25 Nov. 1966, "re: Claire Middlemiss & John Birch Society," in "Hugh B. Brown's File on the John Birch Society."

79. Eugene Campbell's typed draft of Hugh B. Brown biography, chapter titled, "Responsibility Without Authority—The 1st Counselor Years," 11, Campbell papers.

80. "The Movement to Impeach Earl Warren," *The John Birch Society Bulletin,* Aug. 1961, 5; George T. Boyd (associate director of the LDS Institute of Religion in Los Angeles) to the First Presidency (with copy to Benson), 14 Dec. 1961, carbon copy in fd 6, box 40, Poll papers, regarding "'Hang Earl Warren' Then—an Apology," *Salt Lake Tribune,* 14 Dec. 1961, A-4. In answer to Boyd's similar letter to Brown, 22 Sept. 1961, Brown replied on 6 October that the entire First Presidency "hope some action can be taken to reduce or control the unwise actions of some of our people there [in Los Angeles] and in other parts of the Churchap." Copies of both 1962 letters are in Lee Library and LDS archives.

81. Quoted in Frederick S. Buchanan diary, 10 Apr. 1963.

82. J. D. Williams to James M. Whitmire, 21 May 1963, carbon copy in Williams papers.

83. George T. Boyd to "Dick" [Richard D. Poll], undated but written ca. 18 Oct. 1961 and answered 24 Oct., fd 15, box 39, Poll papers. Gibbons, *David O. McKay,* 381, affirms: "And the Latter-day Saints on both sides of it [the Birch controversy]—members of goodwill who had differing perceptions of the problem and its solution—felt both free and obligated to press their views, as long as doing so did not run afoul of the doctrines of the Church or the directives of the Prophet."

84. Ezra Taft Benson, *"Let Us Live to Keep Men Free": An Address . . . at a Patriotic Testimonial Banquet for Robert Welch, sponsored by Friends and Members of The John Birch Society at the Hollywood Palladium, Los Angeles, California, September 23, 1963* (Los Angeles: N.p, 1963); "2000 Hail Welch As 'Great Patriot,'" *Los Angeles Herald-Examiner,* 24 Sept. 1963, A-18; "Birch Society Dinner: Elder Benson Hits A-Treaty," *Deseret News,* 24 Sept. 1963, A-4; "Benson Extols Founder of John Birch Society," *Salt Lake Tribune,* 24 Sept. 1963, 2; "Birch Chief Applauded by Benson," *Ogden Standard-Examiner,* 24 Sept. 1963, 4; Richard Swanson, "McCarthyism in Utah," M.A. thesis, Brigham Young University, 1977, 138-39. For an earlier example of Benson's public endorsement of Robert Welch, see his remarks to students at the University of Washington in "Ezra Taft Benson Sees Reds 'Everywhere,' Lauds Birchers," *Seattle Times,* 1 May 1963, 15.

85. "Benson Urges Americans: 'Stand Up For Freedom No Matter What The Cost," *The Freedom Press,* 9 Oct. 1963, 7-8, reprint (Belmont, MA: John Birch Society, 1963), copy in fd 4, box 245, Moss papers.

86. Robert Welch, *The Politician* (Belmont, MA: Belmont Publishing Co., 1963), 278; William P. Hoar, "Welch and Eisenhower," in the John Birch Society's *American Opinion* 28 (Mar. 1985): 54-55. Eisenhower never sued Welch for libel or defamation of character, but for a libel suit against the Birch Society, see Elmer Gertz, *Gertz v. Robert Welch, Inc.: The Story of a Landmark Libel Case* (Carbondale: Southern Illinois University Press, 1992).

87. Ezra Taft Benson to Joseph Fielding Smith, 31 July 1963, in copy of Welch's *The Politician*, Lee Library; Hansen, "Analysis of the 1964 Idaho Second Congressional District Election Campaign," 50. Nevertheless, at Eisenhower's death in 1969 Benson wrote: "May God bless his memory" (Dew, *Ezra Taft Benson*, 404).

88. Ralph W. Harding speech, *Congressional Record* 109 (25 Sept. 1963): 17208-209, reprinted as *Ezra Taft Benson's Support of John Birch Society Is Criticized* (Washington, D.C.: U.S. Government Printing Office, 1963); "Idaho Congressman Hits Benson Speech," and "Birch Official Gives Statement on Benson Talk," *Deseret News,* 26 Sept. 1963, A-3; "Legislator, a Mormon, Scores Benson for Birch Activities," *New York Times,* 26 Sept. 1963, 29; "Mr. Harding's Risk," *Idaho State Journal,* 27 Sept. 1963, 4; "Idaho Congressman Hits Benson Speech," *Deseret News,* 26 Sept. 1963, A-6; "Ezra Benson And The Mormon Church," *Lewiston Morning Tribune,* 29 Sept. 1963, 4; Hansen, "Analysis of the 1964 Idaho Second Congressional District Election Campaign," 51; Anderson, "Church and Birch In Utah," 11-12, 54.

89. For example, Ralph Harding to Richard Poll, 30 Sept. 1963, fd 15, box 39, Poll papers.

90. Dwight D. Eisenhower to Ralph R. Harding, 7 Oct. 1963, photocopy in fd 3, box 42, Poll papers, in fd 2, box 4, David S. King papers, Marriott Library, and in fd 22, box 5, Buerger papers, Marriott Library. Eisenhower's letter was first quoted in "Ike, LDS Leaders Thank Harding For Anti-Birch, Benson Speech," *Idaho State Journal,* 20 Feb. 1964, 1; "Ike Praises Idaho Solon For Benson Criticism," *Salt Lake Tribune,* 21 Feb. 1964, A-4.

91. "Birchers Reply to Harding On Benson's Coast Talk," *Salt Lake Tribune,* 26 Sept. 1963, A-3.

92. "Rep. Harding Of Idaho Replies To Reed Benson's Charge," *Logan Herald Journal,* 20 Nov. 1963, 6.

93. Rex E. Lee to Ralph R. Harding, 30 Sept. 1963, and Ralph A. Britsch to Ralph R. Harding, 8 Oct. 1963, photocopies in fd 2, box 4, King papers.

94. Reported in Richard D. Poll to Ralph Harding, 31 Oct. 1963, fd 15, box 39, Poll papers.

95. "Harassment Campaign Follows Political Argument," *Provo Daily Herald,* 24 Nov. 1963, 10. For the Bircher tactic of harassment phone calls, see Peterson, "Ideology of the John Birch Society," 115.

96. Ezra Taft Benson, "Be Not Deceived," *Improvement Era* 66 (Dec. 1963): 1063-1065; Dew, *Ezra Taft Benson*, 372.

97. Ernest L. Wilkinson diary, 4 Oct. 1963; Hugh B. Brown to Gustive O. Larson, 2 Oct. 1963, copy in fd 15, box 11, Larson papers, also copies in fd 1, box 51, Poll papers, and in Campbell papers. Aside from Benson, Brown resented the influence on McKay by Clare Middlemiss and Thorpe B. Isaacson, both of whom apparently shared much of Benson's philosophy.

98. "Elder Benson To Direct Europe Mission," *Deseret News,* 24 Oct. 1963, A-1; *Improvement Era* 66 (Dec. 1963): 1065; "Mormons To Send Benson Overseas," *New York Times,* 25 Oct. 1963, 18; "Apostle Benson Denies Being Sent Into 'Exile' for Political Views," *Ogden Standard-Examiner,* 29 Oct. 1963, A-7; "Mormon Church Sends Benson to Europe," *U.S. News and World Report* 55 (Nov. 1963): 12; "Mormon Church Is Gaining in Strength Despite Tensions," *New York Times,* 27 Dec. 1965, 18; Hansen, "Analysis of the 1964 Idaho Second Congressional District Election Campaign," 52; Dew, *Ezra Taft Benson,* 372.

99. "Church Leader Rebuffs Self-Styled Patriots," *Ogden Standard-Examiner,* 26 Oct. 1963, 9; also "President Brown Supports U.N., Hits Extremists," *Deseret News,* 26 Oct. 1963, B-1.

100. "Stake Conference Assignments," *Deseret News "Church News,"* 19 Oct. 1963, 4; "Benson, Graham Rip Wheat Sale," *Deseret News,* 28 Oct. 1963, A-6; "Benson Says Black is Red," *Daily Utah Chronicle,* 29 Oct. 1963, 1.

101. "Harding Says Benson Move 'Wise,'" *Idaho Daily Statesman,* 1 Nov. 1963, 20.

102. Ralph Harding to Richard D. Poll, 6 Nov. 1963, fd 15, box 39, Poll papers.

103. "Benson Says: New Duties Not 'Rebuke," *Salt Lake Tribune,* 29 Oct. 1963, A-4; "Church Denies Mission Rumors," *Deseret News,* 21 Feb. 1964, A-8; "Letter Denies Rebuke in Benson Call," *Salt Lake Tribune,* 22 Feb. 1964, C-11.

104. Robert R. McKay to Ralph R. Harding, 18 Oct. 1963, photocopy in fd 2, box 4, King papers, and in fd 22, box 5, Buerger papers; quotes from letter first published in "Ike, LDS Leaders Thank Harding," 1; "Ike Praises Idaho Solon," A-4; also Anderson, "Church and Birch In Utah," 12. Robert McKay's letter was printed in full in "Bill Hall's Political Scratchpad," *Idaho State Journal,* 23 Feb. 1964, 4. For 18 October as the date on which McKay told Benson of his mission assignment, see Dew, *Ezra Taft Benson,* 372. For Robert R. McKay, see Gibbons, *David O. McKay,* 333; *Improvement Era* 69 (Dec. 1966): 1131, 1152; *Improvement Era* 70 (June 1967): 22, 80, 109; *Improvement Era* 70 (Dec. 1967): 33, 87, 107; *Improvement Era* 71 (Dec. 1968): 34, 108; *Improvement Era* 72 (June 1969): 116; *Improvement Era* 72 (Dec. 1969): 24, 110.

105. "Ike, LDS Leaders Thank Harding," 1.

106. Hugh B. Brown statement to W. Averill Harriman and Richard D. Poll in Salt Lake City, 25 Oct. 1963, quoted in Poll's letter to D. Michael Quinn, 13 Aug. 1992, copy in fd 15, box 39, Poll papers. For the visit of Harriman, Brown, and Poll in Provo, see photograph in *Provo Daily Herald,* 27 Oct. 1963, 3.

107. "President Brown Supports U.N., Hits Extremists," *Deseret News,* 26 Oct. 1963, B-1.

108. Joseph Fielding Smith to Ralph R. Harding, 30 Oct. 1963, photocopy in fd 2, box 4, King papers, and in fd 22, box 5, Buerger papers.

109. *Daily Utah Chronicle,* 30 Oct. 1963, 4; 4 Nov. 1963, 2; 6 Nov. 1963, 4; 8 Nov. 1963, 4; 14 Nov. 1963, 2. Editorially, the *Daily Utah Chronicle* published a cartoon (31 Oct. 1963, 4) which depicted Benson's mission assignment as a banishment by Uncle Sam, followed by an even more insulting cartoon (21 Nov. 1963, 2).

110. Hugh B. Brown to Ernest Cook, 22 Nov. 1963, photocopy in my possession.

111. "Group Decides Against Picketing Benson Talk," *Ogden Standard-Examiner,* 3 Dec. 1963, A-7.

112. Dew, *Ezra Taft Benson,* 372-73.

113. Ezra Taft Benson, "We Must Become Alerted and Informed: An Address by Ezra Taft Benson At A Public Patriotic Meeting," Logan, Utah, 13 Dec. 1963, transcript, Utah State Historical Society, Salt Lake City, 2.

114. B. Delworth Gardner, N. Keith Roberts, E. Boyd Wennergren preface to an annotated typescript of Benson's "We Must Become Alerted and Informed," Utah State Historical Society. In the margins are the page numbers of the *Blue Book* from which Benson's talk quoted or paraphrased.

115. Ezra Taft Benson, "We Must Become Alerted and Informed," 10; also, "Elder Benson Links Reds to [Civil] Rights Furor," *Deseret News,* 14 Dec. 1963, B-5; "Communism Moving In on U.S., Benson Warns," *Salt Lake Tribune,* 14 Dec. 1963, 28. Compare Ross R. Barnett, governor of Mississippi, "The Rape Of Our Constitution and Civil Rights," in the Birch Society's *American Opinion* 6 (Sept. 1963): 20-23; John Rousselot, "Civil Rights: Communist Betrayal Of A Good Cause," *American Opinion* 7 (Feb. 1964): 1-11.

116. J. Edgar Hoover, remarks to the Pennsylvania Society in New York City, 12 Dec. 1964, in *J. Edgar Hoover on Communism* (New York: Random House, 1969), 130, emphasis in original. He added, *"But there are notable exceptions—dangerous opportunists and morally corrupt charlatans who would form an alliance with any organization, regardless of its nature, to advance their own power and prestige"* (emphasis in original). Also see "Hoover Asks Vigil Over Extremists: Warns on 'Opportunists' in the Rights Movement," *New York Times*, 13 Dec. 1964, 79.

117. For publicity of this issue shortly before Benson's remarks, see "NAACP Calls S.L. Protest Over Rights," *Salt Lake Tribune*, 5 Oct. 1963, 32; "Give Full Civil Equality to All, LDS Counselor Brown Asks," and "Negro Group Lauds LDS Rights View," *Salt Lake Tribune*, 7 Oct. 1963, 1, 6; Jeff Nye, "Memo from a Mormon: In Which a Troubled Young Man Raises the Question of His Church's Attitude Toward Negroes," *Look* 27 (22 Oct. 1963): 74-79. For studies of the historical background and 1960s controversy over the church's priesthood restriction, see Armand L. Mauss, "Mormonism and Secular Attitudes Toward Negroes," *Pacific Sociological Review* 9 (Fall 1966): 91-99; Dennis L. Lythgoe, "Negro Slavery in Utah," *Utah Historical Quarterly* 39 (Winter 1971): 40-54; Brian Walton, "A University Dilemma: B.Y.U. and the Blacks," *Dialogue: A Journal of Mormon Thought* 6 (Spring 1971): 31-36; Lester E. Bush, Jr., "Mormonism's Negro Doctrine: An Historical Overview," *Dialogue: A Journal of Mormon Thought* 8 (Spring 1973): 11-68; Ronald K. Esplin, "Brigham Young and Denial of the Priesthood to Blacks: An Alternative View," *Brigham Young University Studies* 19 (Spring 1979): 394-402; William G. Hartley, "Saint Without Priesthood: The Collected Testimonies of Ex-Slave Samuel D. Chambers," and Newel G. Bringhurst, "Elijah Abel and the Changing Status of Blacks within Mormonism," *Dialogue: A Journal of Mormon Thought* 12 (Summer 1979): 13-21, 22-36; Newell G. Bringhurst, *Saints, Slaves, and Blacks: The Changing Place of Black People Within Mormonism* (Westport, CT: Greenwood Press, 1981); Armand L. Mauss, "The Fading of the Pharoah's Curse: The Decline and Fall of the Priesthood Ban against Blacks in the Mormon Church," *Dialogue: A Journal of Mormon Thought* 14 (Fall 1981): 10-45; Lester E. Bush, Jr., and Armand Mauss, eds., *Neither White Nor Black: Mormon Scholars Confront the Race Issue in a Universal Church* (Salt Lake City: Signature Books, 1984); Bergera and Priddis, *Brigham Young University*, 297-303; Jessie L. Embry, "Separate but Equal?: Black Branches, Genesis Groups, or Integrated Wards?," and Mark L. Grover, "The Mormon Priesthood Revelation and the Sao Paulo, Brazil Temple," *Dialogue: A Journal of Mormon Thought* 23 (Spring 1990): 11-37, 39-53.

118. Benson, "We Must Become Alerted and Informed," 8, 9, 10.

119. Drew Pearson, "Benson's Cure for Communism," *Washington Post*, 4 Jan. 1964, D-31, reprinted as "Ezra Taft Benson Hints: 'It Is Time To Revolt,'" in such newspapers as the *Times-Democrat*, 4 Jan. 1964.

120. "Setting The Record Straight," *Fullerton News Tribune*, 11 Jan. 1964, 24, quoted in Salt Lake City Citizens Information Committee, *Comments and Corrections*, No. 3 (15 Jan. 1968): 8.

121. Benson, "We Must Become Alerted and Informed," 10-11; also summarized in "Face Facts of Red Peril, Benson Asks," *Ogden Standard-Examiner*, 14 Dec. 1963, 6; "Benson Urges Vigorous Battle On Communism," *Logan Herald-Journal*, 15 Dec. 1963, 1, 3.

122. Frank E. Moss to Ray R. Murdock, 19 Feb. 1964, and Moss to Hugh B. Brown, 19 Feb. 1964, fd 3, box 122, Moss papers.

123. "CROSS REFERENCE SHEET," Raoul P. Smith, Keith L. Seegmiller, and Ralph Harding letters, Feb. 1964, in "Hugh B. Brown's File on the John Birch Society."

124. Ernest L. Wilkinson diary, 14 Dec. 1963; Dew, *Ezra Taft Benson*, 372, gives a very different view of the Bensons' reaction to this mission assignment.

125. Ernest L. Wilkinson diary, 14 Dec. 1963; Joseph Fielding Smith to Congressman Ralph Harding, 23 Dec. 1963, photocopy in fd 2, box 4, King papers, in fd 3, box 42, Poll papers, and in fd 22, box 5, Buerger papers. Apostle Smith's letter was first quoted in "Ike, LDS Leaders Thank Harding," 1; "Ike Praises Idaho Solon," A-4; also Anderson, "Church and Birch In Utah," 12.

126. Dew, *Ezra Taft Benson*, 373.

127. "Ike Praises Idaho Solon," A-4.

128. "Birch Society Reviewed By Prof. Louis Midgley," *Brigham Young University Daily Universe*, 22 May 1964, 2; McKay to Earl C. Crockett, 4 June 1964, Wilkinson papers, Lee Library, photocopy in my possession; Louis Midgley to Ray C. Hillam, 11 Aug. 1966, fd 10, Hillam papers, Lee Library, and box 34, Buerger papers; Bergera and Priddis, *Brigham Young University*, 196-97.

129. Ezra Taft Benson, *An Internal Threat Today* (Belmont, MA: American Opinion [1964]); *American Opinion* 7 (Oct. 1964): cover page and 43-44, 97; Ezra Taft Benson, "The Christ and the Constitution," *American Opinion* 7 (Dec. 1964): 41-45.

130. Jack Anderson, "Reed Benson Spreads Birch Gospel," *Washington Post*, 15 Jan. 1965, B-13.

131. Ezra Taft Benson, *Title of Liberty*, comp. Mark A. Benson (Salt Lake City: Deseret Book Co., 1964), with references to Welch on 1, 12, 36, 39, and 40. Compare Ezra Taft Benson, *So Shall Ye Reap*, comp. Reed A. Benson (Salt Lake City: Deseret Book Co., 1960), with references to Communism on 163, 208, and 328.

132. "Solon Embarrassed By Letter Publication," *Deseret News*, 21 Feb. 1964, A-8; "'Release Unauthorized,' Solon Says of Letters," *Salt Lake Tribune*, 22 Feb. 1964, C-11; "Idaho Writers Say Letters Were Widely Circulated," and "Bill Hall's Political Scratchpad," *Idaho State Journal*, 23 Feb. 1964, 1, 4; "How Could He Lose?" *Idaho Daily Statesman*, 5 Nov. 1964, 1-2; Ralph R. Harding to Frank H. Jonas, 8 Dec. 1964, Jonas papers; Jack Anderson, "Birch Society Influence Defeated Ralph Harding," *Blackfoot News*, 15 Jan. 1965, 4, also printed as "Reed Benson Spreads Birch Gospel," *Washington Post*, 15 Jan. 1965, B-13; Lynn Broadhead to Dean M. Hansen, 15 June 1967; Swanson, "McCarthyism in Utah," 143.

133. "Rep. Harding Of Idaho Replies To Reed Benson's Charge," *Logan Herald Journal*, 20 Nov. 1963, 6.

134. Hansen, "Analysis of the 1964 Idaho Second Congressional District Election Campaign," 53, 57, 183, 185-86, 206-10.

135. Anderson, "Reed Benson Spreads Birch Gospel," B-13.

136. Clare Middlemiss to Kent Brennan (ca. 20 Jan. 1965), quoted in Anderson, "Church and Birch In Utah," 14; also published in "No Church Rebuke Given to Bensons," *Spokane Daily Chronicle*, and reprinted by the Salt Lake City Citizens Information Committee, *Comments and Corrections*, No. 3 (15 Jan. 1968): 8, which inaccurately dates the *Chronicle* article as 15 January 1965, three days before Brennan's original letter to McKay.

137. Hugh B. Brown to Mrs. W. E. Daddow, 23 Feb. 1965, LDS archives.

138. "NAACP Calls March for LDS Appeal," *Salt Lake Tribune*, 7 Mar. 1965, A-18; "Marchers Pray At LDS Doorstep," *Daily Utah Chronicle*, 8 Mar. 1965, 1.

139. "Give Full Civil Equality to All, LDS Counselor Brown Asks," *Salt Lake Tribune*, 7 Oct. 1963, 1; Hugh B. Brown, "The Fight Between Good and Evil," *Improvement Era* 66 (Dec. 1963): 1058; Sterling M. McMurrin, "A Note on the 1963 Civil Rights Statement," *Dialogue: A Journal of Mormon Thought* 12 (Summer 1979): 60-63.

140. "Benson Ties Rights Issue to Reds in Mormon Rift," *Washington Post*, 13 Apr. 1965, A-5.

141. "President McKay Emphasizes Individual," with subheading for Elder Benson's talk: "Restored Gospel," *Salt Lake Tribune*, 7 Apr. 1965, A-5; compare *Improvement Era* 68 (June 1965): 539. In 1968 Deseret Book Co. published (and reprinted in 1969) Benson's *Civil Rights: Tool of Communist Deception*, 3, which stated: "The so-called civil rights

movement as it exists today is used as a Communist program for revolution." The addition of "used as" softened his original words as reported in "Mormon Leaders Heard By 25,000," *New York Times,* 2 Oct. 1967, 52.

142. Ernest L. Wilkinson diary, 7 Apr. 1965; Edwin B. Morrell, chair, Department of Political Science, John T. Bernhard, dean, College of Social Sciences, Ray C. Hillam, associate professor of political science, Larry T. Wimmer, assistant professor of economics, Louis C. Midgley, associate professor of political science, Richard B. Wirthlin, associate professor of economics, "Events Related To the Covert Surveillance of Faculty Members, Subsequent Investigations of and Accusations Against Said Faculty, and Attempts to Resolve the Matter 'Within the Family,'" 1, fd 1, Hillam papers, and box 34, Buerger papers; John P. Sanders statement, 5 Aug. 1966, fd 10, Hillam papers, and box 34, Buerger papers.

143. Richard Douglas Poll's "Personal Service Contract," 6 Feb. 1958, and Poll's copy of his "Personal History Statement," Form 444 [for a security clearance], both in fd 21, box 26, Poll papers; Robert S. Wattles, Director of Personnel, Central Intelligence Agency, to Richard D. Poll, 5 Aug. 1968, notifying him of "the discontinuance of the University Associates Program as such," but expressing "our interest in continuing our association with you in the future" on an individual basis, fd 22, box 26, Poll papers. As a U.S. counterintelligence agent, I conducted interviews in 1969-70 concerning the names, residences, schools, employment, and organizations named on the "Personal History Statement" of individuals who were seeking security clearances.

144. David J. Whittaker and Chris McClellan, "The Collection: Description," 1, register of the Hillam papers; Stephen Hays Russell to Ernest L. Wilkinson, 26 Apr. 1965, Wilkinson papers, photocopy in my possession. Without identifying their source, Wilkinson's diary also referred on 11 July 1965 to "papers" which were "proof of accusations against Richard Poll."

145. Richard D. Poll, *This Trumpet Gives An Uncertain Sound: A Review of W. Cleon Skousen's THE NAKED COMMUNIST* (Provo, UT: By the author, 1962), 3, listed his objections to the book as "the inadequacy of its scholarship. The incorrectness of its analysis of Communism. The inaccuracy of its historical narrative. The unsoundness of its program for governmental action. The extreme partisanship of its program for individual action. The objectionable character of the national movement of which it is a part." On the ultra-conservative, anti-Communist movement, Poll wrote (12-13): "Much of the market for *The Naked Communist* is in connection with 'Anti-Communist Seminars,' 'Freedom Forums,' and 'Project Alerts,' in which inaccurate history and negative programs are expounded in an evangelical blend of fear, hatred and pulse-pounding enthusiasm. Participants are admonished to study Communism, and they end up buying tracts by Gerald L. K. Smith and his racist cohorts, confessionals of ex-Communists, spy stories and other volumes which excite more than inform. They are aroused to *fight Communism,* and they end up demanding U.S. withdrawal from the UN and the firing of teachers who advocate federal aid to education. They are solicited to contribute to the Anti-Communist crusade, and they end up subsidizing pamphlets calling for the repeal of the income tax and the impeachment of Chief Justice Warren."

146. Hugh B. Brown to Richard D. Poll, 10 Jan. 1962, fd 15, box 39, Poll papers; Brown's role in this anti-Skousen publication also appears in Poll to George T. Boyd, 24 Oct. 1961, Poll to Hugh B. Brown, 18 Dec., 23 Dec. 1961, 6 Jan. 1962, and Poll memorandum to Ernest L. Wilkinson, "Subject: Correspondence with President Brown on the Anti-Communist Problem," 23 Dec. 1961, all in fd 15, box 39, Poll papers; Brown to Poll, 9 Nov. 1961, fd 13, box 48, Poll papers.

147. David O. McKay, "Preach the Word," *Improvement Era* 62 (Dec. 1959): 912.

148. "Faculty Members Deplore 'Fanaticism' of Booklet," *Provo Daily Herald,* 23 July 1964, 14; "None Dare Call It Treason Causes Sincere Concern," *Daily Universe,* 23 July 1964, 2; "Students Take Issue With 'None Dare Call It Treason' Critics," *Daily Universe,* 28 July

1964, 2; "Poll Answers Student Letters," *Daily Universe,* 30 July 1964, 2; also "Hate Book 'None Dare Call It Treason,' A Hoax and Fraud," *Congressional Record* 110 (17 Sept. 1964): 22296-97; "Stormer Book Draws Criticism," *Christian Science Monitor,* 19 Sept. 1964, 4; "A Report and Analysis of Chapter VII of *None Dare Call It Treason,* by John A. Stormer, Prepared by Henry M. Bullock, Editor of Methodist Church School Publications," Sept. 1964, fd 20, box 39, Poll papers; Julian Foster, *None Dare Call It Reason: A Critique of John Stormer's "None Dare Call It Treason"* (Placentia, CA: By the author, 1964).

149. "Birchers Extend Membership Drive to East Coast," *New York Times,* 25 Oct. 1964, 81.

150. Ernest L. Wilkinson to Mark Benson, 27 Apr. 1965, Wilkinson papers, photocopy in my possession; also Bergera and Priddis, *Brigham Young University,* 203, for another quote from the letter.

151. Richard D. Poll, "Addendum on earlier items," 27 Apr. [1965], fd 1, box 12, Poll papers.

152. *1966 Banyan* (Provo, UT: Associated Students of Brigham Young University, 1966), 293; see discussion of 1966 BYU spy ring, to follow.

153. Poll, "Addendum on earlier items," 25 Apr. [1965], also Poll, "Notes on conversation with Stephen Russell, 4/27/65: 11:15 [a.m.]-12:10 [p.m.], 436 JRCL," and "REPORT ON THE DOROTHY MARSHALL AFFAIR AND RELATED MATTERS," 2-3, all in fd 1, box 12, Poll papers; "S.H." Russell [as an *agent provocateur*] to Richard Poll, 16 Apr. 1965: "Some L.D.S. 'radicals' have confronted me with statements in the new book 'Prophets, Principles, and National Survival.' It is hard for me to believe some of these quotations. Would you be kind enough to inform me whether or not this book is authentic, what you know about the compiler, and what your opinion of the book is," in fd 3, box 12, Poll papers.

154. Leon Johnson, "Benson Told A 'Damned Lie,'" *Daily Utah Chronicle,* 12 Apr. 1965, 2, which he admitted was "too intemperate," in 16 Apr. 1965, 2, but then reaffirmed by asking, "did Elder Benson violate the Ninth Commandment when he said the civil-rights movement is being used by the Communists." The *Chronicle* did not print a response to Johnson's letters but did publish on 14 Apr. 1965, 2, two long letters in defense of Benson's speechap. For Benson's remarks which sparked this controversy, see "President McKay Emphasizes Individual," A-5.

Among general histories of the NAACP available to Benson at this time was Langston Hughes, *Fight for Freedom: The Story of the NAACP* (New York: W. W. Norton & Co., 1962). Benson maintained this view despite the previously published findings of Wilson Record, *Race and Radicalism: The NAACP and the Communist Party in Conflict* (Ithaca, NY: Cornell University Press, 1964), 170, that the Communist party "continued its ambivalent attitude toward the NAACP, sometimes eagerly seeking support, at other times bitterly attacking the Association and its leaders. The NAACP increasingly has regarded the party not as a challenger but as an irritant and a source of embarrassment. Particularly has this been the case since 1955."

155. Harold B. Lee, "Be Ye Not Deceived," *Speeches of the Year* (Provo, UT: Extension Publications, Division of Continuing Education, Brigham Young University, 1965), 9.

156. "Reed Benson Says Welch Was Correct in Calling Eisenhower Communist," *Provo Daily Herald,* 22 Apr. 1965, 2.

157. Dew, *Ezra Taft Benson,* 391.

158. "Critical of Church: NAACP Studies Action," *Deseret News,* 2 July 1965, A-6.

159. "Benson Ties Rights Issue to Reds," A-5; *Seattle Times,* 5 May 1965, 13; "NAACP Asks Foreign Bar of Missionaries," *Daily Utah Chronicle,* 6 May 1965, 1, 3, 4; Journal History of the Church of Jesus Christ of Latter-day Saints (1830-1972), 246 reels, microfilm, Special Collections, Marriott Library, 6 May 1965, 6.

160. For discussion (some of it hysteric) of the African-American riot at Watts in 1965 from various perspectives, see California Governor's Commission on the Los Angeles Riots, *Violence in the City: An End or a Beginning? A Report* (Los Angeles: Governor's Commission, 1965); Gerald L. K. Smith, *Guerrilla Warfare in Los Angeles: Black Revolution Launched: 21,000 Troops and Officers Required to Save Whites from Wholesale Slaughter* (Los Angeles: By the author, 1965); *Police Malpractice and the Watts Riot* (Los Angeles: American Civil Liberties Union, Southern California Branch, 1966); Jerry Cohen, *Burn, Baby, Burn! The Los Angeles Race Riot, August, 1965* (New York: Dutton, 1966); David O. Sears, *The Los Angeles Riot Study: The Politics of Discontent: Blocked Mechanisms of Grievance Redress and the Psychology of the New Urban Black Man* (Los Angeles: University of California at Los Angeles, 1967); Robert E. Conot, *Rivers of Blood, Years of Darkness: The Unforgettable Classic Account of the Watts Riot* (New York: Morros, 1968); U.S. Congress, *Subversive Influences in Riots, Looting, and Burning: Hearings Before the Committee on Un-American Activities, House of Representatives, Ninetieth Congress, First (Second) Session,* 7 vols. (Washington, D.C.: Government Printing Office, 1968-69), vols. 1 and 3 on the Watts riot; United States, Kerner Commission, *Report* (Washington, D.C.: Government Printing Office, 1968); Lillian R. Boehme, *Carte Blanche For Chaos* (New Rochelle, NY: Arlington House, 1970); Ralph W. Conant, *The Prospects for Revolution: A Study of Riots, Civil Disobedience, and Insurrection in Contemporary America* (New York: Harper's Magazine Press, 1971); David O. Sears, *The Politics of Violence: The New Urban Blacks and the Watts Riot* (Boston: Houghton Mifflin, 1973); James W. Button, *Black Violence: Political Impact of the 1960s Riots* (Princeton, NJ: Princeton University Press, 1978); Gerald Horne, *Fire This Time: The Watts Uprising and the 1960s* (Charlottesville: University Press of Virginia, 1995).

161. Reed A. Benson, "Memo to the Utah Chapters," 2 Sept. 1965, on letterhead of the Birch Society, photocopy in Williams papers; Quinn G. McKay to J. D. Williams, 20 May 1966, Williams papers.

162. Quinn G. McKay statement, 25 Apr. 1966, in J. Kenneth Davies, *Political Extremism Under the Spotlight* (Provo, UT: Young Democrats and Young Republicans of Brigham Young University, 1966), 21.

163. D. Richard Pine and Charles R. Armour to "All Coordinators, Section Leaders and Chapter Leaders in California," 17 Aug. 1965, and D. Richard Pine to "Coordinators, Section Leaders and Chapter Leaders—L.A. County," 1 Sept. 1965, in Harvey B. Schechter, *How To Listen to a John Birch Society Speaker,* 3d ed. rev. (New York: Anti-Defamation League of B'nai B'rith, 1967), 25-26; Benjamin R. Epstein and Arnold Forster, *The Radical Right: Report on the John Birch Society and Its Allies* (New York: Random House, 1967), 12; Lipset and Raab, *Politics of Unreason,* 268. For the position of Major Coordinator, see Welch, *Blue Book of the John Birch Society,* 152.

164. *The John Birch Society Bulletin* (Sept. 1965): cover and 23. The October *Bulletin* (dated 30 Sept. 1965): 2, concluded its reminder about the Birch battle with the African-American civil rights movement: "And in setting out seriously on this gigantic endeavor, we have really stirred up the animals."

165. David Leslie Brewer, "Utah Elites and Utah Racial Norms," Ph.D. diss., University of Utah, 1966, 143.

166. L. Brent Goates, *Harold B. Lee: Prophet & Seer* (Salt Lake City: Bookcraft, 1985), 378.

167. "NAACP Says 'Too Fantastic' Rumors of Demonstrations," *Ogden Standard-Examiner,* 27 Sept. 1965, 20; "Race Riots in Utah?" *Daily Utah Chronicle,* 28 Sept. 1965, 5.

168. "NAACP Chapter Claims Riot Report 'Malicious,'" *Ogden Standard-Examiner,* 28 Sept. 1965, A-6; "Rumors of Riot Hit By Area NAACP," *Deseret News,* 28 Sept. 1965, B-1; "NAACP Assails Rumors of Protest at LDS Meet," *Salt Lake Tribune,* 29 Sept. 1965, 18.

169. Schechter, *How To Listen to a John Birch Society Speaker,* 24; also Barbara Hogan, *The Shake-Up America Campaign: Who's Who and What's What in the Massive John Birch Society Propaganda Effort to Fan the Flames of Racial Tension* (Washington, D.C.: Institute for American Democracy [1967]). The bias of these publications is as strident as that of Birch Society publications. Their value lies in the quotes from Birch writings to demonstrate the society's approach toward the American civil rights movement.

170. Reed Benson and Robert W. Lee, "The Federalist" (concerning Watts), and Robert H. Montgomery, "From the North," (concerning immigration), in *American Opinion* 8 (Oct. 1965): 65-66, 69-70; also Gary Allen and Bill Richardson, "Los Angeles: Hell In The City of The Angels," *American Opinion* 8 (Sept. 1965): 1-14.

171. *The John Birch Society Bulletin* (Oct. 1965): 2.

172. "Birchers As Group, Unwelcome," *Deseret News,* 27 Oct. 1965, F-1; "Bennett Joins in Rebuke of John Birch Society," *Salt Lake Tribune,* 27 Oct. 1965, A-4.

173. *Congressional Record* 109 (6 Aug. 1963): 14172; Anderson, "Church and Birch In Utah," 10-11.

174. Clare Middlemiss to Russell F. Dickey, 8 Dec. 1965, photocopy in Anderson, "Church and Birch In Utah," appendix.

175. Anderson, "Church and Birch In Utah," 15.

176. Board of Trustees, Executive Committee minutes, 16 Dec. 1965, Brigham Young University, photocopy in my possession; Wilkinson diary, 21 Dec. 1965; Bergera and Priddis, *Brigham Young University,* 197; N. Eldon Tanner statement in the mid-1960s to J. Kenneth Davies as reported in Davies interview by Gary James Bergera, 24 Dec. 1984, photocopy in my possession; identical quote in Davies telephone conversation with me, 6 Jan. 1993. Stapley's vote against the Birch Society president should not be construed as disagreement with Benson's conservative views. See Stapley to Mrs. W. E. Daddow, 19 Feb. 1965, LDS archives.

177. "LDS Apostle Backs Up Birch Group," *Salt Lake Tribune,* 16 Jan. 1966, B-14; "Speak Up! Says Ezra to Save Your Soul and Maybe Your Country," *Fact Finder* 24 (28 Feb. 1966); Anderson, "Church and Birch In Utah," 6.

178. Wallace F. Bennett to David Lawrence McKay, 21 Jan. 1966, fd 3, box 24, Bennett papers, Marriott Library; also Wallace F. Bennett, *Why I Am A Mormon,* 3d ed. (Salt Lake City: Deseret Book Co., 1964).

179. *The John Birch Society Bulletin* (Feb. 1966): 30.

180. Ezra Taft Benson, "Stand Up For Freedom," address to the Utah Forum for the American Idea, Assembly Hall, Temple Square, Salt Lake City, 11 Feb. 1966, typescript, 9, 11, Vertical File, Special Collections, Marriott Library; "Benson Hits Liberals' 'Conspiracy': Assails Plots, Propaganda," *Salt Lake Tribune,* 12 Feb. 1966, 17.

181. Compare Ezra Taft Benson, *An Internal Threat Today* (Belmont, MA: American Opinion, [1964]), with Benson, "An Internal Threat Today," (paid advertisement by Concerned Citizens and Treasure Valley Freedom Forum) *Idaho Statesman,* 19 Jan. 1964, B-7, and with typescript of the address prepared for the Treasure Valley Freedom Forum, Boise, Idaho, 19 Dec. 1963, 6-7, 10, fd 1, box 122, Moss papers.

182. Joseph Fielding Smith to Ralph Harding, 30 Oct. 1963, photocopy in fd 2, box 4, King papers, and in fd 22, box 5, Buerger papers.

183. Benson, "Stand Up For Freedom," 13-14; "Benson Hits Liberals' 'Conspiracy': Assails Plots, Propaganda"; "Socialism Warning Sounded: Elder Benson Hits Liberals," *Deseret News,* 12 Feb. 1966, B-1; Dew, *Ezra Taft Benson,* 385.

184. "Copy of First Presidency minutes digest 2-18-66," in "Hugh B. Brown's File on the John Birch Society."

185. Reported by U.S. senator Frank E. Moss to U.S. representative Ken W. Dyal, 2 Mar. 1966, fd 5, box 184, Moss papers. Although Moss referred to "the Brethren," his Daily Activity Log refers to meeting with only Hugh B. Brown, on 22 February (box 713).

186. "Stand Up For Freedom: Partial Text Of Talk Given to S.L. Group By Elder Benson," *Deseret News "Church News,"* 26 Feb. 1966, 10-12; Duane Price to D. Michael Quinn, 9 Aug. 1992, summarizing his meeting with Benson in April 1966. Price was a supporter of Benson's position on the Birch Society. Anderson, "Church and Birch In Utah," 35n29, alluded to the censorship in the *Church News*.

187. Mr. and Mrs. W. D. Luke, "Motives Unquestioned," *Salt Lake Tribune,* 10 Apr. 1966, A-16.

188. Ernest L. Wilkinson diary, 19-22 Aug. 1965; W. Cleon Skousen, *The Communist Attack on the John Birch Society* (Salt Lake City: Ensign Publishing Co., 1963), and list of speakers of the "American Opinion Speakers Bureau" in the Birch Society's *American Opinion* 9 (May 1966): 109. Skousen stated: "I am not a member of the John Birch Society and never have been," in *Behind the Scenes: A Personal Report to Pledged Freemen from W. Cleon Skousen* (Salt Lake City: The Freemen Institute, 1980), 1, photocopy in fd 25, box 17, Buerger papers. See also Skousen's *My Reply to Dr. Richard D. Poll and His Critique of The Naked Communist* (Salt Lake City: Ensign Publishing Co. [1962]).

189. Ernest L. Wilkinson diary, 13 Apr. 1966.

190. Dew, *Ezra Taft Benson,* 374.

191. *The John Birch Society Bulletin* (Mar. 1966): 22-24; "CROSS REFERENCE SHEET," 2 Mar. 1966, in "Hugh B. Brown's File on the John Birch Society."

192. Ezra Taft Benson to Joseph Fielding Smith, 3 Mar. 1966, LDS archives. This was Benson's defense against a letter to all general authorities from Ken W. Dyal, LDS congressman from California.

193. "Copy of First Presidency minutes digest 3-3-66," in "Hugh B. Brown's File on the John Birch Society."

194. J. Reese Hunter to "Dear Brethren," 8 Mar. 1966, LDS archives, photocopy in Williams papers; Utah Forum For the American Idea, "Program," 11 Feb. 1966, Williams papers.

195. Philip K. Langan to "All Friends of *American Opinion* in Utah," Mar. 1966, quoted in Anderson, "Church and Birch In Utah," 27-28.

196. "OPERATION CHECKMATE," original typed document, Williams papers, also photocopy inscribed, "J D Williams, March 14, 1966," fd 2, box 124, Robert H. Hinckley papers, Marriott Library. Although undated, this document was drafted after the J. Reese Hunter letter of 8 Mar. 1966 (which "OPERATION CHECKMATE" referred to) and before the First Presidency statement of 17 Marchap. In September 1993 Williams told me that he authored it.

197. Campbell and Poll, *Hugh B. Brown,* 259; minutes of meeting on 15 Mar. 1966 with David O. McKay, N. Eldon Tanner, Joseph Fielding Smith, and Mark E. Petersen in Huntsville, Utah. In view of his access to these minutes and those of 3 Mar. 1966, First Presidency secretary Francis M. Gibbons has made the curiously emphatic overstatement that McKay gave Benson "unqualified support, which included agreement with Elder Benson's strong views about the dangers of international Communism, an agreement that continued without change until the time of his death and that included encouragement for his associate to continue to speak out on the subject" (Gibbons, *David O. McKay,* 372).

198. "Church Tells Position On Dinner for Bircher," *Ogden Standard-Examiner,* 17 Mar. 1966, A-10; "Notice To Church Members," *Deseret News "Church News,"* 19 Mar. 1966, 2; "So Much For Mr. Welch," *Rocky Mountain Review,* 17 Mar. 1966, 4.

199. See Ernest L. Wilkinson diary, 22 Mar. 1966; "Birch Dinner in Salt Lake City Vexes Mormons," *New York Times,* 8 Apr. 1966, 28; "Mormons and Politics: Benson's Influence Helps Keep Growing Church on Conservative Track," *Wall Street Journal,* 8 Aug. 1966, 1; J.D. Williams, "Separation of Church and State in Mormon Theory and Practice," *Dialogue: A Journal of Mormon Thought* 1 (Summer 1966): 50; J.D. Williams, "Reply to Letter of Garn E. Lewis," *Dialogue: A Journal of Mormon Thought* 1 (Winter 1966): 8; Epstein and

Forster, *The Radical Right,* 200-201; Anderson, "Church and Birch In Utah," 15-16, 22-25, 27-29; Bethke, "BF, EB," 15-16; Gibbons, *David O. McKay,* 381-82, 383.

200. *American Opinion* 9 (Apr. 1966): cover page, and 112.

201. Ernest L. Wilkinson diary, 22 Mar. 1966; "Welch Raps 'Senseless' U.S. Policy," *Salt Lake Tribune,* 8 Apr. 1966, B-1, with photo on B-2; "Birch Dinner in Salt Lake City Vexes Mormons," 28; Hugh W. Gillilan, "500 Misled Americans," and Mrs. Calvin L. Rampton, "JBS's Tasteless Violation," *Salt Lake Tribune,* 10 Apr. 1966, A-16, with reply by J. Reese Hunter, "Answers Mrs. Rampton," *Salt Lake Tribune,* 13 Apr. 1966, 18; also Anderson, "Church and Birch In Utah," 1, 16.

202. Robert Welch, "Dinner Meeting at Hotel Utah Introductory Remarks—April 7th, 1966 by Robert Welch," mimeograph, 1, Special Collections, Lee Library; Anderson, "Church and Birch In Utah," 25-26, 35n32.

203. "Birch Dinner in Salt Lake City Vexes Mormons," 28, published as "Welch Says Mormons Make Good Birchers," *Minneapolis Tribune,* 9 Apr. 1966.

204. Meeting minutes of 15 Mar. 1966.

205. "Let Us Not Be Carried Away," *Deseret News "Church News,"* 29 July 1961, 16; "What Americanism Must Mean," *Deseret News,* 28 Oct. 1961, A-10; also "A Question For Americans," *Deseret News,* 30 Nov. 1961, A-18. Welch's views on Eisenhower as a "conscious agent" of Communism, circulated in manuscript until 1963, were cited in the media as early as 1960.

Deseret News "Church News," 15 Jan. 1984, 3, said that Mark E. Petersen "had written the editorials since the beginning of the weekly publication in 1931." Peggy Petersen Barton's *Mark E. Petersen: A Biography* (Salt Lake City: Deseret Book Co., 1985), 114, also noted this.

206. Richard D. Poll to Hugh B. Brown, 23 Dec. 1961, referred to their previous discussions of the "substantial involvement on your [Brown's] part in the *Deseret News* editorials and other aspects of this question."

207. "Politics and Religion," *Deseret News "Church News,"* 26 Mar. 1966, 16. Although opposed to the Birch Society, Petersen also warned Mormons against "creeping socialism and its companion, insidious, atheistic communism." See his "New Evidence For the Book of Mormon," *Improvement Era* 65 (June 1962): 457.

208. Mark E. Anderson to David O. McKay, 5 Apr. 1966, LDS archives; also Anderson, "Church and Birch In Utah," 17. Compare Mark Anderson, letter to the editor, *Deseret News,* 14 Apr. 1966, A-18. For Mark Anderson's role as a Birch Society "chapter leader," as a "section leader" over several chapters, and for his promotion to state coordinator four months after his letter to McKay, see "Welch Raps 'Senseless' U.S. Policy," *Salt Lake Tribune,* 8 Apr. 1966, B-1; Mark E. Anderson to Robert Welch, 5 June 1966, with copies to Ezra Taft Benson, Reed Benson, John Rousselot, and Frank Marisch, photocopy in Williams papers; "Birch Society 'Signs Up' LDS Leader," *Salt Lake Tribune,* 7 Aug. 1966, B-3; "Who Is Mark E. Anderson?" *Utah Independent,* 2 June 1972, 8. For the Birch Society's organizational structure, see Welch, *Blue Book of the John Birch Society,* 151-52; "The John Birch Society: A Report," *Advertising Supplement to Los Angeles Times,* 27 Sept. 1964, 7-8; Gerald Schomp, *Birchism Was My Business* (New York: Macmillan Co., 1970), 158.

209. Joe H. Ferguson to "All General Authorities," 16 Apr. 1966, 4, with postscript to "Mark" (Mark E. Anderson), photocopy in my possession; excerpts from Blaine Elswood to the editor of the *Deseret News,* 29 Mar. 1966, files of the *Deseret News* offices, cited in Anderson, "Church and Birch In Utah," 4-6, and in Frank H. Jonas typed document, 81. Also "Letters to the Editor," *Deseret News,* 28 Mar. 1966, A-18, 13 Apr. 1966, A-8.

210. Harold B. Lee introduction to Benson, *So Shall Ye Reap,* vii.

211. Ernest L. Wilkinson diary, 13 May 1963.

212. *April 1966 Conference Report* . . . (Salt Lake City: Church of Jesus Christ of Latter-day Saints, 1966), 64-65, 66, 67, 68. Dew, *Ezra Taft Benson,* 372, 385, observes that Benson saw no difference between his religious beliefs and his political convictions.

213. My telephone conversation, 7 Nov. 1992, with L. Brent Goates, who described his father-in-law's April 1966 address as "an insinuation" concerning Benson but declined to comment further. Goates, *Harold B. Lee,* makes no reference to the dispute.

214. H. Grant Ivins, "Most Divisive Influence," *Salt Lake Tribune,* 11 Apr. 1966, 18. His father was Anthony W. Ivins, First Presidency counselor from 1921 to 1934.

215. Walter Scott, "Personality Parade," *Parade,* 15 May 1966, 2, copy in Special Collections, Lee Library.

216. Quinn G. McKay statements in Davies, *Political Extremism Under the Spotlight,* 12, 19, 20-21. The "standing-room-only" reference is from the description of the meeting on the inside front cover. A BYU-Birch student reminisces: "I also attended the anti-Birch meeting held on the BYU campus wherein Quinn [McKay] and Robert McKay publicly accused ETB's son Reed of deliberately fomenting unrest and strife by asking Birchers the previous summer to spread rumors that the NAACP and others were going to picket the October 1965 sessions of General Conference. It was held in the Joseph F. Smith Family Living Center Lounge area. Their accusations bothered me greatly, and coupled with the [BYU] spy scandal, they led to my eventual disaffection with the YAF [Young Americans for Freedom] and the JBS." See Curt E. Conklin letter (E-Mail) to "Mormon List" electronic bulletin board, 1 July 1993, 2, printout in my possession. The published version by Davies deleted McKay's references to Reed Benson by name.

217. Robert H. Hinckley, "The Politics of Extremism," in *Congressional Record* 112 (13 July 1966): 15584, 15583; Hinckley, *The Politics of Extremism* (Salt Lake City: University of Utah, 1966); "Hinckley Blasts Extremists," *Provo Daily Herald,* 25 May 1966, 14; "Says Birchers Copy Reds," *Deseret News,* 25 May 1966, A-12. For Hinckley's background in Mormonism, civil government, and business, see Robert H. Hinckley and JoAnn Jacobsen Wells, *"I'd Rather Be Born Lucky Than Rich": The Autobiography of Robert H. Hinckley* (Provo, UT: Brigham Young University Press, 1977), 1, 15-22, 75, 78, 125, 139; Billy Wayne Winstead, "Robert Henry Hinckley: His Public Service Career," Ph.D. diss., University of Utah, 1980.

218. Dew, *Ezra Taft Benson,* 252; also Ezra Taft Benson to Robert H. Hinckley, 27 May 1966: "I cannot believe that a man with your background and experience would make the errors attributed to you in the attached item from the Deseret News of May 25th" (fd 2, box 124, Hinckley papers).

219. *Deseret News "Church News,"* 16 Apr. 1966, 7; *Improvement Era* 69 (June 1966): 477 as "nonchurchap."

220. *Bulletin of The John Birch Society* (Jan. 1967): 24-25.

221. Gordon B. Hinckley to Ezra Taft Benson, 21 June 1966, LeGrand Richards to Benson, 8 May 1969, both in Dew, *Ezra Taft Benson,* 390, 405-406; Delbert L. Stapley to Mrs. W. E. Daddow, 19 Feb. 1965, LDS archives.

222. "Authoritative Answers To Questions Concerning Anti-Communism," mimeographed statement (after April 1966), Americanism Discussion Group, 3624 56th Avenue, S.W. Seattle, Washington, 98116, copy in Special Collections, Lee Library. Jerreld L. Newquist lived in Seattle during this period and may have been the source of this mimeographed statement. See Newquist to Richard Poll, 7 Mar. 1967, fd 15, box 39, Poll papers.

223. *The John Birch Society Bulletin* (Feb. 1966): 30.

224. Quoted in Frederick S. Buchanan diary, 7 Oct. 1966.

225. Whittaker and McClellan, "The Collection: Description," 1-2; Stephen Hays Russell to Ernest L. Wilkinson, 26 Apr. 1965; Richard D. Poll to Wilkinson, 24 June 1965, defending himself against complaints by Russell and E. Eugene Bryce, fd 2, box 12, Poll

papers; Poll to Wilkinson, 1 May 1965, fd 1, box 12, Poll papers; Edwin B. Morrell et al., "Events Related To the Covert Surveillance of Faculty Members," 1-2; "Birch Society Reviewed By Prof. Louis Midgley," 2; "Faculty Members Deplore 'Fanaticism' of Booklet," 14; "None Dare Call It Treason Causes Sincere Concern," 2; also Bergera and Priddis, *Brigham Young University,* 207-208.

226. Stephen Hays Russell, "Y Center Activity Schedule," 20 Apr. 1966; and interview of Ronald Ira Hankin by Ray C. Hillam and Louis C. Midgley, 17 Sept. 1966, Provo, Utah, transcript, 4-5, signed at the bottom of each page by Ronald I. Hankin, fds 1, 5, Hillam papers, and box 34, Buerger papers; "Birchers Spied On Professors, Hialeah Student Said," *Miami Herald,* 3 Mar. 1967, A-32; Bergera and Priddis, *Brigham Young University,* 208.

227. Conklin to "Mormon List," 1. He also wrote (3): "I wish I hadn't been involved with either the YAF or the JBS. I wish I had refused to involve myself in the spy ring. I was young, foolish, immature, naive and too trusting of certain individuals," with similar statement in Curt E. Conklin, "Uncannily Accurate," *Dialogue: A Journal of Mormon Thought* 26 (Winter 1993): vii.

228. Russell acknowledged choosing ten students to assist in the "monitoring," yet his reservation for the room was for twenty persons and chairs. Ronald Ira Hankin consistently claimed that Russell selected fifteen to twenty students, though only eleven have been identified: Russell, Michel L. Call (president of BYU's Young Americans for Freedom), Everett Eugene Bryce, Lyle H. Burnett (not Barnett), Curt E. Conklin, Hankin, Edward ("Ted") G. Jacob (not Jacobs), Lloyd L. Miller, Mark Andrew Skousen, Lisle C. Updike, and James H. Widenmann (not Weidenman). See Conklin to "Mormon List"; Russell, "Y Center Activity Schedule," 20 Apr. 1966; Russell statement, 13 Mar. 1967, 4; Hankin interview, 4, 14; Ray C. Hillam to Clyde D. Sandgren, 22 July 1966, "Re: Reports by Vandygriff and Russell"; Russell N. Horiuchi "To Whom it may concern," 11 Aug. 1966; Ray C. Hillam "To Whom It May Concern," 15 Aug. 1966; Larry T. Wimmer statement, 30 Jan. 1968; Morrell, et al., "Events Related To the Covert Surveillance of Faculty Members," 2; Ben E. Lewis, Earl C. Crockett, and Clyde D. Sandgren to Ray C. Hillam, 15 May 1969, 3, in fds 1, 3, 5, 9, 10, Hillam papers, and box 34, Buerger papers; *B.Y.U. Directory, 1965-66*; *1966 Banyan,* 293, and "Student Index," 500-29; *1967 Banyan* (Provo, UT: Associated Students of Brigham Young University, 1967), 464; Bergera and Priddis, *Brigham Young University,* 208.

Byron Cannon Anderson and James C. Vandygriff were also listed by BYU professors. In his telephone conversation with me in 1993, Anderson volunteered that he monitored students and faculty at BYU. He was there in 1964-65 and in summer of 1965, when he was also a member of Young Americans for Freedom. However, Anderson was a student at the University of Utah in 1965-66 and therefore concluded his BYU monitoring before the organization of the 1966 spy ring ("Quinn Responds," xi-ii). Vandygriff, "former officer and member of the John Birch Society," was apparently taking only evening classes when he participated in the spy ring's 1966 activities (Morrell, et al., "Events Related To the Covert Surveillance of Faculty Members," 1, 3).

Mark A. Skousen, son of Cleon Skousen's brother Leroy (*1966 Banyan,* 523; *Skousens in America: James Niels Skousen and His Two Wives . . .* [Mesa, AZ: Lofgreen Printing Co., 1971], 85, 87), later authored such publications as *Tax Free: All the Legal Ways to Be Exempt From Federal State, and Social Security Taxes* (1982) and *Dissent on Keynes: A Critical Appraisal of Keynesian Economics* (New York: Praeger, 1992). Michel L. Call's 1973 BYU master's thesis in political science was "The National Education Association as a Political Pressure Group." A year later Vandygriff completed a master's degree in BYU's Department of Church History and Doctrine.

229. H. Verlan Andersen became Russell's attorney in his dealings with BYU's administration after public exposure of the spy ring. Andersen was the faculty sponsor of BYU's Young Americans for Freedom, of which all the student-spies were members as well as being Birchers (*1966 Banyan,* 293; Conklin to "Mormon List"). After becoming church president, Ezra Taft Benson appointed Andersen as a general authority (*Deseret News 1995-1996 Church Almanac,* 71).

230. E. Eugene Bryce, "Campus Speaker Affiliated With Subversive Groupings," *Provo Daily Herald,* 20 Apr. 1965, 10; Bryce, "Denies Questioning Ability To Distinguish the Truth," *Provo Daily Herald,* 29 Apr. 1965, A-6; Jim C. Vandygriff, "Vandygriff Takes Turn In Word Duel With Davies," *Provo Daily Herald,* 30 Apr. 1965, A-4; Poll to Wilkinson, 24 June 1965; and Lisle Updike to Ernest L. Wilkinson, 5 May 1965, Curt Conklin to David O. McKay, 29 Jan. 1965 [1966], also referred to in Clare Middlemiss to Ernest L. Wilkinson, 3 Feb. 1966, Conklin to Wilkinson, 16 Feb. 1966, all in Wilkinson papers, photocopies in my possession. Conklin explains that his January letter was not part of a coordinated effort ("Mormon List," 2; "Uncannily Accurate," viii).

231. Whittaker and McClellan, "The Collection: Description," 2; Stephen Hays Russell to Ernest L. Wilkinson, 26 Apr. 1965; Morrell, et al., "Events Related To the Covert Surveillance of Faculty Members," 5; Richard D. Poll to Ray C. Hillam, 12 Sept. 1966, fd 10, Hillam papers, also box 34, Buerger papers; minutes of meeting of BYU administrative officers with Ray C. Hillam and Stephen Hays Russell, 16 Sept. 1966, 5, fd 4, Hillam papers, also box 34, Buerger papers; Hankin interview, 17 Sept. 1966, 30; "Birchers Spied On Professors, Hialeah Student Said," A-32; Bergera and Priddis, *Brigham Young University,* 209. For similar tactics, see "Hell Breaks Loose in Paradise: This 'Textbook' Hides a Tape Recorder to Trap a Teacher," *Life* 54 (26 Apr. 1963): 73-84.

232. Stephen Hays Russell, *Personal History of Stephen Hays Russell* (N.P, 1983), 99, photocopy in my possession. In his letter to me, 4 Feb. 1994, Russell wrote: "Much of your narrative on The 1966 BYU 'Spy Ring' in this article [*Dialogue: A Journal of Mormon Thought* 26 (Summer 1993): 50-55] is outrageously false." Compare Conklin, "Uncannily Accurate," vii-ix.

233. Hankin interview, 17 Sept. 1966, 6-7; also David M. Sisson statement, 17 Sept. 1966, fd 10, Hillam papers, and box 34, Buerger papers.

Admitting his involvement in the BYU spy ring, Russell signed a 1967 statement which made no reference to the Birch Society or to Benson. See Stephen Hays Russell statement, 13 Mar. 1967, typescript, signed at the bottom of each page by Stephen Hays Russell, fd 9, Hillam papers, and box 34, Buerger papers. Nineteen years later "Statements By Stephen Hays Russell on 'The 1966-67 Student "'Spy Ring' Section of the Book *Brigham Young University: A House of Faith* by Bergera," 23 Dec. 1986 (photocopy in my possession) did not challenge the Birch Society connection, and Russell referred (1) to his association with the Birch chapter leader in Provo.

There are clearly factual discrepancies in Russell's various statements. During the university inquiry on 16 Sept. 1966, 7 (fd 4, Hillam papers, also box 34, Buerger papers), Russell denied that he was a member of the Birch Society. Ernest L. Wilkinson memorandum, 20 Sept. 1966, 3, photocopy in my possession, shows that Russell told Wilkinson he had resigned from the Birch Society, whereas he told Wilkinson's assistant that he had never been a member. Russell's 1983 *Personal History,* 99-110, acknowledges that he had been a Birch member since January 1965 and makes no reference to his withdrawal from membership prior to the spy scandal. In a letter to Jeff D. Blake on 1 July 1994, "Russell states that he was the only Birch Society member among the [student] spies," cited in Blake, "Ernest L. Wilkinson and the 1966 BYU Spy Ring: A Response to D. Michael Quinn," *Dialogue: A Journal of Mormon Thought* 28 (Spring 1995): 164n9, 168n42. That is clearly false by Hankin's statement, 4-5, and Conklin, "Uncannily Accurate," vii-viii. During the September 1966 inquiry, Russell denied (5) that he was "part of an organized group of students," yet his 1967 statement, 1983 *Personal History,* and 1986 "Statements" describe how he organized such a group. Russell's 1986 "Statements" claimed that students submitted two reports "within two weeks of each other," but his *Personal History,* 109, claimed that "reports were submitted just once." To the contrary, Wilkinson's diary shows that he received the first report on 29 April, and his papers contain a written report, dated 24 May 1966, on J. Kenneth Davies by students Lyle Burnett and Stephen Hays Russell. Seven other professors were monitored as well. After the 1966 spying scandal Russell also claimed that he had only "met Benson once, but this meeting was very informal" (Blake, "Ernest L. Wilkinson and the 1966 BYU Spy Ring," 169), whereas in April 1965 Russell "boasts of frequent meetings with ETB in the last month" (Poll, "Addendum on earlier items," 25 Apr. [1965]).

Russell's 1967 statement (3) acknowledged that "if I 'got caught' at this, official university reactions would be that I was acting on my own," and added (9) that Wilkinson expected Russell to be the "scapegoat" (also Bergera and Priddis, *Brigham Young University,* 211). Although he implicated Wilkinson and two of Wilkinson's assistants already named by Hankin, all of Russell's other statements were intended to shield others beyond the BYU administrators. Nor did he name the students he selected to assist him. Although Blake's "Ernest L. Wilkinson and the 1966 BYU Spy Ring" seeks to be Russell's advocate, Blake apparently disbelieved some of Russell's own statements. See D. Michael Quinn, "A Reply," *Dialogue: A Journal of Mormon Thought* 28 (Spring 1995): 175.

234. My interview, 16 Dec. 1992, with a highly placed official at LDS headquarters in 1966 (name withheld by request). While I was asking about other matters involving Benson, this source volunteered Stephen Russell's name as the person who forwarded the "spy ring's findings" to Benson. This was also implied in Hankin interview, 17 Sept. 1966, 6-7, and Sisson statement, 17 Sept. 1966, fd 10, Hillam papers, and box 34, Buerger papers.

In a letter to me on 4 February 1994 Russell wrote: "Benson had nothing to do whatever with this unfortunate 1966 'spy' incident, I did not in any manner forward or communicate this or any information to Elder Benson—ever, and further, as far as I know, no 'highly placed official at LDS church headquarters' has known of me nor have I known of them." In my reply on 9 February 1994 I promised that I would include his denial. I also relayed to Russell a statement given to me on 9 February 1994 by my anonymous source: "After all these years since my conversations with Stephen Hays Russell, a direct quote of his words is not possible. However, he said words to the effect that 'this' (referring to his own involvement in the BYU spy ring) went beyond Wilkinson and went to Church headquarters, and to a person there that Stephen said he would not identify. It was the conclusion of several people closely involved in the investigation of the BYU spy ring that the person was Ezra Taft Benson."

235. Ernest L. Wilkinson diary, 29 Apr. 1966. This verifies the statement of Ronald Ira Hankin and David M. Sisson on 17 Sept. 1966, fd 10, Hillam papers, and box 34, Buerger papers: "During the last week of April we visited Stephen Hays Russell in his dorm in Deseret Towers. . . . During our visit Stephen told us he would be visiting President Wilkinson soon. . . . Later the same evening Stephen told me, Ron Hankin, that he was going to turn the report over to the President within the next three or four days."

236. Statement of BYU vice-president Earl C. Crockett, 9 Nov. 1966, to Edwin B. Morrell, Richard B. Wirthlin, and Louis C. Midgley, reported in Midgley to Ray C. Hillam, 11 Nov. 1966. However, in November 1993 Midgley claimed that this letter was merely "speculating on a possible connection with Benson. This speculation was based on Benson's political stance and its possible similarities with those involved in the spying. Midgley now believes that no connection existed with Benson" (Blake, "Ernest L. Wilkinson and the 1966 BYU Spy Ring," 169).

Midgley's explanation in 1993 bears no resemblance to his 1966 letter which reported what Crockett indicated he had learned through conversations with Wilkinson, Apostle Lee, and Counselor Tanner. Midgley's letter also continued: "I told Earl [Crockett] as passionately as I could that I thought that, at the very least and inspite [sic] of anything and everything, the whole story should be made clear to Elder Lee and Elder Tanner so that ETB's activities will be known when we have a new president."

In his 1993 reconstruction of his knowledge of Ezra Taft Benson's connection with the BYU spy ring, Louis C. Midgley (LCM) also neglected to mention his 1966 interview of one of the student-spies, Ronald Ira Hankin (RIH):

"LCM: Was there any attempt to suggest that the General Authorities of the Church were behind this?

"RIH: Yes, this was suggested to us two or three times, and later in private conversation with me, Steve [Russell] said that Brother Benson was behind this, but in the meeting [he] mentioned that the Church and the General Authorities were wanting to check on this.

"LCM: Do you remember the occasion on which he identified Benson as being behind this or knowing of it.

"RIH: He mentioned it on two occasions that I remember of. He mentioned it to me when I was up in his room, at least that he was behind it, because he was a friend of President Benson, he might find that he supported it if he was to speak with him, or claim to support it and also we were at a [Birch] Society meeting about a week or two later and he said that he had been speaking to President Benson about some stuff relating to accreditation and all and we weren't going to be accredited possibly because of not having enough liberal professors on the campus. President Benson said in replying to him that he didn't care if this would hold up our accreditation or anything, that we had gotten along before without this" (interview of Ronald Ira Hankin by Ray C. Hillam and Louis C. Midgley, 17 Sept. 1966, Provo, Utah, transcript, 6-7, signed at the bottom of each page by Ronald I. Hankin, fd 5, Hillam papers, and box 34, Buerger papers).

237. Midgley to Hillam, 11 Nov. 1966, and comment on this letter in the inventory of Whittaker and McClellan, "The Collection: Description."

238. Whittaker and McClellan, "The Collection: Description," 5.

239. "Free Forum Filled With 'Charges,'" *Daily Universe,* 1 Mar. 1967, 1; "BYU Denies Campus 'Spy' Story," *Salt Lake Tribune,* 1 Mar. 1967, C-4; "Birchers Spied on Professors, Hialeah Student Says," *Miami Herald,* 3 Mar. 1967, A-32; "Wilkinson Admits 'Spy Ring' Existence at 'Y,'" *Provo Daily Herald,* 14 Mar. 1967, 1, 4; "Patriots On the Campus," *The New Republic* 156 (25 Mar. 1967): 12; "Spies, J[unior]. G[rade].," *Newsweek* 69 (27 Mar. 1967): 112; also "Y. Teachers Blast 'Spy Scandal Coverup,'" *Salt Lake Tribune,* 24 Dec. 1976, B-3; Ron Priddis, "BYU Spy Case Unshelved," *Seventh East Press,* 14 Mar. 1982, 1, 11-12; Bergera and Priddis, *Brigham Young University,* 207-17; Robert Gottlieb and Peter Wiley, *America's Saints: The Rise of Mormon Power* (New York: G. P. Putnam's Sons, 1984), 232-33.

240. Ezra Taft Benson, reading copy of general conference talk, 2 Oct. 1966, photocopy in "Hugh B. Brown's File on the John Birch Society."

241. Frederick S. Buchanan diary, 3 Oct. 1966.

242. N. Eldon Tanner to Joseph Fielding Smith, 31 Oct. 1966, Hugh B. Brown to David O. McKay, 9 Nov. 1966, with notation in Brown's handwriting of First Presidency decision on 16 Nov. 1966, all attached to Benson's reading copy of his October 1966 conference talk, and all in "Hugh B. Brown's File on the John Birch Society."

243. Ezra Taft Benson, "Protecting Freedom—An Immediate Responsibility," *Improvement Era* 69 (Dec. 1966): 1144-46.

244. Audio tape of Ezra Taft Benson, "Our Immediate Responsibility," devotional address to students of Brigham Young University, 25 Oct. 1966, available from BYU Media Services.

245. Ezra Taft Benson, "Our Immediate Responsibility," *Speeches of the Year* (Provo, UT: Extension Publications, Division of Continuing Education, Brigham Young University, 1966), esp. 8, 13-14.

246. Midgley to Hillam, 11 Nov. 1966, fd 12, Hillam papers, and box 34, Buerger papers; Ernest L. Wilkinson diary, 25 Oct. 1966. For Wilkinson's statements in support of Benson, see his diary entries for 3 June 1962, 6 Apr. 1965, 25 Oct. 1966, 23 Sept. 1975, 18 Sept. 1976.

247. "Presidential Draft for Elder Benson?" in *Deseret News,* 3 May 1966, A-1; "Group Seeks Benson for Race in '68," *Salt Lake Tribune,* 3 May 1966, 6; "Benson Hints Door Open In '68 Race," *Salt Lake Tribune,* 4 May 1966, A-14; Dew, *Ezra Taft Benson,* 383. Also Epstein and Forster, *The Radical Right,* 53-55, 142; Bethke, "BF, EB," 16-17; "Mormons and Politics: Benson's Influence Helps Keep Growing Church on Conservative Track," *Wall Street Journal,* 8 Aug. 1966, 1.

248. For the pre-1978 LDS policy of denying ordination to persons of black African ancestry, see n117; for U.S. senator Thurmond's defense of segregation and opposition to African-American voting rights, see Milton R. Konvitz, *A Century of Civil Rights* (New York: Columbia University Press, 1961), 36, 74-75; Robert D. Loevy, *To End All Segregation: The Politics of the Passage of the Civil Rights Act of 1964* (Lanham, MD: University Press of America, 1990), 130, 164-65; Orville Vernon Burton, Terence R. Finnegan, Peyton McCrary, and James W. Loewen, "South Carolina," in Chandler Davidson and Bernard Grofman, eds., *Quiet Revolution in the South: The Impact of the Voting Rights Act, 1965-1990* (Princeton, NJ: Princeton University Press, 1994), 209.

249. Schomp, *Birchism Was My Business,* 159-60.

250. Of thirty-four officers and members of this campaign committee in 1966, fourteen were members of the national council of the John Birch Society, its "top advisory body in matters of organization and policy." The Birch council members on Benson's election committee were Thomas J. Anderson, T. Coleman Andrews, John T. Brown, Laurence E. Bunker, William J. Grede, Augereau G. Heinsohn, Fred C. Koch, Dean Clarence Manion, N. Floyd McGowin, W. B. McMillan, Robert H. Montgomery, Thomas Parker, Robert W. Stoddard, and Charles B. Stone. In addition, K. G. Bentson, Robert B. Dresser, and Charles Edison were on the editorial advisory committee for *American Opinion.* John W. Scott was a Birch Society member in 1966 and joined the editorial advisory committee in 1978. Bonner Fellers and Edgar W. Hiestand had been on the Committee of Endorsers in 1962 and continued to be heavily involved with the Birch Society throughout the 1960s. See *The Team You Can Trust To Guide America, the Best Team for '68: Ezra Taft Benson for President, Strom Thurmond for Vice-President* (Holland, MI, [1966]), 12, and compare national Council members in Robert W. Lee to J. Bracken Lee, 17 Jan. 1966, on letterhead of The John Birch Society, fd 18, box 70, Lee papers, and with editorial staff and advisory committee *American Opinion* 9 (Jan. 1966): inside front cover, (May 1966): inside front cover, (Oct. 1966): inside front cover, 21 (Sept. 1978): inside front cover; John H. Rousselot, "Honorable Edgar W. Hiestand," *American Opinion* 8 (Nov. 1965): 113. *The Team You Can Trust To Guide America,* 15, noted that its list of books in support of this candidacy was available "from any American Opinion bookstore." Probably typical of the committee members who had no national Birch office, William L. McGrath was identified as a member of the John Birch Society in Group Research Reports, "Individual Index—Cumulative (7/1/63)," copy in fd 4, box 9, King papers.

251. Welch, *Blue Book of The John Birch Society,* 73: "We would organize fronts—little fronts, big fronts, temporary fronts, permanent fronts, all kinds of fronts."

252. Hugh B. Brown interview by Richard Wirthlin and Ray Hillam, 9 Aug. 1966, 3, transcribed 11 Oct. 1966 "from Rough Draft Notes," fd 6, Hillam papers, and box 34, Buerger papers.

253. Ezra Taft Benson diary, 24 June 1966, quoted in Dew, *Ezra Taft Benson,* 386; "Benson's Influence Helps Keep Growing Church On Conservative Track," *Wall Street Journal,* 8 Aug. 1966, 1: "But just in case a draft movement does catch fire, he has obtained

from David McKay, the 92-year-old prophet and president of the Mormon Church, an unpublished letter giving full approval to any campaign that Mr. Benson might make."

254. David O. McKay office diary, 25 Feb. 1949, LDS archives. Some readers might suggest that by 1966 McKay had reversed his earlier endorsement of racial segregation in the "Jim Crow" southern states. McKay was better known among Mormon liberals of the 1960s (including his counselor Hugh B. Brown) for the church president's private expressions of appreciation about their support of full civil rights for African-Americans. However, this reflected McKay's desire to be "lauded and lionized" by everyone (Gibbons, *David O. McKay*, 263). His formal endorsement of an apostle becoming a political partner with a known segregationist shows that the church president's racial views had not significantly changed by 1966.

255. Dew, *Ezra Taft Benson*, 383-84, 386, 392-93.

256. "'Strictly a draft'—Elder Benson," *Deseret News "Church News,"* 28 Jan. 1967, 6.

257. "Benson Finds Draft Crusade 'Humbling,'" *Ogden Standard-Examiner*, 11 Mar. 1967, 9; "Benson Says No Interest in '68 Draft," *Salt Lake Tribune*, 12 Mar. 1967, C-6.

258. "Tendency Toward Extremes," *Deseret News "Church News,"* 15 Apr. 1967, 20.

259. "Group Acts to Draft Benson in '68 Race," *Ogden Standard-Examiner*, 1 Nov. 1967, A-12.

260. "Ezra Taft Benson Addresses Rally," *Deseret News*, 7 Jan. 1963, A-3. For Benson's participation with Hargis and his Christian Crusade, see "This Week! 5 Great Nights of Christian Leadership Training: Christian Crusade Leadership School—Feb. 20-24," advertisement in *Tulsa Daily World*, 19 Feb. 1967, photocopy in Williams papers. For background on Hargis, see John Harold Redekop, *The American Far Right: A Case Study of Billy James Hargis and Christian Crusade* (Grand Rapids, MI: William B. Eerdmans Publishing Co., 1968).

261. Hugh B. Brown to Burns S. Hanson, 11 May 1967, carbon copy cross-referenced to "Hargis, Billy James," in "Hugh B. Brown File on the John Birch Society."

262. Ezra Taft Benson, "Prepare, Then Fear Not," *Improvement Era* 70 (June 1967): 57, for "Christian constitutionalists," and 58-59, for longer quote; Goates, *Harold B. Lee*, 387.

263. Ezra Taft Benson address, 29 Sept. 1967, in his *Civil Rights: Tool of Communist Deception*, 3; "Mormon Leaders Heard By 25,000," *New York Times*, 2 Oct. 1967, 52; *Improvement Era* 70 (Dec. 1967): 35, softened his position about the civil rights movement. His original, uncensored 1967 statement was almost identical to the *Deseret News*, 14 Dec. 1963, B-5, report of Benson's assessment of civil rights.

264. Wes Andrews and Clyde Dalton, *The Black Hammer: A Study of Black Power, Red Influence and White Alternatives* (Oakland, CA: Desco Press, 1967), 13, copy in library, Historical Department, Church of Jesus Christ of Latter-day Saints.

265. Ezra Taft Benson, "Trade and Treason," *Christian Crusade* 19 (Apr. 1967): 22-24. Benson re-delivered this address on 14 April 1967 to a joint meeting of Rotary, Lions, and Optimist clubs in Yakima, Washington. A transcript, with accompanying letter from Benson to Frank H. Jonas, 18 Aug. 1967, is in Jonas papers; also printed after Benson re-delivered it at the Highland High School, Salt Lake City, 9 June 1967. See "Benson Talk To Close 'Idea' Series," *Salt Lake Tribune*, 4 June 1967, B-13.

266. Dew, *Ezra Taft Benson*, 392.

267. Ibid., 392.

268. Ibid., 397-98; *The Team You Can Trust To Guide America*; Epstein and Forster, *The Radical Right*, 53-55, 142; Bethke, "BF, EB," 16-17.

269. J. Earl Coke, "Reminiscences on People and Change in California Agriculture, 1900-1975," 111, interviews by Ann Foley Scheuring, 1976, Oral History Center, Shields Library, University of California at Davis, copy in Special Collections, Lee Library. While Benson was Secretary of Agriculture, Wilkinson observed: "Apparently, however, Benson

stands aloof from all his advisors, and they are afraid to tell him [what they think]" (Wilkinson diary, 13 Sept. 1957).

270. Willard S. Voit announcement, 17 Nov. 1967 in *The John Birch Society Bulletin* (Dec. 1967): 26-28; "Wallace In Race; Will 'Run To Win,'" *New York Times*, 9 Feb. 1968, 1; "Benson Backs Wallace Stand," *Christian Science Monitor*, 13 Feb. 1968, 3, based on an undated interview with Benson by a reporter with Reuters news service; also Dew, *Ezra Taft Benson*, 397.

271. George C. Wallace to David O. McKay, 12 Feb. 1968, and McKay to Wallace, 14 Feb. 1968, photocopies in Wilkinson papers and my possession; Dew, *Ezra Taft Benson*, 397; also Lewis Chester, Godfrey Hodgson, and Bruce Page, *An American Melodrama: The Presidential Campaign of 1968* (New York: Viking Press, 1969), 694; Dennis Wainstock, *The Turning Point: The 1968 United States Presidential Campaign* (Jefferson, NC: McFarland & Company, 1988), 164; Dan T. Carter, *The Politics of Rage: George Wallace, the Origins of the New Conservatism, and the Transformation of American Politics* (New York: Simon and Schuster, 1995), 354, 356; Bergera and Priddis, *Brigham Young University*, 221.

272. Dew, *Ezra Taft Benson*, 397.

273. Ezra Taft Benson, "Re: Martin Luther King," 6 Apr. 1968, copy attached to letter of Benson to J. Willard Marriott, 1 May 1969, J. Willard Marriott papers, Marriott Library; compare Jim Lucier, "King of Slick," *American Opinion* 6 (Nov. 1963): 1-11; Alan Stang, "The King And His Communists," *American Opinion* 8 (Oct. 1965): 1-14; Gary Allen, "America: How Communist Are We?" *American Opinion* 10 (July-Aug. 1967): 9. For a variety of perspectives on King, see Lionel Lokos, *House Divided: The Life and Legacy of Martin Luther King* (New Rochelle, NY: Arlington House, 1969); William R. Miller, *Martin Luther King, Jr.: His Life, Martyrdom and Meaning for the World* (New York: Wybright and Talley, 1968); David L. Lewis, *King: A Biography* (Urbana: University of Illinois Press, 1978); Stephen B. Oates, *Let the Trumpet Sound: The Life of Martin Luther King, Jr.* (New York: Harper and Row, 1982); James P. Hanigan, *Martin Luther King, Jr., and the Foundations of Nonviolence* (Lanham, MD: University Press of America, 1984); David J. Garrow, *Bearing the Cross: Martin Luther King, Jr., and the Southern Christian Leadership Conference* (New York: W. Morrow, 1986); James A. Colaiaco, *Martin Luther King, Jr.: Apostle of Militant Nonviolence* (New York: St. Martin's Press, 1988); Taylor Branch, *Parting the Waters: America in the King Years, 1954-63* (New York: Simon and Schuster, 1988); Richard Donald Ouellette, "The Southern Christian Leadership Conference and Martin Luther King, Jr., 1965-1968," senior honors thesis, University of Utah, 1992.

274. Hugh B. Brown to John W. Bennion, LDS bishop of the Elgin Ward, Chicago Stake, 29 May 1968, photocopy in my possession.

275. George S. Tanner journal, 130 (16 Apr. 1968), Marriott Library; also "Gary" to "Dear Dad," 9 Apr. 1968, Poll papers.

276. Ezra Taft Benson, "The Book of Mormon Warns America," address at BYU devotional, 21 May 1968, transcript, 4, 5, 6, 7, 10, Vertical File, Special Collections, Marriott Library, and transcript in Moss papers; also "Road to Anarchy: Benson Blisters Supreme Court," *Ogden Standard-Examiner*, 22 May 1968, A-11; "Benson Warns on Commies in Talk at BYU Assembly," *Provo Daily Herald*, 22 May 1968, 24.

277. Ezra Taft Benson to the First Presidency and the Quorum of the Twelve Apostles, 10 Apr. 1968, in Dew, *Ezra Taft Benson*, 400.

278. George S. Tanner journal, 132 (11 June 1968), and 76, for a summary of Tanner's experience as institute teacher and director.

279. Robert O. Trottier to David O. McKay, 22 May 1968, copies to Hugh B. Brown, N. Eldon Tanner, and Ezra Taft Benson, photocopy in Vertical File for Ezra Taft Benson, Special Collections, Marriott Library.

280. Afton Olson Miles, "Mormon Voting Behavior and Political Attitudes," Ph.D. diss., New York University, 1978, 164-65. Broken down by political affiliation, this anti-Birch view was shared by 86 percent of Mormon Democrats, 64 percent of Mormon independents, and 43 percent of Mormon Republicans.

281. Hugh B. Brown to Trottier, 24 May 1968, photocopy in Vertical File for Ezra Taft Benson, Special Collections, Marriott Library.

282. Campbell and Poll, *Hugh B. Brown*, 259-60.

283. J. Edgar Hoover statement to the U.S. House appropriations subcommittee, 10 Feb. 1966, in *Congressional Record* 112 (27 Sept. 1966): 24028. The Anti-Defamation League of B'nai B'rith analyzed Birch anti-Semitism in "The John Birch Society," *Facts: Domestic Report* 14 (Nov.-Dec. 1961). In the 1940s-50s J. Reuben Clark, Ezra Taft Benson, and Ernest L. Wilkinson were exchanging anti-Semitic publications and views (D. Michael Quinn, *J. Reuben Clark: The Church Years* [Provo, UT: Brigham Young University Press, 1983], 226, 321n24).

284. Hugh B. Brown journal, 21 Aug. 1968, photocopy in box 49, Poll papers.

285. Ezra Taft Benson, "The Proper Role of Government," *Vital Speeches* 24 (15 June 1968): 514-20, also reprinted in *Agricultural Engineering* 49 (Aug. 1968): 469-71; Dew, *Ezra Taft Benson*, 367.

286. Dew, *Ezra Taft Benson*, 398.

287. Charles M. Brown interview, 7 June 1973, page c-1-14, fd 25, box 48, Poll papers; R. Tom Tucker, "Remembering Hugh Brown," *Sunstone* 12 (May 1988): 4; Gottlieb and Wiley, *America's Saints*, 108.

288. Ernest L. Wilkinson diary, 13 May 1969.

289. For example, in his rebuttal to the talk Benson had given at BYU, Brown clearly indicated that he did not think Benson had "maturity of mind and emotion and a depth of spirit . . . to differ with others on matters of politics without calling into question the integrity of those with whom you differ" (Campbell and Poll, *Hugh B. Brown*, 259).

290. My telephone interview, 8 Dec. 1992, with Karl D. Butler, special assistant to Benson as Secretary of Agriculture. The two remained friends thereafter. See Benson, *Cross Fire*, 13-14, 23, 25, 38, 69.

291. Ezra Taft Benson, "Americans Are Destroying America," *Improvement Era* 71 (June 1968): 69.

292. Ezra Taft Benson, "The Proper Role of Government," *Improvement Era* 71 (Dec. 1968): 53.

293. Hugh B. Brown to Philip D. Thorpe, Director of the Community Action Program in Provo, Utah, 18 Oct. 1968, carbon copy in Campbell papers, with attached copy of Benson's October 1968 conference address, "The Proper Role of Government," *Improvement Era* 71 (Dec. 1968): 51-53, with underlined passage (53), also typed copy of letter in fd 1, box 51, Poll papers.

294. *Improvement Era* 72 (Dec. 1969): 69.

295. Ernest L. Wilkinson diary, 12 Apr. 1968; also Bergera and Priddis, *Brigham Young University*, 215. Benson had first suggested Glenn L. Pearson as dean.

296. Phares Woods statement, 27 May 1969, 1-2, fd 16, Hillam papers, and box 34, Buerger papers; *BYU Directory, 1968-69,* s.v. "Phares Quincy Woods." Daughter of Cleon Skousen's brother Ervin M., Cynthia Skousen was a first cousin of the 1966 student-spy Mark A. Skousen (*Skousens In America,* 86). She wrote me on 24 June 1993: "[M]y uncle, W. Cleon Skousen *never* asked me to spy on professors at BYU or to join any kind of a student spy ring. I was not a member of any student spy ring." However, she added: "Now regarding the alleged quote, I don't recall making any statement regarding the potential destruction of BYU by 1970. But then, when one is a teenager, one makes all kinds of statements . . . most of which don't come back 25 years later in quotes!" While I quote her 1993 letter here to satisfy Cynthia Skousen's request for a published acknowledgement of

her denial, I regard the 1969 statement by Phares Woods as the "best evidence" of these 1969 events.

297. Undated, handwritten memo from "M.G.F." (probably Merwin G. Fairbanks, director of student publications) to "Cleon Skousen," with copies to ELW (Ernest L. Wilkinson), RKT (Robert K. Thomas), BEL (Ben E. Lewis), RJS (Robert J. Smith), and "Dan Ludlow," fd 16, Hillam papers, emphasis in original.

298. Phares Woods statement, 27 May 1969, 4.

299. George S. Tanner journal, 150 (30 Oct. 1969); also William E. Berrett to Richards Durham, 26 May 1969, quoted on pp. 5, 8, 10 of Durham to Berrett, 28 May 1969, in Durham papers, Marriott Library.

300. "Statement by Thomas Jerold Stirland (concerning a faculty meeting at the Ogden L.D.S. Institute–April 22, 1969–and related matters)," 1, Durham papers.

301. Durham to Berrett, 28 May 1969, 6; Durham to "Dear Brother _____," 21 Aug. 1969, 11, Durham papers.

302. Richards Durham to Ezra Taft Benson, 11 Dec. 1969, 5, and Benson to Durham, 10 Apr. 1970, quoted in Durham to "Dear [eradicated name]," 18 Feb. 1972, 1, and Durham's "Dialectical Materialism–the Religion of Satan," Durham papers.

303. Dew, *Ezra Taft Benson*, 233, 372, 385; Dew, "Ezra Taft Benson," in Daniel H. Ludlow, ed., *Encyclopedia of Mormonism: The History, Scripture, Doctrine, and Procedure of the Church of Jesus Christ of Latter-day Saints,* 5 vols. (New York: Macmillan Publishing Co., 1992), 1:102-103.

304. Firmage, *An Abundant Life,* 142.

305. See J. Reuben Clark office diary, 22 May 1961; Ernest L. Wilkinson diary, 25 May 1967; Neal A. Maxwell oral history, 1976-77, 24-25, LDS archives; also Quinn, *J. Reuben Clark,* 128, 141-42. Eugene Campbell's typed draft of the Brown biography likewise stated: "Unfortunately some of those who seemed to favor the John Birch Society were close to President McKay . . . [who] . . . with his mental difficulties at times was not always able to see the issues as clearly as he would have done had he been younger" (chapter titled, "Responsibility Without Authority–The 1st Presidency Years," 13, Campbell papers).

306. *October 1959 Conference Report* . . . (Salt Lake City: Church of Jesus Christ of Latter-day Saints, 1959), 5; also David O. McKay, *Statements on Communism and the Constitution of the United States* (Salt Lake City: Deseret Book Co., 1964).

307. David O. McKay office diary, 17 Aug., 24 Aug., 19 Sept. 1961, LDS archives; Quinn, *J. Reuben Clark,* 190, 216; *Deseret News "Church News,"* 16 Apr. 1966, 7; Anderson, "Church and Birch In Utah," 18-19; James B. Allen, "David O. McKay," in Ludlow, *Encyclopedia of Mormonism* 2:874. As early as May 1961 the *Deseret News* indicated the split developing among Mormons regarding the Birch Society. See editorial "How to Become a Millionaire: Start An 'Anti-Commie' Society," *Deseret News,* 2 May 1961, A-12, which Mark E. Petersen re-emphasized in "Let Us Not Be Carried Away," *Deseret News "Church News,"* 29 July 1961, 16; and contrast with Jerrald [sic] L. Newquist, "Liberty Vs. Creeping Socialism: Warns Of Internal Threats," *Deseret News,* 21 Dec. 1961, A-12. Also George T. Boyd to Hugh B. Brown, 22 Sept. 1961, with Brown's answer of 6 Oct., copies in Special Collections, Lee Library. Contrast the 1961 views of Petersen and Brown with the following announcement in the church's *MIA Stake Leader* 13 (Dec. 1961): 3 of anti-Communist publications that "may be obtained from the All American Society, P.O. Box 8045, Foothill Station, Salt Lake City, Utah." At that time Skousen was a director of this All American Society office. See Stewart, "Analysis of the Celebrity Structure of the American Right," 29; All American Society of Utah, "What You Should Know About the All-American Society of Utah," 3, in Williams papers.

308. Gibbons, *David O. McKay,* 382.

309. J. Reuben Clark office diary, 18 June 1951; Ernest L. Wilkinson diary, 3 Jan. 1962, 27 June 1963; Marion G. Romney oral history, 1976, 18, LDS archives.

310. Francis M. Gibbons, *Harold B. Lee: Man of Vision, Prophet of God* (Salt Lake City: Deseret Book Co., 1993), 193; James B. Allen and Glen M. Leonard, *Story of the Latter-day Saints*, 2d ed. rev. (Salt Lake City: Deseret Book Co., 1992), 593-623; Gottlieb and Wiley, *America's Saints*, 15, 59-62, 81-82; Goates, *Harold B. Lee*, 363-77; Richard O. Cowan, *The Church in the Twentieth Century* (Salt Lake City: Bookcraft, 1985), 305-17; Wilburn D. Talbot, *The Acts of the Modern Apostles* (Salt Lake City: Randall Book Co., 1985), 294-95; Frank O. May, Jr., "Correlation of the Church: Administration," James B. Allen and Richard O. Cowan, "History of the Church: 1945-1990," and L. Brent Goates, "Harold B. Lee," in Ludlow, *Encyclopedia of Mormonism*, 1:324, 2:642-43, 822; Gibbons, *Harold B. Lee*, 389-92; Jan Shipps, "Making Saints in the Early Days and the Latter Days," paper given in a plenary session of the Society for the Scientific Study of Religion, Salt Lake City, 27 Oct. 1989, in Marie Cornwall, Tim B. Heaton, and Lawrence A. Young, eds., *Contemporary Mormonism: Social Science Perspectives* (Urbana: University of Illinois Press, 1994), 77, 80.

311. Ernest L. Wilkinson diary, 31 Mar. 1965, also entries about Lee on 6 June, 5 Sept. 1962, 4 Dec. 1963, 7 Sept. 1966, 3 Jan. 1968, 7 Jan. 1970, 31 July, 3 Aug. 1971. On Lee's "fiery temper," see Goates, *Harold B. Lee*, 618; Gibbons, *Harold B. Lee*, 493.

312. Goates, *Harold B. Lee*, 169-403, for service as an apostle, 403-557, for service in First Presidency; Gibbons, *Harold B. Lee*, 146-419, for service as an apostle, 420-93, for service in First Presidency; Talbot, *Acts of the Modern Apostles*, 317; *Deseret News 1995-1996 Church Almanac*, 43.

313. However, the Mormon-Birch *Utah Independent* announced Benson's addresses at Boston rallies "for the American Idea" in 1970 and 1972 where all the other speakers were either staff members of *American Opinion* or longtime authors of its articles. See "Benson, Skousen Speak at New England Rally," *Utah Independent*, 9 July 1970, 1, and "Benson Is Guest of Honor," *Utah Independent*, 30 June 1972, 8, and compare to table of contents pages in previous issues of *American Opinion*, also list of the Birch Society's national council in "The John Birch Society: A Report," *Advertising Supplement to Los Angeles Times*, 27 Sept. 1964, 7.

314. Hugh B. Brown to John W. Bennion, 29 May 1968.

315. "Shun Vigilante Groups, LDS Urges Members," *Salt Lake Tribune*, 4 Mar. 1970, B-1.

316. "TO ALL STAKE PRESIDENTS INTERESTED IN TRUTH AND LIBERTY THIS CALL IS MADE," photocopy of typed document, undated, in fd 22, box 5, Buerger papers, with signed copies by J. Wilson Bartlett in LDS archives, and in fd 3, box 124, Hinckley papers.

317. Harold B. Lee, "To the Defenders of the Faith," 4 Apr. 1970, *Improvement Era* 73 (June 1970): 64.

318. Goates, *Harold B. Lee*, 414; Harold B. Lee, "The Day in Which We Live," and photograph of "Council of the Twelve" vote in "The Solemn Assembly," *Improvement Era* 73 (June 1970): 28, 20.

319. Frederick S. Buchanan diary, 21 July 1970; Ezra Taft Benson, "A World Message," *Improvement Era* 73 (June 1970): 95-97, whose only political reference was prophetic: "The time must surely come when the Iron Curtain will be melted down and the Bamboo Curtain shattered."

320. Byron Cannon Anderson, "LDS General Conference Sustains Pres. Smith," *Utah Independent*, 9 Apr. 1970, 1, 4.

321. Byron Cannon Anderson interview, 18 Jan. 1993. For Anderson's revised version of what he told me on the telephone, see his "Spy Reply," x, and "Quinn Responds," xii.

322. Statement of Henry D. Taylor to his friend Mark K. Allen as reported in Allen interview, 3 May 1984, by Alison Bethke Gayek, photocopy in my possession.

323. Harold B. Lee to Ezra Taft Benson, 12 Feb. 1972, in Dew, *Ezra Taft Benson,* 422.

324. Ernest L. Wilkinson to Ezra Taft Benson, 13 Apr. 1971, also follow-up letter of 4 May 1971, Wilkinson papers, photocopies in my possession; Bergera and Priddis, *Brigham Young University,* 190.

325. Gary Allen, *None Dare Call It Conspiracy* (Rossmoor, CA: Concord Press, 1971). For Allen's prominent role in the Birch Society, see his "The Life and Character of Robert Welch," *American Opinion* 28 (Mar. 1985): 127, and Allen's permanent position as a "Contributing Editor" of *American Opinion* since September 1967.

326. Ezra Taft Benson, "Civic Standards for the Faithful Saints," *Utah Independent,* 14 Apr. 1972, 4; compare with censored version in *Deseret News "Church News,"* 8 Apr. 1972, 12, and *Ensign* 2 (July 1972): 59-61.

On 12 December 1972 BYU professor J. Kenneth Davies reported that he had seen the original letter of Harold B. Lee, N. Eldon Tanner, and Marion G. Romney about this matter to Bishop Delbert Warner (to whom Davies was a counselor). The Lee presidency stated that Benson had requested that his endorsement of Allen's book be deleted from the published version of his conference (Duane E. Jeffery memorandum, 12 Dec. 1972, photocopy in Jeffery's letter to me, 9 Dec. 1992). It is also possible that in April 1972 the Joseph Fielding Smith presidency (in which Lee was a counselor) had asked Benson to request this censorship.

327. Dew, *Ezra Taft Benson,* 421. For the Birch connection with these rallies and forums for the American Idea, see discussion above of his February 1966 talk in Utah and the previous Boston rallies.

328. Ibid., 439.

329. "Support for Candidate Possible Some Day, LDS Apostle Says," *Salt Lake Tribune,* 22 Feb. 1974, B-1; "Benson Tells Party Support," *Salt Lake Tribune,* 4 Nov. 1974, 29; "Church Says Elder's Speech on Third Party 'Unauthorized,'" *Ogden Standard-Examiner,* 4 Nov. 1974, A-10; "American Party told, 'Stand Firm,'" *Deseret News,* 4 Nov. 1974, B-14.

330. Mark E. Petersen, "Ezra Taft Benson: 'A Habit of Integrity,'" *Ensign* 4 (Oct. 1974): 21.

331. David O. McKay to Earl C. Crockett, 4 June 1964, and Crockett memorandum, 11 Dec. 1965, Wilkinson papers, photocopies in my possession; LaVarr G. Webb, "In John Birch Society[,] Fanatics Are Hard to Find," *Daily Universe "Monday Magazine,"* 25 Nov. 1974, 4-6, 10; Bergera and Priddis, *Brigham Young University,* 196, 262-63.

332. BYU President's meeting, 22 Jan. 1975, archives, Lee Library, photocopy in my possession.

333. Bergera and Priddis, *Brigham Young University,* 221-22. However, Oaks (after his appointment as an apostle) told Benson's biographer: "I've always felt that he was the greatest friend BYU had during that period" (Dew, *Ezra Taft Benson,* 468).

334. Ezra Taft Benson, "Problems Affecting the Domestic Tranquility of Citizens of the United States of America: Sovereign Remedies For Our Diseases," *Vital Speeches* 42 (1 Feb. 1976): 236-43; "Elder Benson Warns of Communism's Threat," *Daily Universe,* 25 Feb. 1976, 2; "Inflation, Reds Pose Peril, Benson Warns," *Salt Lake Tribune,* 5 Mar. 1976, B-5; "Ezra Benson: Will Mormons Go Political?" *Los Angeles Times,* 1 Apr. 1976, Pt. I, 5; "LDS Apostle Warns of Communism," *Salt Lake Tribune,* 20 Apr. 1976, A-8; "Benson Attacks Welfare as 'Legal Plunder,'" *Salt Lake Tribune,* 27 June 1976, B-1; "Benson Deplores 'U.S. Support' of Communism," *Salt Lake Tribune,* 28 June 1976, 18; "Pres. Benson Hits Detente: Policy Called Aid to Communism," *Deseret News,* 23 Aug. 1976, B-11; "Benson Lambastes Detente, Support of Communism," *Salt Lake Tribune,* 28 Aug. 1976, Pt. II, 17.

335. Ernest L. Wilkinson diary, 18 Sept. 1976; "Pres. Ezra Taft Benson Speaks At Freeman Institute," *Utah Independent,* 23 Sept. 1976, 5.

336. "Freemen Institute a Burgeoning Political Force," *Deseret News,* 14 June 1980, A-7; *Behind the Scenes: A Personal Report to Pledged Freemen from W. Cleon Skousen* (Salt Lake City: Freemen Institute, 1980), 2, photocopy in fd 25, box 17, Buerger papers. Also John Harrington, "The Freemen Institute," *Nation* 231 (16 Aug. 1980): 152-53; Linda Sillitoe and David Merrill, "Freemen America," *Utah Holiday* 10 (Feb. 1981): 34-43, 66-67, 70-75, (Mar. 1981): 33-40, 52-54; "Cleon Skousen: Humble Teacher or Apostle of the Right?" *Salt Lake Tribune,* 2 Aug. 1981, B-6; Bergera and Priddis, *Brigham Young University,* 220-21, 454n88; "Cleon Skousen: Controversial Dean of Utah's Conservatives," *Deseret News Utah Magazine,* 9 Mar. 1986, 4; "Commission Stops Selling Skousen Text," *Deseret News,* 6 Feb. 1987, B-2; "Skousen's Flock Spreading the Word on Constitution," *Salt Lake Tribune,* 22 Apr. 1987, B-2; "Skousen Isn't About to Break His Ties to Rev. Moon," *Salt Lake Tribune,* 29 Apr. 1987, B-1; "Skousen Stepping Down as President of Institute," *Deseret News,* 17 Sept. 1989, B-3; "Skousen Retires From Constitutional Studies Center," *Salt Lake Tribune,* 20 Sept. 1989, B-8; *Encyclopedia of Associations,* 27th ed. (Detroit: Gale Research, Inc., 1993), s.v. National Center for Constitutional Studies (#14805); also Freemen Institute papers, Marriott Library.

337. Ernest L. Wilkinson diary, 18 Sept. 1976; "Pres. Ezra Taft Benson Speaks At Freeman Institute," 5. There was no advance notice of this Freeman Institute dedicatory service in local papers, and coverage was limited to a news release published identically as "Benson Chides Fiscal Policies," *Salt Lake Tribune,* 19 Sept. 1976, B-2, and "Benson Calls For Sounder Fiscal Policy," *Ogden Standard-Examiner,* 19 Sept. 1976, A-10. The news release referred only to "the opening of a private political research organization in Provo" and to Benson's talk.

338. Ernest L. Wilkinson diary, 18 Sept. 1976; also D. Arthur Haycock's identical statement in his interview with me, 3 Aug. 1979.

339. Ezra Taft Benson to Ernest L. Wilkinson, 2 May 1969, photocopy in fd 3, box 42, Poll papers.

340. Dew, *Ezra Taft Benson,* 262; Edward L. Kimball, ed., *The Teachings of Spencer W. Kimball . . .* (Salt Lake City: Bookcraft, 1982), xvii; Jack Walsh, "D. Arthur Haycock: Aide to Four Prophets," *Ensign* 14 (Aug. 1984): 22-27; Dell Van Orden and Gerry Avant, "Secretary to Five Prophets Called As Temple President," *Deseret News "Church News,"* 19 Jan. 1986, 6, 11; my interview, 5 Sept. 1992, with Rodney P. Foster, assistant secretary in the First Presidency's Office from 1974 to 1981.

341. "Party Qualifies For Utah Ballot," *Salt Lake Tribune,* 6 Mar. 1976, B-5; "LDS Official Says 'No' to Politics," *Salt Lake Tribune,* 25 Mar. 1976, B-4, and "Party Clarifies Stand on Benson Selection," *Salt Lake Tribune,* 29 Mar 1976, 38.

342. Dew, *Ezra Taft Benson,* 394, 446.

343. Duane E. Jeffery memorandum, 26 Oct. 1977, fd 28, box 6, Buerger papers. For Nelson as Benson's secretary, see "LDS Official Acknowledges Church Monitors Critics," *Salt Lake Tribune,* 8 Aug. 1992, D-1; "LDS Leaders Say Scripture Supports Secret Files on Members," *Salt Lake Tribune,* 14 Aug. 1992, B-1.

344. Dew, *Ezra Taft Benson,* 477.

345. Minutes of Combined Boards of Trustees, 7 Dec. 1977, archives, Lee Library, photocopy in my possession; Bergera and Priddis, *Brigham Young University,* 223.

346. Spencer W. Kimball, N. Eldon Tanner, and Marion G. Romney to All Stake Presidents, Bishops, and Branch Presidents in the United States, 15 Feb. 1979, photocopy in fd 25, box 17, Buerger papers.

347. "Free Enterprise Endangered, President Benson Warns," *Deseret News,* 17 May 1977, B-3; "Benson Hails Free Enterprise in 'Hill Cumorah Address,'" *Salt Lake Tribune,* 13 July 1977, A-9; "LDS Leader Offers Interpretation of Church and State Separation," *Salt Lake Tribune,* 25 July 1977, 19; "Socialism Growth in US Rapped by LDS Leader," *Salt Lake Tribune,* 25 Sept. 1977, A-24; "Pres. Benson Defends Free Market," *Deseret News,* 10 Dec.

1977, A-9; "Nation 'Spending Into Oblivion,' Pres. Benson Warns at LDS Meet," *Salt Lake Tribune,* 26 Mar. 1979, D-2; "Benson Rakes U.S. 'Subversives,'" *Ogden Standard-Examiner,* 4 July 1979, A-14; Ezra Taft Benson, "A Warning to America," address to the California Constitutional Crusade, 9 Oct. 1979, transcript in fd 23, box 5, Buerger papers; "LDS Official Decries Spread of Marxism," *Deseret News,* 27 Oct. 1979, A-7; "Apostle Calls For Return to Gold Standard," *Ogden Standard-Examiner,* 20 Jan. 1980, A-12; Ezra Taft Benson, "A Moral Challenge," *American Opinion* 23 (Feb. 1980): 41-54.

348. "Benson Urges Monetary Step: Re-Establish Metal Standard," *Salt Lake Tribune,* 25 Feb. 1980, B-2; "Gathering of Freemen Institute Draws Crowd to Arizona Resort," *Ogden Standard-Examiner,* 25 Feb. 1980, A-12.

349. Ezra Taft Benson, "Fourteen Fundamentals In Following the Prophets," transcript, 26 Feb. 1980, fd 24, box 5, Buerger papers; Benson, "Fourteen Fundamentals in Following the Prophet," *1980 Devotional Speeches of the Year: BYU Devotional and Fireside Addresses* (Provo, UT: Brigham Young University Press, 1981), 26-30; "Prophet's Word 'Law' Benson Tells Group," *Ogden Standard-Examiner,* 26 Feb. 1980, A-2; "Benson Backs Prophet on Politics," *Salt Lake Tribune,* 27 Feb. 1980, B-3; "Mormon Leader's Word Is Law—Benson," *San Jose Mercury News,* 27 Feb. 1980, A-2; "Interpretation of Speech Not Correct, Church Says," *Ogden Standard-Examiner,* 27 Feb. 1980, C-1; "Mormon Professor Says Benson Speech Was Plea Anticipating Rise to LDS Presidency," *Idaho State Journal,* 28 Feb. 1980, A-2; "U. Teacher Replies To Benson" and "Savant Hits 'Theocracy' He Says Benson Wants," *Salt Lake Tribune,* 28 Feb. 1980, B-1, B-3; "Pres. Benson Outlines Way to Follow Prophet," *Deseret News "Church News,"* 1 Mar. 1980, 14; "No. 2 Mormon Says Leader's Word is Law," *Los Angeles Times,* 1 Mar. 1980, Pt. I, 35; "Benson Speech Stirs Speculation on LDS Changes," *Ogden Standard-Examiner,* 2 Mar. 1980, A-1, A-5; Sterling M. McMurrin, "Case for Vigilance," *Salt Lake Tribune,* 18 Mar. 1980, A-9; Dew, *Ezra Taft Benson,* 468-69.

350. First Presidency statement, 5 Mar. 1980, *Deseret News "Church News,"* 8 Mar. 1980, 3; "Church Policies and Announcements," *Ensign* 10 (Aug. 1980): 79.

351. *Salt Lake Tribune,* 9 Mar. 1980, C-31.

352. Edward L. Kimball to D. Michael Quinn, 14 Aug., 20 Aug. 1992. In 1980 Kimball's wife Camilla also described "his displeasure with the speech" to her brother-in-law George T. Boyd (Boyd to Quinn, 24 Sept. 1992).

353. In 1980 a general authority reported to George T. Boyd the apologies which Kimball required of Benson. Boyd's letter to me, 24 Sept. 1992, requested that I not identify his source. Boyd (an in-law of Spencer and Camilla Kimball) also reported this conversation to BYU professor Duane Jeffery early in 1980. Telephone interview of Jeffery in David John Buerger diary, 14 Aug. 1980, fd 4, box 1, Buerger papers. These reproofs were also reported in "What Mormons Believe," *Newsweek* 96 (1 Sept. 1980): 71, in "Thus Saith Ezra Benson," *Newsweek* 98 (19 Oct. 1981): 109; in Allen interview (with Henry D. Taylor as a general authority source different from the above), 3 May 1984, by Alison Bethke Gayek, and in my interview, 5 Sept. 1992, with Rodney P. Foster, assistant secretary in the First Presidency's Office from 1974 to 1981.

354. Dew, *Ezra Taft Benson,* 469. For Mark Benson's position in 1980, see "Mark Benson Becomes Our New Vice President in Charge of Development," *Behind the Scenes,* Jan. 1980, [4].

355. Ezra Taft Benson to "John Birch Society Staff," 30 May 1980, archives, Birch Society, photocopy in my possession. This was in response to a get-well card with messages from each Birch staff member.

356. Dew, *Ezra Taft Benson,* 486-87.

357. "John Birch: Beware the One-Worlders," *Newsweek* 99 (15 Mar. 1982): 17; "The Lonely McCarthyites," *Newsweek* 103 (28 May 1984): 11; "The Birchers After Welch," *Newsweek* 105 (21 Jan. 1985): 38; "Robert Welch, RIP," *National Review* 37 (8 Feb. 1985): 20; "Once a Red, Always a Red: For Birchers, No Peace," *Newsweek* 116 (17 Sept. 1990): 36.

358. "John Birch Society Is Out of Spotlight, But It's Still Alive and Well in Utah," *Salt Lake Tribune*, 16 July 1989, B-10. The BYU library continues to receive copies of *The John Birch Society Bulletin* and its new magazine, *The New American*.

359. Dew, *Ezra Taft Benson*, 469-70. For the national context of the 1980s, see Robert Dallek, *Ronald Reagan: The Politics of Symbolism* (Cambridge, MA: Harvard University Press, 1984); David G. Green, *The New Conservatism: The Counter-Revolution in Political, Economic, and Social Thought* (New York: St. Martin's Press, 1987); Gary Wills, *Reagan's America: Innocents At Home* (Garden City, NY: Doubleday, 1987); Sidney Blumenthal, *Our Long National Daydream: A Political Pageant of the Reagan Era* (New York: Harper and Row, 1988); Steve Bruce, *The Rise and Fall of the New Christian Right: Conservative Protestant Politics in America, 1978-1988* (New York: Oxford University Press, 1988); Martin Anderson, *Revolution: The Reagan Legacy* (Stanford, CA: Hoover Institute Press, Stanford University, 1990); Haynes Johnson, *Sleepwalking Through History: America in the Reagan Years* (New York: W. W. Norton, 1991); Michael Schaller, *Reckoning With Reagan: America and Its President in the 1980s* (New York: Oxford University Press, 1992).

360. John H. Rousselot in *American Opinion* 7 (July-Aug. 1964): inside front cover, 10 (July-Aug. 1967): inside front cover; "Reagan's New Lobbyists to Business," *Fortune* 107 (30 May 1983): 36; Anderson, "Church and Birch In Utah," 21.

361. Dew, *Ezra Taft Benson*, 470.

362. Bob Gottlieb and Peter Wiley, "Mormons to the Right," *San Jose Mercury News*, 1 Dec. 1985, 9; also "Possibility of Benson Heading Mormons Worries Some With Different Views," *Los Angeles Times*, 1 Apr. 1976, Pt. I, 32; "Mormon Church Faces A Fresh Challenge . . . But Now, A Change of Leaders May Bring A Split In Its Ranks," *U.S. News & World Report* 95 (21 Nov. 1983): 61; "Conservative Seeking Leadership Worries Some Mormons," *Baltimore Sun*, 11 Dec. 1983, A-3; Gottlieb and Wiley, *America's Saints*, 247, 257; "Mormon Church Council Meets To Pick New Leader," *Dallas Morning News*, 11 Nov. 1985, A-4.

363. "New Chief of Mormons: Ezra Taft Benson," *New York Times*, 19 Nov. 1985, A-16; Dew, *Ezra Taft Benson*, 475; also Robert Lindsey, "The Mormons: Growth, Prosperity and Controversy," *New York Times Magazine*, 12 Jan. 1986, 46.

364. "President Benson's Fiery Conservatism Remains Quiet," *Salt Lake Tribune*, 30 Mar. 1986, B-2; "President Benson's First Year: Leader Stresses God, Not Politics," *Salt Lake Tribune*, 6 Oct. 1986, A-7.

365. "New Head of Mormon Church," *The New American* 1 (25 Nov. 1985): 9; Evans-Raymond Pierre, "The True Man of Principle: Ezra Taft Benson," *The New American* 1 (9 Dec. 1985): 56.

366. *The Constitution: The Voice of the National Center for Constitutional Studies*, Nov. 1985, 4, Dec. 1986, 3.

367. Benson, "An Internal Threat Today," B-7, 11th para.; also typescript of the address to the Treasure Valley Freedom Forum, Boise, Idaho, 19 Dec. 1963, transcript, 2, Moss papers.

368. Conversation in 1980 with Wayne Owens, recently returned LDS mission president, Democratic leader, and former U.S. congressman from Utah. Packer became an apostle in 1970, Faust in 1978.

369. *Deseret News 1995-1996 Church Almanac*, 15, 19-20; "Benson Heads Mormons, Enlists 2 Key Moderates," *Los Angeles Times*, 12 Nov. 1985, Pt. I, 6; my interviews, 29-30 Aug. 1992, with Alan Blodgett, managing director of the LDS church financial department from 1969 to 1980 and managing director of the investment department from 1980 to 1985; my interview, 2 Nov. 1992, with Lowell M. Durham, Jr., vice-president (and then president) of Zion's Co-operative Mercantile Institution (ZCMI) from 1982 to 1990.

370. "Benson Ties Rights Issue to Reds in Mormon Rift," *Washington Post*, 19 May 1963, E-1, E-7. Benson told BYU students that the American civil rights movement was "Communist inspired" and that its unnamed leader was a Communist sympathizer, if not

an actual Communist. The publication of this talk identified King in the index as this Communist civil rights leader. See Benson, *An Enemy Hath Done This,* ed. Jerreld L. Newquist (Salt Lake City: Parliament Publishers, 1969), 310, 361.

371. Ezra Taft Benson to J. Willard Marriott, 1 May 1969, Marriott papers.

372. Willard Woods, "Martin Luther King Day," *Freemen Digest,* Jan. 1984, 23. Also Skousen and R. Stephen Pratt emphasized King's association with Marxists and Communists in their two articles, "The Early Life of Martin Luther King, Jr.," and "Reverend King's Ministry: Thirteen Years of Crisis," *Freemen Digest,* Jan. 1984, 11, 13, 16, 17, 18, 20. Aside from guilt-by-association, the concluding sentence of Skousen's and Pratt's first article (14) was guilt-by-similar-interest: "As the King program got under way, Gus Hall, head of the Communist party USA, declared: 'For us, by far the most significant development is the escalation of mass protest movements by the American people.'"

In his telephone conversation with me, 15 Jan. 1993, D. Arthur Haycock brought up Martin Luther King Day as an example of "false historical perspective." He stated that the nation had chosen to dishonor two admirable presidents—Washington and Lincoln—by eliminating their holidays and by substituting in their place a holiday for "a man who had sex with three different women the day he died."

373. See *Deseret News,* 14 Oct. 1985, A-2, 13 Feb. 1986, A-1; *Salt Lake Tribune,* 14 Feb. 1986, A-1, 28 Feb. 1986, A-5, 18 Mar. 1986, B-1; "Martin Luther King Holiday or Not, Utah Lawmakers Convene Today," *Salt Lake Tribune,* 18 Jan. 1993, B-1; "Utah's Mix of Church and State: Theocratic or Just Homogenized?" *Salt Lake Tribune,* 18 Jan. 1993, B-2.

374. *Bulletin of the University of Utah: General Catalog, 1987-88* (Salt Lake City, 1987), 4; *Brigham Young University Bulletin: General Catalog, 1987-1988* (Provo, UT: Brigham Young University, 1987), 18; *1988-1989 General Catalogue: Brigham Young University Bulletin* (Provo, UT: Brigham Young University, 1988), ix.

375. For example, Thomas R. Eddlem, "Bolshevism With a New Name," *The New American* 6 (3 Dec. 1990): 22, said that newly non-Communist Czechoslovakia's president Vaclav Havel, formerly imprisoned as a dissident by the Communist regime there, was actually "a key actor in one of the greatest deceptions of all time."

376. Ezra Taft Benson, "I Testify," *Ensign* 18 (Nov. 1988): 87.

377. "LDS Official Acknowledges Church Monitors Critics," *Salt Lake Tribune,* 8 Aug. 1992, D-1; "LDS Leaders Say Scripture Supports Secret Files on Members," *Salt Lake Tribune,* 14 Aug. 1992, B-1; "Secret Files," *New York Times,* 22 Aug. 1992, 9. Such files have occasionally been compiled by the First Presidency's office, Presiding Bishopric Office, Mark E. Petersen's special committee, the Correlation Committee, the Special Affairs Committee, and Ezra Taft Benson's office. Only the Church Security Department has had an on-going responsibility to maintain dossiers on "disloyal" or "potentially dangerous" Mormons and to conduct physical and photographic surveillance. Such intelligence gathering is conducted through what Church Security calls "Confidential Services."

378. My interview, 5-6 Sept. 1992, with Rodney P. Foster, assistant secretary in the First Presidency's office from 1974 to 1981, and member of the Temple Department from 1981 to 1989.

379. *The John Birch Society Bulletin* (May 1989): 30; "Birch Dinner in S.L.," *Salt Lake Tribune,* 16 June 1989, E-5; "Are We Hearing Death Rattle of Communism?" *Salt Lake Tribune,* 18 June 1989, A-3.

380. *Deseret News 1991-1992 Church Almanac* (Salt Lake City: Deseret News, 1990), 315. This information was omitted from the *1995-1996 Church Almanac,* 394.

381. John F. McManus, "'A New World Order' Means World Government," *The John Birch Society Bulletin* (Nov. 1990): 3-14; "Birch Society Lauds 'Fertile Soil' In Utah," *Deseret News,* 13 May 1991, B-2; "Utah's Birchers' Organizing To Fight Bush 'Conspiracy,'" *Salt Lake Tribune,* 27 May 1991, B-1; "John Birch Society Skeptical of Communist Party Demise,"

Salt Lake Tribune, 8 Sept. 1991, B-1; "'John Bircher' Recruits Join Fight Against New World Order," *Salt Lake Tribune,* 21 June 1992, B-1.

382. "Longtime Doomsayer Seeks 'Safety' Back in LDS Fold," *Salt Lake Tribune,* 24 Jan. 1993, B-6; also reference to the American Study Group in Malcolm S. Jeppsen, "We Shall Not Be Led Astray," p. 8 of his computer printout, 25 Oct. 1992, photocopy in my possession.

383. *Ensign* 20 (May 1990): 1, 20 (Nov. 1990): 1, 21 (May 1991): 1, 21 (Nov. 1991): 1, 22 (May 1992): 1, 22 (Nov. 1992): 1; photographs in "LDS Historian Says Benson's Right-Wing Beliefs Caused Infighting, Church To Censure Speeches," *Salt Lake Tribune,* 8 Aug. 1992, A-7, and in "Age Taking Its Toll On President Benson," *Salt Lake Tribune,* 16 Jan. 1993, C-1.

384. "It's Judgment Day for Far Right: LDS Church Purges Survivalists," *Salt Lake Tribune,* 29 Nov. 1992, A-1, A-2. In "LDS Deny Mass Ouster of Radicals," *Salt Lake Tribune,* 4 Dec. 1992, 1, an official LDS spokesman denied only the estimate of "hundreds" of excommunications. See also "LDS Church Downplays Reports On Discipline," *Deseret News,* 4 Dec. 1992, B-1.

385. "Profile of the Splinter Group Members or Others with Troublesome Ideologies," photocopy in my possession. This was based on instructions to stake presidents by Second Quorum of Seventy member Malcolm S. Jeppsen in his "We Shall Not Be Led Astray," especially on p. 8 of his computer printout, 25 Oct. 1992.

386. Also statements of Jack Lewis and D. Michael Quinn in KUER's broadcast of *All Things Considered,* National Public Radio, 4 Dec. 1992.

387. Gordon B. Hinckley, "The Church Is On Course," *Ensign* 22 (Nov. 1992): 53.

388. See, for instance, Gottlieb and Wiley, *America's Saints,* 59, 61.

389. Wilbur Zelinsky, "An Approach to the Religious Geography of the United States: Patterns of Church Membership in 1952," *Annals of the Association of American Geographers* 51 (June 1961): 163-64, 193; D.W. Meinig, "The Mormon Culture Region: Strategies and Patterns in the Geography of the American West, 1847-1964," *Annals of the Association of American Geographers* 55 (1965): 191-220; Samuel S. Hill, "Religion and Region in America," *Annals of the American Academy of Political and Social Science* 480 (July 1985): 137; D. Michael Quinn, "Religion in the American West," in William Cronon, George Miles, and Jay Gitlin, eds., *Under An Open Sky: Rethinking America's Western Past* (New York: W. W. Norton and Co., 1992), 146, 160; Lowell C. "Ben" Bennion, "The Geographic Dynamics of Mormondom, 1965-95," *Sunstone* 18 (Dec. 1995): 21, 27-32.

390. "Hero-Turned Heretic? Gritz May Be Leading LDS Flock Into Wilderness," *Salt Lake Tribune,* 29 Nov. 1992, A-2.

391. "Ultraconservative Gritz Remains as Bold as Ever," *Salt Lake Tribune,* 7 Dec. 1992, B-2; also "LDS Zealots Muzzling Outspoken to Protect Tax Status, Gritz Says," *Salt Lake Tribune,* 22 Jan. 1993, B-1.

392. See Ken Noorlander, letter to the editor, "Stand Fast For Freedom," *Salt Lake Tribune,* 22 Dec. 1992, A-13.

393. "John Birch Director Calls Utah Fertile Ground for His Society," *Salt Lake Tribune,* 14 May 1993, D-1.

394. "Mormon Church Has Begun To Expel Many Extremists," *New York Times,* 21 Dec. 1992, 10. See Eric Hoffer, *The True Believer: Thoughts on the Nature of Mass Movements* (New York: Harper and Row, 1951).

Notes to Chapter Four

1. Except when otherwise indicated, biographical sketches of all general authorities named in this chapter can be found either in the present volume or in D. Michael Quinn, *The Mormon Hierarchy: Origins of Power* (Salt Lake City: Signature Books/Smith Research Associates, 1994).

2. Quinn, *Mormon Hierarchy: Origins of Power,* 53-55; Irene M. Bates and E. Gary Smith, *Lost Legacy: The Mormon Office of Presiding Patriarch* (Urbana: University of Illinois Press, 1996), 66-67.

3. Brigham Young office journal, 24 Feb. 1860, archives, Historical Department, Church of Jesus Christ of Latter-day Saints, Salt Lake City, Utah (hereafter LDS archives), copies in Donald R. Moorman papers, archives, Donnell and Elizabeth Stewart Library, Weber State University, Ogden, Utah, and in H. Michael Marquardt papers, Manuscripts Division, J. Willard Marriott Library, University of Utah, Salt Lake City (hereafter Marriott Library).

4. Heber C. Kimball and Lyman Wight to Joseph Smith, 24 June 1844, in Joseph Smith et al., *History of The Church of Jesus Christ of Latter-day Saints. Period I: History of Joseph Smith the Prophet, and . . . Period II: From the Manuscript History of Brigham Young and Other Original Documents,* ed. B. H. Roberts, 7 vols. (Salt Lake City: Church of Jesus Christ of Latter-day Saints, 1902-32; 2d ed. rev. [Salt Lake City: Deseret Book Co., 1978]), 7: 157 (hereafter *History of the Church*).

5. E. Gary Smith, "The Patriarchal Crisis of 1845," *Dialogue: A Journal of Mormon Thought* 16 (Summer 1983): 35; also Quinn, *Mormon Hierarchy: Origins of Power,* 213-26, Bates and Smith, *Lost Legacy,* 72-103, for William Smith as patriarchap.

6. Bates and Smith, *Lost Legacy,* 95.

7. Heber C. Kimball diary, 7 Dec. 1845, in Stanley B. Kimball, ed., *On the Potter's Wheel: The Diaries of Heber C. Kimball* (Salt Lake City: Signature Books/Smith Research Associates, 1987), 164.

8. *History of the Church,* 6:173; Scott G. Kenney, ed., *Wilford Woodruff's Journal: 1833-1898 Typescript,* 9 vols. (Murray, UT: Signature Books, 1983-85), 3 (6 Dec. 1847): 295; Journal History of the Church of Jesus Christ of Latter-day Saints (1830-1972), 246 reels, microfilm, Special Collections, Marriott Library, 27 Dec. 1847, also 1848-54; Manuscript History of the Church (1848-54), LDS archives; Bates and Smith, *Lost Legacy,* 115, 123.

9. John Smith (b. 1781) 1846-54 diary, 1 Jan. 1849, LDS archives, with photocopy in George A. Smith Family papers, Marriott Library.

10. *History of the Church,* 2:509, 3:249-56; John Smith to George A. Smith, 1 Jan. 1838, LDS archives, quoted in Max H. Parkin, "The Nature and Cause of Internal and External Conflict of the Mormons in Ohio Between 1830 and 1838," M.A. thesis, Brigham Young University, 1966, 319; Bates and Smith, *Lost Legacy,* 108-115; Quinn, *Mormon Hierarchy: Origins of Power,* 63-64.

11. Quinn, *Mormon Hierarchy: Origins of Power,* 201, 528.

12. Leonard J. Arrington, *Great Basin Kingdom: An Economic History of the Latter-day Saints, 1830-1900* (Cambridge, MA: Harvard University Press, 1958), 72-76; Bates and Smith, *Lost Legacy,* 116, although neither source comments on John Smith as "a Counsilor" to Young.

13. John Smith (b. 1781) diary, 20 Sept. 1853; Bates and Smith, *Lost Legacy,* 117, quote other words from this blessing which they do not interpret as I do.

14. John Smith (b. 1781) diary, 4 May 1854.

15. Bates and Smith, *Lost Legacy,* 117.

16. *History of the Church,* 6:173; also Quinn, *Mormon Hierarchy: Origins of Power,* 32-33, for explanation of Oliver Cowdery's statement that Joseph Smith, Jr. was "the first patriarch of the church."

17. Bates and Smith, *Lost Legacy*, 124-25.

18. Robert J. McCue, "Did the Word of Wisdom Become a Commandment in 1851?" *Dialogue: A Journal of Mormon Thought* 14 (Autumn 1981): 66-77. Enforcement was haphazard throughout most of the nineteenth century. The Word of Wisdom's early definitions did not prohibit beer (and in fact recommended barley drinks) or wine (which was both a sacramental and social drink of the Mormon hierarchy and rank-and-file). See Leonard J. Arrington, "An Economic Interpretation of the Word of Wisdom," *Brigham Young University Studies* 1 (Winter 1959): 37-49; Lester E. Bush, Jr., "The Word of Wisdom in Early Nineteenth-Century Perspective," and Thomas G. Alexander, "The Word of Wisdom: From Principle to Requirement," *Dialogue: A Journal of Mormon Thought* 14 (Autumn 1981): 47-65, 78-88; Joseph Lynn Lyon, "Word of Wisdom," in Daniel H. Ludlow, ed., *Encyclopedia of Mormonism: The History, Scripture, Doctrine, and Procedure of the Church of Jesus Christ of Latter-day Saints*, 5 vols. (New York: Macmillan Publishing Co., 1992), 4:1584-85.

19. Joseph Smith, Sr., patriarchal blessing to Hyrum Smith, 9 Dec. 1834, in Marvin S. Hill, *Quest for Refuge: The Mormon Flight from American Pluralism* (Salt Lake City: Signature Books, 1989), 190n5; compare with David Stafford affidavit, 5 Nov. 1833, and Barton Stafford affidavit, 3 Nov. 1833, in Eber D. Howe, *Mormonism Unvailed* (Painesville, OH: By the author, 1834), 249, 250. Concerning Joseph Sr.'s reference that people "laughed him to scorn," one neighbor described such an incident (Lorenzo Saunders interview, 12 Nov. 1884, E. L. Kelley papers, Library and Archives, Reorganized Church of Jesus Christ of Latter Day Saints, Independence, Missouri [hereafter RLDS archives]).

20. Benjamin Saunders interview, ca. 17 Sept. 1884, W. H. Kelley Collection, P 19, RLDS archives; also Orlando Saunders statement: "Everybod[y] drank in those days and the Smith[s] drank also. but they never got drunk," in Rodger I. Anderson, *Joseph Smith's New York Reputation Reexamined* (Salt Lake City: Signature Books, 1990), 171.

21. W. J. Rorbaugh, *The Alcoholic Republic: An American Tradition* (New York: Oxford University Press, 1979).

22. Church Historian's office journal, 18 Feb. 1855, LDS archives; Bates and Smith, *Lost Legacy*, 123, 125.

23. Samuel W. Richards diary, 19 Feb. 1855, LDS archives, with copy at Henry E. Huntington Library, San Marino, California (hereafter Huntington Library).

24. John Smith to Joseph F. Smith, 31 May 1856, quoted in Bates and Smith, *Lost Legacy*, 127; First Presidency and Twelve Apostles prayer circle roll book, 1856-65, LDS archives.

25. First Presidency and Twelve Apostles prayer circle roll books, 1856-65, 1865-74; John Taylor prayer circle roll book, 1858-77, LDS archives; D. Michael Quinn, "Latter-day Saint Prayer Circles," *Brigham Young University Studies* 19 (Fall 1978): 97-98. I have examined the minutes and attendance rolls of prayer circles organized in Utah from the 1850s to the 1950s, LDS archives.

26. Brigham Young office journal, 19 Mar. 1862; also Bates and Smith, *Lost Legacy*, 128-31, and John Smith (b. 1832) missionary diary (1862-64), in Joseph Smith, Sr. Family Collection, Department of Special Collections and Manuscripts, Harold B. Lee Library, Brigham Young University, Provo, Utah (hereafter Lee Library).

27. Kenney, *Wilford Woodruff's Journal* 6 (28 Jan. 1867): 323.

28. Appendix, "Appointments to the Theocratic Council of Fifty through 1884."

29. Joseph F. Smith diary, 8 Apr. 1873, LDS archives, with transcriptions in Scott G. Kenney papers, Marriott Library; Kenney, *Wilford Woodruff's Journal* 7 (9 Oct. 1875): 249-50; Quorum of the Twelve Apostles minutes, 7-8 Oct. 1875, LDS archives; statement of Brigham Young, Jr., in Abraham H. Cannon diary, 4 Oct. 1894, copies at Lee Library, at Marriott Library, and at Utah State Historical Society, Salt Lake City, Utah; Heber J. Grant letterbook-journal, 4 Oct. 1894, LDS archives; statement of Heber J. Grant in minutes of First Presidency and Quorum of the Twelve, 17 Sept. 1942, excerpt from First Presidency

office journal, LDS archives. While "diary" is the standardized term I use to identify personal documents with daily entries, Grant kept several different kinds of such records, which must be identified separately in order to locate the quotations.

30. Brigham Young's prayer circle roll, 1874-77, shows attendance by the First Presidency, Quorum of Twelve Apostles, and Presiding Patriarchap. John Taylor's prayer circle roll, 1877-85, shows the same attendance until February 1884 when William B. Preston was admitted two months before he was sustained as the church's Presiding Bishop. Also Franklin D. Richards diary, 6 Oct. 1880, 19 Jan. 1881, LDS archives.

31. John Taylor, "Patriarchal," *Times and Seasons* (1 June 1845): 921; excerpt from First Presidency office journal, 31 Oct. 1877, LDS archives; John Taylor to George Q. Cannon, 7 Nov. 1877, quoted in Bates and Smith, *Lost Legacy,* 136; Franklin D. Richards statement in Anthon H. Lund diary, 10 Jan. 1899, microfilm, LDS archives. The Lund diary is available to all researchers at LDS archives by stipulation of its donor.

32. Bates and Smith, *Lost Legacy,* 127, 143, 147n12; Hyrum Smith family Bible, "Marriages," eradicated entry for marriage of John Smith and Nancy Lemmon, LDS archives.

33. Franklin D. Richards diary, 22 Apr. 1880. For the text of this revelation, see Kenney, *Wilford Woodruff's Journal* 7 (28 Dec. 1880): 615-21, 9 (17 Apr. 1897): 463-69; Fred C. Collier, ed. *Unpublished Revelations of the Prophets and Presidents of The Church of Jesus Christ of Latter Day Saints,* 2 vols. (Salt Lake City: Collier's Publishing Co., 1979-93), 1:123-29; David M. Reay and Vonda S. Reay, *Selected Manifestations: Being an Unofficial Collection of Temple Dedicatory Prayers, Revelations, Visions, Dreams, Doctrinal Expositions, and other Inspired Declarations Not Presently Included in The Official Canon of Scripture Known as the Four Standard Works of the Church of Jesus Christ of Latter-day Saints* (Oakland, CA: By the authors, 1985), 93-97; Thomas G. Alexander, *Things in Heaven and Earth: The Life and Times of Wilford Woodruff, a Mormon Prophet* (Salt Lake City: Signature Books, 1991), 237-38.

34. Merle Graffam, ed., *Salt Lake School of the Prophets Minute Book, 1883* (Palm Desert, CA: ULC Press, 1981), 48 (12 Oct. 1883); Bates and Smith, *Lost Legacy,* 134-35.

35. Bates and Smith, *Lost Legacy,* 135.

36. Excerpt from First Presidency office journal, 31 Mar. 1884.

37. John Henry Smith to "J. Mack" [Joseph F. Smith], 24 Aug. 1886, John Henry Smith 1884-94 letterbook, 594, George A. Smith Family papers.

38. John Smith to Joseph F. Smith, 6 June 1887, quoted in Bates and Smith, *Lost Legacy,* 136; Franklin D. Richards diary, 30 Jan. 1888.

39. Heber J. Grant journal, 13 Sept., 2, 7 Oct. 1894; Joseph H. Dean diary, 7 Oct. 1894, LDS archives; Thomas A. Clawson diary, 4 Oct. 1894, Utah State Historical Society.

40. Heber J. Grant journal, 7 Oct. 1894; Abraham H. Cannon diary, 4 Oct., 7 Oct. 1894; Franklin D. Richards diary, 7 Oct. 1894; *Salt Lake Tribune,* 8 Oct. 1894, 5; Bates and Smith, *Lost Legacy,* 139.

41. Anthon H. Lund diary, 10 Jan. 1899.

42. This poses problems for the claim of polygamously-oriented Mormon fundamentalists that John Smith (b. 1832) held an office higher in authority than the church president. Joseph Smith made that suggestion in 1836, 1841, and 1843, and Joseph F. Smith renewed that suggestion in 1901 (see below). However, there is no evidence in actual administrative experience that the Presiding Patriarch held higher authority than the president. It is also difficult to understand the claim that before his death in 1911, John Smith conferred patriarchal authority on John W. Woolley to continue polygamous marriages, since John Smith was indifferent (even hostile) toward plural marriage. For these claims, see Jesse B. Stone, *An Event of The Underground Days* (Salt Lake City: By the Author, [1931]), 8; *Priesthood Expounded, The Principles of Succession in Priesthood Authority and the True Pattern of Priesthood Government* (Galeana, Mex.: Mexican Mission of the Church of the Firstborn of the Fullness of Times, 1956), 46; John G. Butchereit, *Priesthood and Prophecy*

(Galeana, Mex.: Church of the Firstborn of the Fulness of Times, 1956), 46; Lynn L. Bishop and Stephen L. Bishop, *The Keys of the Priesthood Illustrated* (Draper, UT: Review and Preview Publishers, 1971), 88-89.

43. Anthon H. Lund diary, 9 Nov. 1901; Journal History, 10 Nov. 1901, 4.

44. *October-November 1901 Conference Report* . . . (Salt Lake City: Church of Jesus Christ of Latter-day Saints, 1901), 71, 80-81; Joseph Fielding Smith, *Life of Joseph F. Smith* . . . (Salt Lake City: Deseret News Press, 1938), 318-19; Steven C. Heath, "Notes on Apostolic Succession," *Dialogue: A Journal of Mormon Thought* 20 (Summer 1987): 51; Bates and Smith, *Lost Legacy,* 142-43. For the succession argument of Daniel H. Wells, see chap. 2.

45. Elias H. Blackburn diary, 10 Nov. 1901, Utah State Historical Society, with microfilm copy at Huntington Library.

46. Anthon H. Lund diary, 17 Oct. 1901; Journal History, 17 Oct. 1901; Bates and Smith, *Lost Legacy,* 142.

47. John Henry Smith diary, 24 Oct. 1901, in Jean Bickmore White, ed., *Church, State, and Politics: The Diaries of John Henry Smith* (Salt Lake City: Signature Books/Smith Research Associates, 1990), 497; Rudger Clawson diary, 7 Nov., 21 Nov. 1901, in Stan Larson, ed., *A Ministry of Meetings: The Apostolic Diaries of Rudger Clawson* (Salt Lake City: Signature Books/Smith Research Associates, 1993), 349, 358.

48. Brigham Young, Jr., diary, 6 Apr. 1902, Rare Book and Manuscript Division, New York Public Library, New York City; John Henry Smith diary, 6 Apr. 1902, in White, *Church, State, and Politics,* 505; Bates and Smith, *Lost Legacy,* 143.

49. Quorum of the Twelve Apostles minutes, 24 June 1902, LDS archives.

50. Emmeline B. Wells diary, 5 Jan. 1902, Lee Library.

51. *History of the Church,* 4:286; E. Gary Smith, "The Office of Presiding Patriarch," 44; Seymour B. Young diary, 6 Oct. 1902, LDS archives; James B. Allen and Glen M. Leonard, *The Story of the Latter-day Saints,* 2d ed. rev. (Salt Lake City: Deseret Book Co., 1992), 461.

52. Ralph G. Smith interview, 17 June 1977, transcript in my possession and also my handwritten notes of the interview at his apartment in Salt Lake City; *Improvement Era* 15 (Dec. 1911): 97.

53. George F. Richards diary, 6 Apr. 1912, LDS archives; Heber J. Grant journal sheets, 6 Apr. 1912; James E. Talmage diary, 9 May 1912, Lee Library; Joseph E. Robinson diary, 18 Apr. 1912, LDS archives; Bates and Smith, *Lost Legacy,* 151-57.

54. Transcription of ordination of Hyrum G. Smith, in excerpt from First Presidency office journal, 9 May 1912; Hyrum G. Smith diaries, 18 July, 20 July, 5 Oct. 1912, 5 Apr., 5 Oct. 1913, 29 Jan., 31 Jan., 1 Feb., 5 Apr. 1914, 30 Apr. 1916; Hyrum G. Smith to Joseph F. Smith, 7 Apr. 1915, LDS archives; Anthon H. Lund diary, 17 Feb. 1916; Bates and Smith, *Lost Legacy,* 158-60, 169.

55. Hyrum G. Smith to Joseph A. West, 30 Dec. 1915, in Bates and Smith, *Lost Legacy,* 163.

56. Minutes of meeting of First Presidency, Quorum of the Twelve, and Presiding Patriarch, 2 Jan. 1919, in excerpt from First Presidency office journal.

57. Heber J. Grant journal sheets, 3 July 1918; Thomas G. Alexander, *Mormonism in Transition: A History of the Latter-day Saints, 1890-1930* (Urbana: University of Illinois Press, 1985), 116-17.

58. Bates and Smith, *Lost Legacy,* 164, 176.

59. Ibid., 160, 163.

60. James E. Talmage diary, 2 Jan. 1919; Anthon H. Lund diary, 2 Jan. 1919; Bates and Smith, *Lost Legacy,* 164.

61. Anthon H. Lund diary, 2 Dec. 1918, 2 Jan. 1919; James E. Talmage diary, 2 Jan. 1919; minutes of meeting, 2 Jan. 1919; Bates and Smith, *Lost Legacy,* 164.

62. George F. Richards diary, 5 Dec. 1922; B. H. Roberts, *A Comprehensive History of the Church of Jesus Christ of Latter-day Saints, Century I,* 6 vols. (Salt Lake City: Deseret News Press and the Church, 1930), 1:387.

63. Bates and Smith, *Lost Legacy,* 229, 232n20; Gloria Wallis Rytting, *James H. Wallis: Poet, Printer and Patriarch* (Salt Lake City: R. & R. Enterprises, 1989), 152-54, 176, 182-91.

64. Bates and Smith, *Lost Legacy,* 165, 177, and 144, for number of John Smith's blessings.

65. Francis M. Gibbons, *Joseph Fielding Smith: Gospel Scholar, Prophet of God* (Salt Lake City: Deseret Book Co., 1992), 342; minutes of meeting of First Presidency and Quorum of the Twelve, 7 Apr. 1932, in excerpt from First Presidency office journal.

66. Bates and Smith, *Lost Legacy,* 180, 187; also this study's biographical sketches of George F. Richards, Nicholas G. Smith, John M. Whitaker.

67. Heber J. Grant to J. Reuben Clark, 4 Nov. 1934, Clark papers, Lee Library and LDS archives; Heber J. Grant journal sheets, 7 Apr. 1937, 10 Feb. 1941, 20 Aug. 1942.

68. Rudger Clawson to Heber J. Grant, 22 Mar. 1933, LDS archives, also summarized in Bates and Smith, *Lost Legacy,* 183.

69. Heber J. Grant journal sheet, 23 Mar. 1933.

70. Heber J. Grant journal sheets, 13 Sept., 2 Oct. 1894, 6 Apr. 1912, 3 July 1918, 23 Mar. 1933; George F. Richards diary, 4 July, 10 July 1942; Ralph G. Smith interview, 17 June 1977; Bates and Smith, *Lost Legacy,* 140, 178, 189.

71. Full quotes in Irene May Bates, "Transformation of Charisma in the Mormon Church: A History of the Office of Presiding Patriarch, 1833-1979," Ph.D. diss., University of California at Los Angeles, 1991, 323, with partial quote in Bates and Smith, *Lost Legacy,* 191. Heber J. Grant journal described his conversation with Eldred on 2 October 1942 as "unpleasant."

72. Heber J. Grant journal sheets, 23 Mar. 1933, 26 Sept. 1935, 7 Apr. 1937. However, that unified resistance developed after the temple council meeting of 7 April 1932 when six apostles voted in favor of Willard R. Smith, Grant's son-in-law. By 1933 the Twelve unanimously recommended Eldred G. Smith.

73. Minutes of meeting of First Presidency and Quorum of the Twelve Apostles, 17 Sept. 1942; also chap. 2 for discussion of Grant's approachap.

74. J. Reuben Clark office diary, 4 Feb. 1943, Clark papers, Lee Library; meeting of 8 Apr. 1943, LDS archives; Joseph Fielding Smith diary, 20 Jan., 7 Oct. 1943, LDS archives; George F. Richards diary, 20 Dec., 31 Dec. 1942; also Bates and Smith, *Lost Legacy,* 193.

75. *October 1944 Conference Report . . .* (Salt Lake City: Church of Jesus Christ of Latter-day Saints, 1944), 110; James R. Clark, ed., *Messages of the First Presidency of the Church of Jesus Christ of Latter-day Saints, 1833-1964,* 6 vols. (Salt Lake City: Bookcraft, Inc., 1965-71), 6:194-96. However, Bates and Smith, *Lost Legacy,* 193-95, interprets Patriarch Smith's conference address as a description of his own office and (193) cites 1942 as the unannounced end of the presiding dimensions of the office.

76. J. Reuben Clark office diary, 29 May 1946; Frank Evans diary, 27 May 1946, LDS archives; Joseph Fielding Smith diary, 29 June 1946.

77. *Deseret News 1995-1996 Church Almanac* (Salt Lake City: Deseret News, 1994), 57-58; "Grey Matters: The Office of Patriarch," *Seventh East Press* 2 (17 Nov. 1982): 15, 17; Bates and Smith, *Lost Legacy,* 195-96, 200n49; Rocky O'Donovan, "'The Abominable and Detestable Crime Against Nature': A Brief History of Homosexuality and Mormonism, 1840-1980," in Brent Corcoran, ed., *Multiply and Replenish: Mormon Essays on Sex and Family* (Salt Lake City: Signature Books, 1994), 146; and D. Michael Quinn, *Same-Sex Dynamics among Nineteenth-Century Americans: A Mormon Example* (Urbana: University of Illinois Press, 1996), 369-71, for the known details of this case.

78. George F. Richards diary, 6 Dec. 1947; Frank Evans diary, 19 Mar., 23 Sept. 1947, 15 Mar. 1948; George Albert Smith diary, 16 Aug. 1950, George A. Smith Family papers; Bates and Smith, *Lost Legacy*, 196.

79. David O. McKay office diary, 10 Apr., 9 May, 10 July, 9 Dec. 1957; Ruth Pingree Smith to David O. McKay, 13 Apr. 1958, both in LDS archives; Bates and Smith, *Lost Legacy*, 196.

80. *Deseret News 1995-1996 Church Almanac*, 58; Bates and Smith, *Lost Legacy*, 202.

81. Pre-publication transcription of Eldred G. Smith talk, 6 Apr. 1947, LDS archives, deleted from Eldred G. Smith, "Response to a Call," *Improvement Era* 50 (May 1947): 275, 278; Bates and Smith, *Lost Legacy*, 201-202.

82. George F. Richards diary, 10 Apr. 1947; Francis M. Gibbons, *Harold B. Lee: Man of Vision, Prophet of God* (Salt Lake City: Deseret Book Co., 1993), 238. Bates and Smith do not interpret the remarks of Richards as a stern rebuke and therefore view Eldred's tears differently than I do: "Patriarch Smith did not recall thanking Elder Richards, nor did he recall weeping in gratitude for his [Richards's] remarks" (*Lost Legacy*, 204).

83. Bates and Smith, *Lost Legacy*, 206.

84. Irene Bates to D. Michael Quinn, 19 Mar. 1991; Bates and Smith, *Lost Legacy*, 204.

85. Quinn, *Mormon Hierarchy: Origins of Power*, 5, 15, 31, 46-47, 156-57, 161, 273-74.

86. Joseph Fielding Smith diary, 24 Jan. 1948, 8 Oct. 1950, 22 Jan., 14 May 1955; Bates and Smith, *Lost Legacy*, 206-207.

87. Bates and Smith, *Lost Legacy*, 207-208, 211.

88. David O. McKay office diary, 12 Mar. 1953; Stephen L Richards office diary, 15 Jan. 1954, LDS archives.

89. Henry D. Moyle diary, 26 Sept. 1951; Spencer W. Kimball and LeGrand Richards to David O. McKay, 9 Jan. 1953, 19 Mar. 1954, 20 June 1957, 28 Sept. 1961; Spencer W. Kimball diary, 6 Jan. 1953; minutes of meeting, 22 Oct. 1954; David O. McKay office diary, 12 Dec. 1952, 22 Sept. 1954, 22 May, 11 July 1957; Eldred G. Smith to David O. McKay, 7 Nov. 1961; minutes of meeting, 2 Jan. 1962, excerpt from First Presidency office journal, all in LDS archives; Bates and Smith, *Lost Legacy*, 208-209; E. Gary Smith to D. Michael Quinn, 6 Dec. 1990.

90. Bates and Smith, *Lost Legacy*, 210; *Deseret News 1995-1996 Church Almanac*, 56, for Evans.

91. Bates and Smith, *Lost Legacy*, 212-14; *Deseret News 1995-1996 Church Almanac*, 44, 56, for Kimball and Richards.

92. Bates and Smith, *Lost Legacy*, 174, 176, 222, 227.

93. Ibid., 1-3, 216, 221; *Ensign* 9 (Nov. 1979): 18; William G. Hartley, "Organization: Contemporary," uses the term "discontinued," while Calvin R. Stephens, "Patriarch: Patriarch to the Church," uses the term "retired" for the office, in Ludlow, *Encyclopedia of Mormonism*, 3:1038, 1066.

94. Bates and Smith, *Lost Legacy*, 216.

95. Richard O. Cowan, *The Church in the Twentieth Century* (Salt Lake City: Bookcraft, 1985), 408.

96. Kenney, *Wilford Woodruff's Journal* 3 (27 Dec. 1847): 300-301.

97. Quinn, *Mormon Hierarchy: Origins of Power*, 73-76.

98. Juanita Brooks, ed., *On the Mormon Frontier: The Diary of Hosea Stout, 1844-1861*, 2 vols. (Salt Lake City: University of Utah Press, 1964), 1:142-43, 208, 245; Willard Richards diary, 4 Apr. 1847, LDS archives; Journal History, 16 Apr. 1847. See also Hartley, "Bishop: History of the Office," and Burton and Dyer, "Presiding Bishopric" in Ludlow, *Encyclopedia of Mormonism*, 1:118, 3:1128, both acknowledge Whitney's appointment as the first Presiding Bishop, but neither mentions the 1841 revelation.

99. Hyrum Smith and Orson Hyde to Edward Partridge, [after 15 Dec. 1832], in *Frontier Guardian* 1 (31 Oct. 1849): [1]; also Quinn, *Mormon Hierarchy: Origins of Power,* 70-71.

100. Donald Gene Pace, "The LDS Presiding Bishopric, 1851-1888: An Administrative Study," M.A. thesis, Brigham Young University, 1978, 114, 119-21; Brigham Young office journal, 8 Oct. 1860; Kenney, *Wilford Woodruff's Journal* 7 (8 Apr. 1873): 130.

101. Orson F. Whitney, "The Aaronic Priesthood," *Contributor* 6 (Sept. 1885): 441.

102. Journal History, 8 Sept. 1851, 1. At the October 1844 conference Young established the office of traveling bishop "to visit the churches." A meeting of the Twelve appointed John M. Bernhisel to this new position on 14 February 1845 (William Clayton diary, 14 Feb. 1845, in George D. Smith, *An Intimate Chronicle: The Journals of William Clayton* (Salt Lake City: Signature Books/Smith Research Associates, 1991), 158; *History of the Church,* 7:374). Neither Bernhisel nor the better known Amos M. Musser in Utah had a presiding role as a traveling bishop. In fact, Musser, who served from 1858 to 1876, was not even formally ordained to the office of bishop until six years after his release. The traveling bishops actually functioned as clerks and auditors who counseled ward bishops and collected funds from them for church headquarters. See Pace, "LDS Presiding Bishopric," 29-30, 32, 43, 54n54; D. Gene Pace, "Changing Patterns of Mormon Financial Administration: Traveling Bishops, Regional Bishops, and Bishop's Agents, 1851-88," *Brigham Young University Studies* 23 (Spring 1983): 184-86. Not until 1851 did Brigham Young give three traveling bishops a presiding role.

103. Kenney, *Wilford Woodruff's Journal* 4 (6 Oct. 1851): 74.

104. Journal History, 7 Apr. 1852, 1; 7 Oct. 1852, 1; 6 Apr. 1853, 1; also Pace, "The LDS Presiding Bishopric," 22-24.

105. Kenney, *Wilford Woodruff's Journal,* 4 (11 Apr. 1852): 134; Hosea Stout diary, 11 Apr. 1852, in Brooks, *On The Mormon Frontier,* 1:435. The conference also sustained the following men as traveling bishops: Seth Taft, David Pettegrew, Abraham Hoagland, David Fullmer, and Daniel Spencer. In commenting on this event the Seventh General Epistle from the First Presidency, dated 18 April 1852, referred to these five men as "assistant Presiding Bishops." However, since the conference did not sustain them, they were only traveling bishops subordinate to Felt, Banks, and Cordon who were sustained as "Presiding Bishops" from 1851 to 1853. See Clark, *Messages of the First Presidency,* 2:97.

106. Uneven efforts to organize the Presiding Bishopric are evidence of the quorum's late development. See also Dale Beecher, "The Office of Bishop," *Dialogue: A Journal of Mormon Thought* 15 (Winter 1982): 103-15; Pace, "Changing Patterns of Mormon Financial Administration," 183-95.

107. Pace, "The LDS Presiding Bishopric," 58-72; Donald Gene Pace, "Community Leadership on the Mormon Frontier: Mormon Bishops and the Political, Economic, and Social Development of Utah Before Statehood," Ph.D. diss., Ohio State University, 1983, 63-64.

108. Andrew Jenson, *Church Chronology . . . ,* 2d ed. rev. (Salt Lake City: Deseret News, 1914), 14 Nov. 1859.

109. *Deseret Evening News,* 3 Dec. 1869.

110. Pace, "The LDS Presiding Bishopric," 25, 38.

111. *Deseret Evening News,* 26 Apr. 1876.

112. Ibid., 2 Aug. 1876-3 July 1877, usually on the last page of each issue.

113. Clark, *Messages of the First Presidency* 2:287; *Journal of Discourses,* 26 vols. (London and Liverpool: Latter-day Saints' Book Depot, 1854-86), 22:34 (O.Pratt/1880); Pace, "Changing Patterns of Mormon Financial Administration," 184-90; Pace, "Community Leadership on the Mormon Frontier," 65-68; Pace, "The LDS Presiding Bishopric," 76-102.

114. George Q. Cannon diary, 17 Jan. 1878, quoted in the official LDS magazine *Instructor* 80 (June 1945): 259.

115. Pace, "The LDS Presiding Bishopric," 114; Church Historian's office journal, 24 Jan. 1878.

116. L. John Nuttall diary, 24 Nov. 1879, copies at Lee Library, at Marriott Library, and at Huntington Library.

117. Pace, "The LDS Presiding Bishopric," 142, 146.

118. Ibid., 149.

119. Franklin D. Richards diary, 13 Aug. 1887.

120. L. John Nuttall diary, 23 Sept. 1887.

121. Ibid., 23 Jan. 1889.

122. Abraham H. Cannon diary, 10 Oct. 1889; Heber J. Grant letterbook-journal, 10 Oct. 1889; also Franklin D. Richards diary, 10 Oct. 1889.

123. Journal History, 2 Apr. 1896, 2-9.

124. Ibid., 12 Apr. 1897, 2-3, 15 Dec. 1897, 2.

125. Anthon H. Lund diary, 10 July 1901.

126. Heber J. Grant statement in minutes of meeting, 8 Apr. 1943.

127. Clark, *Messages of the First Presidency,* 5:36; Heber J. Grant diary book, 31 Jan. 1919.

128. "Presiding Bishopric Minutes of Meetings with First Presidency—1920," LDS archives; Alexander, *Mormonism in Transition,* 120.

129. Seymour B. Young diary, 8 Oct. 1914.

130. John Wells diary, 22 Jan. 1915, 19 May, 6 June 1933, 2 May 1934, 25-26 June, 20 Sept. 1937, LDS archives.

131. D. Michael Quinn, *J. Reuben Clark: The Church Years* (Provo, UT: Brigham Young University Press, 1983), 263-64, 268-69.

132. Sylvester Q. Cannon diary, 31 Dec. 1930, LDS archives.

133. Quinn, *J. Reuben Clark,* 256, 261-63, 269; Garth L. Mangum and Bruce D. Blumell, *The Mormons' War on Poverty: A History of LDS Welfare, 1830-1990* (Salt Lake City: University of Utah Press, 1993), 90, 104-105, 110-114, 119-20, and 122-28, 142-43 on Cannon-Clark dispute; John Wells diary, 30 July, 24, 28, 31 Oct., 2, 22 Nov. 1933, 6 Nov. 1935, 11 Aug. 1936, 17 Apr., 18 May 1937; Heber J. Grant journal sheets, 20 July 1933, 7 Apr. 1935; J. Reuben Clark memorandum, "Church Security Plan," 19 Oct. 1937, Clark papers; Sylvester Q. Cannon diary, 31 Dec. 1930, 31 Dec. 1933, 5 Apr. 1938.

134. *Deseret News 1995-1996 Church Almanac,* 76-78; Lucile C. Tate, *LeGrand Richards: Beloved Apostle* (Salt Lake City: Bookcraft, 1982), 195-96, 200. This account refers to the release of Presiding Bishop Sylvester Q. Cannon but does not mention his counselors whom Richards did not want.

135. Charles M. Brown interview, 7 June 1973, page d-4-1, fd 25, box 48, Richard Douglas Poll papers, Marriott Library. Brown, who knew him personally, added that David A. Smith's bitterness was "something like Carl Buehner" who was also released as counselor by a new Presiding Bishop in 1961; *Deseret News 1995-1996 Church Almanac,* 77-78, for Smith and Buehner; also Smith's biographical sketch in Appen. 2.

136. Quinn, *J. Reuben Clark,* 271-72.

137. Ibid., 272-73; minutes of meeting, 8 Apr. 1943.

138. Tate, *LeGrand Richards,* 221.

139. Marion G. Romney diary, 23 Jan., 30 Jan. 1942, LDS archives; Quinn, *J. Reuben Clark,* 269 and 327n68.

140. Joseph Fielding Smith diary, 11 July 1946, 18 July 1949.

141. Tate, *LeGrand Richards,* 287; *Deseret News 1995-1996 Church Almanac,* 56, for Richards; J. Reuben Clark office diary, 24 Mar. 1959; Quinn, *J. Reuben Clark,* 150. The dust jacket of Wilburn D. Talbot, *The Acts of the Modern Apostles* (Salt Lake City: Randall Book Co., 1985), had large illustrations of the faces of only two twentieth-century apostles, the then-current church president and the deceased LeGrand Richards.

142. Gibbons, *Harold B. Lee*, 341-43.

143. J. Reuben Clark office diary, 4 Dec. 1959.

144. Harold B. Lee diary, 3 Nov. 1960, quoted in L. Brent Goates, *Harold B. Lee: Prophet & Seer* (Salt Lake City: Bookcraft, 1985), 367, emphasis added here.

145. Tate, *LeGrand Richards*, 200.

146. My interviews, 29-30 Aug. 1992, with Alan Blodgett, managing director of the LDS church's Financial Department from 1969 to 1980, and managing director of the LDS Investment Department from 1980 to 1985.

147. Ibid.; *Descendants of Nathan Tanner (Sr.)* (Salt Lake City: Nathan Tanner Family Association, 1968), 75, 78, 316, 434, 465; George S. Tanner, *John Tanner and His Family* (Salt Lake City: John Tanner Family Association, 1974), 350-53; D. Michael Quinn, "From Sacred Grove to Sacral Power Structure," *Dialogue: A Journal of Mormon Thought* 17 (Summer 1984): 22.

148. Alan Blodgett interviews, 29-30 Aug. 1992.

149. G. Homer Durham et al., *N. Eldon Tanner: His Life and Service* (Salt Lake City: Deseret Book Co., 1982), 277.

150. Alan Blodgett interviews, 29-30 Aug. 1992.

151. My interviews, 5-6 Sept. 1992, with Rodney P. Foster, assistant secretary in the First Presidency's office from 1974 to 1981.

152. *Deseret News 1976 Church Almanac* (Salt Lake City: Deseret News, 1977), 13; *Deseret News 1991-1992 Church Almanac* (Salt Lake City: Deseret News, 1990), 35, for Lynn A. Sorensen's pre-hierarchy positions; *Deseret News 1995-1996 Church Almanac*, 389, for 14 January 1977; Burton and Dyer, "Presiding Bishopric," in Ludlow, *Encyclopedia of Mormonism*, 3:1130; Alan Blodgett interview, 30 Aug. 1992.

153. Rodney P. Foster interviews, 5-6 Sept. 1992.

154. *Deseret News "Church News,"* 23 May 1981, 15, and 13 Feb. 1983, 11; "Area Presidencies Called as Church Modifies Geographical Administration," *Ensign* 14 (Aug. 1984): 75; Burton and Dyer, "Presiding Bishopric," in Ludlow, *Encyclopedia of Mormonism*, 3:1130.

155. *The Doctrine and Covenants of The Church of Jesus Christ of Latter-day Saints*, published at Salt Lake City in various editions, sec. 107:24-26, hereafter D&C with numbers of section and verse(s). There was also an equality with stake high councils. See discussion in Quinn, *Mormon Hierarchy: Origins of Power*, 59-61, 68-69, 157-60.

156. *History of the Church*, 2:476-77.

157. Hazen Aldrich to James J. Strang, 15 Apr. 1846, Strang Manuscripts, Beinecke Rare Book and Manuscript Library, Yale University, New Haven, Connecticut; Orson Pratt statement in Quorum of the Twelve Apostles minutes, 30 Nov. 1847.

158. *History of the Church*, 2:139, 142, 164, 165.

159. Franklin D. Richards diary, 6 Feb. 1892; Joseph F. Smith statement in *October 1903 Conference Report . . .* (Salt Lake City: Church of Jesus Christ of Latter-day Saints, 1903), 87; First Council of Seventy minutes, 4 Jan. 1909, LDS archives; Thomas A. Clawson diary, 8 Apr. 1918.

160. Brigham Young sermon, 25 May 1877, in *Deseret Evening News,* 2 June 1877, 1.

161. *History of the Church,* 7:279, 303, 305, 307-308; First Council of Seventy minutes, 8 Oct. 1844; James Norman Baumgarten, "The Role and Function of Seventies in L.D.S. Church History," M.A. thesis, Brigham Young University, 1960, 31-33.

162. Quinn, *Mormon Hierarchy: Origins of Power*, 173-74.

163. Manuscript History of the Church, 14 Dec. 1845; Kenney, *Wilford Woodruff's Journal*, 5 (17 Feb. 1857): 22, 6 (27 Jan. 1868): 392; James Beck notebook, 27 Apr. 1861, LDS archives; Brigham Young statements in First Council of Seventy minutes, 4 Jan. 1861, 11 July 1877.

164. Certificate to Joseph Young, 10 Feb. 1846, signed by Brigham Young, Heber C. Kimball, Orson Hyde, Parley Pratt, Orson Pratt, John Taylor, Amasa M. Lyman, and Willard Richards, LDS archives, which *History of the Church,* 7:584, summarizes without reference to apostleship; *Deseret News 1995-1996 Church Almanac,* 329.

165. Examples in Hosea Stout diary, 4 Oct., 26 Nov. 1846 in Brooks, *On the Mormon Frontier,* 1:214; Robert T. Burton diary, 2 Sept. 1875, LDS archives (compare his bishop's service since 1867).

166. Brigham Young sermon, 25 May 1877, in *Deseret Evening News,* 2 June 1877, 1.

167. George Goddard diary, 5 Nov. 1874, LDS archives.

168. Journal History, 29 Aug. 1901, 1-2; ordination certificate of Joseph F. Smith, 1858, signed by Joseph Young, LDS archives. A certificate of 1869, also signed by Joseph Young (LDS archives), verified that Smith had been ordained "one of the Seventy Elders."

169. There is still no book about this interesting phase of Utah Mormonism, but the following are useful: Roberts, *Comprehensive History of the Church,* 4:118-36; Howard C. Searle, "The Mormon Reformation of 1856-57," M.A. thesis, Brigham Young University, 1956; Gustive O. Larson, "The Mormon Reformation," *Utah Historical Quarterly* 26 (Jan. 1958): 45-63; Michael Orme, "The Causes of the Mormon Reformation, 1856-57," *Tangents,* Spring 1975, 15-40; Paul H. Peterson, "The Mormon Reformation," Ph.D. diss., Brigham Young University, 1981; Gene A. Sessions, *Mormon Thunder: A Documentary History of Jedediah Morgan Grant* (Urbana: University of Illinois Press, 1982), 205-42; Eugene E. Campbell, *Establishing Zion: The Mormon Church in the American West, 1847-1869* (Salt Lake City: Signature Books, 1988), 181-200; Paul H. Peterson, "The Mormon Reformation, 1856-1857," *Journal of Mormon History* 15 (1989): 59-87; Peterson, "Reformation (LDS) of 1856-1857," in Ludlow, *Encyclopedia of Mormonism,* 3:1197.

170. Kenney, *Wilford Woodruff's Journal* 4 (7 Oct. 1856): 467-69.

171. Kenney, *Wilford Woodruff's Journal* 4 (22 Dec. 1856): 519-20; Hosea Stout diary, 22 Dec. 1856, in Brooks, *On the Mormon Frontier,* 2:611; First Council of Seventy minutes, 16 Jan. 1878.

172. Brigham Young sermon, 6 Apr. 1861, in *Deseret News* [weekly], 10 Apr. 1861.

173. First Council of Seventy minutes, 28 Feb. 1880, 17 Apr. 1881, 25 Nov. 1882; Abraham H. Cannon diary, 14 Apr. 1883.

174. Franklin D. Richards diary, 13-14 Apr. 1883; excerpts from First Presidency office journal, 13-14 Apr. 1883, 61, 63; B. H. Roberts, *The Seventy's Course in Theology: First Year* (Salt Lake City: Deseret News, 1907), 9-10; also in Collier, *Unpublished Revelations,* 1:140; Reay and Reay, *Selected Manifestations,* 108-109; Rudger Clawson diary, 2 July 1903, in Larson, *A Ministry of Meetings,* 632; William G. Hartley, "The Seventies in the 1880s: Revelations and Reorganizing," *Dialogue: A Journal of Mormon Thought* 16 (Spring 1983): 79-83.

175. Franklin D. Richards diary, 26 Oct. 1882.

176. Reed Smoot diary, 7 Oct. 1926, copies at Lee Library and at Marriott Library.

177. For example, see Rudger Clawson diary for his remarks at the meeting of 2 July 1903 in Larson, *A Ministry of Meetings,* 632; also Richard R. Lyman and John A. Widtsoe in minutes of First Presidency and Quorum of the Twelve, 13 Mar. 1941, excerpt from First Presidency office journal; and Talbot, *Acts of the Modern Apostles,* 245.

178. J. Golden Kimball diary, 30 Sept. 1896, Marriott Library.

179. Abraham H. Cannon diary, 18 Sept. 1889, also 5 Dec. 1888; First Council of Seventy minutes, 12 Dec. 1888.

180. Journal History, 16 Jan. 1896, 3.

181. J. Golden Kimball diary, 15 May, 30 Sept. 1896.

182. Ibid., 4-5 Oct. 1897; Anthon H. Lund diary, 29 Jan. 1897.

183. Seymour B. Young diary, 19 Nov. 1887, 13 Dec. 1896, 22 Jan., 12 Mar. 1898; Cassia Stake History, 20 Nov. 1887, LDS archives; Abraham H. Cannon diary, 19 Nov. 1891. John Albert Phillips traced his line of authority as a high priest back to Seymour B. Young's ordination of Myron Busnell Durfee as a high priest on 20 November 1887.

184. First Council of Seventy minutes, 4 Apr. 1899; Rudger Clawson diary, 13 Apr. 1899, in Larson, *A Ministry of Meetings*, 46; Journal History, 13 Apr. 1899, 2-7, 19 Apr. 1899, 2; J. Golden Kimball diary, 8 Aug. 1900; George F. Richards diary, 16 Sept. 1908; First Council of Seventy minutes, 17 Sept., 14 Oct. 1908, 6 Jan. 1925.

185. Seymour B. Young diary, 7-9 Aug. 1900; D. Michael Quinn, "LDS Church Authority and New Plural Marriages, 1890-1904," *Dialogue: A Journal of Mormon Thought* 18 (Spring 1985): 86-88.

186. Joseph F. Smith to John T. Nattress of Payson, Utah, 24 Feb. 1900, my reconstruction of abbreviated notes in fd 1, box 6, Kenney papers, emphasis in original.

187. Rudger Clawson diary, 27 Feb. 1902, 19 May 1904, in Larson, *A Ministry of Meetings*, 401, 740; First Council of Seventy minutes, 18 Apr. 1906.

188. Rudger Clawson diary, 2 July 1903, in Larson, *A Ministry of Meetings,* 632.

189. Rudger Clawson manuscript diary, 6 Oct. 1903, Manuscripts Division, Marriott Library, entry not in Larson, *A Ministry of Meetings*. Anthony W. Ivins diary, 6 Oct. 1903 (Utah State Historical Society), quoted Joseph F. Smith as saying, "A Seventy can ordain a high priest or a high p[rie]st could ordain a Seventy." The official version appeared in *October 1903 Conference Report*, 87: "If it were necessary, the Seventy, holding the Melchisedek Priesthood, as he does, I say IF IT WERE NECESSARY—he could ordain a High Priest; and if it were necessary for a High Priest to ordain a Seventy, he could do that."

190. J. Golden Kimball diary, 29 June 1900, 29-30 May 1901.

191. Ibid., 30 Nov., 5 Dec. 1902.

192. Claude Richards, *J. Golden Kimball: The Story of a Unique Personality* (Salt Lake City: Deseret News Press, 1934), 88, 97-98, 100-101; Thomas E. Cheney, *The Golden Legacy: A Folk History of J. Golden Kimball* (Santa Barbara: Peregrine Smith, 1974), 5, 37, 38, 39, 40, 43-44, 48, 80-81, 99, 101-102, 103, 114-15, 115-16, 120-21.

193. J. Golden Kimball diary, 7 Oct. 1902, 2-6 May 1905; also "J. Golden Kimball," in Howard R. Lamar, ed., *Reader's Encyclopedia of the American West* (New York: Thomas Y. Crowell, 1977).

194. Seymour B. Young diary, 8 Apr. 1912.

195. Minutes of the conference of the Seventies, 4 Oct. 1907, 6, and Seymour B. Young to Joseph F. Smith and counselors, 27 Nov. 1907, both in fd 10, box 12, Kenney papers.

196. J. Golden Kimball diary, 6 Nov., 29 Nov. 1898; Andrew Jenson diary, 3 Aug. 1901, LDS archives.

197. J. Golden Kimball diary, 20 Mar. 1901; Joseph E. Robinson diary, 18 Jan. 1906, LDS archives; undated entry in Seymour B. Young 1908 notebook; also Richard S. Van Wagoner and Steven C. Walker, *A Book of Mormons* (Salt Lake City: Signature Books, 1982), 246. Truman G. Madsen, *Defender of the Faith: The B.H. Roberts Story* (Salt Lake City: Bookcraft, 1980), 379, acknowledged that Roberts used alcohol early in life but interpreted later symptoms as diabetes wrongly viewed by others as alcohol breath.

198. J. Golden Kimball diary, 15 May 1901, 6 July 1904, 10 Apr., 27 Nov. 1901, also 13 May 1903.

199. Seymour B. Young 1912 datebook, 16 May 1912; Young 1921 datebook, 3 Nov. 1921; Young diary, 12 June 1920.

200. William W. Slaughter, *Life In Zion: An Intimate Look at the Latter-day Saints, 1820-1995* (Salt Lake City: Deseret Book Co., 1995), 129.

201. Seymour B. Young 1920 datebook, 14 Oct. 1920.

202. James E. Talmage diary, 8 Jan., 11 Apr., 13 Apr. 1923; First Council of Seventy minutes, 14 Apr. 1923, 15 Jan. 1925.

203. First Council of Seventy minutes, 24 June, 7 Oct. 1926; Heber J. Grant journal, 7 Oct. 1926.

204. First Council of Seventy minutes, 14 Oct. 1926; Rudger Clawson to Heber J. Grant and Counselors, 9 Dec. 1926, LDS archives.

205. First Council of Seventy minutes, 9 Apr. 1931; B. H. Roberts to Heber J. Grant, 27 Apr. 1931, Utah State Historical Society, emphasis in original, also copy in fd 10, box 12, Kenney papers; B. H. Roberts to Anthony W. Ivins, 15 Nov. 1932; David O. McKay and Joseph Fielding Smith to Rudger Clawson, 27 Jan. 1933, latter two in LDS archives.

206. B. H. Roberts to "The First Presidency," 30 Aug. 1932, fd 10, box 12, Kenney papers; First Council of Seventy minutes, 1 Sept. 1932; B. H. Roberts to Anthony W. Ivins, 15 Nov. 1932; David O. McKay and Joseph Fielding Smith to Rudger Clawson, 27 Jan. 1933.

207. *Deseret News 1995-1996 Church Almanac,* 380.

208. *Journal of Discourses* 22:36 (O. Pratt/1880).

209. J. Reuben Clark office diary, 19 Feb. 1941; Heber J. Grant journal sheets, 13 Mar. 1941; minutes of 13 Mar. 1941.

210. Heber J. Grant journal sheets, 13 Mar. 1941; minutes of 13 Mar. 1941; Gibbons, *Joseph Fielding Smith,* 325.

211. J. Reuben Clark office diary, 14 Mar. 1941; Quinn, *J. Reuben Clark,* 87; Heber J. Grant journal sheets, 13 Mar. 1941; minutes of 13 Mar. 1941; Talbot, *Acts of the Modern Apostles,* 245.

212. "The 111th Annual Conference" and John A. Widtsoe, "Assistants to the Twelve," *Improvement Era* 44 (May 1941): 269, 288; Cowan, *Church in the Twentieth Century,* 172-73. Four days after the conference, the Seventy's most junior member, Richard L. Evans, presented Heber J. Grant with scriptural evidence about "the Seventies being assistants to the Twelve." Heber J. Grant journal sheets, 9, 24 Apr. 1941.

213. Conway B. Sonne, *A Man Named Alma: The World of Alma Sonne* (Bountiful, UT: Horizon Publishers, 1988), 123, also 180; with similar statement of authority and identical exceptions in David O. McKay's 1954 setting apart of Sterling W. Sill in *The Nine Lives of Sterling W. Sill: An Autobiography* (Bountiful, UT: Horizon Publishers, 1979), 121, 140. Gibbons, *Harold B. Lee,* 386, did not specify what the "two exceptions" were.

214. Francis M. Gibbons, *Heber J. Grant: Man of Steel, Prophet of God* (Salt Lake City: Deseret Book Co., 1979), 226. A general authority from 1986 until 1991, Gibbons was previously secretary to the First Presidency for sixteen years (*Deseret News 1991-1992 Church Almanac,* 30).

215. *Deseret News 1995-1996 Church Almanac,* 49-50, 63-65; Talbot, *Acts of the Modern Apostles,* 284-85. Byron R. Merrill, "Assistants to the Twelve," in Ludlow, *Encyclopedia of Mormonism,* 1:81, lists assistants who became apostles or counselors in the First Presidency (up to 1992), omitting Alvin R. Dyer and Thorpe B. Isaacson.

216. Neal A. Maxwell oral history, 1976-77, 76, LDS archives. For descriptions of their duties and activities, see Sonne, *A Man Named Alma,* 123, 134, 148, 174-76, 186-98; and Lucile C. Tate, *David B. Haight: The Life Story of A Disciple* (Salt Lake City: Bookcraft, 1987), 234-59.

217. F. Burton Howard, *Marion G. Romney: His Life and Faith* (Salt Lake City: Bookcraft, 1988), 169; J. Reuben Clark office diary, 3 Nov. 1944.

218. Sonne, *A Man Named Alma,* 177.

219. Heber J. Grant journal sheets, 14 Aug. 1942.

220. Benson Y. Parkinson, *S. Dilworth Young: General Authority, Scouter, Poet* (American Fork, UT: Covenant Communications, 1994), 306.

221. Cowan, *Church in the Twentieth Century,* 405; Francis M. Gibbons, *David O. McKay: Apostle to the World, Prophet of God* (Salt Lake City: Deseret Book Co., 1986), 403.

222. *History of the Church*, 2:476; *Deseret News 1995-1996 Church Almanac*, 58.

223. David O. McKay office diary, 14 June 1961.

224. Rudger Clawson manuscript diary, 6 Oct. 1903.

225. David O. McKay office diary, 9 June 1961, also 2 Feb., 30 Mar., 19 Apr., 9 June, 14-15 June 1961; David O. McKay deceased membership record, LDS archives.

226. David O. McKay office diary, 14 June 1961.

277. See weekly reports of the apostles to the temple meeting each Thursday in Journal History from 1901 onward. For numbers of wards and stakes each year, see *Deseret News 1995-1996 Church Almanac*, 418-20.

228. Sheri L. Dew, *Ezra Taft Benson: A Biography* (Salt Lake City: Deseret Book Co., 1987), 241.

229. Gibbons, *Joseph Fielding Smith*, 429, also 449.

230. *Deseret News 1995-1996 Church Almanac*, 388, 389.

231. Gibbons, *Harold B. Lee*, 307-308; Harold B. Lee, "Meeting the Needs of a Growing Church," *Improvement Era* 71 (Jan. 1968): 29-38; *Deseret News 1995-1996 Church Almanac*, 386; Allen and Leonard, *Story of the Latter-day Saints*, 599-600; Cowan, *Church in the Twentieth Century*, 417-19; William E. Berrett, *The Latter-day Saints: A Contemporary History of the Church of Jesus Christ* (Salt Lake City: Deseret Book Co., 1985), 349-50.

232. Douglas L. Callister and Gerald J. Day, "Region, Regional Representative," in Ludlow, *Encyclopedia of Mormonism*, 3:1198; also Tate, *David B. Haight*, 231-33.

233. Parkinson, *S. Dilworth Young*, 306.

234. Goates, *Harold B. Lee*, 436; Allen and Leonard, *Story of the Latter-day Saints*, 604-605.

235. Gibbons, *Joseph Fielding Smith*, 489-90; Cowan, *Church in the Twentieth Century*, 418; Gibbons, *Harold B. Lee*, 432.

236. Parkinson, *S. Dilworth Young*, 307-308; *Deseret News 1995-1996 Church Almanac*, 21, 24, 63.

237. First Presidency circular letters to church officers, 15 Dec. 1969, 23 July 1975, 27 Feb. 1981, LDS archives, with copies in my possession, provided by a local LDS leader; Stan L. Albrecht, "Stake," in Ludlow, *Encyclopedia of Mormonism*, 3:1414.

238. Jay M. Todd, "The First Quorum of the Seventy," *Ensign* 5 (Nov. 1975): 134; Cowan, *Church in the Twentieth Century*, 404-406; *Deseret News 1995-1996 Church Almanac*, 63, 388; Berrett, *Latter-day Saints*, 350.

239. Cowan, *Church in the Twentieth Century*, 406.

240. *Deseret News "Church News,"* 6 Jan. 1979, 19; Talbot, *Acts of the Modern Apostles*, 340.

241. Dean L. Larsen, "Seventy: Quorums of Seventy," in Ludlow, *Encyclopedia of Mormonism*, 3:1304.

242. Parkinson, *S. Dilworth Young*, 308. Parkinson erroneously wrote 1975 in reference to this April event between October 1975 and October 1976, but *Deseret News 1995-1996 Church Almanac*, 63, shows that the four new seventies were appointed in April 1976.

243. Alan K. Parrish, "Seventy," in Ludlow, *Encyclopedia of Mormonism*, 3:1302.

244. Parkinson, *S. Dilworth Young*, 311.

245. *Ensign* 6 (Nov. 1976): 102.

246. *Deseret News 1995-1996 Church Almanac*, 56, 68; Talbot, *Acts of the Modern Apostles*, 332-33.

247. "The Lee Letters," *Sunstone* 13 (Aug. 1989): 51, 55; *Salt Lake Tribune*, 2 Sept. 1989, B-1; "Mormons Oust First Indian in the Hierarchy," *New York Times*, 3 Sept. 1989, A-29; *Deseret News 1995-1996 Church Almanac*, 68.

248. *Deseret News 1993-1994 Church Almanac* (Salt Lake City: Deseret News, 1992), 60-65, compare with *Deseret News 1991-1992 Church Almanac*, 54-56.

249. Cowan, *Church in the Twentieth Century*, 419; Talbot, *Acts of the Modern Apostles*, 340; *Deseret News "Church News,"* 6 Jan. 1979, 19; Gordon B. Hinckley, "This Work Is Concerned with People," *Ensign* 25 (May 1995): 51-52 for release of regional representatives and announcement of new position of "area authority."

250. Perry H. Cunningham, "Area, Area Presidency," William S. Evans, "District, District President," in Ludlow, *Encyclopedia of Mormonism*, 1:65-66, 390-91; *Deseret News 1995-1996 Church Almanac*, 98-107; "First Presidency Names Area Authorities," *Deseret News "Church News,"* 5 Aug. 1995, 3. As of 1 July 1977 the descending regional hierarchy was announced as "Zones," "Areas," and "Regions" but by 24 June 1984 had been simplified to Areas and Regions.

251. My interview, 2 Nov. 1992, with Lowell L. Durham, Jr., who served as assistant editor with LDS church magazines (1972-76); became vice-president and then president of church-owned Deseret Book Company to 1982; and, finally, vice-president and then president of church-controlled Zion's Co-operative Mercantile Institution (ZCMI) until 1990.

252. Goates, *Harold B. Lee*, 241.

253. Rodney Stark, "The Rise of a New World Faith," *Review of Religious Research* 26 (Sept. 1984): 22; Stark, "Modernization and Mormon Growth: The Secularization Thesis Revisited," in Marie Cornwall, Tim B. Heaton, and Lawrence A. Young, eds., *Contemporary Mormonism: Social Science Perspectives* (Urbana: University of Illinois Press, 1994), 14.

254. Alan K. Parrish, "Seventy: Overview," in Ludlow, *Encyclopedia of Mormonism*, 3:1302. At present Second Quorum members have five-year assignments as general authorities, after which they return to the rank-and-file. This temporary calling as a general authority began in 1984. *Ensign* 19 (May 1989): 1; *Deseret News 1995-1996 Church Almanac*, 73, 391, 393-94.

255. *Deseret News 1995-1996 Church Almanac*, 392; Parrish, "Seventy: Overview," in Ludlow, *Encyclopedia of Mormonism*, 3:1300.

256. General authorities are reluctant to acknowledge the existence of a church bureaucracy or bureaucrats. The preferred terms are "church departments," "administrative departments," "church administrators," or "church administrative officers." The overall concept and organization received slight mention in Ludlow, *Encyclopedia of Mormonism*. In 3:1040, William G. Hartley, "Organization: Organizational and Administrative History," uses the secular term: "an extensive bureaucracy was not necessary until rapid international growth began in the 1960s." His coverage (1042) simply observes that by the 1960s there were "professional services and departments for education, social work, legal affairs, building, communications, accounting, etc." In 3:1047-48, Lee Tom Perry, Paul M. Bons, and Alan L. Wilkins, "Organization: Contemporary," gives a paragraph description to each of eight departments in the LDS bureaucracy.

257. Alexander, *Mormonism in Transition*, 99.

258. *History of the Church*, 1:343, 4:205.

259. Richard D. Poll, "Henry D. Moyle: Man of Action," unpublished 1983 biography, fd 16, box 67, chapter, "Missionary Apostle," 9, Poll papers.

260. J. Reuben Clark office diary, 12 June 1948; Quinn, *J. Reuben Clark*, 106.

261. David O. McKay office diary, 22 Dec. 1960, quoted in Quinn, "From Sacred Grove to Sacral Power Structure," 30.

262. Heber J. Grant journal sheets, 18, 22 Apr. 1936; J. Reuben Clark office diary, 15 Sept. 1950; Quinn, *J. Reuben Clark*, 72-73, 111.

263. I have examined hundreds of such documents with these secretary-prepared cover sheets; also Rodney P. Foster interviews, 5-6 Sept. 1992.

264. Gibbons, *David O. McKay*, 419; Joseph Anderson oral history, 1975, 5, LDS archives.

265. Interview with First Presidency secretary A. Hamer Reiser, 1 Mar. 1980; Quinn, *J. Reuben Clark*, 128; Alan Blodgett interviews, 29-30 Aug. 1992; Rodney P. Foster interviews, 5-6 Sept. 1992.

266. Keith Terry, *David O. McKay: Prophet of Love* (Santa Barbara, CA: Butterfly Publishing, 1980), 183, 99-100; also see Dorothy O. Rea, "Secretary to a Prophet," *Deseret News "Church News,"* 21 May 1966, 13.

267. Ernest L. Wilkinson diary, 29 June 1962, also 9 Dec. 1953, 14 Sept. 1960, 7 Mar. 1967, photocopy, Marriott Library.

268. U.S. Senator Frank E. Moss to U.S. Representative Ken W. Dyal, 2 Mar. 1966, Moss papers, Marriott Library. Moss's observation was based on interviews with "the Brethren" in Salt Lake City a week earlier.

269. Gibbons, *David O. McKay*, 419.

270. Charles M. Brown interview, 7 June 1973, c-3-13.

271. Gibbons, *Joseph Fielding Smith*, 460; emphasis added; also Heidi S. Swinton, *In the Company of Prophets: Personal Experiences of D. Arthur Haycock with Heber J. Grant, George Albert Smith, David O. McKay, Joseph Fielding Smith, Harold B. Lee, Spencer W. Kimball, and Ezra Taft Benson* (Salt Lake City: Deseret Book Co., 1993), viii-ix.

272. Rodney P. Foster interviews, 5-6 Sept. 1992. This signature machine is manufactured by International Auto-Pen Company of Arlington, Virginia.

273. Don LeFevre statements in "Documents Show Counselors Now Control LDS Assets," *Salt Lake Tribune*, 15 Aug. 1993, C-2.

274. Heber J. Grant journal, 13 Oct. 1898.

275. Rodney P. Foster interviews, 5-6 Sept. 1992.

276. Swinton, *In the Company of Prophets*, xvi. However, Swinton also noted (ix): "Arthur was not involved in making a name for himself or in formulating policies for the Churchap."

277. *General Church Offices Telephone Directory, 1984* (Salt Lake City: Corporation of the President of The Church of Jesus Christ of Latter-day Saints, 1984); *Deseret News 1995-1996 Church Almanac*, 420. In addition to the staff of the five presiding quorums, the departments of the central LDS bureaucracy in 1984 were Auditing, Budget, Church Educational, Correlation, Curriculum, Finance and Records, Genealogical, Historical, Information Systems, International Mission, Investments, Materials Management, Missionary, Personnel, Physical Facilities, Presiding Bishopric Administrative Services, Presiding Bishopric International Offices, Priesthood, Public Communications, Security, Temple, and Welfare Services.

278. U.S. Bureau of Census, *Statistical Abstract of the United States, 1984* (Washington, D.C.: U.S. Government Printing Office, 1983), 333, Table 536, "Paid Civilian Employment in the Federal Government," excludes employees of the Central Intelligence Agency (CIA), of the National Security Agency (NSA), and temporary Christmas help of the U.S. Postal Service. The table listed 2,092,000 white collar employees for the entire nation. This compared to the U.S. population of 226,545,805 (*Statistical Abstract*, 6).

However, unlike the federal government, the LDS church functions primarily through the unpaid services of a lay ministry of religious officers (general, regional, and local). For a more realistic comparison with the federal bureaucracy, the number of these unpaid LDS religious officers (95,104) should be added to the number of employees in the LDS central bureaucracy (2,971) as of January 1984. This gives a ratio of one LDS bureaucrat/church officer per each 56 Latter-day Saints throughout the world as of the 31 December 1983 church population of 5,351,734. Thus, total LDS administration was almost double the per capita extent of the federal bureaucracy the same year.

This was calculated according to the norm of three men per temple presidency, three men per mission presidency, sixteen per district (presidency, clerk, and district council), three per branch (rather than the ideal of president, two counselors, and clerk), five per ward (bishopric, clerk, and executive secretary), and nineteen per stake (presidency, clerk, executive secretary, twelve high councilmen, and two alternate high councilmen). Any active Latter-day Saint knows that the administrative officers of the above units are more numerous than the highest echelon for which I have limited this computation. In addition to those local officers, the *Directory of General Authorities and Officers, 1984* listed 56 general authorities, 12 international area directors, and 440 regional representatives. As of 31 December 1983, there were 26 temples (including one closed for the year), 178 missions, 353 districts, 1,991 branches in missions, 9,326 wards and 2,677 branches in stakes, and 1,458 stakes ("Church Growth," *Deseret News "Church News,"* 22 Apr. 1984, 8-9, and information about branches and districts provided by LDS church headquarters in January 1984).

279. "Church Office Personnel," *General Church Offices Telephone Directory, January 1996* (Salt Lake City: Church of Jesus Christ of Latter-day Saints, 1996), 33-104 (excluding the general authorities); "Church Growth," *Deseret News "Church News,"* 3 Apr. 1996, 6; Sheri L. Dew, *Go Forward With Faith: The Biography of Gordon B. Hinckley* (Salt Lake City: Deseret Book Co., 1996), 408.

By 1996, there were some changes in the twenty-two departments that existed in 1984. Two were dropped (and regionalized outside the United States): the International Mission and the Presiding Bishopric International Offices (with the director of "International Affairs" located in the Presiding Bishopric Administrative Services at headquarters). AudioVisual, LDS Foundation, Social Services, and Translation were added as departments. Three had been renamed: Family History Department (formerly Genealogical), Human Resource (formerly Personnel), Public Affairs (formerly Public Communications). The Investment Department was unlisted, but its two divisions (Investment Properties and Investment Securities) were each listed as if they had the status of separate departments (possibly indicating massive growth in their responsibilities and/or staffs).

The thirty-four facilities which housed the LDS headquarters bureaucracy in 1996 were the Assembly Hall, the Beehive Clothing Mills Building, the Bishops' Central Storehouse, the Beehive House Building, the Beneficial Life Tower, the BYU Continuing Education Building, the Church Administration Building, the I.S. Production Division, the Church Office Building, the Distribution Center Building, the Deseret Industries Manufacturing, the Eagle Gate Tower (including the General Counsel suite), the Exhibits Building, the Family History Library, the Granite Mountain Vault, the Deseret Gym, Joseph Smith Memorial Building, the Kennecott Building, Deseret Mills, the Museum of Church History and Art, the Motion Picture Studio, the Utah Salt Lake City Mission, the Salt Lake Printing Center, the Relief Society Building, the Sort Center Building, the Sandy Bishops' Storehouse, the Sandy LDS Social Services Building, the Social Services Building, the Salt Lake Tabernacle, the Jordan River temple, the Salt Lake temple, the Temple Square security outpost, the Visitor's Center North, the Visitor's Center South, and Welfare Square.

280. *General Church Offices Telephone Directory, January 1996,* 11-12, for "area offices" in American Samoa, Argentina, Australia, Bolivia, Brazil, Chile, Colombia, Costa Rica, Denmark, Dominican Republic, Ecuador, England, Fiji, Finland, France (including the "Mediterranean" area office), Germany, Ghana, Guam, Guatemala, Hong Kong, Iceland, Indonesia, Italy, Japan, Korea, Mexico, Netherlands, New Zealand, Nigeria, Norway, Peru, Philippines, Portugal, Puerto Rico (U.S. territorial office for the Caribbean area), Singapore, South Africa, Spain, Sweden, Tahiti, Taiwan, Thailand, Tonga, Uruguay, Venezuela, Western Samoa. Canada's provinces are included in three North American administrative areas, all of which are headquartered in Salt Lake City (see *Deseret News 1995-1996 Church Almanac,* 104-106). See David Clark Knowlton, "Mormonism in Latin America: Towards the Twenty-first Century," and Marjorie Newton, "Mormons in Australia," *Dialogue: A Journal of Mormon Thought* 29 (Spring 1996): 172 (on recruitment of local leaders from the

Latin American LDS bureaucracy), 202 (for quote about Australia). For positions in regional bureaucracy, see "New Mission Presidents" and "New Stake Presidencies," in *Deseret News "Church News,"* 18 Mar., 16 Sept., 14 Oct., 21 Oct. 1995, 23 Mar., 30 Mar., 20 Apr., 27 Apr., 4 May, 1 June, 6 July 1996.

    General Church Offices Telephone Directory, January 1996, 105-106, list the following international "Administrative Offices" and their locations: Africa (in Lonehill, Republic of South Africa), Asia (in Hong Kong), Asia North (in Tokyo), Brazil (in Sao Paulo), Central America (in Guatemala City), Europe Central (in Frankfurt am Main), Europe North (in Solihull, England), Mexico (in Mexico City), North America Southeast (in Rio Piedras, Puerto Rico), Pacific (in Carlingford, NSW, Australia), Philippines/Micronesia (in Pasig, Philippines), South America North (in Quito, Ecuador), South America South (in Buenos Aires). Page vii listed "Europe East Area Office" and "Europe West," but page 105 listed "Europe Central" Administrative Office in place of those two. However, the latter page was apparently in error because "Area Authorities Chart," *Deseret News "Church News,"* 5 Aug. 1995, 8, and "Area Presidencies Assigned," *Deseret News "Church News,"* 15 June 1996, 8, both listed areas for "Europe West," "Europe North," and "Europe East."

    281. Burton and Dyer, "Presiding Bishopric," and Dean L. Larsen, "Quorums of Seventy," also the description in Perry, Bons, and Wilkins, "Organization: Contemporary," in Ludlow, *Encyclopedia of Mormonism* 3: 1130, 1304, also 1047-48.

    282. For more information about the LDS bureaucracy, consult Allen and Leonard, *Story of the Latter-day Saints,* 602-606, 614-16, 651-55; Leonard J. Arrington and Davis Bitton, *The Mormon Experience: A History of the Latter-day Saints* (New York: Alfred A. Knopf, 1979), 262-94; Randall Hatch, "The Mormon Church: Managing the Lord's Work," *MBA* (June 1977), 33-37; David J. Whittaker, "An Introduction to Mormon Administrative History," *Dialogue: A Journal of Mormon Thought* 15 (Winter 1982): 14-19; Robert Gottlieb and Peter Wiley, *America's Saints: The Rise of Mormon Power* (New York: G.P. Putnam's Sons, 1984), 15, 54, 97, 102, 108-109, 118, 123, 127-28; Cowan, *Church in the Twentieth Century,* 301-304; Warren P. Wadsworth, "Brave New Bureaucracy," *Dialogue: A Journal of Mormon Thought* 20 (Fall 1987): 33-34.

    283. Gottlieb and Wiley, *America's Saints,* 128.

    284. Dew, *Go Forward With Faith,* 531; Alan L. Frohman and Leonard W. Johnson, *The Middle Management Challenge: Moving from Crisis to Empowerment* (New York: McGraw-Hill, 1993), 11: "In the 1960s and early 1970s . . . to deal with the growing complexities of operations, senior management added middle managers to their staffs. As these fiefdoms expanded, so did the volume of analyses and reports they produced. Middle managers functioned in vertical roles. They were message carriers. Senior managers expected them to pass the word to those in the lower ranks who, in turn, had messages they wanted senior managers to hear. Their roles and responsibilities were supervisory, controlling the vertical flow of directions and information within departmental channels. They compiled data and prepared reports for those at the top."

    285. Talbot, *Acts of the Modern Apostles,* 282.

    286. Abraham H. Cannon diary, 29 Jan. 1891; also George Q. Cannon diary, 7 Jan. 1898, in Stanley B. Kimball, *Heber C. Kimball: Mormon Patriarch and Pioneer* (Urbana: University of Illinois Press, 1981), xvn1.

    287. Ernest L. Wilkinson diary, 23 Feb. 1965, quoted slightly differently in Gary James Bergera and Ronald Priddis, *Brigham Young University: A House of Faith* (Salt Lake City: Signature Books, 1985), 25.

    288. *Journal of Discourses* 1:189 (B. Young/1853), 5:329 (B. Young/1857), 352 (B. Young/1857), 6:77 (B. Young/1857), 174 (B. Young/1858), 7:334 (B. Young/1859), 8:132 (B. Young/1860), 10:295 (B. Young/1864), 11:107 (B. Young/1865), 250 (B. Young/1866), 15:142 (B. Young/1872).

Notes to Chapter Five

1. Herbert Ray Larsen, "'Familism' in Mormon Social Structure," Ph.D. diss., University of Utah, 1954, 146.

2. "LETTER VII. To W. W. Phelps, Esq.," *Latter Day Saints' Messenger and Advocate* 1 (July 1835): 156. Except when otherwise indicated, biographical sketches of all general authorities named in this chapter can be found either in an appendix of the present volume or in D. Michael Quinn, *The Mormon Hierarchy: Origins of Power* (Salt Lake City: Signature Books/Smith Research Associates, 1994).

3. *Elders' Journal* 1 (July 1838): 43, in Joseph Smith et al., *History of The Church of Jesus Christ of Latter-day Saints. Period I: History of Joseph Smith the Prophet, and . . . Period II: From the Manuscript History of Brigham Young and Other Original Documents,* ed. B. H. Roberts, 7 vols. (Salt Lake City: Church of Jesus Christ of Latter-day Saints, 1902-32; 2d ed. rev. [Salt Lake City: Deseret Book Co., 1978]), 3:29 (hereafter *History of the Church*); also Michael Guy Bishop, "The Celestial Family: Early Mormon Thought on Life and Death, 1830-1846," Ph.D. diss., Southern Illinois University, 1981.

4. *The Doctrine and Covenants of The Church of Jesus Christ of Latter-day Saints,* published at Salt Lake City in various editions, sec. 124:29-42, hereafter D&C with numbers of section and verse(s); M. Guy Bishop, "'What Has Become of Our Fathers': Baptism for the Dead at Nauvoo," *Dialogue: A Journal of Mormon Thought* 23 (Summer 1990): 85-96.

5. H. David Burton, "Baptism for the Dead," V. Ben Bloxham, "Family History Centers," Raymond S. Wright III, "Family History Library," George D. Durrant, "Genealogical Society," Steven W. Baldridge, "Granite Mountain Record Vault," Kahlile Mehr, "Name Extraction Program," Elma Fugal, "Salvation of the Dead," in Daniel H. Ludlow, ed., *Encyclopedia of Mormonism: The History, Scripture, Doctrine, and Procedure of the Church of Jesus Christ of Latter-day Saints,* 5 vols. (New York: Macmillan Publishing Co., 1992), 1:95-96, 2:492-95, 537-38, 563-64, 3:979-80, 1257-58; James B. Allen, Jessie L. Embry, and Kahlile B. Mehr, *Hearts Turned To the Fathers: A History of the Genealogical Society of Utah, 1894-1994* (Provo, UT: BYU Studies/Brigham Young University, 1995).

6. Scott G. Kenney, ed., *Wilford Woodruff's Journal, 1833-1898: Typescript,* 9 vols. (Midvale, UT: Signature Books, 1983-85), 3 (16 Feb. 1847): 131; John D. Lee diary, 16 Feb. 1847, in Charles Kelly, ed., *Journals of John D. Lee, 1846-47 and 1869* (Salt Lake City: Western Printing Co., 1938), 79-81.

7. Oliver Cowdery to Brigham Young, 27 Feb. 1848, in Stanley R. Gunn, *Oliver Cowdery: Second Elder and Scribe* (Salt Lake City: Bookcraft, 1962), 263.

8. Wilford Woodruff, Historian's Private Journal, 17 Apr. 1864, archives, Historical Department, Church of Jesus Christ of Latter-day Saints, Salt Lake City, Utah (hereafter LDS archives); also typescript titled, "Minutes of the Quorum of the Twelve Apostles," in fd 8, box 16, Donald R. Moorman papers, archives, Donnell and Elizabeth Stewart Library, Weber State University, Ogden, Utah.

9. Dean C. Jessee, ed., *Letters of Brigham Young to His Sons* (Salt Lake City: Deseret Book Co., 1974), xxiii and 357-58, for the names of his fifty-seven children, listed with each mother. This is misstated as forty-six (which is actually the number who lived to adulthood) in Leonard J. Arrington, *Brigham Young: American Moses* (New York: Alfred A. Knopf, 1985), 223.

10. Larsen, "Familism," 146.

11. John Smith diary, photocopy of holograph, 20 July 1839, George A. Smith Family papers, Manuscripts Division, J. Willard Marriott Library, University of Utah, Salt Lake City (hereafter Marriott Library).

12. Orson Pratt to Parley P. Pratt, 11 Oct. 1853, in Archibald F. Bennett, *Saviors on Mount Zion* (Salt Lake City: Deseret Sunday School Union Board, 1950), 36.

13. "A Family Meeting in Nauvoo," *Utah Genealogical and Historical Magazine* 11 (July 1920): 104-105, 107.

14. "History of Brigham Young," *Latter-day Saints Millennial Star* 25 (3 Aug. 1863): 504, for reference to his fourth cousin as simply "cousin A. P. Rockwood"; Francis M. Lyman to Richard R. Lyman, 15 Apr. 1904, LDS archives; also Joseph F. Smith to his second cousin John Henry Smith ("My Dear Kinsman"), 27 Mar. 1902, in 1902-1905 letterbook, 47, LDS archives.

15. This chapter does not give the same percentages or charts from the previous analysis of family relationships in my "Organizational Development and Social Origins of the Mormon Hierarchy, 1832-1932: A Prosopographical Study," M.A. thesis, University of Utah, 1973, or my "The Mormon Hierarchy, 1832-1932: An American Elite," Ph.D. diss., Yale University, 1976. Further research identified more interrelationships during that first century, and the format of the original charts was probably too detailed for general readers. Since publishing the biographical sketches in my 1994 *Mormon Hierarchy: Origins of Power*, I have also discovered kinship relationships for men that I thought had no family connections to the hierarchy at their appointment. Newly appointed Seventy's president Salmon Gee in 1837 was a third cousin of then-current LDS president Joseph Smith, First Presidency counselor Hyrum Smith, and Apostle William Smith; newly appointed apostle John E. Page in 1838 was a third cousin once-removed to recently appointed Seventy's president Zerah Pulsipher; newly appointed apostle Lyman Wight in 1841 was a third cousin once-removed of former apostle Thomas B. Marsh. I have also recently discovered an additional kinship for one man whose family relationships listed in *Origins* were not as complete as I had thought: newly appointed apostle Heber C. Kimball in 1835 was also a third cousin once-removed of then-current First Presidency counselor Frederick G. Williams.

16. Heber J. Grant's father Jedediah was not a member of the Twelve, but was ordained an apostle when he became Brigham Young's counselor. Since no apostle appointed before 1849 was born earlier than 1796, Franklin D. Richards (b. 1821) was the first new apostle to be a contemporary of the Twelve's sons. *Deseret News 1995-1996 Church Almanac: The Church of Jesus Christ of Latter-day Saints* (Salt Lake City: Deseret News, 1994), 47, 50-52.

17. John Henry Smith diary, 24 Oct. 1901, in Jean Bickmore White, ed., *Church, State, and Politics: The Diaries of John Henry Smith* (Salt Lake City: Signature Books/Smith Research Associates, 1990), 497.

18. Often a new appointee had several of these relationships to other general authorities, living and dead. Each of these separate relationships is counted as one occurrence of a kinship relation. When a new appointee had identical relationships (e.g., brother) to more than one current or former general authority, that is counted as only one occurrence of the particular relation. When related men were advanced to the hierarchy simultaneously (e.g., Luke and Lyman Johnson in 1835), their separate relationships to each other are counted separately. In other words, the advancement of the Johnson brothers to the hierarchy is counted here as two incidents of the brother relationship of new appointees. On the other hand, the advancement of Joseph F. Smith to the hierarchy in 1866 is counted as only one relationship of brother, since his brother was already a general authority. Joseph Smith, Jr. is excluded from these calculations because he was LDS president before the hierarchy existed.

19. J. Golden Kimball diary, 9 Oct. 1898, 10 Dec. 1903, Marriott Library.

20. Oliver Cowdery to Brigham Young, 27 Feb. 1848, in Gunn, *Oliver Cowdery*, 268-69; for explanation of Cowdery's "deep mortification" concerning William Smith's apostleship, see Quinn, *Mormon Hierarchy: Origins of Power*, 219-24.

21. Brigham Young, Jr., diary, 28 Sept., 30 Sept., 5 Oct. 1897, LDS archives.

22. Cowdery to Young, in Gunn, *Oliver Cowdery*, 268.

23. Brigham Young, Jr., diary, 5 Apr. 1900; also Davis Bitton, "The Ordeal of Brigham Young, Jr.," in Bitton, *The Ritualization of Mormon History and Other Essays* (Urbana: University of Illinois Press, 1994), 141-42.

24. Abraham H. Cannon diary, 7 Oct. 1889, Department of Special Collections and Manuscripts, Harold B. Lee Library, Brigham Young University, Provo, Utah (hereafter Lee Library), with photocopies in Marriott Library and in Utah State Historical Society, Salt Lake City.

25. Brigham Young, Jr., diary, 5 Oct. 1898.

26. J. Golden Kimball diary, 2 July 1899.

27. John Henry Smith diary, 24 Oct. 1901, 6 Oct. 1903, in White, *Church, State, and Politics*, 497, 526.

28. Heber J. Grant journal sheets, 30 Mar., 1 Apr. 1932, 23 Mar. 1933, LDS archives; minutes of the First Presidency and Quorum of the Twelve Apostles, 7 Apr. 1932, excerpt in LDS archives; Heber J. Grant to J. Reuben Clark, 4 Nov. 1934, fd 2, box 352, Clark papers, Lee Library; Francis M. Gibbons, *Heber J. Grant: Man of Steel, Prophet of God* (Salt Lake City: Deseret Book Co., 1979), 33, 225. While "diary" is the standardized term I use to identify personal documents with daily entries, Grant kept several different kinds of such records, which must be identified separately in order to locate the quotations.

29. *Webster's Third New International Dictionary of the English Language, Unabridged* (Springfield, MA: G. & C. Merriam Co., 1968), 1518.

30. John Henry Smith diary, 24 Oct. 1901, in White, *Church, State, and Politics*, 497.

31. J. Golden Kimball diary, 24 Oct. 1901, 4-6 Oct. 1903.

32. Joseph E. Robinson diary, 6 Oct. 1903, LDS archives.

33. William H. Smart diary, 10 Apr. 1910, Marriott Library.

34. Joseph Fielding Smith, Jr., and John J. Stewart, *The Life of Joseph Fielding Smith: Tenth President of The Church of Jesus Christ of Latter-day Saints* (Salt Lake City: Deseret Book Co., 1972), 176; Francis M. Gibbons, *Joseph Fielding Smith: Gospel Scholar, Prophet of God* (Salt Lake City: Deseret Book Co., 1992), 174.

35. John Henry Smith diary, 4 Oct. 1903, in White, *Church, State, and Politics*, 526.

36. Church Historian's office journal, June-Dec. 1859 Book, 283-84 (23 Oct. 1859), LDS archives, with copy in fd 9, box 11, Moorman papers.

37. *History of the Church*, 2:195-97; chap. 1

38. "The Law of Adoption," *Deseret Evening News*, 14 Apr. 1894, 9.

39. Gordon Irving, "The Law of Adoption: One Phase of the Development of the Mormon Concept of Salvation, 1830-1900," *Brigham Young University Studies* 15 (Spring 1974): 291-314; Juanita Brooks, *John Doyle Lee, Zealot-Pioneer Builder-Scapegoat* (Glendale, CA: Arthur H. Clark Co., 1961), 73-74, 121-22. When he was adopted to Apostle Willard Richards, Thomas Bullock recorded that he changed his "name to Thomas Bullock Richards." See Thomas Bullock Apr. 1845-Feb. 1846 diary (25 Jan. 1846), LDS archives, and Greg R. Knight, ed., *Thomas Bullock Nauvoo Journal* (Orem, UT: Grandin Book Co., 1994), 44-45. However, within two years this name-adoption practice ended, and men such as Lee and Bullock stopped referring to themselves by their adopted surnames.

40. Nauvoo Temple Book of Adoptions and Sealings of Parents to Children (11 Jan.-3 Feb. 1846), 26, LDS archives, with copy in box 129, H. Michael Marquardt papers, Marriott Library; computerized Ancestral File for Brigham Young and Albert P. Rockwood, Family History Library, Church of Jesus Christ of Latter-day Saints, Salt Lake City, Utah (hereafter LDS Ancestral File and LDS Family History Library).

41. Nauvoo Temple Book of Adoptions; George Teasdale diary, 1 Mar. 1881, microfilm, Marriott Library; Anthon H. Lund diary, 16 Apr. 1893; Gibbons, *Heber J. Grant*, 13; Ronald W. Walker, "Rachel R. Grant: The Continuing Legacy of the Feminine Ideal," *Dialogue: A Journal of Mormon Thought* 15 (Autumn 1982): 109, 111. Use of the term "proxy" in marriage sealings had two meanings. First, a living man became the proxy "for time" in

a literal marriage for a deceased former husband. Any children born to the wife in this proxy marriage were regarded as belonging eternally to the first husband, to whom the woman had been sealed for eternity. That was Grant's situation. Although technically only the living husband served as a proxy, it was common for Mormons to refer to the living woman as "a proxy wife" (J. Golden Kimball diary, 26 Dec. 1896). Second, two living persons (sometimes with no family relationship to each other) served as proxies for a deceased husband and deceased wife in a sealing ordinance of marriage "for eternity." The first type of proxy ordinance established a living relationship between the two persons serving as proxies, while the second type did not. Though far less common, the first type of proxy sealing has continued in the twentieth century. The second type of proxy sealing continues to occur in every temple ordinance of sealing on behalf of deceased couples.

42. *Deseret News 1995-1996 Church Almanac,* for the appointments and brief biographical sketches of these men, whose kinship connections can be determined through the LDS Ancestral File.

43. Sheri L. Dew, *Ezra Taft Benson: A Biography* (Salt Lake City: Deseret Book Co., 1987), 175.

44. Benson Y. Parkinson, *S. Dilworth Young: General Authority, Scouter, Poet* (American Fork, UT: Covenant Communications, 1994), 220.

45. Francis M. Gibbons, *Harold B. Lee: Man of Vision, Prophet of God* (Salt Lake City: Deseret Book Co., 1993), 250, emphasis in original.

46. Bennett, *Saviors on Mount Zion,* 85.

47. *Webster's International Dictionary of the English Language, Unabridged,* s.v. "dynasty."

48. W. W. Phelps to Sally Waterman Phelps, 26 May 1835, 1, Journal History of the Church of Jesus Christ of Latter-day Saints (1830-1972), 246 reels, microfilm, Special Collections, Marriott Library; also quoted in Walter Dean Bowen, "The Versatile W. W. Phelps: Mormon Writer, Educator, and Pioneer," M.S. thesis, Brigham Young University, 1958, 68; W. W. Phelps, "Letter No. 8," *Latter Day Saints' Messenger and Advocate* 1 (June 1835): 130; John Corrill's holographic letter to Margaret Raymond Corrill, 20 July 1835, on the top half of a sheet of paper, the rest of which was used by W. W. Phelps for a holographic letter to his wife Sally, Phelps letters, microfilm 110, item 3, LDS Family History Library. Some authors have cited this same microfilm collection for a letter (allegedly written on 9 Sept. 1835) from Phelps to his wife Sally, where he referred to Joseph Smith's recent preaching and told Mrs. Phelps "thus you will be mine, in this world and in the world to come." This is an important reference for dating Smith's first sermons about eternal marriage, but those quotes are absent from the microfilmed letter of 9 September in which Phelps gave lengthy instructions on her wifely duties, "so that you may know your place and stand in it, beloved, admired and rewarded, in time and in eternity." The alleged quotes are also missing from the microfilmed letters of 11 September and October 1835. When microfilmed, the pages of the correspondence were numbered, and there were missing pages of some letters and page-gaps where entire letters had once been. It is possible that some authors have examined the original Phelps letters and cited this microfilm collection on the assumption that it contained what they examined elsewhere.

49. William Clayton diary, 20 Oct. 1843, in George D. Smith, ed., *An Intimate Chronicle: The Journals of William Clayton* (Salt Lake City: Signature Books/Smith Research Associates, 1991), 122-23; *History of the Church,* 6:60; Jason W. Briggs testimony in *Complainant's Abstract of Pleading and Evidence, In the Circuit Court of the United States, Western District of Missouri, Western Division at Kansas City: The Reorganized Church of Jesus Christ of Latter Day Saints, Complainant, vs. The Church of Christ at Independence, Missouri* [often informally titled "Temple Lot Case"] (Lamoni, IA: Herald Publishing House, 1893), 399; Robert Bruce Flanders, *Nauvoo: Kingdom on the Mississippi* (Urbana: University of Illinois Press, 1965),

267-68; Andrew F. Ehat, "Joseph Smith's Introduction of Temple Ordinances and the 1844 Mormon Succession Question," M.A. thesis, Brigham Young University, 1982, 61-63.

50. D&C 27:6, 77:9, 14, 86:10, 132:40, 45; Joseph Fielding Smith, *The Restoration of All Things* (Salt Lake City: Deseret News Press, 1945); Cory Hinckley Maxwell, "Restoration of All Things," in Ludlow, *Encyclopedia of Mormonism,* 3:1218-19.

51. Jacob 2:30 in *The Book of Mormon,* published at Salt Lake City in various editions, with verse citations (similar to the Bible) according to name of its constituent books.

52. Ezra Booth letter in *Ohio Star* (Ravenna, OH), 8 Dec. 1831, also printed in Eber D. Howe, *Mormonism Unvailed* (Painesville, OH: By the author, 1834), 220. I dislike the sex-object implication of a man "taking" a wife, but I adopt this usage because it was almost universal in nineteenth-century American sources. Mormon polygamous wives frequently used the take-a-wife phrasing in regard to their own marriages. See the upcoming quote by Mary Elizabeth Rollins Lightner.

53. William W. Phelps to Brigham Young, 10 Aug. 1861, LDS archives, with full text published in Fred C. Collier, comp., *Unpublished Revelations of the Prophets and Presidents of the Church of Jesus Christ of Latter-day Saints,* 2 vols. (Salt Lake City: Collier's Publishing Co., 1979-93), 1:57-58; the 1861 letter has been discussed in Donna Hill, *Joseph Smith: The First Mormon* (Garden City, NY: Doubleday, 1977), 340; Lawrence Foster, *Religion and Sexuality: Three American Communal Experiments of the Nineteenth Century* (New York: Oxford University Press, 1981), 134-35, and Richard S. Van Wagoner, *Mormon Polygamy: A History* (Salt Lake City: Signature Books, 1986), 3, 223; Quinn, *Mormon Hierarchy: Origins of Power,* 617.

54. *Journal of Discourses,* 26 vols. (London and Liverpool: Latter-day Saints' Book Depot, 1854-86), 13:192 (O. Pratt/1869).

55. Benjamin F. Johnson to George S. Gibbs, 1903, in Dean R. Zimmerman, ed., *I Knew the Prophets: An Analysis of the Letter of Benjamin F. Johnson to George F. [sic] Gibbs, Reporting Doctrinal Views of Joseph Smith and Brigham Young* (Bountiful, UT: Horizon, 1976), 38; Max H. Parkin, "The Nature and Cause of Internal and External Conflict of the Mormons in Ohio Between 1830 and 1838," M.A. thesis, Brigham Young University, 1966, 163-74; Danel Bachman, "New Light on an Old Hypothesis: The Ohio Origins of the Revelation on Eternal Marriage," *Journal of Mormon History* 5 (1978): 19-32; Van Wagoner, *Mormon Polygamy,* 3-13; Quinn, *Mormon Hierarchy: Origins of Power,* 44-45.

56. Lawrence Foster, "A Little-Known Defense of Polygamy from the Mormon Press in 1842," *Dialogue: A Journal of Mormon Thought* 9 (Winter 1974): 21-34; Danel W. Bachman, "A Study of the Mormon Practice of Plural Marriage Before the Death of Joseph Smith," M.A. thesis, Purdue University, 1975; Foster, *Religion and Sexuality,* 142-80; Van Wagoner, *Mormon Polygamy,* 17-79; Lawrence Foster, *Women, Family, and Utopia: Communal Experiments of the Shakers, the Oneida Community, and the Mormons* (Syracuse, NY: Syracuse University Press, 1991), 123-69; Kathryn M. Daynes, "Family Ties: Belief and Practice in Nauvoo," *John Whitmer Historical Association Journal* 8 (1988): 63-75.

57. Andrew Jenson, "Plural Marriage," *Historical Record* 6 (May 1887): 233-34; Joseph F. Smith, Jr. [Joseph Fielding Smith, who later served as the publicly sustained Church Historian for fifty years], *Blood Atonement and the Origin of Plural Marriage* (Salt Lake City: Deseret News Press, 1905), 81-105, hereafter *Origin of Plural Marriage;* "Individual Record" of the Ancestral File for Joseph Smith (AFN:9KGL-W2), authorized printout obtained from LDS Family History Library, 4 Oct. 1996, which list omits Fanny Alger, Lucinda Pendleton Morgan Harris, Sarah M. Kingsley Cleveland, Flora A. Woodworth, Maria Lawrence, Hannah Ells, and Olive Frost who were in Jenson's list; also see the conservative numbering in Todd Compton, "A Trajectory of Plurality: An Overview of Joseph Smith's Thirty-three Plural Wives," *Dialogue: A Journal of Mormon Thought* 29 (Summer 1996): 1-38; and his *In Sacred Loneliness: The Plural Wives of Joseph Smith* (Salt Lake City: Signature Books, 1997).

58. Fawn M. Brodie, *No Man Knows My History, The Life of Joseph Smith the Mormon Prophet*, 2d ed., rev. (New York: Alfred A. Knopf, 1971), 457-88; Bachman, "Study of the Mormon Practice of Plural Marriage Before the Death of Joseph Smith," 113-15, 333-36; Jerald Tanner and Sandra Tanner, *Joseph Smith and Polygamy* (Salt Lake City: Modern Microfilm Co., n.d.), 41-47; Quinn, *Mormon Hierarchy: Origins of Power*, 587-88; also a slightly lower number (based, in part, on research-in-progress I furnished on request) in George D. Smith, "Nauvoo Roots of Mormon Polygamy, 1841-46: A Preliminary Demographic Report," *Dialogue: A Journal of Mormon Thought* 27 (Spring 1994): 5n14, 13-15, 30, 32-34.

59. Mary E. R. Lightner, remarks at Brigham Young University, 14 Apr. 1905, transcript, 5, Lee Library, also copy signed by Lightner in microfilm reel 3, N. B. Lundwall papers, LDS archives; also quoted in Compton, "Trajectory of Plurality," 16.

60. Josephine Rosetta Fisher statement, 24 Feb. 1915, witnessed by Joseph H. Grant, Andrew Jenson, and I. F. Fisher, LDS archives; also Bachman, "Study of the Mormon Practice of Plural Marriage Before the Death of Joseph Smith," 141-42; Richard S. Van Wagoner, "Mormon Polyandry in Nauvoo," *Dialogue: A Journal of Mormon Thought* 18 (Fall 1985): 67-83, gives an overview but barely mentions Sylvia Sessions Lyon on the last page; Van Wagoner, *Mormon Polygamy*, 41; Quinn, *Mormon Hierarchy: Origins of Power*, 642; Smith, "Nauvoo Roots of Mormon Polygamy," 11; Compton, "Trajectory of Plurality," 17, 29-30, 34.

61. D&C 132; Stanley S. Ivins, "Notes on Mormon Polygamy," *Utah Historical Quarterly* 35 (Fall 1967): 309-21; Kenneth W. Godfrey, "The Coming of the Manifesto," *Dialogue: A Journal of Mormon Thought* 5 (Autumn 1970): 11-25; James E. Smith and Phillip R. Kunz, "Polygyny and Fertility in Nineteenth-Century America," *Population Studies* 30 (September 1976): 465-480; Vicky Burgess-Olson, "Family Structure and Dynamics in Early Mormon Families, 1847-1885," Ph.D. diss., Northwestern University, 1976; Phillip R. Kunz, "One Wife or Several?: A Comparative Study of Late Nineteenth Century Marriage in Utah," in Thomas G. Alexander, ed., *The Mormon People: Their Character and Traditions* (Provo, UT: Brigham Young University Press, 1980), 53-73; Joan Iversen, "Feminist Implications of Mormon Polygyny," and Julie Dunfey, "'Living the Principle' of Plural Marriage: Mormon Women, Utopia, and Female Sexuality in the Nineteenth Century," *Feminist Studies* 10 (Fall 1984): 505-22, 523-36; Kahlile Mehr, "Women's Response to Plural Marriage," Jessie L. Embry and Martha S. Bradley, "Mothers and Daughters in Polygamy," *Dialogue: A Journal of Mormon Thought* 18 (Fall 1985): 84-97, 99-107; Van Wagoner, *Mormon Polygamy*, 1-146; David J. Whittaker, "The Bone in the Throat: Orson Pratt and the Public Announcement of Plural Marriage," *Western Historical Quarterly* 18 (July 1987): 293-314; Jessie L. Embry, *Mormon Polygamous Families: Life in the Principle* (Salt Lake City: University of Utah Press, 1987); Thomas G. Alexander, "The Odyssey of a Latter-day Prophet: Wilford Woodruff and the Manifesto of 1890," *Journal of Mormon History* 17 (1991): 169-206; E. Leo Lyman, "The Political Background of the Woodruff Manifesto," and B. Carmon Hardy, "Self-Blame and the Manifesto," *Dialogue: A Journal of Mormon Thought* 24 (Fall 1991): 21-39, 43-57; Kathryn M. Daynes, "Plural Wives and the Nineteenth-Century Mormon Marriage System: Manti, Utah, 1849-1910," Ph.D. diss., Indiana University, 1991; B. Carmon Hardy, *Solemn Covenant: The Mormon Polygamous Passage* (Urbana: University of Illinois Press, 1992), 1-166; Lola Van Wagenen, "Sister-Wives and Suffragists: Polygamy and the Politics of Woman Suffrage, 1870-1896," Ph.D. diss., New York University, 1994; also chaps. 8-9.

62. For discussion of the prophet's intentions for sons of his first wife Emma Hale Smith to serve in the LDS hierarchy, see Quinn, *Mormon Hierarchy: Origins of Power*, 226-43.

63. LDS Ancestral File.

64. Ivins, "Notes on Mormon Polygamy," 311; Dean L. May, "People on the Mormon Frontier: Kanab's Families of 1874," *Journal of Family History* 1 (Winter 1976): 172; Lowell "Ben" Bennion, "The Incidence of Mormon Polygamy in 1880: Dixie versus Davis Stake,"

Journal of Mormon History 11 (1984): 29-38; Larry M. Logue, *A Sermon in the Desert: Belief and Behavior in Early St. George, Utah* (Urbana: University of Illinois Press, 1988), 50-51; Daynes, "Plural Wives and the Nineteenth-Century Mormon Marriage System," 157, 159; Jessie L. Embry, "Polygamy," in Allan Kent Powell, ed., *Utah History Encyclopedia* (Salt Lake City: University of Utah Press, 1994), 428-29; Dean L. May, *Three Frontiers: Family, Land, and Society in the American West, 1850-1900* (Cambridge, Eng.: Cambridge University Press, 1994), 121.

65. D. Gene Pace, "Wives of Nineteenth Century Mormon Bishops: A Quantitative Analysis," *Journal of the West* 21 (Apr. 1982): 49-57.

66. *Journal of Discourses*, 11:221 (J. Taylor/1866) for Nauvoo statement of Joseph Smith, 1:64 (O. Pratt/1852) for the public announcement.

67. Ivins, "Notes on Mormon Polygamy," 312; Paul H. Peterson, "The Mormon Reformation of 1856-1857: The Rhetoric and the Reality," *Journal of Mormon History* 15 (1989): 71-72; Thomas G. Alexander, "Wilford Woodruff and the Mormon Reformation of 1855-57," *Dialogue: A Journal of Mormon Thought* 25 (Summer 1992): 33-36.

68. *Journal of Discourses*, 20:353, 356 (J. Taylor, 1879); John Taylor, *Revelation Given Through President John Taylor at Salt Lake City, Utah Territory . . .* (Salt Lake City, 1882); Abraham H. Cannon, Journal, 5 Apr. 1884; A. C. Lambert, *The Published Editions of the Book of DOCTRINE AND COVENANTS of the Church of Jesus Christ of Latter-day Saints In All Languages, 1833-1950* (N.p.: By the author, 1950), [3-4, 7]; Collier, *Unpublished Revelations*, 1:138; Van Wagoner, *Mormon Polygamy*, 117-18; Hardy, *Solemn Covenant*, 51.

69. Minutes of the Quorum of the Twelve Apostles, 30 Jan. 1888, LDS archives; Hardy, *Solemn Covenant*, 221, for Taylor's 1888 marriage aboard ship.

70. D. Michael Quinn, "LDS Church Authority and New Plural Marriages, 1890-1904," *Dialogue: A Journal of Mormon Thought* 18 (Spring 1985): 9-105; Hardy, *Solemn Covenant*, 167-319, and 208-209 for Owen Woodruff.

71. David S. Hoopes and Roy Hoopes, *The Making of a Mormon Apostle:The Story of Rudger Clawson* (Lanham, MD: Madison Books, 1990), 68-69, 91, 111, 216-18, 227-28, 279-80.

72. Quinn, "LDS Church Authority and New Plural Marriages," 105; Hardy, *Solemn Covenant*, 291-95, 311-28; Dean C. Jessee, "A Comparative Study and Evaluation of the Latter-day Saint and 'Fundamentalist' Views Pertaining to the Practice of Plural Marriage," M.A. thesis, Brigham Young University, 1959; Jerold A. Hilton, "Polygamy In Utah and Surrounding Area Since the Manifesto of 1890," M.A. thesis, Brigham Young University, 1965; Ken Driggs, "After the Manifesto: Modern Polygamy and Fundamentalist Mormons," *Journal of Church and State* 32 (Spring 1990): 367-89; Ken Driggs, "Fundamentalist Attitudes toward the Church: The Sermons of Leroy S. Johnson," *Dialogue: A Journal of Mormon Thought* 23 (Summer 1990): 39-60; Ken Driggs, "Twentieth-Century Polygamy and Fundamentalist Mormons in Southern Utah," *Dialogue: A Journal of Mormon Thought* 24 (Winter 1991): 44-58; D. Michael Quinn, "Plural Marriage and Mormon Fundamentalism," in Martin E. Marty and R. Scott Appleby, eds., *Fundamentalisms and Society: Reclaiming the Sciences, the Family, and Education*, vol. 2 of the Fundamentalism Project of the American Academy of Arts and Sciences (Chicago: University of Chicago Press, 1993), 240-93; Martha Sonntag Bradley, *Kidnapped From that Land: The Government Raids on the Short Creek Polygamists* (Salt Lake City: University of Utah Press, 1993), 18-39, 182-95; Martha Sonntag Bradley, "Joseph W. Musser: Dissenter or Fearless Crusader for Truth?" in Roger D. Launius and Linda Thatcher, eds., *Differing Visions: Dissenters in Mormon History* (Urbana: University of Illinois Press, 1994), 262-78.

73. I use this qualifier because Orson F. Whitney, appointed an apostle in 1906, had been courting various women as prospective new wives since the mid-1890s. His 1900 proposal as a local bishop to Vilate Peart failed because she had just become the polygamous wife of Hugh J. Cannon, a member of the Sunday School General Board. The First

Presidency's counselor had arranged for Apostle Cowley to perform his son's marriage. If Whitney's polygamous courtships in 1901-1903 resulted in an actual marriage, it was of short duration because the women married other men civilly about the time of Whitney's appointment to the Twelve. As an apostle Whitney jeopardized his church membership by continuing polygamous courtship while his quorum was investigating and excommunicating men for entering into such marriages. Whitney obviously could trust no one to officiate in the polygamous marriage he was contemplating. Therefore, it is uncertain whether cryptic diary entries in December 1910 were describing a mutual covenant of marriage between him and the woman he had been courting for years. In either case, the strains on the relationship caused the woman to end it shortly thereafter. This was the last known instance of Apostle Whitney's polygamous courtships.

74. J. Reuben Clark office diary, 2 Nov. 1943, Lee Library; Joseph Fielding Smith diary, 2 Nov., 4 Nov., 11-12 Nov. 1943, LDS archives; George Albert Smith diary, 9 Nov., 12 Nov. 1943, Marriott Library; George F. Richards diary, 12 Nov. 1943, LDS archives; "Notice of Excommunication," *Deseret Evening News*, 13 Nov. 1943, 1; Richard R. Lyman to Stephen L Richards, 12 Nov. 1949, 10 Apr. 1956, LDS archives; Edward L. Kimball and Andrew E. Kimball, Jr., *Spencer W. Kimball: Twelfth President of the Church of Jesus Christ of Latter-day Saints* (Salt Lake City: Bookcraft, 1977), 209, 346; L. Brent Goates, *Harold B. Lee: Prophet & Seer* (Salt Lake City: Bookcraft, 1985), 183; John R. Sillito, "Enigmatic Apostle: The Excommunication of Richard R. Lyman," paper given at Sunstone Symposium, Salt Lake City, Aug. 1991. For extensive discussion of the 1845 precedent for an authorized solemn covenant of polygamous marriage, see D. Michael Quinn, *Same-Sex Dynamics among Nineteenth-Century Americans: A Mormon Example* (Urbana: University of Illinois Press, 1996), 139-40. Before her relationship with Apostle Lyman, Anna Jacobsen married Victor C. Hegsted polygamously in 1907. Hegsted had already married a polygamous wife in May 1904 (after the Second Manifesto), as described in Julie Hemming Savage, "Hannah Grover Hegsted and Post-Manifesto Plural Marriage," *Dialogue: A Journal of Mormon Thought* 26 (Fall 1993): 102-17, which made no reference to Jacobsen.

75. Larsen, "Familism," 143-49, 155-59; John A. Widtsoe, *Joseph Smith: Seeker After Truth, Prophet of God* (Salt Lake City: Deseret News Press, 1952), 240; Kimball Young, *Isn't One Wife Enough?* (New York: Henry Holt & Co., 1954), 32.

76. Jeffery Ogden Johnson, "Determining and Defining 'Wife': The Brigham Young Households," *Dialogue: A Journal of Mormon Thought* 20 (Fall 1987): 58.

77. Susa Young Gates, "My Father's Wives," typescript, 5, fd 1, box 12, Gates papers, Utah State Historical Society.

78. Augusta Adams Cobb Young to Brigham Young, 2 Feb. 1850, Brigham Young papers, LDS archives.

79. Brooks, *John Doyle Lee*, 380, concerning Abigail Sheffer Woolsey (b. 1785); also Nauvoo Temple record of sealing, LDS Family History Library.

80. Mrs. T. B. H. [Fanny] Stenhouse, *Expose of Polygamy in Utah, A Lady's Life Among the Mormons* (New York: American News Co., 1872), 91-92; Stanley B. Kimball, *Heber C. Kimball: Mormon Patriarch and Pioneer* (Urbana: University of Illinois Press, 1981), 227.

81. Patty Bartlett Sessions holographic 1856-66 diary, LDS archives, entry between 16 June and 17 June 1860, which has a later addition in another person's handwriting of the words "time and all" before the word "Eternity." Brodie, *No Man Knows My History*, 445, and Claire Noall, *Intimate Disciple: A Portrait of Willard Richards, Apostle to Joseph Smith-Cousin of Brigham Young* (Salt Lake City: University of Utah Press, 1957), 611, quoted the edited phrase as if those were original words in the Sessions diary. This change was probably made by a member of the Sessions family before the diary's donation to the old Church Historian's Office or by a CHO staff member after the diary's donation. The apparent purpose of the addition was to defeat the argument of the Reorganized Church of Jesus Christ of Latter Day Saints that any woman "sealed" to Joseph Smith during his

lifetime was for "eternity only" and was not an actual wife. Whoever added the phrase "time and all eternity" did not apparently realize that this revision did more than disprove RLDS claims: the revised diary asserts that as an already married woman, her 1842 sealing allowed sexual intercourse with Joseph Smith.

Although nearly eleven years older than Smith, Patty B. Sessions was passionate in her marriage relationships for another decade. When left to sleep alone while David Sessions was with his plural wife in 1847, she wrote in the morning, "I am so full of grief that there is no room for food and I soon threw it up." Tired of sharing her husband, she left Sessions and became the monogamist wife of another man in 1851. Three years later, at age fifty-nine, Patty Bartlett Sessions Smith Parry "felt betrayed" when her husband married a plural wife. See Susan Sessions Rugh, "Patty B. Sessions," in Vicky Burgess-Olson, ed., *Sister Saints* (Provo, UT: Brigham Young University Press, 1978), 311.

82. Lightner remarks, 7; Mary E. R. Lightner statement, 23 Mar. 1877, original manuscript in Joseph F. Smith papers, LDS archives, also a photocopy in fd 14, box 11, Scott G. Kenney papers, Marriott Library; Mary E. Lightner to John Henry Smith, 25 June 1892, emphasis in original, George A. Smith Family papers, Marriott Library; also Van Wagoner, "Mormon Polyandry in Nauvoo," 77; Van Wagoner, *Mormon Polygamy*, 39-40; Smith, "Nauvoo Roots of Mormon Polygamy," 11; Martha Sonntag Bradley and Mary Brown Firmage Woodward, "Plurality, Patriarchy, and the Priestess: Zina D. H. Young's Nauvoo Marriages," *Journal of Mormon History* 20 (Spring 1994): 84-118; Quinn, *Mormon Hierarchy: Origins of Power*, 587, 607; Compton, "Trajectory of Plurality," 23, 28, for Jacobs, and 19, 30, for the apologetical use of Lightner's "for Eternity" statement.

83. Arrington, *Brigham Young*, 120-21, echoes that view; Mabel Young Sanborn, *Brigham Young's Wives, Children and Grandchildren* (Salt Lake City: By the author, 1940), 2, 4, 10, itemized Augusta Adams, Olive G. Frost, Susan Snively, Ellen Rockwood, Maria Lawrence, Martha Bowker, Namaah K. Carter, and Mary J. Bigelow each as a "wife for eternity only," and Eliza R. Snow as a "wife in name only" because her eternal relationship was with Joseph Smith. Despite identifying only nine wives as having celibate marriages, Sanborn stated (10): "Ten of the above named wives were wives in name only." She intended the tenth as either Ann Eliza Webb (who divorced her father) or the childless Amelia Folsom (who was her father's favorite and "public" wife during his last years). Despite basing her publication on Sanborn's list, Kate B. Carter, "Brigham Young: His Wives and Family," *Our Pioneer Heritage* (Salt Lake City: Daughters of Utah Pioneers, 1958), 409-56, did not accept Sanborn's categories for the above wives, instead simply noting that those wives bore Young no children. Carter's article was reprinted as an undated pamphlet.

84. John J. Stewart, *Brigham Young and His Wives and the True Story of Plural Marriage* (Salt Lake City: Mercury Publishing Co., 1961), began the revisionist trend by documenting fifty-three marriages from official LDS genealogical records; Johnson, "Determining and Defining 'Wife,'" 58, 65-70, acknowledged fifty-five such unions, as did Dean C. Jessee, "Brigham Young's Family: The Wilderness Years," *Brigham Young University Studies* 19 (Summer 1979): 476, although Jessee insisted that most of the lesser-known wives "were married primarily with an 'other-world' spiritual relationship in mind"; Quinn, *Mormon Hierarchy: Origins of Power*, 607-608, lists fifty-six wives, including Maria Lawrence in 1844. Jessee (472n3) and Johnson omitted Maria Lawrence because the Nauvoo temple record shows her 1846 sealing to Almon W. Babbitt, not Young. However, Maria Lawrence was listed as Brigham Young's wife in Susa Young Gates and Mabel Young Sanborn, "Brigham Young Genealogy," *Utah Genealogical and Historical Magazine* 11 (July 1920): 131; Sanborn, *Brigham Young's Wives, Children and Grandchildren*, [4], and Carter, "Brigham Young: His Wives, and Children," 429-30. My research indicates that families may omit polygamous wives, but never invent a marital relationship that did not exist with the father or ancestor. Therefore, I do not agree with Jessee's and Johnson's dismissal of the claim by Brigham Young's own daughters that their father married Maria Lawrence in Nauvoo, even though

the 1846 date is wrong. Also, Maria Lawrence is listed among the thirty-four wives acknowledged in the Individual Record of the Ancestral File for Brigham Young (AFN:3ZDB-KC), authorized printout obtained from LDS Family History Library, 4 Oct. 1996.

I believe that Heber C. Kimball's diary provides a resolution for the conflict between Young family sources and the Nauvoo temple record concerning Maria Lawrence. Johnson noted (60-61) that the diaries of Brigham Young and Heber C. Kimball record several instances in 1844-45 when the two apostles performed polygamous marriages for each other on the same day. My examination of the Young and Kimball diaries shows that sometimes they both mentioned the other's respective new wife, and sometimes each diarist mentioned only his own new wife even though both men married wives to each other on that occasion, and sometimes one diary was silent about a marriage involving one apostle as officiator and the other as new husband. Heber C. Kimball's 1844-1845 diary, 12 Oct. 1844, LDS archives, has a lined-through entry that he was "combined" to two of Joseph Smith's former wives, including "Sarah L." Stanley B. Kimball, ed., *On the Potter's Wheel: The Diaries of Heber C. Kimball* (Salt Lake City: Signature Books/Smith Research Associates, 1987), 90, published the revised entry, but not the lined-through entry. The original 1844 entry obviously referred to Smith's widow Sarah Lawrence, who was resealed to Heber C. Kimball in the Nauvoo Temple in 1846, as were most marriages performed before the temple opened. The Lawrence sisters apparently married Joseph Smith on the same day in 1843. It would have been consistent for Maria Lawrence to be sealed "for time" to Brigham Young on the same occasion he united Sarah and Kimball in a similar proxy marriage in 1844. This would explain why Brigham Young's daughters consistently included Maria Lawrence as one of their father's Nauvoo wives, even though they got the date wrong. The Nauvoo temple record did not show her sealing to Young, because by January 1846 Maria Lawrence chose not to continue her marriage with Young. Instead he allowed her to be sealed in the temple as a proxy wife to Babbitt, by whom she bore a child.

85. As cited above, both Stewart and Johnson provide the exact dates of each wife's sealing/marriage ceremony, while Stewart gives the woman's age and Johnson gives her year of birth; Divorce Certificates (1847-1867), Brigham Young papers, LDS archives; also Eugene E. Campbell and Bruce L. Campbell, "Divorce Among Mormon Polygamists: Extent and Explanations," *Utah Historical Quarterly* 46 (Winter 1978): 4-23.

86. LDS Ancestral File for Brigham Henry Roberts; Truman G. Madsen, *Defender of the Faith: The B.H. Roberts Story* (Salt Lake City: Bookcraft, 1980), 199, 249, 200; Robert Henry Malan, *B.H. Roberts: A Biography* (Salt Lake City: Deseret Book Co., 1966), 42, claimed that Margaret Curtis Shipp (b. 17 Dec. 1849) was thirty-nine when she married Roberts, a year too young even for the April 1890 marriage date claimed by Malan. She actually married Roberts shortly after the church president's September 1890 proclamation publicly ended the possibility of such a marriage.

87. Ellis Reynolds Shipp to "My Beloved Son," 18 Apr. 1892, fd 1, box 3, Shipp papers, Utah State Historical Society; Malan, *B.H. Roberts,* 118; also Madsen, *Defender of the Faith,* 201, noted that Margaret was less physically attractive than Roberts' younger wives. Madsen did not state whether this was his own conclusion based on examination of their photographs or if this was the view of the first two wives and/or their children. Either way, Madsen's comment reflected a bias of someone other than Roberts himself.

88. Related by Salt Lake Stake President Angus M. Cannon in "Statement of an Interview with Joseph Smith, President of the 'Reorganites,' by Elder Angus M. Cannon, Oct. 12*th* 1905," typescript, 23, LDS archives, quoted fully in Compton, "Trajectory of Plurality," 17; also the quoted sentence in Linda King Newell and Valeen Tippetts Avery, *Mormon Enigma: Emma Hale Smith,* 2d ed. (Urbana: University of Illinois Press, 1994), 136.

89. Augusta Cobb Young to Brigham Young, 22 Jan., 20 July 1850, with 24 Mar. 1852 reference to "Emily [D. Partridge Young] who is much in Same condition," Theodore Schroeder papers, Manuscript and Rare Book Division, New York Public Library, New York City, New York; Emily D. Partridge Young diary, 16 Apr. 1874, 1 Feb. 1875, 29 July 1881, typescript, Lee Library; Ann-Eliza Young, *Wife No. 19* . . . (Hartford, CT: Dustin, Gilman, & Co., 1875), 457, 460, 488, 489, 490, 491, 493, 494, 500, 512, 513, 514; Gates, "My Father's Wives," 2, concerning the sexually frustrated "gnawing desire" of Harriet Cook Young; Quinn, *Same-Sex Dynamics among Nineteenth-Century Americans*, 111.

90. "Annie" [pseudonym for Augusta Adams Cobb Young] to "Br Brigham," 11 Mar. 1846, and "Augusta A." to "President B Young," 22 Jan. 1850, Schroeder papers.

91. Unsigned letter to "Beloved Friend," 9 Aug. 1846, filed with "Mary Ann" [Clark Powers] to Brigham Young, 18 June 1851, Brigham Young papers, LDS archives, with spelling corrections.

92. James B. Woodward to Brigham Young, 1 Feb. 1847, and "Mary" [Ellen de la Montague Woodward Young] to "dear B," with notation by Thomas Bullock on back of the letter, "about 1st. August 1851," both in Brigham Young papers, LDS archives.

93. Jenson, "Plural Marriage," 233; Quinn, *Mormon Hierarchy: Origins of Power*, 45, 550, 587; Todd Compton, "Fanny Alger Smith Custer: Mormonism's First Plural Wife?" *Journal of Mormon History* 22 (Spring 1996): 174-207.

94. Joseph Smith revelation to Newel K. Whitney, 27 July 1842, LDS archives, published unofficially in Collier, *Unpublished Revelations*, 1:95-96, and Joseph Smith to Newel K. Whitney, Elizabeth Smith Whitney, "&c." [Sarah Ann Whitney,] 18 Aug. 1842, LDS archives, with transcription and photocopy of holograph in Dean C. Jessee, ed., *The Personal Writings of Joseph Smith* (Salt Lake City: Deseret Book, 1984), 539-42, both of which documents were described (with their history and provenance at the time of being donated to the LDS Church Historian's Office) in Orson F. Whitney to Joseph F. Smith, 1 Apr. 1912, box 1, Whitney papers, Lee Library; also Willard Richards diary, 12 June 1843, transcription of shorthand entry, LDS archives; Joseph Smith, Jr., diary, page following entry for 14 July 1843, LDS archives, with microfilm copies at Lee Library, Utah State Historical Society, and archives, Reorganized Church of Jesus Christ of Latter Day Saints, Independence, Missouri; J. Gibson Divine letter, 24 Mar. 1845, in delayed publication of *Latter Day Saints' Messenger and Advocate* (Pittsburgh) 1 (15 Mar. 1845): 156; Wilford Woodruff's Historian's Private Journal, entry after 1 July 1866; Rhoda Richards affidavit, 1 May 1869 in Plural Marriage Affidavit Book (June-Aug. 1869), 17, and Harriet Cook Young affidavit, 4 Mar. 1870, witnessed by "Fanny Murray Smith," in Plural Marriage Affidavit Book (1870-1903), 12, both in LDS archives as original manuscripts, with copies in fds 17-18, box 21, Linda King Newell papers, Marriott Library; Jenson, "Plural Marriage," 221-40; Smith, *Origin of Plural Marriage*, 83, 86-87, 88, 90-91; Carter, *Brigham Young, His Wives, and Children*, 424-25; Bachman, "Study of the Mormon Practice of Plural Marriage Before the Death of Joseph Smith," 114, 150-53, 334-35; Hill, *Joseph Smith*, 352, 355; Van Wagoner, "Mormon Polyandry in Nauvoo," 78; Lyndon W. Cook, *Joseph C. Kingsbury: A Biography* (Provo, UT: Grandin Book Co., 1985), 75-76; Newell and Avery, *Mormon Enigma*, 125, 137-39, 145-47; also Smith, "Nauvoo Roots of Mormon Polygamy," 14-15, which contains some problems in dating.

95. F. Mark McKiernan, *The Voice of One Crying in the Wilderness: Sidney Rigdon, Religious Reformer, 1793-1876* (Lawrence, KS: Coronado Press, 1971), 115-19; Newell and Avery, *Mormon Enigma*, 111-12; Richard S. Van Wagoner, *Sidney Rigdon: A Portrait of Religious Excess* (Salt Lake City: Signature Books, 1994), 294-97.

96. Sarah M. Kimball, "Auto-Biography," *Women's Exponent* 12 (1 Sept. 1883): 51, fully reprinted in Augusta Joyce Crocheron, *Representative Women of Deseret: A Book of Biographical Sketches* (Salt Lake City: J. C. Graham & Co., 1884), 26; also Jill C. Mulvay, "The Liberal Shall Be Blessed: Sarah M. Kimball," *Utah Historical Quarterly* 44 (Summer 1976): 209; Van Wagoner, "Mormon Polyandry in Nauvoo," 77.

97. Horace Cummings, "Conspiracy of Nauvoo," *Contributor* 5 (Apr. 1884): 254-45; Dr. W. Wyl [Wilhelm Ritter von Wymetal], *Mormon Portraits, or the Truth About the Mormon Founders from 1830 to 1886* (Salt Lake City: Tribune Printing and Publishing Co., 1886), 70-71; Breck England, *The Life and Thought of Orson Pratt* (Salt Lake City: University of Utah Press, 1985), 77, 80-81; Richard S. Van Wagoner, "Sarah M. Pratt: The Shaping of an Apostate," *Dialogue: A Journal of Mormon Thought* 19 (Summer 1986): 71-72, 76-78; Lyndon W. Cook, *William Law: Biographical Essay, Nauvoo Diary, Correspondence, Interview* (Orem, UT: Grandin Book Co., 1994), 26.

98. Brigham Young 1840-1844 diary, 2 Dec. 1843, LDS archives; Orson F. Whitney, *Life of Heber C. Kimball: An Apostle, the Father and Founder of the Britain Mission* (Salt Lake City: The Kimball Family, 1888), 333-35; John M. Whitaker, edited journal, 1, 242, 1 Nov. 1890, Marriott Library; Van Wagoner, "Mormon Polyandry in Nauvoo," 76; my unpublished researchap.

99. *Journal of Discourses*, 2:14 (J. M. Grant/1854).

100. *Journal of Discourses*, 11:207 (A. M. Lyman/1866); Quinn, *Mormon Hierarchy: Origins of Power*, 161, 163, 192, 561-63, for Lyman.

101. Peter Dobkin Hall, "Family Structure and Economic Organization: Massachusetts Merchants, 1700-1850," in Tamara K. Hareven, ed., *Family and Kin in Urban Communities, 1700-1930* (New York: New Viewpoints/Franklin Watts, 1977), 43. Anthropologists use the term "sister exchange" to describe this marriage pattern in various cultures, as in Claude Levi-Strauss, *The Elementary Structures of Kinship*, trans. James Harle Bell and John Richard von Sturmer (Boston: Beacon Press, 1969), 433-34; Mark William Busse, "Sister Exchange among the Wamek of the Middle Fly," Ph.D. diss., University of California at San Diego, 1987.

102. Florence Smith Jacobsen interview, 24 Aug. 1972, 6, LDS archives.

103. Although ten general authorities were released in October 1996, this discussion includes those who served during the first nine months of the year. Except where otherwise noted, all data in this section are contained in the LDS Ancestral File; *Deseret News 1995-1996 Church Almanac* has biographical sketches of all general authorities mentioned here.

104. In order of their marriage dates they were Apostle John W. Taylor (1890), Seventy's president Brigham H. Roberts (1891), Apostle Abraham H. Cannon (1896), LDS president Wilford Woodruff (1897), Apostle George Teasdale (1897), Apostle Matthias F. Cowley (1899), Apostle Abraham Owen Woodruff (1901), Apostle Marriner W. Merrill (1901), Apostle Brigham Young, Jr. (1901), Apostle John W. Taylor (1901, 1901), Apostle Rudger Clawson (1904), Apostle Matthias F. Cowley (1905), and Apostle Richard R. Lyman (1925). The last of these post-Manifesto polygamists to serve in the hierarchy were Apostle Clawson, who died in June 1943, and Apostle Lyman, who was excommunicated in November when the hierarchy discovered his second marital relationship. The above based on my unpublished research; also Hoopes and Hoopes, *Making of a Mormon Apostle*, 68-69, 91, 111, 216-18, 227-28, 279-80; Hardy, *Solemn Covenant*, 206-32, 247.

105. Victor W. Jorgensen and B. Carmon Hardy, "The Taylor-Cowley Affair and the Watershed of Mormon History," *Utah Historical Quarterly* 48 (Winter 1980): 4-36; Kenneth L. Cannon II, "After the Manifesto: Mormon Polygamy, 1890-1906," *Sunstone* 8 (Jan./Apr. 1983): 27-35; James B. Allen and Glen M. Leonard, *The Story of the Latter-day Saints*, 2d ed. rev. (Salt Lake City: Deseret Book Co., 1992), 449; Hardy, *Solemn Covenant*, 262-67, 280n133.

106. In order of their highest positions/seniority and with the dates of their performing polygamous marriage: Joseph F. Smith (1896, also his verified instructions for certain persons to enter or perform polygamous marriages, 1892-1907), Heber J. Grant (1897), Anthon H. Lund (1897-98), John Henry Smith (his verified instructions to perform polygamous marriages, 1897-98), Anthony W. Ivins (1897-1904), Francis M. Lyman (1890, 1894), George Teasdale (1891-96), Marriner W. Merrill (1894-1905), and Rudger Clawson

(1903). Grant, who died in 1945, was the last survivor of these officiators. The above list of post-Manifesto officiators is based on my unpublished research; Hardy, *Solemn Covenant*, 169-70, 206-209, 220, has some references to the above.

107. In alphabetical order, these are their ancestors who married polygamous wives between the Manifesto of September 1890 and the Second Manifesto of April 1904, with year of birth and polygamous marriage indicated: George H. Brimhall (b. 1852, md. ca. 1903), Willard Call (b. 1862, md. 1902), Edward C. Eyring (b. 1868, md. 1903), Heber E. Farr (b. 1875, md. 1904), Winslow Farr (b. 1837, md. 1899), George M. Haws (b. 1858, md. 1900), Philip Hurst (b. 1836, md. 1892), Ben E. Rich (b. 1855, md. two in 1898, one in 1899), Miles P. Romney (b. 1843, md. 1897), Daniel Skousen (b. 1865, md. 1901), Walter W. Steed (b. 1858, md. 1897), John J. Walser (b. 1849, md. 1903), Edward J. Wood (b. 1866, md. 1904), Newell K. Young (b. 1877, md. 1900). Much, but not all, of the above information appears in the partial list of post-Manifesto polygamists and their wives in Hardy, *Solemn Covenant*, following p. 393.

108. In alphabetical order, these are their ancestors who married polygamous wives after the Second Manifesto of 1904, with year of birth and polygamous marriage indicated: Nathan Clayson (b. 1847, md. 1906), John T. Smellie (b. 1863, md. 1905), Walter W. Steed (b. 1858, md. 1918), and Ernest L. Taylor (b. 1852, md. 1910). With some variation in details, all the above marriages except Steed's appear in Hardy, *Solemn Covenant*, 319-20, and appendix following p. 393.

109. Hardy, *Solemn Covenant*, 168, 187, 317, 194n26, for the general pattern; my unpublished research has the details of Macdonald's activities.

110. Quinn, "LDS Church Authority and New Plural Marriages, 1890-1904," 104.

111. Sheri L. Dew, *Go Forward With Faith: The Biography of Gordon B. Hinckley* (Salt Lake City: Deseret Book Co., 1996), 467.

112. Phillip R. Kunz, "Family Organizations," in Ludlow, *Encyclopedia of Mormonism*, 2:497-98; Allen, Embry, and Mehr, *Hearts Turned To The Fathers*, 109, 202-203, 275-76.

113. By this I do *not* mean that every member of the First Presidency is currently related to every member of the Twelve. Appendix 4 shows how each man is related to current and former general authorities, either himself or through his wife. In that total context, 100 percent of the First Presidency and Twelve sustain relationships either to former general authorities or to current general authorities.

114. Abbie Hyde Cowley diary, 28 July 1895, LDS archives; Henry A. Smith, *Matthew Cowley: Man of Faith* (Salt Lake City: Bookcraft, 1954), 31-32.

115. Gibbons, *Joseph Fielding Smith*, 326.

Notes to Chapter Six

1. The standard work on nineteenth-century Mormon economics is Leonard J. Arrington, *Great Basin Kingdom: An Economic History of the Latter-day Saints, 1830-1900* (Cambridge, MA: Harvard University Press, 1958, reprinted in paperback by University of Nebraska Press since 1966). There is no equivalent for the twentieth century. However, as a balance to Arrington's institutional focus, more demographically and econometrically focused studies have appeared in Marvin S. Hill, C. Keith Rooker, and Larry T. Wimmer, "The Kirtland Economy Revisited: A Market Critique of Sectarian Economics," *Brigham Young University Studies* 17 (Summer 1977); Lee Soltow and Dean L. May, "The Distribution of Mormon Wealth and Income in 1857," *Explorations in Economic History* 16 (Apr. 1979): 151-62; James R. Kearl, Clayne T. Pope, and Larry T. Wimmer, "Household Wealth in a Settlement Economy: Utah, 1850-1870," *Journal of Economic History* 40 (Sept. 1980): 477-96.

2. Cornelius Krahn, *Dutch Anabaptism: Origin, Spread, Life, and Thought (1450-1600)* (The Hague: Martinus Nijhoff, 1968); Kennelm Burridge, *New Heaven, New Earth: A Study of Millenarian Activities* (New York: Schocken Books, 1969); Norman Cohn, *The Pursuit of*

the Millennium: Revolutionary Millenarians and Mystical Anarchists of the Middle Ages, rev. ed. (New York: Oxford University Press, 1970); B. S. Capp, *The Fifth Monarchy Men: A Study in Seventeenth-century English Millenarianism* (London: Faber, 1972); Claus-Peter Clasen, *Anabaptism: A Social History, 1525-1618* (Ithaca, NY: Cornell University Press, 1972); Lowell H. Zuck, ed., *Christianity and Revolution: Radical Christian Testimonies, 1520-1650* (Philadelphia: Temple University Press, 1975); James M. Stayer, *Anabaptists and the Sword,* 2d ed. (Lawrence, KS: Coronado Press, 1976); Stephen A. Marini, *Radical Sects of Revolutionary New England* (Cambridge, MA: Harvard University Press, 1982); Lawrence Foster, *Sexuality and Religion: The Shakers, the Mormons, and the Oneida Community* (Urbana: University of Illinois Press, 1984); D. Michael Quinn, "Socio-Religious Radicalism of the Mormon Church: A Parallel to the Anabaptists," in Davis Bitton and Maureen Ursenbach Beecher, eds., *New Views on Mormon History: A Collection of Essays in Honor of Leonard J. Arrington* (Salt Lake City, University of Utah Press, 1987); Abraham Friesen, *Thomas Muentzer, a Destroyer of the Godless: The Making of a Sixteenth-century Religious Revolutionary* (Berkeley: University of California Press, 1990); Michael G. Baylor, trans. and ed., *The Radical Reformation* (Cambridge, Eng.: Cambridge University Press, 1991).

3. Concerning the conflicts caused by these Mormon views in the nineteenth century, see Stephen C. LeSueur, *The 1838 Mormon War in Missouri* (Columbia: University of Missouri Press, 1987); Marvin S. Hill, *Quest for Refuge: The Mormon Flight from American Pluralism* (Salt Lake City: Signature Books, 1989); Kenneth H. Winn, *Exiles in a Land of Liberty: Mormons in America, 1830-1846* (Chapel Hill: University of North Carolina Press, 1989); D. Michael Quinn, *The Mormon Hierarchy: Origins of Power* (Salt Lake City: Signature Books/Smith Research Associates, 1994), 79-141; John E. Hallwas and Roger D. Launius, eds., *Cultures in Conflict: A Documentary History of the Mormon War in Illinois* (Logan: Utah State University Press, 1995); chaps. 7-8.

4. *The Doctrine and Covenants of The Church of Jesus Christ of Latter-day Saints,* published at Salt Lake City in various editions, sec. 29: 34, hereafter cited as D&C with numbers of section and verse(s); Leonard J. Arrington, "Economic History of the Church," in Daniel H. Ludlow, ed., *Encyclopedia of Mormonism: The History, Scripture, Doctrine, and Procedure of the Church of Jesus Christ of Latter-day Saints,* 5 vols. (New York: Macmillan Publishing Co., 1992), 2:435.

5. James R. Clark, ed., *Messages of the First Presidency of The Church of Jesus Christ of Latter-day Saints,* 6 vols. (Salt Lake City: Bookcraft, 1965-71), 4:147-48.

6. Robert Gottlieb and Peter Wiley, *America's Saints: The Rise of Mormon Power* (New York: G. P. Putnam's Sons, 1984), 97, 128.

7. Quinn, *Mormon Hierarchy: Origins of Power,* 13-14, 59-61, 70-72. Except when otherwise indicated, biographical sketches of all general authorities named in this chapter can be found either in the above book or in an appendix of the present volume.

8. Donald Q. Cannon and Lyndon W. Cook, eds., *Far West Record: Minutes of The Church of Jesus Christ of Latter-day Saints, 1830-40* (Salt Lake City: Deseret Book Co., 1983), 131; compare to Howard D. Swainston, "Tithing," in Ludlow, *Encyclopedia of Mormonism,* 4:1481.

9. Arrington, *Great Basin Kingdom,* 134-36, 409.

10. Meeting of seven members of the Quorum of the Twelve Apostles with English immigrant Joseph Fielding at Nauvoo, Illinois, 31 Nov. 1841, minutes, archives, Historical Department, Church of Jesus Christ of Latter-day Saints, Salt Lake City, Utah (hereafter LDS archives); Arrington, *Great Basin Kingdom,* 18, and Swainston, "Tithing," in Ludlow, *Encyclopedia of Mormonism,* 4:1482, overlooked this as a liberalization of the requirement in the 1838 revelation.

11. Joseph Smith et al., *History of the Church of Jesus Christ of Latter-day Saints. Period I: History of Joseph Smith, the Prophet, and . . . Period II: From the Manuscript History of Brigham Young and Other Original Documents,* ed. B. H. Roberts, 7 vols. (Salt Lake City: Church of

Jesus Christ of Latter-day Saints, 1902-32; 2d ed. rev. [Salt Lake City: Deseret Book Co., 1978]), 7:251 (hereafter *History of the Church*). Arrington, *Great Basin Kingdom*, 18, 428n58, overlooked the double-jeopardy dimension of the epistle's tithing requirement.

12. *History of the Church*, 7:358.

13. Heber C. Kimball diary, 29 Jan. 1845, in Stanley B. Kimball, ed., *On the Potter's Wheel: The Diaries of Heber C. Kimball* (Salt Lake City: Signature Books/Smith Research Associates, 1987), 94; Nauvoo Trustee-in-Trust Tithing and Donation Record, 220-222 (29 Jan. 1845), LDS archives. For the term general bishop and its meaning in early LDS history, see *Journal of Discourses*, 26 vols. (Liverpool and London: Latter-day Saints' Book Depot, 1854-86), 22: 34 (O. Pratt/1880); D. Michael Quinn, "Evolution of the Presiding Quorums of the LDS Church," *Journal of Mormon History* 1 (1974): 34; Dale Beecher, "The Office of Bishop," *Dialogue: A Journal of Mormon Thought* 15 (Winter 1982): 103; Quinn, *Mormon Hierarchy: Origins of Power*, 69-71.

14. John E. Page statement at meeting of Strangite high council, Voree, Wisconsin, 6 Apr. 1846, Document 6, James J. Strang Manuscripts, Western Americana, Beinecke Rare Book and Manuscript Library, Yale University, New Haven, Connecticut. For a history of Strang and his schismatic alternative to Brigham Young, see Roger Van Noord, *King of Beaver Island: The Life and Assassination of James Jesse Strang* (Urbana: University of Illinois Press, 1988).

15. Hosea Stout diary, 9 Sept. 1851, in Juanita Brooks, ed., *On the Mormon Frontier: The Diary of Hosea Stout, 1844-1861*, 2 vols. (Salt Lake City: University of Utah Press, 1964), 2:403; Robert J. McCue, "Did the Word of Wisdom Become a Commandment in 1851?" *Dialogue: A Journal of Mormon Thought* 14 (Fall 1981): 66-77. For enforcement of the Word of Wisdom, see Lester E. Bush, Jr., "The Word of Wisdom in Early Nineteenth-Century Perspective," and Thomas G. Alexander, "The Word of Wisdom: From Principle to Requirement," *Dialogue: A Journal of Mormon Thought* 14 (Fall 1981): 46-65, 78-88.

16. "Notice," *Deseret News* [weekly], 26 Oct. 1854, [3]; Bishops' meeting minutes, 28 Oct. 1858, LDS archives. Arrington, *Great Basin Kingdom*, 456n21, argued that excommunication for delinquent tithing was an unfulfilled threat.

17. John D. Lee diary, 25 Jan. 1868, in Robert Glass Cleland and Juanita Brooks, eds., *A Mormon Chronicle: The Diaries of John D. Lee, 1848-1876*, 2 vols. (San Marino, CA: Huntington Library, 1955), 2:96.

18. *Journal of Discourses*, 13:279 (B. Young/1870).

19. Leonard J. Arrington, "The Mormon Tithing House: A Frontier Business Institution," *Business History Review* 28 (Mar. 1954): 29, and Arrington, *Great Basin Kingdom*, 137. Larry M. Logue, *A Sermon in the Desert: Belief and Behavior in Early St. George, Utah* (Urbana: University of Illinois Press, 1988), was a demographic analysis that gave brief discussion of tithing (18, 120).

20. For example, *Journal of Discourses*, 15:308 (O. Hyde/1873), 15:359 (O. Pratt/1873), 16:157 (O. Pratt/1873).

21. *Journal of Discourses*, 19:337 (E. Snow/1878).

22. Brigham Young sermon, 8 Oct. 1875, in "Semi-Annual Conference," *Deseret Evening News*, 9 Oct. 1875, [2].

23. Arrington, *Great Basin Kingdom*, 355.

24. Journal History of the Church of Jesus Christ of Latter-day Saints (1830-1972), 246 microfilm reels, Special Collections, J. Willard Marriott Library, University of Utah, Salt Lake City, Utah (hereafter cited as Marriott Library), 8 Jan. 1881, 5, quoted John Taylor's statement about the lump-sum tithing requirement of Utah "new comers," but did not mention the similar requirement for new converts; George Goddard diary, 8 Jan. 1881, LDS archives, emphasized the lump-sum tithing upon conversion, but did not mention the tithing requirement for new immigrants to Utah; *Journal of Discourses*, 22:5-16 (J. Taylor/1881), was the church president's sermon on 9 January 1881 as an addition to his

"remarks yesterday afternoon, in answer to certain questions which have been put to me in relation to the principle of Tithing." This second sermon did not refer to the obligations of tithing upon baptism or emigration to Zion.

25. Journal History, 8 Jan. 1881, 5; quote from Heber J. Grant diary, 2 Apr. 1881, LDS archives; *Journal of Discourses,* 22:207-208 (Woodruff/1881); Swainston, "Tithing," in Ludlow, *Encyclopedia of Mormonism,* 4:1482. While "diary" is the standardized term I use to identify personal documents with daily entries, Grant kept several different kinds of such records, which must be identified separately in order to locate the quotations.

26. Richard O. Cowan, *The Church in the Twentieth Century* (Salt Lake City: Bookcraft, 1985), 16-17; Richard Edgley and Wilford G. Edling, "Finances of the Church," and Maureen Ursenbach Beecher and Paul Thomas Smith, "Lorenzo Snow," in Ludlow, *Encyclopedia of Mormonism,* 2:508, 3:1370; E. Jay Bell, "The Windows of Heaven Revisited: The 1899 Tithing Revelation," *Journal of Mormon History* 20 (Spring 1994): 45-83.

27. Swainston, "Tithing" in Ludlow, *Encyclopedia of Mormonism,* 4:1481.

28. Presiding Bishopric 1909 cumulative report, 58, LDS archives. Before 1894 the report did not itemize the percentage of tithepayers in the stakes. The PBO did not receive tithing from missions. I calculated those percentages by comparing itemized numbers of tithepayers from 1890 through 1893 with stake membership for those years as contained in *Deseret News 1995-1996 Church Almanac* (Salt Lake City: Deseret News, 1994), 419.

29. Journal History, 29 Mar. 1900, 2.

30. Anthon H. Lund diary, 2 May, 27 June 1901, microfilm, LDS archives, available to all researchers by stipulation of its donor.

31. William H. Smart diary, 5 Apr. 1910, Manuscripts Division, Marriott Library. Smart was a stake president in Utah.

32. Presiding Bishopric Office 1909 cumulative report, 58, 1910 report, 32, 1915 cumulative report, 1916 report, 1924 cumulative report, 1925 report.

33. Presiding Bishopric Office cumulative report for 1915. The rest were "exempt" by reason of being non-wage earning children or adults, impoverished, or full-time missionaries. By this time the PBO reports implied (but did not specifically state) that the itemized figures applied to tithepayers for the stakes only. Each report compared those numbers with the total church membership of stakes and missions. Percentages here consistently reflect the population of the church's stakes and wards, rather than its missions and branches.

34. Neil Morgan, "Utah: How Much Money Hath the Mormon Church?: A million dollars a day . . . what with tithing, real estate and commerce," *Esquire,* Aug. 1962, 86-91.

35. *Condensed Financial Report to the Corporation of the President* (Salt Lake City: LDS Church Financial Department, 12 Apr. 1961) and *Condensed Financial Report to the Corporation of the President* (Salt Lake City: LDS Church Financial Department, 20 Dec. 1962), copies in LDS archives.

36. Morgan, "Utah: How Much Money Hath the Mormon Church?" 90.

37. "Income of Mormon Church Is Put at $4.7 Billion a Year," *New York Times,* 2 July 1991, A-14. The headline amount included income from sources other than tithing.

38. *Condensed Financial Report to the Corporation of the President* [12 Apr. 1961]; *Condensed Financial Report to the Corporation of the President* [20 Dec. 1962]; the 1990 dollar amounts were calculated according to the Consumer Price Index for December 1990, as derived from *Statistical Abstract; Economic Trends: August 1991* (St. Louis: Federal Reserve Bank of St. Louis, Aug. 1991).

39. Don LeFevre's statement in "Income of Mormon Church Is Put at $4.7 Billion a Year," *New York Times,* 2 July 1991, A-14.

40. *History of the Church,* 2:221.

41. Cannon and Cook, *Far West Record,* 131, 187, 188n6.

42. *History of the Church,* 2:273. For examples of frequent *ad hoc* financial appropriations to the First Presidency, see ibid., 4:46, 137-38, 412-13.

43. Irene May Bates, "Transformation of Charisma in the Mormon Church: A History of the Office of Presiding Patriarch, 1833-1979," Ph.D. diss., University of California at Los Angeles, 1991, 302-304; Patriarch John Smith statement in Rudger Clawson diary, 10 July 1902, in Stan Larson, ed., *A Ministry of Meetings: The Apostolic Diaries of Rudger Clawson* (Salt Lake City: Signature Books/Smith Research Associates, 1993), 463.

44. Zadock Knapp Judd reminiscences, photocopy of typescript, 13, Henry E. Huntington Library, San Marino, California.

45. John Smith's 1846-1854 diary and autobiography, 55, LDS archives, with copy in George A. Smith Family papers, Marriott Library.

46. John Taylor to George Q. Cannon, 7 Nov. 1877, in Samuel W. Taylor and Raymond W. Taylor, eds., *The John Taylor Papers: Records of the Last Utah Pioneer,* 2 vols. (Redwood City, CA: Taylor Trust, 1984-85), 2:16; also quoted in Irene M. Bates and E. Gary Smith, *Lost Legacy: The Mormon Office of Presiding Patriarch* (Urbana: University of Illinois Press, 1996), 136.

47. Journal History, 25 Jan. 1899, 2. Elias H. Blackburn's diary referred to performing blessings of healing but made no reference to a gratuity. However, he noted on 10 June 1895, as if it were an exception, his healing administration to a woman with cancer: "I done my part In Administering to her *all for no consideration.*" Emphasis in original at Utah State Historical Society, Salt Lake City, Utah, with copy at Huntington Library.

48. Rudger Clawson diary, 10 July 1902, in Larson, *Ministry of Meetings,* 462-63; Bates and Smith, *Lost Legacy,* 160.

49. First Presidency circular letter, "Suggestions for Stake Patriarchs," 25 May 1943, cited in Bates, "Transformation of Charisma in the Mormon Church: A History of the Office of Presiding Patriarch, 1833-1979," 306.

50. Church Historian's office journal, 13 Jan. 1859, LDS archives, with copy in fd 9, box 11, Donald R. Moorman papers, archives, Donnell and Elizabeth Stewart Library, Weber State University, Ogden, Utah.

51. Brigham Young office journal, 8 Oct. 1860, LDS archives, with copies in fd 2, box 26, Moorman papers, and in fd 1, box 93, H. Michael Marquardt papers, Marriott Library. That quote was deleted from "REMARKS By President BRIGHAM YOUNG, Bowery, October 8, 1860," *Deseret News* [weekly], 28 Nov. 1860, 305, and from *Journal of Discourses,* 8:201 (B. Young/1860).

52. First Council of Seventy minutes, 28 June 1879, LDS archives.

53. Journal History, 7 Apr. 1896, 4; Marriner W. Merrill diary, 2 Apr. 1896, LDS archives, for quote; also Journal History, 2 Apr. 1896, 2-9, for minutes of the meeting which discussed salaries for church officers.

54. Journal History, 30 Dec. 1896, 2; 7 Apr. 1897, 2; 27 Oct. 1898, 3.

55. J. Golden Kimball diary, 19 Feb. 1904, Marriott Library.

56. Presiding Bishopric Office 1910 annual report, 32.

57. George R. Blake to D. Michael Quinn, 7 Aug. 1991. His father Samuel Henry Blake was bishop of Vineyard Ward, Sharon Stake, Utah, from 1920 to 1929.

58. L. John Nuttall's First Presidency office journal, 22 Jan., 25 Jan. 1887, 30 Dec. 1889, LDS archives.

59. Anthon H. Lund diary, 16 May 1901, 2 July 1903.

60. John D. Lee diary, 21 Mar. 1847, in Charles Kelly, ed., *Journals of John D. Lee, 1846-47 and 1859* (Salt Lake City: Western Printing Co., 1938), 129.

61. Scott G. Kenney, ed., *Wilford Woodruff's Journal: 1833-1898 Typescript,* 9 vols. (Murray, UT: Signature Books, 1983-85), 5 (22 Feb. 1859): 294.

62. Salt Lake County assessment books, 1853, 1859-66, Utah State Archives, Salt Lake City; also chart, "Comparative Wealth of the Hierarchy, 1850-1869: Salt Lake County Assessed Property Valuations," in D. Michael Quinn, "The Mormon Hierarchy, 1832-1932: An American Elite," Ph.D. diss., Yale University, 1976, 103, and in Quinn, "From Sacred Grove to Sacral Power Structure," *Dialogue: A Journal of Mormon Thought* 17 (Summer 1984): 27.

63. Kenney, *Wilford Woodruff's Journal,* 6 (22 Dec. 1865): 265.

64. Salt Lake County's 1859 assessment book.

65. Brigham Young 1858-63 office journal, 18 Mar. 1860, 62, LDS archives, with copy in fd 1, box 26, Moorman papers.

66. Brigham H. Roberts, *A Comprehensive History of The Church of Jesus Christ of Latter-day Saints, Century I,* 6 vols. (Salt Lake City: Deseret News Press and "the Church," 1930), 5:443; *Journal of Discourses,* 15:208 (G. Q. Cannon/1872).

67. My unpublished calculations of annual property assessments for all general authorities in Salt Lake County (1850-90), summarized in Quinn, "Mormon Hierarchy, 1832-1932: An American Elite," 110-11, 113-14.

68. George Q. Cannon diary, 17 Jan. 1878, in Joseph J. Cannon, "George Q. Cannon," *Instructor* 80 (June 1945): 259.

69. Joseph F. Smith to Henry W. Naisbitt, 2 Dec. 1877, Quinn's narrative reconstruction of the abbreviated notes in fd 21, box 5, Scott G. Kenney papers, Marriott Library.

70. Joseph F. Smith diary, 3 May 1880, LDS archives, with copy in box 6, Kenney papers; Franklin D. Richards diary, 3 May 1880, LDS archives.

71. Heber J. Grant letterbook-journal, 8 Sept. 1887.

72. Abraham H. Cannon diary, 6 Apr. 1888, Department of Manuscripts and Special Collections, Harold B. Lee Library, Brigham Young University, Provo, Utah (hereafter Lee Library), with copies at Marriott Library and Utah State Historical Society; J. Golden Kimball diary, 5 May 1898.

73. Journal History, 2 Apr. 1896, 3-6; Brigham Young, Jr., diary, 7 Apr. 1896, LDS archives.

74. Heber J. Grant journal sheets, 13 Nov. 1920.

75. Kenney, *Wilford Woodruff's Journal,* 8: 146, 452, for 10 Jan. 1883, 12 Aug. 1887; Heber J. Grant journal, 8 Sept. 1887; Franklin D. Richards diary, 31 Jan. 1888.

76. Records of the Trustee-in-Trust and Corporation of the President, LDS archives.

77. My interviews, 29-30 Aug. 1992, with Alan Blodgett who was the LDS church's Assistant Comptroller (1965-69), Comptroller and Managing Director of the Financial Department (1969-80), and Managing Director of the Investment Department (1980-85).

78. *Journal of Discourses,* 8:202 (B. Young/1860); Wilford Woodruff record of divorces (1889-98), LDS archives.

79. Anthon H. Lund diary, 19 Oct. 1899.

80. Clark, *Messages of the First Presidency,* 6:284.

81. J. Reuben Clark to Otto Norman Olsen, 21 Sept. 1949, Clark papers, Lee Library.

82. F. Burton Howard, *Marion G. Romney: His Life and Faith* (Salt Lake City: Bookcraft, 1988), 165.

83. Francis M. Gibbons, *Harold B. Lee: Man of Vision, Prophet of God* (Salt Lake City: Deseret Book Co., 1993), 148.

84. Table, "Percent of Mean Wealth Growth For New General Authorities, 1860-1889," in Quinn, "Mormon Hierarchy, 1832-1932: An American Elite," 117-18.

85. Francis M. Gibbons, *Joseph Fielding Smith: Gospel Scholar, Prophet of God* (Salt Lake City: Deseret Book Co., 1992), 370; Joseph Fielding Smith estate file #59189, Salt Lake County Probate Court records, Utah State Archives.

86. Lucile C. Tate, *LeGrand Richards: Beloved Apostle* (Salt Lake City: Bookcraft, 1983), 236-37, 255; my interview on 30 Oct. 1992 with Lowell L. Durham, Jr., former president of Deseret Book Company and former president of ZCMI.

87. Gordon B. Hinckley, "Questions and Answers," *Ensign* 15 (Dec. 1985): 50.

88. Estate file #59189; Gibbons, *Joseph Fielding Smith.*

89. "Organizational Chart, 31 Dec. 1995," at end of chap. 4.

90. Newel K. Whitney, "Memo. of Balances Vs. Individuals Balanced 23*d* day of Apl. 1834 without Value Recd. because Joseph said it must be done," Document 113, Newel K. Whitney Family papers, Lee Library.

91. Franklin D. Richards diary, 4 Aug. 1877.

92. Kenney, *Wilford Woodruff's Journal,* 7 (10 Nov. 1880): 604; Joseph F. Smith diary, 10 Nov. 1880. Smith's diary, 17 July 1879, also showed that John Taylor, as president of Zion's Savings Bank and Trust, had the vice-president of the bank destroy two notes for $50,000. I have regarded this as Taylor's personal indebtedness, but Taylor and Taylor, *John Taylor Papers,* 2:22, stated: "Taylor cancelled $50,000 in debts incurred by missionaries, and initiated a policy of paying their return fare from Church funds so that they would not have to 'return with a load of debt upon their shoulders.'" They cited *Journal of Discourses,* 20:47, which was John Taylor's announcement in August 187*8* that he and the apostles "decided to cancel such indebtedness." Since this referred to a debt-cancellation eleven months before the one described in Smith's diary, I am still inclined to view the latter as Taylor's personal debt whose cancellation Smith recorded without explanation as one of the frequent dissents expressed in Smith's diary against Taylor's decisions. However, because of the ambiguity of the evidence, I moved this discussion into this note.

93. W. W. Riter, August W. Carlson, John C. Cutler, and Heber Scowcroft to the First Presidency (Joseph F. Smith, Anthon H. Lund, Charles W. Penrose), 3 Apr. 1911, 14-16; W. W. Riter, John C. Cutler, Joseph S. Wells, H. H. Rolapp, Heber Scowcroft to the First Presidency, 3 Apr. 1912, 30, both in LDS archives.

94. Anthony W. Ivins diary Oct. 1909-May 1910 diary, 4 Jan. 1910, Utah State Historical Society.

95. G. Homer Durham, comp., *Gospel Standards: Selections from the Sermons and Writings of Heber J. Grant, Seventh President of the Church of Jesus Christ of Latter-day Saints* (Salt Lake City: Deseret News, 1942), 59.

96. Legal notices, dated 28 Apr. 1842, of bankruptcy petitions by Joseph Smith, Sidney Rigdon, Hyrum Smith, Vinson Knight, and others, in *THE WASP* (Nauvoo, IL), 7 May 1842, [4], reprinted in issues of 14 May, 21 May, 4 June, 11 June, 26 June 1842.

97. Bankruptcy case 467, U.S. District Court of Utah, Salt Lake City, Utah State Archives; J. Golden Kimball diary, 19 Apr., 15 May 1899.

98. Anthon H. Lund diary, 27 Mar. 1902.

99. Minutes of First Presidency meeting, 27 Dec. 1919, LDS archives.

100. Anthony W. Ivins diary, 4 Sept. 1930.

101. Cannon and Cook, *Far West Record,* 233, Appendix A, also 233.

102. *Journal of Discourses,* 8:201 (B. Young/1860).

103. LDS Church Historian's office journal, 24 Jan. 1878.

104. John Taylor statement in "Fifty-Fourth Annual Conference," *Deseret Evening News,* 7 Apr. 1884, [2]; chaps. 8-9.

105. Journal History, 5 Jan. 1899, 3.

106. *April 1907 Conference Report . . .* (Salt Lake City: Church of Jesus Christ of Latter-day Saints, 1907), 39-40; compare with "The Church Audit Committee Report," *Ensign* 26 (May 1996): 21.

107. *April 1915 Conference Report . . .* (Salt Lake City: Church of Jesus Christ of Latter-day Saints, 1915), 8.

108. Arrington, *Great Basin Kingdom,* 12.

109. Kenney, *Wilford Woodruff's Journal* 6 (7 Oct. 1870): 574; Fred C. Collier, comp., *Unpublished Revelations of the Prophets and Presidents of the Church of Jesus Christ of Latter-day Saints*, 2 vols. (Salt Lake City: Collier's Publishing Co., 1979-93), 1:113.

110. John Taylor revelation, 28 Apr. 1883 in Collier, *Unpublished Revelations*, esp. 1:142; Heber J. Grant letterbook journal, 5 Oct. 1887; Abraham H. Cannon diary, 5 Aug. 1889; Journal History, 27 Apr. 1899, 4; Charles O. Card diary, 10 Feb. 1890, in Donald G. Godfrey and Brigham Y. Card, eds., *The Diaries of Charles Ora Card: The Canadian Years, 1886-1903* (Salt Lake City: University of Utah, 1993), 109-10.

111. Arrington, *Great Basin Kingdom*, 388-89.

112. My unpublished historical sketches of each company; Riter, Cutler, Wells, Rolapp, and Scowcroft to the First Presidency, 3 Apr. 1912, 2-3, provided these categories.

113. Brigham Young, Jr., diary, 30 May 1890.

114. James E. Talmage diary, 14 Jan. 1919, 10 Jan. 1921, Lee Library.

115. George Albert Smith's financial papers, box 110, George A. Smith family papers, Marriott Library.

116. Neil K. Coleman, "A Study of the Church of Jesus Christ of Latter-day Saints as an Administrative System: Its Structure and Maintenance," Ph.D. diss., New York University, 1967, 177, citing documents in the office of the Insurance Department, State of Utah, Salt Lake City.

117. Minutes of meeting of First Presidency and Quorum of the Twelve, 8 Apr. 1943, LDS archives; J. Reuben Clark office diary, 26 May 1943, 3 Feb. 1961; J. Reuben Clark to John A. Widtsoe, 1 May 1946; J. Reuben Clark memorandum of conversation with William F. Edwards, financial secretary to the First Presidency, 22 May 1957, all at Lee Library; D. Michael Quinn, *J. Reuben Clark: The Church Years* (Provo, UT: Brigham Young University Press, 1983), 275.

118. George Q. Cannon, *The Life of Joseph Smith, The Prophet* (Salt Lake City: Juvenile Instructor Office, 1888), 211.

119. *Journal of Discourses*, 10:77-78 (Kimball/1862).

120. Arrington, *Great Basin Kingdom*, 323-34; D. Paul Sampson and Larry T. Wimmer, "The Kirtland Safety Society: The Stock Ledger Book and the Bank Failure," and Scott H. Partridge, "The Failure of the Kirtland Safety Society," and Davis Bitton, "The Waning of Mormon Kirtland," *Brigham Young University Studies* 12 (Summer 1972): 427-36, 437-54, 455-64; Hill, Rooker, and Wimmer, "The Kirtland Economy Revisited: A Market Critique of Sectarian Economics"; Leonard J. Arrington, "Utah and the Depression of the 1890's," *Utah Historical Quarterly* 29 (Jan. 1961): 3-18; Leonard J. Arrington, *From Wilderness To Empire: The Role of Utah in Western Economic History* (Salt Lake City: Institute of American Studies, University of Utah, 1961), 17; Elroy Nelson, *Utah's Economic Patterns* (Salt Lake City: University of Utah Press, 1956), 201-02; Dean L. May, "Towards a Dependent Commonwealth," Thomas G. Alexander, "From War to Depression," and John F. Bluth and Wayne K. Hinton, "The Great Depression," in Richard D. Poll, ed., *Utah's History* (Provo, UT: Brigham Young University Press, 1978), 228, 237-38, 463-69, 472, 481-96; Wayne K. Hinton, "The Economics of Ambivalence: Utah's Depression Experience," *Utah Historical Quarterly* 54 (Summer 1986): 270-71; Brian Q. Cannon, "Struggle against Great Odds: Challenges in Utah's Marginal Agricultural Areas, 1925-39," *Utah Historical Quarterly* 54 (Fall 1986): 308-27.

121. Cowan, *Church in the Twentieth Century*, 15; Edgley and Edling, "Finances of the Church," in Ludlow, *Encyclopedia of Mormonism*, 2:508.

122. Ronald W. Walker, "Crisis in Zion: Heber J. Grant and the Panic of 1893," *Arizona and the West* 21 (Autumn 1979): 257-78, reprinted with less documentation in *Sunstone* 5 (Jan.-Feb. 1980): 26-34.

123. Arrington, *Great Basin Kingdom,* 402; Journal History, 2 Dec. 1898, 2. The church investment of $216,800 appears in Rudger Clawson manuscript diary, 7 Mar. 1899, Marriott Library, which entry is omitted from Larson, *Ministry of Meetings,* 30.

124. Journal History, 8 June 1899, 6.

125. Anthony W. Ivins, "Memoranda Relative to Utah State National Bank," 25 Nov. 1927, fd 5, box 13, Ivins papers, Utah State Historical Society; J. Reuben Clark, "What Has the Utah State National Bank Cost the Church?" 31 Dec. 1932, Clark papers, Lee Library.

126. Anthony W. Ivins diary, 4 Sept. 1930.

127. J. Reuben Clark remarks to presidencies and superintendents of all church auxiliaries, 1 Apr. 1940, Clark papers, Lee Library; also his less detailed reference in *April 1940 Conference Report...* (Salt Lake City: Church of Jesus Christ of Latter-day Saints, 1940), 14. In Clark's office diary for 23 January 1939, he confided to Brigham Young University's president that the church had spent "between $800,000 and $900,000 more than our revenues . . ."; also Quinn, *J. Reuben Clark,* 272. Ronald W. Walker and Richard W. Sadler are clearly wrong in their assertion that the "Church never again resorted to deficit spending [after the 1890s], not even during the Great Depression." See their "History of the Church: 1898-1945, Transitions: Early-Twentieth-Century Period," in Ludlow, *Encyclopedia of Mormonism,* 2:630.

128. J. Reuben Clark memorandum, 21 Sept. 1956, Clark papers, Lee Library.

129. *April 1959 Conference Report . . .* (Salt Lake City: Church of Jesus Christ of Latter-day Saints, 1959), 91-92.

130. Ernest L. Wilkinson diary, 4 Dec. 1959, Marriott Library; *Condensed Financial Report to the Corporation of the President* [12 Apr. 1961] for summary from 1950 to 1960. The above diary entry said that the Budget Committee announced "the Church last year had spent $8,000,000 in excess of its income," which leaves the impression that he referred to 1958. However, the Financial Department reports show that deficit in 1959, which means Wilkinson's diary reference to "last year" referred to the year which was just ending in December 1959.

131. L. Brent Goates, *Harold B. Lee: Prophet & Seer* (Salt Lake City: Bookcraft, 1985), 381.

132. *Condensed Financial Report to the Corporation of the President* [20 Dec. 1962]; Goates, *Harold B. Lee,* 382.

133. Gottlieb and Wiley, *America's Saints,* 101-02, 135; Ernest L. Wilkinson diary, 6 Mar. 1963.

134. G. Homer Durham et al., *N. Eldon Tanner: His Life and Service* (Salt Lake City: Deseret Book Co., 1982), 208.

135. Ibid., 257: "He was noted for being the guiding genius behind Church investments and finances," also 208-209, for quotes.

136. Ernest L. Wilkinson diary, 29 Mar. 1966.

137. Ibid., 6 Jan., 3 Feb. 1965, 16 Apr. 1969.

138. Alan Blodgett interviews, 29-30 Aug. 1992.

139. Those "financial controls" are summarized by Edgley and Edling, "Finances of the Church," in Ludlow, *Encyclopedia of Mormonism,* 2:509.

140. "Ward Teachers' Message for June, 1945," *Improvement Era* 48 (June 1945): 354. In his negative review of Anson D. Shupe's polemic, *The Darker Side of Virtue: Corruption, Scandal, and the Mormon Empire,* Mormon sociologist Armand L. Mauss criticized Shupe's use of this 1945 ward teaching message, "without mentioning that the president of the Church immediately repudiated it." See Mauss, "The Darker Side of Scholarship," *Sunstone* 15 (Nov. 1991): 54. Mauss was referring to the letter George Albert Smith wrote to Unitarian minister, J. Raymond Cope, 7 Dec. 1945, in part, "the passage quoted *does not express* the true position of the Church," as published in "A 1945 Perspective," *Dialogue: A Journal of Mormon Thought* 19 (Spring 1986): 38. However, President Smith's conciliatory view was in

a private letter to a Protestant minister, while the general church membership received no such information from the *Improvement Era* or any of the general conference addresses George Albert Smith gave from 1945 to his death in 1951. Therefore, contrary to Mauss, it is legitimate for Shupe and anyone else to regard this 1945 statement ("when our leaders speak, the thinking has been done") as officially published and unretracted by LDS church headquarters. The 1945 statement has been expressed in a variety of ways by general authorities during the last two decades, including the version by First Presidency counselor N. Eldon Tanner, widely regarded as a liberal: "When the prophet speaks the debate is over." See Tanner, "The Debate Is Over," *Ensign* 9 (Aug. 1979): 2. This was an extended endorsement of an earlier statement ("When the prophet speaks, sisters, the debate is over") originally made by Elaine Cannon, Young Women's general president, in "If We Want to Go Up, We Have to Get On," *Ensign* 8 (Nov. 1978): 108; see chap. 10.

141. "First Presidency Amends Policy on Corporations," *Deseret News "Church News,"* 7 June 1975, 14; *Deseret News 1995-1996 Church Almanac,* 420.

142. "LDS General Authorities To Withdraw From Boards," *Deseret News,* 18 Jan. 1996, B-1. For the financial role of the bishopric, see Quinn, *Mormon Hierarchy: Origins of Power,* 69-76.

143. "Latter-Day Saints: Leaders of Mormonism Double as Overseers of a Financial Empire," *Wall Street Journal,* 9 Nov. 1983, 1.

144. Annual reports of individual corporations, Lt. Governor's office, Utah State, Salt Lake City; *Best's Insurance Reports, Life-Health, 1984* (Oldwick, NJ: A. M. Best Co., 1984); *Best's Insurance Reports, Property-Casualty, 1984* (Oldwick, NJ: A. M. Best Co., 1984); *Billion Dollar Directory, 1983* (Parsippany, NJ: Dun's Marketing Services, 1983); *Directory of Corporate Affiliations, 1984: "Who Owns Whom"* (Wilmette, IL: National Register Publishing Co./Macmillan, 1984); *Million Dollar Directory, 1984* (Parsippany, NJ: Dun & Bradstreet Corporation, 1984); *Moody's Bank and Finance Manual, 1984* (New York: Moody's Investors Service/Dun & Bradstreet Corporation, 1984); *Moody's Transportation Manual, 1984* (New York: Moody's Investors Service/Dun & Bradstreet Corporation, 1984); *Rand McNally International Banker's Directory, 1984,* 2 vols. (Chicago: Rand McNally & Co., 1984); *Reference Book of Corporate Managements: 1984, America's Corporate Leaders* (New York: Dun & Bradstreet, 1983); *Standard & Poor's Register of Corporations, Directors and Executives, 1984,* 2 vols. (New York: Standard & Poor's Corporation, 1984); *Walker's Manual of Western Corporations, 1984,* 2 vols. (Garden Grove, CA: Walker's Manual, Inc., Nov. 1983); *Who's Who in America, 1984-1985,* 2 vols. (Chicago: Marquis Who's Who, Inc., 1984); *Who's Who in the West, 1984-85* (Chicago: Marquis Who's Who, Inc., 1983).

145. Gibbons, *Joseph Fielding Smith,* 201.

146. Sheri L. Dew, *Go Forward With Faith: The Biography of Gordon B. Hinckley* (Salt Lake City: Deseret Book Co., 1996), 304 (first quoted phrase), 303 (second) 304 (third).

147. *Who's Who in America, 1984-1985,* 2:2306, for Apostle Thomas S. Monson who became a counselor in the First Presidency a year after this was published. As indicated above, this entry did not list all of his corporate responsibilities.

148. Gottlieb and Wiley, *America's Saints,* 108. Their source was Alan Blodgett, managing director of the LDS church's Financial Department (1969-80) and managing director of the Investment Department (1980-85), who made similar statements to me during interviews on 29-30 Aug. 1992.

149. J. Reuben Clark office diary, 12 June 1948; David O. McKay office diary, 22 Dec. 1960, LDS archives; Quinn, *J. Reuben Clark,* 106-07; Quinn, "From Sacred Grove to Sacral Power Structure," 30; chap. 4.

150. Marvin S. Hill, "Quest for Refuge: An Hypothesis as to the Social Origins and Nature of the Mormon Political Kingdom," *Journal of Mormon History* 2 (1975): 3-20; also his more recent book *Quest for Refuge,* previously cited.

151. For extensive discussion of these characteristics, see Arrington, *Great Basin Kingdom;* Hill, Rooker, and Wimmer, "Kirtland Economy Revisited: A Market Critique of Sectarian Economics"; Quinn, *Mormon Hierarchy: Origins of Power,* 79-103, 105-41; see also chaps. 7-8.

152. *Mormon Inc.: Finances & Faith: A Series About the Church of Jesus Christ of Latter-day Saints that Appeared in THE ARIZONA REPUBLIC, June 30-July 3, 1991* (Phoenix: Series Reprint, The Arizona Republic, 1991), 4-5, identified the location, number of employees, and annual income for most of the following corporations (listed alphabetically here, with Salt Lake City locations abbreviated as SLC and with locations deleted if in the company's name): Agri-Northwest (Washington state), Applied Technology Group (SLC), Beehive Clothing (SLC), Beneficial Development Co. (SLC), Beneficial Life Insurance Co. (SLC), BLIC Agency (SLC), Bluestem Co. (Oklahoma), Bonneville Broadcasting System (SLC), Bonneville Entertainment (SLC), Bonneville Holding Co. (SLC), Bonneville International Corp. (SLC), Bonneville Media Communication (SLC), Brigham Young University (Provo, Utah), Brown & Co. (SLC), BYU-Hawaii (Laie, Oahu), Columbia Ridge Farms (Tri-Cities, Washington), Continental Western Life Insurance Co. (Des Moines, Iowa), Corporation of the President (SLC), Corporation of the Presiding Bishop (SLC), Cultural Centers Properties, Inc. (Oahu, Hawaii), Descal & Co. (California), Desco & Co. (Colorado), Deseret Book Co. (SLC), Deseret Farms (SLC), Deseret Farms of California, Deseret Grain ("nationwide"), Deseret Gymnasium (SLC), Deseret Industries (SLC and "national, similar to Goodwill Industries"), Deseret International Charities (SLC), Deseret Land and Livestock Co. (Utah and Wyoming), Deseret Management (SLC), Deseret Mutual Insurance Corp. (SLC), Deseret News Publishing Corp. (SLC), Deseret Ranches of Florida (Orlando), Deseret Ranches of Wyoming (Cody), Deseret Transportation (SLC), Deseret Trust (SLC), Deseret Trust of California (Los Angeles), Eagle Gate Apartments (SLC), Elberta Farms (Provo, Utah), Eleven Bar Ranch (Nephi, Utah), Farm Management Co. (SLC), Foreign Lands Corp. (SLC), Garrison Welfare Farm (Garrison, Utah), Genealogical Society of Utah (SLC), Grain Handling, Inc. (Washington state), Hotel Temple Square Corp. (SLC), Islands Foundation (Oahu, Hawaii), KAAM-AM (Dallas), KBIG-Radio (Los Angeles), KBYU-FM and KBYU-TV (Provo, Utah), Keystone Communications (SLC), KIRO-AM and KIRO-TV (Seattle), KMBZ-Radio (Kansas City), KMEO-Radio (Phoenix), KOIT-Radio (San Francisco), KRIC-Radio (Ricks, Idaho), KSEA-FM (Seattle), KSL-Radio and KSL-TV (SLC), K2H Farms, Inc. (Washington state), KZPS-FM (Dallas), Laie Resorts (Oahu, Hawaii), LDS Business College (SLC), LDS Foundation (SLC), LDS Social Services (SLC), LDS Social Services of Massachusetts, LDS Social Services of New York, LDS Social Services of Virginia, Mormon Temples (SLC), Magnolia Management Corp. (Orlando, Florida), Mormon Handicraft (SLC), Mortgage Loan Services (SLC), Nauvoo Restoration (Illinois), Newspaper Agency Corp. (SLC), Office Management of Utah (SLC), Pacific Heritage Life Insurance Co. (Portland, Oregon), Polynesian Cultural Center (Laie, Oahu, Hawaii), Promised Valley Playhouse (SLC), Property Reserve of Arizona, Proprietary Holding, Inc. (SLC), Ricks College (Rexburg, Idaho), Salt Lake Macaroni & Noodle Co., Shadow Mountain Press (SLC), Sooner Land & Livestock Co. (Oklahoma, Nebraska, and Kansas), Third Avenue Productions (Seattle), Utah Home Fire Insurance Co. (SLC), Video West Network (SLC), Western American Life Insurance Co. (SLC), WNSR-FM (New York City), WTMX-Radio (Chicago), ZCMI (SLC and national), Zion's Securities Corp (SLC).

153. Reprinted in "Church at Fortune 500 Level," *Salt Lake Tribune,* 30 June 1991, A-4, A-5; see also Ludlow, *Encyclopedia of Mormonism,* for articles on Business, Broadcasting, Bonneville International Corporation, Deseret Book Company, Deseret Industries, Deseret News, Distribution Centers, Farms Management Corporation, Hospitals, KSL, and LDS Foundation.

154. For example, Sheri L. Dew, *Ezra Taft Benson: A Biography* (Salt Lake City: Deseret Book Co., 1987), 416, noted that Temple View Farms controls "the Church's properties in Hamilton, New Zealand." Aside from Antarctica, I excluded Africa because I have not yet heard of the church having established holding companies on that continent. That will undoubtedly occur eventually.

155. James B. Allen, "On Becoming a Universal Church: Some Historical Perspectives," *Dialogue: A Journal of Mormon Thought* 25 (Spring/Mar. 1992): 14, "a kind of cultural imperialism"; also Sterling M. McMurrin, "Problems in Universalizing Mormonism," *Sunstone* 4 (Dec. 1979): 14-17; LaMond Tullis, "The Church Moves Outside the United States," and Jiro Numano, "How International Is the Church in Japan?" *Dialogue: A Journal of Mormon Thought* 13 (Spring 1980): 67-70, 87; Murray Boren, "Worship Through Music: Nigerian Style," *Sunstone* 10 (May 1985): 64-65; Garth N. Jones, "Spiritual Searchings: The Church On Its International Mission," *Dialogue: A Journal of Mormon Thought* 20 (Summer 1987): 64-66; F. LaMond Tullis, *Mormons In Mexico: The Dynamics of Faith and Culture* (Logan: Utah State University Press, 1987), 202-04; David Knowlton, "Missionaries and Terror: The Assassination of Two Elders In Bolivia," *Sunstone* 13 (Aug. 1989): 10-11, 13-14; Michael Hicks, *Mormonism and Music: A History* (Urbana: University of Illinois Press, 1989), 221-22; David Martin, *Tongues of Fire: The Explosion of Protestantism in Latin America* (Oxford, Eng.: Basil Blackwood, 1990), 208-209; Marjorie Newton, "'Almost Like Us': The American Socialization of Australian Converts," *Dialogue: A Journal of Mormon Thought* 24 (Fall 1991): 9-20; David Knowlton, "Thoughts on Mormonism in Latin America," *Dialogue: A Journal of Mormon Thought* 25 (Summer 1992): 42-43; Lawrence A. Young, "Confronting Turbulent Environments: Issues in the Organizational Growth and Globalization of Mormonism," in Marie Cornwall, Tim B. Heaton, and Lawrence A. Young, eds., *Contemporary Mormonism: Social Science Perspectives* (Urbana: University of Illinois Press, 1994), 50-56; Marjorie Newton, "Towards 2000: Mormonism in Australia," Ian G. Barber and David Gilgen, "Between Covenant and Treaty: The LDS Future in New Zealand," Jiro Numano, "Mormonism in Modern Japan," and Armand L. Mauss, "Mormonism in the Twenty-first Century: Marketing for Miracles," *Dialogue: A Journal of Mormon Thought* 29 (Spring 1996): 195-96, 214-16, 219-20, 230-32, 241-42, 245-48; J. Michael Cleverly, "Mormonism on the Big Mac Standard," *Dialogue: A Journal of Mormon Thought* 29 (Summer 1996): 72-73.

Notes to Chapter Seven

1. William Jarman, *U.S.A. Uncle Sam's Abscess, or, Hell Upon the Earth for U.S. Uncle Sam* (Exeter, Eng.: H. Leduc's Steam Printing Works, 1884); also J. H. Beadle, "The Mormon Theocracy," *Scribner's Monthly* 14 (July 1877): 391-97; M. Paul Holsinger, "Senator George Graham Vest and the 'Menace' of Mormonism," *Missouri Historical Review* 65 (Oct. 1970): 23-36.

2. George Q. Cannon diary, 17 Jan. 1878, in Joseph J. Cannon, "George Q. Cannon," *Instructor* 80 (June 1945): 259. Except when otherwise indicated, biographical sketches of all general authorities named in this chapter can be found either in an appendix of the present volume or in D. Michael Quinn, *The Mormon Hierarchy: Origins of Power* (Salt Lake City: Signature Books/Smith Research Associates, 1994).

3. Quinn, *Mormon Hierarchy: Origins of Power,* 173-76, 192-98.

4. Richard E. Bennett, *Mormons at the Missouri, 1846-1852: "And Should We Die"* (Norman: University of Oklahoma Press, 1987), 232.

5. Quinn, *Mormon Hierarchy: Origins of Power,* 138-39.

6. William Clayton diary, 7 Aug., 8 Sept. 1844, in George D. Smith, ed., *An Intimate Chronicle: The Journals of William Clayton* (Salt Lake City: Signature Books/Smith Research Associates, 1991), 141, 148; Quinn, *Mormon Hierarchy: Origins of Power,* 195, 525, 659; Richard S. Van Wagoner, *Sidney Rigdon: A Portrait of Religious Excess* (Salt Lake City:

Signature Books, 1994), 338-39, 354-57, 362n30, 385n43, 388. Joseph Smith et al., *History of The Church of Jesus Christ of Latter-day Saints. Period I: History of Joseph Smith the Prophet, and . . . Period II: From the Manuscript History of Brigham Young and Other Original Documents,* ed. B. H. Roberts, 7 vols. (Salt Lake City: Church of Jesus Christ of Latter-day Saints, 1902-32; 2d ed. rev. [Salt Lake City: Deseret Book Co., 1978]), 7:269 (hereafter *History of the Church*), deletes reference to the excommunication and disfellowshipping of Samuel James and Rigdon's other followers.

    7. *History of the Church,* 7:213.

    8. William Clayton diary, 30 June, 19 Dec. 1844, in Smith, *An Intimate Chronicle,* 136, 152; *History of the Church,* 7:159; John Hardy, *Startling developments . . . or Two Mormon apostles exposed, in practising the spiritual wife system in Boston* (Boston: Conway and Company, 1844), 3, 4, 9; Wilford Woodruff to Brigham Young, 9 Oct., 3 Dec. 1844, archives, Historical Department, Church of Jesus Christ of Latter-day Saints, Salt Lake City, Utah (hereafter LDS archives); Quinn, *Mormon Hierarchy: Origins of Power,* 228, 232.

    9. William Clayton diary, 27 Aug. 1844, in Smith, *An Intimate Chronicle,* 146; also Valeen Tippets Avery and Linda King Newell, "The Lion and the Lady: Brigham Young and Emma Smith," *Utah Historical Quarterly* 48 (Winter 1980): 81-97; Quinn, *Mormon Hierarchy: Origins of Power,* 151-52, 157-60, 170, 173.

    10. *History of the Church,* 6:269-70, 377-78, 383-84; John A. Forgeus to Samuel L. Forgeus, 22 Sept. 1844, in *Latter Day Saint's Messenger and Advocate* (Pittsburgh) 1 (15 Oct. 1844): 5; Dale L. Morgan, ed., "The Reminiscences of James Holt: A Narrative of the Emmett Company," *Utah Historical Quarterly* 23 (Jan. 1955): 7n16, "This was the Council of the Fifty Princes of the Kingdom of God, organized in Nauvoo, in March, 1844, as not least among the astonishing developments of that winter"; William G. Hartley, *My Best for the Kingdom: History and Autobiography of John Lowe Butler, a Mormon Frontiersman* (Salt Lake City: Aspen Books, 1993), 137-45; Quinn, *Mormon Hierarchy: Origins of Power,* 197-200.

    11. *History of the Church,* 6:71, 149; 7:350.

    12. Ibid., 7:370. The newly elected, non-Fifty municipal officers were Daniel Spencer, George W. Harris, David Fullmer, John Pack, Jonathan C. Wright, Phineas Richards, James Sloan, and Edward Hunter. Richards entered the Fifty in December 1848, Hunter in January 1867, while Harris, Wright, and Sloan never did. See appendix, "Appointments To the Theocratic Council of Fifty Through 1884."

    13. Thus a recently published and revised analysis is still an overstatement: "Under his practical leadership [after 1844], the Council of Fifty assumed the responsibility of directing both the politics and administration of the government of Nauvoo." See Klaus J. Hansen, "The Political Kingdom of God as a Cause of Mormon-Gentile Conflict," in Roger D. Launius and John E. Hallwas, eds., *Kingdom on the Mississippi Revisited: Nauvoo in Mormon History* (Urbana: University of Illinois Press, 1996), 69.

    14. William Clayton diary, 4 Feb. 1845, in Smith, *An Intimate Chronicle,* 157.

    15. Quinn, *Mormon Hierarchy: Origins of Power,* 229-32.

    16. In Andrew F. Ehat, "'It Seems Like Heaven Began on Earth': Joseph Smith and the Constitution of the Kingdom of God," *Brigham Young University Studies* 20 (Spring 1980): 260-61, the first and last "Rules of the Kingdom" state the necessity of the LDS church president being the Council of Fifty's standing chair. However, there is no evidence that this succession was stated as a necessity before Young's ascendance. Ehat derived the "rules" regarding the standing chair from Council of Fifty minutes and references dating after the spring of 1844.

    17. William Clayton diary, 4 Feb. 1845, in Smith, *An Intimate Chronicle,* 157.

    18. *History of the Church,* 6:412, 488-90, 500, 576.

    19. Ibid., 6:488-90, 554; Phillip D. Jordan's introduction to Edward Bonney, *Banditti of the Prairies* (Norman: University of Oklahoma Press, 1963), 18-20.

20. Bonney, *Banditti of the Prairies,* xi, 15-22, 33-35, 66-73, 82-85, 214-17 (for the confession by Robert Birch); *History of the Church,* 7:486; Heber C. Kimball diary, 12 Nov. 1845, in Stanley B. Kimball, ed., *On the Potter's Wheel: The Diaries of Heber C. Kimball* (Salt Lake City: Signature Books/Smith Research Associates, 1987), 141. Kimball erroneously referred to Edward Bonney as "Edwin Bonny."

21. *History of the Church,* 6:576; 7:169; William Clayton diary, 7 July 1844, in Smith, *An Intimate Chronicle,* 138.

22. Illinois Executive Record (1843-47), 4:208, Illinois State Archives, Springfield.

23. *History of the Church,* 5:210; Uriah Brown to Brigham Young, 3 Nov. 1845; Council of Fifty minutes, 25 Aug., 13 Sept. 1851, both in LDS archives.

24. Klaus J. Hansen, *Quest for Empire: The Political Kingdom of God and the Council of Fifty in Mormon History* (Lansing: Michigan State University Press, 1967), 61-63, suggested plausibly (but inaccurately) that Daniel H. Wells was a member of the Fifty while he was a non-Mormon at Nauvoo and that Thomas L. Kane later became a Fifty non-Mormon during or after the exodus to Utah. Council of Fifty minutes and rolls demonstrate that Kane was never initiated into the Fifty. Mormon schismatic Lorin C. Woolley told his followers during the 1920s that the Council of Fifty had admitted U.S. presidents Theodore Roosevelt and Calvin Coolidge. The diary of the last surviving member of the Council of Fifty refutes Woolley's claim. See Mark J. Baird and Rhea A. Baird, *Reminiscences of John W. Woolley and Lorin C. Woolley,* 4 vols. (Draper, UT: N.p., n.d.), 3:9.

25. *History of the Church* repeatedly refers to Cahoon's role in Smith's return, which resulted in his death (see *History of the Church,* 6:549, 552; 7:81); William Clayton diary, 27 Oct. 1844, in Smith, *An Intimate Chronicle,* 151.

26. Richard L. Anderson, "Christian Ethics in Joseph Smith Biography," in Susan Easton Black, ed., *Expressions of Faith: Testimonies of Latter-day Saint Scholars* (Salt Lake City: Deseret Book Co.; Provo, UT: Foundation for Ancient Research and Mormon Studies, 1996), 167. This appeal to the official *History of the Church,* a fallacy of irrelevant proof, would invalidate the William Clayton diary as a source for suspicions about Cahoon, Phelps, and Babbitt. Anderson uses this deeply flawed, yet officially published source to attack the reminiscent statements about criticisms of Jonathan Dunham for refusing Joseph Smith's military order to have the Nauvoo Legion rescue the prophet from Carthage Jail. Anderson is responding to the discussion in Quinn, *Mormon Hierarchy: Origins of Power,* 141, 179-80. For some of the problems and retroactive changes in the official *History of the Church,* see Quinn, *Origins,* 5, 15, 31, 46, 48, 59, 69, 88, 108, 118, 156-57, 161, 164, 178, 274, 289n134, 306n70, 311n105, 315n130, 337n77, 353n54, 387n68, 393n111, 393n114, 395n132, 412n33, 413n33, 451n7, 492, 495, 501, 503, 506, 513, 515, 640, 642, 650-51, 653.

27. For the Anointed Quorum, see Quinn, *Mormon Hierarchy: Origins of Power,* 54, 55, 114, 115-16, 118-19, 139, 146, 149-52, 171-72, 176, 198, 206, 209, 230-31, 247, 399-402, 491-519, 634, 640, 641, 642, 644, 646-47, 648, 654.

28. Statement of Joseph Smith's polygamous brother-in-law Lorenzo Snow in Abraham H. Cannon diary, 9 Apr. 1890, Department of Special Collections and Manuscripts, Harold B. Lee Library, Brigham Young University, Provo, Utah (hereafter Lee Library), with copies in Manuscripts Division, J. Willard Marriott Library, University of Utah, Salt Lake City (hereafter Marriott Library), and in Utah State Historical Society, Salt Lake City; George A. Smith statement in Scott G. Kenney, ed., *Wilford Woodruff's Journal: 1833-1898 Typescript,* 9 vols. (Murray, UT: Signature Books, 1983-85), 4 (22 Dec. 1852): 157.

29. William Clayton diary, 19 Dec. 1844, in Smith, *An Intimate Chronicle,* 152; Wilford Woodruff to Brigham Young, 9 Oct., 3 Dec. 1844, LDS archives.

30. "Minutes of a Conference held in Pittsburgh, Oct. 12th 1844," *Latter Day Saint's Messenger and Advocate* (Pittsburgh) 1 (15 Oct. 1844): 11; Samuel Bennett, "To the Members of the Church of Jesus Christ of Latter Day Saints," *Latter Day Saint's Messenger and Advocate*

(Pittsburgh) 1 (1 Nov. 1844): 12; "NAUVOO AND THE LEADING MEN OF THAT CITY," *Latter Day Saint's Messenger and Advocate* (Pittsburgh) 1 (2 Dec. 1844): 47.

31. William Clayton diary, 1 Mar., 11 Mar., 18 Mar., 11 Apr., 15 Apr. 1844, in Smith, *An Intimate Chronicle*, 158-59, 160, 163. In ranking by age they were: Isaac Morley, Shadrach Roundy, Daniel Spencer, John W. Farnham, Joseph Young, Phineas H. Young, John E. Page, Jonathan Dunham, Theodore Turley, David Fullmer, Cyrus Daniels, Lewis Dana, Albert Rockwood, Charles Shumway, Lucien R. Foster, John S. Fullmer, John Pack, John D. Lee, and Albert Carrington.

32. George Miller to James J. Strang, 1 July 1855, in "Correspondence," *Northern Islander* 5 (20 Sept. 1855): [1]. Miller was specifically complaining about the council's condition in late 1846.

33. Ehat, "'It Seems Like Heaven Began on Earth,'" 273. Ehat notes that "William Clayton mentions all these failures in his 1845 New Year's day entry." However, Ehat imposes a mood of failure on Clayton's enthusiastic entry for January 1845. See Smith, *An Intimate Chronicle*, 153-54.

34. For Robert F. Kennedy's campaign, see Jules Witcover, *85 Days: The Last Campaign of Robert F. Kennedy* (New York: Putnam, 1969).

35. William Clayton diary, 1 Mar. 1845, in Smith, *An Intimate Chronicle*, 158, emphasis added.

36. Quinn, *Mormon Hierarchy: Origins of Power,* 79-88.

37. Joseph Smith diary, 10 Mar. 1844, in Scott H. Faulring, ed., *An American Prophet's Record: The Diaries and Journal of Joseph Smith* (Salt Lake City: Signature Books/Smith Research Associates, 1987), 458, deleted in *History of the Church,* 6:254-60.

38. Quinn, *Mormon Hierarchy: Origins of Power,* 176-81, 216-18, 647-54; Marshall Hamilton, "From Assassination to Expulsion: Two Years of Distrust, Hostility, and Violence," in Launius and Hallwas, *Kingdom on the Mississippi Revisited,* 214-30.

39. The westward exodus would have the greatest national impact of any council decision. Significant studies are Bernard DeVoto, *The Year of Decision, 1846* (Boston: Little, Brown and Co., 1943), 86-98, 148-50, 431-54; Preston Nibley, *Exodus to Greatness: The Story of the Mormon Migration* (Salt Lake City: Deseret News Press, 1947); Philip A. M. Taylor, "The Mormon Crossing of the United States, 1840-1870," *Utah Historical Quarterly* 25 (Oct. 1957): 319-37; LeRoy R. Hafen and Ann W. Hafen, *Handcarts To Zion: The Story of a Unique Western Migration* (Glendale, CA: Arthur W. Clark, 1960); Wallace Stegner, *The Gathering of Zion: The Story of the Mormon Trail* (New York: McGraw-Hill Book Co., 1964); William J. Petersen, "Mormon Trails in Iowa," *Palimpsest* 47 (Sept. 1966): 353-84; Frederick A. Norwood, *Strangers and Exiles: A History of Religious Refugees,* 2 vols. (Nashville: Abingdon Press, 1969), 2:235-46; Lewis Clark Christian, "A Study of the Mormon Westward Migration Between February 1846 and July 1847," Ph.D. diss., Brigham Young University, 1976; W. Turrentine Jackson, "The Mormon Trail," in Howard R. Lamar, ed., *Reader's Encyclopedia of the American West* (New York: Thomas Y. Crowell Co., 1977), 772-73; Fred Douglas Duehlmeier, "The 1847 Mormon Migration," M.A. thesis, University of Utah, 1977; Richard H. Jackson, "The Overland Journey to Zion," in Jackson, ed., *The Mormon Role in the Settlement of the West* (Provo, UT: Brigham Young University Press, 1978), 1-27; John D. Unruh, Jr., *The Plains Across: The Overland Emigrants and the Trans-Mississippi West, 1840-60* (Urbana: University of Illinois Press, 1979), 18-19, 253-59, 302-37; Joseph E. Brown, *The Mormon Trek West* (Garden City, NY: Doubleday & Co., 1980); Jeffery O. Johnson, "Women Among the Wagons: The Mormon Migration From Another Perspective," *Pioneer* 29 (May/June 1982): 12-13; Ronald K. Esplin, "'A Place Prepared': Joseph, Brigham and the Quest for Promised Refuge in the West," *Journal of Mormon History* 9 (1982): 85-111; Bennett, *Mormons at the Missouri;* Stanley B. Kimball, *Historic Sites and Markers Along the Mormon and Other Great Western Trails* (Urbana: University of Illinois Press, 1988); Stanley B. Kimball, "Mormon Pioneer Trail," in Daniel H. Ludlow, ed., *Encyclopedia of Mormonism:*

The History, Scripture, Doctrine, and Procedure of the Church of Jesus Christ of Latter-day Saints, 5 vols. (New York: Macmillan Publishing Co., 1992), 2: 942-46; Stanley B. Kimball, "From Nauvoo To Council Bluffs," and Wayne L. Wahlquist, "Mormon Trail," in S. Kent Brown, Donald Q. Cannon, and Richard H. Jackson, eds., *Historical Atlas of Mormonism* (New York: Simon & Schuster, 1994), 79-71, 86-87; Stanley Kimball, "The Mormon Trail in Utah," in Allan Kent Powell, ed., *Utah History Encyclopedia* (Salt Lake City: University of Utah Press, 1994), 380-81; Susan Arrington Madsen, *I Walked To Zion: True Stories of Young Pioneers on the Mormon Trail* (Salt Lake City: Deseret Book Co., 1994); William E. Hill, *The Mormon Trail: Yesterday and Today* (Logan: Utah State University Press, 1996).

40. Danite initiates in 1845 were Isaac Morley, Phineas H. Young, Jonathan Dunham, Cyrus Daniels, Albert P. Rockwood, John D. Lee, and George D. Grant. Grant was the last initiate, replacing William Smith who was expelled from the council in September. Some secondary sources also identify another 1845 member of the Fifty as a former Danite, but I have not yet verified that Shadrach Roundy was a Danite. See Missouri General Assembly, *Documents Containing the Correspondence, Orders, &c In Relation to the Disturbances With the Mormons . . .* (Fayette, MO: Boon's Lick Democrat, 1841), 97-98, 106; John D. Lee, *Mormonism Unveiled; or the Life and Confessions of . . . John D. Lee* (St. Louis: Bryan, Brand and Co., 1877), 57-58, 72; Juanita Brooks, *John Doyle Lee: Zealot-Pioneer Builder-Scapegoat* (Glendale, CA: Arthur H. Clark Co., 1962), 32; Hansen, *Quest for Empire,* 199n45; Stephen C. LeSueur, *The 1838 Mormon War in Missouri* (Columbia: University of Missouri Press, 1987), 118, 178, 125n35, 261-62; Albert Rockwood diary, 29 Oct. 1838, Western Americana, Beinecke Rare Book and Manuscript Library, Yale University, New Haven, Connecticut, which document is dated 22 October in later copies transcribed by fellow member of the Council of Fifty, Phineas Richards; Dean C. Jessee and David Whittaker, "The Last Months of Mormonism in Missouri: The Albert Perry Rockwood Journal," *Brigham Young University Studies* 28 (Winter 1988): 6-7, 11-15, 23 (which does not mention that Rockwood later became a member of the Council of Fifty); *History of the Church,* 6:149-50; Quinn, *Mormon Hierarchy: Origins of Power,* 480-90, 528-530.

41. Ehat, "'It Seems Like Heaven Began On Earth,'" 276; entries for 4 Feb., 1 Mar., 11 Mar., 18 Mar., 22 Mar., 25 Mar., 5 Apr., 11 Apr., 15 Apr., 22 Apr., 29 Apr., 6 May, 10 May 1845, in Kimball, *On the Potter's Wheel,* 95, 97, 98, 99, 102, 103, 105 [for "14. of Apriel"], 106, 109, 110, in Smith, *An Intimate Chronicle,* 157-65, and same dates in Willard Richards diary, LDS archives.

42. William Clayton diary, 1 Mar.-10 May 1845, in Smith, *An Intimate Chronicle,* 158-65; *History of the Church,* 7:379-80.

43. William Clayton diary, 11 Mar., 22 Mar. 1845, in Smith, *An Intimate Chronicle,* 160-61; compare *History of the Church,* 7:383, 427, 431.

44. Ehat, "'It Seems Like Heaven Began on Earth,'" 275.

45. *History of the Church,* 7:408, 417, 428.

46. Ibid., 7:433-34; Willard Richards diary, 2 Aug. 1845; John Taylor diary, 4 Aug. 1845, in Dean C. Jessee, "The John Taylor Nauvoo Journal, January 1845-September 1845," *Brigham Young University Studies* 23 (Summer 1983): 80-81.

47. Willard Richards diary, 27 Feb. 1845; minutes of meeting, 27 Feb. 1845, LDS archives; *History of the Church,* 7:377-79.

48. William Clayton diary, 12 Aug. 1845, in Smith, *An Intimate Chronicle,* 177; Church Historian's office journal, 12 Aug. 1845, LDS archives; *History of the Church,* 7:435; Hartley, *My Best for the Kingdom,* 169-71.

49. *History of the Church,* 7:439; compare William Clayton diary, 9 Sept. 1845, in Smith, *An Intimate Chronicle,* 180; John Taylor diary, 9 Sept. 1845, in Jessee, "John Taylor Nauvoo Diary," 88; Brigham Young diary, 13 Sept. 1845, LDS archives. *History of the Church,* 7:442-43, omits all reference to the meeting's discussion of the California coast.

50. William Clayton diary, 30 Sept. 1845, in Smith, *An Intimate Chronicle,* 183-84.

51. *History of the Church,* 7:447.

52. See Heber C. Kimball diary, 11 Dec. 1845, in Jerald and Sandra Tanner, eds., *Heber C. Kimball's Journal: November 21, 1845 to January 7, 1846* [photocopy of original manuscript] (Salt Lake City: Modern Microfilm Co. 1987), 30-32; also "THE REMOVAL OF THE MORMONS," *Illinois State Register,* 12 Dec. 1845. In order of seniority, the excluded members of the Fifty were John Smith, Alpheus Cutler, Isaac Morley, Reynolds Cahoon, William W. Phelps, Joseph Fielding, Joseph Young, Cornelius Lott, Orson Spencer, Lucien R. Foster, Charles C. Rich, and John D. Lee.

53. Brigham Young to W[illiam]. L. Marcy, U.S. Secretary of War, 17 Dec. 1845, photocopy in Russell R. Rich, *Ensign to the Nations: A History of the Church From 1846 to the Present* (Provo, UT: Brigham Young University Publications, 1972), 53; Milo Milton Quaife, ed., *The Diary of James K. Polk During His Presidency, 1845-1849,* 4 vols. (Chicago: A. C. McClurg & Co., 1910), 1:205 (31 Jan. 1846), 444 (2 June 1846), 446 (3 June 1846), with the quote from 450 (5 June 1846); Leland Hargrave Creer, *Utah and the Nation* (Seattle: University of Washington Press, 1929), 31-39; DeVoto, *Year of Decision,* 235-38; Charles Grier Sellers, Jr., *James K. Polk: Continentalist, 1843-1846* (Princeton, NJ: Princeton University Press, 1966), 397, 406-409, 425-26; Alan E. Haynes, "The Federal Government and Its Policies Regarding the Frontier Era of Utah Territory, 1850-1877," Ph.D. diss., Catholic University of America, 1968, 15-19; W. Ray Luce, "The Mormon Battalion: A Historical Accident?" *Utah Historical Quarterly* 42 (Winter 1974): 27-38; James B. Allen and Glen M. Leonard, *The Story of the Latter-day Saints,* 2d ed. rev. (Salt Lake City: Deseret Book Co., 1992), 238-39; Clark V. Johnson, "Government Responses to Mormon Appeals, 1840-1846," in H. Dean Garrett, ed., *Regional Studies in Latter-day Saint Church History: Illinois* (Provo, UT: Department of Church History and Doctrine, Brigham Young University, 1995), 196-97.

54. Daniel Tyler, *A Concise History of the Mormon Battalion in the Mexican War, 1846-1847* (N.p., 1881; Glorietta, NM: Rio Grande Press, 1969); Brigham H. Roberts, *The Mormon Battalion: Its History and Achievements* (Salt Lake City: Deseret News Press, 1919); Frank Alfred Golder, Thomas A. Bailey, and J. Lyman Smith, eds., *The March of the Mormon Battalion From Council Bluffs to California, Taken from the Journal of Henry Standage* (New York: Century, 1928); Creer, *Utah and the Nation,* 40-55; DeVoto, *Year of Decision,* 239-42; 312-18, 368-75; Leonard J. Arrington, *Great Basin Kingdom: An Economic History of the Latter-day Saints, 1847-1900* (Cambridge, MA: Harvard University Press, 1958), 21; Pauline Udall Smith and Alison Comish Thorne, *Captain Jefferson Hunt of the Mormon Battalion* (Salt Lake City: Nicholas G. Morgan, Sr. Foundation, 1958); Juanita Brooks, ed., "Diary of the Mormon Battalion Mission," *New Mexico Historical Review* 42 (July-Oct. 1967): 165-209, 281-332; Rich, *Ensign to the Nations,* 55-82; John F. Yurtinus, "A Ram in the Thicket: The Mormon Battalion in the Mexican War," Ph.D. diss., Brigham Young University, 1975; John R. Wunder, "Freedom From Government, Case Study: The Mormon Frontier Experience," in Carl Ubbelohde and Jack R. Fraenkel, eds., *Values of the American Heritage: Challenges, Case Studies, and Teaching Strategies* (Arlington, VA: National Council for the Social Studies, 1976), 94-95; Stanley B. Kimball, "The Mormon Battalion March, 1846-47," *Ensign* 9 (July 1979): 57-61; John F. Yurtinus, "The Mormon Volunteers: The Recruitment and Service of a Unique Military Company," *Journal of San Diego History* 25 (Summer 1979): 242-61; John F. Yurtinus, "'Here is One Man Who Will Not Go, Dam'um': Recruiting the Mormon Battalion in Iowa Territory," *Brigham Young University Studies* 21 (Fall 1981): 475-87; Eugene E. Campbell, "Pioneers and Patriotism: Conflicting Loyalties," in Davis Bitton and Maureen Ursenbach Beecher, eds., *New Views of Mormon History: A Collection of Essays in Honor of Leonard J. Arrington* (Salt Lake City: University of Utah Press, 1987), 314; Eugene E. Campbell, *Establishing Zion: The Mormon Church in the American West, 1847-1869* (Salt Lake City: Signature Books, 1988), 19-20; Bruce A. Van Orden, "The March of the Mormon Battalion in Its Greater American Historical Setting," in H. Dean Garrett and Clark V.

Johnson, eds., *Regional Studies in Latter-day Saint Church History: Arizona* (Provo, UT: Department of Church History and Doctrine, Brigham Young University, 1989), 159-76; Dan Talbot, *A Historical Guide to the Mormon Battalion and Butterfield Trail* (Tucson: Westernlore Press, 1992); John F. Yurtinus, "Mormon Battalion," in Ludlow, *Encyclopedia of Mormonism*, 2:933-36; Susan Easton Black, "The Mormon Battalion," in Brown, Cannon, and Jackson, *Historical Atlas of Mormonism*, 80-81; Susan Easton Black, "Mormon Battalion," in Powell, *Utah History Encyclopedia*, 376-78; Sandy M. Sanders, "In 1846, During the War With Mexico, Was President Polk's Decision To Employ a Battalion of Mormons a Military or Political Decision?" M.M.A.S. thesis, U.S. Army Command and General Staff College, 1994; Richard O. Cowan and William E. Homer, *California Saints: A 150-Year Legacy In The Golden State* (Provo, UT: Religious Studies Center, Brigham Young University, 1996), 59-78; Norma B. Ricketts, *The Mormon Battalion: United States Army of the West, 1846-1848* (Logan: Utah State University Press, 1996).

55. "Names of Those in the Mormon Battalion," in Frank Esshom, *Pioneers and Prominent Men of Utah, Comprising Photographs-Genealogies-Biographies* (Salt Lake City: Utah Pioneers Book Publishing Co., 1913), 43-45; "List of Members of the Mormon Battalion," in David Parry Wilson, "The Mormon Battalion," M.A. thesis, University of Utah, 1941, 103-14; appendix, "Appointments To the Theocratic Council of Fifty Through 1884." Battalion member Christopher Layton was not admitted to the Council of Fifty until 1883.

56. Brigham Young sermon, 1 Oct. 1848, quoted in Hubert Howe Bancroft, *History of Utah, 1540-1887* (San Francisco: History Co., 1890), 286, citing Young's manuscript history; also *Journal of Discourses,* 26 vols. (London and Liverpool: Latter-day Saints Book Depot, 1854-86), 2:173-74 (B. Young/1855), 8:335-36 (B. Young/1861), 10:106-107 (B. Young/1863), 16:19 (B. Young/1873).

57. A convenient listing of the 1847 captains appears in Duehlmeier, "The 1847 Mormon Migration," 123-59. The captains of the 1846 Mormon migration from Nauvoo to Winter Quarters appear in scattered references in the diaries of Hosea Stout, William Clayton, John D. Lee, Willard Richards, and others.

58. Willard Richards diary, 2 Apr. 1846; also similar entry in John D. Lee diary, 2 Apr. 1846, LDS archives, with a copy in Henry E. Huntington Library, San Marino, California.

59. Willard Richards diary, 18 Apr. 1846. He and John D. Lee were the only council members who spelled Fifty backwards when identifying the organization.

60. George Miller to James J. Strang, 1 July 1855.

61. Willard Richards diary, 12 Nov. 1846; Ehat, "'It Seems Like Heaven Began On Earth,'" 276-77; Quinn, *Mormon Hierarchy: Origins of Power,* 567.

62. George Miller to James J. Strang, 1 July 1855; Richard E. Bennett, "Winter Quarters," in Ludlow, *Encyclopedia of Mormonism,* 4:1,568-69.

63. Kenney, *Wilford Woodruff's Journal* 3 (29 May 1847): 188-89; William Clayton diary, 29 May 1847, in Smith, *An Intimate Chronicle,* 325-31; Norton Jacob record, 29 May 1847, Huntington Library. Clayton and Jacob also recorded Young's sentiments about other religions, but they did not give the kingdom's name, and Woodruff left out some words from the name. The full phrase appears in Clayton diary, 1 Jan. 1845, in Smith, *An Intimate Chronicle,* 153, with a singular "power," which is also the version of the name in Joseph F. Smith diary, 16 Mar. 1880, LDS archives, with copy in fd 6, box 6, Scott G. Kenney papers, Marriott Library. Other statements of the Fifty's long name appear in John D. Lee diary, 3 Mar. 1849, in Robert Glass Cleland and Juanita Brooks, eds., *A Mormon Chronicle: The Diaries of John D. Lee, 1848-1876,* 2 vols. (San Marino, CA: Huntington Library, 1955), 1:98; in John Taylor revelation, 27 June 1882, Annie Taylor Hyde notebook, 67, LDS archives; in Franklin D. Richards diary, 16 Mar. 1880, LDS archives; in Abraham H. Cannon diary, 9 Oct. 1884; in Council of Fifty minutes, 10 Apr. 1880, Lee Library.

64. James R. Clark, ed., *Messages of the First Presidency of the Church of Jesus Christ of Latter-day Saints,* 6 vols. (Salt Lake City: Bookcraft, 1965-71), 1:334. On Young's ecumenical view of the Mormon kingdom, see Hansen, *Quest for Empire,* 37.

65. "Lo! the Gentile chain is broken," *Sacred Hymns and Spiritual Songs for the Church of Jesus Christ of Latter-day Saints,* 15th ed. (Liverpool: Latter-day Saints' Book Depot, 1871), 103; also restatement of this view in *Journal of Discourses* 17:156 (B. Young/1874).

66. Hosea Stout diary, 26 Sept. 1845, in Juanita Brooks, ed., *On the Mormon Frontier: The Diary of Hosea Stout, 1844-1861,* 2 vols. (Salt Lake City: University of Utah Press, 1964), 1:73-74.

67. *History of the Church,* 7:515; Kenneth H. Winn, *Exiles in a Land of Liberty: Mormons in America, 1830-1846* (Chapel Hill: University of North Carolina Press, 1989), 236-38.

68. *Times and Seasons* 6 (1 Feb. 1846): 1,114.

69. Creer, *Utah and the Nation,* 80; William Cecil Carr, "Utah Statehood: Its Background and Development to 1865," Ph.D. diss., University of California, Berkeley, 1963, 263-65. In other words, from 1848 to 1850 the Anglo-European inhabitants of Salt Lake Valley and adjacent areas were living in a U.S. possession that was not formally organized as U.S. territory. For example, the United States purchased the city of New Orleans and all of Louisiana from France in December 1803, but waited until May 1805 to establish Louisiana as an organized U.S. territory. Likewise, the U.S. acquired Florida and its several Spanish settlements as a U.S. possession in February 1819, but waited until March 1822 to organize its inhabitants into a territory. See Joe Gray Taylor, *Louisiana: A Bicentennial History* (New York: W. W. Norton and Co., 1976), 47; Federal Writers' Project, *Florida: A Guide to the Southernmost State* (New York: Oxford University Press, 1939), 55-56. U.S. law sometimes adopts the international usage of "territory" to refer to a nation's entire domain (including coastal waters and uninhabited lands). However, in U.S. law and history "territory" usually refers to the intermediate step between nationally acquired lands and a state of the Union. See Robert F. Berkhofer, Jr., "The Northwest Ordinance and the Principle of Territorial Evolution," in John Porter Bloom, ed., *The American Territorial System* (Athens: Ohio University Press, 1973), 45-55.

70. Bernard A. DeVoto, *The Course of Empire* (Boston: Houghton Mifflin, 1952); Edward H. Spicer, *Cycles of Conquest: The Impact of Spain, Mexico, and the United States On the Indians of the Southwest, 1533-1960* (Tucson: University of Arizona Press, 1962); Vine Deloria, *Custer Died For Your Sins: An Indian Manifesto* (New York: Macmillan, 1969); Wilcomb E. Washburn, *Red Man's Land–White Man's Law* (New York: Charles Scribner's Sons, 1971); Vine Deloria, *Of Utmost Good Faith* (San Francisco: Straight Arrow Books, 1971); Virgil J. Vogel, ed., *This Country Was Ours: A Documentary History of the American Indian* (New York: Harper & Row, 1972); Kirk Kickingbird and Karen Ducheneaux, *One Hundred Million Acres* (New York: Macmillan, 1973); Wilcombe E. Washburn, ed., *The American Indian and the United States: A Documentary History,* 4 vols. (New York: Random House, 1973); Francis Jennings, *The Invasion of America: Indians, Colonialism, and the Cant of Conquest* (Chapel Hill: University of North Carolina Press, 1975); Wilcomb E. Washburn, *The Assault On Indian Tribalism: The General Allotment Law (Dawes Act) of 1887* (Philadelphia: J. B. Lippencott Co., 1975); Robert A. Hecht, *Continents In Collision: The Impact of Europe On the North American Indian Societies* (Lanham, MD: University Press of America, 1980); William M. Rieske, *Territorial Growth On Indian Lands Map: Eastern States From Colonial Times to 1800* (Salt Lake City: Historic Indian Publishers, 1981); William M. Rieske, *Territorial Growth On Indian Lands, 1800-1860, Showing Claims and Statehood Dates* (Salt Lake City: Historic Indian Publishers, 1981); William M. Rieske, *Treaties, Agreements, and Land Cessions, 1778-1909: Eastern States, Trans-Mississippi West* (Salt Lake City: Historic Indian Publishers, 1981); James Axtell, *The Invasion Within: The Contest of Cultures in Colonial North America* (New York: Oxford University Press, 1985); Imre Sutton and Theodore S. Jojola, eds., *Irredeemable America: The Indians' Estate and Land Claims* (Albuquerque: University of New Mexico Press,

1985); Patricia Nelson Limerick, *The Legacy of Conquest: The Unbroken Past of the American West* (New York: Norton, 1987); L. C. Green and Olive P. Dickason, *The Law of Nations and the New World* (Edmonton, Alberta, Can.: University of Alberta Press, 1988); Robert A. Williams, *The American Indian in Western Legal Thought: The Discourses of Conquest* (New York: Oxford University Press, 1990); Janet A. McDonnell, *The Dispossession of the American Indian, 1887-1934* (Bloomington: Indiana University Press, 1991); Francis Jennings, *The Founders of America . . .* (New York: Norton, 1993); Ian K. Steele, *Warpaths: Invasions of North America* (New York: Oxford University Press, 1994).

71. Leonard J. Arrington and Davis Bitton, *The Mormon Experience* (New York: Alfred A. Knopf, 1979), 145-46; also Spencer W. Kimball, "Of Royal Blood," *Ensign* 1 (July 1971): 6-10; George P. Lee, "My Heritage Is Choice," *Ensign* 5 (Nov. 1975): 100-101; Bruce A. Chadwick and Thomas Garrow, "Native Americans," in Ludlow, *Encyclopedia of Mormonism*, 3:981-82.

72. Brigham D. Madsen, *The Northern Shoshoni* (Caldwell, ID: Caxton Printers, 1980), 30, also 29-42, 90-93, 95-100; also Dale L. Morgan, "The Administration of Indian Affairs in Utah, 1851-1858," *Pacific Historical Review* 17 (Nov. 1948): 383-409; Lawrence G. Coates, "Mormons and Social Change Among the Shoshoni, 1853-1900," *Idaho Yesterdays: The Quarterly Journal of the Idaho Historical Society* 15 (Winter 1972): 2-11; Lawrence G. Coates, "Brigham Young and Mormon Indian Policies: The Formative Period, 1836-1851," *Brigham Young University Studies* 18 (Spring 1978): 428-36; Shirley Greenwood Jones, "Brigham Young's Rhetoric: A Critical and Cultural Analysis of Key Sermons In Five Rhetorical Events," Ph.D. diss., University of Utah, 1992, 140-200.

73. Creer, *Utah and the Nation,* 164-91; Albert R. Lyman, "A Relic of Gadianton: Old Posey as I Knew Him," *Improvement Era* 26 (July 1923): 791-801; Josiah F. Gibbs, "Black Hawk's Last Raid—1866," *Utah Historical Quarterly* 4 (Oct. 1931):99-108; "Daniel H. Wells' Narrative," *Utah Historical Quarterly* 6 (Oct. 1933): 125-32; Carling I. Malouf, "A Study of the Gosiute Indians of Utah," M.S. thesis, University of Utah, 1940, 63, 68-77; Angus M. Woodbury, "A History of Southern Utah and Its National Parks," *Utah Historical Quarterly* 19 (July-Oct. 1944): 167-78; Coulson Wright and Geneva Wright, "Indian-White Relations in the Uintah Basin," *Utah Humanities Review* 2 (Oct. 1948): 324-37; William E. Berrett and Alma P. Burton, eds., *Readings In L.D.S. History from Original Manuscripts,* 3 vols. (Salt Lake City: Deseret Book Co., 1953-58), 2: 355-92; Conway B. Sonne, *World of Wakara* (San Antonio, TX: Naylor Co., 1962), 51-52, 90-97, 161-73; Frederick Ross Gowans, "A History of Brigham Young's Indian Superintendency (1851-1857): Problems and Accomplishments," M.S. thesis, Brigham Young University, 1963, 26-38; Joseph Gilbert Jorgensen, "The Ethnohistory and Acculturation of the Northern Ute," Ph.D. diss., Indiana University, 1964, 71-78; Joel E. Ricks, *Forms and Methods of Early Mormon Settlement in Utah and Surrounding Region, 1847-1877* (Logan: Utah State University Press, 1964), 37-38, 83-89, 94, 97, 100; David L. Bigler, "The Crisis At Fort Limhi, 1858," and L. A. Fleming, "The Settlements on the Muddy, 1865 to 1871: 'A God Forsaken Place,'" *Utah Historical Quarterly* 35 (Spring 1967): 121-36, 159-63; James D. Matthews, "A Study of the Cultural and Religious Behavior of the Navaho Indians Which Caused Animosity, Resistance, or Indifference To the Religious Teachings of the Latter-day Saints," M.R.E. thesis, Brigham Young University, 1968; Deloy J. Spencer, "The Utah Black Hawk War, 1865-1871," M.A. thesis, Utah State University, 1969; Floyd A. O'Neil, "The Reluctant Suzerainty: The Uintah and Ouray Reservation," James B. Allen and Ted J. Warner, "The Gosiute Indians in Pioneer Utah," *Utah Historical Quarterly* 39 (Spring 1971): 137-39, 164; Floyd A. O'Neil, "A History of the Ute Indians of Utah Until 1890," Ph.D. diss., University of Utah, 1973, 25-99; Beverly P. Smaby, "The Mormons and the Indians: Conflicting Ecological Systems in the Great Basin," *American Studies* 16 (Spring 1975): 35-48; Brigham D. Madsen, "The Northwestern Shoshoni in Cache Valley," in Douglas D. Alder, ed., *Cache Valley: Essays on Her Past and People* (Logan: Utah State University Press, 1976), 28-44; Floyd A. O'Neil, "The Utes, Southern Paiutes,

and Gosiutes," in Helen Z. Papanikolas, ed., *The Peoples of Utah* (Salt Lake City: Utah State Historical Society, 1976), 36-38, 47-48; Thomas G. Alexander, *A Clash of Interests: Interior Department and Mountain West, 1863-96* (Provo, UT: Brigham Young University Press, 1977), 6, 36, 46; Coates, "Brigham Young and Mormon Indian Policies," 436-52; Howard Allan Christy, "Mormon-Indian Relations In Utah, 1847-1852," M.A. thesis, Brigham Young University, 1978; John Frederick Bluth, "Confrontation With an Arid Land: The Incursion of the Gosiutes and Whites Into Utah's Central West Desert, 1800-1978," Ph.D. diss., Brigham Young University, 1978; Howard A. Christy, "Open Hand and Mailed Fist: Mormon-Indian Relations in Utah, 1847-1852," and Floyd A. O'Neil and Stanford J. Layton, "Of Pride and Politics: Brigham Young as Indian Superintendent," *Utah Historical Quarterly* 46 (Summer 1978): 216-35, 236-50; S. Lyman Tyler, "The Indians in Utah Territory," in Richard D. Poll, ed., *Utah's History* (Provo, UT: Brigham Young University Press, 1978), 357-66; Lynn A. Rosenvall, "Defunct Mormon Settlements, 1830-1930," in Jackson, *Mormon Role in the Settlement of the West*, 53; Howard A. Christy, "The Walker War: Defense and Conciliation as Strategy," *Utah Historical Quarterly* 47 (Fall 1979): 395-420; Dennis Ray Defa, "A History of the Gosiute Indians to 1900," M.S. thesis, University of Utah, 1980, 41-44, 47-48, 53-60; Gregory C. Thompson, "The Unwanted Indians: The Southern Utes in Southeastern Utah," *Utah Historical Quarterly* 49 (Spring 1981): 189-203; Howard A. Christy and Kathryn L. MacKay, "Indian-White Encounters," in Wayne L. Wahlquist and Howard A. Christy, eds., *Atlas of Utah* (Ogden and Provo, UT: Weber State College/Brigham Young University Press, 1981), 103; Fred A. Conetah, *A History of the Northern Ute People* (Salt Lake City: Uintah-Ouray Ute Tribe, 1982), 37-42, 51-54; Lawrence G. Coates, "Cultural Conflict: Mormons and Indians in Nebraska," *Brigham Young University Studies* 24 (Summer 1984): 279-80, 290-99; Stanley B. Kimball, "The Captivity Narrative on Mormon Trails," *Dialogue: A Journal of Mormon Thought* 18 (Winter 1985): 81-88; Robert S. McPherson, "Paiute Posey and the Last White Uprising," *Utah Historical Quarterly* 53 (Summer 1985): 248-67; Floyd A. O'Neil, "The Mormons, the Indians, and George Washington Bean," in Clyde A. Milner II and O'Neil, eds., *Churchmen and the Western Indians, 1820-1920* (Norman: University of Oklahoma Press, 1985), 77-107; Brigham D. Madsen, *The Shoshoni Frontier and the Bear River Massacre* (Salt Lake City: University of Utah Press, 1985), 22, 36-39, 87, 140-43, 171-76.

Also, Newell G. Bringhurst, *Brigham Young and the Expanding American Frontier* (Boston: Little, Brown and Co., 1986), 108-109, 113-17; Brigham D. Madsen, *Chief Pocatello: The "White Plume"* (Salt Lake City: Bonneville Books/University of Utah Press, 1986), 8, 29-38; Donald Callaway, Joel Janetski, and Omer C. Stewart, "Ute," Isabel T. Kelly and Catherine S. Fowler, "Southern Paiute," Carling I. Malouf and John M. Findlay, "Euro-American Impact Before 1870," in Warren L. D'Azevedo, ed., *Great Basin* (Washington, D.C.: Smithsonian Institution, 1986), vol. 11 of *Handbook of North American Indians*, 339, 356, 387, 508-10; Albert Winkler, "The Circleville Massacre: A Brutal Incident in Utah's Black Hawk War," *Utah Historical Quarterly* 55 (Winter 1987): 4-21; Pamela A. Bunte and Robert J. Franklin, *From the Sands to the Mountain: Change and Persistence in a Southern Paiute Community* (Lincoln: University of Nebraska Press, 1987), 53-55, 90-98; Campbell, *Establishing Zion*, 93-110, 132, 266-68, 329-30; Robert S. McPherson, *The Northern Navajo Frontier, 1860-1900: Expansion through Adversity* (Albuquerque: University of New Mexico Press, 1988), 6, 22, 31-37; Warren Metcalf, "A Precarious Balance: The Northern Utes and the Black Hawk War," *Utah Historical Quarterly* 57 (Winter 1989): 24-35; Ronald W. Walker, "Toward a Reconstruction of Mormon and Indian Relations, 1847-1877," *Brigham Young University Studies* 29 (Fall 1989): 26-28, 33-36; Albert Winkler, "Justice in the Black Hawk War: The Trial of Thomas Jose," *Utah Historical Quarterly* 60 (Spring 1990): 124-36; Craig Woods Fuller, "Land Rush in Zion: Opening of the Uncompahgre and Uintah Indian Reservations," Ph.D. diss., Brigham Young University, 1990, 154-74, 209-48; Howard A. Christy, "'What Virtue There Is in Stone' and Other Pungent Talk on the Early Utah Frontier," *Utah Historical Quarterly* 59 (Summer 1991): 300-19; Albert Winkler, "The Ute

Mode of War in the Conflict of 1865-68," *Utah Historical Quarterly* 60 (Fall 1992): 300-18; Chadwick and Garrow, "Native Americans," in Ludlow, *Encyclopedia of Mormonism* 3:982-83; Ronald L. Holt, *Beneath These Red Cliffs: An Ethnohistory of the Utah Paiutes* (Albuquerque: University of New Mexico Press, 1992), 3, 12-15, 24-41; Donald R. Moorman and Gene A. Sessions, *Camp Floyd and the Mormons: The Utah War* (Salt Lake City: University of Utah Press, 1992), 178-91, 199-200, 203-205, 221-222, 227-30; John Alton Peterson, "Mormons, Indians, and Gentiles and Utah's Black Hawk War," Ph.D. diss., Arizona State University, 1993; John A. Peterson, "Black Hawk War," Dennis R. Defa, "Goshute Indians," Paul Pailla, "Kanosh," David Rich Lewis, "Native Americans in Utah," Ronald L. Holt, "Paiute Indians of Utah," Brigham D. Madsen, "Shoshoni Indians (Northwestern Bands)," David Rich Lewis, "Uintah-Ouray Indian Reservation," and David Rich Lewis, "Ute Indians-Northern," Tina Kelley and Kathryn L. MacKay, "Wakara," in Powell, *Utah History Encyclopedia*, 44, 228-29, 297-98, 390, 409, 497-98, 572, 608, 615; John W. Heaton, "'No Place To Pitch Their Teepees,': Shoshone Adaptation To Mormon Settlers in Cache Valley, 1855-70," *Utah Historical Quarterly* 63 (Spring 1995): 158-71; Robert S. McPherson, *A History of San Juan County: In the Palm of Time* (Salt Lake City: Utah State Historical Society/San Juan County Commission, 1995), 121-69; Thomas G. Alexander, *Utah: The Right Place, The Official Centennial History* (Salt Lake City: Gibbs-Smith Publisher/Utah Division of State History, 1995), 103, 108-116, 142-46, 246-49, 449-50; Robert E. Parson, *A History of Rich County* (Salt Lake City: Utah State Historical Society/Rich County Commission, 1996), 47-48, 71-76; Jessie L. Embry, *A History of Wasatch County* (Salt Lake City: Utah State Historical Society/Wasatch County Commission, 1996), 36-37; Richard A. Firmage, *A History of Grand County* (Salt Lake City: Utah State Historical Society/Grand County, 1996), 82-100, 125-29.

Despite all evidence and LDS publications in conflict with his views, LDS institute teacher Rhett Stephens James, "150 Years of Mormon-Indian Relations: A Synthesis," in *Sidney B. Sperry Symposium, January 26, 1980: A Sesquicentennial Look At Church History* (Provo, UT: Religious Instruction, Brigham Young University/Church Educational System, 1980), claimed that problems occurred only because (172) some Mormons "resented Indian reluctance to accept help," because (172) Brigham Young was replaced by non-Mormons as Indian Superintendent, and because "to 1877 Utah Indians had proved to be reluctant prodigals" (176). Instead James argued that (187) "negative Anglo-attitudes have been resisted and fought against by the official Church and by ever increasing numbers of individual Latter-day Saint Anglos."

74. *The Book of Mormon*, published at Salt Lake City in various editions, with verse citations (similar to the Bible) according to name of its constituent books, Ether 2:3; Stephen Parker, "Deseret," in Ludlow, *Encyclopedia of Mormonism*, 1:370-71, citing Alan Gardiner, *Egyptian Grammar*, 3rd ed. (Oxford: Oxford University Press, 1982), 73-74; Richard D. Poll, "Deseret," in Powell, *Utah History Encyclopedia*, 138-39.

75. Alexander, *Utah*, 118; also Wayne L. Wahlquist, "Political Development: State of Deseret," in Wahlquist and Christy, *Atlas of Utah*, 160; Dale L. Morgan, *The State of Deseret* (Logan: Utah State University Press, 1987), 2-3; Campbell, *Establishing Zion*, 204-205; Glen M. Leonard, "The Mormon Boundary Question in the 1849-50 Statehood Debates," *Journal of Mormon History* 18 (Spring 1992): 118-21; Jeffery Ogden Johnson, "Deseret, State of," in Ludlow, *Encyclopedia of Mormonism*, 1:371-72; Dean L. May, "The State of Deseret," in Brown, Cannon, and Jackson, *Historical Atlas of Mormonism*, 90-91. I was unable to locate BYU's copy of Roger Milton Barrus, "Religion, Regime, and Politics: The Founding and Political Development of Utah," Ph.D. diss., Harvard University, 1984.

76. John D. Lee diary, 9 Dec. 1848, 4 Mar. 1849, in Cleland and Brooks, *Mormon Chronicle*, 1:80, 98-99; Hosea Stout diary, 12 Mar. 1849, in Brooks, *On the Mormon Frontier*, 2:348; Thomas Bullock diary, 12 Mar., 21 Mar. 1849, LDS archives; Journal History of the Church of Jesus Christ of Latter-day Saints (1830-1972), 246 reels, microfilm, Special Collections, Marriott Library, 4 Mar., 12 Mar. 1849; Morgan, *State of Deseret*, 30-33;

Campbell, *Establishing Zion,* 205; Bringhurst, *Brigham Young,* 103-104; Leonard, "The Mormon Boundary Question," 119-20; Peter Crawley, "The Constitution of the State of Deseret," *Brigham Young University Studies* 29 (Fall 1989): 9-10; contrast with the "State of Deseret" by University of Utah historian Leland Hargrave Creer, *The Founding of an Empire: The Exploration and Colonization of Utah, 1776-1856* (Salt Lake City: Bookcraft, 1947), 303-38, which was silent about several details, including the Council of Fifty. Although Fawn M. Brodie, *No Man Knows My History: The Life of Joseph Smith, The Mormon Prophet* (New York: Alfred A. Knopf, 1945), 356, should have alerted Creer to examine the role of the Council of Fifty, he did not. In reaction against Creer's kind of history, historians Juanita Brooks, James R. Clark, Dale L. Morgan, and Klaus J. Hansen launched what I have called "the kingdom school" of Mormon historiography which heavily emphasized the secretive role of the Council of Fifty. However, this had no effect on Creer who published "The Evolution of Government in Early Utah," *Utah Historical Quarterly* 27 (Jan. 1958): 23-42, without a single reference to the Council of Fifty. In response, James R. Clark published "The Kingdom of God, The Council of Fifty and the State of Deseret," *Utah Historical Quarterly* 27 (Apr. 1958): 131-48.

77. See especially Crawley, "The Constitution of the State of Deseret," 7-22, also summarized in Leonard, "Mormon Boundary Question," 120-21, both of which correct the traditional misreading of documents in Morgan, *State of Deseret,* 25-26; also Ehat, "'It Seems Like Heaven Began On Earth,'" 277; Alexander, *Utah,* 117.

78. Quinn, *Mormon Hierarchy: Origins of Power,* 5, 6, 9, 15, 16, 17, 26, 31, 33, 35, 38, 39, 40, 41-42, 46, 48, 49, 59, 69, 70-71, 88, 108, 118, 156-57, 161, 164, 178, 198, 274.

79. Although apparently unaware of the non-existent events claimed by the 1849 *Constitution of the State of Deseret,* Marvin S. Hill, *Quest for Refuge: The Mormon Flight from American Pluralism* (Salt Lake City: Signature Books, 1989), 129, noted that the document "was either *prima facie* evidence of the disingenuousness of the Council of Fifty or of its inability to recognize the inherent contradiction of this democratic document with the manner in which it had been created and the conditions under which it would operate."

80. Hansen, *Quest For Empire,* 68.

81. Carr, "Utah Statehood," 346-57, 362-64; Haynes, "Federal Government and Its Policies Regarding the Frontier Era of Utah Territory," 24-39; Michael F. Holt, "Compromise of 1850," in Lamar, *Reader's Encyclopedia of the American West,* 251-52; also Edwin C. Rozwenc, ed., *The Compromise of 1850* (Boston: D. C. Heath, 1957); Holman Hamilton, *Prologue to Conflict: The Crisis and Compromise of 1850* (Lexington: University of Kentucky Press, 1964); Michael F. Holt, *The Political Crisis of the 1850s* (New York: Wiley, 1978).

82. Campbell, *Establishing Zion,* 205-209; with revisionist insights provided by Crawley, "The Constitution of the State of Deseret."

83. Morgan, *State of Deseret,* 186.

84. Council of Fifty rolls (1845-82), LDS archives, and Ehat, "'It Seems Like Heaven Began On Earth,'" 277.

85. John D. Lee diary, [6] Dec. 1848, in Cleland and Brooks, *Mormon Chronicle,* 1:80. Lee's entry appeared at the end of a now-missing portion of his diary describing the Council of Fifty meeting on 6 December 1848. His next reference was a summary of its 9 December meeting; Brooks, *John D. Lee,* 73, for his adoption to Young.

86. John D. Lee diary, 24 Feb., 3-4 Mar., 10 Mar. 1849, in Cleland and Brooks, *Mormon Chronicle,* 1:95, 97-100; Horace S. Eldredge diary, 4 Mar. 1849, LDS archives; Joseph Fielding diary, 11 Mar. 1849, LDS archives.

87. Jack Ericson Eblen, *The First and Second United States Empires: Governors and Territorial Government, 1784-1912* (Pittsburgh: University of Pittsburgh Press, 1968), 160.

88. Minutes of meeting of Quorum of the Twelve Apostles, 12 Feb. 1849, 3, LDS archives.

89. *Journal of Discourses* 5:219 (H. C. Kimball/1856), emphasis added; Council of Fifty rolls (1845-82) and Ehat, "'It Seems Like Heaven Began On Earth,'" 277, contain the dates of meetings.

90. "THE SALT LAKE BANDITTI," *Melchizedek and Aaronic Herald* 1 (Feb. 1850): 1; also "IS MORMONISM TREASON? . . . Independent Political Power," *Salt Lake Daily Tribune,* 8 Mar. 1885, [4], that Brigham Young "was himself crowned as both 'King and Priest.'" Gordon C. Thomasson, "Foolsmate," *Dialogue: A Journal of Mormon Thought* 6 (Autumn-Winter 1971): 148-51, is the best known effort to explain away the descriptions of Smith and Young as theocratic kings.

91. Quinn, *Mormon Hierarchy: Origins of Power,* 124, 138-39; William Clayton diary, 11 Apr. 1844, 1 Jan. 1845, in Smith, *An Intimate Chronicle,* 129, 154; chap. 8 for Taylor's ordination as king.

92. George Miller to James J. Strang, 12 June 1850, in *Gospel Herald* 4 (16 Aug. 1849): 99; George Miller to James J. Strang, 1 July 1855.

93. Quinn, *Mormon Hierarchy: Origins of Power,* 203-209; Danny L. Jorgensen, "The Old Fox: Alpheus Cutler," in Roger D. Launius and Linda Thatcher, eds., *Differing Visions: Dissenters in Mormon History* (Urbana: University of Illinois Press, 1994), 158-79; Danny L. Jorgensen, "Conflict in the Camps of Israel: The 1853 Cutlerite Schism," *Journal of Mormon History* 21 (Spring 1995): 25-64.

94. [George A. Smith and Ezra T. Benson] to Brigham Young, Heber C. Kimball, and Willard Richards, 27 Mar. 1849, 13, LDS archives, concerning a meeting with Peter Haws in February. The original words "nothing but" were lined through in the manuscript.

95. Minutes of the Council of Fifty, 22 Aug.-13 Sept. 1851; Ehat, "'It Seems Like Heaven Began On Earth,'" 277. "The Quorum of 50" was the designation in Willard Richards diary, 21-23 Aug., 25 Aug., 30 Aug., 13 Sept. 1851; and Phineas Richards diary, 25 Aug. 1851, 23 Jan. 1867, LDS archives.

96. Rich, *Ensign to the Nations,* 197; Creer, *Utah and the Nation,* 91, called them "so-called 'foreign'" officials; also Everett L. Cooley, "Carpetbag Rule: Territorial Government in Utah," *Utah Historical Quarterly* 26 (Apr. 1958): 107-31.

97. Creer, *Utah and the Nation,* 93-104; Richard D. Poll, "The Mormon Question Enters National Politics, 1850-1856," *Utah Historical Quarterly* 25 (Apr. 1957): 118; Leland Homer Gentry, "The Brocchus-Young Speech Controversy of 1851," M.S. thesis, University of Utah, 1958; Norman F. Furniss, *The Mormon Conflict, 1850-1859* (New Haven: Yale University Press, 1960), 24-29, 31-33; Carr, "Utah Statehood," 394-99; Howard Roberts Lamar, *The Far Southwest, 1846-1912: A Territorial History* (New Haven: Yale University Press, 1966), 328-29; Haynes, "Federal Government and Its Policies Regarding the Frontier Era of Utah Territory," 43-51; Wunder, "Freedom From Government," in Ubbelohde and Fraenkel, *Values of the American Heritage,* 99-100; David Lee Washburn, "The First Eight Years: The Deterioration of Mormon-Federal Relations in Utah, 1850-1857," M.A. thesis, University of Utah, 1980, 11-24; Michael W. Homer, "The Judiciary and the Common Law in Utah Territory, 1850-61," *Dialogue: A Journal of Mormon Thought* 21 (Spring 1988): 98-101; Clifford L. Ashton, *The Federal Judiciary In Utah* (Salt Lake City: Utah Bar Foundation, 1988), 1-4; Campbell, *Establishing Zion,* 211-15; Alexander, *Utah,* 119-20.

98. Minutes of the Council of Fifty, 22 Aug.-4 Oct. 1851; Ehat, "'It Seems Like Heaven Began On Earth,'" 277.

99. Homer, "The Judiciary and the Common Law in Utah," 102; Shane Swindle, "The Struggle Over the Adoption of the Common Law in Utah," *Thetean: A Student Journal of History* (Provo, UT: Beta Iota Chapter of Phi Alpha Theta, Brigham Young University, 1981), 76-97.

100. Jerrold S. Jensen, "The Common Law of England in the Territory of Utah," *Utah Historical Quarterly* 60 (Winter 1992): 21.

101. "Discourse By President BRIGHAM YOUNG, Tabernacle, July 8th, 1855," *Deseret News* [weekly], 1 Aug. 1855, 162.

102. Furniss, *Mormon Conflict*, 95-123; Lamar, *Far Southwest*, 338-45; Campbell, "Pioneers and Patriotism," in Bitton and Beecher, *New Views of Mormon History*, 316-17; Campbell, *Establishing Zion*, 233-38; William Mackinnon, "125 Years of Conspiracy Theories: Origins of the Utah Expedition of 1857-58," *Utah Historical Quarterly* 52 (Summer 1984): 212-30; Moorman and Sessions, *Camp Floyd and the Mormons*, 3-24; Charles S. Peterson, "Alfred Cumming," and Richard D. Poll, "The Utah War," in Powell, *Utah History Encyclopedia*, 607-608; Alexander, *Utah*, 125-26; discussion below.

103. Kenney, *Wilford Woodruff's Journal* 5 (26 Aug., 26 Oct. 1857): 82-83, 114-15.

104. Church Historian's office journal, 14 Sept. 1857; appendix, "Appointments To the Theocratic Council of Fifty Through 1884." Then-current non-Fifty in this meeting were: William H. Kimball, Joseph A. Young, Hosea Stout, Feramorz Little, Evan M. Greene, and Hiram B. Clawson, and two clerks Leo Hawkins and Robert L. Campbell. The excluded, yet faithful, members of the Fifty were: Thomas Bullock, Reynolds Cahoon, William Clayton, Horace S. Eldredge, Amos Fielding, Joseph Fielding, David Fullmer, John S. Fullmer, Joseph L. Heywood, Benjamin F. Johnson, Philip B. Lewis, Isaac Morley, John Pack, John D. Parker, William W. Phelps, Levi Richards, Phineas Richards, Orrin Porter Rockwell, Albert P. Rockwood, Shadrach Roundy, Charles Shumway, Willard Snow, Daniel Spencer, John Young, Joseph Young, and Phineas H. Young.

105. Church Historian's office journal, 18 Mar. 1858. Aside from John S. Fullmer and Albert Rockwood, see the previous note for the uninvited members of the Fifty.

106. Quinn, *Mormon Hierarchy: Origins of Power*, 81-85, 91-92, 93-100, 113, 117, 176-78, 179-81.

107. *History of the Church*, 1:265, 431n, 3:171, 182-86, 6:618, 7:523; Josiah E. Hickman, "The Banishment of the Mormon People," third-prize winner of oratorical contest at University of Michigan in Mar. 1895, in *Brigham Young University Studies* 11 (Spring 1971): 311-16; Lycurgus Arnold Wilson, *The Life of David W. Patten: The First Apostolic Martyr* (Salt Lake City: Deseret News, 1900); Brigham H. Roberts, *The Missouri Persecutions* (Salt Lake City: George Q. Cannon & Sons, 1900); Brigham H. Roberts, *A Comprehensive History of The Church of Jesus Christ of Latter-day Saints, Century I*, 6 vols. (Salt Lake City: Deseret News Press and "the Church," 1930), 1:280, 345, 475, 480-83, 2:314, 3:45-46, 4:155n; Richard L. Bushman, "Mormon Persecutions in Missouri, 1833," *Brigham Young University Studies* 3 (Autumn 1960): 11-20; Warren A. Jennings, "Zion is Fled: The Expulsion of the Mormons From Jackson County, Missouri," Ph.D. diss., University of Florida, 1962; Leland H. Gentry, "A History of the Latter-day Saints in Northern Missouri from 1836 to 1839," Ph.D. diss., Brigham Young University, 1965, 39-51, 430-66; Warren A. Jennings, "The Expulsion of the Mormons From Jackson County, Missouri," *Missouri Historical Review* 64 (Oct. 1969): 41-63; Alma R. Blair, "The Haun's Mill Massacre," *Brigham Young University Studies* 13 (Autumn 1972): 62-67; Patricia A. Zahniser, "Violence in Missouri, 1831-1839: The Case of the Mormon Persecution," M.A. thesis, Florida Atlanta University at Boca Raton, 1973; Steven Pratt, "Eleanor McLean and the Murder of Parley P. Pratt," *Brigham Young University Studies* 15 (Winter 1975): 225-56; Max H. Parkin, "A History of the Latter-day Saints In Clay County, Missouri, From 1833 to 1837," Ph.D. diss., Brigham Young University, 1976, 242-79; Ronald K. Esplin, ed., "Life in Nauvoo, June 1844: Vilate Kimball's Martyrdom Letters," *Brigham Young University Studies* 19 (Winter 1979): 231-40; Dean C. Jessee, "Return to Carthage: Writing the History of Joseph Smith's Martyrdom," *Journal of Mormon History* 8 (1981): 3-19; Davis Bitton, "The Martyrdom of Joseph Smith in Early Mormon Writings," *John Whitmer Historical Association Journal* 3 (1983): 29-30; William G. Hartley, "Almost Too Intolerable A Burden: The Winter Exodus from Missouri," *Journal of Mormon History* 18 (Fall 1992): 7-40; Alma R. Blair, "Haun's Mill Massacre," Joseph I. Bentley, "Martyrdom of Joseph and Hyrum Smith," Robert C. Patch, "Martyrs," Clark V. Johnson, "LDS Commu-

nities in Jackson and Clay Counties," and Max H. Parkin, "Missouri Conflict," in Ludlow, *Encyclopedia of Mormonism,* 2:577, 860-62, 862-63, 922-25, 927-28; Clark V. Johnson, ed., *Mormon Redress Petitions: Documents of the 1833-1838 Missouri Conflict* (Provo, UT: Religious Studies Center, Brigham Young University, 1992); Kenneth W. Godfrey, "Remembering the Deaths of Joseph and Hyrum Smith," and Danel W. Bachman, "Joseph Smith, a True Martyr," in Susan Easton Black and Charles D. Tate, Jr., eds., *Joseph Smith: The Prophet, the Man* (Provo, UT: Religious Studies Center, Brigham Young University, 1993), 301-15, 317-22; chaps. titled "Expulsion from Jackson County," "Missouri Persecutions and Expulsion," and "The Martyrdom," in *Church History In the Fulness of Times,* rev. ed. (Salt Lake City: Church of Jesus Christ of Latter-day Saints, 1993), 127-39, 193-210, 272-88; Kenneth W. Godfrey, "A Time, A Season, When Murder Was In the Air: The Martyrdoms of Joseph and Hyrum Smith After 150 Years," *Mormon History Magazine,* July/Aug 1994, 34-39; Quinn, *Mormon Hierarchy: Origins of Power,* 82, 99-100, 141, 618, 620, 629, 646, 651; Alma R. Blair, "Conflict in Missouri," and Sean J. Cannon, "Expulsion From Missouri," in Brown, Cannon, and Jackson, *Historical Atlas of Mormonism,* 46-47, 48-49; Davis Bitton, *The Martyrdom Remembered: A One Hundred-Fifty Year Perspective on the Assassination of Joseph Smith* (Salt Lake City: Aspen Books, 1994); Alexander L. Baugh, "The Battle Between Mormon and Missouri Militia at Crooked River," Alvin K. Benson, "The Haun's Mill Massacre: Some Examples of Tragedy and Superior Faith," Kenneth W. Godfrey, "New Light on Old Difficulties: The Historical Importance of the Missouri Affidavits," Clark V. Johnson, "A Profile of Mormon Missouri, 1834-1839," Max H. Parkin, "Latter-day Saint Conflict in Clay County," Keith W. Perkins, "DeWitt—Prelude to Expulsion," Bruce A. Van Orden, "Causes and Consequences: Conflict in Jackson County," in Arnold K. Garr and Clark V. Johnson, eds., *Regional Studies in Latter-day Saint Church History: Missouri* (Provo, UT: Department of Church History and Doctrine, Brigham Young University, 1994), 85-103, 105-18, 206-14, 219-31, 241-60, 261-80, 341-46; Reed H. Blake and Spencer H. Blake, *The Carthage Tragedy: The Martyrdom of Joseph Smith* (Provo, UT: LDS Book Publications, 1994).

108. Bennett, *Mormons at the Missouri, 1846-1852,* 137, estimated 1,003 deaths only within the settlements on the pioneer trail for the first two years; Stanley B. Kimball, *Historic Resource Study: Mormon Pioneer National Historic Trail* (Washington, D.C.: U.S. Department of the Interior/National Park Service, 1991), 21, 134-35, estimated a 10 percent death rate, which would equal 6,800 deaths for the total 68,028 Mormon pioneers to Utah before the arrival of the transcontinental railroad in 1869; also see Susan W. Easton, "Suffering and Death on the Plains of Iowa," *Brigham Young University Studies* 21 (Fall 1981): 431-39.

109. Quinn, *Mormon Hierarchy: Origins of Power,* 84, 117, 135, 477-48; Paul H. Peterson, "The Mormon Reformation," Ph.D. diss., Brigham Young University, 1981, 189.

110. John A. Peterson, "Warren Stone Snow, a Man In Between: The Biography of a Mormon Defender," M.A. thesis, Brigham Young University, 1985, 3; also Lynn M. Hilton and Hope A. Hilton, "Danites," in Powell, *Utah History Encyclopedia,* 126.

111. Brigham Young, Jr., diary, 8 Apr. 1902, Rare Book and Manuscript Division, New York Public Library, New York City, and microfilm at Utah State Historical Society; also biographical perspective in Charles S. Peterson, "'A Mighty Man Was Brother Lot': A Portrait of Lot Smith—Mormon Frontiersman," *Western Historical Quarterly* 1 (Oct. 1970): 393-414; Ray Hunter, "Early Law Enforcement: Lot Smith, Outlaw or Lawman, Which?" *Utah Peace Officer* 62 (Winter 1985-Spring 1986): 8-11, 14-17; Charles S. Peterson, "Lot Smith," in Powell, *Utah History Encyclopedia,* 506.

112. *History of the Church,* 5:260-61, 267, 7:446; Quinn, *Mormon Hierarchy: Origins of Power,* 180-81, 484, 527, 652-53; Harold Schindler, *Orrin Porter Rockwell: Man of God, Son of Thunder* (Salt Lake City: University of Utah Press, 1966), 43, 145, 185, 185n37; Richard S. Van Wagoner and Steven C. Walker, *A Book of Mormons* (Salt Lake City: Signature Books, 1982), 250-53; Harold Schindler, "Orrin Porter Rockwell," in Powell, *Utah History Encyclopedia,* 473-74.

113. Municipal High Council minutes, 17 Mar. 1848, Brigham Young papers, LDS archives. For Stout's pride in his membership of the Mormon-organized Danites, see Hosea Stout diary, 22 Sept. 1846, in Brooks, *On the Mormon Frontier,* 1:197; also Andrew Jenson, *Latter-day Saint Biographical Encyclopedia,* 4 vols. (Salt Lake City: Andrew Jenson History Co. and Deseret News, 1901-36), 3:530-34; Quinn, *Mormon Hierarchy: Origins of Power,* 92-99.

114. Hosea Stout diary, 8 Mar. 1858, in Brooks, *On the Mormon Frontier,* 2:653; William Allan Neilson, ed., *Webster's New International Dictionary of the English Language, With Reference History,* 2d ed., 3 vols. (Springfield, MA: Merriam Co., 1949), 1:262; Lester V. Berrey and Melvin Van Dern Bark, *The American Thesaurus of Slang,* 2d ed. (New York: Thomas Y. Crowell, 1960), 461n7.

115. Ivan J. Barrett, *Eph Hanks: Fearless Mormon Scout* (Salt Lake City: Covenant Communications, 1990), 107; William A. Hickman, *Brigham's Destroying Angel: Being the Life, Confession, and Startling Disclosures of the Notorious Bill Hickman, The Danite Chief of Utah. Written by Himself, with Explanatory Notes by J. H. Beadle, Esq., of Salt Lake City* (New York: Geo. A. Crofutt, 1872), 47, 128; Quinn, *Mormon Hierarchy: Origins of Power,* 481; appendix, "Appointments To the Theocratic Council of Fifty Through 1884"; Hope A. Hilton, *"Wild Bill" Hickman and the Mormon Frontier* (Salt Lake City: Signature Books, 1988), 31, added George Boyd to the list of Brigham's "boys."

116. Aaron Johnson autobiography, 95-96, LDS archives, quoted in Peterson, "Mormon Reformation" (1981), 189, with quote of Peterson's own view (188), also his discussion of the Parrish murders (194-96), which did not mention that Johnson was the Springville bishop identified by court witnesses as ordering the murders.

117. "COURT DOINGS AT PROVO," *Deseret News* [weekly], 6 Apr. 1859, 1. Since the issue of 16 March, the *News* had quoted almost no testimony, but quoted full transcripts of federal judge John Cradlebaugh's statements to the jury. Quinn, *Mormon Hierarchy: Origins of Power,* 484, 525, for Elias Smith; also Hosea Stout diary, 22 Mar., 29 Mar., 31 Mar., 1 Apr., 2 Apr. 1859, in Juanita Brooks, *On The Mormon Frontier,* 2:692, 2:692n51, 2:693, 2:693-94, 2:694n52, 2:694n53; Alan P. Johnson, *Aaron Johnson: Faithful Steward* (Salt Lake City: Publishers Press, 1991), 560-85, which remarkably omitted the fully published affidavits and courtroom testimony of Mrs. Alvira L. Parrish, Orrin E. Parrish, Joseph Bartholomew, Zephaniah J. Warren, Alva A. Warren, James W. Webb, Abraham Durfee, Thomas O'Bannion, and Mr. Phillips, Mar.-Aug. 1859, as published in "The Murder of the Parrishes and Potter at Springville, on Sunday night, March 14, 1857," *Kirk Anderson's Valley Tan* (Salt Lake City), 5 Apr. 1859, [1]; "THE PARRISH MURDER," *Kirk Anderson's Valley Tan* (Salt Lake City), 19 Apr. 1859, [1-2], and by Judge Cradlebaugh, *Utah and the Mormons: Speech of Hon. John Cradlebaugh, of Nevada, on the Admission of Utah As a State. Delivered in the House of Representatives, February 7, 1863* ([Washington, D.C.], 1863), 43-61; Moorman and Sessions, *Camp Floyd and the Mormons,* 102-21; Davis Bitton, "The Cradlebaugh Court (1859): A Study in Early Mormon-Gentile Misunderstanding," in Clark S. Knowlton, ed., *Social Accommodation in Utah,* bound mimeograph (Salt Lake City: American West Center Occasional Papers, University of Utah, 1975), 71-97, discussed the environment surrounding Cradlebaugh's activities and only mentioned (90) "the so-called Potter-Parrish murders."

118. Hartley, *My Best For the Kingdom,* 322.

119. Monte Burr McLaws, *Spokesman for the Kingdom: Early Mormon Journalism and the DESERET NEWS, 1830-1898* (Provo, UT: Brigham Young University Press, 1977), 54.

120. Brigham Young to Aaron Johnson at Springville, 30 July 1857, and Young to Lysander Gee, 30 July 1857, Young letterbook 3:730, 731, transcripts in fd 6, box 21, Donald R. Moorman papers, Donnell and Elizabeth Stewart Library Weber State University, Ogden, Utah; Mrs. Alvira L. Parrish affidavit, 26 Mar. 1859, in *Kirk Anderson's Valley Tan* (Salt Lake City), 19 Apr. 1859, [1], and in Cradlebaugh, *Utah and the Mormons,* 44-45.

121. "Another Man Killed," *Deseret News* [weekly], 1 Feb. 1860, 380, with no correction of the story's details or new information in any of the issues through 4 April. Richard S. Van Wagoner, *Lehi: Portraits of a Utah Town* (Lehi: Lehi City Corporation, 1990), 55, claimed that there was a second story in the "4 February 1860 *Deseret News,*" that Rockwell fired the fatal shot after Oats "renewed his knife threats" and "thrust at him." However, Van Wagoner's source note (417n18) showed that this added version appeared in the *Mountaineer,* a newspaper co-published by fellow "Be'hoy" Hosea Stout (diary, 27 Aug. 1859, in Brooks, *On the Mormon Frontier,* 2:701). See "THE SHOOTING AFFAIR AT THE HOT SPRING BREWERY," *Mountaineer* (Salt Lake City), 4 Feb. 1860, 94, which also claimed that Oats "was standing on the road, evidently awaiting his approach," a significant departure from the earlier report by *Deseret News* that Rockwell "overtook Oats, who had not made good speed, or had been loitering along by the way for no good . . ."

122. Carlos A. Badger diary, 14 July 1902, LDS archives, quoted in Rodney J. Badger, *Liahona and Iron Rod: The Biography of Carl A. and Rose J. Badger* (N.p.: Rodney J. Badger Family History Publishers, 1985), 193; Jenson, *Latter-day Saint Biographical Encyclopedia,* 1:604; Esshom, *Pioneers and Prominent Men of Utah,* 729.

123. "PRIESTLY DEFAMERS OF THE DEAD," *Deseret Evening News,* 21 June 1878, [2]. For Rockwell's alleged murder of the Aiken father, son, and relatives who had been arrested as "supposed spies" during the Utah War, see Hosea Stout diary, 8 Nov. 1857, in Brooks, *On the Mormon Frontier,* 2:644, also 644n15; Alice Lamb affidavit, 30 May 1859, in Cradlebaugh, *Utah and the Mormons,* 65-66; "THE AIKEN MURDER. The Collett Trial Commenced," *Salt Lake Daily Herald,* 9 Oct. 1878, [3]; "THE AIKEN MURDER," *Salt Lake Daily Herald,* 10 Oct. 1878, [3]; "THE AIKEN MURDER," *Salt Lake Daily Herald,* 11 Oct. 1878, [3]; "THE COLLETT TRIAL," *Salt Lake Daily Herald,* 12 Oct. 1878, [3]; "THE COLLETT TRIAL," *Salt Lake Daily Herald,* 13 Oct. 1878, [3]; "ALL IN. The Last Testimony in the Collett Case," *Salt Lake Daily Herald,* 15 Oct. 1878, [1]; "THE ARGUMENTS," *Salt Lake Daily Herald,* 16 Oct. 1878, [1]; "NOT GUILTY," *Salt Lake Daily Herald,* 17 Oct. 1878, [1]; A[nthony]. Metcalf, *Ten Years Before the Mast . . . How I Became a Mormon and Why I Became An Infidel* (Malad, ID: By the author, 1888), 36-37; Orson F. Whitney, *History of Utah,* 4 vols. (Salt Lake City: George Q. Cannon & Sons, 1892-1904), 3: 27-35; Schindler, *Orrin Porter Rockwell,* 268-79; Hilton, *"Wild Bill" Hickman,* 69-70; Richard Lloyd Dewey, *Porter Rockwell: The Definitive Biography* (New York: Paramount Books, 1986), 397-401, stresses the inconsistencies in the court testimony.

124. "THE COLLETT CASE," *Deseret Evening News,* 10 Oct. 1878, [2].

125. Sonne, *World of Wakara,* 56.

126. Whitney, *History of Utah,* 2:630-38; Roberts, *Comprehensive History,* 4:133, 5:405-406; Susa Young Gates and Leah Young Dunford Widtsoe, *The Life Story of Brigham Young* (New York: Macmillan, 1930), 315; Van Wagoner and Walker, *Book of Mormons,* 123; Moorman and Sessions, *Camp Floyd and the Mormons,* 239, 243-44. Moorman was non-LDS, Sessions a Mormon.

127. Hickman, *Brigham's Destroying Angel,* 96-98; Hosea Stout diary, 9 Apr., 1 May, 3 May 1854, in Brooks, *On the Mormon Frontier,* 2:512, 514; also R. N. Baskin, *Reminiscences of Early Utah* (Salt Lake City: By the author, 1914), 152-54; Hilton, *"Wild Bill" Hickman,* 43-44.

128. Hilton, *"Wild Bill" Hickman,* 62; appendix, "Appointments To the Theocratic Council of Fifty Through 1884." Leonard J. Arrington, "William A. ('Bill') Hickman: Setting the Record Straight," *Task Papers in LDS History,* No. 28 (Salt Lake City: Historical Department, The Church of Jesus Christ of Latter-day Saints, 1979), 12, observed: "Bill may have wrongfully interpreted this phrase as sanction for some of the activities in which he later engaged."

129. Brigham Young office journal, 3 Apr. 1860, LDS archives, with typescript in fd 10, box 11, Moorman papers; also in Peterson, "Mormon Reformation" (1981), 188-89, in Paul H. Peterson, "The Mormon Reformation of 1856-1857," *Journal of Mormon History* 15 (1989): 73, in Moorman and Sessions, *Camp Floyd and the Mormons,* 242; Allan Kent Powell, "Abraham Owen Smoot," in Powell, *Utah History Encyclopedia,* 507; appendix, "Appointments To the Theocratic Council of Fifty Through 1884."

130. Statements of Louide Noble Badger whose widowed mother and sister both married George Stringham's brother, in Carlos A. Badger diary, 14 July 1902, quoted in Badger, *Liahona and Iron Rod,* 194; Hilton, *"Wild Bill" Hickman,* 117. For Stringham's admission of plotting Pike's murder with Hickman, the Mormon jury's acquittal of the man who admitted killing Pike, and for the dismissal of charges against Stringham, see "THE EXAMINATION. The Closing Testimony on Behalf of the Prosecution," *Deseret Evening News,* 16 Aug. 1888, [3]; "A JUST VERDICT," and "VERDICT OF NOT GUILTY. What the Jury Say in the Spencer Case," *Deseret Evening News,* 11 May 1889, [2, 3]; "Third District Court," *Deseret Evening News,* 13 Sept. 1889, [3]. For Robinson, Pike, and their murders, see Roberts, *Comprehensive History,* 5: 194-99, 202-206, 503-505; and Thomas G. Alexander and James B. Allen, *Mormons & Gentiles: A History of Salt Lake City* (Boulder, CO: Pruett Publishing Co., 1984), 54, neither of which mentions that Brigham Young withdrew his publicly announced reward for Robinson's murderers after Mormons were accused of the crime. See Brigham Young, "PUBLIC NOTICE," *Deseret Evening News,* 3 Feb. 1872, [1].

131. Nathaniel George Stringham, ed., *Briant Stringham and His People* (Salt Lake City: Stevens & Wallis Press, 1949), 95.

132. "To Whom It May Concern," *Deseret Evening News,* 29 May 1874, [3]; "Chips," *Salt Lake Daily Herald,* 11 July 1879, [3]; "The Stringams Arrested," *Deseret Evening News,* 2 July 1890, [3]; "The Stringam Case," *Deseret Evening News,* 5 July 1890, [3]; "Died," *Deseret Evening News,* 3 Sept. 1906, 2.

133. John Bennion diary, 13-14 Oct. 1860, Utah State Historical Society; Hilton, *"Wild Bill" Hickman,* 96, 119; Lynn M. Hilton and Hope A. Hilton, "William Adams Hickman," in Powell, *Utah History Encyclopedia,* 253.

134. Hosea Stout diary, 26 May 1845, 21 Sept. 1851, in Brooks, *On the Mormon Frontier,* 1: 46, 404; "Plea of George A. Smith, Esq., *Deseret News* [weekly], 15 Nov. 1851, [3]; *Journal of Discourses* 1:97 (G.A. Smith/1851); Franklin D. Richards, comp., *Latter-day Saints in Utah . . . Plea of George A. Smith and Charge of the Hon. Judge Z. Snow Upon the Trial of Howard Egan Before the United States District Court On Indictment For the Murder of James Monroe . . .* (Liverpool, Eng.: F. D. Richards, 1852); also J. Raman Drake, "Howard Egan: Frontiersman, Pioneer and Pony Express Rider," M.S. thesis, Brigham Young University, 1956, 33-34, 37-38, 112-13; Kenneth L. Cannon II, "'Mountain Common Law': The Extralegal Punishment of Seducers in Early Utah," *Utah Historical Quarterly* 51 (Fall 1983): 310-17; Homer, "The Judiciary and the Common Law in Utah," 100.

135. William M. Egan, ed., *Pioneering the West, 1847 to 1878: Major Howard Egan's Diary* (Richmond, UT: Howard R. Egan Estate, 1917), 283; Ann W. Engar, "Beehive and Lion Houses," in Powell, *Utah History Encyclopedia,* 38.

136. Hosea Stout diary, 27 Sept. 1845, in Brooks, *On the Mormon Frontier,* 1: 76; Elden J. Watson, ed., *MANUSCRIPT HISTORY of Brigham Young, 1846-1847* (Salt Lake City: By the author, 1971), 480 (20 Dec. 1846), 530 (24 Feb. 1847); "DISCOURSE By Jedediah M. Grant, Tabernacle, G.S.L. City, March 12th, 1851 [1854]," *Deseret News* [weekly], 27 July 1854, [2]; "REMARKS By President J. M. Grant, Bowery, Sunday Morning, Sept. 21, 1856," *Deseret News* [weekly], 1 Oct. 1856, 235; *Journal of Discourses* 1:73 (Hyde/1853), 1: 83 (B. Young/1853), 1:97 (G.A. Smith/1851), 1:108 (B. Young/1853), 3:246-47 (B. Young/1856), 4:49-51 (J.M. Grant/1856), 4:53-54 (B. Young/1856), 4:173-74 (Kimball/1857), 4:219-20 (B. Young/1857), 4:375 (Kimball/1857), 6:38 (Kimball/1857), 7:20 (Kimball/1854), 7:146 (B. Young/1859), 10:110 (B. Young/1863); Gene A. Sessions, *Mormon Thunder: A Docu-*

mentary History of Jedediah Morgan Grant (Urbana: University of Illinois Press, 1982), 125-30, 211; John W. Welch and John William Maddox, "Reflections on the Teachings of Brigham Young," in Susan Easton Black and Larry C. Porter, eds., *Lion of the Lord: Essays on the Life & Service of Brigham Young* (Salt Lake City: Deseret Book Co., 1995), 393, listed two of these sermons on "Blood Atonement."

137. Joseph F. Smith, Jr. [Joseph Fielding Smith], *Blood Atonement and the Origin of Plural Marriage* (Salt Lake City: Deseret News Press, 1905), 15-16, 36-37, 42-43, 47-48; Lowell M. Snow, "Blood Atonement," in Ludlow, *Encyclopedia of Mormonism*, 1:131.

138. Joseph Fielding Smith, *Doctrines of Salvation*, Bruce R. McConkie, comp., 3 vols. (Salt Lake City: Bookcraft, 1954), 1:134; also Charles W. Penrose, *Blood Atonement, As Taught By Leading Elders of the Church of Jesus Christ of Latter-day Saints* (Salt Lake City: Juvenile Instructor Office, 1884), 23-29; Roberts, *Comprehensive History*, 4:128-29; Bruce R. McConkie, *Mormon Doctrine*, 2d ed. (Salt Lake City: Bookcraft, 1966), 92.

139. Roberts, *Comprehensive History*, 4:126; Peterson, "Mormon Reformation" (1981), 177; Peterson, "Mormon Reformation of 1856-1857," (1989), 66-67, 73-75; Penrose, *Blood Atonement*, 35; Alexander, *Utah*, 124; Lowell M. Snow, "Blood Atonement," in Ludlow, *Encyclopedia of Mormonism*, 1:131; Paul H. Peterson, "Brigham Young and the Mormon Reformation," in Black and Porter, *Lion of the Lord*, 251. Peterson's essay in this Deseret Book Company publication (contrary to his previous writings) does not even mention the phrase "blood atonement" in the text or notes (244-61). Compare with the less defensive Keith E. Norman, "A Kinder Gentler Mormonism: Moving Beyond the Violence of Our Past," *Sunstone* 14 (Aug. 1990): 10-11. Without specific reference to blood-atonement sermons, Eugene England, *Brother Brigham* (Salt Lake City: Bookcraft, 1980), 169, commented on Young's "hyperbolic rhetoric," and "his more acute aversion to bloodshed than many of his frontier-conditioned associates" (182).

140. *History of the Church*, 5:296; Joseph Smith's statement, "I'll wring a thief's neck off if I can find him. if I cannot bring him to justice any other way," first manuscript version (10), minutes of general conference on 6 Apr. 1843, LDS archives, but rendered simply as "I despise a thief above ground," in *Times and Seasons* 4 (1 May 1843): 183-84; Sidney Rigdon statement, "There are men standing in your midst that you cant do anything with them but cut their throat & bury them," 6 Apr. 1844, compiled on 24 Apr. 1844 by Thomas Bullock, LDS archives, but deleted from the published report; Quinn, *Mormon Hierarchy: Origins of Power*, 112, 182, 637, 643, also 94, for a faithful Mormon's claim that Rigdon made a similar statement in 1838.

141. *History of the Church*, 7:597.

142. Thomas Bullock diary, 13 Dec. 1846.

143. Willard Richards diary, 20 Dec. 1846; also Watson, *MANUSCRIPT HISTORY of Brigham Young, 1846-1847*, 480 (20 Dec. 1846); Hosea Stout diary, 13 Mar. 1847, in Brooks, *On the Mormon Frontier*, 1:241. For Brigham Young's being publicly sustained as church president in 1845 and using that title in copyrights of LDS scripture that year, see Quinn, *Mormon Hierarchy: Origins of Power*, 178-79.

144. John D. Lee diary, 21 Nov. 1846, in Charles Kelly, ed., *Journals of John D. Lee, 1846-47 and 1859* (Salt Lake City: Western Printing Co., 1938), 21, which was overlooked in Eugene E. Campbell, "Authority Conflicts in the Mormon Battalion," *Brigham Young University Studies* 8 (Winter 1968): 132-34. Unlike Campbell, Susan Easton Black, "The Mormon Battalion: Religious Authority Clashed with Military Leadership," in Black and Porter, *Lion of the Lord*, 158, referred to the conflict between Lee and Lt. Smith but did not refer to Lee's diary reference in the text or notes (168-71). For Lt. Smith, see Hamilton Gardner, "The Command and Staff of the Mormon Battalion in the Mexican War," *Utah Historical Quarterly* 20 (Oct. 1952): 346-47.

145. Minutes of the Quorum of the Twelve Apostles, 3 Dec. 1847, 6, Miscellaneous Minutes, Brigham Young papers, LDS archives; Mary Haskin Parker Richards diary, 16 Apr. 1848, in Maurine Carr Ward, ed., *Winter Quarters: The 1846-1848 Life Writings of Mary Haskin Parker Richards* (Logan: Utah State University Press, 1996), 212; Daniel Davis diary, 8 July 1849, LDS archives.

146. John D. Lee diary, 3 Mar., 4 Mar., 17 Mar. 1849, in Cleland and Brooks, *Mormon Chronicle*, 1:98, 102.

147. "CRIMINAL LAWS OF THE STATE OF DESERET, *Passed* January 16, 1851," sec. 10, in Morgan, *State of Deseret*, 177; Martin R. Gardner, "Mormonism and Capital Punishment: A Doctrinal Perspective, Past and Present," *Dialogue: A Journal of Mormon Thought* 12 (Spring 1979): 13.

148. Winslow Farr diary, LDS archives, quoted in Peterson, "Mormon Reformation" (1981), 195; Davis Bitton, *Guide to Mormon Diaries & Autobiographies* (Provo, UT: Brigham Young University Press, 1977), 105.

149. Fellowship Meeting minutes, Salt Lake Fifth Ward Historical Record, 31 May 1857, quoted in Peterson, "Mormon Reformation" (1981), 185; "DISCOURSE By Jedediah M. Grant, Tabernacle, G.S.L. City, March 12th, 1851 [1854]," *Deseret News* [weekly], 27 July 1854, [1-2]; Kenney, *Wilford Woodruff's Journal* 4 (12 Mar. 1854): 254, "Jedediah M. Grant Preached to the People Concerning executing the Law of God upon all persons who broke their Covenants."

150. George A. Hicks to "Eds. TRIBUNE," 12 Aug. 1874, in "SOME STARTLING FACTS. A Saint of Thirty Years' Standing Unburdens His Bosom," *Salt Lake Daily Tribune*, 20 Aug. 1874, [4]; George A. Hicks, "A History of Spanish Fork," typescript dated 13 June 1913, 13, Lee Library, does not have the above quote but said: "The church was to be purified; undesirable people were to be removed."

151. Mary L. Campbell to Andrew Jenson, 24 Jan. 1892, LDS archives, quoted in Moorman and Sessions, *Camp Floyd and the Mormons*, 142.

152. John Smith patriarchal blessing to John Smith (b. 1832), 22 Jan. 1845, quoted in Irene M. Bates, "Patriarchal Blessings and the Routinization of Charisma," *Dialogue: A Journal of Mormon Thought* 26 (Fall 1993): 12, 12n45, also 21.

153. Elisha H. Groves patriarchal blessing to William H. Dame, 20 Feb. 1854, photocopy of handwritten manuscript, in Harold W. Pease, "The Life and Works of William Horne Dame," M.A. thesis, Brigham Young University, 1971, 64-66, 192; Elisha H. Groves patriarchal blessing to William Leany, 23 Feb. 1854, in Leany autobiography, 8, typescript, Utah State Historical Society; Juanita Brooks, *The Mountain Meadows Massacre*, rev. ed. (Norman: University of Oklahoma Press, 1962), 80, 92, 95; Moorman and Sessions, *Camp Floyd and the Mormons*, 134, 137-38, for Dame's role in the massacre, and 126-31, for the significance of the Arkansas origin of these emigrants and of the Mormon-baiting by the Missourians who joined the Arkansas families on route to Utah; also Roger V. Logan, Jr., "New Light on the Mountain Meadows Caravan," *Utah Historical Quarterly* 60 (Summer 1992): 224-27.

154. Anna Jean Backus, *Mountain Meadows Witness: The Life and Times of Bishop Philip Klingensmith* (Spokane: Arthur H. Clark Co., 1995), 118, 124, 124n17, 125; also Elisha H. Groves patriarchal blessing to Joseph Fish, 30 Jan. 1857, in Peterson, "Mormon Reformation" (1981), 192, to "become an avenger of the blood of innocence upon them that dwell upon the earth."

155. Samuel L. Sprague's prayer circle minutes, 21 Sept. 1857, LDS archives; see also D. Michael Quinn, "Latter-day Saint Prayer Circles," *Brigham Young University Studies* 19 (Fall 1978): 79-105; George S. Tate, "Prayer Circle," in Ludlow, *Encyclopedia of Mormonism*, 3:1121.

156. Abraham H. Cannon diary, 6 Dec. 1889; also Quinn, *Mormon Hierarchy: Origins of Power*, 179.

157. Iron County Court Minute Book B, 8, 19-20 July 1854, quoted in Brooks, *John Doyle Lee*, 189.

158. James H. Martineau record of Parowan, Utah, 20 (19 Oct. 1856), William Rees Palmer and Kate Vilate Palmer papers, Special Collections, Library, Southern Utah University, Cedar City, quoted in Backus, *Mountain Meadows Witness*, 123.

159. Isaac C. Haight to Brigham Young, 29 Oct. 1856, LDS archives, cited in Peterson, "Mormon Reformation" (1981), 198n66, as part of a general summary of this attitude; Peterson, "Mormon Reformation of 1856-1857" (1989), 75, summarized Haight's letter specifically and quoted Brigham Young's reply 5 Mar. 1857, as cited on 85n125. Peterson made no comment about the four-month delay in Young's reply about this man's request to be blood-atoned. For Haight's enthusiastic role in the Mountain Meadows Massacre, see Brooks, *Mountain Meadows Massacre*, 93, 192, 197-98; Brooks, *John Doyle Lee*, 211, 221; Moorman and Sessions, *Camp Floyd and the Mormons*, 131, 134, 135; Backus, *Mountain Meadows Witness*, 134, 275; L. W. Macfarlane, *Yours Sincerely, John M. Macfarlane* (Salt Lake City: By the author, 1980), 64-65.

160. Alexander Neibaur diary, 22 Jan. 1862, LDS archives.

161. At least regarding blood atonement, the evidence does not support Ronald W. Walker, "Raining Pitchforks: Brigham Young As Preacher," *Sunstone* 8 (May-June 1983): 8, "The Saints also understood that there was little bite to his celebrated bark."

162. "The Reformation: Sung in the 17th Ward School House by P. Margetts," *Deseret News* [weekly], 26 Nov. 1856, 302.

163. "Up, awake, ye defenders of Zion!", "Lift up your heads, ye scattered Saints," "Awake, ye Saints of God, awake!", "Wake, O wake, the world from sleeping!", "O! ye mountains high," "Deseret, Deseret!", *Sacred Hymns and Spiritual Songs* (1871), 73-74, 314, 330, 332, 377, 385.

164. Hosea Stout diary, 17 Mar. 1851, in Brooks, *On the Mormon Frontier*, 2:396; "Served Him Right," *Deseret Evening News*, 5 Mar. 1868, [3]; also Cannon, "Mountain Common Law," 310; Homer, "The Judiciary and the Common Law in Utah Territory," 100.

165. William Leany, Sr., at Harrisburg, Utah, to John Steele, 17 Feb. 1883, fd 21, box 1, Steele papers, Lee Library, quoted and discussed in Wesley P. Larsen, "The 'Letter' or Were the Powell Men Really Killed by Indians?" *Canyon Legacy: A Journal of the Dan O'Laurie Museum–Moab, Utah* 17 (Spring 1993), 12-19 (esp. 16-17); Kerry William Bate, "John Steele: Medicine Man, Magician, Mormon Patriarch," *Utah Historical Quarterly* 62 (Winter 1994): 87, which quoted the letter's final reference to "the killing of the three in one room in our own ward . . ." Also Paul Dean Proctor and Morris A. Shirts, *Silver, Sinners & Saints: A History of Old Silver Reef, Utah* ([Sandy, UT]: Paulmar, Inc., 1991), 4, for 1860s map of Harrisburg showing William Leany's residence and, 75, for residence of John Steele in nearby Toquerville; also Andrew Karl Larsen, *"I Was Called To Dixie": The Virgin River Basin: Unique Experiences In Mormon Pioneering* (St. George, UT: Dixie College Foundation, 1992), 78, "The peak of Harrisburg's growth was reached about 1868 when twenty-five families lived there"; Firmage, *History of Grand County*, 101-102, that "three members of his [Powell's] first expedition were killed in southern Utah or northern Arizona when they left the expedition in the Grand Canyon and attempted to walk to the Mormon settlements."

Leany's letter could also be interpreted as referring to the alleged killing of three men a decade earlier than the Powell case, but near Leany's residence. In his testimony during the trial of John D. Lee in 1875, Philip Klingensmith spoke of "three other men said to have been put out of the way [in Cedar City] when I was in Salt Lake, that I didn't know anything about" (Backus, *Mountain Meadows Witness*, 120). Lee, *Mormonism Unveiled*, 273, claimed that stake president Isaac C. Haight and Philip Klingensmith, bishop of Cedar City, approved the killings. Lee said the perpetrators were John M. Higbee, John Weston, James Haslam, William C. Stewart, "and I think another man, but if so I have forgotten his name." However, there are four significant variations from the case Leany's letter described. According to Lee, the three men were killed in a distillery (not a ward house), in Cedar City (not Harrisburg or Toquerville), by a group of men (rather than one "murderer"). Also, the named perpetrators died of natural causes decades later instead of being "killed to stop the shed[d]ing of more blood."

166. Eliot Porter, ed., *Down the Colorado: Diary of the First Trip Through the Grand Canyon, 1869* (New York: E. P. Dutton, 1969), 139 (28 Aug. 1869); William Culp Darrah, *Powell of the Colorado* (Princeton, NJ: Princeton University Press, 1951), 145. Darrah described (157) the August 1870 meeting of LDS scout Jacob Hamblin and Powell with Shivwit Indians who acknowledged (according to Hamblin's translation) that they killed the three men and expressed regret to Powell. In "Did Murders Happen in Mormon Ward? 1883 Letter May Solve Mystery of Trio," *Salt Lake Tribune,* 28 Nov. 1993, B-3, professor emeritus Wesley P. Larsen observed that "Hamblin could have told Powell anything since the explorer didn't know the language," and the scout may have invented a translation that exonerated his fellow Mormons while still satisfying Powell's inquiries.

167. "Geo. C. L." to editor, 1 Jan. 1870, in *Deseret Evening News,* 18 Jan. 1870, [1], about "passing on my way Washington, Harrisburg and Leeds"; Larsen, *I Was Called To Dixie,* 517.

168. "Jack Sumner's Account," and "William Hawkins' Story" in Robert Brewster Stanton, *Colorado River Controversies,* ed. James M. Chalfant (New York: Dodd, Mead, & Co., 1932), 203, 161. Sumner (b. 1840) became suspicious (208-209) during the visit of Bishop James Leithead and his counselor Andrew V. Gibbons to the exploring camp on the Colorado River, because the two Mormons showed sudden interest in the recently departed men after learning of the valuable equipment the three had taken with them. Several years later Sumner saw someone in the area with a watch Sumner had given to one of the victims, and he concluded (209) that "the Indians were not at the head of the murder, if they had anything to do with it." In publishing his river-exploring friend's suspicions, Stanton (b. 1846) had no personal animosity toward the Mormons. Two years before his own death Stanton wrote: "I wish that all of my Christian friends had the spirit of kindness and charity that it has been my good fortune to find among the Mormons in northern Arizona and *southern* Utah" (emphasis in original), from his *Down the Colorado,* ed. Dwight L. Smith (Norman: University of Oklahoma Press, 1965), 122; also "EXPLORATION OF THE COLORADO FINISHED," *Deseret Evening News,* 15 Sept. 1869, [2], for Bishop Leithead's visit to the Powell group.

169. Larsen in "The 'Letter,'" 16, and "Did Murders Happen in Mormon Ward? 1883 Letter May Solve Mystery of Trio," *Salt Lake Tribune,* 28 Nov. 1993, B-3, theorized that Eli N. Pace committed the murders because he thought the three men were actually federal deputies trying to arrest his father-in-law John D. Lee for the Mountain Meadows Massacre. Shot in the heart under mysterious circumstances in January 1870, Pace's death was declared a suicide by an inquest jury of three Mormons from Toquerville, including Isaac C. Haight. See previously cited references for Haight's role in the massacre, also John D. Lee diary, 29 Jan. 1870, in Cleland and Brooks, *A Mormon Chronicle,* 2:133-34, for Pace's death and inquest. Leany's letter did not exclude the possibility of a five-month interval between the death of the three men and the killing of the perpetrator, but the letter clearly indicated that the perpetrator was killed to avoid retribution on the LDS community.

170. Peterson, "Warren Stone Snow," 112-15, citing Thomas Pitchforth diary, 31 May 1857, and Brigham Young to Warren Snow, 7 July 1857, also Kenney, *Wilford Woodruff's Journal* 5 (2 June 1857): 55, for Young's initial reaction.

Various LDS sources indicate that Thomas Lewis was twenty-three, twenty-four, or twenty-five at this 1857 incident, so my text discussion uses the middle one. He was listed as age 16 when his mother Elizabeth emigrated to Utah with her six children in 1849. The 1860 census listed Thomas as a twenty-eight-year-old Welch bachelor living with his mother in Manti. The LDS International Genealogical Index gives only the year 1833 as the birth date of Thomas Lewis, while the LDS Ancestral File for his father David Thomas Lewis (who never came to Utah) gave his son Thomas's birth year as 1834, and indicated that the son died unmarried in 1854, the latter date being an obvious error. His actual death date is presently unknown, but Thomas Lewis lived long enough to join his younger brother Lewis Lewis and two friends in an attempt to castrate Warren Snow in revenge in March 1872. Snow used a pistol to shoot two of his attackers, and perhaps this was when Thomas Lewis actually died. See Elizabeth Lewis and children in Utah Overland Immigration Index (1847-68), the Manti Ward Record of Members (1850-75), 18, 19, 20, Ancestral File for David Thomas Lewis (b. 1809), and Thomas Lewis in International Genealogical Index (IGI) for Wales, Family History Library, Church of Jesus Christ of Latter-day Saints, Salt Lake City, Utah (hereafter LDS Family History Library); 1860 Census of Manti, Sanpete County, Utah, 23 (p. 656 of entire census); Peterson, "Warren Stone Snow," 120-21. Some historians have also confused the castrated and never-married Welshman Thomas Lewis (born ca. 1832-34) with a decade-younger Englishman of the same name who married, fathered children, and first appeared with his wife and one-year-old child in the 1870 Utah census of Salt Lake City. Aside from the significant age disparity, the Utah census consistently distinguished Wales from England as a birthplace. See U.S. 1870 Census of Salt Lake City, Salt Lake County, Utah, sheet 724-B, microfilm, LDS Family History Library.

Some reminiscent accounts confused this 1857 incident involving a Welshman with an 1859 incident in which a diary referred to an unnamed bishop who had just castrated a young Danish man so that the bishop could marry his girlfriend (see below). Some reminiscent accounts claimed the bishop in this 1859 castration was Warren Snow. This indicates either that Bishop Snow committed a second castration (not inconceivable in view of Brigham Young's approval of the 1857 castration) or that later accounts mistakenly blamed him for a castration performed by someone else two years later.

171. Bringhurst, *Brigham Young,* 133, also on aftermath of Drummond's complaints (134-48); Creer, *Utah and the Nation,* 117-23; Haynes, "Federal Government and Its Policies Regarding the Frontier Era of Utah Territory," 75-77; Rich, *Ensign to the Nations,* 219-24; Ashton, *Federal Judiciary In Utah,* 10-11.

172. Moorman and Sessions, *Camp Floyd and the Mormons,* 10-20, for background of the Utah War, 21 for quotes; Brigham Young diary, 24 July, 11 Aug., 16 Aug. 1857, in Everett L. Cooley, ed., *Diary of Brigham Young, 1857* (Salt Lake City: Tanner Trust Fund/University of Utah Library, 1980), 49, 58, 60; Brigham Young and Daniel H. Wells to William H. Dame at Parowan, Utah, 14 Sept. 1857, typescript in fd 6, box 21, Moorman papers; also Creer, *Utah and the Nation,* 126-35; Furniss, *Mormon Conflict,* 18, 55-124; Haynes, "Federal Government and Its Policies Regarding the Frontier Era of Utah Territory," 82-92, 105-11; Allen and Leonard, *Story of the Latter-day Saints,* 305-11; MacKinnon, "125 Years of Conspiracy Theories," 212-30; Clifford L. Stott, *Search For Sanctuary: Brigham Young and the White Mountain Expedition* (Salt Lake City: University of Utah Press, 1984), 28-29; Jones, "Brigham Young's Rhetoric," 201-40; Ashton, *Federal Judiciary In Utah,* 12-13; Richard D. Poll and William P. MacKinnon, "Causes of the Utah War Reconsidered," *Journal of Mormon History* 20 (Fall 1994): 16-44.

173. *Journal of Discourses* 5:223 (G.A. Smith/1857); Brooks, *Mountain Meadows Massacre,* 36-40; Backus, *Mountain Meadows Witness,* 98-101; Church Historian's office journal, 8-26 Aug. 1857, for references to George A. Smith's sermons in southern Utah.

174. John D. Lee diary, 29 Dec. 1870, in Cleland and Brooks, *Mormon Chronicle,* 2:152; Abraham H. Cannon diary, 11 June, 13 June 1895; Benjamin Knell statement in Joseph E. Robinson diary, 25 July 1906, LDS archives; Creer, *Utah and the Nation,* 192-214; Brooks, *Mountain Meadows Massacre,* 52-56, 69-108, 192, 224-41; Claude Thomas Boring, "The Mountain Meadows Massacre: A Reassessment," M.A. thesis, University of Southern California, 1961; Brooks, *John D. Lee,* 202-15; Van Wagoner and Walker, *Book of Mormons,*

158; Moorman and Sessions, *Camp Floyd and the Mormons,* 131-36; Backus, *Mountain Meadows Witness,* 103-118, 129-38; Robert Kent Fielding, *The Unsolicited Chronicler: An Account of the Gunnison Massacre: Its Causes and Consequences, Utah Territory, 1847-1859* (Brookline, MA: Paradigm Publications, 1993), 404-405, 413-17; Jay M. Haymond, "John D. Lee," and Morris A. Shirts, "Mountain Meadows Massacre," in Powell, *Utah History Encyclopedia,* 321, 384-85.

175. Watson, *MANUSCRIPT HISTORY of Brigham Young, 1846-1847,* 359 (31 Aug. 1846); Quinn, *Mormon Hierarchy: Origins of Power,* 657; Brigham Young to Jeter Clinton, 12 Sept. 1857, Young letterbook 3:841, LDS archives, with transcription in fd 6, box 21, Moorman papers; Brigham Young diary, 1 Sept. 1857, in Cooley, *Diary of Brigham Young, 1857,* 71; also Madsen, *Northern Shoshoni,* 30.

176. Francis M. Gibbons, *Brigham Young: Modern Moses, Prophet of God* (Salt Lake City: Deseret Book Co., 1981), 210; compared with Roberts, *Comprehensive History,* 4:153, 155-57; McLaws, *Spokesman for the Kingdom,* 75; Allen and Leonard, *Story of the Latter-day Saints,* 312-13; Ronald K. Esplin and Richard E. Turley, Jr., "Mountain Meadows Massacre," in Ludlow, *Encyclopedia of Mormonism,* 2:966-67.

177. Kenney, *Wilford Woodruff's Journal,* 5 (29 Sept. 1857): 102; "MOUNTAIN MEADOWS MASSACRE. New Indictments Against the Alleged Murderers. The Statement of John D. Lee which was Refused by the Prosecution," *Salt Lake Herald,* 21 July 1875, [3], also similar description in Brigham Young to Thomas L. Kane, 15 Dec. 1859, quoted in Moorman and Sessions, *Camp Floyd and the Mormons,* 139.

178. Francis M. Lyman diary, 19 Sept. 1895, LDS archives; David O. McKay diary, 27 July 1907, LDS archives.

179. In answer to the inquiry about destroying the emigrant train, Brigham Young wrote Isaac C. Haight, 10 Sept. 1857: "In regard to emigration trains passing through our settlements we must not interfere with them untill they are first notified to keep away. You must not meddle with them. The Indians we expect will do as they please but you should try and preserve good feelings with them. There are no other trains going south that I know of if those who are there will leave let [sic] them go in peace" (Young letterbook 3:827-28, transcription in fd 6, box 21, Moorman papers). However, Fielding, *Unsolicited Chronicler,* 405, regards even this emphatic letter as containing an authorization for Indian allies to destroy the emigrant train.

180. Kenney, *Wilford Woodruff's Journal,* 5 (25 May 1861): 577; John D. Lee diary, [30] May 1861, in Cleland and Brooks, *Mormon Chronicle,* 1:314. The accuracy of this sermon quote is supported by the fact that at the end of this entry Lee correctly reported Young's statement five days earlier as: "Vengeance is Mine Saith the Lord, & I have taken a litle of it."

181. Gustive O. Larson, "The Mormon Reformation," *Utah Historical Quarterly* 26 (Jan. 1958): 62n39.

182. Ben Brown, ed., *The Journal of Lorenzo Brown, 1823-1900* ([St. George, Utah]: Heritage Press, n.d.), 92, 93 (1 Dec., 13 Dec. 1857); Frederick Kesler diary, 1 Dec. 1857, Marriott Library, for second quotation which described the previous day's court martial on 30 November and the next day's general assembly and ratifying vote; Daniel H. Wells general order, 28 Nov. 1857, providing for a general court martial on 30 November, Document 628, fd 41, box 1, Series 2210, Territorial Militia Records (1849-1877), Utah State Archives, Salt Lake City; Patriarchal Blessing Index (1833-1963) and Ancestral File for Willis Drake (b. 10 July 1836, with no death date or marriage date listed), LDS Family History Library. However, I was unable to locate the minutes or other reference to Drake's court martial in this collection of military records.

183. Brigham Young to Daniel H. Wells, 1 Dec. 1857, transcription of Young's unnumbered letterbook (12 Aug. 1857-Jan. 1859), 210, box 24, Moorman papers.

184. John M. Higbee history, Southern Utah University Library, as quoted in Backus, *Mountain Meadows Witness*, 134; also "painted like Indians" in Higbee (alias, "Bull Valley Snort"), typescript, 1, Utah State Historical Society, also quoted in Brooks, *Mountain Meadows Massacre*, 227; Moorman and Sessions, *Camp Floyd and the Mormons*, 133, that "John D. Lee joined the Indians, disguised as one of the war party" against the Arkansas-Missourian emigrant train.

185. Hosea Stout diary, 27 Feb. 1858, 17 Aug. 1858, 26 Mar. 1859, in Brooks, *On the Mormon Frontier*, 2:635, 663 , 692; Homer, "The Judiciary and the Common Law in Utah Territory," 105.

186. Affidavits of Nathaniel Case, Andrew J. Moore, Thomas Hollingshead, Abner M. Hollingshead, Amos B. Moore, Mar.-Apr. 1859, in "Murder of Henry Jones and his Mother," *Kirk Anderson's Valley Tan* (Salt Lake City), 19 Apr. 1859, [2], and in Cradlebaugh, *Utah and the Mormons*, 61-64; indictment of People vs. George Washington Hancock, Lycurgus Wilson, James Bracken, Price Nelson, Alvin Crockett, Daniel B. Rawson, George Patten, Charles B. Hancock, filed on 26 August 1859, older document filed with the 1889 re-indictment, Case 23, First District Court (Utah County), Criminal Case Files, Utah State Archives. The killings and castration of the infant's father-brother were reported in "ARRESTED FOR MURDER. Reviving a Tragedy of Thirty-two Years Ago," *Deseret Evening News*, 6 Nov. 1889, [3]; "The Payson Killing," *Salt Lake Herald*, 21 Mar. 1890, 5; "THE HANCOCK TRIAL. Drawing to a Close," *Deseret Evening News*, 21 Mar. 1890, [3]; "THE JONES KILLING. Mr. Hancock Denies Firing the Fatal Shot," *Deseret Evening News*, 22 Mar. 1890, [3]. The witnesses did not mention whether he was alive or dead when castrated.

187. Entries for Thomas Hancock (b. 1763), his sons Solomon (b. 1793) and Levi W. Hancock (b. 1803), and their sons Charles B. Hancock (b. 1823), George W. Hancock (b. 1826), and Mosiah Lyman Hancock (b. 1834) in Ancestral File, LDS Family History Library; Dennis A. Clegg, "Levi Ward Hancock: Pioneer and Religious Leader of Early Utah," M.A. thesis, Brigham Young University, 1966; Quinn, *Mormon Hierarchy: Origins of Power*, 550-51. For the residence of Levi W. Hancock and his son Mosiah in Payson, see Payson Ward Membership Record (Early to 1871), 5, 24, LDS Family History Library; Mosiah Lyman Hancock autobiography, typescript, 52, 58, Utah State Historical Society; Bryan Lee Dilts, comp., *1856 Utah Census Index: An Every-Name Index* (Salt Lake City: Index, 1983), 109. The 1856 census of Utah was a name-and-place only census authorized by Gov. Brigham Young.

188. "The Usual Dish of Sensations," *Deseret Evening News*, 22 Nov. 1889, [2]; "G.W. HANCOCK SENTENCED. His Term is Fixed at Ten Years in the Penitentiary," *Deseret Evening News*, 23 Apr. 1890, [3]; also "BELIEVES HIM INNOCENT. Mrs. Hancock Declares Her Husband is Guiltless," *Salt Lake Tribune*, 25 Mar. 1890, 7, for charges being dropped against Charles B. Hancock, the former bishop.

189. Brigham Young to "the officers North of Great Salt Lake City, Ecclesiastical, Civil, Military," 24 Mar. 1858, and Young to Warren S. Snow, 26 June 1858, Young letterbook 4:110, 271-72, transcriptions in fd 7, box 21, Moorman papers; Thomas L. Kane diary, 28 Mar.-10 May 1858, in Oscar Osburn Winther, ed., *The Private Papers and Diary of Thomas Leiper Kane: A Friend of the Mormons* (San Francisco: Gelber-Lilienthal, 1937), 77-79; Lot Smith, "The Echo Canyon War: Lot Smith's Narrative," *The Contributor* 4 (Oct. 1882-Mar. 1883), 27-29, 47-50, 167-69, 224-26; Otis G. Hammond, ed., *The Utah Expedition, 1857-1858: Letters of Capt. Jesse A. Gove, 10th Inf., U.S.S., of Concord, N.H., to Mrs. Gove, and Special Correspondence of the New York Herald* (Concord: New Hampshire Historical Society, 1928); Creer, *Utah and the Nation*, 136-59; Roberts, *Comprehensive History*, 4:273-451; E. Cecil McGavin, *U.S. Soldiers Invade Utah* (Boston: Meador Publishing Co., 1937), 107-62, 205-45; M. Hamlin Cannon, "The Mormon War: A Study in Territorial Rebellion," M.A. thesis, George Washington University, 1938, 35-51; Leonard J. Arrington, "Mormon Finance and the Utah War," *Utah Historical Quarterly* 20 (July 1952): 219-37; LeRoy R. Hafen and Ann

W. Hafen, eds., *The Utah Expedition, 1857-1858: A Documentary Account . . .*, vol. 8 of Hafen and Hafen, eds., *The Far West and the Rockies: Historical Series, 1820-1875*, 15 vols. (Glendale, CA: Arthur H. Clark Co., 1954-61); Don Richard Mathis, "Camp Floyd in Retrospect," M.S. thesis, University of Utah, 1959; Furniss, *Mormon Conflict*, 125-201; Haynes, "Federal Government and Its Policies Regarding the Frontier Era of Utah Territory," 93-104; Lamar, *Far Southwest*, 347-51; Charles P. Roland, *Albert Sidney Johnston: Soldier of Three Republics* (Austin: University of Texas Press, 1964), 190-214; Albert L. Zobell, Jr., *Sentinel In the East: A Biography of Thomas L. Kane* (Salt Lake City: Nicholas G. Morgan/Utah Printing Co., 1965), 101-71; Thomas G. Alexander and Leonard J. Arrington, "Camp in the Sagebrush: Camp Floyd, Utah, 1858-1861," *Utah Historical Quarterly* 34 (Winter 1966): 3-21; Rich, *Ensign to the Nations*, 243-65; Reba Lou Keele, "A Doctrinal Group Counterattacks: An Analysis of the Oral Rhetoric of the Mormons in the Utah War, 1855-1859," Ph.D. diss., Purdue University, 1974, 60-152; Gene A. Sessions and Stephen W. Stathis, "The Mormon Invasion of Russian America: Dynamics of a Potent Myth," *Utah Historical Quarterly* 45 (Winter 1977): 22-35; Leonard J. Arrington, "'In Honorable Remembrance': Thomas L. Kane's Services to the Mormons," *Brigham Young University Studies* 21 (Fall 1981): 395-98; Stott, *Search For Sanctuary*, 33-202; Wilford Hill LeCheminant, "A Crisis Averted?: General Harney and the Change in Command of the Utah Expedition," *Utah Historical Quarterly* 51 (Winter 1983): 30-45; Richard D. Poll, *Quixotic Mediator: Thomas L. Kane and the Utah War* (Ogden, UT: Weber State College Press, 1985); Moorman and Sessions, *Camp Floyd and the Mormons*, 25-56; Richard D. Poll, "The Move South," *Brigham Young University Studies* 29 (Fall 1989): 65-88; Audrey M. Godfrey, "A Social History of Camp Floyd, Utah Territory, 1858-1861," M.A. thesis, Utah State University, 1989; Richard D. Poll, "Thomas L. Kane and the Utah War," *Utah Historical Quarterly* 61 (Spring 1993): 112-35; "Utah War," *Church History In the Fulness of Times*, 368-79; Audrey M. Godfrey, "Camp Floyd," Scott Nielson, "Albert Sidney Johnston," David McAllister, "Thomas Leiper Kane," Richard D. Poll, "Utah War, in Powell, *Utah History Encyclopedia*, 66-67, 287, 295-96, 607-608.

190. Albert Sidney Johnston to William Preston Johnston, 4 Sept. 1858, Johnston papers, in Mrs. Mason Barret Collection, Manuscripts Division, Howard-Tilton Library, Tulane University, New Orleans, Louisiana, quoted in Moorman and Sessions, *Camp Floyd and the Mormons*, 292n9.

191. Church Historian's office journal, 12 Sept. 1858.

192. J. Cecil Alter and Robert J. Dwyer, eds., "Journal of Captain Albert Tracy, 1858," *Utah Historical Quarterly* 13 (1945): 32, for date of 31 July 1858. Like this discovery, a dog also found a woman's head in September. Nevertheless, these were two separate findings—the first head was "mummified" with age, whereas the second woman's head was found within days after she was last seen alive in the army camp.

193. *Journal of Discourses* 7:19-20 (Kimball/1854).

194. Smith, *Blood Atonement and the Origin of Plural Marriage*, 13.

195. John W. Phelps diary, 28 March 1859, Utah State Historical Society. Mormon apologists have disputed as unreliable the reminiscent accounts of this castration incident as found in Lee, *Mormonism Unveiled*, 285-86, and Johanna Christina Neilson Averett history, 20, Elijah Averett history, Utah State Historical Society. They both identified the castrating bishop as Warren Snow of Manti, Sanpete County, Utah, where many Danish immigrants settled. However, it seems difficult to dispute the daily diary of a soldier who recorded what the young man said on the day he told him about his being castrated. In addition, the Phelps diary did not claim that Snow was the perpetrator. Brigham Young had approved Bishop Snow's castrating a non-Danish male two years earlier. Warren Snow may not have been the bishop involved in this 1859 castration, but the incident itself apparently occurred as described in the Phelps diary. See previous discussion.

196. "REMARKS By President HEBER C. KIMBALL, delivered in Springville, Saturday morning, June 22, 1861," *Deseret News* [weekly], 20 Aug. 1862, 58.

197. "REMARKS By President BRIGHAM YOUNG, Tabernacle, Feb. 9th, 1862," *Deseret News* [weekly], 26 Mar. 1862, [305]; A. R. Mortensen, ed., "Elias Smith: Journal of a Pioneer Editor, March 6, 1859-September 23, 1863," *Utah Historical Quarterly* 21 (Oct. 1953): 350.

198. Church Historian's office journal, 4 Aug. 1862; Journal History, 4 Aug. 1862, 1.

199. John Devitry-Smith, "The Saint and the Grave Robber," *Brigham Young University Studies* 33, No. 1 (1993): 50n97, for "folklore" that Ephraim Hanks killed Baptiste. A description of Hanks killing Baptiste was in John R. Young to Francis M. Young, 20 Nov. 1924, John R. Young Scrapbook, LDS archives.

200. "A GRUESOME TALE. How Jean Baptiste, the Grave Robber, Was Branded and Banished," *Salt Lake Herald*, 2 Apr. 1893, 8; "Robber of the Dead. Story of Jean Baptiste's Grave Desecration," *Deseret Evening News*, 27 May 1893, 8; also Allen D. Roberts, "History of Antelope Island in the Great Salt Lake, Utah," bound mimeograph, [1983], 40-42, Utah State Historical Society. Devitry-Smith, "The Saint and the Grave Robber," 8, 22-29, 49n73-50n99, made no reference to the *Salt Lake Herald*'s claim of finding the decapitated skeleton of Baptiste, even though 49n74 cited the *Deseret News* reply to the *Herald*.

201. Albert Winkler, "The Circleville Massacre: A Brutal Incident in Utah's Black Hawk War," *Utah Historical Quarterly* 55 (Winter 1987): 4-21 (esp. 18-20).

202. Brigham Young, Jr., diary, 11 Dec. 1866, LDS archives; "Recent Murder," *Daily Union Vedette* (Salt Lake City), 13 Dec. 1866, [3], gave this version of the inscription: "Notice to all Niggers! Warning!! Leave white women alone!!!" There were no other newspapers in the city at this time. The entire month of December 1866 is missing on the microfilm of the *Deseret News* at Brigham Young University, LDS archives, University of Utah, and Utah State Historical Society.

203. "REMARKS By President BRIGHAM YOUNG, Tabernacle, March 8, 1863," *Deseret News* [weekly], 18 Mar. 1863, 298; *Journal of Discourses* 10:110 (B. Young/1863).

204. "SHOT THE SEDUCER OF HIS SISTER," *Deseret Evening News*, 10 Jan. 1868, [2]; "A SEDUCER SHOT," *Deseret Evening News*, 4 Feb. 1868, [3].

205. *Journal of Discourses* 14:58 (G.Q. Cannon/1869).

206. Peterson, "Mormon Reformation of 1856-1857" (1989), 84n69; also BYU history professor Thomas G. Alexander's "Wilford Woodruff and the Mormon Reformation of 1855-57," *Dialogue: A Journal of Mormon Thought* 25 (Summer 1992): 27, "Though Young's references to blood atonement were probably hyperbole, they may have prompted some overzealous members to put the doctrine into practice"; Fielding, *Unsolicited Chronicler*, 471, concerning the Mountain Meadows Massacre: "This ritualistic mass murder was the direct consequence of instructions by the Governor [Brigham Young] to the Indians and the result of years of preaching by Young and other Mormon leaders, that vengeance was due against their enemies for shedding the blood of the Prophets."

207. "DISCOURSE By President Brigham Young, Tabernacle, Feb. 8, 1857," *Deseret News* [weekly], 18 Feb. 1857, 397; *Journal of Discourses* 4:219 (B. Young/1857).

208. Peterson, "Mormon Reformation" (1981), 191; also Andrew Love Neff, *History of Utah, 1847 to 1869* (Salt Lake City: Deseret News Press, 1940), 413; Howard Clair Searle, "The Mormon Reformation of 1856-1857," M.A. thesis, Brigham Young University, 1956, 85, 96.

209. McLaws, *Spokesman for the Kingdom*, 76.

210. In addition to the sources already cited, see Hosea Stout diary, 15 Feb., 17 Mar., 21 Sept., 18 Oct. 1851, 1-3 May 1854, 14 Apr. 1856, in Brooks, *On The Mormon Frontier*, 2:393, 396, 404, 407, 514, 545; Kenneth L. Cannon II, "'Mountain Common Law': The Extralegal Punishment of Seducers in Early Utah," *Utah Historical Quarterly* 51 (Fall 1983): 308-27.

211. Alter and Dwyer, "Journal of Captain Albert Tracy, 1858," 43, 45, and 44 (14 Oct. 1858).

212. "Wholesale Shooting Affair," *Deseret News* [weekly], 23 May 1860, 92.

213. John Ward Christian reminiscences, Bancroft Library, University of California at Berkeley, quoted in Moorman and Sessions, *Camp Floyd and the Mormons,* 125; also Aird G. Merkley, ed., *Monuments to Courage: A History of Beaver County* (Beaver, UT: Daughters of Utah Pioneers of Beaver County, Utah, 1948), 91.

214. Statement by "seceding Mormons" in John W. Phelps diary, 23 July 1857, in Hafen and Hafen, *Utah Expedition,* 8:96; Welch convert's statement in Alter and Dwyer, "Journal of Captain Albert Tracy, 1858," 44-45 (18 Oct. 1858); Lee, *Mormonism Unveiled,* 157-59, 269-70, 272-75, 278-86, 288.

215. A. J. Simmonds, "Cause of Death—LYNCHING," *The West* 17 (Jan. 1974): 26-27, 48; A. J. Simmonds, *The Gentile Comes To Cache Valley: A Study of the Logan Apostasies of 1874 And the Establishment of Non-Mormon Churches In Cache Valley, 1873-1913* (Logan: Utah State University Press, 1976), 9-10.

216. Ian Craig Breaden, "Poetry, Polity, and the Cache Valley Pioneer: Polemics in the Journal of Aaron DeWitt, 1869-96," *Utah Historical Quarterly* 61 (Fall 1993): 329, for circumstances of Ricks killing prisoner Elisha David Skeen, and 335 for quote.

217. "OFFICIAL DECLARATION," *Deseret Evening News,* 14 Dec. 1889, [2]; Clark, *Messages of the First Presidency,* 3:185.

218. Abraham H. Cannon diary, 2 Dec. 1890.

219. "Assault and Battery," *Deseret Evening News,* 14 Nov. 1878, [3]; "HOT SHOT FROM CANNON," *Deseret Evening News,* 12 Feb. 1878, [2].

220. "CHASTISED. The 'Tribune' Local Editor Soundly Thrashed," *Salt Lake Herald,* 1 Nov. 1884, 9; "A REPORTER RAWHIDED. ENCOUNTER BETWEEN A RESPECTABLE CITIZEN AND A 'TRIBUNE' REPORTER," *Deseret Evening News,* 10 Nov. 1884, [3].

221. "A BLISSFUL LOT. Another of the 'Tribune' Crew Rewarded," *Salt Lake Herald,* 9 Dec. 1884, 8; "A HAMMERED 'HERO.' A 'TRIBUNE' REPORTER COMES TO GRIEF," *Deseret Evening News,* 8 Dec. 1884, [3].

222. "THRASHING A REPORTER. Don Carlos Young Remodels the Phiz [sic] of C.T. Harte to Suit His Fancy," *Salt Lake Herald,* 11 Mar. 1886, 8; "The Battery Case," *Deseret Evening News,* 11 Mar. 1886, [3].

223. Larry R. Gerlach, "Vengeance vs. the Law: The Lynching of Sam Joe Harvey in Salt Lake City," in Jessie L. Embry and Howard A. Christy, eds., *Community Development in the American West: Past and Present, Nineteenth and Twentieth Century Frontiers* (Provo, UT: Charles Redd Center for Western Studies, Brigham Young University, 1985), 202 for quote, 204-14 for the incident; also for similar lynching in 1925 of an African-American man in Castle Gate, southern Utah, where the grand jury refused to indict the accused lynchers who included prominent local Mormons Joseph Parmley and Warren S. Peacock (b. 1881, the city marshal), see "Mob Lynches Negro Slayer of Castlegate Deputy Sheriff After He Is Captured by Officers: 1000 Citizens Take Part In Price Hanging," *Deseret News,* 18 June 1925, [1]; "Eleven Arrested on Charge of Murder in Lynching of Negro: Apprehension of Prominent Citizens Follows Investigations by F. W. Keller and O. K. Clay," *News-Advocate* (Price, UT), 25 June 1925, [1]; Steve Lacy, *The Lynching of Robert Marshall: Last In the West* (Price, UT: Castle Press, 1978); Warrum, *Utah Since Statehood,* 4:173-74 for Parmley; Esshom, *Pioneers and Prominent Men of Utah,* 1,092, for Peacock; Thursey Jessen Reynolds, comp., *Centennial Echoes From Carbon County* ([Price, UT]: Daughters of Utah Pioneers of Carbon County, 1948), 37, 42, 59, 77, 114, 118, 148, 153, 168, 184, for other accused men and their families.

224. Heber J. Grant 1883 journal, 126 (26 Aug. 1883), LDS archives. While "diary" is the standardized term I use to identify personal documents with daily entries, Grant kept several different kinds of such records, which must be identified separately in order to locate the quotations.

225. "A JUST VERDICT," *Deseret Evening News,* 11 May 1889, [2], referring to Howard Spencer's acquittal for the murder of Sergeant Ralph Pike in 1859; Moorman and Sessions, *Camp Floyd and the Mormons,* 252-56.

226. Hubert Howe Bancroft, *Popular Tribunals,* 2 vols. (San Francisco: A. L. Bancroft, 1887); Wayne Gard, *Frontier Justice* (Norman: University of Oklahoma Press, 1949); Richard Hofstadter and Michael Wallace, eds., *American Violence: A Documentary History* (New York: Alfred A. Knopf, 1970); Irving J. Sloan, *Our Violent Past: An American Chronicle* (New York: Random House, 1970); Richard Slotkin, *Regeneration Through Violence: The Mythology of the American Frontier* (Middletown, CT: Wesleyan University Press, 1973); W. Eugene Hollen, *Frontier Violence: Another Look* (Oxford University Press, 1974); Richard M. Brown, *Strain of Violence: Historical Studies of American Violence and Vigilantism* (New York: Oxford University Press, 1975); Gary L. Roberts, "Violence and the Frontier Tradition," in Forrest R. Blackburn et al., eds., *Kansas and The West* (Topeka: Kansas State Historical Society, 1976), 96-111; W. Eugene Hollen, "Vigilantism," in Lamar, *Reader's Encyclopedia of the American West,* 1,227-28; Bill O'Neal, *Encyclopedia of Western Gunfighters* (Norman: University of Oklahoma Press, 1979); Michael Feldberg, *The Turbulent Era: Riot and Disorder in Jacksonian America* (New York: Oxford University Press, 1980); Llewellyn L. Callaway, *Montana's Righteous Hangmen: The Vigilantes in Action* (Norman: University of Oklahoma Press, 1982); Donald Curtis Brown, "The Great Gun-Toting Controversy, 1865-1910: The Old West Gun Culture and Public Shootings," Ph.D. diss., Tulane University, 1983; Roger D. McGrath, *Gunfighters, Highwaymen, & Vigilantes: Violence on the Frontier* (Berkeley: University of California Press, 1984); William John McConnell, *Idaho's Vigilantes* (Moscow: University Press of Idaho, 1984); Henry Sinclair Drago, *The Great Range Wars: Violence on the Grasslands* (Lincoln: University of Nebraska Press, 1985); Robert M. Senkewicz, *Vigilantes in Gold Rush California* (Stanford, CA: Stanford University Press, 1985); Richard Patterson, *Historical Atlas of the Outlaw West* (Boulder, CO: Johnson Books, 1985); Paul I. Wellman, *A Dynasty of Western Outlaws* (Lincoln: University of Nebraska Press, 1986); Bill O'Neal, *Cattlemen vs. Sheepherders: Five Decades of Violence in the West, 1880-1920* (Austin, TX: Eakin Press, 1989); R. E. Mather and F. E. Boswell, *Vigilante Victims: Montana's 1864 Hanging Spree* (San Jose, CA: History West Publishing Co., 1991).

227. Cannon, "Mountain Common Law," 327.

228. Robert M. Ireland, "The Libertine Must Die: Dishonor and the Unwritten Law in the Nineteenth-Century United States," *Journal of Social History* 23 (Fall 1989): 31-32, 40; Homer, "The Judiciary and the Common Law in Utah Territory," 101, noted that this was statutory law in Utah as of 1852.

229. Ronald W. Walker review of Fielding, *Unsolicited Chronicler* in *Journal of Mormon History* 20 (Spring 1994): 170, 173.

230. P. A. M. Taylor, "The Life of Brigham Young: A Biography Which Will Not Be Written," *Dialogue: A Journal of Mormon Thought* 1 (Autumn 1966): 107; Moorman and Sessions, *Camp Floyd and the Mormons,* 231-46. Taylor and Moorman were non-LDS, Sessions a Mormon.

231. Bringhurst, *Brigham Young,* 130.

232. Ephraim Edward Ericksen, *The Psychological and Ethical Aspects of Mormon Group Life* (Chicago: University of Chicago Press, 1922), 42-43; Lowry Nelson, *The Mormon Village: A Pattern and Technique of Land Settlement* (Salt Lake City: University of Utah Press, 1952), 86-87; Judson Harold Flower, Jr., "Mormon Colonization of the San Luis Valley, Colorado, 1878-1900," M.A. thesis, Brigham Young University, 1966, 36-74; Milton R. Hunter, *Brigham Young: The Colonizer,* rev. ed. (Santa Barbara, CA: Peregrine Smith, 1973), 377-82;

Ricks, *Forms and Methods of Early Mormon Settlement*, 19-20, 51, 65-66, 73; Wayne L. Wahlquist, "Settlement Processes In the Mormon Core Area, 1847-1890," Ph.D. diss., University of Nebraska, 1974, 85-88, 201; Dean L. May, "The Making of Saints: The Mormon Town as a Setting for the Study of Cultural Change," *Utah Historical Quarterly* 45 (Winter 1977): 76-77; Michael Scott Raber, "Religious Polity and Local Production: The Origins of a Mormon Town," Ph.D. diss., Yale University, 1978, 147-63, which also analyzes instances of splits between local leaders at initial settlement; Larry M. Logue, *A Sermon in the Desert: Belief and Behavior in Early St. George, Utah* (Urbana: University of Illinois Press, 1988), 4-5; Dean L. May, "Expansion Along the Wasatch Front," and Lynn A. Rosenvall, "Expansion Outside the Wasatch Front," in Brown, Cannon, and Jackson, *Historical Atlas of Mormonism*, 88-89, 96-97; Dale F. Beecher, "Colonizer of the West," in Black and Porter, *Lion of the Lord*, 172, 176-77; Parson, *History of Rich County*, 67-119, 274-77; also Lowell "Ben" Bennion, "A Geographer's Discovery of *Great Basin Kingdom*," in Thomas G. Alexander, ed., *Great Basin Kingdom Revisited: Contemporary Perspectives* (Logan: Utah State University, 1991), 116-31, which distinguishes these pioneer settlements as "compact," "dispersed," and a mixture of the two.

233. Thomas E. Austin and Robert S. McPherson, "Murder, Mayhem, and Mormons: The Evolution of Law Enforcement on the San Juan Frontier," *Utah Historical Quarterly* 55 (Winter 1987): 43, also 42, 44, 49.

234. Van Wagoner, *Lehi*, 54; Moorman and Sessions, *Camp Floyd and the Mormons*, 110; "THE COLLETT CASE," *Deseret Evening News*, 10 Oct. 1878, [2]; "The Usual Dish of Sensations," *Deseret Evening News*, 22 Nov. 1889, [2].

235. For example, Samuel H. Rogers, a member of the Parowan militia, made no entries in his diary from 31 August 1857 until 12 September, just after the massacre. His diary did not mention that event until 18 July 1860. See Samuel H. Rogers diary, microfilm, Huntington Library; also William Leany's autobiography of his residence in Parowan, Utah, skipped from 1855 to 1860.

236. George A. Hicks to "Eds. TRIBUNE," 12 Aug. 1874; also Hicks, "History of Spanish Fork," 14; Hartley, *My Best For the Kingdom*, 476n16.

237. Samuel Knight statement in Abraham H. Cannon diary, 13 June 1895; Carlos A. Badger diary, 26 Sept. 1905, quoted in Badger, *Liahona and Iron Rod*, 275, 276; John C. Chatterley to assistant church historian Andrew Jenson, 18 Sept. 1919, LDS archives, quoted in Moorman and Sessions, *Camp Floyd and the Mormons*, 125-26, also 130; Johanna Christina Neilson Averett history, 20-21; Commodore Perry Liston autobiography, 8, Utah State Historical Society; Brooks, *Mountain Meadows Massacre*, 54, 55, 90; Brooks, *John Doyle Lee*, 206. However, Liston's autobiography failed to mention an incident in which he was on the other side of a death-threat: "There was one named Liston who lived in St. George in 1874-5 who was regarded by all the Mormons as a shifty character. Jacob [Hamblin] told me that once, on the old trail down the Virgin when the Church had set up a post for the protection of the emigrants, a young man arrived travelling alone. Jacob came shortly after. Liston said 'This man has got to go up'—meaning die. Jacob said, 'No—I'll die first.' Liston did not molest the man.'" See Frederick S. Dellenbaugh to Charles Kelley, 16 Aug. 1934, in C. Gregory Crampton, ed., "F. S. Dellenbaugh of the Colorado: Some Letters Pertaining to the Powell Voyages and the History of the Colorado River," *Utah Historical Quarterly* 37 (Spring 1969): 243.

238. Clark, *Messages of the First Presidency*, 3:186.

Notes to Chapter Eight

1. *Journal of Discourses*, 26 vols. (London and Liverpool: Latter-day Saints' Book Depot, 1854-86), 2:189 (B. Young/1855).

2. Franklin D. Richards editorial, "Union," *Latter-day Saints' Millennial Star* 17 (5 May 1855): 274. Except when otherwise indicated, biographical sketches of all general authorities named in this chapter can be found either in an appendix of the present volume or in D. Michael Quinn, *The Mormon Hierarchy: Origins of Power* (Salt Lake City: Signature Books/Smith Research Associates, 1994).

3. *Latter-day Saints' Millennial Star* 16 (18 Nov. 1854): 725-26; *Journal of Discourses* 14:92 (B. Young/1871). This tradition became a constitutional limit after Republicans gained control of Congress following the election of Franklin D. Roosevelt to his fourth consecutive term as Democratic president in 1944.

4. Richards, "Union," 174.

5. Abbe Guilliame Thomas Raynal's statement, quoted in Leonard Krieger, *An Essay on the Theory of Enlightened Despotism* (Chicago: University of Chicago Press, 1975), 86-87. Raynal's complete *Philosophical and Political History* appeared in seventeen British editions (1771-1811) and was excerpted in his *Revolution of America* in five British and four U.S. editions from 1781 to 1792. See *National Union Catalog of Pre-1956 Imprints,* 754 vols. (London: Mansell, 1968-81), 483:118-22; also Vernon Bogdanor, ed., *The Blackwell Encyclopedia of Political Institutions* (Oxford, Eng.: Basil Blackwell, 1987), 171, for "enlightened despotism" views common among other eighteenth-century writers.

6. *Journal of Discourses* 6:346-47 (B. Young/1859).

7. Brigham Young to Thomas L. Kane, 1 Sept. 1858, Western Americana, Beinecke Rare Book and Manuscript Library, Yale University, New Haven, Connecticut (hereafter Beinecke Library). Kane supported that view, for he had written Heber C. Kimball on 7 April 1851 about "your *Nation,*" archives, Historical Department, Church of Jesus Christ of Latter-day Saints, Salt Lake City, Utah (hereafter LDS archives); chap. 7 for the Utah War.

8. William C. Staines to George Reynolds, 19 Sept. 1879, Department of Special Collections and Manuscripts, Harold B. Lee Library, Brigham Young University, Provo, Utah (hereafter Lee Library).

9. John D. Lee diary, 12 Jan. 1846, LDS archives and Henry E. Huntington Library, San Marino, California.

10. The most comprehensive discussion of the "Flag of Deseret," its gradual development, its relation to the pioneer entry into Utah, and this flag's sometimes joint display with the American flag is Ronald W. Walker, "'A Banner is Unfurled': Mormonism's Ensign Peak," *Dialogue: A Journal of Mormon Thought* 26 (Winter 1993): 71-91, which refers to its public display at Utah pioneer celebrations (84-85, 86-87). For illustrations of this theocratic flag's variant forms and for emphasis on other occasions of its public display, see D. Michael Quinn, "The Flag of the Kingdom of God," *Brigham Young University Studies* 14 (Autumn 1973): 105-14; "Flags of the Kingdom," in *Deseret News 1980 Church Almanac: Church of Jesus Christ of Latter-day Saints* (Salt Lake City: Deseret News, 1980), 334, also p. 297 of 1981 edition. As Walker demonstrates, the colors of the Deseret Flag were not fixed for several years. The Deseret Flag's colors evolved from Brigham Young's use of white flags and blue flags to summon council meetings in Nauvoo and during the pioneer trek. Young recorded in September 1845, "I gave orders that when the officers [of the Nauvoo Legion] were wanted we should hoist a striped flag on the Temple, and when all the companies were wanted, we would hoist a white flag in the daytime." By February 1846, when Young "wanted to see all the Brethren together he would raise a white flag [and] that when he wanted to see the captains he would raise a blue or colored flag" (Brigham Young diary, 19 Sept. 1845, LDS archives; Willard Richards diary, 18 Feb. 1846, LDS archives).

11. This is the extended argument of Marvin S. Hill, "Quest for Refuge: An Hypothesis as to the Social Origins and Nature of the Mormon Political Kingdom," *Journal of Mormon History* 2 (1975): 3-20; Marvin S. Hill, *Quest for Refuge: The Mormon Flight from American Pluralism* (Salt Lake City: Signature Books, 1989).

12. Orson Pratt, "A Prophecy and Its Fulfilment," *The Seer* 2 (July 1854): 304; *Journal of Discourses* 3:16 (O. Pratt/1855), 4:106 (Kimball/1856), 5:9-10 (Kimball/1857), 5:329-30 (B. Young/1857), 9:342-43 (J. Taylor/1862), 17:156-57 (B. Young/1874), 18:10 (G. Q. Cannon/1875), 21:8 (J. Taylor/1879), 25:222-23 (Penrose/1884).

13. "Discourse by Elder Orson Pratt, delivered in the Twentieth Ward Meeting House, Sunday evening, September 26th, 1875," *Deseret Evening News,* 2 Oct. 1875, 1; *Journal of Discourses* 9:8-10 (J. Taylor/1861), 10:189-90 (B. Young/1863), 14:92-93 (B. Young/1871), 15:124-25 (B. Young/1872), 19:332-34 (O. Pratt/1878), 20:59-60 (J. Taylor/1878).

14. "NOTHING IF NOT ILLOGICAL,"*Deseret Evening News,* 7 Feb. 1883, [2]; also "Our Unity—Its Causes and Antagonisms," *Deseret News* [weekly], 19 July 1865, 332; "Church Influence in Politics," *Deseret Evening News,* 16 July 1880, [2]; and "Counsel and Coercion," *Deseret Evening News,* 16 Mar. 1889, [2].

15. "A WORD OF WARNING," *Deseret Evening News,* 4 Feb. 1878, [2]; also similar phrasing in "AN UNWISE ACT," *Deseret Evening News,* 3 Apr. 1878, [2].

16. Ronald Collett Jack, "Utah Territorial Politics: 1847-1876," Ph.D. diss., University of Utah, 1970, 69, 71, 99, 101, 104, 106, 108, 110-11, 114, 117; also Philip A. M. Taylor, "Early Mormon Loyalty and the Leadership of Brigham Young," *Utah Historical Quarterly* 30 (Spring 1962): 103-32.

17. "Election Day," *Deseret News* [weekly], 9 Aug. 1865, 357.

18. "ELECTION RETURNS FOR BEAR LAKE COUNTY," *Bear Lake Democrat* (Paris, ID), 13 Nov. 1880, [2].

19. "Vote for John T. Caine, 23,239; vote for P.T. VanZile, 4,908," *Salt Lake Daily Herald,* 19 Nov. 1882, 4.

20. Charles S. Peterson, *Take up Your Mission: Mormon Colonizing Along the Little Colorado River, 1870-1900* (Tucson: University of Arizona Press, 1973), 222, 226.

21. "FRANKLIN," *Idaho Tri-Weekly Statesman* (Boise), 6 Oct. 1874, [1]; Grenville H. Gibbs, "Mormonism In Idaho Politics, 1880-1890," *Utah Historical Quarterly* 21 (Oct. 1953): 286, 288-93; Merrill C. Hansen, "The Role of Rhetoric in the Mormon Suffrage Debate in Idaho, 1880-1906," Ph.D. diss., Stanford University, 1958, 19-26, 52-59, 66-68, 104-107, 119-21, 125-47; Dennis L. Thompson, "Religion and the Idaho Constitution," *Pacific Northwest Quarterly* 58 (Oct. 1967): 169-78; Merle W. Wells, *Anti-Mormonism in Idaho, 1872-92* (Provo, UT: Brigham Young University Press, 1978), 4, 13, 15, 38, 45, 48, 50, 52n24, 54n48, 57-58, 105-106, 137-44; Merle W. Wells, "Law in the Service of Politics: Anti-Mormonism in Idaho Territory," *Idaho Yesterdays: The Quarterly Journal of the Idaho Historical Society* 25 (Spring 1981): 33-43; Dennis C. Colson, *Idaho's Constitution: The Tie That Binds* (Moscow: University of Idaho Press, 1991), 148-59; Lawrence G. Coates, Peter G. Boag, Ronald Hatzenbuehler, and Merwin R. Swanson, "The Mormon Settlement of Southeastern Idaho, 1845-1900," *Journal of Mormon History* 20 (Fall 1994): 58-60; Leonard J. Arrington, *History of Idaho,* 2 vols. (Moscow and Boise: University of Idaho Press and Idaho Historical Society, 1994), 1:369-72, 379-80, 419-21; chap. 9 for the Liberal Party in Utah.

22. Eric N. Moody, "Nevada's Anti-Mormon Legislation of 1887,"; Andrew Jenson, *Church Chronology,* 2d ed., rev. (Salt Lake City: Deseret News, 1914), 13 Jan. 1887.

23. "Membership of Religious Denominations in Utah, 1870-1975," in Richard D. Poll, ed., *Utah's History* (Provo, UT: Brigham Young University Press, 1978), 692.

24. Rutherford B. Hayes diary, 9 Jan. 1880, in T. Harry Williams, ed., *Hayes: The Diary of a President, 1875-1881* (New York: David McKay Co., 1964), 259; also Thomas G. Alexander, "Federal Authority Versus Polygamic Theocracy: James B. McKean and the Mormons, 1870-1875," *Dialogue: A Journal of Mormon Thought* 1 (Autumn 1966): 85-100; Gustive O. Larson, "Federal Efforts to 'Americanize' Utah Before Admission to Statehood," *Brigham Young University Studies* 10 (Winter 1970): 218-232; Thomas G. Alexander, "A Conflict of Perceptions: Ulysses S. Grant and the Mormons," *Ulysses S. Grant Association*

Newsletter 8 (July 1971): 29-42; Edwin B. Firmage, "The Judicial Campaign Against Polygamy and the Enduring Legal Questions," *Brigham Young University Studies* 27 (Summer 1987): 91-117; Ken Driggs, "The Mormon Church-State Confrontation in Nineteenth Century America," *Journal of Church and State* 30 (Spring 1988): 273-89.

25. Kenneth Gordon Crider, "Rhetorical Aspects of the Controversies Over Mormonism in Illinois, 1839-1847," Ph.D. diss., University of Illinois, 1956, 285-308; Robert Bruce Flanders, *Nauvoo: Kingdom on the Mississippi* (Urbana: University of Illinois Press, 1965), 211-40; Kenneth W. Godfrey, "Causes of Mormon Non-Mormon Conflict in Hancock County, Illinois, 1839-1846," Ph.D. diss., Brigham Young University, 1967, 43-63; J. Keith Melville, *Conflict and Compromise: The Mormons in Mid-Nineteenth Century American Politics* (Provo, UT: Brigham Young University Printing Service, 1974), 27-29; Stephen C. LeSueur, *The 1838 Mormon War in Missouri* (Columbia: University of Missouri Press, 1987), 17, 59; Richard E. Bennett, *Mormons at the Missouri, 1846-1852: "And Should We Die"* (Norman: University of Oklahoma Press, 1987), 220-21; Kenneth H. Winn, *Exiles in a Land of Liberty: Mormons in America, 1830-1846* (Chapel Hill: University of North Carolina Press, 1989), 5, 85-95; John E. Hallwas and Roger D. Launius, eds., *Cultures in Conflict: A Documentary History of the Mormon War in Illinois* (Logan: Utah State University Press, 1995), 67-68, 83-87, 103-104.

26. "RESULT OF THE ELECTION," *Deseret News* [weekly], 13 Aug. 1862, 52; also "Provo Items," *Deseret Evening News*, 8 Aug. 1878, [3].

27. "The Election," *Salt Lake Daily Herald*, 3 Aug. 1880, [3]; "Exemplary," *Deseret Evening News*, 2 Aug. 1881, [3].

28. "The Election," *Deseret Evening News*, 5 Aug. 1884, [3].

29. "THE ELECTION TO-DAY," *Salt Lake Daily Herald*, 5 Nov. 1878, [2].

30. "THE MUNICIPAL CONVENTION," *Salt Lake Daily Herald*, 9 Feb. 1882, 4. See chap. 9 for discussion of the People's Party, the LDS church's political organization.

31. "AN ACT REGULATING ELECTIONS," *Journals of the House of Representatives, Council, and Joint Sessions of the First Annual and Special Sessions of the Legislative Assembly of the Territory of Utah, Held at Great Salt Lake City, 1851 and 1852* (Salt Lake City: Brigham Young, Printer, 1852), 105; "PEOPLE'S MUNICIPAL CONVENTION," *Deseret Evening News*, 29 Jan. 1878, [2]; "THE NEW ELECTION LAW," *Deseret Evening News*, 25 Feb. 1878, [2]; "THE ELECTION LAW," *Salt Lake Daily Herald*, 26 Feb. 1878, [2]; R. N. Baskin, *Reminiscences of Early Utah* (Salt Lake City: By the author, 1914), 73; Everett L. Cooley, "Carpetbag Rule: Territorial Government in Utah," *Utah Historical Quarterly* 26 (Apr. 1958): 118; Jack, "Utah Territorial Politics," 76-77, 365-68, 519; Jean Bickmore White, "The Right to Be Different: Ogden and Weber County Politics, 1850-1924," *Utah Historical Quarterly* 47 (Summer 1979): 254-55.

32. L. E. Fredman, *The Australian Ballot: The Story of an American Reform* (Lansing: Michigan State University Press, 1968), 21-22; Morton Keller, *Affairs of State: Public Life in Late Nineteenth Century America* (Cambridge, MA: Belknap Press/Harvard University Press, 1977), 529.

33. "THE ELECTION SYSTEM OF UTAH," *Salt Lake Daily Tribune*, 16 Nov. 1873, [2]; also "THE LATE ELECTION AND ITS LESSON," *Salt Lake Daily Tribune*, 11 Aug. 1871, [2].

34. "THE GOVERNOR'S MESSAGE," *Deseret Evening News*, 13 Jan. 1876, [2]; "MORE PROSCRIPTIVE LEGISLATION SOUGHT," *Deseret Evening News*, 11 Dec. 1877, [2].

35. "THE UTAH ELECTION LAW," *Deseret Evening News*, 29 Jan. 1878, [2].

36. Dale L. Morgan, *The State of Deseret* (Logan: Utah State University Press, 1987), 33-36.

37. Wayne K. Hinton, "Millard Fillmore: Utah's Friend in the White House," *Utah Historical Quarterly* 48 (Spring 1980): 112-28; Leonard J. Arrington, *Brigham Young: American Moses* (New York: Alfred A. Knopf, 1985), 227, 231; Eugene E. Campbell, *Establishing Zion: The Mormon Church in the American West, 1847-1869* (Salt Lake City: Signature Books, 1988), 68, 208; Jenson, *Church Chronology,* 29 Oct. 1851, 18 Dec. 1858.

38. Brigham Young diary, 16 July 1857, in Everett L. Cooley, ed., *Diary of Brigham Young, 1857* (Salt Lake City: Tanner Trust Fund/University of Utah Library, 1980), 45.

39. Utah Legislature, *Journals* [published under varying titles] (Salt Lake City, 1851-95); Utah Territory, Secretary of State, Election Papers, 1850-95, Utah State Archives, Salt Lake City; Jack, "Utah Territorial Politics," 546-697; Gordon Irving, "Roster of Members of the Legislative Assembly, Utah Territory, 1851/2 to 1894," *Task Papers in LDS History,* No. 5 (Salt Lake City: History Division, Historical Department, The Church of Jesus Christ of Latter-day Saints, 1975). Some discrepancies in the listings of legislators in these various records had to be reconciled in order to arrive at the calculations in the table.

40. *Journal of Discourses* 8:105 (O. Pratt/1860).

41. *Journals of the House of Representatives, Council, and Joint Sessions of . . . the Territory of Utah, Held at Great Salt Lake City, 1851 and 1852,* 5, compare with *Journals* (1853-94).

42. *Journals of the House of Representatives, Council, and Joint Sessions of . . . the Territory of Utah, Held at Great Salt Lake City, 1851 and 1852,* 67 (13 Jan. 1852), 85 (23 Jan. 1852), 89 (27 Jan. 1852), 116 ([2]9 Jan. 1852), 39 (24 Jan. 1852); *Acts, Resolutions and Memorials, Passed By the First Annual, and Special Sessions, of the Legislative Assembly, of the Territory of Utah, Begun and Held at Great Salt Lake City on the 22nd Day of September, A.D. 1851* (Salt Lake City: Brigham Young, Printer, 1852), 93.

43. *Journals of the House of Representatives, Council, and Joint Sessions of the Second Annual and Adjourned Sessions of the Legislative Assembly of the Territory of Utah, Held at Great Salt Lake City, 1852 and 1853* (Salt Lake City: George Hales, 1853), 13 (17 Dec. 1852).

44. *Journal of the Legislative Assembly of the Territory of Utah, For the Fourth Annual Session: Convened At Great Salt Lake City, 1854-6* (Salt Lake City: Joseph Cain, Public Printer, 1856), 27 (9 Jan. 1855); *Journals of the Legislative Assembly of the Territory of Utah, For the Tenth Annual Session, For the Years 1860-61* (Salt Lake City: Elias Smith, Public Printer, 1861), 166 (18 Jan. 1861).

45. Dale A. Bolingbroke, "A History of the Utah Territorial Legislature, 1851-1861," M.A. thesis, Utah State University, 1971, 27.

46. *Journals of the Legislative Assembly of the Territory of Utah, For the Fifteenth Annual Session, For the Years 1865-66* (Salt Lake City: Henry McEwan, Public Printer, 1866), 176 (19 Jan. 1866).

47. *House Journal of the Twenty-Fifth Session of the Legislative Assembly of the Territory of Utah* (Salt Lake City: By authority, 1882), 71 (16 Jan.), 81 (19 Jan.), 112 (31 Jan.), 119 (2 Feb.), 130 (7 Feb.), 144 (10 Feb.), 145 (10 Feb.), 160 (16 Feb.), 161-62 (17 Feb.), 171 (18 Feb.), 175 (20 Feb.), 183 (21 Feb.), 188 (23 Feb.), 193 (24 Feb.), 200 (25 Feb.), 203 (27 Feb.), 203-204 (27 Feb.), 219 (28 Feb.), 288 (1 Mar.), 230 (2 Mar.), 236 (2 Mar.), 239 (3 Mar.), 259 (6 Mar.), 260-61 (6 Mar.), 274 (7 Mar.), 276-77 (7 Mar.), 281 (8 Mar.), 285 (8 Mar.), 290-91 (8 Mar.), 293-94 (9 Mar.), 296-97 (9 Mar.), 301-302 (9 Mar.), 308 (9 Mar.), 318-19 (9 Mar. 1882); compared with no record of split-voting in *Council Journal of the Twenty-Fifth Session of the Legislative Assembly of the Territory of Utah* (Salt Lake City: By authority, 1882).

48. *Council Journal of the Twenty-Sixth Session of the Legislative Assembly of the Territory of Utah* (Salt Lake City: Tribune Printing and Publishing Co., 1884), 75 (25 Jan.), 96 (7 Feb.), 100 (7 Feb.), 139-40 (23 Feb.), 222 (8 Mar.), 225 (10 Mar.), 246 (11 Mar.), 263 (12 Mar.), 265 (12 Mar.), 286 (13 Mar.), 315 (13 Mar.), 317 (13 Mar. 1884).

49. Church Historian's office journal, 13 Jan. 1862, LDS archives.

50. First Council of Seventy minutes, 31 Dec. 1859, 3, LDS archives.

51. Brigham Young office journal, 5 Jan., 11 Jan., 17 July 1861, 29 Jan. 1862, LDS archives, with copy in fd 2, box 26, Donald R. Moorman papers, archives, Donnell and Elizabeth Stewart Library Weber State University, Ogden, Utah; Lynn M. Hilton and Hope A. Hilton, "John M. Bernhisel," in Allan Kent Powell, ed., *Utah History Encyclopedia* (Salt Lake City: University of Utah Press, 1994), 41-42.

52. "PROGRESS OF SECESSION," *Deseret News* [weekly], 5 Dec. 1860, 317; Brigham Young to William H. Hooper, 27 Dec. 1860, 1-2, Young-Hooper Correspondence, Beinecke Library, with microfilm copy in Microforms, J. Willard Marriott Library, University of Utah, Salt Lake City, and typed transcript in box 25, Moorman papers.

53. "INTERESTING FROM THE EAST. (By Pony Express): SPECIAL CORRESPONDENCE FOR THE 'NEWS,'" *Deseret News* [weekly], 26 Dec. 1860, [337]. The letter was dated 11 December, signed by "VERITAS," and its last paragraph concluded: "Col. Hooper is in excellent health, but very much occupied. His lady is expected here tomorrow."

54. William H. Hooper to George Q. Cannon, 16 Dec. 1860, in "Extract of a Letter From Hon. W. H. Hooper," *Latter-day Saints' Millennial Star* 23 (12 Jan. 1861): 30.

55. Brigham Young to William H. Hooper, 3 Jan. 1861, 3, Young-Hooper Correspondence; Allen Johnson and Dumas Malone, eds., *Dictionary of American Biography*, 20 vols. (New York: Charles Scribner's Sons, 1928-36), 3:592-93. C. Vann Woodward, ed., *Mary Chestnut's Civil War* (New Haven, CT: Yale University Press, 1981), 601n6, mistakenly claimed that Mary Boykin Chestnut's 1864 diary should have identified the nephew rather than her description of "Governor Cumming, a Georgian, late governor of Utah" as having been confined for two years "in prison" before being allowed to travel to the Confederacy with "his wife" (601). However, Ray R. Canning and Beverly Beeton, eds., *The Genteel Gentile: Letters of Elizabeth Cumming, 1857-1858* (Salt Lake City: Tanner Trust Fund/University of Utah Library, 1977), 101, quoted Cumming's relative that President Lincoln would not permit the former Utah governor to leave the Union's capital until 1864 when he allowed Cumming to return to Georgia, "weighing over 400 pounds." Chestnut's eyewitness account (601) was an obvious description of the sixty-one-year-old former governor: "huge and with snow-white hair, fat as a prize ox—no sign of Yankee barbarity or starvation about him" during his imprisonment.

56. Brigham Young to William H. Hooper, 17 Jan. 1861, 2, Young-Hooper Correspondence.

57. E. B. Long, *The Saints and the Union: Utah Territory During the Civil War* (Urbana: University of Illinois Press, 1981), 37-38; Donald R. Moorman and Gene A. Sessions, *Camp Floyd and the Mormons: The Utah War* (Salt Lake City: University of Utah Press, 1992), 275-76.

58. James M. McPherson, *Ordeal By Fire: The Civil War and Reconstruction*, 2d ed. (New York: McGraw-Hill, 1992), 131; Brigham Young to William H. Hooper, 7 Feb. 1861, 5, Young-Hooper Correspondence.

59. Gustive O. Larson, "Utah and the Civil War," *Utah Historical Quarterly* 33 (Winter 1965): 63; Gustive O. Larson, *Outline History of Utah and The Mormons* (Salt Lake City: Deseret Book Co., 1965), 206, also without documentation; Long, *Saints and the Union*, 17n28, 56n37, cited Larson's article before and after this quote but made no reference to Larson's claim. I quote Larson's statements because of their wide circulation, but I have found no evidence of such "overtures" to Utah from the Confederacy.

60. Scott G. Kenney, ed., *Wilford Woodruff's Journal: 1833-1898 Typescript*, 9 vols. (Murray, UT: Signature Books, 1983-85), 5 (10 Mar. 1861): 559.

61. List of requested appointments as attachment to letter of Brigham Young to William H. Hooper, 4 Apr. 1861, Young-Hooper Correspondence.

62. "REMARKS By President BRIGHAM YOUNG, Tabernacle, a.m. of April 6, 1861," *Deseret News* [weekly], 1 May 1861, 66; *Journal of Discourses* 9:4-5 (B. Young/1861).

63. Heber J. Grant letterbook-journal, 12 Aug. 1887, LDS archives. While "diary" is the standardized term I use to identify personal documents with daily entries, Grant kept several different kinds of such records, which must be identified separately in order to locate the quotations.

64. L. John Nuttall's First Presidency office journal, 19 Jan. 1887, LDS archives.

65. Brigham Young Hampton diary, 22 Jan. 1886, LDS archives; Abraham H. Cannon diary, 20 Sept. 1888, 18 Oct. 1890, Lee Library, with copies in Manuscripts Division, Marriott Library, and in Utah State Historical Society, Salt Lake City.

66. Abraham H. Cannon diary, 24 Jan. 1890, 4 Apr., 14 Nov. 1895.

67. Ibid., 24 Aug., 20 Oct. 1893.

68. Heber J. Grant diary, 6 Sept. 1887.

69. Abraham H. Cannon diary, 17 Dec. 1892.

70. Ibid., 19 Dec. 1889, 30 Jan. 1891; First Presidency office journal, 19 Dec. 1889, excerpt in LDS archives.

71. The details of this incident appear in Charles W. Penrose diary, 4 Jan.-8 Feb. 1885, Utah State Historical Society, also published in William C. Seifrit, "'To Get U[tah] in U[nion]': Diary of a Failed Mission," *Utah Historical Quarterly* 51 (Fall 1983): 358-81; also Brigham Young, Jr., diary, 4 Jan.-7 Feb. 1885, LDS archives, with references in Franklin D. Richards diary, 7 Jan. 1885, LDS archives. The two emissaries discovered that they were the intended victims of "confidence men" who pretended to be intermediaries for president-elect Cleveland. Young and Penrose had positive meetings with Cleveland and his secretary Daniel S. Lamont who exposed the impostors.

72. George C. S. Benson, *Political Corruption in America* (Lexington, MA: Lexington Books/D. C. Heath Co., 1978), 80; also Wallace D. Farnham, "The Weakened Spring of Government: A Study in Nineteenth-Century American History," *American Historical Review* 68 (Apr. 1963): 662-80; C. K. Yearley, *The Money Machines: The Breakdown and Reform of Government and Party Finance in the North, 1860-1920* (Albany: State University of New York Press, 1970), 257-58; Keller, *Affairs of State,* 244-45; Mark W. Summers, *The Plundering Generation: Corruption and the Crisis of the Union, 1849-1861* (New York: Oxford University Press, 1987); Mark Wahlgren Summers, *The Era of Good Stealings* (New York: Oxford University Press, 1993).

73. Brigham Young to William H. Hooper, 11 Apr. 1861, 1, Young-Hooper Correspondence.

74. Long, *Saints and the Union,* 28.

75. McPherson, *Ordeal By Fire,* 149; Long, *Saints and the Union,* 24, with quotation from Young's office journal, 28 Jan. 1861.

76. Brigham Young to William H. Hooper, 25 Apr. 1861, 2; compare *Journal of Discourses* 8:322 (B. Young/10 Feb. 1861): "And if a State has a right to secede, so has a Territory, and so has a county from a State or Territory . . . and you will have perfect anarchy." Long, *Saints and the Union,* 14, 15, 24, 27, 28, cited some of this correspondence but made no comment about Young's repeated hints of Utah's secession.

77. Brigham Young office journal, 1 May 1861, also quoted in Long, *Saints and the Union,* 31.

78. Brigham Young office journal, 1 Aug. 1861.

79. Alvin M. Josephy, Jr., *The Civil War In the West* (New York: Alfred A. Knopf, 1991), 50; also Ray C. Colton, *The Civil War in the Western Territories: Arizona, Colorado, New Mexico, and Utah* (Norman: University of Oklahoma Press, 1959), 19.

80. Josephy, *Civil War In the West,* 233-38; Benjamin Franklin Gilbert, "The Confederate Minority in California," *California Historical Society Quarterly* 20 (June 1941): 154-70; Aurora Hunt, *The Army of the Pacific: Its Operations in California, Texas, Arizona, New Mexico, Utah, Nevada, Oregon, Washington, Plains Region, Mexico, etc., 1860-1866* (Glendale, CA: Arthur H. Clark Co., 1951), 336-43, 346-48; G. Thomas Edwards, "Holding the Far West

for the Union: The Army in 1861," *Civil War History* 14 (Dec. 1968): 307-24; John W. Robinson, *Los Angeles in Civil War Days, 1860-65* (Los Angeles: Dawson's Book Shop, 1977); Robert J. Chandler, "The Velvet Glove: The Army During the Secession Crisis in California, 1860-61," *Journal of the West* 20 (Oct. 1981): 35-42.

81. *Acts Resolutions and Memorials, Passed At the Several Sessions of the Legislative Assembly of the Territory of Utah* (Salt Lake City: Joseph Cain, Public Printer, 1855), 161 (4 Feb. 1852); Newell G. Bringhurst, *Saints, Slaves, and Blacks: The Changing Place of Black People Within Mormonism* (Westport, CT: Greenwood Press, 1981), 67-70, 226; also Jack Beller, "Negro Slaves In Utah," *Utah Historical Quarterly* 3 (Oct. 1929): 122-26; Dennis L. Lythgoe, "Negro Slavery in Utah," *Utah Historical Quarterly* 39 (Winter 1971): 40-54; Ronald G. Coleman, "Blacks In Utah History: An Unknown Legacy," in Helen Z. Papanikolas, ed., *The Peoples of Utah* (Salt Lake City: Utah State Historical Society, 1976), 116-22; Ronald G. Coleman, "African Americans in Utah," in Powell, *Utah History Encyclopedia,* 2.

82. Acting governor Francis Wootton to U.S. Secretary of State William H. Seward, 5 Sept. 1861, in Long, *Saints and the Union,* 40; "The Completion of the Telegraph," *Deseret News* [weekly], 23 Oct. 1861, 189; Brigham H. Roberts, *A Comprehensive History of The Church of Jesus Christ of Latter-day Saints, Century I,* 6 vols. (Salt Lake City: Deseret News Press and "the Church," 1930), 4:548.

83. Brigham Young office journal, 16 Sept. 1861, also quoted in Long, *Saints and the Union,* 41.

84. "The Governor's Veto," "The Act which the Governor Vetoed," and "Proclamation," *Deseret News* [weekly], 25 Dec. 1861, 205, 208; also Long, *Saints and the Union,* 45.

85. Brigham Young to Dwight Eveloth, 1 Jan. 1862, typescript of Brigham Young letterbook 6 (1 Nov. 1861-15 Apr. 1864), 85, box 22, Moorman papers; "Departure of the Governor," *Deseret News* [weekly], 1 Jan. 1862, 212; Charles L. Walker diary, 3 Jan. 1862, in A. Karl Larson and Katharine Miles Larson, eds., *Diary of Charles Lowell Walker,* 2 vols. (Logan: Utah State University Press, 1980), 1:212; also Nels Anderson, *Desert Saints: The Mormon Frontier in Utah* (Chicago: University of Chicago Press, 1942), 222, "Some say he was emasculated [castrated]."

86. "GOVERNOR DAWSON'S STATEMENT," *Deseret News* [weekly], 22 Jan. 1862, 224; "Disgraceful Outrage," *Deseret News* [weekly], 8 Jan. 1862, 221 for quoted phrase; Thomas A. McMullin and David Walker, *Biographical Directory of American Territorial Governors* (Westport, CT: Meckler Publishing, 1984), 295; also Long, *Saints and the Union,* 46-53; chap. 7 for "Be'hoys."

87. Richard K. Hanks, "Eph Hanks: Pioneer Scout," M.A. thesis, Brigham Young University, 1973, 100.

88. Brigham Young to John M. Bernhisel, 14 Jan. 1862, typescript of Young's letterbook 6 (1 Nov. 1861-15 Apr. 1864): 106, in box 22, Moorman papers, also quoted in Long, *Saints and the Union,* 52.

89. Historian's office journal, 16 Jan. 1862; "Exciting and Terrifying Occurrences," *Deseret News* [weekly], 22 Jan. 1862, 237.

90. *Journal of Discourses* 24:12 (J.F. Smith/1882); also Moorman and Sessions, *Camp Floyd and the Mormons,* 233-37, and L. Kay Gillespie, *The Unforgiven: Utah's Executed Men* (Salt Lake City: Signature Books, 1991), 17-19, for examples.

91. Alexander Neibaur diary, 22 Jan. 1862, LDS archives; also Charles L. Walker diary, 19 Jan. 1862, in Larson and Larson, *Diary of Charles Lowell Walker,* 214n23; "Exciting and Terrifying Occurrences," *Deseret News* [weekly], 22 Jan. 1862, 237, for Isaac Neibaur as one of those who attacked Governor Dawson; "Great Salt Lake County Probate Court," *Deseret News* [weekly], 26 Mar. 1862, 309, for Neibaur's sentence; Theda Lucille Bassett, *Grandpa Neibaur Was a Pioneer* (Salt Lake City: Artistic Printing Co., 1988), 52, for Isaac Neibaur's birth on 30 Mar. 1839.

92. Long, *Saints and the Union,* 60.

93. "ORGANIZATION OF THE CONVENTION FOR THE ESTABLISHMENT OF A STATE GOVERNMENT," *Deseret News* [weekly], 22 Jan. 1862, 237.

94. "PROGRESS OF EVENTS," *Deseret News* [weekly], 26 Feb. 1862, 267.

95. David D. Perrine, "Battle of Valverde, New Mexico Territory, February 21, 1862," *Journal of the West* 19 (Oct. 1980): 26-38; Colton, *Civil War in the Western Territories*, 25, 28-36, 38; Josephy, *Civil War In the West*, 59, 72-75. Remarkably, Long, *Saints and the Union*, made no reference to these military developments south of Utah.

96. William I. Waldrip, "New Mexico During the Civil War," *New Mexico Historical Review* 28 (July 1953): 167; Donald S. Frazier, *Blood & Treasure: Confederate Empire in the Southwest* (College Station: Texas A&M University Press, 1995), 298; Long, *Saints and the Union*, 124, cited a similar view in a letter from New Mexico's governor to U.S. Secretary of State Seward, 13 Dec. 1862.

97. "An Address to the People of Georgia," *Deseret News* [weekly], 5 Mar. 1862, 283.

98. "THE VOICE OF THE PEOPLE," *Deseret News* [weekly], 12 Mar. 1862, 292.

99. "JEFF. DAVIS'S INAUGURAL ADDRESS," and "Message of President Davis to the Confederate Congress," *Deseret News* [weekly], 2 Apr. 1862, 314-15, 320.

100. Brigham Young to John M. Bernhisel, 14 Apr., 15 Apr. 1862, transcriptions in bound typescript of Young's letterbook 6 (1 Nov. 1861-15 Apr. 1864), box 22, Moorman papers; "MESSAGE BY THE GOVERNOR OF THE STATE OF DESERET," *Deseret News* [weekly], 16 Apr. 1862, [329]; Morgan, *State of Deseret*, 96-97.

101. Long, *Saints and the Union*, 82-83; "California Items," *Deseret News* [weekly], 30 Apr. 1862, 318; also Margaret M. Fisher, ed., *Utah and the Civil War: Being the Story of the Part Played by the People of Utah in That Great Conflict, with special reference to the LOT SMITH EXPEDITION and The Robert T. Burton Expedition* (Salt Lake City: Deseret Book Co., 1929).

102. "The Mails," *Deseret News* [weekly], 14 May 1862, 364; also Larson, "Utah and the Civil War," 59; Monte Burr McLaws, *Spokesman for the Kingdom: Early Mormon Journalism and the DESERET NEWS, 1830-1898* (Provo, UT: Brigham Young University Press, 1977), 29-30; Long, *Saints and the Union*, 102-103.

103. "Congressional Items," *Deseret News* [weekly], 14 May 1862, 368; Edwin Brown Firmage and Richard Collin Mangrum, *Zion in the Courts: A Legal History of the Church of Jesus Christ of Latter-day Saints, 1830-1900* (Urbana: University of Illinois Press, 1988), 131-32.

104. *Congressional Globe*, 7 Apr. 1860, 1559, plus index to the volume, for the votes against the Morrill bill by the following number of representatives from each state: Alabama (6), Arkansas (1), California (2), Delaware (1), Florida (1), Georgia (6), Illinois (4), Indiana (3), Louisiana (2), Maryland (1), Massachusetts (1), Michigan (1), Mississippi (2), Missouri (3), New Jersey (1), New York (1), North Carolina (3), Ohio (6), Oregon (1), Pennsylvania (2), South Carolina (6), Tennessee (2), Texas (1), Virginia (3); *Congressional Globe*, 14 June 1860, 2909, for last reference until 1861 to the Morrill bill which had stalled in the Senate's Committee on the Judiciary; Richard D. Poll, "The Legislative Antipolygamy Campaign," *Brigham Young University Studies* 26 (Fall 1986): 108-11; David Buice, "A Stench in the Nostrils of Honest Men: Southern Democrats and the Edmunds Act of 1882," *Dialogue: A Journal of Mormon Thought* 21 (Autumn 1988): 100-101. Morrill had to reintroduce his bill and obtain a second sustaining vote in the House before the Senate approved the bill in 1862.

105. "THE LATEST NEWS," *Deseret News* [weekly], 21 Mar. 1860, 20; "Secessionism on the Pacific Slope," *Deseret News* [weekly], 21 May 1862, 373.

106. Albert L. Zobell, Jr., *Sentinel in the East: A Biography of Thomas L. Kane* (Salt Lake City: Nicholas G. Morgan, Sr., 1965), 194-95.

107. Brigham Young to William H. Hooper, at Washington, D.C., 30 May 1862, 1-2, Young-Hooper Correspondence; Stanford Orson Cazier, "The Life of William Henry Hooper: Merchant Statesman," M.A. thesis, University of Utah, 1956, 51; Robert H.

Sylvester, "Dr. John Milton Bernhisel: Utah's First Delegate to Congress," M.S. thesis, University of Utah, 1947, 85-86.

108. Lythgoe, "Negro Slavery in Utah," 43, 46, 53; Hosea Stout diary, 21 Apr. 1859, Juanita Brooks, ed., *On the Mormon Frontier: The Diary of Hosea Stout, 1844-1861*, 2 vols. (Salt Lake City: University of Utah Press, 1964), 2:695. This was a private transaction, however, since there were too few slave-owners in Utah to support slave auctions.

109. Brigham Young to John M. Bernhisel, 12 Nov., 21 Dec., 30 Dec. 1861, 4 Jan., 14 Jan., 30 Jan., 2 Feb., 15 Feb., 25 Feb., 22 Mar., 14 Apr., 15 Apr., 25 Apr. 1862 in bound typescript of Brigham Young letterbook 6 (1 Nov. 1861-15 Apr. 1864), box 22, Moorman papers; Gwynn W. Barrett, "John M. Bernhisel, Mormon Elder in Congress," Ph.D. diss., Brigham Young University, 1968, 1, 171, 175-76; Richard S. Van Wagoner and Steven C. Walker, *A Book of Mormons* (Salt Lake City: Signature Books, 1982), 18; Quinn, *Mormon Hierarchy: Origins of Power*, 524; appendix, "Appointments To the Theocratic Council of Fifty Through 1884."

110. Brigham Young to William H. Hooper, 20 Dec. 1860, 2, 3 Jan. 1861, 1, Young-Hooper Correspondence.

111. Colton, *Civil War in the Western Territories*, 106; Josephy, *Civil War In the American West*, 90; William I. Waldrip, "New Mexico During the Civil War," *New Mexico Historical Review* 28 (Oct. 1953): 254-58.

112. Roberts, *Comprehensive History*, 5:39-52; John Banks, "A Document History of the Morrisites In Utah," M.S. thesis, University of Utah, 1909, 60 for quote, 56-93 for the military attack and its consequences; Larry J. Halford, "Mormons and Morrisites: A Study in the Sociology of Conflict," Ph.D. diss., University of Montana, 1972; C. LeRoy Anderson and Larry J. Halford, "The Mormons and the Morrisite War," *Montana: The Magazine of Western History* 24 (Oct. 1974): 42-53; G. M. Howard, "Men Motives and Misunderstandings: A New Look at the Morrisite War of 1862," *Utah Historical Quarterly* 44 (Spring 1976): 112-32; C. LeRoy Anderson, *For Christ Will Come Tomorrow: The Saga of the Morrisites* (Logan: Utah State University Press, 1981); Janet Burton Seegmiller, *"Be Kind to the Poor": The Life Story of Robert Taylor Burton* ([Salt Lake City]: Robert Taylor Burton Family Organization/Publishers Press, 1988), 213-27; Kenneth Godfrey, "Morrisites," in Powell, *Utah History Encyclopedia*, 381-82; also for an analysis of the conversion and continued devotion of some Morrisites, see Richard Neitzel Holzapfel, "The Flight of the Doves from Utah Mormonism to California Morrisitism: The Saga of James and George Dove," in Roger D. Launius and Linda Thatcher, eds., *Differing Visions: Dissenters in Mormon History* (Urbana: University of Illinois Press, 1994), 196-219.

113. Brigham Young to Walter M. Gibson, 18 July 1862, typescript of Young's letterbook 6 (1 Nov. 1861-15 Apr. 1864): 339, box 22, Moorman papers.

114. Lyman Clarence Pedersen, Jr., "History of Fort Douglas, Utah," Ph.D. diss., Brigham Young University, 1967, 33; Tom Generous, "Over the River Jordan: California Volunteers in Utah During the Civil War," *California History* 63 (1984): 200-11; James F. Varley, *Brigham and the Brigadier: General Patrick Conner and His California Volunteers in Utah and Along the Overland Trail* (Tucson, AZ: Westernlore Press, 1989), 66; Brigham D. Madsen, *Glory Hunter: A Biography of Patrick Edward Connor* (Salt Lake City: University of Utah Press, 1990), 70; Long, *Saints and the Union*, 38, 107; also Max Reynolds McCarthy, "Patrick Edward Connor and the Military District of Utah: Civil War Military Operations in Utah and Nevada," M.S. thesis, Utah State University, 1976.

115. Long, *Saints and the Union*, 116.

116. Journal History of the Church of Jesus Christ of Latter-day Saints (1830-1972), 246 reels, microfilm, Special Collections, Marriott Library, 30 Oct. 1862, 2; also Long, *Saints and the Union*, 120, for the same quote, and 145-58, 167-71, on Mormon conflicts with Governor Harding.

117. Barrett, "John M. Bernhisel," 168; Roberts, *Comprehensive History,* 5:18n13; Francis Edward Rogan, "Patrick Edward Connor: An Army Officer in Utah, 1862-1866," M.S. thesis, University of Utah, 1952, 41; Ray B. West, Jr., *Kingdom of the Saints: The Story of Brigham Young and the Mormons* (New York: Viking Press, 1957), 290; Leonard J. Arrington and Thomas G. Alexander, "The U.S. Army Overlooks Fort Douglas, 1862-1965," *Utah Historical Quarterly* 33 (Fall 1965): 326-33; McLaws, *Spokesman for the Kingdom,* 81.

118. William Nelson statement in Brigham D. Madsen, *The Shoshoni Frontier and the Bear River Massacre* (Salt Lake City: University of Utah Press, 1985), 196; Fred B. Rogers, *Soldiers of the Overland: Being Some Account of the Services of General Patrick Edward Connor & His Volunteers in the Old West* (San Francisco: Grabhorn Press, 1938), 75, 77; Kenney, *Wilford Woodruff's Journal* 6 (3 Feb. 1863): 96, for the apostle's comment on Lt. Chase's LDS background; Quinn, *Mormon Hierarchy: Origins of Power,* 418, for Chase's Danite affiliation in Missouri during 1838.

119. Long, *Saints and the Union,* 149, 161-63, 171; also Robert J. Dwyer, *Gentile Comes to Utah: A Study in Religious and Social Conflict (1862-1890)* (Washington, D.C.: Catholic University of America Press, 1941), 15; Larson, "Utah and the Civil War," 73-75; Varley, *Brigham and the Brigadier,* 81-83, 120-22; Pedersen, "History of Fort Douglas, Utah," 71, 80. This situation was probably why little-known Mormons claimed to be "a bodyguard for President Brigham Young," in Edith Parker Haddock and Dorothy Hardy Matthew, comps., *History of Bear Lake Pioneers* (Salt Lake City: Daughters of Utah Pioneers/Utah Printing Co., 1968), 291, 407, 819.

120. Long, *Saints and the Union,* 153, quoting from the full transcription in Brigham Young's letterbook, rather than the summary in "GOVERNOR YOUNG'S SPEECH," *Deseret News* [weekly], 4 Mar. 1863, 285.

121. *Journal of Discourses* 10:107 (B. Young/1863).

122. Roberts, *Comprehensive History,* 5:9-12; Morgan, *State of Deseret,* 94-97; Russell R. Rich, *Ensign to the Nations: A History of the Church From 1846 to the Present* (Provo, UT: Brigham Young University Publications, 1972), 294-95; Long, *Saints and the Union,* 15-16, 65, 119-20, 159, 254; Thomas G. Alexander, *Utah: The Right Place, The Official Centennial History* (Salt Lake City: Gibbs-Smith Publisher/Utah Division of State History, 1995), 141.

123. Dwyer, *Gentile Comes to Utah,* 7; D. Michael Quinn, "The Mormon Church and the Spanish-American War: An End to Selective Pacifism," *Pacific Historical Review* 43 (Aug. 1973): 352.

124. Alan E. Haynes, "The Federal Government and Its Policies Regarding the Frontier Era of Utah Territory, 1850-1877," Ph.D. diss., Catholic University of America, 1968, 125, 128; also Franklin D. Daines, "Separatism In Utah, 1847-1870," *Annual Report of the American Historical Association For 1917* (Washington, D.C.: American Historical Association, 1920), 341-42.

125. George U. Hubbard, "Abraham Lincoln as Seen by the Mormons," *Utah Historical Quarterly* 31 (Spring 1963): 103, with variant of this quote in Preston Nibley, *Brigham Young: The Man and His Work* (Independence, MO: Zion's Printing and Publishing Co., 1936), 369; Haynes, "Federal Government and Its Policies Regarding the Frontier Era of Utah Territory," 128; Arrington, *Brigham Young,* 295; Long, *Saints and the Union,* 191-92, for the basic reliability of this account, and 183-84, for Harding's removal; also Dwyer, *Gentile Comes to Utah,* 13-14, 17; Howard Roberts Lamar, *The Far Southwest, 1846-1912: A Territorial History* (New Haven, CT: Yale University Press, 1966), 362-64. Larry Schweikart, "The Mormon Connection: Lincoln, the Saints, and the Crisis of Equality," *Western Humanities Review* 34 (Winter 1980): 1, asserted that "Hubbard's otherwise excellent scholarship wanes in his timid conclusion that the Mormons' intense anti-Lincoln sentiment rather miraculously shifted, simply because of Lincoln's avowed policy to 'let them alone.' This conclusion is at best simplistic and at worst simply false." However, Schweikart's article (1-22) then launched into an irrelevant discussion of the philosophical attitudes of Lincoln

and the Mormons concerning African-Americans, without comparing Mormon rhetoric before and after Lincoln's above statement in 1863.

126. Orson F. Whitney, *History of Utah*, 4 vols. (Salt Lake City: George Q. Cannon & Sons, 1892-1904), 4: 669-70; Dwyer, *Gentile Comes to Utah*, 18; Lamar, *Far Southwest*, 379; Long, *Saints and the Union*, 198-99; Larry Haslam, "Utah's Delegates To Congress, 1851-1896," M.S. thesis, Utah State University, 1962, 83-90; also Michael W. Homer, "The Federal Bench and Priesthood Authority: The Rise and Fall of John Fitch Kinney's Early Relationship with the Mormons," *Journal of Mormon History* 13 (1986-87): 89-108.

127. John Cradlebaugh, *Utah and the Mormons: Speech of Hon. John Cradlebaugh, of Nevada, on the Admission of Utah As a State. Delivered in the House of Representatives, February 7, 1863* ([Washington, D.C.], 1863), 15.

128. McLaws, *Spokesman for the Kingdom*, 81-82; also Larson, "Utah and the Civil War," 75.

129. Gordon M. Bakken, "The English Common Law In the Rocky Mountain West," *Arizona and the West: A Quarterly Journal of History* 11 (Summer 1969): 126-27.

130. Morgan, *State of Deseret*, 96-112; Campbell, *Establishing Zion*, 234-35; Arrington, *Brigham Young*, 252; Richard Neitzel Holzapfel, "The Civil War In Utah," in Powell, *Utah History Encyclopedia*, 94-95.

131. Charles S. Peterson, *Utah: A Bicentennial History* (New York: W. W. Norton & Co.; Nashville: American Association for State and Local History, 1977), 78.

132. Alice Elizabeth Smith, *James Duane Doty: Frontier Promoter* (Madison: State Historical Society of Wisconsin, 1954), 375; also Gustive O. Larson, "Government, Politics, and Conflict," in Poll, *Utah's History*, 245-46.

133. Lamar, *Far Southwest*, 356. This passage referred to the situation in 1861 but is applicable throughout the Civil War period.

134. Kenney, *Wilford Woodruff's Journal* 6 (6 Mar. 1865): 216, which was a restatement of a revelation to Kimball on 30 April 1862, "The Lord told me the North would not overcome the South," in Heber C. Kimball's memoranda, copied into J. Golden Kimball's 1885-87 diary after entry for 21 Feb. 1887, Marriott Library; also McPherson, *Ordeal By Fire*, 158-60, 231, 330, 340, 441-42, 459-63, 466, 471, 475, 479, for condition of the Confederacy in March 1865.

135. Lamar, *Far Southwest*, 367; McPherson, *Ordeal By Fire*, 491-594; Victor B. Howard, *Religion and the Radical Republican Movement, 1860-1870* (Lexington: University Press of Kentucky, 1990).

136. Minutes of the Council of Fifty, 23 Jan. 1867, LDS archives. Alexander, *Utah*, 141, wrongly states that "in 1862, the Mormon leadership revived the Council of Fifty . . ."

137. Manuscript History of the Church, minutes of the Council of Fifty, and diaries of Brigham Young, Jr., Elias Smith, Wilford Woodruff, and Franklin D. Richards for 23 Jan., 25 Jan., 5 Apr., 5 Oct., 10 Oct. 1867, 4 Apr., 9 Apr., 9 Oct. 1868, all in LDS archives; Church Historian's office journal, 9 Oct. 1868; Andrew F. Ehat, "'It Seems Like Heaven Began on Earth': Joseph Smith and the Constitution of the Kingdom of God," *Brigham Young University Studies* 20 (Spring 1980): 278; "Co-operation," editorial, *Deseret Evening News*, 3 Oct. 1868, [2], prepared for the conference vote: "There should be, also, a wholesale house in this city, on the same principle, that all who desired might buy goods here at fair jobbing rates, not exorbitant retail prices with ten per cent off." For the significance of ZCMI, see Leonard J. Arrington, *Great Basin Kingdom: An Economic History of the Latter-day Saints, 1847-1900* (Cambridge, MA: Harvard University Press, 1958), 293-322; Martha Sonntag Bradley, *ZCMI: America's First Department Store* (Salt Lake City: ZCMI, 1991).

138. Minutes of the Provo School of the Prophets, 13 Oct. 1868, microfilm at Lee Library, also in typescript, 106, Utah State Historical Society and Beinecke Library; minutes of the meeting of bishops of Provo, 15 Oct. 1868, microfilm at Lee Library, also typescript,

28, LDS archives, and Huntington Library; Klaus J. Hansen, *Quest for Empire: The Political Kingdom of God and the Council of Fifty in Mormon History* (Lansing: Michigan State University Press, 1967), 145.

139. Orlen Curtis Peterson, "A History of the Schools and Educational Programs of the Church of Jesus Christ of Latter-day Saints in Ohio and Missouri, 1831-1839," M.A. thesis, Brigham Young University, 1972, 13-41; Milton V. Backman, Jr., *The Heavens Resound: A History of the Latter-day Saints in Ohio, 1830-1838* (Salt Lake City: Deseret Book Co., 1983), 264-68.

140. John R. Patrick, "The School of the Prophets: Its Development and Influence in Utah Territory," M.A. thesis, Brigham Young University, 1970, 142-143; Arrington, *Great Basin Kingdom*, 245-51; minutes of the School of the Prophets, Salt Lake City, 1870-74, LDS archives.

141. Patrick, "School of the Prophets," 47, for quote, also 142-43.

142. Minutes of the School of the Prophets, Salt Lake City, 29 Jan. 1870; Joseph F. Smith diary, 29 Jan. 1870, LDS archives, with copy in fd 5, box 6, Scott G. Kenney papers, Marriott Library.

143. For example, "GREAT SALT LAKE COUNTY CAUCUS MEETING," *Deseret News* [weekly], 1 July 1863, 5; "THE NOMINEES FOR OFFICE," *Deseret Evening News,* 18 July 1870, [2]; "PRIMARY ELECTION MEETING," *Salt Lake Daily Herald,* 5 Feb. 1872, [2]; "MEETING FOR NOMINATIONS," *Salt Lake Daily Herald,* 11 Mar. 1872, [3]; "LOCAL AND OTHER MATTERS . . . Political Caucus," *Deseret Evening News,* 13 July 1872, [3]; "The Convention," *Deseret Evening News,* 19 July 1873, [3]; "PUBLIC NOMINATION MEETING," *Deseret Evening News,* 31 Jan. 1874, [3]; Jack, "Utah Territorial Politics: 1847-1876," 97-98, 102, 169-70, 256, 260, 269, 319, 384, 400.

144. Albert Carrington diary, 28 Jan. 1872, Marriott Library; Joseph F. Smith diary, 28 Jan., 3 Feb. 1872; Robert McQuarrie diary, 3 Feb. 1872, LDS archives; minutes of the School of the Prophets, Salt Lake City, 3 Feb. 1872, 26 Jan. 1874.

145. *Journal of Discourses* 17:157 (B. Young/1874). On the Council of Fifty's constitution, see Ehat, "'It Seems Like Heaven Began On Earth,'" 260-61; Quinn, *Mormon Hierarchy: Origins of Power,* 131.

146. LeGrand Young diary and memorandum, 19 Jan. 1878, in David Freed papers, Marriott Library.

147. Franklin D. Richards diary, 16 Jan. 1878.

148. Kenney, *Wilford Woodruff's Journal* 5 (12 July 1857, 20 July 1859): 67, 371; Brigham Young office journal, 17 July 1861, LDS archives, with copy in fd 2, box 26, Moorman papers; Franklin D. Richards diary, 4 Sept. 1878, 2 Feb. 1882; John Henry Smith diary, 5 Oct. 1890, in Jean Bickmore White, ed., *Church, State, and Politics: The Diaries of John Henry Smith* (Salt Lake City: Signature Books/Smith Research Associates, 1990), 242.

149. Franklin D. Richards diary, 17 Dec. 1879, 16 Feb. 1888; Heber J. Grant journal, 13 Jan. 1884.

150. Brigham Young office journal, 29 Jan. 1862; Kenney, *Wilford Woodruff's Journal,* 7 (5 Feb. 1876): 265-66; Albert Carrington diary, 28 Jan. 1872; L. John Nuttall diary, 2 Feb. 1884, 9 July 1889, Lee Library, with copy in Marriott Library and Huntington Library; Joseph F. Smith diary, 22 Jan., 1 Feb., 2 Mar. 1880, 4-5 Feb. 1881; John Henry Smith diary, 13 Jan. 1882, in White, *Church, State, and Politics,* 72-73; Franklin D. Richards diary, 15 Jan., 25 Jan. 1877, 4-5 Feb. 1881; Abraham H. Cannon diary, 21 Jan., 23 Jan. 1890; Richard E. Kotter, "An Examination of Mormon and Non-Mormon Influences in Ogden City Politics, 1847-1896," M.A. thesis, Utah State University, 1967, 35, 44-46.

151. Arrington, *Brigham Young,* 231.

152. Minutes of the School of the Prophets, Parowan, 27 July 1872, typed copy, Beinecke Library; minutes of the School of the Prophets, Salt Lake City, 3 Feb. 1872, 26 Jan. 1874.

153. "'Conservative' Ratification," *Deseret Evening News,* 8 Feb. 1878, [3]; also "Convention," *Deseret Evening News,* 29 July 1876, [3], for Benedict's position with the LDS political party.

154. "THE COUNTY CONVENTION. The People's Party Nominate Their Ticket. Lively Time at the Meeting," *Salt Lake Daily Herald,* 28 July 1880, [3].

155. Brigham Young-William H. Hooper correspondence; John M. Bernhisel papers, Lee Library and Huntington Library; Young-Bernhisel correspondence, Moorman papers; correspondence to and from the territorial delegates with Brigham Young, John Taylor, and Wilford Woodruff papers, LDS archives; Barrett, "John M. Bernhisel," 91-181; Mark W. Cannon, "The Mormon Issue in Congress, 1872-1882, Drawing on the Experience of Territorial Delegate George Q. Cannon," Ph.D. diss., Harvard University, 1960.

156. Alvin Charles Koritz, "The Development of Municipal Government in the Territory of Utah," M.A. thesis, Brigham Young University, 1972, 55-60.

157. Examples of this approach are James R. Clark, "The Kingdom of God, the Council of Fifty, and the State of Deseret," *Utah Historical Quarterly* 26 (Apr. 1958): 145; and Hansen, *Quest for Empire,* 128, 131, 135-37.

158. They are: Alexander Badlam, Abraham H. Cannon, Joseph W. Coolidge, Lewis Dana, Cyrus Daniels, John W. Farnham, Amos Fielding, George F. Gibbs, Samuel James, Charles S. Kimball, David P. Kimball, John E. Page, Ezra Thayer, Lorenzo D. Wasson, and Lucien Woodworth. However, Badlam, Coolidge, Daniels, and Thayer did serve in the Zion's Camp and/or Danite militias. The Council of Fifty admitted a total of 138 members from its first meeting in 1844 to its last meeting in 1884.

159. Morgan, *State of Deseret,* 35-36; Irving, "Roster of Members of the Legislative Assembly, Utah Territory, 1851/2 to 1894," 40-54.

160. Utah Territorial Legislature, *Journals;* Irving, "Roster of Members of the Legislative Assembly, Utah Territory, 1851/2 to 1894."

161. Cannon, "The Mormon Issue in Congress."

162. Irving, "Roster of Members of the Legislative Assembly, Utah Territory, 1851/2 to 1894."

163. Ibid.; Utah Territorial Legislature, *Journals.*

164. Morgan, *State of Deseret,* 36; Irving, "Roster of Members of the Legislative Assembly, Utah Territory, 1851/2 to 1894"; Utah Territorial Legislature, *Journals.*

165. *House Journal of the Twenty-Fifth Session of the Legislative Assembly of the Territory of Utah, 1882,* [5], [9]; *Council Journal . . . of the Territory of Utah* (1882-95); *House Journal . . . of the Territory of Utah* (1882-95); *Senate Journal...of the Legislature of the State of Utah* (1896-1995); *House Journal...of the Legislature of the State of Utah* (1896-1995).

166. Orma Linford, "The Mormons and the Law: The Polygamy Cases," *Utah Law Review* 9 (Winter 1964): 317-18; Lamar, *Far Southwest,* 391; Gustive O. Larson, *The "Americanization" of Utah For Statehood* (San Marino, CA: Huntington Library, 1971), 91-114; Joseph H. Groberg, "The Mormon Disfranchisements of 1882 to 1892," *Brigham Young University Studies* 16 (Spring 1976): 399-408; Edward Leo Lyman, *Political Deliverance: The Mormon Quest for Utah Statehood* (Urbana: University of Illinois Press, 1986), 22-25; Firmage and Mangrum, *Zion in the Courts,* 160-97; B. Carmon Hardy, *Solemn Covenant: The Mormon Polygamous Passage* (Urbana: University of Illinois Press, 1992), 46-47.

167. Franklin D. Richards diary, 15 Mar. 1882.

168. Jerome Bernstein, "A History of the Constitutional Conventions of the Territory of Utah from 1849 to 1895," M.S. thesis, Utah State University, 1961, 97-114.

169. For example, Young's circular letter, 23 Dec. 1861, listed the names of men to be chosen as delegates from Juab, Beaver, Iron, Washington, Sanpete, and Millard counties in an election of 6 January 1862 for the upcoming constitutional convention, in bound typescript of Young's letterbook 6 (1 Nov. 1861-15 Apr. 1864), box 22, Moorman papers.

170. Franklin D. Richards diary, 26 Apr. 1882.

171. Lyman, *Political Deliverance*, 9, 18, 24, 59-60, 280.

172. U.S. Senate, 31st Congress, 1st Session, Miscellaneous Document 10, *Memorial of the Members of the Legislative Council of the Provisional State of Deseret* [Washington, D.C., 1849], 3, copy in Marriott Library; U.S. House of Representatives, 31st Congress, 1st Session, Report No. 219, *ALMON W. BABBITT, DELEGATE FROM DESERET. April 4, 1850* [Washington, D.C., 1850], 4; "ORGANIZATION OF THE CONVENTION FOR THE ESTABLISHMENT OF A STATE GOVERNMENT," *Deseret News* [weekly], 22 Jan. 1862, 237; "Territorial Convention," *Deseret Evening News,* 20 Feb. 1872, [2], and 23 Feb. 1872, [2]; Bernstein, "History of the Constitutional Conventions of the Territory of Utah," 14.

173. *Constitution of the State of Utah, Adopted By the Convention, April 27, 1882* (Salt Lake City: Deseret News Co., 1882), 7, with twenty-one men on the Revision and Consolidation committee (including Daniel H. Wells, Franklin S. Richards, John T. Caine, John R. Winder, William W. Cluff, Silas S. Smith, Abraham O. Smoot). Charles W. Penrose was admitted to the Fifty shortly after this convention.

174. John Taylor to James Jack, 27 Feb. 1887, quoted in Henry J. Wolfinger, "A Reexamination of the Woodruff Manifesto in the Light of Utah Constitutional History," *Utah Historical Quarterly* 39 (Fall 1971): 343; First Presidency office journal, 15 June 1887, excerpt in LDS archives; minutes of the Quorum of the Twelve Apostles, 15 June 1887, LDS archives; Heber J. Grant letterbook-journal, 20 June 1887; *Constitution of the State of Utah, With the Proceedings of the Constitutional Convention, Abstract of Vote on Ratification and Memorial to Congress Asking Admission Into the Union* ([Salt Lake City], 1887), 8; Lyman, *Political Deliverance*, 44-45.

175. Gordon Morris Bakken, *Rocky Mountain Constitution Making, 1850-1912* (New York: Greenwood Press, 1987), 11.

176. Minutes of the consititutional convention, Council House, Salt Lake City, 21-22 Mar. 1856, in "Utah Political Convention Minutes," LDS archives; "CONSTITUTION OF THE STATE OF DESERET," *Deseret News* [weekly], 2 Apr. 1856, 30; William J. Snow, "Utah Indians and Spanish Slave Trade," *Utah Historical Quarterly* 2 (July 1929): 81-86; Juanita Brooks, "Indian Relations On the Mormon Frontier," *Utah Historical Quarterly* 12 (Jan.-Apr. 1944): 8-9; Roldo V. Dutson, "A Study of the Attitude of the Latter-day Saint Church in the Territory of Utah Toward Slavery As It Pertained to the Indian As Well As To the Negro From 1847 to 1865," M.A. thesis, Brigham Young University, 1964; Lythgoe, "Negro Slavery in Utah," 51-52.

177. "THE PRESIDENTIAL CONTEST. Cayuga County Republicans in Council: SPEECH OF WM. H. SEWARD," *New York Times,* 23 Oct. 1856, 2; also quoted with slight variations in Richard D. Poll, "The Mormon Question Enters National Politics, 1850-1856," *Utah Historical Quarterly* 25 (Apr. 1957): 125-26.

178. *Church History In the Fulness of Times,* rev. ed. (Salt Lake City: Church of Jesus Christ of Latter-day Saints, 1993), 435 for quote; Jean Bickmore White, "Prelude to Statehood: Coming Together in the 1890s," *Utah Historical Quarterly* 62 (Fall 1994): 300-15.

179. Utah Secretary of State, Territorial Election Papers.

180. James B. Allen, "The Development of County Government in the Territory of Utah, 1850-1896," M.A. thesis, Brigham Young University, 1956, 15, 168, 169; Haynes, "Federal Government and Its Policies Regarding the Frontier Era of Utah Territory," 212-17; James B. Allen, "The Unusual Jurisdiction of County Probate Courts in the Territory of Utah," *Utah Historical Quarterly* 36 (Spring 1968): 132-42; Jay Emerson Powell, "An Analysis of the Nature of the Salt Lake County Probate Court's Role in Aggravating Anti-Mormon Sentiment, 1852-1855," Senior honors thesis, University of Utah, 1968; Jay E. Powell, "Fairness in the Salt Lake County Probate Court," *Utah Historical Quarterly* 38 (Summer 1970): 256-62; Raymond T. Swenson, "Resolution of Civil Disputes by Mormon Ecclesiastical Courts," *Utah Law Review* (1978): 573-95; Elizabeth D. Gee, "Justice for All or for the 'Elect': The Utah County Probate Court, 1855-72" *Utah Historical Quarterly* 48

(Spring 1980): 129-47; Shane Swindle, "The Struggle Over the Adoption of the Common Law in Utah," *Thetean: A Student Journal of History* (Provo, UT: Beta Iota Chapter of Phi Alpha Theta, Brigham Young University, 1981), 76-97; Michael W. Homer, "The Judiciary and the Common Law in Utah Territory, 1850-61," *Dialogue: A Journal of Mormon Thought* 21 (Spring 1988): 97-108; Firmage and Mangrum, *Zion in the Courts*, 10, 148-51, 229, 264-65.

181. Utah Secretary of State, Territorial Election Papers; Edward W. Tullidge, *Tullidge's Histories, (Volume II.) Containing the History of All the Northern, Eastern and Western Counties of Utah; Also the Counties of Southern Idaho* (Salt Lake City: Juvenile Instructor, 1889), 94, 396; Whitney, *History of Utah*, 4:83; Leonard J. Arrington, *Charles C. Rich: Mormon General and Western Frontiersman* (Provo, UT: Brigham Young University Press, 1974), 272, 366n3.

182. Quinn, *Mormon Hierarchy: Origins of Power*, 106.

183. Salt Lake City Council Minutes, 1851-88, microfilm, Family History Library, Church of Jesus Christ of Latter-day Saints, Salt Lake City, Utah (hereafter LDS Family History Library).

184. Joseph F. Smith diary, 7 Feb., 18 Feb., 30 Feb. 1879.

185. Herbert Lester Gleason, "The Salt Lake City Police Department: 1851-1949, A Social History," M.S. thesis, University of Utah, 1950, 14, 20, 21.

186. Utah Secretary of State, Territorial Election Papers; Koritz, "Development of Municipal Government," 57-58, 61, 64, 96, 97, 142; Tullidge, *Tullidge's Histories*, 97; Hazel Bradshaw, ed., *Under Dixie Sun: A History of Washington County By Those Who Loved Their Forebears* (Panguitch, UT: Daughters of Utah Pioneers, 1950), 296, 326; Marilyn McMeen Miller and John Clifton Moffitt, *Provo, A Story of People in Motion* (Provo, UT: Brigham Young University Press, 1974), 100-101; Albert E. Miller, *The Immortal Pioneers: Founders of the City of St. George, Utah* (St. George, UT: By the author, 1946), 43-45; Joseph S. Wood, "The Mormon Settlement in San Bernardino, 1851-1857," Ph.D. diss., University of Utah, 1968, 165; Edward Leo Lyman, *San Bernardino: The Rise and Fall of a California Community* (Salt Lake City: Signature Books, 1996), 135, Edward L. Sloan, *Gazetteer of Utah and Salt Lake Directory* (Salt Lake City: Salt Lake Herald Publishing Co., 1874) 62; appendix, "Biographical Sketches."

187. Quinn, *Mormon Hierarchy: Origins of Power*, 109-10.

188. Utah Secretary of State, Territorial Election Papers; appendix, "Biographical Sketches."

189. Lamar, *Far Southwest*, 385-86.

190. See Zora Jarvis, *Ancestry, Biography and Family of George A. Smith* (Provo, UT: Brigham Young University Press, 1962); Charles Kent Dunford, "The Contributions of George A. Smith to the Establishment of the Mormon Society in the Territory of Utah," M.A. thesis, Brigham Young University, 1970; Merlo J. Pusey, *Builders of the Kingdom: George A. Smith, John Henry Smith, George Albert Smith* (Provo, UT: Brigham Young University Press, 1981), 80-88.

191. Edward Porritt and Annie G. Porritt, *The Unreformed House of Commons: Parliamentary Representation Before 1832*, 2 vols. (Cambridge, Eng.: Cambridge University Press, 1903), 1:122; George B. Galloway, *History of the House of Representatives*, 2d ed. (New York: Thomas Y. Crowell Co., 1976), 30.

192. Arrington, *Brigham Young*, 192-99, 232, 238, 243-44.

193. Francis M. Gibbons, *Joseph F. Smith: Patriarch and Preacher, Prophet of God* (Salt Lake City: Deseret Book Co., 1984), 89-90, 112.

194. George Teasdale diary, 27 Jan., 21 Feb. 1880, microfilm, Marriott Library.

195. Albert Carrington diary, 10 Apr. 1880; minutes of the Council of Fifty, 10 Apr. 1880, Lee Library.

196. Council of Fifty rolls (1845-82); diaries of Robert T. Burton, Abraham H. Cannon, Albert Carrington, Heber J. Grant, George Reynolds, Franklin D. Richards, Elias Smith, John Henry Smith, Joseph F. Smith, William W. Taylor, Junius F. Wells, Wilford Woodruff for 10 Apr., 21 Apr., 5 Oct., 12 Oct. 1880, 5 Apr., 8 Apr., 18 May, 4 Oct. 1881, 4-5 Apr., 21-24 June, 26-27 June, 10-11 Oct. 1882, 10-11 Apr., 27-29 June, 6 July, 3 Oct., 10 Oct. 1883, 12 Jan., 8 Apr., 8-9 Oct. 1884; also Ehat, "'It Seems Like Heaven Began On Earth,'" 279, which gave the numerical dates but accidentally omitted some of the months and years.

197. Minutes of the Council of Fifty, 12 Oct. 1880, quoted in Ehat, "'It Seems Like Heaven Began On Earth,'" 264-65.

198. Franklin D. Richards diary, 18 May, 12 July 1881.

199. Minutes of the Council of Fifty, 4-5 Apr. 1882, LDS archives.

200. Franklin D. Richards diary, 22 June 1882; John Henry Smith diary, 22 June 1882, in White, *Church, State, and Politics,* 79; minutes of the Council of Fifty, 22 June 1882.

201. Franklin D. Richards diary, 23 June, 10 Oct. 1882; minutes of the Council of Fifty, 23 June 1882.

202. Minutes of the Council of Fifty, 11 Apr. 1883.

203. Franklin D. Richards diary, 24 June 1882. The released members were John D. Parker, Charles Shumway, Charles C. Rich, John S. Fullmer, John Pack, Joseph L. Heywood, and Thomas Bullock. Rich was the apostle; Heywood lived until 1910.

204. *Deseret News 1995-1996 Church Almanac: The Church of Jesus Christ of Latter-day Saints* (Salt Lake City: Deseret News, 1994), 389.

205. Given shortly after the 27 June 1882 meeting adjourned. The next meeting officially adopted the revelation as the "word of the Lord" (Annie Taylor Hyde notebook, 80, LDS archives; Franklin D. Richards diary, 27 June, 10 Oct. 1882).

206. The Council of Fifty did not admit counselors in the Presiding Bishopric until the 1880s, by which time Jesse C. Little had resigned his office as counselor. The Fifty's exclusion of a majority of the First Council of Seventy and of Patriarch John Smith (b. 1832) from 1844 to 1884 is an evidence of their diminished status within the hierarchy. See chap. 4.

207. Robert T. Burton diary, 10 Apr. 1883; compare Albert Carrington diary, 10 Apr. 1883; Franklin D. Richards diary, 10 Apr. 1883.

208. Quinn, *Mormon Hierarchy: Origins of Power,* 127-28.

209. Examples were special presidency counselors Joseph A. Young, Brigham Young, Jr., Joseph F. Smith, and John W. Young; apostles Ezra T. Benson, George Q. Cannon, Franklin D. Richards, Lorenzo Snow, Moses Thatcher, John W. Taylor; Presiding Bishop Edward Hunter; Presiding Bishopric counselor John Q. Cannon; and Seventy's presidents Abraham H. Cannon, William W. Taylor, and Seymour B. Young. Edward Hunter became Presiding Bishop in 1851 when there were no vacancies in the Fifty which voted him in at its next meeting in 1867. Ordained an apostle in 1860, George Q. Cannon entered the Fifty at its next meeting in 1867. Joseph A. Young and Brigham Young, Jr., were secretly ordained apostles and special counselors to Brigham Young in 1864, and Joseph F. Smith was likewise ordained in 1866. The Fifty voted for all three men at its next meeting in January 1867. John W. Young was ordained a special counselor to his father in 1864 but was on a foreign mission when the Fifty next met in January 1867. The Fifty admitted John W. in October 1867, its first meeting after his return. See appendix, "Appointments To the Theocratic Council of Fifty Through 1884."

210. Rockwood entered the Fifty in March 1845 and the First Council of Seventy the following December. Eldredge entered the Fifty in 1848 and the First Council of Seventy in 1854.

211. *Journal of Discourses* 2:317 (B. Young/1855).

212. Franklin D. Richards diary, 3 Mar., 1 Apr. 1880; Joseph F. Smith diary, 16 Mar., 1 Apr. 1880.

213. Franklin D. Richards diary, 1 Apr., 10 Apr. 1880; Junius F. Wells diary, 9-10 Apr. 1880, LDS archives.

214. Minutes of meeting of the First Presidency and the Quorum of the Twelve Apostles, 4 Jan. 1882, LDS archives; also Heber J. Grant journal, 13 Jan. 1884.

215. Franklin D. Richards diary, 4 Oct., 11 Oct. 1882; minutes of the Council of Fifty, 11 Oct. 1882.

216. Heber J. Grant 1884-87 journal, 12 Jan. 1884.

217. Brigham Young, Jr., diary, 10 Oct., 17 Oct. 1883.

218. Quinn, *Mormon Hierarchy: Origins of Power,* 139-40, 176, 193-98, 199-208.

219. Ibid., 120-25; Ehat, "'It Seems Like Heaven Began On Earth,'" 256-67.

220. Ehat, "'It Seems Like Heaven Began On Earth,'" 277-78.

221. Leonard J. Arrington, Feramorz Y. Fox, and Dean L. May, *Building the City of God: Community and Cooperation Among the Mormons,* 2d ed. (Urbana: University of Illinois Press, 1992), 15-32.

222. Hansen, *Quest For Empire,* 3-44; Hyrum L. Andrus, *Doctrines of the Kingdom,* Vol. 3 of *Foundations of the Millennial Kingdom of Christ* (Salt Lake City: Bookcraft, 1973), 352-401; Gordon Pollock, "In Search of Security: The Mormons and the Kingdom of God on Earth, 1830-1844," Ph.D. diss., Queen's University, 1977; Warren David Hansen, "Re-establishing Community: An Analysis of Joseph Smith's Social Thought in the Context of Philosophical Tradition," Ph.D. diss., Rutgers University, 1980; John F. Wilson, "Some Comparative Perspectives on the Early Mormon Movement and the Church-State Question, 1830-1845," *Journal of Mormon History* 8 (1981): 63-77.

223. Clark, "The Kingdom of God," 143; Jo Ann Barnett Shipps, "The Mormons in Politics: The First Hundred Years," Ph.D. diss., University of Colorado, 1965, 165; also Arrington, *Great Basin Kingdom,* 31-32; Cleland and Brooks, *Mormon Chronicle,* 1:xxiii and passim.

224. Klaus J. Hansen, "The Metamorphosis of the Kingdom of God: Toward a Reinterpretation of Mormon History," *Dialogue: A Journal of Mormon Thought* 1 (Autumn 1966): 83; Hansen, *Quest For Empire,* 190. Despite the publication of studies which detailed the decades in which the Fifty never met during Young's presidency, Hansen has reaffirmed the emphasis of his widely known *Quest For Empire.* In his *Mormonism and the American Experience* (Chicago: University of Chicago Press, 1981), 142, he still affirmed that "Young established a political kingdom of God, ruled by the Council of Fifty under the direction of the hierarchy." In Hansen's "The Metamorphosis of the Kingdom of God: Toward a Reinterpretation of Mormon History," in D. Michael Quinn, ed., *The New Mormon History: Revisionist Essays on the Past* (Salt Lake City: Signature Books, 1992), 241n1, Hansen writes that "reports of the death of the kingdom school of Mormon history have been exaggerated." On the other hand, Powell, *Utah History Encyclopedia* (1994) does not even have an entry for the Council of Fifty in the index.

225. Abraham H. Cannon diary, 2 Dec. 1895. This is one of the documentary evidences which refutes the argument of Gordon C. Thomasson, "Foolsmate," *Dialogue: A Journal of Mormon Thought* 6 (Autumn-Winter 1971): 148-51, that the kingly office was the second anointing ceremony of a husband and wife. Since non-Mormons could be members of the Council of Fifty, this theocratic body had no role in approving or disapproving whether anyone received any ordinance of the temple or Endowment House. Also, John Taylor received the second anointing ceremony in 1846.

226. Samuel W. Taylor, *The Kingdom or Nothing: The Life of John Taylor, Militant Mormon* (New York: Macmillan Publishing Co., 1976), 333-85; Paul Thomas Smith, "John Taylor," in Leonard J. Arrington, ed., *The Presidents of the Church: Biographical Essays* (Salt Lake City: Deseret Book Co., 1986), 112-13.

227. Franklin D. Richards manuscript, 4 Feb. 1885, which reads: "At 8. m. attended Council at Endowment House where we had prayers [—] consecrated oil, and Prest. Jno Taylor was anointed K[ing]. P[riest]. R[uler]. of C[hurch]. Z[ion]. & K[ingdom]."

228. "THAT DECLARATION," *Salt Lake Daily Tribune,* 5 May 1885, [2]; John Henry Smith to "J. Mack" [pseudonym for Joseph F. Smith], 28 Aug. 1885, John Henry Smith 1884-94 letterbook, 434-35, George A. Smith Family papers, Marriott Library; also Van Wagoner and Walker, *Book of Mormons,* 358-59.

229. Lamar, *Far Southwest,* 393.

230. Jenson, *Church Chronology,* 5 Dec. 1884, Jan. 1885; Roberts, *Comprehensive History,* 6:120-21, 124; M. Hamblin Cannon, ed., "The Prison Diary of a Mormon Apostle," *Pacific Historical Review* 16 (Nov. 1947): 393-409; "The Raid," in Arrington, *Great Basin Kingdom,* 353-79; Grace Atkin Woodbury, "The Cohabs Go Underground," in William Mulder and A. Russell Mortensen, eds., *Among the Mormons: Historic Accounts by Contemporary Observers* (New York: Alfred A. Knopf, 1958), 411-15; S. George Ellsworth, "Utah's Struggle for Statehood," *Utah Historical Quarterly* 31 (Winter 1963): 66; Robert B. Day, ed., "Eli Azariah Day: Pioneer Schoolteacher and 'Prisoner for Conscience Sake,'" *Utah Historical Quarterly* 35 (Fall 1967): [322]-41; Larson, *"Americanization" of Utah for Statehood,* 115-138; William G. Hartley, ed., "'In Order To Be In Fashion I Am Called On a Mission': Wilford Woodruff's Parting Letter To Emma As He Joins the 'Underground,'" *Brigham Young University Studies* 15 (Autumn 1974): 110-12; JoAnn W. Bair and Richard L. Jensen, "Prosecution of the Mormons in Arizona Territory in the 1880s," *Arizona and the West: A Quarterly Journal of History* 19 (Spring 1977): 32-43; Melvin L. Bashore, "Life Behind Bars: Mormon Cohabs of the 1880's," *Utah Historical Quarterly* 47 (Winter 1979): 22-41; James B. Allen, "'Good Guys' vs. 'Good Guys': Rudger Clawson, John Sharp, and Civil Disobedience in Nineteenth-Century Utah," *Utah Historical Quarterly* 48 (Spring 1980): 148-74; Kimberly Jensen James, "'Between Two Fires: Women on the 'Underground' of Mormon Polygamy," *Journal of Mormon History* 8 (1981): 49-61; Martha Sonntag Bradley, "Hide and Seek: Children on the Underground," *Utah Historical Quarterly* 51 (Spring 1983): 133-53; Ronald W. Walker, "A Mormon Widow in Colorado: The Exile of Emily Wells Grant," *Arizona and the West: A Quarterly Journal of History* 25 (Spring 1983): 5-22; Christa Marie Sophie Ranglack Nelson, "Mormon Polygamy In Mexico," M.A. thesis, University of Utah, 1983, 33-39; David L. Crowder, *Rexburg, Idaho: The First One Hundred Years, 1883-1983* (Caldwell, ID: Caxton Printers, 1983), 86-100; William C. Seifrit, "The Prison Experience of Abraham H. Cannon," *Utah Historical Quarterly* 53 (Summer 1985): 222-36; Rosa Mae McClellan Evans, "Judicial Prosecution of Prisoners for LDS Plural Marriage: Prison Sentences, 1884-1895," M.A. thesis, Brigham Young University, 1986; Richard S. Van Wagoner, *Mormon Polygamy: A History* (Salt Lake City: Signature Books, 1986), 115-27; Rowland M. Cannon, *From Theocracy To Democracy: A Political History of the Mormon Church and the State of Utah, 1830-1906, With Special Emphasis on the Roles of George Q. Cannon and Frank J. Cannon toward Statehood for Utah* (Salt Lake City: "Written expressly for the author's children and their children as well as the sister and brothers of the author," 1986), 134-36; Jessie L. Embry, *Mormon Polygamous Families: Life in the Principle* (Salt Lake City: University of Utah Press, 1987), 17-23; Clifford L. Ashton, *Federal Judiciary In Utah* (Salt Lake City: Utah Bar Foundation, 1988), 40-42; Ken Driggs, "The Prosecutions Begin: Defining Cohabitation in 1885," *Dialogue: A Journal of Mormon Thought* 21 (Spring 1988): 109-121; Constance L. Lieber and John Sillito, eds., *Letters From Exile: The Correspondence of Martha Hughes Cannon and Angus M. Cannon, 1886-1889* (Salt Lake City: Signature Books/Smith Research Associates, 1989); Stephen Cresswell, *Mormons & Cowboys, Moonshiners & Klansmen: Federal Law Enforcement in the South & West, 1870-1893* (Tuscaloosa: University of Alabama Press, 1991), 95-132; Thomas G. Alexander, *Things in Heaven and Earth: The Life and Times of Wilford Woodruff, a Mormon Prophet* (Salt Lake City: Signature Books, 1991), 236-42; Bruce A. Van Orden, *The Life of George*

Reynolds: Prisoner For Conscience' Sake (Salt Lake City: Deseret Book Co., 1992), 61-116; Allen and Leonard, *Story of the Latter-day Saints*, 402-407; Stan Larson, ed., *Prisoner For Polygamy: The Memoirs and Letters of Rudger Clawson At the Utah Territorial Prison, 1884-87* (Urbana: University of Illinois Press, 1993); chapter, "A Decade of Persecution," in *Church History In the Fulness of Times*, 422-34; Tracey E. Panek, "Search and Seizure in Utah: Recounting the Antipolygamy Raids," *Utah Historical Quarterly* 62 (Fall 1994): 316-334; Sarah Barringer Gordon, "'The Twin Relic of Barbarism': A Legal History of Anti-Polygamy in Nineteenth-Century America," Ph.D. diss., Princeton University, 1994. The southern portion of Canada's Northwest Territory (later Alberta) became a polygamous refuge in 1887.

231. "$800 REWARD To be Paid for the Arrest of John Taylor and Geo. Q. Cannon," *Salt Lake Daily Tribune*, 20 Feb. 1887, [1].

232. For other discussions of the symbolic role of the LDS prophet-king, see Andrus, *Doctrines of the Kingdom*, 556-67; Melodie Moench, "Joseph Smith: Prophet, Priest, and King," *Task Papers in LDS History*, No. 25 (Salt Lake City: Historical Department, The Church of Jesus Christ of Latter-day Saints, 1978).

233. "Mrs. Joe Smith: Grand Design of the Prophet," *Upper Mississippian and Rock Island Republican*, 2 Nov. 1844; George T. M. Davis, *An Authentic Account of the Massacre of Joseph Smith, the Mormon Prophet, and Hyrum Smith, His Brother, Together with a Brief History of the Rise and Progress of Mormonism, And All the Circumstances Which Led to Their Deaths* (St. Louis: Chambers and Knapp, 1844), 7.

234. William Smith statement in "THE SALT LAKE BANDITTI," *Melchizedek and Aaronic Herald* 1 (Feb. 1850): 1; [Charles B. Thompson], "THE MISSION OF BANEEMY," *Zion's Harbinger, and Baneemy's Organ* 2 (Jan. 1852): 3; William Marks to "Beloved Brethren," 15 June 1853, in *Zion's Harbinger, and Baneemy's Organ* 3 (July 1853): 53.

235. Hosea Stout diary, 13 Jan. 1846, in Brooks, *On the Mormon Frontier*, 1:105. Stout did not become a member of the Council of Fifty until 1867.

236. Albert King Thurber journal, typescript, 26, Utah State Historical Society; Kate B. Carter, comp., *Treasures of Pioneer History*, 6 vols. (Salt Lake City: Daughters of Utah Pioneers, 1952-57), 3:273, erroneously altered Thurber's original words to read: "as B. J. [sic] Johnson was of the Council of Seventy [sic] . . ." For this "Gold Mission," see Arrington, *Great Basin Kingdom*, 72-76; Eugene E. Campbell, "The Mormon Gold-Mining Mission of 1849," *Brigham Young University Studies* 1 (Autumn 1959-Winter 1960): 19-31.

237. "HISTORY OF JOSEPH SMITH," *Deseret News* [weekly], 17 June 1857, 114; Kenney, *Wilford Woodruff's Journal* 5 (26 Nov. 1857): 124.

238. "HISTORY OF BRIGHAM YOUNG," 11 Mar., 19 Mar. 1844, in *Deseret News* [weekly], 24 Mar. 1858, [17], and in *Latter-day Saints' Millennial Star* 26 (21 May 1864): 328; also examples in Joseph Smith et al., *History of The Church of Jesus Christ of Latter-day Saints. Period I: History of Joseph Smith the Prophet, and . . . Period II: From the Manuscript History of Brigham Young and Other Original Documents*, ed. B. H. Roberts, 7 vols. (Salt Lake City: Church of Jesus Christ of Latter-day Saints, 1902-32; 2d ed. rev. [Salt Lake City: Deseret Book Co., 1978]), 7:381-82, and in Hyrum L. Andrus, *Joseph Smith and World Government* (Salt Lake City: Deseret Book Co., 1958), 4, 5, 9.

239. Minutes of the Provo School of the Prophets, 13 Oct. 1868; minutes of the meeting of bishops of Provo, 15 Oct., 22 Dec. 1868; Hansen, *Quest for Empire*, 145.

240. Philip B. Lewis obituary, "Veteran Departed," *Deseret Evening News*, 28 Nov. 1877, [4], reprinted in *Deseret News Semi-Weekly*, 1 Dec. 1877, [2], and in *Deseret News* [weekly], 5 Dec. 1877, [689].

241. Salt Lake Seventeenth Ward Relief Society Minutes, Jan. 1880, 1868-84 book, 345-46, LDS archives.

242. "THE FIRST COUNCIL," *Salt Lake Daily Tribune*, 15 May 1881, [2]; "THE CASE OF IRA E. WEST," *Salt Lake Daily Tribune*, 5 June 1881, [2]; compare with John D. Lee diary, Dec. 1848, 3-4 Mar., 17 Mar. 1849, in Cleland and Brooks, *Mormon Chronicle*, 1:80-81, 97-99, 102; Ehat, "It Seems Like Heaven Began On Earth," 279, for meeting on 8 Apr. 1881.

243. Henry W. Miller statement, 5 May 1883, minutes of general meetings in St. George Stake, LDS archives.

244. Andrew Jenson, *Latter-day Saint Biographical Encyclopedia*, 4 vols. (Salt Lake City: Deseret News/Andrew Jenson History Company, 1901-36), 1:290, 368.

245. Fawn M. Brodie, *No Man Knows My History: The Life of Joseph Smith, The Mormon Prophet*, 2d ed. rev. and enl. (New York: Alfred A. Knopf, 1976), 356.

246. Heber J. Grant letterbook-journal, 25 Oct. 1887.

247. Lyman, *Political Deliverance*, 1.

248. "The Republican Platform," *Deseret Evening News*, 21 June 1888, [2].

249. "OFFICIAL DECLARATION," *Deseret Evening News*, 14 Dec. 1889, [2]; Clark, *Messages of the First Presidency*, 3:186.

250. Joseph F. Smith diary, 7 Feb. 1879; Franklin D. Richards diary, 24 Jan. 1888; Abraham H. Cannon diary, 11 Oct., 17 Oct. 1889; L. John Nuttall diary, 11 Oct., 18 Oct. 1889, also in Ogden Kraut, comp., *L. John Nuttall Diary Excerpts* (Salt Lake City: Pioneer Press, 1994), 186.

251. Franklin D. Richards diary, 25 May 1876, 20 Jan. 1880, 23 Feb. 1882, 23 Jan., 29 Jan., 31 Jan. 1888; John Henry Smith diary, 17 Jan. 1882, in White, *Church, State, and Politics*, 73; Heber J. Grant journal sheets, 23 Jan. 1888; Bolingbroke, "History of the Utah Territorial Legislature, 1851-1861," 27.

252. "COUNSEL AND COERCION," *Deseret Evening News*, 16 Mar. 1889, [2].

253. Heber J. Grant letterbook-journal, 29 Dec. 1889.

254. Therald N. Jensen, "Mormon Theory of Church and State," Ph.D. diss., University of Chicago, 1938, 26-37; G. Homer Durham, "The Democratic Crisis and Mormon Thought," *Ethics* 52 (Oct. 1941): 110-15; Gaylen L. Caldwell, "Mormon Conceptions of Individual Rights and Political Obligation," Ph.D. diss., Stanford University, 1952, 120-28; Cannon, "The Mormon Issue in Congress," 251-69; Edward A. Warner, "Mormon Theodemocracy: Theocratic and Democratic Elements In Early Latter-day Saint Ideology, 1827-1846," Ph.D. diss., University of Iowa, 1973, 137-207; Arthur Ray Bassett, "Culture and the American Frontier In Mormon Utah, 1850-1896," Ph.D. diss., Syracuse University, 1975, 12; Andrus, *Doctrines of the Kingdom*, 393-394.

255. J. Keith Melville, "Brigham Young's Ideal Society: The Kingdom of God," *Brigham Young University Studies* 5 (Autumn 1962): 12, 13.

256. Quinn, "Mormon Church and the Spanish-American War," reprinted in *Dialogue: A Journal of Mormon Thought* 17 (Winter 1984); also discussion of selective pacifism in Thomas G. Alexander, *Mormonism in Transition: A History of the Latter-day Saints, 1890-1930* (Urbana: University of Illinois Press, 1986), 13-14; Quinn, *Mormon Hierarchy: Origins of Power*, 82-84; Davis Bitton, "The Ordeal of Brigham Young, Jr.," in Bitton, *The Ritualization of Mormon History and Other Essays* (Urbana: University of Illinois Press, 1994), 141.

257. The U.S. House of Representatives excluded Brigham H. Roberts in January 1900, thus refusing to admit him despite his election by Utah's voters. This issue was his continued cohabitation with plural wives by whom he fathered children even during the controversy. The House investigation and vote did not involve theocracy or his position as an LDS general authority. See Roberts, *Comprehensive History*, 6:363-68; Davis Bitton, "The B. H. Roberts Case of 1898-1900," *Utah Historical Quarterly* 25 (Jan. 1957): 27-46; Robert H. Malan, *B. H. Roberts: A Biography* (Salt Lake City: Deseret Book Co., 1966), 62-77; Leonard J. Arrington, "Crisis in Identity: Mormon Responses in the Nineteenth and

Twentieth Centuries," in Marvin S. Hill and James B. Allen, eds., *Mormonism and American Culture* (New York: Harper and Row, 1972), 172-73; William Griffith White, Jr., "Feminist Campaign for the Exclusion of Brigham Henry Roberts from the Fifty-Sixth Congress," *Journal of the West* 17 (Jan. 1978): 45-52; Truman G. Madsen, *Defender of the Faith: The B. H. Roberts Story* (Salt Lake City: Bookcraft, 1980), 241-68; Alexander, *Mormonism in Transition*, 11; Gary James Bergera, ed., *The Autobiography of B. H. Roberts* (Salt Lake City: Signature Books, 1990), 212-19; Davis Bitton, "The Exclusion of B. H. Roberts from Congress," in Bitton, *Ritualization of Mormon History*, 150-70.

258. U.S. Senate, *Proceedings Before the Committee on Privileges and Elections of the United States Senate in the Matter of the Protests Against the Right of Hon. Reed Smoot, a Senator from the State of Utah, to Hold His Seat*, 4 vols. (Washington: Government Printing Office, 1904-1907), 1:1.

259. Jay R. Lowe, "Fred T. Dubois, Foe of the Mormons: A Study of the Role of Fred T. Dubois in the Senate Investigation of the Hon. Reed Smoot and the Mormon Church, 1903-1907," M.A. thesis, Brigham Young University, 1960; Alan Elmo Haynes, "Brigham Henry Roberts and Reed Smoot: Significant Events in the Development of American Pluralism," M.A. thesis, Catholic University of America, 1966, iii-vi, 40-74; Jan Shipps, "Utah Comes of Age Politically: A Study of the State's Politics in the Early Years of the Twentieth Century," *Utah Historical Quarterly* 35 (Spring 1967): 92-99; M. Paul Holsinger, "J. C. Burrows and the Fight Against Mormonism, 1903-1907," *Michigan History* 52 (Fall 1968): 181-95; M. Paul Holsinger, "Philander C. Knox and the Crusade Against Mortmonism, 1904-1907," *Western Pennsylvania History Magazine* 51 (Jan. 1969): 47-56; M. Paul Holsinger, "For God and the American Home: The Attempt to Unseat Senator Reed Smoot, 1903-1907," *Pacific Northwest Quarterly* 60 (July 1969): 154-60; David Brudnoy, "Of Sinners and Saints: Theodore Schroeder, Brigham Roberts, and Reed Smoot," *Journal of Church and State* 14 (Spring 1972): 261-78; Gary James Bergera, "Secretary To The Senator: Carl A. Badger And The Smoot Hearings," *Sunstone* 8 (Jan.-Apr. 1983): 36-41; Richard O. Cowan, *The Church In the Twentieth Century* (Salt Lake City: Bookcraft, 1985), 29-31; Alexander, *Mormonism in Transition*, 16-27; *Church History In the Fulness of Times*, 467-70.

260. Joseph F. Smith, John R. Winder, and Anthon H. Lund, "AN ADDRESS: THE CHURCH OF JESUS CHRIST OF LATTER-DAY SAINTS TO THE WORLD," 26 Mar. 1907, in *Improvement Era* 10 (May 1907): 492-93 for political statement, and "adopted by vote of the Church, in General Conference, April 5, 1907" (495); Clark, *Messages of the First Presidency*, 4:153 for the political statement and (142) for quote about the significance of the conference vote.

261. Allen and Leonard, *Story of the Latter-day Saints*, 445, 490; Alexander, *Mormonism in Transition*, 29-35; Reuben Joseph Snow, "The American Party In Utah: A Study of Political Party Struggles During the Early Years of Statehood," M.A. thesis, University of Utah, 1963; Thomas G. Alexander and James B. Allen, *Mormons & Gentiles: A History of Salt Lake City* (Boulder, CO: Pruett Publishing Co., 1984), 140-48.

262. John W. Taylor to Joseph F. Smith, 17 Feb. 1911, with Smith's handwritten note, LDS archives; John Henry Smith diary, 18 Feb. 1911, in White, *Church, State, and Politics*, 666. For John W. Taylor's initiation at the Fifty's last meeting, see Abraham H. Cannon diary, 9 Oct. 1884; for his circumstances which prompted this letter, see Van Wagoner and Walker, *Book of Mormons*, 364; Hardy, *Solemn Covenant*, 265-66, 291.

263. "Instructions given to Elder Joseph F. Smith Jr., at the Salt Lake Temple, April 7th, 1910, immediately prior to his receiving ordination as an Apostle," LDS archives.

264. For "Living Constitution" as a name for the Council of Fifty, see Daniel Spencer diary, 12 Apr., 18 Apr. 1845, LDS archives; William W. Phelps statement in meeting of apostles on 27 Apr. 1845, LDS archives; *Zion's Harbinger, and Baneemy's Organ* 2 (Jan. 1852): 3; John D. Lee's autobiography in Lee, *Mormonism Unveiled; or the Life and Confessions of the*

Late Mormon Bishop, John D. Lee (St. Louis: Bryan, Brand & Co., 1877), 173; Quinn, *Mormon Hierarchy: Origins of Power,* 131.

265. Heber J. Grant journal, 3 Jan. 1932. This should disprove rumors about other men allegedly initiated but who lived beyond 1931.

266. Francis M. Gibbons, *David O. McKay: Apostle to the World, Prophet of God* (Salt Lake City: Deseret Book Co., 1986), 378-79; also "President David O. McKay, Visits with U.S. Government Officials, General Dwight D. Eisenhower, 34th President of the United States, 1952-1960," bound scrapbook, LDS archives.

267. Quinn, *Mormon Hierarchy: Origins of Power,* 84, 102, 113, 116, 135, 140, 250, 472-74, 477, 621, 627, 636, for Joseph Smith and Brigham Young before 1848; previous discussion and chap. 7 for Young's bodyguards in Utah; Samuel Bateman diaries, 26 Aug. 1886-25 July 1887, Lee Library; Taylor, *Kingdom or Nothing,* 335-74.

268. Abraham H. Cannon diary, 9 Sept. 1887.

269. Seymour B. Young diary, 30 Sept. 1905, 29 July 1913, LDS archives; Anthon H. Lund diary, 3 Jan. 1911, LDS archives; Leonard J. Arrington and Heidi S. Swinton, *The Hotel: Salt Lake's Classy Lady: The Hotel Utah, 1911-1986* (Salt Lake City: Publishers Press/Westin Hotel Utah, 1986), 16; Andrew Hunt, "Beyond the Spotlight: The Red Scare in Utah," *Utah Historical Quarterly* 61 (Fall 1993): 363-66; also Noble Warrum, *Utah Since Statehood,* 4 vols. (Chicago: S. J. Clarke Publishing Co., 1919-20), 2:196-99, 3:894-97, for King and Nebeker. The Lund diary microfilm is available to all researchers at LDS archives by stipulation of their donor, and will be published in edited form by Signature Books, Salt Lake City.

270. Dean C. Jessee, "A Comparative Study and Evaluation of the Latter-day Saint and 'Fundamentalist' Views Pertaining to the Practice of Plural Marriage," M.A. thesis, Brigham Young University, 1959; Jerold A. Hilton, "Polygamy In Utah and Surrounding Area Since the Manifesto of 1890," M.A. thesis, Brigham Young University, 1965; Ken Driggs, "After the Manifesto: Modern Polygamy and Fundamentalist Mormons," *Journal of Church and State* 32 (Spring 1990): 367-89;; Ken Driggs, "Fundamentalist Attitudes toward the Church: The Sermons of Leroy S. Johnson," *Dialogue: A Journal of Mormon Thought* 23 (Summer 1990): 39-60; Ken Driggs, "Twentieth-Century Polygamy and Fundamentalist Mormons in Southern Utah," *Dialogue: A Journal of Mormon Thought* 24 (Winter 1991): 44-58; D. Michael Quinn, "Plural Marriage and Mormon Fundamentalism," in Martin E. Marty and R. Scott Appleby, eds., *Fundamentalisms and Society: Reclaiming the Sciences, the Family, and Education,* vol. 2 of the Fundamentalism Project of the American Academy of Arts and Sciences (Chicago: University of Chicago Press, 1993), 240-93; Martha Sonntag Bradley, "Joseph W. Musser: Dissenter or Fearless Crusader for Truth?" in Launius and Thatcher, *Differing Visions,* 262-78.

271. George F. Richards diary, 15 Apr. 1921, LDS archives.

272. Martha Sonntag Bradley, *Kidnapped From That Land: The Government Raids on the Short Creek Polygamists* (Salt Lake City: University of Utah Press, 1993), 57.

273. Robert A. Tucker, "Temple Recommend," in Ludlow, *Encyclopedia of Mormonism,* 4:1,446.

274. "CHURCH MEMBERS WARNED TO ESCHEW COMMUNISM: Leaders Cite Threat To Home, Nation And Church," and "Warning To Church Members," *Deseret News,* 3 July 1936, [1]; "Editorial: Warning to Church Members," *Improvement Era* 39 (Aug. 1936): 488; Clark, *Messages of the First Presidency,* 6:17-18; D. Michael Quinn, *J. Reuben Clark: The Church Years* (Provo, UT: Brigham Young University Press, 1983), 189.

275. Fraser M. Ottanelli, *The Communist Party of the United States From the Depression to World War II* (New Brunswick, NJ: Rutger's University Press, 1991), 12, 43; "LIST OF NOMINATIONS," *Salt Lake Tribune,* 7 Nov. 1932, 7; "FOR PRESIDENT," *Salt Lake Tribune,* 10 Nov. 1932, 7; also John Sillito, "Third Parties In Utah," in Powell, *Utah History Encyclopedia,* 554.

276. Lester Wire to First Presidency, 20 July, 23 July, 30 July, 12 Aug. 1936, LDS archives; *Municipal Record* 25 (Salt Lake City, July 1936): [1], for Finch as chief of police; Jenson, *Latter-day Saint Biographical Encyclopedia*, 4:726, for Finch; "Retired Police Officer, Inventor Dies In S.L.," *Deseret News*, 15 Apr. 1958, A-16, for Wire.

277. Samuel O. Bennion to the First Presidency, 27 July 1936, LDS archives; Wendell J. Ashton, *Voice in the West: Biography of a Pioneer Newspaper* (New York: Duell, Sloan & Pearce; Salt Lake City: Deseret News Press, 1950), 301-302.

278. *Presidential Elections Since 1789* (Washington, D.C.: Congressional Quarterly, 1987), 137, but the vote-tallies in this source omitted the Communist Party votes in the 1932 election; Ottanelli, *Communist Party of the United States*, 103.

279. Jeremiah Stokes to David O. McKay, 16 Apr. 1940, with "a copy of a secret report of Officer Lester Wire of the City Police force," LDS archives; David O. McKay to Jeremiah Stokes, 19 Apr. 1940, acknowledging receipt of the report "of two communist meetings held recently in Salt Lake City," LDS archives; also Jeremiah Stokes, *Modern Miracles: Authenticated Testimonies of Living Witnesses* (Salt Lake City: Deseret News Press, 1935); Jeremiah Stokes, *Communism on Trial* (Salt Lake City: Federated Libraries, 1939).

280. "Nazis Infest Utah," *Sugar House Post Sentinel–Extra*, 25 May 1940, copy in Special Collections, Lee Library.

281. Frank Evans diary, 17 Mar., 5 Aug. 1942, LDS archives; Horst Scharffs (b. 4 Feb. 1902) in 1935 LDS church census, LDS Family History Library. Grant's presidency publicly encouraged Mormons to feel no hatred for the people of their nation's enemies in "To a World at War," *Improvement Era* 43 (Dec. 1940): 712; Clark, *Messages of the First Presidency*, 115-17, 152-53, 158-59.

282. Heidi S. Swinton, *In the Company of Prophets: Personal Experiences of D. Arthur Haycock with Heber J. Grant, George Albert Smith, David O. McKay, Joseph Fielding Smith, Harold B. Lee, Spencer W. Kimball, and Ezra Taft Benson* (Salt Lake City: Deseret Book Co., 1993), ix, 1, 18; Gibbons, *George Albert Smith*, 283.

283. "First Presidency—Plural Marriage—Investigation of Meetings of 'Fundamentalist' Musser-Darter Groups," Bishop Fred E. H. Curtis and counselors John L. Riley and Ernest Blackmore to J. Reuben Clark, 1 Oct. 1938, Curtis to First Presidency, 10 Nov. 1938, Curtis to First Presidency, with copy to Presiding Bishop LeGrand Richards, 9 June 1939, J. Reuben Clark and David O. McKay to Curtis, 24 June 1939, Curtis to First Presidency, 4 Oct. 1939, Curtis to Clark, 30 Sept. 1940, all in LDS archives; Quinn, *J. Reuben Clark*, 184-85.

284. J. Reuben Clark office diary, 6 May, 15 Oct., 30 Dec. 1940, Lee Library; William Holmes of the Genealogical Society to Clark, 16 Oct. 1940, and Clark to Holmes, 16 Oct. 1940, both in LDS archives; Jenson, *Latter-day Saints Biographical Encyclopedia*, 4:575; *Directory of the General Authorities and Officers of The Church of Jesus Christ of Latter-day Saints* (Salt Lake City: Presiding Bishopric, 1938), 25, 26.

285. J. Reuben Clark to Fred E. H. Curtis, 16 Oct. 1940, Curtis to First Presidency, 25 Feb. 1941, Curtis to First Presidency, attention to Clark, 25 Aug. 1941, all in LDS archives; Quinn, *J. Reuben Clark*, 185; *Municipal Record* 29 (Salt Lake City, Dec. 1940): 4, concerning Vetterli's appointment on 18 November 1940; Warrum, *Utah Since Statehood*, 3:1,139, for Vetterli's LDS background; Gleason, "Salt Lake City Police Department, 1851-1949," for Olson (177), for Vetterli and "the explosive nature of his personality" (200), for a fellow detective's description of Wire as "one of these guys who never married, had nothing to do with women. His whole life and ambitions were to get the dope on the tough guys, then give 'em the business" (308n). Gleason's history made no reference to the surveillance on Mormon fundamentalists in his chapters, "Recent Years, 1940-1949," "Morals Squad," or "Detective Bureau."

286. David O. McKay office diary, 12 Jan. 1944, LDS archives; J. Reuben Clark office diary, 21 Aug. 1944; Bradley, *Kidnapped From That Land*, 64-65, 226n5; *Directory of General Authorities and Officers of The Church of Jesus Christ of Latter-day Saints* (Salt Lake City: Presiding Bishopric, 1944), 31, 253.

287. Van Wagoner, *Mormon Polygamy*, 197; Bradley, *Kidnapped From That Land*, 84-87; also "Cultists Get Jail Terms," *Deseret News*, 10 Nov. 1944, 9.

288. Joseph W. Musser diary, 17 July 1938, 8 May 1939, LDS archives; Quinn, *J. Reuben Clark*, 185.

289. "Polygamy," *Deseret News*, 29 Sept. 1944, 17; "State Rests Cult Case: Recess Follows 4 Days of Testimony," *Deseret News*, 30 Sept. 1944, 12; "Jury Convicts 31 Cultists: Venire Deliberates For Only 90 Minutes," *Deseret News*, 7 Oct. 1944, [11]; also Van Wagoner, *Mormon Polygamy*, 197; Bradley, *Kidnapped From That Land*, 64, 84.

290. "Regional Representatives: 69 Receive Calls," *Deseret News "Church News,"* 7 Oct. 1967, 5.

291. Frank Evans diary, 27 Nov. 1945; Gordon Burt Affleck statement to me after a stake high council meeting in 1979.

292. George Albert Smith, J. Reuben Clark, and David O. McKay to Senator Elbert D. Thomas, 27 Aug. 1946, and Thomas to "The First Presidency," 10 Sept. 1946, both in unnumbered fd "General File—1946—Misc. (Lat-1)," box 99, Thomas papers, Utah State Historical Society.

293. Peggy Petersen Barton, *Mark E. Petersen: A Biography* (Salt Lake City: Deseret Book Co., 1985), 167, for quote; for examples of Petersen's "watchdog" emphasis and activities see J. Reuben Clark office diary, 9-10 Sept., 13 Sept., 27 Nov. 1946, 16 Apr. 1948, 17 May, 31 May 1949, 29 Nov. 1950, 4 Dec. 1951; Lavina Fielding Anderson, "The LDS Intellectual Community and Church Leadership: A Contemporary Chronology," *Dialogue: A Journal of Mormon Thought* 26 (Spring 1993): 22; Armand L. Mauss, *The Angel and the Beehive: The Mormon Struggle with Assimilation*, (Urbana: University of Illinois Press, 1994), 81; also statements to me by J. Max Anderson, whose book against Mormon Fundamentalists was carefully edited by Petersen; my interview with Henry W. Richards concerning Petersen's committee of which Richards was a member.

294. Edward L. Kimball and Andrew E. Kimball, Jr., *Spencer W. Kimball: Twelfth President of the Church of Jesus Christ of Latter-day Saints* (Salt Lake City: Bookcraft, 1977), 381.

295. "Blast Damages S.L. Temple—Believed Work Of Vandals," *Deseret News*, 14 Nov. 1962, B-1.

296. David Leslie Brewer, "Utah Elites and Utah Racial Norms," Ph.D. diss., University of Utah, 1966, 143; also "Race Riots in Utah?" *Daily Utah Chronicle*, 28 Sept. 1965, 5; chap. 3.

297. Benson Y. Parkinson, *S. Dilworth Young: General Authority, Scouter, Poet* (American Fork, UT: Covenant Communications, 1994), 285; "STAKE CONFERENCES," *Deseret News "Church News,"* 2 Sept. 1967, 14, as last such listing of upcoming visits by the general authorities; Gordon B. Hinckley, "Rise, and Stand Upon Thy Feet," *Improvement Era* 71 (Dec. 1968): 69.

298. L. Brent Goates, *Harold B. Lee, Prophet & Seer* (Salt Lake City: Bookcraft, 1985), 25; Francis M. Gibbons, *Harold B. Lee: Man of Vision, Prophet of God* (Salt Lake City: Deseret Book Co., 1993), 424; "Violence Mars BYU-CSU Game," *Deseret News*, 6 Feb. 1970, D-1, D-2; "Violence Mars Cat-Ram Duel," *Salt Lake Tribune*, 6 Feb. 1970, D-1; Brian Walton, "A University's Dilemma: B.Y.U. and Blacks," *Dialogue: A Journal of Mormon Thought* 6 (Spring 1971): 31-36; Gary James Bergera and Ronald Priddis, *Brigham Young University: A House of Faith* (Salt Lake City: Signature Books, 1985), 297-304; also media coverage shortly before this violent protest, "CAMPUS COMMUNIQUE: Outcries of Dissent," *Time* 94 (14 Nov. 1969): 49; "Trouble in Happy Valley," *Newsweek* 74 (1 Dec. 1969): 102-103; "Mormons and

the Mark of Cain," *Time* 95 (19 Jan. 1970): 46-47; "Second Class Mormons," *Newsweek* 75 (19 Jan. 1970): 84; "Pigskin Justice and Mormon Theology," *Christian Century* 87 (21 Jan. 1970): 67; William F. Reed, "The Other Side of 'The Y': Attitude Toward Negroes of the Church of Jesus Christ of Latter-day Saints," *Sports Illustrated* 37 (26 Jan. 1970): 38-39; "Mormons and Blacks: Doctrine Forbidding Black Males From Becoming Priests," *Christianity Today* 14 (30 Jan. 1970): 22.

299. "U of U Police Arrest 85 at Park Building Sit-In," *Deseret News,* 8 May 1970, A-6; "U Building Swept By Blaze," *Deseret News,* 11 May 1970, A-1; "Arson 'Sure' In Burning of U. Building," *Deseret News,* 12 May 1970, B-1; "Bomb Rocks Utah Guard Office in S.L.: Explosion Demolishes Interior," *Deseret News,* 13 May 1970, A-1.

300. Gibbons, *Harold B. Lee,* 424-25.

301. *Telephone Directory: General Church Offices* (Salt Lake City: The Church of Jesus Christ of Latter-day Saints, July 1972), 43; Gibbons, *Harold B. Lee,* 473.

302. "Annual and quarterly reports and summaries, 1952-1960," fd 1, box 1, and "Federal Bureau of Investigation, correspondence, 1970-1972," fd 1, box 3, "Register to the Records of SECURITY POLICE, UA 511," Lee Library; "Captain Nielson [sic]," *Daily Universe,* 23 Feb. 1968, 5, referring to Swen C. Nielsen; "Lies," *Daily Universe,* 29 Feb. 1968, 3; "Y Standards using polygraph," *University Post: The Unofficial Newspaper of Brigham Young University,* 15 Apr. 1983, 1; Bergera and Priddis, *Brigham Young University,* 123; also "Provo Police Chief To Retire in July," *Deseret News,* 7 June 1995, B-1.

303. Robert McQueen, "Mormons Show Fear," *The Advocate* 166 (18 June 1975): 15; McQueen, "BYU Inquisition," *The Advocate* 170 (13 Aug. 1975), 14; McQueen, "Gay Mormons Talking Back," *The Advocate* 175 (22 Oct. 1975): 23; "Homosexuality at BYU," *Seventh East Press* (Provo, UT), 12 Apr. 1982, 1.

304. "Ex-BYU Security Officer Tells of Intrigue, Spying," *Salt Lake Tribune,* 22 Mar. 1975, A-10; "Oaks Supports Security's Police Powers," *Daily Universe,* 18 Sept. 1979, 1; "Brigham Young U. Admits Stakeouts on Homosexuals," *New York Times,* 27 Sept. 1979, A-16; "BYU Security Personnel Can Operate Off Campus: Gays Protest Power," *Salt Lake Tribune,* 23 Oct. 1979, D-2; also "Homosexuality," *Seventh East Press* (Provo, UT), 12 Apr. 1982, 12.

305. *Municipal Record* 60 (Salt Lake City, Nov. 1971): 1; *Municipal Record* 63 (Salt Lake City, Dec. 1974): 1; "Police Chief Jones Retains Police Job," *Salt Lake Tribune,* 21 Mar. 1975, 2; statement of LDS headquarters spokesman Jerry Cahill in "Mormons Accused of 'Mafia' Tactics," *Idaho Statesman,* 10 Apr. 1976, 11; *Telephone Directory: General Church Offices, December 1977* (Salt Lake City: The Church of Jesus Christ of Latter-day Saints, 1977), 98-99.

306. Mason S. Sherwood, "The Potential Threat of Terrorism to Utah," M.A. thesis, Brigham Young University, 1979, 44, 52; Gordon B. Hinckley diary, 4 Mar. 1995, quoted in Sheri L. Dew, *Go Forward With Faith: The Biography of Gordon B. Hinckley* (Salt Lake City: Deseret Book Co., 1996), 506.

307. "LDS Security: Tight and Tight-lipped," *University Post: The Unofficial Newspaper of Brigham Young University,* 15 Apr. 1983, 10.

308. Sherwood, "The Potential Threat of Terrorism to Utah," 44.

309. "Life of Service," *Deseret News "Church News,"* 31 Jan. 1987, 4; "J. Martell Bird, Director of Church Security, Dies at 69," *Deseret News "Church News,"* 7 Feb. 1987, 14.

310. "FBI Agent Is Named Chief of LDS Security," *Deseret News,* 24 Mar. 1988, G-1; "FBI Agent Will Retire to Head Church Security," *Deseret News "Church News,"* 2 Apr. 1988, 2; "Mormon Security Receives Cautious Praise," *Salt Lake Tribune,* 9 Oct. 1990, B-2; also Derin Lea Head, "Richard Bretzing: Games Keeper," *This People* 5 (June/July 1984): 34-36; "Judge Rules FBI Misused Grand Jury Subpoena," *Deseret News,* 4 Dec. 1988, A-11; Journal History, 6 Oct. 1990, 17; "Ex-FBI Agent Gets 20 Years For Spying," *Deseret News,* 5 Feb. 1991, A-3.

311. "LDS Official Acknowledges Church Monitors Critics," *Salt Lake Tribune,* 8 Aug. 1992, D-1, D-2; also sources in next notes.

312. Anderson, "LDS Intellectual Community and Church Leadership," 31.

313. Ibid., 20-21, 22, 32, 38-39, 40, 41, 43, 45, 47, 49, 50, 54, 55; Mauss, *The Angel and the Beehive,* 184.

314. F. Ross Peterson to D. Michael Quinn, 18 Oct. 1990; Anderson, "LDS Intellectual Community and Church Leadership," 33; "LDS Leaders Say Scripture Supports Secret Files on Members," *Salt Lake Tribune,* 14 Aug. 1992, B-1.

315. "Scriptural Mandate Cited for LDS Committee," *Deseret News,* 14 Aug. 1992, B-2; also "First Presidency Statement Cites Scriptural Mandate For Church Committee," *Deseret News "Church News,"* 22 Aug. 1992, 7.

316. Don LeFevre statements in "Mormon Secret Files," *Christian Century* 109 (9 Sept. 1992): 800.

317. Statement of LDS headquarters spokesman Jerry Cahill in "Role in Stakeout Pinned on LDS," *Salt Lake Tribune,* 17 Sept. 1977, D-1; "Did Church Manipulate S.L. Police? Misleading Tip Caused Check of Anti-Mormon," *Salt Lake Tribune,* 29 July 1988, B-1; "Suspect Linked to Guns Left at Square," *Deseret News,* 8 Feb. 1993, A-1; Gibbons, *Harold B. Lee,* 473.

318. Information furnished in 1987 and 1991 by persons wishing to remain anonymous who were significantly connected with Brigham Young University and ZCMI security; Anderson, "LDS Intellectual Community and Church Leadership," 45-46.

319. *General Church Offices Telephone Directory, January 1996* (Salt Lake City: The Church of Jesus Christ of Latter-day Saints, 1996), 25, 37, 40, 41, 42, 45, 49, 55, 57, 58, 59, 61, 62, 63, 68, 70, 71, 72, 74, 75, 76, 78, 79, 80, 82, 85, 87, 88, 89, 93, 95, 96, 97, 100, 103.

320. "Life of Service," *Deseret News "Church News,"* 31 Jan. 1987, 4; also *Protective Recommendations for Home and Abroad* (Salt Lake City: Security Department, n.d.).

321. James B. Allen, "Ecclesiastical Influence on Local Government in the Territory of Utah," *Arizona and the West: A Quarterly Journal of History* 8 (Spring 1966): 35-48; Koritz, "Development of Municipal Government in the Territory of Utah," 74; Timothy L. Taggart, "The Kingdom of God In Early Cache Valley," in Douglas D. Alder, ed., *Cache Valley: Essays on Her Past and People* (Logan: Utah State University Press, 1976), 13-27; Jessie L. Embry, "'All Things Unto Me Are Spiritual': Contrasting Religious and Temporal Leadership Styles in Heber City, Utah," in Embry and Christy, *Community Development in the American West,* 164-65; Bringhurst, *Brigham Young,* 119.

322. Political scientist G. Homer Durham compared the shadow government "before civil machinery appeared" to the secret political control of Number 10 Downing Street, the White House, and the Kremlin. See Durham, "The Development of Political Parties in Utah: The First Phase," *Utah Humanities Review* 1 (Jan. 1947): 125. The comparison is more accurate for the period *after* civil government was established in Utah.

323. Joy Lynn Wood Wetzel, "The Patriotic Priesthood: Mormonism and the Progressive Paradigm," Ph.D. diss., University of Minnesota, 1977, 125; also, D. W. Meinig, "The Mormon Nation and the American Empire," *Journal of Mormon History* 22 (Spring 1996): 33-51.

324. See the chapters "Civilization Threatened: Mormon Polygamy under Siege" and "Blessings of the Abrahamic Household" in Hardy, *Solemn Covenant,* 39-126.

325. *Journal of Discourses* 11:239 (B. Young/1866), 13:166 (Woodruff/1869), 22:147-48 (Woodruff/1881), 22:174 (Woodruff/1881), 23:240-41 (J. Taylor/1882), 25:321-22 (G. Q. Cannon/1884), 26:152 (J. Taylor/1885); "THE ONLY CONSISTENT COURSE," *Deseret Evening News,* 23 Apr. 1885, [2]; George Q. Cannon, "Editorial Thoughts," *Juvenile Instructor* 20 (1 May 1885): 136; George Q. Cannon, "Topics of the Times," *Juvenile Instructor* 20 (15 May 1885): 156; "NO RELINQUISHMENT," *Deseret Evening News,* 5 June 1885, [2].

Notes to Chapter Nine

1. Jean Bickmore White, "Utah State Elections, 1895-1899," Ph.D. diss., University of Utah, 1968, ix.

2. Hosea Stout diary, 7 Aug. 1854, in Juanita Brooks, ed., *On The Mormon Frontier: The Diary of Hosea Stout, 1844-1861,* 2 vols. (Salt Lake City: University of Utah Press, 1964), 2:524; "RESULT OF THE ELECTION," *Deseret News* [weekly], 13 Aug. 1862, 52; Church Historian's office journal, 14 Feb. 1868, archives, Historical Department, Church of Jesus Christ of Latter-day Saints, Salt Lake City, Utah (hereafter LDS archives); Scott G. Kenney, ed., *Wilford Woodruff's Journal: 1833-1898 Typescript,* 9 vols. (Murray, UT: Signature Books, 1983-85), 6 (15 Feb. 1868): 395-96; minutes of the School of the Prophets, Salt Lake City, 26 Jan. 1874, LDS archives; Franklin D. Richards diary, 13 Mar., 3 May 1875, 28 Jan. 1876, 29 Jan., 1-2 Feb. 1879, LDS archives; "Cache Valley," *Deseret Evening News,* 22 May 1876, [3]; "THE ELECTION," *Ogden Junction* (Ogden, UT), 8 Aug. 1876, [2]; "Not Conservative," *Deseret Evening News,* 5 Feb. 1878, [2]; "An Unwise Act," *Deseret Evening News,* 3 Apr. 1878, [2]; "The Tooele Conspiracy," *Deseret Evening News,* 12 Aug. 1878, [2]; "THE MUNICIPAL ELECTION: A Highly Exciting Contest Over One Ticket," *Salt Lake Daily Tribune,* 14 Feb. 1882, [4]; "THE ELECTION," *Salt Lake Daily Herald,* 14 Feb 1882, [8]; "Dangerous Disputes," and "THE SPLIT IN BEAVER," *Salt Lake Herald,* 3 Dec. 1884, 4, 8; "Stand By The People's Party," *Deseret Evening News,* 19 Oct. 1888, [2]; "An Unenviable Step," *Deseret Evening News,* 31 July 1889, [2]; Abraham H. Cannon diary, 6 Feb. 1890, Department of Special Collections and Manuscripts, Harold B. Lee Library, Brigham Young University, Provo, Utah (hereafter Lee Library), with copies in Manuscripts Division, J. Willard Marriott Library, University of Utah, Salt Lake City (hereafter Marriott Library), and in Utah State Historical Society, Salt Lake City; "LOGAN POLITICS. Opposition to the Regular People's Ticket," *Deseret Evening News,* 24 Feb. 1890, [3]; "BEAVER POLITICS. The People's Party Settle Differences, and Will be United at the Polls," *Deseret Evening News,* 2 Aug. 1890, [3]; Rudger Clawson 1887-92 journal, 62-63, regarding election on 2 March 1891, Marriott Library; Joseph S. Wood, "The Mormon Settlement in San Bernardino, 1851-1857," Ph.D. diss., University of Utah, 1968, 209-10; Ronald Collett Jack, "Utah Territorial Politics: 1847-1876," Ph.D. diss., University of Utah, 1970, 78-79, 83-84, 97, 100, 104-105, 108-109, 492; A. J. Simmonds, *The Gentile Comes To Cache Valley: A Study of the Logan Apostasies of 1874 And the Establishment of Non-Mormon Churches In Cache Valley, 1873-1913* (Logan: Utah State University Press, 1976), 28-29; M. Guy Bishop, "Politics, Land, and Apostasy: The Last Days of the San Bernardino Mormon Colony, 1855-57," *Pacific Historian* 30 (Winter 1986): 24-25; David S. Hoopes and Roy Hoopes, *The Making of a Mormon Apostle: The Story of Rudger Clawson* (Lanham, MD: Madison Books, 1990), 148, that "in the spring [actually February-March] of 1891 a maverick group within the People's party [was] led by one of Lorenzo Snow's sons, A. H. Snow"; Edward Leo Lyman, *San Bernardino: The Rise and Fall of a California Community* (Salt Lake City: Signature Books, 1996), 151-57, 335, 380-81.

3. Thomas E. Jeremy diary, 14 Feb. 1868, LDS archives.

4. Church Historian's office journal, 17 Feb. 1868. Except when otherwise indicated, biographical sketches of all general authorities named in this chapter can be found either in an appendix of the present volume or in D. Michael Quinn, *The Mormon Hierarchy: Origins of Power* (Salt Lake City: Signature Books/Smith Research Associates, 1994).

5. Moroni Historical Record, 9 Aug. 1868, LDS archives, quoted in Jack, "Utah Territorial Politics," 114.

6. Hosea Stout diary, 7 Aug. 1854, in Brooks, *On The Mormon Frontier,* 2:524.

7. "THE ELECTION," *Ogden Junction* (Ogden, UT), 8 Aug. 1876, [2], with "Election Returns" on same page; also "THE PEOPLE'S TICKET," *Ogden Junction* (Ogden, UT), 1 Aug. 1876, [2], for the approved ballot and an editorial warning "when we frame a ticket, either in mass meeting or by our delegates, our true policy is to unite on that ticket to a man."

8. Gordon Douglas Pollock, "In Search of Security: The Mormons and the Kingdom of God on Earth, 1830-1844," Ph.D. diss., Queen's University, 1977, 293.

9. Lyman, *San Bernardino,* 155-56, describes the excommunication of political dissenters in California's 1855 election, and comments (159) that Apostle Amasa M. Lyman's "action in the political crisis appears to be an isolated instance, uncharacteristic of the notably tolerant church leader."

10. Moses Thatcher 1888-90 letterbook, 21, Moses Thatcher Family papers, Special Collections, Milton R. Merrill Library, Utah State University, Logan (hereafter Merrill Library).

11. "The God that others worship is not the God for me," *Sacred Hymns and Spiritual Songs for the Church of Jesus Christ of Latter-day Saints,* 15th ed. (London and Liverpool: Latter-day Saints' Book Depot, 1871), 351; also William E. Berrett and Alma P. Burton, eds., *Readings In L.D.S. Church History From Original Manuscripts,* 3 vols. (Salt Lake City: Deseret Book Co., 1953-58), 2:393-407; William Mulder, "Mormonism's 'Gathering': An American Doctrine with a Difference," *Church History* 23 (Sept. 1954): 248-64; Thomas F. O'Dea, *The Mormons* (Chicago: University of Chicago Press, 1957), 41-75; Ronald D. Dennis, "Gathering," in Daniel H. Ludlow, ed., *Encyclopedia of Mormonism: The History, Scripture, Doctrine, and Procedure of the Church of Jesus Christ of Latter-day Saints,* 5 vols. (New York: Macmillan Publishing Co., 1992), 2:537-38; Davis Bitton, *Historical Dictionary of Mormonism* (Metuchen, NJ: Scarecrow Press, 1994), 90-91; Rulon T. Burton, *We Believe: Doctrines and Principles of The Church of Jesus Christ of Latter-day Saints* (Salt Lake City: Tabernacle Books, 1994), 287-97; Bruce A. Van Orden, *Building Zion: The Latter-day Saints in Europe* (Salt Lake City: Deseret Book Co., 1996), 73-91; Maurine Jensen and Scot Facer Proctor, *The Gathering: Mormon Pioneers on the Trail to Zion* (Deseret Book Co., 1996).

12. Joseph Smith et al., *History of The Church of Jesus Christ of Latter-day Saints. Period I: History of Joseph Smith the Prophet, and . . . Period II: From the Manuscript History of Brigham Young and Other Original Documents,* ed. B. H. Roberts, 7 vols. (Salt Lake City: Church of Jesus Christ of Latter-day Saints, 1902-32; 2d ed. rev. [Salt Lake City: Deseret Book Co., 1978]), 1:450 (hereafter *History of the Church*).

13. Max H. Parkin, Mormon Political Involvement in Ohio," *Brigham Young University Studies* 9 (Summer 1969): 488-91; Milton V. Backman, Jr., *The Heavens Resound: A History of the Latter-day Saints in Ohio, 1830-1838* (Salt Lake City: Deseret Book Co., 1983), 334-35.

14. Oliver Cowdery to John A. Bryan, 15 Oct. 1835, Cowdery letterbook, 51-52, Henry E. Huntington Library, San Marino, California; Oliver Cowdery diary, 3 Jan., 8-9 Jan. 1836, in Leonard J. Arrington, ed., "Oliver Cowdery's Kirtland, Ohio, 'Sketch Book,'" *Brigham Young University Studies* 12 (Summer 1972): 414n6.

15. "Extract of a letter to the Editor of the Telegraph, dated, KIRTLAND, April 14, 1835," *Painesville Telegraph,* 17 Apr. 1835, [3].

16. Max H. Parkin, "Nature and Causes of Internal and External Conflict of the Mormons In Ohio Between 1830 and 1838," M.A. thesis, Brigham Young University, 1966, 184-91; Parkin, "Mormon Political Involvement in Ohio," 490.

17. "MEETING!" *Painesville Republican,* 2 Mar. 1837, [3]. Until ratification of the 22d Amendment in 1933, the U.S. president was inaugurated in March following his election.

18. Parkin, "Mormon Political Involvement in Ohio," 492-502.

19. Stephen C. LeSueur, *The 1838 Mormon War in Missouri* (Columbia: University of Missouri Press, 1987), 59.

20. Reed C. Durham, Jr., "The Election Day Battle at Gallatin," *Brigham Young University Studies* 13 (Autumn 1972): 36-61; LeSueur, *The 1838 Mormon War in Missouri,* 60-244; Quinn, *Mormon Hierarchy: Origins of Power,* 96-103.

21. George Churchill to A. Doubleday, 11 Sept. 1838, Railroad papers, Missouri Historical Society, St. Louis.

22. Joseph Smith diary, 6 Aug. 1838, in Scott H. Faulring, ed., *An American Prophet's Record: The Diaries and Journal of Joseph Smith* (Salt Lake City: Signature Books/Smith Research Associates, 1987), 199-201, and in Dean C. Jessee, ed., *The Papers of Joseph Smith,* 2+ vols., with a different subtitle for each volume (Salt Lake City: Deseret Book Co., 1989-92+), 2:265-66; *History of the Church,* 3:55-56; Reed Peck manuscript history, 18 Sept. 1839, 57-59, Huntington Library; John Corrill, *Brief History of the Church of Christ of Latter Day Saints, (Commonly Called Mormons) . . . With the Reasons of the Author For Leaving the Church* (St. Louis: By the author, 1839), 33; Quinn, *Mormon Hierarchy: Origins of Power,* 91-99, 102-103, 479-90.

23. *History of the Church,* 4:40, 80.

24. Walter John Raymond, *Dictionary of Politics: Selected American and Foreign Political and Legal Terms,* 7th ed. (Lawrenceville, VA: Brunswick Publishing Co., 1980), 426, and 431, *"Realpolitik.* In the German language, 'power politics' or 'politics based on realities.'"

25. Robert Bruce Flanders, *Nauvoo: Kingdom on the Mississippi* (Urbana: University of Illinois Press, 1965), 19; Kenneth Gordon Crider, "Rhetorical Aspects of the Controversies Over Mormonism in Illinois, 1839-1847," Ph.D. diss., University of Illinois, 1956, 270-71; Kenneth W. Godfrey, "Causes of Mormon Non-Mormon Conflict in Hancock County, Illinois, 1839-1846," Ph.D. diss., Brigham Young University, 1967, 43-47.

26. Frederick C. Waite, "The First Medical Diploma Mill in the United States," *Bulletin of the History of Medicine* 20 (Nov. 1946): 497-504; James J. Tyler, "John Cook Bennett: Colorful Freemason of the Early Nineteenth Century," *Proceedings of the Grand Lodge of Ohio* (1947); Richard S. Van Wagoner, *Mormon Polygamy: A History* (Salt Lake City: Signature Books, 1986), 15-29, 243n4; Mervin B. Hogan, *John C. Bennett: Unprincipled, Profligate, Cowan* (Salt Lake City: Campus Graphics, 1987); Roger Van Noord, *King of Beaver Island: The Life and Assassination of James Jesse Strang* (Urbana: University of Illinois Press, 1988), 58-64; Andrew F. Smith, "'The Diploma Peddler': Dr. John Cook Bennett and Christian College at New Albany, Indiana," *Indiana History* 90 (Mar. 1994): 26-47; Quinn, *Mormon Hierarchy: Origins of Power,* 536-38; Andrew F. Smith, *The Saintly Scoundrel: The Life and Times of Dr. John Cook Bennett* (Urbana: University of Illinois Press, forthcoming). Raymond, *Dictionary of Politics,* 292: "*Machiavellian Leadership Style.* A manner of managing people and events, in public or private life, characterized by deceitful, unethical, cold-blooded, selfish, and calculated methods, giving no moral consideration to other persons. Named after Niccolo Machiavelli (1469-1527), a political philosopher and author of *The Prince,* who lived in the state of Florence, now part of Italy."

27. Flanders, *Nauvoo,* 217, 220-22; "STATE GUBERNATORIAL CONVENTION," *Times and Seasons* 3 (1 Jan. 1842): 651; *History of the Church,* 4:480.

28. Flanders, *Nauvoo,* 230; Robert Bruce Flanders, "The Kingdom of God in Illinois: Politics in Utopia," *Dialogue: A Journal of Mormon Thought* 5 (Spring 1979): 30-32.

29. "Let Him That Readeth Understand," *Sangamo Journal,* 10 June 1842, 2-3.

30. Marvin S. Hill, *Quest for Refuge: The Mormon Flight from American Pluralism* (Salt Lake City: Signature Books, 1989), 110.

31. William Harris, *Mormonism Portrayed: Its Errors and Absurdities* (Warsaw, IL: Sharp and Gamble, 1841), 15.

32. *History of the Church,* 5:526; Flanders, "Kingdom of God in Illinois," 32-33; "The Prophet and the 1843 Congressional Race," in John E. Hallwas and Roger D. Launius, eds., *Cultures in Conflict: A Documentary History of the Mormon War in Illinois* (Logan: Utah State University Press, 1995), 85-87.

33. Hill, *Quest for Refuge,* 132-33; Flanders, *Nauvoo,* 211-40; Crider, "Rhetorical Aspects," 285-308; Godfrey, "Mormon Non-Mormon Conflict," 43-63; Hallwas and Launius, *Cultures in Conflict,* 79-82, 97-102.

34. "Mormon Matters," *Warsaw Signal,* 28 Feb. 1844, [2]. The editor, Thomas Sharp, later publicly defended the civil necessity of murdering the Smiths in Carthage Jail. See Hallwas and Launius, *Cultures in Conflict,* 247-51.

35. "THE ELECTION," *Nauvoo Neighbor,* 6 Nov. 1844, [2]; "Specta . . ." [torn page], *Nauvoo Neighbor,* 20 Aug. 1845, [2].

36. *History of the Church,* 6:386, 391; "Jeffersonian Democracy," *Salt Lake Herald,* 27 Oct. 1892, 8, reproduction of an 1844 flier for Joseph Smith's candidacy; Quinn, *Mormon Hierarchy: Origins of Power,* 117-41.

37. Hosea Stout diary, 4 Nov. 1844, in Brooks, *On The Mormon Frontier,* 1:8.

38. Brigham Young to David Rogers, 5 Dec. 1844, Western Americana, Beinecke Rare Book and Manuscript Library, Yale University, New Haven, Connecticut (hereafter Beinecke Library). The letter is in the handwriting of Orson Hyde.

39. "Our Political Interest," *Prophet,* 21 Dec. 1844, [2].

40. J. Keith Melville, *Conflict and Compromise: The Mormons in Mid-Nineteenth-Century American Politics* (Provo, UT: Brigham Young University Printing Service, 1974), 6-14 (esp. 10 for photograph of letter to "Rev. Brigham Young").

41. "Whig Corruption—Mormons," *St. Louis Daily Union,* 29 Aug. 1848, "The Mormon Votes," *St. Louis Daily Union,* 19 Sept. 1848, "The Mormon Bribery," *St. Louis Daily Union,* 20 Sept. 1848, "The Mormon Bribe—Whig Corruption," *St. Louis Daily Union,* 12 Oct. 1848, transcriptions in box 2, Dale Morgan, "THE MORMONS AND THE FAR WEST," Huntington Library; Richard E. Bennett, *Mormons at the Missouri, 1846-1852: "And Should We Die. . . "* (Norman: University of Oklahoma Press, 1987), 220-21; Melville, *Conflict and Compromise,* 27-29. These two authors disagree about the vote count. Bennett cites 491 Whig votes to thirty-two Democratic (221), whereas Melville says "only forty-two Democratic votes were cast of a total of over five hundred" (27).

42. Brigham Young to Orson Hyde, 20 July 1849, in J. Keith Melville, "Brigham Young On Politics and Priesthood," *Brigham Young University Studies* 10 (Summer 1970): 489.

43. "WHIG NOMINATIONS," *Frontier Guardian* 2 (10 July 1850): [2]; "State Whig Convention," *Frontier Guardian* 4 (20 Feb. 1852): [3]; "STATE WHIG TICKET," *Frontier Guardian* 4 (25 June 1852): [2]; Melville, *Conflict and Compromise,* 34-37.

44. Lyman, *San Bernardino,* 90, 178-81, 334, 381, 383, 389-95, 415; chap. 7 for Utah War.

45. Melville, *Conflict and Compromise,* 22, 58; Gwynn W. Barrett, "John M. Bernhisel: Mormon Elder in Congress," Ph.D. diss., Brigham Young University, 1968, 70; Jay Donald Ridd, "Almon Whiting Babbitt: Mormon Emissary," M.S. thesis, University of Utah, 1953, 49-62; David Lee Washburn, "The First Eight Years: The Deterioration of Mormon-Federal Relations in Utah, 1850-1857," M.A. thesis, University of Utah, 1980, 6-9.

46. Orson Hyde to Brigham Young, Heber C. Kimball, and Willard Richards, 27 Apr. 1851, in Barrett, "John M. Bernhisel," 83, also 156 for Bernhisel's request for a release in March 1859.

47. William B. Dickinson, ed., *Guide to the Congress of the United States: Origins, History and Procedure* (Washington, D.C.: Congressional Quarterly Service, 1971), 68-69; *Biographical Directory of the United States Congress, 1774-1989: Bicentennial Edition* (Washington, D.C.: Government Printing Office, 1989), 614, 1208; Barrett, "John M. Bernhisel," 159-60, did not seem to recognize the correlation in the service of Hooper and Bernhisel with the political party in control of Congress.

48. Orma Linford, "The Mormons and the Law: The Polygamy Cases," *Utah Law Review* 9 (Winter 1964): 314-16; Edwin Brown Firmage and R. Collin Mangrum, *Zion in the Courts: A Legal History of the Church of Jesus Christ of Latter-day Saints* (Urbana: University of Illinois Press, 1988), 130-34, 149-51; Richard D. Poll, "The Legislative Antipolygamy Campaign," *Brigham Young University Studies* 26 (Fall 1986): 108-11.

49. Barrett, "John M. Bernhisel," 159-167; "UTAH TERRITORIAL OFFICIALS, 1850-1896," in Richard D. Poll, ed., *Utah's History* (Provo, UT: Brigham Young University Press, 1978), 694; *Biographical Directory of the United States Congress*, 726, 739, 1208, 1315-16, 1694, which claims (739) that George Q. Cannon was a Republican during his entire service as territorial delegate. He actually switched from the Democratic Party as soon as he arrived in Washington, then became a Democrat again when the tide turned in D.C. See "A HOPEFUL CONVERT," *Salt Lake Daily Tribune*, 7 Dec. 1873, [1]; "HOT SHOT FROM CANNON. AN INTERVIEW WITH THE UTAH DELEGATE," *Deseret Evening News*, 12 Feb. 1878, [2].

50. "'THE MASS MEETING,'" *Deseret Evening News*, 10 Feb. 1870, [2]; also John S. McCormick and John R. Sillito, "Henry W. Lawrence: A Life in Dissent," in Roger D. Launius and Linda Thatcher, eds., *Differing Visions: Dissenters in Mormon History* (Urbana: University of Illinois Press, 1994), 225-28.

51. Jack, "Utah Territorial Politics," 137-40.

52. Orson F. Whitney, *History of Utah*, 4 vols. (Salt Lake City: George Q. Cannon and Sons Company, 1892-1904), 2:385.

53. "Union Ticket" *Deseret News* [weekly], 13 Feb. 1856, 389; "People's Ticket," *Deseret News* [weekly], 27 July 1859, 164; "ANNUAL ELECTION—1862: PEOPLE'S TICKET," *Deseret News* [weekly], 30 July 1862, 86; "ANNUAL ELECTION—1865: PEOPLE'S TICKET," *Deseret News* [weekly], 5 July 1865, 316; "The People's Ticket," *Deseret Evening News*, 20 July 1868, [2].

54. Jack, "Utah Territorial Politics," 194.

55. "THE NOMINEES FOR OFFICE," *Deseret Evening News*, 18 July 1870, [3]; Jack, "Utah Territorial Politics," 162, 169-70.

56. Dale L. Morgan, *The State of Deseret* (Logan: Utah State University Press, 1987), 114; Edward Leo Lyman, *Political Deliverance: The Mormon Quest for Utah Statehood* (Urbana: University of Illinois Press, 1986), 18.

57. Jack, "Utah Territorial Politics," 275.

58. Ibid., 276-88; "REPUBLICAN CONVENTION," *Salt Lake Daily Herald*, 16 Mar. 1872, [2]; "REPUBLICAN PRIMARY MEETING," *Deseret Evening News*, 1 Apr. 1872, [2]; "Territorial Republican Convention," *Deseret Evening News*, 6 Apr. 1872, [2]; "Republican Convention Last Night," *Salt Lake Daily Herald*, 6 Apr. 1872, [2].

59. "THE DELEGATES TO THE PHILADELPHIA CONVENTION," *Salt Lake Daily Herald*, 30 May 1872, [2].

60. "The Ratification Meeting Last Night," *Salt Lake Daily Herald*, 14 July 1872, [2].

61. Calvin W. Hiibner, "Utah Delegations at the National Nominating Conventions: 1860-1928," M.S. thesis, Utah State University, 1966, 14; Brigham H. Roberts, *A Comprehensive History of The Church of Jesus Christ of Latter-day Saints, Century I*, 6 vols. (Salt Lake City: Deseret News Press and "the Church," 1930), 5:466-67.

62. "Organization of the P.T.C.C.," *Deseret Evening News*, 15 July 1874, [3]; Jack, "Utah Territorial Politics," 403.

63. "PEOPLE'S TERRITORIAL CONVENTION . . . PEOPLE'S CENTRAL COMMITTEE," *Salt Lake Daily Herald*, 8 Oct. 1876, [3]; "Territorial Convention," *Deseret Evening News*, 9 Oct. 1876, [1].

64. "Territorial Convention," *Deseret Evening News*, 8 Oct. 1878, [3]; "County Convention," *Salt Lake Daily Herald*, 28 July 1878, [3]; "Territorial Convention," *Salt Lake Daily Herald*, 8 Oct. 1878, [3]. The three women on the county central committee were

Sarah M. Kimball, Emmeline B. Wells, and Mary Isabella Horne. For these women and Bathsheba Smith, see Jenson, *Latter-day Saint Biographical Encyclopedia*, 1:807-808; Jill Mulvay Derr, "Sarah M. Kimball," Barbara Fluckiger Watt, "Bathsheba B. Smith," Patricia Rasmussen Eaton-Gadsby and Judith Rasmussen Dushku, "Emmeline B. Wells," in Vicky Burgess-Olson, ed., *Sister Saints* (Provo, UT: Brigham Young University Press, 1978), 21-39, 201-21, 457-75.

65. "Territorial Convention," *Salt Lake Daily Herald*, 8 Oct. 1878, [3]; "Territorial Convention," *Salt Lake Daily Herald*, 8 Oct. 1880, [3]; "PEOPLE'S TERRITORIAL CONVENTION," *Deseret Evening News*, 13 Oct. 1882, [2].

66. "Organization of the P.T.C.C.," *Deseret Evening News*, 15 July 1874, [3]; "PEOPLE'S TERRITORIAL CONVENTION," *Deseret Evening News*, 13 Oct. 1882, [2]; "Standard Bearer," *Salt Lake Daily Herald*, 9 Oct. 1884, 8; "John T. Caine," *Salt Lake Daily Herald*, 13 Oct. 1886, 8; "JOHN T. CAINE THE MAN . . . THE CENTRAL COMMITTEE," *Salt Lake Daily Herald*, 9 Oct. 1888, 5.

67. Abraham H. Cannon diary, 21 Jan. 1890.

68. "THE CAUCUS," *Ogden Junction*, 15 July 1874, [3]; "Cache County Caucus and Ticket," *Deseret Evening News*, 21 July 1874, [2]; "Caucus in Cache," *Deseret Evening News*, 8 July 1875, [2]; "Sanpete County," *Salt Lake Herald*, 24 July 1878, [3]; "COUNTY CONVENTION," *Daily Ogden Junction*, 24 July 1879, [2]; "COUNTY CONVENTION," *Ogden Daily Herald*, 15 July 1881, [3]; "WEBER COUNTY CONVENTION," *Ogden Daily Herald*, 16 July 1883, [3]; Richard E. Kotter, "An Examination of Mormon and Non-Mormon Influences in Ogden City Politics, 1847-1869," M.S. thesis, Utah State University, 1967, 55-56.

69. "PEOPLE'S COUNTY CONVENTION," *Utah Journal* (Logan, UT), 18 July 1883, [3]; "COUNTY CONVENTION," *Utah Journal* (Logan, UT), 30 July 1883, [3].

70. "The Convention," *Deseret Evening News*, 19 July 1873, [3]; "Cache County Caucus and Ticket," *Deseret Evening News*, 21 July 1874, [2]; "Caucus in Cache," *Deseret Evening News*, 8 July 1875, [2]; "Convention," *Deseret Evening News*, 29 July 1876, [3]; "The Primaries," *Deseret Evening News*, 26 Sept. 1876, [3]; "Primaries," *Salt Lake Daily Herald*, 26 Sept. 1876, [3]; "Primaries in Logan," and "People's Primaries," *Salt Lake Daily Herald*, 27 Sept. 1876, [3]; "PEOPLE'S COUNTY CONVENTION," *Salt Lake Daily Herald*, 1 Oct. 1876, [3]; "Cache County People's Convention," *Salt Lake Daily Herald*, 3 Oct. 1876, [3]; "County Conventions," *Deseret Evening News*, 3 Oct. 1876, [3]; "Territorial Convention," *Deseret Evening News*, 7 Oct. 1876, [3]; "PEOPLE'S TERRITORIAL CONVENTION," *Salt Lake Daily Herald*, 8 Oct. 1876, [3]; "People's County Convention," *Salt Lake Daily Herald*, 29 July 1877, [3]; "The Primaries," *Salt Lake Daily Herald*, 29 Jan 1878, [3]; "THE MUNICIPAL CONVENTION," *Deseret Evening News*, 2 Feb. 1878, [3]; "Washington County Convention," *Deseret Evening News*, 5 July 1878, [3]; "Territorial Convention," *Salt Lake Daily Herald*, 8 Oct. 1878, [3]; "Territorial Convention," *Deseret Evening News*, 8 Oct. 1878, [3]; "The Municipal Convention," *Deseret Evening News*, 3 Feb. 1880, [3]; "The People's Convention," *Salt Lake Daily Herald*, 3 Feb 1880, [3]; "County Convention," *Logan Leader*, 8 Oct. 1880, [3]; "Territorial Convention," *Deseret Evening News*, 8 Oct. 1880, [3]; "THE PRIMARIES," *Deseret Evening News*, 22 July 1884, [3]; "The Primaries," *Salt Lake Daily Herald*, 22 July 1884, [8]; "THE COUNTY CONVENTION," *Deseret Evening News*, 26 July 1884, [5]; "Standard Bearer," *Salt Lake Daily Herald*, 9 Oct. 1884, 8; "PEOPLE'S PARTY PRIMARIES," *Deseret Evening News*, 2 July 1889, [3]; "THE PEOPLE'S CONVENTION," *Deseret Evening News*, 6 Sept. 1889, [3].

71. *Biographical Directory of the United States Congress, 1774-1989*, 739.

72. "A HOPEFUL CONVERT," *Salt Lake Tribune*, 7 Dec. 1873, [1].

73. "HOT SHOT FROM CANNON. AN INTERVIEW WITH THE UTAH DELEGATE," *Washington Post*, 6 Feb. 1878, reprinted in *Deseret Evening News*, 12 Feb. 1878, [2]; Dickinson, *Guide to the Congress*, 68-69; Gene A. Sessions, ed., *A View of James Henry Moyle: His Diaries and Letters* (Salt Lake City: N.p., 1974), 123.

74. "Oneida County," *Salt Lake Tribune,* 6 Oct. 1874, [2]; Leonard J. Arrington, *Charles C. Rich: Mormon General and Western Frontiersman* (Provo, UT: Brigham Young University Press, 1974), 272, 361n3; "A Voice from the South," *Salt Lake Daily Herald,* 26 Mar. 1876, [3]; "DEMOCRATIC CONVENTION. Delegates Assemble from All Over the Territory," *Deseret Evening News,* 10 Oct. 1891, 8.

75. Linford, "The Mormons and the Law," 331-41; C. Peter Magrath, "Chief Justice Waite and the 'Twin Relic': *Reynolds v. United States,*" *Vanderbilt Law Review* 18 (1965): 507-43; Ray Jay Davis, "Plural Marriages and Religious Freedom: The Impact of *Reynolds vs. United States,*" *Arizona Law Review* 15, No. 2 (1973): 287-306; James L. Clayton, "The Supreme Court, Polygamy, and the Enforcement of Morals in Nineteenth Century America: An Analysis of Reynolds v. United States," *Dialogue: A Journal of Mormon Thought* 12 (Winter 1979): 46-61; Jeremy M. Miller, "A Critique of the Reynolds Decision," *Western State University Law Review* 11 (Spring 1984): 165-98; Mark S. Lee, "Legislating Morality: *Reynolds vs. United States,*" *Sunstone* 10 (Apr. 1985): 8-12; Poll, "The Legislative Antipolygamy Campaign," 113-14; Henry Mark Holzer, "The True Reynolds vs. United States," *Harvard Journal of Law and Public Policy* 10 (Winter 1987): 43-46; Randall D. Guynn and Gene C. Schaerr, "The Mormon Polygamy Cases," *Sunstone* 11 (Sept. 1987): 9-12; Bruce A. Van Orden, *Prisoner for Conscience' Sake: The Life of George Reynolds* (Salt Lake City: Deseret Book Co., 1992), 61-92; Firmage and Mangrum, *Zion in the Courts,* 148-59; also Thomas G. Alexander, "Charles S. Zane—Apostle of the New Era," *Utah Historical Quarterly* 34 (Fall 1966): 290-314; Robert G. Dyer, "The Evolution of Social and Judicial Attitudes Toward Polygamy," *Utah State Bar Journal* 5 (Spring 1977): 35-45; Douglas H. Parker, "Victory In Defeat: Polygamy and the Mormon Legal Encounter With the Federal Government," *Cardozo Law Review* 12 (Feb./Mar. 1991): 805-19.

76. Hübner, "Utah Delegations," 109; Mark W. Cannon, "The Mormon Issue in Congress, 1872-1882, Drawing on the Experience of Territorial Delegate George Q. Cannon," Ph.D. diss., Harvard University, 1960, 72-89; Dickinson, *Guide to the Congress,* 68-69.

77. Richard D. Poll, "Political Reconstruction of Utah Territory," *Pacific Historical Review* 27 (May 1958): 111-26; Linford, "Mormons and the Law," 317-21; Joseph H. Groberg, "The Mormon Disfranchisements of 1882 to 1892," *Brigham Young University Studies* 16 (Spring 1976): 399-408; Thomas G. Alexander, *A Clash of Interests: Interior Department and Mountain West, 1863-96* (Provo, UT: Brigham Young University Press, 1977), 74-75; Poll, "The Legislative Antipolygamy Campaign," 115; Lyman, *Political Deliverance,* 22-23; Firmage and Mangrum, *Zion in the Courts,* 160-97; B. Carmon Hardy, *Solemn Covenant: The Mormon Polygamous Passage* (Urbana: University of Illinois Press, 1992), 46-47.

78. David Buice, "A Stench in the Nostrils of Honest Men: Southern Democrats and the Edmunds Act of 1882," *Dialogue: A Journal of Mormon Thought* 21 (Autumn 1988): 100-101, 105-13; "RAISING A FALSE ISSUE," *Deseret Evening News,* 22 Sept. 1884, [2].

79. Linford, "Mormons and the Law," 322-27; Leonard J. Arrington, *Great Basin Kingdom: An Economic History of the Latter-day Saints, 1847-1900* (Cambridge, MA: Harvard University Press, 1958), 360-61; Gustive O. Larson, *The "Americanization" of Utah for Statehood* (San Marino, CA: Huntington Library, 1970), 208-12; Alexander, *Clash of Interests,* 118, 133-35; Poll, "The Legislative Antipolygamy Campaign," 116-17; Lyman, *Political Deliverance,* 46; Firmage and Mangrum, *Zion in the Courts,* 197-209, 235, 242, 252-56; Lola Van Wagenen, "Sister-Wives and Suffragists: Polygamy and the Politics of Woman Suffrage, 1870-1896," Ph.D. diss., New York University, 1994, 374, for quote.

80. Heber J. Grant letterbook-journal, 20 June 1887, LDS archives; Henry J. Wolfinger, "A Reexamination of the Woodruff Manifesto in the Light of Utah Constitutional History," *Utah Historical Quarterly* 39 (Fall 1971): 328-49; Lyman, *Political Deliverance,* 41-56. While "diary" is the standardized term I use to identify personal documents with

daily entries, Grant kept several different kinds of such records, which must be identified separately in order to locate the quotations.

81. Abraham H. Cannon diary, 22 July, 2 Aug. 1888; Frank J. Cannon and Harvey J. O'Higgins, *Under the Prophet in Utah: The National Menace of a Political Priestcraft* (Boston: The C.M. Clark Publishing Co., 1911), 79-80; Lyman, *Political Deliverance,* 99-100. Charles S. Zane diary, 19 Feb., 23 Feb. 1889, indicates his puzzlement and frustration about his fellow jurist's leniency toward polygamists. See Zane diaries, Manuscript Section, Illinois State Historical Society, Springfield.

82. Franklin D. Richards diary, 7 Aug., 29 Aug. 1888; also Charles W. Watson, "John Willard Young and the 1887 Movement for Utah Statehood," Ph.D. diss., Brigham Young University, 1984; undated manuscript draft, John W. Young papers, LDS archives; Lyman, *Political Deliverance,* 61, for this 13 Feb. 1888 telegram from Young; *Congressional Record* 19:4 (5 Dec. 1887), 16 (12 Dec. 1887), for Senators Shelby M. Cullom and Cushman K. Davis as members of the committee.

83. John W. Young to A. W. Cochran, 31 May 1889, 1888-89 letterbook, 382-83, Young papers; Moses Thatcher letterbook, 18-21; Franklin D. Richards diary, 28 Sept. 1888.

84. "DEMOCRATIC CONVENTION. Preliminary Steps Looking to a Territorial Organization," *Deseret Evening News,* 6 Oct. 1888, [3]; "A Democratic Party," *Salt Lake Daily Herald,* 7 Oct. 1888, 5, for quotes from platform. Notable among the faithful Mormon participants in this independent Democratic organization were Anthony W. Ivins (future member of the First Presidency) and Henry J. Faust (great-grandfather of current First Presidency counselor and Democrat, James E. Faust).

85. "Stand By The People's Party," *Deseret Evening News,* 19 Oct. 1888, [2].

86. Charles S. Peterson, *Take Up Your Mission: Mormon Colonizing Along the Little Colorado River, 1870-1900* (Tucson: University of Arizona Press, 1973), 238-39; John Henry Smith diary, 2 Sept. 1888, in Jean Bickmore White, ed., *Church, State, and Politics: The Diaries of John Henry Smith* (Salt Lake City: Signature Books/Smith Research Associates, 1990), 207.

87. Interview of William Budge with Judge Charles H. Berry, 30 Sept. 1888, Berry papers, Minnesota Historical Society, St. Paul; E. Leo Lyman, "A Mormon Transition in Idaho Politics," *Idaho Yesterdays: The Quarterly Journal of the Idaho Historical Society* 20 (Fall 1976): 5-6, 9-10; also Merrill D. Beal and Merle W. Wells, *History of Idaho,* 3 vols. (New York: Lewis Historical Publishing Co., 1959), 1:600-601. For Budge's transition from Democratic activist to Republican activist, see "Minutes of a Meeting of the Bear Lake County Democratic Convention," *Bear Lake Democrat* (Paris, ID), 26 Aug. 1882, [2]; "DEMO-CRATIC TERRITORIAL CONVENTION," *Bear Lake Democrat* (Paris, ID), 26 Sept. 1884, [2]; Merle W. Wells, *Anti-Mormonism in Idaho, 1872-92* (Provo, UT: Brigham Young University Press, 1978), 167, 169-70.

88. "THE DUTY OF THF HOUR," *Deseret Evening News,* 26 Oct. 1888, [2].

89. Lyman, *Political Deliverance,* 101-10.

90. Junius F. Wells to Joseph F. Smith, 21 Nov. 1888, my narrative reconstruction of the abbreviated notes in fd 7, box 6, Scott G. Kenney papers, Marriott Library.

91. Heber J. Grant letterbook-journal, 31 May 1889.

92. Abraham H. Cannon diary, 8 Oct. 1889.

93. Lyman, *Political Deliverance,* 126-31; "AIMED AT THE MORMONS. Another Bill Introduced In the Senate," *Deseret Evening News,* 1 July 1890, [3]; Abraham H. Cannon diary, 10 July 1890.

94. Abraham H. Cannon diary, 31 July 1890; Jesse N. Smith diary, 14 Aug. 1890, in *Journal of Jesse Nathaniel Smith: The Life Story of a Mormon Pioneer, 1834-1906* (Salt Lake City: Jesse N. Smith Family Association, 1953), 379.

95. Wells, *Anti-Mormonism in Idaho,* 155; Abraham H. Cannon diary, 31 July 1890; Lyman, "Mormon Transition in Idaho Politics," 25-26.

96. Abraham H. Cannon diary, 12 June 1890; Cannon and O'Higgins, *Under the Prophet*, 86-100; Richard S. Van Wagoner and Steven C. Walker, *A Book of Mormons* (Salt Lake City: Signature Books, 1982), 45; Rowland M. Cannon, *From Theocracy To Democracy: A Political History of the Mormon Church and the State of Utah, 1830-1906, With Special Emphasis on the Roles of George Q. Cannon and Frank J. Cannon toward Statehood for Utah* (Salt Lake City: "Written expressly for the author's children and their children as well as the sister and brothers of the author," 1986), 173-79, 214-15; Lyman, *Political Deliverance*, 132; E. Leo Lyman, "The Political Background of the Woodruff Manifesto," *Dialogue: A Journal of Mormon Thought* 24 (Fall 1991): 26-29.

97. *Who's Who in America: A Biographical Dictionary of Notable Living Men and Women of the United States, 1903-1905* (Chicago: A. N. Marquis Co., 1903), 461-62.

98. George Q. Cannon diary excerpt, 12 Sept. 1890, LDS archives; also quoted in D. Michael Quinn, "LDS Church Authority and New Plural Marriages, 1890-1904," *Dialogue: A Journal of Mormon Thought* 18 (Spring 1985): 42-43.

99. George Q. Cannon diary excerpt, 9 Sept. 1889. Lyman's 1987 *Political Deliverance*, 147n39, says that "there is no direct evidence of the church leaders conferring with him [James S. Clarkson] or any other national Republican leader in California" in September 1890. Also Thomas G. Alexander, *Things in Heaven and Earth: The Life and Times of Wilford Woodruff, a Mormon Prophet* (Salt Lake City: Signature Books, 1991), 266, lists Estee among those with whom the First Presidency met in San Francisco but makes no reference to discussions about ending plural marriages. In his "The Odyssey of a Latter-day Prophet: Wilford Woodruff and the Manifesto of 1890," *Journal of Mormon History* 17 (1991): 202-203, Alexander acknowledges Woodruff had six days of "negotiations" with Estee and other Republican leaders about "the very real prospect of losing the temples," but he makes no reference to Cannon's 1890 diary entry (published in 1985) of his reaction to Estee's proposal to lay aside polygamy. Hardy's 1992 *Solemn Covenant*, 130-31, skips over the First Presidency's mid-September meeting with Republican leaders altogether.

100. Kenney, *Wilford Woodruff's Journal* 9 (3-25 Sept. 1890): 109-14; Larson, *"Americanization" of Utah*, 248-264; Kenneth M. Godfrey, "The Coming of the Manifesto," *Dialogue: A Journal of Mormon Thought* 5 (Autumn 1970): 11-25; Gordon C. Thomasson, "The Manifesto Was a Victory," *Dialogue: A Journal of Mormon Thought* 6 (Spring 1971): 37-45; Jan Shipps, "The Principle Revoked: A Closer Look at the Demise of Plural Marriage," *Journal of Mormon History* 11 (1984): 68-72; Quinn, "LDS Church Authority and New Plural Marriages, 1890-1904," 44-46; Lyman, *Political Deliverance*, 135-39; Alexander, *Things in Heaven and Earth*, 267; Hardy, *Solemn Covenant*, 130-48; Edward Leo Lyman, "Manifesto," in Allan Kent Powell, ed., *Utah History Encyclopedia* (Salt Lake City: University of Utah Press, 1994), 342-43.

101. David Brion Davis, "Some Themes in Counter Subversion: An Analysis of Anti-Masonic, Anti-Catholic and Anti-Mormon Literature," *Mississippi Valley Historical Review* 57 (Sept. 1960): 205-224; Mark W. Cannon, "The Crusades Against the Masons, Catholics, and Mormons: Separate Waves of Common Current," *Brigham Young University Studies* 3 (Winter 1961): 23-40.

102. Hill, *Quest For Refuge*, 181, also 36, 70; Kenneth H. Winn, *Exiles in a Land of Liberty: Mormons in America, 1830-1846* (Chapel Hill: University of North Carolina Press, 1989), 5, 99.

103. Dean L. May, "People on the Mormon Frontier: Kanab's Families of 1874," *Journal of Family History* 1 (Winter 1976): 172; Lowell "Ben" Bennion, "The Incidence of Mormon Polygamy in 1880: Dixie versus Davis Stake," *Journal of Mormon History* 11 (1984): 29-38; Larry M. Logue, *A Sermon in the Desert: Belief and Behavior in Early St. George, Utah* (Urbana: University of Illinois Press, 1988), 50-51; Kathryn M. Daynes, "Plural Wives and the Nineteenth-Century Mormon Marriage System: Manti, Utah, 1849-1910," Ph.D. diss., Indiana University, 1991, 157, 159; Jessie L. Embry, "Polygamy," in Powell, *Utah History*

Encyclopedia, 428-29; Marie Cornwall, Camela Courtright, and Laga Van Beek, "How Common the Principle?: Women as Plural Wives in 1860," *Dialogue: A Journal of Mormon Thought* 26 (Summer 1993): 148-49; Dean L. May, *Three Frontiers: Family, Land, and Society in the American West, 1850-1900* (Cambridge, Eng.: Cambridge University Press, 1994), 121; also Phillip R. Kunz, "One Wife or Several? A Comparative Study of Late Nineteenth Century Marriage in Utah," in Thomas G. Alexander, ed., *The Mormon People: Their Character and Traditions* (Provo, UT: Brigham Young University Press, 1980), 53-73.

104. Charles A. Cannon, "The Awesome Power of Sex: The Polemical Campaign Against Mormon Polygamy," *Pacific Historical Review* 43 (Feb. 1974): 61-82; Hardy, *Solemn Covenant,* 59; Lyman, *Political Deliverance,* 2; John Smyth Iversen, "A Debate On the American Home: The Anti-Polygamy Controversy, 1880-1890," *Journal of the History of Sexuality* 1 (Apr. 1991): 585-602. Hardy's analysis (41-60) is the most insightful explanation for the fears and fury directed against Mormon polygamy by nineteenth-century Americans.

105. Klaus J. Hansen, "The Political Kingdom of God as a Cause for Mormon-Gentile Conflict," *Brigham Young University Studies* 2 (Spring-Summer 1960): 241-60; Hansen, *Quest for Empire: The Political Kingdom of God and the Council of Fifty in Mormon History* (Lansing: Michigan State University Press, 1967), 179, and Hansen, *Mormonism and the American Experience* (Chicago: University of Chicago Press, 1981), 144-45. See the qualified dissent from Hansen in Lyman, *Political Deliverance,* 2, 23; Hardy, *Solemn Covenant,* 57.

106. Rutherford B. Hayes diary, 9 Jan. 1880, in T. Harry Williams, ed., *Hayes: The Diary of a President, 1875-1881* (New York: David McKay Co., Inc., 1964), 258-59.

107. "The Republican Platform," *Deseret Evening News,* 21 June 1888, [1]; Hansen, *Quest For Empire,* 145; Poll, "The Legislative Antipolygamy Campaign," 119.

108. *Journal of Discourses,* 26 vols. (London and Liverpool: Latter-day Saints' Book Depot, 1854-86), 11:239 (B. Young/1866), 13:166 (Woodruff/1869), 22:147-48 (Woodruff/1881), 22:174 (Woodruff/1881), 23:240-41 (J. Taylor/1882), 25:321-22 (G. Q. Cannon/1884), 26:152 (J. Taylor/1885); "THE ONLY CONSISTENT COURSE," *Deseret Evening News,* 23 Apr. 1885, [2]; Wilford Woodruff, "To The World, the Nation and the Saints," *Deseret Evening News,* 12 May 1885, [2]; "No Relinquishment," *Deseret Evening News,* 5 June 1885, [2]; George Q. Cannon, "Editorial Thoughts," *Juvenile Instructor* 20 (1 May 1885): 136; George Q. Cannon, "Topics of the Times," *Juvenile Instructor* 20 (15 May 1885): 156; "THE LAW OF GOD IS SUPREME," *Deseret Evening News,* 12 Aug. 1886, [2].

109. Howard Roberts Lamar, *The Far Southwest, 1846-1912: A Territorial History* (New Haven: Yale University Press, 1966), 409.

110. "OFFICIAL DECLARATION," *Deseret Evening News,* 14 Dec. 1889, [2]; James R. Clark, ed., *Messages of the First Presidency of the Church of Jesus Christ of Latter-day Saints, 1833-1964,* 6 vols. (Salt Lake City: Bookcraft, 1965-71), 3:186.

111. Hansen, *Quest For Empire,* [ii]. However, in 1981 Hansen, *Mormonism and the American Experience,* 176, argued that "because its leaders had kept the government of the political kingdom secret, they were able to hang on to it a bit longer" than polygamy. Actually, a year before Hansen's book was published, two publications had documented that the Council of Fifty ceased to function six years before the LDS president officially abandoned polygamy. See D. Michael Quinn, "The Council of Fifty and Its Members, 1844-1945," *Brigham Young University Studies* 20 (Winter 1980): 190-91; Andrew F. Ehat, "'It Seems Like Heaven Began on Earth': Joseph Smith and the Constitution of the Kingdom of God," *Brigham Young University Studies* 20 (Spring 1980): 279.

112. Lyman, *Political Deliverance,* 110-11, 117-18; Jean Bickmore White, "The Right to Be Different: Ogden and Weber County Politics, 1850-1924," *Utah Historical Quarterly* 47 (Summer 1979): 262-63; "NOT DEFEATED BUT ROBBED," and "A Wild Scene Follows the Announcement of 'Liberal' Victory," *Deseret Evening News,* 11 Feb. 1890, [2-3]; Alexander, "Odyssey of a Latter-day Prophet," 199-201.

113. "DISBAND THE PEOPLE'S PARTY," *Salt Lake Tribune,* 3 Nov. 1890, 4.

114. L. John Nuttall diary, 17 Feb., 19 Feb., 25 Feb. 1891, Lee Library, with copy in Marriott Library and Huntington Library.

115. Abraham H. Cannon diary, 19 Mar., 25 May 1891.

116. "A CALL! County Central Committee and Club Officers," and "A CALL. Territorial Central Committee of the People's Party," *Deseret Evening News,* 27 May 1891, 8; "DISSOLVED. The People's Party in Salt Lake County Decided to Disband," *Deseret Evening News,* 1 June 1891, 8; Abraham H. Cannon diary, 10 June 1891; "THE PEOPLE'S PARTY," *Deseret Evening News,* 11 June 1891, 4; Lyman, *Political Deliverance,* 153-54. Ironically, simultaneous with the dissolution of the Mormon People's Party of Utah, the national People's Party of the United States ("Populists") was organized. See "THE NEW NATIONAL PARTY," *Deseret Evening News,* 27 May 1891, 4.

117. For a similar view, see Jack, "Utah Territorial Politics," 517.

118. Compiled from the following sources: newspaper reports of attendance at political conventions; references to political preferences and activities in diaries and correspondence; consultations with descendants; examination of political reminiscences of James H. Moyle, chair of Utah's Democratic Party from 1898 to 1902; and consultation with Charles Smurthwaite, secretary of the Salt Lake County Democratic Committee, 1934-41. Where sources disagreed, I gave preference to the source that seemed to be the most authoritative. Due to recent research on Utah's political conventions from 1891 to 1930, this corrects some of my previous publications on this matter.

119. John Henry Smith diary, 14 May 1891, in White, *Church, State, and Politics,* 253.

120. Gordon B. Hinckley, *James Henry Moyle: The Story of a Distinguished American and an Honored Churchman* (Salt Lake City: Deseret Book Co., 1951), 220.

121. "ASSERTS THAT UTAH WAS SOLD . . . Mr. Woodruff's Early Vote," *Salt Lake Herald,* 18 Feb. 1895, 3; "The Mormon Question," *Standard* (Ogden, UT), 20 Aug. 1895, 2; J. Golden Kimball diary, 7 Oct. 1895, Marriott Library, also commented that Wilford Woodruff publicly voted Republican in 1894. Nevertheless, Alexander, *Things in Heaven and Earth,* 277, claims that "Woodruff himself was a nominal Democrat"; also Leonard Schlup, "Utah Maverick: Frank J. Cannon and the Politics of Conscience in 1896," *Utah Historical Quarterly* 62 (Fall 1994): 335-48; Kenneth M. Godfrey, "Frank J. Cannon: Declension in the Mormon Kingdom," in Launius and Thatcher, *Differing Visions,* 241-61; Kenneth Godfrey, "Frank J. Cannon," in Powell, *Utah History Encyclopedia,* 70.

122. Gustive O. Larson and Richard D. Poll, "The Forty-fifth State," in Poll, *Utah's History,* 390; Alexander, *Things in Heaven and Earth,* 277-82.

123. Frank Esshom, *Pioneers and Prominent Men of Utah, Comprising Photographs-Genealogies-Biographies* (Salt Lake City: Utah Pioneers Book Publishing Co., 1913), 1173, for Republican sons Lorenzo Snow, Jr., and Oliver G. Snow; and Democratic sons Alphonzo H. Snow, Mansfield L. Snow, and Orion W. Snow; for their political participation, see "Box Elder DEMOCRACY: Wednesday's Work of the County Convention," *Brigham City Bugler,* 18 July 1891, [4]; "Primary Meeting at Brigham City," *Logan Leader* (Logan, UT), 22 July 1891, [3]; "THE REPUBLICANS Hold a Stirring County Convention," *Brigham City Bugler,* 25 July 1891, [3]; "THE REPUBLICAN TICKET," *Brigham City Bugler,* 1 Aug. 1891, [4]; "DEMOCRATIC CONVENTION," *Brigham City Bugler,* 21 Oct. 1893, [1]; "JUBILEE. Zion Shaken Up by Triumphant Republicanism," *Salt Lake Tribune,* 13 Nov. 1894, [1]; "The Mormon Question," *Standard* (Ogden, UT), 20 Aug. 1895, 2; "ELECTION JUDGES," *Brigham City Bugler,* 12 Oct. 1895, [1].

124. "HOW ROBERTS STOOD THEN . . . Talked of For Senator," *Salt Lake Herald,* 25 Oct. 1895, 3.

125. Abraham H. Cannon diary, 30 July 1895; "More 'Nuggets of Truth,'" *Salt Lake Herald,* 25 Aug. 1895, 3.

126. "DEMOCRATIC. The Democrats of Boxelder [sic] Precinct Choose Delegates," *Brigham City Bugler,* 19 Sept. 1896, [1].

127. "PRESIDENT SNOW MISREPRESENTED: Declares Neutrality in Weber County Politics," *Salt Lake Herald,* 14 Oct. 1898, [1].

128. "ANTI-POLYGAMY AMENDMENT TO FEDERAL CONSTITUTION," *Salt Lake Herald,* 21 Feb. 1899, [1]; Rudger Clawson diary, 2 Mar., 29 Dec. 1899, in Stan Larson, ed., *A Ministry of Meetings: The Diaries of Rudger Clawson* (Salt Lake City: Signature Books/Smith Research Associates, 1993), 30, 127; Journal History of the Church of Jesus Christ of Latter-day Saints (1830-1972), 246 reels, microfilm, Special Collections, Marriott Library, 22 Nov. 1899, 2; *New York Journal,* 5 Dec. 1899; "Reasons For and Objections To a Constitutional Amendment," *The Kinsman: The Organ of the Campaign for the Anti-Polygamy Constitutional Amendment* 2 (Jan. 1900): 72-76; "MINISTERS URGE THE AMENDMENT: Want a Sixteenth Article Added to the United States Constitution to Prohibit Polygamy," *Deseret Evening News,* 13 Feb. 1900, 8.

129. John Henry Smith diary, 12 Feb., 14 Feb. 1900, in White, *Church, State, and Politics,* 448; "FITCH CHARMS A MULTITUDE: Magnificent Gathering of Republicans Responds Enthusiastically to the Eloquence of the Great Orator," *Salt Lake Tribune,* 31 Mar. 1900, [1].

130. Anthon H. Lund diary, 3 Jan. 1901, LDS archives; Abraham Owen Woodruff diary, 17 Jan. 1901, LDS archives, with copy in Lee Library; also following discussion. The Lund diary microfilm is available to all researchers at LDS archives by stipulation of its donor, and will be published in edited form by Signature Books, Salt Lake City.

131. "IT WAS DEMOCRACY'S DAY: Twelve Hundred Delegates at the Great Convention," *Salt Lake Herald,* 14 July 1895, [1]; "HOW ROBERTS STOOD THEN . . . Talked of For Senator," *Salt Lake Herald,* 25 Oct. 1895, 3; B. H. Jones to John Henry Smith, 18 Dec. 1896, fd 13, box 8, George A. Smith Family papers, Marriott Library; "FITCH CHARMS A MULTITUDE. Magnificent Gathering of Republicans Responds Enthusiastically to the Eloquence of the Great Orator," *Salt Lake Tribune,* 31 Mar. 1900, [1]; Hoopes and Hoopes, *Making of a Mormon Apostle,* 149, 153.

132. Heber J. Grant 1891 letterbook-journal (7 July 1891), 125; John M. Whitaker edited journal 1:271 (June 1892), Marriott Library; "More 'Nuggets of Truth," *Salt Lake Herald,* 25 Aug. 1895, 3.

133. Abraham H. Cannon diary, 13 July 1892, 4 Apr. 1895. "The Mormon Question," *Standard* (Ogden, UT), 20 Aug. 1895, 2, did not list Taylor among the Republican members of the Quorum of the Twelve. However, this Republican newspaper mistakenly claimed that Brigham Young, Jr., was a Republican apostle, which Young disproved by attending Democratic conventions before and after this published list of Republican general authorities.

134. Lyman, *Political Deliverance,* 261; Samuel W. Taylor to D. Michael Quinn, 15 Jan. 1976.

135. Abraham Owen Woodruff diary, 8 Nov. 1898; "SENATOR CANNON PLEADS FOR UTAH'S SALVATION," *Salt Lake Tribune,* 10 Feb. 1899, [1]; "FITCH CHARMS A MULTITUDE," *Salt Lake Tribune,* 31 Mar. 1900, [1]; Abraham Owen Woodruff diary, 17 Jan., 21-23 Jan. 1901; "KEARNS AND CANNON MEET WITH APOSTLES: Hold Session with Cowley and Woodruff in State Bank of Utah," *Salt Lake Herald,* 21 Jan. 1901, 8; Anthon H. Lund diary, 17 Dec. 1903; Abraham Owen Woodruff to Heber J. Grant, 5 Feb. 1902, LDS archives; J. F. Gibbs, *Lights and Shadows of Mormonism* (Salt Lake City: Salt Lake Tribune Publishing Co., 1909), 321; Gene A. Sessions, ed., *Mormon Democrat: The Religious and Political Memoirs of James Henry Moyle* (Salt Lake City: Historical Department, Church of Jesus Christ of Latter-day Saints, 1975), 208.

136. Abraham H. Cannon diary, 25 Oct. 1894.

137. Heber J. Grant journal sheets, 2 Nov. 1920; "A Statement From Prest. Heber J. Grant," *Deseret News,* 13 Oct. 1928, II, 1; Dan E. Jones, "Utah Politics, 1926-1932," Ph.D. diss., University of Utah, 1968, 108.

138. "THE BIRTH. Real Democracy Born," *Salt Lake Herald,* 16 May 1891, 8; "DEMOCRACY!: Call For a County Convention," *Salt Lake Herald,* 7 June 1891, 8; "JEFFERSON CLUB. First Democratic Club Organized in Cache Valley," *Logan Journal,* 24 June 1891, [8]; "REPUBLICAN GATHERINGS," *Logan Journal,* 1 July 1891, [4]; "REPUB-LICAN CONVENTION," *Deseret Evening News,* 8 July 1891, 8; "DEMOCRATIC. The Convention Met at the Court House Over a Hundred Strong," *Logan Journal,* 8 July 1891, [1]; "THE CONVENTION. Republican League Organized," *Daily Enquirer* (Provo, UT), 11 July 1891, [4]; "DEMOCRATIC CONVENTION. Delegates Assemble from All Over the Territory," *Deseret Evening News,* 10 Oct. 1891, 8; "THE PRIMARIES. Dems. Hold Forth in the Wards," *Daily Enquirer* (Provo, UT), 29 Jan. 1892, [2]; "CONVENTION: Hundreds of Delegates Present," *Daily Enquirer* (Provo, UT), 1 Apr. 1892, [1]; "UTAH REPUBLICANS," *Salt Lake Herald,* 2 Apr. 1892, 3; "DEMOCRATIC Territorial Convention to be Held in Ogden Saturday, May 14," *Journal* (Logan, UT), 11 May 1892, [2]; "UTAH SHOUTS DEMOCRACY!" *Salt Lake Herald,* 15 May 1892, 1, 5; "COUNTY CONVENTION. Delegates Chosen to the Territorial Convention," *Journal* (Logan, UT), 1 Oct. 1892, [8]; "J.L. Rawlins For Delegate," *Salt Lake Herald,* 6 Oct. 1892, 6; "REPUBLICAN CONVENTION," *Salt Lake Herald,* 15 Oct. 1893, 8; "DEMOCRACY IS BOOMING," *Journal* (Logan, UT), 5 Sept. 1894, [1]; "Rawlins and Victory," *Salt Lake Herald,* 16 Sept. 1894, 5-6; "A GRAND ARRAY OF MEN," *Logan Nation,* 2 Oct. 1894, [1]; "JUBILEE. Zion Shaken Up by Triumphant Republicanism," *Salt Lake Tribune,* 13 Nov. 1894, [1]; "THE REPUBLICAN JUBILEE," *Deseret Evening News,* 13 Nov. 1894, 8; "DELEGATES ELECTED To the Convention at Salt Lake City," *Journal* (Logan, UT), 11 July 1895, [1]; "IT WAS DEMOCRACY'S DAY: Twelve Hundred Delegates at the Great Convention," *Salt Lake Herald,* 14 July 1895, 1; "AT THE PRIMARIES: Democrats Held Spirited Meetings Last Evening," *Journal* (Logan, UT), 27 Aug. 1895, [1]; "PRIMARY MEETINGS Of the Democratic Party—Delegates Elected to the County Convention," *Deseret Evening News,* 30 Aug. 1895, 8; "'RAWLINS AND THATCHER.' Salt Lake Delegation Instructed to Work for them," *Salt Lake Herald,* 1 Sept. 1895, 1, 3; "A BIG CONVENTION. Superb Ticket Nominated By Davis County Demo-crats," *Salt Lake Herald,* 1 Sept. 1895, 6; "GIVES GREAT SATISFACTION," *Salt Lake Herald,* 24 Oct. 1895, [3]; "HOW ROBERTS STOOD THEN . . . Talked of For Senator," *Salt Lake Herald,* 25 Oct. 1895, 3; "UTAH STANDS FOR FREE SILVER," *Salt Lake Herald,* 7 June 1896, 3; "Democratic Primaries," *Journal* (Logan, UT), 10 Sept. 1896, [5]; "WHITNEY AND THOMAS," *Deseret Evening News,* 10 Sept. 1898, 2; "DEMOCRATIC CONVENTION COMMENCES ITS WORK," *Salt Lake Herald,* 10 Sept. 1898, 1; "FITCH CHARMS A MULTITUDE. Magnificent Gathering of Republicans Responds Enthusiastically to the Eloquence of the Great Orator," *Salt Lake Tribune,* 31 Mar. 1900, [1]; "REPUBLICAN LEAGUE IS DEAD," *Salt Lake Herald,* 14 July 1900, 5; "REPUBLICAN CONVENTIONS," *Logan Nation,* 29 Aug. 1900, [1]; "DEMOCRATS NAME THEIR DELEGATES," *Deseret Evening News,* 5 Sept. 1900, 5; "GREAT REPUBLICAN RALLY: Addresses by Senators Thos. Kearns and C.D. Clark, and Hon. John Henry Smith," *Deseret Evening News,* 22 Oct. 1902, 7; "LOCAL DEMOCRATS PAINT TOWN RED," *Deseret Evening News,* 11 July 1904, 5; "DELEGATES TO STATE CONVENTION," *Deseret Evening News,* 24 Aug. 1904, 5; "DEMOCRATS HOLD WARD PRIMARIES," *Deseret Evening News,* 22 Sept. 1905, 5; "DEMOCRATS NAME DELEGATES," and "REPUBLICAN PRIMARIES HELD," *Deseret Evening News,* 2 Oct. 1906, 5; "NAME DELEGATES FOR CONVENTION," *Deseret Evening News,* 13 Sept. 1907, 10; "PRIMARIES ARE WITHOUT COLOR," *Salt Lake Herald,* 25 Sept. 1907, 3; "ENDORSED JESSE KNIGHT: Cache County Democrats Are For The Provo Man For Governor," *Journal* (Logan, UT), 22 Sept. 1908, [1]; "REPUBLICAN PROHIBITION MASS CONVENTION," *Deseret Evening News,* 20 Feb. 1909, 5; "REPUBLICANS TO MEET

TONIGHT: Ward Conventions on Councilmanic Tickets to be Held in Five Wards," *Deseret Evening News,* 28 Sept. 1909, 8; "THE DEMOCRATIC CITY PRIMARIES," *Journal* (Logan, UT), 13 Oct. 1910, [1]; "CHIEF EXECUTIVE HONORED GUEST," *Deseret Evening News,* 5 Oct. 1911, 2; "PRIMARIES HELD BY REPUBLICANS: Delegates to Salt Lake County Convention Are Elected," *Deseret Evening News,* 24 Aug. 1912, 8; "DEMOCRACY OF UTAH MEETS IN CONVENTION," *Deseret Evening News,* 29 Aug. 1912, 1; "DEMOCRATS HOLD THEIR PRIMARIES: Delegates Selected for County Convention Next Thursday," *Deseret Evening News,* 10 Sept. 1912, 6; "DEMOCRATS HOLD THEIR PRIMARIES," *Deseret Evening News,* 16 July 1914, 2; "REPUBLICANS NAME DELEGATES TO LEGISLATIVE CONVENTION," *Deseret Evening News,* 16 Sept. 1914, 9; "POLITICAL POINTERS," *Deseret Evening News,* 17 Sept. 1914, 3; "POLITICAL POINTERS," *Deseret Evening News,* 9 Oct. 1914, 16; "COMMITTEES NAMED FOR ANNUAL OUTING OF REPUBLICAN CLUB," *Deseret Evening News,* 13 Aug. 1915, 10; "DELEGATES FROM COUNTY: Republican Primaries Largest And Most Enthusiastic Held Locally in Years," *Deseret Evening News,* 4 Aug. 1916, 14; "DELEGATES NAMED BY DEMOCRATS," *Deseret Evening News,* 12 Aug. 1916, 5; "DELEGATES CHOSEN FOR CONVENTION: Republican Primaries Are Well Attended," *Deseret Evening News,* 9 Sept. 1916, 14; "NAME DELEGATES TO CONVENTIONS: Democrats and Progressives Hold Their Primaries in Salt Lake City and County," *Deseret Evening News,* 13 Sept. 1916, 12; "BRYAN RECEPTION COMMITTEE NAMED: Commoner Will be Guest of Utah Democrats in Ogden and Salt Lake City," *Deseret Evening News,* 18 Sept. 1916, 2; "CHAIRMAN CHOSEN AND COMMITTEES APPOINTED FOR GOV. COX RALLY," *Deseret Evening News,* 13 Sept. 1920, 3; "Delegates Selected for Republican Conventions Will Go Uninstructed," *Deseret Evening News,* 13 Sept. 1922, 5; "List of Representatives to Ogden," *Deseret Evening News,* 28 May 1924, 1; "DEMOCRATS NAME DELEGATES FREE TO VOTE AT WILL," *Deseret Evening News,* 10 Sept. 1926, 5; "PRIMARIES CENTER ON SENATE FIGHT," *Deseret Evening News,* 14 Aug. 1928, II, 8.

139. John Henry Smith 1884-94 letterbook, 787, George A. Smith Family Collection, Marriott Library; J. Golden Kimball diary, 7 Oct. 1895; also Van Wagoner and Walker, *Book of Mormons,* 300.

140. "THE DEMOCRATIC CONVENTION," *Deseret Evening News,* 29 July 1872, [2]; Sessions, *Mormon Democrat,* 199, 204.

141. Milton R. Merrill, *Reed Smoot: Apostle in Politics* (Logan: Utah State University Press, 1990), 8; Harvard S. Heath, "Reed Smoot: The First Modern Mormon," Ph.D. diss., Brigham Young University, 1990, 1061.

142. Franklin D. Richards diary, 22 June 1882; minutes of the Council of Fifty, 22 June 1882, LDS archives; John Henry Smith diary, 22 June 1882, in White, *Church, State, and Politics,* 79 which says only that "I moved to form a political party," without specifying it was the Democratic Party, as did the above two sources. Compare with Smith's quoted statement in "DEAD FOREVER," *Deseret Evening News,* 21 May 1891, 6.

143. "REPUBLICANS ORGANIZE," *Logan Journal,* 27 June 1891, [8]; "Church Influence at Logan," *Salt Lake Herald,* 16 Mar. 1892, 4. For Nibley as an adviser to the Mormon Democratic delegation in the Idaho legislature in 1885 and as a lobbyist for Democratic state officials in 1888, see Wells, *Anti-Mormonism in Idaho,* 60-61; Lyman, "Mormon Transition in Idaho Politics," 8.

144. For convenience, I do not include the New Deal election of 1932 which changed the political affiliations of many former Republicans and Democrats. This table maintains the national party identification for men who were basically apolitical despite affiliation with a particular national party or leanings that way. From 1918 onward, the church president was a registered Democrat, who had become a Republican in everything but name by 1931. Due to my recent research of the attendance at Utah's political conventions from 1891 to 1930, these percentages vary from some of my earlier publications.

145. Abraham H. Cannon diary, 8 Feb. 1892.

146. James E. Talmage diary, 28 May 1892, Lee Library.

147. Reed Smoot diary, 10 Aug. 1909, Lee Library, with copy in Marriott Library; Brent Grant Thompson, "Utah's Struggle For Prohibition, 1908-1917," M.A. thesis, University of Utah, 1979, 34; Brent G. Thompson, "'Standing between Two Fires': Mormons and Prohibition, 1908-1917," *Journal of Mormon History* 10 (1983): 41; Jan Shipps, "Utah Comes of Age Politically: A Study of the State's Politics in the Early Years of the Twentieth Century," *Utah Historical Quarterly* 35 (Spring 1967): 103-105, 107; Van Wagoner and Walker, *Book of Mormons*, 317; Merrill, *Reed Smoot*, 191-94.

148. Reed Smoot diary, 6 Nov. 1910, 14 Oct. 1920.

149. "HEADS OF THE CHURChap. Interview with President Woodruff and President Cannon on the Present Political Situation in Utah," *Salt Lake Times*, 23 June 1891, [1]; "IMPORTANT INTERVIEW. President W. Woodruff and Geo. Q. Cannon on the Utah Situation," *Deseret Evening News*, 24 June 1891, 5; Clark, *Messages of the First Presidency*, 3:211-17; Roberts, *Comprehensive History*, 6:302-306. Roberts attempted (305-306) to reconcile the statement about the dissolution of the People's Party with acknowledgements of the hierarchy's role in that development.

150. Abraham H. Cannon diary, 16 Mar. 1891; Franklin D. Richards diary, 16 Mar. 1891. The church periodical in England publicly stated the intentional myth by describing the *Salt Lake Times* as "a non 'Mormon' Republican paper" (*LDS Millennial Star* 53 [27 July 1891]: 465).

151. Clark, *Messages of the First Presidency*, 3:233, 4:79-80, 152, 153, 225, 227-28, 5:260-61, 310, 6:155-56.

152. Abraham H. Cannon diary, 9 July 1891; Lyman, *Political Deliverance*, 130-31, 169, 185-246; also Edward Leo Lyman, "Isaac Trumbo and the Politics of Statehood," *Utah Historical Quarterly* 41 (Spring 1973): 128-49.

153. "SECRET BETRAYALS," *Salt Lake Tribune*, 19 May 1891, 4; "JUST A VULGAR TRADE," *Salt Lake Tribune*, 31 July 1891, 4; O. N. Malmquist, *The First 100 Years: A History of THE SALT LAKE TRIBUNE, 1871-1971* (Salt Lake City: Utah State Historical Society, 1971), 166, 235, for the newspaper's support of the Republican Party.

154. Abraham H. Cannon diary, 15 Oct. 1891.

155. Lyman, *Political Deliverance*, 2-3. Apostle John Henry Smith, a Republican, recorded during the Utah legislature's election of a U.S. senator in 1899 that Utah's non-Mormon Supreme Court chief justice, George W. Bartch, "wanted me to convert Democrats but I could not see how it could be done. He was quite confident as to the way it could be reached." See John Henry Smith diary, 26 Feb. 1899, in White, *Church, State, and Politics*, 420. In 1902 Idaho Democrats privately threatened the First Presidency that Idaho Mormons would be disenfranchised if the First Presidency did not insure a Democratic victory in counties with Mormon majorities. Anthon H. Lund diary, 30 Oct., 3 Nov. 1902.

156. George Q. Cannon diary excerpt, 25 Sept. 1894; James S. Clarkson to Wilford Woodruff, 14 Dec. 1895, 1-2, LDS archives; Lyman, *Political Deliverance*, 130-31, 169, 185-245; Edward Leo Lyman, "Statehood, Political Allegiance, and Utah's First U.S. Senate Seats: Prizes for the National Parties and Local Factions," *Utah Historical Quarterly* 63 (Fall 1995): 354.

157. White, "Utah State Elections," 130-31; Richard D. Poll, "The Political Reconstruction of Utah Territory, 1866-1890," *Pacific Historical Review* 27 (May 1958): 124-125; Leonard J. Arrington, "Objectives of Mormon Economic Policy," *Western Humanities Review* 10 (Spring 1956): 184; Thomas G. Alexander, *Mormonism in Transition* (Urbana: University of Illinois Press, 1986), 7-8.

158. Jo Ann Barnett Shipps, "The Mormons in Politics: The First Hundred Years," Ph.D. diss., University of Colorado, 1965, 215; also Alexander, *Mormonism in Transition*, 9-11.

159. "CHURCH AND CHURCH INFLUENCE," *Salt Lake Tribune,* 27 Oct. 1892, 4; "LET STATEHOOD COME," *Salt Lake Tribune,* 17 Nov. 1893, 4; "SHALL THE LIBERALS QUIT? Judge Powers Thinks It Is Time to Rest," *Salt Lake Tribune,* 11 Nov. 1893, 3; "PASSED. The House Almost Unanimous for Utah Statehood," *Salt Lake Tribune,* 14 Dec. 1893, [1]; "THE LIBERAL PARTY QUITS. By Formal Motion It Resolves to Dissolve," *Salt Lake Tribune,* 19 Dec. 1893, 8; Lyman, *Political Deliverance,* 2-3, 201-202, 213; also Howard R. Lamar, "Statehood for Utah: A Different Path," *Utah Historical Quarterly* 39 (Fall 1971): 350-69.

160. "THE CONVENTION," *Salt Lake Herald,* 5 Mar. 1895, 8; "CONSTITUTIONAL CONVENTION . . . Ivins Takes Them By Surprise," *Salt Lake Herald,* 7 Mar. 1895, [1]; Stanley S. Ivins, "A Constitution for Utah," *Utah Historical Quarterly* 25 (Apr. 1957): 100; Jean Bickmore White, "The Making of the Convention President: The Political Education of John Henry Smith," *Utah Historical Quarterly* 39 (Fall 1971): 350-69; Lamar, *Far Southwest,* 407; also Robert Reed Boren, "An Analysis of the Speaking in the Utah Constitutional Convention," Ph.D. diss., Purdue University, 1965.

161. "REPUBLICAN CONVENTION," *Salt Lake Herald,* 21 Dec. 1893, 2; Brigham Young, Jr., diary, 28 Sept. 1895, LDS archives; "AN OPEN LETTER. Hon. George Q. Cannon Defines His Position on the Senatorship," *Salt Lake Herald,* 14 Jan. 1896, 2; John Henry Smith diary, 17 Sept. 1896, 24 Mar., 6 Sept. 1898, 23 Feb. 1899, in White, *Church, State, and Politics,* 358, 393, 406, 419n6, 420; "APOSTLE LUND IS OUT: Would Decline Any Nomination For Congressman," *Salt Lake Herald,* 28 Feb. 1900, [8]; "LOCAL NEWS," *Journal* (Logan, UT), 14 Oct. 1909, 5; Robert H. Malan, *B. H. Roberts: A Biography* (Salt Lake City: Deseret Book Co., 1966), 83. D. Michael Quinn, *J. Reuben Clark: The Church Years* (Provo, UT: Brigham Young University Press, 1983), 61-67; *Deseret News 1995-1996 Church Almanac: The Church of Jesus Christ of Latter-day Saints* (Salt Lake City: Deseret News, 1994), 46, for Clark.

162. *Council and House Journals of the Thirtieth Session of the Legislative Assembly of the Territory of Utah, 1892* (Salt Lake City; Press of Irrigation Age, 1892), 405; *Senate Journal . . . of the Legislature of the State of Utah* (1896-1995); *House Journal . . . of the Legislature of the State of Utah* (1896-1995).

163. Lyman, *Political Deliverance,* 173.

164. *Salt Lake Herald,* 8 Nov. 1894, 3; "The Returns," *Salt Lake Herald,* 9 Nov. 1894, 7.

165. "CANDIDATES FOR POSITIONS," *Salt Lake Tribune,* 30 June 1895, 2; "RAWLINS, THATCHER AND ROBERTS. Three Invincible Candidates Nominated," *Salt Lake Herald,* 6 Sept. 1895, [1]; "THE VICTIMS. Utah Democracy's First State Convention. BIG THREE RUN THINGS," *Salt Lake Tribune,* 6 Sept. 1895, [1]; "A Venomous Attack," *Salt Lake Herald,* 8 Sept. 1895, 4; White, "Utah State Elections," 232; Clark, *Messages of the First Presidency,* 4:133; Stewart L. Grow, "Utah's Senatorial Election of 1899: The Election That Failed," *Utah Historical Quarterly* 39 (Winter 1971): 35-36.

166. Roberts, *Comprehensive History,* 6:363-68; Malan, *B. H. Roberts,* 68-77; R. Davis Bitton, "The B. H. Roberts Case of 1898-1900," *Utah Historical Quarterly* 25 (Jan. 1957): 27-46; Alan Elmo Haynes, "Brigham Henry Roberts and Reed Smoot: Significant Events in the Development of American Pluralism," M.A. thesis, Catholic University of America, 1966, iii-38; David Brudnoy, "Of Sinners and Saints: Theodore Schroeder, Brigham Roberts, and Reed Smoot," *Journal of Church and State* 14 (Spring 1972): 261-78; William Griffith White, Jr., "The Feminist Campaign For The Exclusion Of Brigham Henry Roberts From The Fifty-Sixth Congress," *Journal of the West* 17 (Jan. 1978): 45-52; Truman G. Madsen, *Defender of the Faith: The B.H. Roberts Story* (Salt Lake City: Bookcraft, 1980), 241-68; Alexander, *Mormonism in Transition,* 11; Gary James Bergera, ed., *The Autobiography of B. H. Roberts* (Salt Lake City: Signature Books, 1990), 212-19; Davis Bitton, "The Exclusion of

B. H. Roberts from Congress," in Bitton, *The Ritualization of Mormon History and Other Essays* (Urbana: University of Illinois Press, 1994), 150-70.

167. Jones, "Utah Politics, 1926-1932," 205-10; Heber J. Grant journal sheets, 3 Nov., 7 Nov. 1932; Heath, "Reed Smoot," 1030-31, 1031n21, also 1034, quoting Reed Smoot to John A. Widtsoe, 5 Dec. 1932; Van Wagoner and Walker, *Book of Mormons*, 318.

168. Records of Committee for Armenian and Syrian Relief, Utah State Archives, Salt Lake City; Frank W. Fox, *J. Reuben Clark: The Public Years* (Provo, UT: Brigham Young University Press, and Salt Lake City: Deseret Book Co., 1980), 590-96; Quinn, *J. Reuben Clark*, 57-60; Gene A. Sessions, *Prophesying Upon the Bones: J. Reuben Clark and the Foreign Debt Crisis, 1933-39* (Urbana: University of Illinois Press, 1992).

169. *Public Documents of the State of Utah*; Utah Secretary of State's Executive Record Books (1896-1949); Utah Secretary of State's Commission records (series 352); and records of the Committee for Armenian and Syrian Relief, the Council of Defense, all at Utah State Archives.

170. "Utah Child Health Session Begins In S.L. On Saturday: Governor Dern Scheduled For Opening Talk," *Deseret News*, 13 Mar. 1931, 1, 4; "4,000 Attend Opening Meet on Child Help," *Deseret News*, 7 Apr. 1931, 1; records of the Council for Child Health and Protection and the Utah Centennial Exposition Commission, Utah State Archives.

171. *Public Documents of the State of Utah;* Utah Secretary of State's Executive Record Books; Utah Secretary of State's Commission Records; also records of the Council of Defense, Commission for the Education of Aliens, Commission for the Mormon Battalion Monument, State Industrial School, all at Utah State Archives; Sylvester Q. Cannon diaries, LDS archives.

172. Joel Edward Ricks, *The Utah State Agricultural College: A History of Fifty Years, 1888-1938* (Salt Lake City: Deseret News Press, 1938), 162-63; Ralph V. Chamberlin, *The University of Utah: A History of Its First Hundred Years, 1850 to 1950* (Salt Lake City: University of Utah Press, 1960), 569-71; *University of Utah General Catalog* (Salt Lake City: University of Utah, 1951-96); "Those Who Have Served Utah State University's First Century: Board of Trustees from 1888-1969 and Institutional Council from 1969," in file titled "Membership Lists, Invitations, Proceedings of Final Reception, 1968," Board of Trustees Record Group, Archives, Merrill Library; Richard W. Sadler, ed., *Weber State College: A Centennial History* (Ogden, UT: Weber State University/Publishers Press, 1988), 122, 154n9; Jay L. Nelson, *The First Thirty Years: A History of Utah Technical College at Salt Lake, 1948-49-1977-78* (Salt Lake City: Utah Technical College at Salt Lake, 1982), 519; *Deseret News 1995-1996 Church Almanac*, for Ashton, Bennion, Cowley, Evans, Hales, Hanks, Hansen, Isaacson, Maxwell, Monson, Petersen, Richards, Sonne, and Vandenberg, and appendix, "Biographical Sketches," for the others listed.

173. Ezra Taft Benson, *Cross Fire: The Eight Years With Eisenhower* (Garden City, NY: Doubleday, 1962); Edward L. Schapsmeier and Frederick H. Schapsmeier, *Ezra Taft Benson and the Politics of Agriculture: The Eisenhower Years, 1953-1961* (Danville, IL: Interstate Printers and Publishers, 1975).

174. "Report On Education Stirs Utah Criticism: Objection To Delegates," *Deseret News*, 26 Nov. 1955, B-1; "Ike Appoints Church Official," *Deseret News*, 29 May 1958, B-1; "Is Our Youth Ready?" *Deseret News*, 25 Mar. 1960, A-22; *Deseret News 1995-1996 Church Almanac*, 56, 65, for Bennion and Hanks. The name of the youth committee has varied over the years.

175. L. John Nuttall diary, 19 Feb., 24 Feb. 1891; J. Cecil Alter, *Early Utah Journalism* (Salt Lake City: Utah State Historical Society, 1938), 154, 177, 305, 311, 339-40.

176. Abraham H. Cannon diary, 16 Mar. 1891; Franklin D. Richards diary, 16 Mar. 1891; Malmquist, *First 100 Years*, 146, 157; Monte Burr McLaws, *Spokesman for the Kingdom: Early Mormon Journalism and the DESERET NEWS, 1830-1898* (Provo, UT: Brigham Young University Press, 1977), 216-17; Lyman, *Political Deliverance*, 154-55.

177. Journal History, 29 Apr. 1900, 3-4, 27 July 1900, 1, 28 July 1900, 1.

178. "THE ENQUIRER: Published by The Enquirer Company," *Provo Daily Enquirer,* 5 May 1903, [3].

179. Minutes of meeting, 29 Dec. 1899, 202-204, in Joseph F. Smith papers, LDS archives; Anthon H. Lund diary, 29 Dec. 1899; Reed Smoot diary, 8 Oct. 1915; Merrill, *Reed Smoot,* 139-41.

180. Anthon H. Lund diary, 2 Feb. 1909; Reed Smoot diary, 2 Oct. 1911, 22 Oct. 1922; Alter, *Early Utah Journalism,* 312-15, 337-38; Merrill, *Reed Smoot,* 190; Thompson, "Utah's Struggle For Prohibition," 6; Alexander, *Mormonism in Transition,* 263.

181. Abraham H. Cannon diary, 12-13 Jan. 1892; Franklin D. Richards diary, 12-13 Jan. 1892; and the less revealing entries in John Henry Smith diary, 12-13 Jan. 1892, in White, *Church, State, and Politics,* 267-68.

182. Anthon H. Lund diary, 2 Oct. 1892; Peterson, *Take Up Your Mission,* 240.

183. Reed Smoot diary, 29 Sept. 1910; Merrill, *Reed Smoot,* 190-93; Thompson, "Utah's Struggle For Prohibition," 24, 26-28, 34, and Thompson, "'Standing between Two Fires,'" 36-42, described Grant's zeal during this time.

184. Reed Smoot diary, 29 July 1920; Merrill, *Reed Smoot,* 257-62; James B. Allen, "Personal Faith and Public Policy: Some Timely Observations on the League of Nations Controversy in Utah," *Brigham Young University Studies* 14 (Autumn 1973): 80, 91-96.

185. Franklin D. Richards diary, 29 June 1891; Abraham H. Cannon diary, 29 June 1891; Marriner W. Merrill diary, 29 June 1891, LDS archives.

186. Described in John Henry Smith to Joseph Smith III, 14 Jan. 1892, in John Henry Smith 1884-94 letterbook, 785; also Charles S. Zane diary, 12 May 1891.

187. Joseph F. Smith, *Another Plain Talk: Reasons Why the People of Utah Should be Republicans* (Salt Lake City: Republican Central Committee, 1892); Anthon H. Lund diary, 11 Sept. 1892.

188. White, "Utah State Elections," 29-32; Lamar, *Far Southwest,* 411.

189. Sessions, *Mormon Democrat,* 180-92.

190. Nephi L. Morris to Francis M. Lyman, 28 Mar. 1914, 1, 7, typed copy in Morris papers, Marriott Library.

191. Reed Smoot diary, 17 Feb. 1916; Alexander, *Mormonism in Transition,* 43.

192. Abraham H. Cannon diary, 9 Feb. 1892; Hinckley, *James Henry Moyle,* 219.

193. Abraham H. Cannon diary, 16 Mar. 1892; "Church Influence at Logan," *Salt Lake Herald,* 16 Mar. 1892, 4; Heber J. Grant letterbook-journal, 3-28 Mar. 1892.

194. Roberts, *Comprehensive History,* 6:308-309; Clark, *Messages of the First Presidency,* 3:232-33.

195. Anthon H. Lund diary, 9 Nov. 1900.

196. Francis M. Lyman diary, 5 Apr. 1909, quoted in Thompson, "Utah's Struggle For Prohibition," 33.

197. Joseph F. Smith, "The Presidential Election," *Improvement Era* 15 (Oct. 1912): 1120-21; C. Austin Wahlquist, "The 1912 Presidential Election in Utah," M.A. thesis, Brigham Young University, 1962, 76-79; Donald Bruce Gilchrist, "An Examination of the Problem of L.D.S. Church Influence in Utah Politics, 1890-1916," M.S. thesis, University of Utah, 1965, 90; Alexander, *Mormonism in Transition,* 39-41; Michael Nelson, ed., *Congressional Quarterly's Guide to the Presidency* (Washington, D.C.: Congressional Quarterly, 1989), 1417.

198. Kenneth G. Stauffer, "Utah Politics, 1912-1918," M.S. thesis, University of Utah, 1972, viii; also Darwin Kay Craner, "The Influence of the L.D.S. Church in Utah Politics, 1902-1916," M.S. thesis, University of Utah, 1969.

199. Brad E. Hainsworth, "Utah State Elections, 1916-1924," Ph.D. diss., University of Utah, 1968, 230-32.

200. Alexander, *Mormonism in Transition,* 51, with Grant's 1922 endorsement on 56.

201. Jones, "Utah Politics, 1926-1932," 205-10.

202. Clark, *Messages of the First Presidency,* 3:275-76.

203. White, "Utah State Elections," 133-142; Roberts, *Comprehensive History,* 6:332-35; Alexander, *Mormonism in Transition,* 9-10.

204. Journal History, 29 Sept. 1896, 2. For the original intent, see statement of Wilford Woodruff in Journal History, 9 July 1896, 2.

205. Abraham H. Cannon diary, 9 Feb. 1892.

206. Kenney, *Wilford Woodruff's Journal,* 9 (4 Oct. 1892): 221.

207. Marriner W. Merrill diary, 23 Mar., 3 Apr., 5 Apr. 1893, in Melvin Clarence Merrill, ed., *Utah Pioneer and Apostle: Marriner Wood Merrill and His Family* (Salt Lake City: By the author, 1937), 162, 163; Gilchrist, "Problem of L.D.S. Church Influence," 35-37; Lyman, *Political Deliverance,* 208; Alexander, *Mormonism in Transition,* 8; D. Craig Mikkelsen, "The Politics of B. H. Roberts," *Dialogue: A Journal of Mormon Thought* 9 (1972), 2:27-28.

208. Seymour B. Young diary, 27 Sept. 1895, LDS archives.

209. Gilchrist, "Problem of L.D.S. Church Influence," 37-42; John M. Whitaker edited journal, 1:321-322; White, "Utah State Elections," 42-51, 78-95; Lyman, *Political Deliverance,* 269-72.

210. Abraham H. Cannon diary, 14 Nov. 1895.

211. Marriner W. Merrill, 5 Mar., 19 Mar., 26 Mar. 1896, in Merrill, *Utah Pioneer and Apostle,* 198; Heber J. Grant journal sheets, 5 Mar., 12-13 Mar., 26 Mar. 1896; Brigham Young, Jr., diary, 13 Feb., 5-6 Mar., 14 Mar., 19 Mar., 26 Mar. 1896; Madsen, *Defender of the Faith,* 223-27; Van Wagoner and Walker, *Book of Mormons,* 243-44; Alexander, *Mormonism in Transition,* 9-10; Mikkelsen, "Politics of B. H. Roberts," 32-34; James B. Allen and Glen M. Leonard, *Story of the Latter-day Saints,* 2d ed. rev. (Salt Lake City: Deseret Book Co., 1992), 424.

212. Francis M. Gibbons, *Heber J. Grant: Man of Steel, Prophet of God* (Salt Lake City: Deseret Book Co., 1979), 103.

213. Journal History, 6 Apr. 1896, 2-5. The best study of this is E. Leo Lyman, "The Alienation of an Apostle from His Quorum: The Moses Thatcher Case," *Dialogue: A Journal of Mormon Thought* 18 (Summer 1985): 67-91; also Madsen, *Defender of the Faith,* 227-29.

214. White, "Utah State Elections," 134; Lyman, "The Alienation of an Apostle from His Quorum"; Van Wagoner and Walker, *Book of Mormons,* 368-70.

215. John Henry Smith diary, 4 May, 25 June, 16 July 1896, in White, *Church, State, and Politics,* 350, 352, 354; Journal History, 17 Sept. 1896, 2; Lyman, "The Alienation of an Apostle from His Quorum."

216. Journal History, 15 Oct. 1896, 2; John Henry Smith diary, 15 Oct. 1896, in White, *Church, State, and Politics,* 360.

217. Brigham Young, Jr., diary, 1 Nov. 1895, 7-8 Jan., 23 Jan., 5 Apr., 13 Apr., 29 Apr., 9 July, 25 July, 17 Sept., 15 Oct., 19 Nov. 1896; Kenney, *Wilford Woodruff's Journal,* 9 (17 Sept., 15 Oct., 22 Oct., 12 Nov. 1896): 425, 429, 431, 434; John Henry Smith diary, 4 May, 28 May, 25 June, 9 July, 16 July, 26 July, 17 Sept., 14-15 Oct. 1896, in White, *Church, State, and Politics,* 350-54, 357, 360; Heber J. Grant journal sheets, 28 May, 8-9 July 1896; Anthon H. Lund diary, 19 Nov. 1896; Marriner W. Merrill diary, 12 Nov. 1896, in Merrill, *Utah Pioneer and Apostle,* 209; Calvin Reasoner, *Church and State: The Issue of Civil and Religious Liberty in Utah* (Salt Lake City: N.p., 15 Dec. 1896); Stanley S. Ivins, *The Moses Thatcher Case* (Salt Lake City: Modern Microfilm Co., n.d.); Lyman, "The Alienation of an Apostle from His Quorum"; Benjamin Urrutia, "Moses Thatcher," in Powell, *Utah History Encyclopedia,* 550-51. Reasoner was polemically pro-Thatcher. As discussed previously, Snow and Young were Democrats in 1896 but publicly affiliated with the Republican Party in 1900. *Deseret News 1995-1996 Church Almanac,* 53, dates Thatcher's removal from the Quorum of Twelve as 6 April 1896, when his name was not presented with the rest of the apostles. However, the *Almanac* (52) acknowledges Lyman Wight as a member of the Twelve

until his excommunication in 1848, even though the Twelve had declined to ask Mormons to sustain Wight as an apostle at general conferences since 1845. See Quinn, *Mormon Hierarchy: Origins of Power,* 200-201.

218. See previous note 138 and appendix, "Biographical Sketches."

219. Ben [E. Rich] to John Henry Smith, 4 Oct., 12 Oct. 1902, fd 20, box 9, George A. Smith Family papers.

220. Anthon H. Lund diary, 5 July 1916. In addition, Smith and Smoot in a private meeting with Utah governor William Spry in 1916 tried to persuade him against seeking reelection. They were unsuccessful and Spry was defeated. Reed Smoot diary, 16 June 1916; William L. Roper and Leonard J. Arrington, *William Spry: Man of Firmness, Governor of Utah* (Salt Lake City: University of Utah Press, 1971), 199-205.

221. "APPEAL TO THE VOTERS OF IDAHO: Chairman H. W. Lockhart of Democratic Central Committee Issues Letter," *Salt Lake Herald,* 1 Sept. 1906, 5.

222. George Q. Cannon diary excerpt, 25 Sept. 1894; C. H. Hoebeke, *The Road to Mass Democracy: Original Intent and the Seventeenth Amendment* (New Brunswick, NJ: Transaction Publishers, 1995).

223. John Henry Smith diary, 26 Nov. 1896, in White, *Church, State, and Politics,* 362; compare John Henry Smith diary, 20 Oct. 1896 (ibid., 360); Abraham H. Cannon diary, 20 Nov., 26 Dec. 1895.

224. Franklin D. Richards diary, 24 Oct. 1896; Journal History, 26 Nov. 1896, 5; John Henry Smith diary, 27 Jan. 1897, in White, *Church, State, and Politics,* 366; Kenney, *Wilford Woodruff's Journal,* 9 (20 Jan. 1897): 444; Whitney, *History of Utah,* 4: 679-80; White, "Utah State Elections," 160-72; Joan Ray Harrow, "Joseph L. Rawlins: Father of Utah Statehood," M.A. thesis, University of Utah, 1973, 116-25; also Harrow's article by same title in *Utah Historical Quarterly* 44 (Winter 1976): 64-72.

225. Brigham Young, Jr., diary, 24 Feb. 1899.

226. Grow, "Utah's Senatorial Election of 1899," 30-39; White, "Utah State Elections," 218-34; Cannon and O'Higgins, *Under the Prophet in Utah,* 220-34.

227. Abraham Owen Woodruff diary, 9 Mar. 1899.

228. Anthon H. Lund diary, 3 Jan. 1901; Alexander, *Mormonism in Transition,* 17.

229. Abraham Owen Woodruff diary, 17 Jan., 20-23 Jan. 1901; also Miriam B. Murphy, "Thomas Kearns," in Powell, *Utah History Encyclopedia,* 299.

230. Nephi L. Morris to Francis M. Lyman, 20 Mar. 1914.

231. Carl A. Badger diary, 6 Jan. 1905, LDS archives; also summary in Alexander, *Mormonism in Transition,* 17; Kent Sheldon Larsen, "The Life of Thomas Kearns," M.A. thesis, University of Utah, 1964, 58, claimed that bribery "at this late date, would be impossible to verify." Larsen dismissed allegations in the *Salt Lake Herald* because "neither the *Herald* nor the *Tribune* had ever been very friendly to the Mormons," despite the fact that the *Herald* was the church's political newspaper until 1891 and was governed by Mormon apostles and church leaders until the mid-1890s.

232. Journal History, 28 Apr. 1896, 2.

233. Abraham H. Cannon diary, 25 Jan. 1894.

234. "LET THE PEOPLE SPEAK," *Salt Lake Tribune,* 12 Apr. 1896, 5; "WELLS SAYS IT'S FALSE: The Governor Replies to Mr. Critchlow. NOT INFLUENCED BY CHURChap. Had no Knowledge of a Committee Alleged to Have been Appointed to Supervise Legislation," *Salt Lake Tribune,* 13 Apr. 1896, [1]; "CHURCH DIDN'T DICTATE: First Presidency Denies the Junta Story. NO COMMITTEE APPOINTED," *Salt Lake Tribune,* 14 Apr. 1896, [1]; "About That 'Committee': Direct Statement From the First Presidency of the Church," *Salt Lake Herald,* 14 Apr. 1896, [1]; White, "Utah State Elections," 143; Journal History, 12 Apr. 1896, 2-3, 13 Apr. 1896, 2, 14 Apr. 1896, 2-4.

235. Ronald Walker, "Response to [Edward Leo] Lyman's Paper, *Mormon History Association Newsletter* 102 (Summer 1996): 5.

236. Anthon H. Lund diary, 30-31 Jan., 26 Feb., 15 Mar. 1901; John Henry Smith diary, 4 Feb., 7 Feb., 14-15 Mar. 1901, in White, *Church, State, and Politics,* 474-75, 478-79; Abraham Owen Woodruff diary, 19 Feb., 26 Feb., 9 Mar. 1901; Rudger Clawson diary, 26 Feb., 28 Feb. 1901, Marriott Library; "Abel John Evans Favors Polygamous Cohabitation," *Salt Lake Herald,* 13 Feb. 1901, [1]; Hardy, *Solemn Covenant,* 245.

237. Francis M. Lyman diary, 3 Jan., 19 Jan., 16 Mar. 1909, in Thompson, "Utah's Struggle For Prohibition," 14, 18, 29.

238. Anthon H. Lund diary, 5 Mar. 1915; Thompson, "Utah's Struggle For Prohibition," 67; Thompson, "'Between Two Fires,'" 46-47. See also Bruce T. Dyer, "A Study of the Forces Leading to the Adoption of Prohibition in Utah in 1917," M.S. thesis, Brigham Young University, 1958, 88-107; Gilchrist, "Problem of L.D.S. Church Influence," 128-35; Shipps, "Utah Comes of Age Politically," 109-10; Roper and Arrington, *William Spry,* 82-85.

239. John Henry Smith diary, 14-15 Mar. 1901, in White, *Church, State, and Politics,* 478-79; Anthon H. Lund diary, 15 Mar. 1901, 29 June 1904.

240. Reed Smoot diary, 18 Feb. 1913, 29 July 1920; Alexander, *Mormonism in Transition,* 52-53; Merrill, *Reed Smoot,* 251-66; also Allen, "Personal Faith and Public Policy," 77-98; Van Wagoner and Walker, *Book of Mormons,* 317-18. The League of Nations controversy was one of those national issues in which the First Presidency and Quorum of the Twelve limited their views to sermons. However, the evidence in this case does not support Armand L. Mauss, *The Angel and the Beehive: The Mormon Struggle with Assimilation* (Urbana: University of Illinois Press, 1994), 111, "No matter how crucial the issue, or how 'official' the church's initiative, the 'involvement' cannot be considered very serious if it is limited to sermons or passing comments." The Mauss assertion would also not apply to President Heber J. Grant's earnest plea through sermons only for Utah's Mormons to vote against repealing Prohibition in 1933.

241. Heber J. Grant journal, 29 Dec. 1898.

242. Anthon H. Lund diary, 27 Jan. 1909.

243. Reed Smoot diary, 28 Sept., 4-5 Oct., 8 Oct., 6 Nov. 1912, 24 Oct., 27 Oct. 1922.

244. Allen, "Personal Faith and Public Policy"; Merrill, *Reed Smoot,* 251-66; Alexander, *Mormonism in Transition,* 52-53.

245. Reed Smoot diary, 14 Aug. 1910.

246. Reed Smoot diary, 1-2 Nov., 7 Nov. 1922; Alexander, *Mormonism in Transition,* 54-56.

247. Reed Smoot diary, 27-28 Sept. 1928.

248. Alexander, *Mormonism in Transition,* 58.

249. Joseph F. Merrill diary, 22 June 1933, Lee Library; Joseph Lynn Lyon, "Word of Wisdom," in Ludlow, *Encyclopedia of Mormonism,* 4:1584-85.

250. Mauss, *Angel and the Beehive,* 110; also Robert Gottlieb and Peter Wiley, *America's Saints: The Rise of Mormon Power* (New York: G. P. Putnam's Sons, 1984), 66.

251. Heber J. Grant to Morton J. Thieband, 21 Nov. 1936, LDS archives; also Loman Franklin Aydelotte, "The Political Thought and Activity of Heber J. Grant," M.A. thesis, Brigham Young University, 1965, 68-76.

252. James B. Allen, "Joseph F. Merrill," in Kenneth W. Godfrey and Audrey M. Godfrey, eds., "Cache Valley's General Authorities: Twelve Biographical Essays," typescript, 90, Merrill Library.

253. George Harmon Skyles, "A Study of Forces and Events Leading to the Repeal of Prohibition and the Adoption of a Liquor Control System in Utah," M.A. thesis, Brigham Young University, 1962, 70-72, 77, 114; John Kearnes, "Utah, Sexton of Prohibition," *Utah Historical Quarterly* 47 (Winter 1979): 4-21; also Larry Earl Nelson, "Problems of Prohibition Enforcement in Utah, 1917-1933," M.S. thesis, University of Utah, 1970; John Kearnes, "Utah Electoral Politics, 1932-1938," Ph.D. diss., University of Utah, 1972, 89-116; Helen Z. Papanikolas, "Bootlegging in Zion: Making and Selling the 'Good Stuff,'" *Utah Historical*

Quarterly 53 (Summer 1985): 268-91; John D. Wrathall, "Morality and Criminality in Utah County: The Dry Years, 1917-1933," *Thetean: A Student Journal of History* (Provo, UT: Beta Iota Chapter of Phi Alpha Theta, Brigham Young University, 1986): 59-74; *Church History In the Fulness of Times*, rev. ed. (Salt Lake City: The Church of Jesus Christ of Latter-day Saints, 1993), 498-99.

254. Kearnes, "Utah Electoral Politics," 197-200; Wayne Kendall Hinton, "The New Deal Years in Utah: A Political History of Utah, 1932-1940," M.S. thesis, Utah State University, 1963, 183-89; Frank H. Jonas and Garth N. Jones, "Utah Presidential Elections, 1896-1952," *Utah Historical Quarterly* 24 (Oct. 1956): 304-305; Quinn, *J. Reuben Clark*, 74-75, 86-87; Frank H. Jonas, "Utah: The Different State," in Jonas, ed., *Politics In the American West* (Salt Lake City: University of Utah Press, 1969), 332.

255. Charles C. Richards, *A Brief Sketch of the Organization and Growth of the Democratic Party in the Territory of Utah, 1847-1896* (N.p.: Sage Brush Democratic Club, 1942), 31-32, which list included the following LDS general authorities [those appointed after 1896 are noted here by *] among the one hundred names: John R. Winder, *Charles W. Penrose, *Anthony W. Ivins, Moses Thatcher, *Orson F. Whitney, *Charles A. Callis, Brigham H. Roberts, *Charles H. Hart, Rulon S. Wells, William B. Preston, *Orrin P. Miller, Theodore B. Lewis (appointed temporarily in 1882); "The Herald Publishing Co.," *Salt Lake Herald*, 1 May 1896, 4, last issue in which Grant was listed as vice-president.

256. Heber J. Grant letterbook-journal, 19 July 1889; Thomas A. Clawson diary, 22 Nov. 1918, Utah State Historical Society; also Ronald W. Walker, "Heber J. Grant," in Leonard J. Arrington, ed., *The Presidents of the Church: Biographical Essays* (Salt Lake City: Deseret Book Co., 1986), 242-43.

257. J. Reuben Clark statement to General Welfare Committee, 10 Apr. 1938, Clark papers, Lee Library; Quinn, *J. Reuben Clark*, 76-77.

258. Heber J. Grant, J. Reuben Clark, and David O. McKay to Senator Elbert D. Thomas, Senator Abe Murdock, Congressman J. W. Robinson, and Congressman Walter K. Granger, 17 Dec. 1941, "Dear Brethren," in unnumbered fd, "Personal File—1941: Corr, LDS," box 30, Elbert D. Thomas papers, Utah State Historical Society.

259. Mark E. Petersen to J. Reuben Clark, 2 Feb. 1945; J. Reuben Clark office diary, 4 Feb. 1945; J. Reuben Clark manuscript draft, 5 Feb. 1945, of First Presidency statement against peace-time conscription; Mark E. Petersen to J. Reuben Clark, 6 Feb. 1945, all in Clark papers. For Clark's pacifism at this time, see "AMERICAN PEACE SOCIETY (Founded 1828)... Directors," *World Affairs: Published Quarterly By the American Peace Society* 108 (June 1945): [144]; Quinn, *J. Reuben Clark*, 208; *Deseret News 1995-1996 Church Almanac*, 55, for Petersen.

260. Harold B. Lee diary, 7 June 1945, LDS archives; J. Reuben Clark to Tucker Smith of the American Friends Service Committee, 15 June 1945, Clark papers; George Albert Smith, J. Reuben Clark, and David O. McKay to Senator Elbert D. Thomas, 14 Dec. 1945, Thomas papers.

261. "CHURCH OPPOSES MILITARY BILL: Letter Sent Utah Solons December 14," *Deseret News*, 3 Jan. 1946, 1, 5; Clark, *Messages of the First Presidency*, 6:239-42; J. Reuben Clark to U.S. Senator Arthur Vandenberg, 31 Dec. 1947, Clark papers; *April 1948 Conference Report*... (Salt Lake City: Church of Jesus Christ of Latter-day Saints, 1948), 174-75; Quinn, *J. Reuben Clark*, 214; J. D. Williams, "The Separation of Church and State in Mormon Theory and Practice," *Dialogue: A Journal of Mormon Thought* 1 (Summer 1966): 47, reprinted in *Journal of Church and State* 9 (Spring 1976); Q. Michael Croft, "Influence of the L.D.S. Church on Utah Politics, 1945-1985," Ph.D. diss., University of Utah, 1985, 88.

262. For the reasoned views on both sides of the issue at this time, see Robert J. Havighurst, "Against Compulsory Military Training in Peacetime," *School Review: A Journal of Secondary Education* 53 (Feb. 1945): 63-67; Frank L. Wright, "The Case Against Conscription," *Christian Century* 62 (7 Mar. 1945): 299-300; Charles G. Bolte, "Conscription Between

Wars," *Nation* 160 (24 Mar. 1945): 330-32; Felix Morley, President of Haverford College, "The Real Case Against Conscription," *Saturday Evening Post* 217 (24 Mar. 1945): 17, 82-84; William F. Tompkins, "Future Manpower Needs of the Armed Forces," *Annals of the American Academy of Political and Social Sciences* 238 (Mar. 1945): 56-62; Hansen W. Baldwin, "Conscription for Peacetime?" *Harper's Magazine* 190 (Mar. 1945): 289-300; Bernard De Voto, "The Easy Chair," *Harper's Magazine* 190 (Apr. 1945): 410-13; E. J. Kahn, Jr., "A Soldier's Slant On Compulsory Training," *Saturday Evening Post* 217 (19 May 1945): 27, 94; "Do We Want Permanent Conscription?: John J. McCloy, Assistant Secretary of War, 'Yes,' and Robert M. Hutchins, University of Chicago president, 'No,'" *Collier's* 115 (9 June 1945): 14-15; Arthur Kornhauser, "The American Magazine Poll of Experts: Will Compulsory Military Training Be Good or Bad For Our Boys?" *American Magazine* 139 (June 1945): 34-35, 92-95; U.S. senator Robert A. Taft, "Compulsory Military Training In Peace Time," and Ralph A. Bard, Under Secretary of the Navy, "Universal Military Training," *Vital Speeches of the Day* 11 (1 July 1945): 554-57, 559-61; "The Case Against Compulsory Military Service," *Parent's Magazine* 20 (July 1945): 17, 90-91; *Compulsory Peacetime Military Training: Can the United States Avoid It?: A Radio Discussion by Robert Havinghurst, Arthur Rubin and Elbert Thomas* (Chicago: University of Chicago Roundtable/National Broadcasting Co., 16 Sept. 1945); *Now Is the Time To Adopt Universal Military Training* (Indianapolis: Defense Division, American Legion, 1945); Stuart O. Landry, *Shall We Train Our Boys To Worship the God of War?* (New Orleans: Pelican Publishing Co., 1946); Francis L. Bacon et al., *An Analysis of the Report of the President's Advisory Commission on Universal Training* (Washington, D.C.: National Council Against Conscription, 1947); *Resolutions Against Universal Military Training, 1945-1947* (Washington, D.C.: Friends Committee on National Legislation, 1947).

263. Frank H. Jonas, "The Mormon Church and Political Dynamiting In the 1950 Election In Utah," *Proceedings of the Utah Academy of Sciences, Arts, and Letters* 40, Pt. 1 (1963): 98, 107, for chairman Elmer Thomas's reports to Kimball, 108-109, for the list of approved candidates, 110, for the recommended text of the sermon; *Polk's Salt Lake City (Salt Lake County, Utah) Directory, 1949* (Salt Lake City: R. L. Polk & Co., 1949), 1031, for Elmer G. Thomas; *Deseret News 1995-1996 Church Almanac,* 44, for Kimball.

264. "LDS Church Heads Disavow Letter 'Selecting' Candidates," *Salt Lake Tribune,* 2 Nov. 1950, 19; "LDS Officials Deny Link To Election Literature," *Salt Lake Telegram,* 2 Nov. 1950, 21; "Church Denies Political Letter," *Deseret News,* 3 Nov. 1950, B-1; Jonas, "The Mormon Church and Political Dynamiting In the 1950 Election In Utah," 102, for Petersen's role; Beverly B. Clopton, *Her Honor, the Judge: The Story of Reva Beck Bosone* (Ames: Iowa State University Press, 1980), 182-83, described the situation without naming Petersen.

265. Henry D. Moyle diary, 3 Oct. 1950, LDS archives; 19 Jan. 1951 for attorneys Melville and Bird; 23 Feb. 1951 for meeting with LeRoy D. White (D, Rep, Box Elder Co.), Lawrence B. Johnson (R, Rep, Rich Co.), Welby W. Young (R, Rep, Wasatch Co.), J. R. Bagnall (R, Rep, Sanpete Co.), R. Clair Anderson (R, Rep, Sanpete Co.), Archie O. Gardner (R, Rep, Millard Co.), and William W. Brotherson (R, Rep, Duchesne Co.); 24 Feb. 1951 for meeting with Elias L. Day (R, Senator, Salt Lake Co.) and with J. Francis Fowles (D, Senator, Weber Co.), Lorenzo Elggren (D, Senator, Salt Lake Co.), Edward H. Watson (D, Senator, Salt Lake Co.), Luke Clegg (R, Senator, Utah Co.), Grant S. Thorn (R, Senator, Utah Co.), A I Tippetts (D, Senator, Sanpete Co.), Fred J. Milliman (D, Senator, Juab Co.), James E. Burns (D, Senator, Davis Co.), Jaren L. Jones (R, Rep, Salt Lake Co.), Lee W. Dalebout (R, Rep, Salt Lake Co.); 1 Mar. 1951 for meeting with Luke Clegg (R, Senator, Utah Co.) and telephone lobbying with Marl C. Gibson (D, Senator, Carbon Co.), Harold Reese (D, Senator, Box Elder Co.), W.N. Brotherson (R, Rep, Duchesne Co.), Grant Thorne (R, Senator, Utah Co.); 2 Mar. 1951 for telephone lobbying with Alonzo F. "Lou" Hopkins (D, Senator, Morgan Co.) and Elias L. Day (R, Senator, Salt Lake Co.); Wayne Stout, *History of Utah,* 3 vols. (Salt Lake City: By the author, 1960-71), 3:486-89, for political affiliations

of the legislators; *Polk's Salt Lake City (Salt Lake County, Utah) Directory, 1951* (Salt Lake City: R. L. Polk & Co., 1951), 1667-68, for attorneys Richard L. Bird, Jr., and Alton C. Melville; *Deseret News 1995-1996 Church Almanac,* 43, 46, 55, for Lee, Moyle, Bowen, and Matthew Cowley.

266. "Pres. McKay Hails Ike As Good Omen," *Deseret News,* 22 Jan. 1953, A-1; Francis M. Gibbons, *David O. McKay: Apostle to the World, Prophet of God* (Salt Lake City: Deseret Book Co., 1986), 316; "Utahns Join Inaugural Festive Fare," *Deseret News,* 20 Jan. 1953, A-4; *Deseret News 1995-1996 Church Almanac,* 76, for Wirthlin.

267. Henry D. Moyle statement quoted in an interview, 4 Apr. 1956, in Kenneth Holmes Mitchell, "The Struggle for Reapportionment in Utah," M.A. thesis, University of Utah, 1960, 96-97.

268. Quinn, *J. Reuben Clark,* 193; Mitchell, "The Struggle for Reapportionment in Utah," 97-102; J. Reuben Clark office diary, 2 Mar. 1953, 2 Dec. 1954, Clark papers; Henry D. Moyle diary, 29 Jan., 6 Mar., 10 Mar., 12 Mar. 1953; David O. McKay office diary, 12 Mar. 1953, LDS archives.

269. J. Reuben Clark office diary, 2 Mar. 1953, also 2 Dec. 1954.

270. Mitchell, "The Struggle for Reapportionment in Utah," 113-14, 118-19; Frank H. Jonas, "Reapportionment in Utah and the Mormon Church," *Proceedings of the Utah Academy of Sciences, Arts, and Letters* 46, Pt. 1 (1969): 19-20; Croft, "Influence of the L.D.S. Church on Utah Politics," 90, 222-23.

271. Mitchell, "The Struggle for Reapportionment in Utah," 118-19; Jonas, "Reapportionment in Utah and the Mormon Church," 21-25.

272. Henry D. Moyle diary, 29 Jan. 1953.

273. Ibid., 12 Mar. 1953.

274. David O. McKay office diary, 12 Mar. 1953.

275. Croft, "Influence of the L.D.S. Church on Utah Politics," 8.

276. Henry D. Moyle diary, 2 Mar. 1951, 31 Jan. 1953; Dennis L. Lythgoe, *Let 'Em Holler: A Political Biography of J. Bracken Lee* (Salt Lake City: Utah State Historical Society, 1982), 98.

277. J. Reuben Clark office diary, 30 Jan. 1953; Lythgoe, *Let 'Em Holler,* 99.

278. Ross Patterson Poore, Jr., "Church-School Entanglement In Utah: Lanner v. Wimmer," Ed.D. diss., University of Utah, 1983, 158, 164-227; Frederick S. Buchanan, *Culture Clash and Accommodation: Public Schooling In Salt Lake City, 1890-1994* (San Francisco: Smith Research Associates/Signature Books, 1996), 135, 150-7, 186-87; Linda Sillitoe, *Friendly Fire: The ACLU in Utah* (Salt Lake City: Signature Books, 1996), 52-54; also Arthur A. Bailey, "An Analysis of the Problems in Obtaining and Maintaining Released Time For Seminary in the Central Idaho Seminary District," M.R.E. thesis, Brigham Young University, 1975; William E. Berrett, *A Miracle In Weekday Religious Education: A History of the Church Educational System, Being an Account of Weekday Religious Education of The Church of Jesus Christ of Latter-day Saints and Especially of the Seminaries and Institutes of Religion* (Salt Lake City: Salt Lake Printing Center, 1988); John Lessing Fowles, "A Study Concerning the Week-day Religious Educational Program of the Church of Jesus Christ of Latter-day Saints From 1890-1990: A Response To Secular Education," Ph.D. diss., University of Missouri, 1990.

279. F. Ross Peterson, "Utah Politics Since 1945," in Poll, *Utah's History,* 516; chap. 3 and *Deseret News 1995-1996 Church Almanac,* 44, 46, for Benson and Brown.

280. Edward L. Kimball and Andrew E. Kimball, Jr., *Spencer W. Kimball: Twelfth President of The Church of Jesus Christ of Latter-day Saints* (Salt Lake City: Bookcraft, 1977), 387; James B. Allen, "David O. McKay," in Arrington, *Presidents of the Church,* 302; also the emphasis of Gibbons, *David O. McKay,* 136, on McKay's physical appearance and his "charisma, that intangible something that arouses popular loyalty and enthusiasm and sets the one who possesses it apart from others."

281. Gary Huxford (b. 1931), "The Changing Image of Prophet," *Sunstone* 5 (July-Aug. 1980): 38-39, described this "shift" according to his personal observations. He noted that there were occasions at general conferences when pre-McKay presidents were called "the Prophet." However, they were exceptions. The Huxford Hypothesis, as I call it, is consistent with casual observations I have heard over the years by Samuel W. Taylor, George S. Tanner, Richard D. Poll, and numerous others. This shift in usage of the term "prophet" is also indicated by a computerized content analysis of the "prophet" references in the *Journal of Discourses* (1854-86) and *Conference Reports* (1950-70). This was done as a preliminary study in 1995 by Warren C. Jaycox, a history major at Utah State University, and described in Jaycox to Quinn, 1995.

282. *Deseret News "Church News,"* 5 Feb. 1955, cover photo, also 8, 9. I verified the lack of such references previously by reading every issue of the *Church News* from 1931 on.

283. Gibbons, *David O. McKay*, 347, 263.

284. "President Clark's Lecture: When Are Church Leader's Words Entitled to Claim of Scripture?" *Deseret News "Church News,"* 31 July 1954, 11; J. Reuben Clark to Clare Middlemiss, 1 Sept. 1958, Clark papers; Quinn, *J. Reuben Clark*, 168, 172.

285. Photo caption in *Deseret News "Church News,"* 8 Apr. 1961, 3.

286. Gibbons, *David O. McKay*, 375; Nelson, *Congressional Quarterly's Guide to the Presidency*, 1423; Jonas, "Utah: The Different State," 335.

287. Dean E. Mann, "Mormon Attitudes Toward the Political Roles of Church Leaders," *Dialogue: A Journal of Mormon Thought* 2 (Summer 1967): 33-35.

288. To avoid the ecological fallacy in statistics, I have not attempted even a conservative estimate of the total Democratic vote of Mormons from counties with less than 90 percent LDS population. Thus, for example, the 14.6 percent of total non-LDS population in Salt Lake County could not have produced the 45.5 percent of the county's adults who voted Democratic in the 1960 presidential election. Beyond that, however, it is impossible to say with certainty what percentage of Mormons or non-Mormons voted Democratic, even in a county with 85 percent LDS population. Thus the text discussion only concludes that it is reasonable to expect that Mormons cast at least 2,000 of the 122,000 Democratic votes in those counties where Mormons constituted 80-89 percent of the population. However, as LDS population approaches 100 percent in a county, so also does the confidence that the voting percentages also measure the Mormon vote.

Churches and Church Membership in the United States (New York City: National Council of the Churches of Christ in the United States of America, 1956-57), Series C, Tables 117, 119, 124, and Richard M. Scammon, ed., *America At the Polls: A Handbook of American Presidential Election Statistics, 1920-1964* (Pittsburgh: University of Pittsburgh Press, 1965), 122, 291, 462, show the following percentages of LDS members and Democratic votes in the 1960 election:

IDAHO: Bonneville County (81.0 percent LDS; 8,845 Democratic votes), Caribou County (98.4 percent LDS; 1,293 Democratic votes), Cassia County (84.8 percent LDS; 2,445 Democratic votes), Franklin County (100 percent LDS; 1,352 Democratic votes), Fremont County (88.4 percent LDS; 1,887 Democratic votes), Jefferson County (97.6 percent LDS; 2,374 Democratic votes), Madison County (98.5 percent LDS; 1,678 Democratic votes), Oneida County (96.7 percent LDS; 799 Democratic votes);

NEVADA: Lincoln County (90.1 percent LDS; 771 Democratic votes);

UTAH: Beaver County (97.1 percent LDS; 1,156 Democratic votes), Box Elder County (99.2 percent LDS; 3,831 Democratic votes), Cache County (98.9 percent LDS; 4,917 Democratic votes), Davis County (98.2 percent LDS; 10,244 Democratic votes), Duchesne County (97.1 percent LDS; 1,166 Democratic votes), Emery County (99.0 percent LDS; 1,238 Democratic votes), Garfield County (100 percent LDS; 471 Democratic votes), Grand County (87.3 percent LDS; 805 Democratic votes), Iron County (99.2 percent LDS; 1,738 Democratic votes), Juab County (89.2 percent LDS; 1,158 Democratic votes), Kane

County (100 percent LDS; 213 Democratic votes), Millard County (99.9 percent LDS; 1,425 Democratic votes), Morgan County (100 percent LDS; 622 Democratic votes), Piute County (97.9 percent LDS; 247 Democratic votes), Rich County (100 percent LDS; 291 Democratic votes), Salt Lake County (85.4 percent LDS; 75,868 Democratic votes), San Juan County (88.4 percent LDS; 837 Democratic votes), Sanpete County (98.1 percent LDS; 2,180 Democratic votes), Sevier County (99.6 percent LDS; 1,690 Democratic votes), Summit County (89.2 percent LDS; 1,217 Democratic votes), Tooele County (83.9 percent LDS; 3,665 Democratic votes), Uintah County (86.3 percent LDS; 1,380 Democratic votes), Utah County (97.1 percent LDS; 19,626 Democratic votes), Wasatch County (99.3 percent LDS; 1,066 Democratic votes), Washington County (100 percent LDS; 1,290 Democratic votes), Wayne County (100 percent LDS; 382 Democratic votes), Weber County (85.9 percent LDS; 24,239 Democratic votes).

289. Gibbons, *David O. McKay,* 373, with corrections of capitalization.

290. "Congress Spurns Mormon Plea To Keep Taft-Hartley Section," *New York Times,* 15 July 1965, 19; "The Right to Vote," *Newsweek* 66 (26 July 1965): 83; "Mormons Soften Opposition to 'Right-to-work' Section," *New York Times,* 26 July 1965, 11; "LDS Church Stands Firm: Right to Work," *Deseret News,* 27 July 1965, A-1; "LDS View on Work Law Unchanged: Rap Unauthorized Thinking," *Salt Lake Tribune,* 28 July 1965, 19; Robert L. Morlan, "The Mormons and 14(b)," *Frontier* 17 (July 1966): 11; "Utah & the Mormons: As State Bids for Business It Comes Into Conflict With Church," *Wall Street Journal,* 10 Aug. 1965, 12; J. Kenneth Davies, "The Accommodation of Mormonism and Politico-Economic Reality," *Dialogue: A Journal of Mormon Thought* 3 (Spring 1968): 52-54; H. George Frederickson and Allen J. Stevens, "The Mormon Congressmen and the Line Between Church and State," and Richard B. Wirthlin and Bruce D. Merrill, "The L.D.S. Church as a Significant Political Reference Group in Utah—Right to Work," *Dialogue: A Journal of Mormon Thought* 3 (Summer 1968): 124-29, 129-33; Ken W. Dyal, former U.S. Congressman from California, to the editors, *Dialogue: A Journal of Mormon Thought* 3 (Autumn 1968): 11-14; David K. Elton, "The Mormons and the Right to Work Law," M.A. thesis, Arizona State University, 1968; J. Kenneth Davies, "The Right-To-Work Movement," in Powell, *Utah History Encyclopedia,* 468-69; Mauss, *Angel and the Beehive,* 115.

291. "Honors For a Prophet," *Deseret News "Church News,"* 11 Sept. 1965, 3; "Secretary To A Prophet," *Deseret News "Church News,"* 21 May 1966, 13; "The Beloved Prophet, Seer, and Revelator, President David O. McKay," *Deseret News "Church News,"* 3 Sept. 1966, cover; "Voice of a Prophet," *Deseret News "Church News,"* 4 Feb. 1967, 2; "Prophet's Portrait," *Deseret News "Church News,"* 2 Sept. 1967, 8-9; "Timmy Meets The Prophet," *Deseret News "Church News,"* 13 Jan. 1968, 3; "Portrait of a Prophet," *Deseret News "Church News,"* 2 Mar. 1968, 10; "A Prophet's Counsel," *Deseret News "Church News,"* 7 Sept. 1968, 3; "The Prophet of God," *Deseret News "Church News,"* 24 Jan. 1970, 16; "Stake No. 500 Formed: Coincides With the Prophet's Death," *Deseret News "Church News,"* 31 Jan. 1970, 12.

292. "From Pres. McKay: Urges Stand Against Liquor Plan: Statement by President David O. McKay of The Church of Jesus Christ of Latter-day Saints," *Deseret News,* 11 May 1968, A-1; "Law of the Spirit: From Mormon Chief McKay (above), a call to battle against liquor by the drink," *Newsweek* 72 (22 July 1968): 87-89; Gordon B. Hinckley, "Liquor by the Drink," *Improvement Era* 71 (Oct. 1968): 4-7, released just before the election; JeDon A. Emenhisen, "The 1968 Election in Utah," *Western Political Quarterly* 22 (Sept. 1969): 532-33, 535; Croft, "Influence of the L.D.S. Church on Utah Politics, 1945-1985," 91; G. Homer Durham, et al., *N. Eldon Tanner: His Life and Service* (Salt Lake City: Deseret Book Co., 1982), 245; Francis M. Gibbons, *Joseph Fielding Smith: Gospel Scholar, Prophet of God* (Salt Lake City: Deseret Book Co., 1992), 450; Sheri L. Dew, *Go Forward With Faith: The Biography of Gordon B. Hinckley* (Salt Lake City: Deseret Book Co., 1996), 291-94.

However, during the twenty-eight years since the 1968 liquor-by-the drink crusade, LDS headquarters has grudgingly allowed the Utah legislature to legalize liquor-by-the-drink in restaurants and private clubs, as well as the sale of wine coolers and beer in grocery stores. So far this process has been chronicled only by newspaper stories about each change. This is evidence of economic necessities for Utah as a tourist and convention center, as well as the gradual secularization of LDS headquarters culture. Such processes of accommodation will undoubtedly increase due to Salt Lake City's hosting the winter Olympics in 2002.

293. James B. Allen and Glen M. Leonard, *The Story of the Latter-day Saints,* 2d ed. rev. (Salt Lake City: Deseret Book Co., 1992), 620.

294. "Another Prophet Is Sent," *Deseret News "Church News,"* 31 Jan. 1970, 16; "She Wasn't Lost, She Was with the Prophet," *Deseret News "Church News,"* 25 Apr. 1970, 3; also "A Tribute To The Prophet," *Deseret News "Church News,"* 9 May 1970, 8-9; "A Blessing By the Prophet," *Deseret News "Church News,"* 10 Oct. 1970, 11.

295. Harold B. Lee diary, Nov. 1972, quoted in L. Brent Goates, *Harold B. Lee: Prophet & Seer* (Salt Lake City: Bookcraft, 1985), 506. Goates referred to this (467) as "the almost-adoration of the [LDS] people toward the new President."

296. "Another Prophet Now," *Deseret News "Church News,"* 8 July 1972, 16; "Prophet's Brother Recalls Early Days," *Deseret News "Church News,"* 29 Dec. 1973, 3.

297. Kimball and Kimball, *Spencer W. Kimball,* 189, 193, 201, 251, 253, 263, 376, 393; "Everywhere He Goes He Shares Love," *Deseret News "Church News,"* 6 Jan. 1979, 16; Richard O. Cowan, *The Church In the Twentieth Century* (Salt Lake City: Bookcraft, 1985), 384-85; Edward L. Kimball and Andrew E. Kimball, Jr., *The Story of Spencer W. Kimball: A Short Man, A Long Stride* (Salt Lake City: Bookcraft, 1985), 114, 125; Edward L. Kimball, "Spencer W. Kimball," in Arrington, *Presidents of the Church,* 395-96, 400-401, 407, 414-17.

298. Francis M. Gibbons, *Spencer W. Kimball: Resolute Disciple, Prophet of God* (Salt Lake City: Deseret Book Co., 1995), ix.

299. "Chronology of a Prophet," *Deseret News "Church News,"* 19 Jan. 1974, 5; "Prophet Says Worthy Youth Should Serve On Missions," *Deseret News "Church News,"* 15 Mar. 1975, 11; "Prophet in Tennessee," *Deseret News "Church News,"* 2 Aug. 1975, 8-9; "Prophet Visits Methodists," *Deseret News "Church News,"* 6 Dec. 1975, 4; "Members in Georgia Welcome the Prophet," *Deseret News "Church News,"* 17 Jan. 1976, 3; "The Prophet's Visit," *Deseret News "Church News,"* 6 Mar. 1976, 8-9; "Prophet's Birthday," and "A Prophet Declares: Abortion Is Wrong," *Deseret News "Church News,"* 27 Mar. 1976, 4, 6; "The Prophet Returns," *Deseret News "Church News,"* 26 June 1976, 8-9; "Prophet Visits Pres. Ford," *Deseret News "Church News,"* 10 July 1976, 4; "Prophet Helps Open Mall, Hotel," and "Prophet Speaks At Opening of Businesses," *Deseret News "Church News,"* 18 Sept. 1976, 3, 7; "Prophet Testifies of Revelation," and "Prophet Says the Lord's Blessings Follow Obedience," and "Prophet Gets 'World Award,'" *Deseret News "Church News,"* 9 Apr. 1977, 3-4, 13; "Prophet Speaks in Louisiana," *Deseret News "Church News,"* 21 May 1977, 3; "As Father, Prophet Made Time Count," *Deseret News "Church News,"* 11 June 1977, 5; "Prophet Given 'Plate' Award," *Deseret News "Church News,"* 2 July 1977, 5; "Prophet Underscores Need For Genealogy," *Deseret News "Church News,"* 13 Aug. 1977, 5; "Prophet Challenges New Generation," *Deseret News "Church News,"* 8 Oct. 1977, 19; "Prophet There to Welcome Widow Home," *Deseret News "Church News,"* 29 Oct. 1977, 5; "Prophet, Wife Married 60 Years," *Deseret News "Church News,"* 12 Nov. 1977, 8-9; "Prophet Visits San Antonio," *Deseret News "Church News,"* 10 Dec. 1977, 3.

300. George P. Lee, "But They Were In One," *Ensign* 6 (May 1976): 99, for first quotes; Franklin D. Day, "Elijah," in Ludlow, *Encyclopedia of Mormonism,* 2:450, for final quote.

301. Harold T. Christensen and Kenneth L. Cannon, "The Fundamentalist Emphasis at Brigham Young University: 1935-1973," *Journal for the Scientific Study of Religion* 17 (Mar. 1978): 55; Mauss, *Angel and the Beehive,* 178, observed that "it is also probable that much of the drastic change in opinion between the two surveys can be attributed to a strong selective recruitment bias in the 1973 data. Unlike the students in the thirties, recent aspirants to BYU have had to obtain recommendations from their local bishops testifying to their 'worthiness.'"

302. Mauss, *Angel and the Beehive,* 127.

303. Quinn, *J. Reuben Clark,* 208-19; also Quinn, "The Mormon Church and the Spanish-American War: An End to Selective Pacifism," *Pacific Historical Review* 43 (Aug. 1974): 342-366, reprinted in *Dialogue: A Journal of Mormon Thought* 17 (Winter 1984); Quinn, "Conscientious Objectors or Christian Soldiers?: The Latter-day Saint Position on Militarism," *Sunstone* 10 (Mar. 1985): 15-23.

304. "LDS First Presidency Issues MX Statement," *Deseret News,* 5 May 1981, A-1; "LDS First Presidency Rejects MX Plan," *Salt Lake Tribune,* 6 May 1981, B-1; "Mormon Church Opposes Placing MX Missiles in Utah and Nevada," *New York Times,* 6 May 1981, A-1; "Mormon Church Joins Opposition to MX Program," *Washington Post,* 6 May 1981, A-5; "Top Mormons Oppose MX Missile System," *Los Angeles Times,* 6 May 1981, 1; Carl T. Rowan, "Mormon MX Stand Looks 'Convenient,'" *Salt Lake Tribune,* 13 May 1981, A-15; "Mormons and MX," *Nation* 232 (16 May 1981): 588; "Nix to MX," *Time* 117 (18 May 1981): 28; Constance Holden, "Mormons Rebel on MX," *Science* 212 (22 May 1981): 904; "First Presidency Statement on Basing of MX Missile," *Ensign* 11 (June 1981): 76; Fred Esplin, "Missiles, Motherhood and Moral Issues," *Utah Holiday* 10 (June 1981): 46; William F. Buckley, Jr., "The Strange Declaration of the Mormons," *National Review* 33 (26 June 1981): 740-41; Joan Elbert, "Mormons and the MX Missile," *Christian Century* 98 (15 July 1981): 725-26; Stephen W. Stathis, "Mormonism and the Periodical Press: A Change Is Underway," *Dialogue: A Journal of Mormon Thought* (Summer 1981): 61-64; Steven A. Hildreth, "The First Presidency Statement on MX in Perspective," *Brigham Young University Studies* 22 (Spring 1982): 215-25; Steven A. Hildreth, "Mormon Concern Over MX: Parochialism or Enduring Moral Theology?" *Journal of Church and State* 26 (Spring 1984): 227-53; Val Norman Edwards, "A Rhetorical Analysis of Three Policy Statements of the Church of Jesus Christ of Latter-day Saints," M.S. thesis, University of Utah, 1987, 112-22; David B. Magleby, "Contemporary American Politics," *Encyclopedia of Mormonism,* 3: 1108-1109; Matthew Glass, *Citizens against the MX: Public Languages in the Nuclear Age* (Urbana: University of Illinois Press, 1993), 69-72, 78, 104-105, 161-62; also Stan Albrecht, "*Great Basin Kingdom:* A Sociocultural Case Study," in Thomas G. Alexander, *Great Basin Kingdom Revisited: Contemporary Perspectives* (Logan: Utah State University Press, 1991), 68-69, for the MX statement as "an exception" to "the more usual pattern [of] accommodation"; Mauss, *Angel and the Beehive,* 116; John Edwards, *Superweapon: The Making of MX* (New York: Norton, 1982); Robert A. Hoover, *The MX Controversy: A Guide to Issues & References* (Claremont, CA: Regina Books, 1982).

305. "MX Opposition Soars Since LDS Statement," *Deseret News,* 25 May 1981, B-2; "Public Mood in Utah and Nevada Turns Sharply Against MX Plan," *New York Times,* 8 June 1981, A-1; "MX: Most Utahns Will Go Along With Reagan," *Deseret News,* 14 Sept. 1981, A-3.

306. Frances FitzGerald, "A Reporter At Large: A Disciplined, Charging Army," *New Yorker* 57 (18 May 1981): 53, 64, 124; "Why the Mormon Church Speaks Out on 'Moral' Issues," *Christian Science Monitor,* 28 Apr. 1982, B-6; Gabriel Fackre, *The Religious Right and Christian Faith* (Grand Rapids, MI: William B. Eerdmans Publishing Co., 1982), 3; Shirley Rogers Radl, *The Invisible Woman: Target of the Religious New Right* (New York: Delacorte Press, 1983), 4, 32, 34, 104; James T. Richardson, "The 'Old Right' in Action: Mormon and Catholic Involvement in an Equal Rights Amendment Referendum," in David Bromley and

Anson Shupe, eds., *New Christian Politics* (Macon, GA: Mercer University Press, 1984), 213-33; Dinesh D'Souza, *Falwell: Before the Millennium: A Critical Biography* (Chicago: Regnery Gateway, 1984), 115; Anson Shupe and John Heinerman, "Mormonism and the New Christian Right: An Emerging Coalition?" *Review of Religious Research* 27 (Dec. 1985): 146-57; Albert J. Menendez, "Righter Than Thou: Robertson, Religious Right Challenge GOP Regulars For Republican Power," *Church & State* 39 (July-Aug. 1986): 12; O. Kendall White, Jr., "A Review and Commentary on the Prospects of a Mormon-New Christian Right Coalition," *Review of Religious Research* 28 (Dec. 1986): 180-88 (esp. 185-87); Merlin B. Brinkerhoff, Jeffrey C. Jacob, and Marlene M. Mackie, "Mormonism and the Moral Majority Make Strange Bedfellows?: An Exploratory Critique," *Review of Religious Research* 28 (Mar. 1987): 236-51; George M. Marsden, "Afterword: Religion, Politics, and the Search for an American Consensus," in Mark A. Noll, ed., *Religion and American Politics: From the Colonial Period to the 1980s* (New York: Oxford University Press, 1990), 388; Matthew C. Moen, *The Transformation of the Christian Right* (Tuscaloosa: University of Alabama Press, 1992), 157; George Marsden, "The Religious Right: A Historical Overview," in Michael Cromartie, ed., *No Longer Exiles: The Religious Right in American Politics* (Washington, D.C.: Ethics and Public Policy Center, 1993), 10; Michael Lienesch, *Redeeming America: Piety and Politics in the New Christian Right* (Chapel Hill: University of North Carolina Press, 1993), 9-10, 252; Mauss, *Angel and the Beehive*, 180; "Members Help Defeat Lottery Initiative," *Deseret News "Church News,"* 23 July 1994, 12; "LDS and Catholic Coalition Opposes Hawaii Legislation," *Deseret News*, 21 Feb. 1996, B-1.

    307. Radl, *Invisible Woman*, 161; Steve Bruce, *The Rise and Fall of the New Christian Right: Conservative Protestant Politics in America, 1978-1988* (Oxford, Eng.: Clarendon Press, 1988), 127. For expressions of disdain to abhorrence of the LDS church by major evangelical and Catholic publishers, see Dan Gilbert, *Mormonism Unmasked: In the Light of Bible Prophecy* (Grand Rapids, MI: Zondervan Publishing House, 1945); L. Rumble, *The Mormons or Latter-day Saints*, with Imprimatur by the archbishop of St. Paul (St. Paul, MN: Radio Replies Press, 1950); Gordon H. Fraser, *Is Mormonism Christian?: An Examination of Mormon Doctrine As Compared With Orthodox Christianity* (Chicago: Moody Press, 1957); *The Challenge of the Cults: A CHRISTIANITY TODAY Symposium* (Grand Rapids, MI: Zondervan Publishing Co., 1961), 20-27; Walter R. Martin, *The Maze of Mormonism* (Grand Rapids, MI: Zondervan Publishing House, 1962); J. K. Van Baalen, *The Gist of the Cults: Christianity Versus False Religion* (Grand Rapids, MI: William B. Eerdmans Publishing Co., 1964); Gordon R. Lewis, *The Bible, the Christian, and Latter-day Saints* (Philadelphia: Presbyterian and Reformed Publishing Co., 1966); Jerald Tanner and Sandra Tanner, *The Changing World of Mormonism* (Chicago: Moody Press, 1980); Fred Lilly, "How Christians Adjust to Life in Mormon Country," *National Catholic Register* 53 (23 Jan. 1983), 1, 10; Robert F. Baldwin, "Twenty Years a Mormon: She's Catholic Again," *Our Sunday Visitor* 72 (5 June 1983): 3; Robert A. Morey, *How To Answer a Mormon* (Minneapolis: Bethany House Publishers, 1983); John Thomas Rogers, *Communicating Christ To Cults* (Schaumburg, IL: Regular Baptist Press, 1983); William Joseph Whalen, "Don't Get Unhinged by Doorbell Evangelists," *U.S. Catholic* 49 (Mar. 1984): 39-40; Walter Martin, *The Kingdom of the Cults*, rev. ed. (Minneapolis: Bethany House Publishers, 1985), 166-226; J. Gordon Melton, *Encyclopedic Handbook of Cults in America* (New York: Garland Publishing, 1986), 29-34; James R. Spencer, *Have You Witnessed To a Mormon Lately?* (Tarrytown, NY: Chosen Books/Fleming H. Revell Co., 1986); Albert J. Nevins, *Strangers At Your Door: How To Respond to Jehovah's Witnesses, the Mormons, Televangelists, Cults, and More* (Huntington, IN: Our Sunday-[Catholic] Visitor, 1988); Edgar P. Kaiser, *C'omo Responder a Los Santos de los Ultimos Dias* (St. Louis, MO: Concordia, 1991); Kurt Van Gordon, *Mormonism* (Grand Rapids, MI: Zondervan Publishing House, 1995). The above list does not include evangelical publishers (usually former Mormons) who specialize in anti-Mormon ministries.

308. For evidence of the rapid development of partisanship among Mormon women, see Carol Cornwall Madsen, "Schism in the Sisterhood: Mormon Women and Partisan Politics, 1890-1900," in Davis Bitton and Maureen Ursenbach Beecher, eds., *New Views of Mormon History: A Collection of Essays in Honor of Leonard J. Arrington* (Salt Lake City: University of Utah Press, 1987), 212-41.

309. On the several proposed amendments to prohibit polygamy, see *Report of the Utah Commission to the Secretary of the Interior, 1889* (Washington: Government Printing Office, 1889), 18; Abraham H. Cannon diary, 2 Feb. 1892; John Henry Smith diary, 4 Apr. 1896, 15 Jan., 25 Jan.-14 Feb. 1900 in White, *Church, State, and Politics*, 347, 443n9, 444-48; "ANTI-MORMON NIGHTMARE: Slanderous Petition From West Virginia Bigots," *Salt Lake Herald*, 19 Dec. 1897, [1]; "ANTI-POLYGAMY AMENDMENT TO FEDERAL CONSTITUTION," *Salt Lake Herald*, 21 Feb. 1899, [1]; Rudger Clawson diary, 2 Mar., 29 Dec. 1899, 3 Apr. 1902, in Larson, *Ministry of Meetings*, 30, 127, 420; *New York Journal*, 5 Dec. 1899; "Reasons For and Objections to a Constitutional Amendment," *The Kinsman: The Organ of the Campaign for the Anti-Polygamy Constitutional Amendment* 2 (Jan. 1900): 72-76; Journal History, 22 Nov. 1899, 2, 26 Dec. 1901, 1, 6 Mar. 1902, 2, 3 Apr. 1902, 5-6, 27 May 1902, 2-5; "MINISTERS URGE THE AMENDMENT: Want a Sixteenth Article Added to the United States Constitution to Prohibit Polygamy," *Deseret Evening News*, 13 Feb. 1900, 8; "Anti-Polygamy Amendment," *Deseret Evening News*, 12 Dec. 1902, [1]; Anthon H. Lund diary, 4 Mar. 1902, 21 Mar. 1903, 3 Dec. 1906; "ANTI-POLYGAMY AMENDMENT," *Deseret Evening News*, 31 Jan. 1903, [1]; Carl A. Badger to Ed Jenkins, 1 Feb. 1904, and Carl A. Badger to Rose Badger, 4 Dec. 1906, in Badger letterbook 1:432 and 4:105, Lee Library, the latter quoted in Rodney J. Badger, *Liahona and Iron Rod: The Biography of Carl A. and Rose J. Badger* (N.p.: Rodney J. Badger Family History Publishers, 1985), 335-36; "Anti-'Mormon' Crusade Continued," *Deseret Evening News*, 9 Aug. 1911, 4; Reed Smoot diary, 10 Dec. 1913.

310. Reed Smoot diary, 3 Nov. 1920, 8 Dec. 1920, 5 Feb. 1929; also Merrill, *Reed Smoot*, 3, 231, 267-68, 329; Thomas G. Alexander, "Reed Smoot, the L.D.S. Church and Progressive Legislation, 1903-1933," *Dialogue: A Journal of Mormon Thought* 7 (Spring 1972): 47-56; Jeffrey L. Swanson, "That Smoke-filled Room: A Utahn's Role in the 1920 GOP Convention," *Utah Historical Quarterly* 45 (Fall 1977): 369-80; Heath, "Reed Smoot," 1022-24.

311. Raymond, *Dictionary of Politics*, 379, "*Pocket borough*. A term used in England to describe a 'political machine' that controls the government of a borough or a county."

312. Shipps, "Mormons in Politics," 221.

313. Frank Herman Jonas, "Utah: Sagebrush Democracy," in Thomas C. Donnelly, ed., *Rocky Mountain Politics* (Albuquerque: University of New Mexico Press, 1940), 34-35.

314. Raymond, *Dictionary of Politics*, 114, "*Cult of Personality*. An unquestionable [i.e., not to be questioned] loyalty, devotion, and worship of one person during his lifetime"; Gordon Shepherd and Gary Shepherd, *A Kingdom Transformed: Themes in the Development of Mormonism* (Salt Lake City: University of Utah Press, 1984), 122.

315. Dew, *Go Forward With Faith*, ix, photograph opposite 495.

316. *April 1940 Conference Report* . . . (Salt Lake City: Church of Jesus Christ of Latter-day Saints, 1940), 14. The First Presidency also officially published a centennial history which denied that general authorities "are without faults or infallible" (Roberts, *Comprehensive History*, 1:viii).

317. M. Russell Ballard, "What Came from Kirtland," 6 Nov. 1994, in *Brigham Young University 1994-95 Devotional & Fireside Speeches* (Provo, UT: Brigham Young University Publications & Grapics, 1995), 50; "Ballard: Heed LDS Leaders In Faith During 'Last Days,'" *Salt Lake Tribune*, 16 Mar. 1996, C-2; *Deseret News 1995-1996 Church Almanac*, 19, for Ballard; also James E. Faust, "The Prophetic Voice: Continuing Revelation and Leadership for the

Church Come Through the President of the Church, and He Will Never Mislead the Saints,"
Ensign 26 (May 1996): 4-7.

318. Cole R. Capener, "How General the Authority?: Individual Conscience and De
Facto Infallibility," *Sunstone* 9 (Autumn 1984): 26-30.

319. Armand L. Mauss and M. Gerald Bradford, "Mormon Politics and Assimilation:
Toward a Theory of Mormon Church Involvement in National U.S. Politics," in Anson
Shupe and Jeffrey K. Hadden, eds., *Religion and the Political Order* (New York: Paragon
House, 1988), 44-45, which was reduced in Mauss, *Angel and the Beehive*, 111, to: "This
dependence upon collegial consensus obviously provides inherent restraints on official
political involvement in the name of the churchap."

320. "LDS Church's Influence A Myth, Legislators Say," *Deseret News*, 16 Jan. 1993,
B-1.

321. "Church's Word On Guns Packs A Real Wallop," *Salt Lake Tribune*, 9 June 1996,
B-1, B-2.

322. Durham, *N. Eldon Tanner*, 246; Gibbons, *David O. McKay*, 376.

323. Gibbons, *Joseph Fielding Smith*, 468; Jonas, "Utah: The Different State," 336-37;
Frank H. Jonas, "President Lyndon Johnson, the Mormon Church and the 1964 Political
Campaign," *Proceedings of the Utah Academy of Sciences, Arts, and Letters* 44, Pt. 1 (1967): 67-90.

324. Schapsmeier and Schapsmeier, *Ezra Taft Benson and the Politics of Agriculture;*
"New NASA Director Is Active In Church," *Deseret News "Church News,"* 6 Mar. 1971, 3; Lee
H. Burke, "J. Reuben Clark, Jr.: Under Secretary of State," and Martin B. Hickman, "The
Ambassadorial Years: Some Insights," *Brigham Young University Studies* 13 (Spring 1973):
396-404, 405-14; Sessions, *Mormon Democrat*, 237-85; *Deseret News 1977 Church Almanac* (Salt
Lake City: Deseret News, 1977), 233; *Deseret News 1978 Church Almanac* (Salt Lake City:
Deseret News, 1978), 14; *Deseret News 1979 Church Almanac* (Salt Lake City: Deseret News,
1979), 252; Fox, *J. Reuben Clark*, 503-30; "LDS Man May Head Agency," *Deseret News "Church
News,"* 30 May 1981, 6; Ron Hrebenar, "Utah: The Most Republican State In the Union,"
Social Science Journal 18 (Oct. 1981): 112-13; "S.L. Native Given Command of 14th Air
Force," *Salt Lake Tribune*, 15 Dec. 1982, B-5; "Mormons Who Have Served In U.S.
Government (As of October 1982)," in *Deseret News 1983 Church Almanac: The Church of
Jesus Christ of Latter-day Saints* (Salt Lake City: Deseret News, 1982), 283-84; Cindy Nightin-
gale, "Roger Porter: When the President Needs Advice," *This People* 4 (June/July 1983):
31-34; Pat Ashby, "Ambassador Keith Nyborg: An American To the Finish," *This People* 4
(Aug. 1983): 43-46, 58; Kathleen Lubeck, "George M. Romney: Driven," and Norman R.
Bowen, "Ambassador Mark Evans Austad: In a Not-So-Foreign Service," *This People* 5 (May
1984): 20-26, 56-62; Dale Van Atta, "Richard B. Wirthlin: In Highest Regard," *This People*
5 (Aug./Sept. 1984): 21-27, 28-34; Lois Blake, "The Church in Washington: LDS/DC," and
Cydney Peterson Quinn, "Angela Buchanan Jackson: Auditing the Treasurer," *This People*
5 (Oct. 1984): 39-43; Mary Lythgoe Bradford and Alice Allred Pottmyer, "Power People
on the Potomac," *Utah Holiday* 14 (Nov. 1984): 36-49, 75; Lois Blake, "Dodie Livingston:
Commissioner Livingston, I Presume?" *This People* 6 (Oct. 1985): 46-50; Dale Van Atta,
"James C. Fletcher: Star Man," *This People* 7 (Aug./Sept. 1986): 32-39; Larry Morris,
"Stephen Studdert: A Friend in High Places," and Cydney P. Quinn, "Admiral Paul Yost:
At the Helm," *This People* 8 (Apr. 1987): 28-34, 62-68; Heidi A. Waldrop, "Paul Yost: The
Admiral's Anchor Is the Gospel," *Ensign* 17 (Aug. 1987): 38-42; Kathleen Lubeck, "Gregory
J. Newell, United States Ambassador to Sweden," *Ensign* 17 (Oct. 1987): 34-39; Martin
Berkeley Hickman, *David Matthew Kennedy: Banker, Statesman, Churchman* (Salt Lake City:
Deseret Book Co., 1987), 225-313; Terrel H. Bell, *The Thirteenth Man: A Reagan Cabinet
Memoir* (New York: Free Press, 1988); James Coates, *In Mormon Circles: Gentiles, Jack
Mormons, and Latter-day Saints* (Reading, MA: Addison-Wesley Publishing Co., 1991),
121-26; *Deseret News 1993-1994 Church Almanac* (Salt Lake City: Deseret News, 1992), 9;
"Utah Politics: Latter-day Losers," *Economist* 326 (30 Jan. 1993): 28-29; Peter B. Levy,

Encyclopedia of the Reagan-Bush Years (Westport, CT: Greenwood Press, 1996), 320-22; Mario S. DePillis, "The Emergence of Mormon Power since 1945," *Journal of Mormon History* 22 (Spring 1996): 18-21.

325. "LDS First Presidency Opposes Legalization of Gay Marriages," *Deseret News,* 14 Feb. 1994, B-2; "Sex-Sex Marriage: Are LDS Gearing Up for a Holy War?" *Salt Lake Tribune,* 26 Mar. 1994, B-1; "LDS Church Opposing Gay Marriages," *Deseret News,* 30 Mar. 1994, A-10; "Church Joins Hawaii Fight Over Same-Sex Marriages," *Deseret News,* 24 Feb. 1995, A-2; "A Mormon Crusade In Hawaii," *Salt Lake Tribune,* 9 June 1996, B-1; "Your Tithing Dollars At Work: The LDS Church Political Campaign Against Same-Sex Marriage," panel discussion, Sunstone Symposium, 17 Aug. 1996, audio-tape available from *Sunstone Magazine,* Salt Lake City, Utah; chap. 10.

326. Jonas, "Utah: Sagebrush Democracy," 36.

327. Milton R. Merrill, *Reed Smoot: Utah Politician* (Logan: Utah State Agricultural College, 1953), 5; Shipps, "Utah Comes of Age Politically," 110.

328. Charles Lawrence Hermansen, "Two Third Party Elections in Utah, 1912 and 1924," M.A. thesis, University of Utah, 1972, 47.

329. See Jones, "Utah Politics, 1926-1932," 109; Gilchrist, "Problem of L.D.S. Church Influence," 34, 141-143; R. Gary Penrod, "The Election of 1900 in Utah," M.A. thesis, Brigham Young University, 1968, 104-105.

330. Mauss, *Angel and the Beehive,* 109; "Rumors of 'Mormon Conspiracy' Make Church Central Issue in Idaho Campaign," *Los Angeles Times,* 1 Nov. 1978, I, 18. However, I disagree with Mauss (109): "Yet, as an institution, the Mormon church has only rarely injected itself in national political issues since Utah achieved statehood in 1896." First, this statement made the artificial distinction between the church "as an institution" on national issues and his acknowledgement that the hierarchy has acted politically "officially and unofficially" since 1896 on local, state, and regional political matters. Second, even if such a "church" appeal had only been made to Utah voters and elected officials, the distinction Mauss tries to make would require one to agree that the following were not "national political issues": support of the Spanish-American War and subsequent national conflicts since 1898, support of William H. Taft's presidential candidacy in 1912, support of the nationwide prohibition movement from 1908 to 1917, support of the right of conscientious objection to war during U.S. conflicts from 1917 to 1955, support of the U.S. Senate's ratification of the League of Nations in 1919-20, opposition to immigration restrictions during the 1920s, opposition to ending Prohibition in 1932-33, opposition to the New Deal and public "counsel" for voters to vote against Franklin D. Roosevelt in 1936, opposition to Congressional adoption of universal military service in 1945-46, support of Congressional adoption of anti-union legislation in 1954, support of Richard M. Nixon's presidential candidacy in 1960, support of national civil rights legislation in 1963, opposition to Congressional repeal of anti-union legislation in 1965, opposition to the ratification of the Equal Rights Amendment in 1976 to 1982, opposition to Congressional deregulation of the airline industry in 1977, opposition to the MX missile system and other "vast" systems of weaponry in 1981, to name only the well known examples. Mauss (112-19) discussed several of these to support his view that "the history of Mormon political involvements in national politics up to about 1960 provides few, if any, exceptions to dominant national trends," which is a different matter than his statement on page 109.

331. Francis M. Gibbons, *Harold B. Lee: Man of Vision, Prophet of God* (Salt Lake City: Deseret Book Co., 1993), 300. However, for the hierarchy's critics of Benson as Secretary of Agriculture, see chap. 3.

332. Anthon H. Lund diary, 28-29 Nov. 1914.

333. 2 Ne. 2:11-16 in *The Book of Mormon,* published at Salt Lake City in various editions, with verse citations (similar to the Bible) according to the name(s) of its constituent books; Bruce R. McConkie, *Mormon Doctrine* (Salt Lake City, Bookcraft, 1958), 25.

334. J. Reuben Clark remarks to missionary meeting, 4 Apr. 1960, manuscript, 1, Clark papers; *April 1945 Conference Report* . . . (Salt Lake City: Church of Jesus Christ of Latter-day Saints, 1945), 55.

335. Jonas, "Utah: The Different State," 363, 373; Dennis L. Lythgoe, "The Changing Image of Mormonism," *Dialogue: A Journal of Mormon Thought* 3 (Winter 1968): 49, for quotes of this view from *Saturday Evening Post* and *New York Times Magazine*; Elaine Jarvik, "Probing the Power Structure," and Elaine Jarvik and George Buck, "The Powers That Be," *Utah Holiday* 5 (24 May 1976): 4-9, 10-15; "Moslems Join Mormons in Utah Boom," *New York Times*, 27 Dec. 1982, A-12; Thomas G. Alexander and James B. Allen, *Mormons & Gentiles: A History of Salt Lake City* (Boulder, CO: Pruett Publishing Co., 1984), 293-95, 304, 306.

336. J. Bracken Lee's exactly transcribed words in J. Reuben Clark office diary, 10 Apr. 1956; Lythgoe, *Let 'Em Holler*, 103, also in Dennis L. Lythgoe, "A Special Relationship: J. Bracken Lee and the Mormon Church," *Dialogue: A Journal of Mormon Thought* 11 (Winter 1976): 85.

337. "Volunteers Asked to Halt Salt Lake City Flooding," *New York Times*, 7 June 1983, A-18; "Utah: Helping Thy Neighbor," *Newsweek* 101 (20 June 1983): 27; "An Inspired Clean-Up Campaign: Mormon Volunteers Fight the Spring Floods in Utah," *Time* 121 (20 June 1983): 25; Albert L. Fisher, "Utah, the L.D.S. Church, and the Floods of 1983: A Case Study," *International Journal of Mass Emergencies and Disasters* 3 (Nov. 1985): 53-74; Gottlieb and Wiley, *America's Saints*, 12, also 52 on Mormonism's present "autonomous religious culture." "We have a wonderful relationship with the LDS Church," reports Salt Lake City's current mayor, a Roman Catholic woman. "I can't think of a time we have approached them about assisting us that they have not responded in some measure" (Deedee Corradini statement, 13 Sept. 1996, quoted in Dew, *Go Forward With Faith*, 522-23).

338. Frederick S. Buchanan, "Masons and Mormons: Released-Time Politics In Salt Lake City, 1930-56," *Journal of Mormon History* 19 (Spring 1993): 100-101.

339. Robert W. Blair, "Vocabulary, Latter-day Saint," in Ludlow, *Encyclopedia of Mormonism*, 4:1537-38; "Respected Historian Isn't LDS, But She Speaks Mormon," *Salt Lake Tribune*, 20 Aug. 1994, D-4.

Notes to Chapter Ten

1. O. Kendall White, Jr., "Overt and Covert Politics: The Mormon Church's Anti-ERA Campaign in Virginia," *Virginia Social Science Journal* 19 (Winter 1984): 14. White was in an alphabetical list of Mormons who favored the ERA and wrote supportive letters to Sonia Johnson, fd 1, box 11, Sonia Johnson papers, Manuscripts Division, J. Willard Marriott Library, University of Utah, Salt Lake City (hereafter Marriott Library).

2. Jane J. Mansbridge, *Why We Lost the ERA* (Chicago: University of Chicago Press, 1986), 3, limited discussion of the church to half of one sentence in the text: "Opposition to the ERA . . . centered in the fundamentalist South, including southern Illinois, and in the Mormon states of Utah and Nevada, where the Mormon church actively fought the ERA." Mary Frances Berry, *Why ERA Failed: Politics, Women's Rights, and the Amending Process of the Constitution* (Bloomington: Indiana University Press, 1986), 76, reported the LDS church president's official opposition but mentioned nothing of the lobbying efforts, even in Utah.

3. *Deseret News 1995-1996 Church Almanac: The Church of Jesus Christ of Latter-day Saints* (Salt Lake City: Deseret News, 1994), 390; also "ERA Dies Today Amid Ovation, Mourning," *Salt Lake Tribune*, 30 June 1982, A-1, A-2.

4. White, "Overt and Covert Politics," 15-16; White, "Mormonism and the Equal Rights Amendment," *Journal of Church and State* 31 (Spring 1989): 249-67, esp. 252-54, 266-67. For Shupe's conspiracy interpretations of the church, see Shupe and John Heiner-

man, "Mormonism and the New Christian Right: An Emerging Coalition?" *Review of Religious Research* 27 (Dec. 1985): 146-57; Heinerman and Shupe, *The Mormon Corporate Empire* (Boston: Beacon Press, 1985), 144-52; Shupe, *The Darker Side of Virtue: Corruption, Scandal, and the Mormon Empire* (Buffalo, NY: Prometheus Books, 1991).

    5. A significant comparative study is Anne Firor Scott, "Mormon Women, Other Women: Paradoxes and Challenges," *Journal of Mormon History* 13 (1986-87): 3-19. See also Edward W. Tullidge, *The Women of Mormondom* (New York: Tullidge & Crandall, 1877); Augusta Joyce Crocheron, *Representative Women of Deseret* (Salt Lake City: J. C. Graham, 1884); *Heroines of Mormondom* (Salt Lake City: Juvenile Instructor Office, 1884); Susa Young Gates and Leah D. Widtsoe, *Women of the Mormon Church* (Independence, MO: Zion's Printing and Publishing Co., 1926); William Forrest Sprague, *Women and the West: A Short Social History* (Boston: Christopher Publishing House, 1940), 158-70; Blanche E. Rose, "Early Utah Medical Practice," and Claire Noall, "Mormon Midwives," *Utah Historical Quarterly* 10 (Jan.-Oct. 1942): 27-32, 84-144; Keith C. Terry, "The Contribution of Medical Women During the First Fifty Years in Utah," M.A. thesis, Brigham Young University, 1964; Thomas G. Alexander, "An Experiment in Progressive Legislation: The Granting of Woman Suffrage in Utah in 1870," and Jean Bickmore White, "Gentle Persuaders: Utah's First Women Legislators," *Utah Historical Quarterly* 38 (Winter 1970): 20-30, 31-49; Leonard J. Arrington, "Blessed Damozels: Women In Mormon History," *Dialogue: A Journal of Mormon Thought* 6 (Summer 1971): 22-31; Carol Lynn Pearson, *Daughers of Light* (Provo, UT: Trilogy Arts, 1973); Jean Bickmore White, "Woman's Place Is in the Constitution: The Struggle for Equal Rights in Utah in 1895," *Utah Historical Quarterly* 42 (Fall 1974): 344-69; Jill Mulvay Derr, "Our Foremothers and the 1870 Franchise," *Exponent II* 1 (Dec. 1974): 14; Claire Noall, *Guardians of the Hearth: Utah's Pioneer Midwives and Women Doctors* (Bountiful, UT: Horizon Publishers, 1974); Calvin Seymour Kunz, "A History of Female Missionary Activity in The Church of Jesus Christ of Latter-day Saints, 1830-1898," M.A. thesis, Brigham Young University, 1975; Carol Lynn Pearson, *The Flight and the Nest* (Salt Lake City: Bookcraft, 1975); Maureen Ursenbach Beecher, "Three Women and the Life of the Mind," *Utah Historical Quarterly* 43 (Winter 1975): 26-40; Jill C. Mulvay, "Eliza R. Snow and the Woman Question," *Brigham Young University Studies* 16 (Winter 1976): 250-64; Jill C. Mulvay, "The Liberal Shall Be Blessed: Sarah M. Kimball," and Sherilyn Cox Bennion, "The WOMAN'S EXPONENT: Forty-two Years of Speaking for Women," *Utah Historical Quarterly* 44 (Summer 1976): 205-21, 222-39; Beverly Beeton, "Woman Suffrage in the American West, 1869-1896," Ph.D. diss., University of Utah, 1976, 35-152; Judith Rasmussen Dushku, "Feminists," and other relevant essays in Claudia L. Bushman, ed., *Mormon Sisters: Women in Early Utah* (Salt Lake City: Olympus Publishing Co., 1976); Carol Cornwall Madsen, "Remember the Women of Zion: A Study of the Editorial Content of the *Woman's Exponent,* a Mormon Women's Journal," M.A. thesis, University of Utah, 1977; Shauna Adix, "Education for Women: The Utah Legacy," *Journal of Education* 159 (Aug. 1977): 38-49; Maureen Ursenbach Beecher, "A Decade of Mormon Women in the 1870s," *New Era* 8 (Apr. 1978): 34-39; Maureen Ursenbach Beecher, "The Eliza Enigma," *Dialogue: A Journal of Mormon Thought* 11 (Spring 1978): 31-43; Beverly Beeton, "Woman Suffrage in Territorial Utah" and Miriam B. Murphy, "The Working Women of Salt Lake City: A Review of the *Utah Gazetteer, 1892-93,*" *Utah Historical Quarterly* 46 (Spring 1978): 100-20, and 121-35; Jill Mulvay Derr, "Woman's Place in Brigham Young's World," *Brigham Young University Studies* 18 (Spring 1978): 377-95; Chris Rigby Arrington, "The Finest of Fabrics: Mormon Women and the Silk Industry in Early Utah," *Utah Historical Quarterly* 46 (Fall 1978): 376-96; Jill Mulvay Derr and Ann Vest Lobb, "Women in Early Utah," in Richard D. Poll, ed., *Utah's History* (Provo, UT: Brigham Young University Press, 1978); relevant essays in Vicky Burgess-Olson, ed., *Sister Saints* (Provo, UT: Brigham Young University Press, 1978); Linda King Newell and Valeen Tippets Avery, "Jane Manning James: Black Saint, 1847 Pioneer," *Ensign* 9 (Aug. 1979): 26-29; Leonard J. Arrington, "Persons for All Seasons: Women in

Mormon History," *Brigham Young University Studies* 20 (Fall 1979): 39-58; Miriam B. Murphy, "Martha Spence Heywood," and Murphy, "Sarah Elizabeth Carmichael Williamson," in Lina Mainiero, ed., *American Women Writers,* 4 vols. (New York: Frederick Ungar Publishing Co., 1979), 2:292-94, 4:433-35; Maureen Ursenbach Beecher, Carol Cornwall Madsen, and Jill Mulvay Derr, *The Latter-day Saints and Women's Rights, 1870-1920* (Salt Lake City: Historical Department, Church of Jesus Christ of Latter-day Saints, 1979); Sherilyn Cox Bennion, "Lula Greene Richards," *Brigham Young University Studies* 21 (Spring 1981): 155-74; Linda Thatcher, "'I Care Nothing For Politics': Ruth May Fox, Forgotten Suffragist," Maureen Ursenbach Beecher, "Women's Work on the Mormon Frontier," and Sherilyn Cox Bennion, "Enterprising Ladies: Utah's Nineteenth-century Women Editors," *Utah Historical Quarterly* 49 (Summer 1981): 239-53, 276-90, 291-304.

Also, Carol Cornwall Madsen, "Mormon Women and the Struggle for Definition: The Nineteenth Century Church," *Sunstone* 6 (Nov.-Dec. 1981): 7-11, reprinted in *Dialogue: A Journal of Mormon Thought* 14 (Winter 1981): 40-47; Maureen Ursenbach Beecher, "The 'Leading Sisters': A Female Hierarchy in Nineteenth Century Mormon Society," *Journal of Mormon History* 9 (1982): 25-39, reprinted in D. Michael Quinn, ed., *The New Mormon History: Revisionist Essays on the Past* (Salt Lake City: Signature Books, 1992); Karen Preece Neff, "Attitudes Towards Women's Rights and Roles in Utah Territory, 1847-1887," M.S. thesis, Utah State University, 1982; Nancy Briggs Rooker, "Mary Ann Burnham Freeze: Utah Evangelist," Ph.D. diss., University of Utah, 1982; Sandra L. Myres, *Westering Women and the Frontier Experience, 1800-1915* (Albuquerque: University of New Mexico Press, 1982), 221-23, 266; Kenneth W. Godfrey, Audrey Godfrey, and Jill Mulvay Derr, *Women's Voices: An Unwritten History of the Church, 1830-1900* (Salt Lake City: Deseret Book, 1982); Carol Cornwall Madsen, "A Bluestocking in Zion: The Literary Life of Emmeline B. Wells," *Dialogue: A Journal of Mormon Thought* 16 (Spring 1983): 126-40; Christine Croft Waters, "Pioneering Women Physicians, 1847-1890," in John R. Sillito, ed., *From Cottage to Market: The Professionalization of Women's Sphere* (Salt Lake City: Utah Women's History Association, 1983), 47-61; Leonard J. Arrington and Susan Arrington Madsen, *Sunbonnet Sisters: The Stories of Mormon Women and Frontier Life* (Salt Lake City: Bookcraft, 1984); Michael Vinson, "From Housework to Office Clerk: Utah's Working Women, 1870-1900," *Utah Historical Quarterly* 53 (Fall 1985): 326-35; Margaret K. Brady, "Transformations of Power: Mormon Women's Visionary Narratives," *Journal of American Folklore* 100 (Oct.-Dec. 1987): 461-68; Maureen Ursenbach Beecher, "Priestess Among the Patriarchs: Eliza R. Snow and the Mormon Female Relief Society, 1842-1877," in Carl Guarneri and David Alvarez, eds., *Religion and Society in the American West: Historical Essays* (Lanham, MD: University Press of America, 1987), 153-70; Linda King Newell, "Gifts of the Spirit: Women's Share," and Jill Mulvay Derr, "'Strength in Our Union': The Making of Mormon Sisterhood," in Maureen Ursenbach Beecher and Lavina Fielding Anderson, eds., *Sisters in Spirit: Mormon Women in Historical and Cultural Perspective,* (Urbana: University of Illinois Press, 1987), 111-150, 153-207; John Sillito and Constance L. Lieber, "'In Blessing We Too Were Blessed': Mormon Women and Spiritual Gifts," *Weber Studies* 5 (Spring 1988): 61-73; Leonard J. Arrington, "Modern Lysistratas: Mormon Women in the International Peace Movement," *Journal of Mormon History* 15 (1989): 89-104; Martha S. Bradley, "Mary Teasdel: Yet Another American in Paris," and Harriet Horne Arrington, "Alice Merrill Horne: Art Promoter and Early Utah Legislator," *Utah Historical Quarterly* 58 (Summer 1990): 244-60, 261-76; Vella Neil Evans, "Mormon Women and the Right to Wage Work," *Dialogue: A Journal of Mormon Thought* 23 (Winter 1990): 46-49; Joan Iversen, "The Mormon-Suffrage Relationship: Personal and Political Quandaries," *Frontiers: A Journal of Women Studies* 11, Nos. 2-3 (1990): 8-16; Pamela R. Brewster, "Mothers and Goddesses: American Women in the Mormon Subculture," M.A. thesis, California State University at Fullerton, 1990; Leonard J. Arrington, "The Legacy of Early Latter-day Saint Women," Tom Morain, "A Review," and Imogene Goodyear, "A Feminist Critique," *John Whitmer Historical Association Journal* 10

(1990): 3-17, 18-20, 21-23; Carol Cornwall Madsen, "'Feme Covert': Journey of a Metaphor," *Journal of Mormon History* 17 (1991): 43-61.

Also, Beverly Beeton, "A Feminist among the Mormons: Charlotte Ives Cobb Godbe Kirby," *Utah Historical Quarterly* 59 (Winter 1991): 22-31; Lola Van Wagenen, "In Their Own Behalf: The Politicization of Mormon Women and the 1870 Franchise," *Dialogue: A Journal of Mormon Thought* 24 (Winter 1991): 31-43; Maureen Ursenbach Beecher, ed., *Eliza and Her Sisters* (Salt Lake City: Aspen Books, 1991); Suzanne Larson, "An Ideograph Analysis of the Mormon Women and Non-Mormon Women's Public Argument On Polygamy and Suffrage, 1870-1886," Ph.D. diss., University of Oregon, 1992; Linda King Newell, "The Historical Relationship of Mormon Women and Priesthood," Maxine Hanks, "Historic Mormon Feminist Discourse—Excerpts," Ian G. Barber, "Mormon Women as 'Natural' Seers: An Enduring Legacy," in Maxine Hanks, ed., *Women and Authority: Re-emerging Mormon Feminism* (Salt Lake City: Signature Books, 1992), 23-48, 69-86, 167-84; Carol Cornwall Madsen, "'Sisters at the Bar': Utah Women in Law," *Utah Historical Quarterly* 61 (Summer 1993): 217-19; Susan Evans McCloud, "Ellis Shipp: Frontier Doctor and Teacher," *Cameo: Latter-day Women In Profile* 1 (Nov. 1993): 39-49; Carol Cornwall Madsen, "'The Power of Combination': Emmeline B. Wells and the National and International Councils of Women," *Brigham Young University Studies* 33, No. 4 (1993): 646-73; Martha Sonntag Bradley, "'Seizing Sacred Space': Women's Engagement in Early Mormonism," *Dialogue: A Journal of Mormon Thought* 27 (Summer 1994): 57-70; Carol Cornwall Madsen, *In Their Own Words: Women and the Story of Nauvoo* (Salt Lake City: Deseret Book Co., 1994); Rebecca Bartholomew, *Audacious Women: Early British Mormon Immigrants* (Salt Lake City: Signature Books, 1995); Carl V. Larson and Shirley N. Maynes, eds., *Women of the Mormon Battalion* (Providence, UT: Watkins Printing, 1995); Erika Doss, "'I Must Paint': Women Artists of the Rocky Mountain Region," in Patricia Trenton, ed., *Independent Spirits: Women Painters of the American West, 1890-1945* (Berkeley: University of California Press, 1995), 216-18, 237-41; Thomas C. Jepsen, "Women Telegraph Operators on the Western Frontier," *Journal of the West* 35 (Apr. 1996): 75-76, 78; and Colleen Whitley, ed., *Worth Their Salt: Notable But Often Unnoted Women of Utah* (Logan: Utah State University Press, 1996).

6. The classic essay on this is Barbara Welter, "The Cult of True Womanhood: 1820-1860," *American Quarterly* 18 (Summer 1966): 151-74, which she reprinted in her *Dimity Convictions: The American Woman in the Nineteenth Century* (Athens: Ohio University Press, 1976). For other views, see Carl N. Degler, *At Odds: Women and the Family in America from the Revolution to the Present* (New York: Oxford University Press, 1980); Mabel Collins Donnelly, *The American Victorian Woman: The Myth and the Reality* (Westport, CT: Greenwood-Praeger Press, 1986).

7. Carol Cornwall Madsen, "A Mormon Woman in Victorian America," Ph.D. diss., University of Utah, 1985, esp. 164-65; also Carol Cornwall Madsen, "Emmeline B. Wells: 'Am I Not a Woman and a Sister?'" *Brigham Young University Studies* 22 (Spring 1982): 161-178; Carol Cornwall Madsen, "Emmeline B. Wells: A Voice for Mormon Women," *John Whitmer Historical Association Journal* 2 (1982): 11-22; Carol Cornwall Madsen, "Emmeline B. Wells," in Allan Kent Powell, ed., *Utah History Encyclopedia* (Salt Lake City: University of Utah Press, 1994), 626-27; D. Michael Quinn, "Emmeline Blanche Woodward Wells," in John A. Garraty, ed., *American National Biography* (New York: Oxford University Press, forthcoming).

8. Lawrence Foster, "From Frontier Activism to Neo-Victorian Domesticity: Mormon Women in the Nineteenth and Twentieth Centuries," *Journal of Mormon History* 6 (1979): 3-21; Linda King Newell, "A Gift Given, A Gift Taken: Washing, Anointing, and Blessing the Sick Among Mormon Women," *Sunstone* 6 (Sept.-Oct. 1981): 16-25.

9. Joseph Fielding Smith, Harold B. Lee, and N. Eldon Tanner statement, 17 July 1970, photocopy in my possession; statement summarized but not quoted in Jill Mulvay Derr, Janath Russell Cannon, and Maureen Ursenbach Beecher, *Women of Covenant: The Story of Relief Society* (Salt Lake City: Deseret Book Co., 1992), 341.

10. For feminist developments in the 1960s, see Eleanor Flexner, *Century of Struggle: The Woman's Rights Movement in the United States* (Cambridge, MA: Belknap Press/Harvard University Press, 1959); Betty Friedan, *The Feminine Mystique* (New York: W. W. Norton, 1963); William L. O'Neill, *Everyone Was Brave: The Rise and Fall of Feminism in America* (Chicago: Quadrangle Books, 1969); *Voices of the New Feminism* (Boston: Beacon Press, 1970); Cellestine Ware, *Woman Power: The Movement for Women's Liberation* (New York: Tower Publications, 1970); Shulmith Firestone, *The Dialectic of Sex: The Case for Feminist Revolution* (New York: Morrow, 1970); June Sochen, *The New Feminism in Twentieth-Century America* (Lexington, MA: D.C. Heath, 1971); Judith Hole, *Rebirth of Feminism* (New York: Quadrangle Books, 1971); Gloria Martin, *Socialist Feminism: The First Decade, 1966-76*, 2d. ed. (Seattle: Freedom Socialist Publications, 1986); Leila J. Rupp, *Survival In the Doldrums: The American Women's Rights Movement, 1945 to the 1960s* (New York: Oxford University Press, 1987); Nancy F. Cott, *The Grounding of Modern Feminism* (New Haven: Yale University Press, 1987); Cynthia Ellen Harrison, *On Account of Sex: The Politics of Women's Issues, 1945-1968* (Berkeley: University of California Press, 1988); Winifred D. Wandersee, *On the Move: American Women in the 1970s* (Boston: Twayne, 1988); Alice Echols, *Daring To Be Bad: Radical Feminism In America, 1967-1975* (Minneapolis: University of Minnesota Press, 1989); Flora Davis, *Moving the Mountain: The Women's Movement In American Since 1960* (New York: Simon & Schuster, 1991); Blanche Linden-Ward, *American Women In the 1960s: Changing the Future* (New York: Twayne, 1993); and Kathleen Anne Weigland, "Vanguards of Women's Liberation: The Old Left and the Continuity of the Women's Movement in the United States, 1945-1970s," Ph.D. diss., Ohio State University, 1995.

For the social upheaval of the 1960s in America generally, see Kenneth Keniston, *Young Radicals: Notes on Committed Youth* (New York: Harcourt, Brace, and World, 1968); Theodore Roszak, *The Making of a Counter Culture: Reflections on the Technocratic Society and Its Youthful Opposition* (Garden City, NY: Doubleday, 1969);Philip Slater, *The Pursuit of Loneliness: American Culture at the Breaking Point* (Boston: Beacon Press, 1970); David Burner, Robert D. Marcus, and Thomas R. West, *A Giant's Strength: America in the 1960s* (New York: Holt, Rinehart and Winston, 1971); Arthur Bell, *Dancing the Gay Lib Blues: A Year In the Homosexual Liberation Movement* (New York: Simon and Schuster, 1971); William L. O'Neill, *Coming Apart: An Informal History of America in the 1960's* (Chicago: Quadrangle Books, 1971); Laud Humphreys, *Out of the Closets: The Sociology of Homosexual Liberation* (Englewood Cliffs, NJ: Prentice-Hall, 1972); Donald D. Warren, *The Radical Center: Middle Americans and the Politics of Alienation* (South Bend, IN: University of Notre Dame Press, 1976); Morris Dickstein, *Gates of Eden: American Culture in the Sixties* (New York: Basic Books, 1977); Charles R. Morris, *A Time of Passion: America, 1960-1980* (New York: Harper and Row, 1984); Allen J. Matusow, *The Unraveling of America: A History of Liberalism in the 1960s* (New York: Harper and Row, 1984); Todd Gitlin, *The Sixties: Years of Hope, Days of Rage* (New York: Bantam Books, 1987); Kim McQuaid, *The Anxious Years: America in the Vietnam-Watergate Era* (New York: Basic Books, 1989); Stewart Burns, *Social Movements of the 1960s: Searching For Democracy* (Boston: Twayne, 1990); Peter Collier, *Destructive Generation: Second Thoughts About the Sixties* (New York: Simon and Schuster, 1990); Edward P. Morgan, *The 60s Experience: Hard Lessons About Modern America* (Philadelphia: Temple University Press, 1991); Eric R. Nelson, "Breaking Through To the Other Side: The Rhetorical and Ideological Consciousness of Sixties Radicalism," M.A. thesis, University of Ohio, 1992; Margaret Cruikshank, *The Gay and Lesbian Liberation Movement* (New York: Routledge, 1992); Robert S. Ellwood, *The Sixties Spiritual Awakening: American Religion Moving From Modern To Postmodern* (New Brunswick, NJ: Rutgers University Press, 1994);

Craig Cox, *Storefront Revolution: Food Co-ops and the Counterculture* (New Brunswick, NJ: Rutgers University Press, 1994); Melvin Small, *Covering Dissent: The Media and the Anti-Vietnam War Movement* (New Brunswick, NJ: Rutgers University Press, 1994); Meta Mendel-Reyes, *Reclaiming Democracy: The Sixties In Politics and Memory* (New York: Routledge, 1995); Mary C. Brennan, *Turning Right In the Sixties: The Conservative Capture of the GOP* (Chapel Hill: University of North Carolina Press, 1995); David Steigerwald, *The Sixties and the End of Modern America* (New York: St. Martin's Press, 1995); Terry H. Anderson, *The Movement and the Sixties* (New York: Oxford University Press, 1995); Barry D. Adam, *The Rise of a Gay and Lesbian Movement*, rev. ed. (New York: Twayne, 1995); Douglas T. Miller, *On Our Own: Americans In the Sixties* (Lexington, MA: D. C. Heath, 1996); Michael Bibby, *Hearts and Minds: Bodies, Poetry, and Resistance in the Vietnam Era* (New Brunswick, NJ: Rutgers University Press, 1996); Lynn Spigel and Michael Curtin, *The Revolution Wasn't Televised: Sixties Television and Social Conflict* (New York: Routledge, 1996); and Stephen Macedo, *Reassessing the Sixties: The Constitutional Legacy* (New York: W. W. Norton, 1996).

11. "Message from the First Presidency," *Ensign* 1 (Jan. 1971): 1. Val Norman Edwards, "A Rhetorical Analysis of Three Policy Statements of the Church of Jesus Christ of Latter-day Saints," M.S. thesis, University of Utah, 1987, 32-77, gives a perceptive analysis of the ideology and rhetoric of the church's campaign against women's liberation and against the ERA.

12. Gilbert Y. Steiner, *Constitutional Inequality: The Political Fortunes of the Equal Rights Amendment* (Washington, D.C.: The Brookings Institution, 1985), 6-21; Donald Bruce Johnson, comp., *National Party Platforms*, 2 vols. (Urbana: University of Illinois Press, 1978), 1:393, 403, 412, 453, 486, 504, 537, 554, 2:791, 820, 880, 976.

13. *Congressional Record* 96: 861; Joan Hoff-Wilson, ed., *Rights of Passage: The Past and Future of the ERA* (Bloomington: Indiana University Press, 1986), 122; "Mormons Who Have Served In U.S. Government (As of October 1982)," in *Deseret News 1983 Church Almanac: The Church of Jesus Christ of Latter-day Saints* (Salt Lake City: Deseret News, 1982), 284; also Amelia R. Fry, "Conversations With Alice Paul: Woman Suffrage and the Equal Rights Amendment," 24-26 Nov. 1972, 518-24, Suffragists Oral History Project, Bancroft Library, University of California, Berkeley.

14. J. Reuben Clark office diary, 25 Jan. 1950, Clark papers, Department of Special Collections and Manuscripts, Harold B. Lee Library, Brigham Young University, Provo, Utah (hereafter Lee Library). For Clark as a strict constructionist, see Martin B. Hickman, "J. Reuben Clark, Jr.: The Constitution and The Great Fundamentals," *Brigham Young University Studies* 13 (Spring 1973): 255-72.

15. *Congressional Record* 117:35815, 118:9598; "Mormons Who Have Served in U.S. Government (As of October 1982)," in *Deseret News 1983 Church Almanac*, 284.

16. Janet K. Boles, *The Politics of the Equal Rights Amendment: Conflict and the Decision Process* (New York: Longman, 1979), 2-3; Berry, *Why ERA Failed*, 64; Kate Gardner, "What The ERA Will Mean To You," *Exponent II: A Quarterly Newspaper Concerning Mormon Women, Published by Mormon Women, and of Interest to Mormon Women and Others* [Arlington, MA] 1 (July 1974): 2, its first issue; Armand L. Mauss, *The Angel and the Beehive: The Mormon Struggle with Assimilation* (Urbana: University of Illinois Press, 1994), 117.

17. "Gem Legislature Ratifies Amendment to Ensure Women's Equal Rights," *Idaho Statesman* (Boise, ID), 25 Mar. 1972, 14; "Idaho Ratifies Equal Rights," *Post-Register* (Idaho Falls, ID), 25 Mar. 1972, A-11.

18. Kathryn L. MacKay, "Equal Rights Amendment," in Powell, *Utah History Encyclopedia*, 174.

19. *The Woman's Chronicler: The Equal Rights Amendment: Pertinent Issues Affecting Women–Distributed by the Utah Order of Women Legislators–Salt Lake City, Utah* 1 (Sept. 1974), 2 (Oct. 1976); also Delila M. Abbott and Beverly J. White, *Women Legislators of Utah, 1896-1933* ([Salt Lake City]: N.p. 1993); LDS church censuses, 1914-60, Family History

Library, Church of Jesus Christ of Latter-day Saints, Salt Lake City, Utah. Rearranged in alphabetical order, these LDS women were Delila Richards Abbott (R), Sunday Cardall Anderson (D), Algie Eggertsen Ballif (D), Reva Beck Bosone (D), Vervene ("Vee") Carlisle (D), Lois Bowen Christensen (R), Odessa Allred Cullimore (D), Nellie Haynes Jack (D), Cleo Lund Jensen (D), Josephine Scott Jensen (D), Mary Lorraine Haynes Johnson (D), Margot Ralphs Cannon Kimball (D), Della Lisonbee Loveridge (D), Beatrice Petersen Marchant (D), Ivie Vawdrey Mitchell (D), Rebecca Adams Nalder (D), Ethel Pyne (R), Elizabeth Miller Bodell Skanchy (D), Rita Urie (D), Mary Elizabeth Averett Vance (D), and Beverly J. Larson White (D). Beverly B. Clopton, *Her Honor, the Judge: The Story of Reva Beck Bosone* (Ames: Iowa State University Press, 1980), 161, stated that "she was a non-Mormon," yet described at length Bosone's Mormon family background and her father's LDS funeral (20-25, 53). LDS records shows that she was a baptized Mormon who, as a traditional sign of personal faith, obtained her patriarchal blessing on her eighteenth birthday. See Clarence Beck family of Idaho in LDS church census for 1925 and 1930, also Reva Elizabeth Beck in Patriarchal Blessing Index, all at LDS Family History Library, Salt Lake City, Utah.

20. "Most Favor Full Rights For Women," *Deseret News*, 15 Nov. 1974, A-1, A-7.

21. Boles, *Politics of the Equal Rights Amendment*, 2-3; Lorie Winder, "LDS Position on the ERA: An Historical View," *Exponent II* 6 (Winter 1980): 6.

22. As stated to his grandson David L. Goates and reported to me by Goates in December 1978. Without this perspective, Mauss, *Angel and the Beehive*, 118, has written that "it is truly difficult to understand both why the church opposed the ERA at all, especially so late in the ratification process, and why its opposition was so strenuous"; also Armand L. Mauss and M. Gerald Bradford, "Mormon Politics and Assimilation: Toward a Theory of Mormon Church Involvement in National U.S. Politics," in Anson Shupe and Jeffrey K. Hadden, eds., *Religion and the Political Order* (New York: Paragon House, 1988), 59n12.

23. James B. Allen and Glen M. Leonard, *The Story of the Latter-day Saints*, 2d ed. rev. (Salt Lake City: Deseret Book Co., 1992), 659.

24. Robert Gottlieb and Peter Wiley, *America's Saints: The Rise of Mormon Power* (New York: G. P. Putnam's Sons, 1984), 204, and 269, which cites the correspondence of Barbara B. Smith with Doris M. Harker of the law firm of Romney, Nelson, and Cassity as the source for this discussion; also Barbara B. Smith interviews, June-July 1977, cited in Martha Sonntag Bradley, "The Mormon Relief Society and the International Women's Year Conference," *Journal of Mormon History* 21 (Spring 1995): 117; also "LDS Church's Influence A Myth, Legislators Say," *Deseret News*, 16 Jan. 1993, B-1, for Faust as a Democrat and for the Public Affairs Committee, the renamed Special Affairs Committee.

25. "Equal Rights Amendment Is Opposed by Relief Society President," *Deseret News "Church News,"* 21 Dec. 1974, 7; also "Relief Society President Assails ERA," *Salt Lake Tribune*, 14 Dec. 1974, B-1; Winder, "LDS Position on the ERA," 6. The quoted phrases, as well as much of this talk, have the cadences and style of Gordon B. Hinckley. Bradley, "The Mormon Relief Society and the International Women's Year Conference," 115, mistakenly cites the *Tribune* report as a talk by former Relief Society president Belle Spafford. Her very temperate remarks in July 1974 (see below) did not echo the style or dark warnings of the remarks by Barbara Smith and others from December 1974 on.

26. "Mormon Leader Attacks Sexual Revolution," *San Jose Mercury-News* [San Jose, CA], 5 Jan. 1975, 17; also referred to in White, "Overt and Covert Politics," 11; Gottlieb and Wiley, *America's Saints*, 203-204.

27. "Equal Rights Amendment," *Deseret News "Church News,"* 11 Jan. 1975, 16; "Church Stand Apparently Dooms ERA Amendment," *Herald Journal* (Logan, UT), 19 Jan. 1975, 1; "Mormon Opposition Chills Prospects for ERA in Utah," *Washington Post*, 18 Feb. 1975, A-2; Stephen W. Stathis and Dennis L. Lythgoe, "Mormonism in the Nineteen-Seventies: The Popular Perception," *Dialogue: A Journal of Mormon Thought* 10 (Spring 1977):

110. For the quote about Petersen's editorial role, see *Deseret News "Church News,"* 15 Jan. 1984, 3; also Peggy Petersen Barton, *Mark E. Petersen: A Biography* (Salt Lake City: Deseret Book Co., 1985), 114.

28. M. Byron Fisher statement in "ERA Effort Fails to Take Hold, *Salt Lake Tribune,* 22 Jan. 1975, A-4; "Equal Rights Amendment Suffers Defeat Amid Emotional Voting," *Salt Lake Tribune,* 19 Feb. 1975, A-1; "Utah House Rejects ERA by 54-21 Vote," *Deseret News,* 19 Feb. 1975, A-1; White, "Overt and Covert Politics," 11; White, "Mormonism and the Equal Rights Amendment," 251; also Alice Allred Pottmyer, "Sonia Johnson: Mormonism's Feminist Heretic," in Roger D. Launius and Linda Thatcher, eds., *Differing Visions: Dissenters in Mormon History* (Urbana: University of Illinois Press, 1994), 370; Mauss, *Angel and the Beehive,* 117.

29. Minutes and by-laws, 6 May 1975, Collection of the Equal Rights Coalition of Utah, Utah State Historical Society, Salt Lake City; also Beatrice Marchant, "Common Carrier: Questions Church Political Influence," *Salt Lake Tribune,* 21 Nov. 1976, B-14.

30. Boles, *Politics of the Equal Rights Amendment,* 2-3.

31. "LDS Leaders Oppose ERA," *Deseret News,* 22 Oct. 1976, B-1; Peter James Caulfield, "Rhetoric and the Equal Rights Amendment: Contemporary Means of Persuasion," D.A. diss., University of Michigan, 1984, 136-37, regarded the First Presidency's argument as a puzzling "fear" that legislation could alter biology.

32. Ezra Taft Benson to "All Stake and Mission Presidents in the United States," 29 Dec. 1976, emphasis in original, photocopy in my possession.

33. For Benson's ultra-conservative politics, see chap. 3. On 4 March 1979 Benson told males in a fourteen-stake fireside at Brigham Young University: "You are the provider, and it takes the edge off your manliness when you have the mother of your children also be a provider." See Benson, "In His Steps," *1979 Devotional Speeches of the Year* (Provo, UT: Brigham Young University Press, 1980), 64. On 26 September 1981, addressing the women's general meeting, he instructed them that their "first and most important role has been ushering [children] into mortality.... Adam was instructed to earn the bread... —not Eve. Contrary to conventional wisdom, a mother's place is in the home! . . . The responsibilities of motherhood cannot be successfully delegated." See Benson, "The Honored Place of Woman," *Ensign* 11 (Nov. 1981): 105-106.

34. "2,300 Show Up at Meeting to Express ERA Opposition," *Evening Post Register* (Idaho Falls, ID), 10 Jan. 1977, A-2; "Drive to Stop ERA Given LDS Backing," *Idaho State Journal* (Boise, ID), 9 Jan. 1977, 1; "LDS Apostle Sees ERA As 'Threat' to Family," *Salt Lake Tribune,* 9 Jan. 1977, B-4; Winder, "LDS Position on the ERA," 6; "Chronology: The Mormon Anti-ERA Campaign," *Mormons for ERA Newsletter* 5 (Feb. 1983): [5]; Pottmyer, "Sonia Johnson," 372.

35. "Idaho Asks LDS Official to Respond," *Deseret News,* 21 Jan. 1977, D-1; "Idaho Clears Church in Lobby Accusation," *Deseret News,* 22 Jan. 1977, A-4.

36. Boyd K. Packer, "The Equal Rights Amendment," *Ensign* 7 (Mar. 1977): 6-9.

37. "Regional Representatives [1967-82]," *Deseret News 1983 Church Almanac,* 113; "Marion J. Callister Papers: The File on Idaho v. Freeman," MS 1512, Lee Library; chronology of Callister's role in the Equal Rights Amendment, fd 15, box 2, Collection of Utah Women's Issues, 1970s-80s, Marriott Library; also "Judge's Removal Sought in Suit Against ERA," *New York Times,* 26 Aug. 1979, 25; "NOW Renews Effort to Remove LDS Judge," *Deseret News,* 3 Dec. 1979, A-1; "Women Seeking to Disqualify a Mormon Judge In Equal Rights Case," *New York Times,* 4 Dec. 1979, A-13; "NOW Opposes Mormon Judge in ERA Case," *Washington Post,* 4 Dec. 1979, A-6; "8 in House Seek Mormon Judge's Ouster in Rights Amendment Case," *New York Times,* 7 Dec. 1979, A-23; "Mormons, the Judge and ERA," *Washington Post,* 15 Dec. 1979, A-15; Ruth Marcus, "No Appeal on Mormon Judge," *National Law Journal* 2 (24 Dec. 1979): 2; "Idahoans Say Religion Won't Sway Judge on ERA," *New York Times,* 26 Dec. 1979, A-20; "Mormon Ouster of ERA Backer Adds Pressure

on U.S. Judge," *Washington Post,* 7 Dec. 1979, B-3; "Mormon Judge Won't Disqualify Self In ERA Rescission Case," *ADA World* 35 (Winter 1980): 5; "Judge in Equal Rights Suit No Longer Mormon Officer," *New York Times,* 5 Jan. 1980, 8; Ronald Goetz, "Justifiable Exceptions to Religious Freedom?" *Christian Century* 97 (16 Jan. 1980): 38-39; "The Judge Gave Up the Wrong Task," *New York Times,* 29 Jan. 1980, 18; "Judge Refuses to Drop Case on Rights Amendment," *New York Times,* 19 Aug. 1980, 8; Stephen W. Stathis, "Mormonism and the Periodical Press: A Change Is Underway," *Dialogue: A Journal of Mormon Thought* (Summer 1981): 52-55; "Mormon Judge Challenged on Rights Amendment Suit," *New York Times,* 24 Sept. 1980, A-7; Ruth Marcus, "NOW Revives Attempt to Remove Mormon Judge," *National Law Journal* 3 (6 Oct. 1980): 6; "Laws of the Land: Callister's Decision," *Sunstone* 7 (Mar./Apr. 1982): 60-63; Berry, *Why ERA Failed,* 79.

38. "LDS Official's Son Works for Idaho Judge," *Salt Lake Tribune,* 21 Jan. 1980, C-6; *Deseret News 1995-1996 Church Almanac,* 15, 18; Gottlieb and Wiley, *America's Saints,* 92, 257; Steve Benson, "Ezra Taft Benson: A Grandson's Remembrance," *Sunstone* 17 (Dec. 1994): 30; "Elder Gordon B. Hinckley Called to First Presidency, Elder Neal A. Maxwell to Quorum of Twelve," *Ensign* 11 (Sept. 1981): 73. Maxwell A. Miller and Nancie George, "Judicial Activism and the Constitutional Amendment Process," *Journal of Social, Political, and Economic Studies* 9 (Fall 1984): 293-308, presented a seemingly thorough defense of Callister's conduct. However, their Mormon anti-ERA bias was evident in two respects. First, their citation of BYU law professor Rex E. Lee's booklet as the only source for legal interpretations of the ERA's consequences (293, 304n2). Second, their dismissal of the validity of charges of religious bias against Callister (296, 298) without acknowledging that he was a regional representative. Nor did the authors acknowledge the relationship to the hierarchy of the judge's clerk.

39. Patricia Brim, "The IWY Conference in Utah," 4, fd 35, box 4, Collection of Utah Women's Issues; Linda Sillitoe, "Women Scorned: Inside the IWY Conference," *Utah Holiday* 6 (Aug. 1977): 27; Derr, Cannon, and Beecher, *Women of Covenant,* 370.

40. Georgia Peterson interview, 19 Jan. 1992, cited in Bradley, "Mormon Relief Society and the International Women's Year Conference," 132-33; also Gottlieb and Wiley, *America's Saints,* 204; "Dedicated Legal Team Counsels Church Law," *Deseret News "Church News,"* 9 Jan. 1971, 4, for McConkie's position; *Deseret News 1977 Church Almanac* (Salt Lake City: Deseret News, 1977), 224 for Ashton's position; Sillitoe, "Women Scorned: Inside the IWY Conference," 63-64, and Bradley (131) for Peterson's organization; *Between Ring & Temple: A Handbook for Engaged L.D.S. Couples (and others who need a review)* (Salt Lake City: Olympus Publishing Co., 1981), 9, for Moana Ballif Bennett's positions; statement to me on 1 Oct. 1994 by Lavina Fielding Anderson (formerly associate editor of the *Ensign* magazine) about Moana Bennett's role as speech-writer for Relief Society president Barbara B. Smith. Available sources have not yet identified the person who first suggested the tactic, and it is possible that it simply emerged during discussions of the four persons involved in this *ad hoc* committee.

41. Relief Society General Presidency, with no signatures or names, to "All Regional Representatives in Utah," 3 June 1977, copy in collection of Equal Rights Coalition of Utah, also quoted in Bradley, "Mormon Relief Society and the International Women's Year Conference," 127-28, which describes it as "a letter, also from Benson's office . . . on Relief Society letterhead"; Sheri L. Dew, *Ezra Taft Benson: A Biography* (Salt Lake City: Deseret Book Co., 1987), 453-54; "IWY Parley Involvement Urged," *Deseret News "Church News,"* 18 June 1977, 5. Derr, Cannon, and Beecher, *Women of Covenant,* 371: "First came 'a priesthood telephone call' to the Utah regional representatives; then a follow-up letter was sent from the Relief Society to the regional representatives and also to stake Relief Society presidents."

42. "10,000 Jam Hall, Foyer at Women's Sessions," *Deseret News,* 24 June 1977, A-1; "Mormon Turnout Overwhelms Women's Conference in Utah," *New York Times,* 25 July 1977, 26; "Mormon Utah: Where a Church Shapes the Life of a State," *U.S. News and World Report* 83 (19 Dec. 1977): 59; Marilyn Warenski, *Patriarchs and Politics: The Plight of the Mormon Woman* (New York: McGraw-Hill Book Co., 1978), 14-16.

43. Bradley, "Mormon Relief Society and the International Women's Year Conference," 134.

44. Belva Ashton interview, 30 Aug. 1991, quoted in ibid., 124. For her service on the general board (1962-78), see Derr, Cannon, and Beecher, *Women of Covenant,* 438.

45. Linda Sillitoe typed transcript of interview with Dennis Ker, director of the Conservative Caucus in Utah's Second Congressional District, 2 July 1977, fd 10, box 6, Collection of Utah Women's Issues; also Bradley, "Mormon Relief Society and the International Women's Year Conference," 133-34. Although misspelled in some publications, Ker was the spelling of this bishop's name in *The Church of Jesus Christ of Latter-day Saints Directory: General Authorities and Officers, 1978* (Salt Lake City: Deseret News Press, 1977), 115.

46. Bradley, "Mormon Relief Society and the International Women's Year Conference," 134, with the explanation 139n77: "Although some [of the twenty-two films at the IWY conference] touched on sexuality, the majority were not offensive to the general population and none of them could reasonably be called 'pornographic.'"

47. Lisa Bolin Hawkins, "Report on the Utah International Women's Year Meeting," 2, fd 5, box 2, Collection of Utah Women's Issues. For Amy Y. Valentine's general board service (1969-82), see Derr, Cannon, and Beecher, *Women of Covenant,* 439, which gives an inadequate statement of the situation (371) in view of Valentine's instructions at these meetings: "The [Relief Society general] presidency had not sanctioned the pre-conference sessions, but they were sometimes given an aura of authority by being identified with Relief Society."

48. "Stop E.R.A. on June 24-25," *The Utah Independent: Dedicated To The Constitution, Liberty, Morality, and Truth* (23 June 1977): 11. For the Birch connection of this newspaper, see chap. 3.

49. Notes of my telephone interview with Lou Chandler on 10 May 1994.

50. Sillitoe, "Women Scorned: Inside the IWY Conference," 63; Hawkins, "Report on the Utah International Women's Year Meeting," 7-8; Dixie Snow Huefner, "Church and Politics at the Utah IWY Conference," *Dialogue: A Journal of Mormon Thought* 11 (Spring 1978): 64; Bradley, "Mormon Relief Society and the International Women's Year Conference," 139-40.

51. Edith Mayo and Jerry K. Frye, "The ERA: Postmortem of a Failure in Political Communication," in Hoff-Wilson, *Rights of Passage,* 76; Berry, *Why ERA Failed,* 68; Renee Feinberg, *The Equal Rights Amendment: An Annotated Bibliography of the Issues, 1976-1985* (Westport, CT: Greenwood Press, 1986), 115, entry 10-22.

52. "IWY Parley Involvement Urged," and "Salt Lake: Sister Smith Praises Anti-Gay Effort," *Deseret News "Church News,"* 18 June 1977, 5, 11.

53. Hawkins, "Report on the Utah International Women's Year Meeting," 5, 7-8, fd 5, box 2, and Brim, "The IWY Conference in Utah," fd 35, box 4, Collection of Utah Women's Issues; "Papers of the International Women's Year Conference, Utah," Marriott Library; Sillitoe, "Women Scorned: Inside the IWY Conference," 26-28, 63-69; Huefner, "Church and Politics at the Utah IWY Conference," 58-75; Maureen Ursenbach Beecher and Kathryn L. MacKay, "Women in Twentieth-century Utah" in Poll, *Utah's History,* 583-84; Gottlieb and Wiley, *America's Saints,* 201-202; Bradley, "Mormon Relief Society and the International Women's Year Conference," 141, 146.

54. "Sample Ballot," in Vertical File for "International Women's Year," Special Collections, Marriott Library; also Bradley, "Mormon Relief Society and the International Women's Year Conference," 158, 159, 160. The Utah ballot proposals had been extracted from National Commission on the Observance of International Women's Year, *". . . TO FORM A MORE PERFECT UNION . . .": Justice for American Women* (Washington, D.C.: U.S. Government Printing Office, 1976).

55. Bradley, "Mormon Relief Society and the International Women's Year Conference," 144-45, 146; "Women at Utah Meeting Oppose Rights Proposal," *New York Times*, 26 June 1977, 32; "LDS Women Stand Firm at IWY Meet," *Deseret News "Church News,"* 26 Nov. 1977, 5.

56. Sillitoe, "Women Scorned: Inside the IWY Conference," 64, 66; Huefner, "Church and Politics at the Utah IWY Conference," 64; Bradley, "Mormon Relief Society and the International Women's Year Conference," 135, 136.

57. Her statement referred to the national IWY conference at Houston, but it applied equally well to the conference in Utah. See Eleanor Ricks Colton, president of the Washington, D.C., Stake Relief Society, statement in "A Mormon Woman Looks at the ERA," *Washington Post*, 21 Nov. 1977, A-19, quoted in Derr, Cannon, and Beecher, *Women of Covenant*, 370; also Lincoln C. Oliphant, "Is There An ERA-Abortion Connection?" *Dialogue: A Journal of Mormon Thought* 14 (Spring 1981): 65-72.

58. Mary Gaber, "Houston Wasn't Camelot—But There *Was* a Shining Moment," *Utah Holiday* 7 (Jan. 1978): 6-7.

59. "Mormon Turnout Overwhelms Women's Conference in Utah," *New York Times*, 25 July 1977, 26; "IWY Issues Missing As State Meets Take Sides on Abortion, ERA," *Salt Lake Tribune*, 11 July 1977, A-2. For the fifteen-year controversy in the LDS church about the Birch Society, see chap. 3.

60. Form letter from Barbara Smith, Janath R. Cannon, Marian R. Boyer, general presidency of the Relief Society, 11 July 1977, fd 15, box 6, Collection of Utah Women's Issues; "Relief Society Head Sensitive to Women," *Salt Lake Tribune*, 14 Aug. 1977, W-1.

61. In denying a role of "the Mormon male hierarchy" in packing the conference, Derr, Cannon, and Beecher, *Women of Covenant*, 371, emphasized that the local IWY organizers had originally requested the general authorities to encourage attendance. However, this history's discussion makes no reference to the June planning meeting of McConkie, Ashton, Peterson, and Bennett at LDS headquarters to devise strategy.

62. "Honolulu Stake Workshop Assignments," and handout regarding the Hawaii State Women's meeting 8-10 July 1977, fd 1, Collection of Conservative Women Opposed to the Equal Rights Amendment, MSS SC 1827, Lee Library.

63. "Bitter Battle Expected at Women's Meeting," *Honolulu Star-Bulletin and Advertiser*, 8 July 1977; "Conservative Bloc Exceeds Liberals," *Honolulu Star-Bulletin and Advertiser*, 9 July 1977, 2; also "Mormon 'Blitz' Alters Tactics," *Honolulu Star-Bulletin and Advertiser*, 10 July 1977, A-1, A-4; "Mormon Woman Explains Church Opposition to ERA," *Honolulu Star-Bulletin and Advertiser*, 13 July 1977, A-4; "LDS Women Defend Stand," *Deseret News "Church News,"* 16 July 1977, 7.

64. Terry Bosgra and Lissa Atkinson to National Commission on the Observance of International Women's Year, 15 July 1977, 2, fd 1, Collection of Conservative Women Opposed to the Equal Rights Amendment.

65. "Mormon Turnout Overwhelms Women's Conference in Utah," *New York Times*, 25 July 1977, 26, which belatedly reported the Utah IWY meeting along with similar tactics in the subsequent meetings in Montana and Washington.

66. "IWY Issues Missing As State Meets Take Sides on Abortion, ERA," *Salt Lake Tribune*, 11 July 1977, A-2. The newspaper identified him as Jack Piippo.

67. Notes of my telephone interview with Mark Edward Koltko, 24 Mar. 1994, following his briefer statement to me in person, 19 Mar. 1994, concerning his role at the IWY in Albany, New York; also Pottmyer, "Sonia Johnson," 372, for these LDS methods in the IWY meeting for the state of Washington.

68. Elizabeth B. Ricks, "IWY in New York," letter to the editor, *Dialogue: A Journal of Mormon Thought* 11 (Summer 1978): 7; Ellen Morris, "More IWY," *Dialogue: A Journal of Mormon Thought* 11 (Winter 1978): 5. Among the works of the booed-speaker were Judith T. Younger, *Women and the Family: The Rights of Women and Their Needs* (Oswego, NY: State University of New York, 1978).

69. "Honolulu Stake Workshop Assignments," July 1977, fd 1, Collection of Conservative Women Opposed to the Equal Rights Amendment; "Bitter Battle Expected at Women's Meeting," *Honolulu Star-Bulletin,* 8 July 1977; transcript of an untitled talk by Assemblywoman Karen Hayes, at the Las Vegas 2nd and 8th Ward meeting house, 15 Feb. 1978, 4-6, fd 7, box 7, Johnson papers.

70. Karen Hayes statement in Ann Terry, Marilyn Slaght-Griffin, and Elizabeth Terry, *Mormons & Women* (Santa Barbara, CA: Butterfly Publishing, Inc., 1980), 101.

71. "Senators, Mormons Ask Apology in IWY Flap," *Standard-Examiner* (Ogden, UT), 22 Nov. 1977, A-10.

72. "Church Repudiates Charges," *Deseret News,* 19 Nov. 1977, A-1; also "Senators, Mormons Ask Apology in IWY Flap," *Standard-Examiner* (Ogden, UT), 22 Nov. 1977, A-10; "State Department Repudiates IWY Charge," *Deseret News,* 24 Nov. 1977, B-1; "U.S. Labels IWY Statement 'Incorrect,'" *Deseret News* "Church News," 10 Dec. 1977, 11.

73. For examples of alienation, see "Feminists Fighting Mormon Stand on ERA," *Los Angeles Times,* 17 Sept. 1977, 2; "Dissident Mormon Women Tell Why They Defy Church on ERA," *Daily Herald* (Provo, UT), 4 Feb. 1979, 46; "Feminist Mormons Speak Out for ERA: Women's Group Goes Against Church Policy," *Los Angeles Times,* 6 May 1979, VII-1, 14-18; Jan L. Tyler, "Who Is My Sister?: A Discussion of What Women *Do* To, For, With and Against Each Other," presented to the Women's Forum, Provo, Utah, 12 May 1979, fd 7, box 4, Collection of Utah Women's Issues; "Aerial Note Says LDS Back Era: Banner Hovers Temple Square," *Salt Lake Tribune,* 6 Oct. 1979, B-12; "Many Mormon Women Feel Torn Between Rights Plan and Church," *New York Times,* 26 Nov. 1979, A-1; "Feminist Seeking End to Mormon Ties: Excommunication Is Requested By Aide [Arlene Wood] to Leader [Sonia Johnson] of ERA Fight," *Arizona Republic* (Phoenix, AZ), 1 Jan. 1980, B-6; "Oregon Feminist [Linda Sandrock] Requests Ouster," *Salt Lake Tribune,* 16 Jan. 1980, D-3; "Woman [Leanne Boyd], 27, Excommunicated," *Salt Lake Tribune,* 23 Jan. 1980, D-1, reprinted in "ERA Backer Excommunicated," *Arizona Republic* (Phoenix, AZ), 23 January 1980; "Ogden Feminist [Mary Jean Uebelgunne] Joins Sonia, Leaves LDS Church," *Standard-Examiner* (Ogden, UT), 29 Feb. 1980, B-2; flier titled "X-Mormons for ERA invite you to *Picket the Mormon Conference* Sun. Oct. 5, [1980]," and Mary La Brosse, *THE MORMON CONSPIRACY: Highly Organized, Highly Motivated, Directed by Male Leaders in Utah* (Kingston, WA: Mormons for ERA, [1980]), fd 10 and fd 33, box 4, Collection of Utah Women's Issues; "Two ERA Supporters Chain Themselves to Mormon Temple," *Seattle Post-Intelligencer,* 16 Nov. 1980, A-2; "20 Women Arrested in Protests at Mormon Temple," *Seattle Times,* 17 Nov. 1980; "Mormon Temple Protest Leads to the Arrest of 19," *New York Times,* 18 Nov. 1980, A-10; "Mormons Drop Charges Against 15 Who Chained Themselves to Gates," *Seattle Post-Intelligencer,* 17 Jan. 1981, A-11; "Sustaining Vote Gets 5 Nays at Conference," *Salt Lake Tribune,* 5 Apr. 1981, A-4; Cleo Fellers Kocol, "Civil Disobedience at the Mormon Temple," *Humanist* 41 (Sept.-Oct. 1981): 5-14; "Pro-ERA Picketers Becoming Regular Conference Occurrence," *Brigham Young University Daily Universe,* 5 Oct. 1981, 3; "ERA Supporters Protest Outside Mormon Temple," *Washington Post,* 20 Jan. 1982, A-10; "Mormons Drop Proceedings Against ERA Backer [Melissa D. Mowen, age 19]," *Washington Post,* 6 Mar. 1982, B-6; "ERA Rally & Temple Picket: April 3, 1982, [sponsored by Utah

NOW]," flier in collection of the Equal Rights Coalition of Utah; "'Equal Rights' Plays Role in Teen's [Ann Wallace] Decision to Leave the LDS Church," *Daily Herald* (Provo, UT), 8 Sept. 1982, 21; "Mormons to Try Defiant Woman [Ann Wallace]," *Salt Lake Tribune*, 8 Sept. 1982, B-13; "ERA Group Pickets Conference," *Salt Lake Tribune*, 3 Oct. 1982, B-1; Amy L. Bentley, "Comforting the Motherless Children: The Alice Louise Reynolds Women's Forum," *Dialogue: A Journal of Mormon Thought* 23 (Fall 1990): 48-56.

74. F. Charles Graves, LDS Public Communications Department coordinator for New York City, "Cultivation of Media Representatives," 30 Mar. 1976, archives, Historical Department of the Church of Jesus Christ of Latter-day Saints, Salt Lake City, Utah; *The Importance of the Ward Public Communications Director* (Salt Lake City: Public Communications Department, The Church of Jesus Christ of Latter-day Saints, 1977); *Media Relations Training Outline* (Salt Lake City: Public Communications/Special Affairs Department, The Church of Jesus Christ of Latter-day Saints, 1987).

75. Boles, *Politics of the Equal Rights Amendment*, 2-3; Orrin G. Hatch, *Equal Rights Amendment: Myths and Realities* (N.p.: Savant Press, 1983), 89-94.

76. Mark R. Daniels, Robert Darcy, and Joseph W. Westphal, "The ERA Won—At least in the Opinion Polls," *PS* 15 (Fall 1982): 578-84; also "Gallup Poll: More Americans Favor ERA Than Before," *Salt Lake Tribune*, 9 Aug. 1981, A-4. Anti-ERA arguments never achieved the support of more than 34 percent of America's housewives; during the ten-year ratification controversy, only one-fourth of America's housewives expressed consistent opposition to the ERA in various opinion polls.

77. Berry, *Why ERA Failed*, 66-69.

78. Kay Mills, "Groups Split Over ERA: Mormons, Feminists At Odds," *Phoenix Gazette*, 17 Sept. 1977, A-10, wire-service story by Newhouse News Service.

79. Ruth Ann Alexander, "South Dakota Women Stake a Claim: A Feminist Memoir, 1964-1989," *South Dakota History* 19 (Winter 1989): 552; *Deseret News 1995-1996 Church Almanac*, 167, shows that Mormons are still only 1.1 percent of South Dakota's population.

80. Hatch, *The Equal Rights Amendment*, 89-94, provided a useful summary of successful rescissions and formal defeats (by legislative action or voter referendum) of rescission proposals. However, he did not identify states where there were rescission efforts that failed to garner enough support to be placed on the ballot or to receive legislative vote.

81. Karen Mecham memorandum, 5 Oct. 1979, fd 26, box 7, Johnson papers, quoted here as in the original.

82. Ezra Taft Benson to "All Stake and Mission Presidents in the United States," 29 Dec. 1976. This reflected the official position of the First Presidency since the 1960s, as specified in the front-page announcement, "Statement of the First Presidency," *Deseret News*, 23 Aug. 1962, A-1.

83. "A Conversation with Sister Barbara B. Smith, Relief Society General President," *Ensign* 6 (Mar. 1976): 12; "First Presidency Issues Statement Opposing Equal Rights Amendment," *Ensign* 6 (Dec. 1976): 79; Boyd K. Packer, "The Equal Rights Amendment," *Ensign* 7 (Mar. 1977): 6-7; "Leaders Oppose Time Extension for ERA Vote," *Deseret News "Church News,"* 27 May 1978, 5, 14; "First Presidency Opposes U.S. ERA Ratification Extension," *Ensign* 8 (Aug. 1978): 80; "First Presidency Reaffirms Opposition to ERA," *Ensign* 8 (Oct. 1978): 63-64; "The Church and ERA," *Vienna Vision* (ward newsletter, Aug. 1978), and "Prophet Calls For Positive Action Against ERA," *Oakton, Virginia Stake Newsletter* (Nov. 1978), both in fd 10, box 3, Collection of Utah Women's Issues; Gordon Shepherd and Gary Shepherd, *A Kingdom Transformed: Themes in the Development of Mormonism* (Salt Lake City: University of Utah Press, 1984), esp. 38-39, 206-207.

84. *Ensign* 10 (Mar. 1980): insert between pp. 40 and 41; copy of mailing, postmarked 21 Oct. 1980, of anti-ERA materials, "apparently sent to everyone in both St. Louis stakes," according to attached note of Bob Mecham, 3 Nov. 1980, fd 4, box 7, Kent White statement,

[1979], at Las Vegas, Nevada, fd 5, box 7, Sheldon M. Rampton statement, 11 Apr. 1979, fd 7, box 7, Oakton Virginia Stake Presidency (individually signed), "To All Families in the Oakton Virginia Stake," 8 Sept. 1978, fd 27, box 7, Johnson papers; Ken Driggs to the editor, *Dialogue: A Journal of Mormon Thought* 11 (Autumn 1978): 6; White, "Mormonism and the Equal Rights Amendment," 254-55.

85. Charles Dahlquist talk at Sterling Park Ward chapel, Oakton Stake, Virginia, 14 Dec. 1978, transcript, 1, 3, fd 21, box 3, Collection of Utah Women's Issues; Gottlieb and Wiley, *America's Saints*, 205; Pottmyer, "Sonia Johnson," 372.

86. "Many Mormon Women Feel Torn Between Equal Rights Proposal and Church," *New York Times*, 26 Nov. 1979, B-9; also Maurine Ward, *From Adam's Rib To Women's Lib* (Salt Lake City: Bookcraft, 1981), 78.

87. Kent White statement [1979], fd 5, box 7, also Sheldon M. Rampton statement, 11 Apr. 1979, fd 7, box 7, also copy of *Equal Rights–Yes! E.R.A.–NO!*, fd 8, box 7, also typed document "given to every person who attended the Mormon churches in Las Vegas on Sunday Nov. 5 and taken to them at their homes by home teachers (organized in every ward of the church through priesthood quorums) if they did not attend," fd 16, box 7, Johnson papers; Ms. Lou Ann Stoker Dickson to "Sonja" Johnson, undated, with "enclosed sheaf of papers was mailed by the Bishopric of the Tempe 8th Ward, Tempe Stake of the L.D.S. Church, to all families in the Ward," fd 1, box 3, Collection of Utah Women's Issues; Gottlieb and Wiley, *America's Saints*, 205; Pottmyer, "Sonia Johnson," 374; MacKay, "Equal Rights Amendment," in Powell, *Utah History Encyclopedia*, 174.

88. Renee Marchant Rampton statement, 10 Apr. 1979, 3, fd 7, box 7, Johnson papers.

89. Lisa Cronin Wohl, "A Mormon Connection?: The Defeat of the ERA in Nevada," *Ms.* 6 (July 1977): 70; James T. Richardson, "The 'Old Right' in Action: Mormon and Catholic Involvement in An Equal Rights Amendment Referendum," in David Bromley and Anson Shupe, eds., *New Christian Politics* (Macon, GA: Mercer University Press, 1984), 223; "Chronology: The Mormon Anti-ERA Campaign," *Mormons For the ERA Newsletter* 5 (Feb. 1983): [5].

90. Croft, "Influence of the L.D.S. Church on Utah Politics, 1945-1985," 97.

91. Lou Ann Stoker Dickson, Tempe, Arizona, to "Sonja," n.d., fd 1, box 3, Collection of Utah Women's Issues, and fd 1, box 2, Johnson papers.

92. Richardson, "The 'Old Right' in Action: Mormon and Catholic Involvement in An Equal Rights Amendment Referendum," 222, compare 216; Janet Bingham, "Beyond the Glitter: Las Vegas Saints Know the Other Side of Their City," *Ensign* 9 (Feb. 1979): 38.

93. Statements to me, 21 Mar. 1994, by Maxine Hanks who served in the Florida-Tampa Mission during the state's ERA vote. She and her missionary companion participated in this anti-ERA canvassing one evening but declined to do so after that.

94. Lyle M. Ward to "Dear Missionaries," 8 Dec. 1979, fd 27, box 7, Johnson papers.

95. Transcript minutes of meeting of "Latter-day Saint Women's Coalition," in Vienna, Virginia, 8 Nov. 1978, 1, fd 13, box 3, Linda Sillitoe interview with Julian Lowe, an LDS regional representative, 14 Feb. 1979, fd 10, box 5, Linda Sillitoe interview with Don Ladd, an LDS regional representative, 15 Feb. 1979, fd 10, box 5, Collection of Utah Women's Issues; White, "Overt and Covert Politics," 13; Sonia Johnson, *From Housewife to Heretic* (Garden City, NY: Doubleday and Co., 1981), 164-173; Gottlieb and Wiley, *America's Saints*, 81-82; MacKay, "Equal Rights Amendment," in Powell, *Utah History Encyclopedia*, 174; Pottmyer, "Sonia Johnson," 377.

96. "PROPHET CALLS FOR POSITIVE ACTION AGAINST ERA," Oakton Stake, Virginia, newsletter, Nov. 1978, fd 10, box 3, Collection of Utah Women's Issues; Gottlieb and Wiley, *America's Saints*, 205.

97. For example, "ANNOUNCEMENT FOR OAHU BISHOPS TO READ," Dec. [1978], fd 1, Collection of Conservative Women Opposed to the Equal Rights Amendment.

98. Linda Sillitoe, notes of interview with regional representative [W.] Donald Ladd, 15 Feb. 1979, fd 10, box 5, Collection of Utah Women's Issues; "Regional Representatives [1967-82]," *Deseret News 1983 Church Almanac*, 114.

99. David B. Magleby, "Contemporary American Politics," in Daniel H. Ludlow, ed., *Encyclopedia of Mormonism: The History, Scripture, Doctrine, and Procedure of the Church of Jesus Christ of Latter-day Saints*, 5 vols. (New York: Macmillan Publishing Co., 1992), 3:1108.

100. Charter of incorporation for Hana Pono, 26 Aug. 1977, and "HANA PONO ADDS PAC," *Hana Pono Forum* 2 (Feb. 1979): 1, fd 2, Collection of Conservative Women Opposed to the Equal Rights Amendment; documents of Missouri Citizens Council, fd 14, box 3, Collection of Utah Women's Issues; Renee M. Rampton to Spencer W. Kimball, 23 Nov. 1976, copy in fd 7, box 7, Illinois Citizens for Family Life promotional literature showing organization date of 16 November 1977, copy in fd 26, box 7, and memoranda about Pro-Family Unity, Save Our Families Today (SOFT), and about "Mormon Anti-ERA Organizations in Iowa," fd 26, box 7, Johnson papers; "2,500 Protest Women's Conference: Rally at State Capitol," *Arizona Republic* (Phoenix, AZ), 20 Nov. 1977, A-8; Linda Sillitoe, "The New Mormon Activists: Fighting the ERA in Virginia," *Utah Holiday* 8 (Mar. 1979): 12-13; Terry, Slaght-Griffin, and Terry, *Mormons & Women*, 107; "How the Mormons Helped Scuttle ERA," *Miami Herald*, 20 Apr. 1980, A-33; notes of statement to me on 16 October 1992 by George Johannesen, a member of Illinois Citizens for Family Life in the late 1970s. "Mormon 'Front' Organizations," *Sunstone* 5 (May-June 1980): 6-7, mistakenly identified Pro-Family Unity as the LDS organization in North Carolina (which was actually served by North Carolinians Against ERA) and mistakenly identified United Families of America as one of the LDS church's anti-ERA organizations. See next note and Clifford Cumming, the LDS president of United Families of America, to editors, *Sunstone* 5 (Sept.-Oct. 1980): 2.

101. Donald G. Mathews and Jane Sherron De Hart, *Sex, Gender, and the Politics of ERA: A State and the Nation* (New York: Oxford University Press, 1990), 67; memoranda concerning NCAERA and Save Our Families Today (SOFT), fd 26, box 7, Johnson papers; Gottlieb and Wiley, *America's Saints*, 205.

102. "Mormon 'Front' Organizations," *Sunstone* 5 (May-June 1980): 6; "Regional Representatives [1967-82]," *Deseret News 1983 Church Almanac*, 115. This organization was also identified as "SOLPAC."

103. Statement by Doris Enderle of Huntington Beach, California, in Terry, Slaght-Griffin, and Terry, *Mormons & Women*, 109. The book's interviews with pro-ERA activists Sonia Johnson, Marilee Latta, and Nadine Hansen were overwhelmed numerically by anti-ERA interviews, and the book concluded with several testimonials and pleas against ratification.

104. "ANNOUNCEMENT FOR OAHU BISHOPS TO READ," Dec. [1978], fd 1, and bulletin of Hana Pono announcing Ida Smith as speaker on Thursday, 7 June [1979], fd 2, Collection of Conservative Women Opposed to the Equal Rights Amendment.

105. Transcript of untitled talk by Assemblywoman Karen Hayes, at the Las Vegas 2nd and 8th Ward meeting house, 15 Feb. 1978, 4-6 (for lesbian-gay-dyke) and 13, for Citizens for Responsible Government, fd 7, box 7, Johnson papers; Missouri Citizens Council, printed program for Barbara Smith as speaker on 15 Nov. 1979, fd 14, box 3, Collection of Utah Women's Issues.

106. Bingham, "Beyond the Glitter," 38.

107. BYU President's weekly meeting minutes, 23 Jan. 1980, 4, photocopy in my possession; Gary James Bergera and Ronald Priddis, *Brigham Young University: A House of Faith* (Salt Lake City: Signature Books, 1985), 223; also Paul Swenson, "Who Is Beverly Campbell And Why Is Everyone Afraid of Her?" *Utah Holiday* 8 (Feb. 1979): 13; Linda Sillitoe, "The New Mormon Activists in Virginia," *Utah Holiday* 7 (Sept. 1978): 14-15; Linda Sillitoe, "The New Mormon Activists: Fighting the ERA in Virginia," *Utah Holiday* 8 (Mar.

1979): 12-13; Linda Sillitoe, "Fear and Anger in Virginia: The New Mormon Activists," *Utah Holiday* 8 (Apr. 1979): 9-10, 12; Mary L. Bradford, "Beverly Campbell: Dynamic Spokeswoman," *This People* 1 (Summer 1980): 50-54; "A Conversation With Beverly Campbell," *Dialogue: A Journal of Mormon Thought* 14 (Spring 1981): 45-57; Mary Lythgoe Bradford, "Beverly Brough Campbell: Opportunities Beyond My Wildest Imaginings," *Cameo: Latter-day Women in Profile* 1 (Dec. 1993): 21-22; Pottmyer, "Sonia Johnson," 378; Carol Felsenthal, *The Sweetheart of the Silent Majority: The Biography of Phyllis Schlafly* (Garden City, NY: Doubleday & Co., 1981).

108. Linda Sillitoe notes of interview with Julian Lowe, an LDS regional representative in Virginia, 14 Feb. 1979, fd 10, box 5, Collection of Utah Women's Issues; "Regional Representatives [1967-82]," *Deseret News 1983 Church Almanac,* 115.

109. Richardson, "The 'Old Right' In Action: Mormon and Catholic Involvement in An Equal Rights Amendment Referendum," 218; "Regional Representatives [1967-82]," *Deseret News 1983 Church Almanac,* 114.

110. Sheldon M. Rampton statement, 11 Apr. 1979, p. 2, fd 7, box 7, Johnson papers; White, "Mormonism and the Equal Rights Amendment," 255; Gottlieb and Wiley, *America's Saints,* 204-205.

111. Pottmyer, "Sonia Johnson," 372.

112. White "Overt and Covert Politics," 15; White, "Mormonism and the Equal Rights Amendment," 255; "Mormon Muscle: Members' Funds Fought ERA," *Sacramento Bee,* 19 Apr. 1980, A-1; "Mormon Money Worked Against Florida's ERA," *Miami Herald,* 20 Apr. 1980, A-1, A-33; "Church Orchestrated Florida Anti-ERA Drive, Report Details," *Salt Lake Tribune,* 21 Apr. 1980, D-1; "Mormon Church Plays Key Role in Anti-ERA Fight," *Sacramento Bee,* 4 May 1980, A-3, A-4; "Update," *Sunstone* 5 (May-June 1980):6-7; Florida "Campaign Treasurer's Report, Contributions," from "FACT PAC—Families Are Concerned Today Pol. Action Com.," in separately dated reports for 14 Oct. 1978-2 Jan. 1979, copies in fd 5, box 3, Collection of Utah Women's Issues, and in fd 3, box 7, Johnson papers; Gottlieb and Wiley, *America's Saints,* 204; also Cindy Le Fevre, "California State National Organization for Women, Sacramento National Organization for Women, and the Equal Rights Amendment, 1972-82," senior seminar paper, California State University at Sacramento, courtesy of its author. For Carmack, see also "Regional Representatives [1967-82]," *Deseret News 1983 Church Almanac,* 113; *Deseret News 1995-1996 Church Almanac,* 24.

113. Joan S. Carver, "The Equal Rights Amendment and the Florida Legislature," *Florida Historical Quarterly* 60 (Apr. 1982): 475n62.

114. Lybbert statement in "How the Mormons Helped Scuttle ERA," *Miami Herald,* 20 Apr. 1980, A-33, quoted in "Church Orchestrated Florida Anti-ERA Drive, Report Details," *Salt Lake Tribune,* 21 Apr. 1980, D-1 and in "Florida ERA Campaign," *Sunstone* 5 (May-June 1980): 6, with his affiliation in "SOLPAC" on same page of *Sunstone* under "Mormon 'Front' Organizations."

115. "Mormon Money Worked Against Florida's ERA," *Miami Herald,* 20 Apr. 1980, A-1.

116. Linda Sillitoe notes of undated interview with Bill Evans concerning the Special Affairs Committee, fd 10, box 5, Collection of Utah Women's Issues.

117. "State Official Probes Mormon Lobbying," *Reston [Virginia] Times,* 1 Mar. 1979, 1; "Mormon Lobby On ERA Probed," *Alexandria [Virginia] Gazette,* 1 Mar. 1979, 2; "Mormon Anti-ERA Group To Register as a Lobby," *Arlington-Alexandria [Virginia] Star,* 15 Mar. 1979, A-1; "Mormon Money Worked Against Florida's ERA," *Miami Herald,* 20 Apr. 1980, A-1; "Church Orchestrated Florida Anti-ERA Drive, Report Details," *Salt Lake Tribune,* 21 Apr. 1980, D-1; "State to Probe Mormon Contributions," *Miami Herald,* 22 Apr. 1980, II-1; Pottmyer, "Sonia Johnson," 376.

118. Statement by Doris Enderle of Huntington Beach, California, in Terry, Slaght-Griffin, and Terry, *Mormons & Women,* 101.

119. Florida "Campaign Treasurer's Report, Report of Contribution Receipts and Expenditures," for FACT PAC—Families Are Concerned Today PAC, 16-29 Sept. 1978, copies in fd 2, box 7, Johnson papers; "How the Mormons Helped Scuttle ERA," *Miami Herald*, 20 Apr. 1980, A-33.

120. Reported to me by the Relief Society president's brother, Charles R. Davis, 19 Mar. 1994.

121. Dickson to "Sonja."

122. Copy of petition left in foyers of LDS wards in Virginia, "We consider the Equal Rights Amendment a nonpartisan issue and will, in the 1979 elections, vote only for those candidates who oppose ratification of the Equal Rights Amendment," fd 18, box 3, Collection of Utah Women's Issues; also "Chronology: The Mormon Anti-ERA Campaign," *Mormons for the ERA Newsletter* 5 (Feb. 1983): [5]; Gottlieb and Wiley, *America's Saints*, 205.

123. "Mormons Wage Letter-Writing Blitz Against ERA in Va. General Assembly," *Washington Star*, 10 Jan. 1979, A-4; White, "Mormonism and the Equal Rights Amendment," 257.

124. Gottlieb and Wiley, *America's Saints*, 205.

125. Notes of my interview with Ruth Knight, 14 Oct. 1992.

126. Mary Schoggen, President, Macomb Branch Relief Society, to "Dear Sisters," 8 Dec. 1978, mimeographed letter, fd 33, box 42, Richard Douglas Poll papers, Marriott Library.

127. White, "Mormonism and the Equal Rights Amendment," 252; Lisa Cronin Wohl, "A Mormon Connection?: The Defeat of the ERA in Nevada," *Ms.* 6 (July 1977): 68-70, 80, 83-85; Sheldon M. Rampton statement, 11 Apr. 1979, fd 7, box 7, Johnson papers.

128. "Chronology: The Mormon Anti-ERA Campaign," *Mormons For ERA Newsletter* 5 (Feb. 1983): 5; *Deseret News 1995-1996 Church Almanac*, 185.

129. Mathews and De Hart, *Sex, Gender, and the Politics of ERA*, 67; *Deseret News 1995-1996 Church Almanac*, 157.

130. "ERA Appears Dead This Year," *Phoenix Gazette*, 10 Feb. 1978, A-8, which reported that "Mrs. Bess Stinson, a former state senator [is] leading the lobbying effort against ERA." For her Phoenix residence and background, see *Phoenix Metropolitan Telephone Directory, January 1978* (Phoenix: Mountain Bell, 1978), 1230, and "Without Women's Lib," editorial, *Arizona Republic* (Phoenix, AZ), 15 Mar. 1974, both in Arizona Room, Phoenix Public Library.

131. "It's Do or Die for the ERA: Mormon Power Is the Key," *Boston Globe*, 30 June 1981, 2; William Appleman Williams, "Regional Resistance: Backyard Autonomy," *The Nation* 233 (5 Sept. 1981): 179. He was specifically commenting on the MX controversy, but his words applied equally well to the anti-ERA campaign to which he seemed to be referring when he observed that many LDS leaders "are sexist businessmen who also entertain and act upon other unpleasant prejudices." Williams established his reputation with such publications as *American-Russian Relations, 1781-1947* (New York: Rinehart, 1952); *The Tragedy of American Diplomacy* (Chicago: World Publishing Co., 1959), *The Roots of the Modern American Empire* (New York: Random House, 1969), *America Confronts a Revolutionary World, 1776-1976* (New York: Morrow, 1976).

132. Andrew Hacker, "ERA-RIP," *Harper's* 261 (Sept. 1980): 14, 10.

133. George H. Gallup, *The Gallup Poll: Public Opinion, 1982* (Wilmington, DE: Scholarly Resources, Inc., 1983), 143.

134. Derr, Cannon, and Beecher, *Women of Covenant*, 368: "The publicity also served to draw more Latter-day Saint women into political activity. When a state legislature's agenda included possible ratification of the ERA (or rescission of an earlier ratification), Relief Society women became involved."

135. F. Reed Johnson, "The Mormon Church as a Central Command System," *Review of Social Economy* 37 (Apr. 1979): 79-94. His emphasis was on economics.

136. Derr, Cannon, and Beecher, *Women of Covenant,* 373.

137. "Peterson Heads New Women's Group: 'Voice of Moderation,'" *Salt Lake Tribune,* 25 Apr. 1980, C-3; Lou Chandler interview, 10 May 1994; Bradley, "Mormon Relief Society and the International Women's Year Conference," 146.

138. Dallin H. Oaks, memorandum to all BYU faculty and staff, 27 Apr. 1978, quoted in "Pres. Oaks Attacks ERA Groups in Letter," *Brigham Young University Daily Universe,* 2 May 1978, 1.

139. "Regional Representatives [1967-82]," *Deseret News 1983 Church Almanac,* 115.

140. "Boycotts Part of U.S. History: ERA No Different," *Brigham Young University Daily Universe,* 4 May 1978, 14; Dallin H. Oaks to Sybel Alger, 5 May 1978, photocopy in my possession; Bergera and Priddis, *Brigham Young University,* 39.

141. Leneta [Loneta] Murphy, "Cheers Editorial," Dennis Jensen and Robyn Savage Jensen, "Arguments Invalid," *Brigham Young University Daily Universe,* 11 May 1978, 14, referring to First Presidency statement in "Church Leaders Urge TV Boycott Support," *Deseret News "Church News,"* 29 Apr. 1978, 6; also "Leaders Urge Nationwide TV Boycott on May 23," *Deseret News "Church News,"* 13 May 1978, 4.

142. Dallin H. Oaks to Lael Woodbury and Dallas Burnett, 19 May 1978, photocopy in my possession. Alger's next editorial appeared in *Brigham Young University Daily Universe,* 10 Aug. 1978, 8. All student editorials were signed by their authors.

143. BYU President's weekly meeting minutes, 14 June 1978, 2, photocopy in my possession.

144. Edwards, "A Rhetorical Analysis of Three Policy Statements of the Church of Jesus Christ of Latter-day Saints," 59-60; also Caulfield, "Rhetoric and the Equal Rights Amendment," 138-39; Pottmyer, "Sonia Johnson," 375-76; Sonia Johnson testimony before the U.S. Senate Constitutional Rights Subcommittee, 4 Aug. 1978, transcript, fd 1, box 9, Johnson papers; Johnson, *From Housewife to Heretic,* 111, for her decision in 1978 that the label "radical feminist" described her accurately; also Lee Roderick, *Leading the Charge: Orrin Hatch and 20 Years of America* (Carson City, NV: Gold Leaf Press, 1994), 102-17, for his perspective on Johnson's testimony before the Senate committee of which Hatch was a member.

145. "Church Leaders Reaffirm ERA Stand," *Deseret News "Church News,"* 26 Aug. 1978, 2-3; "First Presidency Re-affirms Opposition to ERA," *Ensign* 8 (Oct. 1978): 63; also MacKay, "Equal Rights Amendment," in Powell, *Utah History Encyclopedia,* 174.

146. "LDS Official Raps ERA," *Deseret News,* 24 Mar. 1977, B-16.

147. Edward L. Kimball and Andrew E. Kimball, Jr., *Spencer W. Kimball* (Salt Lake City: Bookcraft, 1977), 272-73, 325-27, 381-83; Spencer W. Kimball, *New Horizons for Homosexuals* (Salt Lake City: The Church of Jesus Christ of Latter-day Saints, 1971); D. Michael Quinn, *Same-Sex Dynamics among Nineteenth-Century Americans: A Mormon Example* (Urbana: University of Illinois Press, 1996), 373-74, 377, 379, 380, 382.

148. Rex E. Lee, *A Lawyer Looks at the Equal Rights Amendment* (Provo, UT: Brigham Young University Press, 1980), xii, 49, 51, 61, 64-65, 81; *Deseret News 1991-1992 Church Almanac: The Church of Jesus Christ of Latter-day Saints* (Salt Lake City: Deseret News, 1990), 8, 312, 317. By contrast Orrin G. Hatch, fellow Mormon and conservative U.S. senator, simply acknowledged the concern about homosexuality laws and discussed the matter once in his *The Equal Rights Amendment: Myths and Realities,* 51-54. Bradley, "Mormon Relief Society and the International Women's Year," 117, noted that in 1974-75 Lee wrote a preliminary statement of his anti-ERA views, "all of which appeared later in addresses by General Authorities or official statements by Church spokespersons."

149. Boles, *Politics of the Equal Rights Amendment,* 26; Jane Dehart-Mathews and Donald Mathews, "The Cultural Politics of the ERA's Defeat," and Edith Mayo and Jerry K. Frye, "The ERA: Postmortem of a Failure in Political Communication," in Hoff-Wilson, *Rights of Passage,* 49, 85.

150. First Presidency statement, *Deseret News "Church News,"* 26 Aug. 1978, 2.

151. *The Woman's Chronicler* 3 (Sept. 1978).

152. . . . *"the Voice of Womankind" . . . An Historical Perspective of Equality in Utah* (Salt Lake City: The League of Women Voters of Utah, Sept. 1978), copy in fd 33, box 42, Poll papers, Marriott Library.

153. Spencer W. Kimball, N. Eldon Tanner, and Marion G. Romney statement, 12 Oct. 1978, copy in collection of Equal Rights Coalition of Utah, and in fd 27, box 7, Johnson papers; compared with "First Presidency Reaffirms Opposition to ERA," *Ensign* 8 (Oct. 1978): 63. The acknowledgement of anti-ERA activities as "political" on 12 October was probably a result of comments the First Presidency received following the distribution of the October issue of the *Ensign.*

154. *Another Mormon View of the ERA* (Salt Lake City: Equal Rights Coalition of Utah, 1979), copy in fd 33, box 4, Collection of Utah Women's Issues. The other signers (listed here in alphabetical order) were Ramona Adams, Margaret B. Adamson, Marlena Ahanin, Algie E. Ballif, Sherilyn Cox Bennion, Gladys Carling, Linda T. Christensen, Rebecca Cornwall, Au-Deane S. Cowley, Louise Davis, Teresa M. Dodge, Kathleen Flake, Afton Forsgren, Suzanna Mae Grua, Dixie Snow Huefner, Rodello Hunter, Virginia Husband, Nancy Stowe Kader, A. W. Kelson, Virginia Kelson, Jane Cannon King, R. Lee Last, Marilee Latta, Betty M. Madsen, Barbara M. Merrill, Loneta Murphy, Kenneth R. Pangborn, Kay Senzee, Paul Swenson, Sharon Lee Swenson, Eldon M. Tolman, and Thelma E. Weight.

155. N. Eldon Tanner, "First Presidency Message: 'The Debate Is Over'," *Ensign* 9 (Aug. 1979): 2-3; Richard D. Poll, "Henry D. Moyle: Man of Action," unpublished 1983 biography, fd 21, box 67, chapter, "Counselor in the First Presidency—I," 2, Poll papers; Gottlieb and Wiley, *America's Saints,* 103.

156. Elaine Cannon, "If We Want to Go Up, We Have to Get On," *Ensign* 8 (Nov. 1978): 108.

157. Karen Mecham memorandum, 5 Oct. 1979, fd 26, box 7, Johnson papers.

158. Robert Mecham [former bishop of the LDS ward in Cambridge, Massachusetts] to Apostle Neal A. Maxwell, 5 Dec. 1979, copy in fd 19, box 3, Collection of Utah Women's Issues.

159. Notes of my telephone interview with Linda Goold, 31 Mar. 1994.

160. "3,000 in Richmond Urge Ratification of ERA," *Washington Post,* 23 Jan. 1978, C-4; "'Utah Mormons for ERA' Solicits Active Support," *Salt Lake Tribune,* 18 Sept. 1978, B-1; "'Dissident' Local Mormons Organize Pro-ERA Group," *Las Vegas Review-Journal,* 25 Oct. 1978; Mormons for ERA organizational materials, fds 1-5, box 10, Johnson papers; also O. Kendall White, Jr., "A Feminist Challenge: 'Mormons for ERA' as an Internal Social Movement," *Journal of Ethnic Studies* 13 (Spring 1985): 29-50; Pottmyer, "Sonia Johnson," 373.

161. For the formation, in-fighting, reorganization, incorporation, and admission of males to the board of Utah Mormons for ERA, see Mary Ann Payne, Executive Director, to "Dear Friends," 9 Apr. 1980, Kathryn L. MacKay to Mary Ann [Payne], with copies to Sonia Johnson, June Fulmer, and Marilee Latta, Kathryn [L. MacKay] to Jan [Tyler], 18 Apr. 1980, Mary Ann Payne to Kathryn [L. MacKay], with copies to Sonia Johnson, Marilee Latta, and June Fulmer, 21 Apr. 1980, Sonia Johnson to Kathryn [L. MacKay], 8 May 1980, fd 7, box 4, undated mimeographed sheet, titled "Proposal for compromise to resolve issues relating to organization of Utah Mormons for the ERA," fd 10, box 4, complete list of names in the address list of "Mormons for E.R.A. [—] February 23, 1980," fd 13, box 4, minutes of the governing board of Utah Mormons for E.R.A. (8 Mar. 1980-1 June 1980), fd 15, box 4, memorandum from June Fulmer, Marilee Latta, and Kathryn MacKay as the executive board of Utah Mormons for E.R.A. to its governing board, 2 May 1980, fd 16, box 4, Collection of Utah Women's Issues; also in fds 29-30, box 9, Johnson papers.

162. Johnson, *From Housewife to Heretic,* 153.

163. Alphabetical list of 484 LDS persons who were pro-ERA correspondents, fd 1, box 11, and alphabetical list of 1,758 non-LDS persons who were pro-ERA correspondents, fd 1, box 16, Johnson papers.

164. Pottmyer, "Sonia Johnson," 385 for quote, 381-83, for her excommunication; also "Religion vs. Politics: ERA Advocate, Facing Mormon Trial, Finds Her Family Life in Disarray," *Washington Post,* 27 Nov. 1979, C-1, C-3; "Mormon Feminist Faces Trial By Church," *Los Angeles Times,* 1 Dec. 1979, I, 26; "Mormon Feminist Awaiting Verdict of Her Church Trial," *New York Times,* 3 Dec. 1979, A-18; "Can a Mormon Support ERA?" *Newsweek* 94 (3 Dec. 1979): 88; Michael J. Weiss, "Irked by Sonia Johnson's E.R.A. Crusade, Church Elders Throw the Book of Mormon at Her," *People Weekly* 12 (3 Dec. 1979): 44-45; "Mormon Church Excommunicates a Supporter of Rights Amendment," *New York Times,* 6 Dec. 1979, A-26; "Mormon Feminist Sonia Johnson," *Christian Science Monitor,* 7 Dec. 1979, 2; "ERA Support Didn't Lead to Ouster, Mormons Say," *Los Angeles Times,* 7 Dec. 1979, 3, 27; "Scholar Says Feminist's Church Trial Aimed at Influencing Other Mormons," *Washington Star,* 8 Dec. 1979, A-9; "Mormons Eject ERA Activist," *New York Times,* 9 Dec. 1979, A-6; "Mormons: Latter-day Bigotry," *Economist* 273 (15 Dec. 1979): 38; "A Woman's Anguish: Her Church or ERA," *Chicago Tribune,* 16 Dec. 1979, 1, 13; "'A Savage Misogyny': Mormonism vs. Feminism and the ERA," *Time* 114 (17 Dec. 1979): 80; "ERA Advocate Asks Mormons to Overturn Excommunication," *Washington Star,* 25 Dec. 1979; Carl Beauchamp, "The Sonia Johnson Trial," *Women's Political Times* 4 (Dec. 1979): 1, 8; "What's At Stake Here Is More Than Liturgy," *Washington Post,* 1 Jan. 1980, C-1, C-10; David Macfarlane, "Equal Rights Meets Its Martyr," *Macleans* 93 (21 Jan. 1980): 37-38; Linda Sillitoe and Paul Swenson, "The Excommunication of Sonia Johnson: A Moral Issue," *Utah Holiday* 9 (Jan. 1980): 18-34; Linda Sillitoe, "Church Politics and Sonia Johnson: The Central Conundrum," *Sunstone* 5 (Jan./Feb. 1980): 35-42; Barbara Howard, "Sonia Johnson and Mormon Political Power," *Christian Century* 97 (6 Feb. 1980): 126-27; "Sonia Johnson's Sea of Troubles," *Washington Post,* 23 Feb. 1980, B-1, B-5; Lisa Cronin Wohl, "Feminist Latter-Day Saint: Why Sonia Johnson Won't Give up on the ERA or the Mormon Church," *Ms.* 8 (Mar. 1980): 39-40; "Sonia Johnson vs. Mormon Church: ERA Fighter on Ropes, Awaits Decision," *Los Angeles Times,* 28 Mar. 1980, V, 1, 8-9; Teresa Carpenter, "Courage and Pain: Women Who Love God and Defy Their Churches," *Redbook,* Apr. 1980, 155-56; "Mormon Church Confirms Ouster of Sonia Johnson," *Washington Post,* 1 July 1980, C-1, C-6; Christine Rigby Arrington, "One Woman Against the Patriarchal Church," *Savvy* 1 (Oct. 1980): 28-33; "A Mormon Rebel Fights For ERA," *Newsweek* 96 (6 Oct. 1980): 16-17E; Mary L. Bradford, "The Odyssey of Sonia Johnson," and Sonia Johnson, "All on Fire: An Interview with Sonia Johnson," *Dialogue: A Journal of Mormon Thought* 14 (Summer 1981): 14-26, 27-47; Stathis, "Mormonism and the Periodical Press," 55-57; Karen Lanlois, "Interview with Sonia Johnson," *Feminist Studies* 8 (Spring 1982): 7-17; Linda Sillitoe, "Off the Record: Telling the Rest of the Truth," *Sunstone* 14 (Dec. 1990): 17-19; Judy Dushku, "Remembering Sonja," *Exponent II* 18, No. 3 (1994): 5; Heather M. Kellogg, "Shades of Gray: Sonia Johnson's Life through Letters and Autobiography," *Dialogue: A Journal of Mormon Thought* 29 (Summer 1996): 85-86.

165. Copy of Heber A. Woolsey, Managing Director of Church Public Communications, to "Public Communications Directors" (in every stake of the United States), 14 Dec. 1979, fd 27, box 7, Johnson papers; Patrick J. Buchanan, "Sonia's Bishop Was the Real Hero," *Salt Lake Tribune,* 13 Dec. 1979, A-17; also for his ultra-conservative political views, see Buchanan, *Conservative Votes, Liberal Victories: Why the Right Has Failed* (New York: Quadrangle Books/New York Times, 1975); Jerome L. Himmelstein, *To the Right: The Transformation of American Conservatism* (Berkeley: University of California Press, 1990), 81; "Pat Buchanan and 'Religious War': Rejecting Extremism," *Church and State* 45 (Oct. 1992): 17; "Buchanan: An Extremist in Moderate Clothing," *Los Angeles Times,* 21 Feb. 1996, B-8.

166. "A Profile of 170 Mormons for ERA," *Mormons for ERA Newsletter* 5 (May 1983): [3].

167. Belle S. Spafford, "The American Woman's Movement," and Emma Lou Thayne, "The Cat Fight and What Matters Most," in Maren M. Mouritsen, ed., *Blueprints for Living: Perspectives for Latter-day Saint Women*, 2 vols. (Provo, UT: Brigham Young University Press, 1980), 1:13-14, 15, 2:60.

168. Tony Kimball, "Church and State: Separation Without Substance," *Exponent II* 6 (Winter 1980): 8-9; compare with the first issue's title page and lead article by Kate Gardner, "What the ERA Will Mean To You," in July 1974.

169. Terry, Slaght-Griffin, and Terry, *Mormons & Women*, 75-82, 103-107, 110-16.

170. Eleanor Ricks Colton, "My Personal Rubicon," *Dialogue: A Journal of Mormon Thought* 11 (Winter 1981): 106, for quote and, 103, for reference to her "angry" 1977 editorial in the *Washington Post*; n57.

171. "NOW Will Take Case to Mormons," *Los Angeles Times*, 7 May 1981, V-22; *ERA Yes: ERA Missionary Project* (Salt Lake City: ERA Missionary Project, [1981]), and quote from *An Appeal to Members of the LDS Church* (Salt Lake City: National Organization for Women, ERA Missionary Project, [1981]) in fd 15, box 1, Collection of Utah Women's Issues; also Patrick Butler, researcher for the NOW Missionary Project, "Mormon Church Against the ERA: 'Full Institutional Involvement' In Politics," 30 Apr. 1981, mimeographed document, 13 pages, collection of Equal Rights Coalition of Utah; "Selling ERA to Mormons," *Newsweek* 93 (13 July 1981): 26; Vera Goodman, "ERA: The New Face of Missionaries," *New Directions for Women* 10 (July/Aug. 1981): 1, 18; "NOW Missionaries in Utah," *Sunstone* 6 (July-Aug. 1981): 5; Lena Serge Zezuilin, "An ERA Missionary in Utah," *Feminist Studies* 8 (Summer 1982): 457-61; MacKay, "Equal Rights Amendment," in Powell, *Utah History Encyclopedia*, 175.

172. "ERA 'Missionaries' Crusade in Utah," *Los Angeles Times*, 4 Sept. 1981, V-7.

173. John U. Zussman and Shauna M. Adix, "Content and Conjecture in the Equal Rights Amendment Controversy in Utah," *Women's Studies International Forum* 5 (1982): 475-486, esp. 484; also the earlier "Voters Opposed to ERA, But Support Its Concept," *Salt Lake Tribune*, 11 May 1980, A-1.

174. *Teachings of the Living Prophets: Student Manual, Religion 333* (Salt Lake City: The Church of Jesus Christ of Latter-day Saints, 1982), 15, 20, 25, 26, 51, 54, 55, 57, 58. In August 1996 I found this publication on display for sale at the church-owned Deseret Book Store in Salt Lake City, and it has apparently continued to be the course manual for the past fourteen years.

175. Val Burris, "Who Opposed the ERA?: An Analysis of the Social Bases of Antifeminism," *Social Science Quarterly* 64 (June 1983): 308-10. See also David W. Brady and Kent L. Tedin, "Ladies in Pink: Religion and Political Ideology in the Anti-ERA Movement," *Social Science Quarterly* 36 (Mar. 1976): 564-75; Kent L. Tedin, "Religious Preferences and Pro/Anti Activism on the Equal Rights Amendment Issue," *Pacific Sociological Review* 21 (Jan. 1978): 55-61; Carol Mueller and Thomas Dimieri, "The Structure of Belief Systems Among Contending ERA Activists," *Social Forces* 60 (Mar. 1982): 657-73; and Donald G. Mathews, "'Spiritual Warfare': Cultural Fundamentalism and the Equal Rights Amendment," *Religion and American Culture* 3 (Summer 1993): 192-54.

176. Linda Sillitoe notes of interviews with Virginia's regional representatives Julian C. Lowe, 14 Feb. 1979, and [W.] Donald Ladd, 15 Feb. 1979, fd 10, box 5, Collection of Utah Women's Issues; also *Deseret News 1995-1996 Church Almanac*, 36.

177. Winder, "LDS Position on the ERA," 7.

178. "Political Involvement Urged," *Deseret News "Church News,"* 8 Mar. 1980, 3, a First Presidency statement of 5 March which was summarized in "Keep Partisan Political Actions Out of Church, Urge LDS," *Salt Lake Tribune*, 6 Mar. 1980, B-1.

179. Mauss, *Angel and the Beehive*, 118.

180. "Mormon Politicians Not Told How to Vote: No Church Conspiracy," *Las Vegas Review-Journal,* 25 Feb. 1978, A-4.

181. "Meeting between Sonia Johnson, Jan Tyler, Gordon Hinckley, and Neal Maxwell as recalled by Jan Tyler," undated description of a private meeting at Salt Lake City [Feb. 1980], fd 1, box 5, Collection of Utah Women's Issues. Johnson, who had been excommunicated two months earlier, felt that Hinckley and Maxwell were "condescending" and "patronizing." Johnson deliberately called both apostles by their first names, a breach of LDS etiquette. "Interview with Gordon Hinckley and Neal Maxwell as recalled by Sonia Johnson," n.d. [Feb. 1980], 2, fd 1, box 8, Johnson papers; Johnson, *From Housewife to Heretic,* 155.

182. Linda Sillitoe notes of interviews with Virginia's regional representatives Julian C. Lowe, 14 Feb. 1979, and [W.] Donald Ladd, 15 Feb. 1979.

183. Tape recordings and transcriptions of my interviews, 5-6 Sept. 1992, with Rodney P. Foster.

184. G. Homer Durham et al., *N. Eldon Tanner: His Life and Service* (Salt Lake City: Deseret Book Co., 1982), 278-79; Edward L. Kimball, "A Time of Reaching Out: The Administration of Spencer W. Kimball," *Sunstone* 11 (Mar. 1987): 8, 13-14; F. Burton Howard, *Marion G. Romney: His Life and Faith* (Salt Lake City: Bookcraft, 1988), 240; *Deseret News 1995-1996 Church Almanac,* 390.

185. George M. McCune, *Gordon B. Hinckley: Shoulder For the Lord* (Salt Lake City: Hawkes Publishing, 1996), 466; Sheri L. Dew, *Go Forward With Faith: The Biography of Gordon B. Hinckley* (Salt Lake City: Deseret Book Co., 1996), 291-94, 371, and 612n1 for his May 1968 appointment in preparation for the November referendum. Both biographers clearly chose to ignore the many published materials about his role in the ERA campaign, including the detailed 1994 article in *Journal of Mormon History.*

186. Tape recordings and transcriptions of my interviews, 29-30 Aug. 1992, with Alan Blodgett, and of my interview, 30 Oct. 1992, with Lowell M. Durham, Jr.

187. Wohl, "A Mormon Connection?" 70; Driggs letter to the editor, *Dialogue: A Journal of Mormon Thought* 11 (Autumn 1978): 5-7; Richardson, "The 'Old Right' in Action," 221-22; White, "Mormonism and the Equal Rights Amendment," 252-53, 254-55, 257-58; Mansbridge, *Why We Lost the ERA,* 174-75.

188. Allen and Leonard, *Story of the Latter-day Saints,* 659; O. Kendall White, Jr., "A Review and Commentary on the Prospects of a Mormon-New Christian Right Coalition," *Review of Religious Research* 28 (Dec. 1986): 184.

189. Norman Sklarewitz, "Interview: Gordon B. Hinckley," *PSA Magazine,* June 1980, 120, copy in Vertical File for Hinckley, Marriott Library, and also in fd 7, box 3, Collection of Utah Women's Issues.

190. Mauss, *Angel and the Beehive,* 8.

191. "LDS Oppose Airline Bill," *Salt Lake Tribune,* 15 July 1977, C-2; "LDS Letter Opposes Airline Bill," *Deseret News,* 15 July 1977, B-4, which (in response to the *Tribune's* morning report)- acknowledged only that the First Presidency letter went to "some Congressmen June 10." The letter actually went to the Congressmen of every western state as part of an effort to protect Western Airlines in which the church was a significant stockholder. See Croft, "Influence of the L.D.S. Church on Utah Politics, 1945-1985," 92; Robert J. Serling, *The Only Way to Fly: The Story of Western Airlines, America's Senior Air Carrier* (Garden City, NY: Doubleday & Co., 1976), 17; and *Moody's Transportation Manual* (New York: Moody's Investors Services, 1976-82) identifying Presiding Bishop Victor L. Brown as one of Western Airline's directors.

192. White, "Overt and Covert Politics," 12-13, 15; White, "Mormonism and the Equal Rights Amendment," 266-67. See chap. 3 for conflicts within the hierarchy during the 1960s about the national campaign for the civil rights of African Americans.

193. Mathews and De Hart, *Sex, Gender, and the Politics of ERA,* 217.

194. Allen and Leonard, *Story of the Latter-day Saints,* 659.

195. Dallin H. Oaks, "Gospel Teachings About Lying," *Clark Memorandum* [of the J. Reuben Clark School of Law, Brigham Young University], Spring 1994, 16-17, acknowledges "lying for the Lord" by early Mormon leaders who found themselves in difficult circumstances. Oaks admitted that he could not predict what he would do in similar circumstances.

196. For example, judicial decisions against the display of a menorah, cross, or Christmas creche on government property are prohibitions against government endorsement of specific religions, not restrictions on the religious groups represented by these symbols.

197. Luke Eugene Ebersole, *Church Lobbying In the Nation's Capital* (New York: Macmillan, 1951); James L. Adams, *The Growing Church Lobby In Washington* (Grand Rapids, MI: William B. Eerdmans, 1970); Daniel John O'Neill, *Church Lobbying In a Western State: A Case Study On Abortion Legislation* (Tucson: University of Arizona Press, 1970); Allen D. Hertzke, *Representing God In Washington* (Knoxville: University of Tennessee Press, 1988); Allen D. Hertzke, "The Role of Religious Lobbies," in Charles W. Dunn, ed., *Religion In American Politics* (Washington, D.C.: Congressional Quarterly Press, 1989), 123-36.

198. Caption of Mike Peters 1979 nationally syndicated editorial cartoon, "And now the Mormon Tabernacle Choir will sing their medley of 'Stout-hearted Men,' 'You're Having My Baby,' and 'Get Your Biscuits In the Oven an' Your Buns In Bed," reprinted in Stathis, "Mormonism and the Periodical Press," 53; also Robert H. Burgoyne and Rodney W. Burgoyne, "Belief Systems and Unhappiness: The Mormon Woman Example," *Dialogue: A Journal of Mormon Thought* 11 (Autumn 1978): 48-53; Louise Degn, "Mormon Women and Depression," *Sunstone* 4 (Mar.-Apr. 1979): 16-26, reprinted in *Sunstone* 10 (May 1985): 19-27; Laurel Thatcher Ulrich, "The Pink DIALOGUE and Beyond," *Dialogue: A Journal of Mormon Thought* 11 (Winter 1981): 28-39; Lavina Fielding Anderson, "Mormon Women and the Struggle for Definition: Contemporary Women," and Francine Bennion, "Mormon Women and the Struggle for Definition: What Is the Church?" *Sunstone* 6 (Nov./Dec. 1981): 12-16, 17-20; Winthrop S. Hudson, *Religion In America,* 3rd ed. (New York: Charles Scribner's Sons, 1981), 456; David Craig Spendlove, "Depression In Mormon Women," Ph.D., University of Utah, 1982; Jeanne Decker Griffiths, "Confessions of a Once Neurotic Mormon," and Alda Jones, "From the Inside Out and Back Again," *Exponent II* 9 (Summer 1983): 6, 15; Shirley Rogers Radl, *The Invisible Woman: Target of the Religious New Right* (New York: Delacorte Press, 1983), 80-84; David Wayne Bush, "Depression Among Women and Their Perception of Power and Status," Ph.D. diss., Utah State University, 1984; Renata Tonks, "Education for Women at Brigham Young University: Students' Perceptions of Opportunities, Problems, and Stereotypes," University Scholar thesis, Brigham Young University, 1984; Linda P. Wilcox, "Crying 'Change' in a Permanent World: Contemporary Mormon Women on Motherhood," in *Mormon Letters Annual, 1984* (Salt Lake City: Association for Mormon Letters, 1985), 22-35; Shane B. Inglesby, "Priesthood Prescription For Women: The Role of Women as Prescribed in Aaronic Quorum Lesson Manuals," *Sunstone* 10 (Mar. 1985): 28-33; Marjorie Draper Conder, "Constants and Changes: Role Prescriptions For Mormon Women As Seen Through Selected Mormon Periodicals: 1883-1884," M.S. thesis, University of Utah, 1985, 71-88; Vella Neil Evans, "Woman's Image in Authoritative Mormon Discourse: A Rhetorical Analysis," Ph.D. diss., University of Utah, 1985, 158-60, 245-51, 254, 266, 305-10, 354-55, 446-47.

Also, Laurel Thatcher Ulrich, "On Appendages," *Exponent II* 11 (Winter 1985): 9; Sharon Presley, Joanne Weaver, and Bradford Weaver, "Traditional and Nontraditional Mormon Women: Political Attitudes and Socialization," *Women & Politics* 5 (Winter 1985/86): 51-77; Kay Webber, "One Woman's Response," *Exponent II* 13 (Spring 1987): 3; Ezra Taft Benson, *To the Mothers in Zion: Address Given at Fireside for Parents* (Salt Lake City: Church of Jesus Christ of Latter-day Saints, 1987); Lavina Fielding Anderson, "A Voice

From the Past: The Benson Instructions for Parents," *Dialogue: A Journal of Mormon Thought* 21 (Winter 1988): 103-13; Susan H. Swetnam, "Turning to the Mothers: Mormon Women's Biographies of Their Female Forebears and the Mormon Church's Expectations for Women," *Frontiers: A Journal of Women Studies* 10 (1988), 1:1-6; Deborah Austin Christensen, "A Qualitative Analysis of the Developmental Process Among Mormon Women," Ph.D. diss., University of Utah, 1988, 55-56, 62-67, 89-96; Janet W. Tarjan, "Reflections On 'An Address To Mothers in Zion,'" *Sunstone* 13 (Aug. 1989): 7-9; Dorice Williams Elliott, "The Mormon Conference Talk as Patriarchal Discourse," *Dialogue: A Journal of Mormon Thought* 22 (Spring 1989): 70-78; Dorice Williams Elliott, "'Unto the Least of These': Another Gender Gap," *Sunstone* 14 (Apr. 1990): 49-51; "The Mormon Gender Gap," *U.S. News and World Report* 108 (14 May 1990): 14; Laurence R. Iannaccone and Carrie A. Miles, "Dealing with Social Change: The Mormon Church's Response to Change in Woman's Roles," *Social Forces* 68 (June 1990): 1231-50; Marie Cornwall, "Mormonism's Difficult Question," and John Richards, "The Mormon Church Into the '90s," *Utah Holiday* 19 (Aug. 1990): 24, 26-27; "From Garland, Texas, Julie J. Paquette Offers a Four-point List that Explains Why She Thinks LDS Women Are Turning Down Callings More Frequently," *Exponent II* 15, No. 3 (1990): 19; Vella Neil Evans, "Mormon Women and the Right to Wage Work," and Lavina Fielding Anderson, "The Grammar of Inequity," *Dialogue: A Journal of Mormon Thought* 23 (Winter 1990): 54-59, 81-95, the latter reprinted in Hanks, *Women and Authority,* 215-30; Goldie Blumenstyk, "Some Leaders in Utah Seek to Overcome Traditions That Inhibit the Educational Progress of Women: State Ranks Last in Proportion of Students Who Are Female," *Chronicle of Higher Education* 37 (17 Apr. 1991): A35-A36; Dorice Williams Elliott, "Women, the Mormon Family, and Class Mobility: Nineteenth-Century Victorian Ideology In a Twentieth-Century Church," *Sunstone* 15 (Dec. 1991): 19-26; Sally Emery, "A Four-Dimensional Analysis of Sex Role Attitudes in a Mormon Population: Personal Control, Self-esteem, Dogmatism, and Religious Affiliation," Ph.D. diss., California School of Professional Psychology, Los Angeles, 1991; Pamela Bookstaber, "Assessing the Forces: Women's Lives," *Exponent II* 16, No. 1 (1991): 3; Claudia L. Bushman, "The Mormon Female Experience," *Exponent II* 16, No. 3 (1991): 2-6; Heather Symmes Cannon, "Still On the Fringe," *Exponent II* 16, No. 4 (1992): 2; Lavina Fielding Anderson, "Landmarks for LDS Women: A Contemporary Chronology," *Mormon Women's Forum: An LDS Feminist Quarterly* 3 (Dec. 1992): 1-20; Maxine Hanks, "Historic Mormon Feminist Discourse—Excerpts," Dorice Williams Elliott, "Let Women No Longer Keep Silent in Our Churches: Women's Voices in Mormonism," and Sonja Farnsworth, "Mormonism's Old Couple: The Motherhood-Priesthood Connection," Maxine Hanks, "Sister Missionaries and Authority," and Margaret Merrill Toscano, "Put On Your Strength O Daughters of Zion: Claiming Priesthood and Knowing the Mother," in Hanks, *Women and Authority,* 86-147, 201-14, 299-314, 315-34, 411-37; Judy Dushku, "This Is My Church, Too," *Exponent II* 17, No. 2 (1993): 10.

Also, "Challenging the Mormon Church: Feminism Cautiously Tries To Find Its Place in a Conservative Faith," *Boston Globe,* 25 Mar. 1993, reprinted in *Exponent II* 17, No. 4 (1993): 5-7; Lavina Fielding Anderson, "Counterpoint 1993," "Voices From BYU," and Lisa Ray Turner, "Requiem For a Typical Mormon Woman," *Exponent II* 18, No. 1 (1993): 5, 6-8, 15; Kristin Rushforth, "A VOICE from the Margins," and Lara Harris, "Subversions within the House: Is Feminist Activism Possible at BYU?" *Mormon Women's Forum: An LDS Feminist Quarterly* 4 (Spring 1993): 1-4, 6-8; "Protesting Patriarchy," *Los Angeles Times,* 16 May 1993, E-1, E-3; Ellen Fagg, "Cecilia Konchar Farr: The Ties That Bind: Can a Devout Mormon From Outside Serve at the Center," *Network: A Monthly Publication For Progressive Utah Women* 16 (Aug. 1993): 6-8; Lavina Fielding Anderson, "The Oppression of Good Men," "Excerpts: Lynne Whitesides," and Lavina Fielding Anderson, "Counterpoint, 1993," *Mormon Women's Forum: An LDS Feminist Quarterly* 4 (Sept. 1993): 14-15, 16-17; Catharine R. Stimpson, "The Farr Case: The Next Chapter in the History of Academic

Freedom?" *Change: The Magazine of Higher Learning* 25 (Sept./Oct. 1993): 70-71; "Growing Mormon Church Faces Dissent By Women Scholars," *New York Times,* 2 Oct. 1993, 1, 7; Jan Shipps, "Dangerous History: Laurel Ulrich and Her Mormon Sisters," *Christian Century* 110 (20 Oct. 1993): 1012-13; Margaret Merrill Toscano, "The Courage to Act, to Speak, to Risk," *Mormon Women's Forum: An LDS Feminist Quarterly* 4 (Dec. 1993): 4-5; Rhonda Seamons, "Achievement and Religiosity as Perceived By Fifty-Five Mormon Women With Doctoral Degrees," Ph.D. diss., Brigham Young University, 1993; Ann B. Sipes, "Cognitive Dissonance Among Traditional Women: How Mormon Women Resolve Conflict," Ph.D. diss., Fielding Institute, 1993; Marleen K. Williams, "Correlates of Beck Depression Inventory Scores in Mormon and Protestant Women: Religious Orientation, Traditional Family Attitudes and Perfectionism," Ph.D. diss., Brigham Young University, 1993; Susan Buhler Taber, *Mormon Lives: A Year in the Elkton Ward* (Urbana: University of Illinois Press, 1993), 70, 117, 125, 335, 342; "Spirituality and Gender," *Mormon Women's Forum: An LDS Feminist Quarterly* 5 (Mar. 1994): 1-8; Laurel Thatcher Ulrich, "Border Crossings," Erin R. Silva, "Matricidal Patriarchy: Some Thoughts Toward Understanding the Devaluation of Women in the Church," Hilda Kathryn Erickson Pack, "I Must Speak Up," and Janine Boyce, "Messages From the Manuals: Twelve Years Later," *Dialogue: A Journal of Mormon Thought* 27 (Summer 1994): 1-7, 139-55, 157-67, 205-17; Maxine Hanks, "Perspective on Mormonism: A Struggle To Reclaim Authority," *Los Angeles Times,* 10 July 1994, M-7; Linda King Newell, "A Time to Speak: Emma Smith, the Church and Me," *Mormon Women's Forum: An LDS Feminist Quarterly* 5 (July 1994): 1, 3-7; Bonnie Bullough, "A Feminist Comparison of Mormonism and Humanism," Martha Sonntag Bradley, "The Struggle to Emerge: Leaving Brigham Young University," and Cecilia Konchar Farr, "Dancing Through the Doctrine: Observations on Religion and Feminism," in George D. Smith, ed., *Religion, Feminism, and Freedom of Conscience: A Mormon/Humanist Dialogue* (Buffalo, NY: Prometheus Books; Salt Lake City: Signature Books, 1994), 117-22, 123-39, 147-51; Nola D. Smith, "Madwomen in the Mormon Attic: A Feminist Reading of *Saturday's Warrior* and *Reunion,*" and Jean Ann Waterstradt, "In Hims of Praise: The Songs of Zion," in *The Association for Mormon Letters Annual, 1994,* 2 vols. (N.p., n.d.), 1: 139-44, 2: 190-95; Lynn Matthews Anderson, "Issues In Contemporary Mormon Feminism," *Mormon Women's Forum: An LDS Feminist Quarterly* 6 (Summer 1995): 1-8; Mario S. DePillis, "The Emergence of Mormon Power since 1945," *Journal of Mormon History* 22 (Spring 1996): 24-31; Mark Gerzon, *A House Divided: Six Belief Systems Struggling for America's Soul* (New York: G. P. Putnam's Sons, 1996), 19.

    199. Helen B. Andelin, *Fascinating Womanhood,* rev. ed. (Santa Barbara, CA: Pacific Press, 1968); Belle S. Spafford, *Women In Today's World* (Salt Lake City: Deseret Book Co., 1971); Duane S. Crowther and Jean D. Crowther, *The Joy of Being a Woman* (Bountiful, UT: Horizon, 1972); Mildred Chandler Austin, "The Lord's Definition of Woman's Role as He Has Revealed It To His Prophets of the Latter Days," M.A. thesis, Brigham Young University, 1972; N. Eldon Tanner, *The Role of Womanhood* (Salt Lake City: Church of Jesus Christ of Latter-day Saints, 1973); Belle S. Spafford, *A Woman's Reach* (Salt Lake City: Deseret Book Co., 1974); Aubrey P. Andelin, *Fascinating Womanhood Principles Applied to Sex* (Santa Barbara, CA: Andelin Foundation for Education in Family Living, 1974); Carol Clark, *A Singular Life: Perspectives For the Single Woman* (Salt Lake City: Deseret Book Co., 1974); Afton Day, *How To Be a Perfect Wife and Other Myths* (Salt Lake City; Bookcraft, 1977); Jay A. Adamson, ed., *The Role of Women: Supplementary Readings for Religion 333, Teachings of Living Prophets* (Provo, UT: Brigham Young University Publications, 1977); Mildred Chandler Austin, *Woman's Divine Destiny* (Salt Lake City; Deseret Book Co., 1978); Oscar W. McConkie, *She Shall Be Called Woman* (Salt Lake City: Bookcraft, 1979); Spencer W. Kimball, *My Beloved Sisters* (Salt Lake City: Deseret Book Co., 1979); *The Latter-day Saint Woman: Basic Manual For Women* (Salt Lake City: Church of Jesus Christ of Latter-day Saints, 1979, with revised editions, 1981, 1988); Spencer W. Kimball [and fourteen other male

contributors], *Woman* (Salt Lake City: Deseret Book Co., 1980); Camilla E. Kimball [and fifteen other women contributors], *Joy* (Salt Lake City: Deseret Book Co., 1980); Maren M. Mouritsen, ed., *Blueprints for Living: Perspectives for Latter-day Saint Women,* 2 vols. (Provo, UT: Brigham Young University Press, 1980).

Also, Leon R. Hartshorn, *A Mother's Love* (Bountiful, UT: Horizon Publishers, 1980); Ida Smith, "The Psychological Needs of Mormon Women," *Sunstone* 6 (Mar./Apr. 1981): 59-66; Maren M. Mouritsen, ed., *Ye Are Free To Choose: Agency and the Latter-day Saint Woman* (Provo, UT: Brigham Young University Press, 1981); Rose Neeleman, *The Joys of Womanhood* (Provo, UT: Brigham Young University Publications, 1981); Anita Canfield, *Self-Esteem and the Physical Self* (Orem, UT: Randall Publishing Co., 1981); Maren M. Mouritsen, ed., *For Such a Time As This* (Provo, UT: Brigham Young University Press, 1982); Mary Lythgoe Bradford, ed., *Mormon Women Speak: A Collection of Essays* (Salt Lake City: Olympus Publishing Co., 1982); Anita Canfield, *Self-Esteem and the Social You* (Orem, UT: Raymont Publishers, 1982); Afton Day, *Don't Trip On Your Clouds of Glory: A Woman's Guide To Self Realization* (Salt Lake City: Bookcraft, 1983); Dorothy L. Nielsen, *How To Look Like a Million Without Spending A Mint* (Salt Lake City: Deseret Book Co., 1983); Anita Canfield, *The Young Woman and Her Self Esteem* (Sandy, UT: Randall Books, 1983); Barbara B. Smith, ed., *A Woman's Choices: The Relief Society Legacy Lectures* (Salt Lake City: Deseret Book Co., 1984); Anita Canfield, *The Power of Being a Woman* (Sandy, UT: Randall Books, 1984); Della Mae Rasmussen, "AMCAP Men and Women: Together in Mutual Respect and Unity," Francine R. Bennion, "Women and Roles: Transcending Definitions," Russell T. Osguthorpe and Ida Smith, "Roles and Role Models: A Survey Of Issues In Gender Equality," *AMCAP: Journal of the Association of Mormon Counselors and Psychotherapists* 11 (Mar. 1985): 29-39, 48-51, 52-56; *Women of Faith: Selected Speeches* (Provo, UT: Brigham Young University Press, [1985]; Ezra Taft Benson, *To the Young Women of the Church: A Message* (Salt Lake City: Church of Jesus Christ of Latter-day Saints, 1986); Gordon B. Hinckley, *The Wonderful Thing That Is You and the Wonderful Good You Can Do* (Salt Lake City: Deseret Book Co., 1986); Marilyn Todd Linford, *Is Anyone Out There Building Mother's Self-Esteem?* (Salt Lake City: Deseret Book Co., 1986); *Woman To Woman: Selected Talks from the Brigham Young University Women's Conferences* (Salt Lake City: Deseret Book Co., 1986); Mary Alice Campbell, "A View of the '80s: What It Means To Be A Latter-day Saint Woman Today," *Ensign* 17 (Mar. 1987): 22-27; Russell M. Nelson, *Motherhood* (Salt Lake City: Deseret Book, 1987); Amy Hardison, *How To Feel Great About Being a Mother* (Salt Lake City: Deseret Book Co., 1987); Carol L. Clark and Blythe Darlyn Thatcher, eds., *A Singular Life: Perspectives on Being Single* (Salt Lake City: Deseret Book Co., 1987); Paul H. Dunn, *Mothers Need No Monuments* (Salt Lake City: Bookcraft, 1987); *Monument to Women* (Salt Lake City: Church of Jesus Christ of Latter-day Saints, 1988); Mary E. Stovall and Carol Cornwall Madsen, eds., *A Heritage of Faith: Talks Selected from the BYU Women's Conferences* (Salt Lake City: Deseret Book Co., 1988); Barbara Barrington Jones and Sharlene Wells Hawkes, *The Inside-Outside Beauty Book* (Salt Lake City: Deseret Book Co., 1989); Patricia T. Holland, *Within Whispering Distance: A Message for Mothers* (Salt Lake City: Deseret Book Co., 1989); Marie Cornwall, "Women: Changing Ideas and New Directions," *Sunstone* 14 (June 1990): 53-55; Elaine Cannon, ed., *As A Woman Thinketh* (Salt Lake City: Bookcraft, 1990); Ardeth Greene Kapp, *My Neighbor, My Sister, My Friend* (Salt Lake City: Deseret Book Co., 1990); Karen Lynn Davidson, *Thriving on Our Differences: A Book for LDS Women Who Feel Like Outsiders* (Salt Lake City: Deseret Book Co., 1990); Marie Cornwall and Susan Howe, eds., *Women of Wisdom and Knowledge: Talks Selected from the BYU Women's Conferences* (Salt Lake City: Deseret Book Co., 1990); Jaroldeen Edwards, *Things I Wish I'd Known Sooner* (Salt Lake City: Deseret Book Co., 1991); Carroll Hofeling Morris, *"If the Gospel Is True, Why Do I Hurt So Much?: Help For Dysfunctional Latter-day Saint Families* (Salt Lake City: Deseret Book Co., 1991); Beppie Harrison, *Needles in the Basket: Looking at Patterns of a Woman's Life* (Salt Lake City: Deseret Book Co., 1991); Sherrie Johnson, *Man, Woman, and Deity* (Salt Lake

City: Bookcraft, 1991); Dawn Hall Anderson and Marie Cornwall, eds., *Women and the Power Within: To See Life Steadily and See It Whole* (Salt Lake City: Deseret Book Co., 1991).

Also, Dawn Hall Anderson and Marie Cornwall, eds., *Women Steadfast in Christ: Talks Selected from the 1991 Women's Conference Sponsored by Brigham Young University and the Relief Society* (Salt Lake City: Deseret Book Co., 1992); Ezra Taft Benson, *Elect Women of God* (Salt Lake City: Bookcraft, 1992); Marilynne Todd Linford, *A Woman Fulfilled* (Salt Lake City: Bookcraft, 1992); Gail Andersen Newbold, *On New Wings: Mormon Women Rediscover Personal Agency and Conquer Codependency* ([American Fork, UT]: Covenant Communications, 1992), 1-3, 119-25, 136-38; Dawn Hall Anderson, Susette Fletcher Green, and Marie Cornwall, eds., *Women and Christ: Living the Abundant Life: Talks Selected from the 1992 Women's Conference Sponsored by Brigham Young University and the Relief Society* (Salt Lake City: Deseret Book Co., 1993); Elaine Cannon, *Mothering* (Salt Lake City: Bookcraft, 1993); Kimberly Grace Andersen, "Employment and Happiness Among Mormon and Non-Mormon Mothers in Utah," M.S. thesis, Brigham Young University, 1993; Leah Graham Koldewyn, "Conflict and Resolution Among Highly Educated LDS Women," M.A. thesis, Brigham Young University, 1993; Janet Peterson and LaRene Gaunt, *Keepers of the Flame: Presidents of the Young Women* (Salt Lake City: Deseret Book Co., 1993); Chieko N. Okazaki, *Cat's Cradle* (Salt Lake City: Bookcraft, 1993); Arlene Bascom, ed., *Sunny Side Up: Breakthrough Ideas for Women From One of the Most Loved Speakers In the Church, Lucile Johnson* (American Fork, UT: Covenant Communications, 1993); Chieko N. Okazaki, *Lighten Up!* (Salt Lake City: Deseret Book Co., 1993); *Cameo: Latter-day Women in Profile* (Nov. 1993-Aug. 1994); Dawn Hall Anderson and Susette Fletcher Green, eds., *Women In the Covenant of Grace: Talks from the 1993 Women's Conference Sponsored By Brigham Young University and the Relief Society* (Salt Lake City: Deseret Book Co., 1994); Richard M. Siddoway, *Mom and Other Great Women I've Known* (Salt Lake City: Bookcraft, 1994); Jamie Glenn, *Walk Tall, You're a Daughter of God* (Salt Lake City: Deseret Book Co., 1994); Barbara B. Smith, ed., *Words for Women: Promises of the Prophets* (Salt Lake City: Bookcraft, 1994); Marie Cornwall, "The Institutional Role of Mormon Women," and Laurence R. Iannaccone and Carrie A. Miles, "Dealing with Social Change: The Mormon Church's Response to Change in Women's Roles," in Marie Cornwall, Tim B. Heaton, and Lawrence A. Young, eds., *Contemporary Mormonism: Social Science Perspectives* (Urbana: University of Illinois Press, 1994), 260-62, 280-83; Susette Fletcher Green and Dawn Hall Anderson, eds., *To Rejoice As Women: Talks From the 1994 Women's Conference* (Salt Lake City: Deseret Book Co., 1995); Michaelene Graessli, *Leader Talk: Insights on Leadership for Women* (Salt Lake City: Bookcraft, 1996); Susette Fletcher Green, Dawn Hall Anderson, and Dlora Hall Dalton, eds., *Hearts Knit Together: Talks From the 1995 Women's Conference* (Salt Lake City: Deseret Book Co., 1996); Janet Peterson and LaRene Gaunt, *The Children's Friends: Primary Presidents and Their Lives of Service* (Salt Lake City: Deseret Book Co., 1996); Marjorie P. Hinckley, *Mothering: Everyday Choices, Eternal Blessings* (Salt Lake City: Deseret Book Co., 1996); Ardeth Greene Kapp, *What Latter-day Stripling Warriors Learn from Their Mothers* (Salt Lake City: Deseret Book Co., 1996).

200. "Horse-Race Petitions To Hit Streets: LDS Battle Plan Afoot? Church Keeping Quiet," *Salt Lake Tribune*, 2 Apr. 1992, A-1; "LDS Leaders Attack Pari-Mutuel Betting," *Deseret News*, 1 June 1992, A-1.

201. *Public Affairs Handbook* (Salt Lake City: Public Affairs Department, The Church of Jesus Christ of Latter-day Saints, 1991); Bruce L. Olsen, "Developing a Non-Profit Public Relations Network," *Public Relations Quarterly* 36 (Spring 1992): 27-29. For Olsen's position as managing director of the Public Affairs Department and its connection with Special Affairs, see "LDS Church Names Director of Special Affairs Department," *Deseret News*, 26 May 1989, B-2.

202. "Members Help Defeat Lottery Initiative," *Deseret News "Church News,"* 23 July 1994, 12. For the background of D. Todd Christofferson and W. Mack Lawrence, see *Deseret News 1995-1996 Church Almanac,* 25, 36. Since this Oklahoma incident, Christofferson was advanced to be president of the Mexico South Area.

203. "LDS First Presidency Opposes Legalization of Gay Marriages," *Deseret News,* 14 Feb. 1994, B-2; "Same-Sex Marriage: Are LDS Gearing Up for a Holy War?" *Salt Lake Tribune,* 26 Mar. 1994, B-1, B-2; "LDS Church Opposing Gay Marriages," *Deseret News,* 30 Mar. 1994, A-10.

204. "Your Tithing Dollars At Work: The LDS Church Political Campaign Against Same-Sex Marriage," panel discussion, Sunstone Symposium, 17 Aug. 1996, audio-tape available from Sunstone Magazine, Salt Lake City, Utah.

205. "LDS Church Opposing Gay Marriages," *Deseret News,* 30 Mar. 1994, A-10.

206. "Church Joins Hawaii Fight Over Same-Sex Marriages," *Deseret News,* 24 Feb. 1995, A-2; "Church Opposes Same-Sex Marriages," *Deseret News "Church News,"* 4 Mar. 1995, 12, for quotes from regional representative Donald L. Hallstrom.

207. "Lawmakers Pass Late Measure To Not Recognize Gay Marriages," *Deseret News,* 2 Mar. 1995, A-19; "Same-Sex-Marriage Bill Ruled Legal," *Deseret News,* 4 Mar. 1995, A-10; "Utah May Ignore Gay Unions: Group Threatens Lawsuits After Governor Signs Bill," *Salt Lake Tribune,* 17 Mar. 1995, C-1; "Don't Condone Discrimination," *Deseret News,* 31 Mar. 1995, A-15, letter to the editor criticizing Utah's legal rejection of the marriage laws of "Denmark, the Netherlands, Norway, Sweden and, maybe soon, Hawaii." Also on a related issue, see "Leavitt Joins Growing Chorus Against a Gay Club At East: Governor, Whose Son Attends School, Says Issue Should Be Decided Locally," *Deseret News,* 10 Feb. 1996, B-3.

208. "Judge Bars LDS Church From Same-Sex Lawsuit," *Deseret News,* 29 Mar. 1995, B-1; "3 LDS Officials Seek To Join Hawaii Suit," *Deseret News,* 14 Apr. 1995, A-10.

209. "Hawaii Court Rejects LDS Request," *Deseret News,* 25 Jan. 1996, A-6.

210. "LDS and Catholic Coalition Opposes Hawaii Legislation," *Deseret News,* 21 Feb. 1996, B-1; also "Officials Aim To Intervene in Same-Sex Case," *Deseret News,* 28 Feb. 1996, A-4.

211. "Hawaii: Church Aims to End Gay Union," *Salt Lake Tribune,* 9 June 1996, B-2.

212. Charter of incorporation for Hana Pono, 26 Aug. 1977; *ANNOUNCEMENT FOR OAHU BISHOPS TO READ* (Honolulu: Hana Pono, [Nov.] 1978); "HANA PONO ADDS PAC," *Hana Pono Forum* 2 (Feb. 1979): [1]; *HANA PONO: DO WHAT IS RIGHT* (Honolulu, n.d.), for quote; *Position of the Church of Jesus Christ of Latter Day [sic] Saints on the Equal Rights Amendment and Abortion* (Honolulu: Hana Pono: Do What Is Right, n.d.), all in fds 1-2, Collection of Conservative Women Opposed to the Equal Rights Amendment, Lee Library, Brigham Young University.

213. "A Mormon Crusade In Hawaii," *Salt Lake Tribune,* 9 June 1996, B-1, B-2.

214. *The Church and the Proposed Equal Rights Amendment: A Moral Issue* (Salt Lake City: ENSIGN Magazine, 1980), 9.

215. "Supreme Court to Rule on Anti-Gay Rights Law in Colorado," *New York Times,* 22 Feb. 1995, A-17; Vera Titunik, "Sidley Braces for Fallout from Colorado Case," *American Lawyer,* Sept. 1995, 13. Lee's opening brief can be found at http://clam.rutgers.edu/remarks/romerpetitioner.html. His responding brief can be found at http://clam.rutgers.edu/remarks/romerreply.html.

216. "Gay Rights Get Major Legal Boost," *Deseret News,* 20 May 1996, A-1; "Top Court Throws Out Efforts to Preserve U.S. Sexual Mores," *Deseret News,* 22 May 1996, A-10; "Ruling on Gay Rights Is An Injustice," *Deseret News,* 23 May 1996, A-29; Dew, *Go Forward With Faith,* 324.

217. Mormons are 1.8 percent of the U.S. population compared with 37 percent of Tonga, 25 percent of American Samoa, 25 percent of Western Samoa, 17 percent of Niue, 6.5 percent of Kiribati, 6.4 percent of Tahiti, 4.4 percent of the Cook Islands or Rarotonga, 4.2 percent of the Marshall Islands, 2.6 percent of Chile, 2.3 percent of New Zealand, 2.3 percent of Micronesia, 2.2 percent of Alberta province, Canada, 2.2 percent of the Palau Islands, and 1.9 percent of Uruguay. See *Deseret News 1995-1996 Church Almanac,* 108, 192, 207, 216, 220, 231, 251, 256, 262, 265, 268, 292, 298, 302, 414-15; LDS population of 4,719,000 in the United States as of 25 February 1996 in "More Members Now Outside U.S. Than in U.S.," *Ensign* 26 (Mar. 1996): 76-77; U.S. population of 264,349,000 as of 1 March 1996 in Bureau of the Census electronic publication, *Monthly Estimates of the United States Population: April 1, 1980 to June 1, 1996,* (http://www.census.gov/population/estimate-extract/nation/intfile1-1.txt).

218. "Diplomatic Affairs Consultant Appointed," *Deseret News "Church News,"* 13 Apr. 1974, 17; Quinn, *Mormon Hierarchy: Origins of Power,* 132-34; M. Dallas Burnett, "David M. Kennedy: Ambassador for the Kingdom," *Ensign* 16 (June 1986): 42-45; Martin Berkeley Hickman, *David Matthew Kennedy: Banker, Statesman, Churchman* (Salt Lake City and Provo, UT: Deseret Book Co. and David M. Kennedy Center for International Studies, Brigham Young University, 1987), 334-65.

219. "Lebed Says He's Sorry For Anti-LDS Remark," *Salt Lake Tribune,* 3 July 1996, A-1, A-10; also "Lebed Sorry For Picking on Mormons—Sort of," *Deseret News,* 2 July 1996, A-1; "Yeltsin Camp Sees Turnout As Key To Runoff Victory," *Washington Post,* 3 July 1996, A-28; "Yeltsin, Act II," *Newsweek* 128 (8 July 1996): 43.

220. Without political activism in Latin America, the LDS church has been suffering such difficulties there for decades. See David Knowlton, "Missionaries and Terror: The Assassination of Two Elders in Bolivia," *Sunstone* 13 (Aug. 1989): 10-15; Lawrence A. Young, "Confronting Turbulent Environments: Issues in the Organizational Growth and Globalization of Mormonism," and David Knowlton, "'Gringo Jeringo': Anglo Mormon Missionary Culture in Bolivia," in Cornwall, Heaton, and Young, *Contemporary Mormonism,* 50-52, 227-28, 231.

Notes to Afterword

1. Diedrich Willers letter, 18 June 1830, in D. Michael Quinn, trans. and ed., "The First Months of Mormonism: A Contemporary View by Rev. Diedrich Willers," *New York History* 54 (July 1973): 331.

2. Josiah Quincy, *Figures of the Past.* . . (Boston: Roberts Brothers, 1883), reprinted in "Two Boston Brahmins Call on the Prophet," in William Mulder and A. Russell Mortensen, eds., *Among the Mormons: Historic Accounts by Contemporary Observers* (New York: Alfred A. Knopf, 1958), 131-32.

3. Harold Bloom, *The American Religion: The Emergence of the Post-Christian Nation* (New York: Simon & Schuster, 1992), 98, 110.

4. Jan Shipps, *Mormonism: The Story of A New Religious Tradition* (Urbana: University of Illinois Press, 1985).

5. Rodney Stark, "The Rise of a New World Faith," *Review of Religious Research* 26 (Sept. 1984): 22; Rodney Stark, "Modernization and Mormon Growth: The Secularization Thesis Revisited," in Marie Cornwall, Tim B. Heaton, and Lawrence A. Young, eds., *Contemporary Mormonism: Social Science Perspectives* (Urbana: University of Illinois Press, 1994), 14. However, Lowell C. "Ben" Bennion and Lawrence A. Young, "The Uncertain Dynamics of LDS Expansion, 1950-2020," *Dialogue: A Journal of Mormon Thought* 29 (Spring 1996): 16-17, 20, 29, reject Stark's projections due to a 50 percent drop in annual LDS growth rates for "every region except Africa since 1990." Restricting their end point to the year 2020, they argue that instead of Stark's projected LDS membership of 121 million

that year, "the First Presidency in 2020 will preside over no more than about 35 million members."

6. Jay M. Shafritz, Phil Williams, and Ronald S. Calinger, *The Dictionary of 20th-Century World Politics* (New York: Henry Holt & Co., 1993), 375.

7. Thomas F. O'Dea, *The Mormons* (Chicago: University of Chicago Press, 1957), 165.

General Officers of the Church of Jesus Christ of Latter-day Saints, 1845-1996

A. Appointments Made by Brigham Young, Church President, 1845-77

First Counselor:
Heber C. Kimball (1847-68)
George A. Smith (1868-75)
John W. Young (1876-77)

Second Counselor:
Willard Richards (1847-54)
Jedediah M. Grant (1854-56)
Daniel H. Wells (1857-77)

Non-sustained Counselor:
John Smith (1849-54)
John W. Young (1864-73)
Brigham Young, Jr. (1864-73)
Joseph A. Young (1864-71)
Joseph F. Smith (1866-67)

Assistant Counselor:
Lorenzo Snow (1873-77)
Brigham Young, Jr. (1873-77)
Albert Carrington (1873-77)
John W. Young (1873-76)
George Q. Cannon (1873-77)

Counselor to Quorum of the Twelve:
Sidney Rigdon (1844)
Amasa M. Lyman (1844-45)

Quorum of the Twelve Apostles:
Ezra T. Benson (1846-69)
Charles C. Rich (1849-83)
Lorenzo Snow (1849-1901)
Erastus [F.] Snow (1849-88)
Franklin D. Richards (1849-99)
George Q. Cannon (1860-1901)
Brigham Young, Jr. (1868-1903)*

Quorum of the Twelve Apostles (cont'd.):
Joseph F. Smith (1867-1918)*
Albert Carrington (1870-85)

*Ranking was switched in 1900

Prophet, Seer, and Revelator:
No one sustained by that title during Young's presidency until 7 April 1851; Young's counselors first sustained by that title on 8 October 1855; title not presented from 8 October 1859 until 9 October 1872; only Young sustained in this way after April 1873 to his death. (History of the Church, "Journal History," and *Deseret News*)

Brigham Young (1851-59, 1872-77)
Heber C. Kimball (1855-59)
Jedediah M. Grant (1855-56)
Daniel H. Wells (1857-59, 1872-73)
George A. Smith (1872-73)

Presiding Patriarch:
William Smith (1845-45)
John Smith, b. 1781 (1845-54)
John Smith, b. 1832 (1855-1911)

First Council of the Seventy:
Roger Orton [Jr.] (1845-45)
Albert P. Rockwood (1845-79)
Benjamin L. Clapp (1845-59)
Jedediah M. Grant (1845-54)
Horace S. Eldredge (1854-88)
Jacob Gates (1860-92)
John [L.] Van Cott (1862-83)

Presiding Bishop:
Newel K. Whitney (1847-50)
Edward Hunter (1851-83)

Assistant Presiding Bishop:
Nathaniel H. Felt (1851-53)
John Banks (1851-53)
Alfred Cordon (1851-53)

Bishopric First Counselor:
Brigham Young (1850-50, 1852-53)
Leonard W. Hardy (1856-84)

Bishopric Second Counselor:
Heber C. Kimball (1850-50, 1852-53)
Jesse C. Little (1856-74)
Robert T. Burton (1874-84)

B. Appointments Made by John Taylor, Church President, 1877-87

First Counselor:
George Q. Cannon (1880-87)

Second Counselor:
Joseph F. Smith (1880-87)

Quorum of the Twelve Apostles:
Moses Thatcher (1879-96)
Francis M. Lyman (1880-1916)
John Henry Smith (1880-1911)
George Teasdale (1882-1907)
Heber J. Grant (1882-1945)
John W. Taylor (1884-1906)

Counselor to Quorum of the Twelve:
Daniel H. Wells (1877-91)
John W. Young (1877-91)

Prophet, Seer, and Revelator:
All members of the Quorum of
the Twelve and its counselors from 6
October 1877 onward, and members
of the First Presidency from 10 Octo-

ber 1880 onward.

First Council of the Seventy:
William W. Taylor (1880-84)
Abraham H. Cannon (1882-89)
Theodore B. Lewis (1882)**
Seymour B. Young (1882-1924)
Christian D. Fjeldsted (1884-1905)
John [H.] Morgan (1884-94)

Presiding Bishop:
William B. Preston (1884-1907)

Bishopric First Counselor:
Robert T. Burton (1884-1907)

Bishopric Second Counselor:
John Q. Cannon (1884-86)
John R. Winder (1887-1901)

**Sustained publicly and not released
publicly, but not set apart due to previous ordination as a high priest.

C. Appointments Made by Wilford Woodruff, Church President, 1887-98

First Counselor:
George Q. Cannon (1889-98)

Second Counselor:
Joseph F. Smith (1889-98)

Quorum of the Twelve Apostles:
Marriner W. Merrill (1889-1906)
Anthon H. Lund (1889-1921)
Abraham H. Cannon (1889-96)

Quorum of the Twelve Apostles (cont'd.):
Matthias F. Cowley (1897-1906)
Abraham Owen Woodruff (1897-1904)

First Council of the Seventy:
B[righam]. H. Roberts (1888-1933)
George Reynolds (1890-1909)
J. Golden Kimball (1892-1938)
Rulon S. Wells (1893-1941)
Edward Stevenson (1894-97)
Joseph W. McMurrin (1897-1932)

D. Appointments Made by Lorenzo Snow,
Church President, 1898-1901

First Counselor:
George Q. Cannon (1898-1901)
Joseph F. Smith (1901)***

Quorum of the Twelve Apostles:
Rudger Clawson (1898-1943)
Reed Smoot (1900-41)

Second Counselor:
Joseph F. Smith (1898-1901)
Rudger Clawson (1901)***

***Sustained publicly but never set
apart nor functioned in that position.

E. Appointments Made by Joseph F. Smith,
Church President, 1901-18

First Counselor:
John R. Winder (1901-10)
Anthon H. Lund (1910-18)

Second Counselor:
Anthon H. Lund (1901-10)
John Henry Smith (1910-11)
Charles W. Penrose (1911-18)

Quorum of the Twelve Apostles:
Hyrum M. Smith (1901-18)
George Albert Smith (1903-51)
Charles W. Penrose (1904-25)
George F. Richards (1906-50)
Orson F. Whitney (1906-31)
David O. McKay (1906-70)
Anthony W. Ivins (1907-34)
Joseph Fielding Smith (1910-72)
James E. Talmage (1911-33)
Stephen L Richards (1917-59)
Richard R. Lyman (1918-43)

Presiding Patriarch:
Hyrum G. Smith (1912-32)

Prophet, Seer, and Revelator:
        Presiding Patriarch John Smith
was sustained with this title on 6 October 1902, and thereafter his successor
as patriarch was sustained as "Prophet,
Seer, and Revelator" with members of
the First Presidency and Quorum of
the Twelve Apostles.

First Council of the Seventy:
Charles H. Hart (1906-34)
Levi Edgar Young (1909-63)

Presiding Bishop:
Charles W. Nibley (1907-25)

Bishopric First Counselor:
Orrin P. Miller (1907-18)
David A. Smith (1918-38)

Bishopric Second Counselor:
Orrin P. Miller (1901-07)
David A. Smith (1907-18)
John Wells (1918-38)

F. Appointments Made by Heber J. Grant,
Church President, 1918-45

First Counselor:
Anthon H. Lund (1918-21)
Charles W. Penrose (1921-25)
Anthony W. Ivins (1925-34)
J. Reuben Clark, Jr. (1934-45)

Second Counselor:
Charles W. Penrose (1918-21)
Anthony W. Ivins (1921-25)
Charles W. Nibley (1925-31)
J. Reuben Clark, Jr. (1933-34)
David O. McKay (1934-45)

Quorum of the Twelve Apostles:
Melvin J. Ballard (1919-39)
John A. Widtsoe (1921-52)
Joseph F. Merrill (1931-52)
Charles A. Callis (1933-47)
J. Reuben Clark, Jr. (1934-61)
Alonzo A. Hinckley (1934-36)
Albert E. Bowen (1937-53)
Sylvester Q. Cannon (1939-43)
Harold B. Lee (1941-73)
Spencer W. Kimball (1943-85)
Ezra Taft Benson (1943-94)
Mark E. Petersen (1944-84)

Associate to Quorum of the Twelve:
Sylvester Q. Cannon (1938-39)

Patriarch to the Church:
Joseph F. Smith (1942-46)

Assistants to the Twelve:
Marion G. Romney (1941-51)
Thomas E. McKay (1941-58)
Clifford E. Young (1941-58)

Assistants to the Twelve (cont'd.)*:*
Alma Sonne (1941-77)
Nicholas G. Smith (1941-45)

First Council of the Seventy:
Rey L. Pratt (1925-31)
Antoine R. Ivins (1931-67)
Samuel O. Bennion (1933-45)
John H. Taylor (1933-46)
Rufus K. Hardy (1934-45)
Richard L. Evans (1938-53)
Oscar A. Kirkham (1941-58)
S. Dilworth Young (1945-76)
Milton R. Hunter (1945-75)

Presiding Bishop:
Sylvester Q. Cannon (1925-38)
LeGrand Richards (1938-52)

Bishopric First Counselor:
Marvin O. Ashton (1938-46)

Bishopric Second Counselor:
Joseph L. Wirthlin (1938-46)

G. Appointments Made by George Albert Smith, Church President, 1945-51

First Counselor:
J. Reuben Clark, Jr. (1945-51)

Second Counselor:
David O. McKay (1945-51)

Quorum of the Twelve Apostles:
Matthew Cowley (1945-53)
Henry D. Moyle (1947-63)
Delbert L. Stapley (1950-78)

Patriarch to the Church:
Eldred G. Smith (1947-79)

First Council of the Seventy:
Bruce R. McConkie (1946-72)

Bishopric First Counselor:
Joseph L. Wirthlin (1946-52)

Bishopric Second Counselor:
Thorpe B. Isaacson (1946-52)

H. Appointments Made by David O. McKay, Church President, 1951-70

First Counselor:
Stephen L Richards (1951-59)
J. Reuben Clark, Jr. (1959-61)
Henry D. Moyle (1961-63)
Hugh B. Brown (1963-70)

Second Counselor:
J. Reuben Clark, Jr. (1951-59)
Henry D. Moyle (1959-61)
Hugh B. Brown (1961-63)
N. Eldon Tanner (1963-70)

Assistant Counselor:

Hugh B. Brown (1961-61)
Joseph Fielding Smith (1965-70)
Thorpe B. Isaacson (1965-70)
Alvin R. Dyer (1968-70)

Quorum of the Twelve Apostles:

Marion G. Romney (1951-88)
LeGrand Richards (1952-83)
Adam S. Bennion (1953-58)
Richard L. Evans (1953-71)
George Q. Morris (1954-62)
Hugh B. Brown (1958-75)
Howard W. Hunter (1959-95)
Gordon B. Hinckley (1961-)
N. Eldon Tanner (1962-82)
Thomas S. Monson (1963-)

Assistants to the Twelve:

George Q. Morris (1951-54)
Stayner Richards (1951-53)
ElRay L. Christiansen (1951-75)
John Longden (1951-69)
Hugh B. Brown (1953-58)
Sterling W. Sill (1954-76)
Gordon B. Hinckley (1958-61)
Henry D. Taylor (1958-76)
William J. Critchlow (1958-68)

Assistants to the Twelve (cont'd.):

Alvin R. Dyer (1958-68, 70-76)
N. Eldon Tanner (1960-62)
Franklin D. Richards (1960-76)
Theodore M. Burton (1960-76)
Thorpe B. Isaacson (1961-65, 1970-70)
Boyd K. Packer (1961-70)
Bernard P. Brockbank (1962-76)
James A. Cullimore (1966-76)
Marion D. Hanks (1968-76)
Marvin J. Ashton (1969-71)

First Council of the Seventy:

Marion D. Hanks (1953-68)
A. Theodore Tuttle (1958-76)
Paul H. Dunn (1964-76)
Hartman Rector, Jr. (1968-76)
Loren C. Dunn (1968-76)

Presiding Bishop:

Joseph L. Wirthlin (1952-61)
John H. Vandenberg (1961-72)

Bishopric First Counselor:

Thorpe B. Isaacson (1952-61)
Robert L. Simpson (1961-72)

Bishopric Second Counselor:

Carl W. Buehner (1952-61)
Victor L. Brown (1961-72)

I. Appointments Made by Joseph Fielding Smith, Church President, 1970-72

First Counselor:

Harold B. Lee (1970-72)

Second Counselor:

N. Eldon Tanner (1970-72)

Quorum of the Twelve Apostles:

Boyd K. Packer (1970-)
Marvin J. Ashton (1971-94)

Assistants to the Twelve:

Joseph Anderson (1970-76)
David B. Haight (1970-76)

Assistants to the Twelve (cont'd):

William H. Bennett (1970-76)
John H. Vandenberg (1972-76)
Robert L. Simpson (1972-76)

Presiding Bishop:

Victor L. Brown (1972-85)

Bishopric First Counselor:

H. Burke Peterson (1972-85)

Bishopric Second Counselor:

Vaughn J. Featherstone (1972-76)

J. Appointments Made by Harold B. Lee,
Church President, 1972-73

First Counselor:
N. Eldon Tanner (1972-73)

Second Counselor:
Marion G. Romney (1972-73)

Quorum of the Twelve Apostles:
Bruce R. McConkie (1972-85)

Assistants to the Twelve:
O. Leslie Stone (1972-76)
James E. Faust (1972-76)
L. Tom Perry (1972-74)

First Council of the Seventy:
Rex D. Pinegar (1972-76)

K. Appointments Made by Spencer W. Kimball,
Church President, 1973-85

First Counselor:
N. Eldon Tanner (1973-82)
Marion G. Romney (1982-85)

Second Counselor:
Marion G. Romney (1973-82)
Gordon B. Hinckley (1982-85)

Assistant Counselor:
Gordon B. Hinckley (1981-82)

Quorum of the Twelve Apostles:
L. Tom Perry (1974-)
David B. Haight (1976-)
James E. Faust (1978-)
Neal A. Maxwell (1981-)
Russell M. Nelson (1984-)
Dallin H. Oaks (1984-)
M. Russell Ballard (1985-)

Patriarch to the Church:
Patriarch to the Church ceased to exist as of 6 October 1979.

Prophet, Seer, and Revelator:
After 6 October 1979, "Prophets, Seers, and Revelators" applied only to First Presidency and Quorum of the Twelve Apostles.

Assistants to the Twelve:
J. Thomas Fyans (1974-76)
Neal A. Maxwell (1974-76)
William G. Bangerter (1975-76)
Robert D. Hales (1975-76)
Adney Y. Komatsu (1975-76)
Joseph B. Wirthlin (1975-76)

Assistants to the Twelve (con't)*:*
Assistants to the Twelve ceased to exist as of 1 October 1976.

First Council of the Seventy:
Gene R. Cook (1975-76)

First Council of the Seventy ceased to exist as of 1 October 1976.

Presidency of the Seventy:
Franklin D. Richards (1976-83)
James E. Faust (1976-78)
J. Thomas Fyans (1976-85)
A. Theodore Tuttle (1976-80)
Neal A. Maxwell (1976-81)
Marion D. Hanks (1976-80)
Paul H. Dunn (1976-80)
William G. Bangerter (1978-80)
Carlos E. Asay (1980-86)
M. Russell Ballard (1980-85)
Dean L. Larsen (1980-93)
Royden G. Derrick (1980-84)
G. Homer Durham (1981-85)
Richard G. Scott (1983-88)
Marion D. Hanks (1984-92)
William G. Bangerter (1985-89)
Jack H. Goaslind, Jr. (1985-87)
Robert L. Backman (1985-92)

First Quorum of the Seventy:
Charles A. A. Didier (1975-)*
William R. Bradford (1975-)*
George P. Lee (1975-89)*
Carlos E. Asay (1976-96)*
M. Russell Ballard (1976-85)*

First Quorum of the Seventy (cont'd):
John H. Groberg (1976-)*
Jacob de Jager (1976-93)*
Franklin D. Richards (1976-87)*
James E. Faust (1976-78)*
J. Thomas Fyans (1976-89)*
A. Theodore Tuttle (1976-86)*
Neal A. Maxwell (1976-81)*
Marion D. Hanks (1976-92)*
Paul H. Dunn (1976-89)*
Alma Sonne (1976-77)*
Sterling W. Sill (1976-78)*
Henry D. Taylor (1976-78)*
Alvin R. Dyer (1976-77)*
Theodore M. Burton (1976-89)*
Bernard P. Brockbank (1976-80)*
James A. Cullimore (1976-78)*
Joseph Anderson (1976-78)*
William H. Bennett (1976-78)*
John H. Vandenberg (1976-78)*
Robert L. Simpson (1976-89)*
O. Leslie Stone (1976-80)*
William G. Bangerter (1976-89)*
Robert D. Hales (1976-85)*
Adney Y. Komatsu (1976-93)*
Joseph B. Wirthlin (1976-86)*
S. Dilworth Young (1976-78)*
Hartman Rector, Jr. (1976-94)*
Loren C. Dunn (1976-)*
Rex D. Pinegar (1976-)*
Gene R. Cook (1976-)*
Vaughn J. Featherstone (1976-)
Dean L. Larsen (1976-)
Royden G. Derrick (1976-89)
Robert E. Wells (1976-)
G. Homer Durham (1977-85)
James M. Paramore (1977-)
Richard G. Scott (1977-88)
Hugh W. Pinnock (1977-)
F. Enzio Busche (1977-)
Yoshihiko Kikuchi (1977-)
Ronald E. Poelman (1978-)
Derek A. Cuthbert (1978-91)
Robert L. Backman (1978-92)

Rex C. Reeve (1978-89)
F. Burton Howard (1978-)
Teddy E. Brewerton (1978-95)
Jack H. Goaslind, Jr. (1978-)
Angel Abrea (1981-)
John K. Carmack (1984-)
Russell C. Taylor (1984-89)
Robert B. Harbertson (1984-89)
Devere Harris (1984-89)
Spencer H. Osborn (1984-89)
Philip T. Sonntag (1984-89)
John Sonnenberg (1984-89)
F. Arthur Kay (1984-89)
Keith W. Wilcock (1984-89)
Victor L. Brown (1985-89)
H. Burke Peterson (1985-93)
J. Richard Clarke (1985-)
Hans B. Ringger (1985-95)
Waldo P. Call (1985-89)
Helio D. Camargo (1985-89)

*Chronological order, rather than ranking

Presiding Bishop:
Robert D. Hales (1985-94)

Bishopric First Counselor:
Henry B. Eyring (1985-92)

Bishopric Second Counselor:
J. Richard Clarke (1976-85)
Glenn L. Pace (1985-92)

Emeritus General Authority:
Sterling W. Sill (1978-94)
Henry D. Taylor (1978-87)
James A. Cullimore (1978-86)
S. Dilworth Young (1978-81)
Joseph Anderson (1978-92)
William H. Bennett (1978-80)
John H. Vandenberg (1978-92)
Eldred G. Smith (1979-)
Bernard P. Brockbank (1980-)
O. Leslie Stone (1980-86)

L. Appointments Made by Ezra Taft Benson, Church President, 1985-94

First Counselor:
Gordon B. Hinckley (1985-94)

Second Counselor:
Thomas S. Monson (1985-94)

638   APPENDIX 1

Quorum of the Twelve Apostles:
Joseph B. Wirthlin (1986-)
Richard G. Scott (1988-)
Robert D. Hales (1994-)

Presidency of the Seventy:
Joseph B. Wirthlin (1986-86)
Hugh W. Pinnock (1986-89)
James M. Paramore (1987-93)
J. Richard Clarke (1988-93)
Rex D. Pinegar (1989-95)
Carlos E. Asay (1989-96)
Charles A. A. Didier (1992-95)
L. Aldin Porter (1992-)
Joe J. Christensen (1993-)
Monte J. Brough (1993-)
W. Eugene Hansen (1993-)

First Quorum of the Seventy:
H. Verlan Andersen (1986-89)
George I. Cannon (1986-89)
Francis M. Gibbons (1986-89)
Gardner H. Russell (1986-89)
George R. Hill III (1987-89)
John R. Lasater (1987-89)
Douglas J. Martin (1987-89)
Alexander B. Morrison (1987-89, 1991-)
L. Aldin Porter (1987-89, 1992-)
Glen L. Rudd (1987-89)
Douglas H. Smith (1987-89)
Lynn A. Sorensen (1987-89)
Robert E. Sackley (1988-89)
L. Lionel Kendrick (1988-89, 1991-)
Monte J. Brough (1988-89, 1991-)
Albert Choules, Jr. (1988-89)
Lloyd P. George, Jr. (1988-89)
Gerald E. Melchin (1988-89)
Joe J. Christensen (1989-)
W. Eugene Hansen (1989-)
Jeffrey R. Holland (1989-94)
Marlin K. Jensen (1989-)
Earl C. Tingey (1991-)
Harold G. Hillam (1991-)
Carlos H. Amado (1992-)
Ben B. Banks (1992-)
Spencer J. Condie (1992-)
Robert K. Dellenbach (1992-)
Henry B. Eyring (1992-95)
Glenn L. Pace (1992-)
F. Melvin Hammond (1993-)
Kenneth Johnson (1993-)
Lynn A. Mickelsen (1993-)

First Quorum of the Seventy (cont'd.):
Neil L. Andersen (1993-)
D. Todd Christofferson (1993-)
Cree-L Kofford (1994-)

Second Quorum of the Seventy:
Russell C. Taylor (1989-89)
Robert B. Harbertson (1989-89)
Devere Harris (1989-89)
Spencer H. Osborn (1989-89)
Phillip T. Sonntag (1989-89)
John Sonnenberg (1989-89)
F. Arthur Kay (1989-89)
Keith W. Wilcox (1989-89)
Waldo P. Call (1989-90)
Helio R. Camargo (1989-90)
H. Verlan Andersen (1989-91)
George I. Cannon (1989-91)
Francis M. Gibbons (1989-91)
Gardner H. Russell (1989-91)
George R. Hill III (1989-92)
John R. Lasater (1989-92)
Douglas J. Martin (1989-92)
Alexander B. Morrison (1989-91)
L. Aldin Porter (1989-92)
Glen L. Rudd (1989-92)
Douglas H. Smith (1989-92)
Lynn A. Sorensen (1989-92)
Robert E. Sackley (1989-93)
L. Lionel Kendrick (1989-91)
Monte J. Brough (1989-91)
Albert Choules, Jr. (1989-94)
Lloyd P. George, Jr. (1989-94)
Gerald E. Melchin (1989-94)
Carlos H. Amado (1989-92)
Ben B. Banks (1989-92)
Spencer J. Condie (1989-92)
F. Melvin Hammond (1989-93)
Malcolm S. Jeppsen (1989-94)
Richard P. Lindsay (1989-94)
Merlin R. Lybbert (1989-94)
Horacio A. Tenorio (1989-94)
Eduardo Ayala (1990-95)
LeGrand R. Curtis (1990-95)
Clinton L. Cutler (1990-94)
Robert K. Dellenbach (1990-92)
Harold G. Hillam (1990-91)
Kenneth Johnson (1990-93)
Helvecio Martins (1990-95)
Lynn A. Mickelsen (1990-93)
J. Ballard Washburn (1990-95)

Second Quorum of the Seventy (cont'd.):
Durrell A. Woolsey (1990-95)
Rulon G. Craven (1990-96)
W. Mack Lawrence (1990-96)
Julio E. Davila (1991-96)
Graham W. Doxey (1991-96)
Cree-L Kofford (1991-94)
Joseph C. Muren (1991-96)
Dennis B. Neuenschwander (1991-94)
Jorge A. Rojas (1991-96)
In Sang Han (1991-96)
Stephen D. Nadauld (1991-96)
Sam K. Shimabukuro (1991-96)
Lino Alvarez (1992-)
Dallas N. Archibald (1992-96)
Merrill J. Bateman (1992-94)
C. Max Caldwell (1992-)
Gary J. Coleman (1992-)
John B. Dickson (1992-95)
John E. Fowler (1992-)
Jay E. Jensen (1992-95)
Augusto A. Lim (1992-)
John M. Madsen (1992-)
V. Dallas Merrell (1992-)
David E. Sorensen (1992-95)
F. David Stanley (1992-)
Kwok Yuen Tai (1992-)
Lowell D. Wood (1992-)
Claudio R. M. Costa (1994-)

Second Quorum of the Seventy (cont'd.):
W. Don Ladd (1994-)
James O. Mason (1994-)
Dieter F. Uchtdorf (1994-96)
Lance B. Wickman (1994-)

Presiding Bishop:
Merrill J. Bateman (1994-95)

Bishopric First Counselor:
H. David Burton (1992-95)

Bishopric Second Counselor:
Richard C. Edgley (1992-95)

Emeritus General Authority:
W. Grant Bangerter (1989-)
J. Thomas Fyans (1989-)
Paul H. Dunn (1989-)
Theodore M. Burton (1989-89)
Robert L. Simpson (1989-)
Royden G. Derrick(1989-)
Rex C. Reeve (1989-)
Victor L. Brown (1989-96)
Marion D. Hanks (1992-)
Robert L. Backman (1992-)
Adney Y. Komatsu (1993-)
Jacob de Jager (1993-)
H. Burke Peterson (1993-)

M. Appointments Made by Howard W. Hunter, Church President, 1994-95

First Counselor:
Gordon B. Hinckley (1994-95)

Second Counselor:
Thomas S. Monson (1994-95)

Quorum of the Twelve Apostles:
Jeffrey R. Holland (1994-)

First Quorum of the Seventy:
Dennis B. Neuenschwander (1994-)
Andrew W. Peterson (1994-)
Cecil O. Samuelson, Jr. (1994-)

Emeritus General Authority:
Hartman Rector, Jr. (1994-)

N. Appointments Made by Gordon B. Hinckley, Church President, 1995-

First Counselor:
Thomas S. Monson (1995-)

Second Counselor:
James E. Faust (1995-)

Quorum of the Twelve Apostles:
Henry B. Eyring (1995-)

Presidency of the Seventy:
Jack H. Goaslind, Jr. (1995-)
Harold G. Hillam (1995-)
Earl C. Tingey (1996-)

First Quorum of the Seventy:
John B. Dickson (1995-)
Jay E. Jensen (1995-)
David E. Sorensen (1995-)
W. Craig Zwick (1995-)
Merrill J. Bateman (1995-)
Dallas N. Archibald (1996-)
Dieter F. Uchtdorf (1996-)
Bruce C. Hafen (1996-)

Second Quorum of the Seventy:
Bruce D. Porter (1995-)
L. Edward Brown (1996-)
Sheldon F. Child (1996-)

Second Quorum of the Seventy (cont'd.):
Quentin L. Cook (1996-)
William Rolfe Kerr (1996-)
Dennis E. Simmons (1996-)
Jerald L. Taylor (1996-)
Francisco J. Vinas (1996-)
Richard B. Wirthlin (1996-)

Presiding Bishop:
H. David Burton (1995-)

Bishopric First Counselor:
Richard C. Edgley (1995-)

Bishopric Second Counselor:
Keith B. McMullin (1995-)

Emeritus General Authority:
Ted E. Brewerton (1995-)
Hans B. Ringger (1995-)
Carlos E. Asay (1996-)

Biographical Sketches of General Officers of the Church of Jesus Christ of Latter-day Saints, Appointed 1849-1932

This appendix provides background on general officers of the LDS church who were appointed from 1849 through 1932, a century after founder Joseph Smith, Jr. began the hierarchy by choosing counselors. A companion volume, *The Mormon Hierarchy: Origins of Power,* provides biographical sketches for Mormon leaders appointed before 1848. No general officers were appointed in 1848. The quoted word "ordained" indicates that "set apart" is the current LDS phrase for this office, or that "set apart" used to be the accepted phrase for this office.

A <u>Relations</u> section describes kinship and marriage within the hierarchy in each biographical profile. These are simplified where possible, so that half-brothers are listed as brothers, for example. Distant cousins, which were valued by the hierarchy but less noticeable to outsiders (chap. 5), are cited more precisely. Initials identify others with main entries in this appendix. Full names identify church leaders appointed before 1849 (see companion volume) and after 1932 (see *Deseret News 1995-1996 Church Almanac* for biographical sketches according to highest office held).

In the <u>Marriage</u> section, an asterisk (*) indicates a wife not recognized in traditional histories, though there was a marriage ceremony, sexual cohabitation, or a formal divorce. Excluded are nominal marriages such as proxy sealings to deceased persons. A surname in parentheses indicates a wife's previous husband(s), and divorce refers to the formal end of a marriage through ecclesiastical or civil pronouncement. Remarriage means marriage to someone other than the subject of the sketch. The reference "ch" is to the number of children born to a union, and "+" means that birth records are incomplete. "Sb" refers to "stillbirths," which in nineteenth-century usage included infants who were born alive but died shortly afterwards.

In the <u>Business</u> section, a bracketed company name indicates stock ownership only, or a possible management role that is currently unverified. Where business enterprises can be social or educational, I have tried to avoid duplicate entries for a person rather than give a final answer to ambiguities.

<u>Social</u> section includes social registers and biographical directories as indication of public status. This excludes sources which by definition list every member of the hierarchy. Some of these sources required fees for inclusion, which may explain why general authorities were omitted. However, omission from other sources seemed to indicate a lack of status within the larger, secular society or a loss of status within Mormon culture itself.

Men listed with a double asterisk (**) are those who have been inaccurately identified as having had a presiding role over the entire church when their jurisdiction was in fact more limited. One man is listed with a triple asterisk (***) because he became a general authority in 1941 after having served during the previous decade in a similar capacity as some men listed with a double asterisk.

Where sources disagree on spelling, dates, or other specifics, discrepancies are resolved on the basis of the best information available. Underlined dates indicate accuracy despite published assertions to the contrary. Sources represent a wide variety of published and unpublished biographies, diaries, autobiographies, archival records, correspondence, minutes, church ordinance records, corporation files, judicial records, family and community histories, newspapers, and civil records of birth, marriage, divorce, and death. To conserve space, source citations are absent.

**Truman O. Angel[l] (1810-1887)

On 31 May 1857, Angel[l] became a member of the prayer circle of the First Presidency and Quorum of Twelve. He attended with ten other non-general authorities until September 1858 when they were assigned to different circles. Angel[l] was Brigham Young's brother-in-law and the church architect but never a general authority.

MELVIN J[OSEPH] BALLARD (MJB)

Birth: 9 February 1873, Logan, Cache Co., Utah
Parents: Henry Ballard and Margaret McNeil
Marriage (monogamist): Martha A. Jones 1896 (8 ch)
Hierarchy Relations: Son md daughter of HMS and niece of DAS and JFS-2 1926; grandfather of future apostle M. Russell Ballard
Education: Graduate, Brigham Young College in Logan 1894; trustee, Brigham Young College (1919-23), Utah State Agricultural College (1935-40)
Prior Occupation: Businessman
Business To 1932: Artogram System; Ballard-Jackson Nash Co.; Ballard Motor Co.; Ballard Orchard and Produce Co.; Cache Valley Mercantile; Daynes-Beebe Music Co.; Deseret Book Co.; [Great Western Mining and Milling Co.]; [Hess-Nash Sales Co.]; Howell-Cardon Co.; *Improvement Era;* Logan Knitting Factory; Oregon Portland Cement Co.; Portland Cement Co.; Salt Lake Knitting Works; Utah-Idaho Hospital; Utah Marble Co.; W. H. Groves LDS Hospital; Wasatch Land and Improvement Co.; Wasatch Lawn Cemetery Association; Zion's Printing and Publishing Co.
Social: Cache Commercial Club (director, 1904-09; president, 1906-08); listed in *Utah's Distinguished Personalities* 1933, *Who's Who In the Clergy* 1935, *Faith of Our Pioneer Fathers* 1956; omitted from *Biographical Record of Salt Lake City and Vicinity* 1902, from *Men of Affairs in the State of Utah* [Press Club of Salt Lake City] 1914
Political/Civic Life: Democratic election judge (1895, 1899); delegate, Democratic conventions (1900, 1904, 1908); defeated as Democratic candidate for Logan city council 1901
Prior Religion: LDS
Mormon Experience: Baptized 1881; patriarchal blessing 1884 promised he would be prophet in Zion; elder 1895; seventy 1896; mission (1896-98); high priest 1900; bishopric counselor (1900-06); stake high council (1906-09); mission president (1909-19); had vivid dream of embracing Jesus Christ 1917; apostle 7 January 1919; general boards, YMMIA and Religion Class (1919-22); chair, General Music Committee (1920-39); president, Salt Lake Elders' Quorum prayer circle (1921-29); mission president (1925-26); Melchizedek Priesthood Committee (1928-37); counselor, YMMIA General Superintendency (1934-35); Church Security Plan chair (1936-37) and committee (1937-39)
Death: 30 July 1939, Salt Lake City, Utah
Estate: $31,952.34 appraised; $31,000.35 net

JOHN BANKS (JB)
Birth: 6 February 1806, Colne, Lancashire Co., England
Parents: Henry Banks and Elizabeth _____
Marriage (polygamist after appointment): Ellen E. Kendell 1836 (6 ch), sealed 1851, divorced 1857; Catherine Mayer 1852 (no ch), separated abt 1860; Fanny E. Jeune 1857 (no ch), separated abt 1860; Hannah _____ abt 1860.
Hierarchy Relations: ?
Education: English grammar schools
Prior Occupation: Stonecutter
Business To 1932: ?
Social: Omitted from *Pioneers and Prominent Men of Utah* 1914; continues to be omitted from official lists of LDS general authorities
Political/Civic Life: Defied warrants for arrest 1862, obstructed efforts to serve warrants on others connected with the Morrisite movement
Prior Religion: Church of England at christening
Mormon Experience: Baptized 1840; elder abt 1841; seventy 1844; mission (1844-50); mission presidency (1845-47); publicly sustained and "ordained" assistant presiding bishop 8 September 1851; honorably released 7 October 1853; mission (1854-56); excommunicated 13 November 1858; rebaptized 18 November 1858; excommunicated 23 December 1859; baptized into Joseph Morris's Church of Jesus Christ of Saints of the Most High 6 April 1861; apostle, Morrisite church, June 1861; second counselor and spokesman for Morris 7 September 1861; baptized by proxy into LDS church April 1944; baptized again by proxy 9 Feb 1961, after which his priesthood was restored before proxy endowment 1 March 1961.
Death: 15 June 1862, Kingston's Fort, Weber Co., Utah; killed by RTB during "Morrisite War."
Estate: No record

**Thomas D. Brown (1807-1874)
In January 1857 Brown became a member of the prayer circle of the First Presidency and Quorum of Twelve Apostles, attended by eight other non-general authorities. Brown attended until September 1858 when he was assigned to a non-general authority prayer circle. In 1859 he became a dissenter, was excommunicated, and joined Utah's anti-Mormon political party in 1872.

ROBERT T[AYLOR] BURTON (RTB)
Birth: 25 October 1821, Amerstberg, Ontario Province, Canada
Parents: Samuel Burton and Hannah Shipley
Marriage (polygamist before appointment): Maria S. Haven 1845 (10 ch); Sarah A. Garr 1856 (12 ch); Susan E. McBride 1856 (5 ch)
Hierarchy Relations: He and Albert P. Rockwood md sisters; grandfather of future Assistant to the Twelve Theodore M. Burton; 2nd-great-grandfather of future Presiding Bishop H. David Burton
Education: Common schools and secondary schools to age 17; regent, University of Deseret (Utah), 1878-86
Prior Occupation: Farmer and stockman
Business To 1932: A. O. Smoot and Co.; Burton and Co.; Burton and Wilcken; [Burton, Gardner and Co.]; Burton-Gardner Co.; Burton, Sons and Young; Burton Stock Co.; Davis County Co-operative Co.; Deseret Bee, Stock and Fish Association; Deseret Dramatic Association; Deseret Irrigation and Navigation Canal Co.; Deseret Tanning and Manufacturing Co.; Deseret Woolen Mills; Home Coal Co.; [Monitor Mining Co.]; Nevada Land and Livestock Co.; Perpetual Emigrating Fund Co.; [Pride of the West Mining Co.]; [Revenue Mining Co.]; Rexburg Milling Co.; [St. Joe Mining Co.]; [Salt

Lake City] Fifteenth Ward Co-operative Mercantile Institution; Salt Lake Literary and Scientific Association; Sells, Burton and Co.; Social Hall Society; South Jordan Canal Co.; Trapper Mining Co.; Utah Eastern Railroad Co.; Utah Soap Manufacturing Co.; Utah Territorial Insane Asylum; W. H. Groves LDS Hospital; Wasatch Woolen Mills; Zion's Central Board of Trade

Social: Mason 1844, Nauvoo lodge; Young Men's Christian Association (YMCA) by 1907; listed in *Blue Book* for Salt Lake City (1895-1907), *Biographical Record of Salt Lake City and Vicinity* 1902, *Utah As It Is* 1904, *Stalwarts of Mormonism* 1954; omitted from *Testimonies of the Church of Jesus Christ of Latter-day Saints by Its Leaders* 1930

Political/Civic Life: Utah's Nauvoo Legion 1st lieutenant (1850-52), captain (1852-54); Salt Lake City and County constable (1852-54); foreman, Utah legislature's upper chamber (1852-53); U.S. deputy marshal (1852-62); sergeant-at-arms, Utah House of Representatives (1853-55); Salt Lake County sheriff (1854-75), assessor and collector (1859-73); Utah's Nauvoo Legion major (1854-57), and colonel (1857-65); indicted for treason, Utah War, December 1857 (pardoned by U.S. president's general amnesty 1858); was sued for false imprisonment 1858 (case dismissed when plaintiff died 1859); Salt Lake City council (1858-1874); U.S. Internal Revenue collector (1862-69); acquitted for four counts of murder in Morrisite War 1862; Utah's Nauvoo Legion major-general (1865-70); Council of Fifty initiation 25 January 1867; nominating committee, LDS People's Party 1870; delegate, People's Party conventions (1870, 1876, 1877, 1878, 1880); arrested 1877 for murder of former general authority JB and a woman in "Morrisite War" (acquitted 1879); Salt Lake County assessor 1880; member of the Council of Fifty's executive "Committee of Seven" (1882-84); indicted 1885 for cohabitation (avoided arrest), convicted and fined 1889; delegate, Democratic Party territorial convention 1892; pre-1891 polygamy pardoned and re-enfranchised by U.S. president's general amnesties (1893, 1894); unsuccessful Democratic candidate for Utah State Constitutional Convention 1894

Prior Religion: Church of England

Mormon Experience: Baptized 1838 (age 17); elder 1843; seventy 1844; prayer circle of Wilford Woodruff (1858-73); bishopric counselor (1859-67); bishop without high priest ordination as one of the "seventy apostles" (1867-75); mission (1869-70, 1873-75); publicly sustained second counselor, Presiding Bishopric 9 October 1874; high priest 2 September 1875; continued as ward bishop (1875-77); first counselor, Presiding Bishopric 31 July 1884; vice-president, LDS Industrial Bureau (1897-98)

Death: 11 November 1907, Salt Lake City, Utah

Estate: $17,647.99 appraised; $13,791.68 net

ABRAHAM H[OAGLAND] CANNON (AHC)

Birth: 12 March 1859, Salt Lake City, Utah

Parents: GQC and Elizabeth Hoagland

Marriage (polygamist before appointment): Sarah A. Jenkins 1878 (4 ch); Wilhelmina M. Cannon 1879 (6 ch); Mary E. Croxall 1887 (6 ch); Lillian Hamlin 1896 (1 ch); possibly also Leah E. Dunford early 1896 (began courting her and Hamlin simultaneously December 1895—see JAW)

Hierarchy Relations: Son of GQC, brother of JQC and SQC, nephew of WWT's 1st wife; md 1887 to step-daughter of GQC, niece of BY-JR and JWY, and 1st cousin, 1 rvd, of SBY; he and DAS md sisters; grandfather of future Seventy George I. Cannon

Education: Prep school and college, University of Deseret (Utah), 1868-75; trustee, Young University at Salt Lake City (1891-95); vice-president and president, Vortbildungs Verein (1894-94)

Prior Occupation: Architect, editor

Business To 1932: Abraham H. Cannon Co.; Alexander Mining Co.; [American Mining and Milling Co.]; Armstrong, Winder and Co.; Blue Bird Mining Co.; [Brigham Young Trust Co.]; Bullion, Beck and Champion Mining Co.; [Burke Mining Co.]; Cannon Brothers (Books); Cannon Brothers (Loan Agency); Cannon Brothers (Insurance); Cannon Gold Mining and Milling Co.; Cannon, Grant and Co.; Cedar and Iron Railroad Co.; [Cedar Sheep Assn.]; Contributor Co.; Co-operative Furniture Co.; Dalton, Nye and Cannon Co.; Deseret and Salt Lake Agricultural and Manufacturing Canal Co.; Deseret Investment Co.; [Deseret Irrigation and Navigation Canal Co.]; *Deseret News;* Deseret News Publishing Co.; Deseret Savings Bank; George Q. Cannon and Sons; Godbe-Pitts Drug Co.; Grand Central Mining Co.; [Grant Brothers Livery and Transfer Co.]; Grant Gold Mining Co.; Hampton, Jones and Co.; [Hydraulic Canal Co.]; Iphigene Horse Co.; Iron Manufacturing Company of Utah; [J. C. Taylor]; *Juvenile Instructor;* Lehi Commercial and Savings Bank; [Nana Mining Co.]; New Year Gold Mining Co.; New York Gold Mining Co.; Ogden Equitable Co-operative Association; Ogden Herald Publishing Co.; Ogden Investment Co.; People's Equitable Co-operative Association; Purchasers Co-operative Association; Riverside Canal Co.; [Salt Lake Amusement Assn.]; Salt Lake and Pacific Railroad Co.; Salt Lake County Stock Association; [Salt Lake Rapid Transit Co.]; [Spanish Fork Co-operative Institution]; State Bank of Utah; Sterling Mining and Milling Co.; Superior Mining Co.; Tontine Investment Association; Utah and California Railway Co.; Utah and Pacific Improvement Co.; Utah Commercial and Savings Bank; Utah Co.; Utah Consolidated Mining Co.; Utah Guano Co.; Utah Loan and Trust Co.; [Utah Sugar Co.]; Zion's Benefit Building Society, ZCMI

Social: Salt Lake Chamber of Commerce (director 1893-96); listed in *Blue Book* for Salt Lake City (1895-96), *Prophets and Patriarchs of the Church* 1902; omitted from biographies in *History of Utah* 1904

Political/Civic Life: Council of Fifty initiation 9 October 1884; spent 6 months in prison for cohabitation 1886, arrested 1888 (charges dismissed); arrested for conspiracy to misappropriate public funds 1889 (charges dropped 1890); avoided arrest for cohabitation 1890 through friend who bribed deputy marshal; speaker, LDS People's Party meeting 1890; undecided about which national party to join at dissolution of People's Party 1891; reported as Democrat 1892; informed that AHC was to be indicted for cohabitation, First Presidency and Twelve voted 20 October 1893 to bribe Utah's non-LDS attorney general who dropped indictment; pre-1891 polygamy pardoned and re-enfranchised by U.S. president's general amnesties (1893, 1894); Republican *Ogden Standard* identified AHC as Republican 20 August 1895, but two days later *Salt Lake Herald* reported that AHC "entered a specific denial to the charge that he is a Republican"; married polygamously in violation of Utah law 1896

Prior Religion: LDS

Mormon Experience: Baptized 1867; elder 1875; mission (1879-82); nominated for Twelve 1882; seventy and "ordained" president, First Council of the Seventy 9 October 1882; offered to resign 6 April 1888; apostle 7 October 1889; Sunday School General Board (1889-96); blessed by LS 1890 to live to see Jesus Christ; blessed by Presiding Patriarch JS to "live to a good old age" 1892; second anointing 7 June 1893; president, own prayer circle 1896

Death: 19 July 1896, Salt Lake City, Utah

Estate: $68,438.74 final appraisal (including $47,996.23 life insurance policy); $23,438.74 net

GEORGE Q[UAYLE] CANNON (GQC)

Birth: 11 January 1827, Liverpool, Lancashire Co., England

Parents: George Cannon and Ann Quayle

Marriage (polygamist before appointment): Elizabeth Hoagland 1854 (11 ch); Sarah J.

Jenne 1858 (7 ch); Eliza L. Tenney 1865 (3 ch); Martha Telle 1868 (9 ch); *Sophia Ramsell 1875 (no ch); *Emily Hoagland (Little) 1881 (no ch); Caroline P. Young (Croxall) 1884 (4 ch)

Hierarchy Relations: Father of AHC, JQC and SQC; nephew of John Taylor's first wife; adopted son of John Taylor; he and JCL md sisters; he and WWT md sisters; md FDR's stepdaughter 1858; wife's nephew md LS's daughter 1868; sister-in-law md John Taylor's son 1874; son md DHW's daughter 1880; md JCL's divorced wife 1881; md (1884) Brigham Young's daughter and sister of BY-JR and JWY and 1st cousin of SBY; son md GQC's step-daughter 1887 who was Brigham Young's granddaughter; step-son md JRW's daughter 1900; son's sister-in-law md JFS-1's son 1901; great-grandfather of future Seventy George I. Cannon; 2nd-great-granduncle of future apostle Jeffrey R. Holland

Education: Negligible; regent, University of Deseret (Utah), 1868-78; chancellor, University of Deseret (1878-81, 1883-86); trustee, Young University at Salt Lake City (1891-95), Brigham Young College in Logan (1895-1901)

Prior Occupation: Editor

Business To 1932: Alberta Irrigation Co.; Armstrong, Winder and Co.; Big Cottonwood Power Co.; Brigham Young Trust Co.; Bullion, Beck and California Mining Co.; Bullion, Beck and Champion Mining Co.; Cannon, Grant and Co.; Cedar and Iron Railroad Co.; Church Onyx Mines; Co-operative Stock Herd Association; Co-operative Wagon and Machine Co.; Deseret Bee, Stock, and Fish Association; Deseret Irrigation and Navigation Canal Co.; Deseret National Bank; *Deseret News;* Deseret News Co.; Deseret News Publishing Co. (1892); Deseret Paper Mill; Deseret Savings Bank; Deseret Telegraph Co.; Deseret Typographical (and Press) Association; First National Bank of Provo; George Q. Cannon and Sons; George Q. Cannon Association; Grand Central Mining Co.; Grass Creek Coal Co.; Grass Creek Terminal Railway Co.; Hampton, Jones and Co.; Holladay Coal Co.; [Inter-Mountain Salt Co.]; Iron Manufacturing Company of Utah; *Juvenile Instructor;* Lambert and Cannon; *Millennial Star;* Mutual Life and Savings Society of the United States; New Year Gold Mining Co.; Ogden Sugar Co.; Pioneer Electric Power Co.; Riverside Canal Co.; Salt Lake and Los Angeles Railway Co.; Salt Lake and Pacific Railroad Co.; Salt Lake Literary and Scientific Association; Saltair Beach Co.; Saltair Railway Co.; Templeton Hotel; Timpanogos Manufacturing Co.; Union Light and Power Co.; Union Pacific Land Co.; Union Pacific Railroad Co.; United Order of Zion; Utah and California Railway Co.; Utah and Pacific Improvement Co.; Utah Co.; Utah Light and Power Co.; Utah Power Co.; Utah Sugar Co.; *Western Standard;* Wonder Gold Mining Co.; World's Fair Transit and Trust Co.; ZCMI; Zion's Co-operative Fish Association; Zion's Savings Bank and Trust Co.

Social: Utah Sons of the American Revolution by 1900; listed in *Blue Book* for Salt Lake City (1895-1901), *Herringshaw's Encyclopedia of American Biography* 1898, *Financial Red Book of America* 1900, *Prophets and Patriarchs of the Church* 1902, *Biographical Record of Salt Lake City and Vicinity* 1902, *National Cyclopaedia of American Biography* 1904, *Utah As It Is* 1904, *Dictionary of American Biography* 1929, *Utah: The Storied Domain* 1932, *Stalwarts of Mormonism* 1954, *Faith of Our Pioneer Fathers* 1956

Political/Civic Life: U.S. citizen 7 December 1854; messenger, Utah House of Representatives (1854-55); Utah's Nauvoo Legion adjutant-general (1858-70); Utah legislature (1865-67, 1870-72); legislator, secretary to governor, State of Deseret's "ghost government" (1865-67); Council of Fifty initiation 23 January 1867; delegate and nominating committee, LDS People's Party conventions (1870-72); arrested for cohabitation 1871 (free on bail until charges dropped); vice-president, Utah's territorial Democratic Party 1872; delegate, Utah's unsuccessful statehood convention 1872; Utah's territorial delegate to Congress (1872-82); Democrat (1872-73); delegate, People's Party convention 1873; Republican (1873-74); Democrat (1874-91); arrested for "lewd and lascivious cohabitation" and polygamy 1874 (case dismissed due to statute of limitations 1875); 3 weeks in prison for contempt of court 1879; Utah delegate, Democratic national convention which refused to seat him 1880; expelled from U.S. House of Representatives as Utah's non-voting delegate due to passage of Edmunds anti-polygamy bill 1882; indicted for cohabitation 1885 and arrested 1886; accused of bribery and flight 1886 (released on bail which GQC forfeited with prior approval of President John Taylor and Quorum of Twelve Apostles); fugitive with $500 bounty for arrest (1886-88), imprisoned 5 months (1888-89), received U.S. presidential pardon 1889; Republican (1891-death); signed authorizations for GT to perform polygamous marriages in violation of Mexican law (1892-96); apparently signed authorizations for Charles O. Card to perform polygamous marriages in violation of Canadian law (1892-94); informed that GQC was to be indicted for cohabitation, First Presidency and Twelve voted 20 October 1893 to bribe Utah's non-LDS attorney general who dropped indictment; pre-1891 polygamy pardoned and re-enfranchised by U.S. president's general amnesties (1893, 1894); signed authorization for polygamous marriage in Logan temple performed by MWM in violation of federal law 1894; governor's delegate, National Irrigation Congress (1894, 1895, 1896, 1898, 1900), Trans-Mississippi Commercial Congress (1894, 1895, 1900; president 1894-95), International Irrigation Congress 1895; Republican *Ogden Standard* identified him as Republican 20 August 1895; delegate, Republican state convention 1896 (withdrew as Republican candidate for U.S. Senate); attended National Arbitration Conference by invitation of Chief Justice of U.S. Supreme Court 1896; signed written authorizations for AWI to perform polygamous marriages in violation of Mexican law (1897-99); authorized MFC 1898 to perform polygamous marriages anywhere in Utah, Idaho, or elsewhere in U.S. in violation of state laws; governor's delegate, International Mining Congress 1898, national Conference on Combinations and Trusts 1899; unsuccessful candidate, U.S. Senate 1899; declined effort to choose him as delegate to Republican National convention 1900 (sat on stand, state Republican convention 1900)

Prior Religion: Methodist

Mormon Experience: Baptized 1840; elder, seventy 1845; adopted to John Taylor 4 February 1846, Nauvoo temple; dream-vision of Joseph Smith 1849; mission and vision of Christ (1849-54); mission (1855-58, 1859-60); prayer circle of Wilford Woodruff (1858-59); apostle (sustained 23 October 1859, ordained 26 August 1860); mission president (1860-62, 1862-64); secretary to Brigham Young (1864-67); prayer circle of John Taylor (1864-66) and own (1866-81); second anointing 1 January 1867; Sunday School General Superintendent (1867-1901); mission (1871-72); secretary, Salt Lake City School of the Prophets (1872-74); assistant counselor, First Presidency, without being set apart (8 April 1873-29 August 1877); sustained as "prophet, seer, and revelator," first time 6 October 1877; assistant Trustee-in-Trust (1877-80); threatened by senior apostle John Taylor (January to March 1878) with being dropped from Twelve if he (as legal trustee) did not agree to transfer bulk of Brigham Young's estate to LDS church (eventually complied); first counselor, First Presidency, without being set apart (10 October 1880-25 July 1887); restored to ranking in Quorum of Twelve 3 August 1887; Church Board of Education (1888-1910); first counselor, First Presidency, without being set apart (7 April 1889-2 September 1898); while speaking at Salt Lake temple dedication 1893 some saw halo of light around his head (later reported that he had seen and talked with Jesus Christ); set apart for first time as First Presidency counselor 13 September 1898; reported 1898 that he had seen God and Jesus Christ and heard their voices; reported 1899 that he had heard audible voice of Holy Ghost as separate personage

Death: 12 April 1901, Monterey, Monterey Co., California

Estate: $201,051.40 appraised; $200,419.08 net

JOHN Q[UAYLE] CANNON (JQC)
Birth: 19 April 1857, San Francisco, California
Parents: GQC and Elizabeth Hoagland
Marriage (monogamist): Elizabeth A. Wells 1880 (12 ch), divorced 1886 but married each other again 1888 after death of second wife; Louisa A. Wells 1886 (1 sb)
Hierarchy Relations: Son of GQC, brother of AHC and SQC; grandnephew of John Taylor's wife; son-in-law of DHW; he, HJG and SBY md sisters; daughter md (1921) DOM's brother
Education: Prep school and college, University of Deseret (Utah), 1869-71, 1874-75; trustee, Brigham Young Academy in Provo (1886-87); regent, University of Deseret (1887-88)
Prior Occupation: Printer
Business To 1932: Alberta Land and Stock Co.; Aurora Mining and Milling Co.; Brigham Young Trust Co.; Buckeye Consolidated Gold and Copper Co.; Bullion, Beck and Champion Mining Co.; Cannon Brothers (Loan Agency); Capitol Coal Co.; *Deseret News;* Deseret News Publishing Co. (1892); George Q. Cannon and Sons; George Q. Cannon Association; Herald Co.; Jordan and Salt Lake Surplus Water Canal; Lambert and Cannon; Nana Mining Co.; Northwestern Construction Co.; Ogden Equitable Co-operative Association; *Ogden Standard;* Old Imperial Mining and Milling Co.; Riverside Canal Co.; Salt Lake Literary and Scientific Association; Standard Publishing Co.; *Der Stern;* Torbanehill Mining Co.; Wedge Extension Gold Mining Co.; Woolley, Young and Hardy Co.
Social: Committee member, Ogden Chamber of Commerce 1891; Utah Sons of the American Revolution 1897 (president 1923-24); listed in *Blue Book* for Salt Lake City (1895-1901); omitted from *Biographical Record of Salt Lake City and Vicinity* 1902, from biographies in *History of Utah* 1904, from *Pioneers and Prominent Men of Utah* 1914, from *Men of Affairs in the State of Utah* [Press Club of Salt Lake City] 1914, from *Testimonies of the Church of Jesus Christ of Latter-day Saints by Its Leaders* 1930
Political/Civic Life: Alternate delegate, LDS People's Party conventions 1881; Council of Fifty initiation 9 October 1884; fined $15 for assault and battery 1884 on *Salt Lake Tribune* reporter who published that Louie Wells was JQC's secret plural wife; Utah legislature (1886-87); embezzled church funds which his father GQC repaid (1886-87); Salt Lake City council (1886-88 when he withdrew his candidacy due to opposition from apostles); arrested for polygamy when first wife's divorce petition charged him with adultery 1886 (charges dropped after death in San Francisco of principal witness Louie Wells Cannon); protected by brother AHC from criminal prosecution for passing bad checks 1890; sat on stand, Democratic territorial convention 1894; founding president, Salt Lake Businessman's Democratic Club 1895; delegate, Democratic county and territorial conventions (1895-96); Utah National Guard adjutant-general (1895-98), and brigadier-general, first brigade (1898-1905); governor's delegate, Trans-Mississippi Commercial Congress 1897; captain, volunteer cavalry regiment ("Torrey's Rough Riders"), Spanish-American War 1898; treasurer, then president and secretary, Utah State commissions, Lewis and Clark Centennial Exposition and Louisiana Purchase Exposition (1902-05); fled United States to avoid indictment for embezzling state funds 1905 (Canadian authorities arrested him but Utah governor refused to extradite); out of legal jeopardy JQC returned to Utah and became Republican 1906; delegate, Progressive Party conventions 1914; advisory committee, Utah veteran's memorial (1919-20); delegate, Republican conventions (1922, 1924, 1926, 1928); at his death *Deseret News* (he had been managing editor) noted: "John Q. Cannon was no paragon of virtue. He never set himself up as one."
Prior Religion: LDS
Mormon Experience: Baptized 1865; elder 1873; prayer circle of GQC (1874-81); sev-

enty 1881; mission (1881-83); nominated for Twelve 1882; mission president (1883-84); stake clerk (1884-86); high priest and second counselor, Presiding Bishopric 5 October 1884; LDS president John Taylor declined to allow JQC to marry his sister-in-law polygamously to protect him from arrest (1884-86); retained April 1886 despite Twelve's knowledge he had embezzled tithing funds; excommunicated 5 September 1886 for adultery and procuring abortion for his sister-in-law; rebaptized and ordained elder 6 May 1888
Death: 14 January 1931, Salt Lake City, Utah
Estate: No record

SYLVESTER Q[UAYLE] CANNON (SQC)
Birth: 10 June 1877, Salt Lake City, Utah
Parents: GQC and Elizabeth Hoagland
Marriage (monogamist): Winnifred I. Saville 1904 (7 ch)
Hierarchy Relations: Son of GQC, brother of AHC and JQC; nephew a son-in-law of HJG; sister-in-law a daughter of GFR; niece a sister-in-law of DOM
Education: LDS College (1889-93); University of Utah (1894-95); B.S., Massachusetts Institute of Technology 1899; American Society of Civil Engineers; trustee, LDS University and LDS Business College (1923-38), McCune School of Music and Art (1925-27), Brigham Young University (1932-39); president, McCune School of Music (1927-43)
Prior Occupation: Engineer
Business To 1932: Amalgamated Sugar Co.; Cannon Brothers (Architects and Engineers); Cannon Investment Co.; Deseret Building Society; Deseret Gymnasium; Deseret News Publishing Co. (1931); East Jordan Irrigation Co.; Foreign Lands Corp.; George Q. Cannon Association; Holland Gold Mining Co.; [Hyland Oil and Refining Co.]; Idaho Falls LDS Hospital; Little Cottonwood Water Co.; North Point Consolidated Irrigation Co.; Old Imperial Mining and Milling Co.; [Palisades Petroleum Corp.]; Pioneer Realty Co.; Radio Service Corporation of Utah; Riverside Canal Co.; Salt Lake Knitting Works; *De Ster;* Temple Square Hotel Co.; Thomas D. Dee Memorial Hospital Association; Tip Top Group Mining Co.; Torbanehill Mining Co.; Trapper Mining Co.; Uintah Basin Construction Co.; United States Fuel Co.; Utah Hotel Co.; W. H. Groves LDS Hospital; [Wasatch Corp.]; ZCMI; [Zion's Savings Bank and Trust Co.]; Zion's Securities Corp.
Social: Bonneville Club 1913; Salt Lake Chamber of Commerce by 1925; Timpanogos Club 1926; Salt Lake Commercial Club by 1932; Utah Sons of the American Revolution 1940; listed in *Men of Affairs in the State of Utah* [Press Club of Salt Lake City] 1914, *Utah Since Statehood* 1919, *Utah: The Storied Domain* 1932, *Utah's Distinguished Personalities* 1933, *Who's Who in America* 1936
Political/Civic Life: Nominal Republican (frequently voted for Democrats); Salt Lake City Water Supply engineer (1912-13); Salt Lake City engineer (1913-1925); chair, Board of Canal Presidents, Associated Canals (1913-25); U.S. Reclamation Service consulting engineer, American Falls (Idaho) Project 1923; supervisor, Salt Lake County Drainage District No. 2 (1925-26); chair, Smokeless City Committee, Salt Lake City Chamber of Commerce 1927; chair, Board of Adjustments (Salt Lake City Zoning Commission) 1927; board of trustees, Salt Lake City Council of Boy Scouts by 1928; Salt Lake City Water Supply consulting engineer 1928; chair, Utah State Flood Commission (1930-31); general committee, Utah's "White House Convention on Child Health and Protection" 1931; chair, Utah State Advisory Council for Unemployment (1931-32); vice-chair, Salt Lake City and County Unemployment Council (1931-32); Utah Advisory Board, U.S. Public Works Administration (1933-34); supported Democratic New Deal for which he was criticized by First Presidency (1933-38); Utah Centennial Exposition Committee (1938-

43); apparently continued voting for Democratic presidential and Congressional candidates until his death
Prior Religion: LDS
Mormon Experience: Baptized 1885; elder 1898; seventy 1899; mission (1899-1900); mission president (1900-02); presiding elder (1903-05); high priest 1904; stake presidency counselor (1904-07); second anointing 30 September 1904; mission president (1907-09); stake president (1917-25); ordained bishop and set apart as Presiding Bishop 4 June 1925; publicly sustained 6 October 1925; president, Zion's Aid Society (1928-32+); released and ordained apostle 6 April 1938 (Associate to the Quorum); admitted to Quorum of the Twelve 6 October 1939
Death: 29 May 1943, Salt Lake City, Utah
Estate: $56,498.70 appraised; $56,300.96 net

ALBERT CARRINGTON (AC-1)
Birth: 8 January 1813, Royalton, Windsor Co., Vermont
Parents: Daniel V. Carrington and Isabella Bowman
Marriage (polygamist before appointment, free-love polygamist after appointment): Rhoda M. Woods 1839 (5 ch); Mary A. Rock 1846 (5 ch); Elizabeth A. Wright (Woolcott) 1851 (no ch), divorced 1858; *Jenetta Edgar Johnson 1871-73 (no ch); *Ruth Worsdale 1875-77 (no ch); *Sarah Kirkman 1880 (no ch) and for 2 years after her legal marriage to Richard Bridge 1883
Hierarchy Relations: Father-in-law of BY-JR
Education: B.A., Dartmouth College 1834 (Phi Beta Kappa); studied law 1830s; regent, University of Deseret (Utah), 1850-55, 1874-75, chancellor (1855-58, 1860-69)
Prior Occupation: Schoolteacher, clerk, newspaper editor, attorney
Business To 1932: Brigham Young Cotton Factory; Carrington and Young; Deseret Currency Association; *Deseret News;* Deseret Typographical (and Press) Association; *Millennial Star;* Perpetual Emigrating Fund Co.; United Order of Zion; ZCMI; Zion's Savings Bank and Trust Co.
Social: Mason 1843, Nauvoo lodge; vice-president, Philosophical Society (1854-55); vice-president, Universal Scientific Society (1855-55); omitted from biographies in *History of Utah* 1904, from *Pioneers and Prominent Men of Utah* 1914, from *Testimonies of the Church of Jesus Christ of Latter-day Saints by Its Leaders* 1930
Political/Civic Life: Council of Fifty initiation 18 or 22 April 1845; deputy postmaster, Salt Lake City (1847-49); delegate, unsuccessful Utah statehood convention 1849 and member of committee to draft its constitution; State of Deseret assessor, collector, and treasurer (1849-51); Utah's Nauvoo Legion 1st lieutenant (1849-55); clerk, Utah House of Representatives (1851-52); Code Commissioner 1852; Utah legislature (1852-69); Salt Lake City Board of Examiners (1855-57); Utah attorney general (1855-57, 1865, 1866); Utah's Nauvoo Legion colonel (1855-70); delegate, unsuccessful Utah statehood convention 1856; indicted for treason, Utah War, December 1857 (pardoned by U.S. president's general amnesty 1858); delegate, nominating convention for LDS "People's Ticket" 1859; delegate, unsuccessful Utah statehood convention 1862 and member of committee to draft its constitution; legislature (1862-69) and attorney general (1866-67), State of Deseret's "ghost government"; cohabitation with multiple partners in violation of English law (1871-73, 1875-77, 1880-82); delegate and nominating committee, LDS People's Party 1872; delegate, unsuccessful Utah statehood convention 1872; Salt Lake City council (1874-75); acquitted, Salt Lake City Police Court, for exceeding his irrigation rights 1875; 3 weeks in prison for contempt of court 1879; adultery with another man's wife in violation of Utah law (1883-85)
Prior Religion: ?
Mormon Experience: Baptized, elder 1841; seventy 1844; trustee, Seventies' Library

and Institute Association (1844-46); high priest 1845; stake clerk (1847-49); bishopric counselor (1849-55); attended First Presidency and Quorum of the Twelve prayer circle (1856-58); second anointing 7 January 1867; mission president (1868-70, 1871-73, 1875-77); apostle 3 July 1870; Church Historian (1871-74); assistant counselor, First Presidency (8 April 1873-29 August 1877); sustained as "prophet, seer, and revelator," first time 6 October 1877; assistant Trustee-in-Trust (1877-80); threatened by senior apostle John Taylor (January to March 1878) with being dropped from Twelve if he (as legal trustee) did not agree to transfer bulk of Brigham Young's estate to LDS church (eventually complied); mission (1880-82); investigated by First Presidency and Quorum of Twelve for sexual misconduct 28 September 1883; excommunicated 7 November 1885; recommended for rebaptism several times (1886-87) by church president John Taylor (majority of apostles voted against each motion); recommended for rebaptism by senior apostle Wilford Woodruff 2 November 1886 and 12 August 1887 (motions failed due to strenuous opposition by minority of Twelve); baptized again 1 November 1887; died moments before his priesthood was to be re-confirmed upon him 1889; rebaptized by proxy 3 October 1968.

Death: 19 September 1889, Salt Lake City, Utah

Estate: No record

**Hiram B. Clawson (1826-1912)

In November 1856 he was a member of the prayer circle of First Presidency and Quorum of Twelve Apostles. He attended with other non-general authorities until September 1858 when they were assigned to different circles. Clawson was a Council of Fifty member but never a general authority.

RUDGER [JUDD] CLAWSON (RC)

Birth: 12 March 1857, Salt Lake City, Utah

Parents: Hiram B. Clawson and Margaret Judd

Marriage (polygamist prior to appointment, monogamist at appointment, polygamist after appointment): Florence Dinwoodey 1882 (1 ch), divorced 1885; Lydia Spencer 1883 (10 ch); *Pearl Udall 1904 (no ch), separated 1913, obtained divorce through church president and remarried 1919; unmarried widower last 2-1/2 years of his life

Hierarchy Relations: Father was Brigham Young's son-in-law and step-son; stepmother was sister of BY-JR; sister was SBY's daughter-in-law; 3rd cousin of future apostle Arza A. Hinckley; uncle of future Seventy's president S. Dilworth Young

Education: Elementary and secondary; University of Deseret (Utah) 1870; trustee, Box Elder Academy (1888-93), LDS University, LDS Business College, and LDS University School of Music (1913-25), Brigham Young University (1939-43)

Prior Occupation: Clerk

Business To 1932: Beehive Film Co.; Beneficial Life Insurance Co.; Brigham City Mercantile and Manufacturing Association; Brigham City Roller Mills Co.; Brigham City Theatre Co.; Clawson and Burrows; Clawson and Rich; Clawson Brothers; Deseret Investment Co.; Diamond Oil Co.; Gustaveson Oil Co.; Lewiston Sugar Co.; *Millennial Star;* Mutual Creamery Co.; Salt Lake Dramatic Association; Salt Lake Knitting Works; Universal Metal Extraction Co.; Utah and California Railway Co.; Utah Light and Power Co.

Social: Charter member, Sons and Daughters of the Pioneers of Utah 1907; listed in *Blue Book* for Salt Lake City (1901-07), *Prophets and Patriarchs of the Church* 1902, *Utah As It Is* 1904, *Utah: The Storied Domain* 1932, *Utah's Distinguished Personalities* 1933, *Who's Who in America* 1942; omitted from *Biographical Record of Salt Lake City and Vicinity* 1902, from biographies in *History of Utah* 1904, from *Pioneers and Prominent Men of Utah* 1914, from *Men of Affairs in the State of Utah* [Press Club of Salt Lake City] 1914

Political/Civic Life: Imprisoned for polygamy (1884-87); territorial central committee,

LDS People's Party (1887-91); delegate, People's Party territorial convention 1888; pre-1891 polygamy pardoned and re-enfranchised by U.S. president's general amnesties (1893, 1894); governor's delegate, Trans-Mississippi Commercial Congress (1894, 1897); Republican member of stake presidency complained that RC was using church position to promote Democratic Party 1896; Democrat to 1900; sat on stand, Republican state convention 1900; Republican from 1900 to death; performed plural marriages in violation of Mexican and Utah laws 1903; married polygamously in violation of Colorado law 1904; cohabited in violation of laws of Utah, Idaho, Arizona, California, and England (1904-13)

Prior Religion: LDS

Mormon Experience: Baptized 1865; no priesthood office until a seventy 1875; mission 1879 (when antagonists murdered his companion); patriarchal blessing 1883 promised he would be "mighty minister of Jesus" and lead church "like unto Moses"; high priest 1888; stake president (1888-1898); director, Logan Temple Association 1892; apostle 10 October 1898 (said it fulfilled phrenologist's prediction); YMMIA General Board (1898-1920); assistant to General Superintendent of Religion Classes (1900-19); Church Literature Revision Committee (1901-02); president, own prayer circle (1901-10, 1913-22); Church Board of Education (1901-43); publicly sustained as second counselor to LS 6 October 1901 (not set apart before church president's death four days later); General Priesthood Committee (1908-22); mission president (1910-13); General Superintendent of Religion Classes (1919-22); president, Quorum of the Twelve Apostles 17 March 1921; chair, Committee on Revision of Seventies' Work (1923-26)

Death: 21 June 1943, Salt Lake City, Utah

Estate: No record

ALFRED CORDON (AC-2)

Birth: 28 February 1817, Liverpool, Lancashire Co., England

Parents: Samson Cordon and Myra Hampson

Marriage (polygamist after leaving hierarchy): Emma Parker 1836 (14 ch); Emma Pridmore 1856 (3 ch); Rebecca E. Collins 1864 (no ch); Mary A. Voss 1865 (4 ch)

Hierarchy Relations: ?

Education: Common schools

Prior Occupation: Potter

Business To 1932: Deseret Pottery; Nauvoo Potters' Association; Willard Mining Co.; Willow Creek Dramatic Association

Social: Probably Mason 1842-44, one of the smaller lodges in Nauvoo, Illinois, or Montrose, Iowa; continues to be omitted from official lists of LDS general authorities

Political/Civic Life: Delegate, proposed "Jeffersonian Democracy" convention 1844; 3rd lieutenant, Utah's Nauvoo Legion 1852; married polygamously in violation of federal law (1864, 1865)

Prior Religion: Church of England; Aikinites

Mormon Experience: Baptized, elder 1839; political mission 1844; mission (1844-45, 1848-50, 1851); publicly sustained and ordained assistant presiding bishop 9 October 1851; honorably released 7 October 1853; ward bishop (1857-71); prayer circle of Wilford Woodruff 1858

Death: 13 March 1871, Willard, Box Elder Co., Utah

Estate: No record

MATTHIAS F[OSS] COWLEY (MFC)

Birth: 25 August 1858, Salt Lake City, Utah

Parents: Matthias Cowley and Sarah Foss

Marriage (polygamist before appointment): Abbie Hyde 1884 (8 ch); Luella Parkinson

1889 (5 ch); Harriet Bennion (Harker) 1899 (1 ch); Mary L. Taylor 1905 (1 ch), separated and remarried 1911; monogamist after 1931
Hierarchy Relations: Nephew of FDR's wife; grandnephew of Wilford Woodruff's
wife; 1st cousin, 1 rvd, of LS's wife; father of future apostle Matthew Cowley
Education: Elementary and secondary; Morgan Commercial College; prep school,
University of Deseret (Utah), 1871, 1873-77
Prior Occupation: Clerk
Business To 1932: Alberta Mining Co.; American Fork Co-operative Institution;
Bigelow Manufacturing Co.; General Reduction and Chemical Co.; Golden Bee Mining Co.; Logan Knitting Factory; Logan-Wyoming Oil Co.; Mexican Colonization and
Agricultural Co.; Omega Investment Co.; Oneida Mercantile Union; Queen Esther
Mining Co.; Sugar Centrifugal Discharger Co.; Thor Power Co.; Utah Knitting Works
Social: Listed in *Blue Book* for Salt Lake City (1901-07), *Prophets and Patriarchs of the
Church* 1902, *Utah As It Is* 1904, *Utah: The Storied Domain* 1932; omitted from *Biographical Record of Salt Lake City and Vicinity* 1902, from biographies in *History of Utah* 1904,
from *Pioneers and Prominent Men of Utah* 1914, from *Men of Affairs in the State of Utah*
[Press Club of Salt Lake City] 1914, from *Testimonies of the Church of Jesus Christ of Latter-day Saints by Its Leaders* 1930
Political/Civic Life: Salt Lake City justice of the peace (1882-1884); alternate delegate,
LDS People's Party county convention 1883; chaplain, Utah House of Representatives
1884; married polygamously in violation of federal law 1889; pre-1891 polygamy pardoned and re-enfranchised by U.S. president's general amnesties (1893, 1894); Republican campaign worker and lobbyist (1898-1902); performed 69 plural marriages and
married one plural wife in violation of the laws of Utah, Idaho, Mexico, Colorado, Canada, Wyoming, and Illinois (1898-1903); in roving "exile" throughout United States,
Canada, and Mexico (1904-06) to avoid subpoena to testify before U.S. Senate regarding polygamy; performed eight plural marriages (1904-05) and married polygamously
1905 in violation of the laws of Utah, Idaho, Colorado, and Canada.
Prior Religion: LDS
Mormon Experience: Baptized 1866; elder 1874; mission (1878-80, 1880-82, 1896);
seventy 1880; promised by JWT 1882 he would be apostle; nominated for Twelve 1882;
prayer circle of Wilford Woodruff (1883-85); high priest 1884; stake presidency counselor (1887-97); apostle 7 October 1897; second anointing 11 April 1898; YMMIA General Board (1898-1906); Religion Class General Board (1901-06); on virtual church
mission, with regular reports to First Presidency (1904-06) to avoid U.S. Senate subpoena for inquiry into post-1890 (church-sanctioned) polygamy; voted against by two
church members at April 1905 general conference, at which RS also declined to vote
for Twelve; submitted resignation to Quorum of Twelve 28 October 1905 to use if politically expedient (publicly released 9 April 1906); referred men to stake patriarch Judson Tolman for performance of their polygamous marriages (1906-10); FML
instructed stake presidents to stop allowing MFC to speak in church meetings 23 September 1909; tried by Twelve 10 May 1911 for performing post-1904 plural marriages
(seven apostles voted that MFC should receive no further punishment for his prior activities regarding post-Manifesto polygamy, but three apostles unsuccessfully urged
that he be disfellowshipped); deprived of the right to exercise priesthood (not actually
disfellowshipped) 11 May 1911 as compromise within Twelve; encouraged John W.
Woolley (stake patriarch and Salt Lake temple ordinance worker) to perform polygamous marriages and referred prospective polygamists to him (1912-14); at urging of
FML the Twelve again investigated MFC 23 January 1914 for promoting polygamy and
prohibited him from participating in high priest quorum; after inconclusive investigations 30 March and 5 April 1914, the Twelve held his last trial 17 June 1914, at which
time FML and other apostles who wanted to excommunicate him admitted the evi-

dence was insufficient to prove MFC promoted new polygamous marriages after 1906; President JFS-1 publicly instructed ward bishops 8 October 1917 not to invite MFC to speak in meetings; officer of corporation which served as financial holding company for Mormon Fundamentalists, including polygamist leader Lorin C. Woolley (1922-28); unsuccessfully petitioned President HJG for reinstatement to full church privileges (1926, 1927, 1929, 1933); reinstated 3 April 1936; unofficial proselytizing mission in Great Britain (1937-38) at invitation of RRL
Death: 21 June 1940, Salt Lake City, Utah
Estate: No record

**John C. Cutler (1846-1928)
On 23 February 1887 Cutler declined invitation to be second counselor in the Presiding Bishopric. In his place, JRW became counselor. Aside from Roger Orton in 1845, Cutler is only man who declined to become a general authority. He was Utah's governor (1905-09), subsequently one of the church's auditors, and committed suicide in 1928.

HORACE S[UNDERLIN] ELDREDGE (HSE)
Birth: 6 February 1816, Brutus, Cayuga Co., New York
Parents: Alanson Eldredge and Esther Sunderlin
Marriage (polygamist before appointment): Betsey A. Chase 1836 (8 ch); Sarah W. Gibbs 1851 (4 ch); Hannah Adams 1855 (6 ch); Chloe A. Redfield 1857 (10 ch); *Susan M. Redfield 1857 (no ch), divorced 1860; Eliza Morgridge (or Mugridge) 1869 (no ch), divorced; Rosetta Robinson (Grant, Grant) 1870 (no ch)
Hierarchy Relations: Daughter md nephew of Brigham Young and Joseph Young, grandnephew of Joseph Young, and 1st cousin, 1 rvd, of SBY 1855; md widow of Jedediah M. Grant 1870; daughter md brother of HJG and son of Jedediah M. Grant 1875
Education: Common schools; regent, University of Deseret (Utah), 1878-86
Prior Occupation: Farmer
Business To 1932: Bank of Deseret (1871); Blackfoot Stock Co.; Brigham Young Woolen Factory; Clark, Eldredge (and) Co.; Deseret Mercantile Association; Deseret National Bank; [Deseret Salt Co.]; Deseret Savings Bank; Eldredge and Clawson; Eldredge, Pratt and Co.; [First National Bank of Nephi]; First National Bank of Ogden; First National Bank of Provo; Globe Bakery; Great Western Iron Mining and Manufacturing Co.; H.S. Eldredge and Co.; Herald Printing and Publishing Co.; Hooper, Eldredge and Co. (1859); Hooper, Eldredge and Co. (1869); Hooper, Sharp, Little and Eldredge; Lehi and Tintic Railroad Co.; [Lion Hill Manufacturing Co.]; *Millennial Star;* Mutual Life and Savings Society of the United States; Osceola Gravel Mining Co.; Perpetual Emigrating Fund Co.; [Salt Lake City] Thirteenth Ward Co-operative Mercantile Institution; Southeastern Railroad Company of Utah; Stringham and Eldredge; Tintic Iron Co.; United Order of Zion; Utah Central Iron Co.; Utah Central Railroad Co.; Utah Iron Manufacturing Co.; Utah Produce Co.; Utah Southern Railroad Extension Co.; [Utah Silk Association]; [Utah Soap Manufacturing Co.]; [Utah Western Railway Co.]; Wasatch and Jordan Valley Railroad Co.; [Zion's Benefit Building Society]; Zion's Central Board of Trade; ZCMI; Zion's Savings Bank and Trust Co.
Social: Mason 1843, Nauvoo lodge; Salt Lake Chamber of Commerce 1887; listed in *Biographical Record of Salt Lake City and Vicinity* 1902; omitted from *Testimonies of the Church of Jesus Christ of Latter-day Saints by Its Leaders* 1930
Political/Civic Life: Constable, Nauvoo (1843-45); delegate, proposed "Jeffersonian Democracy" convention 1844; marshal, Cutler's Park, Iowa (1846-46); marshal, assessor, collector, Winter Quarters, Nebraska (1846-47); Council of Fifty initiation 9 December 1848; marshal, provisional State of Deseret (1849-51); Utah's Nauvoo Legion brigadier-general (1849-70); marshal, assessor, collector, Utah Territory (1852-53);

Utah legislature (1854-55); probably among the 50 men indicted for treason, Utah War, December 1857 (pardoned by U.S. president's general amnesty 1858); nomination as Utah's delegate to Congress was rescinded 1859 (absent from territory); delegate, unsuccessful Utah statehood convention 1862; Utah legislature (1861-62); church's emigration agent 1863; defeated as "scratch" candidate for Utah legislature 1866; married polygamously in violation of U.S. law (1869, 1871); alternate delegate, LDS People's Party conventions 1876; Sugar House constable and election judge (1877-80); delegate, People's Party county convention 1880; incorporator, pro-Democratic *Salt Lake Herald* 1886

Prior Religion: Baptist at age 16

Mormon Experience: Baptized 1836; elder abt 1837; mission (1843, 1852-54, 1857-58); political missionary, seventy 1844; "ordained" president, First Council of the Seventy 7 October 1854, publicly threatened with dismissal 7 October and 22 December 1856 (continued in office); prayer circle of ES-1 (1858-62), of GQC (1866-81); mission president (1870-71); exonerated in trials for "unchristian" conduct (1877, 1882); *de facto* senior president, First Council of the Seventy in Henry Harriman's absence (1882-88); Church Board of Education (1888-88)

Death: 6 September 1888, Salt Lake City, Utah

Estate: $592,397.35 final appraisal; $585,443.72 net

NATHANIEL H[ENRY] FELT (NHF)

Birth: 6 February 1816, Salem, Essex Co., Massachusetts

Parents: Nathaniel Felt and Hannah Reeves

Marriage (polygamist after leaving hierarchy): Eliza A. Preston 1839 (10 ch); Sarah Strange 1854 (4 ch); Mary L. Pile 1856 (3 ch), divorced 1868

Hierarchy Relations: ?

Education: Common schools

Prior Occupation: Merchant, tailor

Business To 1932: Deseret Mining Co.; Deseret Mining Stock Association; Felt and Allen; Felt and Co.; J. C. Little and Co.; N. H. Felt (Tailor); N. H. Felt's Liquor Store

Social: Continues to be omitted from official lists of LDS general authorities

Political/Civic Life: Utah legislature (1851-53); Salt Lake City alderman (1851-54, 1872-74); Utah's Nauvoo Legion chaplain and colonel (1852-70); Salt Lake City council (1862-66, 1874-76); delegate, LDS People's Party county conventions (1876-77)

Prior Religion: Congregationalist baptism at age 9; unaffiliated as adult

Mormon Experience: Baptized, elder 1843; branch president (1843-45); seventy 1845; mission (1847-50); high priest 1851; stake high council (1851-54); publicly sustained and "ordained" assistant presiding bishop 8 September 1851; prayer circle of Zerah Pulsipher 1851; honorably released as assistant presiding bishop 8 October 1853; stake high council (1853-54); mission (1854-56, 1865-67, 1869-70); stake high council (1870-73); one of first "home missionaries" (to Salt Lake County) 1872

Death: 27 January 1887, Salt Lake City, Utah

Estate: No record

CHRISTIAN D[ANIEL] FJELDSTED (CDF)

Birth: 20 February 1829, Amagar, Copenhagen Amt, Denmark

Parents: Hendrik L. Fjeldsted and Ann C. Hendriksen

Marriage (polygamist before appointment): Karen Olsen 1849 (5 ch); Johanne M. Christensen 1859 (4 ch); Catrina M. Christensen 1865 (no ch); Josephine M. Larsen 1871 (6 ch); monogamist after 1891

Hierarchy Relations: ?

Education: Negligible

Prior Occupation: Moulder and foundryman

Business To 1932: *Nordstjernan; Skandinaviens Stjerne; Ungdommens Raadgiver*
Social: Omitted from *Biographical Record of Salt Lake City and Vicinity* 1902, from *Testimonies of the Church of Jesus Christ of Latter-day Saints by Its Leaders* 1930
Political/Civic Life: U.S. citizen 5 May 1865; married polygamously in violation of federal law (1865, 1871); performed polygamous marriage in violation of Denmark's laws 1869; unsuccessful candidate, Logan City alderman 1874; alternate delegate, LDS People's Party conventions (1876, 1880); delegate, Utah Democratic convention 1876; Logan city councilor (1876-82); indicted for cohabitation 1886 (avoided arrest by going on foreign mission); speaker, Republican rallies 1891; pre-1891 polygamy pardoned and re-enfranchised by U.S. president's general amnesties (1893, 1894); alternate delegate, Republican state convention 1900
Prior Religion: Lutheran
Mormon Experience: Baptized 1852; elder 1853; seventy 1859; mission (1859-61, 1865, 1867-70, 1886-88, 1896, 1901-04); one of first "home missionaries" (to northern Utah's Scandinavians) 1872; mission president (1881-84, 1888-90, 1904-05); First Council of the Seventy 6 April 1884 ("ordained" President of Seventy 28 April); Sunday School General Board (1898-1900)
Death: 23 December 1905, Salt Lake City, Utah
Estate: $530.40 appraised and net

**David Fullmer (1803-1879)
A conference of 11 April 1852 sustained Fullmer and four others as traveling bishops, and First Presidency letter a week later referred to them as "assistant Presiding Bishops," though that was not how they were sustained. In contrast, JB, AC-2, and NHF were ordained as "assistant Presiding Bishop" (under EH) from 1851 to 1853. Fullmer was a prominent Council of Fifty member since 1845 but not a general authority.

JACOB GATES (JG)
Birth: 9 March 1811, St. Johnsbury, Caledonia Co., Vermont
Parents: Thomas Gates and Patty Plumby
Marriage (polygamist before appointment): Mary M. Snow 1833 (no ch); Elizabeth C. Hutchin 1846 (1 ch); Emma Forsberry 1853 (6 ch); Lydia C. West 1856 (nc), divorced and remarried 1862; Sarah J. Meredith (Elliot) 1861 (nc); May Ware 1862 (7 ch)
Hierarchy Relations: 4th cousin of Heber C. Kimball; 4th cousin, 1 rvd, of JGK; brother-in-law of ES-1; son md sister of BY-JR and JWY and 1st cousin of SBY 1880; his 4th cousin, 1 rvd, JGK a Seventy's president 1892
Education: Negligible
Prior Occupation: Farmer, carpenter, joiner
Business To 1932: Canaan Co-operative Stock Co.; Grand Gulch Mining Co.; J. Gates and Co.; *Millennial Star;* St. George Co-operative Mercantile Institution; St. George Stake Board of Trade; [South Ash Creek Coal, Iron, and Lumber Co.]; Southern Utah Co-operative Mercantile Association; United Order of St. George; Washington Field Canal Co.; Zion's Co-operative Rio Virgen Manufacturing Co.
Social: Mason 1843, Nauvoo lodge; omitted from biographies in *History of Utah* 1904, from *Pioneers and Prominent Men of Utah* 1914, from *Testimonies of the Church of Jesus Christ of Latter-day Saints by Its Leaders* 1930
Political/Civic Life: Zion's Camp paramilitary campaign 1834; signed "Danite" letter warning dissenters to leave June 1838; Mormon militiaman 1838; imprisoned 3 weeks for arson and treason, charges dismissed 1838-39; Nauvoo Legion captain 1841; married polygamously in violation of Illinois law 1846; Utah's Nauvoo Legion 2nd lieutenant (1849-66) and colonel (1866-70); married polygamously in violation of federal law 1862; St. George city council (1862-66); Washington County selectman (1862-63, 1870-71); legislature, State of Deseret's "ghost government" (1864-68); Utah legislature

(1864-68, 1874-75); St. George mayor (1866-70); Council of Fifty initiation 10 October 1882; convicted for cohabitation and fined 1889; delegate, Democratic city convention 1892

Prior Religion: Methodist to 1828, then unaffiliated

Mormon Experience: Baptized 1833; elder 1836; mission (1836, 1839, 1841, 1843-44, 1849-53, 1859-61); seventy 1838; exonerated in trial for "unchristian" conduct 1843; local president of Seventy's quorum 1844; second anointing 21 January 1846; one of first LDS "pastors" for British branches 1852; appointed First Council of the Seventy 23 October 1859 (publicly sustained 6 April 1860); prayer circle of Orson Pratt 1861; "ordained" President of Seventy 8 October 1862, but rarely attended council meetings (residence in southern Utah, later Provo); not presented for sustaining vote 9 April 1872 (disagreed with colleagues over use of property); while speaking at Manti temple dedication 1888 some saw halo of light around his head; senior president, First Council of the Seventy (1888-92)

Death: 14 April 1892, Provo, Utah Co., Utah

Estate: No record

HEBER J[EDEDIAH, "JEDDY"] GRANT (HJG)

Birth: 22 November 1856, Salt Lake City, Utah

Parents: Jedediah M. Grant and Rachel R. Ivins

Marriage (polygamist after appointment): Lucy Stringham 1877 (6 ch); Hilda Augusta Winters 1884 (1 ch); Emily H. Wells 1884 (5 ch); courted several prospective new wives 1900-03; monogamist after 1908

Hierarchy Relations: Son of Jedediah M. Grant; 1st cousin of AWI; 1st cousin, 1 rvd, of ARI; adopted to Joseph Smith through mother's sealing; md to ES-1's niece; son-in-law of DHW and brother-in-law of RSW; he, JQC, OFW, and SBY md sisters; he and AOW md sisters; two aunts md William Smith; brother was HSE's son-in-law; daughter md JWT's nephew 1899; daughter md AHC's son 1902; daughter md son of JFS-1 and brother of DAS, HMS, and JFS-2 1910; daughter md son of SBY and brother of LEY 1911; wife's nephew md AWI's daughter 1913; appointed his son-in-law John H. Taylor as Seventy's president 1933; appointed his son-in-law Clifford E. Young an Assistant to the Twelve 1941; grandfather of future Seventy George I. Cannon; great-granduncle of future Seventy Monte J. Brough

Education: Prep school (1869-1870) and college (1870-71), University of Deseret (Utah); Morgan Commercial College (1871-72); University of Deseret 1876, without graduation; instructor of penmanship, University of Deseret 1878; regent, University of Deseret (1887-88); trustee, Young University at Salt Lake City (1891-95), LDS College (1900-01), LDS University and LDS Business College (1901-23), Brigham Young University (1918-45), Brigham Young College in Logan (1919-26)

Prior Occupation: Businessman

Business To 1932: B. F. Grant and Co.; Beneficial Life Insurance Co.; Blackfoot Stock Co.; [Bullion, Beck and Champion Mining Co.]; Burt and Carlquist; Canadian Sugar Factories; Cannon, Grant and Co.; Church Onyx Mines; Clayton Investment Co.; [Commercial Underwriters Agency]; Consolidated Music Co.; Consolidated Wagon and Machine Co.; Contributor Co.; Co-operative Wagon and Machine Co.; Delray Salt Co.; Deseret and Salt Lake Agricultural and Manufacturing Canal Co.; Deseret Gymnasium; Deseret Investment Co.; Deseret National Bank; Deseret Savings Bank; Emigration Canyon Improvement Co.; Foreign Lands Corp.; Fremont County Sugar Co.; Grant and Clayton; Grant and Wells; Grant Brothers Livery and Transfer Co.; Grant Gold Mining Co.; Grant, Livingston and Co.; Grant, Odell and Co.; Grant Soap Co.; Groesbeck Co.; Heber J. Grant (Insurance); Heber J. Grant and Co.; Herald Co.; Herald Publishing Co.; Home Benefit Building Society; Home Fire Insurance Company of Utah; Home

Life Insurance Company of Utah; Idaho Sugar Co.; *Improvement Era;* Inland Crystal Salt Co.; Inland Railway Co.; Jennens and Grant; *Juvenile Instructor;* Kimball-Richards Building Co.; Knight Sugar Co.; Knight Woolen Mills; Lynndyl Townsite Co.; Midvale State Bank; *Millennial Star;* Mohave Land and Cattle Co.; Mountain Summer Resort Co.; National Savings and Trust Co.; Nevada Land and Livestock Co.; Oregon Lumber Co.; Pacific Coast Joint Stock Land Bank; Pacific Hedge Co.; Payson Exchange Savings Bank; Prout and Grant; Provo Manufacturing Co.; Provo Woolen Mills; R. K. Thomas Realty Co.; [Salt Lake City] Thirteenth Ward Co-operative Mercantile Institution; Salt Lake Dramatic Association; Salt Lake, Garfield and Western Railroad Co.; Saltair Beach Co.; Sanpete and Sevier Sugar Co.; Sevier Canal Co.; Sevier River Land and Water Co.; Social Hall Society; State Bank of Utah; Sugar City Townsite Co.; Superior Mining Co.; Temple Square Hotel Co.; [Transcontinental and Western Air of California]; Union Pacific Railroad Co.; Utah Arid Farm Co.; Utah Bond and Share Co.; Utah Hotel Co.; Utah-Idaho Sugar Co.; Utah Implement-Vehicle Co.; Utah Independent Telephone Co.; Utah Light and Traction Co.; Utah Manufacturers Association; Utah State National Bank; Utah Sugar Co.; Utah Vinegar Works; [Utida Investment Co.]; Valley View Co.; [Wandamere Amusement Co.]; Wasatch Land and Improvement Co.; Wasatch Lawn Cemetery Association; West Cache Land Co.; [Western Air Express]; Western Idaho Sugar Co.; [Woolley Smokeless Furnace Co.]; Zion's Benefit Building Society; ZCMI; Zion's Savings Bank and Trust Co.; Zion's Securities Corp.

Social: Wasatch Literary Association 1870s; Salt Lake Chamber of Commerce (director 1887-91); Union Club by 1892; charter member and vice-president, Sons and Daughters of the Pioneers of Utah 1907; Salt Lake City Commercial Club by 1911; Bonneville Club 1913; Ensign Club by 1928; honorary member, Salt Lake City Rotary Club abt 1936; Silver Buffalo award, Boy Scouts of America 1939; listed in *Blue Book* for Salt Lake City (1895, 1896, 1898, 1901, 1907, 1911), *Prophets and Patriarchs of the Church* 1902, *Biographical Record of Salt Lake City and Vicinity* 1902, *Utah As It Is* 1904, *Who's Who in America* 1918, *Utah Since Statehood* 1919, *National Cyclopaedia of American Biography* 1922, *Utah: The Storied Domain* 1932, *Utah's Distinguished Personalities* 1933, *Who's Who In the Clergy* 1935; *Faith of Our Pioneer Fathers* 1956; omitted from biographies in *History of Utah* 1904, from *Men of Affairs in the State of Utah* [Press Club of Salt Lake City] 1914; dropped from *Who's Who in America* (1938-39, reinstated 1940)

Political/Civic Life: Notary public (1879-81); delegate, LDS People's Party conventions (1880, 1884); Tooele city council (1881-83); Council of Fifty initiation 10 October 1882; Utah legislature (1884-85); Salt Lake City council (1884-88); vice-president, pro-Democratic *Salt Lake Herald* 1886; vice-president, People's Party city convention 1889; speaker, People's Party rally 1890; chair, finance committee and member of arrangements committee, territorial Democratic Party 1891; informed that HJG was to be indicted for cohabitation, First Presidency and Twelve voted 20 October 1893 to bribe Utah's non-LDS attorney general who dropped indictment; pre-1891 polygamy pardoned and re-enfranchised by U.S. president's general amnesties (1893, 1894); speaker, territorial Democratic convention 1894; defeated as Democratic candidate for Utah State Constitutional Convention 1894; declined Democratic Party offer to be candidate for Utah's first state governor 1895; excused from jury duty 1896; performed two polygamous marriages in violation of Mexican law 1897; governor's delegate, International Gold Mining Convention 1897, International Congress on School Hygiene 1904; delegate, Utah state Democratic convention 1898; indicted for adultery and convicted (fined) for cohabitation 1899; indicted for cohabitation 1903 (avoided arrest by leaving on foreign mission); re-indicted on arrival, New York City 1906 (charges dismissed 1907); delegate, Democratic county convention 1907; national board, Anti-Saloon League (1908-18); president, Salt Lake Prohibition and Betterment League (1914-18); Utah Democratic Party's reception committee for William Jennings Bryan

1916; vice-president, Utah Public Health Association (1916-27); Utah State Council of Defense (1917-18); chair, Utah Liberty Loan Central Committee 1918; executive committee, Federal Reserve Loan Board (12th District) 1918; Utah Committee for Armenian and Syrian Relief (1918-22); delegate, Mountain Congress, national League to Enforce Peace 1919; executive committee, Utah League to Enforce Peace 1919; formally charged by U.S. Justice Department (June 1920) for illegal profiteering (not indicted with other Utah-Idaho Sugar officers August); publicly charged with voting Republican 1926; vice-president, Utah Tuberculosis Association (1927-28); Salt Lake County Farm Bureau 1928; Republican and anti-"New Deal" 1932 to death; national committee, General John J. Pershing monument 1933; omitted from official list of "one hundred prominent Democrats" in Utah's history 1942

Prior Religion: LDS

Mormon Experience: Promised as "a very small child" by Eliza R. Snow (prophesied in tongues) he would be apostle; promised by first counselor Heber C. Kimball "when he was a young boy" he would be apostle and reach higher position than second counselor Jedediah M. Grant; baptized 1864; seventy 1872 (age 15); no pre-hierarchy proselytizing mission; ward YMMIA presidency counselor (1875-80); high priest 1880; stake president (1880-82), despite majority of stake members voting against him (JFS-1 wanted him released when HJG admitted he didn't know if gospel true); promised by Mormon he happened to meet 7 October 1881 he would be apostle within year; apostle by written revelation 13 October 1882 (ordained 16 October); received (1883) "whisperings of the spirit" (not a vision, as later claimed) that the deceased Jedediah M. Grant and Joseph Smith had arranged for his call as an apostle; second anointing 9 October 1885; while speaking at Manti temple dedication 1888 some saw halo of light around his head (also at Salt Lake temple dedication 1893); told apostles 1890 he "had never had an inspired dream in his life" and had never seen his deceased father in vision despite praying for it; Sunday School General Board (1891-1919); president, own prayer circle (1894-1901, 1906-19); reported 1898 that he had never seen Jesus nor heard his voice; assistant to YMMIA General Superintendent (1898-1918); mission president (1901-03; 1904-06); Religion Class General Board (1908-1918); New Polygamy Investigation Committee (1909-18); director, Genealogical Society of Utah (1909-23); president, Quorum of the Twelve Apostles 23 November 1916; sustained and set apart as president of the LDS church 23 November 1918 by Quorum of the Twelve without public conference due to influenza epidemic; several persons reported seeing HJG transfigured into features and form of his predecessor JFS-1 at Salt Lake temple fast meeting 4 May 1919 and at stake conference 25 May; publicly sustained church president 1 June 1919, when a man reported seeing HJG's transfiguration; Church Board of Education (1919-45)

Death: 14 May 1945, Salt Lake City, Utah

Estate: $152,126.30 final appraisal; $150,026.07 net

**Jacob Hamblin (1819-1886)
Ordained "an apostle to the Lamanites [Native American Indians]" 15 December 1876 by Brigham Young, Hamblin was never admitted to Quorum of the Twelve. His calling was evangelical, like those of Orson Pratt in 1830 and George J. Adams in 1844. Hamblin was never a general authority. (See Adams and Pratt in *The Mormon Hierarchy: Origins of Power.*)

LEONARD W[ILFORD] HARDY (LWH)

Birth: 31 December 1805, Bradford, Essex Co., Massachusetts

Parents: Simon Hardy and Rhoda Hardy

Marriage (polygamist before appointment): Elizabeth H. Nichols (Goodridge) 1826 (3 ch); Sophia L. Goodridge (Quimby) 1850 (9 ch); *Mary J. Andrus (Hendricks) 1851 (no

ch?), 5 months after legal marriage to a man she would bear 11 ch; *Alvira L. Smith (Hendricks) 1851 (no ch?), same day of polygamous marriage to another man she would bear 10 ch; Esther S. Goodridge 1854 (5 ch); Harriet A. Goodridge 1858 (1 ch); *Rachel S. Gardner 1871 (no ch)
Hierarchy Relations: Daughter md Wilford Woodruff 1852, but divorced 1853; son md sister of BY-JR and JWY, niece of Joseph Young, and 1st cousin of SBY 1878
Education: Negligible
Prior Occupation: Merchant
Business To 1932: Deseret Express and Road Co.; Deseret Tanning and Manufacturing Co.; Dustin and Amy; Hardy and Goddard; Hardy and Moon; Hardy and Williams; L. W. Hardy and Co.; Little and Hardy
Social: Omitted from *Testimonies of the Church of Jesus Christ of Latter-day Saints by Its Leaders* 1930
Political/Civic Life: Civil offices, Bradford, Mass.; Nauvoo Legion band (1841-46); police captain, Salt Lake City (1851-58); Utah's Nauvoo Legion captain (1851-52), and colonel (1852-[70]); Salt Lake City Meat Inspector (1855-59); probably among the 50 men indicted for treason, Utah War, December 1857 (pardoned by U.S. president's general amnesty 1858); Salt Lake City council (1859-66); delegate and nominating committee, LDS People's Party conventions (1874, 1876); alternate delegate, People's Party territorial conventions (1876, 1878); Council of Fifty 27 June 1882
Prior Religion: ?
Mormon Experience: Baptized, elder 1832; mission (1844-45, 1869-70); seventy 1851; high priest 1856; ward bishop (1856-77); first counselor, Presiding Bishopric 6 October 1856 (set apart 12 October); prayer circle of Wilford Woodruff (1858-73); tried for unchristian conduct 1860; second anointing 11 January 1867; Brigham Young wanted to drop LWH from position April 1870 because of his using tobacco and alcohol (continued as bishopric counselor)
Death: 31 July 1884, Fairview, Sanpete Co., Utah
Estate: $16,473.26 appraised and net

CHARLES H[ENRY] HART (CHH)

Birth: 5 July 1866, Bloomington, Bear Lake Co., Idaho
Parents: James H. Hart and Sabina Scheib
Marriage (monogamist): Adelia Greenhalgh 1899 (11 ch); widower for 2 years; Mary L. Hendricks 1915 (1 ch)
Hierarchy Relations: ?
Education: Graduate, Normal Department, University of Deseret (Utah) 1887; LL.B., University of Michigan 1889; trustee, Brigham Young College in Logan (1906-23)
Prior Occupation: Lawyer and judge
Business To 1932: [Alta Orzone Corp.]; [Auto Electric Signal Co.]; [Caribou Fur Co.]; Charles H. Hart and Co.; [Consumers Warehouse and Storage Co.]; Danielsen Implement Co.; Danielsen Plow Co.; [Golden Age Mining and Reduction Co.]; Hart and Hart; Hart and Nebeker; Hart and Son; Hart and Sons; Hart and Van Dam; Kimball Brothers and Hart Co.; [Logger Mining Co.]; Midget Marvel Mill Construction Co.; Mutual Savings and Loan Association; Nebeker, Hart and Nebeker; Nebeker, Hart, Nebeker and Thatcher; [North Maxfield Mining Co.]; [People's Canal and Irrigation Co.]; [Premier Silver Mining Co.]; Radiant Monolight Co.; Richards, Hart and Van Dam; [Rook Oil Lands]; Salt Lake Knitting Works; [Salt Lake Tungstonia Mines Co.]; [Shamrock Mines Co.]; [Thorne Springs Canal Co.]; Utah Marble Co.; [Utah Queen Leasing and Mining Co.]; [Western Pacific Mining Co.]
Social: Delta Phi fraternity abt 1887 (also president); Salt Lake Chamber of Commerce by 1925; listed in *Blue Book* for Logan 1898, *Who's Who on the Pacific Coast* 1913, *Her-*

ringshaw's American Blue-Book of Biography 1915, *Utah Since Statehood* 1919, *Utah's Distinguished Personalities* 1933; omitted from *Men of Affairs in the State of Utah* [Press Club of Salt Lake City] 1914

Political/Civic Life: Founding member and secretary, Cache County's Democratic Jefferson Club 1891; territorial central committee, Democratic Party (1892-95); chair, Cache County Democratic Committee (1892-95); delegate, Democratic conventions (1892, 1893, 1894, 1895); Cache County prosecuting attorney (18<u>92</u>-95); Utah legislature (1894-95); executive committee and secretary, Utah Democratic Party (1894-95); delegate, Utah State Constitutional Convention 1895; Utah District Court judge (1896-1904); probate judge (1903-12); delegate, Democratic conventions (1904, 1908, 1910, 1916, 1924, 1926); public altercation in Idaho with "a liquor selling Jew who was abusing Jos. F. Smith" 1908 (no charges filed); withdrew as Democratic candidate for city attorney 1909; Utah Democratic Party's reception committee for William Jennings Bryan 1916; Utah State Commission for Mormon Battalion Monument (1925-31); officially listed among "one hundred prominent Democrats" of Utah's history 1942

Prior Religion: LDS

Mormon Experience: Baptized 1874; elder by 1889; seventy 1890; no pre-hierarchy proselytizing mission; president, local Seventy's quorum (1898-1906); First Council of the Seventy 9 April 1906; prayer circle of JFS-2 (1911-12); Sunday School General Board (1912-34); YMMIA General Board (1926-34); mission president (1927-31)

Death: 29 September 1934, Salt Lake City, Utah

Estate: $26,363.16 appraised; $23,637.02 net

**Abraham Hoagland (1797-1872)

A conference of 11 April 1852 sustained Hoagland and four others as traveling bishops. A First Presidency letter referred to them as "assistant Presiding Bishops," but they were not, as were JB, AC-2, and NHF, ordained "assistant Presiding Bishop" and were never considered general authorities. Grandfather of AHC and JQC; 2nd-great-grandfather of future Seventy George I. Cannon

EDWARD HUNTER [JR.] (EH)

Birth: 22 June 1793, Newton (or Newtown), Delaware Co., Pennsylvania

Parents: Edward Hunter and Hannah Maris

Marriage (polygamist before appointment): Ann Standley 1830 (3 ch); Laura L. Shimer Kaufman 1844 (5 ch), divorced 1856; Susannah Wann 1845 (3 ch); Henrietta L. Spencer 1856 (3 ch), divorced 1871; Elsie Brown in ?

Hierarchy Relations: He and ES-1 md sisters 1856; daughter md CCR's son 1869

Education: Common schools; regent, University of the City of Nauvoo (1844-46)

Prior Occupation: Currier to age 20, then surveyor, merchant, and farmer

Business To 1932: Beaumont and Hunter; Deseret Agricultural and Manufacturing Society; Deseret Agricultural Society; Deseret Horticultural Society; Deseret Irrigation and Navigation Canal Co.; Deseret Tanning and Manufacturing Co.; Deseret Telegraph Co.; Edward Hunter Iron and Steel; Hunter and Morris; Nauvoo Mercantile and Mechanical Association; Nauvoo Water Power Co.; Perpetual Emigrating Fund Co.; Price Convention; [Utah Cashmere Goat Co.]; Utah Produce Co.; Zion's Central Board of Trade

Social: Mason 1843, Nauvoo lodge; listed (despite anachronism) in *Utah Since Statehood* 1919; omitted from *Pioneers and Prominent Men of Utah* 1914, from *Testimonies of the Church of Jesus Christ of Latter-day Saints by Its Leaders* 1930

Political/Civic Life: Unsuccessfully sought to serve in War of 1812; Democrat; Delaware County (PA) militia cavalry (1822-29), commissioner (1823-26); Nauvoo Legion herald and armor-bearer (1841-45); Joseph Smith lifeguard (1842-44); Nauvoo city council (pro-tem, 1842-44; regular, 1844-45); delegate, "state convention" to nominate

Joseph Smith for U.S. presidency 1844; married polygamously in violation of Illinois law (1844, 1845); indicted September 1845 for treason (charges dropped); legislature, provisional State of Deseret (1849-51); justice of the peace (1849-51); Utah's Nauvoo Legion major (1850-70); Utah legislature (1851-52); probate judge (1857-58); probably among the 50 men indicted for treason, Utah War, December 1857 (pardoned by U.S. president's general amnesty 1858); declined to run as opposition candidate for Utah legislature 1858; Council of Fifty 25 January 1867; delegate and nominating committee, LDS People's Party 1874

Prior Religion: Society of Friends (Quaker), then Swedenborgian prior to LDS baptism
Mormon Experience: Baptized 1840; elder 1841; "Pay-master General" for Sidney Rigdon's schismatic group September 1844 (brief association); high priest 1844; ward bishop (1844-46); second anointing 29 January 1846; ward bishop (1849-54); mission (1849-50); publicly sustained Presiding Bishop 7 April 1851 (ordained 11 April 1852); prayer circle of Wilford Woodruff (1858-83); local patriarch 17 March 1873; chair, Old Folks Central Committee (1875-83); assistant Trustee-in-Trust (1877-80)
Death: 16 October 1883, Salt Lake City, Utah
Estate: $70,692.59 appraised; $68,494.59 net

ANTHONY W[OODWARD] IVINS (AWI)

Birth: 16 September 1852, Toms River, Ocean Co., New Jersey
Parents: Israel Ivins and Anna L. Ivins
Marriage (monogamist): Elizabeth A. Snow 1878 (9 ch)
Hierarchy Relations: Father of ARI; 1st cousin of HJG; son-in-law of ES-1; wife a 2nd cousin, 1 rvd, of JHS's wife and 2nd cousin, 2 rvd, of GAS; daughter md nephew of the wives of HJG, OFW, and SBY 1913; daughter md MWM's son-in-law
Education: University of Deseret (Utah), 1869-70; board of trustees, Utah State Agricultural College (vice-president 1917-19; president 1919-34); trustee, LDS University, LDS Business College, and LDS University School of Music (1921-23)
Prior Occupation: Rancher
Business To 1932: A. W. Ivins and Co.; Amalgamated Sugar Co.; Beneficial Life Insurance Co.; Blanding Gold Mining Co.; Blue Jay Consolidated Mining Co.; Burt and Carlquist Co.; Canaan Co-operative Stock Co.; Cinco de Mayo Mining Co.; Clayton Investment Co.; [Cowboy Mining and Smelting Co.]; Danielsen Plow Co.; Deseret Savings Bank; [Diaz Colonization Co.]; Dublan Industrial Co.; Dublan Water and Colonization Co.; Enterprise Mercantile Co.; Foreign Lands Corp.; Gold Leaf Mining Co.; [Guynopa Smelting and Reduction Co.]; Home Fire Insurance Company of Utah; [Hyde Gold Mining Co.]; Insulation Manufacturing Co.; Ivins Investment Co.; [Juarez Colonization Co.]; Juarez Power and Manufacturing Co.; Juarez Tanning and Manufacturing Co.; Kaibab Cattle Co.; Knight Sugar Co.; Lynndyl Townsite Co.; Mexican Colonization and Agricultural Co.; Midvale State Bank; [Mineral County Gold Mining Company of Nevada]; Mohave Land and Cattle Co.; [Morelos Development Co.]; [Nevada-Garfield Mining Co.]; Nevada Land and Livestock Co.; New Castle Reclamation Co.; Northwestern Colonization and Improvement Company of Chihuahua; Pacific Coast Joint Stock Land Bank; Palomas Land and Cattle Co.; Provo Reservoir Co.; [Rio Grande Gold Mines]; St. George Social Hall Co.; Salt Lake Dramatic Association; Salt Lake, Garfield and Western Railroad Co.; Salt Lake Zoological Society; [Seven Stars Mining Co.]; Sevier Canal Co.; Sevier River Land and Water Co.; Temple Square Hotel Co.; [Tintic Drain Tunnel Co.]; Tres Amigos Gold Mining Co.; Union Mercantile Co.; United Order of Washington; United States Fuel Co.; United States Fuel Sales Agency; Utah Bond and Share Co.; Utah Coal Sales Agency; Utah Hotel Co.; Utah-Idaho Sugar Co.; [Utah Incorporated Ranches]; Utah Power and Light Co.; Utah Savings and Trust Co.; Utah Savings and Trust Company Building; Utah Savings and Trust Safety Deposit

Co.; Utah State National Bank; Washington Field Canal Co.; ZCMI; Zion's Savings Bank and Trust Co.; Zion's Securities Corp.

Social: Salt Lake City Rotary Club 1922; listed in *Who's Who in America* 1932, *Utah: The Storied Domain* 1932, *Utah's Distinguished Personalities* 1933, *Who's Who In the Clergy* 1935, *Dictionary of American Biography* 1944, *Faith of Our Pioneer Fathers* 1956; omitted from *Men of Affairs in the State of Utah* [Press Club of Salt Lake City] 1914

Political/Civic Life: Delegate, Utah territorial Republican convention 1872; St. George (Utah) "special policeman"/constable (1877-79), deputy sheriff (1879-82), city council (1882-82, 1886-88), city attorney (1884-85), mayor (1890-94); Washington County (Utah) prosecuting attorney (1881-82, 1884-90), assessor and collector (1884-90); Mohave County (Arizona) deputy assessor and collector 1886; LDS People's Party territorial convention delegate (1886, 1888), territorial central committee (1887-91); committee of permanent organization, Democratic Party of Utah 1888; vice-president, Democratic Society of Utah 1891; U.S. Indian Agent (1891-93); delegate, Democratic conventions (1891, 1892, 1894, 1895), president of territorial convention 1894 and vice-chair 1895; territorial central committee, Democratic Party (1894-95); Utah legislature (1894-95); delegate, Utah Constitutional Convention 1895; publicly withdrew as possible Democratic candidate for Utah's governor due to religious calling to preside in Mexico 1895; performed forty-three polygamous marriages in violation of Mexican law (1897-1904); governor's delegate, Irrigation Congress 1904; declined to perjure himself by denying knowledge of post-1890 plural marriages in affidavit prepared by First Presidency for U.S. Senate 1906; Utah State Conservation Commission (1908-09); officially listed among "one hundred prominent Democrats" of Utah's history 1942

Prior Religion: LDS

Mormon Experience: Baptized 1860; elder 1865 (age 13); seventy 1869; mission (1875-76, 1878, 1882-84); high priest 1881; stake high council (1881-88); mission president (1883-84); stake presidency counselor (1888-95); dreamed 1895 he would preside over Mexico and become an apostle; Juarez stake president (1895-1907); promised by St. George temple president 1896 he would be apostle; nominated for Twelve 1898; apostle 6 October 1907; Religion Class General Board (1908-18); president, Salt Lake Elders' Quorum prayer circle (1909-21); director (1909-21), Genealogical Society of Utah (vice-president 1921-25; president 1925-34); YMMIA General Board (1909-29); YM-MIA General Superintendent (1918-21); Church Board of Education (1921-34); second counselor, First Presidency 10 March 1921, first counselor 28 May 1925

Death: 23 September 1934, Salt Lake City, Utah

Estate: $44,202.81 appraised; $43,390.92 net

ANTOINE R[IDGEWAY] IVINS (ARI)

Birth: 11 May 1881, St. George, Washington Co., Utah

Parents: AWI and Elizabeth A. Snow

Marriage (monogamist): Vilate Romney 1912 (no ch); unmarried widower last 3 years of his life

Hierarchy Relations: Son of AWI; 1st cousin, 1 rvd, of HJG; 3rd cousin, 1 rvd, of GAS; sister md nephew of the wives of HJG, OFW, and SBY; 2nd cousin, 2 rvd, of future apostle Jeffrey R. Holland

Education: School of Jurisprudence, Mexico City (1902-05); law school, University of Michigan 1905; B.S., engineering, University of Utah 1909

Prior Occupation: Rancher, business manager

Business To 1932: Dublan Water and Colonization Co.; Enterprise Reservoir and Canal Co.; [Home Fire Insurance Company of Utah]; Ivins Investment Co.; Koolau Agricultural Co.; Koolau Railway Co.; Koolau Water Co.; Laie Plantation; Layton Sugar

Co.; [Utah Power and Light Co.]; [ZCMI]; Zion's Printing and Publishing Co.; [Zion's Savings Bank and Trust Co.]; Zion's Securities Corp.

Social: Sigma Chi; Ensign Club by 1928; listed in *Utah's Distinguished Personalities* 1933, *Who's Who in America* 1960

Political/Civic Life: Democrat; chair, finance committee, Salt Lake Council of Boy Scouts 1936

Prior Religion: LDS

Mormon Experience: Baptized 1889; elder 1901; seventy 1914; no pre-hierarchy prose-lytizing mission; "mission" to manage church sugar plantation, Hawaii (1921-31); First Council of the Seventy 4 October 1931; mission president (1931-34); high priest 1961; senior president, First Council of the Seventy (1963-67)

Death: 18 October 1967, Salt Lake City, Utah

Estate: $139,839.27 appraised; $139,058.73 net

J[ONATHAN] GOLDEN KIMBALL (JGK)

Birth: 9 June 1853, Salt Lake City, Utah

Parents: Heber C. Kimball and Christeen Golden

Marriage (monogamist): Jennie K. Knowlton 1887 (6 ch)

Hierarchy Relations: Son of Heber C. Kimball; step-brother and brother-in-law of JFS-1; 4th cousin, 1 rvd, of JG; 6th cousin of JS, JHS, JFS-1; 6th cousin, 1 rvd, of DAS, GAS, HMS, JFS-2; brother md JRW's daughter; uncle of future LDS president Spencer W. Kimball; great-granduncle of future Seventy Quentin L. Cook

Education: Morgan Commercial College (1868-69); prep school, University of Deseret (Utah), 1869-70; Brigham Young Academy in Provo (1881-83)

Prior Occupation: Rancher

Business To 1932: [Amplion Radio Corp.]; [Artogram System, Inc.]; [Consumers Mutual Coal Co.]; [Diamond Oil Co.]; [Dry Gulch Irrigation Co.]; [Federal Star Oil Co.]; [Humbolt Seven Troughs Mining Co.]; [Iron Blossom Mining Co.]; Jonathan and Elias Kimball; Journal Publishing Co.; Kimball Brothers; Kimball Brothers and Hart Co.; [Lexington Concord Mining Co.]; Montezuma Orange and Banana Co.; [Mountain Lake Mining Co.]; [Rainbow Petroleum Products Co.]; Rich-Cache Mining Co.; [Ridge and Valley Mining Co.]; Silver Banner Mining Co.; Sinaloa Fruit Lands Co.; [South Lilly Mining Co.]; [Utah Texas Oil Co.]

Social: Listed in *Blue Book* for Salt Lake City (1901-07), *Biographical Record of Salt Lake City and Vicinity* 1902, *Utah's Distinguished Personalities* 1933; omitted from biographies in *History of Utah* 1904, from *Men of Affairs in the State of Utah* [Press Club of Salt Lake City] 1914

Political/Civic Life: Sergeant-at-arms, Utah legislature's upper chamber (1886, 1888); appointed delegate for Utah's unsuccessful statehood convention 1887 (did not attend due to misunderstanding and was formally dropped); Meadowville (Rich County) fence viewer (1887-88); founding member, Cache County's Democratic Jefferson Club 1891; delegate, Democratic conventions (1891, 1892, 1894, 1895, 1896, 1898, 1900, 1901, 1905); notary public, Cache County 1892; declared bankruptcy 1899; Republican 1906 to death; beaten publicly by a Salt Lake City grocer who was acquitted 1913; son-in-law murdered a man for alienating the affections of his wife, JGK's daughter 1917

Prior Religion: LDS

Mormon Experience: Baptized abt 1862; elder and endowed 1867 (age 14); "inactive" (1868-1878); rebaptized 1878; mission (1883-85); seventy 1886; mission president (1891-94); First Council of the Seventy 5 April 1892 ("ordained" President of Seventy 8 April); second anointing 19 April 1900; publicly criticized 6 October 1909 by church president JFS-1 for saying "trivial and nonsensical things" in sermons; recommended by colleagues as mission president 1919 (vetoed by First Presidency); wrote church

president HJG 16 September 1919 that "I would rather be taken out and stood up against a wall and shot" than to again receive the "silent discipline" JFS-1 gave JGK for his folksy speaking style; *de facto* senior president, First Council of the Seventy (1924-27) during BHR absence on mission; said during conference radio broadcast 9 April 1933: "God, how I hate prejudice! A man cannot be prejudiced and be just," and that he loved some church leaders a "damn sight better than others," after which church president HJG publicly criticized JGK; HJG refused to approve JGK's revised version of talk 19 May "because there would be nothing there to criticize," and both sermons went unpublished; senior president, First Council of the Seventy (1933-38)
Death: 2 September 1938, near Reno, Nevada
Estate: $8,852.69 appraised; $8,588.32 net

THEODORE B[ELDEN] LEWIS (TBL)
Birth: 18 November 1843, St. Louis, Missouri
Parents: Thomas A. Lewis and Martha J. Bird
Marriage (polygamist before appointment): Martha J. Coray 1870 (10 ch); Ephrana S. Coray 1871 (7 ch)
Hierarchy Relations: ?
Education: Common, secondary schools; Central College and Fairview Academy, Howard Co., Missouri; principal, Ogden High School (1885-97); president, Utah Educational Association (1892-93)
Prior Occupation: School teacher
Business To 1932: ?
Social: *Deseret News 1974 Church Almanac* made first official acknowledgement in twentieth century that TBL was sustained as a general authority.
Political/Civic Life: Confederate Army 1861, prisoner of war (1861-62); married polygamously in violation of federal law 1871; Juab County superintendent of district schools; justice of the peace (1875-[79]); delegate, Utah Democratic convention 1876; Salt Lake County superintendent of district schools (1877-82); delegate, LDS People's Party conventions (1880, 1881, 1882); arrested for cohabitation 1887 (released on bail); Utah Territorial Commissioner of Public Schools (1894-96); delegate, Democratic Party conventions (1891-95); pre-1891 polygamy pardoned and re-enfranchised by U.S. president's general amnesties (1893, 1894); delegate, Utah State Constitutional Convention 1895; trustee, Utah State Industrial [reform] School 1896; officially listed among "one hundred prominent Democrats" of Utah's history 1942
Prior Religion: ?
Mormon Experience: Baptized 1866; elder 1867; seventy 1868; mission (1868-70); high priest abt. 1874; publicly sustained to First Council of the Seventy 8 October 1882 (released 9 October because high priest ordination disqualified him according to then-current definition)
Death: 20 July 1899, Cambridge, Middlesex, Massachusetts
Estate: No record

JESSE C[ARTER] LITTLE (JCL)
Birth: 26 September 1815, Belmont, Waldo Co., Maine
Parents: Thomas Little and Relief White
Marriage (polygamist before appointment): Eliza Greenwood French 1840 (11 ch); Emily Hoagland 1856 (6 ch), divorced prior to 1881; Mary M. Holbrook 1856 (5 ch)
Hierarchy Relations: Daughter md brother-in-law of Brigham Young and Joseph Young 1858; he and WWT md sisters; GQC was wife's brother-in-law; divorced wife md GQC 1881
Education: Common schools
Prior Occupation: Attorney, hotel keeper

Business To 1932: American Hotel; Deseret Carriage and Furniture Depot; Deseret Carriage and Wagon Manufacturing Co.; Deseret Express and Road Co.; Great Salt Lake City Water Works Association; J. C. Little and Co.; J. C. Little (Butcher); Little and Garrett; Little and Hardy; Little and Patten; Little, Hunt and Zitting; Little, Roundy and Co.; Ogden Canyon Road Co.; Placerville, Humbolt and Salt Lake Telegraph Co.; Rush Valley Herd Co.; Utah Manufacturing Co.; Young and Little
Social: Omitted from biographies in *History of Utah* 1904, from *Testimonies of the Church of Jesus Christ of Latter-day Saints by Its Leaders* 1930
Political/Civic Life: Democrat 1844; Mormon Battalion lieutenant-colonel (1846-47); Salt Lake City council (1852-53); Utah's Nauvoo Legion captain (1852-52), colonel and aide-de-camp (1852-70); Salt Lake City marshal (1853-66), assessor and collector (1853-59), fire marshal (1856-71), sexton (1859-64), inspector of provisions (1870-77); Utah legislature (1855-59); probably among the 50 men indicted for treason, Utah War, December 1857 (pardoned by U.S. president's general amnesty 1858); was sued 1858 for false imprisonment (case dismissed due to plaintiff's death 1859) and for theft of property (settled out of court 1859); Utah assessor, U.S. Internal Revenue Service (1863-66); led disruption of anti-Mormon Liberal Party's first meeting 1870; delegate, Utah Republican Party convention and LDS People's Party convention 1872; nominating committee, People's Party 1872; acquitted by Salt Lake Police Court of permitting his cow to run at large 1878; unsuccessful candidate for probate judge 1878; notary public (1878-80); postmaster, Littleton, Utah (1878-83)
Prior Religion: ?
Mormon Experience: Baptized 1839; elder abt 1840; branch president (1844-46); high priest 1845; mission president (1846-47, 1847-48); presiding officer, eastern United States and British Provinces 1850; director, Deseret Theological Institute (1855-56); second counselor, Presiding Bishopric 6 October 1856; prayer circle of Wilford Woodruff (1858-73); objected to by Brigham Young for use of tobacco and alcohol April 1870; resigned from Presiding Bishopric at conference 7 October 1874
Death: 26 December 1893, Salt Lake City, Utah
Estate: No record

ANTHON H[ENRIK] LUND (AHL)
Birth: 15 May 1844, Aalborg, Jutland Amt, Denmark
Parents: Henrik Lund and Anne C. Andersen
Marriage (monogamist): Sarah A. Petersen 1870 (9 ch)
Hierarchy Relations: ?
Education: Common schools, public schools to age 12; trustee, LDS College (1900-01), LDS University, LDS Business College, LDS University School of Music (1901-21), Snow Academy (College), 1911; regent, University of Utah (1903-21); president, Lund School for Boys (1909-21)
Prior Occupation: Schoolteacher, clerk, merchant
Business To 1932: A. H. Lund Store; Alberta Colonization Co.; Amalgamated Sugar Co.; Bar-Ka-Two Stock Co.; Beneficial Life Insurance Co.; Bikuben Publishing Co.; Bullion, Beck and Champion Mining Co.; Church Onyx Mines; [Colorado Consolidated Mines Co.]; Consolidated Salt and Refining Co.; Deseret Investment Co.; [Deseret Irrigation Co.]; Deseret Savings Bank; Emigration Canyon Railroad Co.; Emigration Canyon Rock Co.; Ephraim Co-operative Mercantile Institution; Grass Creek Coal Co.; Hotel Utah Operating Co.; Idaho State and Savings Bank; Inland Crystal Salt Co.; Inland Railway Co.; Knight Ranching Co.; Knight Sugar Co.; Lund and Olsen; [Mascot Copper Co.]; *Millennial Star;* Mt. Pleasant Co-operative Mercantile Institution; Nevada Land and Livestock Co.; *Nordstjernan;* Oolite Stone Co.; Provo Woolen Mills Co.; [Salt Lake Iron and Steel Co.]; Salt Lake Knitting Works; San Pete

White Stone Co.; *Skandinaviens Stjerne;* State Bank of Utah; [Tintic Drain Tunnel Co.]; *Ungdommens Raadgiver;* United Order of Ephraim; *Utah Genealogical and Historical Magazine;* Utah Hotel Co.; [Utah Lake Irrigation Co.]; Utah Light and Railway Co.; Utah National Bank; Utah Savings and Trust Co.; Utah Savings and Trust Company Building; Utah Savings and Trust Safety Deposit Co.; Utah State National Bank; Utah Sulphur Co.; Wood River Live Stock Co.; ZCMI; Zion's Savings Bank and Trust Co.

Social: Charter member, Sons and Daughters of the Pioneers of Utah 1907; listed in *Blue Book* for Salt Lake City 1901, *Prophets and Patriarchs of the Church* 1902, *Biographical Record of Salt Lake City and Vicinity* 1902, *Utah As It Is* 1904, *Who's Who on the Pacific Coast* 1913, *Men of Affairs in the State of Utah* [Press Club of Salt Lake City] 1914, *Herringshaw's American Blue-Book of Biography* 1915, *National Cyclopaedia of American Biography* 1918, *Utah Since Statehood* 1919

Political/Civic Life: Utah's Nauvoo Legion 2nd lieutenant 1860s; Mt. Pleasant city council (1868-70); U.S. citizen 9 May 1870; Ephraim city council (1870-71); Utah legislature (1886-89); unsuccessful Republican candidate, Utah legislature 1892; performed polygamous marriages aboard U.S.-flagged vessels (Pacific Ocean 1897, Great Lakes 1898) in violation of federal law; declined nominations for U.S. Senate 1898, House of Representatives (1898, 1900); sat on stand, Republican state convention 1900; Utah's governor's welcoming committee for Republican president William H. Taft 1911; Utah State Capitol Commission (1911-17); president, State Historical Society of Utah (1915-17)

Prior Religion: Lutheran

Mormon Experience: Baptized 1856 (age 12); elder 1860; mission (1860-62); seventy 1864; mission (1864, 1871-72, 1883-84, 1897-98); high priest 1874; stake clerk and high council (1874-78); mission president (1884-85, 1893-96); temple presidency counselor (1888-1921); Church Board of Education (1888-1921); apostle 7 October 1889; temple president (1891-93); president, Manti Temple Association (1891-93); president, own prayer circle (1900-02); Church Literature Revision Committee (1900-01); General Superintendent of Religion Classes (1900-19); Church Historian (1900-21); president, Genealogical Society of Utah (1900-21); Missionary Committee (1901-[21]); second counselor, First Presidency 17 October 1901; General Priesthood Committee (1908-21); first counselor 7 April 1910; also temple presidency counselor (1910-11) and temple president (1911-21)

Death: 2 March 1921, Salt Lake City, Utah

Estate: $35,624.98 appraised; $33,289.31 net

FRANCIS M[ARION] LYMAN (FML)

Birth: 12 January 1840, Good Hope, McDonough Co., Illinois

Parents: Amasa M. Lyman and Maria L. Tanner

Marriage (polygamist before appointment): Rhoda A. Taylor 1857 (9 ch); Clara C. Callister 1869 (7 ch); Susan D. Callister 1884 (6 ch)

Hierarchy Relations: Son of Amasa M. Lyman; father of RRL; 2nd cousin, 1 rvd, of George A. Smith; 3rd cousin of JHS; 3rd cousin, 1 rvd, of GAS; 4th cousin of ES-1; 5th cousin of FDR and of JFS-1's wife; 5th cousin, 1 rvd, of GFR; wife was 1st cousin of JHS, 1st cousin, 1 rvd, of GAS, and 2nd cousin of JS and JFS-1; great-grandfather of future Seventy's president Marion D. Hanks; great-granduncle of future apostle James E. Faust

Education: Common schools; trustee, Young University at Salt Lake City (1891-95), LDS University, LDS Business College, and LDS University School of Music (1905-16)

Prior Occupation: Farmer, miller, businessman

Business To 1932: Beneficial Life Insurance Co.; Bingham West Dip Tunnel Co.; Black Rock Springs Ranch; Burke Mining Co.; Cannon, Grant and Co.; Church Onyx Mines; [Colombia Land and Investment Co.]; Consolidated Wagon and Machine Co.; Co-operative Furniture Co.; Co-operative Wagon and Machine Co.; Davis County Electrical Power Co.; Deseret Investment Co.; Deseret National Bank; Deseret Savings Bank; Fillmore Co-operative Horse Herd; Fillmore Co-operative Mercantile Institution; Fillmore Co-operative Sheep Herd Association; Fillmore Library Association; Francis M. Lyman Co.; Grant, Odell and Co.; Heber J. Grant and Co.; Home Benefit Building Society; Home Fire Insurance Company of Utah; Home Life Insurance Company of Utah; [Hudson Railroad and Canal Co.]; Inland Salt Co.; [Intermountain Consolidated Railroad Co.]; Kanosh Co-operative Mercantile Institution; Knight Consolidated Power Co.; Knight Power Co.; Lyman and Partridge; Lyman and Robison (Molasses); Lyman and Robison (Flour Mill); Lyman and Son; Lyman and Thompson; Lyman and Wallace; Mexican Colonization and Agricultural Co.; Mill Creek Power Co.; *Millennial Star;* Minnick Automatic Train Controller Co.; National Savings and Trust Co.; Ogden Investment Co.; [O.K. Flour and Grain Co.]; [O.K. Silver Mining and Milling Co.]; Palantic Mining and Milling Co.; Perpetual Emigrating Fund Co.; Provo Woolen Mills Co.; Rocky Mountain Trout Co.; Salt Lake and Deep Creek Railroad Co.; Shoshone Power Co.; [Silver King Coalition Mines Co.]; Superior Mining Co.; Tooele City Co-operative Building Association; Tooele City Water Co.; Tooele Co-operative Mercantile and Manufacturing Institution; Tooele County Co-operative Milling Co.; Tooele County Co-operative Tanning Co.; Utah Consolidated Mining Co.; Utah-Idaho Sugar Co.; Utah Loan and Trust Co.; Utah Pioneers' Book Publishing Co.; [Western States Mortgage Loan Co.]; Zion's Co-operative Home Building and Real Estate Co.; ZCMI; Zion's Savings Bank and Trust Co.

Social: Charter member, Sons and Daughters of the Pioneers of Utah 1907; listed in *National Cyclopaedia of American Biography* 1894, *Prophets and Patriarchs of the Church* 1902, *Utah As It Is* 1904, *Blue Book* for Salt Lake City 1907; omitted from *Biographical Record of Salt Lake City and Vicinity* 1902, from *Men of Affairs in the State of Utah* [Press Club of Salt Lake City] 1914

Political/Civic Life: Assistant assessor, U.S. Internal Revenue Service (1866-67); Millard County pound keeper (1866-68), prosecuting attorney (1867-68); Fillmore city council (1867-73); Utah's Nauvoo Legion lieutenant-colonel (1867-70); Millard County clerk and recorder (1868-73); legislature, Territory of Utah (1868-69), State of Deseret's "ghost government" (1868-69); Millard County superintendent of common schools (1870-73); delegate, Utah Republican conventions (1872, 1876); Millard County clerk, recorder, and assessor (1875-77), probate clerk (1876-77); territorial central committee, LDS People's Party (1876-78, 1880-82); Utah legislature (1876-82); delegate, People's Party territorial convention 1878; Tooele County clerk-recorder (1878-83), notary public (1878-80); Council of Fifty initiation 10 April 1880; speaker, Utah House of Representatives (1882-82); performed polygamous marriage aboard U.S.-flagged vessel in violation of federal law 1888; imprisoned 3 months for cohabitation 1889; performed polygamous marriage in violation of federal law 1890; Republican League of Utah 1891; delegate, Utah Republican Clubs convention 1891; pre-1891 polygamy pardoned and re-enfranchised by U.S. president's general amnesties (1893, 1894); declined nomination for Utah governor 1895; delegate, Independent (silver) Republican and regular Republican conventions 1896; governor's delegate, International Gold Mining Convention 1897; governor's welcoming committee for Republican president William H. Taft 1911; delegate, non-partisan city convention 1911

Prior Religion: LDS

Mormon Experience: Baptized 1848; elder 1856; seventy 1860; mission (1860-62); high priest 1869; stake high council (1869-73); one of first "home missionaries" (to Millard County) 1872; mission (1873-75); stake president (1877-80); patriarchal blessing 1877 promised he would be apostle; nominated for Twelve 1879; apostle 27 October 1880; while speaking at Manti temple dedication 1888 some saw halo of light (fainter than

JWT's) around his head, while others heard FML speak with voice of Brigham Young; Sunday School General Board (1891-1916); FML and third wife were first to receive second anointing in Salt Lake temple 7 June 1893; president, own prayer circle (1894-1916); YMMIA general board (1898-1916); Church Literature Revision Committee (1900-01); mission president (1901-1904); president, Quorum of the Twelve Apostles 6 October 1903; chair, New Polygamy Investigation Committee (1909-16); General Board of Education (1910-16)

Death: 18 November 1916, Salt Lake City, Utah

Estate: $13,198.16 appraised; $5,122.34 net

RICHARD R[OSWELL] LYMAN (RRL)

Birth: 23 November 1870, Fillmore, Millard Co., Utah

Parents: FML and Clara C. Callister

Marriage (polygamist after appointment): Amy C. Brown 1896 (2 ch); *Anna S. Jacobsen (Hegsted) 1925 (no ch), separated 1952

Hierarchy Relations: Great-grandson of Patriarch ("Uncle") John Smith; grandson of Amasa M. Lyman; grandnephew of George A. Smith; son of FML; 1st cousin, 1 rvd, of JHS; 2nd cousin of GAS; 2nd cousin, 1 rvd, of JS and JFS-1; 3rd cousin of DAS, HMS, and JFS-2; 6th cousin of GFR and SLR; brother-in-law's brother was JFM; granduncle of future Seventy's president Marion D. Hanks; 1st cousin, 2 rvd, of future apostle James E. Faust

Education: Brigham Young College in Logan; graduate, Brigham Young Academy in Provo 1891; B.S., University of Michigan at Ann Arbor 1895; principal, Brigham Young Academy high school (1895-96); professor, Brigham Young Academy (1895-96), University of Utah (1896-1922); chair, University of Utah civil engineering department (1900-1918); graduate study, University of Chicago 1902; M.C.E., 1903, Ph.D., 1905, Cornell University; Croes gold medal, American Society of Civil Engineers 1916; Society for Promotion of Engineering Education; Utah Society of Engineers; regent, University of Utah (1923-25); trustee, LDS University, LDS Business College, LDS University School of Music (1921-25), Brigham Young University (1939-44)

Prior Occupation: Professor of engineering

Business To 1932: Acme-United Motor Company of Utah; Acme-United Motor Truck Company of Utah; [Aultorest Memorial Corp.]; Bitner Real Estate and Investment Co.; Bodell Apartment Co.; California State Life Insurance Co.; Community Clinic and Dispensary; Delta State Bank; [Empire Mines Co.]; Ensign Amusement Co.; Francis M. Lyman Co.; General Stoker Sales Co.; Giant Racer Co.; Heber J. Grant and Co.; Home Benefit Building Society; Intermountain Life Insurance Co.; L. C. Investment Co.; Lyman and Pack; Lyman and Wilson; Lyman-Callister Co.; Lyman-Traher Motor Co.; Morgan-Tanner Equipment Co.; Mutual Home Purchasing Co.; Mutual Purchasing Agency; [Oregon Portland Cement Co.]; Pleasant Green Water Co.; Southwestern Fire Insurance Co.; [Tintic Standard Mining Co.]; [United States Fuel and Utilities Co.]; [Utah Electric Radio Co.]; [Utah Pennsylvanian Oil Co.]; Western States Securities Corp.

Social: Sigma Chi 1904; Kappa Phi Kappa; Utah Sons of the American Revolution abt 1917; Salt Lake Chamber of Commerce by 1925; Theta Tau abt 1925; honorary member, Friar's Club 1927; Ensign Club by 1928; life member, Sons of Utah Pioneers 1950; listed in *Blue Book* for Salt Lake City (1901-11), *Who's Who in America* 1920, *Utah: The Storied Domain* 1932, *Utah's Distinguished Personalities* 1933, *National Cyclopaedia of American Biography* 1969

Political/Civic Life: Provo city engineer (1895-96); governor's committee of arrangements, welcoming and award ceremony for Spanish-American War veterans 1899; Democrat to 1902-03 (FML told RRL 1902 he was a political embarrassment to his father); Republican 1904; delegate, Republican conventions (1905, 1906, 1907, 1914,

1916); vice-chair, Utah State Road Commission (1909-18); alternate delegate, non-partisan city convention 1911; governor's delegate, National Irrigation Congress (1910, 1912), Inter-Mountain Good Road Association 1912, Utah Irrigation and Drainage Congress 1913, International Irrigation Congress 1914; Salt Lake Prohibition and Betterment League (1914-18); Utah State Board of Equalization (1917-19); governor's delegate, Irrigation Congress 1919, Western States Reclamation Association (1919, 1920, 1921); Utah-Colorado River Commission (1921-29); vice-president, International Farm Congress 1920 (speaker 1923); vice-chair, Utah State Water Storage Commission (1921-37); regional council, Boy Scouts of America 1923; Columbia Basin Board of Engineers, U.S. Reclamation Service (1923-25); Chicago's Sanitary District Board of Engineers (1923-29); board of governors, American Farm Congress 1925; entered polygamous marriage in violation of Utah law 1925; American Water Works Association abt 1925; Salt Lake City Mayor's Advisory Water Commission 1929; secretary, Colorado River Commission 1929; Board of Consulting Engineers, Southern California's Metropolitan Water District (1929-32); caught with his 71-year-old plural wife in late-night, smashed-door raid by Salt Lake City police chief, Apostles JFS-2 and Harold B. Lee 11 November 1943 (no criminal charges)
Prior Religion: LDS
Mormon Experience: Baptized 1879; elder 1891; seventy; unsuccessfully nominated as stake president 1895; prayer circle of FML (1896-1916); high priest 1897; stake YMMIA superintendent (1897-1902); second anointing 1901; remarks at YMMIA conference 1902 publicly repudiated by JFS-1; mission 1902; FML made deathbed request 18 November 1916 of JFS-1 to ordain RRL as replacement in Twelve; prayer circle of HJG (1916-19)); apostle 7 April 1918; Sunday School General Board (1918-19); Religion Class General Board (1918-22); YMMIA General Board (1918-34); assistant Commissioner of Church Education (1919-24); president, own prayer circle (1919-29); counselor, YMMIA General Superintendency (1919-34); Church Board of Education (1919-43); Correlation Committee 1931; mission president (1936-38); recommended retirement for apostles 1941; excommunicated 12 November 1943; request for reinstatement denied 1949; First Presidency worried that RRL had joined Fundamentalists 1951 and refused to reinstate (June 1952, October 1952, 1953); rebaptized 27 October 1954; requested priesthood restoration 1956 (denied)
Death: 31 December 1963, Salt Lake City, Utah
Estate: $48,421.71 appraised; $48,017.20 net

DAVID O[MAN] McKAY (DOM)
Birth: 8 September 1873, Huntsville, Weber Co., Utah
Parents: David McKay and Jennetta E. Evans
Marriage (monogamist): Emma Ray Riggs 1901 (7 ch)
Hierarchy Relations: Brother md (1921) JQC's daughter and SQC's niece; son md (1928) granddaughter of JFS-1 and niece of DAS, HMS, and JFS-2; his brother Thomas E. McKay an Assistant to the Twelve 1941; uncle of future Seventy George R. Hill; 1st cousin, 2 rvd, of future Seventy Marlin K. Jensen
Education: Graduate, Normal Department, University of Utah 1897; principal, Weber Academy (1902-08); trustee, Weber College (1908-23), Brigham Young University (1939-70), Utah State Agricultural College (1940-41); regent, University of Utah (1921-23); honorary M.A., Brigham Young University 1922; honorary Doctor of Laws, Utah State Agricultural College 1950; honorary Doctor of Humanities, Brigham Young University 1951; honorary Doctor of Letters, University of Utah 1951; honorary Doctor of Letters, Temple University 1951; honorary membership, International College of Surgeons 1954; honorary Doctor of Humanities, Weber State College 1965
Prior Occupation: School teacher and principal

Business To 1932: Beneficial Life Insurance Co.; David McKay Co.; Home Knitting Co.; Intermountain Mausoleum Co.; Layton Sugar Co.; *Millennial Star;* Mount Ogden Stock Farm; New Castle Land Co.; New Castle Reclamation Co.; Ogden Knitting Co.; Ogden Motor Car Co.; Thomas D. Dee Memorial Hospital Association; Utah-Idaho Motor Co.

Social: President, Huntsville Commercial Club 1915; honorary member, Ogden Rotary Club; honorary life member, Sons of Utah Pioneers; honorary member, Friar's Club 1927; Newcomen Society; Blue Key; Bonneville Club; listed in *Utah's Distinguished Personalities* 1933, *Who's Who in America* 1944, biographies of *Utah: A Centennial History* 1949, *Faith of Our Pioneer Fathers* 1956, *National Cyclopaedia of American Biography* 1975; omitted from *Men of Affairs in the State of Utah* [Press Club of Salt Lake City] 1914

Political/Civic Life: Director, State Historical Society of Utah (1905-08); organizer, Prohibition Republican convention 1909; governor's delegate, National Irrigation Congress 1912; president, Ogden Betterment League (1914-18); vice-president, Utah Federation of Prohibition and Betterment Leagues (1916-18); Weber County executive board, American Red Cross 1915; delegate, Republican state convention where he nominated candidate for governor 1928; general chair, Utah's "White House Convention on Child Health and Protection" 1931; chair, Utah Council for Child Health and Protection (1932-33); chair, Utah Centennial Exposition Commission (1938-47); chair, Utah State Advisory Committee, American Red Cross (1942-43); Silver Buffalo award, Boy Scouts of America 1953; commander's cross, Order of Phoenix, from King Paul of Greece 1954; National Council of Boy Scouts of America (honorary) 1957; National Citizens Committee for Community Relations 1964

Prior Religion: LDS

Mormon Experience: Baptized 1881; elder, seventy 1897; mission (1897-99, promised by mission counselor to "sit in the leading councils of the Church"); stake Sunday School superintendency (1899-1906); high priest and apostle 9 April 1906; Church Board of Education (1906-70); Sunday School assistant general superintendent (1906-18), superintendent (1918-34); General Priesthood Committee (1908-22); chair, Correlation Committee (1913-20); Commissioner of Church Education (1919-21); mission (1920-21, had vivid dream of Jesus Christ); mission president (1922-24); Temple Ceremony Revision Committee (1924-27); Correlation Committee 1931; second counselor, First Presidency (6 October 1934-9 April 1951); president, Quorum of the Twelve Apostles 30 September 1950; "ordained" president of church 9 April 1951, first time in LDS history that Quorum of the Twelve used word "ordained" for LDS church president (see *The Mormon Hierarchy: Origins of Power,* 252-53)

Death: 18 January 1970, Salt Lake City, Utah

Estate: $37,893.56 appraised; $37,183.27 net

JOSEPH W[ILLIAM] McMURRIN (JWM)

Birth: 5 September 1858, Tooele, Tooele Co., Utah

Parents: Joseph McMurrin and Margaret Leaing

Marriage (monogamist): Mary Ellen Hunter 1880 (7 ch)

Hierarchy Relations: Brother-in-law of BY-JR's step-brother; granduncle of future LDS president Harold B. Lee

Education: Negligible

Prior Occupation: Farmer

Business To 1932: McMurrin and Co.; *Millennial Star;* Zion's Printing and Publishing Co.

Social: Listed in *Blue Book* for Salt Lake City (1907-11), *Biographical Record of Salt Lake City and Vicinity* 1902; omitted from biographies in *History of Utah* 1904, from *Pioneers and Prominent Men of Utah* 1914, from *Men of Affairs in the State of Utah* [Press Club of Salt Lake City] 1914

Political/Civic Life: Convicted and fined for assault and battery 1878, for disturbing the peace 1881; delegate, LDS People's Party convention 1882; shot by deputy marshal during scuffle over surveillance of polygamists 1885 (deputy was exonerated); indicted for assaulting the officer 1886 (avoided arrest by going on foreign mission), surrendered 1890 (charges dismissed); delegate, Republican city convention (1893, 1894); sat on stand, Republican state convention 1900; organizer, Prohibition Republican meeting 1909
Prior Religion: LDS
Mormon Experience: Baptized 1866; elder 1876; mission (1886-90); nominated for First Council of the Seventy 1894; prayer circle of FML (1895-1916); mission (1896-98); First Council of the Seventy 5 October 1897; "set apart" as President of the Seventy 21 January 1898, first time First Council member not "ordained"; President LS ruled 29 March 1899 that JWM should be "ordained," but accepted 13 April argument of second counselor JFS-1 that "setting apart" was sufficient; nominated for Twelve 1900; YMMIA General Board (1900-12); Religion Class General Board (1901-22); mission (1901-02, 1904-06); Correlation Committee (1913-[19]); prayer circle of HJG (1916-19); mission president (1919-31)
Death: 24 October 1932, Los Angeles, California
Estate: No record

JOSEPH F[RANCIS] MERRILL (JFM)
Birth: 24 August 1868, Richmond, Cache Co., Utah
Parents: MWM and Maria L. Kingsbury
Marriage (monogamist): Annie L. Hyde 1898 (7 ch); widower for 16 months; Emily L. Traub 1918 (no ch); unmarried widower last 10-1/2 years of his life
Hierarchy Relations: Son of MWM; 8th cousin of DAS, HMS, and JFS-1; wife was granddaughter of Orson Hyde and John Taylor; wife's brother md AWI's daughter; brother's brother-in-law was RRL; wife's 1st cousin was HJG's son-in-law
Education: Graduate, Normal Department, University of Deseret (Utah) 1889; B.S., University of Michigan 1893; summers at Cornell University (1893, 1902), University of Chicago (1894-97); professor, University of Utah (1893-1928); Ph.D., Johns Hopkins University 1899 (Phi Beta Kappa); director, School of Mines and Engineering, University of Utah (1897-1928); acting-president, University of Utah 1904; fellow, American Association for the Advancement of Science, American Electrochemical Society, American Institute of Electrical Engineers, American Physics Society, National Education Association, Society for Promotion of Engineering Education; president, Utah Educational Association (1910-11) and Utah Teachers' Association 1911; director, Lund School for Boys 1915; honorary Doctor of Science, University of Utah 1920; council (1926-28), Utah Academy of Sciences (vice-president, 1928-29); trustee, Brigham Young University (1939-52)
Prior Occupation: Professor of physics and engineering, author
Business To 1932: [Amalgamated Sugar Co.]; [General Motors Co.]; [Montana Power Co.]; Mutual Home Purchasing Co.; New Castle Farm Co.; New Castle Reclamation Co.; [Phillips Petroleum Co.]; [Utah-Idaho Sugar Co.]; [Utah Power and Light Co.]; [ZCMI]
Social: Delta Phi fraternity abt 1889; president, Utah Society of Engineers (1907-10); Bonneville Club 1913; Ensign Club by 1928; Phi Gamma Mu 1928; listed in *Blue Book* for Salt Lake City (1901-11), *Who's Who in America* 1912, *Utah: The Storied Domain* 1932, *Utah's Distinguished Personalities* 1933, *National Cyclopaedia of American Biography* 1956
Political/Civic Life: Delegate, Democratic conventions 1906; president, Iron County Irrigation District abt 1907; Utah State Conservation Commission (1908-15; secretary 1909-15); town trustee, Forest Dale (1909-12); unsuccessful candidate for Utah legislature 1910; governor's delegate, National Conservation Congress 1910; advisor, central

committee, Utah Democratic Party (1910-16); delegate, Democratic state convention where unsuccessfully nominated as candidate for governor 1912; delegate, Democratic convention 1914; resigned as candidate for state senator on Democratic-Progressive Party ticket 1914; Salt Lake Prohibition and Betterment League (1914-18); director, State Historical Society of Utah (1916-26); announced candidacy for Utah's governorship 1916 (not nominated at Democratic convention where he was delegate); Utah Democratic Party's reception committee for William Jennings Bryan 1916; Utah director, Wartime Training Program (1917-18); executive committee, Utah League to Enforce Peace (1918-19); program committee, state Democratic rally 1920 (decided not to run as candidate for governor); governing board, Engineering Council of Utah (1921-27) and president (1923-24); consulting engineer, U.S. Bureau of Mines (1921-52); Republican after 1932 because of opposition to Franklin D. Roosevelt's New Deal; chair, General No-Liquor-Tobacco Campaign Committee 1942

Prior Religion: LDS

Mormon Experience: Baptized 1877; elder 1889; seventy 1898; branch president (1898-99); no pre-hierarchy proselytizing mission; prayer circle of FML (1899-1916), of HJG (1916-19); stake Sunday School superintendency (1903-07), superintendent (1907-11); high priest 1911; stake presidency counselor (1911-19); YMMIA General Board (1927-33); Commissioner of Church Education (1927-33); Church Board of Education (1927-52); apostle 8 October 1931; Correlation Committee 1931; Melchizedek Priesthood Committee (1931-33); mission president (1933-36)

Death: 3 February 1952, Salt Lake City, Utah

Estate: $99,386.21 appraised; $95,289.44 net

MARRINER W[OOD] MERRILL (MWM)

Birth: 25 September 1832, Sackville, New Brunswick Province, Canada

Parents: Nathan A. Merrill and Sarah A. Reunolds [sic]

Marriage (polygamist before appointment): Sarah A. Atkinson 1856 (10 ch); Cyrene Standley 1865 (8 ch); Almira J. Bainbridge 1865 (12 ch); Maria L. Kingsbury 1867 (10 ch); Elna Jonsson 1885 (no ch); Jennie Jacobson 1886 (no ch); Anna S. Mangum 1889 (no ch); Hilda M. Erickson 1901 (1 ch)

Hierarchy Relations: Father of JFM; son md JWT's niece 1898; wife was grandniece of Newel K. Whitney's wives, of LS's 5th cousin, 2 rvd, and 7th cousin of JS and JFS-1

Education: Negligible; trustee, Utah State Agricultural College (1896-1900), Brigham Young College in Logan (1896-98, 1900-06)

Prior Occupation: Farmer, stockman

Business To 1932: [Amalgamated Sugar Co.]; [Bullion, Beck and Champion Mining Co.]; Cache Valley Board of Trade; Cache Valley Dairy Co.; M. W. Merrill and Co.; Merrill and Johnson; Richmond Co-operative Mercantile Co.; Richmond Co-operative Mercantile Institution; [Richmond Irrigation District]; Salt Lake and Ogden Railroad Co.; United Order Manufacturing and Building Company of Logan; United Order of Richmond; Utah and Northern Railroad Co.; Utah Condensed Milk Co.; [Utah-Idaho Sugar Co.]; Utah Northern Railroad Co.

Social: Listed in *Blue Book* for Logan 1898, *Prophets and Patriarchs of the Church* 1902, *Utah As It Is* 1904, *Stalwarts of Mormonism* 1954, *Faith of Our Pioneer Fathers* 1956; omitted from *Biographical Record of Salt Lake City and Vicinity* 1902, from biographies in *History of Utah* 1904

Political/Civic Life: Postmaster, Richmond, Utah (1864-75); Utah's Nauvoo Legion major (1865-69) and captain (1869-70); married polygamously six times in violation of federal law (1865-89); U.S. citizen 8 June 1869; delegate, Utah's unsuccessful statehood convention 1872; Cache County selectman (1872-80); Utah legislature (1874-75); delegate, LDS People's Party county caucus 1874; delegate, People's Party conventions

(1876, 1878); Cache County central committee, People's Party (1876-[91]); Utah legislature (1880-81); performed dozens of plural marriages in Logan temple in violation of federal law (1884-89); indicted for cohabitation 1887 (pleaded guilty and fined); pre-1891 polygamy pardoned and re-enfranchised by U.S. president's general amnesties (1893, 1894); delegate, Republican county convention and attended Republican victory celebration 1894; defeated as Republican candidate for Utah State Constitutional Convention 1894; performed four plural marriages in Logan temple and in Salt Lake City in violation of federal and Utah laws (1894-1903); married polygamously in violation of Utah law 1901; perjured himself in U.S. Senate affidavit 1904 that "he has not taken or married any wife, or woman to be his wife, since President Wilford Woodruff's manifesto of September, A.D. 1890" (obtained physician's release to avoid testifying); performed plural marriage in Logan temple in violation of Utah law 1905
Prior Religion: Unaffiliated (mother was LDS)
Mormon Experience: Vision (age 9) of family life in heaven; baptized 1852; elder 1853; seventy 1855; no pre-hierarchy proselytizing mission; high priest 1861; ward bishop (1861-79); one of first "home missionaries" (to Cache County) 1872; stake presidency counselor (1879-90); president, Logan temple (1884-1906); president, Logan Temple Association (1884-1906); apostle 7 October 1889; reported 1892 that deceased Heber C. Kimball appeared to him in Logan temple; stake president (1899-1901); reported 1900 that Satan appeared to him in temple
Death: 6 February 1906, Richmond, Cache Co., Utah
Estate: $40,890 appraised and net

ORRIN P[ORTER] MILLER (OPM)

Birth: 11 September 1858, Mill Creek, Salt Lake Co., Utah
Parents: Reuben G. Miller and Ann Craynor
Marriage (monogamist): Elizabeth M. Morgan 1881 (11 ch)
Hierarchy Relations: Sister-in-law md HJG's brother; nephew md JRW's daughter
Education: Common schools
Prior Occupation: Farmer, rancher
Business To 1932: Alaska Ice and Storage Co.; Danielsen Implement Co.; Danielsen Plow Co.; Eagle Mercantile Co.; Jordan State Bank; Juab Development Co.; Moapa Improvement Co.; Nevada Land and Livestock Co.; Old Emma Mines Co.; Riverside Canal Co.; Riverton Commercial Co.; South Jordan Canal Co.; Trapper Mining Co.; Uintah Land and Water Co.; Utah and Salt Lake Canal Co.; Utah Lake and Jordan Dam Co.; Utah National Bank; Utah Onyx Development Co.; Valley View Co.; W. H. Groves LDS Hospital
Social: Listed in *Utah As It Is* 1904; omitted from *Pioneers and Prominent Men of Utah* 1914, from *Men of Affairs in the State of Utah* [Press Club of Salt Lake City] 1914, from *Testimonies of the Church of Jesus Christ of Latter-day Saints by Its Leaders* 1930
Political/Civic Life: Election judge (1882, 1886, 1891, 1892, 1893); deputy registrar of federally appointed Utah Commission (6 years); delegate, LDS People's Party conventions (1883, 1885, 1886, 1887, 1890); Salt Lake County central committee, People's Party (1887-91); Salt Lake County selectman (1889-91); territorial central committee and vice-president, Democratic Party 1891; unsuccessful Democratic candidate for Salt Lake County selectman 1892; delegate, Democratic conventions (1894, 1895, 1898); unsuccessful Democratic candidate for Utah legislature 1895; Utah Lake Commission 1900; delegate, Utah state Irrigation Convention 1902; governor's delegate, National Irrigation Congress (1902, 1905, 1910), Trans-Mississippi Commercial Congress (1906, 1910, 1911); Utah Democratic Party's reception committee for William Jennings Bryan 1916; officially listed among "one hundred prominent Democrats" of Utah's history 1942

Prior Religion: LDS
Mormon Experience: Baptized 1867; elder 1881; seventy 1884; no pre-hierarchy prose-lytizing mission; high priest 1886; ward bishop (1886-1900); stake president (1900-01); second counselor, Presiding Bishopric 24 October 1901; first counselor 4 December 1907; General Priesthood Committee (1908-18)
Death: 7 July 1918, Salt Lake City, Utah
Estate: No record

**Aurelius Miner (1832-1913)
As one of the "alternate" members of the First Council of the Seventy (24 May 1879-27 May 1883), Miner served as *ad hoc* replacement for absent members, usually at meetings where missionary appointments were processed. He was never a general authority.

JOHN [HAMILTON] MORGAN (JM)
Birth: 8 August 1842, Greensburgh, Decatur Co., Indiana
Parents: Garrard Morgan III and Elizabeth A. Hamilton
Marriage (polygamist before appointment): Helen M. Groesbeck 1868 (11 ch); Annie M. Smith 1884 (5 ch); Mary A. Linton 1888 (3 ch)
Hierarchy Relations: He and JHS md sisters
Education: Graduate, Eastman Commercial College 1866; president, Morgan Com-mercial College (1867-72); principal, Commercial Department, University of Deseret (Utah), 1870-71; regent, University of Deseret 1884
Prior Occupation: Professor of business skills, author
Business To 1932: Deseret Agricultural and Manufacturing Society; Groesbeck Co.; Manassa Co-operative Milling and Manufacturing Co.; Manassa Ditch Co.; Mexican Colonization and Agricultural Co.; Morgan Hotel; Utah Beekeeper's Association; Vic-tor Gold and Silver Mining Co.
Social: Mason abt 1878 (while LDS mission president); listed in biographies of *Utah: A Centennial History* 1949, *Faith of Our Pioneer Fathers* 1956; omitted from biographies in *History of Utah* 1904, from *Testimonies of the Church of Jesus Christ of Latter-day Saints by Its Leaders* 1930
Political/Civic Life: 123rd Illinois Infantry private (1862-63), corporal (1863-65), and sergeant (1865); postmaster, Mill Creek, Utah (1880-90); enrolling and engrossing clerk, Utah House of Representatives 1882; delegate, LDS People's Party convention 1883; Salt Lake County superintendent of schools (1883-84); Utah legislature (1884-85); arrested for cohabitation 1890 (charges dropped); organizer, Utah Republican Club 1891; delegate, Republican conventions (1891, 1892, 1893, 1894); indicted for polygamy 1892 (avoided arrest); executive committee, Utah Territorial Republican League 1892; election judge 1893; pre-1891 polygamy pardoned and re-enfranchised by U.S. president's general amnesties (1893, 1894)
Prior Religion: Unaffiliated
Mormon Experience: Baptized 1867; excommunicated 28 March 1868 (reinstated within weeks); elder 1868; seventy 1875; mission (1875-77, 1890); mission president (1878-88); prayer circle of Wilford Woodruff (1881-81); nominated for Twelve 1882; assistant General Superintendent of Sunday Schools (1883-94); First Council of the Seventy 5 October 1884 ("ordained" President of Seventy 7 October); director, LDS Bureau of Information (1889-94)
Death: 14 August 1894, Preston, Franklin Co., Idaho
Estate: No record

**Amos Milton Musser (1830-1909)
Identified in some histories as traveling bishop (1858-76), Musser actually served (1860-76) as traveling agent for the General Tithing Office, counseling ward bishops

and auditing records. He was not a general authority and did not have the position of JB, AC-2, and NHF. Musser was ordained to the office of bishop 23 April 1882, and worked in Presiding Bishop's office until 1888.

CHARLES W[ILSON] NIBLEY (CWN)

Birth: 5 February 1849, Hunterfield, Midlothian Co., Scotland
Parents: James Nibley and Jane Wilson
Marriage (polygamist before appointment); Rebecca Neibaur 1869 (10 ch); Ellen J. Ricks 1880 (5 ch); Julia Budge 1885 (8 ch)
Hierarchy Relations: Daughter md HJG's brother-in-law; daughter md RS's son; son md RS's niece; daughter-in-law was 1st cousin, 1 rvd, of SBY and 2nd cousin of LEY
Education: Negligible ("self-educated"); trustee, Brigham Young College in Logan (1908-26)
Prior Occupation: Businessman
Business To 1932: [Acme Portland Cement Co.]; [Adams and Sons Co.]; [Adams and Sons Mining Co.]; [Adams Illinois Mining Co.]; [Adams Lumber Co.]; Agency Co.; Amalgamated Sugar Co.; American Sugar Refining Co.; Auto Securities Co.; Baker City Electric Light Co.; Baker Gas and Electric Co.; Baker Improvement Co.; Baldwin Radio Co.; Beneficial Life Insurance Co.; [Bourne Mining and Milling Co.]; Buckhorn Fruit Lands Co.; [Building Books Society]; Cache Valley Board of Trade; Cache Valley Mercantile; Canadian Sugar Factories; Central Lumber Co.; Clayton Investment Co.; [Consolidated Salt and Refining Co.]; Continental Life Insurance and Investment Co.; Cooper Lumber Co.; Danielsen Implement Co.; Danielsen Plow Co.; [David Wilson's Mine]; Deep Creek Railroad Co.; Deseret National Bank; Deseret News Company; Deseret Savings Bank; Eagle Mines Co.; Ely Lumber and Coal Co.; Emigration Canyon Railroad Co.; Emigration Canyon Rock Co.; [Enamel Brick and Concrete Company of Utah]; Eureka Hill Railway Co.; F. S. Murphy Lumber Co.; First National Bank of Logan; Foreign Lands Corp.; [Glendale Heights Investment Co.]; Glenn Lumber Co.; [Goldwyn Park Investment Co.]; Grande Ronde Lumber Co.; Guardian Casualty and Guaranty Co.; [Haddock-Nibley Investment Co.]; Herald-Republican Publishing Co.; Hilgard Lumber Co.; Hoge and Nibley; Hoge, Cole and Nibley; Home Benefit Building Society; Home Fire Insurance Company of Utah; Hotel Utah Operating Co.; Iron Manufacturing Company of Utah; Jennings-Nibley Warehouse Co.; Juab Development Co.; Juab Lake Irrigation Co.; Knight Consolidated Power Co.; [Knight Power Co.]; Knight Woolen Mills; Layton Sugar Co.; Letha Townsite Co.; Lewiston Sugar Co.; Logan and Smithfield Canal Co.; Logan Co-operative Pasture Co.; Logan Power, Light and Heating Co.; [Logan Republican Publishing Co.]; Logan Sugar Co.; Mecham Lumber Co.; Mercantile Investment Co.; Mount Hood Railroad Co.; [Mountain Lion Mining Co.]; Mountain States Telephone and Telegraph Co.; [Mowray Electrical Co.]; [Nathan Neibaur Mine]; National Savings and Trust Co.; Nevada Land and Livestock Co.; Nibley and Hammond; Nibley and Monson; Nibley-Channel Lumber Co.; Nibley Co.; Nibley Investment Co.; Nibley-Mimnaugh Lumber Co.; [Nibley Mine]; Nibley-Stoddard Lumber Co.; Ogden Publishing Co.; [Ogden Rapid Transit Co.]; [Ogden Street Railroad Co.]; Ogden Sugar Co.; Ogden Water Works Co.; [Oregon Cement Quarries]; Oregon Land Co.; Oregon Lumber Co.; Oregon Lumber Yard; Oregon Portland Cement Co.; Oregon Sugar Co.; Oregon-Utah Sugar Co.; [Pacific Land and Water Co.]; Pacific Provision Co.; Palace Building, Inc.; Palace Operating Co.; Paris Mercantile Co.; Payette Valley Extension Railroad Co.; Payette Valley Railroad Co.; [Pendleton Lumber Co.]; Peterson, Card and Nibley; Portland Cement Co.; Portland Cement Securities Co.; [Portland Coal and Coke Co.]; [Prudential Building Society]; Quincy Lumber Co.; Rio Grande Lumber Co.; [Rogue River Land and Investment Co.]; Rosenbaum and Co.; Salt Lake and Los Angeles Railway Co.; Salt Lake and Ogden Railroad Co.; Salt Lake Knitting Works; Salt

Lake Potash Co.; Saltair Beach Co.; San Vincente Lumber Co.; [Skamania Lumber Co.]; Sloat Lumber Co.; [Spokane Portland Cement Co.]; [Squires Mining Co.]; Standard Investors; State Bank of Utah; [Sumpter Hotel Co.]; Sumpter Valley Railroad Co.; Telegram Publishing Co.; Temple Square Hotel Co.; Tintic Lumber Co.; Tintic Smelting Co.; Trapper Mining Co.; Union Portland Cement Co.; United Order Building and Manufacturing Company of Logan; United States Sugar Manufacturers Association; Utah and Pacific Railroad Co.; Utah Associated Industries; Utah Bag Co.; [Utah Bond and Share Co.]; Utah Conservation Co.; Utah Construction Co.; Utah Hotel Co.; [Utah-Idaho Hospital]; Utah-Idaho Sugar Co.; Utah Lime and Stone Co.; Utah Lumber Co.; Utah National Bank; Utah Northern Railroad Co.; Utah Power and Light Co.; Utah Smelting Co.; Utah State National Bank; [Vineyard Land and Stock Co.]; [Volker Scowcroft Lumber Co.]; W. H. Groves LDS Hospital; [Wandamere Amusement Co.]; Wellsville Co-operative Mercantile Institution; Western Pacific Railroad Co.; White Pine Lumber Co.; [Wilson Mining Co.]; [Wyoming Coal and Coke Co.]; ZCMI; Zion's Savings Bank and Trust Co.; Zion's Securities Corp.

Social: Old Time Telegraphers and Historical Association 1873; Salt Lake City Commercial Club (member 1911, board of governors 1914-17); Bonneville Club 1913; Salt Lake Country Club 1915; Brentwood (CA) Country Club 1915; Salt Lake Chamber of Commerce by 1925; honorary, Salt Lake City Rotary Club 1928; listed in *Financial Red Book of America* (1903-07), *Blue Book* for Salt Lake City (1907-11), *Sketches of the Inter-Mountain States* 1909, *Utah Since Statehood* 1919, *Who's Who in America* 1926, *Utah: The Storied Domain* 1932, *Stalwarts of Mormonism* 1954; omitted from *Who's Who in the Northwest* [1910 and 1917, despite CWN's many incorporations of lumber companies there], from *Men of Affairs in the State of Utah* [Press Club of Salt Lake City] 1914

Political/Civic Life: Refused to be candidate on non-LDS "Reform Party Ticket" 1871; delegate, LDS People's Party municipal convention 1873; Cache County central committee, Democratic Party 1876; delegate, Democratic convention 1876; alternate delegate, People's Party conventions 1876; U.S. citizen 7 May 1877; Cache County assessor and collector (1879-81); trustee and secretary, East Logan Irrigation District before 1880; delegate, People's Party conventions 1880; notary public (1880-82); elected Logan City alderman 1882 (resigned two days after taking oath of office); delegate, Utah's unsuccessful statehood convention 1882; Logan municipal central committee, People's Party (1883-85); adviser to Mormon Democratic legislators in Idaho 1885; arrested for cohabitation but case dismissed (1885, 1888); lobbied Idaho's Democratic state officers 1888; arrested for adultery 1891 (case dismissed); Democrat to 1891; founder, Logan, Utah's Lincoln Republican Club 1891 (declined to be president); Utah Republican League 1891; delegate, Utah Republican conventions (1891, 1892); governor's delegate, American Bi-Metallic League 1893; pre-1891 polygamy pardoned and re-enfranchised by U.S. president's general amnesties (1893, 1894); organizer, Prohibition Republican meeting 1909; Utah governor's reception committee for Republican president William H. Taft 1909; delegate, non-partisan city convention 1911; Utah governor's welcoming committee for President William H. Taft 1911; testified before U.S. Senate about Sugar Trust 1911; Utah State Council of Defense (1917-18); charged with conspiracy in restraint of trade by U.S. Department of Justice and indicted by federal grand jury August 1920 for illegal profiteering in connection with Utah-Idaho Sugar Co. (charges dropped); finance committee, Utah State Republican Party 1922

Prior Religion: Raised Baptist by parents (LDS converts) until family moved to Utah

Mormon Experience: Baptized 1860 (age 11); elder 1865; mission (1869-70, 1877-79); seventy 1877 (local president 1883); HJG blocked appointment as stake president because CWN not "spiritually minded enough" 1899; high priest 1901; stake presidency counselor (1901-07); Presiding Bishop 4 December 1907; General Priesthood Committee (1908-22); chair, Old Folks Central Committee (1908-25); prayer circle of JET

(1921-25); second counselor, First Presidency of HJG 28 May 1925; Church Board of Education (1925-31)
Death: 11 December 1931, Salt Lake City, Utah
Estate: $19,010.75 appraised; $18,831.36 net

CHARLES W[ILLIAM] PENROSE (CWP)

Birth: 4 February 1832, Camberwell, London, England
Parents: George W. Penrose and Matilda Sims
Marriage (polygamist before appointment): Lucetta Stratford 1855 (18 ch); Louisa E. Lusty 1863 (10 ch); Romania Bunnell (Pratt) 1886 (no ch)
Hierarchy Relations: Daughter was sister-in-law of HJG's wife; daughter's brother-in-law was OFW
Education: Common schools; trustee, Salt Lake Stake Academy (1886-89), LDS College (1889-91), LDS University, LDS Business College, and LDS University School of Music (1912-25); professor, Brigham Young Academy in Provo (1896-99, 1901-02); honorary Doctor of Law, Brigham Young University 1921
Prior Occupation: Newspaper editor, author
Business To 1932: [Beneficial Life Insurance Co.]; [Consolidated Wagon and Machine Co.]; *Deseret News;* [Dragon Consolidated Mining Co.]; Farmers and Stockgrowers Bank; [Home Benefit Building Society]; Inland Crystal Salt Co.; [Iron Blossom Consolidated Mining Co.]; Knight Sugar Co.; Logan Co-operative Mercantile Institution; [Lowland Tunnel, Water and Transportation Co.]; *Millennial Star;* [Mount Nebo Marble Co.]; National City Bank of Salt Lake City; *Ogden Junction;* Ogden Publishing Co.; *Ogden Standard;* [People's Sugar Co.]; *Salt Lake Herald;* [Salt Lake Iron and Steel Co.]; Shearman and Penrose; [Tintic Drain Tunnel Co.]; [Utah-Idaho Sugar Co.]
Social: Listed in *Blue Book* for Salt Lake City (1895-1907), *Biographical Record of Salt Lake City and Vicinity* 1902, *Utah As It Is* 1904, *Who's Who in America* 1918, *National Cyclopaedia of American Biography* 1918, *Utah Since Statehood* 1919; omitted from *Men of Affairs in the State of Utah* [Press Club of Salt Lake City] 1914
Political/Civic Life: Probate clerk, Davis County (1864-64); Ogden city council (1871-79); beaten publicly by a Logan attorney 1872; delegate and secretary, Utah Democratic Party convention 1872; delegate, Utah's unsuccessful statehood convention 1872; delegate, LDS People's Party conventions (1872, 1876, 1880, 1881, 1882, 1884); delegate, Democratic convention 1876; Weber County central committee, Democratic Party 1876; Utah legislature (1876-77, 1880-82); Council of Fifty initiation 26 June 1882; delegate, Utah's unsuccessful statehood convention 1882; indicted for cohabitation 1885 (avoided arrest by going on foreign mission); territorial central committee, People's Party (1887-88); U.S. marshals searched Salt Lake tithing office for CWP 1888 (avoided arrest until presidential pardon 1889); imprisoned for five days for contempt of court 1889; city central committee and convention delegate, People's Party 1889; speaker, People's Party meeting 1890; delegate, Utah Democratic conventions (1892, 1895, 1896, 1898, 1899); attended national Democratic convention 1892; pre-1891 polygamy pardoned and re-enfranchised by U.S. president's general amnesties (1893, 1894); sat on stand, Democratic territorial convention 1894; defeated as Democratic candidate, Utah State Constitutional Convention 1894; unsuccessful nominee for Utah legislature 1894; governor's delegate, National Irrigation Congress 1904; delegate, international Peace Congress 1908; Utah Peace Society (1911-14); executive committee, Utah League to Enforce Peace 1919; delegate, Mountain Congress, national League to Enforce Peace 1919; officially listed among "one hundred prominent Democrats" of Utah's history 1942
Prior Religion: Baptist
Mormon Experience: Baptized 1850; elder 1851; mission (1851-61, 1865-68, 1877-79,

1885-87); seventy 1861; stake high council, without high priest ordination as one of the "seventy apostles" (1869-70); high priest 1871; stake high council (1871-77); one of first "home missionaries" (to Weber County) 1872; nominated for Twelve 1882; stake presidency counselor (1884-1904); required by First Presidency to confess 31 March 1893 error in his Democratic Party activities in order to attend dedication of Salt Lake temple; assistant Church Historian (1896-1904); director (1896-1909), Genealogical Society of Utah (vice-president 1909-21; president 1921-25); apostle 7 July 1904; Church Board of Education (1904-25); Religion Class General Board (1906-22); mission president (1906-10); president, own prayer circle (1910-12); second counselor, First Presidency 7 December 1911; general boards, Sunday School and YMMIA (1912-19); first counselor 10 March 1921
Death: 16 May 1925, Salt Lake City, Utah
Estate: $24,112.73 appraised; $24,000.00 net

**David Pettiegrew (1791-1863)
A conference of 11 April 1852 sustained Pettiegrew [or Petteigrew] and four others as traveling bishops, later described in First Presidency letter as "assistant Presiding Bishops," but they were not ordained to this position as were JB, AC-2, and NHF.

**William W. Phelps (1792-1872)
By November 1856, Phelps was a member of the prayer circle of the First Presidency and Quorum of Twelve Apostles. He attended with seven other non-general authorities until September 1858 when they were assigned to different circles. Phelps was prominent as an original member of the Council of Fifty but was not a general authority.

REY L[UCERO] PRATT (RLP)
Birth: 11 October 1878, Salt Lake City, Utah
Parents: Helaman Pratt and Emeline V. Billingsley
Marriage (monogamist): Mary Stark 1900 (13 ch)
Hierarchy Relations: Grandson of Parley P. Pratt; grandnephew of Orson Pratt; 7th cousin, 1 rvd, of JS and JFS-1; 8th cousin of DAS, HMS, and JFS-2; 1st cousin, 2 rvd, of future Seventy Russell C. Taylor; granduncle of future Seventy Waldo P. Call
Education: Elementary and secondary schools
Prior Occupation: Rancher
Business To 1932: Zion's Printing and Publishing Co.
Social: ?
Political/Civic Life: Republican
Prior Religion: LDS
Mormon Experience: Baptized 1886; elder abt 1898; mission (1906-07); mission president (1907-31); seventy 1911; First Council of the Seventy 29 January 1925 (set apart 7 April)
Death: 14 April 1931, Salt Lake City, Utah
Estate: No record

WILLIAM B[OWKER] PRESTON (WBP)
Birth: 24 November 1830, Halifax, Franklin Co., Virginia
Parents: Christopher Preston and Martha M. Clayton
Marriage (polygamist before appointment): Harriet A. Thatcher 1858 (4 ch); Bertha M. Anderson 1871 (5 ch); monogamist after 1889
Hierarchy Relations: Brother-in-law of MT
Education: Common schools; trustee, Brigham Young College in Logan (1877-1908)
Prior Occupation: Farmer
Business To 1932: Ashley Coal, Asphault, and Gilsonite Co.; [Benson Drug Co.]; Black-

foot Stock Co.; Bullion, Beck and Champion Mining Co.; Cache Valley Board of Trade; Central Mining and Elevator Co.; Church Onyx Mines; Consolidated Implement Co.; Co-operative Drug Co.; Deseret Investment Co.; Gold Leaf Mining Co.; Herald Co.; [Ima Consolidated Mining and Milling Co.]; Iron Manufacturing Company of Utah; [Lakeside Mining Co.]; Lehi Commercial and Savings Bank; Lewiston Sugar Co.; Logan and Smithfield Canal Co.; Logan Co-operative Mercantile Institution; Mexican Colonization and Agricultural Co.; Nevada Land and Livestock Co.; Provo Manufacturing Co.; Provo Milling and Manufacturing Co.; Provo Woolen Mills Co.; Rexburg Milling Co.; Salt Lake City Railroad Co.; [Shoshone Power Co.]; Social Hall Society; State Bank of Utah; [Sundown and LaPlata Mining Co.]; Thatcher Sawmill; Trapper Mining Co.; [Union Knitting Co.]; United Order of Cache Valley; Utah and Northern Railroad Co.; Utah Journal Printing and Publishing Co.; Utah-Mexican Rubber Co.; Utah Northern Railroad Co.; Utah Sugar Co.; W. H. Groves LDS Hospital; Wasatch Co-operative Lumber and Manufacturing Co.; Woodruff, Farr and Preston

<u>Social:</u> Listed in *Blue Book* for Salt Lake City (1895-1907), *Biographical Record of Salt Lake City and Vicinity* 1902, *Utah As It Is* 1904, *Utah Since Statehood* 1919, *Stalwarts of Mormonism* 1954; omitted from *Testimonies of the Church of Jesus Christ of Latter-day Saints by Its Leaders* 1930

<u>Political/Civic Life:</u> Utah's Nauvoo Legion aide-de-camp (1860-70); Logan, Utah postmaster (1861-66); Cache County selectman (1861-65); delegate, Utah's unsuccessful statehood convention 1862; Utah legislature (1862-65); legislature, State of Deseret's (1862-65); Logan mayor (1870-82); married polygamously in violation of federal law 1871; Cache County assessor and collector (1871-78); president, municipal Republican Party 1872; delegate, Utah's unsuccessful statehood convention 1872; Utah legislature (1872-82); delegate, LDS People's Party conventions (1874, 1876, 1878, 1880); justice of the peace (1876-[82]); Cache County central committee, People's Party, chair (1876-78, 1880-[86]), member only (1878-80); Council of Fifty initiation 10 April 1880; territorial central committee, People's Party 1878; indicted for cohabitation 1886 (avoided arrest); denied right to vote by local registrars as former polygamist, even though currently a monogamist 1890; delegate, Utah Democratic conventions (1892, 1895); pre-1891 polygamy pardoned and re-enfranchised by U.S. president's general amnesties (1893, 1894); delegate, Utah State Constitutional Convention 1895; unsuccessfully nominated at Democratic convention as candidate for Utah governor 1895; Utah state's Pioneer Jubilee Commission (1896-97); delegate, Democratic county conventions (1896, 1906); local committee, National Irrigation Congress 1897; officially listed among "one hundred prominent Democrats" of Utah's history 1942

<u>Prior Religion:</u> Methodist

<u>Mormon Experience:</u> Baptized, elder 1857; mission (1857, 1865-68); high priest 1859; ward bishop (1859-61, 1868-71); regional "presiding bishop" for Cache Valley (1871-77); one of first "home missionaries" (to Cache County) 1872; stake presidency counselor (1877-79, president 1879-84); First Presidency and Quorum of Twelve prayer circle February 1884; Presiding Bishop 6 April 1884; director, Logan Temple Association (1884-1907); chair, Old Folks Central Committee (1884-1907); president, LDS Industrial Bureau (1897-98); released 5 December 1907 for health reasons

<u>Death:</u> 2 August 1908, Salt Lake City, Utah

<u>Estate:</u> $45,975.36 appraised; $37,428.44 net

GEORGE REYNOLDS [JR.] (GR)

<u>Birth:</u> 1 January 1842, Marylebone, London Co., England

<u>Parents:</u> George Reynolds and Julia A. Tautz

<u>Marriage</u> (polygamist before appointment): Mary A. Tuddenham 1865 (11 ch); Amelia Schofield 1874 (12 ch); Mary G. Gould 1885 (9 ch)

Hierarchy Relations: Daughter md (1908) JFS-2 who was son of JFS-1, nephew of JS, and brother of DAS and HMS

Education: Schools in England and France until age 13; regent, University of Deseret (Utah), 1869-79; trustee, Brigham Young Academy in Salt Lake City (1876-91), Young University at Salt Lake City (1891-95); lecturer, LDS College (1890-96); professor, Brigham Young Academy in Provo (1893-1902)

Prior Occupation: Clerk

Business To 1932: Bullion, Beck and Champion Mining Co.; Deseret Museum; Deseret Telegraph Co.; Grass Creek Terminal Railway Co.; *Juvenile Instructor; Millennial Star;* Perpetual Emigrating Fund Co.; Reynolds and Parry; [Reynolds Feed Co.]; Salt Lake Literary and Scientific Association; [Salt Lake City] Twentieth Ward Co-operative Mercantile Institution; Salt Lake Theatre; ZCMI; Zion's Savings Bank and Trust Co.

Social: Listed in *Blue Book* for Salt Lake City 1901; omitted from *Biographical Record of Salt Lake City and Vicinity* 1902, from biographies in *History of Utah* 1904

Political/Civic Life: Republican; arrested for polygamy 1874, sentenced to prison 1875, decision reversed by Utah Supreme Court, re-arrested and re-sentenced 1875 (freed on bail pending appeal); Salt Lake City council (1875-79); lost appeal to U.S. Supreme Court which ruled in *Reynolds v. the U.S.* that First Amendment did not protect polygamy 1879; imprisoned (1879-81); Council of Fifty initiation 8 April 1881; pre-1891 polygamy pardoned and re-enfranchised by U.S. president's general amnesties (1893, 1894); performed polygamous marriage in violation of federal law 1907; legally committed to Utah State Insane Asylum 3 November 1908 for "Dementia" from "Over Work" (discharged 7 February 1909)

Prior Religion: Church of England

Mormon Experience: LDS convert (age 9); baptized 1856 (age 14); elder 1860; mission (1861-65); branch president (1864-65); seventy 1866; prayer circle of John Taylor (1867-82); mission (1871-72); president, local Seventy's quorum (1875-90); Sunday School General Board (1879-1909); nominated for Twelve 1882; nominated for Council of the Seventy 1888; First Council of the Seventy 5 April 1890 ("ordained" President of Seventy 10 April); secretary, First Presidency (1890-1909); director, Genealogical Society of Utah (1894-1909); secretary, Church Board of Education (1899-1901); Sunday School assistant General Superintendent (1899-1909); Church Literature Revision Committee (1900-01)

Death: 9 August 1909, Salt Lake City, Utah

Estate: $200 appraised and net

**Ben E. Rich (1855-1913)

Unanimously recommended by the First Council of the Seventy as its new member, which was approved by the Quorum of Twelve and First Presidency 22 September 1909. However, on arrival from Washington, D.C. seven days later, Apostle-Senator RS persuaded JFS-1 to cancel this decision because Rich had married three plural wives after 1890. A mission president from 1898 to his death, Rich never became a general authority.

CHARLES C[OULSON] RICH (CCR)

Birth: 21 August 1809, Campbell Co., Kentucky

Parents: Joseph Rich and Nancy O'Neal

Marriage (polygamist before appointment): Sarah D. Pea 1838 (9 ch); Eliza A. Graves 1845 (3 ch); Mary A. Phelps 1845 (10 ch); Sarah J. Peck 1845 (11 ch); Emeline Grover 1846 (8 ch); Harriet Sargent 1847 (10 ch); *Hulda L. Fisk 1870 (no ch); *Ruth Walkup 1873 (no ch)

Hierarchy Relations: He and Amasa M. Lyman md sisters; son md EH's daughter 1869; 2nd-great-granduncle of future Seventy's president L. Aldin Porter

<u>Education:</u> Common schools, secondary school training; regent, University of the City of Nauvoo (1841-46); Nauvoo warden for common schools (1841-[44])

<u>Prior Occupation:</u> Cooper, farmer, school teacher

<u>Business To 1932:</u> C. C. Rich and Co.; Lyman and Rich; Lyman, Rich and Co.; Lyman, Rich, Hopkins and Co.; *Millennial Star;* Nauvoo Mercantile and Mechanical Association; Perpetual Emigrating Fund Co.; Salamander Sawmill; United Order of Bear Lake; United Order of Zion

<u>Social:</u> Mason 1842, Nauvoo lodge; listed in *Prophets and Patriarchs of the Church* 1902, *Utah: The Storied Domain* 1932, biographies of *Utah: A Centennial History* 1949

<u>Political/Civic Life:</u> Captain, Zion's Camp paramilitary campaign 1834; signed "Danite" letter warning dissenters to leave June 1838; Mormon militiaman 1838; fled state to avoid indictment for killing Missouri militiaman 1838-39; committee to "search out [anti-Mormon] offenders and bring them to justice" 1840; Nauvoo city council (1841-43); Nauvoo Legion captain (1841-41), colonel (1841-41), brigadier-general (1841-44); Nauvoo warden for common schools (1841-1843); Nauvoo University building committee (1841-43); "Relief Expedition" with other known Danites to rescue Joseph Smith from arrest 1843; Nauvoo police 1st lieutenant (1843-44); Council of Fifty initiation bet. 14 March and 11 April 1844; Nauvoo Legion major-general (1844-46); married polygamously four times in violation of Illinois law (1845-46); Nauvoo alderman and associate justice of Nauvoo Municipal Court (1845-45); trustee, "Town of Nauvoo" (1845-46); indicted for treason September 1845 (charges dropped); commander-in-chief, LDS military force, Winter Quarters, Nebraska 1847; Salt Lake City municipal council (1847-48); delegate, Utah's unsuccessful statehood convention and member of committee to draft constitution 1849; legislature, [provisional] State of Deseret (1849-51); city council, San Bernardino, California (1854-55); San Bernardino mayor (1855-56); probate judge (1857-58); probably among the 50 men indicted for treason, Utah War, December 1857 (pardoned by U.S. president's general amnesty 1858); Utah legislature (1858-60, 1863-73); legislature, State of Deseret's "ghost government" (1863-70); married polygamously in violation of federal law (1870, 1873); delegate, Utah Republican convention 1872; vice-president and territorial central committee, Utah Republican Party (1872-74); delegate, Utah's unsuccessful statehood convention 1872; territorial central committee, LDS People's Party (1872-75); presided, Idaho Democratic convention 1874 (remained Democrat); polygamy indictment dismissed by Idaho court 1875 (offense did not occur in Idaho); Bear Lake County treasurer (1875-76); Bear Lake County commission (1876-80); released, Council of Fifty 24 June 1882 (physically incapacitated)

<u>Prior Religion:</u> Unaffiliated

<u>Mormon Experience:</u> Baptized, elder 1832; vivid dream of Jesus Christ 1833; mission (1833, 1835, 1842, 1843, 1846, 1851-52); high priest 1836 (quorum president 1837-38); stake high council (1839-41, 1843-44); stake presidency counselor (1841-43, 1844-46, 1847-48); president, political mission to Michigan 1844; church tithing agent (1845-46); second anointing 15 January 1846; stake president (1846-47, 1848-49); nominated for Twelve (1846, 1847); apostle 12 February 1849; mission president (1849-51, 1853-54, 1860-62); director, Deseret Theological Institute (1855-56); president, own prayer circle (1858-60); president, School of the Prophets, Paris, Idaho (1869-74); one of first "home missionaries" (to Rich County, Utah) 1872; sustained as "prophet, seer, and revelator," first time 6 October 1877; assistant Trustee-in-Trust (1877-80)

<u>Death:</u> 17 November 1883, Paris, Bear Lake Co., Idaho

<u>Estate:</u> $19,530 appraised and net

FRANKLIN D[EWEY] RICHARDS (FDR)

<u>Birth:</u> 2 April 1821, Richmond, Berkshire Co., Massachusetts

Parents: Phine(h)as Richards and Wealthy Dewey

Marriage (polygamist before appointment): Jane Snyder 1842 (6 ch); Elizabeth McFate 1846 (no ch); Sarah Snyder (Jenne) 1849 (1 ch); Charlotte Fox 1849 (6 ch); Susan S. Peirson 1853 (3 ch); Laura A. Snyder 1854 (1 ch); Josephine de la Harpe 1857 (no ch), divorced 1859; Nanny Longstroth (Richards) 1857 (3 ch); Mary Thompson (Richards) 1857 (4 ch); Susannah Bayliss (Richards) 1857 (no ch); Rhoda H. Foss (Richards) 1857 (4 ch); *Ann Davies (Dalley) 1857 (no ch)

Hierarchy Relations: Father of GFR; nephew of Willard Richards; 1st cousin, 1 rvd, of SLR; 1st cousin, 1 rvd, of Brigham Young and Joseph Young; 2nd cousin of BY-JR, JWY, JAY, SBY; 3rd cousin, 2 rvd, of John Smith and Joseph Smith, Sr.; 4th cousin, 1 rvd, of Hyrum Smith, Joseph Smith, and William Smith; 5th cousin of JS, JHS, and JFS-1; 5th cousin, 1 rvd, of Amasa M. Lyman; 6th cousin of FML; md four of Willard Richards's widows 1857; wife's nephew was MFC; step-daughter md GQC; md niece of Wilford Woodruff's wife 1857; 1st cousin md JFS-1 1868; 1st cousin md John Taylor's niece 1876; 1st cousin, 1 rvd, md John Taylor's son and JWT's brother; daughter md ES-2's son; grandfather of future apostle LeGrand Richards; grandfather of future Assistant to the Twelve Franklin D. Richards

Education: Common schools; Lennox Academy (1834-35); regent, University of the City of Nauvoo (1844-46), University of Deseret (Utah), 1853-60

Prior Occupation: Carpenter, joiner

Business To 1932: Deseret Iron Co.; Deseret News Co.; Deseret Pastoral Co.; F. D. Richards Mill; Ferris Gold and Silver Mining and Milling Co.; *Millennial Star; Ogden Junction;* Ogden Publishing Co.; Perpetual Emigrating Fund Co.; Pioneer Electric Power Co.; United Order of Weber; United Order of Zion; Utah Loan and Trust Co.; Utah Northern Railroad Co.; Utah Vinegar Works; ZCMI

Social: Mason 1843, Nauvoo lodge; listed in *National Cyclopaedia of American Biography* 1897, *Blue Book* for Ogden 1898, *Herringshaw's Encyclopedia of American Biography* 1898, *Biographical Record of Salt Lake City and Vicinity* 1902, *Utah As It Is* 1904, *Stalwarts of Mormonism* 1954

Political/Civic Life: Married polygamously in violation of Illinois law 1846; Council of Fifty initiation 17 March 1849; legislature, [provisional] State of Deseret (1849-51); Utah legislature (1852-54, 1856-66, 1870-75); Utah's Nauvoo Legion captain (1852-52), colonel and chaplain (1852-57), brigadier-general (1857-70); probably among the 50 men indicted for treason, Utah War, December 1857 (pardoned by U.S. president's general amnesty 1858); probate judge (1869-83); Speaker of the House, State of Deseret's "ghost government" (1870-72); justice of the peace (1870-82); delegate, Utah Republican convention 1872; president, Utah Republican Party and chair of its territorial central committee (1872-76); delegate, Utah's unsuccessful statehood convention 1872; voted against by 39 percent of Mormons as candidate for Weber County probate judge 1876; Weber County prosecuting attorney (1876-78); delegate, LDS People's Party conventions (1876, 1878); territorial central committee, People's Party (1876-82); Weber County central committee, People's Party (chair 1876-84, member only, 1884-85); in hiding to avoid arrest for cohabitation 1878; performed dozens of polygamous marriages to 1889 in violation of federal law; sat on stand, Democratic territorial convention 1891; pre-1891 polygamy pardoned and re-enfranchised by U.S. president's general amnesties (1893, 1894); offered opening prayer, Democratic territorial convention 1895; president, State Historical Society of Utah (1897-99); performed polygamous marriage in violation of Oregon law 1898

Prior Religion: Congregational

Mormon Experience: Baptized 1838; brother was murdered by Missouri anti-Mormons at Haun's Mill 1838; elder, seventy 1840; mission (1840, 1841, 1841-42, 1844-45, 1846-48, 1849-51, 1867-68); political missionary, high priest 1844; church tithing agent (1845-

46); second anointing 23 January 1846; dreamed 1847 that he would become member of Twelve; mission presidency counselor (1847-48); nominated for Twelve 1847; apostle 12 February 1849; mission president (1851-52, 1854-56); after Willie-Martin handcart disaster 1856, FDR as mission president was repeatedly blamed by Brigham Young in sermons and private comments (1856-77); prayer circle of John Taylor (1859-62); stake president (1870-77); one of first "home missionaries" (to Weber County) 1872; sustained as "prophet, seer, and revelator," first time 6 October 1877; assistant Trustee-in-Trust (1877-80); Church Auditing Committee (1878-87); vision/"manifestation" of children's condition after death and resurrection 1878; vivid dream of deceased Brigham Young 1882; assistant Church Historian (1884-89); Church Historian (1889-99); president, Genealogical Society of Utah (1894-99); president, own prayer circle (1897-99); president, Quorum of the Twelve Apostles 13 September 1898
Death: 9 December 1899, Ogden, Weber Co., Utah
Estate: $1,416 appraised and net

GEORGE F[RANKLIN] RICHARDS (GFR)
Birth: 23 February 1861, Farmington, Davis Co., Utah
Parents: FDR and Nanny Longstroth
Marriage (monogamist): Alice A. Robinson 1882 (15 ch); convinced that his eternal exaltation required obedience to polygamy, he was sealed to several deceased women after 1890 Manifesto prohibited polygamous marriage; widower for 15 months; Betsy Hollings 1947 (no ch)
Hierarchy Relations: Grandnephew of Willard Richards; son of FDR; nephew (also 2nd cousin) of SLR; 1st cousin, 1 rvd, of JFS-1's wife; 2nd cousin, 1 rvd, of SBY; 3rd cousin of LEY; 3rd cousin of JAW's wife; 5th cousin, 1 rvd, of JS, JHS, JFS-1, and wife of FML; 6th cousin of DAS, GAS, HMS, JFS-2, OFW; 6th cousin, 1 rvd, of HGS; daughter's brother-in-law was SQC; his son LeGrand Richards appointed Presiding Bishop 1938
Education: Graduate, University of Deseret (Utah) 1881
Prior Occupation: Farmer
Business To 1932: Heber J. Grant and Co.; Inland Railway Co.; *Millennial Star;* Oregon Portland Cement Co.; Richards Implement and Machinery Co.; Taylor-Richards Motor Co.; Tooele City Agricultural Society; Tooele City Water Co.; Tooele County Farmer's Institute; Tooele Creamery Co.; Utah Implement-Vehicle Co.
Social: Listed in *Blue Book* for Salt Lake City (1907-11), *Who's Who in America* 1950; omitted from *Men of Affairs in the State of Utah* [Press Club of Salt Lake City] 1914
Political/Civic Life: Trustee (1889-96), Tooele City Irrigation District (president 1896-99); Tooele County school board (1890-93), treasurer (1890-97); Democrat to 1891; unsuccessful Republican candidate for Utah legislature, justice of the peace, and Tooele City alderman 1891; delegate, Utah Republican conventions (1891, 1892); speaker, Republican rallies 1892; declined Republican nomination for Tooele City mayor and school trustee 1893; Utah legislature (1898-1900); unsuccessful Republican candidate for Tooele City mayor 1899; governor's committee of arrangements, welcoming and award ceremony for Spanish-American War veterans 1899; delegate, Republican state convention 1904
Prior Religion: LDS
Mormon Experience: Baptized 1873; elder 1876 (age 15); seventy 1884; no pre-hierarchy proselytizing mission; high priest 1890; stake presidency counselor (1890-1906); local patriarch 1893; second anointing 12 March 1897; dreamed 1900 that he would become member of the Twelve; "dream or Visit" in which Jesus Christ embraced him March 1906; apostle 9 April 1906; prayer circle of FML (1906-16); Religion Class General Board (1908-22); YMMIA General Board (1911-22); mission president (1916-19); president, Salt Lake temple (1921-37); Temple Ceremony Revision Committee (1923-

27); Acting Patriarch to the Church (4 May 1937-3 October 1942); superintendent of temples 1937; president, Quorum of the Twelve Apostles 21 May 1945; Temple Ordinance Committee (1946-47)
Death: 8 August 1950, Salt Lake City, Utah
Estate: No record

**Levi Richards (1799-1876)
By November 1856 (until late 1858) Richards and seven other non-general authorities attended the prayer circle of the First Presidency and Quorum of Twelve. He was an original member of the Council of Fifty, but not a general authority.

STEPHEN L[ONGSTROTH] RICHARDS (SLR)
Birth: 18 June 1879, Mendon, Cache Co, Utah
Parents: Stephen L. Richards and Emma L. Stayner
Marriage (monogamist): Irene S. Merrill 1900 (9 ch)
Hierarchy Relations: Grandson of Willard Richards; nephew (also 2nd cousin) of GFR; 1st cousin, 1 rvd, of JFS-1's wife; 2nd cousin, 1 rvd, of SBY; 3rd cousin of LEY and JAW's wife; 5th cousin, 1 rvd, of JS and JFS-1; 6th cousin of RRL, DAS, GAS, HMS, JFS-2, and OFW; 6th cousin, 1 rvd, of HGS; wife was 1st cousin of GAS; his brother Stayner Richards appointed Assistant to Twelve 1951; 3rd cousin of future Seventy W. Eugene Hansen
Education: St. Mary's Academy (Roman Catholic); Davis Academy (LDS); University of Michigan at Ann Arbor 1892; University of Utah (1897-99); principal, Malad (Idaho) School (1900-01); University of Michigan (1902-03); LL.B., University of Chicago 1904; professor, University of Utah law school (1907-22); regent, University of Utah (1939-41); trustee, Brigham Young University (1939-59)
Prior Occupation: Attorney, law professor
Business To 1932: Amalgamated Sugar Co.; Central Bank of Bingham; Community Clinic and Dispensary; Copperfield State Bank; Deseret Book Co.; Deseret Gymnasium; Foreign Lands Corp.; Granite Drug Co.; Granite Furniture Co.; Granite Investment Co.; Granite Realty Co.; Hyland Motor Co.; Ima Consolidated Mining and Milling Co.; Industrial Loan and Investment Co.; Kimball and Richards Co.; Kimball and Richards Securities; Kimball-Richards Building Co.; Lower Mill Creek Irrigation Co.; [Mt. Air Private Road Co.]; Mountain States Petroleum Co.; National Food Co.; Nevada Land Sales Co.; Paradise Valley Land and Ranch Co.; Provident Loan Society; Raymond-Bracken Automobile Co.; Revier Motion Picture Co.; Richards, Hart and Van Dam; Richards, Moffat, Porter and Ashton; Richards Motor Co.; Richards, Porter and Van Dam; Salt Lake Amusement Co.; Salt Lake Iron and Steel Co.; Saltair Amusement Co.; [Standard Oil Company of Indiana]; [Standard Oil Company of New Jersey]; Sugar Beet Finance Corp.; Temple Square Hotel Co.; Trenton Orchard Co.; Truth Publishing Co.; *University of Utah Chronicle;* Utah Adjustment Bureau; Utah Fuel Co.; [Utah-Idaho Sugar Co.]; Utah Oil Refining Co.; Utah State National Bank; Wasatch Land and Improvement Co.; Wasatch Lawn Cemetery Association; West Cache Land Co.; Western Oil Co.; Whitmore Oxygen Co.; ZCMI; [Zion's Savings Bank and Trust Co.]; Zion's Securities Corp.
Social: Delta Phi fraternity abt 1897; Salt Lake Commercial Club by 1911; director, Weber Rod Club 1916; Utah Sons of the American Revolution abt 1917; president, Timpanogas Rod Club (1917-18); Salt Lake Country Club by 1930; Ft. Douglas Country Club by 1933; Salt Lake City Rotary Club 1937; listed in *Blue Book* for Salt Lake City 1911, *Who's Who in America* 1930, *Utah's Distinguished Personalities* 1933, *Who's Who In the Clergy* 1935, *National Cyclopaedia of American Biography* 1966
Political/Civic Life: Notary public, Salt Lake County 1905; city attorney, Murray, Utah (1905-06); delegate, Democratic conventions and unsuccessful candidate for Utah leg-

islature 1906, for Salt Lake County attorney 1907; delegate, Citizens Party convention and unsuccessful candidate for Salt Lake City attorney 1909; delegate, Democratic conventions and unsuccessful candidate for Salt Lake County attorney and for Utah legislature 1910; secretary, Utah State Bar Association (1910-12); alternate delegate, non-partisan convention 1911; delegate, Democratic conventions (1912, 1914, 1916); American Bar Association (ABA) 1915; Utah Democratic Party's reception committee for William Jennings Bryan 1916; Utah State Board of Corrections (1917-21); ABA's vice-president for Utah (1919-21); director, Social Welfare League (1919-28); delegate, ABA 1922 (withdrew membership 1927); chair, federal New Deal's Civil Works Administration (1934-35); vice-chair, governor's advisory committee, emergency relief (1934-35)

Prior Religion: LDS

Mormon Experience: Baptized 1893; elder 1900; no pre-hierarchy proselytizing mission; Sunday School General Board (1906-34); General Priesthood Committee (1908-22); Religion Class General Board (1908-22); assistant General Superintendent, Sunday Schools (1909-34); Correlation Committee (1913-[22]); chair, Social Advisory Committee (1916-22); apostle 18 January 1917; president, own prayer circle (1918-28); Church Board of Education (1919-59); assistant Commissioner of Church Education (1919-24); Temple Ceremony Revision Committee (1923-27); Committee on Revision of Seventies' Work (1923-26); delivered sermon at conference 9 April 1932 critical of over-emphasis on Word of Wisdom, refused to recant and offered to resign from Quorum of Twelve 5 May; apologized to church president HJG 26 May 1932 (sermon not published); Temple Ordinance Committee (1946-47); first counselor, First Presidency 9 April 1951

Death: 19 May 1959, Salt Lake City, Utah

Estate: $374,579.45 final appraisal; $297,204.45 net

BRIGHAM H[ENRY] ROBERTS (BHR)

Birth: 13 March 1857, Warrington, Lancashire, England

Parents: Benjamin Roberts and Ann R. Everington

Marriage (polygamist before appointment): Sarah Louisa Smith 1878 (7 ch); Celia A. Dibble 1884 (8 ch); Margaret Curtis (Shipp) 1891 (no ch); monogamist after 1926

Hierarchy Relations: Brothers-in-law md 2nd cousins, 1 rvd, of JS, JHS, and JFS-1 and 3rd cousins of DAS, GAS, HMS, JFS-2

Education: Morgan Commercial College; graduate (valedictorian), Normal Department, University of Deseret (Utah) 1878; lecturer, LDS College (1893-96); trustee, Utah State Agricultural College (1895-96); director, Modern Stenographic Institute (1912-17)

Prior Occupation: Blacksmith, school teacher, editor, author

Business To 1932: *Contributor;* Contributor Co.; *Improvement Era; Millennial Star; Salt Lake Herald;* Union Savings and Investment Co.; Zion's Printing and Publishing Co.

Social: Ananias Club 1910; Bonneville Club 1913; listed in *Who's Who in America* 1899, *Biographical Record of Salt Lake City and Vicinity* 1902, *Utah As It Is* 1904, *Blue Book* for Salt Lake City (1907-1911), *Utah's Distinguished Personalities* 1933, *The Dictionary of American Biography* 1935; omitted from *Men of Affairs in the State of Utah* [Press Club of Salt Lake City] 1914

Political/Civic Life: Deserted British army (enlisted by foster father); married polygamously in violation of federal law 1884; indicted for cohabitation 1885, arrested 1886 (forfeited bail and remained at large), imprisoned for 4 months 1889; married polygamously in violation of federal law 1891; delegate and speaker, Democratic territorial convention 1892, despite receiving instructions from First Presidency not to participate; pre-1891 polygamy pardoned and re-enfranchised by U.S. president's general amnesties (1893, 1894); delegate, Democratic conventions (1894, 1895, 1896, 1908, 1912, 1916); governor's delegate, Western States Conference Convention 1895; delegate, Utah State Constitutional Convention 1895; unsuccessful Democratic candidate for U.S. House of Representatives 1895; elected as Utah's representative to Congress 1898; indicted for cohabitation 1899 and excluded 1900 by U.S. House from taking his seat; tried for cohabitation (hung jury), retried 1900 (convicted and fined), decision reversed by Utah Supreme Court 1901 (on technicality); speaker, Democratic meetings (1904, 1906, 1910, 1914); chair, Democratic state convention 1912; Utah Democratic Party's reception committee for William Jennings Bryan 1916; Utah State Board of Equalization (1917-17; chair 1919-<u>23</u>); chaplain, 145th Field Artillery Regiment, American Expeditionary Force (1917-19); publicly defended U.S. joining League of Nations (1919-20), position supported by entire First Presidency and most of Twelve; withdrew as candidate for Democratic nomination as Utah's governor 1920; chair, Utah State Commission for Mormon Battalion Monument (1925-31); chaplain, Utah veterans organization (1928-33); officially listed among "one hundred prominent Democrats" of Utah's history 1942

<u>Prior Religion:</u> LDS

<u>Mormon Experience:</u> Baptized, elder 1867 (age 10); disfellowshipped temporarily 1874; seventy 1877; mission (1880-82, 1883-88); First Council of the Seventy 7 October 1888 ("ordained" President of Seventy 8 October); mission (1889-90 and dream-vision of angel); declined to participate in sustaining vote for polygamy Manifesto, October conference 1890; required by First Presidency to confess error 31 March 1893 in his Democratic Party activities in order to attend dedication of Salt Lake temple; his political role condemned by second counselor JFS-1 at general priesthood meeting October 1895; told Quorum of the Twelve and First Council of the Seventy 13 February 1896 he would resign his position rather than apologize for Democratic activities; temporarily suspended from office until confessed 26 March 1896; mission (1896-97); temporarily refused to vote for Republican activist RS as newly announced apostle at conference April 1900; declined First Council's request that he be more active in Seventy's work 18 December 1901; YMMIA General Superintendency (1901-1922); assistant Church Historian (1902-33); refused 29 October 1902 to attend future meetings of First Council of the Seventy, and next attended 7 January 1903 only to break established rule by voting in opposition to rest of Council (resolved situation with public apology 4 March 1903); instructed by First Council of the Seventy 10 January 1906 to take alcoholism cure in Los Angeles; treatment unsuccessful and senior president SBY reported BHR "has been many times much the worse for Liquor" 1908; FML instructed BHR "live or die, keep the Word of Wisdom" 5 January 1909; tried by hierarchy 5-6 January 1909 for publicly maligning RS and showing disrespect for First Presidency; refused to apologize and urged entire First Council of the Seventy to submit their resignations 10 February 1909 (Seventy and Twelve asked First Presidency to disfellowship him, but no action for 8 months); denounced by church president JFS-1 at general conference 6 October 1909 (led to BHR's apology and reconciliation); conference talk 5 October 1912 criticized JFS-1 for using church magazine to endorse Republican candidate for U.S. president (JFS-1 repudiated BHR at same conference); assistant General Superintendent of YMMIA (1919-22); presented hierarchy with plea for vigorous research and response to detailed list of textual "problems" in *Book of Mormon* 1922; mission president (1922-27); senior president, First Council of the Seventy (1924-33); criticized by senior apostle RC in letter to First Presidency 9 December 1926 for BHR's "indelicate and unbecoming statements" about apostles supervising work of the Seventy; preached in Salt Lake Tabernacle 22 September 1929 that "the Latter-day Saints are conscious of receding from that zenith [of early Mormonism] in that they are no longer flooded with revelation" (criticized by hierarchy and apologized 3 October);

his 6-volume centennial history of Mormonism published "by the Church" 1930; wrote HJG 30 August 1932 objecting to censorship of historical documents; delegate and speaker ("representing the Church"), World Fellowship of Faith 1933; according to diary of his former missionary, BHR stated 7 August 1933 that for more than 10 years he believed *Book of Mormon* was product of Joseph Smith's imagination rather than ancient record divinely translated from gold plates. (Although some have viewed this as consistent with BHR's detailed analysis of *Book of Mormon* historicity problems in 1922, this alleged statement conflicted with the rest of BHR's public and private statements of faith. It is possible that BHR simply described the 1922 study to this former missionary who mistakenly understood that as expressing his mentor's personal disbelief.)
Death: 27 September 1933, Salt Lake City, Utah
Estate: $1609.32 appraised; $348.00 net

DAVID A[SAEL] SMITH (DAS)
Birth: 24 May 1879, Salt Lake City, Utah
Parents: JFS-1 and Julina Lambson
Marriage (monogamist): Emily Jenkins 1901 (10 ch)
Hierarchy Relations: Great-grandson of Joseph Smith, Sr.; great-grandnephew of John Smith; grandson of Hyrum Smith; grandnephew of Joseph Smith and William Smith; son of JFS-1; nephew of JS; brother of HMS and JFS-2; 1st cousin, 1 rvd, of HGS; 1st cousin, 2 rvd, of George A. Smith; 2nd cousin, 1 rvd, of JHS and FML's wife; 3rd cousin of GAS and RRL; 6th cousin of GFR, SLR, and OFW; 6th cousin, 1 rvd, of JGK; 7th cousin, 1 rvd, of AOW; 8th cousin of RLP; he and AHC md sisters; brother md GR's daughter 1908; niece md MJB's son 1926; niece md DOM's son 1928; uncle of future patriarch Joseph F. Smith (b. 1899); granduncle of future apostle M. Russell Ballard
Education: Graduate, LDS College 1900
Prior Occupation: Clerk
Business To 1932: Acme Shirt Co.; [American Mutual Building and Loan Co.]; Baldwin Radio Co.; Beneficial Laboratories; Beneficial Life Insurance Co.; Bonneville Oil and Gas Co.; Community Clinic and Dispensary; Consolidated Wagon and Machine Co.; Delray Salt Co. (Chicago-Detroit); Delray Salt Co.; Deseret National Bank; Emigration Canyon Railroad Co.; Emigration Canyon Rock Co.; Fielding Investment Co.; Foreign Lands Corp.; Growers' Market; [Heber J. Grant and Co.]; Home Benefit Building Society; [Home Fire Insurance Company of Utah]; Hotel Utah Operating Co.; [Interstate Guano Co.]; Juab Development Co.; Juab Lake Irrigation Co.; Knight Wool Industries; Knight Woolen Mills; Lambert Manufacturing Co.; Lambert Paper Co.; Lambert Roofing Co.; Layton Sugar Co.; Liberty Investment Co.; Liberty Oil Co.; Mount Nebo Marble Co.; [Mountain Mines Co.]; Mutual Creamery Co.; Nevada Land and Livestock Co.; New Yankee Manufacturing Co.; Oregon-Utah Sugar Co.; Provo Reservoir Co.; Radio Service Corporation of Utah; Riverside Canal Co.; Salt Lake and Utah Railroad Co.; Salt Lake Iron and Steel Co.; Salt Lake Knitting Works; [State Reclamation Co.]; Temple Square Hotel Co.; Thomas D. Dee Memorial Hospital Association; Tip Top Group Mining Co.; Trapper Mining Co.; [Union Chief Mining Co.]; Union Portland Cement Co.; Utah Cereal Food Co.; [Utah Galena Corp.]; Utah Hotel Co.; Utah-Idaho Sugar Co.; Utah Light and Traction Co.; Utah Manufacturers Association; [Utah Oil Refining Co.]; [Utah Power and Light Co.]; [Utah State National Bank]; Verona Water Co.; W. H. Groves LDS Hospital; ZCMI; Zion's Printing and Publishing Co.; [Zion's Savings Bank and Trust Co.]; Zion's Securities Corp.
Social: Bonneville Club 1913; Salt Lake City Rotary Club (1915, vice-president 1919-24); Utah Sons of the American Revolution abt 1917; Salt Lake Chamber of Commerce by 1933; listed in *Utah Since Statehood* 1919, *Utah's Distinguished Personalities* 1933; omitted from *Men of Affairs in the State of Utah* [Press Club of Salt Lake City] 1914

Political/Civic Life: Salt Lake County deputy clerk (1902-07); delegate, Republican conventions (1902, 1904, 1906, 1907, 1916, 1922, 1928); organizer, Prohibition Republican meeting 1909; governor's delegate, International Dry Farming Congress 1912; Salt Lake County Republican Committee 1914; committee, Republican Club 1915; Utah Army Reserve (1916-17); director, Charity Organization Society of Salt Lake City 1923
Prior Religion: LDS
Mormon Experience: Baptized 1887; elder 1897; secretary, Salt Lake Elders' Quorum prayer circle (1900-04); seventy 1904; no pre-hierarchy proselytizing mission; second counselor, Presiding Bishopric 4 December 1907 (high priest 11 December); General Priesthood Committee (1908-22); president, Salt Lake Tabernacle Choir (1908-1938); prayer circle of JFS-2 (1910-13), of RC (1913-15); first counselor, Presiding Bishopric 18 July 1918; prayer circle of JET (1921-25), of JAW (1925-27), of JET (1928-29); vice-president, Zion's Aid Society (1922-32+); unsuccessfully nominated for Presiding Bishop 1925; Sunday School General Board (1928-43); honorably released from Presiding Bishopric 6 April 1938; mission (1938-44)
Death: 6 April 1952, Salt Lake City, Utah
Estate: $22,742.10 appraised and net

GEORGE ALBERT SMITH (GAS)

Birth: 4 April 1870, Salt Lake City, Utah
Parents: JHS and Sarah Farr
Marriage (monogamist): Lucy E. Woodruff 1892 (3 ch); widower 14 years
Hierarchy Relations: Great-grandson of John Smith; great-grandnephew of Joseph Smith, Sr.; grandson of George A. Smith; son of JHS; 1st cousin, 1 rvd, of FML's wife; 1st cousin, 2 rvd, of Hyrum Smith, Joseph Smith, and William Smith; 2nd cousin of RRL; 2nd cousin, 1 rvd, of JS and JFS-1; 2nd cousin, 2 rvd, of AWI's wife; 3rd cousin of DAS, HMS, and JFS-2; 3rd cousin, 1 rvd, of ARI and HGS; 6th cousin of GFR, SLR, and OFW; md Wilford Woodruff's granddaughter and AOW's niece; 1st cousin md SLR; his brother Nicholas G. Smith appointed Assistant to the Twelve 1941; 3rd cousin, 2 rvd, of future Presidency counselor James E. Faust
Education: Brigham Young Academy in Provo (1882-83); University of Deseret (Utah), 1885-89; Sprague Correspondence School of Law (1898-99); trustee, Brigham Young University (1945-51); honorary Doctor of Humanities, University of Utah 1950
Prior Occupation: Clerk
Business To 1932: Amalgamated Sugar Co.; Beneficial Life Insurance Co.; [Big Piney Oil and Refining Co.]; Bonneville Oil and Gas Co.; Consolidated Wagon and Machine Co.; Danielsen Plow Co.; Daynes-Beebe Music Co.; Decker Jewelry Co.; Detachable Plowshare Edge Manufacturing Co.; [Dugway Mining Co.]; Eagle Mercantile Co.; Emigration Canyon Railroad Co.; Equitable Life Insurance Co.; [Golden Eagle Mining Co.]; Heber J. Grant and Co.; Home Benefit Building Society; Home Finding Association of Utah; Home Fire Insurance Company of Utah; Insulation Manufacturing Co.; Kanab Co-operative Stock Co.; Libby Investment Co.; *Millennial Star;* Mutual Creamery Co.; Nancy B. Farr Estate; Pacific Nut Butter Co.; Salt Lake Dramatic Association; Spanish Fork Co-operative Institution; Utah Commercial and Savings Bank; Utah-Idaho Sugar Co.; Utah National Bank; Utah Savings and Trust Co.; Utah Savings and Trust Company Building; Utah Savings and Trust Safety Deposit Company; [Utah State Gold Mining Co.]; Utah State National Bank; Utah Sugar Co.; W. H. Groves LDS Hospital; Woodruff Family Association; ZCMI
Social: Utah Sons of the American Revolution 1900 (president 1918-20); charter member, Sons and Daughters of the Pioneers of Utah 1907; Salt Lake Commercial Club by 1911; vice-president general, Sons of the American Revolution (1922-27); Salt Lake Chamber of Commerce 1922 (withdrew membership for "financial reasons" 1928); So-

ciety of Mayflower Descendants; listed in *Blue Book* for Salt Lake City (1901-07), *Utah As It Is* 1904, *Utah's Distinguished Personalities* 1933, *Who's Who in America* 1934, *Who's Who In the Clergy* 1935, biographies of *Utah: A Centennial History* 1949, *National Cyclopaedia of American Biography* 1954, *Faith of Our Pioneer Fathers* 1956, *Dictionary of American Biography* 1977; omitted from *Men of Affairs in the State of Utah* [Press Club of Salt Lake City] 1914

<u>Political/Civic Life:</u> Republican; unsuccessfully sought appointment as Salt Lake City postmaster 1897; governor's delegate, Tennessee Centennial Exposition 1897; sergeant, Utah National Guard (1897-98); delegate, Republican conventions (1898, 1899, 1906, 1907, 1908, 1909, 1912); receiver, U.S. Land Office (1898-1903); delegate, National Convention of Republican Clubs 1900; declined Republican candidacy for Utah legislature 1902; speaker, Republican rallies 1904; vice-president, Society For the Aid of the Sightless (1904-32+); vice-president, International Irrigation Congress (1914-16, president 1916, 1918); vice-president, Utah Federation of Prohibition and Betterment Leagues (1916-18); Utah Council of Defense (1917-18); president, International Dry Farming Congress (1917, 1918); chair, Utah Committee for Armenian and Syrian Relief (1918-19); executive committee, Utah League to Enforce Peace (1918-19); delegate, Mountain Congress, national League to Enforce Peace 1919, International Housing Convention 1919; vice-president, Western States Reclamation Association (1921-23); director, American Flag Association 1923; director, Charity Organization Society of Salt Lake City 1923; executive committee, American Farm Congress 1925; life member, Oregon Trail Memorial Association 1926; president, Utah Pioneer Trails and Landmarks Association (1930-45); national executive board, Boy Scouts of America (1932-51); Silver Buffalo award, Boy Scouts of America 1934; director, Oregon Trail Memorial Association 1937; Utah Centennial Exposition Committee (1938-47); home was burglarized 1945; Certificate of Civic Service, Fraternal Order of Eagles 1948; Award of Merit, U.S. Treasury Department 1950

<u>Prior Religion:</u> LDS

<u>Mormon Experience:</u> Baptized 1878; patriarchal blessing 1884 promised he would be apostle and prophet; elder 1888; mission (1891, 1892-94); seventy 1892; prayer circle of JHS (1894-1906); stake YMMIA superintendent (1902-03); high priest and apostle 8 October 1903; YMMIA General Board (1904-34); president, own prayer circle (1906-26); Religion Class General Board (1906-22); inactive as general authority (1909-13) due to nervous breakdown (2 months in sanitarium); mission president (1919-21); YMMIA General Superintendent (1921-34); Correlation Committee 1931; president, Quorum of the Twelve Apostles 1 July 1943; set apart as president of the church 21 May 1945

<u>Death:</u> 4 April 1951, Salt Lake City, Utah

<u>Estate:</u> $83,080.14 appraised; $80,676.03 net

HYRUM G[IBBS] SMITH (HGS)

<u>Birth:</u> 8 July 1879, South Jordan, Salt Lake Co., Utah

<u>Parents:</u> Hyrum F. Smith and Annie M. Gibbs

<u>Marriage</u> (monogamist): Martha E. Gee 1904 (8 ch)

<u>Hierarchy Relations:</u> Great-great-grandson of Joseph Smith, Sr.; great-great-grandnephew of John Smith; great-grandson of Hyrum Smith; great-grandnephew of Joseph Smith and William Smith; grandson of JS; grandnephew of JFS-1; 1st cousin, 1 rvd, of DAS, HMS, JFS-2; 2nd cousin, 2 rvd, of FML's wife; 3rd cousin, 1 rvd, of RRL and GAS; 6th cousin, 1 rvd, of GFR and SLR; wife was Salmon Gee's great-granddaughter; father of future (and last) patriarch Eldred G. Smith

<u>Education:</u> Graduate, Normal Department, Brigham Young Academy in Provo 1900; D.D.S., University of Southern California 1911

<u>Prior Occupation:</u> School teacher, dentist

Business To 1932: ?
Social: Utah Sons of the American Revolution abt 1917; listed in *Utah: The Storied Domain* 1932; omitted from *Men of Affairs in the State of Utah* [Press Club of Salt Lake City] 1914
Political/Civic Life: Republican; delegate, Republican county convention 1912
Prior Religion: LDS
Mormon Experience: Baptized 1891; elder 1901; seventy 1907; mission (1908-09); branch president (1911-12); high priest and set apart as "Presiding Patriarch" 9 May 1912; Sunday School General Board (1912-20); YMMIA General Board (1912-32); Religion Class General Board (1918-22); director, Genealogical Society of Utah (1918-32)
Death: 4 February 1932, Salt Lake City, Utah
Estate: $250 appraised and net

HYRUM M[ACK] SMITH (HMS)
Birth: 21 March 1872, Salt Lake City, Utah
Parents: JFS-1 and Edna Lambson
Marriage (monogamist): Ida E. Bowman 1895 (5 ch)
Hierarchy Relations: Great-grandson of Joseph Smith, Sr.; great-grandnephew of John Smith; grandson of Hyrum Smith; grandnephew of Joseph Smith and William Smith; son of JFS-1; nephew of JS; brother of DAS and JFS-2; 1st cousin, 1 rvd, of HGS; 1st cousin, 2 rvd, of George A. Smith; 2nd cousin, 1 rvd, of JHS and FML's wife; 3rd cousin of GAS and RRL; 6th cousin of GFR, SLR, and OFW; 6th cousin, 1 rvd, of JGK; 7th cousin, 1 rvd, of AOW; 8th cousin of RLP; brother md GR's daughter 1908; father of future patriarch Joseph F. Smith (b. 1899); grandfather of future apostle M. Russell Ballard
Education: Graduate, LDS College 1894
Prior Occupation: Clerk
Business To 1932: Deseret Gymnasium; Fielding Investment Co.; Juab Development Co.; Lewiston Sugar Co.; *Millennial Star;* Nevada Land and Livestock Co.; Salt Lake and Los Angeles Railway Co.; Sterling Mining and Milling Co.; Utah National Bank; Utah State National Bank; Utah Sulphur Co.; ZCMI; Zion's Savings Bank and Trust Co.
Social: Director, Timpanogas Rod Club (1917-18); listed in *Prophets and Patriarchs of the Church* 1902, *Utah As It Is* 1904; omitted from *Men of Affairs in the State of Utah* [Press Club of Salt Lake City] 1914
Political/Civic Life: Delegate, Republican conventions (1893, 1909)
Prior Religion: LDS
Mormon Experience: Baptized 1880; elder by 1895; mission (1895-98); seventy 1898; stake mission (1900-01); high priest and apostle 24 October 1901; YMMIA General Board (1901-18); Religion Class General Board (1901-18); assistant General Superintendent of Religion Classes (1906-18); mission president (1913-16); Church Board of Education (1917-18)
Death: 23 January 1918, Salt Lake City, Utah
Estate: No record

JOHN SMITH (JS)
Birth: 22 September 1832, Kirtland, Geauga Co., Ohio
Parents: Hyrum Smith and Jerusha Barden
Marriage (polygamist after appointment): Helen M. Fisher 1853 (9 ch); Nancy M. Lemmon 1857 (1 ch), separated 1860s (JS scratched her name from family Bible, unsuccessfully sought church divorce 1886, remained separated from her 40 years); unmarried widower last 4 years of his life
Hierarchy Relations: Grandson of Joseph Smith, Sr.; grandnephew of John Smith; son of Hyrum Smith; brother of JFS-1; nephew of Joseph Smith and William Smith; uncle of DAS, HMS, JFS-2; 1st cousin, 1 rvd, of George A. Smith; 2nd cousin of JHS and FML's wife; 2nd cousin, 1 rvd, of RRL and GAS; 5th cousin of FDR; 5th cousin, 1 rvd,

of Heber C. Kimball, GFR, and OFW; 6th cousin of JGK; 6th cousin, 1 rvd, of Orson Pratt, Parley P. Pratt, LS, Wilford Woodruff, Brigham Young, and Joseph Young; 7th cousin of AOW, BY-JR, JWY, JAY, SBY, and MWM's wife; 2nd cousin md Wilford Woodruff's son 1867; 2nd cousin md FML 1869; nephew md GR's daughter 1908; nephew md HJG's daughter 1910; grandfather of his immediate successor HGS; granduncle of future patriarch Joseph F. Smith (b. 1899); great-grandfather of future (and last) patriarch Eldred G. Smith

Education: Negligible

Prior Occupation: Farmer

Business To 1932: ?

Social: Listed in *Blue Book* for Salt Lake City 1901, *Prophets and Patriarchs of the Church* 1902, *Utah As It Is* 1904; omitted from *Biographical Record of Salt Lake City and Vicinity* 1902, from biographies in *History of Utah* 1904, from *Pioneers and Prominent Men of Utah* 1914

Political/Civic Life: Mormon Battalion private (1846-47); Utah's Nauvoo Legion cavalry 1849 (to protect Salt Lake City from Indian attacks); ceremonial escort battalion, "Lifeguards" (1855-59); probate judge (1857-58); sergeant-at-arms, Utah legislature (upper chamber, 1861-62, 1865-67; House of Representatives, 1864-65, 1876-82); watchman, Utah House of Representatives 1874; Republican; pre-1891 polygamy pardoned and re-enfranchised by U.S. president's general amnesties (1893, 1894)

Prior Religion: LDS

Mormon Experience: Baptized 1841; elder and endowed 1846 (age 13); no pre-hierarchy proselytizing mission; ordained and set apart "to be the first in the Church of Jesus Christ among the Patriarchs" 18 February 1855; prayer circle of First Presidency and Quorum of Twelve Apostles (1856-58, 1874-85), of John Taylor (1858-74); Brigham Young asked George A. Smith to become Presiding Patriarch so that JS could be dropped from office (the apostle declined 19 March 1862); mission (1862-64); second anointing 28 January 1867; not presented for sustaining vote of general conference April 1873 and nearly replaced by brother JFS-1 (who declined position) October 1875; president, church-wide "Quorum of Patriarchs" 31 October 1877 (declined to function for 25 years); only general authority who objected 22 April 1880 to canonization of Wilford Woodruff's recent revelation on plural marriage; described by JFS-1 as unworthy to participate in washing of feet ceremony (School of Prophets) and unworthy of patriarch's office 12 October 1883; learned by rumor (rather than by seeking to enter Endowment House) that had been barred from temple ordinances 1887 (JFS-1 had been informed); warned publicly by LDS president Wilford Woodruff 7 October 1894 that he would be released as patriarch if continued to use alcohol and tobacco; set apart his brother as new LDS church president 17 October 1901; voting participant, temple council of First Presidency and Quorum of Twelve (1901-11); sustained as "prophet, seer, and revelator" 6 October 1902; allegedly conferred authority to perform polygamous marriages on John W. Woolley 1911 (unlikely because of JS lifelong hostility toward polygamy)

Death: 6 November 1911, Salt Lake City, Utah

Estate: No record

JOHN HENRY SMITH (JHS)

Birth: 18 September 1848, Carbunca, Pottawattamie Co., Iowa

Parents: George A. Smith and Sarah A. Libby (Smith)

Marriage (polygamist before appointment): Sarah Farr 1866 (11 ch); Josephine Groesbeck 1877 (8 ch)

Hierarchy Relations: Son of George A. Smith; father of GAS; grandson of John Smith; grandnephew of Joseph Smith, Sr.; 1st cousin, 1 rvd, of Hyrum Smith, Joseph Smith, and William Smith; 1st cousin of FML's wife; 2nd cousin of JS and JFS-1; 2nd cousin, 1 rvd, of DAS, HMS, and JFS-2; 3rd cousin of FML; 5th cousin of FDR; 5th cousin, 1 rvd, of GFR; 6th cousin of JGK; his mother a former wife of William Smith; he and John Taylor's son md sisters; 2nd cousin of Wilford Woodruff's daughter-in-law; wife was 1st cousin of MT's wife; he and JM md sisters; wife was niece of wives of Heber C. Kimball and Brigham Young; wife was 2nd cousin, 1 rvd, of AWI's wife; wife was 6th cousin, 1 rvd, of LS; son md OFW's daughter 1906; father of future Assistant to the Twelve Nicholas G. Smith

Education: Common schools; trustee, Young University at Salt Lake City (1891-95), Brigham Young Academy (University 1901-11)

Prior Occupation: Clerk

Business To 1932: Bear River Water Co.; Beneficial Life Insurance Co.; Cannon, Grant and Co.; Church Onyx Mines; Consolidated Wagon and Machine Co.; Co-operative Furniture Co.; Co-operative Wagon and Machine Co.; Deseret Investment Co.; Deseret Tanning and Manufacturing Co.; Deseret Telegraph Co.; [Duquesne Oil and Gas Co.]; Emigration Canyon Railroad Co.; The Enquirer Co.; Equitable Life Insurance Co.; Fremont County Sugar Co.; Grant Brothers Livery and Transfer Co.; Grant Gold Mining Co.; Grant, Odell and Co.; Grant Soap Co.; Groesbeck Co.; Heber J. Grant and Co.; Home Fire Insurance Company of Utah; Home Life Insurance Company of Utah; Idaho Sugar Co.; Intermountain Cement and Brick Co.; Kanab Co-operative Stock Co.; Mexican Colonization and Agricultural Co.; *Millennial Star;* National Savings and Trust Co.; Nevada Land and Livestock Co.; [North Jordan Irrigation Co.]; Salt Lake and Los Angeles Railway Co.; Salt Lake City Water and Electric Power Co.; Salt Lake Dramatic Association; Salt Lake Gas Co.; Salt Lake Knitting Works; [*Salt Lake Times*]; Saltair Beach Co.; Sanpete and Sevier Sugar Co.; Shoshone Power Co.; Standard Publishing Co.; [Sugar City Improvement Co.]; Sugar City Townsite Co.; Tobasco-Utah Development Co.; Utah Home Telephone Co.; Utah-Idaho Sugar Co.; Utah Independent Telephone Co.; Utah-Mexican Rubber Co.; Utah National Bank; Utah Sugar Co.; Western Idaho Sugar Co.; ZCMI; Zion's Savings Bank and Trust Co.

Social: Listed in *Blue Book* for Salt Lake City (1895-1907), *Herringshaw's Encyclopedia of American Biography* 1898, *Prophets and Patriarchs of the Church* 1902, *Biographical Record of Salt Lake City and Vicinity* 1902, *Utah As It Is* 1904, *Herringshaw's American Blue-Book of Biography* 1915, *National Cyclopaedia of American Biography* 1918; omitted from biographies in *History of Utah* 1904

Political/Civic Life: Assistant clerk, Utah House of Representatives (1870-72); Republican 1872; postmaster, Terrace, Utah (1872-74); alternate delegate, LDS People's Party territorial convention, 1876; Salt Lake City council (1876-82); delegate, People's Party conventions (1877, 1878, 1879, 1880, 1881, 1889); Council of Fifty initiation 10 April 1880; sergeant-at-arms, People's Party territorial convention 1880; unsuccessfully asked Council of Fifty to adopt national Democratic Party as the church's party 1882; Utah legislature (1882-83); arrested and tried for cohabitation 1885 (charges dropped); temporary central committee, Utah Republican Party 1891; Republican League of Utah and Central Republican Club of Utah 1891; delegate, Republican conventions (1891, 1892, 1893, 1894, 1896, 1898, 1900); defeated as candidate for chaplain, Utah House of Representatives 1892; pre-1891 polygamy pardoned and re-enfranchised by U.S. president's general amnesties (1893, 1894); declined nomination for Utah territorial delegate to U.S. House of Representatives 1893; delegate, National Republican League convention 1893; governor's delegate, Trans-Mississippi Commercial Congress (1893, 1894, 1897, annually 1899-1910), National Irrigation Congress (1894, 1895, 1900, annually 1902-10), International Irrigation Congress 1895; Republican delegate and president, Utah State Constitutional Convention 1895; served on jury 1896; declined to become candidate for U.S. Senate or U.S. House of

Representatives 1896; required reluctant HJG to perform two polygamous marriages in violation of Mexican law 1897; unsuccessful Republican candidate for U.S. Senate 1898; instructed JWT to perform six polygamous marriages in violation of Mexican law 1898; lobbied nation's leaders against effort to have constitutional amendment prohibiting polygamy 1900; declined unsolicited election as president, Utah League of Republican Clubs 1900; vice-president, Trans-Mississippi Commercial Congress 1900 (president, 1901-02; vice-president, 1903); lobbied nation's leaders against renewed effort for constitutional amendment prohibiting polygamy 1902; chaplain, Utah Republican convention 1902; risked perjury indictment by testifying before U.S. Senate 1904 that he had no knowledge of authorized plural marriages after 1890 Manifesto; director, Utah Peace Society (1908-11); governor's delegate, National Farmland Congress 1909, National Civic Confederation 1910, Trans-Missouri Dry Farming Congress 1910, International Dry Farming Congress 1911; Utah State Capitol Commission 1911; governor's welcoming committee for Republican president William H. Taft 1911

Prior Religion: LDS

Mormon Experience: Baptized 1856; elder 1864; seventy abt 1866; ward bishopric counselor, without high priest ordination as one of the "seventy apostles" (1867-69); mission (1874-75); high priest 1875; ward bishop (1875-80); high council (1876-82); appointment as stake president blocked by JFS-1 April 1880; apostle 27 October 1880; second anointing 27 April 1881; mission president (1882-85); while speaking at Manti temple dedication 1888 some saw halo of light around his head; president, own prayer circle (1894-1911); reported 1898 he had seen and heard Jesus Christ; YMMIA General Board (1898-1911); promised by Mormon 1901 he would be counselor, First Presidency; Church Literature Revision Committee (1901-02); examined 1902 the Jupiter talisman that once belonged to Joseph Smith, Jr.; Sunday School General Board (1908-11); New Polygamy Investigation Committee (1909-10); second counselor, First Presidency 7 April 1910

Death: 13 October 1911, Salt Lake City, Utah

Estate: $22,092.49 appraised; $19,210.00 net

JOSEPH F[IELDING] SMITH (JFS-1)

Birth: 13 November 1838, Far West, Caldwell Co., Missouri

Parents: Hyrum Smith and Mary Fielding

Marriage (polygamist prior to appointment): Levira A. C. Smith 1859 (no ch), church divorce 1867, civil divorce 1869; Julina Lambson 1866 (11 ch); Sarah E. Richards 1868 (11 ch); Edna Lambson 1871 (10 ch); Alice A. Kimball (Rich) 1883 (4 ch); Mary T. Schwartz 1884 (7 ch)

Hierarchy Relations: Son of Hyrum Smith; step-son of Heber C. Kimball; brother of JS; step-brother of JGK; father of DAS, HMS, and JFS-2; nephew of Joseph Smith and William Smith; grandson of Joseph Smith, Sr.; grandnephew of John Smith; 1st cousin, 1 rvd, of George A. Smith; 2nd cousin of JHS; 2nd cousin, 1 rvd, of RRL and GAS; 5th cousin of FDR; 5th cousin, 1 rvd, of Heber C. Kimball, GFR, and OFW; 6th cousin of JGK; 6th cousin, 1 rvd, of Orson Pratt, Parley P. Pratt, LS, Wilford Woodruff, Brigham Young, and Joseph Young; 7th cousin of AOW, BY-JR, JWY, JAY, SBY; nephew of John Taylor's divorced wife; 2nd cousin md Wilford Woodruff's son 1867; md (1868) Willard Richards's daughter and FDR's 1st cousin; 2nd cousin md FML 1869; md (1883) Heber C. Kimball's daughter and JGK's sister; md (1884) John Taylor's niece and 1st cousin of JWT and WWT; wife's 1st cousins, 1 rvd, were GFR and SLR; wife's 2nd cousin, 1 rvd, was LEY; 7th cousin md MWM; son md AHC's sister-in-law 1901; son md GR's daughter 1908; son md HJG's daughter 1910; grandfather of future patriarch Joseph F. Smith (b. 1899); great-grandfather of future apostle M. Russell Ballard

Education: Common schools; regent, University of Deseret (Utah), 1880-82; trustee,

Young University at Salt Lake City (1891-95), Brigham Young College in Logan (1898-1918), Brigham Young Academy (University 1901-18)
Prior Occupation: Clerk
Business To 1932: [Alaska Ice and Storage Co.]; Alberta Colonization Co.; Amalgamated Sugar Co.; [Amazon Mining Co.]; Armstrong, Winder and Co.; [Bank of Moroni]; [Bank of Randolf]; Bar-Ka-Two Stock Co.; Bear River Water Co.; [Beck Tunnel Consolidated Mining Co.]; Beneficial Life Insurance Co.; Big Cottonwood Power Co.; Bullion, Beck and Champion Mining Co.; Burke Mining Co.; [Calder's Park Co.]; Cannon, Grant and Co.; [Casto Springs Irrigation Co.]; Cedar and Iron Railroad Co.; Cement Securities Co.; Church Onyx Mines; [Cochrane Ranch Live Stock Co.]; [Colorado Consolidated Mines Co.]; Consolidated Wagon and Machine Co.; Co-operative Wagon and Machine Co.; Davis County Co-operative Co.; [Daynes-Beebe Music Co.]; [Daynes Jewelry Co.]; Delray Salt Co.; [Denver and Salt Lake Railroad Co.]; [Deseret Building Society]; Deseret Gold and Silver Mining Co.; [Deseret Investment Co.]; [Deseret News Bookstore]; Deseret News Co.; Deseret Savings Bank; Deseret Telegraph Co.; Enamel Brick and Concrete Company of Utah; [Equitable Life Insurance Co.]; [Farmers and Stockgrowers Bank]; First National Bank of Logan; [Franklin Milling Co.]; Fremont County Sugar Co.; [Grande Ronde Lumber Co.]; Grant Gold Mining Co.; Grant, Odell and Co.; Grass Creek Coal Co.; Grass Creek Terminal Railway Co.; [Great Western Collection Agency]; [Grizzly Mining Co.]; Hampton, Jones and Co.; Heber J. Grant and Co.; Home Benefit Building Society; Home Fire Insurance Company of Utah; Home Life Insurance Company of Utah; Idaho Sugar Co.; *Improvement Era;* Inland Crystal Salt Co.; Inland Railway Co.; Inter-Mountain Salt Co.; [Iosepa Agricultural and Stock Co.]; Iron Manufacturing Company of Utah; [Jumbo Plaster and Cement Co.]; *Juvenile Instructor;* [Kimball and Richards Co.]; Knight Ranching Co.; Knight Sugar Co.; Knight Woolen Mills; Lee's Ferry; [Lucky Deposit Mining Co.]; *Millennial Star;* [Mount Hood Railroad Co.]; [National City Bank of Salt Lake City]; [Nevada Sulphur Co.]; Ogden Woolen Mills Co.; [Oregon Lumber Co.]; [Oregon Portland Cement Co.]; Perpetual Emigrating Fund Co.; Pioneer Electric Power Co.; Provo Woolen Mills Co.; Rexburg Milling Co.; [Rio Virgen Raisen and Fruit Growing Co.]; Salt Lake and Los Angeles Railway Co.; Salt Lake and Pacific Railroad Co.; Salt Lake Dramatic Association; [Salt Lake Iron and Steel Co.]; Salt Lake Knitting Works; Saltair Beach Co.; Saltair Railway Co.; Sanpete and Sevier Sugar Co.; [San Vincente Lumber Co.]; [Silver Brothers Iron Works Co.]; Social Hall Society; State Bank of Utah; [South Jordan Canal Co.]; Sterling Mining and Milling Co.; Sugar City Townsite Co.; [Sumpter Valley Railroad Co.]; [Sundown and LaPlata Mining Co.]; [Tintic Drain Tunnel Co.]; [Torbane Hill Mining Co.]; Touring Salt Lake City Co.; Trapper Mining Co.; [Union Fuel Co.]; Union Light and Power Co.; Union Pacific Railroad Co.; Union Portland Cement Co.; United Order of Zion; Utah and California Railway Co.; Utah and Pacific Improvement Co.; Utah and Pacific Railroad Co.; Utah and Pleasant Valley Railroad Co.; [Utah Bond and Share Co.]; Utah Co.; Utah Eastern Railroad Co.; Utah Hotel Co.; Utah-Idaho Sugar Co.; [Utah Lake Irrigation Co.]; Utah Light and Power Co.; Utah Light and Railway Co.; Utah Loan and Trust Co.; Utah-Mexican Rubber Co.; Utah National Bank; [Utah Oil Refining Co.]; Utah Power Co.; Utah State National Bank; Utah Sugar Co.; [W. J. White Chicle Vending Co.]; [Wandamere Amusement Co.]; Wasatch Coal Mining Co.; Wasatch Land and Improvement Co.; Wasatch Lawn Cemetery Association; [West States Mortgage Loan Co.]; Western Idaho Sugar Co.; [Zion's Aid Society]; ZCMI; Zion's Savings Bank and Trust Co.
Social: Salt Lake Commercial Club by 1915; listed in *Blue Book* for Salt Lake City (1895-1911), *National Cyclopaedia of American Biography* 1897, *Herringshaw's Encyclopedia of American Biography* 1898, *Who's Who in America* 1899, *Prophets and Patriarchs of the Church* 1902, *Biographical Record of Salt Lake City and Vicinity* 1902, *Financial Red Book*

of America (1903-07), *Utah As It Is* 1904, *Men of Affairs in the State of Utah* [Press Club of Salt Lake City] 1914, *Herringshaw's American Blue-Book of Biography* 1915, *Who's Who in the Northwest* 1917, *Utah Since Statehood* 1919, *Faith of Our Pioneer Fathers* 1956

Political/Civic Life: Sergeant-at-arms, Utah legislature's upper chamber (1858-59); Republican 1864; Utah legislature (1865-75); legislature, State of Deseret's "ghost government" (1865-70); Salt Lake City council (1866-84); Council of Fifty initiation 25 January 1867; Provo city council (1868-69); confessed to assault and battery 1872 (charges dropped 1873, neighbor-victim withdrew complaint); nominating committee, LDS People's Party (1870, 1872, 1873, 1874); delegate, People's Party conventions (1870-76, 1881, convention vice-president 1876); territorial central committee, People's Party (1876-77); Utah legislature (1880-82); president, Utah legislature's upper chamber (1882-82); delegate and president, Utah's unsuccessful statehood convention 1882; indicted for cohabitation 1885 (avoided arrest by going on foreign mission), indicted again 1889 (evaded arrest until U.S. president pardoned him 1891); informed that JFS-1 was to be indicted for cohabitation, First Presidency and Twelve voted 20 October 1893 to bribe Utah's non-LDS attorney general who dropped indictment; re-enfranchised by U.S. president's general pardon 1894; speaker, Utah Republican victory rally 1894; authorized AHC to seek a plural wife 1894 (performed this marriage in violation of Utah law 1896); delegate, Independent Republican (silver) convention 1896; authorized polygamous marriages (1897-1904) performed by AWI, SBY, and stake patriarch in Mexico, by MFC in United States, by stake patriarch in Canada; sat on stand, Republican state convention 1900; first LDS president to testify before U.S. Senate 1904 (risked indictment for perjury by giving misleading testimony about post-1890 polygamy); authorized about 10 polygamous marriages (1904-07); Beehive House bedroom burglarized while he and wife slept 1905; indicted for cohabitation, pleaded guilty, and paid fine 1906; testified before U.S. Senate about Sugar Trust 1911; Utah governor's welcoming committee for Republican President William H. Taft 1911; editorialized in church magazine for reelection of President Taft 1912

Prior Religion: LDS

Mormon Experience: Baptized 1850; elder and endowed 1854 (age 16); mission (1854-58, and vivid dream of Celestial Kingdom and deceased Joseph Smith); seventy 1858; high priest 1859; stake high council (1859-61, 1866-67); prayer circle of George A. Smith (1859-65); mission (1860-63); told by Heber C. Kimball 1864 that he would become an apostle; mission president (1864, 1874-75); as non-general authority, prayer circle of First Presidency and Quorum of Twelve Apostles June 1865; apostle and assistant counselor, First Presidency 1 July 1866 (without public acknowledgement); second anointing 4 January 1867; admitted, Quorum of Twelve 8 October 1867 (BY-JR entered Twelve 1868, but ranked ahead of JFS-1 because of earlier ordination as apostle); assistant Trustee-in-Trust (1873-75); declined office of Presiding Patriarch 8 October 1875; mission president 1877 as exile by Brigham Young for criticizing JWY; after Young's death, sustained as "prophet, seer, and revelator," first time 6 October 1877; nominated by DHW to be new church president (October 1877, October 1880, March 1888) but the other apostles declined all such proposals for the junior apostle; assistant Trustee-in-Trust (1877-80); Church Auditing Committee (1878-87); probably the "young man" in the Twelve proposed by Orson Pratt 7 October 1880 to be church president; second counselor, First Presidency, without being set apart (10 October 1880-25 July 1887); counselor, YMMIA General Superintendency (1880-1901); publicly designated by Wilford Woodruff at stake conference 4 February 1881 as a future church president; foreign mission with wife to avoid arrest (1885-87); proposed by HJG to be new church president 25 July 1887; second counselor, First Presidency, without being set apart (7 April 1889-2 September 1898); woman and FML both saw unearthly light over head of JFS-1 in Salt Lake temple 13 April 1893; Church Board of Education

(1893-1918); Sunday School General Board (1898-1918); second counselor, First Presidency 13 September 1898 (first time set apart); temple president (1898-1911); ranked ahead of BY-JR 5 April 1900, first time in 32 years; first counselor, First Presidency 6 October 1901 (not set apart nor functioned before LS died), and stake president saw JFS-1 transfigured into image of church president LS; set apart as church president by Presiding Patriarch JS 17 October 1901 (publicly sustained 10 November 1901); General Superintendent, YMMIA and Sunday Schools (1901-18); testified before U.S. Senate 1904 that he had received no revelations as church president; voted against by church member October 1907 because of criminal conviction for cohabitation; dictated written revelation to restructure church finances 1918; vision of God, Jesus Christ, and spirits of deceased 1918
Death: 19 November 1918, Salt Lake City, Utah
Estate: $415,180.35 appraised and net

JOSEPH FIELDING SMITH [JR.] (JFS-2)
Birth: 19 July 1876, Salt Lake City, Utah
Parents: JFS-1 and Julina Lambson
Marriage (monogamist): Louie E. Shurtliff 1898 (2 ch); widower for 7 months; Ethel G. Reynolds 1908 (9 ch); widower for 8 months; Jessie E. Evans 1938 (no ch); widower for last 11 months of his life
Hierarchy Relations: Great-grandson of Joseph Smith, Sr.; great-grandnephew of John Smith; grandson of Hyrum Smith; grandnephew of Joseph Smith and William Smith; son of JFS-1; nephew of JS; brother of DAS and HMS; 1st cousin, 1 rvd, of HGS; 1st cousin, 2 rvd, of George A. Smith; 2nd cousin, 1 rvd, of JHS and FML's wife; 3rd cousin of RRL and GAS; 6th cousin of GFR, SLR, and OFW; 6th cousin, 1 rvd, of JGK; 7th cousin, 1 rvd, of AOW; 8th cousin of RLP; niece md MJB's son 1926; niece md DOM's son 1928; his nephew Joseph F. Smith (b. 1899) became church patriarch 1942; his son-in-law Bruce R. McConkie became President of Seventy 1946 and apostle 1972; granduncle of future apostle M. Russell Ballard
Education: LDS College (1896-98); trustee, Brigham Young University (1912-72); honorary doctor of letters, Brigham Young University 1951
Prior Occupation: Clerk
Business To 1932: Beneficial Life Insurance Co.; Consolidated Salt and Refining Co.; [Daynes-Beebe Music Co.]; Deseret Building Society; Fielding Investment Co.; [Heber J. Grant and Co.]; Independent Electric Co.; Inland Crystal Salt Co.; [McFarland, Inc.]; [Martin Coal Co.]; [Medical Arts Building]; [Tintic Drain Tunnel Co.]; *Utah Genealogical and Historical Magazine;* [Utah Hotel Co.]; [Utah-Idaho Sugar Co.]; [Utah Power and Light Co.]; [ZCMI]; Zion's Savings Bank and Trust Co.
Social: Utah Sons of the American Revolution abt 1917; Philosophical Society of Great Britain; listed in *Utah: The Storied Domain* 1932, *Utah's Distinguished Personalities* 1933, *Who's Who in America* 1958; omitted from *Men of Affairs in the State of Utah* [Press Club of Salt Lake City] 1914
Political/Civic Life: Delegate, Republican city convention 1901; notary public, Salt Lake County 1905; organizer, Prohibition Republican meeting 1909; delegate, Citizens Party city and county conventions 1909; Utah National Guard honorary colonel 1955, honorary brigadier-general 1962, and Minuteman Award 1964
Prior Religion: LDS
Mormon Experience: Baptized 1884; patriarchal blessing 1896 promised he would be presiding church leader; elder 1897; seventy 1899; mission (1899-1901); stake missionary (1901-10); YMMIA General Board (1903-19); president, local seventy's quorum (1903-04); high priest 1904; stake high council (1904-10); assistant Church Historian (1906-21); Genealogical Society of Utah; vice-president (1907-09, 1925-32+), Genea-

logical Society of Utah (secretary-treasurer 1907-23; director only 1909-25); Religion Class General Board (1909-22); told by mission president Ben E. Rich 1909 that he would become an apostle; apostle 7 April 1910; president, own prayer circle (1910-16); temple presidency counselor (1915-35); Church Board of Education (1917-72); first assistant, Religion Class General Superintendency (1919-22); Church Historian (1921-70); Temple Ceremony Revision Committee (1923-27); Committee on Revision of Seventies' Work (1923-26); Sunday School General Board (1927-35); Melchizedek Priesthood Committee (1928-37); Literature Censorship Committee (1940-44); chair, Publications Committee (1944-53); temple president (1945-49); Temple Ordinance Committee (1946-47); acting president, Quorum of the Twelve Apostles 30 September 1950 (president, 9 April 1951); acted as "mouth" when Quorum of the Twelve "ordained" new church president 9 April 1951, first time in LDS history (see *The Mormon Hierarchy: Origins of Power,* 252-53); Missionary Committee (1951-63; chair, 1954-58); chair, Committee for Filming Temple Ordinances (1953-55); chair, General Priesthood Committee (1961-63); chair, Priesthood Missionary Committee (1963-65); assistant counselor, First Presidency (29 October 1965-18 January 1970); "ordained and set apart," president of the church 23 January 1970
Death: 2 July 1972, Salt Lake City, Utah
Estate: $509,484.69 appraised; $509,029.59 net

***Nicholas G. Smith (1881-1945)
Ordained stake patriarch 19 June 1932, Smith was also authorized to bless missionaries "and people who come in from outside of stakes" while there was no church patriarch. He was not in patriarchal line of descent from Joseph Smith Sr. and did not have general authority status. He continued in that position until bedridden with heart condition in 1934, at which time First Presidency appointed John M. Whitaker to serve as Acting Patriarch. Neither was ever sustained as patriarch by general conference. Smith became an Assistant to the Quorum of Twelve Apostles in 1941.

REED SMOOT (RS)
Birth: 10 January 1862, Salt Lake City, Utah
Parents: Abraham O. Smoot and Anne K. Morrison
Marriage (monogamist): Alpha M. Eldredge 1884 (7 ch); widower for 20 months; Alice Taylor (Sheets) 1930 (no ch)
Hierarchy Relations: 1st cousin of Wilford Woodruff's wife; 1st cousin, 1 rvd, of AOW; brother-in-law of OFW; he and HJG's brother md sisters; sister md son of DHW, brother of RSW, and brother-in-law of HJG and SBY; son md CWN's daughter 1910
Education: Graduate, Brigham Young Academy in Provo 1879; trustee, Brigham Young Academy (University), 1893-1938
Prior Occupation: Businessman
Business To 1932: [Albion Mining Co.]; [Allied Mines and Exploration Co.]; Almo Mining and Milling Co.; [American Crystal Sugar Co.]; [American Fork Co-operative Institution]; American Institute of Provo; Auto Securities Co.; [Automatic Transmission Corporation of America]; Bank of Heber City; Baxter, Straw and Storrs Construction Co.; Big Indian Copper Co.; [Carisa Copper and Gold Mining Co.]; Church Onyx Mines; Clark, Eldredge (and) Co.; Commercial Bank of Spanish Fork; Continental Life Insurance and Investment Co.; Decker Mortgage Co.; Deseret National Bank; Deseret Savings Bank; [Dixon-Taylor-Russell Co.]; [Dragon Consolidated Mining Co.]; [Electric Bond and Share Co.]; The Electric Co.; Empire Construction Co.; [Empire Mines Co.]; First National Bank of Provo; [George E. Merrill Co.]; Gold Chain Mining Co.; Golden Chariot Mining Co.; [Goshen Valley Irrigation Co.]; Grand Central Mining Co.; Grand River Toll Road Co.; Great Basin Oil Co.; [Greely Gold and Silver Mines Co.]; Guardian Casualty and Guaranty Co.; Harold R. Smoot Co.; Harold R. Smoot Se-

curities Co.; *Herald-Republican;* Herald Republican Publishing Co.; Home Fire Insurance Company of Utah; Ibex Gold Mining Co.; Idaho-Utah Electric Co.; Iron King Consolidated Mining Co.; [Knight Woolen Mills]; [Lang-Wall, Inc.]; [Lion Hill Mining Co.]; [Logan Land and Drainage Co.]; [Monroe State Bank]; [Mountain Dell Consolidated Mining Co.]; [Mountain States Petroleum Co.]; National City Bank of Salt Lake City; New Bodie Mining Co.; Northern Spy Mining Co.; Pacific Provision Co.; [Post Publishing Co.]; Provo Book and Stationery Co.; Provo Canning Co.; Provo Commercial and Savings Bank; Provo Co-operative Institution; Provo Lumber, Manufacturing and Building Co.; Provo Manufacturing Co.; Provo Milling and Manufacturing Co.; Provo Woolen Mills Co.; [S.G.S. Industries; Inc.]; San Pedro, Los Angeles and Salt Lake Railroad Co.; [Silver Park Mining Co.]; Sioux Consolidated Mining Co.; Sioux Mines Co.; Smoot and Co.; Smoot and Deal Coal Co.; Smoot and Larson; Smoot and Spafford; Smoot Drug Co.; Smoot Investment Co.; Smoot, Richards and Co.; [Smoot's Inc.]; [Spanish Fork Co-operative Institution]; [Telluride Power Co.]; Tintic Central Mining Co.; [Tintic Drain Tunnel Co.]; Union Portland Cement Co.; Utah Book and Stationery; Utah Consolidated Mining Co.; Utah County Abstract Co.; Utah County Savings Bank; [Utah Hotel Co.]; [Utah-Idaho Sugar Co.]; [Utah Independent]; Utah Lake Irrigation Co.; [Utah Mortgage Co.]; Utah Onyx Development Co.; [Utah Power and Light Co.]; Utah Territorial Insane Asylum; Victoria Consolidated Mining Co.; Victoria Mining Co.; [Wasatch Construction Co.]; Wasatch Grading Co.; Western Hardware Co.; [Western Monthly Co.]; Western Utah Copper Co.; ZCMI

Social: Charter member and president, Provo's Sons and Daughters of the Pioneers of Utah 1897; associated member, Salt Lake Newspaper Press Club 1903; charter member and president, statewide Sons and Daughters of the Pioneers of Utah 1907; Salt Lake City Commercial Club by 1907; Salt Lake Chamber of Commerce by 1925; listed in *Blue Book* for Provo 1898, *Prophets and Patriarchs of the Church* 1902, *Who's Who in America* 1903, *Financial Red Book of America* 1903, *Utah As It Is* 1904, *National Cyclopaedia of American Biography* 1906, *Who's Who on the Pacific Coast* 1913, *Men of Affairs in the State of Utah* [Press Club of Salt Lake City] 1914, *Herringshaw's American Blue-Book of Biography* 1915, *Who's Who in the Northwest* 1917, *Utah Since Statehood* 1919, *Utah: The Storied Domain* 1932, *Utah's Distinguished Personalities* 1933, *Who's Who In the Clergy* 1935, *Faith of Our Pioneer Fathers* 1956

Political/Civic Life: Organized local Republican club 1888; delegate, LDS People's Party convention 1890 (led unsuccessful revolt against proposed Provo mayoral candidate); president, Provo Central Republican League and executive committee, Utah Republican League 1892; defeated as mayoral candidate 1892; delegate, Utah Republican conventions (1892, 1893, 1894, 1895, 1898, 1900); Utah's official Pioneer Jubilee Commission (1896-97); governor's committee of arrangements, welcoming and award ceremony for Spanish-American War veterans 1899; told apostles he would not run for U.S. Senate 1900 (unsuccessful candidate 1901); U.S. Senator (1903-1933); governor's delegate, Trans-Mississippi Commercial Congress 1903, American Mining Congress (1904, 1905), National Conference on Divorce 1906, National Convention for Extension of U.S. Foreign Commerce 1906; risked indictment for perjury 1904 by giving misleading testimony to U.S. Senate about polygamy discussions at Quorum of Twelve's meetings; chair, forestry section, U.S. Conservation Commission 1907; chief Utah delegate, Republican national conventions (1908, 1912, 1916, 1920, 1924, 1928, 1932); Republican National Committee (1912-20); executive committee, Utah League to Enforce Peace 1918; Utah Committee for Armenian and Syrian Relief (1918-22); chair, U.S. Senate's Public Lands Committee (1919-23); Republican Senatorial Campaign Committee (1919-33); declined Warren G. Harding's offer 1920 to be U.S. Secretary of the Treasury; World War Foreign Debt Commission 1922; chair, U.S. Senate's Finance Committee (1923-33); regent, Smithsonian Institution (1924-33); chair, Platform Committee, Republican National Convention 1928; helped president-elect Herbert Hoover finalize cabinet selections 1929; defeated for U.S. Senate 1932 (blamed Democrat AWI who persuaded HJG not to ask Mormons to vote for RS); declined directorship, U.S. Board of Trade 1933 (Democratic administration)

Prior Religion: LDS

Mormon Experience: Baptized 1870; elder 1880; mission (1880-81, 1890-91); seventy 1884; high priest 1895; stake presidency counselor (1895-1900); director, LDS Industrial Bureau (1897-98); apostle 8 April 1900; threatened to resign apostleship if church leaders did not stop performing secret plural marriages 16 March 1904; publicly refused to vote for Quorum of Twelve Apostles at general conference October 1905 because of post-1890 polygamy by MFC, GT, and JWT; threatened to resign apostleship if First Presidency did not publicly punish MFC and JWT (28 October, 8 December 1905, 21 January 1906); told by church president HJG 28 May 1925 that his importance as U.S. senator was only reason he was not new counselor in First Presidency; after 1932 expressed bitterness toward Utah Mormons for voting him out of office

Death: 9 February 1941, St. Petersburg, Pinnellas Co., Florida

Estate: $109,897.80 appraised; $68,000.42 net

ERASTUS [FAIRBANKS] SNOW (ES-1)

Birth: 9 November 1818, St. Johnsbury, Caledonia Co., Vermont

Parents: Levi Snow and Lucina Streeter

Marriage (polygamist before appointment): Artemesia Be[a]man 1838 (11 ch); Minerva White 1844 (8 ch); *Achsah Wing (White) 1846 (no ch); *Louisa Wing (Aldrich) 1846 (no ch); Elizabeth R. Ashby 1847 (10 ch); Julia J. Spencer 1856 (6 ch); *Mary J. Farley 1866 (no ch); *Ann McMenemy 1867 (no ch); *Ane Hansen (Beckstrom) 1870 (no ch); *Margaret Earl (Loudenbach) 1877 (nc); *Rebecca A. Farley 1880 (no ch); *Fanny Porter 1882 (no ch); *Matilda Wells (Streeper, Wadsworth) 1882 (no ch); *Inger Nielsen (Andersen) 1884 (nc)

Hierarchy Relations: 3rd cousin, 1 rvd, of Amasa M. Lyman; 4th cousin of FML; 5th cousin, 1 rvd, of LS; 6th cousin, 1 rvd, of David W. Patten; he and Brigham Young md sisters; wife was Joseph Smith's sister-in-law; he and EH md sisters 1856; daughter md Brigham Young's son 1875; son md Orson Pratt's daughter 1878; son md JG's daughter 1882; daughter md MT 1885; father-in-law of future apostle and presidency counselor AWI; 2nd-great-granduncle of future apostle Jeffrey R. Holland

Education: Common schools; regent, University of Deseret (Utah), 1853-57

Prior Occupation: Farmer, merchant, schoolteacher

Business To 1932: Arizona Cattle and Wool Co.; Canaan Co-operative Stock Co.; Consolidated Implement Co.; Deseret Iron Co.; Deseret Pastoral Co.; Deseret Typographical (and Press) Association; E. Snow and Co. (Merchants); E. Snow and Co. (Wool Manufacturing); E. Snow Flour Mill; [Grand Gulch Mining Co.]; [Mountain Chief Mining Co.]; Nauvoo Mercantile and Mechanical Association; Pickett and Snow; [Pratt & Snow]; St. George Co-operative Mercantile Institution; St. George Co-operative Tanning and Manufacturing Co.; St. George Hall Co.; St. George Library Association; St. George Stake Board of Trade; St. George Water Co.; *St. Louis Luminary;* [Salt Lake Thirteenth Ward Co-operative Mercantile Institution]; *Skandinaviens Stjerne;* Snow, Holbrook and Co.; Southern Utah Co-operative Mercantile Association; United Order of St. George; [South Ash Creek Coal, Iron, and Lumber Co.]; [Southern Utah Stock Protection Association]; United Order of Zion; Utah Cashmere Goat Co.; Washington Field Canal Co.; Winsor Castle Stock Growing Co.; Zion's Central Board of Trade; Zion's Co-operative Rio Virgen Manufacturing Co.

Social: Mason 1843, Nauvoo lodge; listed in *Prophets and Patriarchs of the Church* 1902, *Stalwarts of Mormonism* 1954

Political/Civic Life: Imprisoned 1839 (one week) for aiding attempted escape of Hyrum Smith (acquitted); Council of Fifty initiation 11 March 1844; president, political missionaries to Vermont 1844; delegate, proposed "Jeffersonian Democracy" convention 1844; married three polygamous wives in violation of Illinois law (1844-46); delegate, Utah's unsuccessful statehood convention and committee to draft its constitution 1849; legislature, [provisional] State of Deseret (1849-51); Utah's Nauvoo Legion colonel (1852-66); Utah legislature (1853-54); probate judge (1857-58); probably among the 50 men indicted for treason, Utah War, December 1857 (pardoned by U.S. president's general amnesty 1858); circuit judge, State of Deseret's "ghost government" (1862-70); St. George city council (1863-81); legislature, Territory of Utah (1863-71), State of Deseret's "ghost government" (1863-71); married polygamously eight times in violation of federal law (1866-84); Utah's Nauvoo Legion brigadier-general (1866-70); delegate, Utah Republican convention 1872; vice-president, Utah Republican Party (1872-76); delegate, LDS People's Party (1876-78, and vice-president 1876); chair, Washington County Democratic Party 1876; Utah legislature (1876-83); major-general, St. George military district 1877

Prior Religion: Methodist

Mormon Experience: Baptized 1833; mission (1834, 1835, 1836, 1837, 1838, 1839, 1840, 1841-43, 1847-48, 1854-55, 1856-57, 1860-61, 1873); elder 1835; seventy 1836; saw tongues of fire, vision of Peter, James, and John at Kirtland temple dedication 1836; high priest 1839; stake high council (1839-40); political missionary 1844; church tithing agent (1845-46); second anointing 23 January 1846; stake presidency counselor (1848-49); nominated for Twelve 1847; apostle 12 February 1849; mission president (1849-52); president, own prayer circle (1858-62); sustained as "prophet, seer, and revelator," first time 6 October 1877; assistant Trustee-in-Trust (1877-80); Church Auditing Committee (1878-87); pro-tem temple president (1878-81); president, School of the Prophets, St. George, Utah (1883-84)

Death: 27 May 1888, Salt Lake City, Utah

Estate: $14,891.38 appraised and net

LORENZO SNOW (LS)

Birth: 3 April 1814, Mantua, Portage Co., Ohio

Parents: Oliver Snow III and Rosetta L. Pettibone

Marriage (polygamist before appointment): Mary Adeline Goddard (Hendrickson) 1844 (3 ch); Charlotte Squires 1844 (2 ch); Harriet A. Squires 1844 (5 ch); *Hannah M. Goddard 1845 (no ch), separated 1845, remarried 1849 but not divorced until 1882; Sarah A. Prichard 1845 (5 ch); Eleanore Houtz 1848 (8 ch); Caroline Horton 1853 (3 ch); Mary E. Houtz 1857 (6 ch); Phebe A. Woodruff 1859 (5 ch); Minnie S. Jensen 1871 (5 ch)

Hierarchy Relations: 5th cousin, 1 rvd, of ES-1; 6th cousin of Hyrum Smith, Joseph Smith, and William Smith; 6th cousin, 1 rvd, of JS and JFS-1; brother-in-law of Joseph Smith and Brigham Young; md Wilford Woodruff's daughter 1859; daughter md GQC's nephew 1868; daughter md Brigham Young's son 1875; wife was 1st cousin, 1 rvd, of MFC; 5th cousin, 1 rvd, md JG; 5th cousin, 2 rvd, md MWM; 6th cousin, 1 rvd, md JHS

Education: Oberlin College (1835-36); principal, Salt Lake High School 1853; regent, University of Deseret (Utah), 1853-57; trustee, Brigham Young Academy in Provo, LDS University, LDS Business College, and LDS University School of Music 1901

Prior Occupation: School teacher

Business To 1932: Brigham City Flouring Mill Co.; Brigham City Mercantile and Manufacturing Association; Brigham City Roller Mills Co.; Brigham City Theatre Co.; [Causey-Snow Lumber Co.]; Deseret Pastoral Co.; Deseret Telegraph Co.; Ferris Gold and Silver Mining and Milling Co.; Grass Creek Coal Co.; Inland Crystal Salt Co.; Iron

Manufacturing Company of Utah; *Juvenile Instructor;* L. Snow and Co.; Lee's Ferry; Lorenzo Snow and B. H. Snow; Lorenzo Snow Carding Co.; Lorenzo Snow Mill; Lorenzo Snow Tannery; [Pratt & Snow]; Salt Lake and Los Angeles Railway Co.; Saltair Beach Co.; Snow, Smith and Co.; United Order of Box Elder County; United Order of Brigham City; United Order of Zion; Utah Coal Co.; Utah Light and Power Co.; Utah Northern Railroad Co.; Utah Sugar Co.; [Victoria Mining Co.]; ZCMI; Zion's Savings Bank and Trust Co.

Social: Mason 1843, Nauvoo lodge; vice-president, Philosophical Society (1854-55); vice-president, Universal Scientific Society (1855-55); president, Polysophical Society (1855-56); listed in *National Cyclopaedia of American Biography* 1897, *Herringshaw's Encyclopedia of American Biography* 1898, *Who's Who in America* 1899, *Blue Book* for Salt Lake City 1901, *Appleton's Cyclopaedia of American Biography* 1901, *Prophets and Patriarchs of the Church* 1902, *Biographical Record of Salt Lake City and Vicinity* 1902, *Utah As It Is* 1904, *Dictionary of American Biography* 1935, *Faith of Our Pioneer Fathers* 1956

Political/Civic Life: Nauvoo Legion captain (1843-45); delegate, proposed "Jeffersonian Democracy" convention 1844; married polygamously four times in violation of Illinois law (1844-45); Council of Fifty initiation 10 March 1849; legislature, [provisional] State of Deseret (1849-51); Utah legislature (1852-82; president, upper chamber, 1872-80); delegate, Utah's unsuccessful statehood convention 1856; probably among the 50 men indicted for treason, Utah War, December 1857 (pardoned by U.S. president's general amnesty 1858); delegate, Utah's unsuccessful statehood convention 1862; legislature (1862-70) and associate justice (1866-70), State of Deseret's "ghost government"; delegate, Utah's unsuccessful statehood convention 1872; arrested for cohabitation 1885 (imprisoned, 1886-87); first wife Mary Adeline published statement 1888 that she did not testify at trial because LS asked her to commit perjury by testifying that she and his second wife Charlotte were married to him simultaneously; arrested for conspiracy to misappropriate public funds 1890 (charges dropped 1890); pre-1891 polygamy pardoned and re-enfranchised by U.S. president's general amnesties (1893, 1894); attended Republican victory rally with activist Republican sons 1894; listed by Republican *Ogden Standard* as Republican 20 August 1895 (declared himself a Democrat at Democratic territorial convention October 1895); charged with cohabitation 1899 (charges were dropped); sat on stand, Republican state convention 1900 (part of agreement with national Republican leaders for stopping polygamy amendment to U.S. constitution); instructed apostles to pressure LDS legislators into electing non-Mormon Republican as U.S. senator 1901

Prior Religion: Presbyterian

Mormon Experience: Baptized, elder 1836; mission (1837, 1838-39, 1840-42, 1847, 1872-73); seventy, high priest 1840; mission presidency counselor (1842-43); president, political missionaries to Ohio 1844; church tithing agent (1845-46); second anointing 24 January 1846; apostle 12 February 1849; mission president (1849-52, 1864); director, Deseret Theological Institute (1855-56); stake president (1855-77); one of first "home missionaries" (to Box Elder County) 1872; assistant counselor, First Presidency (8 April 1873-29 August 1877, not set apart); sustained as "prophet, seer, and revelator," first time 6 October 1877; assistant Trustee-in-Trust (1877-80); director, Logan Temple Association 1884; while speaking at Manti temple dedication 1888 some saw halo of light around his head; Church Board of Education (1888-1901); president, Quorum of the Twelve Apostles 7 April 1889; while leading "Hosanna shout" at Salt Lake temple dedication 1893 some saw halo of light around his head; temple president (1893-98); vision/appearance of Jesus Christ in Salt Lake temple, after which he was "set apart" as president of the church 13 September 1898, first ordinance for new apostle-president (see *The Mormon Hierarchy: Origins of Power,* 252-53); YMMIA General Superintendent (1898-1901); Sunday School General Superintendent 1901

Death: 10 October 1901, Salt Lake City, Utah
Estate: $18,845.38 appraised and net

**Daniel Spencer (1794-1868)
A conference of 11 April 1852 sustained Spencer and four others as traveling bishops, later referred to in First Presidency letter as "assistant Presiding Bishops." However, they were never ordained to that position as were JB, AC-2, and NHF. From 1856 to 1858, Spencer and seven other non-general authorities attended prayer circle of First Presidency and Quorum of the Twelve. In September 1858 Spencer and the other non-general authorities were assigned to different circles. Although a prominent member of the Council of Fifty since 1845, Spencer was not a general authority.

EDWARD STEVENSON (ES-2)
Birth: 1 May 1820, Gibraltar, Spain
Parents: Joseph Stevenson and Elizabeth Stevens
Marriage (polygamist before appointment): Nancy A. Porter 1845 (5 ch), divorced 1869; Elizabeth J. DuFresne 1855 (8 ch); Emily E. Williams 1857 (11 ch); Louisa Yates 1872 (3 ch)
Hierarchy Relations: Son md FDR's daughter; son md 1st cousin, 1 rvd, of JFS-1's wife; son md RTB's daughter
Education: Common schools
Prior Occupation: Farmer, turner
Business To 1932: Deseret Stock Mining Association; Deseret Tin-Shop; E. Stevenson Store; Stevenson and Jones; Stevenson and Lewis; Utah Colonization and Improvement Co.; [ZCMI]; [Zion's Savings Bank and Trust Co.]
Social: Listed in *Stalwarts of Mormonism* 1954; omitted from *Testimonies of the Church of Jesus Christ of Latter-day Saints by Its Leaders* 1930
Political/Civic Life: U.S. citizen 2 February 1866; Utah's Nauvoo Legion captain (1867-70); arrested for cohabitation 1888 (charges dropped); pre-1891 polygamy pardoned and re-enfranchised by U.S. president's general amnesties (1893, 1894); Democrat
Prior Religion: Methodist
Mormon Experience: Baptized 1833 (age 13); elder abt 1840; seventy 1845; mission (1852, 1858-59, 1869-70, 1872, 1877-78, 1883-84, 1886, 1888, 1896); mission president (1853-54); prayer circle of ES-1 (1860-62), of GQC (1866-81); second anointing 7 June 1867; "alternate" member, First Council of the Seventy, with no status as general authority (7 June 1879-27 May 1883); First Council of the Seventy 7 October 1894 ("ordained" President of Seventy 9 October)
Death: 27 January 1897, Salt Lake City, Utah
Estate: $18,542.14 appraised; $18,023.00 net

**Seth Taft [III] (1796-1863)
Taft was sustained, along with four others, as a traveling bishop 11 April 1852. Although First Presidency letter referred to them as "assistant Presiding Bishops," they were never ordained to this position as were JB, AC-2, and NHF. Taft became a local patriarch in 1856 but was never a general authority.

JAMES E[DWARD] TALMAGE (JET)
Birth: 21 September 1862, Hungerford, Berkshire Co., England
Parents: James J. Talmage and Susannah Preater
Marriage (monogamist): Mary M. Booth 1888 (8 ch)
Hierarchy Relations: ?
Education: Graduate, Normal Department, Brigham Young Academy in Provo 1879; professor, Brigham Young Academy (1879-91); student, Lehigh University (1882-83)

and Johns Hopkins University (1883-84); trustee, Brigham Young Academy (1886-91); president, Salt Lake Stake Academy (1888-89); honorary Doctor of Science and Didactics, LDS Board of Education 1889; M.S. and Ph.D., correspondence "university" in Chicago 1889 (returned the degrees 1891); president (1889-92) and professor (1889-93), LDS College; B.S., Lehigh University 1891; fellow, Royal Microscopical Society 1891; trustee, Young University at Salt Lake City (1891-95); professor, University of Utah (1893-1907); fellow, Royal Society of Edinburgh and the Geological Society of London 1894; president (1894-97) and regent (1896-97), University of Utah; president, Microscopical Association of Utah 1895; National Education Association 1895; Ph.D. (nonresident), Illinois Wesleyan University 1896; Geological Society of America 1897; fellow, Philosophical Society of Great Britain (Victoria Institute) 1899; honorary fellow, Society of Biological Chemistry of London 1900; life member, American Association for the Advancement of Science abt 1909; life member, National Geographic Society abt 1909; honorary Doctor of Law, Brigham Young University and University of Utah 1922
Prior Occupation: Author, professor, university president
Business To 1932: [Amalgamated Sugar Co.]; [Big Five T. O. & T. C.]; [Colorado Consolidated Mining Co.]; [Columbus Consolidated Mining Co.]; Deseret Book Co.; Deseret Museum; [Grant Gold Mining Co.]; [Great Western Mining and Milling Co.]; [Heber J. Grant and Co.]; [Idaho Springs Sanitarium Co.]; [Idaho Tungsten Co.]; Ima Consolidated Mining and Milling Co.; [International Securities and Bond Co.]; [Lemhi Opal Mining Co.]; *Millennial Star;* [Monitor Mining Co.]; [Mountain View Mining and Milling Co.]; Palantic Mining and Milling Co.; [Park Utah Consolidated Mining Co.]; [Salt Lake Zoological Society]; [Sioux Mines Co.]; [Tintic Drain Tunnel Co.]; [Tintic Mining and Milling Co.]; [Utah-Idaho Sugar Co.]; [Utah Karns Tunneling Machine Co.]; Utah State National Bank
Social: Salt Lake City Commercial Club by 1911; listed in *Blue Book* for Salt Lake City (1895-1907), *Who's Who in America* 1901, *Utah As It Is* 1904, *Herringshaw's American Blue-Book of Biography* 1915, *National Cyclopaedia of American Biography* 1918, *Utah Since Statehood* 1919, *Utah's Distinguished Personalities* 1933, *Dictionary of American Biography* 1936; omitted from *Men of Affairs in the State of Utah* [Press Club of Salt Lake City] 1914
Political/Civic Life: U.S. citizen 1884; Provo city council (1884-88), alderman and justice of the peace 1888; unsuccessful effort to obtain nomination of LDS People's Party for Utah legislature 1889; delegate, People's Party city conventions (1889, 1890); Republican after 1891; Utah State Board of Education (1896-97); governor's delegate, International Geological Congress 1897, International Mining Congress (1901, 1902), American Mining Congress 1904, National Conference of Charities and Corrections 1906; president, Society For the Aid of the Sightless (1904-33); director, State Historical Society of Utah 1908 (president 1909-12); Utah Committee for Armenian and Syrian Relief (1918-22); delegate, Mountain Congress, National League to Enforce Peace 1919, Third Christian Citizenship Conference 1919 (rejected)
Prior Religion: LDS
Mormon Experience: Baptized 1873; elder 1880; high priest 1884; stake high council (1884-88); blessed by LS 1892 to reach high church office; nominated for Council of the Seventy 1894; second anointing 25 May 1899; patriarchal blessing 1899 promised he would be apostle; revision committee, *Pearl of Great Price* 1900-01; no pre-hierarchy proselytizing mission; Sunday School General Board (1901-19); prayer circle of GAS (1906-11); apostle 8 December 1911; YMMIA General Board (1912-22); president, own prayer circle (1912-15, 1928-29); Correlation Committee (1913-[22]); Religion Class General Board (1914-22); revision committee, *Book of Mormon* and *Doctrine and Covenants* 1920-21; Committee on Revision of Seventies' Work (1923-24); Temple Ceremony Revision Committee (1924-24); chair, New Polygamy Investigation Committee (1924, 1927-33); mission president (1924-27)

<u>Death:</u> 27 July 1933, Salt Lake City, Utah
<u>Estate:</u> $29,936.91 appraised; $29,575.99 net

JOHN W[HITTAKER] TAYLOR (JWT)

<u>Birth:</u> 15 May 1858, Provo, Utah Co., Utah
<u>Parents:</u> John Taylor and Sophia Whittaker
<u>Marriage</u> (polygamist after appointment): May L. Rich 1882 (6 ch); Nellie E. Todd 1888 (8 ch); Janette M. Woolley <u>1890</u> shortly after Manifesto (8 ch); Eliza Roxey Welling 1901 (4 ch); Rhoda Welling 1901 (5 ch); Ellen G. Sandburg 1909 (4 ch)
<u>Hierarchy Relations:</u> Son of John Taylor; brother of WWT; father md GQC's aunt; brother and GQC md sisters; brother md JVC's daughter; 1st cousin of JFS-1's wife; brother md FDR's 1st cousin, 1 rvd, 1887; niece md MWM's son 1898; nephew md HJG's daughter 1899; uncle of future Seventy's president John H. Taylor
<u>Education:</u> Elementary schools; regent, University of Deseret (Utah), 1887-88
<u>Prior Occupation:</u> Clerk
<u>Business To 1932:</u> Alberta Colonization Co.; [Alberta Irrigation Co.]; Alberta Land and Colonization Co.; Alberta Railway and Coal Co.; Alta Co.; Alta Stock Co.; Ariel Fruit Lands Co.; Border Ranch and Stock Co.; Buckhorn Irrigation Co.; [Canadian Northwestern Irrigation Co.]; Chinook Stock Co.; Croff Consolidated Mining Co.; Deseret Paper Mill; Fillmore Fruit and Grain Lands Co.; [Hub Mining Co.]; Ima Consolidated Mining and Milling Co.; John W. Taylor and Co.; John W. Taylor Lime Works; [Lethbridge and Cardston Telegraph Co.]; National Gypsum Co.; The Noble Co.; [Ophir Consolidated Mining Co.]; People's Implement Co.; Promontory Ranch Co.; Raymond Milling and Elevator Co.; Taylor Brothers; Tintic Humbolt Mining Co.; Tres Amigos Gold Mining Co.; Union Stock Association; Utah Manufacturing and Building Co.
<u>Social:</u> Listed in *Blue Book* for Salt Lake City 1898, *Prophets and Patriarchs of the Church* 1902, *Utah As It Is* 1904; omitted from *Biographical Record of Salt Lake City and Vicinity* 1902, from biographies in *History of Utah* 1904, from *Pioneers and Prominent Men of Utah* 1914, from *Testimonies of the Church of Jesus Christ of Latter-day Saints by Its Leaders* 1930
<u>Political/Civic Life:</u> Messenger, Utah House of Representatives 1876; Ogden street supervisor (1883-84); chaplain, precinct meeting, LDS People's Party 1884; minute clerk, Utah legislature's upper chamber 1884; Council of Fifty initiation 9 October 1884; sergeant-at-arms, Weber County convention, People's Party 1886; Utah legislature (1886-87); arrested "inciting to rebellion" against the laws of Idaho 1886 (released on bail, charges dismissed 1887); Salt Lake City council (1886-88); justice of the peace (1887-88); published apology 1889 for sermon attacking Utah's territorial delegate for calling polygamy "a dead issue in Utah"; married polygamously twice in violation of federal law (1888, 1890); nominal Democrat 1891; pre-1891 polygamy pardoned and re-enfranchised by U.S. president's general amnesties (1893, 1894); not listed by Republican *Ogden Standard* among Republican apostles 20 Aug. 1895; performed eight polygamous marriages in violation of Mexican, Colorado, and Utah laws (1898-99); First Presidency approved his absence from general conference 1899 to avoid arrest for cohabitation; Republican abt 1900; married polygamously twice in violation of Utah law 1901; instead of declaring bankruptcy 1902, his $140,000 debts were settled with creditors by RS at 10 cents on dollar; in "exile" by permission of First Presidency in Canada (1904-06) to avoid federal subpoena to testify before U.S. Senate; performed three polygamous marriages in violation of Canadian law 1904; married polygamously in violation of Utah law 1909
<u>Prior Religion:</u> LDS
<u>Mormon Experience:</u> Baptized 1867; elder 1876 (and vision of Jesus Christ); prayer circle of President John Taylor (1877-80); mission (1880-82, 1884-86); apostle 9 April 1884; while speaking at Manti temple dedication 1888 many saw halo of light around his head, some saw "shadowy form" of personage behind him, while others heard his

voice transformed into distinctive sound of martyred Joseph Smith; offered 13 March 1889 to resign apostleship for publicly speaking against First Presidency policy (wrote retraction); reported 1890 that he had seen Jesus Christ and deceased Joseph Smith, Brigham Young, and John Taylor; after telling Twelve that Wilford Woodruff's announcement conflicted with revelation given 1886 to his father John Taylor about plural marriage, JWT declined to participate in sustaining vote for polygamy Manifesto, October conference 1890; while speaking at Salt Lake temple dedication 1893 some saw halo of light around his head; reprimanded for neglecting church duties (1894, 1895); mission president (1896-1901); Sunday School General Board (1898-1906); voted against by Tabernacle Choir members 9 October 1898 after his conference talk referred to immorality in the choir; criticized by First Presidency and Twelve for not paying tithing December 1901; in Canadian "exile" by permission of First Presidency (1904-06) to avoid federal subpoena to testify about post-Manifesto plural marriages; voted against by two church members April 1905 conference, at which RS also declined to vote for Twelve; according to GAS, as JWT prepared to leave Canada to "tell the truth" to U.S. Senate about his post-Manifesto polygamy, FML instructed him not to do so 1905; submitted resignation to Quorum of Twelve 28 October 1905 to use if politically expedient (publicly released 9 April 1906); began circulating copies of his father John Taylor's 1886 polygamy revelation 1906; FML instructed stake presidents to stop allowing JWT to speak in church meetings 23 September 1909; claimed 1910 that he caused mental problems of GAS by priesthood curse on his former friend for calling JWT's most recent marriage adultery; unsuccessfully appealed to JFS-1 to protect him from Quorum of Twelve February 1911; excommunicated 28 March 1911 by Twelve; secretly baptized again and reinstated by local stake presidencies August 1916 (action repudiated by published statement of First Presidency 25 August 1917); on deathbed allegedly said he would ask God to summon FML from this life to answer for disloyalty to polygamy and for persecuting JWT and MFC (FML died 6 weeks later); buried 1916 in temple robes allegedly given to his temple-worker wife by JFS-1 who allegedly said original excommunication was invalid; officially baptized by proxy into LDS church 19 May 1965; restored by proxy 21 May 1965 to all priesthood ordinances by JFS-2
Death: 10 October 1916, Salt Lake City, Utah
Estate: $1,382.70 appraised and net

WILLIAM W[HITTAKER] TAYLOR (WWT)

Birth: 11 September 1853, Salt Lake City, Utah
Parents: John Taylor and Harriet Whittaker
Marriage (polygamist after appointment): Sarah T. Hoagland 1875 (6 ch); Selma Van Cott 1884 (no ch)
Hierarchy Relations: Son of John Taylor; brother of JWT; father md GQC's aunt; he, GQC and JCL md sisters; md JVC's daughter; 1st cousin of JFS-1's wife; uncle of future Seventy's president John H. Taylor
Education: Elementary schools
Prior Occupation: Clerk
Business To 1932: [Brighton and North Point Irrigation Co.]; Bullion, Beck and Champion Mining Co.; Deseret Paper Mill; Iron Manufacturing Company of Utah; [Utah and Salt Lake Canal Co.]; Workingmen's Co-operative Association
Social: Omitted from biographies in *History of Utah* 1904, from *Pioneers and Prominent Men of Utah* 1914, from *Testimonies of the Church of Jesus Christ of Latter-day Saints by Its Leaders* 1930
Political/Civic Life: Election judge (1878-79); assistant clerk and minute clerk, Utah legislature's upper chamber (1880-82); Council of Fifty initiation 10 April 1880; constable 1880; alternate delegate, LDS People's Party county convention 1882; executive

"Committee of Seven," Council of Fifty (1883-84); Utah legislature (1883-84); delegate, People's Party county convention 1884; Salt Lake City assessor and collector 1884
Prior Religion: LDS
Mormon Experience: Baptized abt 1862; elder 1872; seventy 1875; mission (1875-77); stake clerk (1877-84); John Taylor prayer circle (1878-82); "ordained" president, First Council of the Seventy 7 April 1880
Death: 1 August 1884, Salt Lake City, Utah
Estate: $4,915.00 appraised; $855.50 net

GEORGE TEASDALE (GT)

Birth: 8 December 1831, London, England
Parents: William R. Teasdale and Harriet H. Tidey
Marriage (polygamist before appointment): Emily E. Brown 1853 (7 ch); Lillas Hook 1875 (no ch), divorced 1900 but stayed occasionally at her home for next 7 years; Matilda E. Picton 1878 (2 ch); Mary L. Picton 1883 (3 ch); Marion E. Scholes 1897 (1 ch); legally a monogamist after 1898; Dollie Letitia Thomas 1900 (no ch), and after GT's death she married his son
Hierarchy Relations: ?
Education: London University's preparatory school
Prior Occupation: Upholsterer, clerk, schoolteacher
Business To 1932: [Co-operative Mercantile Institution of Levan]; Isabella Mining and Milling Co.; [Juarez Tanning and Manufacturing Co.]; Mexican Colonization and Agricultural Co.; *Millennial Star;* Nephi Co-operative Mercantile and Manufacturing Institution; Nephi Mill and Manufacturing Co.; [Provo Commercial and Savings Bank]; Skull Valley Mining and Milling Co.; Zion's Central Board of Trade
Social: Listed in *Blue Book* for Salt Lake City 1901, *Prophets and Patriarchs of the Church* 1902, *Utah As It Is* 1904; omitted from *Biographical Record of Salt Lake City and Vicinity* 1902, from *Pioneers and Prominent Men of Utah* 1914
Political/Civic Life: Delegate, LDS People's Party conventions (1876, 1880, 1882); indicted 1879 for cohabitation, not arrested; Utah legislature (1880-82); territorial central committee, People's Party 1882; Council of Fifty initiation 10 October 1882; indicted for polygamy 1885 (avoided arrest by going on mission), charges dismissed 1892 after formal request by First Presidency and Quorum of Twelve; Republican after 1891; performed fifteen polygamous marriages in violation of Mexican law (1891-96); took oath before U.S. border officer 1893 that he was not a polygamist; pre-1891 polygamy pardoned and re-enfranchised by U.S. president's general amnesties (1893, 1894); Republican *Ogden Standard* identified him as Republican 20 Aug. 1895; married polygamously on U.S.-flagged vessel in violation of federal law 1897; authorized OFW 1900 to marry polygamous wife; "exile" in Mexico (1904-06) at First Presidency request to avoid federal subpoena to testify before U.S. Senate
Prior Religion: Church of England (christened, unconfirmed)
Mormon Experience: Baptized 1852; branch clerk (1853-54); elder 1854 (rumors circulated for 3 years that he paid money to be ordained); district presidency counselor 1854; president, district and branch (1854-57); LDS "pastor" for British branches (1857-60); prayer circle of George A. Smith (1862-64, 1867-75); second anointing 4 April 1867; mission (1868-69, 1875-76, 1886-87); seventy 1875; president, local seventy's quorum (1875-77); high priest 1877; stake president (1877-82); adopted to Joseph Smith and Eliza R. Snow Smith by proxy 1881; his stake presidency counselor told him April 1882 that GT would soon become apostle; apostle by written revelation 13 October 1882 (ordained 16 October); mission president (1883, 1887-90); diplomatic mission (1885-86); met with Presidency and apostles March 1893, first time in 8

years; president, own prayer circle (1896-1904); Sunday School General Board (1896-1907)
Death: 9 June 1907, Salt Lake City, Utah
Estate: $2,508.42 appraised; $2,262.02 net

MOSES THATCHER (MT)

Birth: 2 February 1842, Sangamon, Macon Co., Illinois
Parents: Hezekiah Thatcher and Alley Kitchen
Marriage (polygamist before appointment): Celestia A. Farr 1861 (7 ch); Lydia A. Clayton 1868 (4 ch); Georgina Snow 1885 (4 ch)
Hierarchy Relations: Brother md daughter of Brigham Young and sister of BY-JR, JWY, and JAY; brother-in-law of WBP; md ES-1's daughter 1885; wife's 1st cousin md JHS
Education: Student (1860-61), regent (1878-79, 1894-1903), University of Deseret (Utah); trustee, Young University at Salt Lake City (1891-95), Brigham Young College in Logan (1877-97)
Prior Occupation: Merchant
Business To 1932: A. D. and M. Thatcher; Alaska Gold Mining Co.; [Bank of Randolf]; Beck's Salt Co.; Bullion, Beck and California Mining Co.; Bullion, Beck and Champion Mining Co.; Cache Valley Land and Stock Co.; Cardon and Thatcher; Consolidated Implement Co.; Continental Life Insurance and Investment Co.; Contributor Co.; Co-operative Drug Co.; [Copper King Mining Co.]; Copper Mountain Mining and Milling Co.; Copper Ranch Mining Co.; Deseret National Bank; Deseret Savings Bank; Ensign Knitting Factory; Farmers Utah Loan Association; Herald Co.; Hercules Power Co.; Homansville Water Co.; Home Life Insurance Company of Utah; Idaho Milling; Grain and Power Co.; [Ima Consolidated Mining and Milling Co.]; Iron Manufacturing Company of Utah; Juarez Manufacturing Co.; [Keystone Nevada Mining Co.]; Logan Amusement and Investment Co.; Logan Branch, ZCMI; Logan Co-operative Mercantile Institution; Logan Island Irrigation Co.; Logan Power, Light and Heating Co.; Logan United Order Foundry; Machine and Wagon Manufacturing Co.; Mexican Colonization and Agricultural Co.; Ogden Co.; Oneida Mercantile Union; Oregon Lumber Co.; Perpetual Emigrating Fund Co.; Rancho Rio Verde; [Rich-Cache Mining Co.]; [Rush Valley Farm Co.]; Salt Lake and Ogden Railroad Co.; Salt Lake City Railroad Co.; Salt Lake Literary and Scientific Association; Shearman and Thatcher; State Bank of Richmond; Sundown and LaPlata Mining Co.; [Telluride Power Co.]; Thatcher and Sons; Thatcher Brothers Banking Co.; Thatcher Milling and Elevator Co.; [Thatcher Music Co.]; Thatcher Opera House; Thatcher Sawmill; Tobasco-Utah Development Co.; Union Flour Mills; [Union Knitting Co.]; Union Mercantile Co.; United Order of Zion; Utah and Northern Railroad Co.; Utah and Northern Railway Co.; Utah and Oregon Lumber and Manufacturing Co.; Utah-Idaho Hospital; [Utah-Idaho Sugar Co.]; Utah Journal Printing and Publishing Co.; Utah Marble Co.; Utah-Mexican Rubber Co.; Utah Mortgage Loan Corp.; Utah Northern Railroad Co.; Utah Sugar Co.; [Western Camera Manufacturing Co.]; [Western Cement Block Co.]; World's Fair Transit and Trust Co.; Zion's Central Board of Trade; ZCMI
Social: Listed in *Blue Book* (Logan 1898, Salt Lake City 1896-1901), *National Cyclopaedia of American Biography* 1897, *Herringshaw's Encyclopedia of American Biography* 1898, *Who's Who in America* 1899, *Financial Red Book of America* (1900-07), *Utah As It Is* 1904, *Herringshaw's Blue-Book of Biography* 1915; omitted from *Biographical Record of Salt Lake City and Vicinity* 1902, from *Testimonies of the Church of Jesus Christ of Latter-day Saints by Its Leaders* 1930
Political/Civic Life: Cache County superintendent of schools (1863-64); Utah's Nauvoo Legion captain (1865-70); Utah legislature (1870-79); Logan City alderman (1870-80); delegate, Utah Democratic Party convention 1872; delegate, Utah's unsuccessful state-

hood convention 1872; arrested 1874 for "subornation of perjury" for instructing Franklin, Idaho residents to file land claims for him in their names (apparently acquitted); delegate, LDS People's Party conventions (1874, 1876, 1878, 1880); chair, Cache County central committee, People's Party (1874-76, 1878-80); Cache County central committee, Utah Democratic Party 1876; territorial central committee, People's Party (1878-82); Council of Fifty initiation 10 April 1880; vice-president, People's Party convention 1880; Utah legislature (1882-82); executive "Committee of Seven," Council of Fifty (1882-84); indicted 1886 for cohabitation (injured while escaping arresting officers); performed polygamous marriages in violation of Mexican law 1888; arrested 1888 for cohabitation (charges dropped); delegate and vice-chair, Democratic territorial convention 1892; pre-1891 polygamy pardoned and re-enfranchised by U.S. president's general amnesties (1893, 1894); governor's delegate, Trans-Mississippi Commercial Congress 1894, Western States Conference Convention 1895; delegate, Democratic conventions (1894, 1895, 1897, 1900, 1902, 1904, 1906, 1908); withdrew as delegate to Utah territorial convention in protest against candidate 1894 (sat on stand); unsuccessful Democratic candidate for U.S. Senate (1894, 1896, 1897); delegate, State Constitutional Convention 1895; 2nd vice-president, Democratic Society of Utah 1895; chief Utah delegate, national Democratic convention 1896; declined nomination for election to U.S Senate 1898; director, State Historical Society of Utah (1904-09); officially listed among "one hundred prominent Democrats" of Utah's history 1942
Prior Religion: LDS
Mormon Experience: Baptized 1856; elder 1857 (age 15); mission (1857, 1866-68, 1882-83, 1883, 1885-86); seventy 1860; one of first "home missionaries" (to Cache County) 1872; assistant Trustee-in-Trust (1873-75, 1879-80); high priest 1877; stake president (1877-79); apostle 9 April 1879; mission president (1879-80, 1880-81); YMMIA General Superintendency counselor (1880-96); second anointing 22 October 1880; temple presidency counselor (1884-85); disfellowshipped by Twelve 23 March 1893 for his Democratic activities (restored 4 April 1893 by confession necessary for attending Salt Lake temple's dedication); criticized by Twelve 11 July 1894 for neglecting meetings; omitted from sustaining of general authorities and "suspended from the Apostleship" 6 April 1896 (dropped from Twelve and disfellowshipped 19 November); said 9 February 1897 he regretted ever being Mormon; tried by local church court 13 August 1897 (avoided excommunication by publicly confessing error); prohibited by First Presidency and Twelve 7 December 1899 from speaking at church meetings; regarded by JFS-1 19 May 1904 as apostle (though not in quorum) because not excommunicated
Death: 21 August 1909, Logan, Cache Co., Utah
Estate: $98,580.23 appraised; $93,857.41 net

**Enoch B. Tripp (1823-1909)
As one of the "alternate" members of the First Council of the Seventy (24 May 1879-27 May 1883), Tripp served as *ad hoc* replacement for absent members, usually at meetings where missionary appointments were processed. Never a general authority, Tripp was excommunicated in 1898 for marrying unauthorized plural wife by mutual covenant, rebaptized in 1903 and ordained high priest.

JOHN [LOSEE] VAN COTT (JVC)
Birth: 7 September 1814, Canaan, Columbia Co., New York
Parents: Losee Van Cott and Lovinia J. Pratt
Marriage (polygamist before appointment): Lucy F. Sackett 1835 (7 ch); Jemima Morris 1849 (1 ch); Laura C.P. Lund 1857 (6 ch); Caroline A. Pratt 1857 (9 ch) Caroline C. Erickson 1862 (5 ch)
Hierarchy Relations: 1st cousin of Orson Pratt and Parley P. Pratt; wife was Orson

Pratt's niece; daughter md Orson Hyde's brother-in-law; daughter md Brigham Young 1865; granddaughter md DHW's son 1880; daughter md John Taylor's son WWT 1884
Education: Negligible
Prior Occupation: Farmer
Business To 1932: *Skandinaviens Stjerne;* United Order of Zion
Social: Omitted from biographies in *History of Utah* 1904, from *Testimonies of the Church of Jesus Christ of Latter-day Saints by Its Leaders* 1930
Political/Civic Life: Salt Lake City marshal (1847-48); legislature, [provisional] State of Deseret (1849-51); Salt Lake City council (1847-48, [1850]-52), assistant superintendent of streets (1849-[50]), fence viewer (1852-53), street supervisor 1859; performed polygamous marriage in violation of English law 1853; under military arrest several hours for resisting the trespass of U.S. cavalry on his wheat field 1859; married polygamously in violation of new federal law 1862; legislature, Territory of Utah (1863-67), State of Deseret's "ghost government" (1863-67); Utah territorial land commission (1868-75, 1880-82); nominating committee, LDS People's Party 1872; Salt Lake City alderman (1872-74), superintendent of "the farm interests" 1874; rejected as juror because a polygamist 1879; Council of Fifty initiation 12 October 1880; sergeant-at-arms and doorkeeper, Utah legislature's upper chamber 1882
Prior Religion: ?
Mormon Experience: Baptized 1843; elder abt 1844; seventy 1847; prayer circle of Zerah Pulsipher 1851; mission (1852-53, 1859-60); one of first LDS "pastors" for British branches 1852; mission president (1853-56, 1860-62); local president of seventy 1857; nominated for Twelve 1859; prayer circle of Orson Pratt 1861; "ordained" president, First Council of the Seventy 8 October 1862; one of first "home missionaries" (to Salt Lake County) 1872; assistant Trustee-in-Trust (1873-75)
Death: 18 February 1883, Salt Lake City, Utah
Estate: $8,608.45 appraised; $7,006.15 net

DANIEL H[ANMER] WELLS (DHW)
Birth: 27 October 1814, Trenton, Oneida Co., New York
Parents: Daniel Wells and Catherine Chapin
Marriage (polygamist before appointment): Eliza R. Robison 1837 (1 ch), separated 1847; Louisa E. Free (Lee) 1849 (7 ch); Martha G. Harris 1849 (7 ch); Lydia A. Alley 1851 (6 ch); Susan H. Alley 1852 (4 ch); Hannah C. Free (Hotchkiss) 1852 (8 ch); Emmeline B. Woodward (Harris, Whitney) 1852 (3 ch); *Clara Gorder 1863 (no ch); *Sarah Gomber 1869 (no ch); *Sarah C. Nielson 1870 (no ch); *Elizabeth Harper 1871 (no ch); *Jane Smith 1871 (no ch), separated and remarried 1874; *Charlotte Foreman (Griggs) 1871 (no ch); *Margaret E. N. Edwards 1871 (no ch); *Caroline C. Raleigh 1879 (no ch); *Eliza Foscue (Lee) 1889 (no ch)
Hierarchy Relations: Father of RSW; 5th cousin, 1 rvd, of Wilford Woodruff; md Newel K. Whitney's widow; he and Brigham Young md sisters; son md JVC's granddaughter 1874; daughter md GQC's son JQC 1880; daughter md HJG 1884; daughter md SBY 1884; daughter md JQC 1886; daughter md OFW 1888
Education: Negligible; Nauvoo warden of common schools (1841-[46]); regent, University of the City of Nauvoo (1841-46), University of Deseret (Utah), 1850-60; chancellor, University of Deseret (1869-78)
Prior Occupation: Farmer, judge
Business To 1932: Big Cottonwood Lumber Co.; Brigham Young Cotton Factory; Brigham Young Express Co.; D. H. Wells Lumber Mills; Deseret Currency Association; Deseret Telegraph Co.; Howard Distillery; Jordan Irrigation Co.; Juab, Sanpete and Sevier Railroad Co.; *Millennial Star;* Mutual Life and Savings Society of the United States; Nauvoo Agricultural and Manufacturing Association; Perpetual Emigrating

Fund Co.; Salt Lake Gas Co.; Seventies' Hall Association; United Order of Zion; Utah
Central Railroad Co.; Utah Southern Railroad Co.; Wells, Grant and Woolley; Young
and Little Distillery; Zion's Savings Bank and Trust Co.

Social: Probably Mason 1842-44, in one of smaller Nauvoo lodges; listed in *Prophets and
Patriarchs of the Church* 1902, *Biographical Record of Salt Lake City and Vicinity* 1902, *National Cyclopaedia of American Biography* 1918, *Stalwarts of Mormonism* 1954, *Faith of Our
Pioneer Fathers* 1956

Political/Civic Life: Sergeant, Illinois state militia (1835-38); justice of the peace (1838-
41, 1843-45); Nauvoo alderman and associate justice (1841-45), warden of common
schools (1841-43); Nauvoo University building committee (1841-43); Nauvoo Legion
commissary-general (1841-45) and brevet brigadier-general (1843-45); declared in contempt of court by Nauvoo's chief justice Joseph Smith who then excused him 1843;
delegate, Whig convention 1843; Hancock County coroner (1844-45); Utah's superintendent of public works (1848-70); Council of Fifty initiation 6 December 1848; [provisional] State of Deseret's attorney general (1849-50), legislature (1849-51), chief
justice (1850-51); Utah's Nauvoo Legion major-general (1849-52), lieutenant-general
(1852-70); Utah legislature (1851-64); secretary, Deseret Theological Institute (1855-
56); delegate, Utah's unsuccessful statehood convention (1856, 1862, 1882); indicted
for treason, Utah War, December 1857 (pardoned by U.S. president's general amnesty
1858); president, Utah legislature's upper chamber (1858-64); was sued 1858 for false
imprisonment (case dismissed 1859 due to death of plaintiff); legislature (1862-64) and
secretary of state (1862-70), State of Deseret's "ghost government"; married polygamously nine times in violation of federal laws (1863-89); mayor, Salt Lake City (1866-
76); nominating committee, LDS People's Party (1870-72); delegate, People's Party
conventions (1870-76, president 1876); arrested for cohabitation 1871 (remained free
on bail until case dismissed); imprisoned two days 1871 for murder (remained free on
bail until case dismissed); territorial central committee, People's Party (1872-76), Utah
Republican Party (1872-76); arrested 1874 for disturbing the peace (charges dropped);
imprisoned for contempt of court one day 1875, two days 1879; Utah legislature (1880-
82); delegate, People's Party district convention 1881; Salt Lake City council (1882-84);
performed dozens of polygamous marriages in violation of federal law (1882-89,
1891); advocate of national Republican Party before dissolution of local parties

Prior Religion: Unaffiliated

Mormon Experience: Baptized, elder 1846; high priest abt 1848; assisted First Presidency and apostles in nominating stake high councilmen 1849; no pre-hierarchy proselytizing mission; had revelation 1854 that Brigham Young would select him as second
counselor (believed Young was not led by God to choose Jedediah M. Grant instead);
non-general authority member, prayer circle of First Presidency and Quorum of the
Twelve November 1856; apostle (not member of the Twelve) and "ordained" second
counselor, First Presidency 4 January 1857 (replaced Grant); mission president (1864-
65, 1884-87); second anointing 31 December 1866; vice-president, Salt Lake City's
School of the Prophets (1867-74); president, Endowment House (1868-77); sustained
as "prophet, seer and revelator" with first counselor and Brigham Young 9 October
1872 (counselors not sustained that way, April 1873 to Young's death); while reading
dedicatory prayer at St. George temple 1877 some saw halo of light around his head;
tried by stake high council and condemned by Brigham Young 8 May 1877 for entering
civil suit with Salt Lake City's mayor (no further discipline); released from First Presidency at Young's death 29 August 1877 (appointed counselor to Quorum of the
Twelve 4 September); sustained to that position and "prophet, seer and revelator" 6
October 1877 to his death; unanimously recommended by Twelve as one of two new
members of Quorum April 1882 (church president John Taylor declined making ap-

pointments and dictated revelation 6 months later appointing instead HJG and GT); temple president (1888-91); president, Manti Temple Association (1888-91)
Death: 24 March 1891, Salt Lake City, Utah
Estate: $3,156.22 appraised and net

JOHN WELLS (JW)
Birth: 16 September 1864, Carlton, Nottinghamshire Co., England
Parents: Thomas P. Wells and Sarah Cooke
Marriage (monogamist): Almena Thorpe 1886 (9 ch); widower nearly 2 years; Margaret Ann Newman 1931 (no ch)
Hierarchy Relations: None
Education: Elementary (to age 10)
Prior Occupation: Clerk
Business To 1932: Aurora Mining and Milling Co.; Baldwin Radio Co.; Bonneville Mining Co.; Community Clinic and Dispensary; Co-operative Investment Association; Foreign Lands Corp.; Gold Leaf Mining Co.; Home Benefit Building Society; Juab Development Co.; Juab Lake Irrigation Co.; LDS University School of Music; McCune School of Music and Art; Maynes, Wells, Scofield and Co.; Nevada Land and Livestock Co.; Riverside Canal Co.; Salt Lake Iron and Steel Co.; Salt Lake Knitting Works; Temple Square Hotel Co.; Trapper Mining Co.; Uvada Mining and Exploration Co.; W. H. Groves LDS Hospital; Wheatland Development Co.; Zion's Securities Corp.
Social: Listed in *Blue Book* for Salt Lake City 1907, *Utah's Distinguished Personalities* 1933
Political/Civic Life: Delegate, LDS People's Party city convention 1890; Democratic election judge (1893, 1894, 1895); Republican 1900s; secretary, Society for the Aid of the Sightless (1917-32+)
Prior Religion: Church of England
Mormon Experience: Baptized 1882; elder 1885; branch president (1886-89); no prehierarchy proselytizing mission; clerk, Presiding Bishopric's office (1890-1918); high priest 1911; stake high council (1914-16); stake presidency counselor (1916-18); ordained bishop and set apart as second counselor, Presiding Bishopric 18 July 1918; General Priesthood Committee (1918-22); Religion Class General Board (1918-22); prayer circle of JFS-2 (1913-13), of RC (1913-14), of JET (1921-25), of JAW (1925-27), of JET (1928-29); trustee, Zion's Aid Society (1928-32+); honorably released from Presiding Bishopric 6 April 1938
Death: 18 April 1941, Salt Lake City, Utah
Estate: $15,540.38 appraised; $15,250.97 net

RULON S[EYMOUR] WELLS (RSW)
Birth: 7 July 1854, Salt Lake City, Utah
Parents: DHW and Louisa E. Free (Lee)
Marriage (monogamist): Josephine E. Beatie 1883 (7 ch); remained unmarried widower for last 18 years of his life
Hierarchy Relations: Son of DHW; brother-in-law of JQC, HJG, OFW, and SBY; brother md RS's sister; nephew md AWI's daughter 1913
Education: Morgan Commercial College (1868-69); University of Deseret (Utah), 1869-72; president, Vortbildungs Verein (1894-94)
Prior Occupation: Clerk
Business To 1932: *Beobachter;* Beobachter Publishing Co.; *Bikuben;* Bingham Centennial Mining Co.; Charmer Manufacturing Co.; Commercial Discount Co.; Co-operative Wagon and Machine Co.; Deseret Building Society; Forest Dale Water Co.; Gold Bug Mining Co.; Gold Reserve Co.; Grant, Odell and Co.; Heber J. Grant and Co.; Home Benefit Building Society; Home Fire Insurance Company of Utah; Hot Salt Lake Improvement Co.; Hydraulic Canal Co.; Lynndyl Townsite Co.; *Millennial Star;*

Mutual Life Insurance Company of New York; Salt Lake Rock Co.; Sevier Canal Co.; Sevier River Land and Water Co.; *Utah-Nederlander; Utah Posten;* Zion's Benefit Building Society
Social: Delta Phi fraternity abt 1874; Salt Lake City Commercial Club by 1907; charter member, Sons and Daughters of the Pioneers of Utah 1907; listed in *Blue Book* for Salt Lake City (1901-11), *Biographical Record of Salt Lake City and Vicinity* 1902, *Utah: The Storied Domain* 1932, *Utah's Distinguished Personalities* 1933; omitted from biographies in *History of Utah* 1904, from *Men of Affairs in the State of Utah* [Press Club of Salt Lake City] 1914
Political/Civic Life: Foreman, Utah legislature's upper chamber 1872 (engrossing clerk 1874); delegate, LDS People's Party conventions (1884, 1885, 1886, 1888, 1889, 1890); executive committee, Democratic Jefferson Club of Utah (1891-92); delegate, Utah's Democratic conventions (1891, 1892, 1895, 1900, 1901, 1906, 1907, 1910); Democratic election judge 1892, when assaulted and battered; unsuccessful Democratic candidate for Utah legislature (1894, 1895, 1902); Salt Lake Businessman's Democratic Club 1895; Utah legislature (1900-02); Salt Lake City council (1904-08); Utah Democratic Party's reception committee for William Jennings Bryan 1916; Utah State Commissioner of Insurance (1917-21); committee, Democratic rally 1920; officially listed among "one hundred prominent Democrats" of Utah's history 1942
Prior Religion: LDS
Mormon Experience: Baptized 1862; elder 1866; seventy 1875; mission (1875-77); nominated for First Council of the Seventy 1892; "ordained" president, First Council of the Seventy 5 April 1893; prayer circle of HJG (1894-96); mission president (1896-98); nominated for Twelve (1898, 1900); YMMIA General Board (1899-1929); Religion Class General Board (1901-22); senior president, First Council of the Seventy (1938-41)
Death: 7 May 1941, Salt Lake City, Utah
Estate: $9,711.18 appraised; $9,445.76 net

**John M. Whitaker (1863-1960)
Ordained a local patriarch in 1914, Whitaker was authorized 18 June 1934 to serve the entire church in place of Acting Patriarch Nicholas G. Smith whose health was bad. Neither was sustained by general conference, and both were told their position would not be permanent. Whitaker continued until 1937 when GFR was publicly sustained as Acting Patriarch to the Church. Whitaker was secretary to the First Council of the Seventy (1889-97) but never a general authority.

ORSON F[ERGUSON] WHITNEY (OFW)
Birth: 1 July 1855, Salt Lake City, Utah
Parents: Horace K. Whitney and Helen Mar Kimball (Smith)
Marriage (polygamist before appointment): Zina B. Smoot 1879 (2 ch); Mary M. Wells 1888 (2 ch); monogamist after 1900, when he began polygamous courting of several women for next decade
Hierarchy Relations: Grandson of Heber C. Kimball and Newel K. Whitney; mother a widow of Joseph Smith; nephew of JGK; 5th cousin, 1 rvd, of JS, JHS, JFS-1; 6th cousin of RRL, GFR, SLR, DAS, GAS, HMS, and JFS-2; brother-in-law of RS and RSW; he, HJG and SBY md sisters; aunt md JFS-1; daughter md JHS's son 1906; wife's nephew md (1913) daughter of AWI and 1st cousin, 1 rvd, of HJG
Education: Morgan Commercial College; prep school and college, University of Deseret (Utah), 1868-71, 1874, 1880; University of Deseret regent (1882-83), chancellor (1886-90); lecturer, LDS College (1890-92); trustee, Young University at Salt Lake City (1891-95); professor of philosophy, Brigham Young College in Logan (1896-97); director, Modern Stenographic Institute (1912-17)
Prior Occupation: Clerk, reporter, editor, author, professor, poet

Business To 1932: Contributor Co.; *Deseret News;* Deseret News Co.; *Millennial Star;* Social Hall Society; [Zion's Benefit Building Society]

Social: Delta Phi fraternity 1873; Wasatch Literary Association (president 1874-76 and 1878); vice-president of Dicennial Philadelphian Society 1876; president, Home Dramatic Club (1880-81); listed in *Blue Book* for Salt Lake City (1895-1911), *Herringshaw's Encyclopedia of American Biography* 1898, *Utah As It Is* 1904, *Herringshaw's American Blue-Book of Biography* 1915, *Faith of Our Pioneer Fathers* 1956; omitted from *Men of Affairs in the State of Utah* [Press Club of Salt Lake City] 1914

Political/Civic Life: Salt Lake City council (1880-82); delegate, LDS People's Party conventions (1880, 1881, 1884); Salt Lake City treasurer (1884-90); elected Utah territorial superintendent of district schools 1885 (denied office by federally appointed Utah Commission); minute clerk, Utah House of Representatives 1888; married polygamously in violation of Mexican law 1888; denied right to vote by registrars 1890 (published absolute denial that he had "entered into the relationship of bigamy or polygamy"); unsuccessful Democratic candidate for Salt Lake County clerk (1892, 1902); pre-1891 polygamy pardoned and re-enfranchised by U.S. president's general amnesties (1893, 1894); sat on stand, Democratic territorial convention 1894; delegate, Democratic county convention and Utah State Constitutional Convention 1895; Utah legislature (1898-1902); president, State Historical Society of Utah (1902-08); officially listed among "one hundred prominent Democrats" of Utah's history 1942

Prior Religion: LDS

Mormon Experience: Baptized 1866; no priesthood office until elder 1873; seventy 1876; mission (1876-78 and vivid dream of Jesus Christ); high priest 1878; ward bishop (1878-1906); promised by Mormons (1878, 1879) he would be Presiding Bishop; mission (1881-83); nominated for Twelve 1882; leader in spiritualist seances (1883-1900); promised by JWT 1885 he would be apostle "when all things will be shaken" (month later his seance associate Arthur Stayner wrote Twelve's counselor JWY that OFW would be next apostle); gathered information 1885 leading to excommunication of AC-1; patriarchal blessing 1886 promised he would be apostle; stake high council 1886; friend wrote First Presidency 1887 recommending OFW as next apostle; dreamed 1889 that he would become church president; three days later told by father-in-law DHW that he was being considered for Twelve (apostles decided against OFW because of his seance activities, belief in reincarnation, and alcohol use, which decision OFW reported to others 1890s); warned by HJG against polygamous courtship 1895; told LS October 1898 that spiritualist Charles W. Stayner "is a prophet of God and that I had been sent of God on his behalf" to deliver instructions to LS (who took no offense but expressed disbelief in Stayner); asked by LS to become assistant church historian November 1898 (began serving without public acknowledgement January 1899); criticized by JHS 1900 for association with Stayners and soon ended seance activities; prayer circle (1900-04) of GT who authorized him to seek polygamous wife; sustained assistant Church Historian (1902-06); apostle 9 April 1906 to replace JWT (dropped from Twelve for public knowledge of his post-Manifesto polygamy); Church Board of Education (1906-31); Religion Class General Board (1906-22); promised by Susa Young Gates 1906 he would be counselor, First Presidency; identified by apostle's dream 1910 as obstructing Twelve's investigations of recent plural marriages; stopped seeking polygamous wife 1911; mission president (1921-22)

Death: 16 May 1931, Salt Lake City, Utah

Estate: $8,197.80 appraised; $7,159.12 net

JOHN A[NDREAS] WIDTSOE (JAW)

Birth: 31 January 1872, Daloe, Island of Froyen, Trondjem, Norway

Parents: John Andersen Widtsoe and Anna K. Gaarden

Marriage (monogamist): Leah E. Dunford 1898 (7 ch)
Hierarchy Relations: Wife was Brigham Young's granddaughter, niece of BY-JR, 1st cousin, 1 rvd, of SBY, 2nd cousin of LEY, and 3rd cousin of GFR and SLR, and prospective wife of AHC
(After BY-JR performed polygamous marriages 1894, niece Leah Dunford expressed interest in becoming plural wife of AHC. In December 1895, with encouragement of her mother Susa Young Gates, he began courting Dunford and the woman he married June 1896. AHC may have also married Dunford in first months of 1896 but unlikely).
Education: Graduate, Normal Department, Brigham Young College in Logan 1891; B.S. (*summa cum laude*), Harvard University 1894; professor, Utah Agricultural College (1894-1905); traveling Parker fellow, Harvard University (1898-1900); M.S. and Ph.D. (*magna cum laude*), University of Goettingen, Germany, 1899; post-doctoral, Polytechnicum at Zurich, Switzerland 1900; director, Experimental Station, Utah State Agricultural College (1900-05); principal (1905-07) and professor (1906-07), School of Agriculture, Brigham Young University; president, Utah State Agricultural College (1907-16); vice-president, Utah Academy of Sciences (1908-09); honorary Doctor of Laws, Utah State Agricultural College 1914; president, University of Utah (1916-21); president, Utah Educational Association (1918-19); honorary Doctor of Laws, University of Utah 1921; fellow, Philosophical Society of Great Britain (Victoria Institute) 1921; professor (1921-26) and trustee (1939-52), Brigham Young University
Prior Occupation: Professor of chemistry and agriculture, university administrator, author
Business To 1932: Beneficial Life Insurance Co.; *Beobachter;* [Big Four Consolidated Mining and Milling Co.]; *Bikuben;* [Crescent Eagle Oil Co.]; *Deseret Farmer;* Deseret Farmer Publishing Co.; Eddington-Cope Radio Corp.; First National Bank of Logan; Hotel Logan Co.; Inland Fertilizer Co.; Juab Development Co.; Logan Rapid Transit Co.; Marysville Potash Co.; *Millennial Star;* National Savings and Trust Co.; Nitrate Exploration Co.; [Phillips Petroleum Co.]; Rocky Mountain Pure Food Co.; [State Savings and Loan Assn.]; [Silver Lake Co.]; Utah Arid Farm Co.; Utah Cereal Food Co.; Utah Fertilizer and Chemical Manufacturing Co.; Utah Fruit Growers Association; *Utah-Nederlander; Utah Posten*
Social: Delta Phi fraternity abt 1891; Bonneville Club 1913; Salt Lake City Chamber of Commerce by 1925; honorary member, Friar's Club 1927; grand president, Delta Phi fraternity (1937-52); listed in *Who's Who in America* 1905, *Men of Affairs in the State of Utah* [Press Club of Salt Lake City] 1914, *Herringshaw's American Blue-Book of Biography* 1915, *Utah Since Statehood* 1919, *Utah's Distinguished Personalities* 1933, *Who's Who In the Clergy* 1935, *National Cyclopaedia of American Biography* 1970
Political/Civic Life: Republican; delegate, Utah Irrigation Congress 1902; governor's delegate, National Irrigation Congress (1905, 1910, 1912; vice-president 1912), Trans-Missouri Dry Farming Congress (annually 1907-1910), International Dry Farming Congress (annually 1911-15; president 1911; board of governors 1913-17), Utah Irrigation and Drainage Congress 1913, International Irrigation Congress (1914, 1915); Utah State Conservation Commission (1909-19); Utah governor's welcoming committee for Republican president William H. Taft 1911; Utah State Board of Education, also secretary (1911-18); director (1914-20), State Historical Society of Utah (vice-president 1920-21; president 1921-22); Utah State Council of Defense (1917-18); Utah Committee for Armenian and Syrian Relief (1918-22); Utah State Committee for Commemorating Irrigation by the Anglo-Saxon Race (1919-21); executive committee, Utah League to Enforce Peace 1919; delegate, Mountain Congress, national League to Enforce Peace 1919, Western States Reclamation Association (1919-21, 1923), Santa Fe Conference (co-formulator of Colorado River Compact) 1922; Utah State Water Storage Commission (1921-27); president, Utah Public Health Association 1923; Com-

mittee of Special Advisors, U.S. Bureau of Reclamation (vice-chair, 1923-24; chair 1925); president, Utah Tuberculosis Association 1927; Utah State Water and Power Board (1947-52); Royal Commission on the South Saskatchewan Project (1951-52)
Prior Religion: Lutheran
Mormon Experience: Baptized 1884; elder 1891; seventy 1898; no pre-hierarchy prose-lytizing mission; YMMIA General Board (1906-36); prayer circle of HJG (1917-19), of RRL (1919-21); high priest and apostle 17 March 1921; director, Genealogical Society of Utah (1921-32+); Commissioner of Church Education (1921-24, 1934-36); Church Board of Education (1922-52); Temple Ceremony Revision Committee (1924-27); president, own prayer circle (1925-27); mission president (1927-33); Melchizedek Priesthood Committee (1933-37); Publications Committee (1944-52); Temple Ordi-nance Committee (1946-47)
Death: 29 November 1952, Salt Lake City, Utah
Estate: $42,826.00 appraised; $42,116.93 net

JOHN R[EX] WINDER (JRW)

Birth: 11 December 1821, Biddenden, Kent Co., England
Parents: Richard Winder and Sophia Collins
Marriage (polygamist before appointment): Ellen Walters 1845 (10 ch); Hannah B. Thompson 1855 (3 ch), divorced 1864; Elizabeth Parker 1857 (10 ch); widower 11 months; Mira Burnham 1893 (no ch); monogamist after 1893
Hierarchy Relations: Divorced wife was niece of John Taylor's wife; md LEY's grand-daughter and SBY's niece 1893; daughter md Heber C. Kimball's son and JGK's brother; daughter and JFS-1 md siblings; daughter md GQC's stepson 1900
Education: Negligible
Prior Occupation: Tanner, merchant
Business To 1932: [Alaska Ice and Storage Co.]; Alberta Colonization Co.; [Amalga-mated Sugar Co.]; Armstrong, Winder and Co.; [Bank of Garland]; [Bank of Randolf]; Bar-Ka-Two Stock Co.; Bear River Water Co.; Beneficial Life Insurance Co.; B[ig]. K[anyon]. Tannery; Blackfoot Stock Co.; Cedar and Iron Railroad Co.; Collinson's Boots and Shoes; [Consolidated Music Co.]; [Consolidated Wagon and Machine Co.]; Daynes Jewelry Co.; Deseret Agricultural and Manufacturing Society; Deseret Invest-ment Co.; Deseret Meat and General Provision Store; Deseret National Bank; Deseret Savings Bank; Deseret Tanning and Manufacturing Co.; Emigration Canyon Railroad Co.; Emigration Canyon Rock Co.; [First National Bank of Murray]; Fremont County Sugar Co.; Grass Creek Coal Co.; [Heber J. Grant and Co.]; Herald Co.; Herald Pub-lishing Co.; Holladay Coal Co.; [Home Fire Insurance Co.]; Hydraulic Canal Co.; [Idaho State and Savings Bank]; Idaho Sugar Co.; Inland Crystal Salt Co.; Iron Manu-facturing Company of Utah; Jennings and Winder; Knight Ranching Co.; Knight Sugar Co.; Mulliner and Winder; Ogden Sugar Co.; P. W. Madsen and Co.; Perpetual Emi-grating Fund Co.; Pioneer Electric Power Co.; [Portland Cement Securities Co.]; Provo Woolen Mills Co.; Rexburg Milling Co.; Salt Lake and Pacific Railroad Co.; Salt Lake Dramatic Association; Salt Lake Knitting Works; Saltair Beach Co.; Sanpete and Sevier Sugar Co.; [San Vincente Lumber Co.]; [Silver Brothers Iron Works Co.]; Sugar City Townsite Co.; Trapper Mining Co.; [Union Fuel Co.]; Union Light and Power Co.; Utah and California Railway Co.; Utah and Pacific Improvement Co.; Utah Hotel Co.; Utah-Idaho Sugar Co.; Utah Iron Manufacturing Co.; Utah Light and Power Co.; Utah Light and Railway Co.; Utah Sugar Co.; Utah Territorial Insane Asylum; Western Idaho Sugar Co.; [Woolley Smokeless Furnace Co.]; Young, Little and Winder; Zion's Central Board of Trade; ZCMI; Zion's Savings Bank and Trust Co.
Social: Listed in *Blue Book* for Salt Lake City (1901-07), *Prophets and Patriarchs of the*

APPENDIX 2

Church 1902, *Biographical Record of Salt Lake City and Vicinity* 1902, *Utah As It Is* 1904, *National Cyclopaedia of American Biography* 1918
Political/Civic Life: Utah's Nauvoo Legion captain (1855-66) and lieutenant-colonel (1866-70); U.S. citizen 30 May 1862; U.S. gauger, Internal Revenue Service (1862-72); Salt Lake City assessor and collector (1870-84), city council (1870-78); nominating committee, LDS People's Party 1872; vice-chair, territorial central committee, People's Party (1874-87); Salt Lake County central committee, People's Party (1874-91; chair, 1887-91); delegate, People's Party conventions (1876, 1877, 1878, 1879, 1880, 1881, 1882); Council of Fifty initiation 8 April 1881; delegate, Utah's unsuccessful statehood convention (1882, 1887); executive "Committee of Seven," Council of Fifty (1882-84); Salt Lake City watermaster (1884-87); director, pro-Democratic *Salt Lake Herald* 1886; chair, territorial central committee, People's Party (1887-91); failed to obtain People's Party nomination for Utah legislature 1889; arrested 1889 for conspiracy to misappropriate public funds (charges dropped 1890); attended mass meeting, Utah Democratic Party 1891; delegate, Democratic convention 1892; pre-1891 polygamy pardoned and re-enfranchised by U.S. president's general amnesties (1893, 1894); officially listed among "one hundred prominent Democrats" of Utah's history 1942
Prior Religion: Church of England (confirmed)
Mormon Experience: Baptized 1848; elder abt 1848; seventy 1854; no pre-hierarchy proselytizing mission; prayer circle of John Taylor (1859-82); high priest 1872; acting-bishop of ward (1872-73); stake high council (1873-87); second counselor, Presiding Bishopric shortly after John C. Cutler declined office February 1887 (sustained 8 April); temple presidency counselor (1893-1910); vice-president, LDS Industrial Bureau (1897-98); first counselor, First Presidency 17 October 1901; Sunday School General Board (1901-10); Church Board of Education (1901-10); YMMIA General Board (1909-10)
Death: 27 March 1910, Salt Lake City, Utah
Estate: $146,710.17 appraised; $145,805.82 net

ABRAHAM OWEN WOODRUFF (AOW)

Birth: 23 November 1872, Salt Lake City, Utah
Parents: Wilford Woodruff and Emma Smith
Marriage (polygamist after appointment): Helen M. Winters 1897 (4 ch); Eliza Avery Clark 1901 (1 ch)
Hierarchy Relations: Son of Wilford Woodruff; 1st cousin, 1 rvd, of RS; 7th cousin of JS and JFS-1; 7th cousin, 1 rvd, of GAS and HMS; brother-in-law of LS; he and HJG md sisters; md ES-2's grandniece 1901; mother-in-law was Parley P. Pratt's step-daughter; sister-in-law was 2nd cousin of JS, JHS, and JFS-1; step-mother was MFC's grandaunt; step-mother's niece md FDR
Education: Elementary and secondary schools; LDS College
Prior Occupation: Clerk
Business To 1932: Big Horn Basin Colonization Co.; Church Onyx Mines; Deseret and Salt Lake Agricultural and Manufacturing Canal Co.; Inland Crystal Salt Co.; Lewiston Sugar Co.; Logan Knitting Factory; Wood River Live Stock Co.; Zion's Savings Bank and Trust Co.
Social: Listed in *Blue Book* for Salt Lake City 1901, *Prophets and Patriarchs of the Church* 1902, *Biographical Record of Salt Lake City and Vicinity* 1902, *Utah As It Is* 1904; omitted from biographies in *History of Utah* 1904, from *Pioneers and Prominent Men of Utah* 1914
Political/Civic Life: Democrat to 1899; attended Republican meeting with partisan apostles AHL and FML February 1899; performed eight polygamous marriages in violation of Mexican law (1899-1903); sat on stand, Utah Republican state convention 1900; persuaded Utah legislators to vote for two non-LDS senators (Republican) 1901; married polygamously in violation of Idaho law 1901; witnessed plural marriage in vio-

lation of Utah law 1904; died 1904 while preparing to leave United States to avoid subpoena to testify about post-Manifesto polygamy

Prior Religion: LDS

Mormon Experience: Baptized 1881; elder, seventy 1894; mission (1894-96); high priest and apostle 7 October 1897; second anointing 11 April 1898; YMMIA General Board (1898-1904); reported 1899 he had seen Joseph Smith in vision; Church Colonization and Employment Agent (1900-04); Sunday School General Board (1903-04); advised by church president JFS-1 not to attend general conference April 1904 to avoid subpoena to testify before U.S. Senate about post-1890 polygamy (also spared from publicly voting for "Second Manifesto" to which AOW was opposed because had JFS-1 authorization to marry a third wife); died while preparing to be mission president in Germany

Death: 20 June 1904, El Paso, El Paso Co., Texas

Estate: $4,107.92 appraised; $2,388.42 net

**Edwin D. Woolley (1807-1881)

By November 1856, Woolley had joined the prayer circle of the First Presidency and Quorum of the Twelve Apostles, attended by seven other non-general authorities. In September 1858 he and other non-general authorities were assigned to different circles. A prominent ward bishop, he was never a general authority. Grandfather of future LDS president Spencer W. Kimball and of future Presidency counselor J. Reuben Clark; 2nd-great-grandfather of future Seventy Robert E. Wells

BRIGHAM YOUNG JR. (BY-JR)

Birth: 17 December 1836, Kirtland, Geauga Co., Ohio

Parents: Brigham Young and Mary Ann Angel

Marriage (polygamist before appointment): Catherine C. Spencer 1855 (11 ch), separated 1888 but reconciled 1889; Jane Carrington 1857 (8 ch), separated 1886, requested divorce (he consented) 1887 but not formalized; Mary Elizabeth Fenton 1868 (3 ch); Rhoda E. Perkins 1886 (1 ch); Abbie Stevens 1887 (7 ch); Helen Armstrong 1890 (1 ch); *Kisty M. Willardsen 1901 (no ch)

Hierarchy Relations: Son of Brigham Young; brother of JWY and JAY; nephew of Joseph Young; 1st cousin of SBY; 1st cousin, 1 rvd, of Willard Richards; 2nd cousin of FDR; 4th cousin, 1 rvd, of Albert P. Rockwood; 7th cousin of JS and JFS-1; son-in-law of AC-1; brother md Jedediah M. Grant's niece 1856; 2nd cousin md JFS-1 1868; sister md LWH's son; sister md JG's son; sister md MT's brother; sister's step-son was RC; brother-in-law's son was RS; step-brother's brother-in-law was JWM; niece md AHC 1887; another niece being courted by AHC (1895-96); 1st cousin, 1 rvd, of future Assistant to the Twelve Clifford E. Young; granduncle of future Seventy's president S. Dilworth Young; great-granduncle of future Seventy LeGrand R. Curtis

Education: Negligible; regent, University of Deseret (Utah), 1868-71; trustee, Brigham Young College in Logan (1877-1903), Brigham Young Academy in Salt Lake City (1876-91), Young University at Salt Lake City (1891-95), Brigham Young Academy in Provo (1895-1903)

Prior Occupation: Stockman

Business To 1932: Anti-Friction Journal Box and Divided Car Axle Co.; Brigham Young Trust Co.; Burton, Sons and Young; Cache Valley Board of Trade; Carrington and Young; Chase Mill; Church Onyx Mines; City Creek Foundry and Machine Shop; Deseret Agricultural and Manufacturing Society; Deseret Investment Co.; *Deseret News;* Deseret Woolen Mills; East Canyon Coal Co.; Forest Farm; *Millennial Star;* Salt Lake City Railroad Co.; Salt Lake Gas Co.; Salt Lake Rock Co.; Social Hall Society; United Order of Cache Valley; United Order of Zion; Utah Central Railroad Co.; Utah Northern Railroad Co.; Utah Southern Railroad Co.; Utah Western Railway Co.; Young and Young; ZCMI; Zion's Savings Bank and Trust Co.

Social: Listed in *Blue Book* for Salt Lake City 1901, *Prophets and Patriarchs of the Church* 1902, *Biographical Record of Salt Lake City and Vicinity* 1902, *Utah As It Is* 1904; omitted from biographies in *History of Utah* 1904

Political/Civic Life: Utah's Nauvoo Legion major (1852-66); injured while assaulting U.S. soldiers with a club in Salt Lake City 1854 (acquitted 1855); messenger, Utah House of Representatives (1856-58); probably among the 50 men indicted for treason, Utah War, December 1857 (pardoned by U.S. president's general amnesty 1858); was sued 1858 for theft of property (case settled out of court 1859); Utah's Nauvoo Legion brigadier-general (1866-70); Council of Fifty initiation 23 January 1867; legislature, State of Deseret's "ghost government" (1868-70); Utah legislature (1868-79); delegate and nominating committee, LDS People's Party territorial caucus 1870; Cache County clerk (1873-75); delegate and chair, People's Party county caucus (1874, 1875); Logan city council (1874-78); Cache County recorder (1874-77); arrested 1876 for "kidnapping" his daughter, on complaint of her estranged husband whom she had left (charges dropped); delegate and vice-president, People's Party territorial convention 1876; Cache County central committee, People's Party 1876; territorial central committee, People's Party (1876-78); imprisoned three weeks for contempt of court 1879; indicted six times 1886 for cohabitation (avoided arrest); married polygamously in violation of Mexican law 1890; polygamy indictments dismissed by court after formal request by First Presidency and Quorum of Twelve 1892; pre-1891 polygamy pardoned and re-enfranchised by U.S. president's general amnesties (1893, 1894); attended Utah Democratic conventions (1894, 1895); performed seven polygamous marriages in violation of Mexican law (1894-95); identified by Republican *Ogden Standard* as Republican 20 August 1895, but *Salt Lake Herald* claimed two days later that he "openly declares that he is a Democrat"; declined offers 1895 to nominate him as Utah's first state governor; governor's delegate and vice-president, National Irrigation Congress 1896; sat on stand, Republican state convention 1900 and apparently Republican thereafter; married polygamously in violation of Utah law 1901

Prior Religion: LDS

Mormon Experience: Baptized 1845; apostle (without Twelve's knowledge) 13 November 1855 (when endowed) or 22 November (same day as JWY's endowment and ordination, according to Andrew Jenson's *Church Chronology*); seventy 1857 (publicly known); high priest abt 1861 (publicly known); stake high council (1861-62); mission (1862-63, 1864-65, 1867); secretly re-ordained apostle and "ordained" assistant counselor, First Presidency 4 February 1864 (without Twelve's knowledge for 2 months); mission president (1865-1866); prayer circle of First Presidency and Quorum of Twelve Apostles 11 November 1866; second anointing 3 January 1867; admitted to Quorum of Twelve Apostles 9 October 1868 (ranked ahead of previously admitted JFS-1 because of BY-JR's earlier ordination date); regional president (1872-77); publicly sustained as assistant counselor, First Presidency 8 April 1873 (not set apart because now a member of Twelve; released at father's death 29 August 1877); sustained as "prophet, seer and revelator," first time 6 October 1877; assistant Trustee-in-Trust (1877-80); threatened by senior apostle John Taylor (January to March 1878) with being dropped from Twelve if he (as legal trustee) did not agree to transfer bulk of Brigham Young's estate to LDS church (eventually complied); mission president (1890-93); reported 1899 an angel showed him vision of future destructions in America; apostolic ranking changed 5 April 1900 to reflect entry into quorum (this decision deprived BY-JR of becoming church president 1901); president, Quorum of the Twelve Apostles 17 October 1901

Death: 11 April 1903, Salt Lake City, Utah

Estate: $1,200 appraised and net

**[Brigham] Heber Young (1845-1928)

Ordained an apostle by his father Brigham Young, Heber was never made a special counselor to his father as was JAY, not admitted to Quorum of the Twelve as was BY-JR, nor publicly sustained to the First Presidency as was JWY. Despite his apostleship, Heber Young (like Jacob Hamblin) was never a member of the formal hierarchy, nor has the date of his ordination been retained. As the Twelve's president FML included Heber Young in a list of ordained apostles and gave that information to other members of the Twelve. BY-JR indicated that his half-brother was ordained after 1864, and Heber Young's diary for 29 April 1872 may refer to this apostolic ordination: "father pronounced his dearest blessings upon my head."

JOHN W[ILLARD] YOUNG (JWY)

Birth: 1 October 1844, Nauvoo, Hancock Co., Illinois

Parents: Brigham Young and Mary Ann Angel

Marriage (polygamist after appointment): Lucy M. Canfield 1864 (4 ch), separated by 1871 and divorced 1873; Clara L. Jones 1865 (4 ch), separated by 1879; Elizabeth Canfield 1867 (4 ch), separated 1870, reconciled 1871, divorced 1873; Lucy Luella Cobb 1877 (4 ch), divorced 1890; Bertha Christine Damcke 1879 (2 ch), separated abt 1887 and divorced 1890; engagement with a New York City debutante cancelled by her mother 1903 due to scandal about his son; remained unmarried (and ridiculed by LDS general authorities for dyeing his totally white hair black)

Hierarchy Relations: Son of Brigham Young; brother of BY-JR and JAY; nephew of Joseph Young; 1st cousin of SBY; 1st cousin, 1 rvd, of Willard Richards; 2nd cousin of FDR; 4th cousin, 1 rvd, of Albert P. Rockwood; 7th cousin of JS and JFS-1; brother md Jedediah M. Grant's niece 1856; 2nd cousin md JFS-1 1868; sister md LWH's son 1878; sister md JG's son; md JVC's granddaughter; niece md AHC 1887; sister md JG's son; sister md MT's brother; sister's step-son was RC; brother-in-law's son was RS; stepbrother's brother-in-law was JWM; niece md AHC 1887; 1st cousin, 1 rvd, of future Assistant to the Twelve Clifford E. Young; granduncle of future Seventy's president S. Dilworth Young; great-granduncle of future Seventy LeGrand R. Curtis

Education: Negligible; trustee, Brigham Young Academy in Salt Lake City (1876-91), Brigham Young College in Logan (1888-97), Young University at Salt Lake City (1891-95)

Prior Occupation: Clerk

Business To 1932: Anti-Friction Journal Box and Divided Car Axle Co.; Arizona Cattle and Wool Co.; Bingham Placer Mining Co.; Bridesburg Manufacturing Co.; Brigham Young Trust Co.; Canaan Co-operative Stock Co.; [Canda Manufacturing Co.]; [Canfield Manufacturing Co.]; Chase Mill; Chihuahua and Sierra Madre Railroad Co.; City Creek Foundry and Machine Shop; Consolidated Stock and Petroleum Exchange; Deming, Sierra Madre and Pacific Railroad Co.; Deseret Irrigation and Navigation Canal Co.; Deseret Museum; [Eastern Shipbuilding Co.]; Empire State Securities Co.; [Exempt Firemen's Benevolent Fund Association]; Forest Farm; *General Garfield* (Lake Steamboat); Great Salt Lake Salt Co.; Great Western Iron Mining and Manufacturing Co.; Holbrook Co-operative Store; J. W. Young and Co.; Kaibab Cattle Co.; L. W. Hardy and Co.; *Lady of the Lake* (Steamboat); Liberty Park Roller Mill Co.; Mexican North-Western Railway Co.; Mexican Pacific Railway Co.; Moen Copie Woolen Factory; North American Exchange Co.; North Mexican Construction Co.; Northwest Colonization and Improvement Company of Chihuahua; [Pacific Investment Co.]; Perpetual Emigrating Fund Co.; Postal Life Insurance Co.; [Provo City Railroad Co.]; Rapid Transit Cable Co.; Salt Lake and Eastern Railway Co.; Salt Lake and Fort Douglas Railroad Co.; Salt Lake and Ogden Railroad Co.; Salt Lake and Tooele Valley Railroad Co.; Salt Lake City Railroad Co.; Salt Lake Rock Co.; Salt Lake, Sevier Valley and Pioche Railroad Co.; Salt Lake Supply and Forwarding Co.; Salt Lake Theatre; Salt Lake Warehouse Co.; Saturday Globe Publishing Co.; Simpson, Spence and Young Co.; Sonora, Sinaloa, and Chihuahua Railway and Development Co.; [Southport, Northern and Western Railroad Co.]; Texas Transport and Terminal Co.; Tri-State Development Co.; United States Shipbuilding Co.; United States Terminal Co.; Utah Central Railroad Co.; Utah Central Railway Co.; Utah Commercial Exchange; [Utah Land Co.]; Utah Northern Railroad Co.; Utah Western Railway Co.; Wasatch Wagon Road Co.; [Western National Bank]; Winsor Castle Stock Growing Co.; Young and Thatcher; Young, Smith and Tenney; Zion's Savings Bank and Trust Co.

Social: Member 1887 of New York City's "principal clubs, where all the newspaper men, the better class of leading politicians, financiers and private gentlemen" met; Salt Lake Chamber of Commerce 1890; Alta Club by 1892 (dropped); Salt Lake Sportman's Club by 1892; Metropolitan Museum of Art by 1893; Marine and Field Club [NYC] 1903; listed in *Salt Lake City Blue Book* 1895, *Financial Red Book of America* 1900; omitted from biographies in *History of Utah* 1904, from *Pioneers and Prominent Men of Utah* 1914, from *Testimonies of the Church of Jesus Christ of Latter-day Saints by Its Leaders* 1930

Political/Civic Life: Democrat; sergeant-at-arms, Utah legislature's upper chamber (1862-63); Utah's Nauvoo Legion 1st lieutenant 1865; Council of Fifty initiation 5 October 1867; evaded arrest for cohabitation 1877; his Salt Lake City property seized by court order for non-payment of debts 1877; Utah legislature (1878-79); indicted for bigamy 1879, remained at large until arrest 1881 (case dismissed 1884); First Presidency's agent in New York City and Washington, D.C. for bribing Democratic newspaper editors, U.S. senators, and Congressmen to speak and act favorably toward statehood for Utah (1885-89); incorporator, pro-Democratic *Salt Lake Herald* 1886, Democratic *New York Globe* 1889; intervened with Democratic president Grover Cleveland to pardon fellow Democrat CWP 1889; pre-1891 polygamy pardoned and re-enfranchised by U.S. president's general amnesties (1893, 1894); declared bankruptcy in London, England, 1898; attempted to create $400 million syndicate in France to end War of 1898 (prior to Admiral Dewey's naval victory) by purchasing Philippines from Spain; New York City apartment used in his absence by son 1902 to murder a woman (*New York Times* implied she was a prostitute, even though married) whose abdomen was slit diagonally in room where son inscribed the words "Blood Atonement"; maintained frequent contact on son's behalf with New York City's former police chief who apparently persuaded prosecutor to accept plea-bargain (second-degree murder) 1903; sued and counter-sued, U.S. circuit court 1905 ($61 million dollar losses from shipbuilding project); personal property and real estate in Chihuahua, Mexico sold at auction for unpaid debts 1907; attempted to involve U.S. senator RS and former U.S. solicitor J. Reuben Clark in scheme to profiteer from American participation in World War (1917-18)

Prior Religion: LDS

Mormon Experience: Baptized 1852; apostle (without Twelve's knowledge) and endowed 22 November 1855 (age 11); seventy 1858 (publicly known); secretly re-ordained apostle and "ordained" assistant counselor, First Presidency 4 February 1864 (without Twelve's knowledge for 2 months); prayer circle of First Presidency and Twelve 27 December 1864; mission (1866-67); second anointing abt 1868; stake high council (1868-69); stake president (1869-74); publicly sustained as assistant counselor, First Presidency 8 April 1873 (remained stake president despite several contrary votes 8 October); sustained as first counselor, First Presidency 7 October 1876 ("ordained" to that office 8 October because not member of Twelve; released at father's death 29 August 1877); counselor, Quorum of the Twelve 4 September 1877 (sustained to that position and "prophet, seer and revelator," first time 6 October 1877); assistant Trustee-in-Trust (1877-80); not presented for sustaining vote 6 April 1881 (reconciled with Presidency and Twelve 25 May after five-day trial); interrogated by Twelve two days for

business infractions (publicly confessed and sustained at conference 8 April 1883); threatened with church discipline 29 April 1884 concerning use of church funds; nearly dropped as Twelve's counselor 27 May, 7 November 1885 (retained position by confessing errors); nearly dropped from position in his absence 5 April 1889; asked for mission assignment to Palestine 1890 (First Presidency told him to pay debts first); submitted letter of resignation 3 October 1891 (publicly released as Twelve's counselor 6 October); regarded by first counselor GQC 31 October 1893 as outranking GQC and JFS-1 in succession to LDS presidency (JFS-1 disagreed; resolved by decision 5 April 1900 that apostolic ranking only by entry into Quorum of the Twelve); rushed to Utah at death of LS October 1901 (according to newspapers) to be available as most likely candidate for new president (apostle with longest seniority); continued attending LDS services in Brooklyn and Manhattan until his death; his body brought to Utah for funeral at expense of President HJG who offended mourners with eulogy stating that JWY lived and died as a failure
Death: 11 February 1924, New York City, New York
Estate: No record (impoverished)

JOSEPH A[NGEL] YOUNG (JAY)
Birth: 14 October 1834, Kirtland, Geauga Co., Ohio
Parents: Brigham Young and Mary Ann Angel
Marriage (polygamist before appointment): Mary A. Ayers 1852 (10 ch); Athalia E. Grant 1856 (no ch), divorced 1858; Margaret Whitehead 1857 (2 ch); Clara F. Stenhouse 1867 (4 ch)
Hierarchy Relations: Son of Brigham Young; brother of BY-JR and JWY; nephew of Joseph Young; 1st cousin of SBY; 1st cousin, 1 rvd, of Willard Richards; 2nd cousin of FDR; 4th cousin, 1 rvd, of Albert P. Rockwood; 7th cousin of JS and JFS-1; md Jedediah M. Grant's niece 1856; 2nd cousin md JFS-1 1868; 1st cousin, 1 rvd, of future Assistant to the Twelve Clifford E. Young; granduncle of future Seventy's president S. Dilworth Young; great-granduncle of future Seventy LeGrand R. Curtis
Education: Negligible ("a passionate reader, and at the time of his death had, perhaps, the finest private library in the Territory"); regent, University of Deseret (Utah), 1857-75
Prior Occupation: Lumberman, railroad contractor
Business To 1932: City Creek Sawmill; D. O. Calder and Co.; Deseret Bee, Stock and Fish Association; Deseret Irrigation and Navigation Canal Co.; Jordan Irrigation Co.; Joseph A. Young Lumber; Joseph A. Young Sawmill; Juab, Sanpete and Sevier Railroad Co.; Pacific Telegraph Co.; Richfield Co-operative Grist Mill; Richfield Co-operative Mercantile Institution; Richfield Co-operative Sheep Herd Co.; Salt Lake and Tooele Valley Railroad Co.; Salt Lake Theatre; Sevier Co-operative Horse Herd; Sharp and Young; Summit County Railroad Co.; United Order of Richfield; United Order of Sevier; Utah Central Railroad Co.; Utah Southern Railroad Co.; West and Young; Zion's Savings Bank and Trust Co.
Social: *Deseret News 1974 Church Almanac* made first official acknowledgement in twentieth century that JAY was ordained an apostle, but official LDS sources remain silent about his role as one of Brigham Young's special counselors in 1864
Political/Civic Life: Utah's Nauvoo Legion 2nd lieutenant (1849-52) and colonel (1852-70); messenger, Utah's House of Representatives (1852-54); probably among the 50 men indicted for treason, Utah War, December 1857 (pardoned by U.S. president's general amnesty 1858); was sued 1858 for theft of property (settled out of court 1859); Utah legislature (1856-60, 1861-63, 1864-75); legislature, State of Deseret's "ghost government" (1862-70); Council of Fifty initiation 23 January 1867; married polygamously in violation of federal law 1867; indicted for murder 1871 (charges dropped); nominating committee, LDS People's Party 1873

Prior Religion: LDS
Mormon Experience: Baptized 1842; elder 1852; mission (1854-56, 1864-65); seventy 1857; prayer circle of First Presidency and Quorum of Twelve Apostles March 1857 (assigned with other non-general authorities to different circles September 1858); rumored to be in apostasy 1859; secretly ordained an apostle and assistant counselor, First Presidency 4 February 1864 (without Twelve's knowledge for 2 months); mission (1864-65); readmitted, prayer circle of Presidency and Twelve 11 November 1866; second anointing 2 January 1867; served as Presidency assistant counselor without public acknowledgement until 9 April 1871 (last date attended prayer circle of Presidency and Twelve); stake president (1872-75)
Death: 5 August 1875, Manti, Sanpete Co., Utah
Estate: No record

LEVI EDGAR YOUNG (LEY)
Birth: 2 February 1874, Salt Lake City, Utah
Parents: SBY and Ann E. Riter
Marriage (monogamist): Valeria E. Brinton 1907 (3 ch)
Hierarchy Relations: Son of SBY; grandson of Joseph Young; grandnephew of Brigham Young; 3rd cousin of GFR and SLR; brother md HJG's daughter 1911; sister-in-law's brother was RC; 2nd cousin's father-in-law was CWN; 2nd cousin, 1 rvd, md JFS-1; his brother Clifford E. Young appointed Assistant to the Twelve 1941; his nephew S. Dilworth Young appointed Seventy's President 1945; 2nd cousin, 2 rvd, of future Seventy LeGrand R. Curtis
Education: Prep school, University of Deseret (Utah), 1890-92; lecturer, LDS College (1896-98); student, Harvard College (1898-99); professor, University of Utah (1899-1939); student, University of Strassburg (1904-05); M.A., Columbia University 1910; trustee, Utah State Industrial [reform] School (1917-23); American Academy of Political and Social Science before 1919; American Ethnological Society before 1919; president, Pacific Coast Branch, American Historical Association (1919-20); department chair, Western History (1919-37), History and Political Science (1936-39), University of Utah; emeritus professor 1955
Prior Occupation: Professor of history
Business To 1932: [Amalgamated Sugar Co.]; [Columbia Gas Co.]; [Kearns Improvement Co.]; [Pacific Power and Light Co.]; [South Pacific Co.]; *University of Utah Chronicle;* [Utah Power and Light Co.]; [ZCMI]
Social: Delta Phi fraternity abt 1890; Timpanogos Club 1913; Bonneville Club (1913, board of governors 1915, vice-president by 1919); Utah Sons of the American Revolution 1914 (president 1953-54); education committee, national Sons of the American Revolution 1915; grand president, Delta Phi fraternity (1934-37); listed in *Blue Book* for Salt Lake City 1907, *Who's Who in America* 1920, *Utah: The Storied Domain* 1932, *Utah's Distinguished Personalities* 1933; omitted from *Men of Affairs in the State of Utah* [Press Club of Salt Lake City] 1914
Political/Civic Life: Republican; delegate, International Education Association convention 1904; governor's delegate, International Congress on School Hygiene 1904; director (1909-32+), State Historical Society of Utah (secretary 1913-18; president 1923-24); governing board, Utah State Art Institute (1913-16); delegate, national League to Enforce Peace 1918; executive committee, Utah League to Enforce Peace (1918-19); advisory committee, Utah veteran's memorial (1919-20); Utah State Commission on the Education of Aliens 1920; Utah state committee for monument "In Memory of White People Killed In Battles With Indians of This State" 1923; charter member, Utah chapter, National Conference of Christians and Jews 1936 (president 1937); Utah Centennial Exposition Committee (1938-47); chair, Religion Committee,

Utah Association for the United Nations 1946; delegate, American Association for the United Nations 1948; Council of Churches 1950
Prior Religion: LDS
Mormon Experience: Baptized 1882; elder abt 1884; seventy 1897; mission (1897, 1898, 1901-02); mission president (1902-04, 1939-41); First Council of the Seventy 6 October 1909 (set apart 23 January 1910); YMMIA General Board (1913-29); Religion Class General Board (1919-22); president, Salt Lake Temple Block (Square) Mission (1922-32); senior president, First Council of the Seventy (1941-63); threatened by church president with dismissal 6 July 1942 for delivering secular sermons (reconciled 13 August); not ordained high priest with other members of the First Council of the Seventy 1961, because not being assigned to organize bishoprics or stake presidencies
Death: 13 December 1963, Salt Lake City, Utah
Estate: $186,780.30 appraised; $186,632.56 net

**Lorenzo D. Young (1807-1895)
By November 1856 Young was a member of the prayer circle of the First Presidency and Quorum of the Twelve. Attended until 1858 when he and seven other non-general authorities were assigned to different circles. Lorenzo was Brigham's brother and a prominent Mormon but never a general authority.

SEYMOUR B[ICKNELL] YOUNG (SBY)
Birth: 3 October 1837, Kirtland, Geauga Co., Ohio
Parents: Joseph Young and Jane Bicknell
Marriage (polygamist after appointment): Ann Elizabeth Riter 1867 (11 ch); Abbie C. Wells 1884 (2 ch), separated abt 1890 and withdrew her application for divorce (1910) in exchange for financial settlement (arranged by First Presidency with SBY)
Hierarchy Relations: Son of Joseph Young; father of LEY; nephew of Brigham Young; 1st cousin of BY-JR, JWY, JAY; 2nd cousin of FDR; 2nd cousin, 1 rvd, of GFR and SLR; 7th cousin of JS and JFS-1; son-in-law of DHW; brother-in-law of RSW; he, JQC, HJG, and OFW md sisters; daughter-in-law's brother was RC; 1st cousin md Jedediah M. Grant's daughter and HJG's sister; uncle md JVC's daughter; 1st cousin md Parley P. Pratt's daughter and Orson Pratt's niece; 1st cousin md ES-1's daughter; 1st cousin md LS's son; 1st cousin md LWH's son; 1st cousin md JG's son; 2nd cousin md JFS-1; daughter md DHW's son and RSW's brother; son md HJG's daughter 1911; father of future Seventy's president Clifford E. Young; grandfather of future Seventy's president S. Dilworth Young
Education: University of Deseret (Utah), 1870-71; M.D., University Medical College of New York 1874; lecturer, LDS College (1890-94)
Prior Occupation: Physician
Business To 1932: Border Ranch and Live Stock Co.; Canaan Co-operative Stock Co.; Deseret and Salt Lake Agricultural and Manufacturing Canal Co.; Deseret Investment Co.; [East Crown Point Consolidated Mining Co.]; East Side Co-operative Mercantile Co.; Grow Gold Mining and Milling Co.; Lion Hill Mining Co.; Maxfield Mining Co.; [North Standard Mining Co.]; [Opohongo Mining Co.]; Rexburg Milling Co.; Salt Lake and Fort Douglas Railroad Co.; Salt Lake City Insane Asylum; Salt Lake City Railroad Co.; Salt Lake Fish and Dairy Co.; Salt Lake Literary and Scientific Association; Salt Lake Rock Co.; Social Hall Society; Utah Commercial and Savings Bank; Utah Western Railway Co.; Young and Benedict; Young and Spencer; Young and Williams
Social: Charter member, Sons and Daughters of the Pioneers of Utah 1907; listed in Blue Book for Salt Lake City (1895-1907); omitted from Biographical Record of Salt Lake City and Vicinity 1902, from biographies in History of Utah 1904, from Men of Affairs in the State of Utah [Press Club of Salt Lake City] 1914, from Utah Since Statehood 1919
Political/Civic Life: Messenger, Utah House of Representatives (1859-60); Utah's Nau-

voo Legion corporal (1860-70); volunteer, U.S. Army (1862-63); Salt Lake City quarantine physician (1875-86); delegate and sergeant-at-arms, LDS People's Party conventions (1880, 1884; delegate only 1889); Council of Fifty initiation 9 October 1884; incorporator, pro-Democratic *Salt Lake Herald* 1886; arrested for cohabitation 1886 (escaped), surrendered 1887 (charges dismissed), arrested 1888 (charges dismissed); Republican after 1891; pre-1891 polygamy pardoned and re-enfranchised by U.S. president's general amnesties (1893, 1894); governor's delegate, National Irrigation Congress (1899, 1900, 1903, 1904, 1910, 1911; president 1899); performed two polygamous marriages in violation of Mexican law 1900; sat on stand, Republican state convention 1900; delegate, Utah Irrigation Congress 1902; governor's delegate, Trans-Missouri Dry Farming Congress 1909; delegate, Citizens Party city convention 1909; delegate, Republican convention 1916

Prior Religion: LDS

Mormon Experience: Survived Haun's Mill Massacre 1838; baptized 1848; elder 1856; seventy 1857; mission (1857-58, 1870, 1873); second anointing 30 July 1867; "alternate" member, First Council of the Seventy (10 May 1879-13 October 1882), with no status as general authority; prayer circle of Wilford Woodruff (1880-81); designated in deathbed request July 1881 to President John Taylor by senior president Joseph Young to be his replacement in First Council; vivid dream of God and Jesus Christ 18 September 1882; nominated for Twelve 6 October 1882; not chosen by Taylor for Council of the Seventy 8 October 1882 (appointed by written revelation 13 October after newly sustained TBL was found to be ineligible); "ordained" president, First Council of the Seventy 14 October (publicly sustained 8 April 1883); allowed by JWT, MT and other apostles to ordain high priests and bishops (1883-91); instructed by First Presidency to stop ordaining high priests 19 November 1891; senior president, First Council of the Seventy (1892-1924); allowed by LS, AOW and other apostles to assist in ordaining high priests (1892-98); Sunday School General Board (1899-1924); given sealing power 1900 by second counselor JFS-1 and instructed to perform two polygamous marriages (one of which had been specifically forbidden by church president LS, aside from his general policy against allowing such marriages, even in Mexico)

Death: 15 December 1924, Salt Lake City, Utah

Estate: $1,824.49 appraised; $2921.10 debts; (-$1,096.61) net

Appointments to the Theocratic Council of Fifty through 1884

This is an alphabetical list of all members of the theocratic Council of Fifty, originally organized on 11 March 1844. Its final meeting was on 9 October 1884. No new members were added from then until its last surviving member, LDS church president Heber J. Grant, died in 1945. For ranking of the Council of Fifty in 1844-1845, see the appendix in companion volume *The Mormon Hierarchy: Origins of Power*. LDS general authorities are listed in CAPITALS.

Adams, George J. (1810-1880). Admitted between 14 March and 11 April 1844. Dropped 4 February 1845.

Babbitt, Almon W. (1812-1856). Admitted between 14 March and 11 April 1844. Remained a member until his death.

Badlam, Alexander (1808-1894). Admitted 11 March 1844. Dropped 4 February 1845. Readmitted to Council and attended its 1851 meetings. Disfellowshipped by church in 1858, and dropped again from the Council of Fifty when it reconvened in January 1867.

BENSON, EZRA T. (1811-1869). Admitted 25 December 1846.

Bent, Samuel (1778-1846). Admitted 19 March 1844.

Bernhisel, John M. (1799-1881). Admitted 11 March 1844

Bonney, Edward (1807-1864). Admitted between 14 March and 11 April 1844. *Non-LDS*. Dropped 4 February 1845.

Brown, Uriah (1784-). Admitted 19 March 1844. *Non-LDS*. Dropped 4 February 1845. Council voted 25 August 1851 to readmit him but rescinded that vote 13 September 1851.

Budge, William (1828-1919). Considered 10 April 1880. Was voted in 24 June 1882. Admitted 26 June 1882.

Bullock, Thomas (1816-1885). Admitted 25 December 1846. Reporter for the Council meetings from 1848. Released due to old age 24 June 1882.

BURTON, ROBERT T. (1821-1907). Admitted 25 January 1867.

Cahoon, Reynolds (1790-1861). Attended provisional meeting of 10 March 1844. Admitted 11 March 1844.

Caine, John T. (1829-1911). Admitted 8 April 1881.

CANNON, ABRAHAM H. (1859-1896). Admitted 9 October 1884.

Cannon, Angus M. (1834-1915). Admitted 10 April 1880.

CANNON, GEORGE Q. (1827-1901). Admitted 23 January 1867. Elected recorder 23 January 1867.

CANNON, JOHN Q. (1857-1931). Admitted 9 October 1884.

CARRINGTON, ALBERT (1813-1889). Admitted 18 or 22 April 1845. Reporter for Council meetings in 1848.

Clawson, Hiram B. (1826-1912). Admitted 27 June 1882.

Clayton, William (1814-1879). Attended provisional meeting 10 March 1844. Appointed clerk 10 March 1844. Officially admitted 11 March 1844. Officially reappointed Clerk of the Kingdom 13 March 1844.

Clinton, Jeter (1813-1892). Admitted 25 January 1867.

Cluff, William W. (1832-1915). Admitted 10 April 1880.

Coolidge, Joseph W. (1814-1871). Admitted 18 April 1844. Dropped after 1848.

Cutler, Alpheus (1784-1864). Attended provisional meeting 10 March 1844. Admitted 11 March 1844. Dropped (probably in 1848-1849 period).

Dana, Lewis (1805-1885). Admitted 1 March 1845. American Indian. Dropped after 1848.

Daniels, Cyrus (1803-1846). Admitted 11 March 1844.

Dunham, Jonathan (1800-1845). Admitted 1 March 1845.

Eaton, Marinus G. (1811-). Admitted between 14 March and 11 April 1844. *Non-LDS.* Dropped 4 February 1845.

ELDREDGE, HORACE S. (1816-1888). Admitted 9 December 1848.

Emmett, James (1803-1852). Admitted 13 March 1844. Dropped 4 February 1845.

Farnham, John W. (1794-1846). Admitted 18 or 22 April 1845.

Farr, Lorin (1820-1909). Admitted 12 October 1880.

Fielding, Amos (1792-1875). Attended provisional meeting 10 March 1844. Admitted 11 March 1844.

Fielding, Joseph (1797-1863). Admitted between 14 March and 11 April 1844.

Foster, Lucien R. (1806-). Admitted 1 March 1845. Dropped 12 November 1846.

Fullmer, David (1803-1879). Admitted 1 March 1845.

Fullmer, John S. (1807-1883). Admitted 18 or 22 April 1845. Released due to old age 24 June 1882.

GATES, JACOB. (1811-1892). Admitted 10 October 1882.

Gibbs, George F. (1846-1924). Appointed reporter, but not member, 5 April 1882. Admitted 24 June 1882.

Grant, George D. (1812-1876). Admitted 9 September 1845.

GRANT, HEBER J. (1856-1945). Was voted in 26 June 1882. Admitted 10 October 1882. Last surviving member of the Council of Fifty.

GRANT, JEDEDIAH M. (1816-1856). Admitted 6 May 1844.

Greene, John P. (1793-1844). Admitted 26 March 1844.

HARDY, LEONARD W. (1805-1884). Admitted 27 June 1882.

Hatch, Abram (1830-1911). Admitted 29 June 1883.

Haws, Peter (1796-1862). Admitted 11 March 1844. Dropped sometime after 13 November 1846.

Heywood, Joseph L. (1815-1900). Admitted 6 December 1848. Released due to old age 24 June 1882.

Hollister, David S. (1808-1858). Admitted 18 April 1844. Possibly dropped after 25 December 1846.

Hooper, William H. (1813-1882). Was voted in 5 October 1867. Admitted 10 October 1867.

HUNTER, EDWARD (1793-1883). Was voted in 23 January 1867. Admitted 25 January 1867.

HYDE, ORSON (1805-1878). Admitted 13 March 1844.

James, Samuel (1806-). Admitted 19 March 1844. Dropped 4 February 1845.

Jennings, William (1823-1886). Admitted 10 April 1880.

Johnson, Benjamin F. (1818-1905). Admitted between 14 March and 23 March 1844.

Kimball, Charles S. (1843-1925). Was voted in 23 January 1867. Admitted 25 January 1867.

Kimball, David P. (1839-1883). Was voted in 23 January 1867. Admitted 25 January 1867.

KIMBALL, HEBER C. (1801-1868). Attended provisional meeting 10 March 1844. Admitted 11 March 1844.

Kimball, Heber P. (1835-1885). Was voted in 23 January 1867. Admitted 5 April 1867.

Layton, Christopher (1821-1898). Admitted 29 June 1883.

Lee, John D. (1812-1877). Admitted 1 March 1845.

Lewis, Philip B. (1804-1877). Admitted between 14 March and 11 April 1844.

Little, Feramorz (1820-1887). Admitted 21 April 1880.

Lott, Cornelius P. (1798-1850). Admitted between 14 March and 11 April 1844.

LYMAN, AMASA M. (1813-1877). Admitted between 14 March and 23 March 1844. Possibly dropped after 25 January 1867; otherwise remained a technical member until death.

LYMAN, FRANCIS M. (1840-1916). Admitted 10 April 1880.

Marks, William (1792-1872). Admitted 19 March 1844. Dropped 4 February 1845.

Miller, George (1794-1856). Attended provisional meeting 10 March 1844. Admitted 11 March 1844. Dropped after 26 December 1846.

Morley, Isaac (1786-1865). Was voted in 1 March 1845.

Murdock, John R. (1826-1913). Considered as new member on 10 April 1880. Admitted 28 June 1883.

Nuttall, L. John (1834-1905). Admitted 10 April 1880. Elected clerk 10 April 1880.

Pack, John (1809-1885). Admitted 1 March 1845. Released due to old age 24 June 1882.

PAGE, JOHN E. (1799-1867). Admitted 1 March 1845. Dropped 12 November 1846.

Parker, John D. (1799-1891). Admitted 19 March 1844. Released due to old age 24 June 1882.

PENROSE, CHARLES W. (1832-1925). Admitted 26 June 1882.

Peterson, Canute (1824-1902). Was voted in 27 June 1882. Admitted 10 October 1882.

Phelps, John (1800-1883). Attended provisional meeting 10 March 1844 but not admitted to Council of Fifty once formal meetings began 11 March 1844.

Phelps, William W. (1792-1872). Attended provisional meeting 10 March 1844. Admitted 11 March 1844.

PRATT, ORSON (1811-1881). Attended provisional meeting 10 March 1844. Admitted 11 March 1844.

PRATT, PARLEY P. (1807-1857). Attended provisional meeting 10 March 1844. Admitted 11 March 1844.

Pratt, Parley P., Jr. (1837-1897). Admitted 25 January 1867.

PRESTON, WILLIAM B. (1830-1908). Admitted 10 April 1880.

REYNOLDS, GEORGE (1842-1909). Admitted 8 April 1881.

RICH, CHARLES C. (1809-1883). Admitted between 14 March and 23 March 1844. Released due to old age 24 June 1882.

Rich, Joseph C. (1841-1908). Admitted 25 January 1867.

RICHARDS, FRANKLIN D. (1821-1899). Admitted 17 March 1849.

Richards, Franklin S. (1849-1934). Admitted 10 April 1880.

Richards, Heber John (1840-1919). Was voted in 23 January 1867. Admitted 5 October 1867.

Richards, Levi. (1799-1876). Admitted 11 March 1844.

Richards, Phinehas (1788-1874). Admitted 6 December 1848.

RICHARDS, WILLARD (1804-1854). Attended provisional meeting 10 March 1844 and appointed chairman. Admitted officially 11 March 1844. Released as provisional chairman and made recorder 13 March 1844.

RIGDON, SIDNEY (1793-1876). Admitted 19 March 1844. Dropped 4 February 1845.

Rockwell, Orrin Porter (1815-1878). Admitted 19 March 1844.

ROCKWOOD, ALBERT P. (1805-1879). Admitted 1 March 1845.

Roundy, Shadrach (1789-1872). Was voted in 1 March 1845.

Sharp, John (1820-1891). Admitted 25 January 1867.

Shumway, Charles (1806-1898). Admitted 18 or 22 April 1845. Released due to old age 24 June 1882.

Shurtliff, Lewis W. (1835-1922). Admitted 10 April 1883.

Smith, Elias (1804-1888). Admitted between 14 March and 11 April 1844.

SMITH, GEORGE A. (1817-1875). Attended provisional meeting 10 March 1844. Admitted 11 March 1844.

SMITH, HYRUM (1800-1844). Attended provisional meeting 10 March 1844. Admitted 11 March 1844.

SMITH, JOHN (1781-1854). Admitted between 14 March and 23 March 1844.

SMITH, JOHN HENRY (1848-1911). Admitted 10 April 1880.

SMITH, JOSEPH (1805-1844). Attended provisional meeting 10 March 1844. Admitted 11 March 1844. Appointed standing chairman 13 March 1844. Ordained and anointed Prophet, Priest, and King over Israel on Earth 11 April 1844.

SMITH, JOSEPH F. (1838-1918). Was voted in 23 January 1867. Admitted 25 January 1867.

Smith, Silas S. (1830-1910). Admitted 10 April 1880.

SMITH, WILLIAM (1811-1894). Admitted 25 April 1844. Dropped 9 September 1845.

Smith, William R. (1826-1894). Admitted 10 April 1880.

Smoot, Abraham O. (1815-1895). Admitted 25 January 1867.

SNOW, ERASTUS (1818-1888). Admitted 11 March 1844.

SNOW, LORENZO (1814-1901). Admitted 10 March 1849.

Snow, Willard (1811-1853). Admitted 6 December 1848.

Spencer, Daniel (1794-1868). Was voted in 1 March 1845. Admitted 18 March 1845.

Spencer, Orson (1802-1855). Admitted 19 March 1844.

Stout, Hosea (1810-1889). Admitted 25 January 1867.

Taylor, George J. (1834-1915). Was voted in 23 January 1867. Admitted 25 January 1867.

TAYLOR, JOHN (1808-1887). Attended provisional meeting 10 March 1844. Admitted 11 March 1844. Elected standing chairman 10 April 1880. Anointed and ordained as King, Priest, and Ruler over Israel on Earth on 4 February 1885.

TAYLOR, JOHN W. (1858-1916). Admitted 9 October 1884.

TAYLOR, WILLIAM W. (1853-1884). Admitted 10 April 1880. Elected assistant clerk 10 April 1880.

TEASDALE, GEORGE (1831-1907). Was voted in 26 June 1882. Admitted 10 October 1882.

THATCHER, MOSES (1842-1909). Admitted 10 April 1880.

Thayer, Ezra (1790-). Admitted between 14 March and 11 April 1844. Dropped sometime after 22 April 1845.

Turley, Theodore (1801-1871). Admitted 1 March 1845.

VAN COTT, JOHN (1814-1883). Admitted 12 October 1880.

Wasson, Lorenzo D. (1819-1857). Attended provisional meeting 10 March 1844. Admitted 11 March 1844. Dropped 4 February 1845.

WELLS, DANIEL H. (1814-1891). Admitted 6 December 1848.

Wells, Junius F. (1854-1930). Admitted 10 April 1880.

WHITNEY, NEWEL K. (1795-1850). Attended provisional meeting 10 March 1844. Admitted 11 March 1844.

WIGHT, LYMAN (1796-1858). Was voted in 18 April 1844. Admitted 3 May 1844. Dropped 4 February 1845.

WINDER, JOHN R. (1820-1910). Admitted 8 April 1881.

WOODRUFF, WILFORD (1807-1898). Admitted 13 March 1844.

Woodworth, Lucien (1799-1867). Admitted 11 March 1844. Dropped after 1848.

Yearsley, David D. (1808-1849). Admitted between 14 March and 11 April 1844.

YOUNG, BRIGHAM (1801-1877). Attended provisional meeting 10 March 1844. Admitted 11 March 1844. Appointed standing chairman 4 February 1845. Anointed and ordained King, Priest, and Ruler over Israel on Earth before 12 February 1849.

YOUNG, BRIGHAM, JR. (1836-1903). Admitted 23 January 1867.

Young, John (1791-1870). Admitted 9 Feburary 1849.

YOUNG, JOHN W. (1844-1924). Admitted 5 October 1867.

YOUNG, JOSEPH (1797-1881). Admitted 1 March 1845.

YOUNG, JOSEPH A. (1834-1875). Admitted 23 January 1867.

Young, Phineas H. (1799-1879). Admitted 15 April 1845. His "fellowship" in the Council of Fifty was challenged 22 August 1851, but he reconciled himself with the Council on that date.

YOUNG, SEYMOUR B. (1837-1924). Admitted 9 October 1884.

Family Relationships among 101 Current General Authorities and Their Wives, 1996

All serving in September 1996 (*released in October); U.S. born, except where noted; main entries only for names in CAPITALS; data unavailable on marriages of children.

ABREA, ANGEL, Argentinean (First Quorum of the Seventy)
—none
    wife Maria Victoria Chiapparino de Abrea
        —none

ALVAREZ, LINO, Mexican (Second Quorum of the Seventy)
—none
    wife Angelia de Villanueva de Alvarez
        —none

AMADO, CARLOS H., Guatemalan (First Quorum of the Seventy)
—none
    wife Mayavel Pineda Amado
        —none

ANDERSEN, NEIL L. (First Quorum of the Seventy)
—none
    wife Kathy Sue Williams Andersen
        —none

ARCHIBALD, DALLAS N. (First Quorum of the Seventy)
—1st cousin, 1 rvd, of Keith W. Wilcox, a former Seventy
—3rd cousin, 1 rvd, of wife of W. DON LADD
—4th cousin of wife of WILLIAM ROLFE KERR
—4th cousin, 1 rvd, of MERRILL J. BATEMAN
    wife Linda Ritchie Archibald
        —3rd cousin, 1 rvd, of W. EUGENE HANSEN

*ASAY, CARLOS E. (First Quorum of the Seventy)
—2nd cousin, 1 rvd, of former LDS president Ezra Taft Benson
—3rd cousin of ROBERT D. HALES
—3rd cousin, 1 rvd, of wife of GARY J. COLEMAN
—2nd-great-grandson of former apostle Ezra T. Benson
    wife Colleen Webb Asay
        —3rd cousin of wife of LOWELL D. WOOD
        —3rd cousin, 1 rvd, of wife of GENE R. COOK

AYALA, EDUARDO, Chilean (Second Quorum of the Seventy)
—none
    wife Blanca Espinoza de Ayala
        —none

BALLARD, M. RUSSELL (Quorum of the Twelve Apostles)
—nephew of former patriarch Joseph F. Smith (b. 1899)
—grandson of former apostles Melvin J. Ballard and Hyrum M. Smith
—grandnephew of former LDS president Joseph Fielding Smith
—3rd cousin of emeritus patriarch Eldred G. Smith
—4th cousin, 1 rvd, of wife of JAMES O. MASON
—great-grandson of LDS president Joseph F. Smith
—2nd-great-grandson of Presiding Patriarch Hyrum Smith
—3rd-great-grandson of Presiding Patriarch Joseph Smith, Sr.
    wife Barbara Bowen Ballard
          —2nd cousin, 1 rvd, of JOHN H. GROBERG
          —3rd cousin, 1 rvd, of THOMAS S. MONSON
          —3rd cousin, 1 rvd, of GRAHAM W. DOXEY
          —4th cousin of wife of CECIL O. SAMUELSON
          —4th cousin of BRUCE D. PORTER

BANKS, BEN B. (First Quorum of the Seventy)
—3rd cousin, 1 rvd, of wife of JERALD L. TAYLOR
    wife Susan Kearnes Banks
          —2nd cousin of LOWELL D. WOOD
          —4th cousin of wife of ROBERT D. HALES

BATEMAN, MERRILL J. (First Quorum of the Seventy)
—3rd cousin of Glen L. Rudd, a former Seventy
—4th cousin of Keith W. Wilcox, a former Seventy
—4th cousin, 1 rvd, of DALLAS N. ARCHIBALD
    wife Marilyn Scholes Bateman
          —3rd cousin of GLENN L. PACE
          —3rd cousin of Russell C. Taylor, a former Seventy
          —3rd cousin, 1 rvd, of wife of KEITH B. McMULLIN
          —4th cousin of LYNN A. MICKELSEN

BRADFORD, WILLIAM R. (First Quorum of the Seventy)
—2nd cousin of W. MACK LAWRENCE
—2nd cousin, 1 rvd, of wife of DALLIN H. OAKS
—3rd cousin of wife of JACK H. GOASLIND
—3rd cousin of wife of MARLIN K. JENSEN
—3rd cousin, 1 rvd, of EARL C. TINGEY
    wife Mary Ann Bird Bradford
          —1st cousin, 1 rvd, of wife of DENNIS B. NEUENSCHWANDER
          —2nd cousin, 1 rvd, of JAY E. JENSEN
          —2nd cousin, 2 rvd, of wife of JAY E. JENSEN
          —3rd cousin of former Seventy's president A. Theodore Tuttle
          —3rd cousin, 1 rvd, of Sterling W. Sill, former Assistant and Seventy
          —3rd cousin, 1 rvd, of wife of ROBERT D. HALES
          —4th cousin of Francis M. Gibbons, a former Seventy

BROUGH, MONTE J. (Presidency of the Seventy)
—2nd cousin, 1 rvd, of George I. Cannon, a former Seventy
—great-grandnephew of LDS president Heber J. Grant
—2nd-great-grandson of First Presidency counselor Jedediah M. Grant
    wife Ada Lanette Barker Brough
          —none

BROWN, L. EDWARD (Second Quorum of the Seventy)
—none
    wife Carol Ewer Brown
          —none

BURTON, H. DAVID (Presiding Bishop)
—1st cousin, 2 rvd, of Theodore M. Burton, former Assistant and Seventy
—2nd-great-grandson of Presiding Bishopric counselor Robert T. Burton
> wife Barbara Matheson Burton
>> —2nd cousin, 1 rvd, of former LDS president Spencer W. Kimball
>> —3rd cousin, 1 rvd, of DENNIS B. NEUENSCHWANDER

BUSCHE, F. ENZIO, German (First Quorum of the Seventy)
—none
> wife Jutta Baum Busche
>> —none

CALDWELL, C. MAX (Second Quorum of the Seventy)
—3rd cousin, 1 rvd, of W. MACK LAWRENCE
> wife Bonnie Lee Adamson Caldwell
>> —2nd cousin, 2 rvd, of first wife of L. TOM PERRY
>> —3rd cousin of BOYD K. PACKER
>> —3rd cousin, 1 rvd, of JOHN H. GROBERG

CARMACK, JOHN K. (First Quorum of the Seventy)
—2nd cousin of wife of JAMES O. MASON
> wife Shirley Fay Allen Carmack
>> —1st cousin, 1 rvd, of DAVID B. HAIGHT
>> —3rd cousin of H. Verlan Andersen, a former Seventy
>> —4th cousin of F. Arthur Kay, a former Seventy
>> —4th cousin of wife of W. CRAIG ZWICK

CHILD, SHELDON F. (Second Quorum of the Seventy)
—3rd cousin, 1 rvd, of wife of LOWELL D. WOOD
> wife Joan Haacke Child
>> —none

CHRISTENSEN, JOE J. (Presidency of the Seventy)
—none
> wife Ida Barbara Kohler Christensen
>> —none

CHRISTOFFERSON, D. TODD (First Quorum of the Seventy)
—none
> wife Katherine Thelma Jacob Christofferson
>> —2nd cousin, 1 rvd, of wife of RICHARD G. SCOTT
>> —4th cousin of wife of W. CRAIG ZWICK
>> —4th cousin, 1 rvd, of DENNIS B. NEUENSCHWANDER

CLARKE, J. RICHARD (First Quorum of the Seventy)
—none
> wife Barbara Jean Reed Clarke
>> —2nd cousin, 1 rvd, of J. Thomas Fyans, a former Seventy's president
>> —2nd cousin, 2 rvd, of former apostle Albert E. Bowen

COLEMAN, GARY J. (Second Quorum of the Seventy)
—none
> wife Judith Rene England Coleman
>> —3rd cousin, 1 rvd, of CARLOS E. ASAY

CONDIE, SPENCER J. (First Quorum of the Seventy)
—2nd cousin of RICHARD C. EDGLEY
—3rd cousin, 1 rvd, of THOMAS S. MONSON
—3rd cousin, 1 rvd, of wife of JACK H. GOASLIND
> wife Brigitte Dorthea Speth Condie
>> —none

COOK, GENE R. (First Quorum of the Seventy)
—none
    wife Janelle Schlink Cook
        —3rd cousin, 1 rvd, of wife of CARLOS E. ASAY

COOK, QUENTIN L. (Second Quorum of the Seventy)
—1st cousin, 2 rvd, of former LDS president Spencer W. Kimball
—3rd cousin of BRUCE D. PORTER
—great-grandnephew of Seventy's president J. Golden Kimball
—2nd-great-grandson of First Presidency counselor Heber C. Kimball
    wife Mary Gaddie Cook
        —1st cousin, 2 rvd, of former Seventy's president Oscar A. Kirkham;
        —2nd cousin of wife of ANDREW W. PETERSON
        —3rd cousin of wife of REX D. PINEGAR
        —2nd-great-granddaughter of Presiding Bishop Edward Hunter

COSTA, CLAUDIO R. M., Brazilian (Second Quorum of the Seventy)
—none
    wife Margareth Fernandes Morgado Mendes Costa
        —none

*CRAVEN, RULON G. (Second Quorum of the Seventy)
—4th cousin of RUSSELL M. NELSON
    wife Donna Lee Lunt Craven
        —1st cousin, 2 rvd, of JERALD L. TAYLOR

*DAVILA, JULIO E., Colombian (Second Quorum of the Seventy)
—none
    wife Mary Zapata Davila
        —none

DELLENBACH, ROBERT K. (First Quorum of the Seventy)
—none
    wife Mary Jayne Broadbent Dellenbach
        —1st cousin, 1 rvd, of former Presidency counselor Stephen L Richards
        —1st cousin, 1 rvd, of former Assistant Stayner Richards
        —3rd cousin of former apostle LeGrand Richards
        —3rd cousin of former Assistant and Seventy's president Franklin D.
            Richards
        —3rd cousin, 1 rvd, of former Seventy's president Clifford E. Young
        —4th cousin of former Seventy's president S. Dilworth Young
        —4th cousin of wife of JOSEPH B. WIRTHLIN
        —great-granddaughter of First Presidency counselor Willard Richards

DICKSON, JOHN B. (First Quorum of the Seventy)
—4th cousin of wife of V. DALLAS MERRELL
    wife Delores Ann Jones Dickson
        —4th cousin of wife of RICHARD B. WIRTHLIN
        —4th cousin of Waldo P. Call, a former Seventy
        —4th cousin of Russell C. Taylor, a former Seventy
        —2nd-great-grandniece of Apostle Orson Pratt
        —2nd-great-grandniece of Apostle Parley P. Pratt

*DOXEY, GRAHAM W. (Second Quorum of the Seventy)
—2nd cousin, 1 rvd, of THOMAS S. MONSON
—2nd cousin, 1 rvd, of Bernard P. Brockbank, former Assistant and Seventy
—3rd cousin, 1 rvd, of wife of M. RUSSELL BALLARD

wife Mary Louise Young Doxey
   —2nd cousin of former Seventy's president S. Dilworth Young
   —2nd cousin, 1 rvd, of former Seventy's president Clifford E. Young
   —2nd cousin, 1 rvd, of LeGrand Curtis, a former Seventy
   —3rd cousin of wife of JOSEPH B. WIRTHLIN
   —3rd cousin of HENRY B. EYRING
   —3rd cousin of wife of LANCE B. WICKMAN
   —3rd cousin, 1 rvd, of former Presidency counselor Stephen L Richards
   —3rd cousin, 1 rvd, of former Assistant Stayner Richards
   —3rd cousin, 1 rvd, of wife of W. DON LADD
   —4th cousin of former apostle LeGrand Richards
   —great-granddaughter of LDS president Brigham Young
   —great-granddaughter of LDS president Lorenzo Snow

DUNN, LOREN C. (First Quorum of the Seventy)
—son-in-law of former Assistant John Longden
   wife Frances Sharon Longden Dunn
   —2nd cousin of EARL C. TINGEY

EDGLEY, RICHARD C. (First Counselor to Presiding Bishop)
—2nd cousin of SPENCER J. CONDIE
—3rd cousin, 1 rvd, of wife of JACK H. GOASLIND
   wife Pauline Nielson Edgley
   —4th cousin of L. ALDIN PORTER
   —4th cousin of DEAN L. LARSEN
   —4th cousin of DENNIS B. NEUENSCHWANDER
   —4th cousin, 1 rvd, of L. TOM PERRY

EYRING, HENRY B. (Quorum of the Twelve Apostles)
—1st cousin, 1 rvd, of former Presidency counselor Marion G. Romney
—2nd cousin of wife of LANCE B. WICKMAN
—2nd cousin, 1 rvd, of RONALD E. POELMAN
—2nd cousin, 1 rvd, of former apostle Adam S. Bennion
—2nd cousin, 1 rvd, of former Presiding Bishop Victor L. Brown
—2nd cousin, 1 rvd, of former Seventy's president Samuel O. Bennion
—3rd cousin of Richard P. Lindsay, a former Seventy
—3rd cousin of wife of GRAHAM W. DOXEY
   wife Kathleen Johnson Eyring
   —2nd cousin, 1 rvd, of wife of F. DAVID STANLEY
   —3rd cousin of H. Burke Peterson, former Bishopric counselor and member
      of the Seventy
   —3rd cousin, 1 rvd, of MARLIN K. JENSEN

FAUST, JAMES E. (Second Counselor to Church President)
—1st cousin, 2 rvd, of former apostle Richard R. Lyman
—3rd cousin of former Seventy's president Marion D. Hanks
—3rd cousin, 1 rvd, of GORDON B. HINCKLEY
—3rd cousin, 1 rvd, of former Seventy's president S. Dilworth Young
—3rd cousin, 2 rvd, of former LDS president George Albert Smith
—3rd cousin, 2 rvd, of former Assistant Nicholas G. Smith
—great-grandnephew of former apostle Spencer W. Kimball
—2nd-great-grandson of former apostle Amasa M. Lyman
   wife Ruth Wright Faust
   —3rd cousin of former Presidency counselor Marion G. Romney
   —3rd cousin, 1 rvd, of wife of HUGH W. PINNOCK
   —3rd cousin, 1 rvd, of V. DALLAS MERRELL
   —3rd cousin, 1 rvd, of wife of LANCE B. WICKMAN

FEATHERSTONE, VAUGHN J. (First Quorum of the Seventy)
—none
    wife Merlene Miner Featherstone
        —great-grandniece of former apostle Orson Hyde

FOWLER, JOHN E. (Second Quorum of the Seventy)
—2nd cousin, 2 rvd, of wife of RICHARD G. SCOTT
—2nd cousin, 2 rvd, of wife of LANCE B. WICKMAN
—3rd cousin, 2 rvd, of wife of GLENN L. PACE
    wife Marie Spilsbury Fowler
        —3rd cousin of DAVID B. HAIGHT
        —granddaughter of former apostle Charles A. Callis

GOASLIND, JACK H. (Presidency of the Seventy)
—3rd cousin of wife of W. CRAIG ZWICK
    wife Gwen Caroline Bradford Goaslind
        —2nd cousin, 1 rvd, of former apostle Matthew Cowley
        —3rd cousin of WILLIAM R. BRADFORD
        —3rd cousin, 1 rvd, of SPENCER J. CONDIE
        —3rd cousin, 1 rvd, of wife of CREE-L KOFFORD
        —3rd cousin, 1 rvd, of RICHARD C. EDGLEY
        —4th cousin of JEFFREY R. HOLLAND
        —great-granddaughter of First Presidency counselor John R. Winder

GROBERG, JOHN H. (First Quorum of the Seventy)
—1st cousin, 2 rvd, of GORDON B. HINCKLEY
—2nd cousin, 1 rvd, of wife of NEAL A. MAXWELL
—2nd cousin, 1 rvd, of wife of M. RUSSELL BALLARD
—3rd cousin, 1 rvd, of wife of C. MAX CALDWELL
—4th cousin of ROBERT D. HALES
—4th cousin of wife of KEITH B. McMULLIN
—4th cousin, 1 rvd, of EARL C. TINGEY
—great-grandnephew of Apostle Arza A. Hinckley
    wife Jean Sabin Groberg
        —4th cousin of wife of DALLIN H. OAKS
        —4th cousin, 1 rvd, of wife of W. EUGENE HANSEN

HAFEN, BRUCE C. (First Quorum of the Seventy)
—2nd cousin, 1 rvd, of former Seventy's president A. Theodore Tuttle
—3rd cousin of Lloyd P. George, a former Seventy
—3rd cousin of wife of W. DON LADD
    wife Gael Marie Kartchner Hafen
        —1st cousin, 1 rvd, of wife of ROBERT E. WELLS
        —2nd cousin, 1 rvd, of JERALD L. TAYLOR
        —2nd cousin, 1 rvd, of Waldo P. Call, a former Seventy
        —2nd cousin, 1 rvd, of Lloyd P. George, a former Seventy
        —3rd cousin, 1 rvd, of wife of W. DON LADD

HAIGHT, DAVID B. (Quorum of the Twelve Apostles)
—1st cousin, 1 rvd, of wife of JOHN K. CARMACK
—2nd cousin, 1 rvd, of H. Verlan Andersen, a former Seventy
—3rd cousin of wife of JOHN E. FOWLER
—3rd cousin of F. Arthur Kay, a former Seventy
    wife Ruby Mildred Olson Haight
        —none

HALES, ROBERT D. (Quorum of the Twelve Apostles)
—3rd cousin of CARLOS E. ASAY
—3rd cousin of GLENN L. PACE
—3rd cousin, 1 rvd, of EARL C. TINGEY
—4th cousin of L. ALDIN PORTER
—4th cousin of JOHN H. GROBERG
—4th cousin of BRUCE D. PORTER
—4th cousin of wife of KEITH B. McMULLIN
—4th cousin of H. Verlan Andersen, a former Seventy
—4th cousin, 1 rvd, of CECIL O. SAMUELSON
    wife Mary Elene Crandall Hales
        —3rd cousin, 1 rvd, of wife of WILLIAM R. BRADFORD
        —4th cousin of wife of BEN B. BANKS
        —4th cousin of wife of DENNIS B. NEUENSCHWANDER

HAMMOND, F. MELVIN (First Quorum of the Seventy)
—3rd cousin of LYNN A. MICKELSEN
—2nd-great-grandnephew of Apostle John F. Boynton
    wife Evona Bonnie Sellers Hammond
        —none

*HAN, IN SANG, Korean (Second Quorum of the Seventy)
—none
    wife Kyu In Lee
        —none

HANSEN, W. EUGENE (Presidency of the Seventy)
—2nd cousin, 1 rvd, of former apostle LeGrand Richards
—3rd cousin of former Presidency counselor Stephen L Richards
—3rd cousin of former Assistant Stayner Richards
—3rd cousin, 1 rvd, of wife of DALLAS N. ARCHIBALD
    wife Jeanine Showell Hansen
        —4th cousin, 1 rvd, of wife of JOHN H. GROBERG

HILLAM, HAROLD G. (Presidency of the Seventy)
—none
    wife Carol Lois Rasmussen Hillam
        —none

HINCKLEY, GORDON B. (Church President)
—1st cousin of JOSEPH B. WIRTHLIN
—1st cousin of RICHARD B. WIRTHLIN
—nephew of former apostle Arza A. Hinckley
—1st cousin, 1 rvd, of wife of NEAL A. MAXWELL
—1st cousin, 2 rvd, of JOHN H. GROBERG
—2nd cousin, 1 rvd, of Albert Choules, a former Seventy
—3rd cousin, 1 rvd, of former apostle Rudger Clawson
—3rd cousin, 1 rvd, of JAMES E. FAUST
    wife Marjorie Pay Hinckley
        —none

HOLLAND, JEFFREY R. (Quorum of the Twelve Apostles)
—2nd cousin, 1 rvd, of wife of CREE-L KOFFORD
—3rd cousin of wife of EARL C. TINGEY
—3rd cousin of ROBERT E. WELLS
—2nd cousin, 2 rvd, of former Seventy's president Antoine R. Ivins
—2nd cousin, 2 rvd, of former Seventy's president Robert L. Backman
—3rd cousin, 1 rvd, of George I. Cannon, a former Seventy

—4th cousin of wife of JACK H. GOASLIND
—2nd-great-grandnephew of former apostle Erastus Snow
—2nd-great-grandnephew of former Presidency Counselor George Q. Cannon
    wife Patricia Terry Holland
        —2nd-great-granddaughter of Seventy's president Zerah Pulsipher

HOWARD, F. BURTON (First Quorum of the Seventy)
—2nd cousin of WILLIAM ROLFE KERR
—2nd cousin, 1 rvd, of wife of JOHN E. FOWLER
—4th cousin of CREE-L KOFFORD
    wife Caroline Heise Howard
        —none

JENSEN, JAY E. (First Quorum of the Seventy)
—2nd cousin, 1 rvd, of wife of WILLIAM R. BRADFORD
—3rd cousin of wife of DENNIS B. NEUENSCHWANDER
—3rd cousin, 1 rvd, of former Seventy's preseident A. Theodore Tuttle
    wife Lona Lee Child Jensen
        —2nd cousin, 2 rvd, of wife of WILLIAM R. BRADFORD
        —3rd cousin, 1 rvd, of wife of DENNIS B. NEUENSCHWANDER

JENSEN, MARLIN K. (First Quorum of the Seventy)
—1st cousin, 2 rvd, of former LDS president David O. McKay
—1st cousin, 2 rvd, of former Assistant Thomas E. McKay
—2nd cousin, 1 rvd, of George R. Hill, a former Seventy
—3rd cousin, 1 rvd, of wife of HENRY B. EYRING
—4th cousin of BRUCE D. PORTER
    wife Kathleen Bushnell Jensen
        —2nd cousin, 1 rvd, of Bernard P. Brockbank, former Assistant and Seventy
        —3rd cousin of WILLIAM R. BRADFORD
        —3rd cousin, 1 rvd, of BRUCE D. PORTER

JOHNSON, KENNETH, English (First Quorum of the Seventy)
—none
    wife Pamela Violet Wilson Johnson
        —none

KENDRICK, L. LIONEL (First Quorum of the Seventy)
—none
    wife Myrtis Lee Noble Kendrick
        —none

KERR, WILLIAM ROLFE (Second Quorum of the Seventy)
—2nd cousin of F. BURTON HOWARD
—2nd cousin, 1 rvd, of wife of JOHN E. FOWLER
    wife Janeil Raybould Kerr
        —3rd cousin, 1 rvd, of Keith W. Wilcox, a former Seventy
        —4th cousin of DALLAS N. ARCHIBALD
        —4th cousin of F. DAVID STANLEY

KIKUCHI, YOSHIHIKO, Japanese (First Quorum of the Seventy)
—none
    wife Toshiko Koshiya Kikuchi
        —none

KOFFORD, CREE-L (First Quorum of the Seventy)
—4th cousin of F. BURTON HOWARD
    wife Ila Jean Macdonald Kofford
        —2nd cousin, 1 rvd, of JEFFREY R. HOLLAND
        —3rd cousin, 1 rvd, of wife of JACK H. GOASLIND

LADD, W. DON (Second Quorum of the Seventy)
—none
    wife Ruth Lynne Pearson Ladd
        —3rd cousin of BRUCE C. HAFEN
        —3rd cousin of Lloyd P. George, a former Seventy
        —2nd cousin, 2 rvd, of former Seventy's president Clifford E. Young
        —3rd cousin, 1 rvd, of former Seventy's president S. Dilworth Young
        —3rd cousin, 1 rvd, of wife of JOSEPH B. WIRTHLIN
        —3rd cousin, 1 rvd, of DALLAS N. ARCHIBALD
        —3rd cousin, 1 rvd, of wife of BRUCE C. HAFEN
        —3rd cousin, 1 rvd, of wife of GRAHAM W. DOXEY
        —2nd-great-grandniece of LDS president Brigham Young

LARSEN, DEAN L. (First Quorum of the Seventy)
—4th cousin of wife of RICHARD C. EDGLEY
    wife Geneal Johnson Larsen
        —none

*LAWRENCE, W. MACK (Second Quorum of the Seventy)
—2nd cousin of WILLIAM R. BRADFORD
—3rd cousin, 1 rvd, of C. MAX CALDWELL
    wife Jacqueline Elsie Young Lawrence
        —2nd cousin of CECIL O. SAMUELSON

LIM, AUGUSTO A., Filipino (Second Quorum of the Seventy)
—none
    wife Myrna Garcia Morillo Lim
        —none

McMULLIN, KEITH B. (Second Counselor to Presiding Bishop)
—none
    wife Carolyn Jean Gibbs McMullin
        —2nd cousin of LYNN A. MICKELSEN
        —3rd cousin, 1 rvd, of wife of MERRILL J. BATEMAN
        —4th cousin of ROBERT D. HALES
        —4th cousin of JOHN H. GROBERG
        —4th cousin, 1 rvd, of EARL C. TINGEY

MADSEN, JOHN M. (Second Quorum of the Seventy)
—none
    wife Diane Dursteler Madsen
        —none

MASON, JAMES O. (Second Quorum of the Seventy)
—4th cousin, 1 rvd, of wife of HUGH W. PINNOCK
    wife Lydia Marie Smith Mason
        —2nd cousin of JOHN K. CARMACK
        —3rd cousin, 1 rvd, of former LDS president George Albert Smith
        —3rd cousin, 1 rvd, of former LDS president Joseph Fielding Smith
        —3rd cousin, 1 rvd, of former apostle Hyrum M. Smith
        —3rd cousin, 1 rvd, of former Assistant Nicholas G. Smith
        —4th cousin of emeritus patriarch Eldred G. Smith
        —4th cousin, 1 rvd, of M. RUSSELL BALLARD
        —1st cousin, 3 rvd, of LDS president Joseph Smith
        —1st cousin, 3 rvd, of Presiding Patriarch Hyrum Smith
        —2nd-great-grandniece of Presiding Patriarch Joseph Smith, Sr.

MAXWELL, NEAL A. (Quorum of the Twelve Apostles)
—1st cousin, 2 rvd, of O. Leslie Stone, former Assistant and Seventy
        wife Colleen Fern Hinckley Maxwell
                —1st cousin, 1 rvd, of GORDON B. HINCKLEY
                —2nd cousin, 1 rvd, of JOHN H. GROBERG
                —3rd cousin, 1 rvd, of former Presidency counselor N. Eldon Tanner
                —4th cousin of H. Burke Peterson, former Bishopric counselor and Seventy
                —grandniece of former apostle Arza A. Hinckley

MERRELL, V. DALLAS (Second Quorum of the Seventy)
—2nd cousin of Merlin R. Lybbert, a former Seventy
—3rd cousin of W. Grant Bangerter, a former Seventy
—3rd cousin, 1 rvd, of wife of JAMES E. FAUST
        wife Karen Dixon Merrell
                —3rd cousin of wife of DALLIN H. OAKS
                —4th cousin of JOHN B. DICKSON

MICKELSEN, LYNN A. (First Quorum of the Seventy)
—2nd cousin of wife of KEITH B. McMULLIN
—3rd cousin of F. MELVIN HAMMOND
—4th cousin of wife of MERRILL J. BATEMAN
        wife Jeanine Anderson Mickelsen
                —2nd cousin of H. Verlan Andersen, a former Seventy

MONSON, THOMAS S. (First Counselor to Church President)
—2nd cousin, 1 rvd, of GRAHAM W. DOXEY
—3rd cousin, 1 rvd, of wife of M. RUSSELL BALLARD
—3rd cousin, 1 rvd, of SPENCER J. CONDIE
        wife Frances Beverly Johnson Monson
                —none

MORRISON, ALEXANDER B., Canadian (First Quorum of the Seventy)
—none
        wife Shirley Edith Brooks Morrison
                —none

*MUREN, JOSEPH C. (Second Quorum of the Seventy)
—none
        wife Gladys Elizabeth Smith Muren
                —none

*NADAULD, STEPHEN D. (Second Quorum of the Seventy)
—none
        wife Margaret May Dyreng Nadauld
                —none

NELSON, RUSSELL M. (Quorum of the Twelve Apostles)
—4th cousin of RULON G. CRAVEN
        wife Dantzel White Nelson
                —none

NEUENSCHWANDER, DENNIS B. (First Quorum of the Seventy)
—2nd cousin, 2 rvd, of James A. Cullimore, former Assistant and Seventy
—3rd cousin, 1 rvd, of wife of H. DAVID BURTON
—4th cousin of former apostle Delbert L. Stapley
—4th cousin, 1 rvd, of former Seventy's president A. Theodore Tuttle
—4th cousin, 1 rvd, of wife of D. TODD CHRISTOFFERSON

wife Le Ann Clement Neuenschwander
> —1st cousin, 1 rvd, of wife of WILLIAM R. BRADFORD
> —3rd cousin of JAY E. JENSEN
> —3rd cousin, 1 rvd, of wife of JAY E. JENSEN
> —4th cousin of wife of ROBERT D. HALES
> —4th cousin of wife of RICHARD C. EDGLEY

OAKS, DALLIN H. (Quorum of the Twelve Apostles)
—2nd-great-grandnephew of Martin Harris, *Book of Mormon* witness
> wife Verda June Dixon Oaks
> > —2nd cousin of Waldo P. Call, a former Seventy
> > —2nd cousin, 1 rvd, of WILLIAM R. BRADFORD
> > —2nd cousin, 2 rvd, of EARL C. TINGEY
> > —3rd cousin of wife of V. DALLAS MERRELL
> > —4th cousin of wife of JOHN H. GROBERG

PACE, GLENN L. (First Quorum of the Seventy)
—3rd cousin of wife of MERRILL J. BATEMAN
> wife Jolene Clayson Pace
> > —3rd cousin of wife of RICHARD G. SCOTT
> > —3rd cousin of wife of LANCE B. WICKMAN
> > —3rd cousin, 2 rvd, of JOHN E. FOWLER

PACKER, BOYD K. (Quorum of the Twelve Apostles)
—3rd cousin of wife of C. MAX CALDWELL
> wife Donna Edith Smith Packer
> > —3rd-great-granddaughter of Apostle Luke S. Johnson

PARAMORE, JAMES M. (First Quorum of the Seventy)
—none
> wife Helen Heslington Paramore
> > —none

PERRY, L. TOM (Quorum of the Twelve Apostles)
—nephew of former Seventy's president Alma Sonne
—4th cousin, 1 rvd, of EARL C. TINGEY
—4th cousin, 1 rvd, of wife of RICHARD C. EDGLEY
> wife (deceased) Virginia Clare Lee Perry
> > —2nd cousin, 2 rvd, of wife of C. MAX CALDWELL
> wife (current) Barbara Taylor Dayton Perry
> > —1st cousin, 2 rvd, of former Seventy's president John H. Taylor
> > —2nd-great-granddaughter of LDS president John Taylor

PETERSON, ANDREW W. (First Quorum of the Seventy)
—1st cousin, 2 rvd, of former Seventy's president Samuel O. Bennion
> wife Christine Ann Swensen Peterson
> > —2nd cousin of wife of QUENTIN L. COOK
> > —4th cousin, 1 rvd, of wife of KEITH B. McMULLIN
> > —2nd-great-granddaughter of Presiding Bishop Edward Hunter

PINEGAR, REX D. (First Quorum of the Seventy)
—none
> wife Bonnie Lee Crabb Pinegar
> > —1st cousin, 2 rvd, of former Seventy's president Oscar A. Kirkham
> > —3rd cousin of wife of QUENTIN L. COOK

PINNOCK, HUGH W. (First Quorum of the Seventy)
—none
    wife Anne Hawkins Pinnock
        —3rd cousin, 1 rvd, of former Presidency counselor Marion G. Romney
        —3rd cousin, 1 rvd, of wife of JAMES E. FAUST
        —4th cousin of wife of LANCE B. WICKMAN
        —4th cousin, 1 rvd, of JAMES O. MASON

POELMAN, RONALD E. (First Quorum of the Seventy)
—2nd cousin, 1 rvd, of HENRY B. EYRING
    wife (deceased) Claire Howell Stoddard Poelman
        —none
    wife (current) Anne Gregory Osborn Poelman
        —none

PORTER, BRUCE D. (Second Quorum of the Seventy)
—3rd cousin of L. ALDIN PORTER
—3rd cousin of QUENTIN L. COOK
—3rd cousin of H. Verlan Andersen, a former Seventy
—3rd cousin, 1 rvd, of wife of MARLIN K. JENSEN
—4th cousin of wife of M. RUSSELL BALLARD
—4th cousin of ROBERT D. HALES
—4th cousin of MARLIN K. JENSEN
—4th cousin of wife of CECIL O. SAMUELSON
        wife Susan Elizabeth Holland Porter
        —3rd cousin of wife of CECIL O. SAMUELSON

PORTER, L. ALDIN (Presidency of the Seventy)
—3rd cousin of BRUCE D. PORTER
—3rd cousin, 1 rvd, of wife of RICHARD G. SCOTT
—4th cousin of ROBERT D. HALES
—4th cousin of wife of RICHARD C. EDGLEY
—4th cousin of H. Verlan Andersen, a former Seventy
—2nd-great-grandnephew of Apostle Charles C. Rich
    wife Shirley Faye Palmer Porter
        —none

*ROJAS, JORGE A., Mexican (Second Quorum of the Seventy)
—none
    wife Marcela Burgos Perez de Rojas
        —none

SAMUELSON, CECIL O., JR. (First Quorum of the Seventy)
—2nd cousin of wife of W. MACK LAWRENCE
—4th cousin, 1 rvd, of ROBERT D. HALES
    wife Sharon Giauque Samuelson
        —3rd cousin of wife of BRUCE D. PORTER
        —4th cousin of wife of M. RUSSELL BALLARD
        —4th cousin of BRUCE D. PORTER
        —2nd-great-grandniece of Apostle Matthias F. Cowley

SCOTT, RICHARD G. (Quorum of the Twelve Apostles)
—none
    wife Jeanene Watkins Scott (recently deceased)
        —2nd cousin of wife of LANCE B. WICKMAN
        —2nd cousin, 1 rvd, of wife of D. TODD CHRISTOFFERSON
        —2nd cousin, 2 rvd, of JOHN E. FOWLER
        —3rd cousin, 1 rvd, of L. ALDIN PORTER
        —3rd cousin of wife of GLENN L. PACE
        —great-granddaughter of Apostle Charles C. Rich

*SHIMABUKURO, SAM K. (Second Quorum of the Seventy)
—none
        wife Amy Michiko Hirose Shimabukuro
                —none

SIMMONS, DENNIS E. (Second Quorum of the Seventy)
—none
        wife Carolyn Thorpe Simmons
                —none

SORENSEN, DAVID E. (First Quorum of the Seventy)
—none
        wife Verla Anderson Sorensen
                —none

STANLEY, F. DAVID (Second Quorum of the Seventy)
—4th cousin of wife of WILLIAM ROLFE KERR
        wife Annette Shewell Stanley
                —2nd cousin, 1 rvd, of wife of HENRY B. EYRING

TAI, KWOK YUEN, Hong Kong Chinese (Second Quorum of the Seventy)
—none
        wife Hui Hua Tai
                —none

TAYLOR, JERALD L. (Second Quorum of the Seventy)
—1st cousin, 2 rvd, of wife of RULON G. CRAVEN
—2nd cousin of Waldo P. Call, a former Seventy
—2nd cousin of Russell C. Taylor, a former Seventy
—2nd cousin of wife of ROBERT E. WELLS
—2nd cousin, 1 rvd, of wife of BRUCE C. HAFEN
—4th cousin of wife of W. CRAIG ZWICK
        wife Sharon Elizabeth Willis Taylor
                —3rd cousin, 1 rvd, of BEN B. BANKS

TINGEY, EARL C. (Presidency of the Seventy)
—2nd cousin of wife of LOREN C. DUNN
—2nd cousin, 2 rvd, of wife of DALLIN H. OAKS
—3rd cousin, 1 rvd, of ROBERT D. HALES
—3rd cousin, 1 rvd, of WILLIAM R. BRADFORD
—4th cousin, 1 rvd, of JOHN H. GROBERG
—4th cousin, 1 rvd, of wife of KEITH B. McMULLIN
—4th cousin, 1 rvd, of L. TOM PERRY
        wife Joanne Wells Tingey
                —1st cousin of ROBERT E. WELLS
                —1st cousin, 1 rvd, of former LDS president Spencer W. Kimball
                —1st cousin, 1 rvd, of former Presidency counselor J. Reuben Clark
                —3rd cousin of JEFFREY R. HOLLAND
                —2nd cousin, 2 rvd, of former Seventy's president Robert L. Backman

UCHTDORF, DIETER F., Sudetenland German-Czech (First Quorum of the Seventy)
—none
        wife Harriet Reich Uchtdorf
                —none

VINAS, FRANCISCO J., Uruguayan (Second Quorum of the Seventy)
—none
        wife Christina Gaminara Vinas
                —none

WELLS, ROBERT E. (First Quorum of the Seventy)
—1st cousin of wife of EARL C. TINGEY
—1st cousin, 2 rvd, of former LDS president Spencer W. Kimball
—1st cousin, 2 rvd, of former Presidency counselor J. Reuben Clark
—3rd cousin of JEFFREY R. HOLLAND
—2nd cousin, 2 rvd, of former Seventy's president Robert L. Backman
     wife Helen Walser Wells
               —1st cousin of Waldo P. Call, a former Seventy
               —1st cousin, 1 rvd, of wife of BRUCE C. HAFEN
               —2nd cousin of JERALD L. TAYLOR

WICKMAN, LANCE B. (Second Quorum of the Seventy)
—3rd cousin of former Seventy's president Robert L. Backman
     wife Patricia Farr Wickman
               —1st cousin, 1 rvd, of former Presidency counselor Marion G. Romney
               —1st cousin, 1 rvd, of former Seventy's president G. Homer Durham
               —2nd cousin of wife of RICHARD G. SCOTT
               —2nd cousin, 2 rvd, of JOHN E. FOWLER
               —3rd cousin of wife of GLENN L. PACE
               —3rd cousin, 1 rvd, of wife of JAMES E. FAUST
               —4th cousin of wife of HUGH W. PINNOCK
               —2nd great-grandniece of Seventy's president Jacob Gates

WIRTHLIN, JOSEPH B. (Quorum of the Twelve Apostles)
—son of former Presiding Bishop Joseph L. Wirthlin
—brother of RICHARD B. WIRTHLIN
—1st cousin of GORDON B. HINCKLEY
—2nd cousin, 1 rvd, of Albert Choules, a former Seventy
     wife Elisa Young Rogers Wirthlin
               —niece of former Seventy's president Clifford E. Young
               —1st cousin of former Seventy's president S. Dilworth Young
               —granddaughter of former Seventy's president Seymour B. Young
               —great-granddaughter of Seventy's president Joseph Young
               —3rd cousin of wife of GRAHAM W. DOXEY
               —3rd cousin of wife of LOWELL D. WOOD
               —3rd cousin, 1 rvd, of LeGrand Curtis, a former Seventy
               —3rd cousin, 1 rvd, of wife of W. DON LADD
               —3rd cousin, 1 rvd, of former LDS president Spencer W. Kimball
               —3rd cousin, 1 rvd, of former Presidency counselor J. Reuben Clark
               —3rd cousin, 1 rvd, of former Presidency counselor Stephen L Richards
               —3rd cousin, 1 rvd, of former Assistant Stayner Richards
               —4th cousin of former apostle LeGrand Richards
               —4th cousin of wife of ROBERT K. DELLENBACH

WIRTHLIN, RICHARD B. (Second Quorum of the Seventy)
—son of former Presiding Bishop Joseph L. Wirthlin
—brother of JOSEPH B. WIRTHLIN
—1st cousin of GORDON B. HINCKLEY
—2nd cousin, 1 rvd, of Albert Choules, a former Seventy
     wife Jeralie Mae Hilton Chandler Wirthlin
               —4th cousin of Waldo P. Call, a former Seventy
               —4th cousin of Russell C. Taylor, a former Seventy
               —4th cousin of wife of JOHN B. DICKSON
               —2nd-great-granddaughter of Apostle Orson Pratt
               —2nd-great-grandniece of Apostle Parley P. Pratt

WOOD, LOWELL D. (Second Quorum of the Seventy)
—2nd cousin of former Presidency counselor Hugh B. Brown
—2nd cousin of wife of BEN B. BANKS
—2nd cousin, 1 rvd, of former Presidency counselor N. Eldon Tanner
—2nd cousin, 1 rvd, of former Presiding Bishop Victor L. Brown
    wife Lorna Cox Wood
        —2nd cousin, 1 rvd, of former LDS president Harold B. Lee
        —3rd cousin of wife of JOSEPH B. WIRTHLIN
        —3rd cousin of wife of CARLOS E. ASAY
        —3rd cousin, 1 rvd, of SHELDON F. CHILD
        —3rd cousin, 1 rvd, of former Presiding Bishop Victor L. Brown

ZWICK, W. CRAIG (First Quorum of the Seventy)
—3rd cousin of JACK H. GOASLIND
—3rd cousin, 1 rvd, of Russell C. Taylor, a former Seventy
—3rd-great-grandnephew of Seventy's president Sylvester Smith
    wife Janet Kaye Johnson Zwick
        —2nd cousin, 2 rvd, of former Seventy's president Milton R. Hunter
        —3rd cousin, 1 rvd, of emeritus patriarch Eldred G. Smith
        —4th cousin of wife of JOHN K. CARMACK
        —4th cousin of wife of D. TODD CHRISTOFFERSON
        —4th cousin of JERALD L. TAYLOR

Selected Chronology of the Church of Jesus Christ of Latter-day Saints, 1848-1996

1848

14 Jan., Brigham Young instructs Seventy's meeting: "For the first act of adultery you may forgive a man, but if a man beds with [a] woman & does it 10 times he [is] guilty."

17 Jan., bishop's court orders Salt Lake City marshal to give horse thief "39 lashes on the bare back."

24 Jan., Mormons discharged from Mormon Battalion and now working at John Sutter's mill participate in discovery of gold there. This leads to Gold Rush of 1849 which aids Salt Lake City's economy.

11 Mar., Benjamin Covey is excommunicated for having sexual intercourse with two girls "less than Twelve years of age" who are his foster daughters. He is rebaptized and serves as bishop of Salt Lake City Twelfth Ward from 22 February 1849 until 1856.

17 Mar., Hosea Stout tells Salt Lake high council: "It has been my duty to hunt out the rotten spots in this K[ingdom]. . . . even now I have a list [of] who will deny the faith." Stout reassures the council that "I av tried not to handle a man's case until it was right."

27 May, "Today to our utter astonishment, the crickets came by millions, sweeping everything before them." Seagulls, no strangers to settlers in small numbers, arrive in dense flocks to devour crickets but not in time to save whole fields from destruction. Although published letter by First Presidency and LDS sermons refer to this event in non-miraculous terms for several years, anti-Mormon *Warsaw Signal* of 17 Nov. 1849 shows that Mormons soon describe this experience as divine intervention: "This year, as the story goes—the Lord sent immense numbers of gulls from the Lake, to devour the crickets." Seagulls descend during cricket infestations in 1849 and 1850, but apparently not until 1853 does general authority (Orson Hyde) publicly describe the 1848 seagull visitation as miraculous. The "Miracle of the Seagulls" is now memorialized by statue on Salt Lake Temple Square and by adoption of seagull as Utah's state bird.

20 Sept., Brigham Young returns to Salt Lake City and never again leaves Great Basin.

9 Oct., arsonist burns Nauvoo temple. Its ruins are leveled by tornado on 27 May 1850.

12 Nov., *Book of Mormon* witness Oliver Cowdery is baptized into LDS church.

3 Dec., Apostle Lyman Wight is excommunicated for his pamphlet against succession leadership of Brigham Young over LDS church.

1849

1 Jan., "Uncle John" Smith (b. 1781) is ordained as "Patriarch over the Church." He has served in that capacity since 1845. The newly organized First Presidency privately sustained him to that position on 6 Dec. 1847, and church conference publicly did so on 27 Dec.

2 Jan., Brigham Young and Heber C. Kimball of First Presidency and Presiding Bishop Newel K. Whitney sign first paper bills of "Valley Currency." Second issue three days later includes $1,331 worth of re-issued notes from failed Kirtland Safety Society Bank.

6 Jan., high council at Kanesville, Iowa, excommunicates two Mormons for counterfeiting

coins. Investigations into Feb., but council takes no action against two members of theocratic Council of Fifty involved: John M. Bernhisel (who transports counterfeiting equipment to Iowa) and Theodore Turley (mechanic who works with the dies and press). Apostles George A. Smith and Ezra T. Benson allude to their involvement in letter to First Presidency on 27 Mar. Turley is Brigham Young's father-in-law.

1 Feb., first counselor Heber C. Kimball tells Sunday meeting that plural marriage "would end he said when the Church had gon[e] to the Devil or the Priesthood taken from this people [–] then God would give it to another people."

7 Feb., William A. Hickman's affidavit in first issue of church's *Frontier Guardian:* "I do hereby solemnly declare that Mr. [Orson] Hyde never induced me to commit violence on the person of any man, either white or red." Apostle Hyde is editor.

12 Feb., Twelve ordain new men as apostles to fill administrative vacancies in quorum caused by service of three apostles in First Presidency. Lorenzo Snow is first apostle who has attended college (at Oberlin College).

At this meeting Brigham Young refers to himself as "King & Prest." This shows that Council of Fifty has already ordained Young to theocratic office of King.

3 Mar., at Council of Fifty meeting, Brigham Young speaks concerning thieves, murderers, and sexually licentious: "I want their cursed heads to be cut off that they may atone for their crimes." Next day, Council agrees that man has "forfeited his Head," and decides it would be best "to dispose of him privately." Instead, they allow him to live.

5 Mar., organization of theocratic State of Deseret, which is denied statehood in 1850.

13 Mar., Apostle George A. Smith writes sixteen-year-old Joseph Smith III, asking him to come to Utah, with or without his mother.

17 Mar., Brigham Young instructs Council of Fifty regarding two imprisoned men (one of them referred to on 3 Mar.): "he would show them that he was not afraid to take their Head but do as you please with them." Council allows them to live.

27 Mar., Apostles Orson Hyde, George A. Smith, and Ezra T. Benson write Young that Council of Fifty member Peter Haws complains that "Twelve men had swallowed up thirty eight." Council members George Miller, Lyman Wight, and Lucien Woodworth also claim that Quorum of Twelve usurped Fifty's theocratic prerogatives after 1844. Today Smith retorts that Council of Fifty is "nothing but a debating School."

28 Mar., at organization of Utah's Nauvoo Legion, Hosea Stout notes: "John Pack & John D. Lee were each put in nomination for Majors by regular authority & both most contemptuously hissed down. When any person is thus duly nominated I never before knew the people to reject it [–] But on this occasion it appears that they are both a perfect stink in every body's nose."

29 Apr., First Presidency and Quorum of Twelve make following decisions concerning sex in marriage: "not to unite with a woman in view of impregnation till 7 days after the cessation of the menstrual discharge in order for the most healthy procreation. also that after childbirth if delivered of a son she should continue 40 days in her purification [without sexual intercourse with her husband]. If a daughter she [the new mother] should be 70 days separated as unclean for a man. As to sexual connexion during pregnancy[, do] just as they please about that [–] suit themselves." This is earliest known LDS discussion of what is appropriate in sexual relations of married couples. These rules are based on Book of Leviticus, rather than on current medical writings.

1 June, Orson Hyde writes Brigham Young, "Brother Hickman ... is sometimes a little rash and may shoot an innocent Indian, mistaking him for an Omaha horse thief."

8 July, Brigham Young preaches, "if any one was catched stealing to shoot them dead on the spot and they should not be hurt for it."

21 July, Addison Pratt, departing missionary, receives endowment given on Ensign Peak.

24 July, first mass celebration of Pioneer Day; first LDS historical event to be "ritualized."

9 Sept., James H. Mulholland writes anti-Mormon Thomas Sharp from Iowa to inform him

that "I was present last fall when I seen a man hired with a promise of five hundred dollars to go to your place [at Warsaw, Illinois] and take your life. . . . the man that hired Bill Hickman to come and murder you was [Apostle] Orson Hyde." Mulholland is already excommunicated, and Hyde publishes denial of his claim in Jan. 1850.

3 Oct., *Frontier Guardian* observes that "Mr. Jonathan Browning is manufacturing some of the most splendid revolving rifles that we ever saw." He invents one of "the earliest known American repeating rifles" when he moves to Nauvoo in 1842. Establishes gunsmith shop in Ogden, Utah where he continues making his unpatented "six-shot repeater." His son John M. Browning is "the father of modern firearms."

7 Oct., Brigham Young instructs his special counselor, Presiding Patriarch John Smith, to select men to go to California on "Gold Mission" for church. Among "Forty-Niners" who travel to California are about fifty gold-digging Mormon missionaries.

17 Oct., *Frontier Guardian* editorial "Dancing" observes: "Among the Saints, it is regarded not only as a civil recreation, but a religious exercise when conducted by the sanction and under the government of the Church."

9 Dec., Richard Ballentyne begins teaching Sunday school as own activity in Salt Lake City. In 1867 Deseret Sunday School Union becomes churchwide, centrally directed program with George Q. Cannon as first general superintendent. In 1934 LDS headquarters adopts junior Sunday school program which was independently established in local wards. Like Sunday schools, churchwide programs for young men, primary children, high school seminary, adult Aaronic priesthood, Welfare Plan, and Indian Placement begin as local innovations without central church direction. All LDS auxiliaries, except Religion Classes in 1890, are modeled on pre-existing programs of Protestant denominations. Only Relief Society, young women's program, and Religion Classes have direction of headquarters at outset.

1850

28 Feb., incorporation of University of Deseret (later Utah).

14 Mar., Senator Thomas H. Benton of Missouri checks out *Book of Mormon* from Library of Congress. He does not return it until 3 June 1851, first national leader to voluntarily show interest in Mormon scriptures.

7 Apr., Brigham Young is Trustee-in-Trust, first time for LDS president since 1844.

15 June, first issue of church's *Deseret News*, which includes astrological almanacs.

8 July, James J. Strang is publicly crowned "King of Zion" at St. James, Beaver Island, Michigan. Ceremony is performed by George J. Adams, former member of Joseph Smith's Council of Fifty. Non-believers and apostates murder Strang in 1856.

9 Sept., official establishment of Territory of Utah by federal government which also appoints Brigham Young as Utah's first governor on 20 Sept.

14 Sept., incorporation of Perpetual Emigrating Company by General Assembly of State of Deseret. Before federal government forces its disincorporation in 1887, PEF assists more than third of all European immigrants to Utah.

1851

15 Jan., first of Brigham Young's five formal divorces from plural wives. He is only one formally divorced while serving as church president. Joseph Smith informally ended several plural marriages, and four LDS presidents are formally divorced as apostles (John Taylor, Wilford Woodruff, Lorenzo Snow, and Joseph F. Smith).

19 Jan., Utah legislature enacts law against "Sodomy" by "any man or boy," but removes sodomy from criminal code on 6 Mar. 1852, without explanation. As governor Brigham Young signs both laws. Due to absence of sodomy statute, Utah judge drops charges against soldier for raping LDS boy in 1864. Young claims Utah's legislators never criminalized sodomy and he declines to instruct them to do so for next twelve years. Utah legislators criminalize sodomy in 1876 only because federally appointed governor asks them to adopt entire criminal code of California which has five-year imprisonment for

sodomy. For next twenty years LDS judges give 3-6 months of imprisonment to those convicted of homosexual rape, the same sentencing given to young males and females convicted of consensual fornication. Mormons of this era give no known explanations for any of these legislative and judicial actions/inactions.

4 Feb., incorporation of The Church of Jesus Christ of Latter-day Saints.

20 Feb., endowment ceremony is again administered on regular basis in such places as Brigham Young's office and upper room of Council House.

17 Mar., Brigham Young speaks in favor of Madison D. Hambleton who is being tried for shooting and killing man at LDS church services, immediately after closing prayer. The man "seduced" wife of Hambleton who is "acquitted by the Court and also by the Voice of the people present." Hambleton later becomes sheriff in Utah.

28 Mar., General Assembly of State of Deseret dissolves itself to accept jurisdiction of Territory of Utah. In most elections from 1851 to 1869, 99 percent of Utah's voters choose church-approved candidates. Ballots are marked to show how persons vote.

7 Apr., Brigham Young is sustained "prophet, seer, and revelator," first time since 1836. He presents himself this way at conferences until 1859 and again, 1872 to his death.

20 Apr., Alpheus Cutler is excommunicated for leading group opposed to Young.

22 Aug., at Council of Fifty meeting Phineas H. Young admits plotting with Indians to kill Apostle Orson Hyde in Iowa, because Hyde ordered someone to kill Phineas. Hyde mentions William A. Hickman but doesn't admit responsibility for an attempt on Phineas' life. Brigham successfully reconciles these two members of the Fifty.

9 Sept., Brigham Young has conference covenant to accept and obey Word of Wisdom as commandment and to accept excommunication for non-payment of tithing. Church leaders do not consistently enforce either practice until 20th century.

4 Oct., Brigham Young signs law legalizing all laws passed previously by State of Deseret. He adjourns poorly attended meeting of Fifty, does not reconvene it for 15 years.

18 Oct., trial of confessed murderer (and newly returned LDS missionary) Howard Egan. His lawyer Apostle George A. Smith popularizes phrase "mountain common law" and argues: "The man who seduces his neighbor's wife must die, and her nearest relative must kill him!" Fifteen minutes later jury finds Egan not guilty of murder. Church authorities print Smith's full closing argument in *Deseret News*, in two pamphlets, and later in *Journal of Discourses* 1:97. Egan is one of Brigham Young's enforcers.

15 Dec., Baron von Gerolt, Prussia's minister to United States, checks out *Book of Mormon* from Library of Congress. He returns it 16 Feb. 1852. This Berlin diplomat is first representative of foreign government to show interest in Mormon scripture. Brigham Young reports to April 1852 conference that this ambassador requests copies of all LDS publications on behalf of Prussian monarch who "wished to investigate our doctrine."

27 Dec., Governor Brigham Young officially proclaims 1 January 1852 as "a day of Praise and Thanksgiving." In 1863 U.S. President Abraham Lincoln does likewise.

1852

23 Jan., Brigham Young instructs Utah Legislature to legalize slavery because "we must believe in slavery."

5 Feb., Brigham Young announces policy of denying priesthood to all those of black African ancestry, even "if there never was a prophet, or apostle of Jesus Christ spoke it before" because "negroes are the children of old Cain. . . . any man having one drop of the seed of Cain in him cannot hold the priesthood." Contrary to Joseph Smith's example in authorizing the ordination of Elijah Abel, this is LDS policy for next 126 years.

Young announces this policy in connection with Utah legislature's legalization of African-American slavery. The law provides for only one interference with property rights of slave-owners: "if any master or mistress shall have sexual or carnal intercourse with his or her servant or servants of the African race, he or she shall forfeit all claim to said servant or servants to the commonwealth; and if any white person shall be guilty of sexual intercourse with any of the African race, they shall be subject, on conviction thereof, to a fine of not exceeding one thousand dollars, nor less than five hundred, to the use of the Territory, and imprisonment not exceeding three years."

7 Feb., Utah's legislature legalizes voluntary indentured servitude, and authorizes county selectmen or probate courts to put into indentured servitude "any idle, vicious or vagrant minor child without his or her consent, or the consent of the parent or guardian of such minor child, if such parent or guardian neglects, refuses, or otherwise fails in properly controlling the actions and education of such minor, and does not train him or her up in some useful avocation."

7 Mar., Utah law allows whites to "purchase" Native Americans from Indian or Mexican slave-owners in order to prevent these captives from being killed. Purchaser must "immediately go" before county selectmen or probate judge who will "bind out the same, by indenture for the term of not exceeding twenty years." Mormons are prohibited from owning Indian slaves, but can own African-American slaves.

6-9 Apr., at conference in England, Apostle Franklin D. Richards calls men to new office of "pastor." Office continues until 1860, when it is changed to "district president."

9 Apr., Brigham Young's first published sermon that Adam "is our Father and our God, and the only God with whom We have to do." For the next twenty-five years, Young speaks about so-called "Adam-God doctrine" in numerous sermons, most of which he publishes. In this same sermon Young says: "The Holy Ghost is the Spirit of the Lord, and issues forth from Himself. . . . The Lord fills the immensity of space."

12 May, William A. Hickman tells Mosiah Lyman Hancock, a loyal Mormon, that Brigham Young instructs him to "kill Gentiles [non-Mormons] and take their property for the good of the Church," but Young denies this to Hancock on 3 July.

29 Aug., first public announcement of previously denied practice of plural marriage. Contemporary reports show this causes extensive disaffection among British Mormons.

12 Nov., all LDS missionaries in Norway are in jail for preaching; released 5 May 1853.

16 Dec., Brigham Young, as Utah governor, issues "free Pardon for Jerome Owens who had been condemned to die for murder in first degree by Judge of first Judicial District."
   Thomas Ellerbeck writes that Young requests "the privilege of going in and out of the House without being molested by their rising" in his honor. About 100 years later this practice reemerges among Mormons to honor LDS president.

1853

19 Jan., first theatrical performance in Social Hall, Salt Lake City. Soon there are full performances of such classic stage productions as *Othello* and *She Stoops to Conquer*.

20 Feb., Brigham Young speaks concerning Mormons who say the judgment of living prophets "is superior to mine, and consequently I let you judge for me." He says that such Latter-day Saints do not possess "the true independence of heaven," and consequently "will never be capable of entering into the celestial glory, to be crowned as they anticipate; they will never be capable of becoming gods." Young says that Mormons should depend on "the influences of the Holy Spirit" and "their own understanding."

28 Feb., Millard Fillmore writes Utah's congressional delegate John M. Bernhisel (a member of Council of Fifty), "my thanks for the beautiful copy of the 'Book of Mormon.'" Fillmore is apparently first U.S. president to accept copy of *Book of Mormon* but may not have even opened it. He appoints Brigham Young as Utah's first governor who gratefully names Fillmore, Utah, as territorial capital from 1851 to 1858.

11 Mar., Church Historian's Office records death of Ike Hatch and notes that "Bill Hickman" ambushes him in "Big Field." Hickman later writes that LDS president expresses satisfaction for his killing a man whom "Brigham wanted to watch."

6 Apr., cornerstone laying ceremony for Salt Lake temple. Brigham Young publishes this description of endowment: "Your endowment is, to receive all those ordinances in the House of Lord, which are necessary to you, after you have departed this life, to enable you

to walk back to the presence of the Father, passing the angels who stand as sentinels, being enabled to give them the key words, the signs and tokens, pertaining to the Holy Priesthood, and gain your eternal exaltation in spite of earth and hell."

12 June, John Taylor: "If there is any truth in heaven, earth, or hell, I want to embrace it."

18 July, beginning of Walker War between Mormons and Indians. Ends in May 1854.

24 July, Brigham Young preaches, "The Father came down in his [bodily] tabernacle and begot Jesus."

4 Aug., Apostle Amasa M. Lyman begins acting as medium in spiritualistic seances in San Bernardino, California. After being dropped from Quorum of Twelve in 1867 and excommunicated in 1870, in seances with such prominent Mormons or former Mormons as T. B. H. Stenhouse, E. L. T. Harrison, William S. Godbe, William H. Shearman, Henry W. Lawrence, Theodore Turley, Sarah B. Pratt, Andrew F. Cahoon, Arthur Stayner, John V. Long, Nathan Tanner, Sr., and Emma Brown Teasdale (wife of future apostle George Teasdale). Founding prophet's son David H. Smith also joins some of these seances while visiting Utah.

11 Sept., Brigham Young says there will be temple in Scotland. Joseph Smith once made similar promise to Apostle Parley P. Pratt.

20 Sept., "Uncle John" Smith, Presiding Patriarch, confers upon his son, Apostle George A. Smith, "all the keys of the Patriarchal Priesthood that ever was sealed upon any man on the Earth." Despite Presiding Patriarch's dying request in 1854 that his son be his successor, Brigham Young instead chooses oldest son of martyred Hyrum Smith.

23 Oct., Brigham Young preaches, "Many received heavenly visions, revelations, the ministering of holy angels, and the manifestations of the power of God . . . before the ordinances of the house of God were preached to the people."

1 Nov., first issue of British Mission's *Journal of Discourses,* most famous collection of Mormon sermons which had been published previously in *Deseret News.*

22 Dec., formation of phonetic Deseret Alphabet, which LDS leaders try to make standard written language of Mormon Utah. Formal announcement is on 19 Jan. 1854.

1854

3 Jan., Brigham Young invites Elijah Abel, free black and ordained Seventy, to party with 98 other men in Social Hall. Some of these parties are male-only dances.

19 Feb., Seventy's president Jedediah M. Grant preaches: "Did the Prophet Joseph want every man's wife he asked for? He did not . . ."

20 Feb., William H. Dame receives patriarchal blessing: "Thou shalt be called to act at the head of a portion of thy brethren and of the Lamanites in the redemption of Zion and the avenging of the blood of the Prophets." He orders Mountain Meadows Massacre.

3 May, month after Brigham Young publicly condemns and excommunicates lawyer Jesse T. Hartley, he starts for eastern states, apparently without Young's safe-conduct pass. William A. Hickman murders him during trip with Apostle Orson Hyde and Hosea Stout in canyon. Stout's diary verifies Hickman's later account of this.

8 June, upon meeting non-Mormon friend, LDS convert of less than two years writes: "He is one of my old Friends, one that I loved and in whose society I have spent many many hours, but now I have nothing to say." Such awkwardness around non-Mormons is common response of many Mormons, whether converted or born into LDS church.

4 July, Brigham Young preaches that U.S. Constitution is not complete, but "it is a progressive—a gradual work."

16 July, first counselor Heber C. Kimball recommends decapitation for adulterers and preaches concerning "unclean" women: "we wipe them out of existence."

21 July, Salt Lake City court "release[s]" Thomas Burke from being "a bound boy" to Mormon man who mistreats him as "white" indentured servant.

27 July, *Deseret News* publishes 12 Mar. sermon of second counselor Jedediah M. Grant:

"But if the Latter Day Saints should put to death the covenant breakers, it would try the faith of the very meek, just, and pious among them, and it would cause a great deal of whining in Israel . . . and it is also their right to kill a sinner to save him, when he commits those crimes that can only be atoned for by shedding his blood."

6 Oct., Orson Hyde preaches, "The world was peopled before the days of Adam, as much so as it was before the days of Noah."

8 Oct., in what Apostle Wilford Woodruff describes as "the greatest sermon that ever was delivered to the Latter day Saints since they have been a people," Brigham Young announces: "I beleive [sic] in Sisters marrying brothers, and brothers haveing [sic] their sisters for Wives. Why? because we cannot do otherwise. There are none others for me to marry but my sisters. . . . Our spirits are all brothers and sisters, and so are our bodies; and the opposite idea has resulted from the ignorant, and foolish traditions of the nations of the earth." Young's secretary George D. Watt has already married his own half-sister as a plural wife. Her letter to Young shows that he was initially "unfavorable" toward allowing them to marry, but this sermon reveals theological basis for Young's authorizing Watt's brother-sister marriage and the three children born of their union.

26 Oct., Bishop publishes notice in *Deseret News* that Enoch M. King is disfellowshipped "for repeatedly refusing to conform to the rules of said Church, in the law of Tithing."

31 Oct., public reading of written revelation to Brigham Young "directing him to sell the Church property here and move south with the Church." Text unavailable.

20 Dec., Polysophical Society organizes with Apostle Lorenzo Snow as president. Women and men lecture and participate in discussions on equal basis. Brigham Young soon organizes male-dominated Deseret Theological Institute as competition.

1855

4 Feb., Apostle Wilford Woodruff describes "some of the strongest preaching ever delivered to the Saints." First rebaptisms of Utah Reformation occur in wards (like Payson) as early as 14 April 1855.

18 Feb., Orson Pratt preaches: "I will tell you what I believe in regard to the Holy Ghost's being a person: but I know of no revelation that states that this is the fact."

7 Apr., Brigham Young establishes Deseret Theological Institute which is open to women who comprise 37 percent of its membership. However, women do not lecture on same equality they experience in non-institutional Polysophical Society.

27 Apr., lieutenant in Colonel E. J. Steptoe's command at Salt Lake City writes friend about his romance and near seduction of wife of Brigham Young's son Joseph (who is on mission): "Mary [Ayers] Young I had to give up. Brigham sent me word—that if I took her away he would have me killed before I could get out of the Territory. He is a man of his word in little matters of this sort and I concluded I had better not do it, although I went back to the city purposely to get her. We wrote each other affectionate notes."

5 May, dedication of Salt Lake Endowment House, and inauguration of first Thursday of each month as day of fasting and prayer, with "testimony meeting" during day.

26 June, Indian Territory Mission established to proselytize among Cherokees and Creeks in what is now Oklahoma. Directed almost exclusively toward Native Americans, mission closes in 1877, reopens in 1883 with increasing efforts toward Anglos.

5 Aug., Brigham Young tells apostles that after final judgment those consigned to terrestrial and telestial kingdoms will "eventually have the privilege of proveing [sic] themselves worthy & advancing to a celestial kingdom but it would be a slow progress."

8 Oct., Young's counselors, Heber C. Kimball and Jedediah M. Grant are each sustained as "Prophet, Seer, and Revelator." Not since 1841 have Presidency counselors been publicly announced in this manner. He has had this public title since April 1851.

22 Nov., Brigham Young secretly ordains his eleven-year-old son John W. an apostle in connection with receiving the endowment. He also ordains his eighteen-year-old son Brigham Jr. as apostle, either this day or (more likely) at his namesake's endowment a

few days earlier. The Twelve doesn't learn of these ordinations for almost nine years. In later years he secretly ordains two other sons as apostles.

1856

23 Feb., Brigham Young exhibits brown seer stone obtained from Oliver Cowdery's widow. He explains that Smith used this stone to find gold plates of *Book of Mormon*.

17 Mar., unsuccessful convention seeking statehood.

6 Apr., Presiding Bishopric given permanent organization (first and second counselors).

9 June, first handcart pioneers leave Iowa City, and arrive by foot in Salt Lake City 26 Sept.

31 Aug., Brigham Young publicly prophesies that by 1882 "Elders of this Church will be as much thought of as the kings."

21 Sept., first counselor Heber C. Kimball preaches: "You cannot see God, you cannot behold Him and hold converse with Him."

24 Sept., due to report that Stephen A. Douglas has called Utah's Mormons "an ulcer on the body politic," *Deseret News* publishes Joseph Smith's 1843 prophecy: "Judge [Douglas], you will aspire to the Presidency of the United States," with his warning of failure if he turns against Mormons. Douglas is defeated for presidency in 1860; dies next year.

1 Oct., typical *Deseret News* report of Reformation meetings. Jedediah M. Grant presides over three days of meetings at Farmington, Utah, where he speaks seven times, prays four times, and during which 450 are rebaptized.

8 Oct., second counselor Jedediah M. Grant declares that Polysophical Society is "a stink in his nostrils," Heber C. Kimball agrees. They regard its equality of female participation as "an adulterous spirit." The society does not survive this general conference.

9 Oct., in midst of Utah Reformation's frenzy, Apostle Wilford Woodruff notes, "The spirit of God is like flame among the Leaders of this people & they are throwing the arrows of the Almighty among the people."

4 Nov., at meeting with stake presidencies, ward bishoprics, and local quorum presidents, Brigham Young presents catechism for every Mormon to answer. Among questions: Have you ever committed murder, shed innocent blood, or given your consent thereto? Have you ever committed adultery? Have you ever spoken evil of the church authorities or anointed of the Lord? Have you ever betrayed your brethren? Have you ever stolen or taken anything that was not your own? Have you ever taken the name of God in vain? Have you ever been drunk? Do you pay all your tithing? Do you teach your children the gospel? Do you pray in your family night and morning? Do you attend your ward meetings? Do you pray in secret? Do you wash your bodies once a week? At this meeting, Young answered only the last question: "Said that he did not. He had tried it. He was well aware that this was not for everybody."

9 Nov., arrival in Salt Lake City of Willie handcart company after loss of sixty-eight persons who freeze or starve to death in mountains. Martin handcart company arrives on 30 Nov. after about 150 similar deaths. This total death rate of 22 percent is worst of any Mormon emigrant companies. With better planning, handcarts bring thousands of European Mormons to Utah for another four years with few deaths.

26 Nov., *Deseret News* publishes new hymn, "The Reformation," with fourth verse: "We ought our Bishops to sustain,/ Their counsels to abide/ And knock down every dwelling/ Where wicked folks reside."

22 Dec., At Seventy's meeting apostles ask six subordinate members of First Council to resign. Some do temporarily but are reinstated. A week later several apostles offer to resign from Quorum of Twelve.

28 Dec., apostles preach that First Presidency has "retired from our midst because the people will not do as they are told," and the apostles also threatened to leave and take the "Holy Priesthood . . . into the wilderness among the Lamanites, or to the Ten tribes." Brigham Young has already stopped administering sacrament to Utah's Mormons.

30 Dec., eight days after his excommunication, Mormons make night raid on office of

Judge George P. Stiles and burn his law library in a privy. Anti-Mormon officials use this incident to falsely claim that Mormons have destroyed federal records.

1857

11 Jan., first counselor Heber C. Kimball preaches "against wild enthusiasm." First official reference that religious zeal of Utah Reformation is getting out of control.

14 Jan., Thomas D. Brown begins "his duties in the President's Office, astonished at the number of applications for permission to take [plural] wives." A month later hard-pressed Brigham Young recites "each [sealing] ceremony requiring about 600 words, which in several instances were spoken in 1 min 48 seconds!"

27 Jan., when ward bishop asks what should be done with Mormons who commit abortions, Brigham Young replies: "Tell them if they have destroyed children heretofore not to do so any longer," but he makes no reference to punishment for abortion.

8 Feb., Brigham Young asks congregation, "Will you love your brothers or sisters likewise, when they have committed a sin that cannot be atoned for without the shed[d]ing of their blood? Will you love that man or woman well enough to shed their blood?" Blood atonement sermons are the most publicized feature of the Reformation. Heber C. Kimball preaches, "My God is a cheerful, pleasant, lively, and good-natured being."

22 Feb., Apostle Wilford Woodruff publicly prophesies that there are "women present who would assist in giving endowments to the Ten Tribes of Israel—for they have to receive their endowments in the New Jerusalem [at Independence, Missouri]."

5 Mar., Brigham Young permits woman to select faithful elder to act as "proxy" to father children for her sexually impotent husband. Young performs polyandrous ceremony "for time," and the relationship lasts several years producing two sons, (1858, 1861). Mother's legal husband raises the boys with her, and later tells them he loves them as much as if they were his natural sons. Both boys grow up to become devoted Mormons and polygamists. This is last known case of authorized polyandry.

6 Apr., Brigham Young restores sacrament, after withholding it from all church members for past six months of Reformation which ends with Utah War.

13 May, murder of Apostle Parley P. Pratt in Arkansas by disgruntled legal husband of his last plural wife. Newspaper accounts of Pratt's murder reach Salt Lake City on 23 June.

28 May, U.S. War Department orders army to suppress what U.S. president James Buchanan regards as Mormon treason and insurrection. One army officer writes on 10 June that Mormon "opposition to government cannot be overcome without the destruction of its cause, which involves the complete destruction of their life as a public body."

2 June, Brigham Young says, "I feel to sustain him," when informed that local bishop Warren S. Snow has castrated twenty-four-year-old Welchman for undisclosed sex crime. "Just let the matter drop, and say no more about it," Young writes Snow in July about the castration, "and it will soon die away among the people." Snow's counselor confides to his diary that this young man "has now gone crazy."

14 June, at prayer circle of First Presidency and apostles, Brigham Young says he refuses to seal three girls (ages 12 to 13) to "Father [James] Allred" (age 73) because they "would not be equally yoked together" in marriage.

25 June, Wilford Woodruff records Brigham Young reminiscing that in 1837 "Joseph slapped him [Apostle David W. Patten] in the face & kicked him out of the yard." Young consistently claims he is a gentler taskmaster than Smith.

28 June, Brigham Young tells Apostle Wilford Woodruff that the church president believes astrology "is true." Young also has bloodstone amulet for his protection.

23 July, officer in U.S. army heading for Utah writes that he met "a number of receding Mormons who found the severity of the Saints intolerable and who left Utah last Apr. They said secret assassinations had occurred during the last winter."

24 July, during tenth anniversary celebration of pioneer arrival, Brigham Young announces the "invasion" of U.S. troops and instructs Mormons to resist militarily.

26 July, first counselor Heber C. Kimball publicly prophesies: "And the President of the United States will bow to us and come to consult the authorities of this Church to know what he had best to do for his people." Latter occurs 31 Jan. 1964.

27 July, Samuel L. Sprague, president of weekly prayer circle in Salt Lake City, instructs its members about "the holy anointing, that those who appreciated those sacred ordinances had in them the spirit and power to avenge the blood of the Prophets."

2 Aug., first counselor Heber C. Kimball prophesies that U.S. president James Buchanan "will die an untimely death." He dies at age 77 in 1868, same year Kimball dies at age 67. Brigham Young preaches, "There are probably but few men in the world who care about the private society of women less than I do."

9 Aug., Apostle John Taylor: "This [Horace] Greeley is one of their popular characters in the East, and one that supports the stealing of niggers and the underground railroad."

15-16 Aug., Apostle George A. Smith preaches fiery sermons at Cedar City in southern Utah. Smith left Salt Lake City on 13 Aug. and brings latest news of U.S. army's "invasion," also report of Apostle Pratt's murder in Arkansas. Smith likes wearing a holstered revolver in public, appeals to memories of Missouri persecutions, and has been preaching "speedy vengeance" for a decade. From all accounts he leaves Mormons of southern Utah filled with hatred and fear of their approaching enemies. A clerk records that in traveling north on 25 Aug. Smith meets "a party of emigrants who seemed to be much excited and placed on a double guard as soon as we arrived." A few days later that emigrant party camps farther south at place called Mountain Meadows.

30 Aug., Apostle John Taylor preaches that Mohammed "might have been a true one [prophet], for aught I know."

11 Sept., members of Parowan's militia participate in killing 120 men, women, and children in Mountain Meadows Massacre. This is largest massacre of wagon train in American history and is unparalleled because killing begins as "whites" are escorting emigrants under flag of truce. After holding prayer circle, local LDS leaders decide not to await word from Brigham Young about whether to help Indians destroy emigrants. At pre-arranged signal, most Mormon participants dutifully kill unarmed emigrant walking beside each militiamen, while some Mormons fire their weapons in air, and a few kill as many emigrants as they can. They spare eighteen small children.

Apostle Amasa M. Lyman crosses the Meadows on route to Salt Lake City from California and meets militia as it returns from burying murdered emigrants. "The twilight had commenced and he knew many of them, but none of them spoke to him or his company." His son says, "The stench was nearly unbearable, and the cattle were nearly crazy smelling blood. . . . it was the most hideous night he has spent."

Decades later participants acknowledge various motivations for destroying this Missouri and Arkansas group which antagonized both Mormons and Indians of southern Utah: war hysteria that belligerent emigrants might incite California to send military force to combine with "invasion" from east by U.S. army; fear that Indians would attack isolated settlements if they didn't assist; "avenging the blood" of Missouri expulsion of 1838 and of Apostle Pratt's recent murder; desire to plunder wagon train's property, which included 1,000 head of cattle, according to Church Historian's Office on 28 Sept. 1857; and intimidation by some Mormon firebrands who threatened to "blood atone" LDS militiamen who didn't want to participate.

Brigham Young gives unsuccessful order to prevent massacre but becomes accessory after fact. He later tells participants that he approves of the massacre and lets them know he expects them to exonerate each other in court of law. He publicly intimidates anyone who is inclined to give evidence against Mormon participants. He refuses to give federal authorities information that would implicate nearly all adults of small Mormon community in massacre and division of victims' property. Then when total denial becomes impossible, Young scapegoats three men through excommunication and arranges for participants to testify against (and jurymen to convict) only John D. Lee, Brigham Young's adopted son and Council of Fifty member.

13 Sept., Apostle George A. Smith preaches in Salt Lake City that there is "a spirit in the breasts of some [at Parowan, southern Utah] to wish that their enemies might come and give them a chance to fight and take vengeance for the cruelties that had been inflicted upon us in the States."

15 Sept., Brigham Young declares martial law in Utah, orders Utah's Nauvoo Legion to prevent U.S. troops from entering, and instructs missionaries to return to Utah.

21 Sept., at weekly prayer circle of Samuel L. Sprague: "Br. *P[hineas]. Richards* [a member of Council of Fifty] spoke of coming in contact with our enemies. We have covenanted to avenge the blood of the Prophets and Saints. Why, then, should we hesitate to go forth and slay them—shed their blood—when called upon. Pres. *Sprague* spoke a few words in answer to the inquiry made by br. Richards; that the Lord had said 'vengeance is mine.' Nevertheless, we shall have blood to shed."

29 Sept., John D. Lee reports Mountain Meadows Massacre to Brigham Young and claims that Indians "cut the throats of their women & children." That is not Indian practice but is consistent with Mormon beliefs about blood atonement. Decades later one participant acknowledges that Mormon men slit throats of women and children.

12 Oct., officer in U.S. army expedition at Fort Laramie, Wyoming writes: "Two men by the name of Hickman, brothers to Bill Hickman who is celebrated in this country as one of the 'Destroying Angels,' came into our camps yesterday. . . . One of them had a sword belt in his possession which had belonged to the man (Vilkins) who went out gunning on the 7th inst and had not been heard from since."

18 Oct., William A. Hickman kills non-Mormon Richard Yates for trying to transport munitions to U.S. army. Hickman later implicates Brigham Young, second counselor Daniel H. Wells, and Joseph A. Young in decision, and Judge Hosea Stout in actual murder. In 1858 Mormon woman says that Yates "disappeared—'used up [killed] in the pocket of the Lord,' we call it—and Bill Hickman—one of the 'Destroyers'—passed through this very town, waving the overcoat of Yates, and riding his bay pony." Hickman later writes that he gave to President Young money he took from Yates's body. Despite arrest and pre-trial detention, all those indicted in 1871 for Yates murder are freed by U.S. Supreme Court in 1872 due to improper impaneling of juries.

20 Oct., as Mormon troops leave to confront U.S. regiment, first counselor Heber C. Kimball "promise[s] them that if they would live the religion of Christ not one of them should fall by the hand of an enemy." There are no military deaths in Utah War.

3 Nov., safe conduct pass signed by Brigham Young that bearer "is hereby granted permission to pass freely and safely through this Territory on his way to California." Since early 1850s there are claims that it is dangerous for Mormons to attempt to leave Salt Lake City for the East without a pass from Brigham Young.

20 Nov., Orrin Porter Rockwell leaves Salt Lake City with four members of Aiken party of six California emigrants whom Mormons arrest as "supposed spies." After camping near Nephi, Utah, Mormon guards murder two, then kill two survivors who had been nursed by Mormons at Nephi. In Salt Lake City William A. Hickman kills one of Aiken party, but last man escapes to California. Hickman claims he reported these killings to Brigham Young afterward. Rockwell is arrested but dies before trial begins for remaining Mormon defendant, who is acquitted due to lack of corpse as evidence.

Russia's ambassador warns Czar's Foreign Minister of newspaper rumors, which U.S. president James Buchanan has implied are true, that Mormons are preparing to abandon Utah and "head North to settle on the lands of the Hudson Bay Company *or in our American possessions*" of Alaska. Russia's ambassador concludes that this "would force us either to offer armed resistance or give up a part of our territory" to Mormons. Czar Alexander II writes on this secret dispatch: "This supports the idea of settling right now the question of our American possessions." Thus, untrue rumor of Mormon intentions causes Czar to decide on disposing of Russia's only colony in North America, which Russia sells to United States in 1868.

6 Dec., Apostle Wilford Woodruff preaches: "God himself is increasing and progressing in knowledge, power, and dominion, and will do so, worlds without end."

18 Dec., Brigham Young says that when Salt Lake temple is completed, "Under the pulpit in the west end will be a place to offer Sacrifices [—] there will be an altar prepared for that purpose so that when any sacrifices are to be offered they should be offered there." This supports reminiscence of Wandall Mace that he heard Joseph Smith give similar instructions to apostles in 1839: "Joseph told them they must go to Kirtland, and cleanse and purify a certain room in the Temple, that they must kill a lamb and offer a sacrifice unto the Lord, which should prepare them to ordain Willard Richards a member of the Quorum of the Twelve Apostles." Young's diary makes no reference to sacrifice while in Kirtland (3-18 Nov. 1839) on route to England.

21 Dec., during prayer circle meeting, Heber C. Kimball says, "tell br. [David] *Pettegrew* to tell the devil to kiss his arse and come to his circle meeting and pray for the welfare of Israel."

30 Dec., Brigham Young and other LDS leaders are indicted for treason. This does not surprise them, since Apostle George A. Smith had told Utah Legislature on 21 Dec.: "we may prepare our neck for the halter if our enemies catch us."

1858

14 Jan., David Fullmer, Fifty's member says all Mormons are "one—black, white or red."

27 Feb., Judge Hosea Stout describes with no disapproval how Mormons "disguised as Indians" drag man "out of bed with a whore and castrated him by a square & close amputation."

8 Mar., Hosea Stout lists "[Howard] Egan, [Orrin Porter] Rockwell, [Ephraim K.] Hanks and several other of the 'Be'hoys'" which was American slang for "gang member" or "thug." William A. Hickman refers to himself as one of "Brigham's boys."

21 Mar., announcement of abandonment of Salt Lake City and all northern Utah settlements due to approach of U.S. troops. Brigham Young tells this special conference that Joseph Smith disobeyed revelation by returning to Nauvoo to stand trial, that church's founding prophet lost Spirit of God the last days of his life, and died as unnecessary martyr. He publishes this talk as pamphlet.

31 Mar., ex-apostle Lyman Wight dies in Texas from alcoholism and opium addiction.

5 Apr. (or 24 Apr. by some accounts), bishop of Payson, his brother (the sheriff), and several members of their LDS congregation join in shooting to death twenty-two-year-old Henry Jones and his mother Mrs. Hannah Jones Hatch for committing incest by which she has a daughter. The men kill infant and also castrate brother/father. Perpetrators are indicted next year, but not brought to trial. When indicted again in 1889, *Deseret News* criticizes trial of this "antiquated Payson homicide" as anti-Mormon crusade against those who were justifiably "disgusted and greatly incensed" against "the brutal mother and son." Former sheriff is convicted of murder, former bishop is acquitted.

26 June, U.S. troops pass peacefully through nearly deserted Salt Lake City under terms of presidential amnesty and truce arranged by non-Mormon Thomas L. Kane.

1 July, First Presidency and others return to homes in otherwise-deserted Salt Lake City.

17 Aug., Apostle George A. Smith, after extensive consultation with leaders of Mountain Meadows Massacre, writes official account which details their movements on day of massacre but not their participation in it. Begins conspiracy to obstruct justice.

1 Sept., Brigham Young writes Thomas L. Kane "that the time is not far distant when Utah shall be able to assume her rights and place among the family of nations."

12 Sept., church historian's office notes discovery this morning of severed head of Provo woman who has been at U.S. military camp for a week. Six weeks earlier another woman's decapitated head is discovered. These are earliest verified examples of some-

one taking literally the repeated teachings of Mormon leaders that apostates and adulterers should have their heads cut off as "blood atonement" for their sins.

15 Dec., in reply to man's request for divorce, "Pres. Young said that when a man married a wife he took her for better or for worse, and had no right to ill use her, and if she shit in bed and laid in it until noon; he must bare it, until he gets power over her to learn her better." Young readily grants divorce to unhappy plural wives but requires husband to pay him $10 fee. Young issues 1,600 certificates of divorce for unhappy polygamous marriages. Civil divorces for monogamous marriages are even more common in pioneer Utah where courts require only statement of incompatibility.

1859

2 Jan., Brigham Young begins custom of having Mormon congregations sit with women on north side of center aisle, men on south side, and children on front benches. This seating arrangement lasts for decades.

1 Feb., nine-year-old Indian boy Samuel is indentured to John Beal for ten-years.

23 Feb., first counselor Heber C. Kimball tells apostles "there are thousands of prophets among the Gentiles and spiritualists that have not repented or obeyed the gospel."

26 Feb., Brigham Young tells church historian that "there had not been a Judge in Utah, that had been so completely taken up and set down on his arse in the mud, and had his ears pissed into as Judge [Charles E.] Sinclair had been."

2 Apr., non-Mormon judge convicts three Mormons (two of them policemen) for conspiracy in Parrish family's murder. Under immunity two LDS men testify that Springville bishop ordered the killings because Parrishes were leaving Utah with unpaid tithing. Shot to death, the bodies are left with slit throats as "blood atonement."

7 Apr., each member of First Presidency is presented as prophet, seer, and revelator; last time general conference sustains anyone with that title until 9 Oct. 1872.

4 June, U.S. army officer writes: "Saw two skulls today from the scene of the Mountain Meadows Massacre[—]One of them was shot through[,] the ball entering the back part of the head and coming out near the right temple. The other had two gashes on the top as if from a sharp knife. They were of young persons."

18 June, "Prest. Young told Br. [Jacob] Hamblin that as soon as a court of Justice could be held, so that men could be heard without the influence of the military he should advise men accused to come forward and demand trial on the charges preferred against them for the Mountain Meadows massacre." Hamblin (who did not participate in massacre) refers to this conversation when he testifies at trial of John D. Lee in 1876.

29 June, *Deseret News* reports that fifteen child-survivors of Mountain Meadows Massacre leave for Fort Smith, with escort of soldiers.

11 Aug., U.S. army sergeant Ralph Pike is shot in Salt Lake City just before his trial for assaulting LDS youth, Howard O. Spencer. A diary notes that murderer is "seen by hundreds and no one knew him and no two gave the same description of him." At trial in 1889, Spencer pleas temporary insanity and jury acquits him. *Deseret News* editorializes 11 May 1889 that murdered man "richly deserved his fate."

20 Aug., *New York Daily Tribune* publishes Horace Greeley's recent interview with Brigham Young: "H. G. What is the position of your church with respect to slavery?" "B. Y. We consider it of divine institution, and not to be abolished until the curse pronounced on Ham shall have been removed from his descendants."

7 Sept., Salt Lake City clerk records sale of twenty-six-year-old "negro boy" for $800 to William H. Hooper, elected month before as Utah's delegate to Congress. Until federal law ends slavery in U.S. territories in 1862, some African-American slaves are paid as tithing, bought, sold, and otherwise treated as chattel in Utah.

8 Oct., Brigham Young tells bishops to give Melchizedek priesthood to eighteen-year-old boys, even if they "have been sowing their wild oats for years."

14 Nov., Peter Maughan is "Presiding Bishop in Cache Valley." He is among first, if not the

first, of nineteenth-century stake bishops who function in most stakes outside Salt Lake Stake. This office does not continue in twentieth century.

1860

20 Jan., concerning Mormon woman who commits suicide due to chronic illness, Brigham Young says, "she had done wrong but by no means had committed the unpardonable sin and in course of time a proxy could be appointed who could be baptized for her."

27 Jan., Quorum of Twelve investigates Apostle Orson Pratt for rejecting Brigham Young's Adam-God teachings. This repeats similar trial in Mar. 1858, and apostles vote to drop Pratt. Young intercedes to prevent Twelve from disfellowshipping or excommunicating Pratt, but apostles do not restore him to full fellowship until 5 Apr. On 25 July *Deseret News* publishes confession as Twelve require Pratt to revise it.

1 Feb., *Deseret News* reports that Orrin Porter Rockwell shoots Martin Oats to death after Oats accuses him of stealing cattle. Rockwell reports incident to Lehi authorities who dismiss him without further action.

22 Feb., *Deseret News* article, "How to Impress Niggers."

4 Mar., Brigham Young: "it floods my heart with sorrow to see so many Elders of Israel who wish everybody to come to their standard and be measured by their measure. Every man must be just so long, to fit their iron bedstead, or be cut off to the right length."

18 Mar., devout Mormon writes: "Sunday preaching by John Taylor [is] long and dry."

3 Apr., Salt Lake City's LDS mayor cautions Brigham Young that William A. Hickman has been useful as a dog to protect Mormon flock but should now be removed because he is also killing Mormons within the fold.

5 Apr., LDS delegate William H. Hooper tells Congress: "From my observation, from ten years' residence in Utah, I can say that not over one half of the people of Utah are polygamists; and that probably not half of that half have more than two wives."

6 Apr., Joseph Smith III is president of Reorganized Church of Jesus Christ of Latter Day Saints (RLDS).

7 Apr. Brigham Young announces: "When I present the authorities of this Church for the Conference to vote upon, there if there is a member here who honestly and sincerely thinks that any person whose name is presented should not hold the office he is appointed to fill, let him speak. I will give full liberty, not to preach sermons, nor to degrade character, but to briefly state objections, and at the proper time I will hear the reasons for any objections that may be advanced." Mormon diarist writes that "a wonder among the Saints" occurs during sustaining, when one man votes against Heber C. Kimball. He remains first counselor, but identity of dissident is unknown.

23 May, *Deseret News* editorial: "Murder after murder has been committed with impunity within the precincts of Great Salt Lake City, till such occurrences do not seemingly attract much attention, particularly when the murdered have had the reputation of being thieves and murderers or of associating with such characters from day to day . . ."

8 July, Brigham Young preaches, "Children are now born who will live until every son of Adam will have the privilege of receiving the principles of eternal life."

He also preaches, "The birth of the Saviour was as natural as are the births of our children; it was the result of natural action." Traditional Christians are infuriated by this rejection (dating to 24 July 1853) of the Virgin Birth and Young's assertion that God has body capable of sexual intercourse. Repeated publication of such assaults on Christian orthodoxy leads to near hysteria in Protestant rhetoric against Mormons.

11 July, *Deseret News* favorably reports lynching of horse-thief A.B. Baker by posse deputized to arrest him. He is "buried by those who thus meted out to him summary justice, not exactly according to law, but upon a more speedy, economical and salutary principle . . ." In territorial Utah, there are eleven judicial executions, and same number of lynchings by mobs (primarily Mormon).

24 Sept., last company of handcart pioneers enters Salt Lake City.

4 Oct., Brigham Young's financial report informs general conference that from 1857 to this date, church spent total of "$70,204 in excess of what has been received in money and Tithing." This is first financial report to acknowledge church's deficit spending.

8 Oct., Brigham Young preaches "he was contending against a principle in many of the Bishops to use up all the Tithing they could for their own families."

13 Oct., Apostle Orson Hyde intervenes to spare William A. Hickman from excommunication and tells bishopric: "a man may steal and be influenced by the spirit of the Lord to do it, that Hickman had done it in years past." The bishop reluctantly acquits him.

18 Nov., Brigham Young: "right where the Prophet Joseph laid the Foundation of the Temple, in the Center Stake of Zion [at Independence, Missouri], was where God commenced the Garden of Eden, & there He will end or Consummate his work."

1861

6 Apr., Brigham Young tells conference it is necessary "to grease the wheels" (bribe federal officials). "To show how minutely corruption prevails where justice should exist," Young gives example where it was necessary to pay $1,300 bribe "to get our claims paid for expenditures in quelling Indian disturbances in 1853." This is first announcement of First Presidency's policy to bribe federal officials when necessary. Historian Wallace D. Farnham once described the frequent graft in nineteenth-century federal government as the "weakened spring of government" in America.

7 May, Brigham Young preaches and publishes: "Three High Priests form a Quorum. . . . Let a Quorum of High Priests go into an upper room, and there appear before the Lord in the garments of the holy Priesthood, and offer up before the Father, in the name of Jesus, the signs of the holy Priesthood, and then ask God to give a revelation."

25 May, church historian records when Brigham Young visits Mountain Meadows he says memorial plaque should read: "Vengeance is mine and I have taken a little."

30 May, Brigham Young preaches to southern Utah congregation filled with participants in Mountain Meadows Massacre: "Pres. Young said that the company that was used up at the Mountain Meadows were the Fathers, Mothers, Bros., Sisters & connections of those that Murdered the Prophets; *they Merit[ed] their fate, & the only thing that ever troubled him was the lives of the Women & children, but that under the circumstances could not be avoided.* Although there had been [some] that want[e]d to betray the Brethren into the hands of their Enemies, for that thing [such] will be Damned & go down to Hell. I would be Glad to see one of those traitors" (emphasis added).

28 July, Concerning U.S. Civil War Brigham Young says: "Will it be over in six months or in three years? No; it will take years and years, and will never cease until the work is accomplished . . . and it will spread and continue until the land is emptied."

7 Oct., Brigham Young changes seniority of apostles Wilford Woodruff and John Taylor and ranks Woodruff after Taylor, first time in 22 years. Says their ranking should be according to ordination date rather than their previous ranking according to age.

8 Oct., Brigham Young preaches that no woman "will never become an angel to the devil, and sin so far as to place herself beyond the reach of mercy."

18 Oct., Brigham Young sends first message on newly completed telegraph line to president of Pacific Telegraph Company in Ohio: "Utah has not seceded, but is firm for the Constitution and laws of our once happy country."

18 Nov., Abraham Lincoln checks out *Book of Mormon* from Library of Congress. He returns it on 29 July 1862, apparently first U.S. president to read *Book of Mormon*.

7 Dec., John W. Dawson arrives in Salt Lake as newly appointed governor. Within three weeks he alienates Mormons by vetoing bill for statehood convention.

23 Dec., unidentified person fires five shots at federal associate justice Henry R. Crosby on Main Street in Salt Lake City.

1862

1 Jan., *Deseret News* reports that Governor John W. Dawson hurriedly left Salt Lake City yesterday at 2 p.m. after "offering a gross insult to a respectable lady of this city." *News* claims governor hired as his bodyguards Lot Huntington, Jason Luce, William Luce, and Moroni Clawson to protect against "his being killed or becoming qualified for the office of chamberlain [castrated eunuch] in the king's palace."

Although it is evening newspaper, *Deseret News* does not report what happened to Dawson the previous night at Ephraim Hanks's coach station at Mountain Dell. The so-called bodyguards beat Dawson "nearly to death" and then stripped him of his clothes and valuables. Governor recovers well enough to write the *News* on 7 Jan.: "Any report stating that I hired these desperadoes to escort me over the mountains, is also untrue." Dawson says he asked for the protection of Ephraim Hanks, who instead sent the others to escort the governor out of the territory. Dawson continues his journey back to his home in Indiana, where he dies of natural causes sixteen years later. His official biography claims he never fully recovers from the beating in Utah.

16 Jan., Orrin Porter Rockwell kills "while attempting to escape" Lot Huntington for Dawson beating. Church Historian's Office notes that Rockwell shoots Huntington eight times in stomach—difficult to do while someone is running away from the shooter. Salt Lake City policemen kill Moroni Clawson and John P. Smith while escorting them to jail on 17 Jan. for the beating. On 22 Jan. bishop's court tries participant Isaac Neibaur who confesses, protests that he "never stole from a Mormon," asks forgiveness, "but if his Blood must atone he is willing to die." Church court forgives Neibaur without blood atonement, but Salt Lake county court on 25 Mar. sentences him and two others to varying prison terms for Dawson incident.

20 Jan., unsuccessful convention seeking statehood.

9 Feb., Brigham Young preaches, "To hang a man for such a deed would not begin to satisfy my feelings." He speaks of discovery that Jean Baptiste has been robbing Mormon graves in Salt Lake City for four years, stripping clothes and valuables from corpses. Judge Elias Smith writes that "the people wo[u]ld have torn him in pieces," and court gives unusual sentence Young recommends—banishment of Baptiste to a deserted island in the Great Salt Lake. On 4 Aug., Church Historian's Office Journal notes that punishment included cutting off his ears and branding his forehead with words "Grave robber," but that he has disappeared from island. Thirty-two years later skeleton is found with ball-and-chain attached to its leg bone and with the decapitated skull lying several feet away. *Salt Lake Herald* claims this is the grave-robber's remains, which *Deseret News* denies. Young's nephew later writes that Ephraim Hanks killed Baptiste.

23 Feb., Brigham Young preaches that concept of Mother in Heaven is as essential as concept of Father in Heaven.

8 Mar., Salt Lake Theatre opens and during sixty years hosts such performers as Maude Adams, Lillian Russell, P. T. Barnum, the Barrymores, Eddie Foy, and Al Jolson.

19 Mar., *Deseret News* reports Heber C. Kimball sermon of 7 July 1861, which says church was organized in Manchester, New York.

14 Apr., first session of "ghost government" of theocratic State of Deseret, which publicly meets, passes its own laws (duplicates of what same legislators have just done in territorial legislature), holds elections, and functions until 1872. Significant as theocratic symbol but unimportant in practice.

13-15 June, with authorization of Utah's acting governor Frank Fuller, military-sized Mormon "posse" attacks schismatic community of Joseph Morris in Weber County, Utah. Mormon forces kill principal leaders of "Morrisite War" for resisting arrest. Rest of community is imprisoned but receive governor's pardon on 31 Mar. 1863.

8 July, enactment of Morrill Act which prohibits polygamy in U.S. territories, disincorporates LDS church and prohibits it from owning more than $50,000 of real estate in U.S.

territory. There are only sporadic arrests of polygamists and no enforcement of disincorporation clause.

13 July, Brigham Young preaches, that "if the *Book of Mormon* were now to be rewritten, in many instances it would materially differ from the present translation."

1 Aug., Brigham Young writes to local bishop: "my advice is for bro James T.S. Allred to marry the Indian girl in question. It is written that 'not many generations shall pass away before they become a white and delightsome people.'" Dozens of Mormon men marry Native Americans as plural wives in pioneer Utah and Arizona.

13 Aug., *Deseret News* editorializes: "The number of votes cast at the annual election in this county, was unusually small—but little interest having been taken in that matter." Apathy of Mormon voters continues until LDS church disbands its political party in 1891.

20 Aug., *Deseret News* reports first counselor Heber C. Kimball's sermon: "Do not fret yourselves; if any man has done a wrong deed, do not undertake to kill him without knowing whether he has done right or wrong; wait till you have ascertained the facts in the case." No sermon requires Mormons to seek permission to blood-atone.

22 Aug., Brigham Young tells Apostle Wilford Woodruff: "I want to hasten with it [Salt Lake temple] so as to get it as near done as I can before we go to Jackson County [—] the way things are going the way will soon be clear [—] I think It will not be more than seven years and I want to get the Temple most done before we go." Then he adds that "no Temple will be finished until the one pointed out in Jackson County by Joseph Smith."

11 Oct., Brigham Young writes his son Brigham Jr.: "It is now going on two years and a half since I have used a particle of tobacco . . ."

12 Nov., *Deseret News* denounces unidentified persons who threw a living cat through glass window of Governor Stephen S. Harding's home.

10 Dec., *Deseret News* reports that Church Historian's Office is displaying sample of tobacco crops grown in Provo during past summer.

1863

24 Jan., Brigham Young marries first of six plural wives in violation of federal Morrill Act.

10 Mar., Brigham Young is arrested for bigamy, but charges are dismissed.

24 May, Brigham Young preaches, "In proportion to our fall through sin so shall we be exalted in the presence of our Father and God."

4 June, passenger ship *Amazon* departs London with 882 Mormon emigrants aboard. British author Charles Dickens observes: "Now, I have seen emigrant ships before this day in June. And these people are so strikingly different from all other people in like circumstances whom I have ever seen." He explains: "Nobody is in an ill-temper, nobody is the worse for drink, nobody swears an oath or uses a coarse word, nobody appears depressed, nobody is weeping . . . they established their own police, made their own regulations, and set their own watches at all hatchways."

7 July, Brigham Young speaks about future complex of twenty-four temples in Independence, Missouri: "A tower upon Each then a main high Tower in the center [with] gardens on the top of the Towers with fruit & flowers growing thereon." On 8 July 1861 he said this temple complex will cover ten acres of land.

6 Oct., Brigham Young prophesies to general conference: "Will the present struggle [of the U.S. Civil War] free the slave? No . . . and men will be called to judgment for the way they have treated the negro." U.S. president Abraham Lincoln has already signed on 20 June 1862 law which prohibits slavery in all federal territories, and this emancipates the few dozen slaves in Utah. On 1 Jan. 1863 Lincoln has also issued his proclamation which emancipated all slaves in Confederacy but does not free slaves in Maryland, West Virginia, Kentucky, and Missouri. The 13th Amendment legally ends slavery everywhere in United States in 1865.

7 Oct., Brigham Young tells conference that Joseph Smith III will never become LDS president but that martyred prophet prophesied this role for David H. Smith.

1864

17 Apr., Brigham Young informs members of Quorum of Twelve that he has ordained sons as apostles and as his unsustained counselors: "You have the same privilege." Joseph A. is one, and Brigham later ordains Heber Young an apostle.

15 May, Brigham Young preaches, "I don't want 'Mormonism' to become popular. . . . we would be overrun by the wicked."

11 June, Brigham Young preaches that part of endowment ceremony can be given to Aaronic priesthood boys to "receive the ordinances pertaining to the Aaronic order of Priesthood." Holders of Melchizedek priesthood would then receive that part of the endowment separately. LDS leaders periodically discuss this change, but continue to require young men (some as young as ten) to be ordained to Melchizedek priesthood.

27 June, strike for higher wages by laborers doing construction on East Temple Street (now Main Street) and on Salt Lake City Hall. *Deseret News* on June 29 criticizes their "coercion . . . when the same end might be obtained in a more agreeable way."

1865

26 Jan., LDS missionary Francis A. Hammond agrees to pay $14,000 for church's purchase of 6,000-acre Laie Plantation on island of Oahu, Hawaii. This fulfills his written instructions from Brigham Young to obtain lands "suitable for growing cotton, sugar, rice, tobacco." Hammond's diary notes: "Everybody says I have made a good bargain."

19 Feb., first counselor Heber C. Kimball testifies of healing people with his special handkerchief, cane, and cloak.

6 Mar., Heber C. Kimball tells Apostle Woodruff: "The North will never have the power to crush the South [—] No never." Confederacy surrenders next month.

10 Apr., special conference agrees to build telegraph line in Utah. At same time Black Hawk War with Native American Indians commences in central Utah and continues for two years.

23 Aug., First Presidency and Twelve publish proclamation against Lucy Mack Smith's *Biographical Sketches of Joseph Smith the Prophet* and against some of Apostle Orson Pratt's published teachings. Concerning Mother Smith's biography of her son: "Every one in the Church, male or female, if they have such a book, to dispose of it." Proclamation threatens excommunication against anyone espousing doctrines such as Pratt's statement: "The Father and Son do not progress in knowledge and wisdom, because they already know all things past, present, and to come." (Oct. 1865 in England.)

20 Sept., *Salt Lake Telegram* reports that Salt Lake City's Jews celebrate Yom Kippur in LDS 14th Ward chapel, as arranged by Brigham Young.

1866

18 Jan., Deseret Telegraph Company chartered by Utah legislature. President Lorenzo Snow sells this church business to Western Union on 8 Mar. 1900.

22 Jan., Brigham Young authorizes J. H. Ellis (Worshipful Master of Mt. Moriah Lodge, U.D., F.&A.M.) to rent Social Hall for "the organization of a Lodge of Masons."

12 Apr., *Deseret News* reports murder of S. Newton Brassfield on 2 Apr. He legally marries plural wife of absent Mormon missionary, and *News* editorializes that "the illegally [sic] married couple would probably have been suffered to pursue their way to their own liking," except that she files for custody of her children. *News* also reports Brigham Young's sermon about Brassfield: "Were I absent from my home [on mission], I would rejoice to know that I had friends there to protect and guard the virtue of my household; and I would thank God for such friends."

23 Apr., "Circleville Massacre," in which local Mormon militia shoots hand-tied Piede Indian men, then slits throats of their women and children one-by-one. Of this incident commanding general Daniel H. Wells (Young's counselor) writes that these "brethren" did what was necessary.

3 June, Brigham Young preaches, "We who are called Latter-day Saints are Gentiles by birth—we are nationally so."

19 Aug., Brigham Young preaches: "Mary the wife of Joseph had another husband. On this account infidels have called the Savior a bastard. . . . He was begotten by God our heavenly Father." She was a polyandrist, like the woman he authorized in 1857.

7 Oct., Brigham Young tells general conference it is right of Joseph Smith's last son, David H. Smith, to be president of LDS church.

11 Oct., during Dr. J. King Robinson's lawsuit against Salt Lake City, mob of twenty to thirty men destroy his "bowling-saloon" in city. Police chief Andrew Burt and two policemen are identified as members of mob, and Robinson tells Mayor Daniel H. Wells on 20 Oct. that he will sue city for damages. He is ejected from the mayor's office.

22 Oct., Dr. J. King Robinson is murdered in Salt Lake City. Witnesses see seven men leaving scene of crime but claim inability to identify them. Brigham Young publicly condemns the act, offers $500 reward on 23 Oct. for arrest of murderers. After three Salt Lake City police officers (all Mormons) are charged with murder, Young withdraws reward on 1 Feb. 1872 because he has "no desire to endanger the lives of innocent men."

11 Dec., Brigham Young, Jr. writes in his diary that "a nigger" is found dead in Salt Lake City with this note pinned to corpse: "Let this be a warning to all niggers that they meddle not with white women."

23 Dec., Brigham Young preaches, "A Jew cannot now believe in Jesus Christ. . . . They cannot have the benefit of the atonement until they gather to Jerusalem."

31 Dec., Brigham Young gives second anointing, first time in nearly twenty-one years.

1867

13 Jan., Brigham Young preaches: "According to his [Apostle Orson Pratt's] theory, God can progress no further in knowledge and power; but the God that I serve is progressing eternally."

23 Jan., Brigham Young reconvenes Council of Fifty, first time in more than 15 years.

10 Feb., Brigham Young preaches that polygamy is practice "of Jesus and his Apostles." He also says, "Men who know nothing of the Priesthood receive revelation and prophecy."

4 May, Quorum of Twelve drops Apostle Amasa M. Lyman due to his refusal to recant his teachings which deny Christ's blood atonement. Next day Brigham Young preaches that Apostle Orson Pratt "would have been cut off from the Church long ago had it not been for me." This refers to their long dispute over Adam-God theory.

4 June, Brigham Young gives "pass" for William A. Hickman to leave Salt Lake Valley and travel east through mountains out of Utah. Exit pass states in part that he "is intending to leave this Territory, and in view of his doing so he should be at liberty to. . . . I know of no reason why he should not be permitted to attend to his business and leave, when he gets ready, in peace and quietness."

6 Oct., first conference in "new" Salt Lake Tabernacle.

9 Dec., Brigham Young organizes School of Prophets in Salt Lake City, thirty-two years after first one at Kirtland closed. More than 900 men belong to Salt Lake City school, and 5,000 join other Schools of Prophets throughout Great Basin.

27 Dec., School of the Prophets in Salt Lake City votes to boycott "outsiders who are our bitter enemies." On 3 Jan. School votes to boycott all non-Mormon merchants.

1868

10 Jan., *Deseret News* editorial: "In this Territory we jealously close the door against adultery, seduction and whoredom. Public opinion here pronounces the penalty of death as the fitting punishment for such crimes."

3 Feb., Brigham Young tells Salt Lake City School of Prophets that "there were witches in the midst of this people, by whose influence suffering and distress were wrought among the people." He reaffirms this to School of Prophets on 11 Dec. 1869: "Witch Craft is

true but not of the Lord but is of the evil one." His remarks lead some faithful Mormons to use well-known magical remedies, such as parchment house-amulets and counter-charm incantations against witchcraft.

4 Feb., *Deseret News* editorializes that "it is a pity" LDS father did not succeed in killing his daughter's seducer when the father "drew a revolver and shot him down in the court room."

12 Feb., *Deseret News* editorial "Marry and Be Happy" says that if men continue to refuse to marry, "we would be inclined to favor the revival of the Spartan custom of treating bachelors [by flogging]."

5 Mar., *Deseret News* article "Served Him Right" reports that a Gentile is given "sound thrashing" when he visits LDS meeting to see young woman.

28 May, Presiding Bishop instructs ward bishops to have "faithful teachers to settle all difficulties that may arise." First Presidency letter of 11 July 1877 urges teachers to bring evidence of wrongdoing to church courts. Monthly meeting of teachers is pre-trial hearing in church court system.

12 June, without trial William A. Hickman is excommunicated about six months after he tries to extort money from Brigham Young with threat of publishing his crimes.

4 July, Apostle Orson Pratt confesses to Salt Lake School of Prophets that he has been wrong to reject Brigham Young's Adam-God doctrine for past sixteen years. This is three days after Pratt writes personal apology to Young.

23 Aug., Apostle Wilford Woodruff tells congregation in Logan, Utah that within thirty years New York City will be destroyed by "the Sea Heaving itself beyond its bounds & washing the inhabitants into the Sea," Albany, New York will be "utterly Destroyed by fire," Boston will be "sunk with an Earthquake," and Chicago will be "burned with fire." As for United States, it will be "broken to peaces [sic]." Brigham Young says Woodruff's remarks are "given By Revelation." Although Mormons regard Chicago Fire of 1871 as fulfillment of this prophecy, they donate "for the relief of the sufferers."

3 Oct., Salt Lake City School of Prophets votes again to sustain Brigham Young's proposal to boycott all "Gentile" merchants, including Jews. General conference publicly sustains this boycott, which continues until 1882 and leads to establishment of ZCMI.

9 Oct., Brigham Young adjourns Council of Fifty. He never reconvenes it again.

1869

12 Jan., *Deseret News* editorial against universal male suffrage for United States: "Education and intelligence should precede the suffrage, otherwise the latter would be like a razor in the hands of a child—more likely to prove destructive than otherwise." Since Utah is not a state, it is unable to cast its vote against 15th amendment (Mar. 1870).

1 Mar., opening of Zion's Co-operative Mercantile Institution (ZCMI).

1 May, church begins obtaining sworn affidavits from persons who have personal knowledge of Joseph Smith instructing, performing, or entering into plural marriage. Unfortunately this is not careful effort at historical reconstruction of pre-1844 plural marriage but is legalist response to RLDS church's denials of founding prophet's involvement in polygamy. The living witness who knows most details of Nauvoo polygamy, Brigham Young, does not add affidavit of his own to this bound collection.

10 May, completion of transcontinental railroad at Promontory Summit, Utah. This ends Mormon pioneer period and begins significant non-LDS population.

15 Aug., Apostle George Q. Cannon preaches: "We close the door on one side, and say that whoredoms, seductions and adulteries must not be committed among us, and we say to those who are determined to carry on such things[:] we will kill you . . ."

28 Sept., *Deseret News* advertises sale of *Book of Mormon* "In Phonetics." Apostle Orson Pratt reports he translated it into Deseret Alphabet in "four months of continuous labor."

27 Oct., Brigham Young preaches at Lehi, Utah, that "by marriage Lot's two daughters were sealed to him, & will be his to all eternity." Young adds that it might one day become nec-

essary to seal a man's daughter to him as a wife, "but it is not likely ever again to occur." There are verified instances of LDS leaders performing polygamous marriages between men and their foster-daughters or step-daughters, but not actual daughters.

28 Nov., Brigham Young organizes Young Ladies' Retrenchment Association among his daughters at Lion House. Aside from Relief Society, this is only other church auxiliary organized by church president at its outset. Renamed Young Ladies' Mutual Improvement Association, its first president is Elmina Shepherd Taylor in 1880. Renamed Young Women's MIA, it is now known simply as Young Women.

9 Dec., ZCMI Drug Store advertises that it has just opened on Main Street with "Liquors, Draught and [by the] Case."

1870

29 Jan., Salt Lake City School of Prophets "turn[s] into a caucus meeting, for the purpose of nominating our City officers, preparatory to the forthcoming Election."

9 Feb., formation of anti-Mormon "Liberal Party" which opposes LDS church's "People's Party" at every Utah election for more than twenty years. Presiding Bishopric counselor Jesse C. Little helps lead group of Mormons who disrupt its first meeting.

12 Feb., Utah enfranchises women, who are among first in nation on 14 Feb., when Miss Seraph Young votes. Wyoming adopted woman's suffrage in 1869. Mormon legislature passes bill knowing this doubles Mormon vote. Non-LDS governor signs bill in mistaken assumption that Utah's women will vote against polygamist power of People's Party. This 1870 law does not allow women to hold elective office, and Utah's governor vetoes bill in 1880 that would give full civil rights to women.

20 Feb., Brigham Young preaches, "Now the Church of Jesus Christ of Latter-day Saints believes every word of truth believed in by the holy Catholic Church."

27 Feb., Thomas C. Griggs, faithful Mormon, writes in his diary: "in the afternoon we had a lengthy if not interesting discourse from Elder Erastus Snow."

5 May, Salt Lake Tabernacle fast and testimony meeting: "Prest. Young spoke 12 minutes, requesting mothers to leave their children at home if possible so as not to disturb the meeting. also that Gentlemen will desist besmearing the floors with tobacco spittle &c." Tabernacle installs dozens of tobacco spittoons.

18 June, first counselor George A. Smith tells Salt Lake School of Prophets about "the evil of Masturbation" among Utah Mormons. Apostle Lorenzo Snow says that "Plural Marriage would tend to diminish the evil of self-pollution," and he believes that "indulgence on the part of men was less in Plural marriage than in Monogamy." Elder George Reynolds (secretary to Brigham Young) also tells the School that "where Monogamy was the Law, it compelled a more frequent [sexual] cohabitation than is right and proper." Medical books advise sexual intercourse only once a month.

3 July, ordination of Albert Carrington as apostle, first general authority with B.A. degree (Dartmouth College, 1834, Phi Beta Kappa). He is also first general authority who attended Ivy League school.

26 July, Apostle Joseph F. Smith performs proxy sealing of Scotland's Queen Maud (or Matilda, b. 1104) as eternal wife to martyred prophet Joseph Smith. Similar ordinances are performed by Apostle Wilford Woodruff on 5 Sept. for eight political heroines or female rulers including Charlotte Corday (who murdered the radical Marat during French Revolution) and Empress Josephine (wife of Napoleon). On 15 Sept. second counselor Daniel H. Wells seals two Catholic saints as wives to founding Mormon prophet: Saint Helena (mother of Roman emperor Constantine) and Saint Theresa (b. 1515 in Spain). These are first women of international prominence sealed as wives to Joseph Smith, but during fifty years after his death hundreds of deceased women are similarly joined to him, even though many had husbands during their lifetimes.

28 July, *Deseret News* reports that on his return to Salt Lake City yesterday, Milando Pratt says

that he and Thomas Rich saw Bear Lake Monster from shore: "The portion of the body out of the water was about ten feet long," with head like walrus.

23 Aug., LDS political newspaper *Salt Lake Herald* reports "The Outrage," in which four unidentified men "discharged the contents of a bottle filled with diluted excrements" upon Mormon apostates T. B. H. Stenhouse and his wife Fanny.

1 Sept., Salt Lake City's 9th Ward reports that only thirty-one of its 181 families attends Sunday services regularly and 50 percent of families are "perfectly indifferent."

28 Sept., baptism at Salt Lake City of Martin Harris, second of three *Book of Mormon* witnesses to return to church as led by Brigham Young.

6 Oct., Brigham Young tells general conference that his published talks are scripture.

7 Oct., at priesthood meeting in Salt Lake Tabernacle, Brigham Young announces revelation about Mormons investing in bonds of Utah Central Railroad Co. Text available but never canonized or officially published.

8 Oct., First Presidency and Quorum of Twelve excommunicate following leaders of Mountain Meadows Massacre: Isaac C. Haight, John D. Lee, and George Wood: "They [are] not to have the privilege of returning again to the Church again in this life."

31 Oct., at death of Utah's governor J. Wilson Schaffer, Apostle Joseph F. Smith writes: "Thank God! He was a low, debauched, vulgar, senseless, ignorant cur, and the Lord be praised that his vile, despicable existence has terminated."

1871

4 Mar., Salt Lake City School of Prophets votes to organize church life insurance company. This Mutual Life and Savings Society of the United States dissolves on 10 Oct. 1873.

25 Mar., at Parowan's School of Prophets, "speaking of the apostacy in the Church," one of local Seventy's presidents says that "there were many who are beginning to think they do not worship the same God that Brigham Young does."

3 June, Salt Lake Tabernacle service: "Prest. D.H. Wells spoke 25 minutes following Prest. Youngs remarks. Not very good attention. Considerable moving about, passing out, & drowsiness."

16 June, Apostle Joseph F. Smith writes of his divorced first wife "Levira [who] arrived from California in a state of insanity." Daughter of founder's brother Samuel H. Smith and first cousin-wife of Apostle Smith, Levira C. Smith is earliest example of mental illness in prominent Mormon. In 1886 she is legally committed to Utah Insane Asylum as its fifty-ninth patient, and remains there for three months.

27 June, Brigham Young: "The Garden of Eden was where Jackson Co. is now in Mo. & when Adam was driven out, he crossed the river into what is now Daviess Co. The City of Enoch stood where the Gulf of Mexico is now, but these things are not written."

28 July, First Presidency's written appointment of Elijah F. Sheets "to act as a Traveling Bishop." Sheets counsels local members and ward bishops and ordains local officers until his release as traveling bishop in 1878. Better-known A. Milton Musser is often described as traveling bishop from 1858 to 1876. However, Musser's service actually begins in 1860 as traveling "agent" of General Tithing Office.

11 Sept., Counselor Daniel H. Wells tells Grantsville School of Prophets that "a great many of our young men, [are] abusing themselves by the habit of self-pollution: or self-abuse, or as the Bible terms it Onanism," which he regards as "one great cause why so many of our young men were not married, and it was a great sin, and would lead to insanity and a premature grave." Polygamy is likelier cause for prevalence of bachelorhood in nineteenth-century Utah. First, every national census lists more males than females in Mormon population. Second, 20-40 percent of Mormon men marry polygamously which demographically requires bachelorhood in Utah's majority population of males.

2-3 Oct., Brigham Young and his counselor Daniel H. Wells are arrested for polygamous cohabitation and subsequently for murder, but charges are dismissed.

16 Dec., Seymour B. Young, son of senior Seventy's president, writes: "Salt Lake City has for the first time in its history houses of Ill fame almost on every corner."

1872

3 Feb., two women are on LDS People's Party "Committee of Seven" which selects nominees for upcoming election.

5 Feb., while in prison, William A. Hickman publishes *Brigham's Destroying Angel*, first Mormon exposé by confessed murderer. He is again excommunicated, this time by church court, on 12 Jan. 1878. On 21 Mar. 1934, First Presidency approves Hickman's rebaptism and "his former blessings restored," which occur by proxy on 5 May 1934.

20 Feb., unsuccessful statehood convention which drafts proposed constitution that allows Congress to add anti-polygamy clause. Of this, his non-Mormon friend Thomas L. Kane writes Brigham Young: "I will not probably be able to recommend the pretended acceptance by your citizens of a Constitution containing features repugnant to their principles. As regards the actual abandonment of polygamy, that is a question between you and your God. And I have naught to say on it. But Duplicity, I see, without a shadow, will not be good policy for you."

27 Feb., *LDS Millennial Star* editorial, "Motherhood Of God," repeats a child's question: "Why don't you tell me 'bout the Heavenly Mother? Don't *she* give us anything?" Editorial speaks of those who "yearn to adore her" and expresses approval of praying to "Father and Mother God." Conclusion: "When we draw nearer the Divine Man, lo! we shall find a Divine Woman smiling upon us. . . . In the Father's many mansions, we shall find her and be satisfied."

9 Apr., conference sustains new calling of "home missionaries," which Counselor George A. Smith explains before presenting names of those assigned for each stake (which is entire county at this time). Calling of home missionaries overlaps with visits of "block teachers." In 1912 term "ward teachers" becomes official, by which time "home missionaries" are known as "stake missionaries."

June, first Mormon women's periodical, *Woman's Exponent*.

3 Aug., Brigham Young dissolves School of Prophets in Salt Lake City and throughout Utah because of breaches in meeting's secrecy that end up in anti-Mormon *Salt Lake Tribune*.

21 Sept., Miss Phoebe W. Cousins and Miss Georgeanna Snow become first women admitted to practice of law in Utah.

7 Oct., Apostle John Taylor tells general conference: "And if we have Presidents or Apostles or anybody that we do not like, let us vote them out, and be free men."

9 Oct., Brigham Young and his counselors are each sustained as "Prophet, Seer and Revelator." This is first conference since 1859 which sustains anyone with that title. Quorum of Twelve Apostles are not presented in this manner at this conference, and from 8 Apr. 1873 until his death Young is only church officer sustained by conferences as "Prophet, Seer and Revelator."

11 Nov., Brigham Young re-establishes School of the Prophets in Salt Lake City, with tighter controls on membership and attendance to protect confidentiality. At this meeting, second counselor Daniel H. Wells says, "The violation of the Word of Wisdom is not a matter of fellowship and will not clip a man in his glory; but he will not have the blessings which are promised."

1873

1 Jan., Apostle Joseph F. Smith strikes his neighbor's head "three times with my cane" for insulting him and letting his livestock trespass on Smith's property. He voluntarily pleads guilty to assault and battery to Mormon justice of the peace. On Christmas night Smith had dreamed of using his cane repeatedly on opponent's head, "intending to kill him, but was partially prevented from striking him with full force by my wives."

10 Feb., Apostle Orson Hyde preaches that church's law of tithing is "one tenth of all we possess at the start, and then ever after one tenth."

18 Feb., Mormon mob lynches Charles A. Benson for murder in Logan, Utah, under circumstances in which his LDS apostasy is contributing factor. He is son of former Cache Valley president, deceased apostle Ezra T. Benson, whose official biography states that "no further record of his life is available" after Charles's endowment date.

27 Feb., Apostle Joseph F. Smith dreams of anti-Mormon who uses bottle of "concentrated essence of S—t" to attack plural marriage. He thinks dream refers to Congress.

4 Mar., Seymour B. Young describes inauguration of Ulysses S. Grant as U.S. president: "Useless S Grant shits in Washingtons chair." Mormons regard Grant as anti-LDS.

8 Apr., Brigham Young resigns as Trustee-in-Trust, and conference sustains his first counselor George A. Smith to that position with twelve "assistants." Apostle Albert Carrington is assistant counselor in Presidency and is first college graduate to serve.

30 May, Catholic Father Damien [Joseph de Veuster] begins his ministry at leper colony of Molokai, Hawaii, five months after equally self-sacrificing Jonathon Napela, president of LDS branch. Napela, who does not have the disease, accompanies his wife Kitty who is required to live there because of her leprosy. Jonathon contracts disease in 1877, and dies in 1879, followed by Kitty in 1881. Father Damien dies of leprosy in 1889.

1 June, Brigham Young tells apostles of revelation he received concerning appearance of future temples. Text available but never canonized or officially published.

1 July, Brigham Young's son Willard is first Mormon admitted as cadet in U.S. Military Academy at West Point. He graduates on 16 June 1875, "second in discipline" and "fourth in over-all standing" within his class. Second Mormon at West Point is Brigham's nephew Richard W. Young in 1878. After two years as first Mormon at U.S. Naval Academy at Annapolis, Maryland, Brigham's son Feramorz L. Young resigns "in good standing" in December 1876 because he decides against military career. In twentieth century, hundreds of Mormons graduate from U.S. military academies.

8 July, incorporation of Zion's Savings Bank and Trust, succeeded nearly century later by Zion's First National Bank.

5 Aug., African-American Samuel Chambers tells meeting of Salt Lake Stake deacon's quorum: "as I have been appointed a deacon I feel to fulfill my mission" On 8 Dec. 1874 he says that gospel "is not only to the Gentiles but also to the African, for I am of that race." Denied priesthood ordination by LDS presidents from 1852 to 1978, some LDS African-Americans in Utah are officially appointed as "acting deacon."

13 Oct., Salt Lake City School of Prophets discusses practice of Patriarch John Smith and others who ordain infant boys to priesthood. Second counselor Daniel H. Wells "said some had ordained children when thought they would die—this had been a comfort to some parents, though there was no law or revelation given for or against it, consequently he could not see any harm or wrong in having it done, neither could he think there was any particular virtue in it."

1874

26 Jan., apparently last meeting of Brigham Young's School of Prophets.

21 Feb., during meeting of Young Ladies Mutual Improvement Association in Assembly Hall on Salt Lake Temple Square, "Mother [Elizabeth A.] Whitney sung in tongues, and Carrie Carter in attempting an interpretation threw her bonnet and muff on the floor, & fell on her knees, remaining for some time in that position."

9 May, general conference speakers promote establishment of communitarian "United Orders." Most successful and well-known is in Orderville, Utah, where no one owns private property, clothing and houses are standardized, and everyone eats in common dining hall after food is prepared in communal kitchen. Orderville continues in this manner until dissolved in 1885 by instruction of Presidency and Twelve.

16 May, Congress establishes Mount Olivet Cemetery in Salt Lake City as only civilian cemetery ever created by federal government. Although some civilians are buried in

Washington, D.C.'s Arlington Cemetery, it is military cemetery. Congressmen do not trust Mormons to give proper respect to graves of non-Mormons.

17 June, Elsa Johnson is first woman to become naturalized citizen in Utah.

23 June, Poland Act removes criminal jurisdiction from Utah's probate judges who have been LDS bishops since 1850. In 1870, 100 percent of jurors are Mormon, compared to their 83 percent share of Utah's population. From now on non-Mormon federal judges rather than LDS bishops preside over criminal trials of Mormons, where juries are now disproportionately non-Mormon.

Emily D. Partridge Young writes: "In the evening several spoke in tong[u]es. Sister E[liza R]. Snow insisted on my speaking in tong[u]es so I complied, but I am not in favor of making use of that gift. I would rather hear speaking in our own language. I think it the safest. The devil is apt to poke his nose in where there is tong[u]es, espesially among the inexperienced. . . . yet the gift of tounges [sic] is one of the gifts of the gospel, but should not be trifled with."

28 June, Brigham Young preaches, "Now brethren, the man that honors his Priesthood, the woman that honors her Priesthood, will receive an everlasting inheritance in the kingdom of God."

9 Aug., Brigham Young publicly dictates revelation on communitarian United Order. Officially published in *Deseret News* and *Journal of Discourses* but never canonized.

25 Sept., *Deseret News* editorial about "immortal seven" Mormons who are excused from grand jury in Beaver because they can not conscientiously indict anyone for polygamy.

1875

1 Feb., Emily D. Partridge Young, Brigham Young's plural wife of thirty years, confides to her diary: "I feel rather dispirited and a good cry might do me good. I feel quite ashamed to be known as a wife of the richest man in the territory, and yet we are so poor. I do not know why he is so loth to provide for me. My children are his children. He provides sumptuously for some of his family. . . . He manifests a desire to cast me off, and I cannot ask him for anything." She is with him at his death two years later and writes: "I believe Pr. Young has done his whole duty towards Joseph Smith's family. They have sometimes felt that their lot was hard, but no blame or censure rests upon him. And I feel grateful to him and bless his name forever."

12 Feb., *Deseret News* editorial comment: "As to a unity of Church and State, or, in other words, a blending of spiritual and temporal matters, what has Congress to do with that?"

22 Feb., first sealing of husband and wife who are both Native American Indians, Olieto Comp ("James Laman") and his wife Minnie, "as man and wife for time and eternity at the altar in the Endowment House."

27 Feb., *Deseret News* reports Orson Pratt sermon: "Little did we suppose when we were driven out from Jackson County, the place where God has promised to give his Saints their inheritances, and in the regions round about, that nearly half a century would pass over our heads before we would be restored back to that land." He adds that a few who were in the church at the time they were driven from Jackson County "will live to behold the day, and will return and receive their inheritances."

7 Mar., Apostle Joseph F. Smith's wife writes him that "you know how brother [Albert] Carrington thinks a deal of women." In Dec. 1882 Apostle John Henry Smith writes President John Taylor that maid at British Mission headquarters "found Bro. Carrington lying upon the lounge and Sarah Kirkman lying upon top of him." Upon Brigham Young's inquiry about other women in 1873 and John Taylor's inquiry about Sarah Kirkman in 1883, Carrington denies serious wrongdoing. He is not excommunicated until 1885 when protests from Sarah's husband become too insistent to ignore.

10 Apr., Brigham Young changes ranking in Quorum of Twelve and demotes Orson Hyde and Orson Pratt beneath John Taylor for first time in nearly thirty-seven years. This makes Taylor senior-ranking apostle after Young. This action also releases Hyde as

president of Quorum of Twelve, office to which he had been publicly sustained since 27 Dec. 1847. However, because of their mutual dislike Young declines to sustain Taylor in Hyde's former office either privately or publicly.

10 June, first organization for young men is local innovation of Salt Lake 13th Ward. It becomes churchwide organization on 8 Dec. 1876.

27 June, Apostle Wilford Woodruff preaches that spirits "come from their eternal Father and their eternal Mother unto whom they were born in the eternal world."

18 July, Apostle Orson Pratt preaches in Salt Lake City that rebaptism "seems to be a kind of standing ordinance for all Latter-day Saints who emigrate here, from First Presidency down; all are rebaptized and set out anew by renewing their covenants."

After his counselor Daniel H. Wells eulogizes Emmeline Free Young, Brigham Young stuns those at funeral by instructing her children and grandchildren not to follow his plural wife's "bad example." In her manuscript "My Father's Wives," Susa Young Gates explains that "Aunt Emmeline became addicted to morphine in the later years of her life."

21 July, LDS political newspaper *Salt Lake Herald* publishes John D. Lee's "confession" that "all who participated in the lamentable transaction, or most of them, were acting under orders that they considered it their duty—their religious duty—to obey." Lee says that when informed of Mountain Meadows Massacre, Brigham Young "wept like a child, walked the floor and wrung his hands in bitter anguish."

28 July, *Deseret News* reports one of meetings where apostles preach United Order: "The vote to renew their covenants by baptism was very general by the people."

1 Aug., George W. Hill baptizes more than 300 Shoshone Indians in Box Elder County, Utah, and performs priesthood administrations which heal many of them. First Presidency establishes Washakie Farm for Indian converts in Box Elder County. Two years later one of Brigham Young's sons writes of these Native American converts: "They practiced polygamy [before LDS baptism] & of course continue it."

3 Oct., Ulysses S. Grant is first U.S. president to visit Utah and meet LDS president there.

8 Oct., Brigham Young is sustained again as Trustee-in-Trust, following death of his replacement, George A. Smith. He has no assistants, and office remains with presiding apostle or church president from now on.

16 Oct., establishment of Brigham Young Academy in Provo, renamed "University" in 1903. This is first of church's thirty-seven academies which until 1900 offer primarily elementary level education with some secondary coursework. However, academies also develop college-level "normal" curriculum for teacher-training. By 1934 only four remain LDS institutions. Other major LDS academies are Brigham Young College at Logan, Utah, in 1877 (closed in 1926), Salt Lake Stake Academy in 1886 (now LDS Business College), Bannock Stake Academy in 1888 (now church-owned Ricks College in Idaho), St. George Stake Academy in 1888 (now Utah state-operated Dixie College), Sanpete Stake Academy in 1888 (now Utah state-operated Snow College), Weber Stake Academy in 1888 (now Utah state-operated Weber State University), St. Joseph Stake Academy in 1891 (now state-operated Eastern Arizona College), and Juarez Stake Academy in 1897 (later Academia Juarez).

21 Nov., local bishop reports that first counselor "George A. Smith preached in Salina, Sevier County last year and said that *The Savior Jesus Christ* will be here on Earth in 1891" (emphasis in original).

1876

5 Apr., Salt Lake City arsenal explodes, killing four people and severely damaging houses in 13th, 14th, 16th, 17th, 18th, 19th, and 20th wards. *Deseret News* reports: "Nearly every building of any size, for a mile and a half or two miles around" is damaged.

11 Apr., stake president Francis M. Lyman spends day studying Buddhism and Confucianism. Four days later he studies Hindu philosophy for half-day.

6 May, General Aaronic Priesthood minutes note that it has "been the custom to ordain boys to the office of deacon and allow them to retain this office till they get their endowments when they [are] ordained Elders."

3 June, *Deseret News* publishes grand jury's audit of Salt Lake City Corporation's financial records which show extensive transactions involving liquor. Municipal funds purchase liquor for Pioneer Day on 24 July and also for party of Mormon Battalion veterans. The city rents Brigham Young's distillery for $2,000 annually from 1861 to 1867, after which city government purchases its liquor directly from Howard Distillery which is owned jointly by Brigham Young and his first counselor Daniel H. Wells. Young is also member of Salt Lake City Council (1872-77), and Wells is mayor from 1866 to 1876. Report observes: "After completion of the railroad, the city continued to buy liquor from Brigham Young at $4.00 per gallon, although they could have gotten better 'States' liquor at $1.25 per gallon."

11 June, at St. George, Utah, Brigham Young preaches, "as to the Mountain Meadows Massacre if he had not been foiled by Judge [John] Cradlebaugh and other federal officials He would have hung every guilty person concerned in the bloody deed." Men in congregation are involved, and by arrangement several testify against John D. Lee.

24 June, Brigham Young confides that it is "a curiosity to him that men could commit adultery and still retain the spirit of the Lord as he had witnessed on one occasion. The man [is] now dead."

6 July, concerning Custer Massacre few days before, *Deseret News* editorializes that it is doubtful if possession of Black Hills country by whites can be justified. If it cannot, "the Indians [rather than Custer's men] must consequently have the sympathy of every just man in the area of the civilized world." Such pro-Indian sentiments contribute to hostility of U.S. army and federal government toward Mormons.

2 Aug., *Deseret News* publishes directory of "PRESIDING ELDERS AND BISHOPS of the Church of Jesus Christ of Latter-day Saints." This is list of twenty-one regional bishops. Cache Valley's "presiding bishop" presides over twenty-four wards, while Iron County's presiding bishop is responsible for two wards.

11 Sept., Jens C.A. Weibye lists number of married LDS men in his home town of Manti, Utah, and calculates that 15.8 percent are polygamists.

14 Oct., "It having been given out at Conference that the Endowment House would be closed after this week, for the past few days hundreds of persons have been going through the House, in fact, great numbers have to be refused, the authorities not having time or room for them." Closing Endowment House in Salt Lake City is Brigham Young's way of guaranteeing use of the distant St. George temple.

1877

1 Jan., Apostle Wilford Woodruff gives first reading of dedicatory prayer for Utah's first temple (at St. George), and temple ordinances begin. He prays that Brigham Young will live to see United States "broken in pieces like a potter's vessel and swept from off the face of the Earth" because this nation "shed the Blood of Prophets and Saints which cry unto God day and night for vengeance."

4 Jan., Joseph Smith's last-born child David is committed to Illinois Hospital for the Insane. Proclaimed by Brigham Young in 1866 as rightful heir of LDS presidency, he has served as counselor in RLDS presidency since 1873. He dies in asylum in 1904.

15 Jan., Brigham Young begins dictating from memory first written version of endowment ceremony. He adds Protestant minister as new character in endowment drama which does not have set dialogue at this time.

7 Feb., Brigham Young gives his last Adam-God sermon as final lecture of endowment ceremony for St. George temple. This "lecture at the veil" remains for many years.

15 Mar., Romania Bunnell Pratt is first Mormon woman to obtain M.D. degree (from

Women's Medical College in Philadelphia). On 1 Nov. she opens school of obstetrics in Salt Lake City where she trains Mormon midwives and nurses for twenty-two years.

23 Mar., execution of John D. Lee at Mountain Meadows, Utah, for his role in massacre almost twenty years earlier.

30 Mar., Brigham Young instructs apostles to re-organize all stakes of Great Basin.

1 Apr., at meeting in St. George, Utah, Brigham Young verbally attacks second-ranked apostle John Taylor for indifference to communitarian United Orders. Young warns that Taylor could lose his standing in Twelve and cancels his administrative assignments. Apostle Lorenzo Snow finally persuades Taylor to apologize, which Snow believes is necessary to preserve Taylor's status in Twelve.

6 Apr., in St. George temple, second counselor Daniel H. Wells reads dedicatory prayer at re-dedication ceremony, during which some see halo of light around his head.

25 May, Brigham Young preaches: "The Seventies are Apostles; and they stand next in authority to the Twelve," as reported in *Deseret News* on June 2.

2 June, *Deseret News* story that reporter for *New York Herald* claims there were two attempts to kill him during past week in Salt Lake City, a knife attack and a shooting. On 2 June, *News* dismisses his claim as "a vile plot gotten up . . . to revive the anti-'Mormon' excitement." On 23 June it editorializes that the New York reporter "is really in mental disorder," but two days later defends the city's investigation as serious effort.

11 July, First Presidency's letter to bishops and stake presidents includes: "It would be excellent for the young men if they had the opportunity of acting in the offices of the lesser priesthood." This mild suggestion does not result in widespread practice of ordaining teenage boys, so adults continue to be deacons, teachers, priests of most wards.

4 Aug., Brigham Young obtains cancellation of his debts in Ogden, Utah, dating back to 1849.

19 Aug., Apostle Wilford Woodruff tells Sunday school meeting that he heard Joseph Smith say: "If the People knew what was behind the vail they would try by every means to commit suicide that they might get there but the Lord in his wisdom had emplanted the fear of death in every person that they might cling to life and thus accomplish the designs of their creator."

21 Aug., Apostle Wilford Woodruff is proxy in vicarious baptisms for all signers of Declaration of Independence (except John Hancock) and for all deceased U.S. presidents, except James Buchanan and Martin Van Buren. This is first baptism for dead on behalf of U.S. president since 1840.

29 Aug., Brigham Young dies. This is exactly twenty-five years after he authorized public announcement of polygamy. His last words are "Joseph, Joseph, Joseph!"

4 Sept., Quorum of Twelve sustains John Taylor as its president.

26 Sept., grand jury describes Salt Lake County probate court as "divorce mill" which granted 300 divorces in previous twelve-month period, primarily on "grounds of incompatibility of temperament, different aims and objects in life." Eighty percent of divorced couples come to Utah for divorces from such places as San Francisco, New York City, Chicago, Terre Haute, and St. Louis. Report finds that 13 percent of divorces are granted same day of complaint, total of 42 percent within week of application, and total of 85 percent are granted within month of application. Report continues, "[A]nd your committee have good reason to believe that other county probate courts of the territory are likewise engaged in this class of divorce business, to an equal if not greater extent." Two months later U.S. senator Dawes introduces bill to remove divorce from jurisdiction of Mormon probate courts and limit divorce cases to federally appointed non-Mormon judges.

3 Oct., in meeting of Twelve with Brigham Young's former counselors, Daniel H. Wells proposes that junior apostle Joseph F. Smith should become church president. Wells denies that Young ever intended for John Taylor to succeed him as church president. First time general authority proposes ending automatic succession of senior apostle. In

1880 Wells and Apostle Orson Pratt again urge this. In 1887 Apostle Heber J. Grant wants lower-ranked apostle Joseph F. Smith to become church president instead of Wilford Woodruff or four other senior apostles.

6 Oct., for first time, conference sustains John Taylor as president of Quorum of Twelve Apostles, office not presented for vote since release of Orson Hyde. Conference also sustains Twelve as "Prophets, Seers and Revelators" for first time in 41 years. John Taylor is sustained as Trustee-in-Trust with rest of Twelve as "Counselors."

7 Oct., John Taylor tells general conference that Trustee-in-Trust's office will begin giving "reasonable recompense for their services" to Twelve and their two counselors.

31 Oct., John Taylor tells apostles it is wrong for some local patriarchs "to be underbidding the others" in giving patriarchal blessings.

11 Nov., Apostle Charles C. Rich preaches: "When I first received the gospel [in 1832] I did not expect forty-seven years to pass away before the prophecies would be fulfilled concerning the second coming of the Savior, and the end of the world." (published in *Deseret News*, 17 Jan. 1878)

15 Nov., at meeting of bishops: "A communication was read from President John Taylor to Pres. Angus M. Cannon, that the Twelve had decided to open the Endowment House on the last Thursday in each month for marriage sealings. President Taylor said this was done because many young people and the aged and infirm could not arrange to go to St. George. The priesthood was not made for Temples, but Temples for the priesthood." This is first of several public reversals by Taylor of Brigham Young's policies.

19 Nov., John Taylor's revelation about Brigham Young estate. Text available but never canonized or officially published.

1 Dec., *Woman's Exponent* publishes Presiding Bishop Edward Hunter's sermon concerning LDS women: "They have the Priesthood," he says, "a portion of the priesthood rests upon the sisters."

2 Dec., Joseph F. Smith writes about the newly limited compensation for apostles: "One man [probably John W. Young], for instance, who has drawn $16,000 per year from the tithing office for his support, has been cut down to 2,000 per year. Thus some of the leaks are plugged up and we hope to be able by and by to build the temple."

16 Dec., vision of destructions in America before Second Coming. Attributed to John Taylor because of reference to reading "the French language" or to Wilford Woodruff who records this "very strange vision" in his diary, neither man claims authorship, which is actually by Mormon astrologer John Steele who sends copy to Woodruff as church historian.

1878

17 Jan., Apostle George Q. Cannon (special counselor and private secretary to Brigham Young) comments that fellow apostles "felt that the funds of the Church have been used with a freedom not warranted by the authority which he [Brigham Young] held."

20 Jan., Llewellyn Harris begins proselytizing Zuni Pueblo at beginning of small pox epidemic. He administers priesthood ordinance of healing to 409 Zunis, all of whom "recovered, excepting five or six that the [Presbyterian] minister gave medicine to, and four or five that the [Zuni] medicine man had tried to cure by magic."

24 Jan., presiding apostle John Taylor tells meeting of local bishops, "He expected to present before the people at least once a year an account of what was done with their means." It becomes policy to present financial report at Apr. general conference.

29 Jan., *Deseret News* editorial denies that marked ballots have been used to ostracize those who vote against church candidates, but then observes: "And while no one should be injured in consequence of his breaking loose from his associates and joining with those who oppose them, it cannot be expected that the dissenter will receive as much cordial friendship, countenance and support from his former fellow-partisans as those who remain in accord with them."

30 Jan., *Deseret News* advertises "WAGNER'S BEER ON DRAUGHT AT 5 CENTS A

GLASS" on same page as its directory of "NAMES OF PRESIDENTS AND BISHOPS OF THE ORGANIZED STAKES OF ZION." The "CITY LIQUOR STORE" ad is also immediately above "GENEALOGICAL" advertisement directed to Latter-days. *Deseret News* previously ran several alcohol ads in each issue for years, but alcohol ads now appear next to directory of church officers from its first publication on 9 Jan. 1878 until 1 Apr. 1878. On 2 Jan. 1879 chewing tobacco ad appears on page with directory of church officers. On 6 Jan. 1880 church directory appears next to ad for "BETTER AND PURER LIQUORS, WINES AND CIGARS Than can be found at any other House in Utah."

Jan.-Mar., under threat of excommunication by John Taylor, apostles George Q. Cannon, Brigham Young, Jr., and Albert Carrington (as Brigham Young's legal executors) agree to transfer 2/3 of his estate to Taylor as Trustee-in-Trust.

4 Feb., first ad in *Deseret News* for "JACKSON'S BEST SWEET NAVY Chewing Tobacco," which appears directly under large advertisement for "St. Louis Excelsior Lager Beer! Which we offer at LOWER RATES than any other first class beer in the market." Ads for chewing tobacco appear in *Deseret News* (sometimes on front page) through 2 Feb. 1880.

7 Feb., at meeting for renegade "Conservative" ticket of People's Party, first speaker is Dr. J. M. Benedict (who is member of People's Central Committee for Salt Lake County). He complains that regular People's convention is "influenced by previous manipulation." Benedict adds: "He was opposed to that unity produced by the bulk of the people doing as two or three men directed."

12 Feb., *Deseret News* reports interview of George Q. Cannon on 6 Feb. in which he tells *Washington Post*: "The Mormons generally on national issues are inclined to be Democrats, and all other things being equal, in the respective candidates of the parties, would vote the Democratic ticket."

22 Feb., Utah adopts election law which for first time since 1849 eliminates marked ballots that allow election officials to know how each person voted.

3 Apr., concerning recent split in church's political party, *Deseret News* editorializes: "'One Lord, one faith, one baptism, one hope of their calling,' are accepted principles in spiritual things; and one platform, one party, and one ticket, acknowledged fundamentals in political things." On 4 Feb *News* editorialized: "One policy, one ticket, one ballot for all. 'Whatever is more or less than this cometh of evil.'"

15 May, John Taylor preaches: "These 'damned Gentiles,' as you are sometimes pleased to call them, are the children of our Heavenly Father."

24 May, John Taylor to Daniel Tyler, 24 May 1878, regarding Tyler's forthcoming *Concise History of the Mormon Battalion*: "All that I have any desire the Church should do in the matter is to have it looked over by someone appointed by the Council of the Apostles before publication, and eliminate from it anything that is deemed undesirable to publish, should it so happen that any such be found."

28 May, Patriarch Joseph Young, senior Seventy's president and member of Joseph Smith's Anointed Quorum, blesses Brigham Young's daughter Zina Young Card: "These blessings are yours, the blessings and the power according to the holy Melchisedek Priesthood you received in your Endowments, and you shall have them."

13 June, LDS political newspaper *Salt Lake Herald*'s editorial on "Unhappy Marriages" begins: "We cannot say how many divorces the Utah probate courts have granted during the last few years, but the number is enormous, amounting perhaps to thousands."

21 June, *Deseret News* editorial in defense of giving Orrin Porter Rockwell a church funeral: "At his death he was under indictment for the killing of some persons by the name of Aiken, in Juab County, over twenty years ago. . . . He was reported honorable in all his dealings, true to his friends and his word, firm in the faith of the gospel, and feared only by cattle-thieves and mobocrats and their supporters."

27 July, Emmeline B. Wells, Isabella M. Horne, and Sarah M. Kimball become first female delegates to county convention of church's People's Party of which they also become

members of Salt Lake County central committee. However, convention has to withdraw nomination for Wells as People's candidate for county treasurer because "though the statute provided for the enfranchisement of women, it does not admit of their holding office." Instead, Wells joins with Bathsheba W. Smith on 7 Oct. as first female members of territorial central committee of the People's Party.

25 Aug., Aurelia Rogers holds first meeting in Farmington, Utah, of her independently devised program for children. Not until 19 June 1880 does this become official, churchwide program with Louie B. Felt as its first president.

5 Nov., LDS political organ, *Salt Lake Herald,* editorial, "The Election To-day," in part: "No apparent interest has been taken in the matter, one side resting serenely in the knowledge that it will be successful."

13 Nov., three unidentified men attack John C. Young, editor of anti-Mormon *Salt Lake Tribune,* as he leaves its office near midnight and breaks his nose with "brass knuckles." On 12 Feb. 1878 *Deseret News* reported Counselor George Q. Cannon's statement about Young: "I consider the fellow without character, who deserves kicking, and who would not resent the insult if kicked."

23 Nov., *Deseret News* reports that Apostle Orson Pratt "declared that sometimes Joseph [Smith] used a seer stone when enquiring of the Lord, and receiving revelations."

24 Dec., Mormon writes John Taylor concerning new United Order at Sunset, Arizona: "We are building a dining room and are calculating to all eat at the same table like they do at Orderville. But the rumor has come here that the Twelve counsel otherwise." He had not learned about Taylor's letter on 26 Nov. advising against "the idea of all eating at one and the same table, and like matter of lesser moment."

1879

6 Jan., U.S. Supreme Court issues its *Reynolds vs. the United States* decision which upholds constitutionality of 1862 Morrill Anti-Bigamy Act, and further rules that not every religious practice is protected by First Amendment. As result of the Supreme Court's first decision about sexual conduct, George Reynolds is imprisoned from 1879 to 1881 for polygamy. As of 1990s this case continues to be Supreme Court's precedent for limiting some practices defined as religious.

16 Jan., editorial comment of LDS political newspaper *Salt Lake Herald:* "We question if seventy-six polygamous marriages have been solemnized in the Endowment house, this city, in a year, or even twice that period." In fact, during 1878, 113 men entered polygamous marriages in Endowment House.

2 Mar., John Taylor preaches: "I think a full, free talk is frequently of great use; we want nothing secret nor underhanded, and I for one want no association with things that cannot be talked about and will not bear investigation."

6 Apr., John Taylor overrides vote of rest of Twelve for new apostle and appoints Moses Thatcher.

6 May, Daniel H. Wells is released from prison for contempt of court in refusing to answer questions about ceremony and clothing of temple endowment. Church authorities organize parade to greet him, as described by *Deseret News:* "about ten thousand persons took part in the procession, and fully fifteen thousand and more were spectators."

18 May, in discussing whether all "colored" people are denied priesthood, John Taylor rules that Chinese are eligible to receive priesthood.

24 May, Apostles Brigham Young, Jr. and George Q. Cannon, as editors of *Deseret News,* write concerning astrology: "It is quite probable that some planets exert a baneful and others a beneficial power on the earth and its inhabitants."

4 June, John Taylor and apostles decline to allow Elijah Abel to receive temple endowment because he is Negroid, even though Abel received Melchizedek priesthood with Joseph Smith's authorization. This African-American regularly attends his Seventy's quorum meetings and serves proselytizing mission just before his death.

17 July, John Taylor, as president of Zion's Savings Bank and Trust, has vice-president of the bank destroy two notes for $50,000 (possibly of Taylor's personal indebtedness).

20 July, Apostle George Q. Cannon preaches, "If plural marriage be divine, as the Latter-day Saints say it is, no power on earth can suppress it, unless you crush and destroy the entire people."

21 July, Joseph Standing is first missionary killed by anti-Mormon mob. Accused murderers are acquitted by Georgia court.

6 Aug., under headline "Another Whipping Affair," *Deseret News* reports that A. Milton Musser (Presiding Bishopric's agent) and others beat U.S. Solicitor's son in Salt Lake City police court in retaliation for his previous assault on Musser. On 8 Aug. *Deseret News* editorial "Let the Issue Come," announces: "We shall protect our lives as best we may from the murderous assaults of imported assassins," and alludes to Musser incident as "one small act of retaliation which, if they do not desist, will be but the first drop of the drenching shower to come."

9 Aug., U.S. Secretary of State William M. Evarts instructs American diplomatic officers to encourage foreign governments to prevent Mormon emigration to United States. With continued defiance of LDS leaders against 1879 Supreme Court decision, U.S. State Department in 1884 instructs diplomatic officers "to refuse protection to Mormon missionaries" from foreign governments or individuals.

6 Sept., other apostles vote against presiding apostle John Taylor's proposal to organize First Presidency.

Deseret News editorial "What Shall the Mormon Church Do?" quotes recommendation of pro-Mormon *Omaha Herald:* "Let the Mormon people renounce all future polygamous marriages by an open and honest declaration, and there are not a baker's dozen of decent people in America who would ask that any such a brand [of abandonment] as is mentioned by the NEWS should be put upon the women and children." *News* replies: "If the authorities of the Church were to take any such stand as some friends suppose possible, their enunciation [pronouncement] would in all probability be repudiated by the people." Apostles restate this fear in 1890.

10 Sept., John Taylor and apostles vote to officially encourage Mormon polygamists to go into hiding ("the Underground") rather than be arrested.

7 Oct., U.S. government grants first patent to Mormon, John M. Browning for rifle. Two years after that invention is marketed as Winchester Single Shot Rifle of 1885, Browning becomes full-time missionary. Among later inventions of this "father of modern firearms," are Winchester Repeating Rifle of 1886, Winchester Lever Action Shotgun Model of 1887, Winchester Pump-action Shotgun of 1890, Winchester .22-caliber Single Shot Rifle of 1900, Colt .45-caliber semiautomatic pistol (standard U.S. military sidearm since 1911), .30-caliber machine gun used in World War I. His Browning automatic rifle (BAR) is later used in World War II.

27 Dec., Apostle Wilford Woodruff tells stake conference in Snowflake, Arizona, "There will be no United States in the year 1890."

1880

4 Jan., Apostle Orson Pratt preaches at Salt Lake Stake conference that "as a general rule it was the children who were attacked by diphtheria, and on investigation it would be found that the parents of such children as had been taken [by death] were neglectful of the word of wisdom or some of the commandments of God."

8 Jan., LDS political newspaper *Salt Lake Herald* reports George Q. Cannon's interview with pro-Mormon Omaha *Herald,* in part: "Polygamous marriages have ceased entirely so far as I know." In fact, in Endowment House alone, 107 men married polygamously in 1879 and 136 in 1880, most performed by general authorities.

9 Jan., Apostle Orson Pratt writes his children that city of New Jerusalem will be constructed by April 1950.

10 Mar., opening session of territory's first medical school, Medical College of Utah in Morgan, Utah. Its first student and first M.D. graduate in 1882 is Emeline Grover Rich, plural wife of Apostle Charles C. Rich. She is mother of eight children.

4 Apr., John Taylor and Twelve vote to accept as "Word of the Lord" a revelation on plural marriage received by Apostle Wilford Woodruff on 26 Jan. 1880. Text available but never canonized or officially published. Presiding Patriarch John Smith (b. 1832) is only general authority to oppose adoption of this revelation.

6 Apr., John Taylor restores Old Testament practice of jubilee celebration, in honor of church's fiftieth birthday. He forgives half of unpaid tithing and debts owed to Perpetual Emigrating Fund and encourages charitable gifts to poor.

7 Apr., conference sustains first Utah-born general authority, William W. Taylor as member of First Council of Seventy.

10 Apr., presiding apostle John Taylor reconvenes Council of Fifty for first time in nearly twelve years.

18 Apr., Apostle Joseph F. Smith writes of his belief that Great Pyramid's measurements predict future events.

3 May, at apostles meeting, "The question of over running salaries was brought up. Several of the brethren had overdrawn their allowance." They vote to forgive overdrafts, to increase their annual allowance, and to give allowance to Presiding Patriarch.

6 July, *Deseret News* reports on "the first non-Mormon Fourth of July celebration ever attempted in Utah." Its editorial next day comments: "The 'Mormons' of Salt Lake City have not celebrated Independence Day in this fashion for several years.... When we can celebrate the day as freemen, as other citizens of our common country celebrate," Salt Lake City "will again come to the front with her popular displays of patriotism."

3 Aug., Mormon *Salt Lake Herald* reports that "not one-fourth of the registered voters" vote.

6 Oct., most of apostles oppose John Taylor's proposal to organize First Presidency during series of meetings but finally accepts his motion evening of 9 Oct.

10 Oct., conference sustains John Taylor as church president with George Q. Cannon and Joseph F. Smith as counselors. None of members of this First Presidency are set apart. Taylor is only church president born outside United States or its territories.

12 Oct., at Council of Fifty meeting, John Pack (age seventy-one) says "lots of our young folks would not vote because they wanted a change." Hosea Stout (age seventy) replies: "I would rather undertake to get 20 young men to the polls than one old fossil."

25 Oct., *Deseret News* editorial, "A Utah Genius," suggests that some of Utah's "public-spirited men who have means to spare for occasional luxuries" order sculpture work by 17-year-old Cyrus Dallin and pay him in advance so he can continue art studies in Boston.

10 Nov., John Taylor persuades Twelve to allow him $10,000 claim for sugar machinery, which claim Brigham Young had refused since 1853.

26 Nov., Rev. Thomas DeWitt Talmage, nationally known Protestant minister, preaches in Brooklyn, New York: "I tell you that Mormonism will never be destroyed until it is destroyed by the guns of the United States government. It would not be war. I hate *war*. It would be national police duty, executing the law against polygamy."

1881

8 Jan., John Taylor preaches that "President Brigham Young had adopted the system of asking one-tenth of the property of the new comers in lieu of the surplus spoken of in the [1838] revelation." Taylor says that from now on tithing should be only "one tenth of our interest annually," and says local bishops must bear responsibility for giving temple recommends to non-tithers. Clerk in Presiding Bishopric's office records that Taylor has meeting vote to continue previous requirement of "one tenth of the property on entering the church." Thus a new convert is required to pay 1/10 of his/her property, but a new arrival in Utah is not required to repeat lump-sum tithing.

16 Jan., Apostle Wilford Woodruff tells conference of Young Men's Mutual Improvement

Association in Ogden, Utah that "there were thousands of young men living among this people now that would live to see the Savior come to the earth." He adds that they will "be changed to immortality in the twinkle of an eye without tasting death."

19 Jan., First Presidency, Quorum of Twelve, Presiding Patriarch, and Presiding Bishop wash their feet in three-hour ordinance against specifically named local and national enemies of church and kingdom of God.

25 Feb., *Deseret News* reports that first counselor Joseph F. Smith and Apostle Wilford Woodruff set apart seven recent graduates of Dr. Romania B. Pratt's course in midwifery.

10 Mar., Eliza R. Snow says that her polygamous husband Joseph Smith told her "that they (10 tribes) were on an orb or planet by themselves."

2 Apr., in meeting of stake presidents with First Presidency and apostles: "Before parties can be recommended to the Temples or house of the Lord, they must be rebaptised & must be tithing payers."

11 June, Heber J. Grant writes that Lysander Gee (b. 1818) "told me that he had known Oliver Cowdery personally & that to his knowledge Cowdrey [sic] had committed adultry [sic] before he lost his faith."

2 July, *Deseret News* reports Apostle Erastus Snow's sermon of 3 Aug. 1880: "Our people are already settling in Idaho, Montana, Wyoming, Colorado, Arizona, Nevada, and are stretching into Old Mexico. . . . He [God] wishes us to occupy the land, because the time is coming when He proposes to give it to us, and give us the rule over it. I suppose you voted at the general election yesterday; it is a part of your duty, because by voting at the polls we establish our rule and government in the land."

25 July, stake president Heber J. Grant writes: "I wanted to waltz very badly but knowing it was contrary to the wishes of the Genl. Church authorities I refrained from doing so."

3 Aug., at St. Charles, Idaho, George Q. Cannon reports "having seen the Bear Lake Monster or something of that kind this evening while strolling along the lake."

25 Aug., organization of Utah Iron Manufacturing Company.

26 Sept., Heber J. Grant expresses his disappointment about his racehorse being disqualified from upcoming race in Salt Lake City: "I had counted considerable, however, on Hyrum's winning the race and the horse becoming enough of a public favorite that I could sell him for a nice round sum." Heber becomes apostle in 1882, and horse racing remains legal in Utah until 1913.

8 Oct., first counselor George Q. Cannon tells general conference: "We hear now of men having to get married to cover up certain things; of children born wonderfully soon after marriage in some of our settlements, and perhaps in this city no less than in our [rural] settlements."

1882

4 Jan., First Presidency and Apostles vote not to allow any "President or Apostle to draw funds from the Church without limit for their own use or any other purpose." This avoids financial abuses they attribute to Brigham Young and John W. Young, but putting fixed limit on financial allowances is a salary system.

7 Jan., Apostle Francis M. Lyman's diary begins recording month-long nervous breakdown of Heber J. Grant, his successor as Tooele Stake president. Physician diagnoses Grant's condition as "nervous convulsions" and warns that condition would lead to "softening of the brain" if Grant continues his stressful pace of activity. Grant becomes apostle ten months later and is first LDS leader with diagnosed history of emotional illness.

22 Mar., enactment of Edmunds Anti-Polygamy law which disfranchises polygamist men and defines polygamous living as "unlawful cohabitation" punishable by $300 fine, six months' imprisonment, or both. This law supplements Morrill Anti-Bigamy Act, which is ineffective due to difficulty of proving polygamous ceremony. Unlike Morrill Act and later Edmunds-Tucker Act, constitutionality of 1882 Edmunds Act is not appealed to U.S. Supreme Court.

25 Mar., Apostle Brigham Young, Jr. preaches, "This Church will go into Sonora [Mexico] before it goes to Jackson County [Missouri]." This is early reference to alleged prophecy by Joseph Smith that church headquarters will trace horse shoe in moving from Nauvoo to Utah to Mexico to Missouri.

31 Mar., John Taylor closes Church Historian's Office to public.

7 Apr., John Taylor refuses to accept unanimous recommendation of Twelve for two men to fill vacancies as apostles.

9 Apr., John Taylor formally announces to general conference that 1880 U.S. census report shows Utah territory has 120,283 Mormons, with 14,155 "Gentiles" and 6,988 "Apostates." Utah is only place in 1880 that U.S. government includes religion in census.

10 Apr., unsuccessful convention seeking statehood.

12 Apr., *Deseret News* editorial comment: "Our readers ought to be able to draw a clear distinction between the advertising and editorial columns of this paper. . . . If a liquor dealer advertises his wares, we do not endorse liquor drinking."

20 Apr., U.S. House of Representatives votes to refuse George Q. Cannon as Utah's delegate, due to his polygamy, according to Edmunds Act. Cannon is first Mormon to be formally denied public office to which he is legally elected. Within months federally-appointed judges remove all known polygamists from civil office in Utah.

26 June, in morning John Taylor finishes dictating revelation he begins previous night concerning Celestial Law of plural marriage. Text available but never canonized.

27 June, Council of Fifty (which includes First Presidency and Twelve) votes to accept as "the word and will of God" yesterday's revelation on polygamy, as well as another revelation John Taylor dictates this day about the Kingdom of God and its Council of Fifty. Texts of both revelations are available, but never canonized or officially published.

28 June, "President Taylor offered another [revelation]," available copy of which is dated "end of June or very early in July, 1882." This revelation, third sustained by the Fifty this month, concerns church leaders who comprise "the Kingdom" (Council of Fifty). Text available, but is never canonized or officially published.

17 July, first LDS-operated hospital is Deseret Hospital, founded by women Eliza R. Snow, Emmeline B. Wells, Zina D. H. Young, Jane S. Richards, Phebe Woodruff, Marinda N. Hyde, Bathsheba W. Smith, Isabella M. Horne, and Dr. Romania B. Pratt.

6 Oct., President Taylor again refuses to accept Twelve's nomination for two men as apostles, with result that another conference passes without filling vacancies.

8 Oct., Theodore B. Lewis is first Civil War soldier and former prisoner to be sustained as general authority, and he is also only Confederate Army veteran appointed. Despite being publicly sustained as new member of First Council of Seventy, Lewis's appointment is cancelled next day when First Presidency learns he is also a high priest.

9 Oct., Apostle Erastus Snow preaches that early Mormons "supposed that our Prophet was going to continue with us until the coming of the Savior."

11 Oct., First Presidency and apostles vote privately that John T. Caine be candidate for Utah's delegate to Congress. Three hours later Council of Fifty convenes, discusses who should be delegate, and also nominates Caine. This is clearest example of hierarchy directing meetings of the Fifty to arrive at pre-determined decisions.

12 Oct., Abram Hatch tells convention of church's People's Party: "If we join either [national] party let us be careful that we go with the party that is on top and that will be sure to stay there."

13 Oct., John Taylor announces revelation appointing two men he had wanted as apostles since the previous April: George Teasdale and Heber J. Grant. Of this appointment, Apostle John Henry Smith complains that newly appointed apostle George Teasdale "is distasteful to me in his sycophantic manner" and that Heber J. Grant does not have "a testimony of the truth."

This revelation requires plural marriage for all presiding officers. Accepted by First

Presidency and Twelve on 14 Oct. 1882. Church authorities publish this as pamphlet in Salt Lake City, and in editions of the *Doctrine and Covenants:* Swedish in 1888; German in 1893, 1903, and 1920; Danish in 1900. The 1882 revelation is never canonized by conference vote and is not added to English language editions of D&C.

14 Oct., Seymour B. Young is "ordained" president in First Council of Seventy. He is first general authority with post-graduate degree (from University Medical College of New York) and first M.D. to serve in hierarchy. No other general authority has M.D. degree until appointments of Russell M. Nelson in 1984, Malcolm S. Jeppson in 1989, J. Ballard Washburn in 1990, James O. Mason in 1994, and Cecil O. Samuelson, Jr. in 1994.

16 Oct., ordination of first Utah-born apostle, Heber J. Grant. Grant is also first general authority who has previously experienced nervous breakdown. As apostle his debts result in chronic insomnia and nervousness that he frequently fears are pushing him toward another breakdown. Grant's concern for his emotional health is underscored by mental problems he later observes in four fellow general authorities.

17 Oct., Annie Gallifant Connelly, despite her pregnancy, is first Mormon woman sentenced to penitentiary for refusing to answer questions from grand jury seeking to indict her polygamous husband. For similar refusal, better-known Belle Harris is in penitentiary with her infant child from 18 May-31 Aug. 1883.

22 Oct., David H. Peery resigns as stake president due to his refusal to accept Oct. 1882 revelation's requirement for polygamous marriage.

29 Oct., second counselor Joseph F. Smith's sermon denies there have ever been Danites in Utah but acknowledges that "a few horse thieves and murderers have perchance been summarily dealt with by officers of the law."

3 Dec., second counselor Joseph F. Smith's sermon says, "I think of two or three hundred thousand people wending their way across the great plain . . . back to Jackson County[, Missouri]." Mormon population in stakes of Utah, Idaho, and Arizona is 128,779 at this time.

1883

31 Mar., Apostle Brigham Young, Jr. tells stake priesthood meeting: "There are many girls in Utah who have never had an offer of marriage from a man in the Church. . . . Girls who marry outsiders are not worthy of the Sacrament."

13 Apr., John Taylor dictates revelation on organizing the Seventies, and First Presidency and Quorum of Twelve accept it on 14 Apr. Church authorities publish revelation as pamphlet in Salt Lake City in 1883 and by its 14 Apr. 1884 reprint in the following editions of the *Doctrine and Covenants:* Swedish in 1888; German in 1893, 1903, and 1920; Danish in 1900. The 1883 revelation is never canonized by conference vote or by inclusion in English language editions of *Doctrine and Covenants.* Taylor defines First Quorum of Seventy as presidents of subordinate local quorums rather than as independent quorum.

28 Apr., John Taylor's revelation concerning "gold and silver and copper and brass and iron" and "a way to raise a fund which should be at your disposal" [Bullion, Beck and Champion Mining Company], and command to organize School of the Prophets. The revelation also chastises "My servant Thomas" [Taylor, no relation to church president] concerning Utah Iron Manufacturing Company. John Taylor presents this to some apostles on 4 Oct. 1883 and to formal meeting of First Presidency and Twelve on 11 Oct. 1883. Text available but never canonized or officially published.

20 May, Salt Lake City police arrest seventeen boys for "breaking the Sabbath" by playing baseball on Sunday.

21 June, accidental explosion of stored gun powder destroys Council House and some minute books of Salt Lake Stake, as well as blowing out windows of Assembly Hall and Tabernacle on Temple Square.

24 June, Parowan 1st Ward membership record and stake history records: "Sister Ellen Banks Wife of W*m* Banks was ordained & Set Apart to administer to the Sick in the ca-

pacity of Midwifery & all other kinds of Sicknesses By Apostle Francis M. Lyman." Hers is first entry in list of "Special Ordinations." Ten other entries (1883-86) are for men to various priesthood offices.

2 Aug., John Taylor and several apostles state their preference for conferring only Aaronic priesthood part of endowment ceremony on newly endowed adults. No decision.

26 Aug., Apostle Heber J. Grant notes in his diary that yesterday a mob lynches "the nigger" who kills LDS bishop and policeman Andrew Burt. On 14 May 1885 jury finds police officer not guilty for his part in "assaulting the negro." However, Grant's political newspaper generally uses respectful terms when referring to African-Americans.

28 Sept., John Taylor re-establishes School of the Prophets in obedience to revelation exactly five months earlier. "A number" of First Presidency and apostles "confessed to breaking the Word of Wisdom" and vote to obey it. However, this vote does not apply to wine which members of School of Prophets drink by glassful at their meeting on 12 Oct.

2 Oct., Bishop Orson F. Whitney begins participating in regular spiritualistic seances about this date. In 1889 Twelve learns of this activity, reverses its decision to call Whitney as new apostle, yet allows Whitney to remain bishop. Among those who attend these seances are Arthur and Charles Stayner and Maud May Babcock. Bishop Whitney continues to participate until 1900.

4 Oct., President Taylor tells some apostles about arrangement with George Q. Cannon and John Beck in Bullion, Beck and Champion Mining Co. Also presents to them his revelation of 28 Apr. 1883 which refers to this financial arrangement.

6 Oct., King David Kalakaua speaks at LDS conference in Laie, Oahu, Hawaii. He is first reigning monarch to speak at Mormon meeting. King Kalakaua's premier (1882-87) is Walter Murray Gibson, former Mormon.

9 Oct., in several hours of meetings with stake presidents, First Presidency and apostles give instructions about "Masturbation . . . self-pollution of both sexes & excessive [sexual] indulgence in the married relation." This is first-known Mormon reference to female masturbation.

12 Oct., John Taylor washes feet of other members of School of Prophets, first time church president performs this ordinance in forty-seven years.

2 Dec., first counselor George Q. Cannon preaches: "It is not the true condition for the Church of Jesus Christ of Latter-day Saints to be in, to be petted by the world, to be fostered by the world, to be spoken well by the world, to be welcomed by the world, to have favor showered upon it by the world, because we ought not to be of the world."

1884

30 Jan., counselor in Salt Lake Stake presidency explains why women anoint and bless women: "There are often cases when it would be indelicate for an Elder to anoint, especially certain parts of the body, and the sisters are called to do this and [their] blessing follows."

22 Mar., James E. Talmage begins using hashish at Johns Hopkins University as "my physiological experiment" of its effects. By 6 Apr. he is using twenty grains, "and the effect was felt in a not very agreeable way." Nevertheless, he intends to "vary the trial in the future." This is last reference in Talmage's diary to using narcotics. Four months later he becomes member of stake high council.

1 Apr., John Taylor allows first commercial program in Salt Lake Tabernacle, operatic performance by Adelina Patti. In later decades Tabernacle hosts Ernestine Schumann-Heink, Lili Pons, Ignace Padewerski, John Philip Sousa, Fritz Kreisler, Vladimir Horowitz, Artur Rubinstein, Marian Anderson, Yehudi Menuhin, Van Cliburn, and others.

5 Apr., John Taylor declines to release church's annual financial report because "it is none of the business of outsiders to know about our financial matters." This is due to federal government's anti-polygamy campaign against church.

6 Apr., conference sustains first continental European general authority, Seventy's president Christian D. Fjeldsted of Denmark.

At conference priesthood meeting, John Taylor says all presiding officers must marry polygamously or resign their positions. He names three monogamous stake presidents.

22 Apr., William W. Cluff resigns as stake president rather than marry polygamously. He retains membership in Council of Fifty.

16 May, Apostle Francis M. Lyman tells priesthood meeting that he "considered that the blood of Cain was more predominant in these Mexicans than that of Israel."

17 May, John Taylor dedicates temple at Logan, Utah, and receives revelation concerning temple (exact date unknown). Text available but not canonized or officially published.

18 May, Apostles instruct stake leaders about President John Taylor's ruling that as payment for their services, bishops will receive 8 percent of tithing they collect, and stake presidents 2 percent of stake tithing.

5 Aug., *Deseret News* editorializes that "as a synonym for quietude and lackadaisical apathy, yesterday's election ought to be placed in the museum and handed down to succeeding ages."

10 Aug., anti-Mormon mob attacks Sunday meeting of Mormons in Tennessee and murders four men, including missionaries William S. Berry and John H. Gibbs.

5 Oct., John Morgan is first Civil War veteran to actually become LDS general authority. He served with Union forces.

9 Oct., last time Council of Fifty formally convenes; its last surviving member dies in 1945.

9 Nov., LDS political newspaper *Salt Lake Herald* reports that it was "a refreshing and pleasing sight to many" when Presiding Bishopric counselor John Q. Cannon assaulted reporter for anti-Mormon *Salt Lake Tribune,* then took out "a riding whip, and struck his victim a couple of times over the head. Then he knocked him down." Mormon judge fines Cannon $15 for battering the reporter, described as "a diminutive individual, with a Hebraic cast of countenance."

14 Nov., *Deseret News* editorial: "The 'Mormon' people lean to Democratic principles because those principles are in consonance with the Constitution and preservation of local and individual rights."

9 Dec., LDS political newspaper *Salt Lake Herald* reports another Mormon's assault and battery on reporter of *Salt Lake Tribune* as "A BLISSFUL LOT. Another of the 'Tribune' Crew Rewarded. A TROUNCING WELL MERITED."

14 Dec., George Q. Cannon preaches, "Now I have heard that there are men among us who are professing to cure witchcraft and other evils of that kind. . . . Do not seek for those who have peepstones, for soothsayers, and for those who profess to be able to counteract the influence of witchcraft." Faithful Mormons continue using counter-charms.

25 Dec., John Taylor's revelation repeating previous requirement for priesthood leaders to live plural marriage, with promise: "I will be your shield and protector, and your strong tower and no man shall be able to hurt you, for I will be your defence." Text available but never canonized or officially published.

30 Dec., Turkish Mission established in response to request of Armenian Christian living in Constantinople (now Istanbul). Nearly all converts are Armenian Christians.

31 Dec., First Presidency authorizes Apostle Brigham Young, Jr. and Charles W. Penrose (also in Council of Fifty) to use $25,000 to bribe incoming administration of U.S. president Grover Cleveland. Quorum of Twelve agrees to these arrangements on 4 Jan. 1885, but effort proves to be attempt by impostors to defraud church.

1885

3 Feb., enactment of "Idaho Test Oath" which prohibits all Mormons from voting.

4 Feb., nine apostles and two other members of Fifty anoint and ordain John Taylor as King, Priest, and Ruler over Israel on Earth. *Salt Lake Tribune* reports this event.

14 May, Apostles Brigham Young, Jr. and Moses Thatcher meet with Don Carlos Pacheco of the Porfirio Diaz cabinet to obtain permission for polygamous Mormons to settle just across border from United States. Although polygamy is illegal under Mexican law, Pacheco says Mexican authorities will not bother a polygamist unless his wife files complaint. Mormon colonies center in Colonia Juarez (named after Mexico's national hero) and include colonies named after President Diaz and cabinet member Pacheco.

3 July, Apostle Heber J. Grant records that First Presidency authorizes half-masting of American flags on Salt Lake city hall, court house, and at church-owned ZCMI on July 4. This causes near-riot by non-Mormons.

16 July, death by self-inflicted morphine overdose of Lavinia Triplett Careless, famous Utah singer and wife of Professor George Careless, director of Mormon Tabernacle Choir.

15 Sept., LDS political newspaper *Salt Lake Herald* describes "FILTHY OUTRAGE" committed against local leaders of anti-polygamy crusade. Late Sunday night unidentified persons threw "a dozen fruit jars filled with a horrible mess of filth taken from privy vaults" through glass windows of residences of Prosecuting Attorney William H. Dickson, his assistant Charles S. Varian, and United States Commissioner William McKay. *Deseret News* describes weapons as "glass jars filled with human excrement and possibly some other nastiness" and blames incident on anti-Mormons.

18 Sept., John Sharp, local bishop, agrees in court to obey anti-polygamy laws. He is first Utah polygamist to be convicted and only fined. Regarded as traitor, he is released as bishop on 1 Oct. However, Sharp remains chair of LDS People's Party central committees for Salt Lake County and Utah territory until 1887. Therefore, it is unlikely he would have been released from Council of Fifty had it convened after Oct. 1884.

7 Nov., Quorum of Twelve excommunicates Apostle Albert Carrington "for the crimes of lewd and lascivious conduct and adultery" with several women dating back to 1871. This is first time since 1842 that general authority is excommunicated for sexual misconduct, and its publication on 10 Nov. stuns the community.

11 Nov., Salt Lake City police fine LDS Deputy Sheriff Andrew J. Burt $25 for assault and battery on U.S. Deputy marshal Henry F. Collin. Three days later district court sentences him to five days' imprisonment for crime.

21 Nov., deputy U.S. marshal is first anti-Mormon to be arrested for complaint of "lewd and lascivious conduct" signed by Brigham Y. Hampton, Salt Lake City policeman. Hampton pays professional madam to operate brothel so that Mormon policemen can obtain evidence against those prominent in anti-polygamy crusade. Hampton conducts this brothel espionage with knowledge of Salt Lake Stake presidency and (he believes) by authority of First Presidency. *Deseret News* editorial of 14 Dec 1885 argues in support of brothel espionage: "It was the only way by which their guilt could be proven beyond question. It was disgusting business, no doubt. But which was the most disgusting, the detestation of their bestiality, or the acts which were witnessed?" Federal judge Charles S. Zane infuriates Mormons by quashing all those indictments with argument: "A private act is not defined by the common law as a crime. When both parties go together out of the sight of everyone under the Connecticut law it is not an offense." Hampton is then tried and sentenced to one year in penitentiary for conspiracy and for operating brothel. First Presidency later compensates him financially.

28 Nov., bodyguard Joseph W. McMurrin is shot twice in stomach and nearly killed by U.S. deputy marshal Collins seeking to arrest polygamists. Collins claims four men with clubs attack him in alley, and one tries to shoot him. Seven witnesses support his account, and McMurrin's club is found at scene. Court finds marshal innocent of attempted murder. McMurrin is active Mormon with history of convictions for assault and battery going back seven years. He is first Mormon bodyguard to be shot and becomes general authority in 1897.

1886

7 Jan., U.S. Supreme Court sustains Utah judges' definition of "cohabitation" as not requiring proof of sexual intercourse but rather of marital relationship. Justices Miller and Field dissent on grounds that Congress intended law to prohibit "unlawful habitual sexual intercourse" with more than one woman. Justice Field is on secret payroll of First Presidency.

25 Jan., federal court begins hearings concerning effort of two men to bribe U.S. deputy marshal E. A. Franks to give advance warning of efforts to arrest Mormon polygamists. Both men are sentenced to three years' imprisonment for attempted bribery, but are released in May 1888. Unknown to court, these men had worked with Brigham Y. Hampton in spying on anti-Mormons in the brothel. By 1888 Deputy Franks is on First Presidency's payroll as bribed informer.

8 Feb., U.S. marshal publishes $500 reward for arrest of first counselor George Q. Cannon. A week later Cannon is arrested in Nevada after unsuccessfully trying to bribe arresting officer and then jumping from moving train to escape. He denies attempted bribery and claims that he accidentally fell from train.

2 Mar., Quorum of Twelve accepts John Taylor's statement that it is "the mind of the Lord" for George Q. Cannon to forfeit $25,000 bond and for that to be paid from church mining revenues. This may be date of second revelation on Bullion, Beck, and Champion Mining Company, which George Q. Cannon describes to apostles on 27 Apr. 1899. Text is unavailable. Cannon skips trial on 17 Mar. and forfeits bond.

11 Mar., LDS political newspaper *Salt Lake Herald* reports another Mormon's assault on reporter for anti-Mormon *Salt Lake Tribune* with this headline: "THRASHING A REPORTER. Don Carlos Young Remodels the Phiz [sic] of C.T. Harte to Suit His Fancy." Mormon judge fines Young $17.50 for this assault and battery.

18 Mar., *Deseret News* editorial in support of George Q. Cannon's forfeiting bond to become fugitive from justice: "No one believes he would have had a fair trial." Editorial adds: "And our slandering enemies need not talk about Church funds being used for this purpose, either. It is none of their business anyhow."

27 Mar., polygamist husband confides to his diary: "How delicate is the position of a man in plural marriage who loves his wives and who in turn is loved by them. Every move he makes, in his relation or intercourse with them, is an arrow that pierces deep into the heart of one or other of them. . . . A thousand thoughts and plans may come into his mind, but there is only one true solution. He must please God. In doing this, it may be hoped that bye and bye, he may also please them."

28 Mar., Abraham H. Cannon, Seventy's president and son of First Presidency counselor, writes: "Bro. Olsen brought word in this evening that President Taylor had received a revelation from the Lord in which it stated that God was satisfied with the sacrifice made by the people in this [anti-polygamy] crusade and that He would now turn their wrath aside. This word, he said, came from Bishop Allen of the 21st Ward, and if, true, we as a people can rejoice at it." This indicates curious situation in which general authorities learn about Taylor's revelations from rank-and-file Mormons.

4 May, Apostle John Henry Smith writes that Presiding Bishopric counselor John Q. Cannon is "getting quite reckless" with church's tithing funds. Cannon is excommunicated four months later, but for adultery not embezzlement. His father, first counselor George Q. Cannon, tells apostles on 3 Aug. 1887 that "he admitted trying to cover up John Q. Cannon's stealings from the Church and that he & his son Abraham had made good John Q's defalcations to the amount of nearly Ten thousand dollars."

10 May, court sentences Frank J. Cannon to three months' imprisonment and $150 fine for instructing his 16-year-old brother Hugh J. Cannon to physically attack Prosecuting Attorney Dickson following arrest of their father, George Q. Cannon. Frank becomes U.S. Senator from Utah (1896-98). Fined $35 dollars in 1886, Hugh grows up to become

general board member (1896-1931), mission president (1901-1904), and stake president (1904-25).

11 May, "There have been two windows left out of the west end of the Salt Lake Temple through an error of the architect which will most likely necessitate the taking down of the wall for 20 feet."

15 July, Apostle Lorenzo Snow says that in future "brothers and sisters would marry each other in this church. All our horror at such a union was due entirely to prejudice, and the offspring of such unions would be as healthy and pure as any other. These were the decided views of Pres. [Brigham] Young, when alive, for Bro. S[now]. talked to him freely on this matter."

31 July, Philo Dibble tells meeting of high priests that "Joseph Smith had been to Prest John Taylor and conversed with him in his body about this crusade against us, and that he felt grieved at the course his son Joseph [III] was taking." Joseph Smith III preaches in Utah (17 June-21 Dec. 1885). This vision occurs during one of the nights Taylor stays at John Carlisle house: 14 July, 28 Sept.-1 Oct. 1885, or 10-19 Jan. 1886.

31 Aug., U.S. officials at Staten Island, New York, send immigrants back to England because they are Mormons. They board next ship, conceal their religion and destination, pass through American customs, and arrive in Salt Lake City on 27 Oct. For next several years, European immigrants conceal their LDS religion and Utah destination.

8 Sept., Isaac C. Haight dies in Arizona, fully reinstated in church sixteen years after his excommunication for ordering Mountain Meadows Massacre.

14 Sept., by appointment of First Presidency, Charles O. Card begins mission to North-West Territories (now Alberta Province), Canada, to find refuge for polygamous Mormons to escape arrest. This is origin of Mormon settlements centering in Cardston, Alberta, Canada, where settlers arrive on 1 June 1887.

27 Sept., John Taylor, in hiding at home of monogamist John W. Woolley, gives revelation about plural marriage: "I have not revoked this law nor will I for it is everlasting." Never formally presented to Twelve, but Apostle John W. Taylor discusses 1886 revelation in meetings of 2 Oct. 1889, 30 Sept. 1890, 1 Apr. 1892, and 22 Feb. 1911. On 15 July 1933 First Presidency accepts custody of 1886 revelation's original text which is in John Taylor's handwriting. The 1886 revelation has never been officially published (and its existence has been officially denied). Photocopies of 1886 revelation have been unofficially published, and Apostle Melvin J. Ballard writes that it is definitely the handwriting of LDS president John Taylor.

11 Oct., John W. Woolley marries his first plural wife just before President Taylor leaves his home. She is mother of future Seventy's president B. H. Roberts.

4 Nov., U.S. deputies raid Church Historian's Office.

16 Dec., U.S. deputy kills unarmed polygamist Edward M. Dalton during arrest attempt, only death on either side during decades of bitter anti-polygamy crusades. Dalton is member of Utah Territorial Central Committee of People's Party and has twice before escaped after being arrested. Court finds deputy not guilty of manslaughter.

19 Dec., John Taylor enters his first plural marriage since passage of 1862 federal law against Mormon polygamy. Performed by bride's father, and witnessed by his counselor George Q. Cannon and bodyguard Charles H. Wilcken.

27 Dec., Sarah M. Granger Kimball, counselor in Relief Society general presidency, says that "her brother Lafayette Granger and the late Bishop [George] Miller in conversation once with the prophet Joseph Smith were told by him that when Mary the mother of Jesus was on her way to the hill country she was met by [God] the Father and the Angel Gabriel and the latter performed the marriage between the Father and Mary."

1887

15 Jan., Arizona's governor signs repeal of "Test Oath," which disfranchised all Mormons.

19 Jan., John Taylor has $40,000 removed from First Presidency's safe to bribe influential members of Congress to oppose Edmunds-Tucker bills and support Utah statehood.

31 Jan., published reward of $300 for John Taylor.

4 Feb., about thirty riveters at Z.C.M.I. Shoe Shop go on strike over change in work assignments. While not first collective bargaining strike in Utah, it is first against church business. *Deseret News* says: "The movement savors too much of the dictatorial style of some of the labor organizations, and should not exist among our people."

7 Feb., U.S. Supreme Court reverses decisions of Utah courts that define as separately punishable crimes each instance of unlawful cohabitation with one wife. This declares "segregation policy" illegal, and therefore allows only one conviction for "continuous crime" of unlawful cohabitation with each plural wife.

26 Feb., Utah Supreme Court rules that legal wife is required to testify against her polygamous husband. As result several legal wives are imprisoned for refusing to testify against their polygamous husbands. U.S. Supreme Court waits to reverse this decision until 22 Dec. 1890, after LDS church has publicly abandoned polygamy.

3 Mar., Edmunds-Tucker Act disincorporates LDS church, provides for confiscation of its assets and properties, dissolves Perpetual Emigrating Fund Company, disfranchises all Utah's women, and dissolves Utah's militia ("Nauvoo Legion").

14 Mar., wife of Seventy's president Abraham H. Cannon goes to "Madam Mizpah," fortune-teller. He opposes this.

8 Apr., general conference sustains Quorum of Twelve Apostles as "prophets, seers & revelators," title "omitted by mistake [for] several conferences past."

24 May, U.S. deputy marshals "ransacked" nearly-finished Manti temple for polygamists.

15 June, John Taylor says other general authorities should not "be too particular or scrupulous" about promoting proposed Utah state constitution which outlaws polygamy.

30 June, unsuccessful convention seeking statehood, even though proposed state constitution has provision outlawing polygamy.

21 July, Apostle Franklin D. Richards: "God, the Father came down in his tabernacle of flesh and bone and had association with Mary, and made her pregnant with Jesus."

25 July, John Taylor's dies on "the Underground." Because of his wounds in Carthage Jail and his death in exile, counselors George Q. Cannon and Joseph F. Smith write: "To-day he occupies the place of a double martyr. *PRESIDENT JOHN TAYLOR has been killed by the cruelty of officials who have, in this Territory, misrepresented the government of the United States* . . . who, with insensate hate, have offered rewards for his arrest and hounded him to the grave."

 After conversation with senior apostle Wilford Woodruff, Apostle Heber J. Grant writes: "Prest. Woodruff said he would be willing to have [junior apostle] Joseph F. Smith made the Prest of the Church provided the quorum of the Apostles should wish it but as near as I could judge he had no idea that such a thing would be done."

3 Aug., Wilford Woodruff and Quorum of Twelve vote to accept George Q. Cannon and Joseph F. Smith into their original ranking following their release as counselors to John Taylor. First time this is necessary at death of church president.

12 Aug., Twelve authorizes First Presidency to complete its arrangements for pro-Mormon coverage from "the leading papers in New York, & other cities" by paying various newspaper editors $75,000 cash in advance, plus added $70,000 after Utah gains statehood.

8 Sept., Wilford Woodruff and Twelve formally establish fixed salaries for themselves. Previous to this apostles negotiated individually with Trustee-in-Trust for allotments according to their needs. At this meeting Joseph F. Smith prefers old system and comments that "it was repugnant to the people to have the 12 draw a salary." Not long after this meeting, apostles set the "annuity" of Presiding Patriarch at rate exactly one-third of annual allotment for each apostle. Church members also give patriarch $2 for each patriarchal blessing.

9 Sept., apostles decide to dispose of "underground vehicles" and to dismiss all bodyguards employed by John Taylor to protect general authorities from arrest.

5 Oct., beginning of series of meetings in which nearly half of Twelve accuse George Q. Cannon of abusing his authority as counselor.

6 Oct., Charles R. Savage, faithful Mormon, writes of general conference: "The instructions were of the usual character—and lacked definiteness of purpose."

1888

20 Mar., Wilford Woodruff officially proposes organizing First Presidency. After three days of meetings in which apostles oppose proposal and criticize George Q. Cannon in particular, Woodruff formally withdraws motion on 23 Mar.

23 Mar., in Quorum of Twelve meeting, Apostle Erastus Snow says that apostles Wilford Woodruff and George Q. Cannon are "men worshippers [and] sycophants." Woodruff replies, "While Brother Cannon is charged with Nepotism, you go to St. George and the offices in that region are nearly all filled by his [Erastus Snow's] boys."

6 Apr., letter of Wilford Woodruff and apostles establish annual salaries for stake presidents and end President John Taylor's provisions for local bishops to receive fixed percentage (8 percent) and stake presidents (2 percent) of collected tithing as salary. Until 1896 stake committee apportions this 10 percent of tithing between stake tithing clerk and bishops. On same day apostles approve salary for First Council of Seventy, to which one of its members responds: "I would prefer to receive no salary."

5 May, Utah territorial Democratic convention excludes all Mormon delegates.

17 May, at dedication of Manti temple, Wilford Woodruff says, "We are not going to stop the practice of plural marriage until the Coming of the Son of Man." During dedication some hear heavenly choir, while others see bright halos of light around apostles Lorenzo Snow, John W. Taylor, Heber J. Grant, John Henry Smith, and Seventy's president Jacob Gates, and dimmer halo around Apostle Francis M. Lyman's head. Some say that John W. Taylor's "voice was exactly like Joseph the Prophet" and that Lyman's voice is that of Brigham Young.

While in temple, Woodruff "Consecrated upon the Altar the [brown] seers Stone that Joseph Smith found by Revelation some 30 feet under the Earth."

24 May, *Deseret News* reports that a polygamist's legal wife "attempted to kill herself by cutting her throat with a razor" when she is subpoenaed to testify against him.

4 July, first joint celebration of Independence Day by prominent Mormons and anti-Mormons. Presided over by non-LDS governor Caleb W. West, ceremonies have LDS participation by Arthur Stayner, Orson F. Whitney, and James E. Talmage, with anti-polygamy leaders: Judge Charles S. Zane, Judge Goodwin, and Commissioner Norrell.

Sept., committee of apostles to Twelve: "The great majority of the Saints respect the advice and counsel of this Quorum in political as in other matters, and obey it in most instances: at times even against their own judgment. In the opinion of your committee it is of the utmost importance that this influence for good be maintained and even increased, for upon it largely depends the political well-being of the Saints of God."

3 Oct., *Deseret News* editorializes that Idaho Mormons who are being voluntarily excommunicated in order to vote are acting without "advice from the constituted authorities as some people foolishly suppose."

8 Oct., Nevada Supreme Court declares unconstitutional Nevada's law which denies vote to anyone "who is a member of or belongs to the 'Church of Jesus Christ of Latter-day Saints,' commonly called the 'Mormon Church'. . ."

12 Oct., Wilford Woodruff and apostles vote to allow Idaho Mormons to be excommunicated in order to vote. They regret this decision within three weeks.

23 Oct., Wilford Woodruff and apostles approve sending $20,000 to bribe Democratic members of Congress to help Utah Mormon cause.

3 Nov., Apostles Francis M. Lyman and John W. Taylor begin meetings with members of

Canada's parliament and cabinet and with Premier John A. Macdonald himself. Canadian government informs them that it doesn't care if Mormon settlers are polygamists, but a man can have only one wife in Canada. Apostles agree to this condition.

26 Nov., Apostle Lorenzo Snow speaks concerning "N. K. Whitney and wife and H. C. Kimball, who, he said, the Prophet Joseph told his sister Eliza [R. Snow], were descendants of the Savior."

12 Dec., release of Rudger Clawson after serving three years and one month in prison, longest any nineteenth-century Mormon is imprisoned for polygamy or unlawful cohabitation. On this same day, Idaho Legislature expels all Mormon legislators.

20 Dec., senior apostle Wilford Woodruff tells meeting of Twelve, "The Lord never will give a revelation to abandon plural marriage."

1889

17 Feb., Abinadi Pratt, son of deceased apostle Parley P. Pratt, prophesies to Salt Lake City congregation that within three weeks God will destroy San Francisco, Chicago, Boston, New York City, and Washington, D.C. One Mormon writes: "None felt concerned about his prophecy."

27 Feb., LDS political newspaper *Salt Lake Herald*'s article, "FAILED MARRIAGES," regarding "the report of Labor Commissioner Wright, presented last week, on the statistics of marriage and divorce in United States from 1867 to 1886 inclusive," with following: In 1870 Utah had second highest rate of divorce out of all states and territories. In 1870 Utah's rate was one divorce per 185 marriages. National average was 1:664. States with lowest divorce rates are South Carolina at 1:133,359, Delaware at 1:23,672, New Mexico at 1:16,077, North Carolina at 1:4,938, and Louisiana at 1:4,579. In 1880 Utah had tenth highest rate of divorce out of all states and territories. In 1880 Utah's rate was one divorce per 219 marriages, which was more than twice national average of 1:479. In twentieth century, divorce rate for LDS temple marriages *starts out* three times higher than this "divorce mill" rate for early Utah civil marriages.

27 Feb., Wilford Woodruff tells his secretary "he would about as soon attend a funeral as one of our council meetings." Several apostles have opposed each of his efforts to organize First Presidency.

2 Mar., Grover Cleveland pardons Charles W. Penrose from arrest for unlawful cohabitation. Penrose is Democrat and special emissary of First Presidency to Washington, D.C. John W. Young, fellow Democrat and Twelve's counselor arranges this.

7 Mar., *New York Times* gives its first theatre review for actress Maude Adams, born of "Gentile" father and Mormon mother. One of era's most popular Broadway actresses, Maude Adams creates and repeats title role of *Peter Pan* (1905, 1912, 1914, 1915).

7 Apr., conference sustains Wilford Woodruff as church president with George Q. Cannon and Joseph F. Smith as counselors. They are not set apart or ordained.

22 Apr., Ida Wright testifies her husband John rose from dead after priesthood administration by elders. He spoke to family four hours and then lay back and died.

8 June, Apostle Lorenzo Snow says that "his sister, the late Eliza R. Snow Smith, was a firm believer in the principle of reincarnation and that she claimed to have received it from Joseph the Prophet, her husband. He said he saw nothing unreasonable in it, and could believe it, if it came to him from the Lord or His oracle."

23 June, at stake conference, "The name of Wm. Marsden was submitted to the Priesthood for Stake Patriarch and 51 voted in his favor and 65 against him." Apostles Francis M. Lyman and John Henry Smith withdraw the unpopular nomination, and "James Dalley was submitted to the people for Patriarch and unanimously received by vote."

3 July, Apostle John W. Taylor prophesies about "the battle when the Negroes rise up against their masters which soon would be the case. The red men would stalk through the land as the battle axe of the Lord and after they had done this work they would be changed to a skin of whiteness in a day."

15 Aug., church purchases ranch in Skull Valley, Tooele County, Utah, for Hawaiian Mormon immigrants. They name community *Iosepa* (Joseph). Colony continues until 1917.

27 Aug., *Deseret News* describes as "Organized Tyranny" a labor strike at construction site of Zion's Savings Bank. "We feel ashamed to know that many of these men who have combined [in] this improper manner are 'Mormons,'" *News* observes. "On general principles we are opposed to 'strikes,' because they usually result in much more harm than good to all parties affected and are often started on incorrect principles."

7 Oct., at priesthood leadership meeting, President Wilford Woodruff prophesies, "In the name of Israel's God there shall be no peace in the nation. There is no need to look for prosperity and peace because it will not come."

9 Oct., Salt Lake stake high council excommunicates elder for having local bishop perform unauthorized plural marriage for him four years earlier. Stake authorities had not authorized marriage because the young woman has "negro blood in her veins." First counselor says her father is "about 1/6 Nigger from his appearance."

14 Nov., First Presidency and apostles consider giving public testimony about endowment's "prayer of vengeance" to refute false testimony about alleged "oath of vengeance." However, they decide not to reveal wording.

24 Nov., after First Presidency discussion about promising there will be no more plural marriages in Utah territory, Wilford Woodruff dictates revelation which instructs First Presidency to make no promises to end plural marriage. Accepted as revelation by First Presidency and Quorum of Twelve but never officially published or canonized.

30 Nov., federal judge in Utah refuses to grant citizenship to Mormon immigrants.

6 Dec., first counselor George Q. Cannon says "when he had his endowments in Nauvoo that he took an oath against the murderers of the Prophet Joseph as well as other prophets, and if he had ever met any of those who had taken a hand in that massacre he would undoubtedly have attempted to avenge the blood of the martyrs." Cannon then relates how second counselor Joseph F. Smith was once about to stab to death man he suspects of approving of the martyrdom after-the-fact.

12 Dec., First Presidency official statement concerning "Blood Atonement."

19 Dec., First Presidency and Twelve accept Wilford Woodruff's revelation of 24 Nov. 1889.

23 Dec., churchwide fast sponsored by First Presidency to ask God's deliverance from federal crusade against polygamy.

1890

20 Jan., Utah Supreme Court rules that polygamous children cannot inherit from their father, even though Utah law since 1852 guaranteed: "Illegitimate children and their mothers inherit in like manner from the father, whether acknowledged by him or not."

3 Feb., U.S. Supreme Court rules in *Davis vs. Beason* that it is constitutional for Idaho to disfranchise all Mormons.

10 Feb., anti-Mormon Liberal Party wins municipal election and takes control of Salt Lake City's government on 18 Feb.

13 Mar., plural wife writes of her husband: "We are more like lovers than husband and wife for we are so far removed from each other [—] there is always the embarrassment of lovers and yet we have been married more than 37 years."

5 Apr., George Reynolds is sustained as first convicted felon to become general authority.

10-11 Apr., both U.S. Senate and House propose bills to disfranchise all Mormons. With delaying tactics by Mormon allies in Congress, these two bills make slow progress into summer, but Supreme Court decision in Feb. 1890 assures eventual enactment.

11 Apr., Canada's Parliament increases penalty for polygamy from two years' to five years.

17 May, LDS political newspaper *Salt Lake Herald* condemns "the scheme of the conspirators to consummate the political debauchery of making Utah a Republican state."

19 May, U.S. Supreme Court upholds the Edmunds-Tucker Act and confiscation of LDS properties; committee of U.S. Senate recommends disfranchisement bill.

30 May, Apostle Lorenzo Snow tells meeting of apostles, "I have thought of the necessity of establishing a mission in Jerusalem and to have a colony established there who should water their lands from the river Jordan."

Heber J. Grant also tells apostles that "he had never had an inspired dream in his life and that although he had always desired to see his father in dream or vision that he had never been allowed to enjoy this great privilege." Decades later as church president, Grant often speaks publicly of 1883 manifestation where he saw and heard a heavenly council meeting of his deceased father with Jesus Christ and Joseph Smith. However, he first describes this experience to other apostles as simply "the whisperings of the spirit to him" that he was called as apostle because of such a meeting.

3 June, First Presidency sets apart John Hafen, Lorus Pratt, and John B. Fairbanks as "art missionaries" to study in France in order to paint murals on interior of Salt Lake temple. They reach Paris on 24 July. They are joined by Edwin Evans and Herman H. Haag. Enrolled in Julian Academy, the art missionaries return to Salt Lake City in 1892 and complete the temple murals. They are not first formally trained Mormon artists, because C. C. A. Christensen (b. 1831) and Danquart A. Weggeland (b. 1827) both trained at Royal Academy of Art in Copenhagen.

Contemporary with these art missionaries are three Julian Academy sculptors of Mormon background. Brigham Young's grandson Mahonri M. Young wins silver medal at Panama-Pacific International Exposition in 1915, creates statue of Brigham Young in U.S. Capitol, and sculpts Salt Lake Temple Square monuments to Joseph Smith, Hyrum Smith, and Miracle of the Seagulls. Cyrus E. Dallin wins gold medal at Panama Exposition and sculpts Angel Moroni statue atop Salt Lake temple and also creates pioneer monument. Least identified with his Mormon parentage of the three, Gutzon Borglum designs and sculpts Mt. Rushmore National Memorial.

Mary Teasdel joins Julian Academy in 1899. She is first female Mormon artist whose work eventually becomes part of collection at National Gallery in Washington, D.C.

6 June, federal grand jury in Idaho indicts 153 ex-Mormons for voting in recent election.

30 June, First Presidency decides to prohibit plural marriages even in Mexico unless new plural wife agrees to remain there.

1 July, U.S. Senate bill to deny all Mormons any right to homestead public lands.

7 Aug., First Presidency and apostles agree to loan $5,000 to Church of Christ, Temple Lot, as mortgage on part of their property in Independence, Missouri. Elder Hall of this "Hedrickite" group originally offers seven lots for $20,000 mortgage.

1 Sept., federal officials indicate that they intend to confiscate LDS temples. Presidents Woodruff and Cannon soon leave for San Francisco to avoid subpoena to testify.

8 Sept., Apostle John Henry Smith preaches that "married people who indulged their passions for any other purpose than to beget children, really committed adultery."

12 Sept., in San Francisco, pro-Mormon Republicans (including "permanent" national chair of Republican Party's national convention) tell Presidents Woodruff and Cannon that LDS church's only hope is to make "some announcement concerning polygamy and the laying of it aside." Republican leaders then promise to promote Utah's statehood in expectation that church will work to have majority of Mormons vote Republican.

24 Sept., Wilford Woodruff's "Manifesto" advises all church members to obey anti-polygamy laws. It is not added to *Doctrine and Covenants* until 1914.

1 Oct., apostle asks "how the Son of God was begotten," and Lorenzo Snow tells apostles, "that he was begotten just the same as you and I were or as our sons are."

6 Oct., general conference votes to sustain Wilford Woodruff's Manifesto. Minority of congregation raises its hands to sustain it, and some general authorities also decline to vote.

Woodruff signs recommends for seven men to have plural marriages performed in Mexico by Alexander F. Macdonald, local president.

18 Oct., Apostle Abraham H. Cannon writes concerning bribery of federal officials: "Thus with a little money a channel of communication is kept open between the government offices and the suffering and persecuted Church members."

25 Oct., First Presidency publicly establishes Religion Classes, America's first experiment in separate weekday religious training for public school students. This elementary level program merges with LDS Primary program in May 1929. Seminaries for LDS high school students are spin-off which lasts longer than the innovative Religion Classes.

5 Nov., U.S. district attorney files suit to confiscate Temple Square and Salt Lake temple, which federal government seizes for five months.

2 Dec., Apostle Lorenzo Snow tells Quorum of Twelve that "he expect[s] to see the day when a man's blood will be shed for the crime of adultery."

1891

1 Jan., Wilford Woodruff writes: "This is New Years day And the year that has been looked upon by many as one of the most important years of the world."

19 Jan., U.S. Supreme Court reverses Utah courts and rules that children born within year after Edmunds Act are legitimate and can inherit from their fathers.

Benjamin F. Johnson (original member of Joseph Smith's Council of Fifty) gives patriarchal blessing to Mary L. Picton Teasdale: "Thou art of Ephraim and are entitled to all the priesthood, exaltations, increase and dominion pertaining to the daughters of Abraham in the New & Everlasting Covenant."

3 Feb., rank-and-file Mormon writes: "Some say and have written that great things are to happen this year. . . . Some even declare that Christ will come and the Millennial Reign be inaugerated. I think some of these things will not happen as stated, but God holds all these things in his hands and at the close of 91 we shall tell more than now."

19 Feb., delegation of Mormon young women and plural wives attends first meeting of National Council of Women, which accepts Relief Society as charter member.

24 Mar., Utah's chief justice Zane writes: "Polygamy has demoralized the people of Utah. I presume there are more sexual crimes here in proportion to the population than anywhere else."

16 Apr., First Presidency learns that U.S. solicitor general and Utah's district attorney have formally agreed "to let loose of our *Temple.*"

14 May, concerning young man who has been endowed and "sealed to his wife without having been ordained to any Priesthood," First Presidency decides to have him ordained as elder, but not to require him to be re-endowed or re-sealed.

10 June, dissolution of church-controlled People's Party which instructs its members to join one of the two national parties, Democratic or Republican.

10 Sept., U.S. president Benjamin Harrison grants pardon to fellow Republican and second counselor Joseph F. Smith for outstanding warrants for his arrest on polygamy.

1 Oct., First Presidency and Quorum of Twelve Apostles consider this question: "Shall the Priesthood nominate and the people accept, or shall the people nominate?" The decision of the meeting: "It is quite proper for the brethren before making appointments to consult with the local authorities and be sure to select men for position whom the people will be glad to sustain" to offices of bishop, stake president, and patriarch.

19-20 Oct., First Presidency and Lorenzo Snow, Twelve's president, and Apostle Anthon H. Lund testify in court that Manifesto prohibits new plural marriages anywhere in world and prohibits cohabitation with wives married before the Manifesto and that the church will excommunicate violators. Although testimony is published in various editions of *Deseret News,* all polygamous general authorities violate this by continuing to cohabit with their plural wives after 1891.

13 Nov., Wilford Woodruff authorizes non-Mormon George L. Miller to tour interior of

Logan temple, "the first Outsider that has ever seen the inside of this Temple." Miller is editor of the *Omaha Herald* and one of several influential allies of First Presidency.

5 Dec., stake president relates "incident of the Prophet Joseph telling Dimic[k] B Huntington . . . that Noah built the Ark in the Land where South Carolina is now."

1892

2 Jan., U.S. district court in Idaho dismisses indictments against Mormons for voting.

21 Jan., First Presidency letter of introduction for assistant church historian Andrew Jenson's effort to interview participants in Mountain Meadows Massacre: "We are anxious to learn all that we can upon this subject, not necessarily for publication, but that the Church may have the details in its possession for the vindication of innocent persons, and that the world may know, when the time comes, the true facts connected with it."

9 Feb., First Presidency sends its secretary "to go quietly to Logan and work to make the Republican ticket successful in the approaching city election." Democratic leaders complain of church influence, Presidency issues carefully worded statement on 25 Mar. which does not deny that Presidency sent its secretary to influence Mormons to vote Republican but denies authorization "to use our names."

6 Mar., stake president "condemn[s] the practice that existed among the Saints to some extent of taking means to restrict the number of their children to two or three."

15 Mar., depositions in Salt Lake City about Nauvoo polygamy and other matters for so-called "Temple Lot Case." Depositions begin on 18 Apr. at Independence, Missouri.

15 June, Anthon H. Lund, apostle and temple president, gives instructions that no proxy endowments should be done for persons who died "under 15 or 16" years of age.

18 July, first verified letter from First Presidency authorizing Apostle George Teasdale, president of Mexican colonies, to perform polygamous marriage there.

2 Aug., first polygamous marriage performed in LDS Canadian settlement by its president Charles O. Card, who performs this marriage by instructions of First Presidency. To end of 1905 only fifteen more post-Manifesto plural marriages occur in Canada (by Card and his successor as polygamy officiator), compared with hundreds performed in Mexico and United States.

11 Sept., St. George, Utah stake leaders proudly report that only 20 percent of its young men smoke tobacco. Apostle Francis M. Lyman preaches to St. George stake conference: "in Prest Brigham Young's time an effort was made to make a certain man as Bp of the 3rd Wd Salt Lake City. Bro Young named him but the people did not want the man for a Bp. and did not have him. Prest Young wanted Bro. Jesse N. Smith to be Prest of Parowan Stake But the people did not want him and would not have him and he was not their President. Prest. Woodruff felt desirous to having a certain man ordained a Patriarch in Parowan Stake but the people did not want him and would not and did not have him. This indicates the liberty of the Latter Day Saints."

At priesthood meeting, Lyman "referred to the disappointment of Pres Woodruff on discovering that there was not influence enough with the Presidency and Twelve to put one Republican in the Legislature. I felt the time would come when we would wish we were not so fanatically Democratic."

13 Oct., at prayer circle of First Presidency and apostles, "Pres. Woodruff was mouth in prayer and he made a very strong appeal to the Lord in behalf of Mrs. [Benjamin] Harrison, who is afflicted with some lung disease. The President of the United States had asked that we pray for his wife."

27 Oct., first counselor George Q. Cannon tells apostles that Utah's newly appointed U.S. marshal has instructions from the Republican administration in Washington, D.C., to "do as he was directed by the heads of the Mormon Church. . . . He had expressed his willingness to do so, and had sent such word to the Presidency."

2 Dec., Wilford Woodruff instructs Lorenzo Snow, next-ranked apostle, to organize new First Presidency immediately after church president's death.

15 Dec., First Presidency informs apostles that "our success in the Church suits was in a great measure due to the fact that we have a partner of Justice Field of the Supreme Court of the United States in our employ, who is to receive a percentage of the money if the suits go in our favor, and the property is returned to us." Aside from Justice Field (1863-97), U.S. Supreme Court justice Samuel Blatchford (1882-93) has also been bribed by the church's intermediaries, even though he is inconsistent ally.

1893

4 Jan., soon to leave office, U.S. president Benjamin Harrison issues amnesty for all who lived in polygamous marriage before 1 Nov. 1890.

12 Feb., Edmund Ellsworth says "he heard Joseph Smith say in Nauvoo that the outsiders would not let the Saints stay there. Said they would remove to the Rocky Mountains . . . and they will finally cast us out from the United States. . . . We shall pass down through Mexico and back up through Texas to build up the center Stake of Zion [at Independence, Missouri]. He marked the profile of the journey in the sand. Bro. Averett [Everett] in speaking of the matter afterward said the route of the journey was shaped like a horseshoe. He haveing seen Joseph mark it out before." The published diary of Jesse N. Smith deletes this reference to Horse Shoe Prophecy.

6 Apr., Wilford Woodruff dedicates Salt Lake temple, forty years after its cornerstone-laying. It is largest LDS temple ever built, with 253,105 square feet of floor space.

Joseph F. Smith "sobbed & wept like a child" as he gives talk that day. Some see halos of light around first counselor George Q. Cannon and around Apostles Lorenzo Snow, John W. Taylor, and Heber J. Grant. Not everyone present sees these manifestations, and future apostle James E. Talmage notes: "There were no strange or bewildering manifestations of 'supernatural' agencies during the service: but the power of God was there, and the entire assembly felt it."

13 Apr., at session of temple dedication, "Pres Woodruff said there would never be an hour when these apostles will be divided from now till the coming of the Son of Man."

Apostle Francis M. Lyman and Mary Ann Burnham Freeze separately record seeing bright light pass over head of second counselor Joseph F. Smith as he speaks. Apostle Lyman also hears heavenly choir.

24 May, suicide of businessman William H. Jennings, first prominent Utah Mormon male to commit suicide. This is during national economic depression which bankrupts many Utahns. George A. Mears, another "financially ruined" Salt Lake City businessman and "a friend of the 'Mormons'" also commits suicide on 8 July.

7 June, Francis M. Lyman and his plural wife Susan Callister Lyman are first persons to receive second anointing in Salt Lake temple's "Holy of Holies."

24 Aug., Presidency and apostles vote to "save Bro. [Leonard G.] Hardy from the penitentiary, and take steps to get the means to meet the amount of his defalcations" from Salt Lake County. Son of former Presiding Bishopric counselor and a local bishop himself, general authorities want to protect embezzler Hardy's appointment by courts as receiver for LDS church's confiscated properties.

8 Sept., first national recognition of Mormon Tabernacle Choir which receives second prize of $1,000 at Chicago World's Fair.

11 Sept., World Parliament of Religions refuses to admit LDS delegates.

17 Oct., Democratic *Salt Lake Herald* (of which Apostle Heber J. Grant is vice-president) reports meeting of "Afro-American Club, recently organized here for the purpose of promoting the social and political interests of the colored people of this city." The club's leader comments that "the [anti-Mormon] Liberal party had always treated the Afro-Americans WITH DISDAIN."

20 Oct., First Presidency and Quorum of Twelve agree to bribe Utah's non-LDS attorney general to prevent indictment of general authorities for unlawful cohabitation.

25 Oct., U.S. president Grover Cleveland signs congressional resolution for return of

church's confiscated monies and personal property. Utah Supreme Court returns these properties to church authorities on 10 Jan. 1894.

31 Oct., first counselor George Q. Cannon "holds that [apostolic] seniority rests with Apostles who have not been of the Twelve as well as the Twelve." Second counselor Joseph F. Smith disagrees. By Cannon's definition, John W. Young outranks both Cannon and Smith. This would make Young the church's presiding apostle after President Snow's death in 1901, even though Young has never been member of the Twelve. Lorenzo Snow rules in 1900 that apostolic ranking is by entry into Twelve and not by ordination date as apostle. This ends Young's hopes.

29 Nov., Presidents Wilford Woodruff and George Q. Cannon meet with three apostles and James E. Talmage: "That there will also be daughters of Perdition there is no doubt in the minds of the brethren."

Presidency and apostles decide that frequent rebaptisms "will not be allowed, and that this sacred ordinance is becoming too common." After 1893 Salt Lake temple performs no rebaptisms for renewal of covenants. Presidency and apostles again discuss on 19 May 1898 whether to stop rebaptisms completely but reach no decision. St. George temple stops rebaptisms after 1900. Manti and Logan temples perform only thirteen in 1910 and continue sporadically until Presidency ends practice in 1922.

7 Dec., First Presidency and Twelve decide that garments worn under clothing should be white. This is first departure of Utah temple garment from contemporary "Union suit" which comes in various colors and upon which Utah "street garment" is based.

18 Dec., anti-Mormon Liberal Party passes resolution to dissolve and have its members join national political parties.

1894

5 Jan., George Q. Cannon comments "on the ambiguity existing in our printed works concerning the nature or character of the Holy Ghost[, and] expressed his opinion that the Holy Ghost was in reality a person. . . . However, the Presidency deemed it wise to say as little as possible on this as on other disputed subjects."

16 Jan., Presidency and apostles vote for church to pay $25,000 to Brigham Young Trust Company to act as intermediary in making "a loan" to repay that amount of monies which Bishop Leonard G. Hardy has embezzled from Salt Lake County.

24 Jan., at Cardston, Canada, Apostle John W. Taylor prophesies that "there would yet be a beautiful Temple here built."

5 Apr., at meeting of First Presidency and apostles, Wilford Woodruff announces revelation which ends practice of adopting men to LDS leaders. He instructs Mormons to seal each generation of ancestors to preceding generation. This results in program of genealogical research. His published sermon is only available text of the revelation. Old form of adoption ordinance continues sporadically in LDS temples with high of fifteen adoption ceremonies in 1910. The revelation is never canonized.

9 Apr., of "O My Father," President Wilford Woodruff tells general conference: "That hymn is a revelation, though it was given unto us by a woman—Sister Eliza R. Snow."

Death of Thomas C. Sharp, principal conspirator in murder of Joseph and Hyrum Smith. He has had successful career as mayor, judge, school principal, and newspaper editor.

15 Apr., *Juvenile Instructor* publishes hymn "Our Mother in Heaven," which is phrased as prayer to the goddess.

26 Apr., Presidency and apostles decide that John D. Lee, Jr. ("a son of the Mountain Meadows murderer") can go on proselytizing mission but must "assume his mother's maiden name."

18 May, in Salt Lake temple, "Jane Elizabeth Manning (a Negro Woman)" is sealed "as a Servitor for eternity to the Prophet Joseph Smith." Joseph F. Smith acts as proxy.

16 July, first post-Manifesto plural marriage performed in United States by (verified) written authorization of First Presidency. Marriage occurs in Logan temple.

19 July, news of failure of Cannon, Grant, and Company, holding company for church finance: "Every dollar we invested is swept away and we are left penniless." General authorities reckon their losses at $100,000 for George Q. Cannon, $75,000 for Heber J. Grant, and $25,000 each for Joseph F. Smith, Francis M. Lyman, John Henry Smith, and Abraham H. Cannon. Unable to shoulder such losses, the men keep company technically afloat until 20 July 1898, when they ask Trustee-in-Trust to save it.

16 Aug., Jewish boy gives his bar mitzvah talk in LDS stake conference "in confirmation of his faith in the Jewish religion."

26 Aug., "first time a woman has spoken in the [Salt Lake] Tabernacle on the Sabbath at the regular service—the people do not know what to make of it—it must bode good for women." The speaker is non-Mormon.

27 Aug., U.S. president Cleveland issues amnesty for previous violations of anti-polygamy laws and restores civil rights to disenfranchised polygamists.

7 Oct., Wilford Woodruff instructs conference priesthood meeting that all presiding officers should live Word of Wisdom, and he threatens to drop Presiding Patriarch John Smith from office if he continues using tobacco and alcohol.

24 Oct., Wilford Woodruff and his two counselors each give approval for Apostle Abraham H. Cannon to marry plural wife. In all, ten general authorities marry post-Manifesto plural wives by permission of church president or his counselors during next ten years.

1895

24 Jan., First Presidency and apostles decide to ordain all bishops as well as set them apart.

3 Feb., Emmeline B. Wells cancels her appointment to speak at Bethel Church in Atlanta, because it is "a colored people's church [and] the Southern people consider it unwise."

1 Mar., some non-Mormons are given tour of dedicated Salt Lake temple interior.

4 Mar., Utah territorial convention (with Apostle John Henry Smith as president) drafts proposed state constitution which includes woman's suffrage. Convention completes proposed constitution on 8 May, and Congress accepts it.

7 Apr., Wilford Woodruff tells conference: "Cease troubling yourselves about who God is; who Adam is, who Christ is, who Jehovah is. For heaven's sake, let these things alone."

2 May, First Presidency and apostles consider request for excommunication by G. C. Williams who "feels to condemn the Church for allowing Isaac Haight, who is said to have been one of the leaders in the Mountain Meadows Massacre to remain [actually, be rebaptized] in the Church after his participation in that terrible crime. In that massacre Williams is said to have lost fourteen relatives."

9 June, first stake outside United States (in Cardston, Alberta, Canada).

13 July, at Utah Democratic convention, "women are delegates in about equal number with men."

22 Aug., First Presidency and apostles decide to deny temple endowment to "Black Jane" Manning (James) because of her "negro blood."

25 Aug., at Salina, Utah, Apostle Francis M. Lyman "denounce[s] the ideas of the world in regard to small families and the use of preventatives to avoid large families."

5 Nov., Utah's first elected state governor is LDS Heber M. Wells who serves (1896-1905). Other Mormon governors of Utah are John C. Cutler (1905-1909), William Spry (1909-17), Charles R. Mabey (1921-25), Henry H. Blood (1933-41), Herbert B. Maw (1941-49), George D. Clyde (1957-65), Calvin L. Rampton (1965-77), Scott M. Matheson (1977-85), Norman Bangerter (1985-93), and Mike Leavitt (1993-).

1896

4 Jan., Democratic president Grover Cleveland proclaims Utah as state. Only two members of U.S. House of Representatives voted against enabling act in 1893.

30 Jan., First Presidency and Quorum of Twelve decide that women should not have their own prayer circles or participate with their husbands in prayer circle meetings.

23 Feb., Apostle Heber J. Grant ordains his dying seven-year-old son to office of elder, "and I blessed him with all the earnestness of my soul, and dedicated him to the Lord to live or die which ever was His will, and covenanted with the Lord if he would spare my only son, and give him life and strength that I would dedicate his time to the service of the Lord and do all in my power to teach him the ways of truth and righteousness." Heber Jr. dies four days later.

27 Feb., court dismisses long-standing indictment against John M. Higbee. Other participants say privately that he was most blood-thirsty man at Mountain Meadows Massacre.

12 Mar., First Presidency gives James E. Talmage "an instruction" to smoke tobacco to relieve his persistent insomnia. Apostle Heber J. Grant is present and gives "his acquiescence" but dates meeting as 11 Mar. Talmage is then president of University of Utah and becomes apostle in 1911. His diary is silent about using this tobacco remedy for insomnia which he occasionally mentions from 1896 on.

28 Mar., U.S. president Cleveland signs act to return confiscated real estate of LDS church.

2 Apr., First Presidency and Presiding Bishop resolve decade of controversy over who controls church finances in practical terms. Trustee-in-Trust resumes governance.

3 Apr., Apostle Franklin D. Richards tells Relief Society conference that women have right "to rebuke disease in the name of the Lord Jesus Christ & by virtue of the Holy Anointing which I have received."

6 Apr., all general authorities except Apostle Moses Thatcher sign political manifesto which requires church officers to obtain permission before seeking political office. Thatcher refuses to sign, and his name is not presented for sustaining vote of conference.

7 Apr., First Presidency announces at conference priesthood meeting the end of salaries for local church officers. On 2 Apr. the temple council decides "to not pay Salaries to any one but the Twelve." However, in 1898, hierarchy returns to fixed allotments for general authorities.

7 May, First Presidency and apostles decide that baptisms for dead and all other baptism ordinances eliminate words "for remission of sins" or "renewal of covenants," and use only the words in *Doctrine and Covenants.*

3 June, Idaho Mormons are still being rebaptized and restored to priesthood blessings eight years after First Presidency allowed them to be excommunicated in order to vote.

18 Aug., Wilford Woodruff receives revelation concerning recent death of Apostle Abraham H. Cannon, which Woodruff relates next general conference. Paraphrased text published in *Deseret News* report of his Oct. 1896 sermon. This revelation's full text is never published or canonized.

23 Aug., Sugar House Ward congregation votes against man proposed as bishop of new ward to be divided from the old. Salt Lake stake president Angus M. Cannon furiously shouts, "Sit down! and shut your mouths, you have no right to speak!" When Cannon engages in shouting match with dissenting congregation, a ward member and policeman threatens to arrest stake president for disturbing the peace. Cannon more calmly repeats his attempt but is voted down "again several times." Secretary of the First Council of Seventy in attendance writes: "I have been taught that the appointing power comes from the priesthood and the sustaining power from the people and that they have the right of sustaining or not sustaining appointees."

26 Aug., Apostle Moses Thatcher begins treatment with Keeley Institute for his addiction to opium and morphine. First Presidency and apostles tolerated Thatcher as a "Morphine fiend" and "opium eater," but on 26 July his family and friends considered involuntary commitment for treatment. He is most prominent drug addict in Mormon history. Twelve drop Thatcher from quorum membership on 19 Nov. because of four-

year conflict over his insubordination in political matters, but Thatcher's drug addiction aggravates that conflict.

20 Sept., Seventy's president J. Golden Kimball preaches: "There are 500 girls who are public prostitutes in Salt Lake City. Some of these are daughters of Latter-day Saints."

7 Oct., at priesthood leadership conference, Wilford Woodruff asks "all those that had money to spare to loan it to the Trustee in Trust to assist the Church."

3 Nov., Utah's first state election uses "Australian ballot" which guarantees confidentiality of person's vote.

Martha Hughes Cannon is elected as Democratic member of Utah State Legislature and defeats her own husband who is Republican candidate. She is first woman in United States to serve as state senator. When newspaper reporter asks how she, as "modern woman," can be plural wife, Cannon replies: "If her husband has four wives, she has three weeks of freedom every single month."

5 Nov., Apostle Lorenzo Snow's youngest plural wife bears his last child in Canada. At age 82 he is oldest general authority to father a child.

6 Dec., First Presidency changes monthly day of fasting from first Thursday of month to first Sunday. This signals secularization in Mormon society (particularly in Salt Lake City) where Mormons can no longer expect employers to close businesses for regular "fast and testimony" meeting or to allow LDS employees to attend without loss of pay.

1897

15 Jan., Apostle Brigham Young, Jr. temporarily resigns as vice-president of Brigham Young Trust Co. because first counselor George Q. Cannon allows its property to become "a first class" brothel on Commercial Street (now Regent Street), Salt Lake City. Apostle Heber J. Grant is invited to its opening reception and is stunned to discover himself inside "a regular whore-house." This situation begins in 1891, and for fifty years church-controlled real estate companies lease houses of prostitution.

25 Jan., Lorin C. Woolley tells congregation "he knew that the Prophets Joseph, Brigham and Heber lived for he had seen them as they appeared to Prest. John Taylor in Bro. John [W.] Woolley's house." This is earliest known statement by Lorin Woolley about miraculous events involving President John Taylor at Woolley house in 1886.

28 Jan., First Presidency and apostles discuss "the subject of building a Temple in Arizona."

4 Mar., Apostle Heber J. Grant writes: "Prest. William McKinley is to take the oath of office today as the Prest. of the United States. . . . I have for some unknown reason been very much depressed in my feelings today. I hope that all is well at home, and that I may not have some bad news at a future date to confirm me in some reason for my feelings." President McKinley is assassinated in 1901.

19 Mar., First Presidency letter: "Where couples living together as man and wife have observed the requirement of their people, tribe or nation, their union should be respected by our brethren," even if it is not a legally performed marriage. Since the 1950s, church policy has reversed that Presidency's ruling in two ways: first by sanctioning and performing temple sealings for long-term relationships of Latin American couples who are living without legal marriage (due to restrictions on divorce) even though these relationships are defined as adulterous by the laws of their nation; second by refusing to "respect" the legitimacy of black African polygamous marriages which are legal by the laws of their tribe and nation.

22 June, first plural marriages performed in Mexico by (verified) written authority of First Presidency since 1892 and the first performed by stake president Anthony W. Ivins. He is the best-known officiator for post-Manifesto polygamous marriages in Mexico.

22 July, organization of State Historical Society of Utah on fiftieth anniversary of arrival of first Mormon pioneer wagons in Salt Lake Valley. Its first president is apostle and church historian Franklin D. Richards. In 1923 general authority Levi Edgar Young becomes first professionally trained historian to serve as president.

4 Aug., Lorenzo Snow tells apostles: "Patriarch Joseph Smith, the father of the Prophet, had stated in his [1836] patriarchal blessing, that he should have power, when not able to visit the sick, to send his handkerchief to them, and that the afflicted by touching it should be made whole." Snow adds "on one occasion" a Mormon in Kaysville, Utah, "was healed immediately upon receipt of the handkerchief."

19 Aug., apparent date Wilford Woodruff marries Lydia Mountford as plural wife aboard U.S. vessel. He authorizes Apostle Anthon H. Lund to perform polygamous marriage for Apostle George Teasdale under same circumstances in October. On Apostle Lund's return from that trip, President Woodruff confides the Mountford marriage to him while authorizing the apostle to perform another shipboard polygamous marriage. Federal law applies to U.S.-flagged vessels, and therefore these shipboard marriages violate letter and spirit of 1890 Manifesto. As Salt Lake temple president and Presidency first counselor, Lund ratifies Woodruff's out-of-temple 1897 sealing by re-performing it as proxy sealing on 23 Nov. 1920. Woodruff's son stands as his proxy, and Woodruff's former sister-in-law stands as proxy for the 1897 polygamous wife.

5 Oct., after President Woodruff's son and Counselor Cannon's grandnephew are announced as new apostles, Apostle Brigham Young, Jr. writes: "I felt almost rebellious for a few minutes." Seventy's president J. Golden Kimball observes that "the brethren feel if they are not represented while living, they may not be after they are dead." Both Young and Kimball are sons of general authorities.

12 Oct., at meeting of Quorum of Twelve, "Pres. [Lorenzo] Snow led out on Adam being our father and God. How beautiful the thought [—] it bro[ugh]t God nearer to us."

24 Nov., after meeting of First Council of Seventy, J. Golden Kimball writes: "Some men will *kiss* a mans *ass* to get to suck a sugar *tit.*"

9 Dec., First Presidency and apostles discuss "subject of building a Temple at [Colonia] Juarez, Mexico." When temple is built, two shifts have occurred in the church in Mexico: its population is primarily ethnic Mexican rather than transplanted Anglos, and its geographic center has shifted deep into Mexico. Therefore, site changes.

16 Dec., First Presidency and apostles agree that "Adam is our father and God and no use to discuss it with [RLDS] Josephites or any one else."

1898

21 Jan., Apostle Anthon H. Lund sets apart First Council of Seventy member Joseph W. McMurrin but mistakenly does not "ordain" him to office of President of Seventy. First Presidency and Quorum of Twelve agree on 13 Apr. 1899 that this is an error but decide not to re-perform it "correctly." This oversight in 1898 eventually leads to decision to stop using word "ordain" for any Seventy's president, local or general.

22 Jan., George Q. Cannon teaches: "There are different degrees of glory. Some attain to a more exalted glory. They must help those who are lower to rise up to their plane. Then there is another degree below them, and they must labor to lift those who are lower than they ... progressing from one degree of glory to another, without end, because there is no end to eternity."

14 Apr., First Presidency and apostles consider "alleged belief of some Elders in the doctrine of reincarnation. . . . the conclusion reached was that every Elder's right to believe what seemed right to him should be respected and that no action should be taken against him while he refrained from teaching his views to others and respected and upheld the authority vested in the Presiding Priesthood." This refers to local bishop Orson F. Whitney who becomes member of Twelve in 1906.

21 Apr., arrival in British Mission of Amanda Inez Knight and Lucy Jane Brimhall, first unmarried women to serve as full-time missionaries. Previously lady missionaries were married women who were set apart as companions to their husbands, usually mission presidents. On 16 Mar. George Q. Cannon had said that through missionary service of

unmarried young women, "some kind of solution would be found to the problem so often discussed, 'What shall we do with our girls?'"

28 Apr., First Presidency announces that Mormons should support their government's call for volunteer soldiers in war. This ends policy of "selective pacifism," in which LDS president (not national leaders) decided whether Mormons participated in war.

5 May, President Woodruff decides against withholding temple recommends for non-compliance with Word of Wisdom.

9 May, first LDS baptisms in Jerusalem, Palestine. Converts are Armenian Christians.

24 Aug., George H. Hudson is first Mormon to die in combat during U.S. War. As private in Battery B of Utah Light Artillery, he is killed by Filipinos during Philippine Insurrection at conclusion of Spanish-American War of 1898. Filipinos want true independence, not to be new colony of the United States

2 Sept., death of Wilford Woodruff, only Utah church president to die outside Utah (in San Francisco, California); buried in Salt Lake City.

13 Sept., Quorum of Twelve Apostles sustains Lorenzo Snow as church president with two counselors.

7 Oct., at general conference Apostle John W. Taylor reports that in one rural area, 80 percent of LDS marriages involve pre-marital sex.

10 Oct., Lorenzo Snow is "set apart" (*not* ordained) as church president, and his counselors are also set apart. This is first time that members of Quorum of the Twelve Apostles are set apart for service in First Presidency. Rudger Clawson is ordained apostle, first convicted felon to become member of Quorum of Twelve.

20 Oct., first plural marriage performed in Salt Lake City by Apostle Matthias F. Cowley by authorization of Counselor George Q. Cannon who allows him to perform plural marriages in U.S. for high-ranking church officers not required to travel to Mexico.

29 Dec., President Lorenzo Snow issues statement that polygamy has ceased in Utah.

1899

5 Jan., First Presidency and Twelve discuss resuming public reporting of church finances. Senior apostle Franklin D. Richards observes that such public accounting should be "presented before the General Conference, thereby correcting false reports and bringing the people to share in the responsibility of the Church's business." Until 1915 these annual reports to Apr. conference do not contain specific dollar amounts.

11 Jan., Apostle Franklin D. Richards tells Quorum of Twelve that there will be "temples in New Zealand & other places."

13 Jan., First Presidency decides that James E. Talmage's *Articles of Faith* will "be published by the Church" due to the review of its contents by the First Presidency and committee which included three apostles. Its discussion of Celestial, Terrestrial, and Telestial Kingdoms (420-21) states that "advancement from grade to grade within any kingdom, and from kingdom to kingdom, will be provided for." Eleventh edition deletes latter phrase in 1919, and twelfth edition in 1924 says: "as to possible progress from one kingdom to another the scriptures make no positive affirmation."

25 Jan., at temple meeting with First Presidency, Apostle Francis M. Lyman praises local patriarch who administers to sick, "without receiving very much pay for his services."

2 Feb., First Presidency and apostles decide that "inasmuch as dancing in moderation was a healthful and grace-giving exercise, and that the style of round-dancing [waltzing] had so changed of late years as to do away with its most objectionable features, and since to prohibit it altogether would be to drive many of our young people to Gentile dancing halls, outside the control of the Priesthood, that it was not wise to attempt to abolish it entirely, but to restrict it as much as possible, and instruct Bishops and Stake Presidents accordingly."

17 Feb., First Presidency and twelve apostles decide against traditional practice of conferring priesthood on dying sons who are infants or small children.

2 Apr., Lorenzo Snow presides at Salt Lake temple monthly fast meeting: "Sister Maria Y Dougall bore her testimony and wound up by speaking in tongues which struck me as the finest expression of that beautiful gift to which I had ever listened and when Aunt Zina [H. Young] interpreted it[,] it was sweet in deed."

4 Apr., Franklin D. Richards tells quarterly meeting of apostles that God "revealed to the Prophet true Masonry as we have it in our temples."

17 May, Lorenzo Snow's revelation at St. George on necessity for church members to pay full 10 percent tithing, which conference votes to accept on 30 May. Tithing is now on annual income only. However, individual general authorities and local leaders continue to differ about whether tithing should be on gross or net income. Text of revelation is part of his published sermon but never canonized by addition to D&C.

29 May, at missionary meeting in Scotland, Charles Woolfenden sees two angels and proclaims that one is "guardian angel" of Elder John Young. Mission counselor James L. McMurrin says that second is guardian angel of missionary D.C. Eccles. Founding prophet Joseph Smith had referred matter-of-factly to "my guardian angel" in sermon of 13 June 1844.

2 July, at solemn assembly in Salt Lake temple, President Lorenzo Snow says if Mormons observe law of tithing, "in 10 or 15 or 20 years a people would be chosen" to build the temple in Jackson County, Missouri. First counselor George Q. Cannon tells men that some of them descend literally from marriages of Jesus Christ.

13 July, Salt Lake temple fast meeting for general authorities: "At 1 P.M. the tables were spread with bread and wine. . . . We then partook of the bread & wine until we were satisfied."

23 July, last plural marriage President Lorenzo Snow permits stake president Anthony W. Ivins to perform in Mexico.

30 Sept., reports that Apostle Franklin D. Richards "is losing his mind, [which] has been known for some time to his own family." First reported instance of mental instability in current general authority. He dies two months after this report.

14 Oct., Salt Lake County attorney declines to issue warrant for President Lorenzo Snow due to insufficient evidence of unlawful cohabitation.

19 Oct., First Presidency and apostles agree to no longer charge fee for giving blessings to departing full-time missionaries.

27 Dec., when Salt Lake temple worker visits President Snow at home, he "brot me a glass of wine also and some cake."

1900

8 Jan., President Lorenzo Snow issues statement against polygamous cohabitation and new plural marriages and says violators of this rule must bear responsibility themselves.

23 Jan., U.S. House of Representatives excludes B. H. Roberts because he is polygamist.

27 Jan., John Steele writes, "I have worked in the Science [of astrology] for the last 40 years." He casts astrological charts before performing priesthood ordinances for the sick. He also inscribes paper charms against thieves and witches, and wax dolls to injure his enemies. Steele has been a Seventy since 1845, member of Mormon Battalion, marshal and mayor of Parowan, stake presidency counselor, participant in Mountain Meadows Massacre, probate judge, and justice of the peace.

14 Feb., U.S. president William McKinley promises Apostle John Henry Smith to defeat proposed U.S. amendment against polygamy and polygamous cohabitation in exchange for Utah's vote in the Nov. election.

21 Feb., George P. Frisby and George D. Cole of Church of Christ, Temple Lot ("Hedrickite"), meet with First Presidency, Quorum of Twelve Apostles, and Presiding Bishopric. Elders Frisby and Cole propose that their church, LDS church, and RLDS church each send four delegates to jointly agree on construction of temple at Independence, Missouri. After discussion of pros and cons, President Lorenzo Snow decides against

proposal because "he naturally feared some trick being played against us." However, he is willing to pay travel expenses of Hedrickite elders.

25 Feb., returned missionary from Southern States Mission speaks in tongues at Salt Lake Tabernacle and gives "the interpretation which was very beautiful." This may not be first time, but is probably the last, that someone speaks in "unknown tongue" (glossolalia) in Tabernacle.

5 Apr., First Presidency and Twelve decide that apostolic ranking is according to entry into quorum, not according to ordination date as apostle. This puts Joseph F. Smith ahead of Brigham Young, Jr.—first time in thirty-three years.

7 Apr., at general priesthood meeting Lorenzo Snow presents "a book containing 10,000 names of non-Tithe payers," including that of Apostle John W. Taylor.

9 Apr., Lorenzo Snow tells priesthood leadership meeting that second anointing "is not only intended for the aged, but also for younger men. We are afraid, however, that Presidents of Stakes do not exercise sufficient care in regard to this matter. The privilege should only be given to those who have been tried and tested, being full of integrity and not likely to fall away."

14 June, First Presidency and apostles agree to give $3,600 to Brigham Y. Hampton for his prior "detective work" in which he paid prostitutes to allow him and nearly thirty LDS "Home Missionaries" and policemen to spy on anti-Mormons engaging in sex acts in Salt Lake City brothel in 1885. Although first counselor denies it at this meeting, in private meetings of First Presidency George Q. Cannon refers to Hampton's brothel work as "services rendered the Church" and "work in behalf of the Church." Hampton has been set apart Salt Lake temple worker since 1893, and another coordinator of brothel-spying is the temple doorkeeper (1893-1910).

28 July, advertisement in *The Logan Nation* for "all wool Garments," with illustration of two men and woman in one-piece underwear from neck to wrist and ankle.

8 Aug., first of two plural marriages in Mexico that second counselor Joseph F. Smith secretly authorizes without knowledge of President Lorenzo Snow, who prohibits polygamous ordinances. Counselor Smith instructs senior Seventy's president Seymour B. Young to perform the polygamous marriages.

12 Aug., while in Mormon colonies of Mexico, Joseph F. Smith instructs men of Brigham Young Academy's expedition to Latin America that theirs is a "scientific not a Church mission." Some return to Utah, but most of original volunteers continue their quest to locate *Book of Mormon* sites. This expedition returns to Provo in February 1902.

25 Aug., when visiting apostles ask congregation how often ward teachers visit them, some "had not seen a Teacher in their homes for years and many not for months."

4 Oct., at temple meeting of First Presidency and apostles: "The subject of round-dancing [waltzing] was discussed and it was decided not to put it down when young people wanted it. The desire is to furnish amusements to the young and not force them to go elsewhere to find them."

21 Oct., Alexander F. Macdonald performs plural marriage in Mexico, his first since 1890. Second counselor Joseph F. Smith authorizes this without knowledge of church president Lorenzo Snow, who later threatens to excommunicate this patriarch.

10 Nov., LDS Bertha Martineau "killed a deer a few days ago and is an expert shot."

23 Nov., editorial in Democratic *Salt Lake Herald:* "It is not likely that the active participation of church apostles in campaigns will ever be abandoned until the church realizes that such participation is injurious to church interests, as their best friends and a host of their own people believe."

16 Dec., second counselor Joseph F. Smith tells Mormons of St. Johns, Arizona, that Jesus was married to the Mary who anointed his feet.

1901

1 Feb., First Presidency decides to suspend ten-year policy of allowing sale of alcohol at church's Saltair amusement park and resort.

7 Feb., Apostle Brigham Young, Jr. writes that proposal to provide Utah's school children with smallpox vaccinations is "Gentile doctors trying to force Babylon into the people and some of them are willing to disease the blood of our children if they can do so, and they think they are doing God's service." Presiding Bishopric counselor had written on 9 Dec. 1900: "Small pox is spreading most all over the State," yet on 22 Feb. 1901 Utah's legislature overrides governor's veto and passes law ending compulsory vaccination of school children. In June 1904 Apostle Abraham Owen Woodruff and his first wife Helen die of smallpox, after declining counsel of LDS president Joseph F. Smith to be vaccinated before young couple goes to Mexico City.

3 Mar., Lorenzo Snow promises Salt Lake temple workers that "some of us would go back to Jackson Co., [Missouri]."

5 Apr., Lorenzo Snow tells general conference that "we will continue on improving, advancing and increasing in wisdom, intelligence, power, and dominion, worlds without end." In 1908 John A. Widtsoe's *Joseph Smith As a Scientist* (137) affirms: "God in 'Mormon' Theology is the greatest intelligence; yet it must of necessity, under the inexorable law of the universe, grow." In his 1910 *Seventies' Course in Theology*, B. H. Roberts writes that "progress is eternal, even for the highest intelligences" (151). In his 1911 *Seventies' Course in Theology*, Roberts writes: "And is it too bold a thought that with this progress, even for the Mightiest, new thoughts, and new vistas may appear, inviting to new adventures and enterprises that will yield new experiences, advancement, and enlargement even for the Most High?"

11 Apr., organization of Daughters of Utah Pioneers, although such statewide organization for both males and females has existed since 1907. Separate organization for male descendants is formed in 1935.

20 May, Mormon's funeral has "white coffin & white horse, flowers." To symbolize their positive view of death, Utah Mormons emphasize white at funerals.

20 June, during social party at home of second counselor Joseph F. Smith, Lorenzo Snow says: "He the Saviour lives and I know it! . . . Many of you will live to go to Jackson Co. and you will see Him there."

25 June, at Koosharem, Utah, Apostle Owen Woodruff writes: "We then held a council of the Indians [—] they chose Mocha Nogitz for their Chief. I ordained him an Elder and set him apart as Chief of the little band of Utes."

7 July, Lorenzo Snow presides at Salt Lake temple's monthly fast meeting, "and Sister Lillie T. Freeze sang in tongues."

10 July, Apostle Anthon H. Lund reports to apostles that during six-month period, 58 percent of LDS marriages in rural ward were "forced."

11 July, First Presidency and apostles agree that Danish beer is not harmful or in violation of Word of Wisdom.

11 Aug., of men attending stake priesthood meeting, one-third admit they do not observe Word of Wisdom.

29 Aug., First Presidency statement against secret orders and organizations. This is official culmination of half-century of estrangement from church's involvement in Freemasonry, which Joseph Smith thought would help protect him and Mormons.

13 Sept., First Presidency agrees with policy of "drawing as much business as possible to the north end of Main Street as against the efforts made by the Gentiles to pull to the South." This results in geographic polarization of Salt Lake City's business district on basis of religion, which geographic pattern lasts until late twentieth century.

6 Oct., when counselor Joseph F. Smith stands to open conference, stake president writes:

"I looked at him and he appeared to me to be Prest. Snow, and I looked several times and each time he appeared like that."

10 Oct., Lorenzo Snow's death. First time church president dies before being able to set apart or function with new counselors publicly sustained at general conference, Joseph F. Smith as first and Rudger Clawson as second counselor.

17 Oct., Quorum of Twelve Apostles sustains Joseph F. Smith as church president with his counselors, and Presiding Patriarch "sets apart" (*not* ordains) church president, only time patriarch does this.

24 Oct., Joseph F. Smith ordains his oldest son Hyrum M. Smith as new member of Twelve. Apostle John Henry Smith writes, "I called attention to the charge that was likely to be made of Nepotism." Before learning of this appointment, Apostle Smith recommends as new apostle "the names of the sons of the dead apostles."

7 Nov., First Presidency decides there is no "rule in the church forbidding cousins to inter-marry" and that first cousins can have temple marriages if they present civil license. General authorities such as Brigham Young, Willard Richards, Joseph F. Smith, and Abraham H. Cannon married their first cousins as legal or as plural wives.

9 Nov., Joseph F. Smith proposes to sustain Presiding Patriarch above Quorum of Twelve, which his counselors and apostles oppose. At special conference next day which sustains him as church president and his half-brother as Presiding Patriarch, Smith says church patriarch technically should be sustained above church president.

10 Nov., special conference votes for new First Presidency and new Relief Society presidency, with men standing by priesthood quorums and women standing as a group. "This was the first time women had been honored in being presented before the solemn assembly in that way." In 1995 solemn assembly females vote according to membership in auxiliaries.

6 Dec., First Presidency discusses "a letter from Sister Hendricksen [–] she is anxious to get word from us in regard to her being the Holy Ghost!" Nevertheless, first counselor Anthon H. Lund regards her as "gentle and good."

1902

2 Jan., First Presidency and Quorum of Twelve decide against allowing temple sealing of young man who is 1/8 African-American.

24 Jan., First Presidency statement that Holy Ghost is spirit personage, while Spirit of God is impersonal influence from God. This resolves quiet dispute that has existed since Joseph Smith's 1833 Lecture on Faith that Holy Ghost "is the mind of God."

4 Feb., First Presidency announces that full-time missionaries need not pay tithing.

27 Feb., Joseph F. Smith rules that stake president has authority to ordain bishops, but only if authorized by First Presidency. He instructs apostle to re-ordain man who has been ordained bishop by his stake president.

6 Mar., Apostle Abraham Owen Woodruff writes: "Had trouble with an insolent 'Nigger' Conductor [on train], told him what I thought of him and wished for a while that the 'Slave Days' might return."

9 Mar., first plural marriage Anthony W. Ivins performs for Juarez Stake residents by authority of President Joseph F. Smith.

1 Apr., First Presidency obtains (at exorbitant prices) last stock certificates in failed Utah Loan and Trust Company in Ogden. Necessary to prevent civil and criminal action against its former president Joseph F. Smith and director, Apostle Francis M. Lyman.

3 Apr., First Presidency and apostles read letter that U.S. president Theodore Roosevelt and Republican Party leader Mark Hanna guarantee they will arrange to defeat proposed constitutional amendment on polygamy and unlawful cohabitation. They expect Mormons to vote Republican in exchange.

5 Apr., "Clyde Felt has confessed to cutting the throat of old man Collins, at his request. The old man was a moral degenerate. The boy is a son of David P. Felt." Grandson of former

general authority, Clyde Felt is fourteen. Despite this blood atonement murder, LDS leaders allow young man to be endowed and married in temple eight years later.

17 Apr., only specifically dated example of Joseph F. Smith as church president authorizing man to marry plural wife. Apostle Abraham Owen Woodruff's daily diary records that President Smith says: "While I can not advise you to do this I will not advise you not to do it." That is the kind of covert authorization that reminiscent accounts by other post-Manifesto polygamists claim Smith gave them.

22 Apr., staff of Church Historian's Office begins unpacking sacks of historical documents kept hidden for sixteen years since anti-polygamy raid.

24 Apr., Joseph F. Smith rules that he does not want to change "usual procedure" of ordaining man to priesthood office without first conferring Melchizedek priesthood, but he prefers *less* common practice of first conferring priesthood before ordaining to office.

10 July, First Presidency and Quorum of Twelve decide that local patriarchs should no longer charge "a fee" ($2 by late-nineteenth century) for patriarchal blessings but simply allow blessed person to make "free will offering" to patriarch.

27 July, *Deseret News* editorial, "Blood Atonement," affirmed: "We take the ground that the only atonement a murderer can make for his guilt is the shedding of his blood according to the divine mandate.

***

"Under the new and everlasting covenant, as well as under the Mosaic law and the patriarchal law which preceded it, an adulterer who is under a sacred vow not to commit that crime is also worthy of death. But this is not sanctioned by modern civil law; therefore, the penalty cannot be executed. For the Church is commanded of God to obey the laws of the land."

6 Sept., Apostle John Henry Smith writes at Nauvoo: "Mr. Chas. E. Bidamon showed us a medal said to have been carved by Joseph Smith with this inscription on it [—] Confirm[o] O Deus Potentissimus." Bidamon is Emma Smith's stepson, and these Latin words are traditional inscriptions for magic talisman of Jupiter.

12 Sept., at meeting of Stirling Ward, Canada: "Apostle Taylor said he had decided to let the people write the name of the man they desired to act as Bishop of the Ward. Bro. Taylor wished them to write 3 names after which a selection would be made. Bro. Taylor put the [minimum] age limit in voting at 20 years. Bro Taylor said that though the people had had a chance to make their choice he wished the final vote to be unanimous." This is also practice of Apostle Francis M. Lyman in choosing new bishops.

17 Sept., Emmeline B. Wells, editor of *Woman's Exponent* and later president of Relief Society, writes, "Sister Walden told Em's [Emmeline B.'s granddaughter] fortune in her hand also Anna Henderson's."

6 Oct., Joseph F. Smith has general conference sustain Presiding Patriarch as prophet, seer, and revelator, first time since Hyrum Smith in 1840s.

8 Nov., Joseph F. Smith tells congregation how he was once ready to stab man to death on suspicion this man approved afterwards of the killing of Joseph and Hyrum Smith.

23 Nov., Apostle John W. Taylor tells stake priesthood meeting that "those who have sexual intercourse with their wives or touch any dead body are unclean until evening, and therefore during that day should not enter the temple or officiate in the ordinances of the gospel."

2 Dec., President Joseph F. Smith issues press release that church does not sanction marriages contracted in violation of laws of land.

1903

20 Jan., Utah legislature elects Apostle Reed Smoot as U.S. Senator. This begins national crusade, led by Salt Lake Ministerial Alliance, to persuade U.S. Senate to reject him.

10 Mar., first polygamous marriage since 1898 for non-resident of Mexico performed by stake president Anthony W. Ivins, by written authorization from First Presidency.

26 Mar., Joseph F. Smith tells apostles "there would be no daughters of perdition" in final judgment. General authorities authorize rebaptism (without church discipline) for young man who confesses "secret crime he committed in having to do with animals."

27 June, incorporation of W. H. Groves Latter-day Saint Hospital, with Presiding Bishop as president. Opened on 1 Jan. 1905, LDS Hospital is first in church's hospital system.

7 July, Apostle Rudger Clawson tells other apostles "that the practice of self-abuse existed to an alarming extent among the boys in our community who attended the district schools, and also, he doubted not, the church schools. He felt that the boys and girls should be properly instructed in regard to this evil."

9 July, First Presidency and Twelve agree that it would be "a disastrous thing for the country, should the time ever come when Senators would be elected by popular vote. The popular vote is a very uncertain quantity." Their primary concern is preserving hierarchy's influence on senatorial elections by Utah's legislature. Amendment to U.S. Constitution in 1913 requires that U.S. Senators be elected directly by U.S. citizens, but by that time Apostle Reed Smoot is in his second term as U.S. senator.

6 Aug., Joseph F. Smith rules that no European Mormons should emigrate unless they have relatives in U.S. to take care of them.

9 Aug., Apostle John Henry Smith attends and President Joseph F. Smith speaks at corner-stone-laying ceremony for orthodox Jewish synagogue Montefiore in Salt Lake City. Two months later First Presidency donates $650 toward its completion.

11 Sept., first polygamous marriage performed in Canada by authorization of President Joseph F. Smith. Patriarch John A. Woolf performs this plural marriage and several others until end of 1905.

6 Oct., George Albert Smith is presented to general conference as new apostle. "A cold wave passed over the congregation," general authority J. Golden Kimball writes, "and many expressed themselves to me as disgusted. . . . It is nepotism of the strongest kind since the days of President Brigham Young."

22 Oct., First Presidency and Twelve authorize purchase of "twenty-five acres of the original temple lot" at Independence, Jackson County, Missouri. Purchase is completed on 14 Apr. 1904. These purchases continue throughout twentieth century.

5 Nov., announcement of purchase of Carthage Jail as historic site.

1904

7 Jan., church president instructs twelve apostles to walk through doorways in order of seniority. Protocol follows technology as church buildings and temples install elevators.

9 Jan., Emmeline B. Wells, editor of *Woman's Exponent,* writes: "Aunts Presendia [H. Kimball] & Zina [D.H. Young] used to interpret dreams for us but now there is no one to do it." This is one of earliest comments about loss of spiritual gifts in Mormonism.

20 Feb., first (verified) suicide of full-time LDS missionary. He shoots himself as he is returning to Utah.

2 Mar., before committee of U.S. Senate, Joseph F. Smith testifies: "I have never pretended to nor do I profess to have received revelations. I never said that I had a revelation except so far as God has shown to me that so-called Mormonism is God's divine truth; that is all." Smith also testifies that by cohabiting with his plural wives, he is in violation of laws of church and state. He is first LDS president to testify before Congress.

29 Mar., last plural marriage performed by stake president Anthony W. Ivins in Mexico.

5 Apr., Joseph F. Smith criticizes ward bishop for giving temple recommend to friendly non-Mormon who uses it to receive endowment ceremony.

6 Apr., Joseph F. Smith's so-called "Second Manifesto," which denies fact that there has been officially sanctioned plural marriages since 1890 Manifesto and threatens excom-

munication for persons entering plural marriage in future. Some apostles continue performing and entering new plural marriages for almost more two years. In 1906 and 1907, Smith himself permits two exceptions to this "Second Manifesto."

14 Apr., First Presidency and apostles decide to resume sale of liquor at church resort of Saltair due to need for non-Mormon patronage.

30 June, LDS church historian decides that publications should acknowledge existence of only Presiding Bishopric and ward bishopric and not acknowledge former offices of regional bishops, traveling bishops, and stake bishops.

20 July, *Deseret News* reports that young man being sent home early from his mission has attempted suicide by taking carbolic acid and slitting his throat and wrists with razor.

8 Oct., Mormon tells Senator Reed Smoot's secretary that "Apostle [Abraham Owen] Woodruff told him that a certain number of worthy people had been commissioned to keep alive the principle of plural marriage." This view is basis of Mormon Fundamentalist movement which does not fully emerge until 1920s. Woodruff, who died in June after visiting his post-Manifesto plural wife and her first baby, is honored as polygamy martyr by these Mormons.

26 Oct., Apostle George Albert Smith instructs Salt Lake stake prayer circle: "Among some women the practice of removing the garments from the neck and arms and tying them behind the back was common. These were serious faults, and might result in the offenders being disfellowshipped."

1905

1 May, Jean Hunter Mulholland, LDS and "first woman ever summoned for jury service" in Salt Lake County, is dismissed by judge because "commissioners thought the name was masculine." Utah's women apparently do not serve on juries until after ratification of women's suffrage amendment to U.S. Constitution in 1920.

5 May, *Deseret News* advertises LDS Bureau of Information's publication of *The Great Temple* also endorsed in this month's *Improvement Era*. Photos of Council Room of First Presidency and Quorum of Twelve show two of room's spittoons for chewing tobacco.

10 May, incorporation of Beneficial Life Insurance Company, church's first successful life insurance enterprise.

16 Sept., last polygamous marriages performed by Canadian patriarch commissioned by President Joseph F. Smith.

30 Sept., as Joseph F. Smith and his wife sleep, burglar robs their bedroom.

25 Oct., public criticism of Joseph F. Smith's remarks that Father Damien of Hawaiian leper colony was immoral before his death. LDS church president is convinced that leprosy is contracted through sexual contact.

28 Oct., after week of Quorum of Twelve meetings so secret that no official minutes are kept, apostles John W. Taylor and Matthias F. Cowley write formal resignations due to their participation in post-Manifesto polygamy. Resignations are held in reserve unless considered necessary to save church from U.S. constitutional amendment or to save Apostle Reed Smoot from expulsion from U.S. Senate.

1906

10 Jan., First Council of Seventy instructs B. H. Roberts to go to Los Angeles for "recuperation" from "a weakness for liquor that had fastened itself upon him." Roberts confessed his problem to Council in 1901, and its senior president writes in 1908 that he "has been many times much the worse for Liquor in so much that his brethren of the Council have had to take up a labor with him."

14 Feb., probable date of first plural marriage performed without claiming authority from current First Presidency. Second and third such marriages are on 13-14 June 1906. This is early stage of what became Mormon Fundamentalist movement.

21 Feb., first verified plural marriage personally authorized by President Joseph F. Smith since 1904 "Second Manifesto."

9 Apr., Francis M. Lyman announces resignations of apostles Taylor and Cowley for being "out of harmony." In priesthood meeting, Lyman is emotional as he says some stake presidents feel he has been out of harmony for his opposition to post-1890 plural marriages.

Charles H. Hart, new Seventy's president, is first general authority with law degree (LL.B. from University of Michigan). LL.B (later J.D.) degree of law eventually is most common graduate degree among general authorities of modern LDS church including, Stephen L Richards (appointed in 1917), J. Reuben Clark (1933), Albert E. Bowen (1937), Marion G. Romney (1941), Matthew Cowley (1945), Bruce R. McConkie (1946), Henry D. Moyle (1947), Marion D. Hanks (1953), Franklin D. Richards (1958), Howard W. Hunter (1959), James E. Faust (1972), W. Grant Bangerter (1975), Ronald E. Poelman (1978), Derek A. Cuthbert (1978), Robert L. Backman (1978), F. Burton Howard (1978), Dallin H. Oaks (1984), John K. Carmack (1984), H. Verlan Andersen (1986), Francis M. Gibbons (1986), W. Eugene Hansen (1989), Marlin K. Jensen (1989), Merlin R. Lybbert (1989), Earl C. Tingey (1991), Cree-L Kofford (1991), Augusto A. Lim (1992), D. Todd Christofferson (1993), Lance B. Wickman (1994), Bruce C. Hafen (1996), Quentin L. Cook (1996), Dennis E. Simmons (1996).

18 Apr., San Francisco earthquake. Room of Matthias F. Cowley, recently dropped from Quorum of Twelve Apostles, "is the only one in [his hotel that is] undamaged."

24 May, *Deseret Evening News* editorial argues against frequent requests to remove section 132 from D&C. This indicates how deeply post-Manifesto polygamy has alienated church members who often refer to themselves as "modern Mormons".

23 June, ex-apostle Matthias F. Cowley gives to mission president a copy of John Taylor's revelation of 27 Sept. 1886. This is first verified date for distributing 1886 revelation, but Cowley has received copy at earlier date from John W. Taylor.

5 July, First Presidency, Quorum of Twelve Apostles, and Presiding Patriarch begin consistently using "water and not wine" in their own sacrament. Joseph F. Smith personally stopped drinking wine at temple meeting sacrament in Dec. 1902. When this first came up for discussion by apostles on 7 Jan. 1903, Hyrum M. Smith criticized this practice. However, most apostles in 1903 preferred to continue using wine in temple.

7 July, ex-Queen Liliuokalani of Hawaii is baptized. Although she is first monarch to convert to Mormonism, she also joins other churches in her last years.

1 Aug., "Fast meeting in 1*st* Ward. . . . Sister Jarrett speaks in tongues and prophesies."

Der Stern reports Joseph F. Smith's statement to conference at Bern, Switzerland: "The time will come when this land [Europe] will be dotted with temples . . ."

6 Aug., Samuel W. Richards tells high priest quorum that he "was the last of the original company of young men organized by Joseph Smith the Prophet to go and explore the Rocky Mountains for a dwelling place for the saints. He spoke of a night vision he had . . . wherein he came west all over these regions down into California, Mexico and back up to Jackson Co where he helped to build the Great Temple there." This is another version of Horse Shoe Prophecy.

30 Aug., at testimony meeting of general board of Young Ladies Mutual Improvement Association invited guests Lillie T. Freeze and Maria Young Dougall speak in tongues and interpret. Sisters Freeze and Dougall are general board members in other auxiliaries and speak in tongues and interpret at such meetings until they die in 1937. By then glossolalia no longer occurs in LDS meetings, since all Mormons with this gift have died without successors. After 1930s LDS leaders redefine "gift of tongues" to be ability to learn unfamiliar language (such as Japanese), rather than spontaneous speaking of "unknown tongues" which correspond to no recognized language.

1 Sept., J. Reuben Clark is first Mormon appointed to federal government service (U.S.

State Department's assistant solicitor). He serves as department's solicitor from 1910 to 1911. No Mormon serves in equivalent legal position until Rex E. Lee's appointment as U.S. Solicitor General (1981-85).

10 Oct., mission president tells Apostle Francis M. Lyman, "President Taylor died in exile for this principle and he gave men authority to perform the ceremony of marriage which authority I have been told was never revoked-etc."

23 Nov., Joseph F. Smith pleads guilty to unlawful cohabitation for which he pays $300 fine.

1907

20 Feb., Apostle Reed Smoot retains his seat in U.S. Senate, after three-year "trial."

7 Apr., general conference votes to send twenty tons of flour to China for famine relief. This comes from Relief Society grain storage program.

21 Apr., last known plural marriage performed with personal knowledge and authorization of President Joseph F. Smith.

18 July, incorporation of church's Utah-Idaho Sugar Company. As successor to church sugar companies formed since 1889, U-I Sugar dominates western sugar economy but puts enormous financial drain on church resources during its early decades.

18 Sept., front-page headline of *The Logan Republican:* "Bear Lake Monster Appears: Leviathan Comes from Lake and Devours Horse While Men Shoot At It."

6 Oct., at sustaining of church officers a man votes against Joseph F. Smith because of his admitted violation of Utah's cohabitation law. Smith has him ejected from Salt Lake Tabernacle. Conference sustains new apostle Anthony W. Ivins, who performed dozens of plural marriages in Mexico after 1890 Manifesto.

Francis M. Lyman instructs newly ordained Ivins: "The Twelve are the Special witnesses of Jesus Christ & should be able to testify that he lives even *as if* he had been seen by them" (emphasis added).

4 Dec., First Presidency and Twelve agree to immediately release Presiding Bishop William B. Preston because he has "been for some time past mentally incapable of attending to the duties of his office." First general authority to be released due to mental illness.

1908

23 Aug., U.S. immigration officials send nine Mormon immigrants back to England because they admit belief in LDS doctrine of plural marriage.

3 Nov., George Reynolds is legally committed to Utah Insane Asylum, first Mormon general authority to be hospitalized in mental institution. Previous June, First Council of Seventy recommended that Reynolds be sent to Oregon "sanitarium" because of his "physical and mental condition." Unknown if he actually spent time in Portland asylum, but Reynolds is patient in Utah asylum 7 Feb. 1909. He dies six months later.

1909

1 Jan., Presiding Bishopric instructions "that as near as circumstances will permit boys be ordained as follows: Deacons at twelve, Teachers at fifteen and Priests at eighteen years of age." For first time, Aaronic Priesthood offices are conferred generally on teenage boys, although age intervals later change to twelve, fourteen, and sixteen.

7 July, Joseph F. Smith, son of Hyrum Smith who led similar effort in 1842-43, instructs Twelve to investigate and suppress new plural marriages.

14 July, Quorum of Twelve appoints apostles Francis M. Lyman, John Henry Smith, and Heber J. Grant to investigate evidence of new plural marriages

3 Oct., at general conference, Apostle George Albert Smith stops speaking after three minutes as he begins to "tremble and perspire." Apostle Reed Smoot referred two weeks earlier as Smith's "mental trouble." Since Jan. Smith's diary has described symptoms of his eventual collapse. At age thirty-nine he is first general authority whose debilitating mental problems cannot be attributed to senility. Hospitalized for ten weeks at Gray's

Sanitarium in Salt Lake City, Smith does not recover from this emotional breakdown until 1913. Problem re-emerges in 1930s and in 1949-51.

14 Oct., "The [First] Presidency read the article on the origin of man written by O. F. Whitney. . . . As it will go out under our names the Presidency made a few changes." Published in Nov., the statement responds to theory of organic evolution by affirming that Adam was first man and progenitor of human race. Statement does not deny possibility of biological evolution preceding Adam. Its author believes in reincarnation.

1910

5 Apr., Joseph F. Smith instructs bishops and stake presidents that payment of tithing and observance of Word of Wisdom are necessary for Mormons to obtain temple recommends. Smith also says: "Suicides who are willful should not be buried in [temple] robes or have public funeral, but local authorities must be the judges of their state of mind when committing the act and act accordingly."

10 Apr., stake president writes of church members "complaining on account of so many Smiths being chosen." Recent conference sustained John Henry Smith as second counselor and President Smith's son, Joseph Fielding Smith, as new apostle. In addition to appointing his son Hyrum M. an apostle in 1901, Smith also appointed his son David A. Smith to Presiding Bishopric in 1907.

18 Apr., on night Halley's Comet is visible in Salt Lake City, bomb explosion causes extensive damage to partially constructed Hotel Utah and to front of Utah State Bank, both owned by LDS church. Perpetrators bomb offices of *Los Angeles Times* six months later, killing twenty-one people. Hotel Utah opens without further incident July 1911.

8 Oct., First Presidency instructs local priesthood leaders to investigate and excommunicate persons who enter recent plural marriages.

1911

11 Feb., *New York Times* gives its first theater review of actress Hazel Dawn. With her debut on London stage in 1910, she is first nationally recognized star of twentieth century who publicly acknowledges Mormonism (e.g. *Who's Who* entry).

12 Feb., BYU professor Ralph V. Chamberlin's "Darwin Centennial Speech" ignites controversy. General authorities (as school's trustees) to fire him and professor Henry Peterson. BYU students protest dismissals with petitions and demonstrations.

17 Feb., John W. Taylor appeals to Joseph F. Smith to re-convene theocratic Council of Fifty to protect Taylor and other "co-religionists" from polygamy investigations by Twelve. Smith's notation on letter: "*Not granted* [—] I think the demand most absurd."

28 Mar., Quorum of Twelve Apostles excommunicates John W. Taylor for marrying plural wife in 1909 and for justifying it by 1886 revelation. His is last excommunication of general authority appointed in nineteenth century and first excommunication of general authority with service in twentieth century.

11 May, Twelve vote as compromise to deprive Matthias F. Cowley of right to exercise priesthood but not to disfellowship him. This resolves two-day deadlock in which seven apostles want to give him no punishment, whereas quorum president Francis M. Lyman and two others want to disfellowship Cowley for performing plural marriage up to 1905 resignation. Cowley regards this as second punishment (double jeopardy) he has received for same acts, which he insists he did by authorization of First Presidency.

16 Sept., public report concerning man who attempts to extort $100,000 from church president to prevent publication of covertly obtained interior photographs of Salt Lake temple. Two days later First Presidency commissions James E. Talmage to write *The House of the Lord.* Published a year later its photographs omit tobacco spittoons from Council Room of First Presidency and Quorum of the Twelve, but include Holy of Holies (photograph deleted from later editions). Ordinance of second anointing is performed for couples in Holy of Holies.

2 Oct., first anti-Mormon film, *Victim of the Mormons* ("Mormonens Offer"), opens in Co-

penhagen, Denmark. Film goes into international distribution, is publicly condemned by Apostle David O. McKay at next general conference. It is target of first censorship effort led by Utah governor (William Spry, LDS).

7 Nov., High point of power for Utah Socialist Party's (founded in 1901). In ten years Socialists elected state legislator, city councilmen in Salt Lake City and Cedar City, and in smaller communities such officers as mayor, councilmen, and sheriffs. Despite Socialist Party's radical reputation, 40 percent of its men are Mormons, including bishop and his first counselor. Of women socialists, 28 percent are Mormons.

7 Nov., Mary Woolley Chamberlain, post-Manifesto polygamous wife, is elected mayor of Kanab, Utah, with all-female town council, first such political event in U.S. Next LDS woman to receive extensive publicity (*New York Times*) for her election as mayor is Dorothy Johnson (Appleton, WI, 1980, three terms). LDS women mayors outside Utah: Faye Myers Dastrup (Ontario, CA, 1985), Lorna Kesterson (Henderson, NV, 1988), Joan Hanet Shoemaker (El Cajon, CA, 1990), Ruth Luke (Choctaw, OK, 1991).

Utah's women mayors (primarily LDS) elected or appointed since 1911: Myrtle Y. Nixon (1951, Holden), Izetta Allred (1953, Loa), Vanda D. Hreinson (1955, Castle Gate), Irene King (1957, Boulder), Marion Ackerman (1961, Marysvale), Edna Cannon (1965, Circleville), Laurie Dea Holley (1976, Cannonville), Beulah Semmens (1976, Virgin), Inez Wilson (1977, Bluff), Vivian Crosby (1977, Bluff), Georgia R. Russell (1977, Ophir), Leah Conover (1977, Salina), Helen B. Excell (1977, Springdale), Donna Wilson (1981, Boulder), Doris Rasmussen (1981, Fillmore), Carole I. Scott (1981, Manila), Amoir Deuel (1981, Mt. Pleasant), Alexia Cooper (1981, Myton), Sue Marie Young (1981, Richfield), Sandra Armstrong (1981, Santaquin), Lola R. Morgan (1981, Washington Terrace), RoJean Addley (1983, Duchesne), Hazel Jean Robinson (1983, Paragonah), Marguerite Sweeney (1985, Castle Valley), Beverly Cannon (1985, Circleville), Ruth Hansen (1985, Delta), Marjorie May Peterson (1985, Manti), Phyllis M. Truman (1985, Minersville), Thelma A. Olsen (1985, Spring City), Connie Putnam (1987, Randolph), Kristin C. Lambert (1988, West Jordan), Elaine J. Barnes (1989, Alpine), Julee C. Lyman (1989, Boulder), Lorna B. Stapley (1989, Koosharem), Patricia J. Braegger (1989, Providence), Kathleen Browning (1989, Roy), Marie W. Huff (1989, Spanish Fork), Delora P. Bertelsen (1989, Springville), Janet Hansen (1989, Torrey), Sue Critchlow (1989, Wellington), Cosetta Castagno (1989, Vernon), Ruth P. Maughan (1989, Wellsville), Connie Dubinsky (1991, Levan), Joyce Johnson (1991, Orem), Stella Welch (1991, Orem), Dee Dee Corradini (1991, Salt Lake City), Carolyn S. Larkin (1992, Snowville), Patsy Hosey (1992, Virgin), Geraldine Rankin (1993, Big Water), Valli D. Smouse (1993, Castle Valley), Martha Spoor (1993, Cedar Hills), Priscilla A. Todd (1993, Centerville), Elaine Redd (1993, Draper), Valerie Hopper (1993, Elsinore), Judy Ann Scott (1993, Green River), Linda L. Malmgren (1993, Gunnison), Darla D. Merrill Clark (1993, Logan), Mary G. Wiseman (1993, Milford), Barbara U. Vanderhoof (1993, Plymouth), Sandra N. Lloyd (1993, Riverton), Carol Bellmon (1993, Sunset), Joy Henderlider (1993, Virgin), Brenda Morgan (1993, Wendover), Flora A. Lamborn (1994, Randolph), Elaine M. Baldwin (1995, Panguitch). Although Utah's male voters have often elected women to executive office on local level, there has been no woman governor and only one lieutenant-governor.

29 Nov., LDS church organizes its first Boy Scout troops. One of Lord Baden-Powell's original English Scout troop is LDS Arthur William Sadler. LDS Young Men's Mutual Improvement Association formally affiliates with Boy Scouts of America in May 1913. In 1932 Apostle George Albert Smith becomes first general authority elected to national executive board of BSA. Boy Scouts of America has conferred its highest award ("Silver Buffalo") on following LDS general authorities: George Albert Smith (1934), Heber J. Grant (1939), David O. McKay (1953), Ezra Taft Benson (1954), Delbert L. Stapley (1961), Harold B. Lee (1963), N. Eldon Tanner (1969), Thomas S. Monson (1978), Spencer W. Kimball (1984), Robert L. Backman (1986), Marion D. Hanks (1988),

Vaughn J. Featherstone (1988), George R. Hill III (1993), Gordon B. Hinckley (1994), Jack H. Goaslind (1995).

8 Dec., James E. Talmage is ordained apostle. Although Apostle Orson Pratt had self-taught interests in mathematics and astronomy, Talmage is first apostle with university training in sciences (geology). He is also first general authority and first apostle with Ph.D. degree (from Illinois Wesleyan University). However, as non-resident, correspondence doctorate, his degree lacks full academic stature.

Nevertheless, Talmage's appointment heralds forty-year era when scientifically-trained intellectuals serve in Quorum of Twelve. Succeeding appointments of Richard R. Lyman, John A. Widtsoe, Joseph F. Merrill, and (to lesser extent) Sylvester Q. Cannon have considerable impact on LDS church administration. From 1921 until 1952 there are always two (and sometimes four) scientifically-trained intellectuals at highest levels of decision-making. There are no scientific doctorates in Twelve from 1952 until 1984, when Russell M. Nelson (physician with Ph.D.) becomes apostle. One nuclear engineer becomes church patriarch in 1947, and another becomes apostle in 1988. Theodore M. Burton (with Ph.D. in chemistry from Purdue) serves as Assistant to Twelve (1960-76) and in First Quorum of Seventy (1976-89), George R. Hill III (with Ph.D. in chemistry from Cornell) serves in First Quorum of Seventy (1987-92), and Alexander B. Morrison (with Ph.D., food sciences, Cornell) serves in Seventy (1987-).

1912

20 Feb., First Presidency letter denies essentials of Brigham Young's Adam-God teachings, by focusing exclusively on his first 1852 sermon, and makes no reference to his Adam-God sermons during remaining twenty-five years of Young's life.

4 Mar., Joseph F. Smith establishes new rule for priesthood ordination: confer priesthood first, then ordain to office. This alters traditional nineteenth-century practice of ordaining to office without specifically conferring priesthood.

21 Mar., First Presidency encourages local leaders to discontinue "common cup" for sacrament and begin using small, individual cups (glass or metal). *Improvement Era* article in Apr. defends this change as prevention against spread of germs.

Apr., first known plural marriage performed by John W. Woolley, Salt Lake temple worker since 1893 and ordained patriarch in 1913. He does not claim authority from President Joseph F. Smith.

15 Apr., passenger liner *Titanic* sinks with loss of 1500 lives including one Mormon fatality, Irene C. Corbett who is returning to Utah from her midwifery study in London.

9 May, ordination of Hyrum G. Smith, first Presiding Patriarch with college degree (from Brigham Young Academy, 1900) and also first with graduate degree (D.D.S. degree from University of Southern California). Other dentists appointed as general authorities are John Sonnenberg (1984), F. Arthur Kay (1984), LeGrand R. Curtis (1990), Harold G. Hillam (1990), Andrew W. Peterson (1994).

12 May, Church Board of Education approves "seminary near Granite High" in Salt Lake City. Innovation recommended by Granite Stake presidency, this first LDS seminary opens following September with seventy LDS high school students. Thomas J. Yates, an engineer, is first teacher in what remains church's only seminary during next four years. In 1916 church's second high school seminary opens in Mt. Pleasant, Utah. This grows into released-time program wherever legal in western states and into early morning seminary program everywhere else (beginning September 1950 in California).

7 July, Alma W. Richards is first Mormon athlete to receive national recognition. He wins gold medal (high jump) at Olympics, and in 1954 is inducted into Helms National Hall of Fame and U.S. Track and Field Hall of Fame. Other Mormon Olympic medalists are Lloyd Butler (1948, gold, eight-oar rowing crew), Jean Saubert (1964, two bronzes, skiing), H. Blaine Lindgren (1964, silver, track hurdles), 17-year-old Jackson S. Horsley (1968, bronze, swimming), L. Jay Silvester (1972, silver, discus), Kresimir Cosic of Yugo-

slavia (1972, bronze; 1976, silver; 1980, gold, basketball team), Bo Gustafsson of Sweden (1984, silver, 50K walk), Tauna Kay Vandeweghe-Mullackey (1984, silver, volleyball team), Cory Snyder (1984, silver, baseball team), Peter Vidmar (1984, two gold and one silver, gymnastics), Troy Dalbey (1988, two gold, swimming), Mike Evans and James Bergeson (1988, silver each, water polo team), Troy Tanner (1988, gold, basketball team), Kristine Quance (1996, gold, swimming). Jean Saubert is inducted into U.S. Ski Hall of Fame (1976), Peter Vidmar is inducted into U.S. Olympic Hall of Fame (1991), Kresimir Cosic is inducted posthumously into Basketball Hall of Fame (1995). Although not Olympic medalists, Alberta Williams Hood is inducted into Women's Basketball Hall of Fame (1967), and Pedro Velasco into National Volleyball Hall of Fame (1970).

In addition, following Olympians receive their medals before joining LDS church: Robert Detweiler (1952), Paula Meyers Pope (1952, 1956, 1960), Jack Yerman (1960), and Kresimir Cosic (1968). The 1976 Olympics also gives gold medal (decathlon) to RLDS Bruce Jenner. He is inducted into U.S. Track and Field Hall of Fame (1980), and into U.S. Olympic Hall of Fame (1988).

Three Mormons become medalists at Olympics for Physically Disabled (Para-Olympiad) in 1976. Michael R. Johnson, double-amputee Vietnam veteran, wins four medals (two gold, one silver, and one bronze). Curtis Brinkman, double amputee since age sixteen, wins three medals (one gold, two bronze), and paraplegic Garry Treadwell wins two medals (silver and bronze). Michael P. Schlappi and John C. Brewster win gold medals at Para-Olympiad (1988), and Schlappi wins her gold medal again (1992). Mandy Kunitz, Down-syndrome Mormon, wins gold medal at Special Olympics (1996).

Other LDS athletes win medals at World Games: Keith Russell (silver, diving, 1973), Wayne Young (gold, gymnastics, 1974), Richard George (bronze, javelin, 1975), Becky Hamblin (bronze, tumbling).

28 July, Mormon families abandon their colonies in Chihuahua, northern Mexico, and "began to pour into El Paso penniless and with little except their clothing." As chaos of Mexican Revolution worsens, Mormon writes that on 18 Aug. "a stampede was on for the border" by those in Sonora. Of several thousand Mormon colonists who leave, most never return to Mexico. Without supportive polygamous environment of colonies, many ex-colonists end previously stable polygamous marriages.

6 Sept., Utah Power and Light Company incorporates in Maine with at least one general authority on its board since then.

Oct., Joseph F. Smith publishes editorial in *Improvement Era* favoring election of Republican William H. Taft as U.S. president. When criticized by Democratic Mormons, Smith replies he is only exercising his rights as private citizen. Utah's vote goes for Taft, but nation elects Democrat Woodrow Wilson.

6 Oct., first written statement by Lorin C. Woolley about circumstances of John Taylor's 1886 revelation at home of his father John W. Woolley. This statement makes no reference to Lorin Woolley's later claim that John Taylor ordained men in 1886 to continue plural marriage no matter what church's official position might be. However, since 1904 diaries have mentioned such claims, though without mentioning 1886 or Woolley.

10 Nov., President John Taylor's brother, Patriarch Joseph E. Taylor, reads entire "White Horse Prophecy" outloud to High Priest quorum meeting of Salt Lake stake. In recent years historians and LDS church leaders have generally regarded as spurious this alleged prophecy by Joseph Smith in 1844.

3 Dec., Joseph F. Smith accepts records of polygamous marriages performed in Mexico (1900-1903) by Patriarch Alexander F. Macdonald and says they were all authorized.

1913

25 Jan., *Deseret News* favorably reviews *One Hundred Years of Mormonism*, first commercial film about Mormons made with cooperation of church officials. The 6-reel, 90-minute silent film features one of Brigham Young's grandsons in role of his grandfather. Dur-

ing Joseph F. Smith presidency, Hollywood produces other silent features which portray Mormonism less favorably: *A Trip To Salt Lake City* (1905), *The Mountain Meadows Massacre* (1912), *The Mormon* (1912), *Deadwood Dick Spoils Brigham Young* (1915), Cecil B. DeMille's *A Mormon Maid* (1917), and *The Rainbow Trail* (1918).

9 May, First Presidency learns that James Dwyer, co-founder of Salt Lake City's LDS University (now LDS Business College), has been "teaching young men that sodomy and kindred vices are not sins . . ." Dwyer's daughter, actress Ada Dwyer Russell, is already in long-term relationship with lesbian poet Amy Lowell. Dwyer's bishop and stake president want to excommunicate him, but First Presidency allows Dwyer, now in his eighties, to voluntarily "withdraw his name" from LDS church membership.

27 July, Seventy's president J. Golden Kimball is publicly beaten in Salt Lake City by grocer. Assailant is acquitted by "jury of grocers."

2 Aug., First Presidency letter against Bishop John Koyle's religious claims for his "Dream Mine." However, he is not excommunicated until 1948, year before his death.

17 Dec., death of Joseph Smith's last surviving plural wife, Mary E. Rollins Lightner. She helped save the still-unbound *Book of Commandments* from printing office set afire by mob in 1833. She witnessed adoption of 1835 D&C, which prohibited polygamy, and became secret plural wife of Joseph Smith at Nauvoo while still living with her non-Mormon husband. She moved with her husband to Utah where she also witnessed polygamy's accepted practice in Mormon society, its "underground" survival despite federal raid, its official prohibition by 1890 Manifesto, renewal of authorized polygamy despite official denials, Second Manifesto and disciplining of two apostles for post-Manifesto polygamy, general disfavor of plural marriage by "modern" Latter-day Saints, and even early stages of Fundamentalist polygamy.

1914

30 Mar., Patriarch John W. Woolley is excommunicated for performing unauthorized plural marriages. Although he advances no schismatic claims, Fundamentalist movement will eventually look to him as one of its founders.

25 Aug., First Presidency cables missionaries to leave France and Germany immediately, due to outbreak of war. LDS missionaries leave in safety.

29 Sept., Quorum of Twelve learns that mission president has "discovered that 15% of the [missionary] Elders in the Netherlands during the past two years, have been guilty of immoral practices, and that a much greater percentage of Elders has been exposed to these evils."

18 Oct., Joseph F. Smith and Apostle Francis M. Lyman publicly state that undergarments worn by endowed persons outside temple must "come high up on the neck and down to the wrists and ankles, for that was the pattern revealed from heaven."

15 Dec., George J. Taylor dies "at his home," according to *Deseret News*, but actually in Utah Insane Asylum, according to its records. Oldest son of LDS president John Taylor, George was also member of theocratic Council of Fifty. He is first prominent Utah Mormon to die in mental asylum (he has been patient since February).

1915

11 Mar., First Presidency letter informs Apostle Francis M. Lyman that Joseph F. Smith recommends "disfellowship or excommunication" for plural wives in polygamous marriages performed by John W. Woolley before his recent excommunication.

6 Apr., church releases its first detailed report to "show how the tithing of the Church for the year 1914 has been disbursed." These annual reports of expenditures continue until last public statement in Apr. 1959.

27 Apr., First Presidency asks LDS families to have "Home Evening" once a month. Mormons generally ignore this and similar appeals for fifty years.

30 May, William Paul Daniels is first black African to join LDS church. Elder in Dutch Reformed Church of South Africa, he accepts baptism in Salt Lake City without opportu-

nity for LDS priesthood. He returns to Cape Town where he dies in 1936. Exactly sixty-five years after his baptism, Daniels receives his temple endowment by proxy.

27 July, revolutionary followers of Emiliano Zapata execute Mexican branch president Rafael Monroy and Vincente Morales, also LDS, after each tells the Zapatistas: "I cannot renounce my religion."

1916

26 Apr., Joseph F. Smith rules that Salt Lake temple have daily limits for proxy ordinances: 240 endowments and 1,200 baptisms for the dead. As example of changes in that policy, Salt Lake temple performs 4,718 endowments on 21 May 1967.

30 June, First Presidency statement on "the Father and the Son," which provides reconciliation of *Book of Mormon* passages which seem to contradict later official teachings about separate character of Godhead's trinity.

7 Sept., Corporation of the Presiding Bishop.

14 Nov., Simon Bamberger, a Jew, is elected as Utah state's first non-Mormon governor. Utah state's other non-Mormon governors are George H. Dern (1925-33) and J. Bracken Lee (1949-57).

16 Dec., *Deseret News* features seventeen Utahns and Mormons who are stars in Hollywood's silent films. Among best known today is Mack Swain of "Keystone Cops" films and other silent comedies. Swain's LDS father helped construct Salt Lake temple. Two other Utahns in Keystone films are actresses Ora Carew and Mary Thurman.

1917

25 Aug., *Deseret News* publishes First Presidency denial that ex-apostle John W. Taylor has been lawfully rebaptized or reinstated in church.

20 Sept., James H. Moyle appointed Assistant Secretary of U.S. Treasury, serving to 1921, and again (1939-40). He is first Mormon to achieve sub-Cabinet appointment in U.S. government. Appointments of similar rank for other Mormons are Assistant Attorney General Frank K. Nebeker (1919-21), Under-Secretary of State J. Reuben Clark (1928-30), Assistant Secretary of Treasury Marriner S. Eccles (1934-36), Assistant Secretary of Commerce Robert H. Hinckley (1940-42), Assistant Secretary of Treasury David M. Kennedy (1953-54), Assistant Secretary of Labor Esther W. Eggertsen Peterson (1961-69), Assistant Secretary of Interior Jack W. Carlson (1974-76), Assistant Attorney General Rex E. Lee (1975-76), Assistant Secretary of State Gregory J. Newell (1982-85), Under-Secretary of Commerce Sidney L. Jones (1984-86), Assistant Secretary of Health and Human Services James O. Mason (1989-93), Assistant Secretary of Treasury Sidney L. Jones (1989-93).

Mormons with equivalent of sub-Cabinet positions in non-U.S. governments are Tevita Mapa as secretary to Tonga's Premier; Alexander B. Morrison as Canada's deputy minister of National Health and Welfare (1972-84). Morrison becomes LDS general authority in 1987.

10 Oct., 145th Field Artillery regiment departs Utah for duty in "Great War" (World War I). Nearly all of its 1,300 to 1,500 officers and enlisted men are LDS, so unit is nicknamed "the Mormon regiment." Seventy's president B. H. Roberts serves regiment as chaplain. He is first active general authority since 1846 to participate in U.S. war and is among first three Mormons to serve as U.S. military chaplains. There are 665 deaths (including missing-in-action) among 21,000 Utahns (primarily Mormons) who serve in World War I.

13 Oct., *Deseret News* reports that "Bishop Robert McQuarrie has resigned from the bishopric of the Ogden Second ward after rendering efficient service as bishop for a period of 40 years." During Mormonism's first century, presiding officers have option to honorably resign for personal reasons such as family stress, business problems, ill health, or simply weariness of the position. It is customary to tell their congregation about leader's request to be released.

25 Dec., according to Apostle David O. McKay, is "one of the most glorious celebrations of

our Lord for over 1600 years," because of British government's Balfour Declaration establishing Palestine as homeland for Jews.

1918

27 Mar., *Deseret News* editorial urges federal government to give non-combat assignments for conscientious objectors.

7 Apr., Richard R. Lyman is ordained apostle. He is first general authority and first apostle who has completed resident Ph.D. degree (in engineering from Cornell University). He is also first general authority with doctorate from Ivy League school.

16 Apr., Richard W. Young, Brigham Young's nephew, is appointed Brigadier General in U.S. Army, first Mormon with general's rank in U.S. military.

3 July, Joseph F. Smith's counselors decline to ask him whether he agrees with Presiding Patriarch's claim that Presiding Patriarch presides over church on President Smith's death.

3 Oct., Joseph F. Smith's written vision of condition of spirits after death and redemption.

1 Nov., Joseph F. Smith dictates "thus saith the Lord" revelation concerning disbursement of tithing funds. This revelation is not presented to meeting of First Presidency and Quorum of Twelve until 8 Apr. 1943. Text available but never published or canonized.

14 Nov., First Presidency and Twelve vote to accept Joseph F. Smith's revelation on spirit world, even though several apostles have misgivings about it. Church officials publish this vision and add it to Standard Works in 1976.

19 Nov., Joseph F. Smith dies. His last words are to Apostle Heber J. Grant: "Always remember this is the Lord's work, and not man's. The Lord is greater than any man. He knows who He wants to lead His Church, and never makes any mistakes." Smith is only LDS president to be buried without public funeral (due to epidemic of "Spanish Influenza").

23 Nov., Quorum of Twelve Apostles sustains Heber J. Grant as church president with Anthon H. Lund and Charles W. Penrose as counselors, and they are "set apart" (*not* ordained). Because of deadly influenza epidemic, conference does not meet to sustain this action until 1 June 1919. Grant is first church president who has previously experienced nervous breakdown, although it was mild by comparison with experience of Apostle-President George Albert Smith. Some Mormons criticize Grant for his relaxed golf games and trips to California resorts, without realizing that these are precautions he has gradually adopted against build up of too much emotional stress.

1919

2 Jan., at temple meeting of First Presidency, Quorum of Twelve, and Presiding Patriarch, President Heber J. Grant rules that patriarch ranks below apostles and has no significant vote in temple council meetings. He orders patriarch's chair removed from its place next to First Presidency and placed after junior apostle's chair.

9 Feb., Thomas C. Neibaur, Mormon from Idaho, is "the first private in the United States Army to receive the Congressional Medal of Honor." Other Mormons who receive America's highest military medal for heroism are Mervyn Bennion (1942, posthumously), William E. Hall (1943), Nathan K. Van Noy, Jr. (1944, posthumously), George E. Wahlen (1944), Leonard C. Brostrom (1945), David B. Bleak (1953), Bernard F. Fisher (1967).

28 Feb., over opposition of Apostle David O. McKay, First Presidency and Twelve vote to "summon" recent plural wives to tell who performed their polygamous marriages. Apostles excommunicate their husbands this day for refusing to answer that question.

22 Mar., "'THE NIGGER' is the new production to be given at the Social Hall," proclaims *Deseret News* with explanation: "'The Nigger' is distinctively Southern. It is a romance based on Southern ideals and the race problem."

1 May, anarchists mail bombs to thirty-six jurists and government leaders across U.S., including Utah's senators William H. King and Reed Smoot, as well as fellow Mormon Frank K. Nebeker, Assistant Attorney General of United States. In 1917-18 Nebeker was federal government's special prosecutor of sensational trial of Industrial Workers

of the World (IWW) leaders. Only two of today's bombs explode, injuring maid and secretary.

25 May, at Salt Lake temple testimony meeting, several report that during recent weeks they saw Heber J. Grant transfigured into appearance of deceased Joseph F. Smith.

4 July, William Harrison ("Jack") Dempsey is first Mormon to be Heavyweight Boxing Champion of world, which title he maintains until 1926. LDS boxers of similar status are Gene Fullmer is (Middleweight Boxing Champion, 1957), Don Fullmer (American Middleweight Champion, 1965), Danny Lopez (Featherweight Boxing Champion of world, 1976-80), Javier Flores (Super Bantamweight Champion of North America, 1978), Albert Kapua (New Zealand's Junior Boxing Champion, 1978). Mormon inductees into Boxing Hall of Fame are Jack Dempsey (1954) and Gene Fullmer (1974).

12 Nov., Apostle James E. Talmage attends Third Christian Citizenship Conference in Pittsburgh as delegate chosen by Utah's governor. Utah delegates are booed and hissed by 4,000 other delegates. Talmage hurriedly leaves after some delegates surround him and threaten to strip off his clothes in order to display his temple garments.

27 Nov., Heber J. Grant dedicates temple at Laie, Oahu, Hawaii, first of many temples outside continental United States as announced by Brigham Young. It is also smallest functioning temple (10,500 square feet of floor space) until 1978, after extensive remodeling more than triples its floor space. Sarah Jenne Cannon also is first woman to speak at temple dedication.

27 Dec., Heber J. Grant obtains approval of his counselors to cancel $30,000 in loans he received as apostle from Trustee-in-Trust in exchange for stock.

1920

10 June, U.S. Department of Justice files charges against church president Heber J. Grant and Presiding Bishop Charles W. Nibley for illegal profiteering on behalf of church's Utah-Idaho Sugar Company. Nibley is already under indictment on related charge of conspiracy in restraint of trade. Federal grand jury excludes Grant but includes Nibley in its indictments on 21 Aug. Grant speaks in Nibley's defense at general conferences, and government eventually drops charges.

14 June, Apostle Reed Smoot turns down offer to be U.S. Secretary of Treasury in President Warren G. Harding's cabinet: "I would prefer to remain in the Senate."

1921

17 Mar., John A. Widtsoe is ordained apostle, first general authority to have Ph.D. degree from non-U.S. school (in chemistry from University of Goettigen, Germany).

Apr., Heber J. Grant telegrams Senator Reed Smoot: "The First Presidency appreciate highly what Mr. [William H.] Hays has done in suppressing the ["Fatty"] Arbuckle and other improper films." Hays Commission becomes famous as Hollywood's self-censorship mechanism.

7 Apr., First Presidency and Quorum of Twelve decide to return to pre-1912 "old form of ordaining" to office without first conferring priesthood.

15 Apr., Apostle George F. Richards formulates loyalty oath for Salt Lake temple workers to detect if they are promoting new plural marriages.

29 July, several apostles "read the revelations which do not appear in the present edition of the Doctrine & Covenants, about twenty in number with the view of recommending to the First Presidency certain of them to be included in the edition we are just now preparing." This refers to uncanonized revelations of Joseph Smith as published in official *History of the Church*, not to uncanonized revelations cited in this chronology.

8 Aug., to rescue church's Utah-Idaho Sugar Company, Heber J. Grant agrees to mortgage Social Hall, Vermont, and Deseret News buildings. However, Counselor Anthony W. Ivins persuades Grant not to mortgage Church Office Building. This is undoubtedly origin of rumor that Grant mortgages Salt Lake Temple Square, including temple.

20 Sept., Apostle Reed Smoot receives letter from president of Fox Films, agreeing to stop

exhibiting movie *Riders of the Purple Sage*, after First Presidency condemned film on 24 Aug. Studio estimates its loss at $300,000 for withdrawing this and *The Rainbow Trail*, which LDS leaders also regard as anti-Mormon. Studio re-edits *Riders*, which Apostle Smoot reviews and approves on 15 Feb. 1925.

1922

4 Jan., from 10 a.m. to 6 p.m., Brigham H. Roberts presents detailed summary of textual and historical problems in *Book of Mormon* to combined meeting of First Presidency, apostles, and Seventy's presidents. He recommends that these problems should be researched and publicly discussed.

9 Feb., Zion's Securities Corporation, to own and manage church real estate properties

6 May, Heber J. Grant speaks first words on Utah's pioneer radio station KZN. His closing statement: "I bear witness to all mankind that Joseph Smith was a prophet of the true and living God." After church buys controlling interest on 21 Apr. 1925, station call sign becomes KSL on 24 June. Still in operation.

9 June, for first time annual conference of LDS youth organizations in Salt Lake City has large scale dancing (at Saltair resort pavilion). Saltair is destroyed by fire three years later, but "all-church dance festival" continues annually in Salt Lake City for fifty years. Regional dance festivals also occur in large Mormon population centers like southern California where 13,000 dancers perform for audience of 100,000 in 1985.

2 Oct., George Sutherland is first U.S. Supreme Court justice of Mormon origins. Raised in LDS church and graduate of Brigham Young Academy in 1881, Sutherland defines himself as non-Mormon long before his election as U.S. Senator in 1905.

1 Nov., day after Heber J. Grant joins in public appeal for election of man as county sheriff, First Presidency issues statement that church feels "free to use its influence in the promotion of good legislation, honest administration of government and matters calculated to benefit the state and its people."

14 Dec., First Presidency and Quorum of Twelve decide to end performance of baptisms for health and renewal of covenants. Official announcement is on 18 Jan. 1923.

1923

17 May, First Presidency and Twelve agree to alter temple undergarment worn outside temple: "buttons instead of strings; no collar; sleeves above the elbow and few inches below the knee and a change in the crotch so as to cover the same." Mormons regard this as dramatic change from endowment garment introduced by Joseph Smith. Few realize that traditional Utah "garment" is based on "Union suit" of last half of nineteenth century, while earlier garment worn under clothing at Nauvoo was based on legless "shirt" or two-piece undergarment current in America from late-eighteenth century to 1840s.

26 Aug., Heber J. Grant dedicates temple in Cardston, Alberta, Canada.

26 Nov., Corporation of the President, successor of Trustee-in-Trust as center of church financial operations.

1924

19 Feb., First Presidency tells Apostle James E. Talmage that church does not want to instigate criminal prosecution of new polygamists but would be happy to see them jailed.

3 Oct., first radio broadcast of general conference on church-owned radio station.

1925

15 Jan., excommunication of Lorin C. Woolley for "pernicious lying," rather than for any specific activities as Fundamentalist leader.

21 Jan., Grand Lodge of Utah officially prohibits Mormons from membership in any of its Masonic lodges and provides for expulsion of any Mormons who are current members of any Utah lodge. Utah is only state with formal Masonic restriction against religious group or denomination. Some Mormons (primarily converts) affiliate or preside in Masonic lodges outside Utah after 1925.

4 Mar., first missionaries enter "Church Missionary Home and Preparatory Training School" in Salt Lake City for week of instruction prior to departing for their mission assignments. This week-long instruction continues until greatly expanded in 1978.

4 Apr., Heber J. Grant warns general priesthood meeting against Ku Klux Klan, and remarks: "It is beyond my comprehension how people holding the priesthood will want to associate themselves with the Ku Klux Klan or any other [similar] organization."

22 May, *Deseret News* editorializes in favor of new Utah law which legalizes horse racing and pari-mutuel betting. Legislature has appointed Brigham F. Grant as chair of Racing Commission. He is manager of *Deseret News* and brother of church president.

17 Sept., Heber J. Grant writes: "Had I had any knowledge of what is known as the Pari betting system I never would have consented to go to the races the opening day. . . . The racing that is now being conducted is licensed gambling under a state law. The law was passed during my absence from the city and I regret exceedingly that it ever got on the statute books, and I am humiliated to think that I attended the races the first day." Four days later First Presidency letter states: "The Church has been and now is unalterably opposed to gambling in any form whatever."

7 Oct., Spencer Adams plays in baseball's World Series for Washington Senators (again in 1926, New York Yankees). First Mormon on major league team of any sport (1923, Pittsburgh Pirates), Adams is only LDS player to participate in consecutive World Series.

9 Nov., Apostle Richard R. Lyman upon his own authority enters plural marriage by mutual covenant. He is almost fifty-five years old, and she is fifty-three. This is first plural marriage of current general authority since 1905.

17 Nov., "Professor [Andrew] Neff, a graduate of the California University, desired to have free access to the original documents in the Historian's office as he was writing a history of Utah." First Presidency rules that "under proper supervision, we had no objections." Although Neff is LDS, this is first occasion in which "outside" scholar and historian has "free access" to manuscripts of LDS archives. Such access remains infrequent and exceptional until appointment of Apostle Howard W. Hunter as church historian in 1970.

1926

10 Sept., Heber J. Grant and his wife Augusta act as proxies for vicarious endowment of Warren G. Harding and wife and for their proxy sealing. Although Apostle Wilford Woodruff was proxy for baptism of deceased U.S. presidents in 1877, Grant is apparently first church president to act as proxy for deceased U.S. president. On 29 Sept. Grant and Apostle Reed Smoot are also proxies for vicarious endowments of Ulysses S. Grant and Theodore Roosevelt. Grant and Harding are known as heavy drinkers and smokers, while Harding's White House mistress has already disclosed their affair.

14 Sept., First Presidency reaffirms "that temple ordinances could not be performed for people who had any Negro blood in their veins."

3 Oct., Counselor Anthony W. Ivins tells conference that measurements of Great Pyramid of Giza foretell LDS church in 1830, start of "Great War" in 1914, and war's end in 1918.

1927

15 Feb., Apostle George F. Richards notifies temples that it is decision of First Presidency and Quorum of Twelve to immediately omit from prayer circles "all reference to avenging the blood of the Prophets. Omit from the ordinance and lecture all reference to retribution." Letter also instructs to "omit the kissing" at end of proxy sealings.

11 Aug., Heber J. Grant says, "There was no other people in the world that has as kindly a feeling toward the Jews as do the Latter-day Saints, as we believe in the final destiny of the Jew." This repeats similar statement to general conference of Apr. 1921. Among Jewish candidates elected by primarily Mormon voters during this period of national anti-Semitism are Simon Bamberger (Utah's governor, 1917-21), Louis Marcus (Salt Lake City mayor, 1931-35), and Herbert M. Schiller (district judge, 1933-39).

23 Oct., Heber J. Grant dedicates temple in Mesa, Arizona.

19 Nov., Harold A. Lafount is appointed chair of Federal Radio Commission, confirmed by U.S. Senate in March 1928, serving to 1935. LDS appointments of similar rank in U.S. government are Edgar B. Brossard (U.S. Tariff Commission, 1930-30), Marriner S. Eccles (Federal Reserve Board, 1936-48), Franklin D. Richards (Federal Housing Administration, 1947-52), Rosel H. Hyde (Federal Communications Commission, 1948, 1953-54), James K. Knudson (Defense Transport Administration, 1950-58), Ellis L. Armstrong (Public Roads Commission, 1958-61), Sterling M. McMurrin (Education Commissioner, 1961-62), Kenneth A. Randall (Federal Deposit Insurance Corp., 1965-70), Rosel H. Hyde (Federal Communications Commission, 1966-69), H. Rex Lee (Federal Communications Commission, 1969-74), Eugene A. Gulledge (Federal Housing Administration, 1969-73), Ellis L. Armstrong (Reclamation Commission, 1969-73), James C. Fletcher (National Aeronautics and Space Administration, 1971-89), Terrel H. Bell (Education Commissioner, 1974-76).

1928

12 Jan., Heber J. Grant comments about lawsuit by native Hawaiians "against the Church having the right to deed its beach property, which it recently sold for something over a quarter of a million dollars, they claiming that the property really belonged to the natives. Inasmuch as the natives never paid for it I do not know whether they can win out, but they have won in the first court in which the case came up."

19-20 Jan., Frederick M. Smith, RLDS president, supervises disinterment of his martyred grandfather and granduncle, Joseph and Hyrum Smith, from coffinless burial place kept secret since 1844. They are reburied in coffins, one on each side of Emma Hale Smith Bidamon, next to Mansion House in Nauvoo.

6 Feb., First Presidency approves $50,000 purchase of Hill Cumorah and farms, Palmyra, N.Y.

30 July, death of ex-governor John C. Cutler from self-inflicted gunshot. He declined First Presidency's call in 1887 to become counselor in Presiding Bishopric. Bishopric's second counselor now describes Cutler as "one of the Church Officers," apparently because he has been auditor of general church funds. Utah's chief executive from 1905 to 1909, Cutler is only Utah governor to commit suicide.

1929

28 Mar., First Presidency and Twelve decide to disband private prayer circle organizations which meet weekly or monthly in temples. Until 1978 local stakes continue to have prayer circle meetings in temples or in special rooms of stake meeting houses.

14 May, first verified date of Lorin C. Woolley's ordination of his priesthood "Council of Friends," from which 90 percent of Mormon Fundamentalists derive authority to continue their "priesthood work." He claims he is last survivor of "Council of Friends" ordained by John Taylor on 27 Sept. 1886 to keep plural marriage alive. On 22 Sept. 1929 Woolley signs detailed account of circumstances surrounding 1886 revelation.

15 July, first network broadcast on radio by Mormon Tabernacle Choir.

14 Aug., Elder Yeates of Church of Christ, Temple Lot, asks Heber J. Grant for permission to solicit donations for construction of temple at Independence, Missouri. President Grant declines "to assist in erecting a temple for a church with which we have no connection whatever."

22 Sept., senior Seventy's president and assistant church historian Brigham H. Roberts tells congregation in Salt Lake Tabernacle that "the Latter-day Saints are conscious of receding from that zenith [of early Mormonism] in that they are no longer flooded with revelation." On 3 Oct. combined meeting of First Presidency, Quorum of Twelve, and Seventy's presidents condemns his statement. He apologizes to them.

24 Sept., Heber J. Grant writes: "I am free to confess that I am disappointed with the Yosemite valley. It seems only about one-half as grand as the American Fork canyon" of Utah.

18 Oct., First Presidency letter urges European Mormons not to emigrate to United States.

1930

6 Apr., "The Message of the Ages" performance in Salt Lake Tabernacle as first historical pageant of LDS church. It involves 1,500 persons. On 24 July "Footprints on the Sands of Time" is first pageant at Hill Cumorah, near Palmyra, New York. Since July 1937 official "Cumorah Pageant" occurs annually. Renamed "America's Witness for Christ," pageant attracts 100,000 people at its fiftieth anniversary in 1987. Similar LDS pageants develop at other sites from Calgary, Canada, to Manti, Utah, to Auckland, New Zealand.

17 May, International Hygiene Exposition at Dresden, Germany, includes LDS exhibit on Word of Wisdom. This is church's first formal participation in national or international exposition. In 1933, church has exhibit which includes sculptures by Avard Fairbanks in Hall of Religion at Century of Progress Exposition in Chicago. In 1935 church has its first exhibit building at California-Pacific International Exposition in San Diego.

18 June, President Heber J. Grant writes that he has no objection to LDS woman receiving temple recommend, despite her self-inflicted abortion three years ago.

16 Aug., Heber J. Grant remarks that Apostle George Albert Smith "is getting very nervous. We don't want him to have another breakdown such as he had years ago, almost costing him his life." Apostle Smith doesn't begin describing his symptoms until Jan. 1932, and year later writes: "My nerves are nearly gone but am holding on the best I know how." Symptoms gradually subside and do not resume until he is church president.

4 Sept., first counselor Anthony W. Ivins computes that church lost $6 million in stock investments and $900,000 in loans and business transactions with Presiding Bishop Charles W. Nibley before his appointment as second counselor in First Presidency in 1925.

3 Oct., J. Reuben Clark is first Mormon to serve as U.S. Ambassador (Mexico). U.S. government appoints other Mormons as ambassadors: Cavendish W. Cannon (Yugoslavia in 1947, Syria in 1950, Portugal in 1952, Greece in 1953, Morocco in 1956), David S. King (Malagasy in 1967, Mauritius in 1968), David M. Kennedy (ambassador-at-large and ambassador to NATO in 1971), Mark Evans Austad (Finland in 1975, Norway in 1980), Keith Foote Nyborg (Finland in 1981), Franklin S. Forsberg (Sweden in 1981), Gregory J. Newell (Sweden in 1985), Jon Huntsman, Jr. (Singapore in 1992).

1931

13 Jan., Deseret Club is organized at UCLA as church's first social organization for LDS college students outside Utah. Current organization is LDS Students Association (LDSSA) for students at every non-church college and university.

4 Apr., Heber J. Grant announces that church will give whatever assistance it can to aid criminal prosecution of polygamists.

7 Apr., First Presidency instructs Apostle Joseph Fielding Smith and Seventy's president B. H. Roberts: "The subject of Pre-Adamites [is] not to be discussed in public by the brethren either for or against the theory, as the Church has not declared itself and its attitude on the question."

23 May, *Deseret News* "*Church Section*" article, "Bishop Released After 31 Years," regarding Joseph C. Cowley.

4 July, *Church Section* article, "Without Purse or Scrip In the Argentine Mission."

7 Nov., *Church Section* report that Church Historian Joseph Fielding Smith, "while rummaging through the manuscripts in the vault," has "discovered" manuscript of Joseph Smith's 1832 prophecy on civil war.

1932

19 Mar., *Deseret News* reports that Dr. Edgar B. Brossard, Congressman Don B. Colton, and mission president James H. Moyle "represented the Church of Jesus Christ of Latter-day Saints at the National Conference of Catholics, Jews, and Protestants" at Washing-

ton, D.C., 7-9 March. *Church Section* article, "Church Extends New Correlation Project To All Priesthood Quorums, Auxiliaries."

2 Apr., Heber J. Grant launches campaign against use of tobacco as part of his emphasis on observing Word of Wisdom by total abstinence from alcohol, tobacco, tea, and coffee.

5 May, Apostle Stephen L Richards tells First Presidency and Quorum of Twelve that he will resign as apostle rather than apologize for his general conference talk which says church is putting too much emphasis on Word of Wisdom. He confesses his error to Heber J. Grant on 26 May and retains his position.

27 July, Heber J. Grant writes: "It makes one's heart ache to see so many people who are willing to work and cannot find positions." Great Depression hits Utah particularly hard because its agricultural economy has also experienced local depression during national "Roaring Twenties." In some urban stakes, 60 percent of previously employed Mormons are without jobs in 1932.

29 July, death of George H. Brimhall from self-inflicted gunshot. He served as BYU president from 1904 to 1921 and is only BYU president to commit suicide.

30 Aug., B. H. Roberts, senior Seventy's president and assistant church historian, writes complaint about censorship. Heber J. Grant requires him to remove from forthcoming volume of *History of the Church* the statement of Brigham Young that Seventies are ordained apostles. "I desire, however, to take this occasion of disclaiming any responsibility for the mutilating of that very important part of President Young's Manuscript," Roberts writes, "and also to say, that while you had the physical power of eliminating that passage from the History, I do not believe you had any moral right to do so."

18 Sept., church's Adult Aaronic Priesthood program begins as local innovation in Salt Lake 28th Ward. It becomes churchwide program next year.

25 Sept., *New York Times* reports that David Abbott ("Ab") Jenkins has set land-speed record during twenty-four hour period, one of many world records in his "Mormon Meteor" cars. He single-handedly turns Utah's Bonneville Salt Flats into national speedway.

8 Nov., Utah Mormons overwhelming vote for Democrat Franklin D. Roosevelt as U.S. president and for all other New Deal candidates. Defeated after nearly thirty years in U.S. Senate, Apostle Reed Smoot is resentful that Heber J. Grant decided not to ask Mormons at October conference to reelect him. He never forgives Democratic counselor Anthony W. Ivins for persuading Grant against official endorsement.

1933

22 Mar., Quorum of Twelve unanimously recommends Eldred G. Smith as new Patriarch to Church. Since 1932, Heber J. Grant has told apostles he wants his son-in-law Willard R. Smith as new patriarch, but he expects them to nominate him. Otherwise "people would say he had set aside Hyrum G. Smith's son in order to give position to his own son-in-law." President Grant refuses to accept Twelve's unanimous recommendation of Hyrum G.'s son in 1933, and stand-off leaves office vacant for another nine years. Excluding patrilineal office of Church Patriarch, twenty-nine sons of general authorities are appointed during first century of Mormon hierarchy. This accounts for 23.6 percent of total appointments. Only eight sons of former general authorities are appointed as general authorities in sixty-four years since 1932: one in 1938, two in 1941, one in 1942, one in 1945, one in 1969, one in 1975, and one in 1996.

6 Apr., J. Reuben Clark, Jr. is sustained as second counselor in First Presidency. As first LDS president since Brigham Young to ask non-general authority to serve as Presidency counselor, Heber J. Grant kept position vacant for sixteen months to allow Clark to complete his service as Ambassador to Mexico. Clark is first general authority who has previously served U.S. government in high office. He is also first member of Presidency with post-graduate degree (from Columbia) and is ordained high priest today.

3 June, *Church Section* reports that, "after years of effort," Mormons have equal rights with

other religions in applying to be military chaplains. This is decision of recently appointed Secretary of War George H. Dern, non-Mormon and former governor of Utah.

7 June, Heber J. Grant tells BYU's graduating class: "If every other state in the Union repeals the Eighteenth Amendment, I hope Utah is the one bright star that remains."

17 June, First Presidency issues its most comprehensive and legalistic statement against post-Manifesto plural marriage and specifically denies legitimacy of claims that John Taylor had 1886 revelation on plural marriage. This statement causes final break between church and its Fundamentalists, who soon become true schismatics.

18 June, Nazi Party newspaper in Berlin publishes "Juden und Mormonen," which criticizes Germans for belonging to LDS church which has "always been very friendly with Jews."

22 June, First Presidency and apostles decide that "the Church as an organization could not take part in the campaign for the repeal of the 18th Amendment since this [is] a partisan political question. It [is] hoped however that all L.D.S. would vote against repeal [of national Prohibition]." Thirty-five years later, LDS hierarchy reverses this decision and participates actively in campaign against liquor-by-the-drink in Utah as "moral issue."

30 July, legal transfer of Gila Junior College from LDS-church ownership to Graham County, Arizona, and E. Edgar Fuller begins service as first LDS president of secular college outside intermountain states. Other Mormons who serve as presidents of junior colleges and colleges outside intermountain states are Monroe H. Clark and William H. Harkness (Gila College, 1940, 1944), Basil Hyrum Peterson (Orange Coast College, Costa Mesa, CA, 1947), Howard S. McDonald (Los Angeles State College, 1949), E. DeAlton Partridge (Monclair State College, NJ, 1951), John T. Wahlquist (San Jose State College, CA, 1952), Lowell F. Barker (Antelope Valley College, Lancaster, CA, 1957), Herman J. Sheffield (San Bernardino Valley College, CA, 1958), Don A. Orton (Lesley College, Cambridge, MA, 1960), Leonard W. Rice (Oregon College of Education, 1962), Dean A. Curtis (Eastern Arizona Junior College, 1965), Burns L. Finlinson (Bakersfield College, CA, 1968), George P. Lee (College of Ganado, Navajo Reservation, 1973), Wayne M. McGrath and Gherald L. Hoopes, Jr. (Eastern Arizona College, 1976, 1984), Harold Heiner (Whatcom Community College, Bellingham, WA, 1984), Clyde B. Jensen (Oklahoma College of Osteopathic Medicine, 1987), Donald P. Kern (Palmer College of Chiropractic, Davenport, IA, 1988), Reed B. Phillips (Los Angeles College of Chiropractic, 1991), James Sloan Allen (Julliard School, New York City, 1992), L. Jackson Newell (Deep Springs College, CA, 1995), Kim B. Clark (Harvard Business School, 1995), David Ferrel (Southern Virginia College, 1996).

16 Sept., *Church Section* full-page article, "The Problem of Isaiah in the Book of Mormon" by Sidney B. Sperry and H. Grant Vest. This is example of LDS leadership's delayed acceptance of B.H. Roberts's recommendation decade earlier to openly confront textual problems in Mormon scriptures. Roberts dies eleven days after this article. On 30 Sept. *Church Section* prints "The Synoptic Problem in Its Relation To Modern Revelation," and "The Johannine Problem In Its Relation To Modern Revelation" on 7 Oct.

26 Oct., at temple council meeting his counselors and Twelve persuade Heber J. Grant not to distribute his Apr. and Oct. conference talks against repeal of national Prohibition. On 7 Nov. Utah's voters elect anti-Prohibition candidates who time their convention on 5 Dec. to make Utah the final state necessary to end Prohibition.

9 Dec., *Church Section* article "Mormonism in The New Germany," enthusiastically emphasizes parallels "between the [LDS] Church and some of the ideas and policies of the National Socialists." First, Nazis have introduced "Fast Sunday." Second, "it is a very well known fact that Hitler observes a form of living which 'Mormons' term the 'Word of Wisdom.'" Finally, "due to the importance given to the racial question [by Nazis], and the almost necessity of proving that one's grandmother was not a Jewess," there no longer is resistance against genealogical research by German Mormons who "now have received letters of encouragement complimenting them for their patriotism."

1934

6 Jan., Leah D. Widtsoe's article "Priesthood and Womanhood" in *Church Section* includes following questions: "5. If a boy of twelve years has this gift [of priesthood ordination] bestowed upon him while his sister has not, does it not tend to make him grow up with a feeling that he is literally a 'lord of creation,' while his sister belongs to 'the common herd?' 6. Does not this discrimination make men more arrogant in their attitude toward women? Do they not necessarily feel themselves the superior and dominant sex?" Perhaps unintentionally, the stridency of her questions outweighs article's effort to deny or downplay gender discrimination in LDS church.

28 Apr., *Church Section* report that general authorities have allowed king of England's official representative to tour temple in Canada from baptistery to celestial room.

7 July, *Church Section* article "The Catawba Indians—A Mormon Tribe" notes that 95 percent of this South Carolina tribe converted after first contact with LDS missionaries fifty-one years earlier. Tribe's chief Samuel Blue is also president of Catawba branch.

4 Sept., Heber J. Grant gives "little or no encouragement" for proposal that LDS church join World Fellowship of Faith.

10 Oct., First Presidency and newly appointed apostle Alonzo A. Hinckley agree that Heber J. Grant should ask Los Angeles stake president Leo J. Muir to "stop working for [Upton] Sinclair," Socialist Party candidate for California governor. Grant publicly opposes Sinclair's election.

27 Nov., gangster George ("Baby Face") Nelson kills Samuel P. Cowley, special agent with recently formed Federal Bureau of Investigation. Cowley, first Mormon FBI agent, is son of former apostle, Matthias F. Cowley. Samuel Cowley helps track down gangster John Dillinger during summer, and is briefly (wrongly) credited with killing Dillinger. Another Mormon FBI agent, J. Robert Porter, is killed in 1979.

9 Dec., New York Stake is first stake east of inter-mountain states since termination of St. Louis Stake in 1858.

1935

14 Mar., Utah makes unlawful cohabitation a felony. Even federal anti-polygamy crusade of 1880s did not do this. With encouragement of First Presidency, stake president Hugh B. Brown writes this bill and Mormon legislators pass it.

31 May, Dr. George W. Middleton and Heber Sears ask "the opinion of the Church regarding sterilization of criminals, incompetents, etc." Heber J. Grant replies that "the Church had taken no stand whatever on this matter up to date."

30 June, first stake outside North America (in Laie, Oahu, Hawaii), as fulfillment of founding prophet's instructions on 8 Apr. 1844 to organize stakes wherever there are sufficient numbers of Mormons.

7 Sept., first excommunication of many Mormon Fundamentalists who refuse to sign loyalty oath that, among other things, denies "any intimation that any one of the Presidency or Apostles of the church is living a double life." Later these excommunicants learn of Apostle Richard R. Lyman's polygamous "double life" at this time.

14 Oct., John Horne Blackmore is elected to Canada's Parliament, serving in House of Commons until 1958. Other non-U.S. Mormons who serve in their nation's parliament are Harry Percival Vette (Tonga, 1940s), Solon E. Low (Canada, 1945), James Gladstone (Canada, 1958), Iofipo R. Kuresa (Samoa, 1970), Manuera Benjamin Riwai-Couch (New Zealand, 1975), Terry Rooney (England, 1990), Moroni Bing Torgan (Brazil, 1991).

1936

25 Jan., *Church Section* photograph of LDS basketball team in Germany giving "Sieg Heil" salute of Nazi Party.

3 Apr., First Presidency restores full church and priesthood blessings to Matthias F. Cowley. He unsuccessfully asked for this since 1926. *Deseret News* publishes announcement.

6 Apr., First Presidency's message is broadcast to European Mormons by shortwave radio.

7 Apr., First Presidency announces Church Security Plan, renamed Church Welfare Program in 1938. This began four years earlier as local innovation by stake president Harold B. Lee in Salt Lake Pioneer Stake.

21 May, Seventy's president Levi Edgar Young represents church at organization of Utah chapter of National Conference of Christians and Jews. He becomes its president in 1937. In 1960s George W. Romney is national director of organization, which gives him its Charles Evans Hughes Gold Medal in 1965.

3 July, First Presidency statement against Communism and Communist Party (which is legal in United States at this time and has candidates in Utah elections).

18 July, *Church Section* photograph of LDS youth conference in Germany with Apostle Joseph F. Merrill in front of Swastika banner of Nazi Party. This is intentional association of visual symbols, since 7 Aug. 1937 issue also prints photograph of church president Heber J. Grant seated in front of Swastika banner at LDS meeting in Frankfurt.

20 July, chief of Salt Lake City's detectives begins sending to First Presidency reports of surveillance and infiltration of Communist Party in Utah.

22 July, first counselor J. Reuben Clark recommends that Communist candidate for U.S. president be denied use of Salt Lake Tabernacle for speech. Also recommends to "confidentially" advise Utah's governor to have Mormon members of American Legion armed with "picks and ax-handles" to attend Communist Party's rally in Liberty Park.

31 Oct., First Presidency publishes unsigned editorial in *Deseret News*, which argues against re-election of Democratic president Franklin D. Roosevelt. Editorial, written by J. Reuben Clark, accuses F.D.R. of unconstitutional and Communist activities. In response one thousand Mormons angrily cancel their subscriptions to *News*. Three days later, 69.3 percent of Utah's voters help re-elect Roosevelt. Utah's electorate re-elects F.D.R. again (1940, 1944), despite First Presidency's opposition.

1937

7 Jan., N. Eldon Tanner is first active Mormon to serve non-U.S. government in position equivalent to U.S. Cabinet. He serves as Minister of Lands and Mines in government of Canada's Premier until 1952. Next Mormons of ministerial rank are Manuera Benjamin Riwai-Couch of New Zealand (for Maori relations and also Postmaster General) in 1978 and Baitika Toum of Kiribati in 1983.

8 Feb., Apostle George F. Richards and Seventy's president Antoine R. Ivins begin seven days of meetings with disaffected LDS Mexicans who demand ethnic Mexican mission president. These nationalist Mexican Mormons hold first meeting of their "Third Convention" on 26 Apr. 1936. After failure of this general authority effort at reconciliation, church leaders on 6 May begin excommunicating dissidents. Third Conventionists foster successful schismatic movement until 1946, when visit of LDS president George Albert Smith to Mexico begins process of reconciliation. Third Convention is first schismatic LDS movement based primarily on ethnicity and national pride.

13 Feb., *Church Section* photograph of LDS missionaries in Tahiti, with all males wearing white suit-and-pants, the custom in Tahiti. Issues of 23 July and 30 July 1938 have similar photographs of missionaries and their mission president in Tonga and Samoa.

13 Mar., *Church Section* article "Introducing The Home Evening," as indication of inability of headquarters for two decades to persuade LDS members to adopt this practice.

26 Aug., death of Apostle Joseph Fielding Smith's wife after four years of acute depression and emotional illness. Ethel Reynolds Smith spent much of that time in Utah State Hospital for the Insane, where her father (a general authority) had also been confined.

18 Sept., *Church Section* full-page article "The Eleusinian Mysteries," which continues as another full-page article on 25 Sept. This is 100 years since LDS periodical at church headquarters first described Eleusinian Mysteries. Through 23 Oct. there are weekly

full-page discussions of "The Mysteries of Bacchus" in two parts, "Orphic Reincarnation," and finally "The Mysteries Of The Great Mother."

1938

5 Jan., Charles E. Bidamon notarizes statement that he has sold [for $50] to collector Wilford C. Wood, Joseph Smith's "silver piece" inscribed "Confirmo O Deus Potentissimus" and that his step-mother frequently said this medallion belonged to Smith. Comparison of this artifact with illustrations for Francis Barrett's 1801 *The Magus* verifies that this is Jupiter talisman inscribed according to instructions in Barrett's book.

6 Aug., first letter to First Presidency from Nigerian S. G. Bada, Baptist minister who for next year requests church publications and information. He is interested in Mormonism because in other Christian churches Nigerian polygamists "are not to be regarded as full members at all." First Presidency politely informs him of church's current ban on polygamy and sends him publications. When he announces he has resigned his pastorate and desires LDS baptism and ordination, First Presidency again sends him publications but does not inform him of church's refusal to ordain black Africans to priesthood.

14 Aug., first Deseret Industries store opens with its dual purposes of providing low-cost used items as well as employment for disabled and elderly persons. Orson H. Hewlett patterns this after Goodwill Industries.

6 Sept., First Presidency appoints coordinator of church's first anti-polygamy surveillance team which obtains information on Mormon Fundamentalists and turns it over to excommunication courts and to law enforcement agencies. Surveillance coordinator reports to first counselor J. Reuben Clark.

24 Sept., *Church Section* article "Are Men of Earth Gods In Embryo?"

8 Nov., Culbert L. Olson is elected California's governor, first Mormon governor outside state of Utah. Other governors with Mormon background: Idaho's Arnold Williams (1945-47), California's Goodwin J. Knight (1953-59), American Samoa's H. Rex Lee (1961-67), Michigan's George W. Romney (1963-69), Idaho's John V. Evans (1977-87), and Arizona's Evan Mecham (1987-88). Knight does not claim Mormonism as politician, and in 1952 *Church News* retracts its statement that he is LDS governor. LDS Luis Alberto Ferrizo is elected to Uruguay's equivalent of governor (1990), and Jien-Nien Chen is elected as governor in Taiwan (1993).

9 Nov., Nazis in Germany begin *Kristallnacht* ("Night of Broken Glass") in which they pillage Jewish businesses, burn synagogues, and arrest thousands of Jews. Max Reschke, non-Jewish Mormon in Hannover, rescues some Jewish friends from armed guards and helps family escape to Switzerland. However, as example of polarization of German Mormons about "the Jewish question," one Hamburg branch president prohibits Jewish Mormons from attending LDS services, while another Hamburg branch welcomes these rejected Mormons, defies Gestapo (Nazi secret police), and gives religious encouragement to Jewish Mormon who refuses to wear yellow Star of David. Later imprisoned for hiding a Jew in his home, Reschke survives Nazi regime.

23 Nov., first Mormon victim of Nazi holocaust, Egon Engelbert Weiss in Vienna, Austria (recently annexed to Nazi Germany), writes desperate letters to eight returned missionaries in Utah and Idaho and to First Presidency: "Conditions here are terrible for us Jewish people." He asks if Presidency can make necessary affidavit to enable his family to escape to America, signing letter "your brother in the Gospel."

1939

22 Jan., Moroni Timbimboo is first Native American Indian ordained and set apart as bishop (Washakie Ward).

23 Jan., first counselor J. Reuben Clark confides to Brigham Young University's president that in 1938 church spent nearly $900,000 more than its revenues. As result Clark begins policy in 1939 of having fixed annual budget for all church expenditures to avoid deficit-spending. On 1 Apr. 1940 Clark informs meeting of all church auxiliary leaders

about the 1939 deficit, as well "a deficit of over $100,000, from the point of income and expenditures" in 1937. He also refers to this deficit-spending in general terms during his remarks to general conference in Apr. 1940.

27 Jan., counselors J. Reuben Clark and David O. McKay write to Jewish non-Mormon who appeals for First Presidency help to escape Nazi regime: "We have so many requests of this sort from various persons, including members of the Church, that we have found it necessary to ask to be excused from making the required guarantee." Letter suggests that he contact American Jewish organizations.

24 Apr., first counselor J. Reuben Clark requests U.S. Department of State to assist immigration of two Mormons: "She and her husband are Aryan natives and nationals of Switzerland." In contrast, Clark privately urges State Department not to help Jewish children to leave Nazi Germany if their parents are trying to send them to United States.

1 July, Nazi Gestapo arrests two American LDS missionaries in Czechoslovakia and put them and two other missionaries into prison. Not released until 23 Aug.

10 July, first counselor J. Reuben Clark "admonished President Grant that people were prone to say to him what people thought he wanted to hear."

21 July, First Presidency agrees to send no more missionaries to Germany due to danger of "having them thrown into concentration camps, with all the horrors that that entails."

18 Aug., First Presidency agrees to allow Southern woman (who looks Caucasian) to be endowed in Salt Lake temple despite fact that her membership record is marked "negro blood." Reason for their decision is that Apostle George F. Richards already gave her patriarchal blessing which declares her lineage as Ephraim through Joseph and Israel.

25 Aug., First Presidency cables mission presidents to have all missionaries leave France and Germany immediately. Mormon missionaries are safely in neutral countries when World War II begins week later with Nazi invasion of Poland and declaration of war by France and England. All missionaries cross Atlantic within three months.

16 Sept., at Salt Lake City's first exhibition of television, Heber J. Grant writes that since "they were not going to mention any names of the men connected with the invention, I decided not to refer to Mr. [Philo] Farnsworth. I did, however, refer to Harvey Fletcher in my brief talk, as one of the greatest scientists, so acknowledged, working in the laboratory of the great Bell Telephone System." Farnsworth and Fletcher are first Mormon inventors to receive national recognition since Jonathan Browning. Member of YM-MIA general board at LDS headquarters, Farnsworth develops stereophonic sound and television.

1940

29 Mar., First Presidency asks Apostle Joseph Fielding Smith to chair "Literature Censorship Committee authorized by the Quorum last Thursday."

5 Apr., in explaining financial decisions of First Presidency to general conference, first counselor J. Reuben Clark observes: "We are not infallible in our judgment, and we err, but our constant prayer is that the Lord will guide us in our decisions, and we are trying so to live that our minds will be open to His inspiration."

21 Apr., Captain William Losey is killed by bomb during Nazi invasion of Norway, first U.S. serviceman to die in World War II. A returned LDS missionary, he is military aide to U.S. ambassador. Despite his and other American deaths in Nazi war zone, United States remains officially neutral until Dec. 1941.

25 May, *Church Section* prints Mrs. Horace Eaton's 1881 account that the prophet's mother Lucy Mack Smith performed various forms of divination, including palmistry.

13 Aug., Heber J. Grant views Hollywood's *Brigham Young*. His reaction: "My eyes were full of tears of gratitude for the fine picture." Dean Jagger, in title role, joins LDS church in 1972.

16 Oct., Salt Lake City police department begins furnishing to First Presidency police surveillance information on suspected polygamists.

30 Oct., first counselor J. Reuben Clark persuades President Grant not to publish statement signed by all general authorities urging defeat of U.S. president Franklin D. Roosevelt's candidacy for third term.

1941

25 Jan., *Church Section* article "If Christ Came To Germany," with photograph of "prisoners in a German concentration camp."

9 Feb., Apostle Reed Smoot dies, and another apostle comments: "I knew he had been afflicted in his mind for some time." President Grant noted this on 13 Nov. 1938.

27 Feb., Leigh A. Harline receives two "Oscars" from the Academy of Motion Picture Arts and Sciences (music score of *Pinocchio* and best song, "When You Wish Upon a Star").

10 Mar., First Presidency orders Clayton Investment Company to get rid of its "whorehouses," no matter the financial loss, so that church-affiliated company can merge with church-owned Zion's Securities Corp. Ends fifty years of church's leases to brothels.

6 Apr., high priests as Assistants to the Twelve are new general authority position. This is also first general conference broadcast outside Utah (to Idaho and southern California).

8 June, first counselor J. Reuben Clark tells annual conference of youth and their leaders: "When I was a boy it was preached from the stand, and my father and my mother repeated the principle to me time and time again. They said, 'Reuben, we had rather bury you than to have you become unchaste.' And that is the law of this Church."

13 June, First Presidency letter against federal payments for not raising crops.

24 June, Counselor J. Reuben Clark advises Mormon "against your assuming as truth the most of the criticism you see leveled against Hitler and his regime in Germany. I visited Germany twice within the last half-dozen years. . . . Hitler is undoubtedly bad from our American point of view, but I think the Germans like him." Because of such statements, federal intelligence agencies investigate Clark in Utah as possible pro-Nazi subversive.

9 Aug., leader of National Reform Association tells annual meeting of Christian Citizenship Institute that LDS church president Heber J. Grant is "the most powerful political individual in America today" because "Grant patronizes presidents, makes bargains with great political parties, dictates the political policies of Utah and at least five surrounding states and wields effective political influence in at least five others." Grant tells the national press that the speaker should "purge himself of falsehood," and entire exchange appears in *Church Section* on 29 Nov.

26 Sept., First Presidency letter in favor of right to work without joining labor union.

7 Dec., Mervyn Bennion is first Mormon to die during U.S. military participation in World War II. As captain of battleship *West Virginia*, Bennion is killed on its bridge during Japanese attack on Pearl Harbor. He is son-in-law of first counselor J. Reuben Clark and receives posthumous Congressional Medal of Honor.

1942

8 Jan., among toasts offered at first party for all general authorities is Amy Brown Lyman's: "Even the apostles are human." This annual social is henceforth held Tuesday after April general conference. At 1946 social, Presiding Bishop LeGrand Richards and Seventy's president Milton R. Hunter perform comic skit in which these nearly bald general authorities wear outrageous-looking wigs.

26 Jan., first counselor J. Reuben Clark tells reporter for *Look* magazine: "Our divorces are piling up." Church Historian's Office in 1968 compiles divorce statistics since 1910 for temple marriages, "church civil" marriages, and "other civil" marriages. Although temple marriages have lowest divorce rate, in 1910 there was one "temple divorce" (cancellation of sealing) for every 66 temple marriages performed that year, 1:41 in 1915, 1:34 in 1920, 1:27 in 1925, 1:30 in 1930, 1:23 in 1935, 1:27 in 1939, 1:17 in 1945, 1:31 in 1950, 1:30 in 1955, 1:19 in 1960 and 1965. Last rate for temple divorce is almost ten times higher than Utah's civil divorce rate century earlier.

12 Mar., First Presidency letter bans foreign-language meetings in United States. Directed

particularly at German-speaking Mormons, this restriction ends thirty years later as conversion and immigration bring to U.S. congregations thousands of Europeans, Latin-Americans, and Asians who speak little or no English.

14 Mar., First Presidency orders bullet-proof glass for windows of its office to protect against air attack by Japanese.

6 Apr., First Presidency's most comprehensive statement on war, upholding patriotic service by Mormons in any country's military but condemning all national leaders who promote war. For first time, Sunday session of general conference is held in assembly room of Salt Lake temple where apostles pass the sacrament to assembled priesthood leaders. Policeman Ray Haight reports that "during the entire morning session an intense, white light flooded the First Presidency . . . and made President Grant's clothes to appear to be white."

May, Peter Vlam, LDS officer in Dutch navy, is imprisoned in Nazi camp in Poland where he preaches to fellow prisoners, seven of whom survive and convert to LDS church.

2 May, First Presidency requests custody of record of monogamous (1896-1907) and plural (1897-1904) marriages which Anthony W. Ivins performed by Presidency authority in Mexico. Now First Presidency has custody of marriage records of three residents of Juarez Stake who had Presidency authorization to perform post-1890 polygamous marriages in Mexico: Alexander F. Macdonald (1888-90, 1900-1903), George Teasdale (1891-96), and Ivins. However, First Presidency furnishes this information only to descendants of marriages performed by Ivins. Through Canadian apostle Hugh B. Brown, First Presidency later obtains custody of record of marriages performed in Canada by Charles O. Card and John A. Woolf.

5 Aug., First Presidency's financial secretary refers to German-born Horst Scharffs as President Heber J. Grant's bodyguard. Apparently this is first time since 1887 that hierarchy has bodyguards.

8 Aug., *Church Section* emphasizes use of handkerchiefs to heal people at great distances, with photograph of "the silk handkerchief blessed and sent by President Lorenzo Snow to Elder [Jacob Charles] Jensen" to heal him in 1899.

17 Aug., *SS Brigham Young* is launched as Liberty Ship for transporting troops, prisoners, and freight. Christened by Lucy Gates Bowen (his granddaughter) in Los Angeles Harbor. On 22 May 1943 *SS Joseph Smith* is launched. Former survives World War II, but latter sinks in heavy seas on 11 Jan. 1944.

8 Oct., general conference sustains Joseph F. Smith (b. 1899) as Patriarch to Church, ending ten-year vacancy.

27 Oct., Helmuth Huebener, age seventeen, is first Mormon the Gestapo executes (by beheading). He leads anti-Nazi resistance group involving two other German LDS teenagers who are sent to concentration camps. To protect other Mormons from Nazi reprisals, Hamburg branch president excommunicates Huebener shortly after his arrest. On 24 Jan. 1948 First Presidency orders following notation to appear on Huebener's membership record: "Excommunication done by mistake."

28 Nov., *Church Section* cover article "L.D.S. Japanese Aid U.S. Soldiers."

24 Dec., Heber J. Grant signs recommends for thirteen general authorities to receive second anointing ceremony. President Grant withdrew all second anointing recommend books from stake presidents in 1928 after Idaho Mormon told priesthood meeting about ordinance. From 1930 to 1942 Grant allows only eight such ordinances, compared with performance of 3,419 living second anointings from 1877 through 1893. This 1942 renewal occurs at strenuous urging of Apostle George F. Richards.

1943

9 Jan., *Church Section* lists non-U.S. rulers who have received *Book of Mormon* since Queen Victoria (1842), King Frederick VII of Denmark (1851), King Kalakaua and Queen Kapiolani of Hawaii (1877), Queen Emma of Holland (1890), King Oscar II of Sweden

(1897), Emperor Mutsuhito of Japan (1900), Empress Haruko of Japan (1909), Crown Prince Yoshihito (later Emperor) of Japan (1909), Queen Liliuokalani of Hawaii, King Albert and Queen Elizabeth of Belgium (1919), President Thomas G. Masaryk of Czechoslovakia (1930), President Jose F. Uriburu of Argentina (1931), President Eduard Benes of Czechoslovakia (1937), and President Getulio Vargas of Brazil (1940).

17 Feb., First Presidency agrees to comply with "request of F.B.I. for missionary information regarding towns and cities in Axis countries, by giving them lists of missionaries and permitting them (FBI) to interview them and get such information as they could. We were to make clear there was to be no espionage in Axis countries by our missionaries." Axis countries are Hitler's Nazi Germany, Mussolini's Fascist Italy, Tojo's Imperial Japan, and territories conquered by them.

7 Mar., establishment of Navaho-Zuni Mission, first mission in twentieth century directed only to Native Americans. This is original intent of 1830 effort to proselytize among Indians.

8 Apr., temple council of First Presidency, Quorum of Twelve, and Presiding Patriarch approves reorganization of administration of church tithing, budget, and expenditures.

12 Nov., excommunication of Apostle Richard R. Lyman for violating "Christian law of chastity," first excommunication of general authority appointed in twentieth century.

13 Nov., *Church Section* article features fifteen "Mormon soldiers of Japanese descent," three already fighting Nazis in Europe and the rest in Mississippi for training.

1944

8 Feb., war correspondent reports during invasion of Kwajalein by U.S. Marines that one LDS marine refuses medical attention until medics help his wounded LDS buddy. Then correspondent records that young man raises his right arm and says: "In the name of Jesus Christ and by virtue of the Holy Priesthood which I hold, I command you to remain alive until the necessary help can be obtained to secure the preservation of your life."

7 Mar., coordinated raid by FBI and local police to arrest polygamist men.

18 Mar., *Church Section* article "Boise Serviceman Writes From Jap Prison Camp." Similar headline on 20 Jan. 1945.

7 Apr., Counselor J. Reuben Clark preaches that "in that inspired document, the Constitution, the Lord prescribed the way, the procedure by which the inspired framework of that Constitution could be changed. Whenever the Constitution is amended in that way, it will be an amendment that the Lord will approve."

18 Apr., *New York Times* announcement of recital by Mormon pianist Grant Johannesen, first of forty such reports during next four decades.

1 May, Daniel DeLuce, war correspondent of Mormon parentage and heritage extending back to 1830s, receives Pulitzer Prize for international reporting. However, not until 1952 does self-acknowledged Mormon receive America's most prestigious publishing award. Two other Pulitzer recipients are non-LDS Utahns who often write about Mormons: Bernard Devoto in 1948 for *Across the Wide Missouri* (history) and Wallace Stegner in 1972 for *Angle of Repose* (fiction). In addition, Nobel Prize winner Haldor Laxness, non-Mormon, publishes novel *Paradise Reclaimed* in Iceland about LDS convert. Utah (specifically Spanish Fork) has largest number of Icelandic immigrants in United States.

16 Aug., First Presidency instructs its Hotel Utah to stop serving liquor.

30 Aug., First Presidency authorizes stake president and bishops to join "*as individuals* a civic organization whose purpose is to restrict and control negro settlement in his stake" (emphasis in original).

9 Sept., *Church Section* article "Primary Boys Make Quilts."

2 Oct., head of church's anti-polygamy surveillance testifies in court.

5 Oct., George E. Wahlen receives Congressional Medal of Honor from U.S. president Harry S Truman for service as Navy corpsman on Iwo Jima. Severely wounded on three

separate days during same week while treating wounded Marines, 19-year-old Wahlen refuses to obey direct orders to leave the injured and seek medical treatment himself.

16 Dec., *Church Section* article from New Orleans: "Negro Members of The Church Display Great Faith."

1945

15 Jan., death of local LDS leader Tevita Mapa, secretary to Tonga's Premier. Similarly respected, Ebenezer Theodore Joshua becomes St. Vincent's Prime Minister in 1969 during this Caribbean island's "associated state" decade prior to independence from Britain. Joshua later converts to Mormonism, and at his death, thousands of non-Mormon admirers attend his funeral at LDS meeting house where he is branch president.

13 Feb., "Saturation-bombing" of Dresden, Germany, non-military cultural target with no heavy industry and no bomb shelters, but with P.O.W. camp of Americans. Planned by England in revenge for similar Nazi raid on Coventry five years earlier, waves of British and U.S. bombers continue pounding Dresden throughout next day (Ash Wednesday) in order to create hurricane-like "firestorms." Inner city is completely incinerated, including LDS branch house which is "destroyed right down to the cellar," while air raid kills 250,000 people. Most are women and children refugees who double Dresden's population due to its being safe-haven during years of Allied bombings elsewhere. Survivor is Dorthea Speth, wife of Spencer J. Condie, current general authority.

17 Feb., *Church Section* article "Meager Report Indicates German Saints Carry On."

24 Feb., *Deseret News* "*Church News*" prints letter concerning LDS captain Denmark C. Jensen of Idaho during U.S. invasion of Philippines: "The next day—Christmas Day—Mark issued the same order [to his men], that they were not to kill any Japs they found but to send for him. During the course of the day another Jap was located with his rifle by his side, bathing his feet in a small mountain stream. They called Mark and unobserved he crept up on the Jap, took his rifle away from him and led his captive down to his waiting men." Captain Jensen explains that "it just didn't seem right to kill even a Jap on Christmas Eve and Christmas Day—the time we have set aside to commemorate the birth of our Lord and Savior."

21 Mar., first counselor J. Reuben Clark says that "one of the reasons why the so-called 'Fundamentalists' had made such inroads among our young people was because we had failed to teach them the truth."

6 Apr., Milton R. Hunter is sustained as first Ph.D. (history) in First Council of Seventy, also first general authority with doctorate in humanities/social sciences. Other general authorities with Ph.D. in humanities/social sciences are G. Homer Durham (appointed in 1977), Jeffrey R. Holland (1989), Spencer J. Condie (1989), Richard P. Lindsay (1989), Dennis B. Neuenschwander (1991), Jay E. Jensen (1992), Lowell D. Wood (1992), Merrill J. Bateman (1992), Bruce D. Porter (1995), Richard B. Wirthlin (1996).

21 Apr., *Church News* reports that due to ward's lack of deacon-age boys, bishop has called young girls (ages 12 to 14) to do work of deacons such as collecting fast offerings.

14 May, death of Heber J. Grant, who is also last surviving member of theocratic Council of Fifty. As his funeral procession passes Roman Catholic Cathedral of the Madeleine, its bells toll and assembled priests bow in respect.

21 May, conference sustains George Albert Smith as church president with J. Reuben Clark and David O. McKay as counselors. He is "set apart" (not ordained) by Apostle George F. Richards, who is also a patriarch. Smith is only unmarried man to become LDS church president and only one who has no marital companion during his entire presidency. He remains unmarried widower last fourteen years of his life.

June, *Improvement Era*, states: "When our leaders speak, the thinking has been done." This is the ward teacher's message to all members for month. To inquiring Unitarian minister George Albert Smith writes that "not a few members of the Church have been upset in their feelings, and General Authorities have been embarrassed" by above statement.

"Even to imply that members of the Church are not to do their own thinking is grossly to misrepresent the true ideal of the Church," he continues. However, church president's retraction reaches one non-Mormon, while original statement reaches entire LDS population without similar correction.

16 June, George Albert Smith rules against LDS meeting houses being used "for meetings to prevent Negroes from becoming neighbors."

11 Sept., *Deseret News* editorial praises "earnest, sincere, loyal conscientious objector[s]" as "better" than military men who praise weapons of mass destruction.

23 Sept., George Albert Smith dedicates temple at Idaho Falls, Idaho.

2 Oct., First Presidency decides to pay expenses of LDS conscientious objectors detained in camps by U.S. government during World War II.

6 Nov., temple endowment ceremony is presented for first time in non-English language (Spanish).

10 Nov., last listing of causes in weekly list of named excommunicants in *Church News*. Up to now most common reasons are apostasy and "violating the law of chastity."

27 Nov., Presiding Bishop LeGrand Richards coordinates continued surveillance of church-owned Belvedere Hotel and Temple Square Hotel to discover and stop "evil practices" of tenants. For financial reasons this does not extend to church's Hotel Utah.

29 Nov., first counselor J. Reuben Clark instructs stake president that First Presidency has no objection to church funerals for suicides, who can also be buried in temple clothing. Clark explains, "[W]e permitted it usually in suicide cases on the theory that no person in his right mind would commit suicide and as he was not in his right mind there was no crime involved." He adds, "I told him that the idea was to be as comforting to the family as possible, in cases of suicide the family had double grief."

1946

20 Jan., Council of Twelve recommends that all stake presidents and bishops engage in "a program of revival and motivation of the 'Home Evening' as a Churchwide project," citing previously unfulfilled instructions in this regard by First Presidency in 1915.

21 June, first shipment of Welfare Plan foodstuffs and essential commodities arrives in Geneva, Switzerland, for distribution to Mormons in war-devastated European cities. This aid totals eighty-five railroad freight cars. Eight months earlier First Presidency reestablished proselytizing missions in Europe.

28 June, First Presidency statement against compulsory military service ("conscription" or "the draft") during peace time. This is extensive version of Presidency's earlier views and of its efforts to persuade LDS congressmen to vote against peacetime draft.

7 July, almost two years after Americans dropped atomic bomb on Hiroshima, U.S. serviceman Boyd K. Packer performs first baptism of Japanese converts in Japan.

25 July, first counselor J. Reuben Clark speaks concerning embezzlement by local bishop: "The Church could not use its funds for such a means as proposed to save any embarrassment to the Church, and it could not and should not require the [local] brethren there to sacrifice unless their friendship for the [bishop's] family prompted them to do so on their own accord, and that he didn't worry about the resultant effect upon the Church if we did not attempt to cover up, but insisted upon justice."

27 July, Saturday, Brazilian Mormons in Sao Paulo celebrate Utah Pioneer Day.

23 Aug., First Presidency tells LDS judge to be cautious about sending LDS "subnormals" to be sterilized in facility at American Fork, Utah.

29 Aug., Apostle George F. Richards asks Alberta temple president to stop "Seances" there.

5 Oct., first counselor J. Reuben Clark's conference talk condemns United States for helping Britain kill 250,000 German civilians in two-day bombing of Dresden. "As the crowning savagery of the war we Americans wiped out hundreds of thousands" of Japanese civilians with two atomic bombs. "This fiendish butchery" by U.S. nuclear weapons

was "wholesale destruction of men, women, and children, and cripples." Still director of national pacifist organization, Clark continues to be focus of federal government's anti-subversive agencies because of his public statements against U.S. participation in World War II, against providing military aid to anti-Communist forces in civil wars of various countries, and against U.S. participation in anti-Soviet North Atlantic Treaty Organization (NATO).

6 Oct., public release of Joseph Fielding Smith (b. 1899) as Patriarch to Church due to "ill health" but actually due to discovery of his recent homosexual activity.

    Bruce R. McConkie is sustained to First Council of Seventy, first veteran of World War II to become general authority.

18 Nov., liberal justice William O. Douglas announces decision of U.S. Supreme Court which upholds conviction of six polygamist Fundamentalists for violating Mann "White Slavery" Act, for driving across Utah border with their plural wives. Congress originally passed Mann Act against interstate transportation of prostitutes. This is first U.S. Supreme Court decision about Mormon polygamy since 1890.

1947

8 Jan., *Deseret News* publishes John H. Koyle's repudiation of his former claims regarding "Dream Mine," in which he urges his followers and stockholders to "regard this mine as a business venture without any religious significance." Despite this statement, Koyle is soon excommunicated, due to pressure from Apostle Mark E. Petersen.

19 Jan., at organization of stake in Jacksonville, Florida, Apostle Charles A. Callis prophesies that temple will be constructed there. In 1994, temple is dedicated in Orlando, 144 miles from Jacksonville, but within original stake boundaries.

15 Mar., *Church News* reports that Charles Davidson, now full-time missionary, has received contract from International Business Machines (IBM) to purchase invention for $5 million, payable over several years. Before his mission Davidson attended Massachusetts Institute of Technology (MIT) on Westinghouse science scholarship.

22 Mar., last weekly list of excommunicated Mormons in *Church News*. Final list gives names in California, Florida, Maine, Massachusetts, Nevada, and Utah.

2 Apr., George Albert Smith's announcement (later described as "a revelation") that mission presidents are to have counselors. Apostle Spencer W. Kimball later says revelation's text exists but is not to be published.

6 Apr., Spencer W. Kimball tells general conference: "When the Indians resisted our encroachments, we called them 'murderous redskins' and continued our relentless aggression." He reminds his listeners that "we [continue to] become fat in the prosperity from the assets we took from them," and concludes that Mormons have religious obligation toward Native American Indians: "to guarantee that they have the education, culture, security, and all other advantages and luxuries that we enjoy."

10 Apr., Eldred G. Smith is ordained patriarch to the church, fourteen years after Quorum of Twelve recommended him. He is nuclear engineer for Manhattan Project at Oak Ridge, Tennessee which helped usher in atomic age at Hiroshima, Japan.

20 May, LDS president George Albert Smith offers official prayer for U.S. Senate, and *Congressional Record* publishes his invocation's full text. Exactly nineteen years later, 20 May 1966, first counselor Hugh B. Brown does likewise. In 1974 Apostle (later LDS president) Gordon B. Hinckley opens U.S. Senate with prayer.

21 July, *Time Magazine* features President George Albert Smith on its cover.

24 July, centennial of arrival of Mormon pioneers in Utah which is celebrated in special ceremonies outside United States by Austrian, Czech, Danish, Dutch, German, and Japanese Mormons according to reports in *Church News*.

29 July, Quorum of Twelve letter to general Relief Society presidency states that women should seek blessings of health from priesthood holders and not from other women.

This officially ends more than century of women's anointing and sealing blessings of health on other women and sometimes on men.

9 Oct., First Presidency and apostles decide to allow faithful African-American Mormons to receive patriarchal blessings, and Patriarch Eldred G. Smith blesses black couple.

1948

3 Jan., organization of LDS Film Council "to appraise motion pictures and decide upon their suitability for entertainment and educational purposes."

16 Apr., Apostle Mark E. Petersen asks for permission to instruct local leaders to begin excommunication trials for persons he suspects of having disloyal attitudes toward LDS church. First counselor J. Reuben Clark warns Petersen "to be careful about the insubordination or disloyalty question, because they ought to be permitted to think, you can't throw a man off for thinking."

10 May, state narcotics officer asks church officials to quietly surrender for destruction the "quantity of opium, an opium pipe, and some other trinkets" in LDS Bureau of Information on Temple Square. Seventy's president Richard L. Evans protests that these materials have been there "since time immemorial." First Presidency cooperates rather than face court order.

26 June, General Mark W. Clark presides at military memorial service at Garland, Utah, for four LDS brothers killed as servicemen during six-month period of World War II: Clyde, LeRoy, and twins Rolon and Rulon Borgstrom. American families are given small service-flag (with gold star in center) to display in window of home for son/daughter killed in war, and Borgstrom "Gold Star Mother" displays flag with four stars. Roman Catholic family suffers similar tragedy when five Sullivan brothers die on day their U.S. ship is torpedoed in World War II.

4 July, *Church News* refers to three significant developments in LDS missionary work. First, report of success of two missionaries "tracting without purse or scrip" in Texas-Louisiana Mission. This practice is newsworthy because it has become so rare and is later prohibited by LDS headquarters. Second, E. Hyde Dunn, age nineteen, has left for special mission in which he volunteers to be construction missionary in Tonga. His voluntarism inspires headquarters to adopt this as regular program for South Pacific. Third, report that missionary Richard L. Anderson's teaching "plan" is now in use by all missionaries of Northwestern States Mission. Fourteen-lesson "Anderson Plan" is soon adopted by many LDS missions as non-memorized outline for teaching investigators. Anderson later becomes distinguished professor of religion at BYU.

2 Nov., Reva Beck Bosone is elected as Democratic member of U.S. House of Representatives, first woman to be U.S. Representative from Utah. Raised as Mormon, she campaigns as non-LDS. Half a century later, Utah has still not elected a woman as U.S. senator, and only two more as U.S. Representatives: Karen Shepherd (1993-95) and Enid Greene Waldholz (1995-97).

11 Nov., Belle Smith Spafford, general president of Relief Society, is elected vice-president of National Council of Women. Subsequent LDS vice-presidents are Florence Smith Jacobson, formerly general president of LDS Young Women (1974) and Elaine Anderson Cannon, general president of Young Women (1982).

1949

20 Jan., President George Albert Smith begins week's stay in California Lutheran Hospital for his "tired nerves," which his diary first refers to at Oct. 1948 general conference. He is first LDS president with history of severe emotional illness and hospitalization. He does not recover from this episode until mid-May 1949, when he is able to be in First Presidency's office at least half day. Smith is absent from church headquarters 12 Jan.-27 Feb. 1950 to stay at Laguna Beach, California, "to rest my nerves." He returns there to recuperate again for ten days in March. Year later his nurse notes that church president

is "very confused, very nervous." Ten days before his death, nurse adds that George Albert Smith is "irrational at times."

5 Feb., first counselor J. Reuben Clark recommends anti-semitic *Protocols of the Elders of Zion* to Ernest L. Wilkinson, soon to be president of Brigham Young University. In Dec. 1957 Clark makes similar recommendation to Apostle Ezra Taft Benson, U.S. Secretary of Agriculture. This may be reason Benson organizes secret surveillance of employees (especially Jews) in U.S. Department of Agriculture.

25 Feb., in discussion of African-American segregation, second counselor David O. McKay says, "the South knows how to handle them and they do not have any trouble, and the colored people are better off down there."

15 Mar., thirty-one-year-old Harold Brown arrives in Buenos Aires as new president of Argentina Mission. He is former FBI agent with experience as U.S. Vice-Consul in Uruguay. Suspicious Argentine authorities arrest him temporarily on 9 Sept. This is beginning of strategic church assignments given to Mormons with training in U.S. intelligence and security services.

16 Mar., *Church News* reports that paraplegic convert Mrs. Luett J. Standliff has been baptized while strapped to stretcher in Salt Lake Tabernacle baptistery.

Apr., Society for Early Historic Archaeology at Brigham Young University, first organized effort to promote study of *Book of Mormon* archaeology since BYA expedition of 1900-02. Similar efforts have been New World Archaeological Foundation (1952), Foundation for Research on Ancient America (RLDS-sponsored, 1966), Foundation for Ancient Research and Mormon Studies (F.A.R.M.S., 1981), Zarahemla Research Foundation (RLDS-affiliated, 1978), and Ancient America Foundation (1994). In 1995, F.A.R.M.S. signs "protocol" to formalize relationship with BYU and allow its publications in tenure ("continuing status") decisions for faculty. F.A.R.M.S. begins construction of its own large office building and research facility in Provo.

5 Apr., first counselor J. Reuben Clark tells meeting of bishops: "I wish that we could get over being flattered into almost anything. If any stranger comes among us and tells us how wonderful we are, he pretty nearly owns us."

26 Apr., first counselor J. Reuben Clark reports that Emily Smith Stewart is prompting her father and church president in making administrative decisions. This is only known period in which a woman has such influence on LDS church administration.

28 Apr., Presidency announces that "there is no truth whatever" in dispatches from Moscow's Tass news agency that "Latter-day Saint missionaries are acting as spies in Finland."

8 June, Reid E. Bankhead is first to receive Master of Theology degree from Brigham Young University where he later becomes professor of religion.

22 June, full-time missionary Robert T. Martin is first American to win grand prize from Conservatory of Music in Nancy, France. In 1975, LDS James Arthur Waite, age sixteen, wins first place in violin from Conservatory of Music in Paris.

27 June, when stake president complains to First Presidency about pari-mutuel betting on horse races, "Pres. Smith said that the position of the Church has always been against horse racing on Sunday." First counselor J. Reuben Clark immediately and emphatically adds, "on any other day, too, where there is betting."

14 July, Presiding Bishop LeGrand Richards approves installation of cigarette vending machine in bus terminal of church's Temple Square Hotel.

24 July, Costa Rican Mormons celebrate Utah Pioneer Day.

Sept., Quorum of Twelve decides that apostles will attend stake conferences semiannually, rather than quarterly, due to increased number of stakes.

18 Sept., *Church News* reports that Ute Indian Albert Harris has been "recently chosen to represent his race and Church on the Roosevelt Stake High Council."

21 Sept., First counselor J. Reuben Clark writes that "the General Authorities of the Church

get precious little from the tithing of the Church. They are not paid as much as a first-class, stenographic secretary of some of the men who run industry."

8 Oct., general conference broadcast on television for first time.

21 Nov., at suggestion of George Albert Smith, first counselor J. Reuben Clark informs representative of Kennecott Copper in Salt Lake City that Guggenheim family's investments in Utah will suffer if Guggenheim Foundation continues to sponsor Dale L. Morgan's proposed multi-volumed history of Mormonism. Guggenheim Foundation agrees to stop funding Morgan, who never finishes even one volume of his history.

1950

7 Jan., at funeral of man who died six weeks after his appointment as stake president, Apostle Joseph Fielding Smith tells Apostle Harold B. Lee: "If you have called a man to a position in this Church and he dies the next day, that position will have a bearing on what he will be called to do when he leaves this earth." Lee will eventually serve barely seventeen months as LDS president.

25 Jan., first counselor J. Reuben Clark advises Relief Society presidency not to oppose "the bill for equal rights for women" because "there will be some of the women who will think it is a fine thing." This day U.S. Senate approves proposed Equal Rights Amendment to U.S. Constitution. It fails to receive vote of U.S. House.

28 Jan., missionaries Stanley E. Abbott and C. Aldon Johnson are arrested by secret police in Communist Czechoslovakia, interrogated for three days as suspected spies, and then each is placed in solitary confinement for twenty-four days. Meanwhile most LDS missionaries are expelled from country, and remainder leave shortly after release of the two from prison.

27 Mar., First Presidency letter to stake presidents: "Since our meetinghouses are tax exempt, it is most important that we should not do anything that would put them into a position where they might be assessed and we be compelled to pay taxes thereon because we were carrying on a merchandising business therein."

18 May, First Presidency letter to make 30 percent increase in living allowances for general authorities.

2 Oct., First Presidency letter: "Where military regulations require the wearing of two-piece underwear, such underwear should be properly marked as if the articles were of the normal [temple garment] pattern." Drafted originally for Korean War, this instruction is reissued during Vietnam War on 31 Aug. 1964 and 17 Mar. 1969.

1951

30 Jan., First Presidency decides that, effective in two days, "no young men of draft age will be recommended for missionary service." As result, there is increase of missionary callings to young, married men who serve two or more years separated from their wives.

4 Apr., George Albert Smith dies.

9 Apr., conference sustains David O. McKay as church president with Stephen L Richards and J. Reuben Clark as counselors. This demotion of Clark from first counselor stuns many Mormons, including Quorum of Twelve Apostles. For first time in its history, Twelve "ordains" church president and then sets apart McKay and his counselors. McKay is also first church president who graduated from college (University of Utah).

7 June, First Presidency appoints three apostles to administer second anointings to designated couples.

25 June, *Deseret News* editorial praises non-combatant conscientious objectors but opposes the "craven draft-dodger."

15 Aug., *Church News* reports that Finland has given its "Silver Cross" to LDS mission president Henry A. Matis for allowing one of his missionaries to coach Finnish National Basketball team for international competition. Other LDS civilians who receive high honors from non-U.S. governments are LDS president David O. McKay (Greece's Cross of Commander of Order of Phoenix from King Paul, 1954), New Zealand physician

Manahi Nitama Paewai (Order of British Empire from Queen Elizabeth, 1967), Julius Andersen (Danish knighthood by authority of Queen Margrethe, 1972), Barton L. Bowen (Brazil's Order of Southern Cross, 1974), Roy W. Oscarson (Sweden's Knight of First Class of Royal Order of Vasa, 1975), J. Earl Jones (Thailand's Order of Royal Crown, 1977), Henry Eyring (Sweden's Berzelius Medal from King Carl XVI Gustav, 1979), Kurt Koehle (Merit Cross from Federal Republic of Germany, 1979), Ernest N. Eklof (Sweden's silver Bicentennial Medal from King Carl XVI Gustav, 1979), Gordon C. Mortenson (Officer's Cross of Order of Merit from Federal Republic of Germany, 1981), John Langeland (Swedish knighthood in Order of St. Olav, 1982), Mark Evans Austad (Sweden's Grand Cross in Order of St. Olav, 1984), Johann Wondra (Austria's Cross of Honor, First Class, 1988), Doreen Sylvia Gilmour (Member of British Empire by Queen Elizabeth, 1989), Mike McPheters (Bolivia's medal of honor, 1990), U. Henry Gerlach (Austrian Medal of Honor in Arts and Sciences, 1991), Chang Young Bo (Citizen's Certificate by South Korea's president, 1992), Thomas Kehoe (Russia's bronze medal for heroism, 1993), Tufuga Samuela Atoa (Western Samoa's Order of Merit, 1995).

17 Aug., First Presidency statement that church's restriction on negroid peoples receiving priesthood "is not a matter of the declaration of policy but of direct commandment from the Lord." However, in his biographies of LDS presidents David O. McKay, Harold B. Lee, and Spencer W. Kimball, First Presidency secretary Francis M. Gibbons repeatedly refers to this priesthood restriction as "policy."

8 Sept., Colleen K. Hutchins is named Miss America. Other Mormon winners of national and international pageants are May Louise Flodin (Miss Sweden and Miss World, 1955), Lavina Christensen Fugal (American Mother, 1955), Charlotte Sheffield (Miss USA, 1957), Linda Bement (Miss USA and Miss Universe, 1960), Shirley Fong (Miss Chinatown USA, 1963), Marie Moua (Miss Tahiti, 1965), Dianna Lynn Batts (Miss USA, 1965), Alice Welti Buehner (Mrs. America, 1965), Lorena Chipman Fletcher (American Mother, 1965), Joan Peterson Fisher (Mrs. America, 1968), Nora Begay (Miss Indian America, 1971), Janene Forsyth (Miss American Teenager, 1971), Susan Merrill (Miss Rodeo America, 1971), Shirley Franklin Casper (National Young Mother, 1971), Marilyn Jones Maw (U.S. Navy Wife, 1972), Connie Della Lucia (Miss Rodeo America, 1974), Phyllis Brown Marriott (National Mother, 1974), Kimberly Ann Jensen (Miss National Teenager, 1975), Sandy Blackwell (Miss Cheerleader USA, 1975), Sherri Magnusson Zirker (National Young Mother, 1975), Kellie Thomson (Miss National Teenager, 1976), Kristine Rayola Harvey (Miss Indian America, 1976), Ann King (Miss United Teenager of America, 1977), Helen Ng Puay Ngoh (Miss Singapore, 1977), Susan Wright Brown (National Young Mother, 1979), Frances Davis Burtenshaw (National Mother, 1979), Vicki Lee (Miss New Zealand, 1980), Gina Durbano (Miss Drill Team USA, 1982), LaDawn Andersen Jacob (National Young Mother, 1982), Tiffani Baker (Miss National Teen Continental, 1983), Becky Hollingsworth (Miss American Teenager, 1983), Catherine Cryer Peterson (National Young Mother, 1983), Laura Baxter (Miss Teenage America, 1984), Jill Thurgood (Miss National Rodeo Queen, 1984), Sharlene Wells (Miss America, 1984), Lezlie Noel Porter (National Young Mother, 1984), Deborah Davis Wolfe (Mrs. America, 1984), Christy Fichtner (Miss USA, 1986), Bobette Kay Wildcat (Miss Indian America, 1988), Corinne Cader (Premier Princess of Mauritius, 1988), Nadine Thomas Matis (National Mother, 1990), Deedra Lybbert (Miss Rodeo Canada, 1991), Wendy Goodrich McKenna (National Mother of Young Children, 1991), Sandra Earnest (Mrs. USA, 1992), Michelle Kay White (National Mother of Young Children, 1993), Roberta Henry Lawler (National Mother of Young Children, 1995), Esther Wright (American Honey Queen, 1995), Carolyn Merrill Shumway (National Mother, 1996), Lisa Vail Phillips (National Mother of Young Children, 1996).

On male side, LDS Larry Scott wins the Mr. America bodybuilding title (1963), Mr.

Universe (1964), and Mr. Olympia (1965, 1966). David W. Checketts, owner of New York Knicks, is National Father (1994).

10 Oct., meeting of Twelve discusses previous "controversy" between President Joseph F. Smith and his second counselor Charles W. Penrose over whether it is necessary to confer priesthood before ordaining to office. This does not become churchwide policy again for almost six years.

16 Oct., temple council of First Presidency, Quorum of Twelve Apostles, and Patriarch to church decides to allow beer commercials on church-owned KSL television station.

29 Oct., John K. Cannon is first Mormon appointed to four-star rank in U.S. military. With this promotion General Cannon is commander of U.S. Tactical Air Command. In World War II he was commander-in-chief of Allied air forces in Europe and later for entire U.S. air force in Europe (1948-51).

5 Nov., First Presidency learns of plans by Warner Brothers to make film about Mountain Meadows Massacre, based on recent scholarly book by LDS Juanita Brooks. Within seven days First Presidency successfully persuades Hollywood studio to kill project.

1952

16 Jan., *Church News* reports that Yotaro Yoshino and Toshio Murakami are first Japanese missionaries to be called from their homeland. Both are converts whose non-LDS parents have agreed to support them financially while proselytizing. These are first native-born Asian missionaries of LDS church, and not until December 1963 are there Chinese missionaries from Hong Kong.

2 Mar., David O. McKay dedicates church's new Primary Children's Hospital in Salt Lake City, with half its cost raised in "penny drive" by children. It began in 1922 as remodeled residence. After Primary Hospital moves near University of Utah, the penny-built hospital is sold to developers in 1995 to be razed so land can be used for condominiums.

14 Mar., First Presidency letter states minimum age for male missionaries is twenty and for female missionaries is twenty-three.

3 May, David O. McKay dedicates first monument to martyred LDS missionary, Joseph Standing.

5 May, Merlo J. Pusey is first actively Mormon recipient of Pulitzer Prize for his biography *Charles Evans Hughes*. Other LDS recipients are John M. Hightower (1952, international reporting), Robert D. Mullins (1962, local reporting), Jack Anderson (1972, national reporting), Laurel Thatcher Ulrich (1991, history *A Midwife's Tale*), Steve Benson (1993, editorial cartoons). In 1952 Pusey also receives nation's most prestigious history award (Bancroft Prize), also conferred on Richard L. Bushman (1968, *From Puritan to Yankee*) and Laurel Thatcher Ulrich (1991, *A Midwife's Tale*). In 1957, Virginia Sorensen receives Newbery Medal from American Library Association for *Miracles on Maple Hill*, and Josefina Febres Cordero is named Argentina's Woman of the Year in 1977 for her autobiography *La Puerta Azul* (The Blue Door). Orson Scott Card is recipient of highest U.S. awards in science fiction: "Nebula" from Science Fiction Writers of America (1098, *Ender's Game*), Nebula and also "Hugo" from World Science Fiction Society (1987, *Speaker for the Dead*), and Hugo (1988, *Eye for Eye*).

14 June, twenty-year-old David B. Bleak, unarmed LDS medic in Korean War, "while attempting to cross the fire-swept area to attend the wounded, he came under hostile fire from a small group of the enemy concealed in a trench. Entering the trench he closed with the enemy, killed 2 with bare hands and a third with his trench knife. Moving from the emplacement, he saw a concussion grenade fall in front of a companion and, quickly shifting his position, shielded the man from the impact of the blast. Later, while ministering to the wounded, he was struck by a hostile bullet but, despite the wound, he undertook to evacuate a wounded comrade. As he moved down the hill with his heavy burden, he was attacked by 2 enemy soldiers with fixed bayonets. Closing with the aggressors, he grabbed them and smashed their heads together, then carried his helpless

comrade down the hill to safety." That is the explanation for Congressional Medal of Honor which Bleak receives in 1953.

25 June, Apostle Albert E. Bowen has debilitating stroke during Council of Twelve's temple meeting. He dies next year.

30 June, First Presidency letter to stake presidents and ward bishops that "we must always be on our guard against false teachings which destroy faith and lead the Church members into forbidden paths." Letter also cautions, "Officers should not be misled by an innocent looking face and a smoothly pious tongue." In restatement of this letter on 22 Feb. 1972, different First Presidency drops latter phrase.

2 Oct., second counselor J. Reuben Clark warns women of Relief Society general conference against "self-pollution," prostitution, and "homosexuality, which, it is tragic to say, is found among both sexes." He cautions LDS women against allowing homosexually oriented males to use them as male-substitutes in dating or marriage: "I wonder if you girls have ever reflected on the thought that was in the mind of the man who first began to praise you for your boyish figures." Clark also tells the ladies, "I forebear to more than mention that abomination of filth and loathsomeness of the ancients—carnal knowledge with beasts." Relief Society magazine publishes this talk in full.

23 Oct., Apostle Henry D. Moyle expresses opposition in meeting of First Presidency and apostles concerning proposal to add lace to temple garments for women. Temple council meeting approves this on 4 Dec.

1953

3 Jan., *Church News* feature story: "Incubator for Freedom: Staff of 'BY Universe' Makes Determined Stand For Hands-Off Policy in Production of Newspaper." That editorial independence lasts sixteen more years at BYU, then falls victim to conservative reaction against student protests nationally.

20 Jan., Apostle Ezra Taft Benson begins his official service as Secretary of Agriculture in cabinet of newly inaugurated U.S. President Dwight D. Eisenhower. Church president David O. McKay already "set apart" Benson as Secretary of Agriculture on 28 Nov. 1952. Subsequent LDS Cabinet members are Stewart Udall (Interior, 1961-69), George Romney (Housing and Urban Development, 1969-72), David M. Kennedy (Treasury, 1969-71, and special cabinet member while ambassador-at-large, 1971-73), Terrel H. Bell (Education, 1981-85).

In addition to this unprecedented appointment of LDS general authority, Eisenhower appoints Mrs. Ivy M. Baker Priest as first Mormon to serve as U.S. Treasurer. In 1981 Republican Ronald Reagan appoints Angela Marie ("Bay") Buchanan as second Mormon to serve as U.S. Treasurer.

11 Feb., First Presidency purchases $5,000 in bonds of State of Israel.

3 Mar., First Presidency secretary answers Mormon's inquiry about receiving blood transfusions from African-Americans: "The L.D.S. Hospital here in Salt Lake City has a blood bank which does not contain any colored blood." This represents five-year effort to keep LDS Hospital's blood bank separate from American Red Cross system in order "to protect the purity of the blood streams of the people of this Church" (Counselor J. Reuben Clark's phrase).

9 Mar., David O. McKay tells president of University of Utah that it "is an LDS Institution."

23 May, Apostle Spencer W. Kimball publishes repudiation of Norman C. Pierce's *The Coming of the Great White Chief*: "If members of the Church would always check the authenticity of such stories, through the Church authorities before spreading them abroad, it would save much embarrassment and deception."

19 June, Leadership Week at Brigham Young University where collector Wilford C. Wood displays "a silver piece that was Emma's most priceless possession, that was taken from the pocket of the Prophet—from his dead body. What do you think it was? In hieroglyphics . . . that the Prophet would save: *Confirmo, O Deus Potentissimus* (Make me, Oh God,

all-powerful)." English texts of magic give the incantation phrase of Jupiter talisman as: "Confirm, O God, thy strength in us."

26 July, Arizona police and national guard raid polygamous commune at Short Creek, Arizona, arrest all its adults, and put its children in foster homes. First Presidency had ten days' advance notice of raid and informed *Deseret News* on 24 July.

26 Aug., David O. McKay informs Utah's Congressional delegation that he does not want them to help European Mormons to immigrate to United States. Instead church president says they should remain and build church in their countries. Unlike earlier statements McKay strengthens this appeal by building European temples, primary motive for moving to Utah.

1954

17 Jan., David O. McKay tells meeting of LDS missionaries in South Africa that he wanted to ordain African-American in 1921 but that is not possible "until the Lord gives us another revelation changing this practice." McKay acknowledges two exceptions to this policy: one African-American (Elijah Abel) received priesthood during Joseph Smith presidency and one other (identity unknown and probably myth) received endowment during Brigham Young's presidency. However, McKay liberalizes church's policy by no longer requiring priesthood eligibility to depend on South African's ability to trace all his ancestral lines to Europe.

15 Mar., O. Meredith Wilson is president, University of Oregon. Other Mormons appointed as university presidents outside intermountain states are Vern O. Knudsen (UCLA, 1959), G. Homer Durham (Arizona State University, 1960), O. Meredith Wilson (University of Minnesota, 1960), Stanford Cazier (California State University at Chico, 1971), E. Gordon Gee (West Virginia University, 1981), David P. Gardner (University of California system, 1984), E. Gordon Gee (University of Colorado, 1985; Ohio State University, 1990), V. Lane Rawlins (Memphis State University, 1990).

12 May, Appointment of A. Sherman Christenson as first active Mormon to be federal judge (U.S. District Court for Utah).

17 May, counselor J. Reuben Clark writes U.S. senator: "I am impressed, as to Indo-China, with this fact.... it is not worth spending our blood for it.... Finally, while unalterably opposed to Communism, I can imagine that an enlightened Communism may be a whole lot better than a decrepit, deficient, corrupt colonial government [in Indo-China]. I feel that that principle could be applied to very much of the situation in the whole Far East." Indo-China soon becomes separate countries of North Vietnam, South Vietnam, Cambodia, and Laos, all of which are part Vietnam conflict, longest war in U.S. history.

7 June, First Presidency letter allows young men and women to be sealed to their parents "at any time prior to their reaching the age of 21. This supersedes the earlier rulings on the question which made a difference between the young men and the young women in respect to the age limits governing them in this matter."

31 July, *Church News* publishes Counselor J. Reuben Clark's talk to all LDS seminary and institute teachers in which he declares that "even the President of the Church has not always spoken under the direction of the Holy Ghost."

18 Aug., First Presidency rules that Apostle Joseph Fielding Smith's anti-evolutionary *Man: His Origin and Destiny* should not be used for study in LDS seminaries and institutes. McKay expresses from 1954 on: "On the subject of organic evolution the Church has officially taken no position. The book 'Man, His Origin and Destiny' was not published by the Church, and is not approved by the Church."

27 Aug., with specific reference to U.S. Supreme Court's recent decision of *Brown vs. Board of Education* which declared segregation unconstitutional, Apostle Mark E. Petersen instructs all LDS "college level" religion teachers: "I would be willing to let every Negro drive a Cadillac if they could afford it. I would be willing that they have all the advantages they can get out of life in the world. But let them enjoy these things among themselves.

I think the Lord segregated the Negro and who is man to change that segregation?" After stating that marriage with African-American is impossible for faithful caucasian Mormons, Apostle Petersen extends his opposition to racial intermarriage by affirming that it is God's will that "the Hawaiians should marry Hawaiians, the Japanese ought to marry the Japanese, and the Chinese ought to marry Chinese, and the Caucasians should marry Caucasians."

24 Sept., CBS television's Edward R. Murrow program features Apostle Ezra Taft Benson's family having "LDS Home Night."

12 Oct., George W. Romney is named president of American Motors in Detroit, Michigan. Other large national corporations (outside intermountain area) and international corporations which have Mormons as president, vice-president, CEO, chair of board, or general manager at various times are Aetna Life and Casualty (D. Lee Tobler), Alexander Hamilton Life Insurance (Richard H. Headlee), American Airlines (Melvin E. Olsen), American Broadcasting Co. (Robert H. Hinckley), American Linen Supply (Paul W. Jespersen, Arnold R. Knapp), American Smelting and Refining (Robert Bradford), American Telecommunications Corp. (Henry Marcheschi), Anaconda Copper (Howard L. Edwards, Charles Jay Parkinson), Asmera Oil Corp. of Canada (Howard S. Rhodes), Associated Dry Goods/Lord & Taylor stores (G. Stanley McAllister), Atari Games (Nolan Bushnell), Atlas Corp. (L. Boyd Hatch), Bank of America (Blair R. Egli, Richard V. Harris), Banker's Trust Co. of New York (William J. Snow), Beatrice Foods (Nolan D. Archibald), Bechtel Corp. and Bechtel Investments (Steven V. White), Beneficial Finance (DeWitt Paul), Bernina Sewing Machine (Richard Clyde Jensen), Black & Decker (Nolan D. Archibald), Black & Decker/Puerto Rico (Guillermo M. Perotti), California Healthcare System (Quentin L. Cook), Canada Loyal Insurance (Lawrence R. Fuller), Century Bank (Robert A. Hinkle), Citibank (Dan C. Jorgensen), Clorox (Robert A. Bolingbroke), Columbia Broadcasting System (Ralph W. Hardy), Columbia Records (James B. Conkling), Conoco (Max G. Pitcher), Consolidated Freightways (Ronald E. Poelman), Continental Grain Corp. (Donald Staehli), Continental Illinois Bank (David M. Kennedy, Paul J. Rands), Credit Data Corp. (Gerald L. Davey), Design Research International (William E. Garbett), Digital Equipment (Ralph N. Christensen), Dow Chemical (Wayne Hancock), Eastman Kodak (Kay R. Whitmore), Edison Brothers Shoes (Roy W. Oscarson, G. Richard Oscarson), Federal Home Loan Mortgage Corp. (Phillip R. Brinkerhoff), First Interstate Bank Corp. (Robert E. Greene), First National City Bank of New York (Wilford Farnsworth), General Mills (Delbert F. Wright, Mark H. Willes, Richard C. Edgley), Goldman-Sachs (A. Kim Smith), B. F. Goodrich (D. Lee Tobler), Gucci Stores (Harmon J. Tobler), Gwerdon Industries (J. Frederick Huckvale), Hallmark Cards of Canada (James R. Bradshaw), Hewlett-Packard (Richard W. Anderson), Hot Shoppes (J. Willard Marriott), Hughes Tool (Rodney H. Brady, Frank William Gay), Industrial Asphalt (T. Conrad Judd), International Container System (Lloyd W. Jones), International Marine Casualty Services (David C. Hatch), Japan Food Storage (Ryo Okamoto), Joseph Magnin Stores (Harmon J. Tobler), Kaiser Steel (Albert P. Heiner), M. W. Kellogg (Alex G. Oblad), Kentucky Fried Chicken (Leon W. Harman), Landa, Inc. (Larry C. Linton), Little Tikes/Rubbermaid (Gary Baughman), Litton Industries (Rudolph E. Lang, Jr.), Lomas & Nettleson (Weston E. Edwards), Los Angeles Times-Mirror (Mark H. Willes), Lufthansa Airlines (Dieter F. Uchtdorf), Madison Square Garden (David W. Checketts), Marriott Hotels (J. Willard Marriott, Sr. and Jr., Richard E. Marriott, Milton A. Barlow, W. Don Ladd, Francis W. Cash, Thomas Hart), McGraw-Hill Publications (David P. Forsyth), Mars Candy (Merrill J. Bateman), Merrill Lynch Real Estate and Insurance Group (Weston E. Edwards), Metromedia (Mark Evans Austad), Metropolitan Life Insurance (Stanley Benfell), Michigan National Bank (Stanford Stoddard), Multiple Zones International (Mark C. Maliwauki), Nabisco (Lee S. Bickmore), Nationwide Insurance (Timothy A. Hoyt, D. Richard McFerson), Nedco of Canada (Earl B. Matthews), *Newsweek* (Llewellyn L. Cal-

laway), New York Clearing House (John F. Lee), NMB Technologies (Myron D. Jones), North American Healthcare (David E. Sorensen), Olson Egg Farms (C. Dean Olson, H. Glenn Olson), Olympic Stain (C. Roger Victor), Ortho Agricultural Products (David B. Barlow), Pacific Corp. (Verl R. Topham), Pacific Mutual Life Insurance (Stanton Hale), Pacific West Yellow Pages (Richard A. Seay), Pay'n Save (Monte L. Bean), J. C. Penney (Oakley S. Evans), Pennzoil Exploration and Production (Rondo Fehlberg), Phillips Petroleum (Robert N. Sears), Prudential Insurance (James B. Jacobson), Range Rover of North America (Joel E. Greer), Republic National Life Insurance (Samuel P. Smoot), Reynolds Metals (Neil W. Zundel), Rose Marie Reid Swimsuits (Rose Marie Reid), Royal Industries (Jay R. Manwaring), Ryder Rental Trucks (M. Anthony Burns), Safeway Stores (O. Leslie Stone), Sambo Restaurants (Sam Battistone, Jr.), Seibi Printing of Japan (Kihachiro Ichimichi), Seiko Time (Donovan H. Larsen), Shaklee (Nevin N. Andersen), Six Flags Amusement Parks (Daniel P. Howells), Skaggs Stores (O. Leslie Stone), Southern California Edison (Thomas F. Bryson, William R. Gould), Sperry Univac (Gerald G. Probst), Stouffer Hotels and Restaurants (Clayne R. Smith), Summa Corp. (Frank William Gay), Sunline Candy and Sunmark (Menlo F. Smith), TAPSA Peruvian Airlines (Frederick S. Williams, Jose S. Ojeda), Topco Associates (W. Steven Rubow), Trans-Canada Pipe Lines (N. Eldon Tanner), Union Carbide (Isaac Stewart), Union Carbide/South Africa (James W. Rawlings), United California Bank (James C. Ellsworth), United Virginia Bankshares (Kenneth A. Randall), UNOCAL (Dennis P.R. Codon), Von's/Arden-Mayfair Markets (J. Earl Garrett), Warner Bros. Records (James B. Conkling), Weight Watchers/Heinz U.S.A. (Douglas C. Haines), Western Airlines (Larry Lee), Western Electric (Stephen H. Fletcher), Winchell's/Denny's Restaurants (John D. Hatch), Woolworth Stores (Robert Kirkwood), Evelyn Wood Reading Dynamics (Evelyn Nielsen Wood), Zero Halliburton Luggage (Jay R. Manwaring).

Intermountain-based companies of national stature (not owned or controlled by LDS church) which have Mormon executives from their inception or at various times are Albertson's Supermarkets, Associated Foods, Evans and Sutherland Computer Corp., First Security Bank, Franklin Quest, Geneva Steel, Huntsman Chemicals, Husky Oil, J.B.'s/Big Boy Restaurants, Little America Hotels, Micron Technology, Morton-Thiokol, Novell, J. R. Simplot Corp., Sinclair Oil, Smith's Food King Stores, Swire Coca-Cola USA, O.C. Tanner Jewelry, Wilson Food Products, WordPerfect.

1955

8 Jan., *Church News* announces that "Duty To God" award is now available for LDS Boy Scouts.

5 Feb., first headline reference in *Church News* since 1931 to living LDS president as the "Prophet." Apparently due to Counselor J. Reuben Clark's criticism of adulation implied by using this title for the living president, "the Prophet" is associated with founder Joseph Smith in *Church News* headlines until after Clark's death in 1961.

30 Mar., Quorum of Twelve Apostles recommends establishment of separate unit or branch for African-American members in Salt Lake City.

25 Apr., official publication of American Jewish Congress notes that "American Jews are proud to join Americans of all faiths in wishing the Mormon Church continued progress and growth."

23 June, *Church News* article, "Church-Approved Formal Evening Gowns Designed: Relief Society Sewing Center."

27 June, First Presidency letter instructs stake presidents that Native American Indian children may be legally taken into LDS homes "in Utah only through the agency of the Relief Society." Established July 1954 this Indian Placement Program seeks to give educational and acculturation advantages to Native Americans by placing their elementary and secondary school age children in homes of LDS Anglo-Americans for each school year. This began in 1947 as innovation of Golden R. Buchanan, member of Sevier Stake presidency, who took first Native American Indian (sixteen-year-old Helen

John) into his home. Later, this program is taken from jurisdiction of Relief Society and given to male church leaders. At its peak in 1972, program places 4,977 Indian children in Anglo-American homes. By 1990 participation declines to 500 because of increased resentment against this well-intentioned effort to "Americanize" native peoples.

28 June, Congress defines full-time LDS missionaries as eligible for ministerial deferments from military service.

11 Sept., David O. McKay dedicates temple near Bern, Switzerland. It is first temple to use filmed version of endowment ceremony.

21 Sept., Joel F. LeBaron incorporates Church of the Firstborn of the Fulness of Times, only Mormon Fundamentalist group to aggressively proselytize.

26 Sept., Church College of Hawaii opens for regular course work. First and largest of LDS schools established in Pacific islands for polynesian Mormons, this becomes Brigham Young University-Hawaii Campus on 1 Sept. 1974.

9 Nov., First Presidency informs Seventy's president Bruce R. McConkie that they have misgivings about his intended publication of multi-volumed *Sound Doctrine* as censored and condensed version of *Journal of Discourses*. Three weeks later Presidency is stunned to find advertisements for McConkie's publication in *Deseret News* (30 Nov. 1955) and in December issue of *Improvement Era*. He writes Presidency on 1 Dec. that ads appeared without his knowledge and "are not intended in any way to embarrass or pressure you Brethren." He then explains that he would "not permit any improper or questionable statements to appear" in his projected ten-volume version of the original twenty-six-volume collection. First Presidency reads page-proofs of first volume and responds on 9 Feb. "Omissions would probably be sought out and magnified" by the church's critics, letter says. "Under this situation we feel constrained to request that you give up the idea of an abridged edition of the Journal of Discourses." Nineteen years later the originally contracted publisher releases *Journal of Discourses Digest*, under editorship of oldest son of McConkie, then a member of Twelve.

22 Nov., Apostle Adam S. Bennion heads Utah's delegation at White House Conference on Education.

1956

28 Jan., *Deseret News* editorializes in favor of forced removal of polygamous children from their Fundamentalist parents and into monogamous foster-homes.

11 Mar., David O. McKay dedicates temple at Los Angeles, California.

15 Mar., First Presidency letter about large number of converts "to be absorbed in the existing stake and mission organizations of the Church. Their assimilation into these organizations has come to be a matter of grave concern." This statement refers to 21,669 convert baptisms in 1955. In 1995 there are 304,330 convert baptisms.

10 Apr., non-LDS governor of Utah, J. Bracken Lee, speaks of his counsel to prominent non-Mormons: "I said to them you are never going to have any success in Utah unless you let the leaders of the Church give you some advice."

21 Sept., second counselor J. Reuben Clark reluctantly agrees not to oppose First Presidency's decision to set aside two-thirds of tithing income to invest in government bonds, even though in previous months church had already lost $1 million on its investments in government securities.

3 Nov., *Church News* full-page repudiation of Annalee Skarin's religious claims, "Self-Styled 'Translated' Person Does Another Disappearing Act." Skarin's book *Ye Are Gods* is metaphysical extension of her early Mormon beliefs, yet relatively few followers know about her LDS background. Likewise, Church of Scientology's members (including Hollywood movie stars Tom Cruise and John Travolta) are generally unaware of the Mormon Fundamentalist background of their current leader Heber C. Jentzsch (Scientology convert in 1961 and church president since 1981).

28 Dec., First Presidency letter urging that all departing missionaries receive Salk vaccina-

tion against polio, which contributes to more rapid decline of this disease in Mormon culture than in U.S. generally. Its recent victims include brother of Seventy's president Bruce R. McConkie and son of Apostle Spencer W. Kimball.

1957

31 Jan., at temple meeting with apostles, First Presidency decides to make universal the previous recommendation of Twelve for priesthood ordinations to first confer priesthood before ordaining to office of deacon or elder. President McKay says that Presidency will give this instruction to temple presidents at their upcoming meeting on 7 Apr. and that all general authorities should announce this policy "when they attend quarterly conferences, and that they should set the example when performing ordinations themselves." This returns to procedure of ordination which existed only in 1912-21.

Oct., general conference is cancelled due to flu epidemic.

1958

20 Apr., David O. McKay dedicates temple near Hamilton, New Zealand.

28 Apr., second counselor J. Reuben Clark advises group of LDS women considering abortions to seek advice of two or three physicians and make their decisions prayerfully.

12 May, James Gladstone ("Many Guns") of Blood Tribe begins his service as first Native American in Canada's national senate.

18 May, first stake beyond North America or its territories (Auckland, New Zealand).

29 May, U.S. president Dwight D. Eisenhower appoints general authority Marion D. Hanks to Citizen's Advisory Committee on Fitness of American Youth. Later various general authorities serve on special White House conferences and committees.

14 July, Apostle Hugh B. Brown formally recommends that First Presidency not ask Salt Lake City Public Library to remove books on list. Brown notes: "Many of the books on this list are only mildly critical or objectionable from the Church standpoint." In 1954 First Presidency assigned Apostle Adam S. Bennion, another well-known liberal within Twelve, to assess this list of books. He delayed fulfilling assignment until his death in 1958. Joseph L. Wirthlin of Presiding Bishopric sent the original 1953 list of books "not favorable to the Church" to the Presidency, "pursuant to your request."

7 Sept., David O. McKay dedicates temple near London, England.

10 Sept., under instructions by First Presidency, Apostle Henry D. Moyle conducts mass excommunication in London, England, of nine American missionaries from French Mission. Led by counselor to mission president, these missionaries converted in France to necessity of continuing polygamy. Immediately after, most affiliate with Church of the Firstborn of the Fulness of Times, headquartered in Mexico.

19 Nov., President David O. McKay says: "I feel that the Lord is opening up the way for a favorable introduction of the Church into Russia." This occurs thirty years later.

1959

28 Jan., Apostle Marion G. Romney writes President David O. McKay that recently published *Mormon Doctrine* by Seventy's president Bruce R. McConkie is discourteous and offensive toward RLDS church, of Christian churches generally, of Catholic church in particular, of Communists, and of evolutionists. Romney also says the book presumes to declare controversial issues and personal interpretations as "Mormon Doctrine."

3 Feb., President David O. McKay writes Dr. A. Kent Christensen: "The Church has issued no official statement on the subject of the theory of evolution. Neither 'Man, His Origin and Destiny' by Elder Joseph Fielding Smith, nor 'Mormon Doctrine' by Elder Bruce R. McConkie, is an official publication of the Church." McKay's secretary Clare Middlemiss restates first sentence in letter of 8 May 1964.

6 Feb., Apostle Mark E. Petersen writes, "We do not associate ourselves with any Protestant organization. We are just 'ploughing our own field' and doing the best we can with it."

17 Feb., in effort to avoid suppression of his book, Elder Bruce R. McConkie drafts letters

to *Improvement Era* and *Church News* stating that *Mormon Doctrine* "contains my personal views only, and I am solely responsible for all statements or opinions expressed in it." He submits these for review of First Presidency, who reply on 18 Feb. that "they do not conform to the ideas that we have that you cannot be disassociated from your official position in the publication of such a manuscript." Presidency concludes that "pending the final disposition of this problem no further edition of the book be printed."

2 Mar., First Presidency letter: "A few years ago we authorized a few inter-stake missions to be set up on an experimental basis to carry the Gospel to the Jews." Letter explains that these "specially prepared missionaries" should not "confine their proselyting effort to searching out the Jews only."

6 Mar., David O. McKay rejects suggestion of opening LDS mission in Israel due to Arab opposition to state of Israel.

7 Mar., *Church News*, after twenty-eight years without advertisements, begins advertising for such diverse enterprises as music stores, mortuaries, furniture stores, insurance agencies, banks, savings and loans, camera stores, jewelers, car dealerships, travel agencies, television repair, optical shops, and movie theaters. As largest single advertisement, American Motors president George W. Romney features himself in one-and-three-fourths-page spread for Kelvinator appliances on 20 June 1959. Commercial ads cease after 24 Sept. 1960.

2 Apr., first temple meeting Apostle Spencer W. Kimball attends since his return from touring missions in South America. He emphasizes to First Presidency and Twelve the special problem in Latin America's "Catholic countries [where] divorce could not be obtained" and "some set up new households without legal sanction. . . . When such people wished to join the [LDS] Church the missionaries would not baptize them, since technically they lived in adultery." Kimball's authorized biography notes that he successfully persuades First Presidency to adopt policy that "such couples could be baptized if they showed that they had done what they could to legalize their relationship, had been faithful to one another, had met responsibility to their previous [and only legal] family, and had conformed to the expectations of custom." From 1959 onward it is LDS church policy to baptize, ordain, and give temple ordinances to any Latin American man complying with above requirements, even though he is living with a woman in legally unmarried relationship defined as adulterous by "the law of the land" where they live.

4 Apr., second counselor J. Reuben Clark tells general conference that "whenever you begin to make great expenditures of money, there is always some lack of wisdom, sometimes a lack of foresight, occasionally, oh so occasionally in this Church, a lack of integrity."

26 Apr., while ordaining local patriarch in windowless room, "a shaft of bright light came onto the back and top of Elder [Harold B.] Lee's head."

21 May, executive committee of Church Board of Education discusses "the growing problem in our society of homosexuality." Spencer W. Kimball reports that President David O. McKay has said "that in his view homosexuality was worse than [heterosexual] immorality; that it is a filthy and unnatural habit."

14 June, Billy Casper is first LDS golfer to win U.S. Open, which he wins again in 1966. Casper is admitted to World Golf Hall of Fame in 1978 and to PGA Hall of Fame in 1982. In 1973 Johnny Miller is second Mormon golfer to win U.S. Open. Miller is first Mormon inducted into new College Golf Hall of Fame in 1974, and two years later is first Mormon to win British Open. Miller enters PGA Hall of Fame in 1996.

27 June, *Church News* headlines, "Sweden's King Is Reading the Book of Mormon," referring to Gustav VI Adolf.

21 Sept., Mormon Tabernacle Choir's recording of "The Battle Hymn of the Republic" enters Top 40. It remains in Top 40 (and on popular radio stations throughout nation) for eleven weeks, during which it reaches its highest ranking of thirteen. National Academy of Recording Arts and Sciences awards Tabernacle Choir a "Grammy" for Best Choral

Performance that year. Other Mormon singers to win individual awards are Donny and Marie Osmond who receive American Music Association award as vocal duo (1976), Marie Osmond who shares vocal duo award from Country Music Association (1986), and Hans Choi who receives Russia's Tchaikovsky Prize (1990).

16 Nov., *Time* magazine article about expulsion of Harry Howard as president of Jewish fraternity B'nai Brith in Pasadena, California because he is Mormon convert. He appeals unsuccessfully to national leadership to reinstate him because he maintains his Jewish identity as a Mormon.

4 Dec., Budget Committee reports that church spent $8 million more than its revenues that year. As result church stops releasing annual reports of expenditures. Counselor J. Reuben Clark opposes deficit-spending and wants complete financial disclosure of deficits to public but is now powerless to change direction of church finances. By end of 1962 church is deficit-spending $32 million annually. This is first factor that leads to censure of first counselor Henry D. Moyle in 1963.

1960

7-8 Jan., First Presidency decides that Bruce R. McConkie's *Mormon Doctrine* "must not be re-published, as it is full of errors and misstatements, and it is most unfortunate that it has received such wide circulation." They are exasperated that McConkie and his publisher released book without pre-publication publicity or notifying First Presidency. Even his father-in-law, senior apostle Joseph Fielding Smith, "did not know anything about it until it was published." This is McConkie's way to avoid repetition of Presidency's stopping his pre-announced *Sound Doctrine* three years earlier.

Committee of two apostles (Mark E. Petersen and Marion G. Romney) reports that McConkie's *Mormon Doctrine* contains 1,067 doctrinal errors. For example, page 493 said: "Those who falsely and erroneously suppose that God is progressing in knowledge and gaining new truths cannot exercise sufficient faith in him to gain salvation until they divest themselves of their false beliefs." However, McConkie is affirming doctrine of omniscience officially condemned by previous First Presidency and Quorum of the Twelve Apostles in 1865. In announcing their decision to the Twelve on 28 Jan. 1960, First Presidency says there should be no revised edition of *Mormon Doctrine*. Presidency reverses its initial decision on 7 Jan. "that the book should be [officially] repudiated." By 28 Jan. Presidency decides against requiring McConkie to make public apology because "it might lessen his influence" as general authority.

In 1966 year after his father-in-law becomes assistant counselor to First Presidency, McConkie publishes second edition of *Mormon Doctrine*. It corrects only a few of first edition's "errors" cited by First Presidency and apostles in 1960. Book becomes bestseller among Latter-day Saints. McConkie becomes member of Quorum of Twelve Apostles to fill vacancy which his father-in-law's death creates in 1972.

31 Jan., LDS Vernon Law receives Cy Young Award for best pitcher in baseball from Baseball Writers Association of America, and he wins Lou Gerig award (1965). Harmon Killebrew is voted Most Valuable Player of American League (1969), and Dale Murphy is MVP of National League (1982, 1983).

24 Feb., Counselor J. Reuben Clark tells BYU's president: "You have got some members of the faculty who are destroying the faith of our students. You ought to get rid of them."

24 Mar., First Presidency writes General Priesthood Committee about "very urgent need of a correlation of studies among the auxiliaries of the Church," which Apostle Harold B. Lee had unsuccessfully advocated to Presidency since 1948 and publicly announces on 30 Sept. 1961. However, Lee expands "Correlation Program" beyond instruction manuals, and throughout 1960s and early 1970s, he revolutionizes church administratively by means of Correlation Program.

27 Mar., first stake in Great Britain (Manchester, England). Seventy's president Marion D.

Hanks gives keynote address at opening session of White House Conference on Children and Youth.

29 Apr., at funeral, first counselor J. Reuben Clark criticizes quartet for leaving out verse concerning Mother in Heaven during their singing of "O My Father."

5 June, first counselor J. Reuben Clark writes, "Sec'y [Ezra Taft] Benson's policies have about extinguished the small farmer and small cattleman."

8 Oct., N. Eldon Tanner and Theodore M. Burton are sustained as Assistants to Twelve. Tanner is first general authority who had prominent office in non-U.S. government, three terms as Minister of Lands and Mines in cabinet of Canada's premier. Burton is first Ph.D. appointed as Assistant.

5 Nov., concerning Gideon Dolo, Fijian whose people had troubled LDS headquarters because of their negroid appearance, *Church News* notes that he is "the first of his race to hold the Melchizedek Priesthood. The first Fijian to receive his temple endowments. The first of his race to serve as a proselyting missionary for the Church."

10 Nov., Brigham Young University's president tells Executive Committee of BYU's trustees "about a colored boy on the campus having been a candidate for the vice presidency of a class and receiving a very large vote." The three apostles present want to exclude all African-Americans from BYU. "If a granddaughter of mine should ever go to the BYU and become engaged to a colored boy," Apostle Harold B. Lee fumes, "I would hold you responsible."

29 Nov., Apostle Ezra Taft Benson proposes verbally and later in writing to appoint his son Reed to faculty of Brigham Young University to uncover unorthodox professors. At this time BYU's president opposes "espionage of that character" and blocks Reed Benson's appointment.

15 Dec., at temple meeting of First Presidency and Quorum of Twelve, first counselor Henry D. Moyle reports on "baseball baptism program," which began targeting pre-adolescent and adolescent boys during summer of 1959. Moyle reports that this is occurring "not only in England but all over the Continent." Missions choose their preferred recreational approach for teenage converts. For example, it is basketball in Northwestern States Mission and beach parties in Gulf States Mission.

20 Dec., Adewole Ogunmokun writes LDS headquarters requesting that LDS missionaries be sent to Nigeria to officially baptize and formally organize Nigerians who have converted to Mormonism after reading LDS publications. In this unprecedented development in Mormonism, a dozen groups of self-converted Nigerians have already organized, calling themselves "Latter-day Saints" and baptizing themselves as sign of their conversion. Within five years one of these Nigerian groups has "seventy-five congregations with nearly ten thousand baptized adult members and six thousand children," many of whom are living in polygamous families and few of whom know about LDS church's policy of denying priesthood to black Africans. This situation creates quandary with which LDS leaders struggle for years.

22 Dec., David O. McKay warns Twelve against growing power of LDS bureaucracy.

1961

4 Feb., *Church News* headlines, "First Presidency Urges Sunday Home Evenings." Like previously unsuccessful efforts, this announcement limits its encouragement to monthly "Home Evening" on Fast Sunday.

12 Mar., first non-English-speaking stake organized at The Hague in Netherlands, which is also first stake in continental Europe.

20 Apr., First Presidency and Twelve approve rebaptism and full reinstatement of priesthood blessings for John D. Lee, only executed participant in Mountain Meadows Massacre. Ordinances occur on 8-9 May 1961.

27 Apr., first counselor J. Reuben Clark tells apostles: "I think it is terrible for any man in the Church to begin to use his Church position, particularly in finances, to his own ad-

vantage. . . . So far as I know there are none of you who are trying to use the Church to your own self-advantage. That cannot be said for all our Church members."

14 May, Apostle Joseph Fielding Smith announces to stake conference in Honolulu: "We will never get a man into space. This earth is man's sphere and it was never intended that he should get away from it." Smith, the Twelve's president and next-in-succession as LDS president, adds: "The moon is a superior planet to the earth and it was never intended that man should go there. You can write it down in your books that this will never happen." In May 1962, he privately instructs that this view be taught to "the boys and girls in the Seminary System." On 20 July 1969 U.S. astronauts are first men to walk on moon. Six months later Joseph Fielding Smith becomes church president.

25 May, several apostles "are gravely concerned about the pressures being put on missionaries to baptize to fill a quota of baptisms. . . . This of course [is] a criticism of President Moyle and many of the mission presidents working under his direction." Extensive abuses in "baseball baptism program" lead to counselor Moyle's censure in 1963, mass excommunications of European "kiddie baptisms" in 1964-65, and more than decade of avoiding baptism quotas for full-time missionaries. General authorities are haunted by memories of baseball baptism era and urge restraint upon youthful missionaries.

30 May, *Church News* describes Duad Sahim as "first Asiatic Indian to be ordained an elder in the Church."

11 June, President David O. McKay begins ordaining members of First Council of Seventy to office of high priest so that they can ordain high priests, bishops, and organize wards and stakes.

14 June, President McKay rejects proposal to merge Assistants to the Twelve with the First Council of Seventy, now that the latter are also high priests.

22 June, First Presidency supports plan to persuade U.S. Army to send its "colored contingents" to California rather than to Utah. At its same meeting Presidency agrees to allow baptism of Nigerians seeking membership in church.

27 June, Musa Bey Alami in company with daughter of Jordanian ambassador to United States expresses gratitude to President David O. McKay and to BYU for their joint donation of large herd of milk cows for Jericho Dairy Project in Jordan. By this time 400 Jordanian boys have graduated from project's dairy school, and 160 are currently enrolled in project which is providing milk to 111 Palestinian and Jordanian villages. Alami says that "there has not been anything done in Jordan, in spite of the millions of dollars spent there that has met the success of this gift." Church called L. Burt Bigler, LDS bishop and dairyman from Jordan, Utah, to select cattle, transport them to Jericho, and supervise dairy in Kingdom of Jordan.

12 Aug., U.S. president John F. Kennedy appoints Esther W. Eggertsen Peterson as assistant secretary of U.S. Labor Department, first Mormon woman in sub-Cabinet position.

4 Oct., first meeting of All-Church Coordinating Council, the Correlation Program's administrative organization for restructuring "almost every program and organization in the Church," according to Harold B. Lee's biographer. This council continues at LDS headquarters as of 1996.

4 Dec., establishment of language-training program known as Language Training Mission (LTM) at Brigham Young University. Originally for Spanish it expands in 1963 to all Spanish-speaking and Portuguese-speaking missions and in 1964 to German-speaking. In 1968 LTM expands to sixteen languages, with branches at Ricks College for Dutch and Scandinavian languages and at Church College of Hawaii for Polynesian and Asian languages. In visiting missions general authorities find LTM graduates to be more disciplined than other missionaries, who have received only one week's orientation and training at Salt Lake Missionary Home since 1925.

1962

3 Feb., *Church News* headlines, "MIA Bans The 'Twist,'" popular dance among teenagers

and young adults. This prohibition is widely ignored by Mormon youth and even by adult leaders in some wards, stakes, and missions, especially in Britain and Europe.

24 Feb., *Church News* reports that 3,500 teams and 50,000 players are involved in all-church basketball tournament. For final playoffs teams come to Salt Lake City from throughout United States, Canada, and Mexico. Basketball is most popular of all-church team sports which also includes softball and volleyball. However, from 1958 to 1971 more than thirty stakes have been organized outside North America, and their youth obviously cannot participate in such tournaments. Also many less affluent, outlying stakes in North American cannot. In 1971 church headquarters ends "all-Church" sports competitions.

Mar., age for full-time proselytizing missions is lowered to nineteen for males, while sixteen-year-old boys can serve as full-time labor missionaries in Pacific islands, Europe, and Latin America. Likewise, while most females continue to wait until age twenty-one for missionary service, mission presidents outside United States can call women as young as seventeen to serve as full-time missionaries within their resident mission area.

8 Apr., Conference is broadcast by television coast-to-coast in United States and Canada, and by shortwave radio to Mexico, South America, Caribbean, Europe, and Africa

25 May, Boyd K. Packer is first to earn regular doctorate while serving as general authority. He receives Ed.D. degree from Brigham Young University. Other general authorities with Ed.D. degree are Carlos E. Asay (appointed in 1976), Joe J. Christensen (1989), L. Lionel Kendrick (1989), John M. Madsen (1992), L. Edward Brown (1996), William Rolfe Kerr (1996).

1 July, Brigadier-General Murray A. Bywater is LDS commander of Strategic Air Command (SAC) in Wichita, Kansas for Titan II underground missiles.

Following release of Lowell L. Bennion as director of LDS institute of religion at University of Utah, George S. Tanner writes in his diary: "The way it looks to me is that the Brethren have suddenly become worried that there is a little too much liberalism among some of our better trained men and they are trying to stamp it out." Tanner was institute director for twenty-eight years in Idaho and has taught continuously in program since 1923.

2 July, Counselor Hugh B. Brown rededicates portions of Alberta (Canada) temple. Extensive remodeling of temple interiors (sometimes involving structural replacement of *everything* except exterior walls and roof) is necessary to accommodate filmed endowment ceremony and to allow larger number of temple patrons. Rededication ceremonies occur for Arizona temple (15 Apr. 1975), St. George temple (11 Nov. 1975), Hawaii temple (13 June 1978), Logan temple (13 Mar. 1979), Manti temple (14 June 1985), Alberta temple (again 22 June 1991), London temple (18 Oct. 1992), Swiss temple (23 Oct. 1992). These temples, sometimes for first time in nearly 100 years, are open to general public for tours prior to rededication ceremonies occurring from 1975 onward.

23 July, Mormon Tabernacle Choir broadcasts from Mt. Rushmore on Telstar, first musical group to use international communications satellite.

Aug., *Esquire* magazine's cover story claims LDS tithing revenues are $1 million daily ($365 million annually). In fact, tithing revenues for 1962 are only about $100 million.

22 Aug., First Presidency letter to stake presidents: "It is contrary to our counsel and advice that ward, branch or stake premises, chapels or other Church facilities be used in any way for political campaign purposes, whether it be for speech-making, distribution of literature, or class discussions." First Presidency finds it necessary to reissue these instructions on 5 Mar. 1980.

19 Sept., First Presidency rules that prominent Egyptian polygamist can be baptized because polygamy is legal in Egypt. This is in reference to "an earlier ruling in the matter of Indians who had married more than one wife and it was decided that they may be baptized, if they were legally married according to their tribal customs." First Presidency

agrees that such legal polygamists cannot be sealed in temples, to avoid confusing LDS policy toward Mormon Fundamentalists.

With regard to black Africa, President David O. McKay says it "is a cruel thing" to require Nigerian polygamists to cease their legally polygamous marriages, yet Presidency decides to forbid baptism of black African polygamists (who are also denied priesthood ordination by LDS policy for all persons of black African descent). By contrast, the Egyptian polygamist, a Coptic Christian, is baptized in London in February 1963 and ordained elder.

22 Sept., *Church News* describes Major Russell L. Rogers as "first Mormon astronaut" who is scheduled to orbit the earth as "one of six Dyna-Soar (X-20) astronauts." At this time Clifford I. Cummings is also LDS director of Lunar Program at CalTech's Jet Propulsion Laboratory. Rogers dies in 1967 crash.

20 Oct., *Church News* announces purchase of church's first shortwave radio station, WRUL, in Boston and New York City. Purchase price is $1,771,850. Church sells its shortwave station in 1974 in response to satellite, cable, and videotape technologies.

27 Oct., in midst of Cuban Missile Crisis, Apostle Ezra Taft Benson publicly endorses John Birch Society as "the most effective non-church organization in our fight against creeping socialism and godless Communism," and his son Reed A. Benson announces that he is Utah coordinator of the society.

14 Nov., unknown persons plant bomb at Salt Lake temple and blow out its east doors and three floors of windows on its east wall.

22 Nov., Yoshihiko Kikuchi, only native missionary at zone meeting in Kyushu, Japan, suddenly begins speaking English (a language he does not know) while bearing his testimony. He becomes general authority in 1977.

19 Dec., David O. McKay privately tells LaMar Williams, church's representative to self-converted Nigerian Mormons, to baptize Nigerian polygamists "and admit them to the Church. They could keep the wives and families that they had at the time of baptism, but they were not to engage further in this practice." Although this is typical example of McKay's pattern of privately reversing First Presidency decisions, circumstances prevent its implementation. Delay in getting visas and subsequent Nigerian civil war prevent Williams and other LDS missionaries from actually being able to perform baptisms until 1978 when official decision of McKay Presidency is enforced prohibiting baptism of polygamists. Black African husbands, wives, and children have to renounce polygamous marriages in order to receive LDS baptism or to receive priesthood. In tribal cultures a divorced wife is an outcast and her children suddenly become illegitimate.

This refusal to recognize legitimacy of black African polygamy contradicts March 1897 letter of First Presidency regarding marriages in non-western cultures. This seems to be race-based policy contrary to First Presidency's recent recognition of polygamy among Arabs ("children of Abraham") and LDS church policy since 1959 to ignore the illegality and "technical adultery" of LDS converted Latin Americans ("blood of Israel") who are living in long-term relationships without legal marriage and without divorce from previous spouse(s).

1963

4 Jan., First Presidency publishes message: "We deplore the presumption of some politicians, especially officers, co-ordinators and members of the John Birch Society, who undertake to align the Church or its leadership with their political views." Apostle Ezra Taft Benson's son Reed is Birch coordinator for Utah.

2 Feb., *Church News* recommends official biography of Hyrum Smith, which describes his family artifacts as including "Emblematic parchments" and steel dagger with "Masonic symbols on blade." Photographs of these artifacts published in 1982 demonstrate that the parchments are "lamens" or parchments of ceremonial magic: one to summon a good spirit, another to ward off evil spirits and witches, and a third against thieves. In-

stead of "Masonic symbols," the Smith family's dagger is inscribed with astrological sign of Mars, the magic sigil or seal for the Intelligence of Mars, and the zodiac sign for Scorpio. In astrology Mars is the governing planet for Joseph Smith, Sr., whose non-Mormon neighbors claim he dug for treasure by drawing magic circles and using books of ceremonial magic.

6 Apr., *Church News* reports explosion of small bomb in LDS chapel at Porto Allegre, Brazil by terrorists who leave anti-American publications nearby.

6 May, Apostle Harold B. Lee is appointed to board of governors for American Red Cross, first LDS general authority in this position.

1 Aug., First Presidency statement that Latter-day Saints should not dance with "grotesque contortions of the body such as shoulder and hip shaking or excessive body jerking." As result Mormon youth generally cease dancing the popular "Twist" at LDS dances throughout world, an adherence that had not uniformly followed the first announced ban two years earlier by youth auxiliaries.

7 Sept., *Deseret News* insert titled *President McKay Birthday Tribute,* with headline on page 2: "Portrait of a Prophet at 90," and caption on page 7: "Huntsville is the Prophet's birthplace." This is not quite two years after the death of Counselor J. Reuben Clark who had opposed using "the Prophet" as reverential title for the living LDS president. However, *Church News* itself continues referring to McKay only as "President McKay" until 1965 after which there are increasing headline references to him as "the Prophet" or "the Beloved Prophet."

19 Sept., First Presidency and apostles decide to prevent performance of BYU professor Clinton F. Larson's play *The Redeemer* because of its portrayal of Mary Magdalene as wife of Jesus. "President McKay [is] very much concerned about it, he having said there was no authoritative basis for such a conclusion—that we just didn't know." Performance occurs because it is sponsored by Provo Recreation Department rather than BYU.

4 Oct., Thomas S. Monson is sustained to Quorum of the Twelve at age thirty-six, youngest man ordained apostle since Joseph Fielding Smith at age thirty-three in 1910. Monson is first World War II veteran to serve as apostle and also first general authority with Master of Business Administration. Other general authorities with MBA or other graduate degree in business are Robert D. Hales (appointed in 1975), Gene R. Cook (1975), John H. Groberg (1976), Ronald E. Poelman (1978), Henry B. Eyring (1985), Glenn L. Pace (1985), Helio R. Camargo (1985), Monte J. Brough (1988), Albert Choules, Jr. (1988), Joseph C. Muren (1991), Stephen D. Nadauld (1991), Dallas N. Archibald (1992), John E. Fowler (1992), V. Dallas Merrell (1992), H. David Burton (1992), Richard C. Edgley (1992), Neil L. Andersen (1993), Dieter F. Uchtdorf (1994).

5 Oct., *Church News* reports that Bruce Behroog Farhangi, Iranian Muslim, has been baptized in Salt Lake City during past week.

6 Oct., first counselor Hugh B. Brown reads statement in favor of full civil rights for all people. BYU's president comments, "This was obviously in response to request that had come to the First Presidency from the National Association for the Advancement of Colored People [NAACP]."

12 Oct., dedication of Polynesian Cultural Center near temple at Laie, Hawaii, which becomes mecca for tourists to Hawaiian Islands.

23 Dec., Apostle Joseph Fielding Smith, president of Twelve, writes: "I am glad to report to you that it will be some time before we hear anything from Brother [Ezra Taft] Benson, who is now on his way to Great Britain."

1964

1 Jan., "Home Teaching" replaces traditional "ward teaching" program of monthly visits of priesthood men to church members. This begins new emphasis on family life which subtly (yet fundamentally) replaces previous priorities of God, church, and family with new ranking of family, church, and God.

18 Jan., *Church News* reports that LDS headquarters has donated $10,000 toward construction of John F. Kennedy Center for Performing Arts in Washington, D.C. In 1974, Mormon Tabernacle Choir performs in Kennedy Center with attendance by newly installed U.S. president Gerald R. Ford.

31 Jan., by request of Lyndon B. Johnson, LDS president David O. McKay meets with U.S. president in White House. Johnson "said that sometimes he felt as he did when he was a little boy when he had more problems than he could handle and would go to his mother and put his head on her breast and get a little sympathy. He mentioned that we have the Panama problem, the matter of the plane that was shot down over East Germany, Viet Nam, etc., and he said he felt the same way now that he did when he was a boy.

"After they went into the dining room, President Johnson turned to President McKay and said, 'I feel that the spiritual and moral fiber of this country need strengthening, and we need it badly. I would like to ask you, President McKay, if you can tell me how we can get it.' He said, 'I have been out to see you [in Utah] on two or three occasions before and each time I left you I came away inspired and I feel I would like to have your advice on this.'"

12 Feb., First Presidency letter that prospective missionaries "found guilty of fornication, of sex perversion, of heavy petting, or of comparable transgressions should not be recommended until the case has been discussed with the bishop and stake president and the visiting [General] Authority."

29 Feb., after forty-one years teaching in Church Educational System, George S. Tanner writes that "a large majority" of CES teachers "are so narrow and ignorant that it is a shame to have them indoctrinating our young people. I would much rather my sons and daughters go to other schools in the state than have them led by these religious fanatics."

15 Apr., Daryl Chase, Mormon president of Utah State University, confides that "the LDS church has a greater strangle hold on the people and institutions of the state now than they had in Brigham's time. Complete academic freedom is actually non-existent."

22 Apr., opening of New York World's Fair which includes LDS church's first major exhibit hall at world's fair, the "Mormon Pavilion." Continues through 1965 season.

24 Oct., Australian judge comments that "it seems a particularly extraordinary way of bringing religion to the notice of the housewife," as he imposes criminal fines on two LDS missionaries for impersonating government inspectors in order to enter the home of potential investigators. From mid-1950s to 1980s there are published complaints in various parts of Australia that LDS missionaries force their way through partly opened doors and refuse to leave until householder listens to message about LDS church.

17 Nov., David O. McKay dedicates temple at Oakland, California.

28 Nov., *Church News* headlines, "Inauguration Steps In Home Evening Plan For December," which describes detailed instructions to stake presidents and subsequently to ward bishops for implementing weekly family home evening program for all Mormons. LDS leaders stress this repeatedly from pulpit and church headquarters eventually enforces it with Monday evening closing of such LDS enterprises in Salt Lake City as Deseret Gymnasium and genealogical library and of temples worldwide. This finally succeeds in achieving widespread compliance of Mormon families in holding home evenings which had not occurred after official announcements in 1915, 1946, and 1961.

1965

18 Jan., Mormon Tabernacle Choir sings at inauguration of U.S. president Lyndon B. Johnson, first of several such inaugural invitations by U.S. presidents.

Feb., Italy's government permits LDS missionaries to proselytize for first time since 1862.

3 Mar., Apostle Harold B. Lee is "protesting vigorously over our having given a scholarship at the B.Y.U. to a negro student from Africa. Brother Lee holds the traditional belief as revealed in the Old Testament that the races ought to be kept together and that there is danger in trying to integrate them on the B.Y.U. campus."

7 Mar., 300 protesters march to Church Office Building on Sunday, "demanding that the Church speak out in favor of civil rights for blacks."

19 May, by authorization of First Presidency, ex-apostle John W. Taylor is baptized into LDS church. On 21 May Apostle Joseph Fielding Smith performs proxy ordinance of restoring all priesthood blessings to the deceased apostle.

1 June, Apostle Richard L. Evans is elected president of Rotary International, with its 560,000 community leaders and business executives in 127 nations.

25 June, *New York Times* reports First Presidency's letters to LDS members of Congress to retain anti-union "right to work" provision of Taft-Hartley Act.

27 June, stake president O. Leslie Stone "represent[s] the Church at the convocation of Religion for World Peace" in San Francisco. He becomes general authority in 1972.

28 Oct., twelve students (at invitation of BYU's president) bring their own rock music and demonstrate contemporary "fad dances" for general authorities in church administration building. Apostle Joseph Fielding Smith says, "I don't know anything about them, and want to see them." Afterwards Apostle Gordon B. Hinckley exclaims, "Nothing like this has ever happened in this building before!" Not long afterwards BYU more strictly enforces its ban against contemporary "rock" dancing.

9 Dec., Shawn Davis is Professional Rodeo Cowboy Association's world champion in saddle bronc riding. He regains that title in 1967 and 1968. After temporary paralysis from riding accident in 1969, he returns to rodeo competition and is inducted into the PRCA's Hall of Champions. Jim Gladstone is world champion in calf roping (1977). Chris Lybbert is the PRCA's All-Around Cowboy (1980) and its world champion in calf roping (1986). Lewis K. Feild is world champion in bareback riding (1985, 1986) and PRCA's All-Around Cowboy (1985-88).

28 Dec., organization of Mormon History Association (MHA) with Professor Leonard J. Arrington as its first president. In 1974 this organization begins publishing its annual *Journal of Mormon History,* which is still active. Prior to MHA the few independent organizations of Mormon professionals or for Mormon studies include Utah Historical Society (1897), Society for Early Historic Archaeology (SEHA, 1949), and "Swearing Elders" (1949). MHA's 1965 organization heralds Dialogue Foundation (1966), [RLDS] Foundation for Research on Ancient America (FRAA, 1966), LDS Composers Association (1969), Genesis (for black Mormons, 1971), [RLDS] Outreach International (1972), [RLDS] John Whitmer Historical Association (1973), Association of Mormon Composers and Performers (AMCAP, 1973), Committee on Mormon Society and Culture (1974), Sunstone Foundation (1974), Mormon Sisters, Inc. (1974), Association of Mormon Counselors and Psychotherapists (also AMCAP, 1975), BYU Management Society (1975), Religious Studies Center of Brigham Young University (1975), Association for Mormon Letters (AML, 1976), Associated Latter-day Media Artists (ALMA, 1977), Utah Women's History Association (1977), Academy of LDS Dentists (1977), Affirmation: Gay/Lesbian Mormons (1977), Mormons for the Equal Rights Amendment (MERA, 1978), Society for the Sociological Study of Mormon Life (SSSML, 1978), Foundation for Ancient Research and Mormon Studies (F.A.R.M.S., 1979), Mormon Pacific Historical Society (1980), B.H. Roberts Society (1980), Joseph Fielding Institute for Church History (1980), Mormon Miscellaneous (1980), Collegium Aesculapium (1980), LDS Booksellers Association (1981), Bay Area Colloquium (1982), LDS Gerontologists (1982), Mormoni Pro Loco Communi (1983), J. Reuben Clark Law Society (1983), Politically Progressive Latter-day Saints (1983), Beehive Foundation (1983), Veterans Assisting Saints Abroad Association (VASAA, 1983), Society for the Study of Mormon Theology (SSMT, 1984), Common Sense Studies Association (1984), Homosexual Education for Latter-day Parents (HELP, 1984), HLT Forum (Germany, 1985), Deseret International Foundation (1986), Canadian Mormon Studies Association (CMSA, 1987), [RLDS] Gay and Lesbian Acceptance (GALA, 1987), Family Cooperative Foundation (1987), Mormon Women's Forum (1988), VOICE: BYU's

Committee to Promote the Status of Women (1988), Latter-day Saint African-Americans for Cultural Awareness (1989), Australian Mormon Studies Association (1989), Early Mormon Research Institute (1989), Mountain Meadows Association (1989), Evergreen International (1989), Enterprise Mentors (1990), Iowa Mormon Trails Association (1992), Mormon Alliance (1992), Gamofites: Gay Mormon Fathers (1992), Family Fellowship (1992), International Action Group (1992), Mormon Peace Gathering (1992), Orson Hyde Gesellschaft (1993), Latter-day Association of Mathematical and Physical Scientists (LAMPS, or James E. Talmage Society, 1993), Danska Mormon Historie (1994), Mormon History Student Association (1995), Single Parent Association (1995).

1966

15 Mar., in special meeting President McKay, second counselor N. Eldon Tanner, and apostles Joseph Fielding Smith and Mark E. Petersen agree to counter Apostle Ezra Taft Benson's preaching of "John Birchism at stake conferences" and his efforts to align LDS church with John Birch Society during upcoming conference. As result *Church News* publishes Petersen's unsigned editorial on 26 Mar. that LDS church has "nothing to do with Birchers. . . . avoid extremes and extremists." Apostle Harold B. Lee's conference talk also attacks Birch Society and indicates that unnamed Benson is not in "harmony" with his quorum.

26 Mar., *Church News* reports that Devendra J. Singh, former Hindu "is the first of his race to be called on a mission, the second East Indian to go through the temple and the fourth of his people to be ordained an elder."

Spring, first issue of *Dialogue: A Journal of Mormon Thought,* longest-running independent publication devoted to Mormonism. Characterized by scholarly historical articles, personal essays on contemporary issues, fiction, poetry, graphic arts, and lively letters to editor. Six men are appointed as general authorities after affiliation with *Dialogue:* Dallin H. Oaks (board of editors, 1966-70; author, 1968), Richard B. Wirthlin (author, 1968), Joseph C. Muren (author, 1969), Ronald E. Poelman (board of advisors, 1970-72), G. Homer Durham (author, 1973), Francis M. Gibbons (author, 1975). Publications of similar scope or related interest are [RLDS] *Courage* (1970), *Journal of Mormon History* (1974), *Sunstone* (1975), *John Whitmer Historical Association Journal* (1981), *Mormon Forum* (Japanese language, 1988), *Wasatch Review International* (1992), *Betrachtungen* ("Reflections," German language, 1993), *La Voz de Cumorah* ("Voice of Cumorah." Spanish language, 1995).

29 Apr., BYU president Ernest L. Wilkinson makes first reference in his diary to receiving reports from student "spy ring" he has authorized and which becomes national scandal within ten months. Among "liberal" professors targeted is economist Richard B. Wirthlin who resigns from BYU in protest, serves as political strategist for conservative U.S. president Ronald Reagan (1980-88), and becomes general authority in 1996.

30 Apr., Lowell L. Bennion hosts several African-American Mormons at his home in Salt Lake City, including LDS converts Ruffin Bridgeforth, Jr. and his Hispanic wife Helen Marie Romero Bridgeforth. She speaks "of the difficulty they have getting their boys to go to church after they get to be deacon age and can't pass the sacrament and do the other things L.D.S. [white] boys do."

1 May, first stake in South America (Sao Paulo, Brazil).

22 June, dedication of church's storage vaults in granite mountains of Little Cottonwood Canyon, which vaults are intended to withstand nuclear explosions in event of war.

9 July, *Church News* reports that general authority Marion D. Hanks recently participated in U.S. Army War College National Strategic Seminar with "100 other civilian and military leaders across the nation."

15 Aug., First Presidency letter that "after the expiration of one year from the date of death, temple ordinances may be performed for all deceased persons, except those of known

Negro blood, without the consideration of worthiness or any other qualification." Until the 1970s LDS Genealogical Department flags records of "those of known Negro blood" to avoid performance of proxy endowment and sealing ceremonies for them. In 1974 church authorities quietly agree to end this practice, after being informed of potential NAACP lawsuit and Congressional investigation of this racially discriminatory use of such federal records as U.S. census.

6 Sept., Deseret Management Corporation as holding company for church's income producing enterprises. "There was criticism from members of the Twelve," second counselor N. Eldon Tanner later comments, "because they couldn't see why the First Presidency would hand that [power] over to the Deseret Management Corporation."

23 Sept., First Presidency letter, "effective immediately," ending "missionary farewells" in LDS meetings. Letter asks local officers "that you counsel families against holding receptions for departing missionaries." Without single reference to war, this letter responds to disparity of holding joyous farewells for young missionaries, while also conducting funerals for young men who are drafted to serve in Vietnam without opportunity to serve mission.

15 Oct., *Church News* article that current non-U.S. LDS chapels "range in architectural style from modern tile and stucco structures in Managua, Nicaragua, to the native-built 'Choza' made from palm trunks, limbs and coconut fronds." However, as part of Correlation Program's drive for church-wide uniformity, headquarters soon requires that chapels throughout world be modeled on those in Utah. In Latin America this makes LDS chapels visual symbols of often-hated "gringo" power and wealth.

1967

28 Jan., *Church News* cover photo and feature-article show LDS females with nose rings in San Blas islands off coast of Panama.

4 Feb., *Church News* honors Max W. Woodbury for fifty years service as branch president.

6 Feb., U.S. president Lyndon B. Johnson confers National Medal of Science on LDS Henry Eyring. Prize-winning chemist since 1932, Eyring authored Absolute Rate Theory and has been among finalists for Swedish Academy's Nobel Prize in chemistry since 1949. He receives Elliot Cresson Medal from Franklin Institute in 1969. Since 1875 Franklin Institute has awarded this prize for inventions and theoretical break-throughs by such notables as Nikola Tesla, Wilhelm C. Roentgen, Madame Curie, Ernest Rutherford, Alexander Graham Bell, Charles P. Steinmetz, Orville Wright, and Henry Ford.

28 Feb., Brigham Young University student publicly admits that under direction of BYU's president, he and ten other undergraduates committed classroom "espionage" on eight professors to document their liberal "political convictions." All student-spies are members of John Birch Society and of BYU's on-campus Young Americans for Freedom. After immediate, official denial by BYU's administration, two weeks later President Ernest L. Wilkinson tells faculty meeting, "I must accept responsibility," but claims "there is misinformation in the charges." Political science professor Edwin B. Morrell resigns as department chair in protest, remains on faculty, and later becomes First Presidency's representative in helping to establish missions in Communist eastern Europe.

11 Mar., BYU's president writes: "Frankly, if they [general authorities] concerned themselves 1/100th as much with teachers as they do with the basketball coach, I would feel much better." Stan Watts is NCAA Basketball Coach of the Year (1957, 1972) and inducted into Naismith Basketball Hall of Fame and into Helms Hall of Fame (1972). Lavell Edwards is NCAA Football Coach of the Year (1984). Beyond BYU, Dick Motta is National Basketball Association's Coach of the Year (1971), and Tom Chambers is NBA's All-Star MVP in 1987.

6 Apr., first television and radio broadcast of conference in Mexico.

18 Apr., first counselor Hugh B. Brown writes of his meeting with full-time missionaries in Taipei, Taiwan, "I was impressed to tell them that there was sitting in that room some

young man who would one day stand in the Council of the Twelve, but before that day he would pass through the very fires of hell, but this great honor would come to one of them if he lives worthy of it." Brown makes similar promises on various occasions, including one in Japan (1965), one in England (1966), and one in Louisiana (April 1970).

23 Apr., BYU entertainers "Y Americans" appear on television program, Ed Sullivan Show.

21 May, front page of *New York Times* business section features LDS convert Florence Doyle, stockbroker with Dupont & Co. since 1941.

24 June, Staff-sergeant Emmo A. Techuban of Tennessee receives six military medals for "heroism in Vietnam," including Silver Star, Soldier's Medal, Bronze Star, Army Commendation Medal, and Purple Heart.

July, *Priesthood Bulletin* prohibits women from praying in sacrament meeting.

6 July, Jose Gabriel Alferez, Benedictine monk for twenty-four years and father-superior, is baptized as Mormon in Costa Rica.

2 Aug., C. Wade Bell wins gold medal (800 meter run) at Pan American Games, also Michael M. Young (gold, wrestling) and Keith Russell (silver, diving). Other LDS medalists are Henry Marsh (2 gold, steeplechase, 1979), Danny Vranes (gold, basketball, 1979), Demetrio Cabanillas of Mexico (bronze, steeplechase, 1979), Mark Fuller (silver, Greco-Roman wrestling, 1983), H. Blaine Lindgren (gold, track), Greg Robbins (silver, wrestling, 1987), Denise Parker (gold, archery, 1987, 1991, 1995), Janet Blomstedt (gold, heptathalon, 1995).

6 Aug., first counselor Hugh B. Brown receives "a call from the Salt Lake City police advising me that four car loads of negroes armed with machine guns and bombs [are] reported coming to Salt Lake City for the purpose of inciting a riot and particularly to destroy property on the temple block." He orders all entrances to Salt Lake Temple Square to remain padlocked, and armed guards turn away all visitors this morning. For first time Choir performs its regular Sunday broadcast in otherwise empty Tabernacle.

21 Aug., First Presidency letter: "It appears that some bishops and branch presidents remove the names of inactive members of their ward or branch from the Church rolls in order that the ward or branch statistical records may present a better showing.... Even the fact that an individual has joined another Church is not always justifiable cause for excommunication. ... some wives of non-members have been excommunicated because their husbands refuse to permit them to be active."

31 Aug., George W. Romney states on national television that U.S. government leaders and senior military officers have "brainwashed" him and every other American about Vietnam War. First Mormon to seek U.S. presidency since 1844, Romney announces: "I no longer believe it was necessary for us to get involved in South Vietnam to stop Communist aggression." U.S. Secretary of Defense Robert McNamara immediately responds: "I don't think Governor Romney can recognize the truth when he sees it or hears it." Three decades later McNamara admits that at this time he privately regards Vietnam War as misguided and unwinnable, despite his public statements to the contrary as U.S. ground troops in Vietnam increase to half a million. Romney's use of word "brainwashed" is ridiculed nationally and he withdraws as presidential candidate in Feb. 1968.

29 Sept., establishment of new position of Regional Representative to the Twelve. At their first training seminar, Apostle Harold B. Lee (rather than member of First Presidency) gives confidential "State of the Church" address, which he continues to do annually.

18 Nov., *Church News* reports that four-year-old Timothy Fass "is '68 Poster Child" for national March of Dimes. Other Mormons who serve likewise are Scott Hafen (1974), Keegan McLoskey (1977), Devin Knight (1995).

27 Nov., New York Metropolitan Museum of Art gives to LDS church the Egyptian papyri upon which Joseph Smith based "Book of Abraham" in *Pearl of Great Price.* Egyptologists, LDS and non-LDS, verify that these papyri are typical "Book of Breathings" in form and content. Their only role was as catalyst for Smith's revelation about Abraham.

7 Dec., First Presidency letter that "we are now reaching over 80 percent of our available boys in Cub Scouting, Boy Scouting, and Exploring."

1968

1 Jan. start of LDS project to microfilm every Polish parish register by permission of Communist government of Poland. Its director, Dennis B. Neuenschwander, becomes general authority in 1991.

Death of Hilda Anderson Erickson at age 108, oldest survivor of 80,000 Mormon pioneers who came to Utah before completion of transcontinental railroad in 1869. She was six when she left Sweden with her parents.

20 Jan., *Church News* reports that LDS Genealogical Society is tape-recording "oral genealogies dating back to the 9th Century among the people of Samoa." Within decade LDS begin recording genealogies memorized by tribal historians of sub-Saharan Africa.

16 Mar., U.S. troops in "Charlie Company" massacre 400-500 civilians at village of My Lai, South Vietnam. One of soldiers later says that he does not participate until he sees his Mormon buddy, recently returned missionary, shooting Vietnamese women and children. Two days earlier, the other Mormon in Charlie Company wrote letter about unrelated incident in which his "friends" shot a woman working in a rice field, "kicked her to death," and then "emptied" their weapons into her head. "It was murder [and] I've seen it many times before," Greg Olsen wrote his father. "My faith in my fellow men is shot all to hell." After remorseful participants and news media unravel military's cover-up, officer-in-charge is court-martialed and imprisoned for giving his troops direct order to kill everyone in My Lai on suspicion that they are Communist sympathizers. Most published accounts emphasize religious background of the two Mormons at My Lai but say nothing about religion of other soldiers involved in massacre.

30 Mar., *Church News* story about two LDS roommates in Salt Lake City, Arab convert Ozzie Shamaly and Jewish convert Jim Loewy.

6 Apr., Hartman Rector, Jr. is sustained to First Council of Seventy as first Korean War veteran to become general authority.

13 Apr., eight African-American athletes from University of Texas at El Paso refuse to compete in track meet with BYU because Mormons "think they are cursed and belong to the devil." George S. Tanner, after forty-one years teaching in LDS institutes of religion, remarks: "The sad part of it is that their charges are not far from the truth."

22 Apr., baptism of Juliet Hulme in California, despite her confession to LDS authorities that she was imprisoned at age 15 for helping to murder the mother of a girlfriend. Her baptism is significant exception to LDS policies and leadership handbooks which prohibit living baptism (or even baptism for the dead) for anyone convicted of murder. While active in LDS women's auxiliaries, she becomes internationally famous as Anne Perry, author of murder mysteries.

18 May, *Church News* report about D.K. Brown, police chief of Jacksonville, Florida. As special-agent-in-charge of FBI office there Brown had succeeded in "breaking the back of a strong Ku Klux Klan by obtaining convictions for bombings of a Negro home."

22 June, BYU's president receives "confidential draft" by Terry Warner, professor of philosophy and religion, that "freedom of speech as it is known today is a secular concept and has no place of any kind at the BYU."

8 Sept., *The Case Against Congress,* co-authored by LDS journalist Jack Anderson, is on *New York Times* list of bestsellers. Other LDS (or raised-as-Mormon) authors on list: Dian Thomas (1975, *Roughing It Easy*); Glen A. Larson (1978, co-author, *Battle Star Galactica*); Howard J. Ruff (1979, *How To Prosper During the Coming Bad Years*); Robert G. Allen (1980, *Nothing Down;* 1983, *Creating Wealth*); Roseanne Barr (1989, *Roseanne*); Stephen R. Covey (1990, *The Seven Habits of Highly Effective People*); Jack Anderson and Dale Van Atta (1991, *Stormin' Norman*); Betty J. Eadie and Curtis Taylor (1993, *Embraced By the Light*); Deborah Laake (1993, *Secret Ceremonies,* for which she was promptly excommu-

nicated); Roseanne Barr Arnold (1994, *My Lives*); Stephen R. Covey, A. Roger Merrill, and Rebecca R. Merrill (1994, *First Things First*); Dave Wolverton (1994, *The Courtship of Princess Leia*); Richard Paul Evans (1995, *The Christmas Box;* 1996, *Timepiece*); Betty J. Eadie (1996, *The Awakening Heart*).

17 Oct., Belle Smith Spafford, general president of Relief Society, is elected president of National Council of Women in its eightieth anniversary year. She serves to 1970.

19 Nov., BYU's administrators discuss possibility of taking legal action to close down off-campus student newspaper.

19 Dec., BYU's *Daily Universe* publishes article in favor of recruiting African-American athletes. BYU's president writes: "This argues all the more in favor of our making the student newspaper an agency of our Communications Department rather than a student publication." *Universe* ceases to be independent student paper on 18 Apr. 1969, but "nothing would be announced about this new policy."

29 Dec., Gallup opinion poll lists David O. McKay as second most admired religious leader in America. Richard James Cushing, Roman Catholic cardinal of Boston, is most admired.

1969

7 Jan., First Presidency secretary Joseph Anderson answers letter about "the Church's stand pertaining to birth control," with the concluding statement: "After all, however, the brethren recognize that this is a personal matter involving the individuals concerned, and concerning which they must make their own decision." First Presidency's official statement on 14 April 1969 omits any reference to their own feelings about birth control as "a personal matter," and states: "We believe that those who practice birth control will reap disappointment by and by," and repeated earlier letter's emphasis on "self-control [as] a dominant factor" in marriage.

26 Feb., BYU's president instructs all bishops and stake presidents of BYU's student stakes to report to campus authorities any students who confess unacceptable conduct. This is way of "eliminating students who do not fit into the culture of BYU so that those [who] would fit into it might be admitted to the institution." This also ends confidentiality of confessions to LDS leaders.

11 Mar., David Ben-Gurion, Israel's former prime minister, tells Apostle Ezra Taft Benson: "There are no people in the world who understand Jews like Mormons." Benson replies: "Mr. Ben-Gurion, there are no people in this world who understand the *world* like the Mormons."

28 Apr., First Annual Mormon Festival of the Arts, held at BYU.

19 May, First Presidency publishes: "We make no statement on how this country can or should try to disengage itself from the present regrettable war in Vietnam. . . . We believe our young men should hold themselves in readiness to respond to the call of their government to serve in the armed forces when called upon." This is the first war in the twentieth century when the church's *Deseret News* does not editorialize in favor of option for conscientious objection.

21 May, First Presidency letter allows LDS servicemen in Vietnam to dye the regular, one-piece, temple garment to match green color of military-issue underwear.

1 June, cigarette ads are henceforth banned on broadcasts of LDS church's radio and television stations in Utah, Washington state, Missouri, California, and New York.

3 June, *New York Times* report that LDS church has preferred charges against LaMar E. Kay for embezzling $604,199.65 while employee of church's Auditing Department. This legal and publicized action is departure from previous church policy not to disclose embezzlements. Kay receives twenty-year sentence.

5 Aug., LDS church's World Conference on Records whose hundreds of participants include representatives of national archives of Soviet Union, Jewish Historical Archives in Jerusalem, UNESCO, U.S. national archives, and Japan's parliamentary library. Inter-

nationally famous for his book *Roots,* Alex Haley (also ghost-writer of *Autobiography of Malcolm X*) speaks at World Conference on Records in 1980.

20 Oct., while BYU's basketball team is playing University of Wyoming at Laramie, fourteen African-Americans are disqualified from Wyoming's team for wearing black armbands in protest of LDS church's priesthood restriction. Game continues despite objects thrown by spectators at playing floor and audience shouting accusations of racism against BYU's athletes.

9 Dec., First Presidency letter to director of seminaries and institutes, with copy to Bruce R. McConkie, that "we know of no justification for claiming that 'man was placed on the earth on the seventh day.'"

13 Dec., *Church News* reports that Mrs. Maria Martinez has been endowed at 114 years of age. By her native name Teoweluy Tetsa, she was among hundreds of Zunis healed in 1878 by Llewellyn Harris, but did not accept LDS baptism until age 107.

15 Dec., First Presidency letter giving stake presidents authority to set apart full-time missionaries. Previously only general authorities did this.

Also separate Presidency letter which begins: "In view of confusion that has arisen, it was decided at a meeting of the First Presidency and the Quorum of the Twelve to restate the position of the Church with regard to the Negro both in society and in the Church." This comes amid newspaper reports of first counselor Hugh B. Brown's statements about imminent change in church's policy toward blacks and priesthood. Apostle Harold B. Lee reversed Twelve's amenability to such a change and drafts this reaffirmation of policy. Brown reluctantly signs it after he adds endorsement of civil rights for African-Americans. It is published on 10 Jan. 1970. In response, Roy Wilkins of NAACP writes guest editorial for *Los Angeles Times* on 26 Jan., which concludes: "The Mormon walls on race will come tumbling down," a prophecy fulfilled in less than eight years.

1970

1 Jan., LDS Church adopts "Computer Age Finance System," and computerizes records of membership as of May 1. These are functions of church-owned Management Systems Corporation (MSC).

15 Jan., *Salt Lake Tribune* publishes statement from David O. McKay's son who verifies accuracy of following statement LDS president made to philosophy professor Sterling M. McMurrin in 1958: "There is no doctrine in this Church and there never was a doctrine in this Church to the effect that the Negroes are under any kind of a divine curse."

18 Jan., David O. McKay's death at age 96, oldest age to which any LDS president has lived, but not oldest general authority. His is longest service as general authority, sixty-three years and nine months. Heber J. Grant and Joseph Fielding Smith have next longest tenures of sixty-two years and a few months as general authorities.

23 Jan., Quorum of Twelve Apostles ordains Joseph Fielding Smith as church president. Some apostles considered by-passing this ninety-three-year-old apostle for the vigorous Harold B. Lee. Smith promised to make Lee his first counselor if he would support automatic succession of elderly apostle. Both keep their promises, and N. Eldon Tanner remains second counselor. Smith is oldest man to become LDS church president.

5 Feb., BYU basketball game is disrupted by protest against LDS church's policy of denying priesthood ordination to African-Americans. While 150 Colorado State University student demonstrators scuffle with campus police and twenty Fort Collins policemen during half-time, someone throws Molotov cocktail on playing floor. When game resumes, spectators throw raw eggs at BYU's players.

14 Feb., First Presidency and Presiding Bishopric launch first organized effort to "provide sufficient security for the Church headquarters buildings." Next day First counselor Lee meets with Salt Lake City officials "to discuss the coordination between Church security personnel and the city police in handling any emergencies that might arise."

7 Mar., *Church News* reports that Ken Shelley and his partner have won U.S. Figure Skating

championship for pairs. They win again (1971, 1972), and Shelley also wins men's national competition (1972). Billy and Cori-Joe Petrunik receive gold medal as LDS pair of figure-skaters at Canada Winter Games (1975). Holly Cook receives bronze medal at World Figure Skating Championships (1990).

15 Mar., first stake in Asia (Tokyo, Japan).

22 Mar., first stake in Africa (Transvaal, South Africa).

30 Mar., First Presidency statement quotes Church Historian's Office against alleged "Horse Shoe Prophecy." It attributes prophecy to John Taylor rather than to Joseph Smith and concludes: "There is no record by any of the General Authorities about it; nor is there anything in the diaries of which we have copies." Current LDS president Joseph Fielding recently ends fifty-year service as church historian.

5 Apr., Brigham Young University publishes full-page newspaper advertisement, "Minorities, Civil Rights, and BYU." This responds to protests about lack of African-Americans on BYU's athletic teams as alleged extension of LDS church's policy of withholding priesthood from blacks. This athletic restriction ends with priesthood restriction.

When bomb threat is phoned during afternoon session of conference, first counselor Harold B. Lee tells police: "There is no bomb here; relax."

6 Apr., in reporting his recent tour of missions in Asia, Apostle Ezra Taft Benson tells general conference of Korean branch of fifty members, including five college professors.

25 Apr. 1970, *Church News* has headline reference to recently sustained LDS president as "The Prophet," which is repeated in May 9 article "A Tribute To The Prophet." Joseph Fielding Smith is first LDS president identified by *Church News* headlines as "The Prophet" throughout his administration. This practice intensifies for his successors.

12 May, after days of student protests at University of Utah against Ohio National Guard's killing of students at Kent State, bomb destroys offices of Utah National Guard.

23 May, *Church News* article about Yoshiko Nakamura, Relief Society president in Hiroshima where her only child was burned to death by atomic blast in 1945 and her husband later died of radiation sickness. She comments: "I have no resentment for America now."

6 June, *Church News* reports advancement to admiral's rank of C. Monroe Hart, MIT graduate who helped develop Polaris missile submarine.

2 July, appointment of Rafael E. Castillo Valdes, BYU graduate and Mormon, as Guatemala's ambassador to United Nations (serving to 1975). David M. Kennedy is appointed United States ambassador to NATO (1972), and newly independent nation of Croatia appoints Kresimir Cosic as its deputy ambassador to United Nations (1992).

17 July, First Presidency letter ends financial independence of Relief Society by stopping payment of dues, prohibiting traditional Relief Society bazaar ("a noisy, carnival-like or commercial atmosphere"), and requiring that individual "Relief Societies should immediately turn over to the appropriate Stake, Mission, Ward, Branch, or District presiding officers all assets which they have accumulated." This clarifies full intent of brief letter of 10 June. Eliminating Relief Society's autonomy is central goal of Harold B. Lee's vision of church "correlation."

24 July, LDS headquarters invites only prominent Republicans to Salt Lake City airport to greet U.S. president Richard M. Nixon who has asked to meet with First Presidency. This excludes Utah's Democratic governor Calvin M. Rampton who "almost had to force his way into receiving line." First Presidency secretary Francis M. Gibbons later acknowledges that this is "a snafu in protocol." *Deseret News* reports that Nixon addresses crowd of 15,000 from steps of Church Office Building at 47 East South Temple Street, but Nixons cancel their scheduled tour of Temple Square because of what Utah's Congressional representative Laurence J. Burton describes as "stupid, crazy, threatening" posters of "dissident groups." Presidency secretary Gibbons later describes these as "militant blacks" and antiwar protestors.

Aug., First Presidency's instruction: "A female Church member married to a nonmember is not permitted to receive a temple recommend for her endowment blessing. The same applies to a female member married to a Church member who has not received his endowment, even though the husband is willing to give his consent in writing for his wife to receive her endowment." On 27 Jan. 1972, First Presidency complained that "from time to time recommends are issued to sisters in accordance with the old provision in the handbook but contrary to and in apparent ignorance of the new instruction contained in the Aug. 1970 *Priesthood Bulletin.*" Since 1845 temple endowment had been available for women to bless their non-LDS husbands. First Presidency repeats this instruction on 25 July 1979 because of "an increasing number of instances in which local leaders issue temple recommends contrary to the express limitations of the General Handbook."

15 Oct., *Deseret News* ceases advertising films rated "X" or "R."

1971

6 Feb., *Church News* reports promotion of Larry M. Killpack as brigadier-general in U.S. Air Force, with comment: "He has flown 165 [combat] missions during the 10 months he has been in Southeast Asia."

8 Feb., arsonists damage stake center of Mill Creek, Utah.

24 Feb., meeting of 150 students on BYU's campus condemns U.S. participation in Vietnam War. Among them is Apostle Spencer W. Kimball's grandson, a registered conscientious objector and returned missionary. He and several members of group soon publish pamphlet, *To the Men of BYU,* which encourages them to consider conscientious objection against this war. Surveys by BYU sociologists find that about 10 percent of BYU students oppose Vietnam War.

2 Mar., First Presidency letter asking "ALL GENERAL AUTHORITIES" to stop "utilizing Church employees and equipment for personal purposes without reimbursement to the Church." Letter specifically refers to maintenance of hierarchy's homes.

3 Mar., demolition begins of old tabernacle at Coalville, Utah, formerly on national register. Mormons and non-Mormons (primarily non-residents of Coalville) waged court battle and petitioned First Presidency not to destroy this meeting house now regarded as obsolete by church authorities. First Presidency publishes statement in defense of demolition, which attracts enough attention to merit feature story in *New York Times.*

17 Mar., James D. Morask, paraplegic for four years after automobile accident, regains feeling and movement in his legs immediately after his LDS baptism. Eight months later, *Church News* reports that he is now walking "with braces to give his legs support and has learned to drive again."

24 Mar., First Presidency shortens "the standard term of service for lady missionaries" from 24 months to 18 months.

28 Mar., Keene Curtis receives "Tony" award from League of American Theatres and Producers as best supporting actor in Broadway musical *The Rothschilds.*

20 May, after BYU's *Wye Magazine* publishes some poetry and fiction which general authorities and others find offensive, the university's administration "confiscated those copies that had not been delivered (1,000 out of 2,000)." Two years later general authorities require BYU Press to destroy its entire press run of Thomas E. Cheney's *Golden Legacy,* because he includes some vulgarisms in J. Golden Kimball's folk tales. Cheney republishes it with independent press and without offending stories.

26 June, BYU's Ballroom Dancers win formation division of British Open Amateur Ballroom Championships. This is first U.S. team of formation dancers to compete abroad.

31 July, *Church News* reports that registered nurse Marilyn Lyons and Dr. Blair L. Bybee, church's first medical missionaries, are departing for assignments in Tonga and Samoa by direction of Welfare Services Missionary Program. First Presidency letter of 22 Jan. 1973 solicits missionaries from U.S., Canada, New Zealand, Australia, and Latin America. Redefined as "welfare missionaries," 768 Mormons without medical degrees are

giving humanitarian aid and instruction throughout world by 1980. Decade later more than 350 "health missionaries" with medical or health degrees are also serving in Africa, Asia, Latin America, Caribbean, Pacific islands, and Eastern Europe.

26 Aug., during church's first area conference in Manchester, England, there is formal meeting of joint council of First Presidency and Quorum of Twelve Apostles. This is first such council meeting outside United States in Mormon history.

14 Sept., Apollo 15 astronauts present to President Joseph Fielding Smith a Utah state flag that has traveled with them to moon.

16 Sept., President Smith faints during First Presidency meeting, and goes to temple council meeting "over the protests of the Brethren." During Thursday meeting on 21 Oct. he becomes ill and has "to be helped from the council room."

9 Oct., *Deseret News* publishes on front page of local section a First Presidency statement which condemns upcoming Salt Lake City performance of Andrew Lloyd Webber's *Jesus Christ Superstar* as "a profane and sacrilegious attack upon true Christianity." Although statement advises everyone to oppose this production, audience fills Salt Palace to "near capacity" for musical's only scheduled performance on 12 Oct.

19 Oct., Genesis Group is organized for Salt Lake Valley's 200 LDS African-Americans to meet for auxiliary organizations, while attending sacrament meetings in their respective wards. Apostle Gordon B. Hinckley sets apart Ruffin Bridgeforth, Jr. as president, with Darius Gray and Eugene Orr as counselors.

21 Oct., First Presidency secretary Joseph Anderson writes that conscientious objectors can teach, partake of sacrament, hold church offices, and receive temple recommends.

1972

14 Jan., First Presidency organizes church's historical department and for first time appoints professional historian, Leonard J. Arrington, as church historian, to which he is sustained by church conferences from 1972 to 1977. Church archives had been open for unrestricted research by scholars of all religious backgrounds since appointment in 1970 of Arrington's predecessor, Apostle Howard W. Hunter. Arrington continues as Church Historian until 1980, during which time First Presidency encourages research and publication.

From 1972 to 1980, historical department has Church History Division. Church Historian Leonard J. Arrington and his staff of trained historians publish articles and books of interpretive history which seek to provide balanced view of Mormonism's controversial past. In 1980 First Presidency eliminates Church History Division and transfers former Church Historian and his staff to Brigham Young University.

Open access to LDS archives gradually diminishes from 1980 to 1986, when historical department begins to claim right of *ex post facto* censorship of previous research. By 1986 historical department has created "public access" computer catalog which omits previously available manuscripts now judged too sensitive for research "patrons." Only staff of historical department has access to uncensored catalog of manuscripts. Procedurally, archival research is further impeded by requiring approval from historical department committee or even from committee of apostles for research access to previously unrestricted manuscripts. By 1990 researchers having signed form since 1986 are required to obtain pre-publication approval from church's Correlation Committee. Efforts at pre-publication censorship prove counterproductive and are officially abandoned in 1992, yet researchers at LDS archives continue to be small fraction of their numbers during years in which people of all backgrounds knew they were welcome there.

18 Jan., Joseph Fielding Smith is unable to finish reading dedicatory prayer for temple at Ogden, Utah, and first counselor Harold B. Lee completes dedication. Some report seeing "a brilliant light at the pulpit whenever the First Presidency members stood to speak in the celestial room of the temple."

Feb., "With reference to cola drinks the Church has never officially taken a position on the matter," begins *Priesthood Bulletin*, yet concludes: "Any beverage that contains ingredients harmful to the body should be avoided."

9 Feb., Joseph Fielding Smith dedicates temple at Provo, Utah. General authority Alvin R. Dyer reports that he "clearly saw [deceased] President David O. McKay in vision."

24 Mar., incorporation of Deseret Trust Company to manage centrally controlled church trusts and endowments (in contrast to church stock and bond portfolios managed by major investment houses in New York City).

6 Apr., Loren C. Dunn tells general conference: "To sustain is to make the action binding on ourselves and to commit ourselves to support those whom we have sustained. . . . If for any reason we have a difficult time sustaining those in office, then we are to go to our local priesthood leaders and discuss the issue with them and seek their help."

13 May, Presidency statement that "fluoridation of public water supplies to prevent tooth decay" is one of the "non-moral issues" that Mormons should vote on "according to their honest convictions." John Birch Society, which Apostle Ezra Taft Benson and many other Mormons support, is condemning fluoridation as Communist "plot."

26 May, Presidency letter that "all existing student wards be converted into student branches" to avoid ordaining men in their twenties to office of high priest. "It also sometimes creates social dislocation where these young men are members of high priests quorums where the age level is much higher than in elders or seventies quorums."

2 July, Joseph Fielding Smith dies.

7 July, Quorum of the Twelve sustains Harold B. Lee as church president with N. Eldon Tanner and Marion G. Romney as counselors and ordains Lee. From 1918 until this day, all LDS church presidents are born in Utah. Lee is first LDS president born in Idaho and first to reach adulthood in twentieth century. Romney is first member of First Presidency born outside U.S. since Charles W. Nibley's death in 1931.

14 July, Jean Miles Westwood is elected national chair of Democratic Party, first Mormon and first woman to head major political party in United States.

20 Aug., Joel F. Lebaron is murdered in Mexico by order of his brother Ervil. This is first fatality involving polygamy since 1886 and first killing of Mormon schismatic leader since 1862. However, it is unfortunately only first of dozen or more murders involving Ervil Lebaron's violent group, The Church of the Lamb of God.

26 Aug., *Church News* article about Mrs. Viola Clawson's recent retirement as supervisor of all-male guides on Salt Lake Temple Square since 1942. She had total discretion in their appointment, assigned days/hours, and release.

30 Sept., during first visit of current LDS president to Jerusalem, Harold B. Lee conducts sacrament meeting in Garden Tomb, and by "inspiration of the moment" organizes branch with David B. Galbraith as president. He "shocked" new branch presidency by denying their request to have branch's worship services on Jewish Sabbath. Months later, Lee relents and authorizes LDS branch in Jerusalem to worship on Saturday.

7 Oct., *Church News* announcement of twelve "fellowship lessons" for new converts.

10 Oct., First Presidency letter: "We are concerned that adequate attention be given to members of the Church who do not speak the language of the majority where they live." It authorizes wards and branches to have priesthood and auxiliary classes taught in foreign languages, or organization of branches/wards for sufficient numbers of Mormons who speak foreign languages. This fulfills Apostle Spencer W. Kimball's earnest proposal to temple meeting on 1 July 1970.

11 Oct., First Presidency letter authorizes young men to be ordained to office of elder at age eighteen, no longer limiting elder's office to age for missionaries.

17 Oct., L. Patrick Gray, FBI director, offers to help LDS church security to protect members of First Presidency against assassination attempts by Ervil LeBaron's followers.

Nov., church's bureaucracy ("administrative departments") begins moving into new 28-story Church Office Building. LDS bureaucracy is already larger than building's capacity, and some units never move in. Other administrative departments stay in "the tower" only until they establish their own separate quarters. Church Office Building is not dedicated (and therefore not paid for) until 1975.

18 Nov., *Church News* reports that one million "family group sheets" have been stolen from LDS genealogical library by researchers: "We appeal to all those who may have archive sheets belonging to the society to return them. No questions will be asked."

1973

6 Jan., Rahman Fatafitah of Beirut is first Muslim to join LDS church in Middle East. Other Muslims had been baptized in Utah decade earlier.

11 Jan., BYU student and returned LDS missionary Thomas Gregory admits to Congress that he was recruited by Watergate co-conspirator E. Howard Hunt to infiltrate and spy on office of Democratic candidate for U.S. presidency, George McGovern from February to June 1972. At time of this political espionage Gregory is student in BYU's intern/study program at Washington, D.C.

3 Feb., church's first agricultural missionaries depart (initially to South America).

10 Feb., Boy Scouts of America's director for Mormon relations reports that one of every twenty Scouts in U.S. is LDS.

13 Feb., twenty-one-year-old Almir S. Dutra is ordained bishop in Porto Allegre, Brazil as one of youngest (if not youngest) bishops in twentieth-century Mormonism.

8 Mar., first stake on mainland Asia (Seoul, South Korea).

10-11 Mar., Major Robert Jeffrey and Captain Larry Chesley, recently released as LDS prisoners-of-war for seven years in North Vietnam, are honored in Texas and Idaho.

28 Apr., *Church News* reports that LDS New Zealander Susan Vickers has won Miss Auckland beauty contest despite her refusal to wear bikini swimming suit.

11 Sept., overthrow and death of Salvador Allende, democratically elected president of Chile where Mormons are higher percentage of population than in U. S. Allende is Marxist, and LDS mission president's non-missionary assistant proclaims that "the Lord played a part in the overthrow of that communist government," possibly a knowing reference to alleged role of Anaconda Copper's LDS executive Charles Jay Parkinson in financing Allende's overthrow. When asked about LDS socialists who are among thousands who soon "disappear" by orders of dictator Augusto Pinochet, Chile's regional representative Robert E. Wells replies: "If he had to shoot anyone the great majority deserved it since they were terrorists. The U.S. bleeding heart press doesn't understand the local situation." Wells becomes general authority in 1976.

21 Oct., First Presidency letter urges 78,800 Mormons in Washington state to vote against referendum to allow nineteen-year-olds to purchase and consume alcoholic beverages.

7 Nov., arsonists damage LDS chapel in Scotsdale, Arizona.

1 Dec., *Church News* story about Amy Moikeha, retired police officer and president of Relief Society on island of Maui, Hawaii.

15 Dec., First Presidency statement, in response to Middle East oil embargo, urges energy conservation and authorizes local wards and branches to hold all auxiliary meetings on single day of week.

26 Dec., death of Harold B. Lee, LDS church president with shortest tenure up to this time, seventeen months and nineteen days. At age seventy-four Lee is youngest LDS president to die since Joseph Smith, and Lee's presidency remains briefest until 1995.

30 Dec., Quorum of Twelve Apostles sustains Spencer W. Kimball as church president with N. Eldon Tanner and Marion G. Romney as counselors, and ordains President Kimball.

1974

7 Jan., Swen Nielsen, head of BYU's security department, is police chief of Provo, Utah. His replacement at BYU, Robert W. Kelshaw, has been assistant police chief since 1966.

13 Jan., three missionaries in Pennsylvania are killed in head-on collision after car repeatedly bumps rear of their car and finally forces them into path of oncoming car.

24 Feb., during his formal presentation to high priest meeting in Salt Lake City ward, Reed C. Durham, Jr. says: "There was a revelation that John Taylor received and we have it in his handwriting. We've analyzed the handwriting. . . . The revelation is dated September 27; that fits this account of a meeting, 1886, and this revelation is very short." Durham is director of LDS institute and president of Mormon History Association.

2 Apr., Academy of Motion Picture Arts and Sciences gives "Oscar" to two Mormons: Keith Merrill (director, documentary *The Great American Cowboy*) and James Payne (set design, *The Sting*). They are the first Mormon winners in 33 years, but LDS nominees are Leigh Harline (music scores, 1943, 1944, 1963), Arnold Friberg (art work, *The Ten Commandments*, 1956), Russ Tamblyn (supporting actor, *Peyton Place*, 1957). Tamblyn also receives Golden Globe award in 1956 as "most promising newcomer," as does LDS Ruth Buzzi in 1973 for her supporting role in television's *Laugh-In*.

Within days, Council on International Non-theatrical Events (CINE) gives its "Golden Eagle" award to Brigham Young University for "Cipher In the Snow," which receives international distribution among schools and various religious denominations. In 1989 LDS church and Bonneville International also receive two Golden Eagle awards for their "Homefront" public-service advertisements. Individual Mormons who win Golden Eagle include Curt Bestor (1988) and Martin L. Andersen (1994).

5 Apr., announcement of appointment of David M. Kennedy as First Presidency's "special representative." Kennedy served as U.S. Secretary of the Treasury (1969-70), as U.S. Ambassador-at-large (1970-72), and as U.S. ambassador to NATO (1972-73). As church's first officially designated foreign ambassador, Kennedy's primary mission is to obtain formal recognition of the LDS church and admission of full-time missionaries wherever they are excluded, especially in Communist Europe and the Near East. He is released on 31 Mar. 1990. Rather than appoint new "special representative," First Presidency delegates those responsibilities to area presidencies and mission presidents.

6 Apr., conference sustains Neal A. Maxwell as Assistant to Twelve, first general authority who previously worked for U.S. government's Central Intelligence Agency (CIA). Maxwell becomes member of Twelve in 1981.

20 Apr., Reed C. Durham, Jr. gives presidential address to Mormon History Association (MHA) at Nauvoo, in which he emphasizes Joseph Smith's Jupiter talisman and its relationship to magic and Freemasonry. As immediate result, officials at LDS information center in Nauvoo remove Angel Moroni from spire of center's detailed model of Nauvoo temple. Following architect's drawings the model shows angel holding Masonic symbols of compass and square, but those symbols are absent when angel-replica is reinstalled on model. Shortly afterward LDS president Spencer W. Kimball releases Durham as institute director and requires him to write letter of apology and retraction. Durham remains faculty member of Salt Lake Institute of Religion but declines to attend future meetings of MHA, even one honoring all of its former presidents.

9 June, Spencer W. Kimball administers second anointing to his heart surgeon Russell M. Nelson and wife Dantzel in Holy of Holies of Salt Lake temple. Nelson becomes member of Twelve in 1984. Dramatic increase of second anointings during Kimball's presidency.

July, first issue of *Exponent II*, "the Spiritual Descendant of the *Woman's Exponent*, 1872-1914." Established in Arlington, Massachusetts, by Mormon Sisters, Inc., to re-invoke the faithful consciousness-raising of original *Woman's Exponent*. Founded by Claudia Lauper Bushman, wife of stake president and later regional representative. Bushman is professor and author of *Mormon Sisters: Women in Early Utah*. Other independent publications emphasizing LDS women are *Mormon Women's Forum: An LDS Feminist Quarterly* (1989), *Voices: A Forum for Feminist Thought at BYU* (1991), *Latter-day Women* (1993).

28 July, *New York Times* reports lawsuit by NAACP against LDS church. Since church's Boy Scout program gives troop and post leadership only to boy-leaders in LDS Aaronic

Priesthood, this discriminates against African-American Boy Scouts, who are denied priesthood ordination by LDS policy. LDS Scout policy changes within months, and lingering discrimination question becomes moot in four years.

This evening Judiciary Committee of U.S. House of Representatives votes to approve first of three articles of impeachment against President M. Nixon. Only Mormon on committee, Democrat Wayne Owens of Utah, votes for all three. As final act of Watergate break-in scandal, Nixon resigns within days rather than wait for certain impeachment by entire House and conviction-expulsion by Senate. Mormon D. Todd Christofferson is clerk for Watergate trial judge John J. Sirica throughout Watergate proceedings, and becomes general authority in 1993.

6 Sept., First Presidency announcement of intention to legally divest church of fifteen hospitals in three western states. Most maintain their "LDS Hospital" titles despite ownership by "non-Mormon" and non-profit corporation, Intermountain Healthcare. This move also represents First Presidency's decision to publicly disengage church from hospital ownership following 1973 U.S. Supreme Court decision *Roe vs. Wade* which legalized abortions on demand. Although Presiding Bishopric signs final divestiture agreement on 1 April 1975, Intermountain Healthcare is listed among "Associated Businesses" of LDS church in *General Church Offices Telephone Directory, January 1996.*

28 Oct., missionary companions Gary S. Darley and Mark F. Fischer are murdered in Texas by LDS convert who had returned to Pentecostal church. In its most sensational coverage ever, *Church News* reports that "body parts" of the missionaries are discovered on 13 Nov. and that murderer is sentenced to death in 1975 for killing the missionaries and "cutting up their bodies with a saw." In 1977, murderer successfully appeals his conviction due to illegal search, but remains in prison on other charges until his parole in 1988.

19 Nov., Spencer W. Kimball dedicates temple near Washington, D.C.

1975

Winter, first issue of *Sunstone: A Quarterly Journal of Mormon Experience, Scholarship, Issues and Art.* This is first Mormon publication with interfaith focus as well as emphasis on controversial Mormon topics. Six years later BYU establishes institutional version of interfaith journal in *Literature and Belief.*

10 Apr., twins Daniel and David Geslison, age twenty-one, begin service as missionaries in Iceland, two days after returning from their first two-year missions, Daniel from Japan and David from Korea. On 20 Aug. 1977, *Church News* refers to their recent "return home" from missionary service in Iceland.

22 May, Association of Catholic Communications gives "Gabriel" award to LDS church for "Homefront" public-service advertising which soon receives this award almost yearly.

30 May, Maxine Conder is second woman in U.S. Navy history to be promoted to admiral. In her biographical sketch for *Who's Who in America,* Admiral Conder writes: "I am eternally grateful for my Mormon heritage."

7 June, President Spencer W. Kimball announces his resignation from management positions of church corporations to more fully serve spiritual needs of church. His associates in Presidency and Twelve continue extensive corporate management roles until 1996.

27 June, announcement of end of conferences at church headquarters for church's auxiliaries. This completes Harold B. Lee's previous efforts to dismantle autonomy of church's five auxiliaries for women, teenage girls, teenage boys, children, and Sunday schools. "Priesthood correlation" eliminates century of administrative autonomy exercised by LDS women over budgetary and administrative decisions in these auxiliaries.

19 July, LDS church and its Bonneville Productions receive national advertising award ("Clio") for its "Homefront" advertising on television. Church also receives Clio awards (1979, 1980, 1984, 1992, 1993).

23 July, First Presidency circular letter authorizes stake presidents to ordain bishops. Previously this was restricted to general authorities.

19 Sept., First Presidency letter instructs that those Mormons who refuse to pay federal income taxes are violating the law and the church's 12th Article of Faith.

2 Oct., conclusion of last Relief Society conference. Primary and Young Women's organizations held their last conferences the previous Apr. and June. Beginning Sept. 1978, there are annual meetings for women, but these lack the several days of training workshops previously directed by women.

3 Oct., organization of First Quorum of the Seventy for first time in 131 years and for first time ever as general authority quorum. Conference also sustains as general authority the first Native American, George P. Lee, a Navajo.

12 Oct., Presidency counselor N. Eldon Tanner dedicates LDS dormitory and classroom building at Michigan State University, "the first of its kind at a non-Church school outside of Utah."

16 Oct., BYU publishes half-page newspaper advertisement, "Notification of Brigham Young University Policy of Non-Discrimination on the Basis of Sex," to counter protests that BYU practices gender discrimination. Two days later BYU places advertisement in various newspapers that the university refuses to comply with six regulations of U.S. Department of Health, Education and Welfare's Title IX regulations for non-discrimination on basis of gender.

1 Nov., *Church News* article about Kathy Devine, LDS shotputter and Olympic aspirant who criticizes those who "think all girls should be out baking cookies somewhere."

8 Nov., *Church News* article about LDS conversion of Moshe A. Ben-Asa, sixteenth-generation rabbi in Sephardic Judaism.

U.S. president Gerald R. Ford appoints Lt.-General Brent Scowcroft to chair National Security Council. He is first Mormon to serve as direct "adviser" to U.S. presidents regarding use of force against foreign nations. Scowcroft serves until Ford's term ends in Jan. 1977 and heralds significant appointments of other Mormons to national military-security positions. Ronald Reagan does not re-appoint Scowcroft but does appoint LDS Michael J. Barrett as Assistant General Counsel to CIA's director.

10 Nov., First Presidency authorizes persons performing temple ordinances to have "the option of wearing either the 'approved style' garment (short sleeve and knee length) or the garment with the long sleeve and long leg."

20 Nov., organization of Jewish Mission Task Committee (JMTC) at LDS headquarters to coordinate proselytizing of Jews

6 Dec., *Church News* features Lillian M. Martin, LDS lieutenant-colonel in U.S. Army. However, on 21 Feb. 1976 article warns that "Women Should Be Cautious About Military."

17 Dec., Robert I. McQueen, returned LDS missionary, begins service as editor-in-chief of *The Advocate*, national magazine for gays and lesbians. He is excommunicated in 1979.

20 Dec., *Church News* feature article about Delores ("Lorie") Watson, national women's motocross champion for 125 cc motorcycles.

1976

1 Jan., LDS church has float in California's Rose Parade, first time in fifty years that invitation is extended to any church by parade organizers.

17 Jan., *Church News* article about Mormon convert Piera Bellaviti, formerly a nun and Vatican secretary to popes Pius XII, John XXIII, and Paul VI.

1 Feb., while speaking to a twelve-stake fireside at BYU about Mormonism and the arts, Apostle Boyd K. Packer says that some LDS musicians are "more temper than mental."

12 Mar., African-American Robert Lee Stevenson is elected vice-president of BYU students.

13 Mar., LaMoin Merkley, LDS high priest, is inducted into Hall of Fame of National Association of Intercollegiate Athletics for wrestling.

3 Apr., adoption of two previously published visions as additions to church's Standard Works. First change in church's official canon since addition of 1890 Manifesto.

21 May, LaVern Watts Parmley receives Silver Buffalo award. Formerly general Primary president, she is first LDS woman to receive this highest honor from Boy Scouts of America. Dwan Jacobsen Young, also former president of Primary, receives award in 1990.

4 June, announcement of new bishopric position of "Presiding Bishopric Area Supervisor." Later called "area director of temporal affairs," this calling represents decentralization of Presiding Bishopric administration in Presiding Bishopric International Offices (PBIO). Several areas, each with its own PBIO, are administered by "zone administrator of temporal affairs." Although implemented outside LDS population centers of U.S. and Canada, these are first intermediate offices in twentieth century between Presiding Bishopric and ward bishops.

5 June, First Presidency statement against legal abortions.

25 June, Missouri's current governor officially rescinds 1838 extermination order.

30 July, Randall Ellsworth, missionary temporarily paralyzed by collapse of LDS chapel during Guatemala's February earthquake, returns to minister among native Indians there. After months of physical therapy in Utah, the twenty-year-old now "walks with short-legged braces and a cane."

14 Aug., *New York Times* reports U.S. patent granted to Mormons G. Richard Jacobs, Cluff Peck, Dean G. Doderquist for "speaking mannequins" at LDS information centers.

28 Sept., First Presidency letter advises Mormons throughout U.S. to obtain immunization against swine flu. Government-sponsored mass inoculations are "a cure without a disease."

1 Oct., dissolution of First Council of the Seventy and Assistants to the Twelve, who merge into First Quorum of the Seventy. After this date there is no permanent ranking or membership for Presidency of the Seventy. Conference also sustains first ethnic Japanese and first former Buddhist as general authority, First Quorum of Seventy's Adney Y. Komatsu, who was born in Hawaii.

2 Oct., at general conference President Spencer W. Kimball says: "We warn you against the dissemination of doctrines which are not according to the scriptures and which are alleged to have been taught by some of the General Authorities of past generations. Such, for instance, is the Adam-God theory. We denounce that theory and hope that everyone will be cautioned against this and other kinds of false doctrine."

16 Oct., "10,000 concerned citizens" attend "Rally for Decency" supported by LDS church in its anti-pornography drive. By assignment from headquarters to local congregations, Mormons are picketing Salt Lake City's X-rated movie houses which soon close.

22 Oct., First Presidency statement against ratification of proposed Equal Rights Amendment to U.S. Constitution, "which could indeed bring them far more restraints and repressions. We fear it will even stifle many God-given feminine instincts." In supplemental letter of 29 Dec. Presidency urges all mission presidents and stake presidents "to join others in efforts to defeat the ERA." This leads to coordinated efforts by Mormons in twenty-one states to lobby state legislators against ratification of ERA or to persuade voters to rescind previous ratification.

1977

15 Jan., *Church News* article about Jack Kong, president of LDS branch at leper colony of Molokai for twenty-five years.

21 Jan., U.S. president Jimmy Carter grants general pardon to Vietnam War's draft resisters, thousands of whom had fled to Canada. Utah's television stations interview draft-resister Richard W. Glade, former LDS missionary and grandson of one of Salt Lake City's mayors. Now a Canadian citizen and university professor, Glade welcomes this as beginning of reconciliation but says he has no intention of returning to United States.

15 Mar., First Presidency letter that "missionaries should not engage in excessive or lengthy fasting."

22 Mar., H. Tracy Hall receives International Prize for New Materials from American Physi-

cal Society for synthesizing diamonds. David M. Grant receives highest award of American Chemical Society in 1990 for his "pioneering work in nuclear magnetic resonance (NMR) spectroscopy." Both are BYU professors.

23 Mar., Jerusalem's mayor Teddy Kollek writes to president of LDS branch there: "We are indeed happy with the great interest shows by the Mormons in Jerusalem. . . . It is in this spirit that we welcome the intentions of the Mormons to build permanent structure in Jerusalem to house center for their activities in the city." This is result of BYU's study abroad program in Jerusalem. Israel's government officially recognizes LDS church as legal association in April. Kollek receives honorary doctorate from BYU in 1995.

2 Apr., Richard G. Scott is sustained to First Quorum of Seventy. He is first general authority with extensive experience in what U.S. president Dwight D. Eisenhower called "the military-industrial complex." Scott served as nuclear engineer at weapons research laboratory in Oakridge, Tennessee, and developed nuclear submarines for twelve years on staff of Admiral Hyman Rickover. Scott becomes member of Twelve in 1988.

9 Apr., death at age eight-one of Mildred T. Pettit, composer of "I Am A Child Of God," most popular twentieth-century hymn of Mormonism.

19 Apr., First Presidency letter solicits contributions for completion of thirteen bronze statues for "Relief Society Monument in Nauvoo, Illinois. The purpose of this monument is twofold: first, to honor the founding of the Relief Society in 1842 by the Prophet Joseph Smith, and second, to portray to the world the role of women in the gospel plan."

29 Apr., *New York Times* reports election of Walter Pearce as first Mormon mayor of Nauvoo, Illinois, since 1846.

10 May, Fundamentalist leader Rulon C. Allred is murdered in his office by two plural wives ("Lambs of God") from Ervil LeBaron's group. This is most publicized of several murders Ervil orders, and his death threats include LDS president Spencer W. Kimball. His actions disenchant all but most devout LeBaron followers. Allred's death leads to close cooperation between law-enforcement agencies and various groups of non-violent Fundamentalist mainstream, which ultimately benefits from this greater understanding. For ordering the murder LeBaron is imprisoned in Utah penitentiary, where he dies of heart attack in 1981. The women who murder Allred are acquitted by Utah jury, and in 1990 one of them publicly admits committing the murder.

14 May, establishment of first bishop's storehouse outside Salt Lake City (in Colton, CA).

30 May, Poland is first Communist regime to grant legal recognition to LDS church, result primarily of LDS microfilming project there. In addition, for five years Croatian basketball hero Kresimir Cosic has persuaded Communist authorities of Yugoslavia to allow LDS missionaries to enter on tourist visas.

3 June, Relief Society's general presidency sends letter to "All Regional Representatives in Utah," restating Apostle Ezra Taft Benson's telephoned instructions for each ward bishop to send ten women to Utah state meeting of International Women's Year. This packs the Salt Lake City meeting with nearly 14,000 women, who have instructions to vote down any proposal which sounds "feminist" or favorable to Equal Rights Amendment, including equal pay for equal work and protections for women who were raped.

20 June, Henry R. Eliason, age 77, is fatally stabbed in El Cajon, California, oldest LDS missionary to be murdered

30 July, *Church News* headline "Church Education System Now In 55 Countries."

1 Oct., conference sustains first Japanese-born general authority as member of First Quorum of the Seventy, Yoshihiko Kikuchi. Also newly appointed F. Enzio Busche is first general authority who has been imprisoned by Americans in POW camp.

15 Oct., *Church News* feature story that "three LDS men serve their community as members of the five-man committee that controls and regulates the state's [Nevada's] billion-dollar-a-year casino industry."

1 Nov., Spencer W. Kimball dedicates Osmond Family Studio in Orem, Utah.

16 Dec., mayor of Sao Paulo, Brazil, approves naming street for Joseph Smith, Jr.

1978

4 Jan., First Presidency announces findings of sociological survey of returned LDS missionaries: 97 percent attend at least one sacrament meeting per month, 95 percent are married or sealed in temple, 89 percent hold current church position, 85 percent have current temple recommend.

7 Jan., *Church News* article that Paul Freebairn, returned LDS missionary, is vice-president of American Surfing Association. Seventeen-year-old Peter Avery becomes U.S. National Body Boarding Champion in 1993.

15 Feb., First Presidency letter that Mohammed and Confucius "received a portion of God's light."

22 Feb., First Presidency letter to all stake and mission leaders: "The fact that there may be some question as to man's ancestry cannot be rightfully considered as evidence that he has Negro blood. . . . If there is no evidence to indicate that a man has Negro blood, you would not be justified in withholding the priesthood and temple blessings from him, if he is otherwise worthy." This stops denial of priesthood merely on the basis of black African appearance and is significant prelude to the end of the ban altogether less than four months later.

25 Feb., *Church News* reports that twenty-three-year-old Lynda McIntosh, fluent in three languages, is Britain's Receptionist of the Year.

31 Mar., announcement of end to quarterly stake conferences, which are impractical due to geometric expansion of church population.

1 Apr., Spencer W. Kimball announces that "we are introducing a Church-wide program of extracting names from genealogical records," program that began on local basis in June 1977.

Apr., *Reader's Digest* publishes first eight-page insert of advertising by the church, unprecedented for this media representative of America's conservative, middle-class values. In May 1982 *Book of Mormon* insert reaches 19.2 million subscribers in U.S. and Europe.

29 Apr., First Presidency letter endorses "Morality in Media Inc., with headquarters in New York City. The Church is represented on its board of directors, which includes men and women of many faiths and from many walks of life."

3 May, First Presidency announces end to all local prayer circle meetings, except those connected with endowment ceremony (and prayer circle meetings of general authorities).

1 June, Spencer W. Kimball's proposal to resolve "the Negro issue," is sustained by apostles after prayer circle in Salt Lake temple. This answer ends policy since 1852 of denying priesthood to those of black African ancestry. Urgency of Kimball's inquiry involves upcoming dedication of temple in Brazil, where centuries of racial intermarriage have always posed problems in administering LDS ban on priesthood to those of black African ancestry. First Presidency announces this change on 9 June, and general conference accepts it on 30 Sept. This announcement becomes "Document 2" in 1981 edition of D&C. First Presidency secretary Francis M. Gibbons writes that this change "seemed to relieve them of a subtle sense of guilt they had felt over the years."

9 June, First Presidency letter instructs that interviews of married persons "should scrupulously avoid indelicate inquiries," yet also emphasizes: "Married persons should understand that if in their marital relations they are guilty of unnatural, impure, or unholy practices, they should not enter the temple unless and until they repent and discontinue any such practices." This reverses position of First Presidency prior to Spencer W. Kimball's ascendancy.

17 June, *Church News* headline "Interracial Marriage Discouraged" in same issue which announces authorization of priesthood for those of black African descent. Sources at headquarters indicate that Apostle Mark E. Petersen requires this emphasis.

25 June, Marcus Helvecio Martins and his father receive priesthood and are ordained eld-

ers in Brazil. The son receives unsolicited missionary calling from First Presidency. Although he and his fiancee have already mailed invitations for their upcoming marriage, they cancel wedding, and in August Marcus H. Martins becomes first full-time missionary of black African descent. His father becomes general authority in 1990.

1 July, Spencer W. Kimball dedicates Relief Society Monument to Women at Nauvoo, Illinois, and assistant to governor formally apologizes for role of Illinois government in expelling Mormons in 1846.

3 Aug., two days after suicide of Mormon schismatic Immanuel David due to collapse of his sect, his wife Rachel throws each of their seven children off eleventh floor of Salt Lake City hotel, then jumps herself. She and six children die in front of dozens of horrified witnesses on street, while her fifteen-year-old daughter is paralyzed.

Sept., James Drake is first Mormon to play pipe organ of Notre Dame in Paris. He receives standing ovation, a rare event at cathedral's musical recitals.

9 Sept., announcement training program for full-time missionaries from Canada and U.S. in new facility at Provo, Utah, Missionary Training Center (MTC). For missionaries from other countries, Area Missionary Training Centers are established adjacent to LDS temples in Latin America, Europe, Asia, and Pacific islands.

16 Sept., first conference for LDS females over age eleven, broadcast over closed-circuit radio to meeting houses. Although not part of general conference, as is male equivalent, this is first step in giving LDS females a meeting similar to that which Mormon males experienced since 1830. In Sept. 1993 this is divided into Relief Society's and Young Women's "general meeting."

23 Sept., Mary Sturlaugson is first African-American lady missionary.

29 Sept., First Presidency allows women to pray in sacrament meetings again.

30 Sept., First Presidency announces emeritus status for general authorities due to age, physical infirmity, or other reasons. Members of First Quorum of Seventy are first general authorities to receive this retirement.

30 Oct., Spencer W. Kimball dedicates temple at Sao Paulo, Brazil. For previous three years Brazilian Mormons have donated their jewelry, including wedding rings, to help pay for constructing this temple. By Apostle Boyd K. Packer's specific instructions, LDS Translation Department renders his address into phonetic *Spanish* which he delivers to Brazilians at the dedication.

3 Nov., Democratic president Jimmy Carter signs repeal of provision in 1862 Morrill antipolygamy law which prohibits the church from owning more than $50,000 worth of real estate in U.S. territory. LDS leaders ask Congressmen to enact this as protection for LDS temple in American Samoa, yet one of bill's Democratic co-sponsors is Roman Catholic Dennis Deconcini of New Mexico.

21 Nov., first official LDS baptisms in Nigeria. LDS missionaries baptize less than 10 percent of previously self-converted Mormon Nigerians from 1960s. Prior to 1978, most former converts tired of waiting for official recognition or abandoned LDS church due to its priesthood restriction against those of black African "blood." Many joined RLDS church which allows ordination of blacks and temporarily baptizes Third World polygamists. Now that LDS proselyting has begun, still other self-converted Nigerians refuse to abandon polygamy as price for LDS baptism or ordination. Since polygamy is legal according to "the laws of the land" in Africa, Nigerian polygamists are in compliance with 1890 Manifesto.

1979

18 Jan., Utah law enforcement officers kill Mormon fundamentalist John Singer as climax to armed stand-off about home schooling of his wives' children. To his adversaries Singer is shot while armed and resisting arrest. To his sympathizers he is polygamy martyr, who is literally shot in back as he flees anti-polygamist Mormon police. Utah courts exonerate police officers.

Feb., start of sociological study of 529 basketball players (182 are LDS) in southern Alberta Province, Canada. University researchers find that Mormon athletes are "significantly more likely to subscribe to superstitions when compared to Catholics and Protestants." Among "magical" practices they employ to guarantee sports-success are double-knotting one's shoelaces, wearing socks inside out, wearing "lucky" item of clothing, or wearing lucky charm (either hidden or observable to others). This study is later published in Canadian *Journal of Sport Behavior.*

10 Feb., *Church News* reports that George Orton has won World Champion Skateboard competition.

15 Feb., *Library Journal* headline "Mormon Book Purges Not Endorsed by Church," regarding LDS missionaries who allegedly remove books they regard as anti-Mormon or non-faith-promoting from public libraries. LDS president Spencer W. Kimball also publicly instructs BYU students to stop cutting out pages from books in campus library even if they regard the content as objectionable.

10 Mar., *Church News* features Bonageres Rubalcava, Ph.D. in biochemistry, university professor, and Mexican stake president.

17 Mar., in one of his nationally syndicated essays political conservative William F. Buckley praises LDS missionary program as "a kind of privately financed peace corps."

16 Apr., LDS amputee Kenneth Archer wins wheelchair division of Boston Marathon. Curt Brinkman wins in 1980.

2 June, *Church News* article "Computers Aid Church" refers to use of computers by Missionary Department. Due to massive increase of missionaries, computers have assigned Mormons to their full-time missions since church-wide computerization in 1970. First Presidency has neither oversight nor review of mission calls. Special committee (LDS bureaucrats and one or two general authorities) reviews computer print-outs of proposed missionary calls and occasionally changes some mission assignments. Signature machine signs church president's name to letter informing LDS missionaries of their assignments. Management Systems Corporation is dissolved in 1979, its functions absorbed by Information Systems Department.

Aug, church's *Ensign* magazine publishes first counselor N. Eldon Tanner's statement: "When the prophet speaks the debate is over," which echoes *Improvement Era*'s message of June 1945.

19 Aug., by authorization of one apostle, Ann Kenney is set apart as stake Sunday School president of University of Utah 2nd Stake. Apostle Ezra Taft Benson, president of Twelve, requires her release month later by his definition that Sunday School president must have Melchizedek priesthood.

29 Sept., publication of first LDS edition of King James Bible.

5 Oct., Apostle Gordon B. Hinckley, chair of Special Affairs Committee, instructs "all of Missouri and Illinois stake presidents and state[wide] ERA coordinators" about how to conduct LDS anti-ERA campaign, including: "Church building[s] may be used for ERA education."

6 Oct., First Presidency vacates office of Patriarch to the Church by giving emeritus status to Eldred G. Smith, ending a hierarchy office in existence since 1834.

24 Oct., Spencer W. Kimball dedicates Orson Hyde Memorial Gardens in Jerusalem.

5 Dec., announcement of excommunication of Sonia Johnson, president of Mormons for the ERA. Charged with apostasy she unsuccessfully appeals decision to First Presidency (which already authorized this "local action"). Johnson's case becomes top story in *New York Times, Christian Science Monitor, Washington Post, Time, Newsweek,* and on network television news. Resulting non-Mormon criticism of church and Johnson's own subsequent radicalization drive many LDS moderates away from their prior support of proposed Equal Rights Amendment and into acceptance of church's anti-ERA position.

15 Dec., First Presidency authorizes two-piece design in temple undergarment for all endowed persons.

22 Dec., first female LDS missionaries to be murdered are sixty-six-year-old Elizabeth W. King and sixty-five-year-old Jane Ruth Teuchner in North Carolina.

1980

10 Jan., N. Eldon Tanner, chair of LDS Personnel Committee, writes all leaders "in Wasatch Front Stakes" to invite members to serve as unpaid volunteers at headquarters. Follow-up letter 16 Apr. 1981 comments: "Their work has resulted in significant savings to the Church" and asks for more volunteers "with managerial, technical, or clerical skills."

Feb., LDS church magazines *Ensign* and *New Era* insert pamphlet *The Church and the Proposed Equal Rights Amendment: A Moral Issue,* which includes previous statements against the ERA and also new set of arguments against it. This same month, *Exponent II* publishes results of survey showing that 66 percent of this feminist periodical's readers define themselves as "very active" in LDS church.

7 Feb., Dallin H. Oaks, president of BYU, is chair of board for television's Public Broadcast Service. He continues as PBS chair after his appointment to Twelve in Apr. 1984.

26 Feb., Apostle Ezra Taft Benson instructs BYU students in televised address "Fourteen Fundamentals In Following the Prophets," including: "1. The Prophet is the only man who speaks for the Lord in everything. 2. The living Prophet is more vital to us than the standard works [of scripture]. 3. The living Prophet is more important to us than a dead prophet. 4. The Prophet will never lead the Church astray. 5. The Prophet is not required to have any particular earthly training or credentials to speak on any subject or act on any matter at any time. 6. The Prophet does not have to say 'Thus saith the Lord' to give us scripture. . . . 11. The two groups who have the greatest difficulty in following the prophet are the proud who are learned and the proud who are rich." In the national publicity resulting from this talk, some Mormon academics interpret this as Benson's way of preparing for his own presidency over the LDS church.

First Presidency's spokesman publicly counters that it is "simply not true" that LDS president's "word is law on all issues—including politics." Privately, church president Spencer W. Kimball is "concerned" about Elder Benson's talk and wants "to protect the Church against being misunderstood as espousing ultraconservative politics, or—in this case—espousing an unthinking 'follow the leader' mentality." However, those concerns have neither the circulation nor publicity of Benson's original talk. Next week Kimball requires Benson to explain himself and his motives to private meeting of all general authorities.

2 Mar., introduction of "Consolidated Meeting Schedule" of three-hours on Sundays. This eliminates week-day meetings of auxiliaries, as well as traditional twice-daily Sunday meetings. This eases transportation and weekly scheduling but erodes fellowshipping opportunities and diminishes tightly-knit social environment of LDS wards. By 1996, this has severely diminished emotional ties of North American Mormon youth to LDS community, eroding what is called "Mormon ethnic identity." Most dramatic manifestation of this trend is fact that for first time in Mormon history, young women cease LDS participation at greater percentages than young men (according to general authority Jack H. Goaslind's statement in *BYU Daily Universe,* 31 Aug. 1992). Likewise, despite absolute increase in missionary numbers, proportion of Mormon males who accept full-time missions has decreased significantly in North America.

4 Mar., Phil Tuckett is first Mormon to receive national "Emmy" from National Academy of Television Arts and Sciences (sports cinematography, 1978-79 season). Lynda Day George is first LDS nominee for Emmy (1973), followed by nominees Robert Brunner (1978) and Merlin Olsen (1979, 1981, 1983). Other LDS Emmy winners include: Phil Tuckett again (1979-80, 1981-82, 1982-83 seasons), Tony Geary (lead actor, daytime drama, 1981-82). LDS church receives Emmy (public service spot, 1987, 1988, 1993), M. Curtis Price for sound-mixing (1988), Kurt Bestor and Sam Cardon for their music

scoring of 1988 Winter Olympics telecast. Raised as both a Jew and a Mormon in Salt Lake City, Roseanne Barr Arnold receives Emmy (best actress in comedy series, 1993). A favorite with Salt Lake City's younger audiences during her early days of stand-up, Roseanne Barr receives American Comedy Awards (Funniest Female Performer, 1988, 1989), People's Choice Awards (Favorite Actress in New Program, 1989; Favorite Female Entertainer, 1990). Above list excludes regional Emmys and similar awards of local, state, or regional status.

10 May, effective date of Utah legislation granting university police statewide jurisdiction. BYU also claims this right, even though it is private institution and its security police take no state oath of office.

1 June, Apostle Bruce R. McConkie preaches at BYU against "Seven Deadly Heresies." First heresy: "There are those who say God is progressing in knowledge and is learning new truths." Second heresy is organic evolution. Fifth heresy: "There are those who say that there is progression from one kingdom to another in the eternal worlds." Sixth "Deadly Heresy" is Adam-God doctrine.

18 June, Apostle Marvin J. Ashton dedicates nondenominational chapel at Utah State prison, constructed with "privately donated" funds, but with significant participation by LDS church and its affiliated businesses. As of 1995, chapel bears his name.

1 July, organization of Africa West Mission, first full-time mission directed specifically to black Africans, especially Nigerians.

3 Aug., three BYU students are injured (Peter Bergstrom, a Swede, critically) in terrorist bombing of railway station of Bologna, Italy.

6 Sept., *Church News* article about Ronald Mead Horton, "newly appointed music director of National Symphony Orchestra of Ecuador."

4 Oct., *Church News* article "Ex-Felon Leads Full Life."

12 Oct., while organizing stake in Brasilia, Brazil, Apostle Ezra Taft Benson gives blessing to new stake president's daughter who "had a large growth on her neck," that "growth would disappear" without surgery recommended by physicians. Five days later the growth is gone.

18 Oct., *Church News* article about LDS institute of religion at university: "Kim R. Rogers was warmly received despite [his] long hair, liberal attitudes."

27 Oct., Spencer W. Kimball dedicates temple at Tokyo, Japan.

4 Nov., Florida elects Paula Hawkins as first LDS women to become U.S. Senator and first female Senator who is not daughter or wife of politician. She is also first prominent LDS woman to publicly acknowledge that she was sexually abused as a child.

17 Nov., Spencer W. Kimball dedicates temple near Seattle, Washington.

24 Dec., national broadcast of "Mr. Krueger's Christmas," dramatic production starring James Stewart and produced by LDS church with proselytizing message at end. It is re-broadcast year later on 125 commercial U.S. stations in all major markets, on PBS in Spanish, on 136 Spanish International Network stations, and on Turner Broadcasting Network. This rebroadcast airs in every Latin American country, as well as in Italy, Australia, the Philippines, and Iceland. Stewart later donates his papers to BYU.

1981

1 Jan., by appointment of First Presidency, BYU professor Edwin B. Morrell begins duties in Vienna as president over central European districts in Communist countries.

16 Jan., Esther W. Eggertsen Peterson receives U.S. Presidential Medal of Freedom. She is first Mormon to receive nation's highest civilian honor, followed by J. Willard Marriott (posthumously, 1988) and Morris K. Udall (1996). No general authority has received Medal of Freedom, but Ezra Taft Benson receives Presidential Citizens Medal (1989).

17 Jan., Richard N. Richards is elected national chair of Republican Party.

24 Jan., *New York Times* reports conversion to LDS church of Eldridge Cleaver, former

Black Panther radical of 1960s. He is first nationally prominent African-American to convert to Mormonism. In 1995 he publicly reaffirms his faith in Mormonism, although he no longer actively attends LDS services.

19 Feb., Apostle Bruce R. McConkie writes to BYU professor Eugene England: "Yes, President [Brigham] Young did teach that Adam was the father of our spirits, and all the related things that the cultists ascribe to him. This, however, is not true [doctrine]. He expressed views that are out of harmony with the gospel."

27 Feb., First Presidency authorizes stake presidents to ordain patriarchs. Previously, the Twelve maintained that as exclusive right, even denying it to the church's patriarch.

1 Apr., announcement of plans to build small temples throughout world, instead of traditionally large temples.

4 Apr., conference sustains first Hispanic Latin American as general authority, First Quorum of Seventy's Angel Abrea.

5 May, First Presidency statement against deployment of MX missile-system in Utah-Nevada desert, including criticism of developing weapons of war.

30 May, *Church News* reports that LDS James B. Conkling is appointed to direct Voice of America. He also serves on board of Bonneville International Corp. and is president of Bonneville International Productions.

3 July, after nearly eleven years of losing advertising revenues, *Deseret News* begins publishing ads for R-rated movies.

24 July, representatives of National Organization of Women march in Salt Lake City's Pioneer Day parade as part of their "mission" to Utah in support of Equal Rights Amendment. *Los Angeles Times* reports that "some spectators heckled, threw fruit and spat on ERA missionaries."

1 Aug., vandal attacks "Christus" statue in Visitor's Center on Salt Lake Temple Square and breaks off its fingers. On 16 Dec. 1982 same vandal breaks off its arms.

15 Aug., LDS *Church News* reports that married couple has been "teaching folk, square and some ballroom dances" to Indians in primarily Christian Goa, while "serving as Church representatives to teach recreation in India." LDS missionary work in India is limited by laws forbidding foreigners to overtly proselytize. Since conversion and baptism in 1965 of S. Paul Thiruthuvadoss, who sought out LDS leaders to teach him, proselytizing on Indian subcontinent is conducted by native converts.

22 Aug., Apostle Boyd K. Packer instructs BYU religion faculty, all seminary and institute teachers, and administrators of Church Education System that Mormon history "if not properly written or properly taught, may be a faith destroyer," and he affirms that Mormon historians are wrong in publicizing controversial elements of Mormon past. *BYU Studies* publishes this address in full. At request of students, BYU history professor gives his perspective on Elder Packer's talk and role of historical inquiry to meeting of BYU's history majors. Summarized within days by off-campus student newspaper *Seventh East Press,* this conflict between some apostles and some Mormon historians is subject of Feb. 1982 *Newsweek* article which quotes BYU professor that "a history which makes LDS leaders flawless and benignly angelic would border on idolatry."

Sept., branch presidents at Missionary Training Center receive 21-point handout to help "both male and female" missionaries avoid masturbation. Point 19: "In very severe cases it may be necessary to tie a hand to the bed frame with a tie in order that the habit of masturbating in a semi-sleep condition can be broken. This can also be accomplished by wearing several layers of clothing which would be difficult to remove while half asleep." In May 1995 article about masturbation, national magazine *Details* publishes seventeen of these recommendations and identifies Apostle Mark E. Petersen as author of *Steps In Overcoming Masturbation: A Guide To Self-Control.* In 1996, spokesman at LDS headquarters denies that Elder Petersen authored this document and denies that it was ever officially distributed.

8 Sept., Utah's Democratic governor names Christine Meaders Durham as first female member of Utah State Supreme Court. Graduate of Wellesley with J.D. degree from Duke University, Durham is Mormon who shares graduate study, housework, and parenting with her physician-husband.

12 Sept., First Presidency announces standardized "Sage Plan" for small meetinghouses, further evidence of financial strains of church growth since 1960s.

1 Oct., *New York Times* reports official announcement that new edition of *Book of Mormon* changes prophecy that Lamanites (Native Americans) will "become white and delightsome." Instead of continuing original reference to skin color, new edition emphasizes inward spirituality: "become pure and delightsome."

3 Oct., establishment of hundreds of satellite dishes in stake centers outside Utah for closed-circuit broadcasts of special LDS meetings and programs.

31 Oct., Apostle Bruce R. McConkie preaches to combined stakes of BYU that second coming of Jesus Christ will not be in his lifetime or in lifetime of his children or his grandchildren. This runs contrary to the common folk belief that Christ will come in year 2000 or shortly thereafter.

16 Nov., second counselor Marion G. Romney dedicates temple at South Jordan, Utah, last LDS temple with more than 150,000 square feet of floor space.

2 Dec., First Presidency letter that divorced persons now "may be granted permission to go to the temple by the stake president without clearance by the First Presidency." Number of LDS divorces is now too large to handle at church headquarters.

1982

5 Jan., First Presidency repeats its 1978 instructions for "interviewing married persons," but adds: "The First Presidency has interpreted oral sex as constituting an unnatural, impure, or unholy practice."

25 Jan., First Presidency formally releases Leonard J. Arrington as Church Historian. Position has been in administrative limbo since 1980, when he and his staff are released from LDS Historical Department and transferred administratively to BYU. Day after this letter Presidency sets apart G. Homer Durham as church historian. He has served as general-authority director of Historical Department since 1976.

28 Jan., Merlin Olsen is inducted into Pro-Football Hall of Fame. He is also inducted into College Football Hall of Fame. Steve Young, Brigham's descendant, is National Football League's MVP (1992, 1994) and Superbowl MVP (1995).

2 Mar., in televised sermon at BYU Apostle Bruce R. McConkie denounces "spiritually immature" students and other Mormons who "devote themselves to gaining a special personal relationship with Christ." He criticizes widely circulated book on that topic by popular religion professor George Pace who writes public letter of apology within days and is released as stake president shortly thereafter.

31 Mar., announcement of temple to be constructed in Guayaquil, Ecuador. Delays in obtaining government permits postpones groundbreaking ceremony until 1996.

2 Apr., First Presidency announces two changes to lessen financial burdens on church members. First, church headquarters henceforth pays for all costs of meetinghouse construction. This relieves local members of requirement to finance construction in addition to paying tithing. Second, service of male missionaries is reduced from 24 months to 18-months. "It is anticipated that this shortened term will make it possible for many to go who cannot go under present [financial circumstances]," counselor Gordon B. Hinckley explains. "This will extend the opportunity for missionary service to an enlarged body of our young men." Instead annual number of new missionaries level off. Annual convert baptisms decline more than 7 percent each year rather than increase by same proportion as before.

4 Apr., Counselor Gordon B. Hinckley tells general conference: "Of course, there are aberrations in our history. There are blemishes to be found, if searched for, in the lives of

all men, including our leaders past and present. But these are only incidental to the magnitude of their service and to the greatness of their contributions. Keep before you the big picture, for this cause is as large as all mankind and as broad as all eternity."

25 May, organization of "Pilgrimage" at Nauvoo, Illinois, by fifty-six Mormon women from across nation. Annual meetings continue in various cities.

23 June, Counselor Gordon B. Hinckley tells Mission Presidents Seminar, "I plead with you to train and motivate your missionaries to the point of view that it is converts they are out to win, rather than numbers of baptisms for the sake of a good statistical record."

30 June, Equal Rights Amendment is defeated. To 1996 no church publication acknowledges Mormon role in its defeat.

24 July, Zion Lutheran Church of Salt Lake City enters float in "Days of '47 Parade," apparently first participation of non-LDS church in this celebration of Mormon Pioneers.

6 Aug., First Presidency letter: "The Church organization formerly identified as The Development Office will henceforth be known as LDS Foundation . . . to encourage and facilitate voluntary philanthropic contributions to The Church of Jesus Christ of Latter-day Saints and its related organizations and activities, with primary fund-raising emphasis relating to Church institutions of higher education."

3 Oct., adoption of subtitle for *Book of Mormon:* "Another Testament of Jesus Christ."

15 Oct., First Presidency instruction to all stake and mission leaders that letters from church members "indicate clearly that some local leaders have been delving into private, sensitive matters beyond the scope of what is appropriate. . . . Also, you should never inquire into personal, intimate matters involving marital relations between a man and his wife." Letter continues that even if a church member volunteers such intimate information, "you should not pursue the matter but should merely suggest that if the member has enough anxiety about the propriety of the conduct to ask about it, the best course would be to discontinue it." In response to widespread complaints from married couples being asked if they have oral sex, this returns First Presidency's stance to what it was prior to presidency of Spencer W. Kimball, now incapacitated.

2 Nov., Idaho votes to rescind its constitutional "Test Oath" which still technically disfranchises all Mormons.

21 Nov., LDS insert appears in *Los Angeles Times.* "The insert will be a missionary tool," according to president of the church's Bonneville International Corporation's two radio stations in California.

2 Dec., LDS physician William C. DeVries performs first successful implant of artificial human heart in Barney B. Clark, also LDS, who survives 112 days.

1983

11 Jan., second counselor Gordon B. Hinckley pays document dealer Mark Hofmann $15,000 for alleged Joseph Smith letter about his treasure-digging activities. He has Hofmann agree not to mention the transaction to anyone else and then he sequesters document in First Presidency's vault. First Presidency does not acknowledge its existence until *Los Angeles Times* is about to release story about document, which Hofmann later admits he forged.

16 Jan., ending policy of 132 years and six months, *Deseret News* (of which Counselor Hinckley is senior director) begins printing Sunday edition.

21 Jan., First Presidency letter: "We are now informed that there are members of the Church who also refuse to pay state income taxes." Provides for denial of temple recommend for any Mormon "who deliberately refuses to pay state or federal income taxes, or to comply with any final judgment rendered in income tax case." Letter also authorizes "Church court" action against those convicted of violating tax laws.

11 Feb., *Seventh East Press,* unofficial BYU student newspaper, is banned from campus due to its interview with LDS philosopher Sterling M. McMurrin. It ceases publication two

months later. BYU's action is widely criticized in media and by president of national journalism society.

4 Mar., *Salt Lake Tribune* reports lawsuit filed in February against LDS church for $28 million. A father blames LDS bishop for contributing to his sixteen-year-old son's suicide for counseling his son "that masturbation is a sin...and being a normal adolescent in the puberty state, KIP ELIASON became increasingly less able to reconcile his sexual desires with the strict doctrines of the said LDS Church. He became filled with self-hate."

15 Apr., *University Post: The Unofficial Newspaper of Brigham Young University* reports interview with director of Standards Department. He acknowledges that students suspected of cheating, illegal drug use, stealing, or homosexuality are expelled from BYU if they refuse to take polygraph examination. BYU Security has licensed polygraph examiner. In separate article, newspaper's photographer reports observing Church Security using specially trained dogs to search for bombs prior to public meetings attended by general authorities in Salt Lake Tabernacle.

7 May, Larry Nielsen is first American to climb Mt. Everest without supplemental oxygen.

23 May, newspapers reveal that Apostle Mark E. Petersen is leading inquisition against Mormons who have written articles for independent publications *Sunstone* and *Dialogue*. Although stake presidents nationally are instructed to interview such contributors, BYU faculty members are focus of special attention. When First Presidency learns of this, second counselor Gordon B. Hinckley tells apostles to stop this investigation immediately.

29 May, Salt Lake City's mayor, by placing one call to local LDS leader, has 2,000 volunteers within hour to create artificial sandbag levees to prevent widespread flooding.

1 June, second counselor Gordon B. Hinckley dedicates temple near Atlanta, Georgia.

5 Aug., second counselor Gordon B. Hinckley dedicates temple at Apia, Western Samoa.

9 Aug., second counselor Gordon B. Hinckley dedicates temple at Nuku'alofa, Tonga.

14 Aug., *Church News* reports that Palestinian Suheil Abu Hadid has arrived in Utah as first Jerusalem Arab to serve full-time LDS mission.

15 Sept., second counselor Gordon B. Hinckley dedicates temple at Santiago, Chile. Before this dedication, Chilean Mormons have prepared 115,000 names for vicarious temple ceremonies.

21 Sept., U.S. postage stamp honors Philo T. Farnsworth for "First Television Camera." His electronic television transmission occurred in San Francisco in 1927.

27 Oct., second counselor Gordon B. Hinckley dedicates temple near Papeete, Tahiti.

30 Oct., *Church News* reports that 70 percent of Gallup Survey respondents have "a highly favorable" view of LDS, and only 10 percent have "a highly unfavorable opinion."

2 Dec., second counselor Gordon B. Hinckley dedicates temple at Mexico City, Mexico.

1984

28 Jan., arson destroys LDS meetinghouse in Marlboro, Massachusetts.

31 Jan., Masonic Grand Lodge of Utah rescinds policy of prohibiting LDS membership.

25 Mar., wards and branches allowed to have microform facilities for genealogical research.

27 Mar., official statement that First Presidency "are disturbed and saddened at the presence of anti-Catholic posters being placed in areas within Salt Lake City."

4 Apr., R. Craig Smith, Mormon CIA agent, is arrested for espionage. Acquitted in 1986, his biographical exoneration is published next year in Utah by manager of Dale Carnegie Training Programs. Four years earlier the government convicted first CIA agent, non-LDS, to be arrested for espionage.

7 Apr., appointment of first general authorities to have stated time-limit on their service. Initially these temporary general authorities served in First Quorum of Seventy. Also Dallin H. Oaks is first general authority and apostle who has served as state supreme court justice.

Dialogue: A Journal of Mormon Thought (an independent scholarly publication with which Oaks had once officially affiliated) publishes survey showing that 88 percent of its subscribers attend LDS services weekly and that two-thirds regard *Book of Mormon* as "an actual historical record of ancient inhabitants."

18 Apr., Bruce L. Christensen is elected president of Public Broadcasting Service. Apostle Dallin H. Oaks is already chair of PBS board of directors. Christensen resigns in 1993 to become dean at BYU.

25 May, second counselor Gordon B. Hinckley dedicates temple at Boise, Idaho.

13 June, first Spanish-speaking stake in U. S. (Huntington Park West Stake in Los Angeles).

12 Aug., Harmon Killebrew is inducted into Baseball Hall of Fame. His career record of 573 home-runs is exceeded only by Hank Aaron, Babe Ruth, Willie Mays, and Frank Robinson. Larry H. Miller enters National Softball Hall of Fame in 1992.

Sept., non-Mormon sociologist Rodney Stark publishes statistical projection that worldwide population of LDS church will reach 265 million by year 2080 A.D. Ten years later he announces that LDS growth is ahead of his projection.

20 Sept., second counselor Gordon B. Hinckley dedicates temple near Sydney, Australia.

25 Sept., Gordon B. Hinckley dedicates temple near Manilla, the Philippines.

5 Oct., psychiatrist Louis A. Moench presents "Mormon Forms of Psychopathology" to annual conference of Association of Mormon Counselors and Psychotherapists. It is published by *AMCAP Journal* in March 1985.

7 Oct., Ronald E. Poelman gives general conference talk stressing need of central headquarters to adapt its programs to cultural diversity of international church, rather than require diverse peoples to conform to Utah Mormon culture. He is required to return to empty Salt Lake Tabernacle to re-deliver censored version of his general conference talk for videotaping which includes pre-recorded track of audience coughs but deletes his endorsement of cultural diversity and decentralization. He is not allowed to speak in general conference again for more than four years.

19 Oct., second counselor Gordon B. Hinckley dedicates temple at Dallas, Texas.

17 Nov., second counselor Gordon B. Hinckley dedicates temple at Taipei, Taiwan.

19 Nov., BYU's football team is ranked "the No. 1 college football team in America" by United Press International, and next day by Associated Press polls of nation's sportswriters and broadcasters.

26 Nov., First Presidency announces that as of 1 Jan., mission service for young men will return to 24 months.

14 Dec., Gordon B. Hinckley dedicates temple at Guatemala City, Guatemala.

17 Dec., David Fowers at age 19 is youngest presidential elector in U.S. history to vote in Electoral College election of U.S. president.

1985

27 Jan., church members in U.S. and Canada hold special fast and donate more than $6.5 million to aid famine victims in Africa. Lacking its own relief network in Africa, LDS church distributes this money primarily to Catholic Relief Services.

7 Feb., First Presidency letter to all presiding officers "on the subject of rape," includes following: "Persons who consciously invite sexual advances also have a share of responsibility for the behavior that follows. But persons who are truly forced into sexual relations are victims and are not guilty of any sexual sin. . . . The extent of resistance required to establish that the victim has not willingly consented is left to the judgment of the victim, who is best acquainted with the total circumstances and their effect on his or her will."

6 Apr., Helio D. Camargo is sustained as member of First Quorum of Seventy, first previously ordained minister (Methodist) to become member of Mormon hierarchy in twentieth century. Hans B. Ringger is also member of Seventy, first general authority who has been high-ranking officer in military of non-U.S. country (Switzerland).

5 May, LDS astronaut Don Lind administers sacrament in zero-gravity Skylab 3.

9 June, church headquarters telephones bishops in Utah, Idaho, and Arizona with instructions to forbid discussion of Linda Newell and Valeen Tippetts Avery's biography *Mormon Enigma: Emma Hale Smith* in Relief Society or other church meetings. Lasting for ten months, this ban is apparently what triples book's sales.

29 June, second counselor Gordon B. Hinckley dedicates temple at Freiberg (then Democratic Republic of Germany). This is only Mormon temple allowed by any Communist regime. It is also smallest LDS temple ever dedicated, with 7,840 square feet of floor space. Before this ceremony, Mormons in Communist East Germany have prepared 35,000 names for vicarious temple work. Since 1960s, apostles have reported that 80-90 percent of East German Mormons attend LDS church services, highest attendance records outside student congregations of Brigham Young University and Ricks College.

2 July, second counselor Gordon B. Hinckley dedicates temple near Stockholm, Sweden. On this date Swedish government issues postage stamp commemorating temple's dedication, and later this year Brazil's government issues stamp commemorating fifty years of Mormon proselytizing among Brazilians.

9 Aug., second counselor Gordon B. Hinckley dedicates temple near Chicago, Illinois.

16 Aug., Apostle (and former Utah Supreme Court Justice) Dallin H. Oaks instructs educators and administrators of LDS Church Educational System: "Balance is telling both sides. This is not the mission of official Church literature or avowedly anti-Mormon literature. Neither has any responsibility to present both sides."

24 Aug., counselor Gordon B. Hinckley dedicates temple at Johannesburg, South Africa.

2 Oct., letter from LDS Church Education System's Zone Administrators of Curriculum and Instruction Division to area directors, associate area directors, teaching support consultants, CES coordinators, institute directors, seminary principals: "Even if the letters [circulated by Mark Hofmann] were to be unauthentic [as they are], such issues as Joseph Smith's involvement in treasure-seeking and folk magic remain. Ample evidence exists for both of these, even without the letters. The publicity surrounding the letters served only to heighten the general public's awareness of these two issues."

5 Nov., Spencer W. Kimball dies.

10 Nov., Quorum of Twelve sustains Ezra Taft Benson as church president with Gordon B. Hinckley and Thomas S. Monson as counselors, and ordains President Benson. Benson is first LDS church president with graduate degree (M.S. from Iowa State University).

Also First Presidency and apostles vote for Howard W. Hunter as Acting President of the Quorum of the Twelve due to incapacity of Marion G. Romney. Although *non compos mentis,* Romney is now next in apostolic seniority to the church president and eligible for automatic succession in the event of Benson's death. This situation continues until Romney's death in 1988, during which time the church president has heart attack.

24 Nov., second LDS fast day for African famine-relief ($4 million more donations).

14 Dec., first counselor Gordon B. Hinckley dedicates temple at Seoul, South Korea.

23 Dec., First Presidency letter inviting all "members of the Church who have become inactive, or who have been disciplined, or who otherwise have become alienated from the Church" to come back to activity and fellowship in church.

1986

10 Jan., first counselor Gordon B. Hinckley dedicates temple at Lima, Peru.

Salt Lake Tribune story, "Mormons Excommunicate Repentant AIDS Victim: He Is Asked Not to Attend Church." First Presidency's spokesman agrees that this young man should not attend LDS services.

17 Jan., second counselor Thomas S. Monson dedicates temple at Buenos Aires, Argentina.

19 Jan., public announcement of First Presidency's approval of "a dyed and specially treated two-piece temple garment for members serving in the U.S. Army that meets both Army and Church standards."

16 Feb., *Church News* announces Lee Roderick is chair of board of National Press Club.

2 Apr., BYU's administration prepares document for its external accreditation review, including: "BYU administrators are advised not to publish in *Dialogue, a Journal of Mormon Thought,* nor to participate in *Sunstone* symposia."

4 May, arsonist destroys LDS stake center in Kirtland, Ohio.

18 May, *Church News* announcement instructs Mormons not to "be parties to" rumors that "the Proctor and Gamble Co. has some connection with satanism and devil worship, based on the firm's moon and stars trademark."

30 May, Paul A. Yost, Jr. is commandant of entire U.S. Coast Guard, only second Mormon to hold four-star rank. First was Air Force General John K. Cannon in 1951. Less than four years earlier, LDS Brig-Gen. Alan G. Sharp was appointed to command Fourteenth Air Force, all AF Reservists east of Mississippi River.

6 July, announcement of "Improved missionary discussions [which] put aside the specific dialogue of the past. Missionaries will now use their own words and follow an outline to share the gospel." This ends twenty-five years of requiring LDS missionaries to memorize and speak word-for-word dialogue when teaching non-Mormons.

4 Oct., end of local Seventy's quorums. Soon church's only Seventies are general authorities.

20 Oct., LDS Lt-Gen. Robert C. Oaks is commander of Allied air forces in southern Europe. He is uncle of recently sustained apostle Dallin H. Oaks.

24 Oct., Ezra Taft Benson dedicates temple near Denver, Colorado.

13 Nov., general authority Loren C. Dunn represents LDS church at conference of Religious Alliance Against Pornography in Washington, D.C.

1987

21 Jan., death of J. Martell Bird, "managing director of Church security worldwide" for previous five years. An FBI agent (1942-69), Bird was also regional representative.

23 Jan., imprisonment of Mark Hofmann for second-degree murder in bombing-deaths of two people in Salt Lake City in October 1985 as his effort to conceal fraudulent business transactions in Mormon documents. As part of plea-bargain, Hofmann also admits forging Mormon documents for several years, including two controversial ones for which he receives greatest financial rewards and notoriety: so-called "Joseph Smith Money Digging Letter" and so-called "Martin Harris Salamander Letter."

11 Mar., Keith B. McMullin, director of LDS Welfare Services, testifies before Subcommittee on Public Assistance of Ways and Means Committee, U.S. House of Representatives. Subcommittee is investigating ways to improve federal assistance programs. He becomes general authority in 1995.

12 Mar., announcement that church's Hotel Utah will be remodeled into additional office building for LDS bureaucracy. When completed in 1991, renamed "Joseph Smith Memorial Building" has 75,000 square feet of floor space.

4 Apr., conference sustains Douglas J. Martin of New Zealand as first general authority from South Pacific. Also John R. Lasater is first Vietnam War veteran and highest-ranking veteran (general) to become general authority.

First counselor Gordon B. Hinckley tells priesthood session of conference that "marriage should not be viewed as a therapeutic step to solve problems such as homosexual inclinations or practices . . ." This reverses decades-long policy formulated by Spencer W. Kimball.

12 Apr., Apostle Boyd K. Packer, native of Brigham City, re-dedicates its tabernacle whose interior has been remodeled in accordance with current LDS chapel usage. Originally dedicated in 1897 Brigham City tabernacle is similar in architecture to Coalville tabernacle, which was demolished amid national controversy.

24 June, U.S. Supreme Court rules that LDS church, as well as any other religious organization, can discriminate against employees on basis of religious persuasion and behavior. This ends $5 million lawsuit against church by five former employees.

25 Aug., National Academy of Television Arts and Sciences gives Emmy for public service

spot "produced for the Church's Missionary Department by Bonneville Media Communications." LDS church is first religious organization to receive national Emmy (again 1988, 1993).

28 Aug., Ezra Taft Benson dedicates temple near Frankfurt, Germany.

7 Nov., convert Maj-General Donald Burdick is appointed director of Army National Guard of more than 452,000 soldiers.

23 Nov., Catholic Community Services of Utah honors LDS church for "sensitive, unselfish and ecumenical response to the needs of the homeless."

1988

Jan., single full-time missionaries arrive in Poland, first Communist nation to officially allow this. In November Communist regime of German Democratic Republic also grants entry to LDS missionaries as well as permitting its own citizens to serve foreign missions. Similar to Yugoslavia's nearly twenty years of unofficial practice, Czechoslovakia's Communist government also allows LDS missionaries in 1988, even though church has no legal recognition there until 21 Feb. 1990 (after Czechoslovakia's democratization).

16 Jan., son-in-law of deceased Fundamentalist John Singer bombs LDS chapel in Kamas, Utah. This begins several-week stand-off between this polygamous clan and law enforcement officers. This results in even more cooperation between law enforcement and Mormon Fundamentalists, who repudiate Singer family's actions and seek peaceful solution. One lawman dies in arresting family.

20 Jan., in his letter of resignation from tenured position as full professor of history at Brigham Young University, D. Michael Quinn writes that "academic freedom merely survives at BYU without fundamental support by the institution, exists against tremendous pressure, and is nurtured only through the dedication of individual administrators and faculty members."

12 Mar., First Presidency statement supports Child Abuse Prevention Month and encourages Mormons to combat this "pernicious problem."

24 Mar., new head of Church Security is Richard Bretzing, twenty-five-year veteran of FBI.

4 Apr., Arizona's state senate convicts Governor Evan Mecham of "high crimes and misdemeanors," thus removing him from office. Mecham is first Mormon office-holder to be impeached (February 1988), and first to be convicted by senate and constitutionally removed from office. Every LDS legislator (all Republicans) voted against his impeachment; there are no Mormons in Arizona senate at this time.

28 Apr., John K. Carmack, of First Quorum of Seventy, testifies in favor of Child Protection and Obscenity Enforcement Act before Subcommittee on Crime, U.S. House.

14 May, 800 Mormon teenagers and young adults participate in dance festival in New Jersey as part of church's centennial in that state. This demonstrates replication of western Mormon culture wherever LDS population is sufficient. LDS dance festivals are discontinued in 1990.

15 May, first African stake where all priesthood leaders are black Africans, at Aba, Nigeria.

18 May, Apostle Howard W. Hunter signs agreement with State of Israel that "the Church will not engage in any missionary activity within the borders of Israel, as long as such activity is not allowed by the government of Israel."

28 May, First Presidency statement on Acquired Immune Deficiency Syndrome (AIDS) which encourages "compassion for those who are ill with AIDS," but with emphasis on abstaining from any homosexual behavior.

1 June, Communist government of Hungary gives legal recognition to LDS church.

4 June, postage stamp by British Commonwealth government of Western Samoa commemorates one hundred years of Mormonism there.

30 July, newspaper reports that Brigham Young University has fired Hebrew professor David P. Wright due to his private disbelief in Book of Mormon as ancient history.

Wright joins faculty of Brandeis University and is excommunicated in 1994 for publishing article which applies biblical textual criticism to *Book of Mormon*. This is reported in national *Chronicle of Higher Education*.

20 Aug., *Church News* article about Aledir Paganelli Barbour, Ph.D. in geology, university professor, and stake president in Sao Paulo, Brazil.

First Presidency statement condemns Hollywood film, *The Last Temptation of Christ*. Opening of film in Salt Lake City is delayed when unknown person(s) use knife to rip theater screen to shreds.

17 Sept., LDS church joins VISN television network (Vision Interfaith Satellite Network) sponsored jointly by different religious organizations; renamed "Faith and Values Channel."

1 Oct., *Deseret News* reports federal judge's decision that FBI has been guilty of systematic discrimination because "Mormon supervisors made personnel decisions which favored members of their church at the expense of Hispanic" FBI agents. Principal offender named is Richard Bretzing, former FBI chief of Los Angeles and current director of LDS Security Department. In December federal judge also rules that FBI used illegal methods to discredit Hispanic FBI agent who had accused Bretzing of protecting Richard N. Miller from arrest as Communist spy because Bretzing was Miller's LDS bishop.

2 Oct., Michaelene P. Grassli, general Primary president, is first woman to speak in general conference in 133 years.

18 Oct., at request of Counselor Gordon B. Hinckley, President Ezra Taft Benson appoints committee of three apostle-lawyers (Howard W. Hunter, James E. Faust, and Dallin H. Oaks) to formally investigate the publicly announced claims that as an apostle Hinckley allegedly had long-term homosexual affair with younger man. Circulated internationally by Protestant evangelicals through anti-Mormon video and book *Godmakers II*, these allegations are repudiated by apostolic committee as "pure fabrication" after "an extensive probe." Hinckley puts formal end to this investigation on 6 May 1993 when he reads statement to Presidency and Twelve. While he is counselor, temple council decides against making any kind of public denial. As church president Hinckley's authorized biography devotes three pages to this matter in 1996 but does not state whether he asked temple council to rescind its previous vote on matter.

23 Nov., president-elect George Bush appoints LDS Lt.-General Brent Scowcroft to his second term as chair of National Security Council. Scowcroft has direct role in decisions involved in 1989 U.S. invasion of Panama and 1991 Persian Gulf War.

14 Dec., church gives $100,000 to Soviet ambassador to United States for relief of earthquake victims in Soviet Armenia.

15 Dec., after more than year of confinement to wheelchair, Twelve's president Howard W. Hunter walks into council room of Salt Lake temple. Apostles stand and clap their hands, apparently first occasion of applause in temple council room.

29 Dec., *New York Times* reports that fertility rate declined in Utah for first time since arrival of Mormons.

1989

19 Jan., president-elect George Bush says that Mormon Tabernacle Choir is "the nation's choir," when it performs at his inaugural gala. Choir performs again at his formal inauguration on 20 Jan.

23 Jan., commercial television stations in eight U.S. cities broadcast church's "Together Forever" production. By end of Apr. commercial stations televise it in every U.S. city with mission headquarters. On 7 Aug. 1989 church's "What Is Real?" has similar commercial broadcast, with similar repetition.

18 Feb., announcement that New York's Macmillan Publishing Company has contracted with BYU to publish multi-volume *Encyclopedia of Mormonism*. Under direct supervision of apostles Neal A. Maxwell and Dallin H. Oaks, church intends this to be public-rela-

tions publication. Published in 1992 encyclopedia's content is so heavily managed by apostles and four other general authorities with "special assignments" that its editor Daniel H. Ludlow (official of Church Correlation Committee) disclaims: "In no sense does the *Encyclopedia* have the force and authority of scripture."

21 Feb., church gives $25,000 to People's Republic of China for earthquake relief.

11 Mar., *Salt Lake Tribune* reports that several Mormon men have telephoned death threats to Edwin B. Firmage for publicly advocating ordination of LDS women to priesthood office. Two days earlier *Tribune* reported those remarks by Firmage, University of Utah law professor, former bishop, and grandson of former First Presidency counselor Hugh B. Brown. However, there are no church sanctions against Firmage.

1 Apr., creation of Second Quorum of the Seventy for those with temporary appointments as general authorities. Announced period of service is five years.

15 Apr., *Church News* article about Brent Peterson, "only active LDS player" in National Hockey League.

16 May, Apostle Howard W. Hunter dedicates Brigham Young University's Jerusalem Center for Near Eastern Studies, despite years of protests by Israel's ultra-orthodox Jews against its construction. For decade Hunter privately urged First Presidency and Twelve to give greater attention to Muslim people through this project. BYU's president signed renewable forty-nine-year lease for property on 18 May 1988.

23 May, First Presidency's office completes documents which give Counselors Gordon B. Hinckley and Thomas S. Monson power of attorney for church president Ezra Taft Benson, which "shall not be affected by [his] disability" or "incompetence." Church president does not sign these legal documents which are instead "signed" by signature machine in First Presidency's office. Identical signature of Ezra Taft Benson also appears on similar document, dated 25 Feb. 1993, and also filed with state of Utah. Although Presidency's office uses its AUTO-PEN machine to create church president's signature on correspondence, missionary calls, and other routine documents, this use of signature machine for legal documents (especially power-of-attorney) is unprecedented. Disclosure of this by *Salt Lake Tribune* fuels speculation that Benson is already in mental decline by 1989.

24 May, political terrorists kill Elders Jeffrey B. Ball and Todd R. Wilson in La Paz, Bolivia. They are first LDS missionaries to be killed for political reasons. FBI agent Mike McPheters, formerly LDS missionary in Bolivia, receives Bolivian national medal of honor for his successful investigation of Ball-Wilson murders.

17 June, *Church News* feature article, "Los Angeles: Hispanics, Other Minorities Strengthen Inner-City Wards."

1 Aug., Kingdom of Jordan grants legal status to LDS church by registering LDS "Center for Cultural and Educational Affairs."

5 Aug., "100 Million Names Processed In Stake Extraction Program," which *Church News* explains "helps keep the Church's 41 operating temples busy" performing vicarious ordinances for the dead. This program includes hundreds of thousands of Jews who died in Nazi holocaust, which Apostle Boyd K. Packer acknowledges to Israeli officials in explaining church's offer to microfilm records of Yad VaShem.

8 Aug., church offers its assistance to government of USSR to build emergency housing.

19 Aug., first counselor Gordon B. Hinckley dedicates temple near Portland, Oregon.

30 Aug., LDS Brent Scowcroft, national security adviser to President George Bush, presents U.S. Presidential Citizens Award to Ezra Taft Benson.

1 Sept., excommunication of Navajo general authority George P. Lee for "apostasy," first excommunication of general authority in almost forty-seven years. He has written letters to First Presidency accusing them of promoting racist policies.

1 Oct., eight men are honorably released from recently established Second Quorum of the Seventy, cease to be general authorities, but do not have the "emeritus" status of those

released from First Quorum of the Seventy. This administrative difference continues to present.

12 Oct., *Deseret News* reports that representative of Eli Lilly pharmaceutical company confirms that Utah has highest per-capita use in nation of anti-depressant Prozac.

24 Oct., Tonga's princess 'Elisiva Fusipala Vaha'i is baptized

1 Nov., announcement that full-time female missionaries will be only guides for traditional tours of Temple Square, Salt Lake City.

16 Dec., first counselor Gordon B. Hinckley dedicates temple at Las Vegas, Nevada.

1990

1 Jan., new budget program eliminates need for local congregations to raise money for operating expenses, all of which are now paid by LDS headquarters.

21 Jan., appointment of David Hsiao Hsi Chen, native of Chinese mainland and professor at BYU-Hawaii, to serve as First Presidency's "traveling elder" for People's Republic of China.

19 Feb., government of Cook Islands issues postage stamp honoring Osborne J.P. Widtsoe, first LDS missionary there in 1899.

31 Mar., conference sustains first general authority of black African descent, Second Quorum of Seventy's Helvecio Martins of Brazil (who is released in 1995). Chieko Nishimura Okazaki is sustained as first counselor in general presidency of Relief Society, first non-Caucasian member of auxiliary presidency in Mormon history.

10 Apr., changes in temple ceremony promote gender equality, de-emphasize symbolic violence, and eliminate Protestant minister from endowment drama. This becomes nationwide news in special reports by *New York Times, Los Angeles Times, Time Magazine, U.S. News and World Report,* and in Associated Press report published in local newspapers.

21 May, U.S. Supreme Court rules that direct donations to LDS missionaries are not deductible under U.S. tax laws. Therefore, First Presidency advises church members to make their donations directly to church, while earmarking funds for individual missionaries.

27 May, missionary Gale Stanley Critchfield, age twenty, is stabbed to death in Dublin by eighteen-year-old Irishman who follows missionaries to their apartment for sole purpose of attack. "We wonder why, when a young man is called to serve the Lord, he isn't watched over so closely [that] his life is protected," says First Presidency counselor Gordon B. Hinckley at funeral. "We don't know why some things happen."

2 July, church sends emergency supplies for earthquake relief in Iran.

5 July, Mormon pianist Kevin Kenner wins bronze in International Tchaikovsky Competition in Moscow, and also wins Rachmaninoff Prize. Hyun Soo Choi, known professionally as Hans Choi, receives first prize in male vocal Tchaikovsky competition. He is first non-Russian, first Asian, and first Mormon to receive this vocal prize.

In Phoenix, Arizona, gunman fires several bullets at 120 LDS young women and their leaders as they board buses for summer camp, wounding one woman adviser. He explains that he wants to kill "religious" people.

7 July, end of Wimbledon tennis tournament where LDS player Rick Leach and partners win men's doubles and mixed doubles. At Wimbledon in 1995 Leach wins his "29th doubles title."

28 July, *Church News* feature article, "Church Brings Hope to Prison Inmates."

22 Aug., LDS missionaries Manuel Antonio Hidalgo and Christian Andreani Ugarte are shot and killed in Peru.

25 Aug., first counselor Gordon B. Hinckley dedicates temple at Toronto, Ontario, Canada.

13 Sept., Soviet Union grants legal registration for LDS branch in Leningrad, renamed St. Petersburg next year.

15 Sept., memorial service at Mountain Meadows, Utah, for descendants of victims and descendants of perpetrators.

6 Oct., newspapers report that LDS Church Security Department is receiving cautious praise from outside security departments and police agencies.

20 Oct., LaRae Orullian is elected national president of Girl Scouts of America. She is Mormon president of Women's Bank in Denver, Colorado.

6 Nov., Larry EchoHawk is elected as Idaho's Democratic attorney general, first Native American Indian to become state attorney general. Within days after his defeat as candidate for governor in 1994 he is appointed as professor in BYU's law school.

5 Dec., leftist guerrillas bomb four LDS chapels in Chile to protest arrival of U.S. president George Bush next day. Later they order congregation to leave LDS chapel in Santiago, burn it to ground, and scatter pamphlets condemning U.S. role in Persian Gulf War.

1991

1 Jan., church headquarters standardizes monthly support for full-time missionaries throughout world at $350 (or 400 Canadian dollars). This equalizes financial burden for U.S. and Canadian families who struggle to support missionaries in cities or countries with far higher cost-of-living than missionary's family. LDS church funds continue to supplement or fully pay for support of 1/3 of LDS missionaries whose families live outside U.S. and Canada.

11 Jan., *Church News* publishes official statement that in special circumstances LDS couples "should consider an abortion only after consulting with each other, and their bishop, and receiving divine confirmation through prayer." This returns to First Presidency's flexible policy on abortion prior to J. Reuben Clark's death thirty years ago.

20 Jan., at LDS interstake center, next to Oakland temple in California, LDS stake president is one of speakers at "An Ecumenical Celebration of the dream of Martin Luther King, Jr." Meeting is sponsored by Interreligious Council of Oakland.

4 Feb., Richard N. Miller, Mormon, is sentenced to twenty years in prison for committing espionage. It requires three trials to convict Miller, first FBI agent arrested as spy.

14 Feb., Amy Baird is president of Brigham Young University's "Student Service Association." In remarks on campus next day, former U.S. president Ronald Reagan praises students for electing first female as president of BYU's student body.

16 Feb., *Arizona Republic* publishes analysis of decades of talks by Seventy's president Paul H. Dunn who has misrepresented his military and baseball careers in order to tell "faith-promoting" stories to LDS youth and young adults. This is based on research of investigative reporter Lynn Packer, whose teaching employment is terminated at BYU after story's publication. In interview Dunn defends himself by saying that parables of Jesus are not literally true either. On 23 Oct. Dunn writes "Open Letter to the Members of the Church," confessing his "inaccurate" sermons and "other activities inconsistent with the high and sacred office which I have held." He acknowledges that general authorities "have censured me and placed a heavy penalty upon me." In addition to receiving emeritus status in 1989, five years before its normal implementation at age seventy, the unnamed "heavy penalty" allegedly now includes Dunn's loss of LDS privileges. Without formal disfellowshipment this would be similar to 1911 decision concerning Matthias F. Cowley, who also had been previously released as general authority before his added punishment.

10 Mar., *Deseret News* publishes report by national Associated Press of first counselor Thomas S. Monson's allowance for conscientious objection against Persian Gulf War. Although emphatic that LDS church leaders and membership support national decisions concerning war, Monson adds that a Mormon conscientious objector "can serve in some capacity that will suit his conscience and country together." This contrasts with LDS hierarchy's position during Vietnam War when only public statement was Boyd K. Packer's condemnation of conscientious objectors.

26 Mar., Utah Supreme Court rules in decision written by Justice Christine Durham: "The fact that our [Utah] constitution requires the state to prohibit polygamy does not necessarily mean that the state must deny any or all civil rights and privileges to polygamists." Therefore, court rules that polygamists have right to adopt children.

1 Apr., student at BYU's commencement offers prayer to "Our Mother and Father in Heaven."

5 Apr., first counselor Gordon B. Hinckley tells meeting of regional representatives: "I regard it as inappropriate for anyone in the Church to pray to our Mother in Heaven" which he defines as one of "small beginnings of apostasy." In response to newspaper stories about these non-public remarks, he repeats them publicly. In his address to general women's meeting following Sept., Hinckley quotes that statement as part of his answer to letter from fourteen-year-old girl he calls "Virginia."

6 Apr., *Church News* statement that "although the Church has issued earlier statements [in 1978 and 1979] advising [LDS] members not to write the FCC regarding the petition [to allegedly stop religious broadcasting], form letters to the FCC regarding the matter continue to circulate among members, even in Church meetings." *News* states that FCC has received 21 million pieces of mail since 1977 about problem that "doesn't even exist." Inability of LDS headquarters for thirteen years to stop Mormons from writing such letters indicates that many American Mormons give greater heed to propaganda by fundamentalist Christians and political ultra-conservatives.

17 Apr., *Chronicle of Higher Education* reports that Utah "ranks last in proportion of students who are female" throughout United States. This is result of Utah's "traditions that inhibit the educational progress of women."

27 Apr., *Church News* feature article about Pulitzer Prize winner Laurel Thatcher Ulrich. However, BYU's administration cancels invitation for her to speak on campus due to her support of Equal Rights Amendment and other feminist causes twenty years ago.

1 May, First Presidency calls 500,000th Mormon to serve full-time mission since 1830.

28 May, LDS church receives legal recognition in Republic of Russia, and Mormon Tabernacle Choir performs concert in Bolshoi Theater on 24 June. *Church News* cover photograph emphasizes that this is "America's Choir" at Red Square in Moscow.

1 June, In Sang Han, first Korean general authority, called to Second Quorum of Seventy.

11 June, BYU students discover bomb disguised as book in Harold B. Lee Library. It is similar to bomb which damages LDS chapel in Provo, Utah, earlier in year.

30 June, *Arizona Republic* begins three-part series on LDS church finances and claims that church receives $4.3 billion in tithing annually. LDS headquarters announces that this estimate is "grossly overstated."

9 Aug., *Salt Lake Tribune* article, "Of LDS Women, 58% Admit Premarital Sex."

19 Aug., legal holiday commemorates one hundred years of Mormon presence in Tonga which issues two postage stamps for occasion. King Taufa'ahau Tupou IV speaks at commemorative services. One-third of Tonga's population is LDS.

21 Aug., *Money* magazine ranks Provo-Orem as America's "No. 1 most-livable metropolitan area." By 1985 it also has highest rate of church membership in nation.

22 Aug., Bode Uale, first judge of Samoan ancestry in United States, is appointed to Family Court of Hawaii.

23 Aug., First Presidency and Quorum of the Twelve Apostles, by infrequently used format of joint declaration, issue statement which refers to the Sunstone Symposium's annual meetings on 7-10 Aug. It condemns "recent symposia" for presentations which are "offensive . . . in bad taste . . . and publicized in such a way as to injure the Church or its members or to jeopardize the effectiveness or safety of our missionaries." In following weeks church authorities instruct local leaders to meet with Mormons, particularly BYU faculty, who participated in Sunstone to persuade them to cease such activities.

24 Aug., *Church News* prints official reassurance of Jack H. Goaslind, Jr. (First Quorum of

Seventy member on executive board of Boy Scouts of America) that LDS church is still in BSA: "'Learning for Life' [program for self-identified homosexual scouts] does not affect the use of traditional Scouting as a tool to further the goals of the Aaronic Priesthood. As far as the Church is concerned, we are still totally supportive of the Boy Scouts of America program as we know it." This is in response to distressed inquiries from parents about Goaslind's previously published statement that LDS church "would withdraw from the Boy Scouts of America" if it permitted membership by self-identified homosexual teenagers. This retraction represents either a reversal of First Presidency decision or repudiation of Goaslind's speaking out of turn.

29 Aug., Arthur K. Smith is first non-LDS president of University of Utah.

6 Sept., LDS leaders give $25,000 to Philippines after eruption of Mt. Pinatubo.

5 Oct., newspaper reports that general authorities have ordered BYU administrators and local church leaders to discipline BYU professor for giving lecture at recent Sunstone Symposium. Persons are dropped from LDS positions and threatened with excommunication for questioning wisdom or necessity of official declaration against symposia.

4 Nov., Julia Mavimbela, black Mormon, is elected as vice-president of South Africa's National Council of Women. She is first black to be executive in organization.

5 Nov., Deedee Corradini is elected as first woman mayor of Salt Lake City. She is non-Mormon as are more than half of city's residents.

1992

18 Jan., Saimoni Tamani is inducted into Fiji's sports Hall of Fame. In 1970 he was first Fijian to win medal in track and field competition at Commonwealth Games.

17 Feb., *Newsweek* reports: "Now the [Central Intelligence] agency recruiters jump at the chance to snare a Mormon. Young Mormons tend to have squeaky-clean backgrounds and, thanks to their work as Third World missionaries, they often have a skill the CIA desperately needs these days: knowledge of a foreign language."

11 Mar., Counselor Gordon B. Hinckley presents copy of five-volume *Encyclopedia of Mormonism* to Vatican Library.

13 Mar., Joseph Anderson dies at age 102, oldest surviving general authority in Mormon history. He had been emeritus member of First Quorum of the Seventy since 1978.

14 Mar., all twenty members of BYU's Department of Sociology sign protest against ecclesiastical sanctions against those who have participated in Sunstone symposium as scholarly forum. Four days later BYU's *Daily Universe* denies Sunstone is academic.

4 Apr., Apostle Richard G. Scott tells general conference that LDS women should avoid "morbid probing into details of past acts, long buried and mercifully forgotten," and that "the Lord may prompt a victim to recognize a degree of responsibility for abuse." Among his concluding remarks: "Remember, false accusation is also a sin," and "bury the past." Unspoken background to his remarks is that in recent years current stake presidents and temple workers have been accused of child abuse by their now-adult children. *Salt Lake Tribune* reports that suicide-prevention lines are swamped with telephone calls by women in days after Scott's remarks.

11 Apr., *Salt Lake Tribune* reports that general authority Loren C. Dunn has censored church display commemorating the sesquicentennial of Relief Society. He orders removal of Joseph Smith's statements regarding priestly role of women.

9 May, *Church News* feature article, "LDS Assist in Aftermath of Riots" in Los Angeles.

13 May, Apostle Dallin H. Oaks testifies before U.S. House Subcommittee on Civil and Constitutional Rights in support of proposed Religious Freedom Restoration Act. This is designed to overturn U.S. Supreme Court's 1990 decision which invoked *Reynolds vs. the United States* to prohibit use of peyote as religious sacrament by Native American Indians. Oaks makes similar appearance on 26 Sept. before Judiciary Committee of U.S. Senate. LDS church joins such diverse religious organizations as Church of Scientology

in promoting this bill for which First Presidency publicly thanks Congress at its passage on 27 Oct. 1993. President Bill Clinton signs it into law on 18 Nov.

16 May, *Deseret News* reports that students at Ricks College, second largest LDS school, elected twin sisters, Kris and Kim Shelley, as president and vice-president of students. First female president there since World War II, during shortage of male students.

20 May, for third time in as many decades, national honor society Phi Beta Kappa rejects BYU's application for membership because BYU does not encourage "a liberal arts education which . . . foster[s] free inquiry."

22 May, First Presidency statement that King James Version of Bible is only English language Bible to be used in LDS church meetings. This codifies position maintained for decades by former First Presidency counselor J. Reuben Clark.

6 June, among those called to Second Quorum of the Seventy are Lino Alvarez (first Mexican general authority), Augusto A. Lim (first Filipino general authority), and Kwok Yuen Tai (first Hong Kong Chinese general authority). Also Gary J. Coleman is first general authority with formal training in counseling (master's and doctorate).

20 June, *Deseret News* reports that Pulitzer Prize historian Laurel Thatcher Ulrich has received MacArthur fellowship, "the genius prize."

1 July, among newly assigned mission presidents are Haitian black Fritzner A. Joseph, Ghanian black Ato K. Dadson, and Nigerian blacks John A. Ehanire and Christopher N. Chukwurah.

21 July, U.S. Department of Health and Human Services presents plaque to Relief Society general president Elaine Low Jack in honor of Society's service for older women.

31 July, counselor Gordon B. Hinckley is speaker with RLDS president Wallace B. Smith at RLDS Auditorium in Independence, Missouri, where Mormon Tabernacle Choir also performs concert "to the sell-out audience of 5200."

8 Aug., *Salt Lake Tribune* reports that First Presidency's spokesman has acknowledged existence of special "Strengthening the Members Committee" that keeps secret files on church members regarded as disloyal. Due to publicity about this matter, including *New York Times,* Presidency issues statement on 13 Aug. defending organization of this apostle-directed committee as consistent with God's commandment to Joseph Smith to gather documentation about non-Mormons who mob and persecute LDS church. Presidency lists Apostles James E. Faust and Russell M. Nelson as leading the Strengthening the Members Committee. Faust becomes counselor in First Presidency in 1995.

9 Aug., general authority Jacob de Jaeger tells Salt Lake City congregation that Latter-day Saints have responsibility "to get along with everybody—and that includes those that read the *Ensign* and those that read *Sunstone.*"

3 Oct., announcement of temple to be constructed for Hartford, Connecticut; this is cancelled on 30 Sept. 1995.

25 Oct., general authority Malcolm S. Jeppsen's prepares talk, which he gives to LDS leaders in Utah during next several weeks, listing twenty warning signs of apostasy. In addition to usual cautions about current polygamy, he includes: "those who advocate a mother in heaven and women holding the priesthood," those who hold special prayer meetings in private, "John Birch membership or leanings," and those who store more than LDS headquarter's recommendation of one-year's supply of food.

29 Dec., first concert of Mormon Tabernacle Choir in Holy Land (at Haifa), with concert in Jerusalem next evening.

3 Nov., Olene S. Walker is elected as Utah's Republican lieutenant governor, highest elective office a woman has achieved in Utah state government.

1993

1 Jan., organization of India Bangalore Mission with Gurcharan Singh Gill as president, thirty missionaries, and 1,150 already-baptized Indian Mormons.

2 Jan., at sacrament meeting in Tiberias, by Sea of Galilee, in Israel, Apostle James E. Faust

tells Tabernacle Choir: "My testimony is like that of the brother of Jared who saw the finger of God and believed no more, for he knew. It has been given to me to know, for I have become acquainted with the Savior."

6 Feb., *Church News*, "Barriers Crumble: Interfaith Activities Build Bridges of Friendship."

7 Feb., man holds Apostle Howard W. Hunter hostage for ten minutes in front of 17,000 students at BYU, as president of the Twelve starts to give Sunday evening sermon at Marriott Center. Man claims to hold a bomb but is physically attacked and subdued by male students and BYU security personnel.

20 Feb., second counselor Thomas S. Monson speaks at rededication ceremony for Roman Catholic church's Cathedral of the Madeleine in Salt Lake City, also attended by Apostles James E. Faust and Neal A. Maxwell.

In response to LDS man and woman separately preparing simplified English versions of *Book of Mormon*, First Presidency officially prohibits such a "translation" as undermining ancient origins of scripture. Man withdraws but Lynn Matthews Anderson publishes her revision in 1994.

4 Mar., First Presidency letter absolutely excludes following persons from possibility of serving full-time missions: "Individuals who have become HIV positive . . . Persons 19 to 26 who have been divorced . . . Young men who have encouraged, paid for, or arranged for an abortion resulting from their immoral conduct . . . Sisters who submit to abortions growing out of their immoral conduct . . . [anyone who] has fathered or given birth to a child out of wedlock." Persons with "homosexual activity" would be eligible only on these conditions: "if there is no current indication of homosexual tendencies" or if "there is strong evidence of complete repentance and reformation, with at least one year free of transgression."

25 Apr., dedication of San Diego, California temple by Gordon B. Hinckley. Its stunning exterior design is post-modern gothic inspiration of its Roman Catholic architects.

2 May, Mormon Tabernacle Choir performs in renovated Cathedral of the Madeleine.

12 May, Regional Representative Jon M. Huntsman, recently released as U.S. ambassador, meets in Vatican with Pope John Paul II who expresses gratitude for Mormon donations to Catholic relief work.

18 May, Apostle Boyd K. Packer tells All-Church Coordinating Council that LDS church faces three major threats: "The dangers I speak of come from the gay-lesbian movement, the feminist movement (both of which are relatively new), and the ever-present challenge from the so-called scholars or intellectuals."

4 June, *Salt Lake Tribune* reports that University of Utah study shows that 61 percent of Utahns "believe bad parenting is the primary cause of severe mental illness." Also 29 percent of Utahns believe that mentally ill persons "would be helped if they repented."

10 June, BYU officials terminate five junior professors, including Cecelia K. Farr (pro-choice feminist) and anthropologist David Knowlton who has published studies of Latin American terrorism against LDS buildings and missionaries. In immediate response more than 100 students rally to protest lack of academic freedom at BYU, first such student demonstration at BYU since 1911. Subsequent rallies include holders of prestigious "Benson Scholarship," and Third World students who compare BYU's current situation with repressive regimes these students have fled. This is reported at length in *Chronicle of Higher Education*, thus worsening BYU's reputation for academic freedom among administrators of nation's universities and grant-giving foundations.

26 June, groundbreaking for temple in Bogota, Colombia; under construction, Nov. 1996.

27 June, counselor Gordon B. Hinckley dedicates former Hotel Utah as new Joseph Smith Memorial Building to serve primarily as additional office space for LDS central bureaucracy. Its large theatres also begin showing devotional film "Legacy" (about Mormon pioneers), scripted by Academy award-winner Keith Merrill according to Hinckley's instruction: "I want them to leave the theater crying."

29 June, Mexico's government grants legal recognition to LDS church and authorizes it to own property for first time in more than one hundred years of settlement.

13 July, *Arizona Republic* reports that First Presidency spokesman Don LeFevre claims "the typical faithful Mormon" already knows that Ezra Taft Benson's mental condition prevents his participation in decision-making. This is in response to continued publicity of Steve Benson's statements during past week that his grandfather is mentally incompetent, and that LDS leaders are exploiting him by giving impression in photographs and official statements that church president is mentally active. Steve Benson withdraws from membership in LDS church in October, after excommunication of several scholars and feminists.

17 July, Counselor Thomas S. Monson presides at memorial service for reinterred bodies of former apostle Abraham Owen Woodruff and his first wife Helen Winters Woodruff. Removed from their original 1904 burial sites in Texas and Mexico, respectively, the couple is buried side-by-side in Salt Lake City. This is first reinterment of Mormon leader and wife since that of Joseph and Emma Smith in 1928.

24 July, Utah Pioneer Day parade has float by "Latter-day Saints for Cultural Awareness," who portray African-American pioneers Elijah Abel (ordained elder and Seventy with Joseph Smith's approval, denied endowment by Brigham Young), Green Flake (Utah pioneer slave), and Jane Elizabeth Manning (sealed as eternal "Servitor" to Smith).

25 July, representatives of University of Jordan and BYU sign agreement for academic and cultural exchanges, which represents Howard W. Hunter's long encouragement for greater LDS out-reach to Arab and Muslim peoples.

30 July, commemorative service at California's Mt. Coray, recently named for Melissa Coray who accompanied Mormon Battalion to California in 1846.

31 July, *Salt Lake Tribune* reports that LDS missionary-couples in Nauvoo, Illinois have worked "for 88 consecutive hours without sleep" to help protect historical properties of RLDS church in Nauvoo from rampaging Mississippi River.

21 Aug., *Church News* article features Egide Nzojibwami, university dean of engineering and branch president in Burundi, Africa.

22 Aug., *Salt Lake Tribune* reports survey showing that 55 percent of Utah's residents favor right of persons to commit suicide under any circumstances. For persons with terminal diseases, 65 percent of Utahns favor physician-assisted suicide.

28 Aug., Apostle Russell M. Nelson represents LDS church at Parliament of the World's Religions in Chicago, exactly 100 years after it rejected first Mormon delegation.

25 Sept., *Church News* article "Jewish Congregations Note High Holy Days in LDS Meetinghouses," with explanation that this practice has continued for twenty years in Southern California because "many synagogues are unable to hold the large numbers wishing to attend Rosh Hashanah and Yom Kippur services."

9 Oct., LDS church-sponsored picnic hosts ambassadors and other diplomats from thirty-three countries at Marriott family's farm in Hume, Virginia. With at least one LDS apostle in cowboy clothing provided to all attenders, this "Ambassadorial Western Family Picnic" is annual event attended by diplomats from ever-larger number of nations.

17 Oct., First Presidency issues statement concerning procedures for disfellowshipment and excommunication. *1995-1996 Church Almanac* states that this was in response to "extensive publicity given to six recent Church disciplinary councils in Utah." Coordinated by instructions from the Strengthening the Members Committee and Apostle Boyd K. Packer to their stake presidents, six scholars and feminists had been excommunicated or disfellowshipped in September.

28 Oct., financed by LDS headquarters and coordinated by resident member of Tabernacle Choir, Hanoi Opera House performs Handel's "Messiah," sung in English by Vietnamese and accompanied by National Vietnam Symphony Orchestra.

30 Oct., groundbreaking for temple near St. Louis, Missouri; under construction Nov. 1996.

1 Nov., Richard A. Searfoss, Mormon lieutenant-colonel, pilots *Columbia* back to earth after fourteen days in orbit, longest space-shuttle flight to this date.

6 Nov., by permission of RLDS church, Utah Mormons hold official meeting in Kirtland temple, first since LDS church established its headquarters in Utah. Principal speaker is Apostle M. Russell Ballard.

18 Dec., *Church News* article "Joseph Smith's Birthday on Dec. 23 Often Overlooked In Holiday Season."

19 Dec., LDS missionary choir sings carols in St. Peter's Basilica during broadcast of Christmas Mass by Vatican Radio. This is spontaneous idea of young missionary, apparently not coordinated by LDS headquarters.

1994

1 Jan., end of congregational hymn-singing and general meeting prior to individual Sunday School classes, as per First Presidency announcement on 25 Sept. 1993.

15 Jan., *Church News* article "Suicide Rates Increasing: Church Members Not Immune."

23 Jan., Colombian rebels blow up LDS chapel in Medellin.

1 Feb., First Presidency endorses appointment of 1994 as "International Year of the Family," by United Nations, organization which currently disabled Ezra Taft Benson has repeatedly denounced as illegal infringement on U.S. sovereignty. This reinforces his grandson's claim that counselors are making decisions without church president's coherent consultation or approval.

10 Feb., Counselor Gordon B. Hinckley withdraws church's financial support from Salt Lake City's Pioneer Memorial Theater (PMT) because of "increasing profanity and vulgarity in its productions." Subsequent explanations in *Deseret News* cite profanity in production of *Conversations With My Father* several months ago. Timing of Hinckley's announcement is unfortunate—day after PMT's premier of Shakespeare's *Romeo and Juliet*, which presents its "star-crossed lovers" as black-white interracial couple.

16 Feb., pipe bomb blows out windows of LDS chapel in Sunland, California.

19 Feb., First Presidency issues statement encouraging church members to actively work against legalization of same-gender marriages. This inaugurates national campaign, similar to centrally directed anti-ERA activities.

21 Feb., LDS headquarters in Bogota, Colombia directs public statement to country's rebel forces denying that LDS chapels represent either U.S. government or American business interests in any way.

21 Mar., Academy of Motion Picture Arts and Sciences gives Oscar to LDS Jerry Molen as co-producer of *Schindler's List*. Because film is "R-rated," BYU refuses to show this dramatization of Jewish Holocaust even though public high school students throughout Utah have seen this film in special screenings as school activity with parental permission.

24 Mar., Jane Partridge, president of her high school seminary class, testifies before U.S. Congress in support of reducing legal limits for blood-alcohol level of teenage drivers.

30 Apr., Tahiti issues postage stamp commemorating 150 years of Mormonism there.

30 May, Ezra Taft Benson's death on Memorial Day. With his internment in Whitney, Idaho, he is first LDS president since Joseph Smith to be buried outside Utah.

3 June, Archibald F. Bennett, former secretary of Genealogical Society and first director of its microfilming, is inducted posthumously into National Genealogical Hall of Fame.

5 June, Quorum of Twelve sustains Howard W. Hunter as church president with Gordon B. Hinckley and Thomas S. Monson as counselors, and ordains President Hunter. He is first LDS church president since founder Joseph Smith who has not served full-time mission before becoming general authority, and first with professional degree (from

Southwestern University Law School in Los Angeles). Hunter is also first LDS president in twentieth century whose wife is previously divorced.

12 June, groundbreaking for temple near Preston, England; under construction Nov. 1996.

23 July, *Church News* story "Members Help Defeat Lottery Initiative" tells how two general authorities coordinate political campaign in Oklahoma where Mormons "make up less than 1 percent of the state's population." LDS Public Affairs officials and their Protestant allies achieve overwhelming defeat of proposal even though "public opinion polls show 75 percent for the initiative" before this Mormon-directed campaign.

28 July, First Presidency sends $760,000 to aid civil-war refugees of Rwanda, Africa.

6 Aug., *Church News* article "Asian LDS Celebrate Pioneer Day."

1 Oct., Utah's Earl Miller is inducted into U.S. National Ski Hall of Fame.

9 Oct., Howard W. Hunter dedicates temple near Orlando, Florida.

6 Nov., Apostle M. Russell Ballard tells 25,000 students at BYU that general authorities "will not lead you astray. We cannot." This claim of infallibility is officially published, and he repeats it to another BYU devotional meeting in March 1996.

12 Nov., announcement of temple to be constructed in Nashville, Tennessee. No groundbreaking ceremony occurs by November 1996.

1995

8 Jan., in his wheelchair Howard W. Hunter dedicates temple in Bountiful, Utah.

3 Mar., death of Howard W. Hunter, whose presidency is briefest in Mormon history—less than nine months. This is half of previously shortest tenure served by any LDS president: Harold B. Lee's seventeen months and nineteen days.

12 Mar., Quorum of Twelve sustains Gordon B. Hinckley as church president with Thomas S. Monson and James E. Faust as counselors, and ordains President Hinckley. Occurring nine days after death of his predecessor, this is longest period without organized First Presidency since 1898. Hinckley is first LDS president since Joseph Fielding Smith who has works his entire adult life in church bureaucracy, church-controlled businesses, and headquarters administration.

13 Mar., LDS president answers questions at press conference, first time in 22 years.

1 Apr., solemn assembly sustains newly ordained Gordon B. Hinckley as LDS president, first time in Mormon history that solemn assemblies have sustained two new presidents within six-month period. For first time, females are asked to vote according to their auxiliary membership, Young Women (ages 12 to 18) and Relief Society (age 18+), in imitation of traditional voting-pattern for males according to their priesthood quorums.

Announcement of end of Regional Representative calling, effective 15 Aug., to be replaced by Area Authorities. These officers will be high priests serving without financial compensation for six years, while they "continue their current employment, [and] reside in their own homes." Number of Area Authorities is intended to be substantially smaller than 284 Regional Representatives serving at this date.

8 Apr., Gordon B. Hinckley dedicates "Tuacahn," outdoor amphitheater seating 2,000 near St. George, Utah, for performances "featuring Mormon themes and values." It hosts Mormon Arts Festival in May 1996.

20 Apr., U.S. postage stamp promoting environment, designed by fourteen-year-old Brian Hailes of Millville, Utah.

3 May, agreement between LDS church and American Gathering of Jewish Holocaust Survivors "over the issue of posthumous baptisms of Jewish Holocaust victims." First Presidency agrees to "remove from next issue of International Genealogical Index [public-access record only] names of all known posthumously baptized Jewish holocaust victims," and "to discontinue any further baptisms of deceased Jews, including all lists of Jewish Holocaust victims who are known Jews, except if they were direct ancestors of living members of the Church."

9 May., announcement that non-LDS Peggy Stock will be president of Westminster College, Salt Lake City, first woman to head Utah institution of higher learning.

10 May, Presiding Bishopric letter informs local LDS leaders to use toll-free telephone number to report cases of child abuse involving Mormons: "This will enable the caller to consult with social services, legal and other specialists who can assist in answering questions and in formulating steps that should be taken."

Excommunication of feminist Janice Merrill Allred for her speaking and publishing about LDS doctrine of Mother in Heaven.

11 May, representatives of LDS church in Denver withdraw their application for institutional "observer status" in Colorado Council of Churches, first step to membership in World Council of Churches. Announcement of application caused firestorm of complaints and letters demanding rejection due to Mormon theology of sexually cohabiting Heavenly Father who progresses by allowing mortals to become gods. Application is withdrawn to avoid bruising confirmation process.

13 May, Gordon B. Hinckley presides at "ground-breaking" ceremony for temple to be constructed by remodeling nearly ninety-year-old Uintah Stake Tabernacle in Vernal, Utah. This is first time new temple is to be created from pre-existing building which had other uses. Still under construction in November 1996.

16 June, International Olympic Committee in Budapest votes overwhelming for Salt Lake City as site of winter Olympics in year 2002. Utahns are divided about economic benefits/losses, and some Mormons have misgivings about long-term secularization of city that Olympics will cause. However, many see this as ideal opportunity to preach Mormonism directly and indirectly to tens of thousands of visitors in short time. LDS headquarters technically remains neutral about this "political matter" during five-year promotional effort. However, Salt Lake Olympic Bid Committee's legally required financial statement shows that during its final year of operation alone, committee received $100,000 from LDS church's "associated business" Intermountain Healthcare, and $100,000 from Deseret Foundation (arm of LDS Hospital). Hospital subsequently denies that it is officially involved in transaction by which "anonymous" party channels donations through Deseret Foundation.

19 June, *Salt Lake Tribune* reports that Utah state task force is trying to understand why suicide is second leading cause of death for Utah's teenage males and young men, and why Utah's suicide rate is sixth highest in nation. Article downplays alleged role of LDS church's "too high expectations on young people," by pointing out that five states (all surrounding Utah) with higher suicide rates have lower percentages of Mormons. However, this is statistical error ("ecological fallacy") because states have not identified religious affiliation of suicides who might actually be disproportionately Mormon. *Tribune* refers to U.S. Health Department's 1989 estimate that homosexual orientation is factor in 30 percent of teenage suicides. *Deseret News* excluded that estimate from its analysis of federal report on 12 Aug. 1989 and has said little about this current Utah task force.

7 July, award-winning young author Brian Evenson announces his resignation as BYU English professor to join faculty at Oklahoma State University. Because of anonymous student's complaint to an apostle about violence and "darkness" in Evenson's published work, BYU's officials were requiring him to cancel his most recent book contract with New York publisher Knopf or face termination. BYU's spokesperson comments: "The University's sense of mission and Brian's sense of mission were quite divergent."

20 July, Presbyterian General Assembly of the United States adopts resolution that LDS church is "a new and emerging religion that expresses allegiance to Jesus Christ in terms used within the Christian tradition." This ecumenical statement is at odds with Protestant denominations which define Mormonism as non-Christian cult. However, in recognition of LDS church's own claim to be neither Catholic nor Protestant, this document adds that LDS church is "not within the historic apostolic tradition of the Christian Church of which the Presbyterian Church (U.S.A.) is a part." This pro-Mor-

mon resolution is drafted and presented by Utah's Presbytery, eighty-five years after it fomented several anti-Mormon campaigns nationally.

5 Aug., *Church News* lists 117 appointments to new position (non-hierarchy) of "Area Authorities," including native-born professors at universities in Brazil, Canada, England, Japan, and Korea.

19 Sept., Wallace B. Smith, president of RLDS church, announces that his successor will be W. Grant McMurray, age forty-eight. Effective as of April 1996, this ends patrilineal succession of Joseph Smith's descendants as presidents of RLDS church since 1860.

23 Sept., at general meeting of LDS Relief Society the First Presidency and Twelve issue "Proclamation on the Family" including the statement: "We further declare that God has commanded that the sacred powers of procreation are to be employed only between man and woman, lawfully wedded as husband and wife." It concludes: "We call upon responsible citizens and officers of government everywhere to promote those measures designed to maintain and strengthen the family as the fundamental unit of society." Aside from this statement's usefulness in LDS campaign against legalization of same-sex marriages, hierarchy's repeated emphasis on importance of its being "proclamation" suggests that this announcement will one day be presented for sustaining vote of general conference and added as numbered document in *Doctrine and Covenants*.

30 Sept., announcement of two temples, one to be constructed for Boston and one for White Plains, New York; no groundbreaking ceremonies occur by November 1996. This day's withdrawal of previous announcement of temple for Hartford, Connecticut is first such cancellation. Even unused (yet dedicated in 1839) temple site of Far West, Missouri, has not been formally cancelled.

Sept., *Ensign* magazine publishes First Presidency message by second counselor James E. Faust which denounces "the false belief of inborn homosexual orientation." Next month's *Ensign* contains what appears as one apostle's direct challenge to First Presidency's unequivocal statement. In his October article "Same-Gender Attraction," Dallin H. Oaks writes: "There are also theories and some evidence that inheritance is a factor in susceptibilities to various behavior-related disorders like aggression, alcoholism, and obesity. It is easy to hypothesize that inheritance plays a role in sexual orientation."

23 Oct., *Salt Lake Tribune* reports that during formal meeting with University of Utah's president, nine Utah legislators from Utah County (home of BYU) criticize coursework at state campus. Utah County legislators (including several members of appropriations committee for University of Utah) complain about "topics being taught that are inconsistent with the beliefs of the predominant religion, particularly in the Graduate School of Social Work and the department of philosophy." These legislators (eight Republicans out of nine) also have "concerns about the Women's Resource Center."

26 Oct., BYU's spokesman announces that university officials have accepted explanation of mathematics professor John Milo Peterson that only "a clerical error" was involved in his claiming for twenty years that University of Georgia had awarded him Ph.D. degree (which would qualify him as specialist in mathematics) rather than his actual degree of Ed.D. (which qualifies him as specialist in educational techniques) from Utah State University. Peterson is currently stake president and his college dean is patriarch of that stake. As stake president, Peterson asks every applicant for priesthood ordination and temple recommends following question: "Are you honest in your dealings with your fellowmen?" In 1993 national *Chronicle of Higher Education* noted that Peterson's annual salary was $103,000 (among BYU's top five) as full professor and director of graduate program in mathematics.

2 Nov., announcement that Presiding Bishop Merrill J. Bateman will be new president of BYU, effective 1 Jan. He is also appointed member of First Quorum of the Seventy. Despite Bateman's Ph.D. in economics from MIT, the appointment of general authority to BYU's helm has appearance of guaranteeing that LDS hierarchy will not need to deal with vigorous advocate for academic freedom at largest LDS campus. This is how *Chron-*

icle of Higher Education views it. Within months Bateman is center of national contro-versy over his speech to BYU students against moral relativism, published version of which lifts numerous phrases (without quotation marks) from recently published arti-cle by neo-conservative scholar Gertrude Himmelfarb. She is cited (with quotation marks) for only one sentence and phrase of many that Bateman's speech/article inter-weaves with slight changes in manner familiar to anyone who has read plagiarized pa-pers by freshman students. Bateman publicly apologizes to Himmelfarb and insists controversy is about "one" misplaced quotation mark, yet public image remains that BYU's president participates in "moral relativism" he condemns.

Nov., five BYU professors submit officially-commissioned, four-year study of LDS appli-cants for freshmen admission (1971-88). Findings show that active Mormons who at-tend BYU "even for only one semester" have significantly higher rates of temple marriage, tithing payment, and belief in LDS doctrines than Mormons who attend other colleges. Although survey participants are age twenty-six to mid-forties, 20 per-cent "of the married respondents in both groups remained childless." BYU's spokes-person says executive committee of Board of Trustees decides to suppress this report because "we already get a lot of pressure about admission to BYU and release of this study would only make that worse." Since 1973 enrollment limit of 27,000 means that "only a small and shrinking minority of Mormon youth" can attend BYU. No spokesper-son at LDS headquarters or at BYU comments on evidence of long-term birth-control by married couples who are actively LDS. Despite contrary statements of BYU's spokes-person and sources at church headquarters, BYU president Bateman denies in Febru-ary 1996 that board has made any decision about circulating this study's findings.

25 Nov., ambassadors from fifty nations attend holiday lighting ceremony at Washington, D.C. temple, and India's ambassador Siddhartha Shankar Ray turns the switch.

23 Dec., 190th birthday of Mormon founder Joseph Smith; First Presidency announces new logo for church's name, with larger letters for JESUS CHRIST.

27 Dec., announcement of temple to be constructed in Monterrey, Mexico. No ground-breaking ceremony occurs by November 1996.

1996

4 Jan., U.S. postage stamp for Utah's statehood centennial. Its image of Delicate Arch is de-sign of McRay Magleby, creative director of BYU's Publication and Graphics.

18 Jan., First Presidency announces that all general authorities are resigning as officers or directors of business enterprises and will not accept such positions in future.

11 Feb., in official editorial against allowing Utah's high schools to have clubs for gay and lesbian students, *Deseret News* comments: "It is still appalling that more than half the identified hate crimes in Utah are aimed at homosexuals." Editorial concludes by af-firming attitude on which such hate crimes are based: "homosexual activities and prac-tices are an abomination, not just some 'alternative lifestyle' no better or worse than others." Within days Salt Lake City's school board prohibits all extracurricular clubs as only way to stop students from forming homosexually oriented clubs and still comply with federal laws against discrimination in public schools. These events are reported by major national newspapers and network television news programs.

21 Feb., *Deseret News* (with follow-up on 28 Feb.) reports that LDS president Gordon B. Hinckley meets with Honolulu's Catholic bishop Francis X. DiLorenzo to coordinate "as part of a grass-roots coalition opposed to same-sex marriage" legalization.

26 Feb., more than half of LDS church's population resides outside U.S.A. as of this date.

5 Mar., former British prime minister Margaret Thatcher accepts honorary doctorate at Brigham Young University

19 Mar., *Church News* story about Chong Youl Kim, LDS director of South Korea's National Institute of Scientific Investigation ("similar to the U.S. Federal Bureau of Investiga-tion," FBI).

10 Apr., Mormon investors announce they are purchasing Southern Virginia College (SVC), four months after it loses accreditation as two-year school and one month before its closing, to turn it into Mormon school without official sponsorship by LDS headquarters. The likely success of this unprecedented idea is indicated by its announcement in *Church News* and choice of David Ferrel as college's new president. He is a senior employee of recently appointed general authority Richard B. Wirthlin who formally endorses school. Having arranged for LDS congressmen to pressure accrediting association to reconsider its decision, newly installed Mormon trustees announce that SVC will be four-year college with starting freshman class of 400 students who meet same standards of conduct and entrance requirements as at BYU.

26 Apr., national news story that Tennessee's Fellowship of Christian Athletes has withdrawn Male Athlete Award of the Year from high school student Aaron Walker because he is member of LDS church.

25 May, *Church News* reports that CIA's director has conferred National Intelligence Medal of Achievement on Robert A. Mills, a Mormon.

26 May, President Gordon B. Hinckley dedicates temple in Hong Kong.

31 May, Apostle Dallin H. Oaks marches in procession honoring Carolyn Tanner Irish's ordination as bishop of Utah's Episcopal diocese. Bishop Irish was LDS member until her Protestant conversion as adult. LDS president Gordon B. Hinckley tells general conference in October: "I know of no other organization [besides LDS church] which affords women so many opportunities . . . for holding positions of leadership and responsibility," even though Mormon women cannot be ordained to ecclesiastical office.

8 June, *Salt Lake Tribune* story that, contrary to recommendation of her department and college, BYU has fired English professor Gail Houston for expressing feminist views off-campus. In support of this decision, university spokesman notes that 5 percent of her student-evaluations complain that Houston's courses in English literature do not offer "gospel insights" and are not "spiritually uplifting," even though 95 percent of student evaluations rank her highly. In October the American Association of University Professors begins investigation of this action in terms of due process and academic freedom.

9 June, *Salt Lake Tribune* reports that LDS headquarters has acknowledged it has been calling specific people (such as advertising executives) on short-term missions to assist in campaign against legalization of same-sex marriages in Hawaii.

11 June, groundbreaking for temple in Madrid, Spain.

2 July, "security leader and de facto second in command" of Russian Republic publicly apologizes week after calling Russia's Mormons "filth and scum." LDS church has no more than 5,000 converts and 300 missionaries there. Apology occurs because LDS members (Republicans) of Republican-controlled U.S. Senate ask Democratic "Clinton administration to reconsider aid to Russia because of [Alekandr] Lebed's stand."

7 July, Northwest Association of Schools and Colleges recertifies BYU's accreditation for ten years, despite committee's acknowledgement of faculty complaints that academic freedom is severely limited on this LDS campus.

10 Aug., groundbreaking for temple in Guayaquil, Ecuador, 14 years after announced.

18 Aug., groundbreaking for temple in Santo Domingo, Dominican Republic.

30 Aug., announcement that Billings, Montana will be site of sixty-third functioning LDS temple. It may be dedicated prior to previously announced temples outside U.S.

2 Sept., Gordon B. Hinckley receives American Legion's "Good Guy Award."

Fall, *Brigham Young University Studies* publishes study by two sociologists who analyze 1,384 questionnaires submitted by LDS "householders," including discovery that LDS men are more likely to think they are going to heaven ("celestial kingdom") than women think of themselves. Men are less likely to attend church or pray privately than women.

13 Oct., Gordon B. Hinckley dedicates Mount Timpanogos temple at American Fork, Utah.

15 Oct., Boyd K. Packer, Twelve's acting-president, tells BYU devotional assembly that

bishops should exercise strict control over LDS funerals because families are conducting funerals where "we hear about the deceased instead of the Atonement." *Deseret News* notes that he speaks about "unwritten laws" of church conduct, but does not quote or paraphrase Apostle Packer's statements against content of LDS funerals by grieving families.

4 Nov., *Publishers Weekly* lists D. Michael Quinn's *Same-Sex Dynamics among Nineteenth-Century Americans: A Mormon Example* as one of six Best Books published in 1996 about religion.

10 Nov., groundbreaking ceremony for Krishna temple in Spanish Fork, Utah, where Hare Krishnas have operated radio station since 1983. One of least likely additions to Utah's religious landscape, the Krishna temple will have 10,000 square feet of floor space, larger than LDS temple in Freiberg, Germany, and equivalent to floor space of LDS temples in Hawaii (original) and Peru.

Groundbreaking ceremony for LDS temple in Cochabamba, Bolivia.

Emotionally disturbed Mormon uses axe to smash through doors of St. George (Utah) temple, where he is physically subdued near celestial room by police officer who does "not want to shed blood in the temple."

13 Nov., BYU-graduate and Utah-native Sharla "Kris" Cook is promoted to brigadier-general in U.S. Air Force.

15 Nov., groundbreaking ceremony for temple in Recife, Brazil.

INDEX

Due to space limitations, this index does not include appendices. It lists persons and selected topics from chapters.

ent on flawed memory, 149-50; dissent, 11, 12, 13, 17-20, 25, 26, 29, 39, 41-42, 45, 46-48, 63, 94-95, 112, 122, 123, 136, 137, 144, 149, 173, 205, 207, 208, 211, 267-69, 286-87, 327, 336, 350-52, 356, 364, 370-71, 393, 394; "end runs," 31, 104; "follow the Brethren," 366; flattery, 17, 157; humor, 12, 18, 23; influenced by seniority, 8-9; influenced by strong-willed subordinate, 20, 46, 105; inspired, 7, 13-14, 16, 17, 20, 25, 33, 51, 173; insufficient information for, 10; lobbying within hierarchy, 10-11, 16, 31, 52, 102, 104; meditation, 33; mental incapacity, 14-15, 54, 56-58, 104; negative votes, 10, 17-18, 42; not by Assistants to the Twelve, 149; not infallible, viii, 7, 141, 363, 368; not limited by written revelation, 148; oligarchy, 408; "pleasing all of the Brethren," 13; punishment for dissent, 19, 38-39, 41, 62-63, 88-89, 193, 265, 250-52, 350-52, 356, 357, 371, 395, 400; repetitive, 8; reversing, 15, 48, 142, 144, 150, 152, 201, 205, 346; Salt Lake temple council, 7, 8, 9, 10, 11-12, 13, 16-17, 18, 19, 20, 21, 24, 34, 50, 52, 54, 59, 61, 63, 65, 108, 122-23, 124, 125-26, 129, 137, 206, 336, 356, 361; secretarial influence, 32, 74, 157-58; snowball voting procedure, 8, 9; split-voting, 11, 62-63, 148; stalemate for years, 41-42, 45-48, 51-53, 126-27, 136; success through absence of opponents, 11-12, 14, 26, 48-49, 52-53; tabling motions, 11, 42; "the thinking has been done," 220; unanimous votes, 7, 10, 11, 12-13, 17-18, 45, 48, 52, 267-68; uninspired, 141, 173, 363, 364; waiting years to inform subordinate quorums about, 146; withdrawing unpopular motions, 47, 122, 123; without discussion, 13, 53, 164

Democratic Independent Party (Idaho anti-Mormon), 264

Democratic Party, 63, 69, 70, 73, 79, 136, 146, 264, 293, 307, 316-22, 324-28, 330-38, 341-44, 345-54, 356-58, 360-61, 363-64, 374, 375, 376, 383, 394. See also Jeffersonian Democracy.

Deregulation of airlines, 399-400

Derrick, Royden G., 222

"Deseret," 236

Deseret, State of (1849-51), 237-38, 242, 265-66, 283, 320; constitution, 237-38; flag, 263; ghost government (1862-70), 278; legislature, 238, 283; secession threats (1862), 274, 275. See also Kingdom of God; Theocracy.

Deseret Book Company, 4, 78, 115, 210, 211, 252, 364, 376, 399

Deseret Gymnasium, 307

Deseret Management Corporation, 224

DeWitt, Aaron, 258

Dickson, John B., 193

Didier, Charles A., 152

DiLorenzo, Francis X., 403

Diplomatic activities, of general authorities, 92; of rank-and-file Mormons, 406. See also Political activities.

Director of Temporal Affairs (DTA). See Bishop(ric), Presiding.

Disciplinary council [recent term]. See Church courts.

Disenfranchisements. See Arizona; Federal government; Idaho; Iowa; Nevada.

Disfellowship (deny LDS privileges to person who remains member of church), examples, 22, 62-63, 197, 200, 235, 351; similar punishment without formal disfellowshipping, 63, 128. See also Church courts; Excommunicate.

Dissenters, 29, 45, 71-73, 74, 75, 78, 83, 90, 105-06, 112, 114-15, 171, 173, 200, 207, 208, 228, 229, 242-43, 244, 258, 265, 311, 314, 327, 336, 350-52, 356, 357, 358, 364, 366, 371, 393, 394. See also Apostasy; Decision-making, dissent; Intimidation of enemies; Killing dissenters; Opposition, loyal; Violence (non-fatal) against enemies.

Faith, 385; despite knowledge of LDS church's problems, viii-ix, 62, 115, 138, 160, 173, 282

Family, "Church family comprised of General Authorities and their kin," 197; extended, 163, 166-67, 173, 174, 192, 195, 195, 197; meetings, 165, 195; theology, 163-64, 176, 178, 196; threatened by minority alternatives, 179, 302, 313, 325, 328, 402-03. *See also* Ancestors; Dynasticism; Hierarchy; Kinship; Marriage; Nepotism; Polyandry; Polygamy.

Faust, James E., 58, 112, 222, 368, 376

Featherstone, Vaughn J., 222

Federal Bureau of Investigation (FBI), 78, 101, 306, 307, 308-09, 310. *See also* Intelligence agencies.

Federal government, 17-18, 303; aid programs, 17-18, 102, 136, 137, 380; anti-polygamy crusade, 179, 181, 213, 264, 284, 285, 325-26, 327; armed rebellion against, LDS leaders consider, 79, 251; bureaucracy compared with LDS bureaucracy, 156, 158-59, 160; confiscated church properties, including Salt Lake temple, 48, 218, 325, 328, 347; corruption, 271; disenfranchised polygamists, 44, 284, 297; disenfranchised Utah women, 44, 297; disincorporated LDS church, 274, 321, 325; limited powers before Civil War, 317; Mormons eagerly expected its downfall, 272, 277, 313; Mormon opposition to federal power, 400; officials in territorial Utah, 239-40, 269, 270, 271, 272-73, 275-78; opposition to Mormon exodus to far west, 233, 234; prepared to deny all Mormons right to homestead, 328; prepared to disenfranchise all Mormons in U.S., 48, 328; subsidy sought by Brigham Young, 234; tried to remove Mormon judge from ERA case, 378; vitality of, 313. *See also* Central Intelligence Agency (CIA); Conscription; Constitution, U.S.; Federal Bureau of Investigation (FBI); House of Representatives, U.S.; Polygamy, raid; Senate, U.S.; Supreme Court, U.S.; War.

Felt, Nathaniel H., 132-33, 284, 288, 290

Fetzer, Percy Kaspar, 306-7

Fielding, Amos, 283

Fielding, Joseph, 283

Fillmore, Millard, 266

Fillmore, Utah, 266

Finch, Harry L., 304

First Council of the Seventy. *See* Seventy.

First Presidency, 371; assistant counselor, 22, 32, 34, 117, 149, 164, 190, 256, 398; associate president, 22, 163, 318; business directorships and income, 217, 220-21, 223; concerned about headquarters bureaucracy, 156, 159, 160, 224; conflicts with apostles, 26, 27, 29-30, 36-59, 126-27, 171; conflicts with Presiding Bishop(ric), 132, 134-38; conflicts with Presiding Patriarch, 119-21, 125-26, 130-31; conflicts with the Seventy, 142-44, 147, 149-50, 151; counselors, 14-15, 22, 30-35, 48, 51, 53, 54-59, 214; created by Quorum of the Twelve, 37-38, 45; debt cancellation, 211, 212; demotion, 23, 25, 30, 32, 33; "deniability," 353; denial of actual events, 339, 340, 355, 361; financial compensation, 204-05, 207-12, 217, 223; first organized, 22, 214; internal conflicts, 18, 22-35, 160, 211; kinship, 163-65, 166-73, 175-77, 192, 194, 195-96; "living constitution," 302-03; marriage relations, 178-92, 195; perceived as ruled by single counselor, 46, 49-50, 53, 56-57; political activities, 265-69, 277, 278, 280-82, 283, 286, 289-92, 316-18, 320, 322-24, 328-36, 339-72, 398-99, 403; political dimensions in choice of counselors, 338, 364; relationship to political action/oversight committees, 355, 359-60, 398; secretaries, 7, 8, 10, 14, 15, 18, 24, 28, 31, 32, 46-47, 47-48, 54, 56, 57, 59, 73, 74, 81, 85-86, 109, 113, 134-35, 139, 149, 157-58, 173, 197, 226, 252, 308-09, 348-49, 351, 363, 365, 366, 369, 370, 398; set apart once by Presiding Patriarch, 122; signature machine, 57-58, 158; supposedly dissolved upon "disability of the President," 57-58; support for Republican Party since 1889, 66, 111-12, 327-29, 333-35,

146; lineal office, 163, 168; membership in (and exclusion from) theocratic Council of Fifty, 120; ordained bishops, 124; ordained stake patriarchs (to 1919 by right of office, 119, 124; after 1919 by "courtesy" only, 125; after 1947 not allowed to, 129-31); "over the whole Church," 117; political activities, 284, 352; polygamy, 121, 182; "Prophet, Seer, and Revelator," 40, 123, 129, 262; relationship to church president, 116-17, 121, 122, 123, 124, 127; relationship to Quorum of the Twelve, 116-17, 118, 119, 122, 123, 125; sealing authority, 116, 124, 130; set apart missionaries, 130; set apart the church president only once, 122, 124; succession potentials, 118, 122, 123, 124-25; ten-year vacancy, 10, 51-53, 126-27, 128; terminated as office, 131; title in ordination, 124; title in public sustaining, 122; voting in temple council with First Presidency and the Twelve, 122-23, 125-26, 127, 137

Patriarchal, blessings, 117, 118, 124, 126, 127, 130, 131, 205, 245, 248, 260; marriage, 118, 182; quorum, 120-21, 123

Patten, David W., 241, 248

Pearson, Drew, 25, 79

Pearson, Glenn L., 72

Penrose, Charles W., 62-63, 124, 141, 285, 332, 341, 350-51, 356

People's Party, 265, 280, 282, 321, 323-24, 326-27, 330-31, 333, 334, 336, 339, 342, 367

Perry, L. Tom, 222

Persecution, 366. *See also* Martyrdom and Martyrs; Mobs.

Petersen, Mark E., 10, 17, 18, 29, 35, 54, 66-67, 88, 89-90, 97, 101, 103, 108, 109, 306, 307, 345, 359, 360, 371, 377

Peterson, Esther Eggertsen, 394

Peterson, Georgia Bodell, 378-79, 381, 391, 393

Peterson, H. Burke, 177, 223

Phelps, Sally Waterman, 178

Phelps, William W., 178, 228, 229-30, 267

Piedes, 256

Pike, Ralph (Sgt.), 245, 259

Pinegar, Rex D., 152

Pinnock, Hugh W., 222

Pioneer Mormons, 193, 197, 200, 249; trail, deaths on, 241. *See also* Railroad, transcontinental.

"Plausible denial," 355

Plural marriage. *See* Patriarchal marriage; Polyandry; Polygamy [a non-derogatory term]

"Pocket borough," 368, 370

Poelman, Ronald E., 222

Poland Act, 288, 325

Political activities, boycotts, 392; concealing Mormon connection, 383, 384, 388, 389, 394, 399, 400, 402; in LDS meeting houses, 71, 74, 359-60, 361, 364, 382, 383, 384-85, 388, 390, 397-98; monolithic, 313, 341, 391; "moral issues," 357-58, 362, 364, 367, 399-400; of general authorities in Mormon Culture Region, 66, 70, 224, 225, 264, 266-67, 269, 280, 282-92, 312-13, 314-72; of general authorities in U.S. nationally, 63, 66-68, 96-99, 110, 114, 225, 342-43, 345, 367-68, 369-70, 399-400; of rank-and-file Mormons in Mormon Culture Region, 263-64, 281, 282, 287, 313, 314-15, 326, 368, 377-81; of rank-and-file Mormons in U.S. nationally, 81, 91, 370, 375, 382-91, 406; of rank-and-file Mormons outside U.S., 73, 406; political action committees, 386-88, 389, 394, 403-04; power of unsigned editorials in *Church News,* 89-90, 377; source of religious disaffection, 370, 384, 391, 395. *See also* Anti-Communism; Bribery; Conscription, peacetime; Deregulation of airlines; Diplomatic activities; Equal Rights Amendment; Gun control; Hierarchy, expectation of political immunity; Interfaith cooperation; Kingdom of God; Liquor-by-the-drink; Lottery; Prohibition; Marriage, same-sex; MX missile; Myths, political; Pari-mutuel betting; Public office; *Quid pro quo;* Reapportionment of legislature; Release-time re-

Progressive Party, 347-48

Prohibition, 63, 347, 349, 355-56, 357-58, 376

Prophecies, 197, 207, 234, 238, 262, 271, 278, 407

Prophet (LDS), adoration of, 363-66, 368, 376, 397; concept of, 21; human weaknesses, viii-ix, 160; infallibility claims concerning, 368, 397; official decisions can be uninspired/wrong, 141, 363; title invoked for political purposes, 355, 364-65, 385; visionary experiences, 4, 5

"Prophet, Seer, and Revelator," as title, 40, 123, 129

Protestants, 301-02, 402, 407; fundamentalists, 367, 387, 393, 399

Protocol, 8-9, 24, 52, 53-54. See also Formal and informal references to LDS leaders.

Provo, Utah, 93, 109, 279, 282, 290, 291, 299, 314, 346

Public Affairs, 203, 312, 401

Public Communications, department and officials, 378-79, 382, 384

Public office, 339; city-town, 269, 281, 282, 288-90, 342; county, 264, 288; life tenure preferred, 262; military, 253, 256; multiple jurisdictions simultaneously, 290-91; national level (U.S.), 63, 66, 96, 99, 110, 230-31, 238, 342-43, 345; non-resident, 291; outside United States, 73; state level, 341-45; territorial level, 241, 253, 266-69, 270, 281, 283-87, 341; theocratic, 265-66, 269, 278. See also Manifesto, political; Political activities.

Pulsipher, Zera(h), 288

Quid pro quo ("exchange of favors"), 317, 328-29, 334-35, 339-40

Quincy, Josiah, 407

Quorum, as attendance requirement to conduct business, 235, 240

Quorum of the Twelve. See Apostles, Quorum of the Twelve.

Race, 13-17, 59, 79, 85, 90, 91, 96, 100-01, 113; miscegenation (interracial inter-

course), 246, 256; segregation, 14, 15, 77, 97, 99

Railroad, transcontinental (arrived in Utah in 1869, official end of pioneer era), 264

Rampton, Lucybeth, 89, 394

Rank-and-file Mormons, viii, 15-16, 34, 58, 69, 115, 155, 198, 200, 207, 208, 211, 214, 217-18, 242, 244, 245, 248, 249, 256-57, 264-65, 282, 314, 326, 338, 347-48, 364, 364, 365, 366, 368, 370, 372, 375-76, 396; aware of hierarchy's internal conflicts, 34, 69-70, 72, 74, 77-78, 79, 81, 91, 92, 97, 102, 106, 115, 160, 170, 262, 338; feel coerced by hierarchy's "counsel," 347-48, 354-55, 377. See also Political voting patterns; Surveys.

Ranking by age, 22. See also Seniority.

Rawlins, Joseph L., 354

Reagan, Ronald, 67, 111-12, 113, 366

Realpolitik ("power politics"), 317

Reapportionment of legislature, 361-62

Redden, Jackson, 228

Reese, Enoch, 286

"The Reformation." See Utah.

Region, 154

Regional Representatives, of the Twelve, 30, 55, 151, 307, 378, 385, 386, 388, 392, 397, 398, 402; of the Seventy, 152, 154

Reiser, A. Hamer, 157

Release-time religious instruction, 362

Relief Society [for women over 18], 36, 106, 374, 375, 376-77, 379, 381, 389-90, 391, 395. See also Auxiliaries.

Religion, Mormonism as new world, 407

Religious freedom, 235-36, 238

Republican Party, 63, 270, 278, 300, 307, 318, 320-43, 345-58, 360-64, 367, 369-70, 374, 375, 376

Resigning church office, 142

"Restoration of all things," 178. See also New Testament as model for Mormonism; Old Testament as model for Mormonism.

Retirement, of elderly Council of Fifty